DATE DUE

			PRINTED IN U.S.A.

Literature Criticism from 1400 to 1800

Guide to Gale Literary Criticism Series

When you need to review criticism of literary works, these are the Gale series to use:

If the author's death date is:

You should turn to:

After Dec. 31, 1959
(or author is still living)

Contemporary Literary Criticism

for example: Jorge Luis Borges, Anthony Burgess,
                William Faulkner, Mary Gordon,
                Ernest Hemingway, Iris Murdoch

1900 through 1959

Twentieth-Century Literary Criticism

for example: Willa Cather, F. Scott Fitzgerald,
                Henry James, Mark Twain, Virginia Woolf

1800 through 1899

Nineteenth-Century Literature Criticism

for example: Fedor Dostoevski, Nathaniel Hawthorne,
                George Sand, William Wordsworth

1400 through 1799

Literature Criticism From 1400 to 1800
(excluding Shakespeare)

for example: Anne Bradstreet, Daniel Defoe,
                Alexander Pope, François Rabelais,
                Jonathan Swift, Phillis Wheatley

Shakespearean Criticism

                Shakespeare's plays and poetry

Antiquity through 1399

Classical and Medieval Literature Criticism

for example: Dante, Homer, Plato, Sophocles, Vergil,
                the Beowulf Poet

Gale also publishes related criticism series:

Black Literature Criticism

This three-volume series presents criticisms of works by major black writers of the past two hundred years.

Children's Literature Review

This series covers authors of all eras who have written for the preschool through high school audience.

Short Story Criticism

This series covers the major short fiction writers of all nationalities and periods of literary history.

Poetry Criticism

This series covers poets of all nationalities and periods of literary history.

Drama Criticism

This series covers playwrights of all nationalities and periods of literary history.

ISSN 0740-2880

Volume 21

Literature Criticism from 1400 to 1800

Excerpts from Criticism of the Works
of Fifteenth-, Sixteenth-, Seventeenth-, and
Eighteenth-Century Novelists, Poets, Playwrights,
Philosophers, and Other Creative Writers,
from the First Published Critical Appraisals
to Current Evaluations

James E. Person, Jr.
Editor

Tina N. Grant
Jelena O. Krstović
Zoran Minderović
Lawrence J. Trudeau
Associate Editors

 Gale Research Inc. • *DETROIT* • *WASHINGTON, D.C.* • *LONDON*

STAFF

James E. Person, Jr., *Editor*

Zoran Minderovic, Lawrence J. Trudeau, *Associate Editors*

Tina Grant, David J. Engelman, Anna J. Sheets, Brian J. St. Germain, *Assistant Editors*

Jeanne A. Gough, *Permissions and Production Manager*

Linda M. Pugliese, *Production Supervisor*
Paul Lewon, Maureen A. Puhl, Camille Robinson, Jennifer VanSickle, *Editorial Associates*
Donna Craft, Rosita D'Souza, Sheila Walencewicz, *Editorial Assistants*

Sandra C. Davis, *Text Permissions Supervisor*
Maria L. Franklin, Josephine M. Keene, Michele M. Lonoconus, Denise Singleton, Kimberly F. Smilay,
Permissions Associates
Brandy C. Merritt, Shalice Shah, *Permissions Assistants*

Margaret A. Chamberlain, *Permissions Supervisor (Pictures)*
Pamela A. Hayes, *Permissions Associate*
Karla A. Kulkis, Nancy M. Rattenbury, Keith Reed, *Permissions Assistants*

Victoria B. Cariappa, *Research Manager*

Maureen Richards, *Research Supervisor*
Robert S. Lazich, Mary Beth McElmeel, Tamara C. Nott, *Editorial Associates*
Andrea B. Ghorai, Daniel J. Jankowski, Julie K. Karmazin, Donna Melnychenko, *Editorial Assistants*

Mary Beth Trimper, *Production Director*
Mary Winterhalter, *Production Assistant*

Cynthia Baldwin, *Art Director*
C. J. Jonik, *Keyliner*

Contents

Preface   vii

Acknowledgments   xi

William Congreve (1670-1729)..1
   English dramatist

John Dryden (1631-1700)...48
   English dramatist

George Farquhar (1678-1707) 124
   Irish-born English dramatist

Restoration Drama 184

Sir John Vanbrugh (1664-1726)..276
   English dramatist

William Wycherley (1640?-1716)..339
   English dramatist

Literary Criticism Series Cumulative Author Index   403

Literary Criticism Series Cumulative Topic Index   469

LC Cumulative Nationality Index   475

LC Cumulative Title Index   477

Preface

Literature Criticism from 1400 to 1800 (LC) presents criticism of world authors of the fifteenth through eighteenth centuries. The literature of this period reflects a turbulent time of radical change that saw the rise of drama equal in stature to that of classical Greece, the birth of the novel and personal essay forms, the emergence of newspapers and periodicals, and major achievements in poetry and philosophy. Much of modern literature reflects the influence of these centuries. Thus the literature treated in *LC* provides insight into the universal nature of human experience, as well as into the life and thought of the past.

Scope of the Series

LC is designed to serve as an introduction to authors of the fifteenth through eighteenth centuries and to the most significant interpretations of these authors' works. The great poets, dramatists, novelists, essayists, and philosophers of this period are considered classics in every secondary school and college or university curriculum. Because criticism of this literature spans nearly six hundred years, an overwhelming amount of critical material confronts the student. *LC* therefore organizes and reprints the most noteworthy published criticism of authors of these centuries. Readers should note that there is a separate Gale reference series devoted to Shakespearean studies. For though belonging properly to the period covered in *LC*, William Shakespeare has inspired such a tremendous and ever-growing corpus of secondary material that the editors have deemed it best to give his works extensive coverage in a separate series, *Shakespearean Criticism.*

Each author entry in *LC* attempts to present a historical survey of critical response to the author's works. Early criticism is offered to indicate initial responses, later selections document any rise or decline in literary reputations, and retrospective analyses provide students with modern views. The size of each author entry is intended to reflect the author's critical reception in English or foreign criticism in translation. Articles and books that have not been translated into English are therefore excluded. Every attempt has been made to identify and include the seminal essays on each author's work and to include recent commentary providing modern perspectives.

The need for *LC* among students and teachers of literature was suggested by the proven usefulness of Gale's *Contemporary Literary Criticism (CLC), Twentieth-Century Literary Criticism (TCLC),* and *Nineteenth-Century Literature Criticism (NCLC),* which excerpt criticism of works by nineteenth- and twentieth-century authors. Because of the different time periods covered, there is no duplication of authors or critical material in any of these literary criticism series. An author may appear more than once in the series because of the great quantity of critical material available and because of the aesthetic demands of the series's *thematic organization.*

Thematic Approach

Beginning with Volume 21, all the authors in each volume of *LC* are organized in a thematic scheme. Such themes include literary movements, literary reaction to political and historical events, significant eras in literary history, and the literature of cultures often overlooked by English-speaking readers. The present volume, for example, focuses upon the Restoration dramatists. Future volumes of *LC* will devote substantial space to the English Metaphysical poets and authors of the Spanish Golden Age, among many others.

Organization of the Book

Each entry consists of the following elements: author or thematic heading, introduction, list of principal works (in author entries only), annotated works of criticism (each followed by a bibliographical citation), and a bibliography of further reading. Also, most author entries contain author portraits and other illustrations.

- The **author heading** consists of the author's full name, followed by birth and death dates. If an author wrote consistently under a pseudonym, the pseudonym is used in the author heading, with the real name given in parentheses on the first line of the biographical and critical introduction. Also located here are any name variations under which an author wrote, including transliterated forms for authors whose native languages use nonroman alphabets. Uncertain birth or death dates are indicated by question marks. The **thematic heading** simply states the subject of the entry.

- The **biographical and critical introduction** contains background information designed to introduce the reader to an author and to critical discussion of his or her work. Parenthetical material following many of the introductions provides references to biographical and critical reference series published by Gale in which additional material about the author may be found. The **thematic introduction** briefly defines the subject of the entry and provides social and historical background important to understanding the criticism.

- Most *LC* author entries include **portraits** of the author. Many entries also contain illustrations of materials pertinent to an author's career, including author holographs, title pages, letters, or representations of important people, places, and events in an author's life.

- The **list of principal works** is chronological by date of first book publication and identifies the genre of each work. In the case of foreign authors whose works have been translated into English, the title and date of the first English-language edition are given in brackets beneath the foreign-language listing. Unless otherwise indicated, dramas are dated by first performance, not first publication.

- **Criticism** is arranged chronologically in each author entry to provide a useful perspective on changes in critical evaluation over the years. For the purpose of easy identification, the critic's name and the composition or publication date of the critical work are given at the beginning of each piece of criticism. Unsigned criticism is preceded by the title of the source in which it appeared. All titles by the author featured in the critical entry are printed in boldface type. Publication information (such as publisher names and book prices) and parenthetical numerical references (such as footnotes or page and line references to specific editions of works) have been deleted at the editors' discretion to provide smoother reading of the text.

- Critical essays are prefaced by **annotations** as an additional aid to students using *LC*. These explanatory notes may provide several types of useful information, including: the reputation of a critic, the importance of a work of criticism, the commentator's individual approach to literary criticism, the intent of the criticism, and the growth of critical controversy or changes in critical trends regarding an author's work. In some cases, these notes cross-reference the work of critics within the entry who agree or disagree with each other.

- A complete **bibliographical citation** of the original essay or book follows each piece of criticism.

- An annotated bibliography of **further reading** appears at the end of each entry and suggests resources for additional study of authors and themes. It also includes essays for which the editors could not obtain reprint rights.

Cumulative Indexes

Each volume of *LC* includes a cumulative **author index** listing all the authors that have appeared in *Contemporary Literary Criticism, Twentieth-Century Literary Criticism, Nineteenth-Century Literature Criticism, Literature Criticism from 1400 to 1800,* and *Classical and Medieval Literature Criticism,* along with cross-references to the Gale series *Short Story Criticism, Poetry Criticism, Children's Literature Review, Authors in the News, Contemporary Authors, Contemporary Authors Autobiography Series, Contemporary Authors Bibliographical Series, Dictionary of Literary Biography, Concise Dictionary of Literary Biography, Something about the Author, Something about the Author Autobiography Series,* and *Yesterday's Authors of Books for Children.* Readers will welcome this cumulative author index as a useful tool for locating an author within the various series. The index, which includes authors' birth and death dates, is particularly valuable for those authors who are identified with a certain period but whose death dates cause them to be placed in another, or for those authors whose careers span two periods. For example, F. Scott Fitzgerald is found in *TCLC,* yet a writer often associated with him, Ernest Hemingway, is found in *CLC.*

Beginning with Volume 12, *LC* includes a cumulative **topic index** that lists all literary themes and topics treated in *LC, NCLC* Topics volumes, *TCLC* Topics volumes, and the *CLC* Yearbook. Each volume of *LC* also includes a cumulative **nationality index** in which authors' names are arranged alphabetically under their respective nationalities and followed by the numbers of the volumes in which they appear.

Each volume of *LC* also includes a cumulative **title index,** an alphabetical listing of the literary works discussed in the series since its inception. Each title listing includes the corresponding volume and page numbers where criticism may be located. Foreign-language titles that have been translated are followed by the titles of the translations—for example, *El ingenioso hidalgo Don Quixote de la Mancha (Don Quixote)*. Page numbers following these translated titles refer to all pages on which any form of the titles, either foreign-language or translated, appear. Titles of novels, dramas, nonfiction books, and poetry, short story, or essay collections are printed in italics, while individual poems, short stories, and essays are printed in roman type within quotation marks.

A Note to the Reader

When writing papers, students who quote directly from any volume in the Literary Criticism Series may use the following general forms to footnote reprinted criticism. The first example pertains to material drawn from periodicals, the second to material reprinted from books.

T. S. Eliot, "John Donne," *The Nation and the Athenaeum,* 33 (9 June 1923), 321-32; excerpted and reprinted in *Literature Criticism from 1400 to 1800,* Vol. 10, ed. James E. Person, Jr. (Detroit: Gale Research, 1989), pp. 28-9.

Clara G. Stillman, *Samuel Butler: A Mid-Victorian Modern* (Viking Press, 1932); excerpted and reprinted in *Twentieth-Century Literary Criticism,* Vol. 33, ed. Paula Kepos (Detroit: Gale Research, 1989), pp. 43-5.

Suggestions Are Welcome

In response to various suggestions, several features have been added to *LC* since the series began, including a nationality index, a Literary Criticism Series topic index, thematic entries, a descriptive table of contents, and more extensive illustrations.

Readers who wish to suggest new features, themes, or authors to appear in future volumes, or who have other suggestions, are cordially invited to write to the editor.

Acknowledgments

The editors wish to thank the copyright holders of the excerpted criticism included in this volume, the permissions managers of many book and magazine publishing companies for assisting us in securing reprint rights, and Anthony Bogucki for assistance with copyright research. We are also grateful to the staffs of the Detroit Public Library, Wayne State University Purdy/Kresge Library Complex, and the University of Michigan Libraries for making their resources available to us. Following is a list of the copyright holders who have granted us permission to reprint material in this volume of **LC**. Every effort has been made to trace copyright, but if omissions have been made, please let us know.

COPYRIGHTED EXCERPTS IN *LC,* VOLUME 21, WERE REPRINTED FROM THE FOLLOWING PERIODICALS:

Comparative Drama, v. 21, Spring, 1987. © copyright 1987, by the Editors of *Comparative Drama.* Reprinted by permission of the publisher.—*Educational Theatre Journal,* v. XXI, October, 1969. © 1969 University College Theatre Association of the American Theatre Association. Reprinted by permission of the publisher.—*ELH,* v. 40, Spring, 1973; v. 51, Fall, 1984; v. 53, Winter 1986. Copyright © 1973, 1984, 1986 by The John Hopkins University Press. All rights reserved. All reprinted by permission of the publisher.—*Genre,* v. VI, September, 1973 for "Sir John Vanbrugh and the Conventions of Restoration Comedy" by Gerald M. Berkowitz. Copyright 1973 by Donald E. Billiar, Edward F. Heuston, and Robert L. Vales. Reprinted by permission of the University of Oklahoma and the author.—*Modern Philology,* v. 72, August, 1974 for "Between Jest and Earnest: The Comedy of Sir John Vanbrugh" by Lincoln B. Faller. © 1974 by The University of Chicago. Reprinted by permission of the University of Chicago Press and the author.—*Mosaic: A Journal for the Interdisciplinary Study of Literature,* v. XVIII, Fall, 1985. © *Mosaic* 1985. Acknowledgement of previous publication is herewith made.—*Papers on Language & Literature,* v. 24, Fall, 1988. Copyright © 1988 by the Board of Trustees, Southern Illinois University at Edwardsville. Reprinted by permission of the publisher.—*PMLA,* v. LXXIX, March, 1964. Copyright © 1964 by the Modern Language Association of America. Reprinted by permission of the Modern Language Association of America.—*Restoration: Studies in English Literary Culture, 1660-1700,* v. 6, Spring, 1982 for "The Idea of Theatre in Wycherley's 'The Gentleman Dancing-Master' " by W. Gerald Marshall; v. 11, Spring, 1987 for "The Royal Harmony: Music and Politics in Dryden's Poetry" by Douglas Murray. Copyright 1982, 1987 © The University of Tennessee, Knoxville. Both reprinted by permission of the publisher and the respective authors.—*Studia Neophilologica,* v. LVII, 1985. Reprinted by permission of the publisher.—*Studies in English Literature, 1500-1900,* v. 27, Spring, 1987 for "Dryden's Poetry and the Language of Magic" by Jack M. Armistead. © 1987 William Marsh Rice University. Reprinted by permission of the publisher and the author.—*Studies in Philology,* v. LXXXIX, Winter, 1992 for "The Limits of Parody in 'The Country Wife' " by Peggy Thompson. © 1992 by The University of North Carolina Press. Reprinted by permission of the publisher and the author.

COPYRIGHTED EXCERPTS IN *LC,* VOLUME 21, WERE REPRINTED FROM THE FOLLOWING BOOKS:

Archer, William. From *The Old Drama and the New: An Essay in Re-Evaluation.* Small, Maynard and Company, 1923. Copyright, 1923 Small, Maynard and Company. Renewed 1950 by Frank Archer.—Atkins, G. Douglas. From *The Faith of John Dryden: Change and Continuity.* University Press of Kentucky, 1980. Copyright © 1980 by The University Press of Kentucky. Reprinted by permission of the publisher.—Burns, Edward. From *Restoration Comedy: Crises of Desire and Identity.* The Macmillan Press Ltd., 1987. © Edward Burns 1987. All rights reserved. Used with permission of St. Martin's Press, Inc. In Canada by Macmillan, London and Basingstoke.—Craik, T. W. From "Congreve as a Shakespearean," in *Poetry and Drama, 1570-1700: Essays in Honour of Harold F. Brooks.* Edited by Antony Coleman and Antony Hammond. The collection © Methuen & Co. Ltd. 1981. The individual contributions © the respective authors 1981. All rights reserved. Reprinted by permission of the publisher.—Dixon, Peter. From an introduction to *The Provoked Husband.* By Sir John Vanbrugh and Colley Cibber, edited by Peter Dixon. University of Nebraska Press, 1973. Copyright © 1973 by the University of Nebraska Press. All rights reserved. Reprinted by permission of the publisher.—Dixon, Peter. From *The Recruiting Officer.* By George Farquhar. Edited by Peter Dixon. Manchester University Press, 1986. © Peter Dixon 1986. All rights reserved. Reprinted by permission of the publisher.—Engell, James. From *Forming the Critical Mind: Dryden to Coleridge.* Cambridge, Mass.: Harvard University Press, 1989. Copyright © 1989 by the President and Fellows of Harvard College. All rights reserved. Excerpted by permission of the publishers and the author.—Farmer, A. J. From *George Farquhar.* Longmans, Green & Co., 1966. © A. J. Farmer 1966.—Fowler, Alastair. From *A History of English*

William Congreve

1670-1729

(Also wrote under pseudonym of Cleophil) English dramatist, poet, librettist, novelist, and translator.

The following entry presents a selection of Congreve criticism from the last decade. For additional information on Congreve's life and works, see *Literature Criticism from 1400 to 1800,* Vol. 5.

INTRODUCTION

Universally acknowledged as the greatest comic dramatist of the Restoration, Congreve is best known for the unflagging wit with which he infused a repertoire of plays still widely performed and read today. His skillful representations of human behavior in society—effected primarily through the brilliant banter of his characters in such celebrated plays as *Love for Love* and *The Way of the World*—have established his prominence within an age which considered intelligent and imaginative wit, particularly in comedy, of premier importance.

Born at Bardsey in Yorkshire, Congreve was the son of a country gentleman. As his family possessed some wealth, he enjoyed the benefits of a private education. After his father received a lieutenant's commission, the family moved to Ireland, where Congreve received his earliest schooling and, at age twelve, entered Kilkenny College, where he met Jonathan Swift. Congreve's curriculum—which included reading, writing, Classical languages, and theology—was rigid, but did not preclude his enjoying school holidays with Swift and other friends or regularly attending local dramatic performances by townsmen and by visiting Dublin players. In 1686 Congreve was admitted into Trinity College, Dublin, where he intensified his studies in theology and, particularly, the classics. Like many a restive student Congreve, disposed to gregariousness and a love of amusement, also availed himself of Dublin's many diversions, such as the theater, though this was officially forbidden to young Trinity residents. Congreve thus became well grounded in the dramatic presentations popular during this time—among them Ben Jonson's *Volpone* and Thomas Durfey's *The Boarding House*—before such performances were suppressed during the reign of James II. He avidly read the established works on dramatic theory as well. It is conjectured that Congreve was probably more familiar with the theater than most young gentlemen of his era by the time he came to London in early manhood, a move precipitated, with James II's accession to the throne, by Irish Protestant fear of a resurgence of Catholic repression.

In 1691 Congreve enrolled in the Middle Temple, London, to study law. He found this pursuit uninspiring, though London afforded him opportunities to meet many men with literary inclinations similar to his own. He soon recommended himself as a wit and promising writer with the novel *Incognita; or, Love and Duty Reconcil'd,* and before long joined the ranks of disciples priviledged to assemble regularly with John Dryden in Will's Coffee House. Congreve soon established himself as Dryden's friend, legal adviser, and literary protégé; his legal acumen enabled him to negotiate arrangements between Dryden and publisher Jacob Tonson, while years of rigorous training allowed him to make numerous important contributions as translator to Dryden's editions of Classical authors. Dryden, recognizing the younger man's sensitivity not only to good translation but to the nuances of his own tongue—evident from his first published work—predicted Congreve's literary success. This came in 1693 with *The Old Batchelour,* which received enthusiastic acclaim. Although some complained that Congreve was merely a creation of his mentor, Dryden, most commentators, echoing the sentiments of English dramatist and translator Peter Motteux, agreed that "the Wit which is diffus'd through

[*The Old Batchelour*], makes it lose but few of those charms in the perusal, which yield such pleasure in the Representation."

Like the majority of plays produced during this period, *The Old Batchelour* was written with specific players in mind; it was performed with a cast of the most popular and accomplished thespians available. Many biographers surmise that Congreve created the role of the virtuous and witty ingenue, Araminta, specifically for actress Anne Bracegirdle, the object of his lifelong, though unrequited, love. In later years, Congreve became romantically involved with Henrietta, Duchess of Marlborough, who became the mother of his daughter and, after Congreve's death, the recipient of his fortune.

Despite ringing endorsements from such notable figures as Dryden and Swift, *The Double-Dealer* inspired much less enthusiasm than its predecessor. Dryden's account of the drama's lukewarm reception includes a faithful summary of some typical audience reactions which also represent perceptions of Congreve's other plays: "The Women think [Congreve] has exposed their Bitchery too much; and the Gentlemen, are offended with him; for the discovery of their Follyes: and the way of their Intrigues, under the notion of Friendship to their Ladyes Husbands." However, the overwhelming success of the subsequent drama, *Love for Love*, both redeemed Congreve's popularity and considerably increased his income, as he was given a full share in a new acting company under William III's protection. In 1696, traveling with dramatist Thomas Southerne, Congreve visited Ireland, where he received a master of arts degree from Trinity College and was briefly reunited with his parents. It is believed that contact with Southerne, the author of several successful tragedies, may have prompted Congreve to test his ability in what most critics of the age considered the higher dramatic form. Ignoring gibes and unsolicited admonitions from fellow coffeehouse wits who were convinced his endeavor would fail, he wrote *The Mourning Bride*, which many critics praised liberally for its morality as well as its literary merit.

Given the prevailing encomiums attending his career thus far, Congreve was unprepared for Jeremy Collier's fervent attack on his work in *A Short View of the Immorality and Profaneness of the English Stage*, published in 1698. Collier, a clergyman, launched indictment after indictment against the profligacy he deemed clearly evident in Congreve's work. Congreve replied with *Amendments to Mr. Collier's False and Imperfect Citations*, which professes the essential morality of all well-crafted art. This lucid rebuttal displays Congreve's characteristic wit but is colored by his own badly disguised contempt for Collier's fervent moralism and social standing—a tack which gave Collier the upper hand in the argument and spawned subsequent skirmishes as well. Weary of being drawn into further confrontations, Congreve concentrated on writing his last comedy, *The Way of the World*. Performed in 1700, it enjoyed moderate success but also revived certain criticisms which Congreve interpreted as indicating his work's opposition to the "general Taste."

Although Congreve's career had passed its apogee, it was by no means over. After several months on the Continent at health spas for treatment of gout and advancing blindness, he turned to the composition of a libretto, *The Judgment of Paris,* which was well received by the public despite the low esteem then accorded opera. Early in the eighteenth century, Congreve collaborated with fellow dramatist John Vanbrugh in the establishment of a new theater, the Haymarket. This project was financed by members of the Kit-Kat Club, a literary-political society which included both Whig nobility and such renowned contemporaries of Congreve as Joseph Addison and Richard Steele. While the Haymarket Theatre shortly failed, Congreve's association with influential members of the Kit-Kat Club proved profitable, enabling him to secure two government posts and a lifelong appointment as Secretary of Jamaica, and also to continue for a time as a man of letters. By 1706, however, ill health compelled Congreve to curtail much of his writing. No longer the prolific artist of his youth, he resided quietly in London until his death, visited to the last by friends and admirers.

Notwithstanding a modest reception by his contemporaries, *The Way of the World* has been long acknowledged as Congreve's masterpiece. Some critics have found the intricate plot difficult, though its derivations from comedic drama in general and comedy of the period in particular are unmistakable. *The Way of the World* relies on the conventional devices of deception and misunderstanding to punctuate the author's wry evaluation of love, human relationships, and the institution of marriage—a favorite butt of Restoration humor. In the play, Millamant wishes to marry Mirabell, the only admirer who can capture her interest and match her wit. The two are denied permission by Millamant's aunt, Lady Wishfort, who does finally yield her consent after numerous events which expose human vanity, avarice, and lust, yet proclaim the existence, amid corruption and marriages of convenience, of genuine values and real love. The play's paramount strength is its dialogue, which prompted Edmund Gosse to remark, "*The Way of the World* is the best-written, the most dazzling, the most intellectually accomplished of all English comedies, perhaps of all the comedies of the world" but, in conceding the almost nonexistent action of the plot, to add judiciously, "The reader dies of a rose in aromatic pain, but the spectator fidgets in his stall, and wishes that the actors and actresses would be doing something. In no play of Congreve's is the literature so consummate, in none is the human interest in movement and surprise so utterly neglected, as in *The Way of the World*."

While acknowledging the amorality of some of Congreve's characters in *The Way of the World* and the other plays, Charles Lamb vigorously opposed blanket condemnation of their actions, deploring the tendency to subject them to moral scrutiny. Lamb advised utter suspension of moral debate for a full appreciation of all of Congreve's works within their proper historical context, a view with which Thomas Babington Macaulay took decided exception, avowing that Congreve's "heroes and heroines . . . have a moral code of their own, an exceedingly bad one, but not, as Mr. Charles Lamb seems to think, a code existing only in the imagination of dramatists." Since the time of this initial schism, critics have not only adopted one position or the other but, like Matthew Arnold, have sometimes straddled both. Writing in the *Pall Mall Gazette* in 1883, Arnold determined Congreve's dramatic world to be entirely of fantasy, but suggests "that in such a world, with a good critic and with good actors, we are not likely to come to much harm."

The libertine sentiments expressed in *Love for Love*, another comedy replete with stock characters and predictable events, reflect the mores of Congreve's age, some of which he doubtless espoused, yet they serve rather to illuminate than to obscure the author's underlying ideals. Gosse has commented that this drama, while "not quite so uniformly brilliant in style as *The Way of the World* . . . has the advantage of possessing a much wholesomer relation to humanity than that play." And, as observed by Bonamy Dobrée, "amid all the flurry and pother and intrigue . . . [appears Congreve's] insistence that the precious thing in life—affection in human relations—must be preserved at all costs," a theme also stressed in *The Way of the World* and elsewhere. *The Mourning Bride*, though a tragedy, utilizes some of the same elements found in Congreve's comedies. The work's popularity has considerably abated since the time when an audience willingly unraveled such complexities of plot. While most critics have considered the drama's plot laborious and its poetry faltering, many have also praised it. If typified almost from its first appearance as poor declamatory tragedy, *The Mourning Bride* does contain several familiar lines (among them, "Music hath charms to soothe the savage breast") which have joined the mainstream of frequently-quoted material.

From the time of Collier's critical assault to the twentieth century, Congreve's critical heritage has been influenced by perception of the morality presented in his works, even though the author's libertinism and antimatrimonial attitudes are considered intrinsic to his milieu. Yet, despite his controversial libertine veneer or shortcomings as a dramatist, Congreve has without contest maintained his supremacy in the English comedy of manners. But because the significance and very concept of "wit" have greatly altered since Congreve's time, some today find his work tedious and trivial.

PRINCIPAL WORKS

Incognita; or, Love and Duty Reconcil'd [as Cleophil] (novel) 1692
The Double-Dealer (drama) 1693
The Old Batchelour (drama) 1693
Love for Love (drama) 1695
The Mourning Bride (drama) 1697
Amendments of Mr. Collier's False and Imperfect Citations from the "Old Batchelour," "Double-Dealer," "Love for Love," "Mourning Bride" (criticism) 1698
The Way of the World (drama) 1700
The Judgment of Paris (libretto) 1701
The Works of Mr. William Congreve. 3 vols. (dramas and poetry) 1710
A Letter to Viscount Cobham (poetry) 1729
The Complete Works of William Congreve. 4 vols. (dramas) 1923

William Congreve: Letters & Documents (letters and documents) 1964

J. C. Ross (essay date 1981)

[*In the excerpt below, Ross offers an overview of the characterization and plot of Congreve's earliest comedy,* The Double-Dealer. *He notes that most scholars have been highly critical of the play, but lauds it as "a genuine comedy" that should be viewed "as a lesser work of a great dramatic artist."*]

> The plot [of *The Double Dealer*] is extremely intricate, and exacts from the spectator very deep attention; without it, he will not be able to see how it is unravelled in the catastrophe.

Thomas Davies, writing [in his *Dramatic Miscellanies*] from a long-standing familiarity with the play in the eighteenth century theatre, points to one side of its central paradox: that despite its avowedly rigorous commitment to classical principles of construction, it pursues the highly unclassical practices of creating surprise by violating generated expectations, and violently shifting in tone and perspective. It demands alertness, not just because the plot is intricate, but also because 'the audience is deliberately confused, refused the security of expectation of what a play ought to do' [Peter Holland in his *The Ornament of Action: Text and Performance in Restoration Comedy,* 1979]. Congreve's second comedy is radically ambitious and experimental, along several diverging paths.

The effect of the Horatian epigraph, together with the claim in the dedicatory epistle that 'the mechanical part' of the play is 'perfect' ('regular' in Q2), is to assert that *The Double-Dealer* complies with the requirements for comedy as laid down by both ancient and more recent classical critics. Yet if the play is arguably 'regular,' by accepted standards, it is less clear that it is the 'true . . . comedy' that its author tried to write.

The epigraph 'Yet at times even comedy raises her voice,' in its original context came within a discussion of generic and stylistic decorum: 'Let each style keep the becoming place allotted to it. Yet . . .' Horace accepted nonetheless the legitimacy of the occasional emergence within a comedy of intensely passionate, serious and elevated speeches, akin to those of tragedy, provided they were appropriate to character and situation. And André Dacier's comment on this line, in a standard critical work of the time ([*Les Œuvres d'Horace,*] referred to in the play) allowed that a more heightened, sublime mode of speech might be introduced not only for moments of rage, but to express any strong passion, even joy. Congreve is involking the authority of Horace and, by implication, the precedent of Terence's comedies . . . to justify his thrusting outward, or actual violation, of the generic boundaries of comedy, by introducing into his main action sequences that approach both the intense passions and the heightened diction of contemporary tragedy. Comparisons can be made with certain of the tragicomedies of John Dryden (e.g. *The*

Spanish Friar) in which the high action was largely serious yet turned out happily, and the low action comic.

The author's declaration that he has 'preserved' the three unities 'to the utmost severity' is not in the strictest sense correct. He complies with them to the generally accepted degree: a time-span of within twenty-four hours, a few places reasonably close to each other, and the pre-eminence of one action, to which lesser actions are related. However the interpretations with which Congreve has tried to comply are far narrower. He has not quite managed to do so, and the play would have suffered badly theatrically if he had placed too high a priority on this. To have made the statement as it stood in the first quarto, 'The SCENE, A Gallery in the Lord *Touchwood*'s House,' literally true, could only have been achieved by reducing the episode in Lady Touchwood's bed-chamber, at the end of Act IV, either to 'noises off' and messenger report, or to a thoroughly implausible intrusion of part of its action out on to the gallery. Either way would have meant a grievous sacrifice of 'beauties' and dramatic values at a point where the play needed an effective crisis. As it is, this brief 'private' scene draws added power and symbolic value from its uniqueness.

Similarly, the statement in Q1 that 'The Time' is 'from Five o'Clock to Eight in the Evening' asserts that the fictive time is equal to the playing-time, and indeed more or less identical with the time of the performance in the Restoration theatre. Here there is an element of *trompe l'oeil*: in the text five references in Acts III and IV to the hour eight o'clock encourage us, despite our growing awareness of Maskwell's true intentions, to anticipate a decisive catastrophe at this time. Instead the events in the bed-chamber multiply the complications, in Jonsonian fashion, and Act V requires approximately one further hour. Maskwell in V, iii. 36-37 tells Mellefont 'meet me in half an hour, yonder in my lady's dressing-room,' and the resultant meetings bring about the true catastrophe. The audience would simply be aware, like Lord Froth, that the final events occur at some time 'past eight' (V,v. 2), as if the clock had accelerated towards eight o'clock and then stopped, leaving them to unfold in a kind of temporal limbo. The time required for events off-stage between the acts would have corresponded, ostensibly, with the duration of the act-intervals, in which the Restoration audience was entertained with music.

Once again, the dramatist claims he has complied with the most stringent version of the unity of action, by making his plot 'single'; this implies that Brisk's cuckolding intrigue with Lady Froth, and Careless's with Lady Plyant, are not intended to be regarded as minor plots at all, but simply as business, the goings-on of the social milieu in relation to which the plot functions and is to be understood. Alternatively the Careless/Plyant strand may be regarded as an aspect of the central plot. But clearly the minor characters' activities are by no means so skillfully woven into a single complex action as in *Love for Love* or *The Way of the World.*

Even allowing that Congreve's proclaimed compliance involves an element of disingenuousness, a conscious manipulation of the reader, the extremely tight limits within which his play works are vital to its nature. They are exceptional for the era, and very difficult to handle with an appearance of naturalness. From the frequent and precise references to time, and to where characters are, or are going, and why, one may glimpse (and reconstruct) a schema in which, as in a detective-story play like Agatha Christie's *The Mousetrap,* the whereabouts of almost every character, in the house or the garden, at crucial times, has been exactly charted. As Peter Holland observes, the narrow time-scheme 'produces in the play an incredible claustrophobic intensity,' and an effect of 'excessive naturalism.'

The virtually constant presence of the ornate gallery setting is likewise claustrophobic. 'No previous Restoration comedy had stayed so firmly in one place, had excluded the outside world so completely' (Holland). It serves to symbolise the closed nature of the upper class society we observe, and also, in its elegance, the privilege, wealth and status which accompany the possession of this great house, that ultimately the conflict is about. One hears further of a bewildering maze of rooms, stairs and back-passages, which give power to those like Maskwell who know them all. Only convention, in the absence of evidence to the contrary, and slight hints like the reference to Sappho's 'chair,' indicate that the house is in the environs of London. The gallery setting thus also takes on a limboesque quality, 'real and unreal at the same time' (Holland); and this is enhanced by the stagey quality of the long soliloquies (emphatically placed as they are), the end-of-act tags, and the more artificially heightened speeches.

Other features of classical regularity include the preservation of *liaison des scènes,* which has been largely though not completely achieved.

That the dramatist was actively conscious of neoclassical critical writings at this time is evidenced not merely by his implicit use of Hédelin and Dryden in his dedicatory epistle. The play's own critical self-consciousness is amusingly revealed in Brisk's questioning Lady Froth in Act III as to whether she has read Rapin, Le Bossu and André Dacier. She has.

As a 'true comedy' the play is committed to satirical instruction by negative example. Not only is there incidental display of a variety of follies; we are told that the central plot is designed to illustrate a moral. What exactly it does demonstrate may be argued about; but Congreve leaves us in no doubt that his intended moral is expressed in Lord Touchwood's closing words: that the treacherous person is inevitably destroyed by his own treachery. The play is not outwardly political; yet treachery (or as those opposed to the regime would call it, Jacobite loyalty) was an intensely relevant political issue amid fears of invasion, subversion and uprising in 1692-3. Some later historians describe Marlborough as one of the arch double-dealers of the time; but there is no clear trace in the play of personal satire.

In the moral the fate of 'secret villainy' is to be like that of Volpone's 'mischiefs,' which 'feed / Like beasts till they be fat and then they bleed.' One of the key images in the play, of the viper in the bosom, is now used to represent Maskwell's treachery as a viper that is emerging and will destroy him, by a process of natural law. It becomes then essential that Maskwell be seen to be defeated not primarily through Mellefont's or anyone else's initiatives, but through the consequence of his own machinations. The dynamic of the central action thus becomes that of Jonsonian 'punitive comedy.' And as the moral governs the plot, so the central plot in its turn takes on a 'set-piece' quality, and to a large degree governs the characterization of the people involved in it.

As Irving Wardle has said [in *The Times,* 23 July, 1969], *'The Double-Dealer* is a double play, combining the usual provisional morality of folly and ill-breeding' of Restoration comedy 'with a fixed morality based on the sense of evil.' In practice the double valuation is all-pervasive. The Froths, the Plyants and Brisk belong firmly in the world normally portrayed by Restoration social comedy; yet their shallow egotism and follies reveal the vulnerability of this realm to the corruptions of serious evil. In the central plot the dynamics and valuations of serious 'punitive comedy' are juxtaposed with the very different expectations and valuations that the social comedy mode generates.

Conventionally the central and normative male figure in the Restoration social comedy was the young rake-wit, and the main action his eventually successful courting of the heroine. The pattern was susceptible of great variation, in particular, in the contrast between a rake-hero and a romantic lead (as reproduced by, e.g., Dorimant and Young Bellair in Etherege's *The Man of Mode*): and in the 1680s the predatory rake was becoming less attractive. Nonetheless the pattern, and the audience expectations it generated, remained extremely potent.

What has happened in *The Double-Dealer* is that the intriguing rake is presented as the 'villain,' the barrier-figure and rival to the love of the romantic lead Mellefont. And Maskwell as a hybrid character carries not only the moral ambivalence of the rake-hero, unscrupulously hunting after sex and a fortune; he also brings with him the double valuation of the Jonsonian rogue, at once hero and villain.

In this play the action begins where the typical social comedy ended: the courting is completed and the rather serious romantic couple, Mellefont and Cynthia, are to marry the following day. The occasion is a celebratory dinner that provides the social framework for a double legal ceremony: Lord Touchwood is to sign the documents constituting his nephew Mellefont as his heir, and putting him in immediate 'possesion of a fair estate' (V,i.76); he and Sir Paul are to sign the writings of settlement and jointure confirming Cynthia's financial status as Mellefont's wife. Brisk and Lord Froth are present not only as guests but as witnesses.

While 'the marriage of Mellefont and Cynthia' remains 'the main business of the play,' the major interest is transferred to the barrier-figures, Maskwell and Lady Touchwood, and to the 'gulling' actions by which they seek to prevent this marriage. Maskwell, the lowborn dependent, is trying to substitute himself in Mellefont's place both as Lord Touchwood's heir and as Cynthia's husband. It is prodigiously difficult: he must dominate the characters concerned when the time arrives for the signing; and he must somehow gain possession of Cynthia, even though this means double-crossing his paranoid ally Lady Touchwood. And all must be done 'before the company break up' (III, 127-8).

He could have settled for the 'fair estate' and presumably got away with it, with audience applause; but whether through avarice, love, the rogue's delight in outrageous deceptions, or all three motives together, he tries to capture Cynthia and her dowry as well, and over-reaches himself. As a rogue-hero like Jonson's Volpone, he may cheat fools with impunity, but when his activities 'threaten the welfare of some good and innocent people, and finally all of society, he must be stopped . . . and . . . punished.' The representatives of the Touchwood and Plyant families, with the exception of Cynthia, are not impressive, either fools or 'honest, well-meaning' but not very perspicacious men. But on Cynthia's marriage with Mellefont depend the survival of not only two aristocratic families, but also, symbolically, their class and their society.

What is unusual is the extent to which Maskwell is depicted (admittedly mainly by the extravagantly-spoken Lady Touchwood) as a figure of outright evil: as 'a sedate, a thinking villain, whose black blood runs temperately bad,' or as a 'mollifying devil' (I,ii, 27-28, 71). Etherege's Dorimant had been accused and cursed in a similar fashion by Mrs Loveit, but with a less exclusively melodramatic effect.

Maskwell is defeated in Act V, yet has come very close to success, which is now redefined in terms of spiriting away Cynthia in a coach with Saygrace and himself for an immediate secret marriage. His defeat comes about apparently by chance: Cynthia's alertness in grasping the potential dangers of the changed rendezvous, and her flukily timely encounters with Careless and Mellefont, lead her to seize the chance to overhear the confrontation between Maskwell and Lady Touchwood. And by chance Lord Touchwood has come along, in a suitable frame of mind, to overhear it with her. The crucial confrontation has itself come about because Lady Touchwood has learnt, too soon, what Maskwell told her husband about his desire to marry Cynthia.

Aubrey Williams [in his *Approach to Congreve,* 1979] is in no doubt that all these chances are brought about through Divine Providence; though (unlike Sir Paul, who appeals to Providence so often) it is necessary to take advantage of the helps that it offers. His position relies on the omnipresence of such ideas about Providence in the sermons and devotional writings of the time, and an equating of providential and poetic justice.

Williams' position on *The Double-Dealer* has been vigorously attacked by John Barnard and B. Eugene McCarthy. Barnard argues [in his "Passion, 'Poetical Justice,' and Dramatic Law in *The Double-Dealer* and *The Way of the World,"* *Mermaid Critical Commentaries: William Congreve,* edited by Brian Horns, 1970] that 'Williams' account seems to me deeply misleading and at odds with the whole ethos of Congreve's world,' and that Congreve's known 'use of the term "poetic justice" . . . is purely affective.' McCarthy argues [in his "Providence in Congreve's *The Double-Dealer*," *SEL* XIX (1970): 407-19] that as well as religious imagery there are many other kinds in the play, and that Maskwell's defeat happens because

> It seems to be of the nature of the evil imagination that since it is uncontrolled it eventually destroys itself; it outwits itself because it operates outside of control. Those who [like Careless or Cynthia] wait with patient ears and eyes for the not entirely understandable . . . events to unwind will succeed. If one wishes to identify this force that exposes villainy as Providence, so be it, but the play itself does not so suggest . . .

The argument has in wider terms been continued by Canfield [in his "Religious Language and Religious Meaning in Restoration Comedy," *SEL* XX (1980): 385-406], who argues that 'the religious language' in four major Restoration comedies that he examines 'is both casual and purposeful, ironic and literal. It is typically casual and ironic in the mouths of the characters but purposeful and ultimately literal in the pen of the author.' The dispute continues. Clearly some uses of religious terms in *The Double-Dealer*, as in Lady Touchwood's furious soliloquy, come very close to literal meaning:

> Oh! That I were fire indeed, that I might burn the vile traitor to a hell of torments,—but he's damnation-proof, a devil already, and fire is his element (V,ii. 27-30)).

A disjunctive private conflict emerges in Cynthia's challenge to Mellefont either to circumvent Lady Touchwood, or to prove that she is indeed assisted by the Devil. If he does neither, she says, she won't marry him. Like several other elements in the plot it is simply lost sight of; even for her (persuaded, offstage, by Maskwell to accept the elopement plan) 'a fundamental discrepancy' is revealed 'between words and action'. And she shares 'the good characters' inability to recognize, let along deal with, evil'.

That it should nonetheless be Cynthia, the primary truewit in the play, who has the key role in the unmasking of Maskwell, exposes the absurdity of his assumption that having got her away from the house he could somehow deceive or compel her to marry him. It is questionable however whether this would be recognized in performance.

Mellefont has the caste-marks of a truewit and certainly talks as one, in his two fine little duets with Cynthia. Yet Congreve's defence of him, in his epistle, as not being proved to be a fool merely because he is cheated by a superlatively cunning opponent, does not dispose of the objection that he lets himself be cheated far too easily. His gushingly naive responses to Maskwell ('Oh see, I see my rising sun! Light breaks through clouds upon me, and I shall live in day,' etc.) demonstrate increasingly an inability to grasp the meaning of what is being said and done. He is shown up damagingly by the greater perspicuity of Careless, Cynthia and even Lord Touchwood. There is a certain aptness in Lady Froth's remark in Act II that 'he is too much a mediocrity'; and Maskwell clearly includes

him in the category of 'fair-faced fools,' embodiments of 'the hungry gudgeon Credulity.' He is then like Maskwell a hybrid, combining features of the truewit, the Jonsonian gull, and the comedy romantic lead (typically nearly till the end unsuccessful in his intrigues). In terms of the standards of good and evil, his moral impeccability may count for more than his lack of efficacy; but he is neither impressive nor very interesting and the play is left without a hero, or anyone to whom our sympathies can firmly attach. Even Cynthia is too cool and restrained, a latent rather than an active force.

Maskwell's true opponent is then not the individual, Mellefont, but the group; and his initial 'shallow device,' of having Lady Plyant persuaded that Mellefont is out to seduce her, has a greater success than he had any right to expect, because it splits the group up. Lady Plyant is impervious to protestations of innocence; and Careless is effectively neutralised for most of the rest of the play by his preoccupation with seducing her in earnest. Until he has won her over, even Cynthia can have only brief consultations with Mellefont. Hence this first device, though not causally connected with Maskwell's later schemes, does make them feasible. Nonetheless Maskwell's dupes are not finally fools, but people of a true though limited wit; and while he can deceive them individually, he cannot indefinitely prevent them from conferring with, or overhearing, each other, or prevent the group from re-uniting against him. That these things should happen in time to frustrate his designs is not inevitable, as I've already mentioned.

Consideration of Lady Touchwood raises in its most acute form the problem of mixed literary idioms. John Barnard has argued that in certain of the serious scenes there is a shift from a naturalistic to an 'affective' mode of dialogue, a heightened, artificial language of passion, as used in much Restoration tragedy. He sees this practice, ostensibly santioned by the Horatian epigraph, as a serious artistic blunder. Now unquestionably Lady Touchwood does at certain crises use such language, but what is uncertain is whether the playgoers of 1693 were instead expected to recognize that she is an instinctive playactor, a self-cast tragedy queen. At certain moments her words clearly reflect those of Roxana in Lee's *The Rival Queens*, though unlike Brisk and Sir Paul in relation to the same play she is not deliberately making direct quotations. Still, the polarity between tragic and comic acting styles at this time was such that to make a character within a comedy adopt an heroic manner and diction would presumably have necessarily involved a calculated creation of a sense of burlesque.

Lady Touchwood can be at once taken seriously and ironically: her passions are intense enough, but her elevated rantings are undercut by the cool cynicism of Maskwell; and in the wider comic context the reflection of them in the gushings of Lady Plyant renders them absurd. Yet she remains a formidable stage-figure, even if, as Harold Love says [in his *Congreve*, 1974], she 'is never permitted to resemble a credible human being.'

The fools, Brisk, the Froths and the Plyants, whose social intercourse and intrigues take up half the stage-time of the first four acts, exhibit a careful graduation from the almost-wit Brisk to the complete ninny Lord Froth. They are fine, not gross, fools, unlike the people at Lady Whiffler's, and exhibit doubtless what many took to be genuine wit, though it is reduced to mere verbal self-display, in which 'figures of speech enlarge the most trivial actions to epic proportions' [Norman N. Holland, *The First Modern Comedies: the Significance of Etherge, Wycherley, and Congreve,* 1967]. Cynthia says, 'these have quality and education, wit and fine conversation, are received and admired by the world . . .'; yet their wit is false, their conversation pretentious and trivial. Congreve is redefining what it is to be a true wit, in the direction of verbal and moral restraint. Notwithstanding the Juvenalian exposure of their follies and failings, they are full of exuberant life.

Despite the relatively rudimentary nature of their intrigues, the triangles Sir Paul—Lady Plyant—Careless and Lord Froth—Lady Froth—Brisk parallel and contrast with the serious cuckolding triangle Lord Touchwood—Lady Touchwood—Maskwell. Where Lady Touchwood's immorality is destructively evil, Lady Froth and Lady Plyant are such butterflies that their promiscuity is merely funny, and such as their husbands richly deserve. A son for Sir Paul may be the best gift Providence can provide. A key (and historically authentic) factor in this society, that makes it so fragile, is its desperate lack of fecundity: there are single offspring only, or none at all. Few were born and fewer still survived. A relatively recent turn towards shows of fondness for children is satirised in Lady Froth's fussing over her Sappho.

The main action is then serious in itself, yet our responses to it are ironically modified by the parallels in the subsidiary plot-strands. Like Lady Touchwood's ranting, Maskwell's villainous double-dealing is matched at the comic level by that of Careless and Brisk. The original casting of the serious actor Kynaston as Lord Touchwood indicates that he was not intended to be seen as, essentially, rendered ridiculous, like the two other cuckolded husbands.

This action is disconcerting in several ways. The opening sequence leads us to expect Mellefont to function as an active intriguer, but his unwillingness to dissimulate, as a means to controlling others, or to recognize Maskwell's dissimulation, renders his schemes almost wholly ineffectual, up to the point where he puts on the physical disguise of the parson's gown, and reverses its intended purpose. The meaning of the action is almost lost when Cynthia and Mellefont in IV, i set up an inner drama of private happiness or rejection independent of considerations of property or status. Maskwell's major plot is frustrated not primarily through a counter-intrigue but an *anagnorisis,* in V, iv. And when the villains are defeated in the bustling final scene they simply vanish, giving place to a brief, optimistic blessing on the lovers, and a dark warning about 'base treach'ry.' In the flawed, pragmatic world of Revolution England, Cynthia and Mellefont together represent the best hope there is for a more wisely governed society.

Much has been said by critics about the shortcomings of this play, by comparison with the masterpieces that followed. Maximilian Novak, who sees it [in his *William Congreve,* 1971] as 'an exciting failure,' considers that

Congreve tried to combine in it too many incompatible elements, creating 'three worlds: a verbal world of grotesque realism, one of high comedy and wit, and another of genuine evil suggested by chthonic imagery.' John Barnard argues that 'the structure is basically affective—moral, character and intrigue are not each inseparably part of the other.' Norman N. Holland believes that 'the play fails because Mellefont is so woefully inadequate as a hero,' though his 'natural goodness' points towards a real happiness beyond the reach either of folly or wisdom, akin to the ethos of eighteenth century sentimentalism. On the contrary side, Brian Corman argues [in his "The Mixed Way of Comedy: Congreve's *The Double-Dealer,*" *MP* LXXI (1974): 356-65] that it does have 'form, unity and coherence,' even if finally it is 'not wholly satisfying.' And Anthony Gosse [in his "Plot and Character in Congreve's *Double-Dealer,*" *MLQ* XXIX (1962): 274-88] has characterised it as 'an ironic, dark comedy,' that achieves a unified complex effect.

I take it to be a frequently dark yet genuine comedy, in which most of the characters are playacting, posturing or creating false appearances, and a few are trying to see truly. If it is a flawed play, its distinguished recent stage history demonstrates that it possesses a unique appeal, and considerable merits, as a lesser work of a great dramatic artist. (xix-xxix)

J. C. Ross, in an introduction to The Double-Dealer *by William Congreve, edited by J. C. Ross, Ernest Benn Limited, 1981, pp. ix-xxix.*

T. W. Craik   (essay date 1981)

[*Craik is an American educator and an acknowledged authority on English drama and the Elizabethan theater. In the following excerpt, he considers Congreve's familiarity with Shakespeare's plays through a comparative study of characterization and language.*]

Congreve is, by general agreement, one of the most conscious stylists among the writers of comedy in English, and his literary expression has received much attention. In this essay I shall confine myself to a single aspect of it, his echoes of Shakespeare. Some of these echoes have the nature of allusions and depend for their full comic effect on their recognition by the audience. Others—by far the greater number—are verbal reminiscences, conscious or unconscious, sometimes evidently prompted by the speaker's character or circumstances, and at other times seemingly springing from Congreve's familiarity with Shakespeare's plays in general and a few of them in particular.

The fact that this aspect of Congreve's style has not—as far as I am aware—been examined as a whole, though some individual examples have been noted by his editors, shows that it is far from being developed into a mannerism. He never makes his *dramatis personae* quote from Shakespeare directly, as Belinda quotes from Cowley, Sir Sampson from Dryden and Millamant from Waller and from 'natural, easy Suckling'. Even his few direct and pointed allusions are integrated into his dialogue, and are uttered by speakers quite unconscious of the Shakespearean origin of their expressions. To attempt to identify them, and still more those of which Congreve himself may not have been fully conscious, is not without such dangers as Johnson humorously points out in the Preface to his edition of Shakespeare:

> I have found it remarked, that, in this important sentence, *Go before, I'll follow,* we read a translation of, *I prae, sequar.* I have been told, that when Caliban, after a pleasing dream, says, *I cry'd to sleep again,* the author imitates *Anacreon,* who had, like every other man, the same wish on the same occasion.

Nevertheless, for the sake of the light which these verbal reminiscences may throw on Congreve's reading, his memory and sometimes his dramatic art, the dangers seem worth risking.

In *The Way of the World,* Sir Wilfull Witwoud's first appearance, at Lady Wishfort's house, is marked by the recurring phrase 'No offence'. He salutes Mrs Marwood, saying, as he does so, 'No Offence, I hope'. His half-brother Witwoud remarks: 'This is a vile Dog, I see that already. No Offence. Ha, ha, ha, to him; to him *Petulant,* smoke him.' Petulant thereupon accosts Sir Wilfull, using the phrase for the third time with ironical intent; presently Sir Wilfull is goaded into asking him 'Do you speak by way of Offence, Sir?', and, when giving his name to Mrs Marwood, adds pointedly, 'No offence to any Body, I hope.' At this stage Mrs Marwood introduces him to his half-brother, who acknowledges him coldly; Sir Wilfull reacts indignantly, and Witwoud, evidently with tongue in cheek, replies 'No offence, I hope, Brother.' At this, Sir Wilfull delivers the retort direct: "Sheart, Sir, but there is, and much offence.' This is the last time the word is used for nearly eighty lines, though it reappears (with the effect of a running joke) at Lady Wishfort's entrance, and again in Sir Wilfull's drunken scene in Act IV.

Only one of Congreve's editors annotates 'No offence', finding it 'possibly reminiscent of Falstaff's attempts to excuse his insults to Hal (*2 Henry IV,* II.iv. 302, 305, 307: 'No abuse, Hal, o' mine honour'). The device of repetition may owe something to this scene, though it should be noticed that Falstaff's insults belonged to the past and not to the present. However, at the climax of Congreve's exchange it is another scene in Shakespeare that is recalled:

> HORATIO. These are but wild and whirling words, my lord.
>
> HAMLET. I am sorry they offend you, heartily; Yes, 'faith, heartily.
>
> HORATIO. There's no offence, my lord.
>
> HAMLET. Yes, by Saint Patrick, but there is, Horatio, And much offence too.

The echo is surely one of which Congreve was conscious and also one which he expected his audience to recognize. (*Hamlet* was in the repertory, Betterton, who played Fainall in Congreve's comedy, acting the Prince.) The humour lies in the incongruity between the two speakers and between the two senses in which they use the phrase (for the 'offence' that Hamlet means is his uncle's crime).

Nothing in the situations or the characterization of this

play recalls *Hamlet.* By contrast, throughout *The Double-Dealer,* Maskwell's behaviour owes a great deal to Iago's in *Othello,* a play which was evidently in the forefront of Congreve's mind when writing the scenes in which the villain persuades Lord Touchwood that his nephew Mellefont is trying to seduce Lady Touchwood. This preoccupation, presumably, threw up the incongruous allusions to *Othello* in the wholly comic scenes involving Sir Paul and Lady Plyant. One of Maskwell's early stratagems is to have Lady Plyant persuaded (by Lady Touchwood) that Mellefont loves her. This is done, and Lady Plyant (with her husband in tow) taxes Mellefont with dishonourable behaviour:

> LADY PLYANT. Have I behaved my self with all the decorum, and nicety, befitting the Person of Sir *Paul*'s wife? Have I preserv'd my Honour as it were in a Snow-House for this three year past? Have I been white and unsulli'd even by Sir *Paul* himself?
>
> SIR PAUL. Nay, she has been an impenetrable Wife, even to me, that's the truth on't.
>
> LADY PLYANT. Have I, I say, preserv'd my self, like a fair Sheet of Paper, for you to make a Blot upon—
>
> SIR PAUL. And she shall make a Simile with any Woman in *England.* (II.i.252-62)

It is not Lady Plyant's role to make similes (the literary set, in this play, consists of the Froths and Brisk), so Sir Paul's admiring comment draws attention to the feeble one she makes here, and hence to the strong Shakespearean metaphor behind it:

> Was this fair paper, this most goodly book, Made to write 'whore' upon?

Congreve soon disentangles this misunderstanding—or, rather, leaves it to disentangle itself—and sets Mellefont's friend Careless in pursuit of the virtuous lady. When Careless's love-letter accidentally falls into Sir Paul's hands, it is Sir Paul's turn to make similes; he exclaims, in soliloquy: 'O my Lady *Plyant,* you were Chaste as Ice, but you are melted now, and false as Water' (IV.i.430-I). Here the echoes of *Hamlet* and *Othello* are not stressed, and though both come from well-known dialogues it would be a quick-minded spectator who would identify them. Congreve seems to have employed them passingly, perhaps instinctively, to exaggerate Sir Paul's passion. Earlier in the same soliloquy he also draws on Shakespeare, this time in *Love's Labour's Lost,* evidently without allusive intent, when Sir Paul is apostrophizing Careless: 'Die and be Damn'd for a *Judas Maccabeus,* and *Iscariot* both.' Here Shakespeare's humorous association of the two Judases is borrowed simply to give a comic heightening. Similarly, Lady Plyant, having already realized that she gave her husband the wrong letter, is made to express her alarm in an idiom of unconscious sexual suggestion derived from Juliet's Nurse: 'I'm all over in a Universal Agitation, I dare swear every Circumstance of me trembles' (IV.i.397-8). As these borrowings show, Congreve's memory was a reservoir of Shakespearean dialogue into which he could dip easily: how easily can be seen from a single speech of Brisk's when he and Lady Froth are anatomizing their social acquaintances:

> I know whom you mean—But Deuce take me,
> I can't hit of her Name neither—Paints de'e say?
> Why she lays it on with a Trowel—Then she has
> a great Beard that bristles through it, and makes
> her look as if she were plaistred with Lime and
> Hair, let me perish.
>
>   (III.i. 583-7)

Here we have Hamlet addressing Yorick's skull ('let her paint an inch thick'), Celia ironically applauding Touchstone's cliché about the destinies, Sir Hugh Evans voicing his misgivings about the fat woman of Brentford, and Theseus commending Snout's performance as Wall. There is, of course, no compulsion to ascribe all or any of these phrases to Shakespearean reminiscence, but, in view of Congreve's demonstrable habit of mind elsewhere, such reminiscence seems highly possible. The following dialogue between Maskwell and Lady Touchwood, for instance, must derive from *2 Henry IV:*

> MASKWELL. You have already been tampering
> with my Lady *Plyant?*
>
> LADY TOUCHWOOD. I have: She is ready for any
> Impression I think fit. (I.i.406-9)

Lady Touchwood's metaphor, of softening wax in order to set one's seal on it, depends on a transitive sense of the verb 'tamper', but the verb is used intrasitively in Maskwell's question. Behind the passage lies Falstaff's plan announced when Bardolph tells him that the army is disbanded after the Gaultree Forest campaign:

> Let them go. I'll through Gloucestershire, and
> there will I visit Master Robert Shallow, Esquire. I have him already temp'ring between my
> finger and my thumb, and shortly will I seal with
> him. Come away.
>
>   (*2 Henry IV,* IV.iii. 125-30)

This is an interesting example of Congreve's indebtedness: apart from the one word 'tampering' ('temp'ring') there is no verbal similarity whatever between the passages, and yet the conclusion seems irresistible, because of Congreve's inconsistent use of this word, that he derived his metaphor from Shakespeare.

Sometimes the Shakespearean reminiscence is a matter of Congreve's retaining a single phrase while transposing the remainder into the idiom of his own times. Thus Bottom's unforgettable 'I have a reasonable good ear in music. Let's have the tongs and the bones' (*Midsummer Night's Dream,* IV.i. 26-7) begets Jeremy's reply to Sir Sampson's indignant question (he does not think a servant is entitled to any tastes, literal or metaphorical) 'and Musick, don't you love Musick, Scoundrell?':

> Yes, I have a reasonable good Ear, Sir, as to
> Jiggs and Country Dances; and the like; I don't
> much matter your *Sola*'s or *Sonata*'s, they give
> me the Spleen.
>
>   (*Love for Love,* II. i. 371-5)

More usually, however, Congreve's Shakespeareanisms are fleeting phrases which bring little if anything of their

original contexts with them. In *The Old Batchelour,* Sir Joseph Wittol repeats Pistol's error of 'Canibal' for 'Hannibal', and in the next speech but one Captain Bluffe repeats Dogberry's 'Comparisons are odorous'. Later, Bluffe makes a Pistolian use of the verb 'ensue'; Heartfree, in love with Silvia against his better knowledge, gloomily foresees himself 'Chronicled in Ditty, and sung in woful Ballad'. and when, near the end of the play, he reacts violently to a taunt of Belinda's, she declares that she has 'only touch'd a gall'd-beast till he winch'd'. In *The Double-Dealer* Mellefont, setting his friend Careless to keep Lady Plyant out of the scheming Lady Touchwood's way, declares 'I'le observe my Uncle my self'; Maskwell, disingenuously letting Mellefont into his intrigue to get him disinherited, says 'I am to turn you a grazing'; and Lord Touchwood, resolving to disinherit him, exclaims 'Death I'll have him stripp'd and turn'd naked out of my house this moment, and let him rot and perish, incestuous Brute'. In *Love for Love* Valentine is reported by Jeremy, as is Hamlet by the Gravedigger, to be 'mad for want of his wits'; Buckram the lawyer is said by Valentine, as is Cassius by Brutus, to have in 'itching Palm'; and Valentine (still in his pretended madness) addresses his father as 'Old Truepenny'. In *The Way of the World,* Fainall (with a materialistic sense alien to Shakespeare's use of the phrase) talks of wearing his horns 'tipt with Gold', and Waitwell as Sir Rowland, pretending to recognize the handwriting of Mrs Marwood's letter as Mirabell's, declares:

> The Rascal writes a sort of a large hand; your
> *Roman* hand—I saw there was a throat to be cut
> presently. If he were my Son as he is my Nephew
> I'd Pistoll him.

This sort of reminiscence is not confined to Shakespeare. Cowley ('Nay the *mute Fish* witness no less his praise') may be behind Sir Sampson's command to Ben ('To your Element, Fish, be mute, Fish, and to Sea'); Bunyan behind Ben's 'For to speak one thing, and to think just the contrary way; is as it were, to look one way, and to row another'; Marston (unless there is some intervening reference which has not been traced) behind Petulant's 'Carry your Mistress's Monkey a spider'. Mirabell's famous metaphor on Millamant's arrival—'Here she comes i'faith full sail, with her Fan spread and her Streamers out, and a shoal of Fools for Tenders'—seems to be Congreve's heightening of Dryden's metaphor on Jacintha by conflating it with Milton's on Dalila; Dryden's *Mac Flecknoe* is echoed in Foresight's abuse of Sir Sampson the traveller ('*Ferdinand Mendez Pinto* was but a Type of thee, thou Lyar of the first Magnitude'). Echoes of Jonson are too numerous to be listed here, but a couple may be mentioned: Lady Plyant's complaisant response to Sir Paul's grovelling request to kiss her hand ('My Lip indeed, Sir *Paul,* I swear you shall'), and (one reminiscence leading to another) Sir Paul's urging of Cynthia to transmit the Plyant family features to her offspring ('our House is distinguish'd by a Languishing Eye, as the House of *Austria* is by a thick Lip').

But it is Shakespeare who most frequently comes to Congreve's mind as he writes, and to ours as we read. In *The Way of the World* Petulant talks of throat-cutting in

Nym's laconic vein, in *Love for Love,* Sir Sampson's back-slapping salutations to Foresight as 'old *Ptolomee*', 'old *Nostrodamus*', 'old *Merlin*', and so on, are in the exuberant style of the Host of the Garter Inn. As Brian Gibbons points out [in his edition of *The Way of the World*], 'the marvellously particular and complete identities of the comic characters [in *The Way of the World*] owe much to Shakespeare's example'; he traces aspects of Lady Wishfort to Juliet's Nurse and to Falstaff, and of the revelling Sir Wilfull Witwoud to Sir Toby Belch. One of Sir Wilfull's drunken protestations, to Millamant, 'If I drunk your Health to day, Cozen—I am a *Borachio*', is Shakespearean in the spirit as well as in the letter. It not only carries an (unconscious?) echo of Falstaff's 'I am a rogue if I drunk today', but also allows us a Shakespearean glimpse into Sir Wilfull's fuddled brain as he triumphantly produces the newly learned term of abuse that his aunt has just bestowed on him.

In his tragi-comedy *The Mourning Bride* Congreve again turns towards Shakespeare, not in the characterization—all these figures breathe only the rarefied air of heroic drama—but in the language. The language is, of course, prevailingly as 'heroic' as the characterization, thus making the Shakespearean echoes, when they occur, the more obvious. *Romeo and Juliet,* as Shakespeare's tragedy of young lovers, is the play on which Congreve chiefly draws. In the second act Almeria's situation, betrothed to Garcia against her will, is so similar to Juliet's, betrothed against her will to Paris, that she naturally applies Juliet's macabre imagery to it:

> Or wind me in the Shroud of some pale Coarse
> Yet green in Earth, rather than be the Bride
> Of *Garcia*'s more detested Bed.

When the action presently shifts to the burial vault, *Romeo and Juliet* continues to furnish imagery and diction. Almeria's attendant says:

> the Iron Grates that lead to Death
> Beneath, are still wide stretch'd upon their
>   Hinge,
> And staring on us with unfolded Leaves.

And Almeria replies:

> Sure, 'tis the Friendly Yawn of Death for
>   me. . . .
>
> Death, grim Death, will fold
> Me in his leaden Arms, and press me close
> To his cold clayie Breast.

However, when Almeria apostrophizes her love Alphonso (whom she supposes lost at sea) and Osmyn ascends from the tomb with the line 'Who calls that wretched thing, that was *Alphonso?*', the seeming apparition of a ghost suggests a different Shakespearean tragedy. Almeria exclaims: 'Angels, and all the Host of heaven support me!' and urges her confidante to 'speak to it quickly, quickly'. Osmyn makes a speech identifying himself, for our information, as Alphonso, and rejoicing that Almeria herself is not a ghost but a living woman: 'It is *Almeria*, 'tis, it is my Wife!' After some time, *Romeo and Juliet* re-surfaces with Osmyn-Alphonso's 'inauspicious Stars', and, Congreve now being again tuned in to Shakespeare's wavelength, Zara shortly demands 'Haste me to know it' and immediately afterwards exclaims: 'O Heav'n! my Fears interpret / This thy Silence'. Zara is the Moorish queen, in whose army the disguised Alphonso has taken service, and whose unreturned passion for him provides most of the play's strongest moments. Meanwhile, Alphonso, languishing in prison, foresees his desperate gestures when Almeria shall marry Garcia; his speech owes something to Romeo's passion over the banishment which will prevent his consummating his marriage to Juliet:

> Then will I . . .
> Break on the flinty Ground my throbbing
>   Breast,
> And grovel with gash'd Hands to scratch a
>   Grave.

It is the non-consummation of his own marriage to Almeria that has just been Alphonso's theme. This scene is shared by Almeria; and Zara, discovering the lovers together, exclaims: 'Perdition catch 'em both, and Ruine part 'em'.

Towards the end of the play, poison becomes a prominent vehicle of the intrigue, and *Romeo and Juliet* resumes its prominence as a source of imagery and diction. Zara, killing herself with one of the two bowls of poison which she intended to share with Alphonso, cries: 'This, to our mutual Bliss when joyn'd above', and then: 'O friendly Draught, already in my Heart!' Almeria, in her turn, believing that the headless body before her (actually her villainous father's, in Alphonso's disguise) is her husband's, decides to take the poison but finds the first bowl empty and cries

> O noble Thirst! and yet too greedy to
> Drink all—O for another Draught of Death.

Besides these reminiscences which are prompted more or less directly by the situations, there are possibly others. When Zara (intending thereby to save Alphonso's life) proposes to substitute a private strangling for a public execution, the King's favourite Gonsalez shrewdly remarks:

> Methinks this Lady's Hatred to the *Moor*
> Disquiets her too much.

Later, having through a misfiring stratagem killed the King with his own hand, Gonsalez apostrophizes himself in terms very like Hamlet's to Polonius: 'O Wretch! O curs'd, and rash, deluded Fool!' Another verbal reminiscence is, unexpectedly, of *2 Henry VI,* one of the less familiar of Shakespeare's plays: 'Confusion, all is on the Rout!' Possibly (as perhaps in the case of the resemblance to Marston's *Malcontent* noted above) some other writer's borrowing of the phrase intervened; however, the scene (in which Young Clifford finds his father dead on the battlefield) contains some of the most memorable verse of the play, and so Congreve may have remembered it for himself.

His favourite plays, it would seem, were what one would expect: for tragedy, *Romeo and Juliet, Julius Caesar, Hamlet* and *Othello;* and for comedy, *Love's Labour's Lost, A Midsummer Night's Dream, Much Ado about Nothing, As You Like It, Twelfth Night, The Merry Wives of Windsor* and the Falstaff scenes of the English histories. Not all of these held the stage in Congreve's time, and it is notable that when Congreve uses allusion allusively it is with reference to those plays—*Hamlet* and *Othello*—which were secure in the theatre. He was himself evidently a reader of Shakespeare. This is further borne out by the handful of Shakespearean allusions in his surviving letters. 'Of my philosophy I make some use' he writes in 1704 (to Joseph Keally), referring to his lack of an official appointment: the metrical word order shows that he is adapting Cassius. In another letter of the same year to the same correspondent he follows a couple of Falstaffian reminiscences with a distorted and witty one of Othello:

> I am grown fat; but you know I was born with somewhat a round belly. I find you are resolved to be a man of this world, which I am sorry for, because it will deprive me of you. However, think of me, as I am nothing extenuate.

Finally (again writing to Keally) he applies a quotation from *The Merry Wives of Windsor* to their fat friend Robert Fitzgerald's proposed Irish voyage:

> Robin talks of going every day. I would have him stay till the weather is a little settled; for if he should be cast away, you know your water swells a man; and what a thing were he if he were swelled?

Both these last quotations illustrate Congreve's thorough familiarity with Shakespearean idiom. In the new sense which he gives to the line from *Othello,* he uses 'nothing' with the Elizabethan meaning 'not at all'; and in quoting Falstaff from memory he substitutes for 'the water' the idiomatic 'your water'—possibly because of yet another spontaneous recollection, this time of the Gravedigger in *Hamlet.* (pp. 186-95)

> *T. W. Craik, "Congreve as a Shakespearean," in* Poetry and Drama, 1570-1700: Essays in Honour of Harold F. Brooks, *edited by Antony Coleman and Antony Hammond, Methuen, 1981, pp. 186-99.*

Paul Salzman   (essay date 1985)

[*Salzman is an Australian educator and the author of several works on English prose fiction. In the excerpt below, he investigates the mixture of influences found in Congreve's novel* Incognita.]

Some time after the Restoration there were important changes in the nature of prose fiction. These changes are not a product of the 1660s—a period . . . during which the antiromance, the picaresque novel, and the last of the long heroic romances, all jostled for attention. The large influx of translations from the French, which critics have seen as exerting an important influence on these changes, reached their peak during the 1680s. But the translations cannot be held entirely responsible for a form which also draws on the native tradition, especially on the English approach to drama.

The most important movement during the period from around 1670 to the end of the century was the replacement

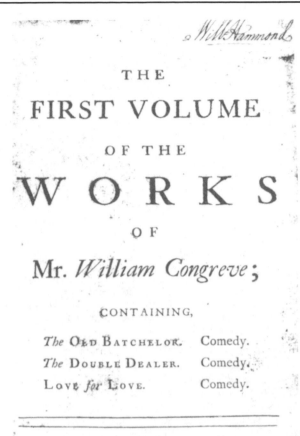

Title page of the first volume of the 1710 edition of Congreve's Works.

of the long romance by the short novella, a change reflected in the use of the word 'novel' on numerous title-pages. This change culminated in Congreve's famous distinction in the preface to ***Incognita*** (1692) between romances and novels, which 'are of a more familiar nature'. (p. 308)

When Congreve wrote ***Incognita,*** he decided to 'imitate Dramatick Writing . . . in the Design, Contexture and Result of the Plot'. . . . [But] he was not as original in this as he claimed to be. Even more important is the fact that he chose to ignore a good many of the new techniques of the Restoration novel. . . . While he shares (and surpasses) Oldys's use of a witty, self-conscious narrator, he does not set his novel in the milieu of the Restoration comedy. Instead, he uses the novella plot, with its surprising turns and contrivances—its attention to action—in a novella setting: a rather stock Italy. Nor is he interested in the tragedy attempted by Behn, or even the tragicomedy of *Clitie.*

Congreve was attracted by the poise a man of true wit might achieve through the use of a witty, detached, but indulgent narrator, who recounts a cleverly contrived story. It is the 'Unity of Contrivance' which Congreve wishes the reader to recognize and admire—so he tells us in the preface. The precedents for this approach have recently been pointed out by Helga Drougge [in her *The Significance of Congreve's* **"Incognita,"** 1976]; the translations (virtually adaptations) of Spanish novellas by Scarron were popular examples, and Congreve owned two editions of *Le Roman Comique* (1655 and 1695). Scarron's 'novels' play a prominent part in **The Old Batchelour** (1693, first draft 1689?), when Bellmour carries a copy instead of a prayerbook during his masquerade as Spintext. Fondlewife discovers the deception, significantly lighting upon 'The Innocent Adultery' when he opens the book (IV.iv.107). Scarron presents the Spanish novellas through the voice of a narrator who is less subtle than Congreve's, but who does comment ironically on the story:

> A Gentleman of *Granada,* whose true name I shall forbear to discover, and on whom I will bestow that of *Don Pedro* of *Casteel, Aragon,* and *Toledo,* or what you please, since that a glorious name in a *Romance* costs no more than another, (which is haply the reason that the *Spaniards,* not content with their own, ever give themselves of the most illustrious . . .

The use of the ironic, detached narrator occurs in various other novels of this period. Charles Mish aptly describes this narrative technique as 'more sophisticated than any other of its period', and two brief, well-written examples, Joseph Kepple's *The Maiden-Head Lost by Moonlight* (1672) and Walter Charleton's *The Cimmerian Matron* (1668), may be examined in Mish's anthology of Restoration fiction. These stories are both, like the novels of Scarron, based on translations (in this case, both from Erycius Puteanus). Using a witty narrator to add spice to an otherwise cliché-ridden story is relatively easy; and such a narrator's comments may mock the devices used by a novelist like Aphra Behn to achieve verisimilitude. This broad type of parody is evident in the style of René Le Pays's *The Drudge* (1673):

> A Cousin of *Zelotide*'s, we called her *Cleonice* in the beginning of this History, was to marry one of her sisters (but truly, Sir, I could never learn what they called her, though I used all possible means to find it out) to a very near kinsman of *Cephisa*'s (but faith, I cannot tell who he was neither).

Such parody may, however, in skilful hands become a device which brings the reader closer to the story. Mish notes the tiny 'novels' written by Peter Motteux for *The Gentleman's Journal* (1692-4), where 'We seem to be listening to an urbane, slightly cynical, and knowing gentleman telling a story to equally urbane listeners.'

It is instructive to remember the much earlier use of a sophisticated narrator commenting on a love story in Gascoigne's *The Adventures of Master F.J.* Of course Gascoigne's work was not reprinted in the seventeenth century, but readers had access to at least half of Sidney's *Old Arcadia,* in the composite version available throughout the century. Sidney's narrator is never as consistently ironic as a Restoration narrator, but he is often digressive, and may at times display a detached humour. However, this humour is not so apparent if one does not read the complete *Old Arcadia,* where the narrator is most obtrusive in the first three books.

While Congreve has many precedents for his use of an ironic narrator, he also has a number of choices to make. Detachment and parody, or the intimacy of, for example, John Dunton's rambler-narrator in *A Voyage Round the World,* which appeared a year before **Incognita**? **Incognita** is neither cynical and completely detached, nor is it overly confidential and formless in the manner of Dunton. Critics attempting to define Congreve's tone have tended to make a firm choice, while **Incognita** is in fact located somewhere between the relatively straight-faced narrative described by Aubrey Williams [in "Congreve's **Incognita** and the Contrivances of Providence", *Imagined Worlds,* edited by M. Mack, 1968] and I. M. Westcott [in "The Role of the Narrator in Congreve's **Incognita,**" *Trivium* 11 (1976): 40-8], and the bewilderingly parodic narrative described by Helga Drougge. While allowing for much more authorial detachment than Westcott does, the following analysis begins from her premiss that 'The effect [of the narrative] is a union of moral seriousness and delicate raillery.'

Incognita is a very tightly-plotted novella—a popular form, as the editions of Scarron and other collections indicate. Aphra Behn's *The Lucky Mistake* (1689) is a good example, in which she avoids, for a change, the darker tragic story. In *The Lucky Mistake,* as in **Incognita,** two couples pass through a series of obstacles before they are able to marry happily and according to their choice: 'all thought themselves happy in this double Union.' **Incognita** presents just such a story, told in a manner that allows us to enjoy its twists and turns, while the narrator also entertains us with comments which recognize just how conventional many of the events are. This is not to say that Congreve asks us to see his story as a complete parody. We should heed his prefatory remarks:

> The design of the Novel is obvious, after the first meeting of Aurelian and Hippolito with Incognita and Leonora, and the difficulty is in bringing it to pass, maugre all apparent obstacles, within the compass of two days.

We know, when we go to see a Restoration comedy, that, for example, Mirabel and Millamant will ultimately marry—the question is, how will the expected end be achieved?

The careful coincidences, the 'design' and 'contrivances' of the plot, have been discussed at length by Aubrey Williams. But to see these as the work of Providence, 'justifications of the ways of God to Man', is to take an over-symbolic and heavy-handed approach, especially as this argument could be applied to any such tightly constructed dramatic plot. Any carefully-plotted novel lures the reader on, anxious to see how the clever manipulation can be kept up, how the puzzle will be solved, the pattern clarified. At the same time, the narrator of **Incognita** also holds us back—at least until the very end. If we share the narrator's sophistication, we may smile at our own impatience:

> Now the Reader I suppose to be upon Thorns at this and the like impertinent Digressions, but let

him alone and he'll come to himself; at which time I think fit to acquaint him, that when I digress, I am at that time writing to please my self, when I continue the Thread of the Story, I write to please him; supposing him a reasonable Man, I conclude him satisfied to allow me this liberty, and so I proceed.

By addressing the 'Reader' in the third person, the narrator allows us to take up his sophisticated position: we are invited to 'let him alone', that is, to let the more naive reader alone. With this preparation, the reader who cavils at a later date will receive short shrift:

> I could find in my Heart to beg the Reader's Pardon for this Digression, if I thought he would be sensible of the Civility; for I promise him, I do not intend to do it again throughout the Story, though I make never so many, and though he take them never so ill.

However, the narrator is not completely impervious to the allure of the plot (and so we may assume that the reader too is expected to share his balance of detachment and concern). When the plot is 'wound up' with the arrival of Don Mario, his daughter Leonora, and her lover Hippolito at Aurelian's lodgings, where Aurelian will discover that Incognita is none other than his destined bride Juliana, the style becomes much less poised than before. The two penultimate paragraphs contain a number of long and quite breathless sentences (one of 144 words). The action is very rapid (perhaps a parallel to the speeded-up action of the last act of *The Way of the World*) and, most significantly, the narrator's comments are absent. Having ensured that we are not too involved, the narrator allows us to enjoy the excitement of the denouement.

The poise of the narrator is most important in relation to sentiment, and to our attitude towards the characters and their situation. Congreve is not writing an anti-romance; he is not consistently parodying the conventions of love. On the other hand, he recognizes how conventional they are. The vision is that of an older, wiser man, regarding the antics of young lovers with wry indulgence. Some of their actions are amusing, but they are also touching. The poise is there from the opening paragraph describing Aurelian's relationship with his father:

> Aurelian was the only Son to a Principal Gentleman of Florence. The Indulgence of his Father prompted, and his Wealth enabled him, to bestow a generous Education upon him, whom, he now began to look upon as the Type of himself; an Impression he had made in the Gayety and Vigour of his Youth, before the Rust of Age had debilitated and obscur'd the Splendour of the Original: He was sensible, That he ought not to be sparing in the Adornment of him, if he had a Resolution to beautifie his own Memory. Indeed Don Fabio (for so was the Old Gentleman call'd) has been observ'd to have fix'd his Eyes upon Aurelian, when much Company has been at Table, and have wept through Earnestness of Intention, if nothing hapened to divert the Object; whether it were for regret, at the recollection of his former self, or for the Joy he conceiv'd in being, as it were, reviv'd in the Person of his

Son, I never took upon me to enquire, but suppos'd it might be sometimes one, and sometimes both together.

This is an urbane view: a paradigm of the narrator's, and the responsive reader's, over-all position. Don Fabio's emotions are a mixture of egoism and genuine involvement, while the humorous 'Rust of Age' holds him away from us, in a faintly amusing pose.

Aurelian and Hippolito are more sympathetic than the older generation, but they have the foibles of youth. They are attractive, but we must not take them too seriously—a point made by our wry introduction to Aurelian: 'Aurelian, at the Age of Eighteen Years, wanted nothing (but a Beard) that the most accomplished Cavalier in Florence could pretend to'. The two friends exist in a sophisticated narrative. The Florentine 'love of Musick' may have been taken from a travel book, but this detail turns to mockery of the conventional serenade:

> Here you should have an affected Vallet, who Mimick'd the Behaviour of his Master, leaning carelessly against the Window, with his Head on one side, in a languishing Posture, whining, in a low, mournful Voice, some dismal Complaint . . .

Incognita is a novel conscious that it relies on novella conventions, and able to smile at them. If Aurelian and Hippolito posture in this way, they are gently mocked. So Hippolito gives rise to a smile when he is prevented from 'Rhyming' when he sees Leonora, thereby saving us from 'a small desert of Numbers to have pick'd and Criticiz'd upon'.

Aurelian's first meeting with Incognita at a grand Masque establishes our interest in him, as well as our amusement. It is here that Congreve's style becomes vital. He already displays the light touch, the flexible elegance, which is a feature of his comedies. James Sutherland [in his *English Literature of the Late Seventeenth Century*, 1969] aptly describes this as 'a cooler and more consciously sophisticated affectation in the manner.' We find it, although at a less mature stage, in the conversation between Aurelian and Incognita, which is a most delicate exchange of compliments. They discuss the relationship between dress and character, Incognita astutely noting:

> there is your brisk fool as well as your brisk man of sense, and so of the melancholick. I confess 'tis possible a fool may reveal himself by his Dress . . . but a decency of Habit (which is all that Men of best sense pretend to) may be acquired by custom and example . . .

Aurelian shows a ready, endearing wit: ' "Look ye there" (says he), pointing to a Lady who stood playing with the Tassels of her Girdle, "I dare answer for that Lady, though she be very well dress'd, 'tis more than she knows" '. Aurelian's compliments almost go too far: 'Aurelian had a little over-strain'd himself in that Complement, and I am of Opinion would have been puzzl'd to have brought himself off readily'. The facility of Congreve's style has lent this conversation a charm which moves the reader in Aurelian's favour.

From this point on, we share the narrator's mixture of amusement and affection. He will not become enamoured, as Aurelian has:

> I should by right now describe her Dress, which was extreamly agreeable and rich, but 'tis possible I might err in some material Pin or other, in the sticking of which may be the whole grace of the Drapery depended.

However, the truth of Aurelian's love is also emphasized:

> our Friend Aurelian had by this time danced himself into a Net which he neither could, nor which is worse desired to untangle.

> His soul was charm'd to the movement of her Body . . .

This is a love affair which begins with a deception. The careful plot turns on such deceptions: Aurelian and Hippolito pretend to be each other after Hippolito has donned Lorenzo's costume to attend the Masque; Juliana maintains her disguise as Incognita. But a sense of the plot as a game predominates—at the end 'it was the Subject of a great deal of Mirth to hear Juliana relate the several Contrivances which she had to avoid Aurelian for the sake of Hippolito'. 'The design of the Novel is obvious'; so the basic emotional situation is serious: 'Aurelian, who was *really* in Love'. Upon this serious base, the game is played, the narrator's wit displayed.

When Aurelian is allowed to see Incognita's face:

> Aurelian (from whom I had every tittle of her Description) fancy'd he saw a little Nest of Cupids break from the Tresses of her Hair, and every one officiously betake himself to his task. Some fann'd with their downy Wings, her glowing Cheeks; while others brush'd the balmy Dew from off her Face, leaving alone a heavenly Moisture blubbing on her Lips, on which they drank and revell'd for their pains; Nay, so particular were their allotments in her service, that Aurelian was very positive a young Cupid who was but just Pen-feather'd, employ'd his naked Quills to pick her Teeth. And a thousand other things his transport represented to him, which none but Lovers who have experience of such Visions will believe.

The smiling asseveration of fact leads to Aurelian's vision. It does have a certain charm, but the narrator's voice, still smiling, intrudes: 'fancy'd', 'blubbing', the cupid picking her teeth. This is Aurelian's 'transport', from which he 'awaked'—it is neither rejected nor embraced by the narrator, but simply put in context. It is important for us to believe in Aurelian's love, but also to see its youthful, amusing extravagance. For this extravagance leads to the contrivances of the plot, by impelling all the lovers to keep up their several disguises.

The same attitude prevails when the two friends discuss the state of being in love, after Hippolito almost kills Aurelian by mistake in the dark. Hippolito

> passionately taking Aurelian by the Hand, cry'd, Ah! my Friend, Love is indeed blind, when it would not suffer me to see you—There arose an-

other Sigh; a Sympathy seiz'd Aurelian immediately: (For, by the Way, Sighing is as catching among Lovers, as yawning among the Vulgar.) Beside hearing the Name of Love, made him fetch such a Sigh, that Hippolito's were but Flyblows in Comparison . . .

When Hippolito pens a perfect, elegant love-letter to Leonora, Leonora's doubts about falling in love with a man intended for Juliana (Hippolito is, of course, pretending to be Aurelian) are quickly overcome, leading to a series of speculations by the narrator:

> I could never get any Body to give me a satisfactory reason, for her suddain and dextrous Change of Opinion just at that stop, which made me conclude she could not help it.

Possible dissatisfaction with the convention by which Leonora's heart is conquered is adroitly turned aside by a piece of witty comment which, for once, does border on cynicism:

> I would not have the Reader now be impertinent, and look upon this to be force, or a whim of the Author's, that a Woman should proceed so far in her Approbation of a Man whom she never saw, that it is impossible, therefore ridiculous to suppose it. Let me tell such a Critick, that he knows nothing of the Sex, if he does not know that a Woman may be taken with the Character and Description of a Man, when general and extraordinary, that she may be prepossess'd with an agreeable Idea of his Person and Conversation; and though she cannot imagine his real Features, or manner of Wit, yet she has a general Notion of what is call'd a fine Gentleman, and is prepar'd to like such a one who does not disagree with that Character.

This is virtually the only example of such cynicism (closer to the tone of Motteux). If the modern reader regrets that Congreve did not follow the example of the vivid Restoration setting seen in the work of Behn and Oldys, he must also recognize that the sophisticated tone of *Incognita* depends upon the tension between the novella form and the narrator's voice.

Incognita's design produces the effect of watching a play. The theatre is perhaps the best vehicle for this balance between involvement and detachment—Congreve wrote no more novels. There are times when a delicate touch by the narrator pulls the reader back into the story, at least as much as it raises an eyebrow at the actors. For example, at the end of the scene with Leonora, 'several Ladies of her acquaintance came to accompany her to the place design'd for the Tilting, where we will leave them drinking Chocolate till 'tis time for them to go'. Here we have a sudden, though still humorous, glimpse of an ongoing reality. On the other hand, after a passionate speech from Aurelian, the narrator 'places' him with a much more broadly humorous image: Aurelian 'stood mute and insensible like an Alarum Clock, that had spent all its force in one violent Emotion'.

As noted above, the narrator does withdraw from the last hurried pages, as the denouement takes over. But the final paragraph leaves us with another recognition of the pleasing artifice which has been so aware of its own construction:

> they all thought it proper to attend upon the
> Great Duke that Morning at the Palace, and to
> acquaint him with the Novelty of what had
> pass'd; while, by the way, the two Young Couple
> entertained the Company with the Relation of
> several Particulars of their Three Days Adventures.

We are pleased by the neat plot, but also by the happiness of 'Our Two Cavalier-Lovers'. The balance has not yet attained the maturity of Congreve's major plays, with their serious purpose, aptly described by Maximillian Novak [in "Love, Scandal, and the Moral Milieu of Congreve's Comedies," in *Congreve Considered*, edited by H. T. Swedenberg, 1971]: 'Congreve's vision is his suggestion of the possibility of genuine love and a good marriage between a few convincingly sensitive and witty couples in a world of fools and knaves.' *Incognita* balances the sophisticated man's detachment with the appeal of a naïve but true love; the appeal of a pattern with the knowledge of its artificiality. At one point, Hippolito is characterized as having 'a Heart full of Love, and a Head full of Stratagem'; this is a most appropriate description of *Incognita* itself. (pp. 328-37)

Paul Salzman, "The Restoration Novel," in his English Prose Fiction, 1558-1700: A Critical History, *Oxford at the Clarendon Press, 1985, pp. 308-37.*

William Congreve (1670-1729). Portrait by Sir Godfrey Kneller.

Richard W. F. Kroll (essay date 1986)

[*In the following essay, Kroll discusses the dynamics of Congreve's* The Way of the World *in terms of three main realms of discourse: natural, social, and legal. He asserts that the function of the characters in the play is to explore the human desire to possesss and comprehend these various levels of interpretation, and simultaneously to attack those who cannot go beyond the level of natural discourse to the detriment of social interaction.*]

Congreve's **The Way of the World** has been regarded as a protosentimental comedy, written partly in response to Collier's attack on its author. Such an assumption receives support from the popularity of the play on the late eighteenth-century stage, despite a disappointing opening in 1700. But I think that we can only accurately call the play sentimental if by that vague term we intend a more essentialist view of character than we find in Wycherley or Etherege. In the portrayal of Dorimant in *The Man of Mode,* the unresolved and morally honest ambivalences of Etherege's ending depend in part on our ignorance of Dorimant's true character or motives; and given his actions through the play, we cannot reasonably prognosticate a satisfactory country retirement. By contrasting Mirabell with Dorimant or Horner, we might feel reasonably safe in predicting how Mirabell will behave in future, because he does not present us with the same conundrum as his older cousins.

Nevertheless, as in **Love for Love,** Congreve is scrupulously unsentimental about the hermeneutical problems of discovering and judging character and motive, and Maximillian E. Novak has recently argued [in "Foresight in the Stars and Scandal in London: Reading the Hieroglyphs in Congreve's **Love for Love,**" *From Renaissance to Restoration,* edited by Lauree Finke and Robert Markley, 1984] that the figure of the hieroglyph in the earlier play portends such difficulties. Moreover, Congreve unhesitatingly confronts the implied political reality that, in the process of sifting through and among the modes of discourse that constitute our social and natural lives, we can never escape from the relations of power in which we are inevitably entangled. Memory and language are the necessary conditions of our social and historical being. Only at the cost of denying our historical condition and finitude can we create fictions of autonomy that appear to free us from social and natural anxiety, that is, the fear of others and the fear of death. It follows, too, that we must obliterate memory and discourse (an impossibility) if we are to escape mortality and purge ourselves of social, legal, and matrimonial obligations. Part of Congreve's intention, indeed, is to force home the impossibility or stupidity of suppressing memory or language in the hope of attaining such autonomy. Only if we cultivate and maintain a studied consciousness can we achieve a kind of relative freedom, while the inescapable nature of memory (both individual and social) and the necessity of discourse always threaten to invade that contingent and hard-won liberty, because they remind us of our mortality and our irrevocably social condition. Our mortality dissipates our fictions of unsullied youth (fictions of "natural" freedom), and our social condition constrains our fictions of social autonomy and political freedom (fictions of "artificial" freedom).

Since Descartes's *Les Passions de l'Ame* (1649), a consciousness of our natural powers was commonly parsed in terms of a discourse of the passions; and, since a knowledge of our social powers requires the apt manipulation of ordinary language, and legal and political discourse, **The Way of the World** is as much a play about reading as anything else. The intelligence of the characters, their studied freedom, can be judged, it is true, according to the rather vague formulas of "wit," but this must entail more than setting off the truewits and witwouds in some tabulated scheme. The characters' manipulation of language—as in all neoclassical discourse—represents their ability to perceive proper distinctions between and among objects and ideas: "wit" thus appears not only as a feature of discourse but as a judgment of discourse that signals apt judgments about the world and entails a proper view of language in relation to persons, things, events, and ideas. Moreover, the reader or spectator must engage in this world of judgment or discrimination because "character" is itself constituted as a feature of discourse. Character thus defines its will, its freedom as against other characters by virtue of manipulating language in distinctive fashion and of being understood—or read—in terms of that manipulation. The ability to understand and wield language, to discriminate among levels of discourse thus becomes an essential tool by which character can win the contingent freedom Congreve offers at the end of the play.

"Reading" assumed a peculiar urgency in the epistemological climate of the Restoration for writers who understood the complex of relations among history, memory, and language, disturbed and heightened by scepticism. Locke typified his age by admitting the sceptical crisis and yet proposing a contingent response in the form of probabilism. "Probability" became the criterion of judging signs, a means of containing the incipient anarchy of unmitigated scepticism. As Locke has it [in *An Essay Concerning Human Understanding*]:

> Upon these grounds depends the *Probability* of any Proposition: And as the conformity of our Knowledge, as the certainty of Observations, as the frequency and constancy of Experience, and the number and credibility of Testimonies, do more or less agree, or disagree with it, so is any Proposition in itself, more or less probable.

To recognize the probabilist milieu in which Congreve worked is to defuse a pertinent debate between two noted Congreve scholars. Aubrey Williams [in his *An Approach to Congreve,* 1979] is right to remind our secular age of the deeply-held or deeply-forged Christian assumptions which pervaded the seventeenth century; but Williams's argument suffers from a number of historical and methodological weaknesses. First, he fails adequately to distinguish those theologies that were more anxious to read the workings of Providence into daily events than others. If McAdoo's and Shapiro's accounts of Anglicanism and broad church sentiment are to be trusted, the majority of orthodox Christians did not seem to suffer from the kind of anxiety that Williams must postulate for most, if not all, of Congreve's audience, particularly if, as he says, Dryden and Pope are "representative." Moreover, Williams tends to conflate aesthetic forms and providential ideas. M. H.

Abrams [in his *Natural Supernaturalism: Tradition and Revolution in Romantic Literature,* 1971] and Frank Kermode [in his *The Sense of an Ending: Studies in the Theory of Fiction,* 1968] have argued for metaphorical relationships between Christian tropes of history and literary form. While the Aristotelian sense of plot may always serve for the Christian reading of history, the Aristotelian *telos* does not necessarily argue for an explicit *eschaton,* as Williams desires.

Second, Williams's dualistic method posits a simple opposition between Epicureanism and Christianity. Not only, however, had Erasmus, Gassendi, Charleton, and others proposed and effected a marriage between Epicurean ethics and Christian dogma, but, more importantly, the methods that the neo-Epicurean canon made available to scientists are the very methods that theologians used to combat complete scepticism about the reliability of the Biblical text. Unwittingly, Williams himself provides examples of those common criteria of judgment, for the search for signs of God's Providence employs the same methods and criteria that men used in other fields of empirical enquiry. Williams cites, for example, Isaac Barrow's *Sermons Preached on Several Occasions,* in which Barrow lists seven "characteristic marks of God's hand." Barrow participates fully in the probabilist method, as these sermons suggest: we must induce God's invisible workings by constructing probable inferences from visible signs. Nor should we forget that Barrow was closely associated with Isaac Newton's early career at Cambridge. So there is good reason to support that, if Congreve were a perfectly orthodox Christian and had read Barrow, he might have been as much interested in the hermeneutical problems of discovering God's workings in the world as in the assertion that God does indeed effect history. Such an interest would make Congreve no less orthodox.

Novak, in his turn [in *Congreve,* 1971], has simplified matters in resisting Williams's thesis. For the notion that Congreve was a libertine only undercuts Williams's emphasis on Christianity if we presume that Congreve was an ethical libertine in the tradition of Théophile de Viau, a tradition which, according to Antoine Adam [in his *Les Libertons au XVII Siecle,* 1964], lost most of its force in 1623, when Viau was arrested. Although in his book Novak allows considerable distance between Viau's libertinism and libertine attitudes of the late seventeenth century, Adam distinguishes more clearly between three different kinds of seventeenth-century libertinism: "le libertinage scandaleux," epitomized by Theophile de Viau; "le libertinage érudit," epitomized in the circle whose mentor was Gassendi; and a vaguer "libertinage subtil et secret" which also characterized a small portion of late seventeenth-century libertine thought. I have argued elsewhere that the kinds of philosophic and reconstructive scepticism we find in Restoration England owe a great deal to Gassendi, who presided over the group which met at the Dupuys. Popkin, writing of these *libertins érudits* [in his *The History of Skepticism from Erasmus to Spinoza,* 1979], quotes a delightful letter describing one of the group's "débauches":

> M. Naudé, librarian of Cardinal Mazarin, intimate friend of M. Gassendy, as he is of mine, has

arranged for all three of us to go and sup and sleep in his home at Gentilly next Sunday, provided that it will be only the three of us, and that we will have a débauche; but God knows what a débauche! M. Naudé regularly drinks only water, and he has never tasted wine. M. Gassendy is so delicate that he would not dare drink it, and believes that his body would burn, if he drank it. This is why I can say of one and the other this verse of Ovid "He avoids wine, the teetotaller praises water without wine." As for me I can only throw powder on the writings of these great men. I drink very little, and nevertheless it will be a débauche, but a philosophical one, and perhaps something more. For all three of us, being cured of superstition and freed from the evils of scruples, which is the tyrant of consciences, we will perhaps go almost to the holy place. A year ago, I made this voyage to Gentilly with M. Naudé, I alone with him. There were no other witnesses, and there should not have been any. We spoke most freely about everything without scandalizing a soul.

We can not easily reach the conclusion that the circle was determinedly antireligious: of Naudé and Patin, Popkin writes, "it is impossible to determine" what their views were; "they may have been true libertins, or they may have been mild fideists, who stayed on the Catholic side out of fear of Protestant dogmatism." Although La Mothe Le Vayer was a total sceptic in regard to secular matters, he was a fideist in matters of faith, such that to doubt the word of God would be to deny God's grace. And Gassendi, we know, though a sceptic, contributed to the mitigated scepticism of the new scientific climate and was never impugned as irreligious. In fact, Isaac Barrow could well have read and understood Gassendi's method and integrated it into his scientific and theological procedures. In short, the contribution of *le libertinage érudit* to the texture of English thought and method after 1650, not least by its contributions to neo-Epicureanism, was probably immense (although difficult to establish by simple historical proofs). Thus, by a curious irony, both Novak's and Williams's positions in their debate seem to depend on a modern—and thus anachronistic—divorce between matters spiritual and secular, a divorce which Isaac Barrow's career, for one, resists.

To effect a rapproachment between Williams and Novak is to reemphasize that Congreve is indeed perfectly typical of his milieu. Both his last plays are about reading in the sense we have been considering. And in both, Congreve permits us to ground the mass of linguistic and semiological uncertainties in a privileged moment of natural action, a gesture, although more obviously and crudely in *Love for Love.* In that play, the world of uncertainties is resolved—at least temporarily—by the crucial moment in which Valentine's and Angelica's uncertainties about each other are dissolved by pure gesture: Valentine attempts to sign the deed relinquishing his claims in order to secure Angelica's happiness (as he believes); and Angelica seizes and "tears the paper," as Congreve's directions have it (*Love for Love,* 5.480-91). Although Williams may be right to propose an eschatological reading of this "judgment" scene, we must also admit a perfectly ordinary forensic concern with evidences. Pure action finally becomes the only trustworthy evidence of individual intentions, all the more so since we have already been prepared for these crucial gestures in act 5 by earlier ones in act 4. After hearing of Valentine's "madness," Angelica arrives to visit him: Scandal carefully scrutinizes her manner and recognizes (despite her assertions) that she is concerned, but she sees him "wink and smile" to Jeremy, and this alerts her to the ruse to entrap her (*Love for Love,* 4.36-47).

In *The Way of the World,* the distinctions among the relative levels of discourse with which we are confronted are not as simply resolved as in the earlier play, and much of its achievement derives from the greater complexity that results. The difficulty of discriminating among levels of discourse, and of discovering and interpreting natural and social signs is as much our problem as the characters', and the consequence is to involve us in the play's world of reading and force home the difficulty of creating a fiction of freedom lying outside, beyond, or above discourse itself. We ourselves must develop the kind of perspicacity that, in the appropriate characters, appears as wit. And, as I have intimated earlier, the constitution of character by his or her language (in that character, in a very real sense, is discourse) also shows us each character's consciousness of the prisonhouse of language and the necessity of using words intelligently. Such a view of representation assumes that knowledge of character is essentially external: we can only infer inner qualities from observing outer qualities; we know character by judging wit, but the externalism of the process also admits other kinds of external signs—in others and in the world—that may prove more reliable in some senses than the way characters speak. Unless guaranteed by an unusual weight of social agreement, words can never be fully trusted.

Congreve's scepticism about the efficacy of ordinary language manifests itself in a kind of linguistic saturation or redundancy. Millamant's magnificent entry is orchestrated by Witwoud's unconsidered and intrusive similes, witty enough perhaps, but disturbingly without regard for appropriateness or genuine discovery or invention. Millamant complains against him and then proceeds to bewail the barrage of letters she must endure: "I am persecuted with letters," she cries, "I hate letters. Nobody knows how to write letters; and yet one has 'em, one does not know why. They serve to pin up one's hair" (2.324-27). Part of her purpose is to deflect the sense of her vulnerability to others' (especially men's) designs, but nevertheless these designs operate in a world in which a superfluity of speech allows Millamant to pin up her hair with verse.

The answer, of course, is not to dispense with language altogether, but rather to propose a social economy (Lady Wishfort speaks of her "economy of face") that can describe and enclose the natural and artificial realms of discourse. To submit entirely to one or the other is either to be trapped in the natural world of human passion and desire or to find oneself caught in an endless web of words. Congreve's social imperative requires a balance: we are indeed animated by common human impulses, while our conscious control of discourse allows us to distance ourselves from the immediacy of our appetites, thus permitting us to engage productively in social rituals, artificial though they may be. This imperative does not assume—or allow— a simple divorce between appearance and nature (as Norman Holland implies [in his *The First Modern Comedies: The Significance of Etherege, Wycherley, and Congreve,* 1959]), but holds that we can codify and understand systems of signification that provide at some level a genuine insight into the natural realm. We are back again with Sextus Empiricus's indicative signs, the most persistent example of which is that blushing is a sign of shame. Since Sextus's model becomes part of a larger Restoration myth for language as a whole, it is striking to find in Congreve's play a peculiar fascination with the act of blushing, given that words can obscure as much as they reveal.

It follows that, almost as much as in *The Plain Dealer,* we begin on the wrong foot if we approach **The Way of the World** primarily as an analysis of individual character psychology. Just as neoclassical forms of knowledge and judgment involve an intelligent, rational appraisal of relations among ideas, so a proper reading of Congreve's masterpiece requires us to conceive character as a method of dramatizing and exploring the various positions that men (more especially women in this play) may adopt— wittingly or unwittingly—in the face of the overwhelming and general facts about human experience Congreve confronts us with. Our judgments of the relative virtues of those positions become increasingly clear as we compare the relationships among the characters, relationships which prevent any single character in the play from failing to contribute to Congreve's overall argument. Thus, to cite a recent article ["Congreve's Way to Run the World," *Papers on Language and Literature* 11 (1975): 379], Jonathan Dietz is completely mistaken to treat Witwoud, Petulant, and Sir Wilfull Witwoud as "intrusions" in the "major themes of the play."

The Way of the World, then, presents us with a dense epistemological and semiological challenge. The well-recognized similarities between Fainall and Mirabell in the opening scene immediately thrust the challenge at the audience, a challenge made all the greater in this case by our coming upon the action *in medias res.* The characters are already situated in a social landscape that we must reconstruct after the fact, while they continue to move through it. The difficulty is further compounded by the notorious prolixity of relationships among the characters, most of whom are relatives, and by the equally notorious and complex sense of plot. One common assumption that follows from an insufficient scrutiny of the play's denouement leads readers to believe that Mirabell is the direct and effective agent in securing Millamant and her fortune intact. This is not true. By a sleight of hand, Congreve allows us to imagine it. But the fact is that Millamant's dowry remains undivided at the end solely because Lady Wishfort is grateful to Mirabell. He has indeed shown genuine legal wisdom, but in order to secure Mrs. Fainall against her husband: the effect on Millamant is indirect and purely fortuitous.

Moreover, we become peculiarly conscious of our own role in reconstructing events by inference, when, at the be-

ginning of act 5, we find that we have to infer for ourselves events that have evidently transpired *between* acts 4 and 5: Fainall has managed to have Waitwell arrested, and Lady Wishfort knows of the whole Sir Rowland scheme. The innocence of the scene tag ("Scene continues") is particularly misleading because it implies a seamless connection between the acts (which we have experienced between acts 3 and 4); and this creates potential confusion even, one imagines, in the process of staging, unless one provides an interact mime of some kind.

The audience's role in such matters is only one part of a broad spectrum of juridical and forensic issues in the play, that Mirabell's legal acumen serves to focus. Williams's point that the black box has no talismanic properties is well taken, but the very ordinariness of the object points up the recurring concern with law, proofs, and witnesses. The resolution of the plot, requiring Mirabell to capture Millamant with all her money, underscores the legal position of women in 1700 in regard to their inheritances. And the successful denouement depends heavily on two sets of witnesses: Foible and Mincing prove reliable observers of Marwood's and Fainall's liaison, and they also prove perspicacious about the status of an oath sworn on a book of verses (5.84-94; 441-53); Petulant and Witwoud have inadvertently assisted Mirabell's scheme by witnessing Mrs. Fainall's deed in trust (5.481-89). (There is a real distinction between these two kinds of witnessing, whose significance I will consider later). Mirabell's success in understanding and manipulating the law is echoed ironically by Fainall's parallel failure; and the irony becomes all the greater because we discover that Witwoud was an attorney's clerk (something Petulant discovers for the first time, [3.490]), and that Sir Wilfull Witwoud is a Justice of the Peace (5.363-64). Witwoud's real failure and Sir Willful's mitigated failure to make adequate judgments of character and events are thus marked by their relative abilities at law. Witwoud was clearly a failure as a clerk— remembering "nothing" about Mrs. Fainall's deed (5.487)—while Sir Wilfull responds sympathetically to Mirabell's plea to Lady Wishfort as if it occurred in the magistrate's court, an act that may demonstrate his rude benevolence, but does not entirely redeem him as an arbiter of character.

The moment the play opens, we recognize a world in which characters scrutinize each other unremittingly, because judgment and knowledge betoken power. The first action we encounter, Fainall's and Mirabell's card game, establishes this world very economically. Moreover, the verbal universe of the play is replete with matters of knowledge, proof, and certainty: Mirabell wants absolute assurance that Waitwell and Foible are indeed married (1.110); Petulant declares of himself that "I know nothing" (1.383); Marwood admits to Mrs. Fainall that "what I have said has been to try you" (2.37); Fainall declares his marriage to Mrs. Fainall should be undeniable proof of his attachment to Marwood, and concludes "Will you yet be reconciled to truth and me?", to which Marwood replies, with some justification, "Truth and you are inconsistent" (2.192-94); and Witwoud and Petulant enter in act 3 and proceed to argue about kinds of proofs:

PETULANT: If I have a humor to prove it, it must be granted.

WITWOUD: Not necessarily must, but it may, it may.

PETULANT: Yes, it positively must, upon proof positive.

WITWOUD. Aye, upon proof positive, it must; but upon proof presumptive it only may. That's a logical distinction now.

(3.361-66)

Sir Wilfull enters for the first time asking not only whether Lady Wishfort's servant knows him, but also whether the servant knows his mistress, raising the question of how we can know people. The servant replies that "I cannot safely swear to her face in a morning, before she's dressed. 'Tis like I may give a shrewd guess at her by this time" (3.407-9). Sir Wilfull's response to the exchange ("this fellow knows less than a starling; I don't think a' knows his own name" [3.418-19]) introduces a peculiar hiatus in which Sir Wilfull and Witwoud fail to recognize each other—the one accidentally, it seems, the other purposefully, and the whole burden of conversation falls on Marwood (3.420ff.). Here Congreve illuminates problems of knowledge in a number of ways at once, not least by exploiting the distinction between the two senses of knowing (as in *"savoir"* and *"connaitre"*).

Fainall has a distinctive concern with jealousy (beginning at 1.135) that is inevitably a concern with ways of knowing, one he expounds at some length at the end of act 3 (629-41). Marwood witnesses Foible's and Mrs. Fainall's conversation and discovers the Sir Rowland plot, and her letter attempting to wreck it in midcourse becomes a magnificent dramatization of the relationships among reading, misreading, evidence, and power. After Waitwell and Foible have successfully negotiated that threat, Waitwell goes off to obtain proofs that he is indeed Sir Rowland as he claims (4.506-80).

Just as act 5 ends with a restoration of Mrs. Fainall's deed in trust "before these witnesses" (5.566)—not with the dance—so each previous act has ended by focussing on matters of knowledge and evidence. Act 1 ends with a debate about the meaning of blushing (Petulant declares "I always take blushing either for a sign of guilt or ill-breeding," and Mirabell concludes the scene by calling Petulant's judgment into question [1.482-86]). Act 2 ends with Waitwell meditating on the nature of the self: is it constituted by title or by some essence, and what does naming do? (2.499-507); act 3, as we have seen, concludes with Fainall's ruminations on the relationship between jealously, belief, and doubt; and act 4, with Waitwell leaving to obtain proofs of his assumed identity.

Act 1 also establishes another relevant feature of the play's procedure. Millamant is conspicuously present by her absence. The male world of this act is fascinated by her. Millamant surfaces several times as a topic of conversation, and the extent to which she is thus constituted by report alerts us to the way in which we inhabit a world of phenomena from which we must make inferences about character and value. Significantly, Witwoud effectively refuses to do this by describing Millamant as "a sort of uncertain woman" (1.422), a judgment that is accidentally appropriate because she is such a consuming and elusive object of Mirabell's desire. Congreve's habit of constituting character by report begins to develop its own momentum and to assume wider symbolic value: by juxtaposing judgment (language, report), with fact (action, stage entry), Congreve disturbs and problematizes the question of how language describes what we observe. Just as there is considerable play with the relationship between Lady Wishfort and her picture, Mirabell and Fainall discuss Witwoud for a while before the "original" enters (1.196-209). The same thing occurs with Petulant (1.308-39), and with Mirabell and Fainall (2.45-71). The implicit argument thus gathers a force sufficient to allow ironic variations upon it and to amplify Millamant's wonderful entry in act 2, surely one of the most dramatic on the English stage. She follows directly on an exchange about Lady Wishfort which has broadened sufficiently to become a discussion about women aging, and this not only frames Millamant's entry but situates one of her and the play's major concerns. Millamant knows she will grow old too.

The occasion for discussing Millamant in act 1 is Lady Wishfort's cabal, which encapsulates the intricate nexus of relationships among reading, signs, judgment, and power. The cabal provides an arena in which members judge not only outsiders but each other: appropriately enough, Fainall compares it to a "coroner's inquest" (1.48). Not only does gossip condemn reputations, but Fainall in particular is conscious of how far Lady Wishfort's position in the cabal betokens her power over Millamant, a power Mirabell overlooks here, and never directly succeeds in breaking (1.39-42). Moreover, Mirabell's anxiety to read and understand Millamant is neatly established, as is her ability to sidestep the kind of control over her he implicitly demands. He is merely left in possession of a cryptic sign: she blushes (1.35).

In seventy lines, Congreve has sketched out the essential symbolic dynamics of his play. We see, for example, how Mirabell is capable of controlled and witty discourse at the level of ordinary language, but is unable to fully control or interpret the realm of the passions (natural discourse): he has failed to interpret Millamant's blush (and thus to break not only her emotional independence, but her control of her own body), and has insufficiently dissembled in his ruse against Lady Wishfort (1.63). In short, he cannot entirely hide his passions and intentions in matters of love, nor can he sufficiently interpret signs of such possible intentions in others. In this light, it is revealing that Mirabell's most characteristic verbal habit in act 1 is the phrase "I confess" (1.16). Moreover, Fainall's evident relish at "the state of nature" (1.63), characterizing Mirabell's designs on Lady Wishfort, helps to remind us that matters of interpretation, openness, secrecy, and so forth have fundamentally to do with power: Hobbes, that great analyst of language and power, beckons briefly from behind the text. In fact, Mirabell tries to exercise his will in order to break Millamant's natural power (her hidden knowledge about her attitude to Mirabell) and to abrogate Lady Wishfort's power over Millamant.

Already we see emerging the three main realms of discourse and interpretation that the characters in *The Way of the World* must seek to understand and control. The purely natural realm includes the hidden drive for love, money, or power, which we cannot hope to purge but must at all events socialize. Although the Restoration required it to provide an ultimate basis for ordinary language, the natural realm constitutes a type of discourse itself because it manifests itself in gesture—notably the act of blushing—pure action, or a significant hiatus in ordinary language characterized by loss of linguistic control. Congreve attacks those who cannot go beyond natural discourse because they have become enslaved to it and cannot—or will not—contribute productively to social intercourse. The realm assumes particular importance in a dramatic world sceptical about ordinary language because it becomes a potential gauge of whether what a character says is true or not.

The level of discourse plagued by the least uncertainties is the purely legal or contractual realm, in which, if parties agree to underwrite the truth of an assertion, it is arbitrarily secured, a position Hobbes desires in the *Leviathan*. Discourse is true merely because there is a general social agreement that particular words and phrases should be accorded a designated force: thus Mrs. Fainall is secured of her inheritance by a purely legal act, "witnessed" in a purely legal sense by Witwoud and Petulant; and her status cannot change in this regard, whatever other social or natural changes occur. We could say that the chief purpose of act 5 is to establish and vindicate the play's action at this level of discourse.

Of course, ordinary language represents the broadest realm of social and human activity, whose uncertainties can only be resolved by fiat or by negotiation with the natural realm. And because methods of analogy ultimately gauge the individual's grasp of the surrounding world, the extent to which a character is capable of negotiating the demands made on ordinary language by the natural and legal worlds appears as wit. Moreover, we can never dispose of this level of discourse because it accompanies and determines all ordinary social activities, such as friendships. We must discover, rather, how to avoid merely being trapped at the natural level (as the Witwouds, Petulant, Marwood, and Fainall ultimately are) or at the legal level (as Mrs. Fainall is). The contrast between the two pairs of friends or lovers in act 2 (Marwood and Fainall / Mirabell and Mrs. Fainall) rather neatly makes the point. The confrontation between Marwood and Fainall is fraught with epistemological difficulties in which neither party is fully in control of the other nor the audience fully appraised of the nature of the relationship until the scene almost collapses in pure physical action and Fainall's sporadic, desperate speech: Fainall seizes Marwood, Marwood begins to cry, and Fainall tries to subdue her with words not only devoid of wit, but quite out of control (2.93-244). These two are ultimately driven by passion that blinds them and fragments language, whereas Mirabell's comparative insight and ease of social control is manifest in the ensuing scene with Mrs. Fainall, in which serious and potentially tragic matters (Mrs. Fainall's marriage, Mirabell's plot, Lady Wishfort's age) are eloquently

conveyed (2.225-89). Without denying the immediacy and power of the natural realm (for Mrs. Fainall reminds him of the fate of all women), Mirabell can still discuss it with a series of finely-chosen similes describing an "old woman's appetite" (2.286-89).

Congreve seems to contend that, despite everything, a satisfactory social level of discourse can be achieved. In act 1, a servant tells Mirabell that his plot is under way because Waitwell and Foible are now married. The brief scene establishes two important facts. Mirabell is evidently legally astute because he demands documented proof of the union (1.112). But, more significantly, by referring to the act of union as "coupling" (1.103), Congreve prefigures the union of all levels of discourse in the great proviso scene in act 4: in one word, Congreve fuses the natural realm of desire and copulation with the social, religious, and legal institution of marriage. That this formulation appears so early in the play, and seems so innocent, is owing to Waitwell's and Foible's status as servants: they are not required to scale the hurdles confronting the gentlefolk. The marriage of desire and law is only easy for a servant who does not, like Millamant, have to husband her reputation. Later, in act 5, Congreve symbolically fragments the relationship between passionate action and legal reality by squaring Fainall and Sir Wilfull Witwoud off against each other around the pun on "instrument." Fainall produces the legal instrument that Lady Wishfort must sign to save her daughter's reputation (5.382-83); Sir Wilfull wants to cut it to shreds with his sword:

> 'Sheart, an you talk of an instrument, sir, I have an old fox by my thigh shall hack your instrument of ram vellum to shreds, sir! It shall not be sufficient for a mittimus or a tailor's measure. Therefore, withdraw your instrument, sir, or by'r Lady, I shall draw mine.
>
>   (5.392-97)

The urgency with which Sir Wilfull's language and logic operate by a kind of furious naturalized metonymy ("old fox," "ram vellum") suggests the inappropriateness of his response to this purely legal threat. Fainall consigns Sir Wilfull to the natural realm by mocking his "bear-garden flourish" (5.408), but, when he himself, disappointed at the failure of his legal trick, *"offers to run at* Mrs. Fainall" (5.513-15), Sir Wilfull in turn welcomes him to that society. Neither Fainall nor Sir Wilfull ever succeed in harmonizing all the realms of discourse.

If, as I have suggested, the action of the plot must give way conceptually to the notion of dramatized positions set up in relationship to a controlling or primary hypothesis about the world and manifested as different forms of discourse, one result of this theoretical orientation is to place Millamant at the center of Congreve's masterpiece. For whatever fascination Mirabell may hold as motivator of plots, as manipulator of others, as wit, Millamant stands unique among the women of Restoration comedy. She must confront the painful and potentially tragic twin recognitions that, in a man's world, a woman must inevitably grow old and lose her natural power over men, and that the price of even partial social and political freedom is the ability to negotiate according to the contracts that maintain the fabric of society. Such negotiation necessarily entails a *quid pro quo,* a benefit yielded for a benefit received, and thus, arguably, the loss of at least two possible fictions of social autonomy. Millamant's intense and delicate intelligence equips her with a peculiar ability to engage with her own passion and the legal realities of marriage while at the same time distancing them. As Alan Roper has remarked her language is defensive inasmuch as it tends to create fictions to keep others at bay—or she may simply laugh aggravatingly ("significant gesture," Marwood calls it [3.213])—without ultimately isolating her from that social relation (courtship and marriage) which has its grounding in natural desire. Thus she can balk so delightfully at the word "breed" without denying the inevitability of her carnal—and thus mortal and confined—existence.

Act 1 shows us the extent to which Millamant is the focus of many masculine desires, and we must believe, given Mirabell's penchant for control, that he presents a powerful threat to her. Act 2 establishes the equality of their relationship at the level of ordinary social discourse—as wits, they are well matched. But Millamant's control of the world of natural discourse results in her obtaining the power of knowledge over Mirabell: he cannot hide the signs of his love for her, a fact that Millamant taunts him with:

> MILLAMANT: Ha! ha! ha! what would you give that you could help loving me?
>
> MIRABELL: I would give something that you did not know I could not help it.
>
> MILLAMANT: Come, don't look grave then. Well, what do you say to me?
>
> MIRABELL: I say that a man may as soon make a friend by his wit, or a fortune by his honesty, as win a woman with plain dealing and sincerity.
>
> MILLAMANT: Sententious Mirabell! Prithee, don't look with that violent and inflexible wise face, like Solomon at the dividing of the child in the old tapestry hanging.
>
> (2.412-22)

Oddly, Mirabell's language here suffers the same fault as Lady Wishfort's: the simile fails to adequately distinguish its various constitutive features from one another. Matters of honesty, fortune, wit, and friendship are not only relevant to, but *part of* the matter at hand; they press immediately on the moment without spatializing, and thus distancing and examining, his problem by carefully measuring it with similar problems outside his situation. The point arises dramatically when Millamant holds Mirabell's seriousness at bay by creating a crystalline divorce between the two terms of her comparison. By an effort of intelligence, she remains free from the febrile immediacy of the argument in a way Mirabell is not. Mirabell's anxiety, his urgency, tends to fuse his terms of comparison, while Millamant's anxiety, her consciousness of her female frailty, urges her to keep those terms discrete. Nevertheless, although Millamant's language thus succeeds in referring to, rather than enacting, her anxiety, its reality looms in the disturbing imbalance between the figure of violence and division (the child cloven asunder as a figure of male power, of rape, literally seizure and apportion-

ment) and its strangely unsuccessful containment (on the one hand, by the Biblical narrative, and, on the other, by its reification as a work of art). We can read Millamant's control of figure as itself a figure for the political ambitions of Congreve's play.

Mirabell's solemn face clinches the issue and delivers him into Millamant's power at this point because she interprets him correctly. (Mirabell also discovers that she knows his plan, which discomforts him [2.434-35]). The import of such gestures has already been established in act 2, and hinted at by Millamant's blushing at the cabal. Marwood's and Mrs. Fainall's opening encounter raises a central issue in the play, and develops a world in which the ability to read others signifies power over them (2.1-71). Marwood confesses to the universal female fear of growing old and determines not to lose out in the pursuit of love. Her speech (2.9-16) renders us sympathetic to her personal tragedy and explains her predatory nature: it must have been the perfect moment for Mrs. Barry, the great tragic actress. Marwood's fears are real, we know, because Millamant also confesses to them, and they echo Lady Wishfort's desperate and pathetic attempts to recuperate her youth, and thus satisfy her desires. And Mrs. Fainall, standing on stage with her, depicts the same dilemma: her status as a married woman prohibits her from satisfying herself as if she were free and still involved with Mirabell. Marwood's desperation is her downfall, and her subjugation to the natural world of desire and passion, her inability to escape or socialize it, is suggested when she changes color on the mention of Mirabell. The atmosphere of intense scrutiny and distrust between the two women causes Mrs. Fainall to notice this sign immediately, and Marwood's explanation does not entirely satisfy her, though Marwood is spared from defending herself further because Mrs. Fainall turns pale. Marwood pounces, but Mrs. Fainall protests that she has just spied her husband (2.55-71). We are thus instructed that blushing and growing pale are sure signs of passion; although we cannot know precisely what they signify, we suspect Marwood of more than she professes. We also recognize that an accurate interpretation of such gestures would lend the interpreter considerable social power, just as Fainall, inferring from Marwood's "warm confession reddening on your cheeks" her partiality for Mirabell, finds himself in control of at least part of their argument (2.122-24).

This argument scene, where purely verbal and socialized combat converts to physical force and the collapse of language, illustrates Marwood's and Fainall's subjection to passion. Millamant is in some sense no less passionate, but her passion is distanced and harmonized with legal discourse and ordinary language; Congreve merely reports, rather than presenting, Millamant's passionate gestures. We hear that she blushed at the cabal, and Mrs. Marwood notices her "color" in act 3, after she breaks her fan in frustration at Petulant (3.254ff.). Even though Petulant is a purely ridiculous object of her anger, Millamant's temper flares in the wings. Typically, Millamant has developed a posture towards her own natural powers by declaring, on the first witty exchange with Mirabell, "One's cruelty is one's power, and when one parts with one's cruelty, one parts with one's power; and when one has parted with that, I fancy one's old and ugly" (2.349-51).

Lady Wishfort stands a living testament to this inescapable reality, wanting to recapture her youth by painting her face to imitate youthful passion in its "complexion" (3.1-24). Unlike younger women, whose natural blushes can inadvertently place them in others' power, Lady Wishfort's nostalgia is registered by her constant references to her own facial gestures. On mention of Mirabell, she cries, "You call the blood into my face with mentioning that traitor" (3.44-45); and she studies her attitudes to capture Sir Rowland, for languishing on the couch and rising in confusion "shows the foot to advantage, and furnishes with blushes, and recomposing airs beyond comparison" (4.26-28). Narcissus-like, perhaps as an ironic reversal of Milton's Eve, for she will tempt no one, she conceives Mirabell in her own image, as constituted by affective gestures (4.455-61; 5.389-81). The conclusion of the play teaches us that Marwood and Fainall are captive to passion, which Lady Wishfort has the good sense to see no longer befits her.

Lady Wishfort discovers what power she has is legal, rather than natural (indeed, "she is the antidote to desire," [4.499]). She controls half of Millamant's fortune. But the extent to which a woman's legal power is circumscribed is illustrated by her inability to overcome Fainall's legal obstacles, and by the fact that she turns to Mirabell (the other real man in the play) to defeat Fainall. At a less serious level, Lady Wishfort signals her dependence upon men when she tells Sir Rowland "you are no novice in the labyrinth of love; you have the clue" (4.469-70), which, by its allusion to the Minotaur legend—to the story of a man who usurps a woman's power and then abandons her—invokes the unmentioned reality of male violence that Millamant remembers. The male is also invested with Ariadne's epistemological function, to which Lady Wishfort submits. Mirabell shows his legal foresight not only by arranging Waitwell's and Foible's marriage, but, most significantly, by providing for Mrs. Fainall, whose sole security at the end of the play is legal: she is precluded by her situation from exercising her passion, and the likelihood of her developing satisfactory liaisons appears slim.

When Marwood admits that "Love will resume his empire in our breasts; and every heart, or soon or late, received him as its lawful tyrant" (2.23-25), she describes passion's predatory force. We lose proper control of the various levels of discourse, and descend into purely natural acts, incoherence, or silence. Witness Marwood's and Fainall's significant linguistic lapses, the failure of Marwood's schemes because she is out of control ("she has a month's mind" [3.196]), and Marwood's and Fainall's legal bungles: Marwood extracts a meaningless oath made on a book of verses, not the Bible (5.91-94), and Fainall's documents prove empty. Act 5 sees Marwood descend into silence (after 448), and Fainall's attack on his wife (513). Their natural drives have blinded them to the role of multiple discourses in a healthy social economy.

Congreve sustains Marwood and Fainall within the broad social realm of discourse for most of the play (though ultimately to exile them) in order to pose a meaningful threat to Mirabell and Millamant; they clearly are not social incompetents. But they finally find themselves in company with Witwoud, Petulant, and Sir Wilfull Witwoud. Congreve invokes *The Tempest* to depict Sir Wilfull as *lusus naturae*: a Caliban, who, with his Stephano and Trinculo, makes confused attempts upon Millamant. They represent a danger that is greater in other quarters, but they deepen our consciousness of Millamant's imperilled and besieged situation. As Millamant implies, though Witwoud has a stock of similes, he is incapable of drawing upon them in order provocatively to illuminate the present (2.304ff.). Because he cannot see what lies before him, his language is not empirically grounded, and plays in its own nominalistic, freewheeling universe. Witwoud and Petulant prove two of a kind (Mirabell implies that they are half-men [1.52-54]), and they condemn each other in act 4:

> WITWOUD: Thou hast uttered volumes, folios, in less than *decimo sexto,* my dear Lacedemonian. Sirrah Petulant, thou art an epitomizer of words.
>
> PETULANT: Witwoud, you are an annihilator of sense.
>
> WITWOUD: Thou art a retailer of phrases and dost deal in remnants, like a maker of pincushions; thou art in truth (metaphorically speaking) a speaker of shorthand.
>
> PETULANT: Thou art (without a figure) just one half of an ass, and Baldwin yonder, thy half-brother, is the rest. A gemini of asses split would make just four of you.
>
> (4.307-16)

As inhabitants of the "natural" realm, Witwoud and Petulant emasculate, truncate and fragment ordinary language: Witwoud annihilates sense, and Petulant speaks shorthand, a cryptic, hieroglyphic mode, which recalls Millamant's reference to the Sybil (3.324-25), and reminds us of the density and obscurity of the codes proliferating in the play. Witwoud is as much if not more a "retailer" of phrases than Petulant, which suggests a wider economic, social and linguistic redundancy: their words are bankrupt, perennially debased. The context of their debate amplifies the social meaninglessness of the verbal atmosphere they import because it occurs immediately after Sir Wilfull's and Petulant's groundless, incoherent, and virtually mute argument. Witwoud reports that "there was no dispute. They could neither of 'em speak for rage, and so fell aspluttering at one another like two roasting apples" (4.298-300). Petulant's fishlike gaping recalls Caliban (4.302).

Though it may be mistaken as merely the result of drunkenness, the speechlessness of this triumvirate primarily indicates a mind sans memory, one of the essential preconditions of Lockean identity. We have already seen how Sir Wilfull and Witwoud forget one another on their first encounter in act 3 (388ff.), and Witwoud reenacts Ben's amnesia in *Love for Love* (Ben forgets his brother is dead) when he admits that "I've almost forgot" Sir Wilfull (3.390). Mirabell has remarked earlier that Witwoud's wit only fails him "as often as his memory fails him, and his commonplace of comparisons" (1.199-200); and Witwoud inadvertently appears to agree by pronouncing, "my memory is such a memory" after forgetting what he is about to say (1.247). Witwoud also discovers Petulant's "natural parts" both by want of learning, and by "want of words" (1.294-98).

Moreover, although Witwoud's and Petulant's contretemps about the ass in act 4 seems to evince a self-consciousness about the difference between "literal" and "metaphorical" applications of words, it succeeds instead by obscuring and collapsing those distinctions, not in the direction of the endlessly figurative nature of language (even the "literal" is subject to *différence / différance* and thus a feature of figuration), but in the arbitrary designation that to be "just one half of an ass" is to be an ass "without a figure," that is, "literally." Congreve finds in the fiction of the "literal" precisely that, a fiction of bad faith: Sir Wilfull's comic courtship of Millamant in the same act is governed by his intentions "to break [his] mind" to Millamant (4.68;118), in an evident belief that a direct representation of the mind's intentions is possible in ordinary language. He cannot see—or will not—that to ask a woman to go for a walk when he is in the posture of courting her means more than it says: "A walk! What then?" exclaims Millamant, to which Sir Wilfull replies, "Nay, nothing. Only for the walk's sake, that's all" (4.103-4). His frustration with the labyrinth of the language whose inheritance he denies provokes the outburst, "Well, well, I shall understand your lingo one of these days, cousin; in the meanwhile, I must answer in plain English" (4.96-97). The yearning for a plain speech accompanies the failure of social responsibility.

Ironically, Sir Wilfull tends to adopt subjunctive rather than indicative terms, so that his intentions are obscure even to himself. Like his courting, his words are already impotent, being merely suspended, potential, chronically hypothetical. He cannot countenance Millamant's contrariness because he cannot see that to make something of contradiction is to invent an illocutionary semantic. To Millamant's protestation that she loathes the country and hates the town. Sir Wilfull replies:

> Ha! that you should hate 'em both! Ha! 'tis like you may; there are some can't relish the town, and others can't away with the country. 'Tis like you may be one of those cousin.
>
> (4.111-14)

Millamant echoes his subjunctive ("Ha! ha! ha! 'tis like I may") before asking whether he has more to add, which precipitates another suspended set of assertions:

> Not at present, cousin. 'Tis like when I have an opportunity to be more private, I may break my mind in some measure. I conjecture you partly guess.
>
> (4.116-18)

The unwillingness to commit to the indicative mood—and thus to action—prefigures Petulant's and Witwoud's final comments in the play. Both resign the responsibility of response to the outcome: Petulant declares, "For my part, I say little; I think things are best off or on" (5.541), and Witwoud admits, "I gad, I understand nothing of the mat-

ter; I'm in a maze yet, like a dog in a dancing school" (5.542-43).

Like his comparison of Sir Wilfull and Petulant to "two roasting apples," Witwoud's final simile is untypically apt; but that is because he has naturalized discourse and rendered it amenable to his limited and "natural" understanding (just as Sir Wilfull compares Lady Wishfort's servant to a "starling"). The Witwouds and Petulant (like Ben and Prue in *Love for Love*) belong to a world also inhabited by dogs, starlings, and roasting apples, resisting integration into the realm of social and artificial discourse signalled by the maze and dancing school.

We can forgive Sir Wilfull his incapacities, however, because, unlike Witwoud and Petulant, a pure action demonstrates that he is good-hearted in a rough and ready way. He is willing to help Millamant outwit Lady Wishfort by appearing to marry her, and he is all too eager to dispatch Fainall's instrument. But these acts of benevolence alone cannot fully integrate Sir Wilfull into society, for we remain uncomfortably aware that for him London is a mere stage on his projected tour of the continent. The prospect of the tour remains as improbable at the end as at the beginning, although Sir Wilfull makes a faint recognition by declaring that "I have thoughts to tarry a small matter in town, to learn somewhat of your lingo first, before I cross the sea" (3.516-18). The project is as empty as Prue's effort (in *Love for Love*) to learn the language of society from Tattle: for her, to respect the discretions of socialized speech is merely to lie. So, because we cannot imagine Sir Wilfull transcending his own natural lingo, we approve of Mirabell serving as interpreter in foreign parts, like Pylades with Orestes (5.324-25). Where we cannot credit Witwoud's claim to interpret for Petulant ("his want of words gives me the pleasure of very often to explain his meaning" [1.297-98]), we can credit Mirabell's responsibility for Sir Wilfull.

If Sir Wilfull's fantasies of escape from social contingencies obey a kind of natural impulse or trope, Lady Wishfort's similar desires are projected onto the most artificial figure conceivable, escape into pastoral solitude, a fantasy Marwood encourages. She tells Marwood, "Well, friend, you are enough to reconcile me to the bad world, or else I would retire to deserts and solitudes, and feed harmless sheep by groves and purling streams. Dear Marwood, let us leave the world, and retire by ourselves and be shepherdesses" (5.121-25). Marwood echoes the sentiment, ironically, in even more fraught circumstances: Fainall is laying down his "savage" conditions to Lady Wishfort (5.243-45).

In contrast to her aunt and cousin, Millamant recognizes that our social, historical, and natural condition prohibits us from denying death and escaping the relations of power that comprise society. We can no more elude the necessity of power than we can the family alliances and the love-chase which supply *The Way of the World* with two of its most basic premises. Where Lady Wishfort desperately seeks to rejuvenate herself, Millamant, in her first witty exchange with Mirabell, recognizes the inevitability of aging; and where Lady Wishfort cultivates fictions of pastoral flight, Millamant, knowing the transience of her first victory over Mirabell, will bargain for a contingent but real social liberty. The central significance of the proviso scene is that she stages a studied and carefully orchestrated withdrawal from her earlier monopoly of knowledge; she now permits herself to be read and obtained. For all Mirabell's insight, the scene begins with Millamant enjoying the superior advantage, because, while Mirabell remains unsure of her, she knows he loves her. By an act of grace on her part, she permits him to enter (4.50-54); and although Mirabell proves his wit by completing the Waller couplet for her as he enters (4.133-34), he treats the locked door as a deliberate ruse, whereas in fact Mrs. Fainall has rather casually locked it on Sir Wilfull (4.77-78; 135-36). Mirabell asks an interpretive question: "is this pretty artifice contrived, to signify that here the chase must end and that my pursuit be crowned, for you can fly no further?" (4.136-38).

The scene amalgamates or plays among all the levels of discourse Congreve deems essential to any satisfactory polity. We miss the full significance of what occurs if we treat it primarily as witty exchange or the creation of a binding legal contract. Of course, it plays with the Restoration convention of proviso scenes, and it makes gestures towards legal force because Mrs. Fainall later arrives as a witness to the agreement (4.256-57). Oral contracts, however, hold an uncertain status in common law, especially if not directly witnessed by a third party, and Mrs. Fainall is only deemed a witness to an event that occurs *in camera*. Rather, the scene symbolizes a social agreement with only potential legal force, one only realized in act 5. In his *Second Treatise of Government* (1689) [edited by Peter Laslett, 1960], Locke writes:

> *Conjugal Society* is made by a voluntary Compact between Man and Woman: and tho' it consist chiefly in such a Communion and Right in one anothers Bodies, as is necessary to its chief End, Procreation; yet it draws with it mutual Support, and Assistance, and a Communion of Interest too, as necessary to their common Offspring, who have a Right to be nourished and maintained by them, till they are able to provide for themselves.

What we witness on the stage is the establishment of a "voluntary compact," which, as Peter Laslett points out, is not exactly contractual in nature:

> It is "compact" or often mere "agreement" which creates a society, a community . . . of political power . . . even law. Now compact and agreement are more general than contract: they are further removed from the language of the law. Vague as Locke is, we seem to have here a deliberate attempt to avoid being specific and to leave legal models on one side. It may imply that the transmutation into the social and political condition must not be looked on in a legal way; it is a variable thing and a pretty loose one too.

Although it partly anticipates the strictly legal resolutions of act 5, the proviso scene invokes "compact," to symbolize the broadly social function of language, not merely its legal applications. It also establishes a traffic between ordinary language and the natural realm, because Millamant and Mirabell agree to banish foolish endearments that (as the Fainalls demonstrate in act 2) can rapidly lose their anchoring in natural affection (4.175ff.), and Mirabell bans Millamant from using cosmetics or wearing corsets during pregnancy (4.221-23; 235-37).

Locke points out that "compact" stands for the forging of all social ties, not only the granting of personal gratification. The proviso scene thus becomes an argument for a patriotic society that surfaces elsewhere in the play. It is infused throughout with the vocabulary of liberty and restraint: Millamant knows she is bargaining away a portion of her "dear liberty," her "darling contemplation" (4.163-65). She will, however, remain "sole empress" of her tea table (199), to which Mirabell agrees in clearly political terms:

> to the dominion of the tea table I submit, but with proviso, that you exceed not your province, but restrain yourself to native and simple tea-table drinks, as tea, chocolate and coffee.
>
> (4.238-41)

True liberty, the argument goes, depends upon a certain constraint which respects the autonomy of the individual. Locke argues that liberty is not unconstrained individual freedom, for that would return us to a state of nature. His view of the balance of power in marriage holds that:

> Husband and Wife, though they have but one common Concern, yet having different understandings, will unavoidably sometimes have different wills too; it therefore being necessary, that the last Determination, *i.e.* the Rule, should be placed somewhere, it naturally falls to the Man's share, as the abler and stronger. But this reaching but to the things of their common Interest and Property, leaves the Wife in the full and free possession of what by Contract is her peculiar Right, and gives the Husband no more power over her Life, than she has over his.

Congreve implies that this true political economy can only be enjoyed by Englishmen because part of the economy of Millamant's dominion over her tea table requires her to use only "native" drinks. This argument is anticipated by sir Wilfull, that most natural Englishman, who wants to "have a spice of your French, as they say, whereby to hold discourse in foreign countries" (3.518-19), which amuses his hearers, while implying that foreign speech is somehow more artificial and constraining than English.

The argument is further elaborated by Mirabell's proviso against "straight-lacing, squeezing for a shape, till you mold my boy's head like a sugar-loaf, and instead of a man-child, make me a father to a crooked billet" (4.235-37). The child in the womb (the "native") enjoys his own natural balance between liberty and restraint: confined within the womb, he is free in his own sphere, which Mirabell is concerned to respect (although he does impose gender on the child, prefiguring its entry into the symbolic order, with which the proviso scene is attempting to negotiate). Mirabell also wants to prevent Millamant from encroaching on the "men's prerogative" and enlisting "foreign forces, all auxiliaries" to the tea table (4.246ff.).

A true balance among all the various levels or applications

of discourse would produce a society that affords all members a contingent liberty, entailing the regulation of an individualistic state of nature (125). Failure to negotiate the complexities of discourse produces various tyrannies. Marwood protests in vain against her subjection to the "natural" realm: "Love will resume his empire in our breasts," she complains, "and every heart, or soon or late, receive and admit his as its lawful tyrant" (2.23-25). Although "in Locke's system it is the power which men have over others, not the power which they have over themselves, which gives rise to political authority," Locke would never admit the "lawfulness" of a "tyrant" whose power was not held in trust (124; 126). The unnaturalness—or oppression—of Marwood's oxymoron matches Fainall's description of her as an Amazon, commenting on her express desire to free herself from men and forget them altogether, a kind of freedom that social reality cannot, and does not, permit (2.39-41). While the proviso scene explicates a theory of mutual benefits (4.148-51), Marwood cites her "obligations to my lady" as the reason for exposing Mirabell's false intentions to Lady Wishfort (2.142). These obligations are neither apparent, nor mutual, and we already suspect Marwood's action flows more from her jealousy of Mirabell than anything else. Lady Wishfort's inability to overcome the legal traps set for her causes her to cry out, "I'll consent to anything to come, to be delivered from this tyranny" (5.422).

Mirabell, of course, helps to set her free. In act 5, he also delivers Waitwell from prison, the most concrete image of confinement. Like Mirabell, who prohibits a corset during pregnancy, Witwoud, commenting on Sir Wilfull's and Petulant's drunken quarrel, also uses a sartorial image: "If I had stayed any longer I should have burst; I must have been let out and pierced in the sides like an insized camlet" (4.292-94).

We can also judge the success of the proviso scene in figuring a social and political compact, because Mirabell can obey Millamant without compromising his autonomy. Obedience is the fruit of a mutual exchange of rights, of relinquishing power over oneself: Mrs. Fainall reminds Mirabell that "there's a necessity for your obedience" (4.270), and Mirabell, on leaving, declares, "I am all obedience" (4.279). His obedience to Millamant in act 5 ("I have laid my commands on Mirabell" [305]) reestablishes Millamant's obedience to Lady Wishfort ("I am somewhat revived at this testimony of your obedience" [311-12]), and helps set the scene for the denouement, whose success depends on Lady Wishfort's obligations to Mirabell for delivering her from Fainall's "tyranny."

The play ends, not with the dance, but with Mirabell restoring Mrs. Fainall's deed in trust "before these witnesses" and with a moral warning against "marriage frauds" (5.566-72). The final lines rehearse the major issues of the play: the appeal for witnesses recalls its epistemological and forensic concerns, and the imperative to scrutinize and control discourse accordingly; Mirabell's gesture returning the deed guarantees his intention to relinquish his power in trust, and so true speech is at once socialized and naturalized. The language of trust and marriage frauds comprehends both narrow legal agreements and the flexible social and political implications of ordinary language. Laslett writes that Locke

> tends to use the language of trust whenever he talks of the power of one man over another, even for fathers and children . . . "Some trust one another" is an assumption of all who join to make up society . . . This must be so if the tendency of men is to be responsible, if governors and governed are interchangeable; we can and must trust one another if natural political virtue is a reality. But there is an easily discovered limit to the trust which can be accorded or assumed, and this limit is implied in the concept of trust itself. Trust is both corollary and the safeguard of natural political virtue.

But Congreve, unlike Locke, does not dogmatically or unthinkingly believe that every person will obey his or her conscience or sense of duty (134). We experience real discomfort at Mrs. Fainall's purely legal settlement; *Love for Love* so clearly shows that relations of power within marriage can too easily go wrong, while a purely legal guarantee of rights is inadequate compensation. To enjoy any meaningful human liberty, we must fully engage with all language, all discourses which comprise social and historical being, and sustain their complexities. That the fates of Mrs. Fainall and Marwood are what they are, that they prove sacrificial victims to the plot, symbolizes the precarious position of any woman in a man's world. After Millamant, that vibrant and complicated creature, has bartered her liberty, she exclaims, "If Mirabell should not make a good husband, I am a lost thing—for I find I love him violently" (4.285-86). She understands the way of the world all too well. (pp. 727-53)

> *Richard W. F. Kroll, "Discourse and Power in 'The Way of the World'," in* ELH, *Vol. 53, No. 4, Winter, 1986, pp. 727-58.*

Albert Wertheim   (essay date 1986)

[*Wertheim is an American educator and authority on Shakespearean and seventeenth-century drama. In the essay which follows, he examines themes of love and money in four of Congreve's comedies, comparing his treatment of these motifs to that of his contemporaries.*]

It is often the case that in the works of second- and third-rate writers we come closest to seeing the preoccupations of an age. For in their works, unalloyed by authorial talent or invention, we find baldly stated the attitudes and ideas artfully and inventively presented in the works of their more gifted contemporaries. Such is the case of *A Wife to be Lett* (1724) by Mrs. Eliza Haywood, whom Pope took to task in *The Dunciad* and whom Swift described as "A stupid, infamous, scribbling woman." The conflict in Mrs. Haywood's play centers around the idea of the union of the sexes as a strictly monetary arrangement rather than as a consummation of romantic love. In the closing couplet of the second act, Toywell, a mercenary fop, asserts:

> When her Fortune's gone, the loveliest of Woman
> In this wise Age is fit Wife for no man.

The contrasting view is given at the close of the fourth act by a reformed rake:

> Ye false-nam'd Pleasures of my Youth farewel,
> They charm'd my Sense, but you subdue my
>   Soul.
> Tho fix'd to you alone, I've pow'r to change,
> While o'er each Beauty of your Form I range.
> Nor to those only need I be confin'd,
> But changing still, enjoy thy beauteous Mind.

With little subtlety, Mrs. Haywood pits extremes of thoroughly crass behavior against extremes of thoroughly romance attitudes. In the plot that gives the play its title, a thoroughly exploitative husband is prepared to rent out his wife for a fee of £2000. In another plot, Celemena has no second thoughts at all about losing her £10,000 portion in order to follow the dictates of her heart:

> Well, let me consider—Here's a Coach and Six
> with my Father's Commands and 10,000*l.* to
> back it—On the other hand, 16 *s.* a Day, and the
> Title of a Captain's Lady, with a reasonable Sus-
> picion of being turn'd out of doors with never a
> Groat—But then, on this side, I've a Fool—on
> that, a Man not disagreeable, and of allow'd
> sense—One marries me upon Compact, the
> other generously runs the risque of a Fortune—
> Well, *Gaylove,* I think you carry the day.

Mrs. Haywood paints her portraits without life, color, or shading.

The conflict of marriage based on romantic feeling versus marriage based on a cash nexus, so flatly and unsubtly presented in *A Wife to be Lett,* is also the one that informs most of the best getting-married plays from the 1690s to Sheridan's *The Rivals* (1775). It is the conflict central to plays like Farquhar's *The Constant Couple* (1700), *The Recruiting Officer* (1706), and *The Beaux' Stratagem* (1707); Steele's *The Tender Husband* (1705) and *The Conscious Lovers* (1722); Gay's *The Beggar's Opera* (1728) and *Polly* (1729); Fielding's *A Modern Husband* (1732); and Colman and Garrick's *Clandestine Marriage* (1766). Viewing Congreve as a transition figure between the love-game comedies of Etherege and Wycherley, which appeared a quarter of a century before *The Way of the World,* and the marriage comedies of the eighteenth century, which so often dwell on questions of portions and jointures, one can see how economic matters make their presence felt in comic drama after 1688, the date usually cited as the onset of England's Commercial Revolution.

The "Glorious Revolution"—the ascension of William and Mary to the throne of England in 1688—is a major landmark in English political, constitutional, and social history. As historians are becoming increasingly aware, however, 1688 is an even more important landmark in English economic history, largely because of the consequences of British commercial interests in the New World and the growing wealth derived from trade as opposed to land. By 1688, as W. W. Rostow [in his *The Stages of Economic Growth,* 1964] and others have shown, England was ready for economic "take-off" and ready to become the first industrial nation. Although in drama before 1688 the opposing claims of romance versus finance had already

made their mark in Elizabethan plays—for example, Shakespeare's *The Taming of the Shrew* (1594) and *The Merchant of Venice* (1596), Middleton's *A Trick to Catch the Old One* (1605), Fletcher's *Wit without Money* (1614), and Shirley's *The Brothers* (1641)—in the period following 1688, the new economic circumstances in England and the new wealth created through entrepôt trade make the economic questions in courtship and marriage comedies particularly acute ones. As the major comic playwright writing in the decade following 1688, Congreve provides us in his four comedies with a useful measure for gauging the growing importance of financial concerns in marriage comedies.

As it is found in the four comedies of Congreve, the question of the conflation of love and money is recognizable but muted. Though financial marriage arrangements are central to the plots of *The Double Dealer* (1693), *Love for Love* (1695), and *The Way of the World* (1700), and though Sir Joseph Wittol's desire to marry Araminta's £12,000 fortune forms one plot interest in *The Old Bachelor* (1693), Congreve's main characters are at once wise enough to know that marriage for money alone is foolish and urbane enough to recognize that London courtship and romance courtship are incongruent. It is only the most excessive of all Congreve's characters, Lady Wishfort, who seems to read romances with any seriousness. Her comparison of her maid to *"Maritornes the Asturian in Don Quixote"* (3.1.37-38), probably in Durfey's version, is only less excessive than her idea that she and Mrs. Marwood head for the nearest pastoral landscape:

> Well Friend, you are enough to reconcile me to
> the bad World, or else I wou'd retire to Desarts
> and Solitudes; and feed harmless Sheep by
> *Groves* and *Purling Streams.* Dear *Marwood,* let
> us leave the World, and retire by our selves and
> be *Shepherdesses.* (5.1.131-35)

The very thought of Lady Wishfort, the foppish, "superannuated" would-be coquette and Mrs. Marwood, the most jaded of all Congreve's town ladies, as shepherdesses is as ludicrous as it is inconceivable. It is, at the same time, only Congreve's two out and out villains, Fainall in *The Way of the World* and Maskwell in *The Double Dealer,* who consider marriage strictly in its nonromantic context, as a means to pecuniary ends.

Though Congreve sees the possibilities of romantic and mercenary excess, he nonetheless maintains an urbane distance from the fundamentally antithetical demands of marriage as the fruition of courtship on the one hand and marriage as the culmination of economic negotiation on the other. This is evident in his first comedy, *The Old Bachelor,* which separates the courtship plots involving Bellmour and Vainlove from the money plot concerning the bilking of the foolish Wittol by the confidence man Sharper. In *The Old Bachelor,* two young men about town, Vainlove and Bellmour, are united by their complementary amoristic tastes. Vainlove relishes only pursuit and courtship; his friend, Bellmour, enjoys the consummation of an affair. They work happily in tandem: the one tracks down agreeable young women and woos them; the other beds them down. It is striking, however, that although Vainlove and Bellmour's activities are not shaped by a profit motive, their association is like a business partnership, as their friend Sharper aptly underlines when he describes their union of Neoplatonic friendship and physical consummation with a monetary image: "He does the drudgery in the Mine, and you stamp your image on the Gold" (1.1.220-21). Throughout **The Old Bachelor,** moreover, the love games of Vainlove and Bellmour are juxtaposed to the confidence game of Sharper, who hopes to fleece Sir Joseph Wittol. Picking up Sharper's monetary imagery, Bellmour says of the Sharper-Wittol relationship, "a little of thy Chymistry *Tom,* may extract Gold from that Dirt" (1.1.345-46). Here as elsewhere, the plots of **The Old Bachelor** are related metaphorically, but metaphorically only. The love plots exist separately from the money plot.

In the main plot or plots, the fortunes of the two women are hardly spoken of. Vainlove pursues the airy Araminta who is described as "a kind of floating Island; sometimes seems in reach, then vanishes and keeps him busied in the search." Bellmour pursues the witty and disdainful Belinda. Although it is known that Araminta is a "great fortune," Vainlove seems unconcerned about Araminta's financial assets. The less idealistic Bellmour is aware of his Belinda's wealth but surely does not treat it with great seriousness:

> SHARPER: Faith e'en give her over for good-and-all; you can have no hopes of getting her for a Mistress, and she is too Proud, too Inconstant, too Affected and too Witty, and too handsome for a Wife.
>
> BELLMOUR: But she can't have too much Mony—There's twelve thousand Pound *Tom*— 'Tis true she is excessively foppish and affected, but in my Conscience I believe the Baggage loves me, for she never speaks well of me her self, nor suffers any Body else to rail at me. Then as I told you there's twelve thousand Pound—Hum— Why faith upon second Thoughts, she does not appear to be so very affected neither—Give her her due, I think the Woman's a Woman, and that's all. As such I'm sure I shall like her; for the Devil take me if I don't love all the Sex.
>
> (1.1.161-75)

These speeches sensitize the audience to Belinda's considerable fortune and make them aware, too, that Bellmour is not entirely ignorant of her £12,000. Still, the pursuit of Belinda is almost entirely an amorous one, and John Harrington Smith rightly asserts [in his *The Gay Couple in Restoration Comedy,* 1948] that Congreve's audience must have delighted in "a love game as had not been seen since the time of Etherege."

The minor plot of **The Old Bachelor** is quite another matter. In it, the foppish Sir Joseph Wittol and his *miles gloriosus* companion, Captain Bluffe, lose their gold in hopes of gaining the rich Araminta. Setter, Bellmour's pimp, ruminating aloud so that Wittol and Bluffe can be sure to hear him, inspires their fortune hunting:

> Were I a Rogue now, what a noble Prize could I dispose of! A goodly Pinnace, richly laden,

and to launch forth under my Auspicious Convoy. Twelve Thousand Pounds, and all her Rigging; besides what lies conceal'd under Hatches. (5.1.221-25)

Both Wittol and Bluffe take the gilded bait, each bribing Setter to match him with Araminta. And in their pursuit of Araminta's £12,000, both Wittol and Bluffe are deprived of courtship and even of the sight of their betrothed. Their comic punishment is that they are married off respectively to Bellmour and Vainlove's shared former mistress, Silvia, and her maid Lucy. Although the love games of Bellmour and Vainlove may be linked metaphorically to the monetary duping of Wittol and Bluffe, Congreve keeps the two plots largely separate, and there seems a distinct reluctance on Congreve's part to recognize the con game and the love game not merely as analogous but as conflated social realities.

In the later comedies, some of that reluctance is overcome, but Congreve's world is, for the most part, homogeneously aristocratic; and neither Mellefont in **The Double Dealer,** nor Valentine in **Love for Love,** nor Mirabell in **The Way of the World** is *forced* to consider a wealthy match either outside or within his class. True, Mellefont and Valentine face the possibility of disinheritance and financial ruin, but Congreve does not have either think of recouping his losses through marriage. Quite the contrary: Mellefont is prepared to marry Cynthia without money, and Valentine hopes to outwit his father so that his own fortune may be commensurate with Angelica's. Mellefont's and Valentine's views are not, however, those of the playwright, and it is the women who must teach them what appears to be Congreve's concept of happiness in marriage.

The Double Dealer is unique among Congreve's comedies, for Mellefont, its hero, is neither rake nor wit. Those traits belong instead to the mercenary villain, Maskwell. Mellefont's innate virtue, his ingenuous and blind trust in the unscrupulous Maskwell, and his near loss of Cynthia bring him dangerously close to sentimentality and to the heroes of sentimental comedy. He is, however, like Valentine in **Love for Love,** both rescued and educated by his more discerning female counterpart. The central difficulty in **The Double Dealer** turns on a financial issue: through the scheming of various characters and of Maskwell in particular, Mellefont stands to lose his own inheritance as well as the hand and fortune of Cynthia. But Mellefont's boyish romantic attitude is such that he is prepared to surrender his monetary interests if he can marry Cynthia. And he is prepared to have her with or without her money. Mellefont's idealistic enthusiasm is, however, significantly adjusted and redirected by a wiser, more pragmatic Cynthia:

> MELLEFONT: I don't know why we should not steal out of the House this moment and Marry one another, without Consideration or the fear of Repentance. Pox o'Fortune, Portion, Settlements and Joyntures.
>
> CYNTHIA: Ay, ay, what have we to do with 'em; you know we Marry for Love.
>
> MELLEFONT: Love, Love, down right very Villanous Love.

CYNTHIA: And he that can't live upon Love, deserves to die in a Ditch—Here, then, I give you my promise, in spight of Duty, any temptation of Wealth, your inconstancy, or my own inclination to change—

MELLEFONT: To run most wilfully and unreasonably away with me this moment and be Married.

CYNTHIA: Hold—Never to Marry any Body else.

MELLEFONT: That's but a kind of Negative Consent.—Why, you wont baulk the Frollick?

CYNTHIA: If you had not been so assured of your own Conduct I would not—But 'tis but reasonable that since I consent to like a Man without the vile Consideration of Money, He should give me a very evident demonstration of his Wit: Therefore let me see you undermine my Lady *Touchwood,* as you boasted, and force her to give her Consent, and then—

MELLEFONT: I'll do't.

CYNTHIA: And I'll do't. (4.1.27-51)

Mellefont's stress upon marriage based on love is applauded, but his easy surrender of both money and wit are not. Of course, Mellefont's proper demonstration of wit, the successful undermining of Lady Touchwood, will, in effect, secure the "Fortune, Portion, Settlements and Joyntures" against which he has just so vocally protested.

Mellefont's education about wit, money, and love is done in the context of Lord and Lady Froth on the one hand and of Machiavellian Maskwell on the other. The Froths are poetasters and false wits, who celebrate their affection by writing "Songs, Elegies, Satires, Encomiums, Panegyricks, Lampoons, Plays, or Heroick Poems" (2.1.1-26), but whose supposed wit has as its end only self-adulation, self-admiration, and self-congratulation. The use of wit—or in this case false wit—merely for egocentric and nonutilitarian purposes is presented and rejected by Congreve as well as by Cynthia (3.1.626-34). Maskwell is a character not as easily rejected, for he has both true wit and utilitarian purpose. For these reasons he is not rendered foolish like the Froths and almost defeats Mellefont. He is a forerunner of Fainall, who is very nearly a match for Mirabell in *The Way of the World,* and like Fainall, he is rendered a Machiavel by the primacy of his utilitarian ends, his acquisitiveness. He tells Mellefont that he has tricked Lady Touchwood and "if I accomplish her designs (as I told you before) she has ingaged to put *Cynthia* with all her Fortune into my Power" (2.1.427-29); and when Mellefont exits, Maskwell, in a long Machiavellian soliloquy, exclaims:

> Success will attend me; for when I meet you [Mellefont], I meet the only Obstacle to my Fortune. *Cynthia,* let thy Beauty gild my Crimes; and whatsoever I commit of Treachery or Deceit, shall be imputed to me as a Merit. (2.1.439-43)

Later, when he seems nearly successful in obtaining Cynthia and the inheritance Lord Touchwood had planned to settle on Mellefont, Maskwell soliloquizes, "This is prosperous indeed—Why let him find me out a Villain, settled in possession of a fair Estate, and full fruition of my Love, I'll bear the railings of a losing Gamester" (5.1.85-88). What makes Maskwell reprehensible and villainous from Congreve's point of view is not that his wit is used to betray others, for certainly this could be said of Bellmour, Valentine, and Mirabell. It is, rather, his concentration upon the acquisition of money. Whether Maskwell has any affection for Cynthia beyond his affection for her fortune is never clear. Even Cynthia's beauty is transmuted into precious metal by Maskwell, for it will "gild" his crimes. He sees, moreover, that Cynthia's money is something to be held and controlled, for he speaks of having Cynthia's fortune put "into my Power" and of being "settled in possession of a fair Estate." Maskwell's possessiveness is such that he wishes to use his wit primarily to bring him a bundle of money and only secondarily the young lady who accompanies it.

To a ruthless business mentality like Maskwell's, a friend like Mellefont is expendable when he becomes a competitor in the economic marketplace. If he can possess Cynthia's estate, says Maskwell, "I'll bear the railings of a losing Gamester." The object of Maskwell's game playing is the possession of money, and here Congreve has Mellefont differ radically and importantly from him. Early in the play, Cynthia and Mellefont describe marriage through the imagery of games. Cynthia quips, "Still it is a Game, and Consequently one of us must be a Loser," to which Mellefont replies, "Not at all; only a Friendly Tryal of Skill, and the Winnings to be Shared between us" (2.1.168-71). For Maskwell, marriage is a game of winners and losers with the former in control of the marriage settlement. For Mellefont, by contrast, marriage and getting married are a game, but the "Tryal of Skill," the play, is more important than any monetary prize; and, furthermore, "the Winnings" are to be *shared* or, as some editions read, "laid out in an Entertainment." What Mellefont and the audience are taught through Cynthia and through Congreve is that the reasons for getting married should be based upon love and should transcend fortune, which is not to say that a loving couple should marry without money if it is in the power of their wit to secure it. In *The Double Dealer* wit must be used to secure the love of a young lady and then to secure the settlement she should bring with her, but step one must greatly outweigh and precede step two.

By making Maskwell such an outright villain and Mellefont so amiable and trusting a fellow, Congreve allows the question of romance versus finance in marriage to be one that need not engage much of the audience's attention. Mellefont's values are after all largely in the right place. He prefers love to settlements and jointures; and he sees any money brought into the marriage by either partner as funds that the married couple may jointly enjoy. Cynthia's task is simply to encourage Mellefont not to lose what, by virtue of the marriage arrangements already drawn up, is nearly his. The questions of money and love are furthermore pushed into the background by Congreve's satiric portraits of three other couples, the Froths, the Plyants, and the Touchwoods. These comic characters and the plots in which they move serve to draw the audience's attention away from the issues besetting the Mellefont-Cynthia-Maskwell triangle. It is in *Love for Love* that Congreve places the questions concerning the relationship between money and love in the foreground and at the center of his comedy. This play abounds in talk of fortunes, inheritances, settlements, deeds of conveyance, and estates. A loan broker and an estate lawyer receive extended comic treatment. And a sometimes nasty, frequently comic, world driven nearly mad by the precedence of material values is the potent image that Congreve has pass before the eyes of his audience.

Love for Love has no fewer than eleven characters of major importance, all of whom are, with the exception of Mrs. Foresight and Scandal, directly affected by the financial state of affairs in the play. Mrs. Foresight, who is financially secure in her marriage to Foresight and who has no children to marry off, has nothing to lose or gain by the monetary transactions of the play. Since, however, she has in the past made a presumably financially advantageous marriage to Foresight, she can use her experience to counsel and abet her sister in Mrs. Frail's attempts to attain financial security through marriage. Likewise, Scandal, whom the play pairs with Mrs. Foresight and who is her worldly-wise male counterpart, has no personal loss or gain at stake in the money that will pass hands in the play; but he serves, nonetheless, to advise and abet his friend Valentine in affairs of the pocketbook as well as of the heart. At the center of Congreve's witty but acquisitive world stand Valentine and Angelica, whose positions toward courtship, marriage, and money create the central interest of the comedy. Those positions not only are treated directly but also are examined indirectly through each of the several other actions of the comedy. In part, the point of *Love for Love* can be located in its title, for although there is much courtship for purely sexual ends and much courtship for purely acquisitive ends, there is no true love for love except that displayed between Angelica and Valentine during the final moments of the play.

The two most patent fortune hunters in *Love for Love* are Mrs. Frail and Mr. Tattle, who, through Congreve's poetic justice, emerge married to each other. Yet Congreve is no harsh judge, for he knows that Mrs. Frail is no mean-spirited, avaricious Maskwell but rather is a victim of the way of the world who must do what she can to mend or make her fortune. Sight unseen, therefore, she is prepared to set her cap for the rough tar, Ben, whose promise of inheritance obliterates his unpromising personality. To her successful sister, she dispassionately explains:

> You have a Rich Husband, and are provided for,
> I am at a loss, and have no great Stock either of
> Fortune or Reputation; and therefore must look
> sharply about me. Sir *Sampson* has a Son that is
> expected to Night; and by the Account I have
> heard of his Education can be no Conjurer: The
> Estate You know is to be made over to him:—
> Now if I cou'd wheedle him, Sister, ha! You un-
> derstand me? (2.2.489-96)

And when the estate is taken from Ben and seems to revert to Valentine, she can just as dispassionately have no

> **Congreve's world is a game board that includes a desired young lady and a bundle of money. To win the game, the male player must bring these two objects to the same square on the board, and the game is not over until there is a winner.**
>
> —Albert Wertheim

qualms about marrying Valentine despite his seemingly demented state. That Ben is crude or that Valentine is mad makes little difference, for it is the estate that matters. As Mrs. Foresight shrewdly comments, "after Consummation, Girl, there's no revoking. And if he should recover his Senses, he'll be glad at least to make you a good Settlement" (4.1.473-75).

As in most love comedies, there are winners and losers in *Love for Love,* but—in a way that sets them apart from Etherege's and Wycherley's characters—the wins and losses are realistically reckoned in pounds sterling rather than in mistresses. This sense of gain and loss informs Tattle's as well as Mrs. Frail's *Weltanschauung.* Valentine's servant Jeremy convinces Tattle that, in return for some tangible rewards, Angelica can be tricked into marrying Tattle. Jeremy's lure is Angelica's fortune, to which Tattle has already shown himself not indifferent. " 'Tis an Act of Charity, Sir," observes Jeremy, "to save a fine Woman with Thirty Thousand Pound, from throwing her self away" (5.1.209-11). Tattle's assurance of success is expressed with images, like Mrs. Frail's, stressing marriage as a game of chance played for monetary stakes:

> I have some taking Features, not obvious to Vul-
> gar Eyes; that are Indications of a sudden turn
> of good Fortune, in the Lottery of Wives; and
> promise a great Beauty and great Fortune re-
> served alone for me, by a private Intrigue of Des-
> tiny. (5.2.267-71)

When Mrs. Frail marries Tattle believing him to be Valentine, and when Tattle married Mrs. Frail believing her to be Angelica, Congreve momentarily allows Tattle and Frail to be comic proxies for Valentine and Angelica in order to project what it would be like for the main couple to marry for fortune and estate only. Despite their dislike for one another, however, the two fortune hunters, Mrs. Frail and Tattle, do not make a bad match; and they will likely survive even more swimmingly than Silvia and Sir Joseph, their forerunners in *The Old Bachelor.*

The economics of getting married are delineated in another key through the marriage preparations for Ben and Miss Prue. Here Congreve presents a radically mismatched couple, he "a Sea-Beast" and she "a Land-Monster," who are brought together by Sir Sampson and Foresight, their parents, to unite jointure and settlement. Sir Sampson is perhaps the character most corrupted by the material values that color the way of *Love for Love's* world, but even the otherworldly astrologer Foresight, comically lost in the stars, seems not completely oblivious to the prime mover, prosperity, that guides the realities of the beau monde:

> SCANDAL: But I fear this Marriage and making over this Estate, this transferring of a rightful Inheritance, will bring Judgments upon us. I prophesie it, and I wou'd not have the Fate of *Cassandra,* not to be believ'd. . . .
>
> FORESIGHT: But as to this marriage I have consulted the Stars; and all Appearances are prosperous—
>
> SCANDAL: Come, come, Mr. *Foresight,* let not the Prospect of Worldly Lucre carry you beyond your Judgment, nor against your Conscience— You are not satisfy'd that you act justly.
>
> (3.1.543-57)

Congreve does not take pains to let us see exactly how much worldly wisdom resides beneath Foresight's otherworldly humour, but he is pellucid in his portrayal of Sir Sampson Legend.

If there is a villain in *Love for Love,* Sir Sampson is it; and he is, appropriately, the one character publicly exposed, disgraced, and punished at the close of the comedy. Sir Sampson not only plans to dispose of Ben as he would a piece of property, but in his treatment of Valentine he replaces the obligations of parental love with loveless legal and monetary obligations. When Valentine sues for his father's blessing, Sir Sampson tellingly replies, "You've had it already, Sir, I think I sent it you to day in a Bill of Four Thousand Pound" (2.1.274-75). Valentine continues to urge the obligations of paternal love; Sir Sampson counters with an argument for paternal despotism and the divine right of the father, unashamedly setting forth the purely capitalistic paradigm of the family as an arrangement of economic exploitation and dependence:

> why Sirrah, mayn't I do what I please? Are not you my Slave? Did not I beget you? And might not I have chosen whether I would have begot you or no? Ouns who are you? Whence came you? What brought you into the World? How came you here, Sir? . . . Did you come a Voluntier into the World? Or did I beat up for you with the lawful Authority of a Parent, and press you to the service? (2.1.323-32)

Valentine rightly terms his father's behavior "Barbarity and Unnatural Usage," an unnaturalness and barbarity bred by a monstrous materialism that allows children to become inanimate goods or property to be disposed of according to the whims of their fathers, the despotic property holders. The monstrosity of Sir Sampson's attitude is brought out to its fullest by Angelica, who wins his favor by feigning to share his materialism, "If I marry, Sir *Sampson,* I'm for a good Estate with any Man, and for any Man with a good Estate" (3.1.253-54). She aphoristically echoes his depersonalization of human relationship in favor of economic egotism. Her trick works so well that Sir Sampson proposes marriage and reveals himself prepared unfeelingly to disinherit both his sons:

> SIR SAMPSON: Odd, Madam, I'll love you as

long as I live; and leave you a good Jointure when I die.

> ANGELICA: Aye; But that is not in your Power, Sir *Sampson;* for when *Valentine* confesses himself in his Senses; he must make over his Inheritance to his younger Brother.
>
> SIR SAMPSON: Odd, you're cunning, a wary Baggage! Faith and Troth I like you the better—But, I warrant you, I have a Proviso in the Obligation in favour of my self—Body o'me, I have a Trick to turn the Settlement upon the Issue Male of our Two Bodies begotten. Odsbud, let us find Children, and I'll find an Estate. (5.1.119-29)

The voice of intelligence, judgment, and wit in *Love for Love* belongs to Angelica, and it is she, therefore, who teases both Valentine and his father to show their best and worst selves respectively. She tests both father and son, and rewards them accordingly:

> I was resolv'd to try him [Valentine] to the utmost; I have try'd you [Sir Sampson] too, and know you both. You have not more Faults than he has Virtues; and 'tis hardly more Pleasure to me, that I can make him and my self happy, than that I can punish you. (5.1.574-78)

For his generous love, Valentine receives a public declaration of Angelica's love for him. For his unnatural and materialistic barbarity, Sir Sampson is publicly exposed; and for his plan to disinherit his sons and marry Angelica, he is rendered a fool open to both the ridicule and scorn of all.

The events involving the Foresights, Mrs. Frail, Ben and Prue, and Sir Sampson and Angelica merely form a dramatic context for the education of the comedy's central character, Valentine. That education is, furthermore, the product of Valentine's two principal teachers, Scandal and Angelica. When at the close of *Love for Love,* Angelica gives heart and hand to Valentine, she says she "was resolv'd to try him to the utmost"; but in the course of that trial, Valentine learns what no character other than Angelica knows: the importance of love for love.

In the first act of the play, Congreve introduces a Valentine impoverished by courtship. At heart a romantic, Valentine takes pleasure in the prospect of becoming a misogynist poet or philosopher, roles his reduced finances will support. He hopes as well to gain Angelica's love, the love he had not gained through prodigality, through the charm of his current romantic poverty. At the same time that he maintains a romantic pose, Valentine also possesses a sharp wit, has fathered a bastard, and has not been untouched by the way of the world. His worldly education has taught him what it has taught the other characters: in this world money triumphs over love. That knowledge, combined with his innate romanticism, has led Valentine first upon a mad course of proving his affection for Angelica by spending vast sums in her behalf and then to a belief that his current resultant poverty is the ultimate demonstration of his love:

> Well; and now I am poor, I have an opportunity to be reveng'd on 'em all; I'll pursue *Angelica* with more Love than ever, and appear more no-

toriously her Admirer in this Restraint, than
when I openly rival'd the rich Fops, that made
Court to her; so shall my Poverty be a Mortification to her Pride, and perhaps, make her compassionate that Love, which has principally
reduc'd me to this Lowness of Fortune. (1.1.49-
56)

This romantic view would justify Valentine's further im-
poverishing himself by signing away his inheritance to his
brother Ben.

Signing a deed of conveyance would be, as Scandal chides,
"A very desperate demonstration of your love to Angelica," and he argues astutely, "you have little reason to believe that a Woman of this Age, who has had an indifference for you in your Prosperity, will fall in love with your
ill Fortune; besides, *Angelica* has a great Fortune of her
own; and great Fortunes either expect another great Fortune, or a Fool" (1.1.343-44, 350-54). The correctness of
Scandal's comment on the monetary basis of love relationships specifically and on social behavior generally is
brought home to Valentine by various characters who are
heard from in act 1. They include the pragmatic, philosophizing Jeremy, who speaks of the need to leave a master
bereft of credit; the past mistress who now writes for child
support; the loan broker Trapland, whose friendliness in
flush times has been replaced by an uncharitable readiness
to clap insolvent debtors into irons; Mrs. Frail, who carries the news of the proposed, economically motivated arranged match between Ben and Prue; and Sir Sampson's
steward, sent to act on his master's barbarous demand for
Valentine's deed of conveyance.

By the end of the first act, Valentine, in the context of the
other characters, does indeed seem to have acted naively,
and Scandal's observation and couplet, which close the
act, are well taken:

> I'll give an account of you, and your Proceed-
> ings. If Indiscretion be a sign of Love, you are
> the most a Lover of any Body that I know: you
> fancy that parting with your Estate, will help
> you to your Mistress.—In my mind he is a
> thoughtless Adventurer,
>
> Who hopes to purchase Wealth, by selling Land;
> Or win a Mistress, with a losing hand.
>   (1.1.675-81)

Apparently, it is Scandal's worldly teaching upon which
Valentine then proceeds to act. His feigned madness is
principled by a pragmatic, materialistic outlook that will
enable him to keep his estate, and provide him with the
land and the winning hand that Scandal asserts are necessary for marriage to Angelica. Valentine's feigned madness is, furthermore, simply his satiric exaggeration of the
mad, unprincipled proceedings of the rest of society. "All
mad, I think—Flesh, I believe all the *Calentures* of the Sea
are come ashore for my part" (4.1.356-57), is, after all,
what the plain-dealing Ben so aptly says of the entire cast
of *Love for Love.*

As the play shows it, Scandal's teaching may have the ring
of truth, but it is, nonetheless, flawed; and as Valentine's
teacher, his *magister ludi,* Congreve replaces Scandal with
Angelica. In act 4, Valentine recites to Angelica the les-

sons he has mastered under Scandal and receives reproof
instead of expected reward. He admits that he "has worn
this Mask of Madness, only as the Slave of Love, and Menial Creature of your Beauty" (4.1.702-4), and that, furthermore, his efforts to retain his estate and inheritance,
to match fortune for fortune (which Scandal has said is
necessary for winning "Women of this Age"), are proof
of his affection. Instead of falling into his arms and ending
the comedy, as Valentine anticipates, Angelica gives him
a telling and heuristic rebuff:

> VALENTINE: The Comedy draws toward an end,
> and let us think of leaving acting, and be our
> selves . . . my seeming Madness has deceiv'd
> my Father, and procur'd me time to think of
> means to reconcile me to him; and preserve the
> right of my Inheritance to his Estate . . .
>
> ANGELICA: How! I thought your love of me had
> caus'd this Transport in your Soul; which, it
> seems, you only counterfeited, for mercenary
> Ends and sordid Interest.
>
> VALENTINE: Nay, now you do me Wrong; for
> if any Interest was considered, it was yours;
> since I thought I wanted more than Love, to
> make me worthy of you.
>
> ANGELICA: Then you thought me mercenary—
> But how am I deluded by this Interval of Sense,
> to reason with a Madman. (4.1.707-8, 715-30)

Angelica here affirms that Valentine has acted as madly
and as badly as the rest of the world. Placing mercenary
interests above love, Valentine has adulterated and transmogrified the love between the sexes in precisely the same
way that Sir Sampson has adulterated and transmogrified
the love between parent and child. In this short exchange,
Angelica successfully reveals that neither prodigality nor
avarice need mix with love and that to posit mercenary
ends as a necessary prelude to marital love, as most of the
characters in *Love for Love* do, is for her nothing short
of madness.

Congreve's title, of course, is the core of Angelica's educational philosophy; and Valentine must come to understand the concept of generosity that avoids and transcends
both prodigality and avarice which is implicit in the title.
It is only when, through Angelica's guidance, he masters
the idea of generosity that Valentine can have both his
woman and his money:

> VALENTINE: I never valu'd Fortune, but as it
> was subservient to my Pleasure; and my only
> Pleasure was to please this Lady: I have made
> many vain Attempts, and find at last, that noth-
> ing but my Ruine can effect it: Which, for that
> Reason, I will sign to—Give me the Paper.
>
> ANGELICA: Generous *Valentine!* . . . Had I the
> World to give you it cou'd not make me worthy
> of so generous and faithful a Passion: Here's my
> Hand, my Heart was always yours, and struggl'd
> very hard to make the utmost Tryal of your Vir-
> tue.
>
>   (5.1.544-64)

Of all his comedies, Congreve's *Love for Love* is the one
that turns most centrally on the conflation of money and

the affairs of the heart. **The Old Bachelor** separates the two concerns by dividing them into two plots, and **The Double Dealer** overwhelms the concern for Mellefont's and Cynthia's fortunes with a strong Machiavel and a constellation of manners comedy stock figures. In **Love for Love,** however, no character is unaffected by the impact of money, yet Congreve seems to shy away from the implications of his own satire. Perhaps this is Congreve's own form of generosity. Clearly Angelica and Valentine rise above the other characters as they affirm a relationship based upon love for love instead of love for money or money for money; but at the same time, the other characters are not, except Sir Sampson, really condemned or punished. Scandal and Mrs. Foresight consummate their affair, Mr. Foresight remains unchanged, Ben happily returns to the sea, and Miss Prue will, as she herself predicts, probably fulfill her destiny and run off with one of the servants. Tattle and Mrs. Frail are married but even they realize that they will likely manage quite well; and though Tattle's fortune is not what Valentine's is or what Ben's would have been, it will nevertheless serve the purpose of rescuing Mrs. Frail from her economic dilemma. Even Sir Sampson, who is condemned and punished, is not in a class with Congreve's out and out villains, Maskwell and Fainall, and his punishment is merely the exposure of his failures as a parent and suitor; there is no concomitant economic punishment as there is for Maskwell and Fainall. Even with Angelica, the central intelligence of the play, Congreve seems to skirt some of the realities of economics by placing Angelica's fortune entirely in her own hands. This rare situation, in short, frees Angelica from any economic control including that of her guardian Foresight. As a totally free agent, absolute mistress of her vast £30,000 fortune, she can enjoy the luxury of teaching Valentine to be generous.

In **The Way of the World,** which is less centrally about money than **Love for Love,** Congreve nonetheless comes closest to treating the question of money convincingly. In **The Double Dealer,** Cynthia's settlement is not in question, it is only a matter of whether it will go to Maskwell or Mellefont; in **Love for Love,** Angelica's considerable fortune is entirely at her own disposal; but in **The Way of the World,** Millamant's £12,000 is only partially in her own hands, for Lady Wishfort controls £6,000, exactly half of it. Millamant, therefore, can only in part be her own mistress and affirm the primacy of love, for she is also in part liable to the loss of half her monies if she marries without her aunt's consent. How Mirabell and Millamant deport themselves, consequently, seems a more true test and more convincing example of Congreve's attitudes toward marriage than those found in his earlier comedies.

Dividing the control of Millamant's £12,000 fortune equally between the heroine and her aunt, Congreve places Millamant at the theoretical center of **The Way of the World.** She could conceivably marry for love thereby forfeiting £6,000; or she could marry the unsuitable Sir Wilfull Witwoud, her aunt's choice, thereby losing Mirabell but keeping her fortune intact. Neither choice is a happy one, but, the conventions of comedy being what they are, an audience has every right to expect that Millamant either alone or together with Mirabell will use her

wit to trick Lady Wishfort and the other blocking characters in such a way that Millamant can have Mirabell as well as her full £12,000 intact. The desired result is achieved, but how it is achieved has not been given enough consideration. It is remarkable indeed that in a society where jockeying for financial position seems so much the way of the world, and in a plot where the disposal of Millamant's fortune is so central an issue, Millamant herself never once discusses her money nor does Mirabell ever once discuss with Millamant his elaborate plotting to secure the £6,000 pounds under Lady Wishfort's control. Millamant is, nonetheless, certainly aware of what is happening around her, as she reveals the one time Mirabell unsuccessfully attempts to broach the subject:

> MIRABELL: Can you not find in the variety of your Disposition one Moment—
>
> MILLAMANT: To hear you tell me that *Foible's* married, and your Plot like to speed—No.
>
> MIRABELL: But how came you to know it—
>
> MILLAMANT: Unless by the help of the Devil you can't imagine; unless she shou'd tell me her self. Which of the two it may have been, I will leave you to consider; and when you have done thinking of that; think of me. *Exit.* (2.2.480-89)

Millamant parries before Mirabell can thrust, at once acknowledging her awareness of Mirabell's doings and forbidding him to speak to her of them. Before the astonished Mirabell can react, she turns with physical and linguistic flourish to exit, but leaves him with the injunction, "think of me." Like so much that happens in **The Way of the World** between Mirabell and Millamant, much of the communication is effected precisely by what is *not* said. Unlike Angelica, Millamant need not stop to reprove the hero's acquisitiveness or remind him to concentrate more on love than on fortune. She merely deflects the topic of conversation, yet wittily and pointedly reminds Mirabell not to lose sight of his real object: "think of me."

The singular and superior relationship between Mirabell and Millamant is made by Congreve to look all the more singular and superior by the characters around them. As everyone who has ever seen or read **The Way of the World** immediately senses, consciously or unconsciously, the foppish Petulant and Witwoud, the plain-spoken but boorish Sir Wilfull, and the passionate Lady Wishfort set off by their various flaws the patently superior wit and style of the lead couple. More discrimination is necessary to measure Mirabell and Millamant against Marwood, Fainall, and Mrs. Fainall, for these three are no fools and fall only slightly short of Mirabell and Millamant's level of intelligence and poise. Yet Mirabell and Millamant do emerge superior and not merely because they are less passionate and less malicious, though that has something to do with placing them above Marwood and the Fainalls. What distinguishes Mirabell and Millamant is, finally, what also distinguishes Valentine and Angelica from the rest of the characters in **Love for Love,** namely their generosity and their attitude toward the relative importance of money as a basis for marriage or love relationships.

If Mirabell and Millamant fail to talk of money, the two

characters who are most closely compared to them, Fainall and Marwood, can think of little else. Their relationship to the other characters and even to each other is repeatedly marked, often dominated, by their prodigality and acquisitiveness. Reminiscent of the union of Jonson's Subtle and Face, the relationship between Fainall and Marwood is an explosive one and one that is a business partnership held together by money:

> MRS. MARWOOD: It shall be all discover'd. You too shall be discover'd; be sure you shall. I can but be expos'd—If I do it my self I shall prevent your Baseness.
>
> FAINALL: Why, what will you do?
>
> MRS. MARWOOD: Disclose it to your Wife; own what has past between us.
>
> FAINALL: Frenzy!
>
> MRS. MARWOOD: By all my Wrongs I'll do't— I'll publish to the World the Injuries you have done me, both in my Fame and Fortune: With both I trusted you, you Bankrupt in Honour, as indigent in Wealth.
>
> FAINALL: Your Fame I have preserv'd. Your Fortune has been bestow'd as the prodigality of your Love would have it, in Pleasures which we both have shar'd. Yet had not you been false, I had e'er repaid it—'Tis true—Had you permitted *Mirabell* with *Millamant* to have stoll'n their Marriage, my Lady had been incens'd beyond all means of reconcilement: *Millamant* had forfeited the Moiety of her Fortune; which then wou'd have descended to my Wife;—And wherefore did I marry, but to make lawful Prize of a rich Widow's Wealth, and squander it on Love and you?
>
> MRS. MARWOOD: Deceit and frivolous Pretence.
>
> (2.1.187-208)

Marwood's passion is conflated with prodigality. Fainall's circuitous plotting to obtain everyone's money is as complex and extravagant as Mirabell's scheme to gain Lady Wishfort's blessing and loosen her grip on Millamant's £6,000 by extricating the aunt from a marriage with a valet. What distinguishes the two schemes, however, is that for Fainall all things and all women are sacrificed to his egotistical desire for money. Any feeling for Marwood is at best an afterthought, as is clear in the priorities revealed in Fainall's declaration that he desires money to "squander it on Love and you." He loves for money, he marries for money, and he plots for money. Mirabell, by contrast, acts with greatest honor toward Mrs. Fainall, his former mistress, and toward the money she has placed in his trust, and he omits all question of money in his discourses with Millamant. His plotting is meant to place at her disposal the money that is rightly Millamant's and not to secure it for himself. Mirabell's elaborate plot is, after all, well under way long before Millamant has given any consent, verbal or written, to marry him.

At the heart of Mirabell and Millamant's relationship is the famous "Contract" or "proviso" scene of act 4. For every critic this scene takes on signal importance as the representation of what the relationship between the hero and heroine actually is and what it will be after marriage. Norman Holland [in his *The First Modern Comedies,* 1959] and Virginia Birdsall [in her *Wild Civility,* 1970] stress the harmony of temperament and the maturation of Millamant; Kathleen Lynch [in her *The Social Mode of Restoration Comedy,* 1926] places the proviso scene in the context of the dramatic sources and analogues Congreve likely knew, and Maximillian Novak [in his *William Congreve*] goes on to show that against the literary background Lynch documents, Mirabell and Millamant play wittily with the proviso convention because their understanding is already such that provisos are superfluous. Ian Donaldson notes in passing [in his *The World Upside-Down,* 1970] that the proviso scene does not touch "upon the cold mercantile facts" raised in Wycherley's *The Gentleman Dancing-Master,* an analogue Lynch overlooked. Donaldson here indicates precisely what is remarkable about the verbal contract Mirabell and Millamant agree to. In the mock formality of its legal language, its *imprimis* and *item,* it calls to mind the usual marriage contracts in which the clauses concerned settlements and jointures, the financial arrangements that were to provide the legal setting for a union officially recognized in a church ceremony. Mirabell and Millamant "convenant" a great many things, most of them trifles that are nonetheless indicative of the social and love relationship they already have and wish to foster in the future. As is often the case, however, in the discourses between Mirabell and Millamant, what is unspoken is as important as what is stated. That the issue of money is never once part of their legalistic convenant, though in the world outside the theater it was always the heart of the legal marriage convenant, shows at once Mirabell and Millamant's awareness of the monetary ways of the world as well as their determination not to define their love verbally by the economic strictures of the traditional marriage contract. The content of the proviso scene italicizes the primacy of love and personal relationships that Mirabell and Millamant affirm as the proper basis for marriage. Money, in not being mentioned, is given a distinctly peripheral place. The actual monetary agreements that would have to have been reached in the written contract, seemingly drawn up off stage somewhere between the fourth and fifth acts, are never either specified or discussed by the principals. Congreve's emphasis upon the importance of love over concerns about money is further italicized by providing Mirabell and Millamant with a real financial issue, namely, Lady Wishfort's control over half of her niece's fortune. For Angelica, whose fortune is entirely in her own hands, her attitudes, however laudable, can be judged a luxury. Millamant's is an attitude that must necessarily be more hard won and, therefore, more credible.

In the concluding scene of *The Way of the World* the avarice of Fainall and the generosity of Mirabell collide. In a proviso scene of his own, Fainall proposes a contract that would enable him to control Lady Wishfort and, consequently, her estate; he demands that Mrs. Fainall "settle on me the remainder of her Fortune, not made over already" (5.1.268-69), and insists upon immediate possession of the half of Millamant's fortune held by Lady Wishfort. Since all things seem to be going Fainall's way, he gives vent to what is for him obviously the optimum social relationship, malevolent economic despotism. Lady Wishfort may enjoy her "own proper Estate during Life; on the condition you oblige your self never to Marry, under such penalty as I think convenient" (5.1.252-54). Mrs. Fainall not only is to make over her fortune to her husband but must, says Fainall, "for her Maintenance depend entirely on my Discretion" (5.1.269-70). As Fainall senses his strength, he revises his demands to insist upon his sole control of Lady Wishfort's estate as well as his wife's (5.1.433-36). His machinations are, however, foiled by Mirabell and the contents of the black box:

> MIRABELL: Mr. *Fainall,* it is now time that you shou'd know, that your Lady while she was at her own disposal, and before you had by your Insinuations wheedl'd her out of a pretended Settlement of the greatest part of her fortune—
>
> FAINALL: Sir! pretended!
>
> MIRABELL: Yes Sir. I say that this Lady while a Widow, having it seems receiv'd some Cautions respecting your Inconstancy and Tyranny of temper . . . she did I say by the wholesome advice of Friends and of Sages learned in the Laws of this Land, deliver this same as her Act and Deed to me in trust, and to the uses within mention'd. You may read if you please—tho perhaps what is inscrib'd on the back may serve your occasions.
>
> FAINALL: Very likely, Sir, What's here? Damnation! *A deed of Conveyance of the whole Estate real of* Arabella Languish *Widdow in trust to* Edward Mirabell. Confusion!
>
> MIRABELL: Even so Sir, 'tis *the way of the World,* Sir: of the Widdows of the World.
> (5.1.535-54)

Why, one is led to ask, should Congreve allow his comic plot to hinge on a providential black box and its hitherto obscure contents? Why, too, is Mirabell's elaborate hoax necessary when he might so easily compel Lady Wishfort to permit his marriage to Millamant by flourishing Mrs. Fainall's deed of conveyance? The obvious answer is that Congreve forces his audience to dwell upon Mirabell's generosity, especially in contrast to the exposition of Fainall's character. There is, however, a still more important answer, namely, that the audience in asking the second question comes to realize that Mirabell could not have won Millamant through blackmail that threatened the financial ruin of her cousin or aunt. In the 162 lines (432-594) comprising Fainall's seeming triumph and his consequent defeat, Millamant remains silent, but consistent with her presentation throughout *The Way of the World,* she is not only present on the stage but eloquent in her silence. Her presence amid the revelations whereby Mirabell saves Mrs. Fainall and Lady Wishfort makes the audience realize that had Mirabell used the black box to obtain Lady Wishfort's consent he would have shown that he sought Millamant's money more than the lady herself, and, more important, would have revealed a culpable, mercenary character, not unlike Fainall's, by the very nature of blackmail based upon economic mastery. In the

last speech of the play, Mirabell relinquishes the deed of conveyance to its owner and projects a new, enlightened view of money in marriage:

> For my part I will Contribute all that in me lies to a Reunion, (*To Mrs.* Fainall) in the mean time, *Madam,* let me before these Witnesses, restore to you this deed of trust. It may be a means well manag'd to make you live Easily together. (5.1.615-19)

Mirabell conveys the sense that in those marriages like the Fainalls' where love does not overshadow economics there is a second best choice, namely, to use economics so that the couple may "live Easily together."

Although in the courtships that take place in his comedies Congreve acknowledges the importance of money in a way that Wycherley and Etherege do not, he finally avoids having his characters make their choices in the context of real monetary pressures. In *The Old Bachelor* marriage for love and marriage for money are separate issues relegated to separate plots; and characters like Mellefont, Valentine, and Mirabell, who acknowledge the need for both love and money, never have to make a serious choice *between* them. Congreve's world is a game board that includes a desired young lady and a bundle of money. To win the game, the male player must bring these two objects to the same square on the board, and the game is not over until there is a winner. Like the witty couples found in the comedies of Elizabethan dramatists such as John Fletcher or in the comedies of Congreve's more immediate forebears, Etherege and Wycherley, Congreve's main couples are primarily expert players of the mating game. Their game has, however, been made more complex and difficult by adding financial obstacles to the sexual ones. And it is precisely those financial obstacles that will increasingly come to occupy the descendents of Valentine and Angelica and of Mirabell and Millamant as they are found in the comedies of Steele, Gay, Fielding, Garrick, and Sheridan. (pp. 255-72)

> *Albert Wertheim, "Romance and Finance: The Comedies of William Congreve," in* Comedy from Shakespeare to Sheridan: Change and Continuity in the English and European Dramatic Tradition, Essays in Honor of Eugene M. Waith, *edited by A. R. Braunmuller and J. C. Bulman, University of Delaware Press, 1986, pp. 255-73.*

Edward Burns   (essay date 1987)

[*In the following excerpt, Burns explores the literary forms and stylistic devices found in Congreve's dramas and his novella,* Incognita. *He maintains that even though Congreve is considered the most classical of the Restoration dramatists, he contributed no new conventions to the genre.*]

Before Congreve's first play, *The Old Batchelour,* reached its final form, Dryden and Southerne had already begun to promote his work as the culmination of Restoration comedy. Not surprisingly in these circumstances, it is he who brings the self-consciousness of the theatre of the nineties to its most dazzling peak. . . . Congreve's consciousness is a consciousness of form, of what it implies and what it must omit. A stylistic device is always more to Congreve than the production of a particular effect. When Dryden first discovered him, he may have seen a first version of *The Old Batchelour;* but he must also have seen *Incognita,* a short novel that explores the theme of disguise through an awareness of the disguise employed in the business of storytelling.

'When I degress' Congreve explains to the reader at one point, 'I am at that time writing to please myself, when I continue the thread of the story, I write to please him; supposing him a reasonable man, I conclude him satisfied to allow me this liberty, and so I proceed.' This gentleman's agreement is already rendered dubious by the use of the third person; if the reader is 'he' then who are we? At the end of his longest and most important digression, the narrator's slightly mad aloofness breaks down into a real comic irascibility—

> I could find it in my Heart to beg the Reader's pardon for this Digression, if I thought he would be sensible of the Civility; for I promise him, I do not intend to do it again throughout the Story, though I make never so many, and though he take them never so ill. But because I began this upon a bare Supposition of his impertinence, which might be somewhat impertinent in me to suppose I do, and hope to make him amends by telling him, that by the time *Lenora* was dress'd, several ladies of her acquaintance came to accompany her to the place designed for the tilting, where we will leave them drinking chocolate till 'tis time for them to go.

Congreve's losing battle with the demands of narrative award it only derisory victories; he may suppress the central fact of his tale and relegate mere event to a flurry of expository speech, mock-apologetic when it is the narrator's and mock-earnest when one of the character's, but he can tell us things whose only interest is that he bothers to us tell them—'By Computation now (which is a very remarkable circumstance) *Hippolito* entered this garden near upon the same instant, when Aurelian wandered into the Old Monestary and found his *Incognita* in distress.' *Incognita* is an anti-narrative; the subtitle deprives us of the usual romantic plot dynamic, for with 'Love and Duty Reconciled' what can a novel be about? About nothing of course. The tilts, amorous encounters and duels are trivialized by their context of 'manners', the nothing of a life where ladies get dressed to drink chocolate until it's time to stop. The tale runs constantly into a kind of narrative hiatus, like Sterne's black page. The same process is at work in the events of the tale;

> Coming by a Light which hung at the Corner of a Street, he join'd the torn papers and collected thus much, that his *Incognita* had written the Note, and earnestly desired him (if there were any reality in what he pretended to her) to meet her at Twelve a Clock that Night at a Convent Gate; but unluckily the Bit of Paper which should have mentioned what Convent, was broken off and lost.

Aurelian walks on 'unwittingly' after this unfortunate lesion in romantic plotting 'till at length a Silence . . . surpriz'd his attention.' Congreve goes on to explain how this might be, but an attentive reader is already aware that the 'Dominions of Silence and of Night' are encroaching; silence disarrays the narrative, as night deranges the events it chronicles; the flimsy characters of banal romance face, with a comic inexpressiveness, vast rents and gaps in their world.

Incognita is a play by negatives. It is based on what, because it is a novel, one cannot see, as plays are based on unspoken feelings, which, because they are plays, cannot be expressed without someone to speak them. It is the presence in a play of real people—actors—that is for Congreve the reason why 'all Traditions must undisputably give place to the Drama.' *Incognita* is what might happen if there were not even an actress behind the mask of the lady-in-disguise, the Incognita. Congreve shrugs off character more insouciantly than he could shake off plot. Aurelian, we are told, is the 'Type' of Fabio, and looks on his friend Hippolito as a 'second self,' so one character is defined by reference to another defined by reference to another still. The only distinguishing moment comes in the tilt scene, when Aurelian, disguised as Hippolito sees Incognita 'and had no other way to make himself known to her, but by saluting and bowing to her after the *Spanish* mode.' Identity, when it is defined by manners, is easily transferred. The novel articulates its range of feeling through a pair of couples contrasted only in the circumstance of intrigue; their dialogue in the ball scene is the high point of its parabolic course. Had the lovers not decided to stay in disguise, 'Love' and 'Duty' could have been reconciled from the start. All their mistakes and adventures, the whole fabric of the book in fact, ramifies from a simple failure to say the obvious. This, I think, is at the root of a fiction itself at the root of Congreve's career. *Incognita* reaches stasis in the convent garden, whose associations enforce purity on the passion conventionally expressed there. But the song in which Leonora expresses her feelings (to be overheard, of course, by the hidden Hippolito) is a graceful parody of the forlorn maiden's lament, a parody by negatives. She is

> Not by Alexis' Eyes undone,
> Nor by his Charming Faithless Tongue,
>   Or Any Practis'd Art;
> Such real Ills may hope a Cure,
> But the sad Pains which I endure
>   Proceed from fansied Smart.

Incognita reaches a pause on this lyric; afterwards it can only rattle through to the end of the intrigue.

The prologue to *The Old Batchelour* (1693) wittily disintegrates as the actress 'dries'.

> He prays—O bless me! What shall I do now!
> Hang me if I know what he prays, or how!
> And 'twas the prettiest Prologue, as he wrote it!
> Well, the Deuce take me, if I han't forgot it . . .
> I shall be hang'd for wanting what to say.
> For my sake then—but I'm in such Confusion.
> I cannot stay to hear your resolution.

She has 'forgotten' that part of the prologue most personal

to its author, the part that, as well as pleading his case, would complete his comparison of the present state of the stage with the 'former days' talked of in the first lines. But the prologue is complete in its rhymes and metrically elegant. It reserves to itself whatever it had to say. It's a piquantly 'impudent' opening to a first play; and it restates aspects of *Incognita* that *The Old Batchelour* locates in a psychological awareness. Congreve's preciosity thins his sense of the unrespectable realities of sexual relationship into the fabric of a brilliant and troubling play.

The Old Batchelour is the most uncompromising of all those plays of the 1690s that centre on a pair of gallants, one 'platonic', the other anti-platonic. Unlike Crowne and Vanbrugh, for example, Congreve explores the possibilities of this conventional contrast through its logical complement in plot; the device, invented by Aphra Behn, by which one gallant consummates the intrigue bagan by another. When the intervention is caused by accident, the upshot is unrespectable but inoffensive farce—as Edward Ravenscroft's *London Cuckolds* (1681) demonstrates, a play derivative in everything but its hilarious energy and solid good nature. Congreve turns over the possibilities of motivation; he moves towards Otway's interest in the darker springs of comic behaviour but withdraws, even more disturbingly, to suggest an impossibility of knowledge, an irrevocable disjunction of behaviour and feeling.

All Congreve's comedies begin with a short scene between the hero and a close associate, which involves an action trivial in itself but encoding something of the movement of the play. (His tragedy begins with the heroine and her attendant—tragedy was by now a feminized genre.) Bellmour meets his friend Vainlove in the street and mocks him for the letters he's carrying; business letters, apparently. His speech is a conventional, and very literary, expansion of the carpe diem topos, but Vainlove brings it, literally, down to earth.

> '. . . Leave Business to Idlers, and Wisdom to Fools . . . wit, be my Faculty; and Pleasure, my Occupation; and let Father Time shake his Glass. Let low and earthy Souls grovel till they have work'd themselves six foot deep into a Grave—Business is not my Element—I rowl in a higher Orb and dwell
>
> VAIN. In Castles i' th' Air of thy own building. . . . well as high a Flyer as you are, I have a Lure may make you stoop. (Flings a Letter.)
>
> BELL. I marry Sir, I have a Hawks Eye at a Womans hand. . . .

It's not even the letter he meant to throw down—a summons to assignation with the banker's wife, Laetitia—but a letter from a previous mistress, Silvia, previously shared as the two men mean to share Vainlove's more recent conquest. The gesture is ambiguous—is it a challenge, or the first move in a game? The other characters in a largely static first act discuss Vainlove's behaviour with a polite but edgy distaste, which Bellmour tries to deflect:

> BELL. He takes as much of an Amour as he cares for, and quits it when it grows stale or unpleasant.
>
> SHARP. An argument of very little Passion, very good Understanding, and very ill Nature.

The play's lightness of tone, the flippant assumption of intimacy set by that initial group of male characters, is achieved by a constant undercutting, as much of the stylistic devices themselves as of the characters who use them. Sharper enters to interrupt Bellmour in an expository speech to the audience, 'I'm sorry to see this, Ned', he says, 'Once a man comes to his Soliloquies I give him for gone.' By the time Heartwell, the play's satirist, enters we are primed to see his attitudes as an essentially defensive presentation of cliches. Satire, in Congreve's plays, is never to be understood simply in the terms it sets itself. 'Wit' is never detachable from character, never 'free', Congreve always sets careful limits to his characters' capacity to make jokes, there is always a qualifying circumstance in motive or plot, a shadow thrown by the movement of the play. Satire, too, is never to be understood in its own terms. When Belinda tells Araminta 'you play the Game and consequently can't see the Miscarriages obvious to every Stander by,' Araminta is easily able to turn the remark back on her. It could be extended to an observation on the play as a whole. The characters seem diminished when set beside those of the later comedies, in that none of them are allowed even the illusion of 'control'. Everyone is placed in the disadvantaged position outlined by Belinda—the play's action *is* a game, and we are the only 'safe' spectators. Heartwell is a 'pretended Woman-hater': his nervous infatuation with Silvia is to be winkled out by the play, whose ironical outcome is to make his woman-

THE

Old Batchelour,

A

COMEDY.

As it is ACTED at the

Theatre Royal,

BY

Their MAJESTIES Servants.

Written by Mr. *Congreve.*

Quem tulit ad Scenam ventoſo gloria Curru,
Exanimat lentus Spectator ; ſedulus inflat.
Sic leve, ſic parvum eſt, animum quod laudis avarum
Subruit, aut reficit——

Horat. Epiſt. I. Lib. II.

LONDON,

Printed for *Peter Buck,* at the Sign of the *Temple* near the *Temple-gate* in *Fleet-ſtreet,* 1693.

Title page of the 1693 quarto of The Old Batchelour.

hating real. Detachment—a fantasy of emotional privilege—turns out to be just as dangerous for Vainlove.

One could summarize the plot of **The Old Batchelour** as Vainlove's attempt to fob off two past attachments, Letitia with Bellmour, and Silvia with Heartwell, the old bachelor of the title, and to come to terms with Araminta, a girl apparently willing to play the game to his rules. Congreve introduces the first female characters unconventionally late, in a scene at the end of act two that serves to focus and to challenge the cool evasive rhetoric of the men.

Araminta assents eagerly to Vainlove's 'romantic' but sexless wooing:

> If Love be the Fever which you mean; kind
> Heav'n avert the cure; Let me have Oil to feed
> that Flame and never let it be extinct, till I my-
> self am Ashes.

The cure of their 'sickly peevish Appetite' (as Sharper calls it) would be, of course, its gratification, and it is this which she is anxious to avert. But Araminta has earlier touched on an idea, introduced by the more sceptical Belinda and Bellmour, that links up to the darker side of Congreve's apprehension of love. 'You are the Temples of Love' says Vainlove. 'Rather poor silly Idols of your own making', she replies, 'which, upon the least displeasure you forsake, and set up new.' The second stanza of the song I quoted from **Incognita** goes on to develop a parallel idea, picking it up from that long 'degression' whose presumed rejection by the reader so irritated the teller of the tale.

> Twas fancy gave Alexis Charms,
>   Ere I beheld his Face;
> Kind Fancy (then) could fold our Arms,
>   And form a soft Embrace.
> But since I've seen the real Swain,
> And try'd to fancy him again,
>   I'm by my Fancy taught,
> Though 'tis a Bliss no Tongue can tell,
> To have Alexis, yet 'tis Hell
> To have him but in Thought.

According to Congreve, love invents its objects. The human disparities to which this gives rise are never wholly comic.

In his brilliant libretto on the Semele story Congreve expands the theme into an ironic divertissement by introducing the pastoral change-of-identity plot, and the Guarinian plotter, in the shape of Juno/Ino. Jupiter, in a slyly blasphemous interpretation, takes on the primary aspect of the Christian God, that of creator. Semele colludes in her role as a mechanism of pleasure. 'With my frailty don't upbraid me' she disingenuously reminds her lover, 'I am Woman as you made me.' 'Frailty in thee is ornament' Jove concedes, with, it will turn out, misplaced complacency, 'In thee perfection / Giv'n to agitate the mind / and keep awake men's passions.' Araminta introduces a song into her first scene in **The Old Batchelour** which, she says, '. . . comes pretty near my own opinion of Love and your Sex.' On one level it fulfils the usual function of songs in Restoration plays. Distanced by their performance by an unnamed or marginal character, they focus our attention on the characters listening to them, and thus become a convention for unspoken thoughts. It is thus a reaction to the received language of passion to parallel Belinda's draconian resolution of her own doubts into her command to Bellmour that she 'would be Ador'd in Silence.' The song is a warning to women to prolong courtship as long as possible—

> Men will admire, adore and die,
> While wishing at your Feet they lie:
> But admitting their Embraces,
>   Wakes 'em from the golden Dream;
> Nothing's new besides our Faces,
>   Every woman is the same.

But its position in the play also lends it a structural weight. Its resonance is as an expression of that reductive quest for more of the same into which male libertinism has dwindled—of that 'sameness' which the women's counterplot is about to explore in its revenge.

In the next scene Silvia and Lucy, her maid, lunch the letter/disguise plot in a variation probably suggested to Congreve by Southerne's handling of the Lady Susan intrigue in *The Maids Last Prayer,* and evidence again of his determination to rethink plot ideas in the terms of his 'platonic' theme. Lucy sends Vainlove an open avowal of love purporting to come from Araminta. The trickster characters set up another impersonation plot to involve Lucy and Silvia in 'witty' marriages, both plots crossing each other in the Park, where one starts and the other finishes. If, as Lucy claims, deceit is second nature to women, it is because the styles that bridge the vast gap of comprehension between men and women in the world of the play are themselves implicitly mendacious. All this layered on to the Behn-derived *male* change-of-identity plot suggests an aspiring virtuosity seemingly intent on exhausting the possibilities of 'impersonation' once and for all, while simultaneously demonstrating the variety of levels on which it can work.

Vainlove confronts Araminta in the Park and tries to give her the letter. She drops it to the ground in unwitting repetition of a moment from the beginning of the play that darkens on recall. He refuses to stoop for it confident that 'she will be unwilling to expose to the censure of the first finder' the false signature at the bottom. That she does eventually stoop for it marks her loss of this little contest. Congreve manages Araminta's crisis with deft understatement. Belinda returns from a circuit of the park to find her gone. When Araminta reappears at the end of the play her primness seems fortified by decision, and her refusal of Vainlove's suit is inevitable.

'As love is a Deity', Vainlove says earlier in the play, 'he must be serv'd by Prayer.' 'O Gad' replies Belinda 'would you would all pray to Love then, and let us alone.' It is precisely as a ploy for letting Araminta alone that Vainlove adopts a style of 'romantic' wooing. The park-scene knits up suggestively a vein of speculation that runs irregularly on the play's polite excluding surface. **The Old Batchelour** seems to suggest that the 'honourable' forms indulged in by Vainlove and Heartwell are paradoxically more indecent than Bellmour's libertinism. But it consistently deflects the possibilities of revealed motivation or confident judgement. When Vainlove at the very start of the play remarks on Bellmour's pursuit of pleasure, his friend answers 'Ay What else has meaning?' The characters all puzzle at meaning; at the feeling behind style, the woman behind the mask. The gallants' double act could be seen to make sexuality unmeaning—as marriage and courtship are rendered unmeaning by Lucy and Silvia's disguise, and the letter-plot, respectively. The play is a kind of teasing out of the implications of disguise plots; there is a parallel to Southerne in the move towards an expression of vacancy, of 'disappointment'. The song on sexual 'disappointment' that Heartwell has sung to Silvia, seems anachronistic in the 1690s; traditionally 'libertine', traditionally 'witty'. But it inserts into the play a lyric expression of the same overriding sense. All four women unmask simultaneously at the end of the play, a coup that drew applause from the first-night audience. The quartet of Incognite state with a fine flourish that apprehension of vacuity which informs both Congreve's novel and his first play.

It would be difficult (and perhaps unrewarding) to establish a kind of ur-*Old Batchelour;* to decide which parts of the play are juvenile Congreve and which are determined by Southerne's and Dryden's tutelage, and the author's adaptation to theatrical conditions.' . . . had it been Acted, when it was first Written', Congreve writes in his Epistle Dedicatory, 'more might have been said in its behalf; Ignorance of the Town and Stage, would then have been excuses in a young Writer, which now, almost four Years experience, will scarce allow of.' On a form so dependent on an idea of social life, it is impossible to say where ignorance of the town might end and ignorance of the stage begin. *The Old Batchelour* is looser in structure than anything else of Congreve's; it is also—a predictable consequence—more lightweight, its characters less imposing. 'Ignorance of the Town' is at the base of this in the simplest sense. The people in the play meet each other by chance in unnamed streets—the play makes less geographical sense than almost any other Restoration comedy. But it is also the result of an attempt at Southerne's 'feel' for open structure and casual insights. Congreve demonstrates a gift for forming his play into moments of emphasis in the congruence of apparently random realistic detail—as in the park-scene. But his mature plays are shaped as wholes, through the imposition of abstract, even 'gratuitous' formal principles. *The Double Dealer* (1694) is an achievement of formal grandeur, the entrance to 'mature' Congreve.

The Double Dealer brings to climax that literary self-consciousness characteristic of the comedy of the 1690s, a self-consciousness often simplified to the decade's equally characteristic idea of theatricality. Southerne's commendatory verses to *The Old Batchelour* carefully place Congreve as the almost inevitable outcome of the tradition of Wit comedy.

> . . . *Wicherly,* in wise Retreat
> Thought it not worth his quiet to be great.
> Loose, wandring, *Etherege,* in wild Pleasures
>   tost,
> And foreign Int'rests, to his hopes long lost;
> Poor *Lee* and *Otway* dead! CONGREVE appears,
> The Darling, and last comfort of his Years.

'His' in this case means Dryden's. Where Southerne is vague, avuncular and only sporadically cogent, Dryden, in his prologue to *The Double Dealer,* creates a 'high' counterpart to *MacFlecknoe,* a movingly serious confirmation of artistic succession. His praise implies a retrospect, precise but large in scope

> Our Age was cultivated thus at length;
> But what we gain'd in skill we lost in strength.
> Our Builders were, with want to Genius, curst:
> The second Temple was not like the first . . .

The firm placing of his metaphor allows Dryden to suggest another history in little of the Restoration settlement. The 'temple' suggests St Paul's; the drift of the poem instates wit and its traditions as equally central to Restoration London. *The Double Dealer* is structurally informed by Congreve's need to validate his claim.

The Double Dealer is an exercise in classical control of a kind very similar to *Incognita's.* In both, the carefully measured space before a marriage is taken up by the overcoming of obstacles. 'I would have mirth continued this day at any rate', Mellefont argues;

> . . . tho' Patience purchase folly, and Attention
> be paid with noise; There are times when Sense
> may be unseasonable, as well as Truth. . . . I
> would have Noise and Impertinence keep my
> Lady Touchwood's head from Working; For
> Hell is not more busie than her Brain, nor contains more Devils than that Imaginations . . .

Comedy is thus evoked from the start as a strategy to head off the possibilities of disaster. 'Plot' is identified as the source of this disaster; 'Imaginations' are equated to 'Devils', and Lady Touchwood is identified as the unpredictable medium of both. The 'good' characters are forced to try to impose a stasis on the play by blocking the 'bad'; the bad provide its dynamic, an inversion which gives the play its sense of diabolic energies, but which also renders the central pair of lovers, Mellefont and Cynthia, so bizarrely numb. Their frozen helplessness is dream-like, or, more accurately, nightmarish. *The Double Dealer,* uniquely in Restoration comedy, obeys all three unities, of place, action and time. Imposition of the unities can have two basic effects—to establish a convention for reality, by skirting the need for more blatant narrative structuring within the play, or, conversely, to achieve a surreality, a dreamlike seamlessness and compression. This last effect, as Anne Barton has pointed out [in her "Introduction" to Congreve's *The Double-Dealer,* 1973], dictates the tone of *The Double Dealer.* It focuses on one time and one place with an hallucinatory intensity heightened by our sense that such limitation is, in terms of Restoration comedy, unconventional, odd.

Congreve's preface defends 'the Hero of the play as they are pleas'd to call him . . .' but this label for Mellefont is carefully evasive. Maskwell, much less ambiguously, he calls 'A Villain.' His accomplice Lady Touchwood's language is fed with the cliches of heroic diction, a high style of low passion. But as their scene together at the end of the first act makes clear, her partnership with Maskwell is riskily unbalanced. The 'heroic' intensity that traps her within the moment of feeling is in contrast to his complete detachment. It is his steady sense of time that emancipates him from that impulse of foresight and memory, of guilt and anticipation, that tug the other characters through a maze of intrigue. It is an awareness, like a neo-classical dramatist's, of the mechanics of action in time, of the effects of proportion and disproportion:

> One Minute gives Invention to Destroy,
> What, to Rebuild, will a whole age Employ.

Maskwell's 'unbuilding' is the building of a classical play. He exists in the present, like theatrical illusion; he has neither future nor past, he is enclosed in a bubble of unity of time, and the plays ending must be his end also. His sense of time is clear in that it is emotionally discontinuous—'I lov'd her once' he says of Lady Touchwood, and then, 'I must dissemble ardour and ecstacies. . . . How easily and pleasantly is that dissembled before Fruition! Pox on't that a Man can't drink without quenching his Thirst. . . .' He *must* oppose 'Fruition', it ends that 'dissimulation' which is the only being he has. It is an impulse that links him back to Vainlove and forward to Angelica; an isolation within individual character of an impulse general to the Etheregean form. Congreve's plays are shaped by an opposing impulse, *towards* a formal consummation. The frequency of soliloquy tends to interiorize the action of the play; Maskwell uses it to offer reflections of the other characters, and implicitly, of the audience. He speaks of motivation as if to place the very idea at a distance. It is a superficiality, a rationale provided by others:

> 'Cynthia, let thy beauty gild my Crimes; and whatsoever I commit of Treachery or Deceit shall be imputed to me as a Merit . . .

His own rationale is to turn the mirror to us:

> Why will Mankind be Fools, and be deciev'd?
> And why are Friends and Lovers Oaths believ'd;
> When each, who searches strictly his own mind,
> May so much Fraud and Power of Baseness find?

Of all the characters in the play, Maskwell lacks individual substance. Existing as he does only within the circle of Mellefont's immediate concerns, he could almost be seen as his dream self.

This, again, suggests a parallel to *Incognita,* the friendship of Aurelian and Hippolito is of the same kind as that of Mellefont and Maskwell, in the overtones of one man's patronage of another whom he takes, unquestioningly, to be his double. As in all the plays, though with different degrees of emphasis, the hero's marriage is preceded by the loosening of this narcissistic bond. Maskwell and Mellefont are more intricately implicated in each other's concerns than a simple hero/villain opposition would allow. In his preface Congreve describes Mellefont's actions in terms of psychological probability, but Maskwell is explained structurally. They are both heroes, one passive, the other active; or they are the halves of a hero, Maskwell the half that acts on the play, and Mellefont the half that reacts to it. Congreve clearly invests more of himself in the latter. 'I have the same Face, the same Words and Accents, when I speak what I do think; and when I speak what I do not think, the very same': says Maskwell 'and

dear dissimulation is the only Art not to be known from Nature.' The arts of deceit, the arts of the theatre, are concerns that Congreve and his 'villain' share; they would seem to share also an apprehension of negativity, the sense that an operation of deceit can make 'reality' unmeaning.

Cynthia closes Act III in meditation on the same problem;

> 'Tis not so hard to counterfeit Joy in the depth of Affliction as to dissemble Mirth in the company of Fools—Why should I call 'em Fools? The World thinks better of 'em; for these have Quality and Education, Wit and fine Conversation, are receiv'd and admir'd by the World—If not, they like and admire themselves—And why is not that true Wisdom, for 'tis Happiness. And for ought I know, we have mis-apply'd the Name of this while, and mistaken the thing . . .

That social fiction embodied by the other couples is a disguise that seems to dislodge meaning from the most immediate emotional concepts. The interim between contract and ceremony is filled for Cynthia by a series of encounters with grotesque parodies of marriage, acted out by the Touchwoods' house-guests. The men had been introduced in Act I in a discussion of the superior wit of *not* laughing at comedy. The first laughter we hear after this is in the context of Maskwell's tricking Mellefont. The laughter of *The Double Dealer* is of a peculiar quality. Highly successful farcical situations are defused and soured by the amusement of characters with whom the audience cannot identify. Lady Froth and Brisk, for example, deceive her husband in double-entendre;

> LADY FROTH. I'll do it with him, my Lord, when you are out of the way.
>
> BRISK. [aside] That's good I'gad, that's good. Deuce take me I can hardly hold Laughing in his Face.

The cheapness of this marks the limit of our assent to the intrigue. The scene where Plyant urges Careless to help him get Lady Plyant with child drifts over depths of pathos by provoking the laughter we give to what we know is not laughable. Cynthia attempts to re-impose order on her and Mellefont's perception of the events around them;

> MELL. . . . Marriage is the Game that we Hunt, and while we think that we only have it in our view, I don't see but we have it in our power.
>
> CYN. . . . Within reach; for example, give me your hand; why have you look'd through the wrong end of the Perspective all this while; for nothing has been between us but our fears.

But as in *The Old Batchelour,* the gesture between lovers echoes, with the consequence of dreams, a gesture from the hero to his friend. 'There's comfort in a hand stretch'd out', Mellefont had said earlier to Maskwell, 'to one that's sinking, though ne'er so far off '. The marriage of Cynthia and Mellefont must be preceded by an exorcism of the nothing that is their fears; the play is, one level, a comedy of the unconscious, in which only the infinitely pathetic Sir Paul can insist that he is not drowning but waving.

> **Congreve invents nothing, his plays are virtuosic rearrangements of received ideas. . . . Alone of any major Restoration dramatist he bequeaths the form no new conventions or types. . . . Of all Restoration dramatists he is the most classical; but it is a classicism of an intensely personal kind.**
>
> —*Edward Burns*

'Guilt is ever at a loss and confusion waits upon it' Maskwell says to Lady Touchwood, at the beginning of the scene in her chamber, the only scene to break the unity of place, 'When Innocence and bold Truth are always ready for expression.' Lady Touchwood's reply touches on the underlying logic of the Etheregean form:

> Not in Love, Words are the weak support of the cold Indifference; Love has no language to be heard.

Her insight has potentially tragic implications. Lady Touchwood is an intensification of the type of an opposite extreme to that evinced in Vanbrugh's Lady Fancyfull. Maskwell however only attains tragedy by imitation, or, more aptly, by 'acting'. The echoes of Shakespeare that recur through the play thicken towards its climax as Maskwell tricks Mellefont into a parody of the closet scene from *Hamlet,* one of the most famous moments of Betterton's celebrated, and very recent, performances of the play. But Maskwell *is* Betterton; he is haunted by ghost-like reminiscences of his Shakespearean roles, tributes to the sinister vacuity of theatrical illusion. It is for this that the play moves out of its other Hamlet-like setting, the gallery where characters walk, soliloquize and accidentally encounter each other. Lady Touchwood as 'plotter' has driven the play, Maskwell as 'actor' steers it. He is able to flatter her into a tragic hubris—' . . . Fortune is your own, and 'tis her interest so to be.' Her fall comes in the frenzy of plotting that constitutes *his* hubris; it explodes in a flurried double version of the impersonation plot, that bursts across the path of the comic characters, as they gather slowly on stage, to return to 'respectability', from the successful upshot of their own little intrigues. The 'tragic' plot recedes in importance. Mellefont's failure to defuse it goes unremarked by Cynthia, though it was a condition of her acceptance. They marry, of course, in the end. Perhaps the plotters cannot be allowed to impose their own values in the play even to the extent of defining virtue by their opposition—they evaporate, but the play of necessity evaporates with them. The play, Congreve's funniest, presents an inverted image of the world, of a kind more familiar to us from tragedy than comedy. It is defined by Congreve with an hallucinatory precision, and a clear awareness of the closeness of hilarity and alarm.

Congreve's next play, *Love for Love* (1695), was again built around a role for Betterton, but in the context of the actor's rebellion from Rich's company and the founding of his own.

> . . . the poor Husbands of the Stage, who found
> Their Labours lost upon the ungrateful Ground,
> This last and only Remedy have prov'd;
> And hope new Fruit from ancient Stocks remov'd.

The extended garden metaphor of Congreve's prologue establishes the new company's style as a 'natural' tradition, and Betterton's tending of it as careful and sensitive cultivation. In terms of the rivalry between the two companies, *Love for Love* makes a conservative, consciously traditional choice of available dramatic styles, a choice that links both play and company back to the traditions of wit comedy and stage libertinism. 'We hope there's something that may please each Taste' the prologue goes on ' . . . of homely Fare we make the Feast.' *Love for Love* is homely fare in a way *The Double Dealer* wasn't. It eschews abstract formal virtuosity for a different kind of literariness, a revival and reappraisal of the conventions of both 'manners' and 'humour' comedy.

The prologue goes on to make the familiar bow in Wycherley's direction, but comparison to *The Plaindealer* shows that this play's satirist, Scandal, operates from no real emotional or moral base. His is simply a more sophisticated version of the narcissism endemic to that society whose news he carries. He employs a cyclic logic that closes and diminishes the conversational essays of the other characters. 'I'm afraid *Jeremy* has Wit' he declares, 'for wherever it is, its always contriving its own Ruin. . . .' The effect is essentially complacent, and easily turned against him. ('You are as inveterate against our Poets as if your Characters had lately been expos'd upon the Stage.)' Scandal has an effect on the play quite opposite to that of the conventional Plaindealer. He cools it down, imposing a disengaged, a 'knowing' tone. 'To converse with *Scandal*' as Valentine realises 'is to play at *Losing Loadum;* you must lose a good Name to him, before you can win it for yourself.'

The play's first scene is itself a kind of prologue; the impoverished Valentine tries to write a play, to take some of 'the Trade' from the 'wits.' Wit is now no more than a trade, its method is a continual anxious transformation of contiguous life, life Congreve presents as rubbish and decay. Jeremy, Valentine's servant, expands the idea into a grand satirical-allegorical panorama. His picture of a 'worn-out Punk with Verses in her Hand, which her Vanity had prefer'd to Settlements' is a warning emblem that writing can dwindle to mere words on paper, the dross that replaces substance. But settlements are words on paper too. Valentine's surname is 'Legend'. The whole play concerns itself with writing and reading, inscription and interpretation. Its literariness is initially of a nightmare kind where words must do for food, and Valentine lives on a 'Paper-Diet'. The imaginary 'pictures' which Scandal offers to show Mrs Frail, 'The satires, descriptions, characters and lampoons' seem by their placing at the end of the act to open up for us the world of the play;

> 'I can show you Pride, Folly, Affectation, Wantonness, Inconstancy, Coventousness, Dissimu-

lation, Malice and Ignorance, all in one Piece. Then I can show you Lying, Foppery, Vanity, Cowardice, Bragging, Lechery, Impotence and Ugliness in another piece; and yet one of these is a celebrated Beauty, and t'other a profest Beau . . .'

'Picturing' is the method of the play's satire. But there is a distance between the world and those for whom it arranges itself in pictures. Scandal's sustained rhetoric suggests mysterious insight and a prophetic stance, but the play undercuts a kind of knowledge that comes to seem dangerously closed and circular. The process of satire is of more interest to Congreve than its product. He uses the idea of satire as he used the idea of theatre in *The Double Dealer,* as a process analogous to the other kinds of process which form the play. In *Love for Love* these are processes of 'knowing'.

'I could heartily wish it yet shorter' Congreve claims in his preface, 'but the Number of Different Characters represented in it would have been too much crowded in less room.' The play works through contrasted character. It is planned symmetrically, organized into encounters, satirical or amorous, and articulated in a systematic pairing of 'humours'. Scandal's counterpart is the beau, Tattle; 'you are light and shadow, and shew one another; he is perfectly thy reverse both in humour and understanding; and as you set up for Defamation, he is a mender of Reputations.' They unfold society, as opposites in the kind of knowledge it offers. Scandal creates a personal secrecy in his revelations, Tattle creates revelation in his secrecy. Old Foresight the astrologer and Sir Sampson, the traveller, match them, to make a square around Valentine. The Restoration 'humour' is more abstract than the Jacobean. Like Shadwell's, Congreve's humours are less self-generated oddity than obsessive strategies for organizing time and awareness. Foresight imaginatively encompasses time as Sir Sampson does place, all within the cramped space of the Foresights' city house. 'The homely fare' offered by the prologue implies a withdrawal from the modish surface of a play like *The Double Dealer,* a quizzical reconsideration of solid Jacobean domesticity. ' . . . if the Sun shine by Day and the Stars by Night', Sir Sampson claims, 'why, we shall know one another's Faces without the help of a Candle, and that's all the stars are good for. . . .' His words touch on the play's central concerns—but when he encounters his son Valentine he is seen to read faces as the same kind of cramped and ludicrous code into which he and Foresight translate the learning they amass: 'Has he not a Rogue's face . . . he has a violent death in his face.' Valentine sets himself up as a philosophical libertine; his father wants to disinherit him, but to become a bare forked animal, is, Valentine claims, impossible; 'you must deprive me of Reason, Thought, Passions, Inclinations, Affections, Appetites, Senses, and the huge Train of Attendants that you begot along with me.' Appetite, for Valentine is a philosophical imperative, and this defines his role in life as sanctioned consumption. This gives him and Scandal a knockdown argument for not paying debts:

> TRAP: I did not value your Sack; but you cannot expect it again when I have drank it.

SCAND: And how do you expect to have your Money again when a Gentleman has spent it?

Congreve establishes Valentine as a libertine by means less picturesque than directly dramatized promiscuity. One demand on his purse is 'Bouncing Margery' with ' . . . one of your children from Twitnam'. Valentine's response to this rude incursion of his past brutally deflates the romantic aloofness of his pose—'she . . . might have overlaid the child a fortnight ago if she had had any forecast in her.' The Libertine cuts himself off from both parents and children. He must play that losing game on which Valentine, at the start of the play seems set.

Even in the Dramatis Personae, Valentine and Angelica are defined in financial terms that mesh suggestively.

> VALENTINE: fallen under his Father's Displeasure by his expensive way of living, in love with *Angelica.*
>
> ANGELICA: Niece to Foresight, of a considerable Fortune in her own Hands.

The obstacle to an apparently inevitable resolution lies in the willed mysteriousness of behaviour with which Angelica advertizes her independence. The callous nonchalance of her behaviour to Foresight at the start of act II sharpens, when he threatens Valentine, into a satirical translation of the old astrologer's occultism into images of a cramped misshapen sexuality. She describes the grotesque obverse of a beauty—magic identification that tinges her own role, and in doing so deepens her enigma; there is no way of knowing whether her anger is at Foresight's cruelty to Valentine, or his assumption that this is of interest to her. *Love for Love* suggests a romantic bargain—it suggests also the provisional contract of a game. The funniest round is that between Tattle and Prue—it is the thinnest part of the play, the most blatantly calculated to entertain, but it is also the most transparent—one sees through it into the links between Angelica's behaviour and the way of the world she lives in. Prue starts from square one—she is the blankest and most biddable of all the country girls. Her thirst for knowledge impels Tattle to spell out the rules that have fogged our sense of relationship in the rest of the play:

> All well-bred Persons lie—Besides, you are a Woman; you must never speak what you Think; Your words must contradict your Thoughts; but your Actions may contradict your words.

Prue reverses those norms of courtship that Angelica protracts to a hazy extreme; she's so willing that it becomes a formality, a decency almost, extended only by Tattle's wit. Angelica presents herself to Valentine as almost wholly passive—

> VAL: Well, you'll come to a Resolution.
>
> ANG: I can't. Resolution must come to me, or I shall never have one.

Reserve, even immobility, may be the only way to remain uncompromised in a social world whose poles are Scandal and Tattle, a world in which Valentine invests to the extent that he can know ' . . . no effectual difference between continued Affectation and Reality.' This scene between the four of them, the first in the play to bring Valentine and Angelica together, builds into an impromptu tribunal, but it resolves nothing. It decorates the fact of Angelica's reserve without explaining it. Her mystery is deepened further in her lie to Sir Sampson—a lie that the audience cannot at this point see through—

> '. . . if ever I cou'd have lik'd anything in him, it should have been his Estate. . . . But since that's gone, the Baits gone off, and the naked Hook appears'

It posits the alarming possibility of a reading of the play in which financial realities are more 'real' than other kinds—a logical extension of a motive we might almost conventionally impute to Valentine. This little exchange is literally and metaphorically central to Congreve's structure. Stressed by our doubts about it, it becomes the climax of both the play's unknowability, and Angelica's.

Valentine attempts to resolve his personal and financial uncertainty by pretending to go mad. Angelica is the first to arrive at his lodging; Scandal engages her in a game of dissimulation, and loses; it recalls the rather unnervingly spirited Angelica of her first scene, and in a favourite card metaphor, echoes the title of the play; '. . . If I don't play Trick for Trick, may I never taste the Pleasure of Revenge.' Scandal is out-manoeuvred by Mrs Foresight when she flatly denies the assignation we saw her make with him at the end of the last act. His exclamations—'You make me mad. You are not serious'—have more than an accidental irony. Mrs Foresight makes him mad by rendering what he knows meaningless; her fortune-hunting sister Mrs Frail seems 'mad' to her former target, Ben; opportunism and deceit scramble and make meaningless her words and behaviour when she changes tack to the re-instated Valentine. His hero's 'madness' allows Congreve another eccentric variant on the impersonation plot; no mask is needed to delude a madman into thinking that Mrs Frail is Angelica. At first he ornaments the plot with the pastoral fantasy of a madman's imagination—

> Endymion and the Moon shall meet us on Mount *Latmos,* and we'll be Marry'd in the dead of Night.

But then he decides to externalize, mockingly, a hypocritical purity in the 'nun' and 'friar' disguise. As a madman Valentine gains privileged access to 'vision'. He has finally become both a 'wit' and a satirist. But Scandal's experience might have warned him that madmen forfeit a claim to meaning. Valentine has evaded the need to complete the document disinheriting him in Ben's favour; but he has pushed further off the possibilities of being known or truly knowing. Angelica has a scene with Tattle to parallel that with Scandal—to demonstrate her mastery of them. Then she challenges Valentine.

> Do you know me, *Valentine?*
> O, very well.
> Who am I?
> You're a Woman—One to whom Heav'n gave Beauty when it grafted Roses on a Briar. You are the reflection of Heav'n in a Pond, and he that leaps at you is sunk. You are all, white, a sheet of lovely spotless Paper, when you first are

Born; but you are to be scrawled and blotted by every Gooses Quill . . .

Valentine insists on woman as something to be 'read', not as something that writes, as something written on. He presumes that disguise can be sloughed off and reality—a reality that *he* defines—simply acknowledged. He pulls in our sense of the play's structure to establish his claim; '. . . the Comedy draws towards an end, and let us think of leaving acting and be ourselves. . . .

Angelica refuses to comply with his expectations of the end of romantic comedy. So does Jeremy, though the genre in which he plays his part is perhaps a degree lower—'Why, you thick-skulled rascal' Valentine rages 'I tell you the farce is done, and I will be mad no longer.' By beating his servant however he contradicts his own word in action, for this is the simplest kind of farce and it seems quite likely to continue. As we saw in Prue's scene, the lie is the basic unit of social currency. Women and servants are parallel in their enforced dependence on that 'Figure of speech' which according to Jeremy 'interlards the great part of my conversation.' But Angelica's parting words are not a 'riddle' as Valentine presumes. Their meaning is in excess of his ability to understand—

> Uncertainty and Expectation are the Joys of Life. Security is an inspid thing, and the overtaking and possessing of a Wish discovers the Folly of the Chase. Never let us know one another better; for the Pleasure of a Masquerade is done when we come to show Faces.

Their resonance can only be placed by an imaginative leap out of the routine misogyny, the mechanical intrigue, of his libertine pose.

Tattle spurns Prue on their next meeting. She has Margery's sense of the permanence of her choice, and this cuts inconveniently across the one other convention of the fashionable world which Tattle now explains to her; that the span of its awareness is no longer than a day. He's off to take Valentine's place in the marriage with Mrs Frail/Angelica—Jeremy has tricked him into the plot. The disguised couple, both duped, burst onto the stage to frame a final unravelling of deceit.

Valentine offers to disinherit himself as a sign of his love for Angelica—apparently on the point of marrying Sir Sampson. The declaration means less at its face value than in the tribute it implies to her—his acceptance to her right to set the conditions of the comedy's true end. When Angelica tears the document she effects the destruction of all the other kinds of 'knowledge' that would lead the play to a different event at this climactic point. Foresight, Sir Sampson Legend, Mrs Frail and Tattle, are all diminished and defeated. Scandal steps in to offer a moral; all the tags at the end of the acts have so far been his; that at the end of act IV, though spoken by Valentine, is a quotation from his 'Satirical Friend . . . ' who says

> That Women are like Tricks by slight of Hand Which, to admire, we should not understand.

It is this complicity in cynicism from which Valentine has broken, and in doing so he has rendered Angelica comprehensible. Angelica gracefully accepts Scandal's 'conversion' as the ground of her assumption to herself of the authority to close the play.

One might trace in Congreve's four comedies a development by which the male characters' strategies for organizing a libertine diversity of experience are replaced as the structuring impulse of the plays by the reserve and dissimulation involved in a woman's attempt to establish a personal reality of feeling. This happens within each play. It happens also over the sequence. Araminta and Cynthia have stubborn strengths and a reserved insight, but the action of the play goes on at some little distance from them. As was the case with *Love for Love,* it is a woman who must bring *The Way of the World* to a close and father the characters to her for an adjudication. The tangle of events that present themselves to Lady Wishfort would bewilder a mind more consistent than hers. *The Way of the World* cuts itself off from audience complicity with a virtuosity so perverse it can seem to mimic the effects of incompetence.

Mirabell loses the card game that ends just prior to the start of the play; he wins that much larger game, whose action concertinas all the possible meanings of 'play'. His method is concealment; to use her husband's description of Mrs Fainall, he throws up his cards, but keeps 'Pam' in his 'pocket.' It would seem to be Congreve's ploy too. Mirabell's 'Sir Rowland' plot is incomprehensible to the audience in act I, vague in act II, and only fully spelt out in act III (by Mrs Fainall, to Foible), as it is about to be spring. There is no surprise effect involved, nor do the concealments reveal individual character. They are a strategy for directing our attention. The play takes great risks (in its game with its audience) to decoy us with plot into confronting relationship. Its style is disturbed sequence. Language, logic and manners are carefully disordered. Everything about the play is, in Mincing's term, 'crips'.

The Way of the World seems to me to be an astonishingly graceful and economical (or 'easy') transmutation of theatrical means into literary form. Fainall, like all Betterton's Congreve roles, is developed out of the libertine tradition but at a distance dictated as much by the actor's age as by the dating of those conventions he had embodied in his roles of the late seventies and eighties. They are comments on that tradition, referential characterizations of ideas *about* the libertine. Fainall is a rake trapped into marriage, who has managed nonetheless to adapt to the new style of libertine behaviour; the half-clandestine style, defined by its 'daring' relationship to society. A society that derives its rules from an idea of 'reputation' implicates its members in a series of gambles. Fainall, who would 'no more play with a Man that slights his ill Fortune than . . . make Love to a Woman who undervalu'd the Loss of her Reputation,' claims to take pleasure in knocking others out of the social game. As villains, Marwood (played by Elizabeth Barry) and Fainall are conceived entirely in terms of the actors' skills. When they exit at the end—after Congreve has made the point that the whole cast are now on stage—they escape from the only sphere of their being, and thus present no lasting threat, or uncomfortable loose ends. An insubstantiality, an improvised identity dictated by 'plot', is common char-

acteristic to all Congreve's villains—and indeed those of many other dramatists, ('motivelessness' is the best dramatic means of suggesting malignancy). When Foible sees Marwood in the park-scene, moving about off-stage, she is vaguely seen, and masked. She has no more reality beyond the feints and disguises of intrigue than had Porcia, Mrs Barry's role in Otway's *The Atheist.* The method of *The Way of the World* is complex, but it is not an overflowing sense of character that complicates it. I stress this because the play can seem untheatrical; anti-theatrical, even. Theatricality—a *perverse* theatricality—seems to me not only to shape the play, but to dictate, through the reminiscence it implies, its content and function. *The Way of the World,* at once so modest and so grandiose in the promise of its title, is a summation of Restoration comedy; the comedy whose history Southerne and Dryden had so carefully recalled, and whose own 'Restoration' they looked on Congreve to effect.

Much is made in the first act of the separate society of the sexes. In act II they meet, on the neutral ground of the park. Congreve continues and elaborates the tortuous retrospect of his expository method into the reminiscence of past amours and deceits germane to its fashionable (and dramatic) function. It is this retrospect that instates the action we *see* as a kind of culmination, and invites us to puzzle over the past, for an explanation of the bewildering 'present'. The opening conversation between Marwood and Mrs Fainall builds a more blatant structure of dissembling and reversal of sense than that of the parallel opening to act I. When the men enter all four are engaged in a game of skirting dangerous admissions, and gracefully turning back. When they split up into *tête-à-têtes* our sense of things becomes clearer, but what is made clear is, paradoxically, the complexity of real and dissembled relationship. 'You are not Jealous?' Fainall asks Marwood at one point. 'Of whom?', she asks, having herself lost track. The subject of these discussions is of course that central preoccupation of the comedies of the nineties, the validity and use of kinds of social contract. Love, friendship and marriage have all become mere masks. 'The Way of the World' is Fainall's phrase, originally. It attaches itself to his wife; our sense of that world's injustice, of Mirabell's smug opportunism, comes to be represented by her.

When Mirabell and Fainall quiz Witwoud as to what might be his friend Petulant's most striking conversational incompetence, Mirabell incidentally allows an insight into his own characteristic style; ' . . . he speaks unseasonable Truths sometimes, because he has not Wit enough to invent an Evasion . . . '. The idea of 'wit' Mirabell posits is bland and defensive, but it *is* basically decent. Congreve seems to propose a new rationale for wit, conciliatory and constructive, in obvious contrast to the personal aggression of the libertines. 'Then ought'st thou to be most asham'd of thyself when thou hast put another out of Countenance' he tells Petulant, who, like Wycherley's Manly, 'makes Remarks'. Mirabell is the master of a cool emotional self-defence. Mrs Fainall's 'Why did you make me marry this man?' hangs over the rest of the play. It finds no answer in his reply—'Why do we daily commit disagreeable and dangerous actions? To save that idol reputation.' The danger and the disagreeableness were hers, not his. If Millamant knows anything of her suitor's involvement with Mrs Fainall she never lets slip any reference to this or any other contingency of the plot. She alone is exempted from retrospect. In a sense, her use of style is as defensive as Mirabell's. Her inversion of cause and effect—'a sort of Poetical Logic' as Congreve called it in *The Old Batchelour*—both deflects an attention to disagreeable fact and blocks, more subtly, the treacherous strategy of romantic language that Mirabell attempts to extend to her. 'One's Cruelty is one's Power', she claims 'and when one parts with ones Cruelty, one parts with ones Power; and when one has parted with that, I fancy ones Old and Ugly.' This may not make sense, but it is, as the fate of her too-susceptible Aunt goes to prove, the way of a world that may not make sense either. It is Millamant who finally and triumphantly inverts that disturbing emotional logic traced earlier in *Incognita, Semele* and *The Old Batchelour.*

> MIR: . . . Beauty is the Lover's Gift; 'tis he bestows your Charms.
>
> MILL: Beauty the Lover's gift—Lord, what is a Lover, that it can give? Why one makes Lovers as fast as one pleases, and they live as long as one leases, and they die as soon as one pleases; And then if one pleases one makes more.

Millamant's meditative reminiscences of scraps of Waller internalize the pastoral fictions of courtship. They clash wittily with the rustic Sir Wilful's attempts to catch that 'critical minute' of successful courtship on which the pastoral lyric is so often built. Real rusticity has no bearing on the fiction whose import for Millamant is as the vehicle of a privacy of feeling. When Mirabell enters to cap her quotation, he demonstrates his right to step inside her bubble of style. Millamant's rudeness to Sir Wilful and Witwoud is sustained by the security of the knowingly loved. The 'proviso scene' is a ceremonial expansion of artifice, seamless with this mock-pastoral 'chase'. That it is not primarily a practical contract is made clear by comparison with its probable model in Sedley's *Bellamira*. The scene between Merryman and Thisbe at a similar point in the play characterizes their relationship as a shrewd respite from the more fraught contracts of mercenary or romantic relationship that the other characters seek. In the Sedley, the provisos balance out equally; in the Congreve they all relate to Millamant's privacy and to Mirabell only as he impinges on it. Merryman may be persuaded to give up ale and to diet, but we have no idea whether there will be more Mrs Fainalls. Millamant draws a veil of ignorance over her future husband's private affairs. As an ideal of marriage, the scene is limited and coy. But its force for Congreve is, in a sense, metaphoric. Their love is real without declaration; it is expressed by how much Millamant can take for granted, how much, in other words, Congreve can leave out. Mirabell has learnt to trust her silence, to respect her privacy. The common-sense contract is freighted with our sense of that image of support and assent, of yielding and trust, into which Congreve has shaped the whole play.

"Tis true he was hearty in his Affection of Angelica' Jeremy Collier had said of Valentine, '. . . Now without ques-

tion, to be in love with a fine Lady of 30,000 Pounds is a great Virtue!' Love is supported by interest even more completely in *The Way of the World.* Mirabell is entirely the 'fine gentleman' whose success Collier laments. The story is built on Collier's premises; it is the story of how a gentleman-sharper wins. Its attitudes are defiantly tough. *The Way of the World* is a diamond-hard summation of the plays written before it. It is built out of a realization and excision of the sentimental or melodramatic potential of the form, by the creation of a perfect dramatic structure within which all the elements of this kind of play find a precisely apt place. There may be a sense in which Congreve is indebted to Collier. *Short View* argues, in effect, that the comedy of the period is amoral in outlook. The foundations of Collier's argument crumble easily, but his observation is clear. The main thrust of his argument is opposed to Restoration comedy's lack of respect for hierarchy;

> . . . has our stage a particular Privilege? Is their *Charter* enlarg'd, and are they on the same Foot of Freedom with the *Slaves* in the *Saturnalia?* Must all Men be handled alike? . . . I hope the Poet's don't intend to revive the Old Project of Levelling, and *vote* down the House of *Peers.*

Lady Wishfort recommends the *Short View* to Marwood. But Collier's supporter is to be cruelly handled by her servants' saturnalian overthrow of rank.

Mirabell's comment on Lady Wishfort in the park-scene colours the setting autumnally, and prepares us for Millamant's immediate entrance in a curiously affecting way.

> An old Woman's Appetite is deprav'd like that of a Girl—Tis the Green Sickness of a second Childhood; and like the faint Offer of a latter Spring, serves but to usher in the Fall; and withers in an affected Bloom.

Lady Wishfort registers the passage of time in the most immediate and personal way. She proves that Collier's values make splendid fuel for the fire they seek to put out. Her fear of offending against decorums makes her, like Wilde's Lady Bracknell, a muse of farce, an embodiment of the rules of the game. It is also an interest more up to date than the ideal of beauty reconstituted from her portrait. That 'sort of dyingness' is a fashion of the earlier Restoration, a measurement of time lapsed more tactful than its hint of a dyingness of another kind. She is catapulted pathetically from hopes of marriage to a helplessness close to a senility. But she is at the centre of the play nonetheless. The last three acts take place in her chamber, and the fortunes of the gamesters come to rely on her flickering insights into their motives. All the other characters come to make deceitful overtures to her; Millamant embellishes her gentle dissimulation with ironical turns of style, Fainall is crudely insolent, and Mirabell treads his usual tightrope of evasive politeness. Lady Wishfort remains undeceived. The mockery of frivolous parent-figures has been a staple of these plays from Sir John Everyoung on. But when the Sir Rowland plot collapses, Lady Wishfort has, if not greatness, at least responsibility thrust upon her.

Mirabell had earlier drawn a careful line between town-society and the inconveniently rural demands of family in his reverberant remark that he would rather be Sir Wilful's relation than his acquaintance. Millamant—who wishes that one could treat acquaintance as one does old clothes—is torn by a similar duality, a loathing of both country and town. The town-world would seem as preclusive of escape as it is for some in *The Man of Mode* or *The Country Wife*— and yet Mirabell benefits from being both Sir Wilful's relation *and* his acquaintance. Millamant steps out of her bubble of nonsensical fancy, into the continuing possibility of a shared life. (It is one of the few Restoration comedy marriages to envisage the production of children.) They do not join in the dance at the end of the play, and in a sense this marks them out as winners in a game for losers. The play ends with reality rediscovered, not transformed. We gain a fuller sense of Mrs Fainall's life history than we do of any other character. Witwoud runs a close second, and in both cases it is because the centre of the play has shifted to Wishfort and that spokesman of plain values, Sir Wilfull, to a reconsideration of family relationship. But the final plot twist fixes the source of Mrs Fainall's 'generosity' for us. Mirabell's protection of her interests tacitly demands her care for his. Sexual opportunism and generous sentiment are equally unrealistic bases for a woman's behaviour. Shared obligations are the way of the world.

Fainall promises Mrs Marwood retreat 'to another World.' Lady Wishfort suggests that the same lady and herself should 'leave the World, and retire by our selves and be *Shepherdesses.*' The ways of the world on stage are so completely realised that other worlds seem impossible—and yet that world is too heavily freighted with the past to pass convincingly into a possible future. The play is full of evocations of a concrete and vigorous life that it admits only in stylistic device—in Witwoud's similes, or Petulant's 'remarks'. Its sense of trivia can also remind it of a side of itself as dilapidated as that 'old peel'd Wall' to which Lady Wishfort compared her face, or the list of items called to her mind by the most deeply felt of all her betrayals, Foible's. The random objects she remembers from Foible's stall form themselves into a soiled still-life, a vanitas;

> . . . an old gnaw'd *Mask,* Two Rows of *Pins* and a *Childs Fiddle; a Glass Necklace* with the Beads broken, and a *Quilted Night-cap* with one Ear . . .

Foible's reward for her trickery is a farm. She, not her mistress, achieves a pastoral retreat.

There is another echo of Sedley, in the praise of 'Terence the most correct Writer in the World . . . ' with which Congreve prefaces his play. Sedley intended a corrective prescription, but Congreve seems to identify with the Roman writer, to use him as a mask from behind which he can lay down the terms in which he himself desires to be judged.

> The Purity of his Style, the Delicacy of his Turns, and the Justness of his characters, were all of them Beauties, which the greater Part of his Audience were incapable of Tasting . . .

By this point analogy has turned by degrees into self-revelation. *Incognita* and the preface to **The Double Dealer** were informed by the same nervous hauteur in relation to their audience. In his dedications he consistently judges himself against an ideal of perfection, projected on to the dedicatee in a way that would seem to mask an anxiety more personal than the straightforward competitive virtuosity normal to seventeenth century writers working in conventional forms. 'As Terence excell'd in his Performances, so had he great Advantages to encourage his Undertakings; for he built most on the Foundations of Menander; His plots were generally modelled and his Characters ready drawn to his Hand.' Congreve invents nothing, his plays are virtuosic rearrangements of received ideas. There is even a sense in which he seems to want to be the *last* Restoration writer. His comedies imply no further comedies. Alone of any major Restoration dramatist he bequeaths the form no new conventions or types. His withdrawal from writing is scarcely unique among dramatists, in any period. But the story sticks to Congreve in its consonance with an aspect of his writing; that withdrawal implied by an artifice almost morbidly conscious of itself. Of all Restoration dramatists he is the most classical; but it is a classicism of an intensely personal kind. (pp. 183-211)

> *Edward Burns, "Congreve," in his* Restoration Comedy: Crises of Desire and Identity, *The Macmillan Press Ltd., 1987, pp. 183-211.*

FURTHER READING

Agate, James, ed. *The English Dramatic Critics: An Anthology, 1660-1932,* pp. 28-9, 32-4. New York: Hill and Wang, 1932.

> Reprints *The London Chronicle's* 1758 reviews of *Love for Love* and *The Way of the World.*

Archer, William. "The Comedies of William Congreve: Parts I and II." *The Forum* XLIII, Nos. 3, 4 (March 1910; April 1910): 276-82, 343-46.

> Sketch of Congreve's life with critical remarks on his work.

Brossman, S. W. "Dryden's Cassandra and Congreve's Zara." *Notes and Queries* CCI (March 1956): 102-03.

> Highlights similarities between the heroine of Congreve's *Mourning Bride* and its prototype.

Canby, Henry Seidel. "Congreve as a Romanticist." *PMLA* n.s. XXIV, No. 1 (1916): 1-23.

> Finds Congreve a "connoisseur in the rare and excellent refinements which he found, or imagined, in the Stuart world."

Corman, Brian. " 'The Mixed Way of Comedy': Congreve's *The Double-Dealer.*" *Modern Philology* 71, No. 4 (May 1974): 356-65.

> Traces dual patterns of punitive and Restoration comedy operative in *The Double-Dealer.*

————. *"The Way of the World* and Morally Serious Comedy." *University of Toronto Quarterly* XLIV, No. 3 (Spring 1975): 199-212.

Attributes Congreve's successful blend of the comic and dramatic to his "consistently effective manipulation of the comic conventions of the Restoration."

Dobrée, Bonamy. *William Congreve: A Conversation between Swift and Gay.* Seattle: University of Washington Book Store, 1929, 24 p.

Imaginary dialogue between Jonathan Swift and John Gay, revealing Congreve as his contemporaries might have known him.

————. *William Congreve.* London: Longmans, Green & Co., 1963, 35 p.

Brief biography with critical overview.

Dobson, Austin. "William Congreve." In *The English Poets,* edited by Thomas Humphry Ward, Vol. III, pp. 10-12. New York: Macmillan Co., 1921.

Presents a brief but balanced appraisal of Congreve's verse.

Frushell, Richard C. "Congreve's Plays and 'The Rape of the Lock'." *American Notes and Queries* XIII, No. 7 (March 1975): 114-16.

Traces Congreve's influence on specific passages of Alexander Pope's "Rape of the Lock."

Gosse, Anthony. "Plot and Character in Congreve's *Double-Dealer.*" *Modern Language Quarterly* XXIX (1968): 274-88.

Maintains the supremacy of the comic in *The Double-Dealer* despite the play's villainous elements.

Harley, Graham D. *"Squire Trelooby* and *The Cornish Squire:* A Reconsideration." *Philological Quarterly* XLIX, No. 4 (October 1970): 520-29.

Inquiry into Congreve's partial authorship of two plays.

Henderson, Anthony G. "Introduction." In William Congreve's *The Comedies of William Congreve,* edited by Anthony G. Henderson, pp. vii-xiii. Cambridge: Cambridge University Press, 1982.

An chronological outline and critical summary of four of Congreve's most popular comedies.

Hinnant, Charles H. "Wit, Propriety, and Style in *The Way of the World.*" *Studies in English* XVII, No. 3 (Summer 1977): 373-86.

An examination of Congreve's wit as more than wordplay in *The Way of the World.*

Jantz, Ursula. *Targets of Satire in the Comedies of Etherege, Wycherley, and Congreve.* Salzburg Studies in English Literature: Poetic Drama and Poetic Theory, edited by James Hogg, no. 42. Salzburg: Institut für Englische Sprache und Literatur, Universität Salzburg, 1978, 242 p.

Studies contrasting approaches to such conventional targets as fops, dupes, women, and marriage.

Kaufman, Anthony. "Language and Character in Congreve's *The Way of the World.*" *Texas Studies in Literature and Language* XV, No. 3 (Fall 1973): 411-27.

Suggests that the distinctive dialogue in *The Way of the World* effectively characterizes its players.

Kimball, Sue L. "Games People Play in Congreve's *The Way of the World.*" In *A Provision of Human Nature: Essays on Fielding and Others in Honor of Miriam Austin Locke,* edited

by Donald Kay, pp. 191-207. University: University of Alabama Press, 1977.

Proposes that the gaming imagery throughout *The Way of the World* is Congreve's "metaphor for life and love."

Kronenberger, Louis. *"The Way of the World."* In his *The Polished Surface: Essays in the Literature of Worldliness,* pp. 55-72. New York: Alfred A. Knopf, 1969.

Claims that "inexorable realism" distinguishes Congreve from his contemporaries.

Krutch, Joseph Wood. "The Utopia of Gallants." *The Nation* CXIX, No. 3100 (3 December 1924): 606-07.

Posits that, unlike his contemporaries, Congreve created "a gallants' Utopia, purged of . . . ugliness and cruelty."

————. *Comedy and Conscience after the Restoration,* 300 p. 1924. Reprint. New York: Columbia University Press, 1949.

Numerous references to and brief comments on Congreve's works.

Lincoln, Stoddard. "The Librettos and Lyrics of William Congreve." In *British Theatre and the Other Arts, 1660-1800,* edited by Shirley Strum Kenny, pp. 116-32. Washington: Folger Books, 1984.

Treats the verse in Congreve's little-known masque, *The Judgment of Paris,* and his libretto for the opera *Semele.*

Lynch, Kathleen M. *A Congreve Gallery.* Cambridge: Harvard University Press, 1951, 196 p.

Illuminates Congreve's life and works through an exploration of his friendships.

Malekin, Peter. " 'Imparadist in One Anothers Arms' or 'The Ecclesiastical Mouse-trap': Marriage in Restoration Comedy." In his *Liberty and Love: English Literature and Society, 1640-88,* pp. 165-95. New York: St. Martin's Press, 1981.

Notes several Restoration dramatists' varying attitudes towards marriage.

McComb, John King. "Congreve's *The Old Bachelour:* A Satiric Anatomy." *Studies in English Literature: 1500-1900* XVII, No. 3 (Summer 1977): 361-72.

Investigates sexual themes in *The Old Bachelour.*

Mueschke, Miriam, and Mueschke, Paul. *A New View of Congreve's "Way of the World."* Ann Arbor: University of Michigan Press, 1958, 85 p.

Detailed study of Congreve's artistry in *The Way of the World.*

Muir, Kenneth. "The Comedies of William Congreve." In *Restoration Theatre,* edited by John Russell Brown and Bernard Harris, pp. 221-37. Stratford-upon-Avon Studies, no 6. London: Edward Arnold, 1965.

Chronicles the evolution of Congreve's skill as a dramatist.

Nolan, Paul T. *"The Way of the World:* Congreve's Moment of Truth." *The Southern Speech Journal* XXV, No. 2 (Winter 1959): 75-95.

Asserts that only in *The Way of the World* does Congreve confront realistic moral issues.

Novak, Maximillian E. "The Artist and the Clergyman: Congreve, Collier, and the World of the Play." *College English* 30, No. 7 (April 1969): 555-61.

Defends Congreve's rebuttal of Jeremy Collier's historic

Short View of the Immorality and Profaneness of the English Stage.

Oates, Mary I. "Jonson, Congreve, and Gray: Pindaric Essays in Literary History." *Studies in English Literature* XIX, No. 3 (Summer 1979): 387-406.

> Considers divergent presentations of the Pindaric ode.

Peters, Julie Stone. *Congreve, the Drama, and the Printed Word.* Stanford: Stanford University Press, 1990, 286 p.

> Investigates the alliance between theater and printed works in the late seventeenth century. In particular, Peters deals with Congreve's struggle to integrate print and performance, his sensitivity to the problems of the book trade, and his attempt to resolve the dichotomy between nature and art.

Simon, John. "Mafia-Something." *New York* 24, No. 22 (3 June 1991): 53-4.

> An unfavorable review of Congreve's *The Way of the World* as staged by David Greenspan at the Public Theater, New York City.

Snider, Rose. "William Congreve." In her *Satire in the Comedies of Congreve, Sheridan, Wilde, and Coward,* pp. 1-40. New York: Phaeton Press, 1972.

> Addresses Congreve's treatment of conventional male and female roles and traditional institutions.

Steele, Richard. Dedication to *Poetical Miscellanies, Consisting of Original Poems and Translations by the Best Hands.* London: Jacob Tonson, 1714.

> Unreserved praise for Congreve's work.

Stephen, Sir Leslie. "Congreve, William." In *The Dictionary of National Biography,* Vol. IV, edited by Sir Leslie Stephen and Sir Sidney Lee, pp. 931-34. London: Oxford University Press, 1921.

> Reprints Stephen's 1887 assessment of Congreve's work as both flawed and essentially base.

Strachey, Lytton. "Congreve, Collier, Macaulay, and Mr. Summers." In his *Portraits in Miniature and Other Essays,* pp. 41-9. New York: Harcourt, Brace and Co., 1931.

> Investigates the essence of Congreve's dramatic comedy and its attendant moral issues.

Symons, Arthur. "The Final Congreve." *The Outlook* LII, No. 1349 (8 December 1923): 425-26.

> Proclaims Congreve "the only dramatist of his time who had touches of genius."

Teyssandier, H. "Congreve's *Way of the World:* Decorum and Morality." *English Studies* 52, No. 2 (2 April 1971): 124-31.

> Affirms that characters in *The Way of the World* are governed by propriety.

Turner, Darwin T. "The Servant in the Comedies of William Congreve." *CLA Journal* I, No. 2 (March 1958): 68-74.

> Illustrates the diversified roles of confidant, arch-deceiver, and wit played by servants in Congreve's comedies.

Tynan, Kenneth. "The British Theatre." In his *Curtains,* pp. 3-241. New York: Atheneum, 1961.

> Critical and dramatic review of Congreve's *The Way of the World.*

Whibley, Charles. "Congreve and Some Others." In his *Literary Studies,* pp. 240-97. London: Macmillan and Co., 1919.

> Critical outline of Congreve's major works in relation to those of other Restoration dramatists.

Williams, Aubrey. "Poetical Justice, the Contrivances of Providence, and the Works of William Congreve." *ELH* 35, No. 4 (December 1968): 540-65.

> Argues that "the major works of Congreve are brilliant demonstrations of a providential order in human events."

Woolf, Virginia. "Congreve." *The New Statesman* XVI, No. 416 (2 April 1921): 756.

> Primarily a performance review of *Love for Love.*

Zeidberg, David S. "Fainfall and Marwood: Vicious Characters and Limits of Comedy." *Thoth* 12, No. 1 (Fall 1971): 33-8.

> Explores Congreve's expansion of stock characters and its consequent effect on *The Way of the World.*

John Dryden

1631-1700

INTRODUCTION

English poet, critic, dramatist, and translator.

The following entry presents a selection of Dryden criticism for the last decade. For additional information on Dryden's life and works, see *Literature Criticism from 1400 to 1800,* Vol. 3.

Regarded by many scholars as the father of modern English poetry and criticism, Dryden dominated literary life in England during the last four decades of the seventeenth century. Through deliberate, comprehensive refinement of language, Dryden evolved an expressive, universal diction which has had immense impact on the development of speech and writing in the English-speaking world. Although initially famous for his numerous comedies and heroic tragedies, Dryden is today most highly regarded for his critical writings as well as his satirical and didactic poems. In the former, particularly *Of Dramatick Poesie,* he originated the extended form of objective analysis that has come to characterize most modern criticism. In the latter, notably *Absalom and Achitophel, The Hind and the Panther,* and *Religio Laici,* he displayed an irrepressible wit and forceful line of argument which later satirists adopted as their model. Dryden is also remembered as an inventive translator of the works of Vrgil, Geoffrey Chaucer, and Giovanni Boccaccio. A precise, graceful, and vigorous style distinguishes nearly all his work and has helped earn him lasting fame as one of the greatest practitioners of English literature.

The eldest son of a large, socially prominent Puritan family, Dryden was born in Aldwinkle, Northamptonshire. Little is known of his early years, though it is known that at a young age he received a classical education at Westminster School through a royal scholarship. While there he published his first poem, "Upon the Death of the Lord Hastings," commemorating the life of a schoolmate who had recently died of smallpox. In 1650 Dryden was elected to Trinity College, Cambridge, where he earned a bachelor of arts degree. Shortly afterward, his father died, leaving him to oversee the affairs of his family and of his own small estate. Dryden's activities and whereabouts during the next several years are unknown; in 1659, however, following the death of Oliver Cromwell, Lord Protector of England, Dryden returned to writing and published "Heroique Stanzas," a group of complimentary verses which portray Cromwell as architect of a great new age. In the following years Dryden continued to publish politically oriented poems, of which the most notable are *Astraea Redux* and *Annus Mirabilis: The Year of Wonders, 1666.* The former, which celebrated the exiled Charles II's restoration to the English crown, incited attacks in later years by Dryden's literary enemies, who charged him with political inconsistency and selfish motivation. But histori-

ans agree that Dryden maintained throughout his life a belief in religious tolerance and moderate government and switched allegiances from the republicans to the royalists at this time just as did the majority of the English people.

In 1663, following his marriage to Lady Elizabeth Howard, Dryden debuted as dramatist, a career which at the time held the most financial promise for an aspiring writer in England. His first play, the comedy *The Wild Gallant,* combined the English comedy of humors with an emphasis on intricate plot structure characteristic of the Spanish theater. It was performed at the newly established Theatre Royal but was unsuccessful. Dryden soon adopted a more sophisticated form of verse drama in collaboration with his brother-in-law Sir Robert Howard, and produced the heroic tragedy *The Indian Queen.* The two writers subsequently engaged in a lengthy literary debate on the merits of rhymed versus unrhymed plays, a dialogue which engendered Dryden's first critical essays and established him as a champion of rhymed verse drama. The sequel to *The Indian Queen, The Indian Emperour,* was written wholly in rhymed couplets. First performed in 1665, the play was extremely popular and gave Dryden standing in a field which he increasingly dominated during the next fifteen years. With the death of Sir William Davenant—the inventor of the English heroic play and, like Ben Jonson, a major influence on Dryden's dramas—Dryden assumed the post of poet laureate in 1668. The same year there appeared his most extended piece of literary criticism, *Of Dramatick Poesie.* Shortly thereafter Dryden reconsidered his earlier arguments in favor of the rhymed play and adopted blank verse, which he now recognized as a less constraining form for drama, and produced *All for Love; or, The World Well Lost.* The play, adapted from Shakespeare's *Antony and Cleopatra,* was a great success and solidified Dryden's reputation as the most talented and accomplished writer of the time.

By then Dryden had wearied of writing for the stage (though a decade later he returned to the theater for financial reasons), and had publicly acknowledged his belief that his talents were ill-suited to the field. The Popish Plot (1678-81), a thwarted attempt by the Earl of Shaftesbury and others to exclude Charles's Catholic brother, James, from his right of succession to the throne, provided Dryden with the topic for what critics consider his greatest work, *Absalom and Achitophel,* a satirical attack on Shaftesbury and his confederates. This work inaugurated a phase of satirical and didactic verse which directly influenced the development of Augustan poetry in the next century, especially that of Alexander Pope. Dryden's first major satire was followed in 1682 by *Mac Flecknoe,* a mock-heroic poem which had been circulating in manuscript for approximately four years and which was directed at the poet Thomas Shadwell, a literary antagonist of Dryden. Allied to *Absalom and Achitophel* in tone, *Mac Flecknoe* displays Dryden's mastery of rhythm and cunning verbal attack. The same year there also appeared a shorter, more serious satiric poem titled *The Medall,* which again was aimed at Shaftesbury, who escaped sentencing for treason despite Dryden's supposed attempt to influence the Grand Jury.

As political and religious matters repeatedly overlapped in Dryden's time, an era much concerned with the question of whether Protestant or Roman Catholic monarchs were the legitimate rulers of Britain, it is not surprising that Dryden also began to address religious issues during this period of national turmoil. *Religio Laici; or, A Laymans Faith* appeared when Whig plots to assassinate the king were being formed. In this didactic poem, which also contains religious and metaphysical insights, Dryden promulgated a compromise between Anglican exclusivism and Roman Catholic belief in absolute papal authority, articulating the king's stance in favor of religious toleration. In 1685 James II ascended the English throne and soon enacted a policy of toleration while placing many of his sympathizers in high government positions. Within the first year of James's reign, Dryden converted to Catholicism, once again inciting his literary detractors to disparage his reputation as a man of conviction. But the question of any underhanded motives by Dryden has been dismissed, as scholars have demonstrated that the renewal of his laureateship by James occurred months before his conversion. The fact that he did not renounce his conversion following James's abdication also supports the sincerity of Dryden's conversion. Known for its remarkable symbolism, *The Hind and the Panther,* stemmed from this occa-

sion. Written in beast-fable form, the poem presents a long theological debate between a milk-white hind, representing the Roman church, and a spotted panther, representing the Anglican church. During his last years, in addition to completing five more plays, Dryden wrote the widely anthologized odes *A Song for St. Cecilia's Day, 1687* and *Alexander's Feast; or The Power of Musique,* which attest to his ability—described as extraordinary by critics such as James Anderson Winn—to successfully incorporate elements of musical compositional technique into his creative procedures. However, it was as a translator that he spent most of his time, completing, in addition to several small projects, *The Works of Virgil* and *Fables Ancient and Modern.* Dryden died in London in 1700 and was buried in Westminster Abbey, having been recognized as an exceedingly popular literary figure who had heavily influenced the tastes of his era.

Samuel Johnson, who first deemed Dryden the father of English criticism, also considered him the English poet who crystallized the potential for beauty and majesty in the English language: according to Johnson's paraphrase of Augustus's encomium to himself, "he found it brick, and he left it marble." In his early complimentary verses Dryden first began developing the language while experimenting with the traditional hexameter form. Although recognized for their artistic promise and innovation, these poems have been faulted for misplaced or excessive conceits and similes. *Annus Mirabilis,* an inspirational, heroic treatment of the great fire in London and of the Anglo-Dutch naval war, represents the capstone of Dryden's early period as a poet. With *Absalom and Achitophel* Dryden displayed his mastery of the heroic couplet and the suitability of his streamlined verse for political satire. Cloaked in allusive language and based on the biblical story of King David's rebellious son, the mock-heroic poem addresses the explosive political climate of the time through a string of character portraits, narrative, and speeches. Dryden's portrayals of Charles II, an inveterate philanderer; his illegitimate son Monmouth, who planned to dethrone his father; and Shaftesbury, the chief orchestrator of the Popish Plot; are admired by critics not only for their liveliness but for the judicious manner in which they are presented. The relentless movement of the poem, its delightful yet pointed commentary on the crucial situation, and its timeless appeal, establish it as one of the highest achievements in the heroic couplet form. That Dryden was an exemplary poet of the public event and was able to infuse even the most ordinary incident with dignified, original art is not disputed. But his poems have been charged with displaying a disturbing impersonality. Several modern critics, however, have revealed a clear, confessional tone in the later poems *Religio Laici* and *The Hind and the Panther.* Although the theological viewpoints in them are disparate, these works forcefully document Dryden's personal reactions to the political milieu and to the power of religious faith in his age.

As translator, Dryden's greatest achievement is his *The Works of Virgil.* His intent, in all his translations, was less to reproduce than to paraphrase, while still capturing the individuality of the original. Hence, Vergilian and Chaucerian purists, for instance, have harshly criticized him for continually changing word order and narrative sense. Yet his translation of Vergil's works, particularly the *Aeneid*, is regarded as a monumental undertaking which, if not always meticulous, is largely representative of the Latin original. *Fables Ancient and Modern* is similarly regarded as a lasting work of translation. Critics agree that it embodies the finest examples of Dryden's narrative verse. Furthermore, scholars such as Paul Hammond regard Dryden's translations as a metaphor for his inquisitive, open-minded approach to literature.

Of all Dryden's works, his dramas have been accorded the least acclaim since his death. With the exception of a few of his thirty-odd plays, such as *All for Love, Don Sebastian,* and *Marriage-à-la-Mode,* his productions have vanished from the English stage. This, according to critics, is perhaps largely due to his devotion to the heroic play, a form which attained its greatest expression through him but which has since radically declined in public appeal. In addition, Dryden's comedies, though held to possess fine examples of witty repartee and many memorable characters, have been found wanting in truly comic scenes or effective explorations of human emotion. Not until the early twentieth century, when studies by T. S. Eliot and Mark Van Doren as well as Montague Summers's six-volume collection of Dryden's *Dramatic Works* appeared, did the plays receive favorable reassessments, with Summers, in particular, extolling Dryden for his monumental contribution to Restoration drama. Dryden also played an important role in the history of English music as the close collaborator of Henry Purcell, for whom he provided the text for the acclaimed musical drama *King Arthur; or The British Worthy.* Yet, of most interest to the majority of critics of his plays are the numerous prologues, prefaces, and dedications, in which Dryden expounded on the English theater, discussed the difficulties of representing life on the stage, assessed the merits and drawbacks of rhyme, and, most perceptively, criticized the works of John Fletcher, Francis Beaumont, Jonson, Shakespeare, and himself. In so doing he inaugurated the English tradition of practical criticism. While critics of his time were characteristically preoccupied with issues of morality, immorality, and the edification of the reader or audience, Dryden wrote objectively and systematically of literature itself. Through a natural, conversational prose style—consummately demonstrated in *Of Dramatick Poesie,* a dialogue written in the skeptical tradition—he discussed works in the context of literary tradition, generic form, technical innovation, and effectiveness of presentation. Hence, his method has been the standard for literary investigations to the present day.

In all his fields of literary endeavor, though least so in drama, Dryden is considered to have attained a level of achievement rarely equalled or surpassed in English literature. Frequent comparisons with his most celebrated literary descendant, Pope, almost unanimously affirm Dryden's superiority in metrical innovation, imagination, and style, though the works of Pope are more widely known. But Dryden's importance is acknowledged to transcend the merits of any individual work. Through his lengthy, varied career he fashioned not only many memorable dramas, poems, and satires, but a vital, concise, and refined language which served as the foundation for the writers

of English prose and verse who followed him. For this reason Dryden has for centuries been considered one of the greatest forces in English literary history.

PRINCIPAL WORKS

"Upon the Death of the Lord Hastings" (poetry) 1649; published in *Lachrymae Musarum; The Tears of the Muses: Exprest in Elegies*

"Heroique Stanzas" (poetry) 1659; published in *Three Poems upon the Death of his Late Highnesse Oliver Lord Protector of England, Scotland, and Ireland*

Astraea Redux. A Poem on the Happy Restoration & Return of his Sacred Majesty Charles the Second (poetry) 1660

The Wild Gallant (drama) 1663

The Indian Queen [with Sir Robert Howard] (drama) 1664

The Rival Ladies (drama) 1664

The Indian Emperour; or, The Conquest of Mexico by the Spaniards. Being the Sequel of the Indian Queen (drama) 1665

Annus Mirabilis: The Year of Wonders, 1666. An Historical Poem: Containing the Progress and Various Successes of our Naval War with Holland, under the Conduct of His Highness Prince Rupert, and His Grace the Duke of Albamarl, and Describing the Fire of London (poetry) 1667

Sir Martin Mar-All; or, The Feign'd Innocence [with the Duke of Newcastle] (drama) 1667

The Tempest; or, The Enchanted Island [adaptor; from the drama *The Tempest* by William Shakespeare; with Sir William Davenant] (drama) 1667

An Evening's Love; or, The Mock-Astrologer [adaptor; from the drama *Le feint astrologue* by Thomas Corneille] (drama) 1668

*Of Dramatick Poesie (criticism) 1668

Tyrannick Love; or, The Royal Martyr (drama) 1669

The Conquest of Granada by the Spaniards, Part I (drama) 1670

The Conquest of Granada by the Spaniards, Part II (drama) 1671

Marriage-à-la-Mode (drama) 1672

Aureng-Zebe (drama) 1675

All for Love; or, The World Well Lost [adaptor; from the drama *Antony and Cleopatra* by William Shakespeare] (drama) 1677

"The Author's Apology for Heroic Poetry and Poetic License" (criticism) 1677; published in *The State of Innocence, and Fall of Man*

The State of Innocence, and Fall of Man [adaptor; from the poem *Paradise Lost* by John Milton; first publication] (drama) 1677

"The Grounds of Criticism in Tragedy" (criticism) 1679; published in *Troilus and Cressida; or, Truth Found Too Late*

Troilus and Cressida; or, Truth Found Too Late [adaptor; from the drama *Troilus and Cressida* by William Shakespeare] (drama) 1679

Absalom and Achitophel (poetry) 1681

The Duke of Guise [with Nathaniel Lee] (drama) 1682

Mac Flecknoe; or, A Satire upon the True-Blew-Protestant Poet, T. S. (poetry) 1682

The Medall. A Satyre against Sedition (poetry) 1682

Religio Laici; or, A Laymans Faith (poetry) 1682

The Second Part of Absalom and Achitophel [with Nahum Tate] (poetry) 1682

Miscellany Poems (poetry) 1684

Sylvae: or, The Second Part of Poetical Miscellanies (poetry) 1685

Threnodia Augustalis: A Funeral-Pindarique Poem Sacred to the Happy Memory of King Charles II (poetry) 1685

"To the Pious Memory of the Accomplisht Young Lady Mrs. Anne Killigrew" (poetry) 1686; published in Killigrew's *Poems*

The Hind and the Panther. 3 Vols. (poetry) 1687

A Song for St. Cecilia's Day, 1687 (poetry) 1687

Don Sebastian, King of Portugal (drama) 1689

King Arthur: or, The British Worthy (drama) 1691

Examen Poeticum: Being the Third Part of Miscellany Poems (poetry) 1693

Alexander's Feast; or, The Power of Musique. An Ode in Honour of St. Cecilia's Day (poetry) 1697

The Works of Virgil: Containing his Pastorals, Georgics, and Æneis. Translated into English Verse [translator] (poetry) 1697

Fables Ancient and Modern; Translated into Verse, from Homer, Ovid, Boccace, & Chaucer: with Original Poems [translator and adaptor] (poetry) 1700

The Works of John Dryden. 18 Vols. (poetry, criticism, and dramas) 1808; revised 1882-93

Dryden: The Dramatic Works. 6 Vols. (dramas and criticism) 1931-32

The Letters of John Dryden (letters) 1942

*This work is commonly referred to as *Essay of Dramatic Poesy.*

G. Douglas Atkins (essay date 1980)

[*In the following excerpt, Atkins comments on the religious ideas in Dryden's writings from 1677 to 1684, the year of his conversion to Roman Catholicism. According to Atkins, Dryden sought "to reestablish a proper, that is, pious, relationship to God and thereby to all authority outside the self."*]

When we turn from a reading of the works Dryden wrote in the 1660s and early and mid-1670s to *Mac Flecknoe, Absalom and Achitophel, The Medall,* and *Religio Laici,* we are struck at once by the differences in his understanding. Evidently a major intellectual conversion had occurred, no doubt induced in part by a growing awareness of the ramifications of the new thought. Whenever and for whatever specific reasons it came about, it produced in Dryden a new insistence on the primacy of the moral in literary invention and on the moral function of poetry. It also led to his greatest literary achievements. I shall try here to describe the nature of Dryden's change in understanding as reflected in the poems (excluding *Religio*

Laici), plays, and prose works written between 1677 and his conversion to Roman Catholicism. A major failure of commentary on Dryden's religious thinking has been the almost total neglect of the works I discuss in this [essay]. (p. 33)

Published in 1682 but almost certainly composed by 1678, *Mac Flecknoe* is one of the first works to reflect Dryden's new outlook. As a satire it represents a new departure for Dryden. Prior to the late 1670s, possessing a tolerant, even optimistic view of man and believing in the inevitability of progress, he was more likely to praise than to blame. When he did ridicule, the abuse was mainly *à la mode* and aimed at the institutions the witty and enlightened thought to be in need of their lashes for old-fashioned, tyrannical, and hypocritical beliefs and actions. Beginning around the time of *Mac Flecknoe,* however, the satire is directed not haphazardly at obvious targets, but at particular and immediate situations generated by the vices and follies of individual men. Dryden's concerns are indeed more moral than before, for he now seems better to understand man's wicked heart.

If in moving from the early and exuberant Charleton poem and *Annus Mirabilis* to *Mac Flecknoe* praise has become satire, the prospect of immediate and unlimited progress has been transformed into a vision of unrelieved decay. The pervasive sense of absolute ruin, apparent from the opening line ("All humane things are subject to decay") to the scatological "subterranean wind" at the close, may be best illustrated with reference to the important account of the Nursery. What appears to be merely a spatial description turns out on closer examination to be an image of the process of historical decay.

> Close to the Walls which fair *Augusta* bind,
> (The fair *Augusta* much to fears inclin'd)
> An ancient fabrick, rais'd t' inform the sight,
> There stood of yore, and *Barbican* it hight:
> A watch Tower once; but now, so Fate ordains,
> Of all the Pile an empty name remains.
> From its old Ruins Brothel-houses rise,
> Scenes of lewd loves, and of polluted joys;
> Where their vast Courts the Mother-Strumpets keep,
> And, undisturb'd by Watch, in silence sleep.
> Near these a Nursery erects its head,
> Where Queens are form'd, and future Hero's bred;
> Where unfledg'd Actors learn to laugh and cry,
> Where infant Punks their tender Voices try,
> And little *Maximins* the Gods defy.
> Great *Fletcher* never treads in Buskins here,
> Nor greater *Johnson* dares in Socks appear.
> But gentle *Simkin* just reception finds
> Amidst this Monument of vanisht minds:
> Pure Clinches, the suburbian Muse affords;
> And *Panton* waging harmless War with words.
> Here *Fleckno,* as a place to Fame well known,
> Ambitiously design'd his *Sh——*'s Throne.
> (ll. 64-86)

Behind this description of the Nursery stands the well-known seventeenth-century tradition of eulogizing "a great public monument for its embodiment and continuation of tradition." But whereas the structures described in

Jonson's "To Penshurst" and Marvell's *Upon Appleton House,* for example, point to the accumulated wisdom of mankind in bodying forth a magnificent order, Shadwell's coronation place is a "Monument of vanisht minds" and so represents absence instead of living presence. As Edward Pechter shrewdly observes [in *Dryden's Classical Theory of Literature*], "The dream of the new science, sprung from Bacon's progressivist hopes, turns here into nightmare. Rather than legitimately extending tradition by refining it, the Nursery represents a radical alienation from all the values of the past."

It would be a mistake, I think, to conclude that Dryden's gloom results simply from disappointment over crushed hopes, now that the promise of the early years of Charles's reign has ushered in bourgeois mediocrity. The reasons for the pessimism of *Mac Flecknoe* cut much deeper. If the present is fallen, the decline is measured not by the halcyon days of the early 1660s, but rather by the standards of traditional understanding formerly supported by art but now subverted. Moreover, ancient wisdom looms impressively, and in particular Dryden's view of the Ancients and the nature they "read" differs from the sanguine picture of "a new nature" he extolled a few years earlier. His optimistic faith in Moderns diminished, he now offers a new estimation of the Ancients in the Preface to *All for Love,* where he calls them "our masters," and in **"The Grounds of Criticism in Tragedy,"** prefixed to *Troilus and Cressida* (1679), which contrasts vividly with the position taken in *Of Dramatic Poesy: An Essay;* here he advises imitation of Shakespeare and Fletcher "so far only as they have copied the excellencies of those who invented and brought to perfection dramatic poetry." As Dryden put it in the dedication of *Plutarch's Lives* (1683) in "powerful periods that roll over the reader like tidal waves" and that constitute "one of the most fervent manifestos in English literature for believers in a golden age of the past and one of the most magnificent admissions of individual and corporate inferiority in his contemporary world":

> Not only the Bodies, but the Souls of Men, have decreas'd from the vigour of the first Ages; . . . we are not more short of the stature and strength of those gygantick Heroes, than we are of their understanding, and their wit. . . . How vast a difference is there betwixt the productions of those Souls, and these of ours! How much better *Plato, Aristotle,* and the rest of the Philosophers understood nature; *Thucydides,* and *Herodotus* adorn'd History; *Sophocles, Euripides* and *Menander* advanc'd Poetry, than those Dwarfs of Wit and Learning who succeeded them in after times!

Without neglecting the Puritan and Whiggish background of the city, its crass materialism and its unruly mobs, Dryden focuses on the deterioration of art in the hands of the poets the city prefers and the loss of understanding that results from that decay. Opposed to the impulse toward earthy realism and the naturalistic in poets like Shadwell, Dryden insists that literature reflect "perfect nature." What Shadwell provides is not Nature but a severely limited and distorted approximation, a parody, void of presence, not altogether different perhaps from the "new nature" drawn by the scientists. "What share have we in Na-

ture or in Art?" asks Flecknoe (1. 176), innocent of the key terms' meaning. Dryden's reiterated conflation of distinct kinds of reality in the poem is evidently intended to dramatize Shadwell's confusion of art with life naturalistically interpreted and his ultimate reduction of both to one dead level. In the final six lines, of course, characters from *Psyche* step out of the play to effect Flecknoe's departure and to enthrone their author.

Shadwell's failure to transform life into art leads inexorably in those who absorb his work to the same leveling of sensibility and deadening of consciousness that he represents so well. Nowhere is the significance of Shadwell's dullness clearer than in the remarks on wit:

> Some Beams of Wit on other souls may fall,
> Strike through and make a lucid intervall;
> But *Sh*——'s genuine night admits no ray,
> His rising Fogs prevail upon the Day.
>
> (ll. 21-4)

Drawing on the ancient tradition which equates light with Being and darkness with nonbeing, Dryden carefully establishes the consequences of Shadwell's parody of art. "Born for a scourge of wit, and flayle of Sense" (l. 89), Shadwell must swear "Ne'er to have peace with Wit, nor truce with Sense" (l. 117). Instead he is to "wage immortal War with Wit" (l. 12) and thus destroy the human faculty which can perceive the physical creation as not wholly material but potentially intelligible as "the manifestation . . . of the Order and Reason behind all things, a reflection of the medieval view that the likeness of God is implanted in the very matter and organization of the universe." Unaware that everything is itself and at the same time a reflection of something more than itself, Shadwell's realism can only celebrate things for what they seem, not for what they mean.

The effects of the spread of dullness are, of course, already observable in the world of the poem. Partly as a result of the penchant for "tortur[ing] one poor word Ten thousand ways" (l. 208) and so "waging harmless War with words" (l. 84), "vanisht minds" are everywhere. Instead of reflecting the light visible in Nature, heightening consciousness, and fulfilling the poet's responsibilities as caretaker of language, tradition, and morality, Shadwell will create "Some peacefull Province in Acrostick Land" (l. 206). Like Flecknoe, "flourishing in Peace" (l. 7), Shadwell will secure accommodation with human nature, rather than encourage discipline, control, and the correction of follies and vices. For as Flecknoe proudly proclaims, asserting the importance of gentleness:

> Like mine thy gentle numbers feebly creep,
> Thy Tragick Muse gives smiles, thy Comick sleep.
> With whate'er gall thou sett'st thy self to write,
> Thy inoffensive Satyrs never bite.
>
> (ll. 197-200)

Dryden aptly summarizes Shadwell's perversion of the poet's public responsibility in comparing "the hopefull boy" (l. 61) with Hannibal, sworn enemy of Rome:

> The hoary Prince in Majesty appear'd,
> High on a Throne of his own Labours rear'd.

At his right hand our young *Ascanius* sate,
Rome's other hope, and pillar of the State.
His Brows thick fogs, instead of glories, grace,
And lambent dullness plaid around his face.
As *Hannibal* did to the Altars come,
Sworn by his *Syre* a mortal Foe to *Rome;*
So *Sh*—— swore, nor should his Vow bee vain,
That he till Death true dullness would maintain;
And in his father's Right, and Realms defence,
Ne'er to have peace with Wit, nor truce with
        Sense.

(ll. 106-17)

As the frequent political references and analogies suggest, Dryden is drawing too on the tradition in which "the lawgiver is . . . named beside the poet, and the formulas which define the law beside the wise utterances of the poet " [Werner Jaeger, *Paideia: The Ideals of Greek Culture,* 1939].

The civil and religious functions of the poet, as Dryden images them, may finally be inseparable. For if, as Sanford Budick has recently argued [in *Poetry of Civilization: Mythopoeic Displacement in the Verse of Milton, Dryden, Pope, and Johnson,* 1974], Dryden, like Milton before and Pope and Johnson afterwards, accepted the biblical notion of the poet as *keryx,* the true poet may be a prophet, that is, one who speaks for God and who has been chosen in some sense to lead his people. Though the several references in the poem to prophets and prophecy have usually been interpreted as simply another strike at Flecknoe and Shadwell, particularly as they are linked to Dissenting attitudes, Dryden may not be reviling at all the idea of the poet's prophetic function but rather the parody of that idea by bad poets. Given the evident foundation of *Annus Mirabilis* in prophecy, this seems plausible.

Not unrelated, I believe, is the fact that beginning in 1678 Dryden increasingly scored the clergy for failing to adhere to their duties and responsibilities. From *Troilus and Cressida* (1679) through *The Duke of Guise* (1683) Dryden's works, dramatic and nondramatic, may be seen as attempting to fulfill at least part of the function traditionally performed by churchmen but now being neglected. *Religio Laici* is the culmination of this effort to supplement and correct those who, like Shadwell, fail to do the necessary work of maintaining access to Being itself. The particular way in which Dryden now treats the clergy is one manifestation of his increasing interest in matters religious and spiritual, which exists alongside growing doubts regarding the world and especially the realm of politics.

For whatever reasons, Dryden's antipathy toward priests increased markedly in the late 1670s, and for the next several years he treated them with a violence unmatched even in an era of anticlericalism. Jeremy Collier's outraged cry that "the English *Oedipus* makes the Priesthood an Imposturous Profession, and rails at the whole Order" contains more truth than one likely expects. For during these years, invoking the concept anathematized by churchmen, Dryden wastes few opportunities to expose *priestcraft.* In his treatment that term, so often used by Deists and freethinkers, is defined as a failure to adhere to the spiritual function, resulting from a self-interested desire for money, place, and power that has led to various forms of worldly engagement, including political intrigue. Maintaining that "Priests of all Religions are the same" (l. 99), Dryden begins *Absalom and Achitophel* by insinuating that priestcraft makes piety virtually impossible (l. 1). The "pious times" Dryden there longingly recalls, soon replaced by moral, political, and religious corruption, evidently understood and practiced what the Ancients called *pietas,* that is, dutiful conduct toward the gods, one's parents, family, benefactors, and country. Now, as a direct result of the ungodly example of priests, piety, understood as the *pietas* for which Aeneas is the best-known exemplar, is hardly possible. Most important, of course, is the lack of respect for, indeed the insult to, God. It is precisely this sense of piety that Dryden, now committed to ancient ideals, works to restore as he exposes priestcraft as well as the directions of modern thought, accepting the responsibilities he evidently felt the clergy had neglected.

Beginning with *All for Love* in 1677 Dryden consistently and successfully integrated his anticlericalism into theme and structure, emphasizing priestly perfidy and revealing the significance he attached to such clerical failure. If we are to understand the nature, extent, and significance of Dryden's opposition to the clergy in this important period of his life, we must attend to the role churchmen play in his art, a role that has not been sufficiently recognized.

All for Love and its subtitle, *The World Well Lost,* spotlight Dryden's focal concerns in the play. As exemplified in the brilliant imagery, it is in at least one sense about transcendence of the Heraclitean flux and of the depersonalizing and soul-enclosing intrigue that characterizes the "worlds" of both Egypt and Rome. Antony well loses that world in choosing instead the constancy Dryden embodies in Cleopatra's love, "the jewel of great price." More so than is ordinarily realized, *All for Love's* distinction between transcendent and worldly—if conventional—values, between the private and public, reflects Dryden's own important development: he comes to place his faith not in politics and hopes for scientific and secular progress but rather in the realm of the spirit, which reveals the imprint of God. If this is so, we may readily understand his vituperative treatment of priests, whom he sees as surrogates of Christ in the service of the powers of the world and thus betrayers of the Christ-role they fill.

Though in this play the attention devoted to the clergy is limited, Dryden makes effective use of the priest Serapion. Evidently Serapion has the faults endemic in the priesthood, for Alexas claims that his primary concern is "His offerings" (V.i.). The characterization of Serapion, in the opening scene, as an intriguer foreshadows the play's general theme:

And dreamed you this? or did invent the story?
To frighten our Egyptian boys withal,
And train them up, betimes, in fear of priest-
        hood?
. . . .
A foolish dream,
Bred from the fumes of undigested feasts,
And holy luxury.

More particularly, Serapion assists in directing the audience's acceptance of Antony and of his rejection of certain orthodoxies. For if following the dictates of one's rational nature is to be approved, conventional obedience to unnatural forms, such as a religion dominated by priests, must appear unworthy. By presenting the representative of religion as corrupt, Dryden helps us accept the unconventional. Further, it is important that Serapion both opens and closes the play. The choice of the priest, rather than the highest ranking surviving character, to take charge at the end may be dramatically unconventional, but it effectively achieves several purposes. It completes the frame and, because Serapion is a symbol of the intrigue and self-interest of the way Antony rejects, Dryden is able to establish the permanence of the world "well lost." Moreover, by framing and in a sense enclosing the tragic pair, Dryden suggests the way they are entrapped in an unfeeling world of self-seeking manipulators. Within the contexts Serapion helps establish, Antony's choice of Cleopatra rather than "the world" appears justified. Dryden's dramatic advocacy of world-transcendence is thus pointedly independent of established religion, which here fosters, rather than retards, the success of the "world."

More striking and more important dramatically is Dryden's use of the priest in *Troilus and Cressida.* In his version, unlike Chaucer's or Shakespeare's, Cressida is completely faithful to her naive Trojan lover. Cressida's father, a priest and "a fugitive to the Grecian camp," becomes the instrument or material cause of the eventual tragedy. The truth found too late is that Cressida is not a whore—Calchas is. (pp. 33-42)

Why Dryden radically revised the story of Troilus and Cressida, making Calchas rather than his daughter the faithless one, is puzzling. Such a transformation, though,

Portrait of Dryden by James Maubert, ca. 1695.

extreme as it is, is in line with Dryden's evident intention at the time to expose clerical treachery whenever and wherever possible. A primary reason for this effort was his growing concern with social unrest and political rebellion and especially a belief that greed and thirst for power made the clergy ready instruments in any cause that promised preferment and "lusty benefices." Whether or not it induced the attention directed to Calchas, Dryden's interest in the worsening political situation appears in *Troilus and Cressida;* by shifting the order of the opening scenes, for example, he, unlike Shakespeare, stresses the civil problems besetting the Greeks and establishes a relevance to England, a point reiterated in the play's last lines: e.g., "since from home-bred factions ruin springs, / Let subjects learn obedience to their kings."

Whenever Dryden focuses on the political situation in the late 1670s and early 1680s, the clergy is treated at some length. In *Absalom and Achitophel,* to take a prominent example, he connects the present upheaval with the "Good old Cause," claims the Dissenting clergy form the vanguard of this movement, and contends that their motivation is the same as that of their predecessors in the 1640s:

> With them Joyn'd all th' Haranguers of the
>   Throng,
> That thought to get Preferment by the Tongue.
> . . . .
> Hot *Levites* Headed these; who pul'd before
> From th' *Ark,* which in the Judges days they
>   bore,
> Resum'd their Cant, and with a Zealous Cry,
> Pursu'd their old belov'd Theocracy:
> Where Sanhedrin and Priest inslav'd the Nation,
> And justifi'd their Spoils by Inspiration;
> For who so fit for Reign as *Aaron*'s Race,
> If once Dominion they could found in Grace?
> These led the Pack; tho not of surest scent,
> Yet deepest mouth'd against the Government.
>   (ll. 509-10, 519-28)

The attack is by no means limited to the "fanatical" clergy, however; as Leon M. Guilhamet notes [in "Dryden's Debasement of Scripture in *Absalom and Achitophel,*" in *Studies in English Literature,* 9, 1969], Dryden includes even the Anglican priesthood in the sweeping condemnation. After charging that "Priests of all Religions are the same" (l. 99), Dryden asserts:

> The *Jewish Rabbins* thô their Enemies,
> In this conclude them honest men and wise:
> For 'twas their duty, all the Learned think,
> T' espouse his Cause by whom they eat and
>   drink.
>   (ll. 104-07)

A few lines later Dryden again directs the charge of materialistic concern at the Established clergy: the Catholics' "busie Teachers," he says,

>   mingled with the *Jews;*
> And rak'd, for Converts, even the Court and
>   Stews:
> Which *Hebrew* Priests the more unkindly took,
> Because the Fleece accompanies the Flock.
>   (ll. 126-29)

The Second Part of *Absalom and Achitophel,* written in collaboration with Nahum Tate and published in 1682, is even more direct in its denunciation of Anglican churchmen. . . . In the context of the widespread belief that Catholic priests had long been engaged in the most sinister plots against the king, the government, and the Protestant religion, Dryden's emphasis in both poems on the Dissenting and Anglican clergy, to the virtual exclusion of the Catholic, seems remarkable. The implication seems to be that if Jesuits are unscrupulous, power-hungry, and seditious, they are no different from priests of other religions. Indeed, lines 85-97 appear sympathetic toward the plight of English Catholics.

At any rate, the anticlerical passages are thematically functional in *Absalom and Achitophel.* At the center of the poem and of the current unrest is "the threat of a specific new force in English life: economic, religious, and political individualism." What has happened, as Ronald Paulson puts it [in *The Fictions of Satire,* 1967], is that a "single ambitious man is willing to overthrow the state in order to gain more power for himself; so he seduces the king's illegitimate son (a pseudo-Christ) into rebelling against his father and master (God), and by means of a plot he turns the crowd into his ally." But the role of the clergy in duping the crowd must not be overlooked. In this regard they are presented as like Shaftesbury and Titus Oates, himself "a *Levite*" (l. 644). Indeed, priests are the corporate manifestation of the evil force represented by Shaftesbury. What Paulson concludes about Shaftesbury applies to the clergy as well: the Satanic focus of the poem "is presented not only as a tempter but as a hypocritical pretender to religion or to public reform: a memory of the fanatic Puritan and the mercenary London merchants who, professing piety, overthrew Charles I." The churchmen satirized in *Absalom and Achitophel* subvert their priestly function as they participate in, and in some cases guide, unholy actions that would, if successful, usher in the reign of man rather than of God.

In *The Duke of Guise,* first performed in 1682, Dryden again depicted the priesthood as agents of sedition and rebellion. He wrote the play in collaboration with Nathaniel Lee, but only those parts he claimed to be his (the first scene, the entire fourth act, and about half of Act Five) expose the central role of the clergy in the Guisard uprising in sixteenth-century France. The play goes far toward justifying the loyalist Crillon's claim that "when the preachers draw against the king, a parson in a pulpit is a devilish fore-horse" (V.i.) (pp. 43-6)

The Spanish Fryar (1681) focuses sharply on clerical corruption. Because the usual interpretation of this play challenges the pattern we have seen developing in Dryden's treatment of the clergy, it deserves considerable attention. I think we will see that this artfully constructed tragicomedy reinforces our understanding of the remarkable degree to which the priesthood was then preying on Dryden's mind as it provides for a better understanding of the exact nature of that concern.

The title would seem to establish the centrality of the unscrupulous friar, but in the most thorough study to date [*Dryden's Major Plays,* 1966], Bruce King claims that

Dominic's role is unrelated to the theme, which, he says, points to "a basic incoherence of parts within the play." Commentators by and large have viewed Dominic as an excrescence on what is otherwise agreed to be one of Dryden's most successful plays. Taking their cue from the phrase "a Protestant play" which Dryden wittily employs in the dedication to "a Protestant patron" (John Lord Haughton), scholars have usually seen the depiction of the friar as "an attack upon an obnoxious priesthood whom [Dryden], in common with all the nation, believed to have been engaged in the darkest intrigues against the King and Government." This "crude caricature of Catholicism" thus reflects, says [Walter Scott in his edition of *The Works of John Dryden* (revised and corrected by George Saintsbury, 1883-1892)], the poet's participation in "the general ferment which the discovery of the Popish Plot had excited."

In fact, however, the "Popish Plot" did not produce any such "ferment" in Dryden. In *Absalom and Achitophel* he blames Anglican and Dissenting churchmen for promoting sedition while extenuating Jesuit blame. Though the clergy depicted in *The Duke of Guise* necessarily is Catholic, Dryden's primary interest lies in a general issue of which the situations in sixteenth-century France and seventeenth-century England are particular instances. In *Absalom and Achitophel,* moreover, with admirable balance Dryden attempts to place the "Plot" in perspective:

> From hence began that Plot, the Nation's Curse,
> Bad in it self, but represented worse:
> Rais'd in extremes, and in extremes decry'd;
> With Oaths affirm'd, with dying Vows deny'd:
> Not weigh'd, or winnow'd by the Multitude;
> But swallow'd in the Mass, unchew'd and
>   Crude.
> Some Truth there was, but dash'd and brew'd
>   with Lyes;
> To please the Fools, and puzzle all the Wise.
> Succeeding times did equal folly call,
> Believing nothing, or believing all.
>
>   (ll. 108-17)

Earlier, when almost the entire nation believed Titus Oates's malicious allegations, Dryden seems to have been no surer of any such plot. Certainly his casual reference to the "plot" in the dedication of *The Kind Keeper,* produced when excitement was at fever pitch, does not suggest the degree of involvement and even frenzy that Scott claims.

Neither does *The Spanish Fryar.* As [Louis I. Bredvold observes in *Essays and Studies in English and Comparative Literature,* 1932], the play "is not ornamented . . . with topical allusions to the Popish Plot and its ramifications." The couple of references to plotting, in fact, seem wittily topical, rather than framed to remind the audience of grave dangers outside the theatre. If Dryden were caught up in the "ferment" excited by the "Popish Plot," he strangely failed to take advantage of the excellent opportunity *The Spanish Fryar* afforded him to condemn Catholic political intrigue. For the thoroughly corrupt friar is relegated to the comic plot where his intrigues are pointedly limited to amorous rather than political causes. The Catholic priesthood here as elsewhere is the obvious vehicle of

Dryden's assault on the clergy, rather than the sole or perhaps even the primary object of a partisan attack. As in Dryden's other major treatments of churchmen (*The Indian Emperour, Troilus and Cressida, The Duke of Guise, Don Sebastian,* and "The Character of a Good Parson"), the priesthood satirized is not limited to the clergy directly presented. Dryden's strategy and purpose in *The Spanish Fryar* have not been correctly perceived.

Without attempting a full-scale vindication of Dryden's own view, supported by Dr. Johnson, that the serious and comic plots fit well together, I think we can appreciate Dominic's relation, indeed centrality, to the whole. As King has noted, *The Spanish Fryar* is designed in part to show that "rebellion, for any reason, is against the will of God." But in addition to answering the central political and theological questions raised by demonstrating that, contrary to earlier appearances, a providential power exists that, according to the play's conclusion, "guards the sacred lives of kings" and involves itself in the daily affairs of men, the play also dramatizes the human tendencies that often conflict with the moral order built into the nature of things. Leonora's soliloquy in III.iii. poses exactly the question of the relationship of men's actions to the Divine Will. Leonora admits the evil with which human activity is tainted, though she denies responsibility for her own actions, maintaining that they have been determined by Heaven; her own consent to Sancho's death, she rationalizes, is proof of Heaven's concurrence:

> . . . I would not do this crime,
> And yet, like heaven, permit it to be done.
> The priesthood grossly cheat us with free-will:
> Will to do what—but what heaven first decreed?
> Our actions then are neither good nor ill,
> Since from eternal causes they proceed;
> Our passions,—fear and anger, love and hate,—
> Mere senseless engines that are moved by fate;
> Like ships on stormy seas, without a guide,
> Tossed by the winds, and driven by the tide.

I would contend that, rather than merely an argument against political rebellion, *The Spanish Fryar* is in large part about these passions in relation to the existing moral order. The play suggests the necessity of restraining, rather than indulging, the self-seeking and impetuous will. (pp. 49-52)

It seems plain that *The Spanish Fryar* carries a generalized attack on the clergy, rather than a militant anti-Catholicism excited by recent events and rumors. The numerous abusive statements made about the clergy by various characters certainly extends the ridicule to the clergy generally, though some of the abuse admittedly is directed at friars in particular. (pp. 54-5)

An excellent gloss on the play's strategy is provided by the Epilogue, which extends the attack on the clergy and where the opening focus on the Catholic priesthood soon broadens to take in all churchmen. Whether or not Dryden himself wrote the lines is immaterial for our purposes.

> How are men cozened still with shows of good!
> The bawd's best mask is the grave friar's hood;
> Though vice no more a clergyman displeases,
> Than doctors can be thought to hate diseases.

> 'Tis by your living ill, that they live well,
> By your debauches, their fat paunches swell.
> 'Tis a mock war between the priest and devil;
> When they think fit, they can be very civil.
> As some, who did French counsels most advance,
> To blind the world, have railed in print at France,
> Thus do the clergy at your vices bawl,
> That with more ease they may engross them all.
> By damning yours, they do their own maintain;
> A churchman's godliness is always gain:
> Hence to their prince they will superior be;
> And civil treason grows church loyalty.
> They boast the gift of heaven is in their power;—
> Well may they give the god, they can devour!
> Still to the sick and dead their claims they lay;
> For 'tis on carrion that the vermin prey.

The end result in both Epilogue and play is a demeaning and diminishing of the clergy.

The final and most devastating blow to the priesthood comes at the end of the play with the necessary intervention of Providence to undo the friar's roguery: "How vainly man designs, when heaven opposes" (IV.ii.). In one of the double discoveries alluded to in the subtitle, Providence, working through secondary means, thwarts the unwitting and licentious lovers and saves them from incest, just as it brings about in the political sphere what rash men like Raymond, depending on their own power, endanger. Indeed, the final discovery (regarding Sancho) appears in the last few lines of the play, which thus blatantly exploits the *deus ex machina* in order to stress providential intervention. Providence works, moreover, not to punish those who rail at the church, as Dominic would have his many antagonists believe, but rather to punish the churchman who violates and undermines the laws of Heaven. The play thus shows that Providence must sometimes work without and even despite priests, whose responsibility it is to make clear and assist the Will of God. Pedro's comment in the opening scene, "O religion and roguery, how they go together!," both anticipates the first line of *Absalom and Achitophel* and foreshadows an important dramatized point of the play. *The Spanish Fryar,* I suggest, is "a Protestant play" not because it abuses the Catholic religion but because, in the antisacerdotal spirit fundamental to Protestantism, it minimizes the priesthood.

In its emphasis on fallen man's willful inclinations, *The Spanish Fryar* points to the major themes of the works Dryden wrote during the years immediately following the "Popish Plot." Suggested in this play and explored from the political and theological perspectives in *Absalom and Achitophel* and *Religio Laici,* the issue at bottom is the fateful question, in whom does final authority and power reside, man or God?

Having finally recognized that Dryden was no hireling who merely wrote on demand for the party in power, many of us are now likely to agree that characteristically Dryden's real subject in his most famous political poem is [as David M. Vieth wrote in "Concept as Metaphor: Dryden's Attempted Stylistic Revolution" in *Language and Style* 3, 1970] "a tertium quid, an abstract, general statement of which the English and biblical situations are merely particular instances." Indeed, there is a growing—and quite proper—understanding that Dryden wrote less for Charles than for a transcendent order imaged, though imperfectly, by his reign. Dryden's work in this period is often political, at least in appearance, because politics was the arena in which the fundamental human drama was then being played out. Paradoxically, Dryden's most political work, superficially speaking, came about when he had lost faith in the world as the realm wherein man might achieve some form of redemption and salvation. At any rate, in the final analysis his argument is that the current "rebellion" against the king, reflected in the agitation to exclude his Catholic brother from the throne, manifests opposition to God. According to *The Medall* (1682):

> If Sovereign Right by Sovereign Pow'r they
>   scan,
> The same bold Maxime holds in God and Man:
> God were not safe, his Thunder cou'd they shun
> He shou'd be forc'd to crown another Son.
>   (ll. 214-17)

Dryden is not, I think, simply rehearsing the traditional *jure divino* contention that rebellion against the monarch as God's vicegerent on earth, divinely appointed for that purpose, serving by his express wish, and enjoying his special protection, violates God's Will. More than this, he finds forces at work which seem to threaten destruction of obligation to and reliance on external authority generally; these forces appear bent on toppling God himself in order to enthrone self-sufficient man. The aim of the new reformers, Dryden claims in *Absalom and Achitophel,* is nothing less than "At once Divine and Humane Laws [to] controul" and so "To change Foundations, cast the Frame anew" (ll. 807, 805). In like manner he wrote in *His Majesties Declaration Defended,* also in 1681, that the king's enemies "will lose their time no more, in cutting off the Succession, altering the course of Nature, and directing the providence of God."

Appropriately, therefore, Dryden associates the current reformers with Satan, the archetypal rebel against God's established order. Thus in *The Spanish Fryar* when Raymond sophistically asks, "What treason is it to redeem my king, / And to reform the state" (his real aim, he has admitted, is to "ruin" the queen and her lover), the heroic Torrismond replies: "That's a stale cheat; / The primitive rebel, Lucifer, first used it, / And was the first reformer of the skies" (V.ii.). The Miltonic echoes throughout *Absalom and Achitophel* help to establish "the false *Achitophel,*" "A Name to all succeeding Ages Curst" (ll. 150-51), as "the intrepid Devil himself emerging from Hell to destroy Eden and to devote man to death." The poem's central passage is replete with images of the Garden as Achitophel employs Satan's arguments both there and in the desert, infusing in Absalom-Adam-Christ the deadly poison and precipitating as the event of the temptation another fall. Attempting "with studied Arts to please," Achitophel "sheds his Venome" (ll. 228-29) as follows:

> Auspicious Prince! at whose Nativity
> Some Royal Planet rul'd the Southern sky;
> Thy longing Countries Darling and Desire;
> Their cloudy Pillar, and their guardian Fire:
> Their second *Moses,* whose extended Wand

> Divides the Seas, and shews the promis'd Land:
> Whose dawning Day, in every distant age,
> Has exercis'd the Sacred Prophets rage:
> The Peoples Prayer, the glad Deviners Theam,
> The Young-mens Vision, and the Old mens
>   Dream!
> Thee, *Saviour,* Thee, the Nations Vows confess;
> And, never satisfi'd with seeing, bless:
> . . . .
> Believe me, Royal Youth, thy Fruit must be,
> Or gather'd Ripe, or rot upon the Tree.
> Heav'n, has to all allotted, soon or late,
> Some lucky Revolution of their Fate:
> Whose Motions, if we watch and guide with
>   Skill,
> (For humane Good depends on humane Will,)
> Our Fortune rolls, as from a smooth Descent,
> And, from the first Impression, takes the Bent:
> But, if unseiz'd, she glides away like wind;
> And leaves repenting Folly far behind.
>   (ll. 230-41, 250-59)

If Absalom becomes savior—Dryden's later use of this terminology in ironically describing the "Progress" of the "young *Messiah*" through "the promis'd Land" (ll. 723 ff.) diminishes the possibility that the rhetoric is merely fanciful—politics has evidently replaced religion as the instrument of man's redemption and salvation.

To effect the subversion of order Achitophel has in mind, other hands are needed. Thus he who "Disdain'd the Golden fruit to gather free, / [Also] lent the Croud his Arm to shake the Tree" (ll. 202-03). In fact, it is the argument of the later, darker, and more bitter *Medall* that Shaftesbury, there diminished in stature but still Satanic, has "pox'd" the nation (l. 266). Like Friar Dominic, Flecknoe, and Shadwell a false legislator, he is

> . . . the Pander of the Peoples hearts,
> (O Crooked Soul, and Serpentine in Arts,)
> Whose blandishments a Loyal Land have
>   whor'd,
> And broke the Bonds she plighted to her Lord.
>   (ll. 256-59)

Having seduced "the Croud" as he "ruined" Absalom, Shaftesbury encourages self-sufficient individualism and its ultimate social consequence, political chaos:

> . . . this new *Jehu* spurs the hot mouth'd horse;
> Instructs the Beast to know his native force;
> To take the Bit between his teeth and fly
> To the next headlong Steep of Anarchy.
>   (ll. 119-22)

But Dryden makes clear that the consequences are not simply social and political. Now infused with his poison and set "in the Papal Chair" (l. 87), the people reflect Achitophel—Satan's false image: "So all are God-a'mighties" (l. 110).

The clergy's role in this grand enterprise of uncreation must not be forgotten. In light of the foregoing, Dryden's identification of the priesthood with the Devil in *The Duke of Guise* appears to be of substance. The same suggestion of priestly complicity in the subversion of order results from the links *Absalom and Achitophel* establishes between the arch-tempter and the clergy. The "Hot *Le-*

vites," important in crying up "Religion, and Redress of Grievances, / Two names, that always cheat and always please" (ll. 747-48), pursue "their old belov'd Theocracy" (l. 522); leading "the Pack," they are "deepest mouth'd against the Government" (ll. 527-28). Of the "numerous Host of dreaming Saints" who follow these priests Dryden says, " 'Gainst Form and Order they their Power employ; / Nothing to Build and all things to Destroy" (ll. 529, 531-32), invoking the Satanic determination expressed in Beelzebub's famous declaration [in John Milton's *Paradise Lost*] "either with Hell fire / To waste his whole Creation, or possess / All as our own."

A major weapon of those who plead the cause of "Religion" is Scripture. In the Preface to **Religio Laici** Dryden charges that "those Texts of Scripture, which are not necessary to Salvation, [have been 'detorted'] to the damnable uses of Sedition, disturbance and destruction of the Civil Government." As he demonstrates in **The Duke of Guise,** Scripture is particularly dangerous in the hands of unscrupulous clergymen, who

> With impious glosses ban the holy text,
> And make it speak rebellion, schism, and murder;
> So turn the arms of heaven against itself.
>
> (IV.ii.)

"False *Achitophel*" also perverts scriptural meaning. In work after work during the early 1680s Dryden focuses on such manipulation of Holy Scripture, which becomes a central element in his "pious" concern with the proper relationship of man to God. This concern is a crucial but largely neglected context for **Religio Laici.**

Abuse of Scripture is nothing new, Dryden maintains. The holy text has perhaps always been a ready weapon for any self-seeking party to use. In the Preface to **Religio Laici,** the structural center of which poem is the "digression" on the new English translation of Father Simon's *Critical History of the Old Testament,* Dryden declares that "While we were Papists, our Holy Father rid us, by pretending authority out of the Scriptures to depose Princes; when we shook off his Authority, the Sectaries furnish'd themselves with the same Weapons; and out of the same Magazine, the Bible." Scripture itself, he admits, is partly to blame; because of its ambiguity on certain nonessential points of faith, it can easily be made to say whatever one pleases. As he put it in the Dedication of **Plutarch's Lives,** "the same Reasons, and Scriptures, which are urg'd by Popes for the deposition of Princes, are produc'd by Sectaries for altering the Succession." Dryden's concern at this time, however, is not with Catholic manipulation of Scripture but with the "Sedition, disturbance and destruction of the Civil Government" threatened by the Whiggish and Dissenting reformers who effectively wield Scripture. The origin of this particular abuse Dryden traces to the Reformation, claiming in the Preface to his layman's faith, "Since the Bible has been Translated into our Tongue, ['the Fanaticks, or Schismaticks, of the *English* Church'] have us'd it so, as if their business was not to be sav'd but to be damned by its Contents." He goes on in the Preface to charge that "never since the Reformation, has there wanted a Text of [the Fanaticks'] interpreting to authorize

a Rebel." His conclusion is not heartening to a Protestant: "If we consider onely them, better had it been for the *English* Nation, that it had still remain'd in the original *Greek* and *Hebrew,* or at least in the honest *Latine* of St. *Jerome,* than that several Texts in it, should have been prevaricated to the destruction of that Government, which put it into so ungrateful hands."

Though he repeatedly abjures the sectarians' convenient habit of neglecting the plain sense of Scripture in favor of undue emphasis on those obscure passages which should be left alone because unnecessary to salvation, Dryden's primary quarrel seems to be with the premise from which such effects follow. That is the fundamental Protestant insistence not only on the availability of Scripture in English translation for every person learned or ignorant but also on Bible reading accompanied by the doctrine of private interpretation. Without at all wishing to imply that Dryden was crypto-Catholic by the early 1680s, I submit that his objection is essentially that of Catholicism to Protestantism. In the Postscript to his translation of Maimbourg's **History of the League** (1684), for example, Dryden speaks contemptuously of the "gift of interpreting Scriptures by private Persons, without Learning" and proceeds to argue that this "was certainly the Original Cause of such Cabals in the Reform'd Churches: So dangerous an instrument of Rebellion is the Holy Scripture, in the hands of ignorant and bigoted men." As he echoes numerous Catholic apologists, Dryden thus opposes the Protestant position as expressed in this representative statement by John Tillotson in his sermon "The Necessity of the Knowledge of the Holy Scriptures": "though there be many difficulties and obscurities in the Scriptures, enough to exercise the skill and wit of the learned, yet are they not therefore either useless or dangerous to the People." Compare this with John Vincent Canes's Catholic position in *Fiat Lux:* "Experience hath now taught us clear enough, that the Scripture is a dangerous edged tool to put into the hands of the rude and boisterous vulgar. . . . [T]he whole and very text now in this last age put into vulgar hands . . . hath filled the land with so much wretchlesness and divisions." Dryden's reiterated point is similar. Perhaps more pessimistic than a year or so earlier, Dryden in 1684 concludes that as long as private interpretation is allowed, Scripture will be manipulated and distorted for selfish ends: "the Scriptures interpreted by each to their own purpose, is always the best weapon in the strongest hand: Observe them all along, and Providence is still the prevailing Argument: They who happen to be in power, will ever urge it against those who are undermost; as they who are depress'd, will never fail to call it Persecution."

Individual interpretation of Scripture is especially dangerous, according to Dryden, when the means is the private spirit. In the Postscript to the **History of the League** he asserts:

> ["Gods people" have] had the impudence to pretend to Inspiration in the Exposition of Scriptures; a trick which since [the Reformation] has been familiarly us'd by every Sect, in its turn, to advance their interests. Not content with this, they assum'd to themselves a more particular intimacy with Gods Holy Spirit; as if it guided

them, even beyond the power of the Scriptures, to know more of him than was therein taught: For now the Bible began to be a dead Letter, of it self; and no virtue was attributed to the reading of it, but all to the inward man, the call of the Holy Ghost, and the ingrafting of the Word, opening their Understanding to hidden Mysteries by Faith: And here the Mountebank way of canting words came first in use: as if there were something more in Religion than cou'd be express'd in intelligible terms, or Nonsence were the way to Heaven. This of necessity must breed divisions amongst them; for every mans Inspiration being particular to himself, must clash with anothers, who set up for the same qualification.

This important passage summarizes Dryden's concern in the early 1680s with approaches to Scripture, makes clear the atomistic individualism and proliferation of sects that he sees resulting from private interpretation, and suggests that a man's way of treating Scripture reflects his relationship to God, whose Revealed Word the Bible is. The sectarians' approach to Scripture, by means of which God's Word becomes "a dead Letter, of it self " and thus subordinate to the intervening private spirit, emerges as symptomatic of the general tendency Dryden has been concerned with to remove God and install an unholy substitute of man's own devising.

Exactly this point Dryden vigorously asserted two years earlier in *The Medall,* where he contends that Scripture will almost certainly be victimized because helpless before willful interpreters. After observing that the Protestant sects "rack ev'n Scripture" and "plead a Call to preach, in spight of Laws" (ll. 156-57), he writes:

> But that's no news to the poor injur'd Page;
> It has been us'd as ill in every Age:
> And is constrain'd, with patience, all to take;
> For what defence can *Greek* and *Hebrew* make?
> Happy who can this talking Trumpet seize;
> They make it speak whatever Sense they please!
> 'Twas fram'd, at first, our Oracle t' enquire;
> But, since our Sects in prophecy grow higher,
> The Text inspires not them; but they the Text inspire.
>
> (ll. 158-66)

Displacing God in obliterating his Word, these private interpreters turn Scripture into an image of themselves, a counterfeit.

Impetuous and tyrannized by the self, the sectarians create a meaning that reflects themselves, rather than seeking to find the meaning visible to those who take no private road. Their obtrusion upon God's Word bodies forth their usurpation of his authority and place and thus participates in the work of uncreation carried on by the reformers who set out "To change Foundations, cast the Frame anew" as well as by false prophets like Flecknoe and Shadwell, whose "art" denies access to Nature, imaging only its antithesis. Believing in the failure of both poet and priest at once to expose the Satanic inversions and to keep open access to Being, Dryden lashes both groups in works that point to the eternal struggle imaged in the current religiopolitical conflict. Dryden's most complex, and least appreciated, contribution to this effort was *Religio Laici,*

where, through a focus on Scripture as God's Revealed Word, he seeks to reestablish a proper, that is, pious, relationship to God and thereby to all authority outside the self. (pp. 55-65)

> *G. Douglas Atkins, in his* The Faith of John Dryden: Change and Continuity, *The University Press of Kentucky, 1980, 194 p.*

Robert P. Maccubbin   (essay date 1985)

[*In the excerpt below, Maccubbin analyzes Dryden's poem "Alexander's Feast," commenting on the poet's ability to turn musical symbolism into an effective vehicle for irony.*]

Though universally regarded by the eighteenth century as the greatest English specimen of the grand, or Pindaric, ode, and though praised in almost reverential terms after it was set to music by Handel in 1736, Dryden's **"Alexander's Feast; or The Power of Musique. An Ode, in Honour of St. Cecilia's Day"** (1697) is today generally regarded as ironic in its treatment of the Macedonian King and/or the musician Timotheus. Even though its ironic tenor is now apparently assumed, the **"Ode"** has never been rigorously examined by reference to the contexts that informed it: namely, baroque theories about music's effects, legends of ancient musical modes, and the figure of Alexander in history, tradition and baroque art—as well as, of course, the annual St. Cecilia Day celebrations.

During the seventeenth century the Platonic explanation of musical effects on the innately harmonic soul was supplanted by empirical study of the more mundane operation of sound impulses on the body. George Sandys, Descartes, Robert Boyle, Kenelme Digby, Abraham Cowley and John Wallis—whose works were certainly known to Dryden—agreed that music creates vibrations of air which strike the ear and are transmitted to the brain, exciting the passions so immediately that reason has little time to prevent the resultant bodily motions corresponding to the passions. To Descartes and his successors each passion was thought to effect a characteristic visible external bodily reaction: for example, "gestures of the eyes and face, changes of color, tremblings, languishing, swouning, laughter, tears, groans, and sighs [Descartes, *The Passions of the Soule,* 1650].

Thus, Dryden's Alexander, celebrating at Persepolis the defeat of Darius, reacts without rational reflection to the music of Timotheus, which moves him through a series of passions depicted by Dryden according to their external bodily signs, such as "glowing cheeks . . . ardent eyes." The tearful Alexander sighs as he contemplates the death of his vanquished foe:

> With down-cast Looks the joyless Victor sate,
>   Revolveing in his alter'd Soul
>   The various Turns of Chance below;
>   And, now and then, a Sigh he stole;
>   And Tears began to flow.
>
> (ll. 84-88)

And in the next stanza, "unable to conceal his Pain," a passion which Descartes too had associated with that of love, Alexander gazes on his lovely consort, Thais, and continues to sigh until sinking senseless upon her breast.

Not only could music arouse the passions, but baroque music conventionalized certain rhythms, keys and graces as the scientifically correct ones for arousing particular passions. By using music, therefore, Timotheus not only prevents the operation of Alexander's reason, but knowingly moves Alexander through a succession of emotions by varying pitch, rhythm and volume:

> The trembling Notes ascend the Sky,
> And Heav'nly Joys inspire.
>
> (ll. 23-24)
>
> . . . .
>
> The Master saw the Madness rise:
> His glowing Cheeks, his ardent Eyes;
> And while He Heav'n and Earth defy'd
> Chang'd his Hand, and check'd his Pride.
>   He chose a Mournful Muse
>   Soft Pity to infuse:
>
> (ll. 69-74)
>
> . . . .
>
> Now strike the Golden Lyre again:
> A lowder yet, and yet a lowder Strain.
>
> (ll. 123-24)

The baroque era—which rationally examined acoustics and music's mathematical proportions, which found scientific reasons for sounds' being pleasing or unpleasing, and which declared the passions to be distinguishable, separable and expressible motions of the soul—saw a natural relation between certain sounds and certain passions, and therefore anxiously sought to determine what aspects and kinds of music were most effective in moving the passions. Harmony or rhythm? Polyphony or monody? The learned and subtle Timotheus perceives the effects of monody and rhythm as well as the consanguinity of different passions and different musical modes:

> The Mighty Master smil'd to see
> That Love was in the next Degree:
> 'Twas but a Kindred-Sound to move;
> For Pity melts the Mind to Love.
>   Softly sweet, in *Lydian* Measures,
>   Soon he sooth'd his Soul to Pleasures.
>
> (ll. 93-98)

As important as "measures" were to the baroque musician, however, they were generally considered most successful when they danced opposite a poetic text. For fullest effect, therefore, Timotheus sings as he plays his lyre (and later as he plays his flute!—impossible even in music hall). Singing first a song of Alexander's lineage, then songs of bacchic joy, the sad fate of Darius, the futility of war and honor, and finally a song of revenge, Timotheus, an ancient bard using the ancient musical modes, also uses baroque scientific method, joining rhythms and words to create effects unequalled by either alone. More importantly, however, the effective strains of Timotheus, though originally prompting the gentle passions of pity and love (though the latter is qualified, as we shall see), ultimately urge the drunken mob vengefully to burn down Persepolis. The occasion for which the ode was written—the annual 22 November music festival in honor of the patron saint of music, Cecilia—would lead us to expect an unam-

biguous honoring of music, but here a pagan bard subverts the traditional Christian humanist expectation that artistic (and scientific?) powers ought to operate for the good. Baroque musical theory seems to be abused by the occasional bard, who is, moreover, ironically analogous to the official state poet, the laureate.

Accounts of the distinctive emotional effects of the ancient modes, exemplified by tales of their usage, were readily available, especially after the appearance of Marcus Meibomius' *Antiquae Musicae Auctores Septem* (Amsterdam, 1652) and Caspar Bartholini's *De Tibiis Veterum* (Rome, 1677), both packed with such tales reiterated frequently thereafter: tales of Orpheus, Amphion and Arion; or Achilles' fierceness' being allayed by the harp, Asclepides' reducing seditious multitudes to temperance and reason, Pythagoras' stopping a young man's fury, David's curing Saul, and Timotheus' enflaming and then appeasing Alexander the Great.

Four of the five prime sources for the life of Alexander the Great—Plutarch's *Lives,* Justin's *History of the World from the Assyrian Monarchy down to the Time of Augustus Caesar,* Diodorus of Sicily's *Library of History,* and Arrian's *Anabasis of Alexander*—do not even mention the Timotheus episode; and the fifth—Quintus Curtius Rufus' *History of the Life and Death of Alexander the Great*—mentions only the effects of the warlike Phrygian mode. Nevertheless, the Timotheus/Alexander tale, together with those about Orpheus and David, formed a tonic triad as the most important instances of ancient musical effects. (pp. 33-5)

[In Dryden's work], instead of having a destructive urge calmed by music, Alexander, having been first moved to pity and love is, in the dramatic climax of the poem, driven to an apocalyptic and fanatical "zeal to destroy" (l. 147). Dryden's drastic departure from traditional legend is one of the poem's fundamental shaping ironies, and it may have had satiric political ramifications inasmuch as the poem was performed hard on the heels of peace.

By reversing the traditional order of Alexander's musically effected moods, Dryden's ode, which may be an allusive soured statement on the militarism of King William, emphasizes the worst of Alexander's passionate excesses, and obscures his virtues, which according to Plutarch included judgment, compassion and determination. Judgment is entirely lacking in the ode; compassion takes up all of stanza III only to be obliterated by the spirit of vengeance; and Alexander's determination, encouraged by Timotheus' music, is misused to destructive ends.

In both Rufus' and Plutarch's "Life," Alexander's compassion is most notable when he visits Darius' despairing mother, wife and children, and of all the Alexander subjects in renaissance and baroque painting, this was by far the most popular. In 1661, as he began to rule personally, Mazarin having died, Louis XIV commissioned Charles LeBrun to do an Alexander painting on any subject, the result being the "Tent of Darius," a lengthy description of which was soon to be found in André Felibien's *Receuil de Descriptions de Peintures et d'Autres Ouvrages faits pour Le Roy* (Paris, 1689). This, the most famous and frequently alluded to of any of the baroque representations of Alexander, is called by Donald Posner a "lesson in formalized gallantry, in the ethic of royalty," that is, in not just compassion, but self-control as well ["Charles LeBrun's Triumphs of Alexander," *Art Bulletin* 41, 1959].

Another of Alexander's virtues, the magnanimity expressed toward the conquered Porus—and portrayed in Racine's *Alexandre le Grand* (1665), dedicated to the new Alexander, Louis XIV—was perhaps an amplification of the compassion and self-control expressed in LeBrun's painting. Both the play and the painting, later to become one of a series of five allegories of Louis as Alexander, were "a statement of the ideological premises of Louis' reign," that is, says Posner, "the just and undeniable triumph of unlimited ambition through inherent, monarchical virtue." Dryden almost certainly knew Racine's play, and because of his keen interest in painting probably knew Felibien's flattering commentary and LeBrun's paintings as engraved by Gerhard Edelinck and Gerard Audran for the *Cabinet du Roi* volumes sent out to all the world in glorification of Louis. But Dryden's Alexander, lacking self-control and magnanimity, is much closer to the Alexander of Nathaniel Lee's heroic tragedy, *The Rival Queens* (1677), for which Dryden wrote several commendatory verses. Richard Steele's complaint against *The Rival Queens* illuminates Lee's intentions, of which Dryden apparently approved: "instead of representing that hero in the glorious character of generosity and chastity in his treatment of the beauteous family of Darius, he is drawn all along as a monster of lust or of cruelty, as if the way to raise him to the degree of an hero were to make his character as little like that of a worthy man as possible" (*The Tatler,* #191 [June 27-29, 1710]).

Like Lee's Alexander, Dryden's can be judged by his falling short of Louis XIV, who at least in French art was the grandest model of baroque heroism. The fame of LeBrun's allegories almost guarantees that a comparison would have been made, and that the result would be denigration of the inferior example. Not only has Dryden rearranged the Timotheus tale to emphasize Alexander's natural inclination to anger, moreover; he has rearranged the chronology of Alexander's life by placing the Darius episode *before* the burning of Persepolis; and in so doing Dryden has placed in the most emphatic position that episode traditionally demonstrative of Alexander's worst excesses.

The two rearrangements—of the Timotheus tale and of the chronology of Alexander's life—may have had satiric political ramifications, especially when one considers that the poem was performed only two months after the Treaty of Ryswick. By the Treaty, England's Alexander had triumphed over France's Darius. No more could Louis be compared to Alexander without irony. But if **"Alexander's Feast"** alludes to William's Protestant victories, the Catholic Dryden's distress was even more severe than has been suspected. Until 1701 peace was to reign in Europe. Is Dryden, the deposed Jacobin poet laureate, contrarily prophesying resumption of hostilities, the blame for which would be the monomaniacal passion of a madman urged on by a perverse court and a flunky laureate? To answer that question one needs to consider that Dryden would

Portrait of Charles II, studio of John Michael Wright, ca. 1661.

not have dared to make a comparison of Alexander and William in a public, occasional poem—unless the comparison were allusive enough to escape prosecution. It escaped not only prosecution, however; for if it was a satire on William, as two recent critics argue [Bessie Proffitt, in "Political Satire in **'Alexander's Feast'**," *Texas Studies in Literature and Language* 11, 1970; and Howard Erskine–Hill, in "John Dryden: Poet and Critic," in *Dryden to Johnson,* edited by Roger Lonsdale, 1971], such historically specific satire may have escaped "all the town" that so esteemed the poem.

Nevertheless, since 1688 William's detractors and defenders alike had occasionally compared him to Alexander, though more frequently to Caesar; so such an analogy would not have been unique to Dryden. Furthermore, the St. Cecilia odes of Shadwell (1690), Wesley (1691), Nicholas Brady (1692), Motteux (1695), and the anonymous "Ode" for 1696 mention war (some only because Dryden had done so in his admired and therefore imitated 1687 **"Song for St. Cecilia's Day"**), and Shadwell's and Wesley's odes make quite apparent that the occasional ode for St. Cecilia's day was considered a legitimate political forum. Such usage by Dryden, therefore, would not have been unique. Intriguingly, the obscure and heretofore unnoticed 1696 "Ode," performed at the height of international hostility, is the only St. Cecilia ode besides Dryden's in which the dramatic conclusion prefatory to the Grand Chorus is a warrior's excitation to destructiveness:

The trembling Slave, tho pale with Fears,

When the loud Trumpet's Voice he hears
Feels a strange Fire his Soul invade,
Collects his new-born Courage to his Aid.
    The warlike Notes impart
Strength to his Limbs, and Boldness to his
    Heart.
Dauntless to fight he goes,
Stalks thro the Field, and swells to meet his
    Foes.

As in **"Alexander's Feast,"** the musical excitation to destructiveness is prefaced by an account of music's ability to soothe the warrior's passions. That pattern of emotions, so appropriate in 1696, hardly seems so a year later, after the Treaty of Ryswick.

Whatever the political ramifications of the ode, however, they seem not so pervasive or simple as Bessie Proffitt has argued, and I concur with Ruth Smith's assessment [in "The Argument and Context of Dryden's **'Alexander's Feast'**," *Texas Studies in Literature and Language* 18, 1978] that it is dangerous to impose an allegorical politic on such an ambiguous poem. The issues at hand are larger than mere events. Dryden's ingenious manipulations of the entire body of accumulated lore associated with Alexander (and Timotheus) has as its end not the debasement of William, a King almost beneath Dryden's contempt, but a whole mode of baroque glorification and representation in need of ironic exposure.

In the light of these informing contexts, we may now move to the poetic text itself, noting first that Alexander's gradual collapse under the effects of music, love and wine is a decadent parody of Darius' "severe . . . fate" (l. 76)—the perhaps sarcastic periphrasis, "vanquish'd victor" (l. 115), suggesting not only Alexander's ultimate fate, but also a disparaging contrast between Darius' heroic martial death and Alexander's drunken stupor. Similarly disparaging of Alexander are lines implicitly comparing Darius' haunting stare into the lonely blankness of death—"On the bare Earth expos'd He lyes, / With not a Friend to close his Eyes" (ll. 83-84)—and Alexander's rhythmically silly, repetitious and empty staring at his whore: "[He] sigh'd and look'd, sigh'd and look'd, / Sigh'd and look'd, and sigh'd again" (ll. 112-13). He then sank, not onto "bare Earth" but soft bosom.

The draught of love is itself given a twist of irony: the "fair / Who caused . . . [Alexander's] care" is not, as tradition had it, either Statira or Roxanna, the rival queens of Lee's drama, neither of whom was at Persepolis, but Thais, who though an Athenian whore is likened to Alexander's "blooming bride" (l. 10). In a letter to his publisher, Tonson, Dryden directed, "Remember in the Copy of Verses for St. Cecilia, to alter the name of Lais, which is twice there, for Thais; those two ladyes were contemporaryes, which caused that small mistake." According to Pierre Bayle's article on her life in his *Dictionnaire Historique et Critique* (Rotterdam, 1697), Lais was a famous Sicilian courtesan falsely said by Amyot to have been a visitor to Alexander's camp. Whatever the source of Dryden's original error (perhaps Amyot's misunderstanding of Plutarch's *Treatise of Love*), his awareness that Alexander's companion was a whore is certain. Apparently unwilling to accept the irony, or thinking that Dryden had uncon-

sciously erred, John Hughes, in revising the ode in 1711 for musical setting by Thomas Clayton, removed the reference to Thais' being a bride, making only more obvious Dryden's sarcasm.

Dryden also creates irony by re-shaping the formal expectations of the St. Cecilia ode genre. Remembering that many such odes began with an opening "welcome" song or declaration that the day was to be one of public celebration, Dryden begins his poem with a description that appears to be not only a grandly painted baroque victory celebration, but a wedding feast:

'Twas at the Royal Feast, for *Persia* won,
        By *Philip's* Warlike Son:
    Aloft in awful State
    The God-like Heroe sate
            On his Imperial Throne:
    His valiant Peers were plac'd around;
Their Brows with Roses and with Myrtles
    bound.
        (So shou'd Desert in Arms be Crown'd:)
The Lovely *Thais* by his side,
Sate like a blooming *Eastern* Bride
In Flow'r of Youth and Beauty's Pride.
                                    (ll. 1-11)

The royal whore, Thais, is only "like" a bride, however. Furthermore, what appears to be a fitting subject of an epithalamic hymn, the lineage of Alexander, the supposed bridegroom, becomes, in part, an ironic analogue to the accounts in other St. Cecilia odes of God's giving form to matter at Creation:

The Song began from *Jove;*
Who left his blissful Seats above,
(Such is the Pow'r of mighty Love.)
A Dragon's fiery Form bely'd the God:
Sublime on Radiant Spires He rode,
        When He to fair *Olympia* press'd:
Then, round her slender Waste he curl'd,
And stamp'd an Image of himself, a Sov'raign of
    the World.
                                    (ll. 25-33)

Jove, assuming a dragon's form that belies his identity, and motivated by "mighty Love," rapes Olympia, thereby creating Alexander, "an Image of himself." In imagery at once reminiscent of the biblical creation of man and of Eve's temptation, Dryden has created an action simultaneously creative and destructive. The language and structure contain other ironies. The rape scene is preceded by the statement that Timotheus' notes will inspire "Heav'nly Joys" (l.24). And so they do—the heavenly lust of Jove, who because of the ambiguity of Dryden's syntax seems to leave his "blissful Seats above" only after Timotheus' "trembling Notes ascend the Sky" (l. 23). Increasing the damage to Timotheus is the last line of the ode, which praises St. Cecilia for drawing an *angel* down to earth, not the rapacious Jove—an act of incomparably greater merit.

Timotheus, however, is merely playing his role as true-blue poet laureate—flattering Alexander's vanity. According to tradition, Olympia confessed that Alexander was begotten by Jove, after which Alexander demanded to be called Son of Jove. "From this very moment," said Justin, "he became insupportably insolent and haughty, and forgot that affability of behaviour, which had been instilled into him by his Grecian education." Furthermore, continued Rufus, the Macedonians, "reserving a greater show of liberality than other nations, did withstand him more obstinately in his affectation of immortality, than was either expedient for him or them." The response to Timotheus' song of Alexander's begetting, though precisely traditional in declaring Alexander's vanity and his warriors' docility, is uniquely sarcastic:

> The list'ning Crowd admire the lofty Sound,
> A present Deity, they shout around:
> A present Deity the vaulted Roofs rebound.
>   With ravish'd Ears
>   The Monarch hears,
>   Assumes the God,
>   Affects to nod,
> And seems to shake the Spheres.
>
> (ll. 34-41)

The iambic dimeter and such terms as "ravish'd," "Assumes," "Affects" and "seems" make the accolade, "A present Deity," as hollow as its own echo.

Thais, the blushing "bride," and Jove, the dragon—neither figure is what she/he seems to be. And Timotheus and Alexander are not what they ought to be. And none of them sees the implications for the future inherent in the tale of Alexander's being made in Jove's image: that the rape of Olympia is a precursor of later actions by Alexander, specifically the burning down of Persepolis. The destruction of the temple of the Ephesian Diana by fire on the night of Alexander's birth had been interpreted by the magi as a sign that the orient would be destroyed by fire. But foreseen or not, Jove's fiery descent in stanza II is a sign of the firing of "another Troy" in stanza VI. Meanwhile, the mindless revels career with abandon.

Ushered in by trumpets and drums (1. 50), as though a conquering military hero, Bacchus now enters as a triumphant god. Hughes' revision of this stanza drops the military instruments, but five completely new lines reinforce the sense of Bacchus as a conquering general:

> As when, by Tigers drawn, o'er India's Plains he rode,
>   While loud with Conquest and with Wine,
> His jolly Troop around him reel'd along,
>   And taught the vocal Skies to join
>   In this applauding Song.

The analogy between Bacchus and Alexander is in each libretto ironic: Alexander feasts after conquering Persia, and Bacchus enters into Alexander's feast in martial triumph over Alexander himself or as a parody.

In the primary accounts, the abandon at Persepolis was invariably cited as the worst example of Alexander's bacchic excess. During the winter at Persepolis, said Rufus, Alexander's uncontrollable desire for women and feasts defaced his excellent qualities. The accounts by Diodorus and Plutarch fully describe the debauch: "Here Alexander made a sumptuous feast for the entertainment of his friends in commemoration of his victory, and offered magnificent sacrifices to the gods. At this feast were entertained whores, who presented their bodies for hire, where the cups went so high, and the reins so let loose to drunkenness and debauchery, that many were both drunk and mad." At Thais' suggestion they all jumped onto tables to celebrate "a victorious festival to Bacchus. Hereupon, multitudes of fire-brands were presently got together, and all the women that played on musical instruments, which were at the feast, were called for, and then the king, with songs, pipes, and flutes, bravely led the way to this noble expedition, contrived and managed by this whore, Thais. . . . " Plutarch's account varies only slightly, and also regards the burning down of Persepolis as an act of barbaric vengeance. At Persepolis, then, Alexander was at his worst, his self-control entirely dissipated and his will subject to that of a whore and wine, both of which in Dryden's ode are made especially potent by Timotheus' reinforcing musical accompaniment.

None of the earlier St. Cecilia odes is as narrative as **"Alexander's Feast,"** and none uses so specific a setting or so dramatic a personage as does Dryden's theatrical ode. To explain why he chose to represent this luxuriant, barbaric, but dramatic episode in an ode honoring St. Cecilia—who makes an appearance only in the undramatic seventh, and seemingly irrelevant, stanza—we need to examine the circumstances of the St. Cecilia's Day festivals, considering first whether the feast at Persepolis was designed to correspond to the St. Cecilia's feast in Stationers' Hall.

Since 1683, the "Society of Gentlemen, Lovers of Music" had assembled ritualistically on 22 November to address St. Cecilia, attending a divine service of sermon and sacred music in the morning but then retiring to Stationers' Hall later in the day for a secular feast of food and music. Information on the conduct of these affairs is scanty, the fullest being the account in Peter Motteux's *The Gentleman's Journal* for January 1692:

> This feast is one of the genteelist in the world. There are no formalities nor gatherings like at others, and the appearance there is always very splendid. Whilst the company is at table, the hautbois and trumpets play succesively. Mr. Showers [John Shore] hath taught the latter of late years to sound with all the softness imaginable; they plaid us some flat tunes, made by Mr. [Godfrey] Finger, with a general applause, it being a thing formerly thought impossible upon an instrument design'd for a sharp key. (p. 7)

Motteux was one of the stewards of the feast; and his account reads like a public whitewashing of the event, especially in light of the very different account in the "Court Records" of the Company of Stationers: "in consideration of the damage that may be done to the Hall by setting up and fastening to the floors and wainscott scaffolds, tables, and benches. . . . the Hall should not be lett upon that occasion under five pounds" (Book F, fol. 194). The Hall must have been severely mauled in 1693 for the rent to have jumped so sharply—by one hundred fifty percent! . . . These are intriguing records, urging us to speculate, with a smile, as to the cause of the damage: press of sheer numbers; weight of singers, musicians and instruments; or general mirth and abandon?

Just as in earlier St. Cecilia odes the celebrants were often described as sons of Apollo gathered at the foot of Mt. Parnassus as muses, so here they are gathered around the elevated figures of Alexander, Thais, Timotheus and their choral retinue—all of whom were apparently on scaffolding. The masque qualities of the action, most notably of course the rollicking entrance of Bacchus and his pards (stanza III) and the surging exit of flaming torches (stanza VI), indicate that the text was acted as well as sung. Many lines describe other performed actions; for example, "The Prince, unable to conceal his Pain, / Gaz'd on the Fair," then "sigh'd and look'd," and finally "sunk upon her Breast" (ll. 109-15). And in stanza VI the audience is actually directed to observe performers:

> See the Furies arise!
> See the Snakes that they rear,
> How they hiss in their Hair,
> And the Sparkles that flash from their Eyes!
> Behold a ghastly Band,
> Each a Torch in his Hand!
>
> (ll. 132-37)

Even the use of the passive voice indicates a staging of the action: Timotheus is "plac'd on high / Amid the tuneful Quire" (ll. 20-21). In fact, then, the opening eleven lines describe the stage set and arrangement of the cast as the action begins. The extent to which Dryden has been commenting on, as well as appealing to, the bacchic qualities of the St. Cecilia feast, cannot be established. What is clear, however, is the uniquely dramatic quality of Dryden's ode compared to its predecessors and successors in the genre. But we still have not satisfactorily accounted for the last stanza—the analytical and retrospective epilogue—in which St. Cecilia is finally mentioned.

The dramatic action of the lyric concludes in stanza VI with an unredeeming antimasque, one of the last and most ferocious outbursts of seventeenth-century baroque violence. But its demonic paganism is abruptly de-energized in the final stanza by the narrator's formal apostrophe which places the just-now-concluded action at a safe distance in the past, freezing the action as it was frozen in stanza I:

> Thus, long ago
> 'Ere heaving Bellows learn'd to blow,
>   While Organs yet were mute;
> *Timotheus,* to his breathing Flute,
>   And sounding Lyre,
> Cou'd swell the Soul to rage, or kindle soft Desire.
>
> (ll. 155-60)

The second and sixth stanzas, which open and close the narrative of Timotheus' role, parody biblical accounts of the creation of man, the Fall and the Apocalypse, and suggest the movement of history. In his earlier **"Song for St. Cecilia's Day"** (1687), Dryden began with an account of the Creation; then, after depicting both past and present human history, he closed with an account of the Dissolution. Just as in that poem human discord was judged against the spiritual concord of St. Cecilia and the harmony of the macrocosm, so here Alexander's unredeemable history is judged against the redemptive biblical pattern, and Timotheus' pagan lyre and flute are judged against the Christian organ:

> At last Divine *Cecilia* came,
> Inventress of the Vocal Frame;
> The sweet Enthusiast, from her Sacred Store,
>   Enlarg'd the former narrow Bounds,
>   And added Length to solemn Sounds,
> With Nature's Mother-Wit, and Arts unknown before.
>
> (ll. 161-66)

Timotheus yields the crown, or at least divides it with Cecilia (ll. 167-68); but mere division of honors would seem to prevent a thoroughly Christian reading of the concluding stanza. That, however, is mere paradox: Dryden's point is that Christianity builds upon, but grows out of and improves upon, the pagan world—under the aegis of divine grace.

As in his **"Secular Masque"** of 1700, Dryden presents us with figures of Mars and Venus, and agrees with Momus' judgment that they are vanities. Similarly, just as the final chorus of the **"Secular Masque"** indicates optimism that mutability and action may operate for the good, so the final apostrophe of **"Alexander's Feast"** reminds us that the history of musical art is a progression, not a regression. The Christian possesses "Arts unknown before." And as a progression mimetic of the advent of Christian grace to post-lapsarian man, music ought to be glorified annually, in what must have become by 1697, however, a gloriously secular bash! (pp. 37-44)

> *Robert P. Maccubbin, "The Ironies of Dryden's 'Alexander's Feast; or The Power of Musique': Text and Contexts," in* Mosaic: A Journal for the Interdisciplinary Study of Literature, *Vol. XVIII, No. 4, Fall, 1985, pp. 33-47.*

David Hopkins   (essay date 1986)

[*In the following excerpt, Hopkins interprets Dryden's poetic works of the 1680s as the outcome of a spiritual awakening.*]

In 1681, the year in which *Absalom and Achitophel* was published and in which Dryden reached the age of fifty, his greatest period as a writer was, according to his earlier admirers, only just beginning. This [essay] investigates the extraordinary burst of new energy which can be seen in Dryden's poetry in the early and middle 1680s, and the events and thinking which lay behind that burst of energy.

The 1680s, I shall suggest, were years in which Dryden underwent what might be called a 'spiritual metamorphosis', in which, as in the metamorphoses of Ovid's poem, or those observed by biologists, he was both utterly altered and yet simultaneously preserved in his new shape recognisable elements of his former self. The poetic byproducts of this period of metamorphosis were of an extraordinarily varied kind—so varied that they seem at times mutually contradictory.

But within these apparent contradictions and contrarieties, there is an essential unity. In an attempt to locate and define this unity, it will first be necessary to chart in some detail the movements in Dryden's career and thinking which have a direct bearing on his period of spiritual metamorphosis.

The 1680s were, from any point of view, a period of prodigious and diverse activity for Dryden. On one level, his career continued in the pattern set by *His Majesties Declaration Defended* and *Absalom and Achitophel.* Dryden continued to propagandise for the royal cause, to attack the Whigs, and to celebrate and advise the Stuart monarchy in verse.

Absalom and Achitophel was followed the next year by two further contributions to the pamphlet war against the king's enemies: *The Medall: A Satire against Sedition* and *The Second Part of Absalom and Achitophel.* The first of these was occasioned by the striking of a medal by Shaftesbury's supporters to celebrate the verdict of *ignoramus* ('no charge to answer') passed by the Whig-packed Grand Jury before whom Shaftesbury appeared in November 1681. The second was substantially written by Nahum Tate, but contains some very lively interpolated lines by Dryden. The most famous of these are the satirical portraits of the two Whig poets 'Og' (Shadwell) and 'Doeg' (Elkanah Settle). Also in 1682 came the first performance of *The Duke of Guise,* a play written by Dryden in collaboration with Nathaniel Lee. *The Duke of Guise* suggests parallels between the Whigs' opposition to Charles and the struggles in the sixteenth century between the French king, Henry III, and the so-called 'Holy League'.

Dryden's activity as a court writer continued further into the 1680s. In 1684 he translated at the king's request a long prose work, again on the subject of the French religious wars, and again with parallels in the events of recent English history: Louis Maimbourg's *History of the League.* In 1685, on Charles's death, Dryden celebrated the king's achievement and heralded in the reign of James II with *Threnodia Augustalis: A Funeral-Panegyric Poem Sacred to the Happy Memory of King Charles II* and *Albion and Albanius.* The latter was an opera depicting the troubles and triumphs of Charles's reign and welcoming the new king in a series of quasi-allegorical tableaux. In the new reign, Dryden celebrated the birth of the king's son (the future 'Old Pretender') in *Britannia Rediviva: A Poem on the Birth of the Prince* (1688) and lent his support to James's propaganda-campaign for the Roman Catholic faith by translating (also in 1688) a second French prose work: Dominique Bouhours' *Life of St Francis Xavier,* an account of the expeditions of a pious sixteenth-century Jesuit missionary to China.

Though none of the works mentioned so far has ever been thought to rank as a whole among Dryden's finest achievements, this body of public work represents a considerable expenditure of personal commitment and professional skill. But during the very same years in which Dryden was so fully occupied with political controversy and with his official work as Poet Laureate and Historiographer Royal, other thoughts were preoccupying his mind and soul, and at a different and deeper level. These thoughts were not entirely new ones. From various pieces of evidence it is clear that for some years before the 1680s Dryden had been beginning to entertain serious misgivings about some aspects of the course which his earlier life and literary ca-

reer had taken. In particular, he seems to have come to regret having squandered so much of his talent trying to please the tastes of a public whom he increasingly despised as shallow and fickle, and on having spent so much of his time flattering members of a court which he was coming to see as a breeding-ground for malice, hypocrisy, ambition and envy. At first these thoughts only surfaced occasionally and were either forgotten or suppressed. Dryden certainly underwent no sudden or immediate transformation as a result of his slowly-forming convictions. He continued for some time to flatter his courtier-patrons, and, long after first expressing doubts about the worth of his career as a dramatist, went on writing weak plays—though it is true that some of the plays of the later 1670s contain more serious matter and are less tainted with modishness than any he had written previously. Nevertheless, though Dryden's critical reflections produced no sudden *volte-face,* they were to increase in intensity, and eventually came to affect his work in crucial ways.

There are many passages in the prologues and epilogues where Dryden jeers at his theatre audiences or expresses dissatisfaction with his plays. Taken individually these remarks might perhaps not seem significant. The dual gambit of insulting one's audience and proclaiming one's own incompetence was, in the Restoration theatre (as now) a standard comic ploy. But the cumulative effect of such passages is telling, and they receive confirmation from remarks in several of Dryden's prefaces where the poet admits the extravagance and absurdity of some of his heroic plays, and expresses his annoyance and weariness at having for so long been forced to please an undiscerning audience. (pp. 90-2)

By 1686 it is clear that Dryden had come to regard some areas of his earlier work not merely as regrettable but as a *desecration* of his sacred calling as a poet. For Dryden cast the following lines which he included in an elegy written in that year on the death of a young poetess, Mrs Anne Killigrew, in the language of vehement religious repentance:

> O Gracious God! How far have we
> Prophan'd thy Heav'nly Gift of Poesy?
> Made prostitute and profligate the Muse,
> Debas'd to each obscene and impious use,
> Whose Harmony was first ordain'd Above
> For Tongues of Angels, and for Hymns of Love?
> O Wretched We! why were we hurry'd down
>   This lubrique and adult'rate age,
>   (Nay added fat Pollutions of our own
>   T' increase the steaming Ordures of the
> Stage?

What had led Dryden to such a pitch of feeling? Why was he prompted to use language with such a specifically religious charge to reflect on earlier activity which might at first seem a purely literary matter? And what was the upshot of such feelings for his subsequent literary development?

The dynamics of Dryden's writing life were as often shaped by his reading as they were by historical or public events. From the mid 1670s onwards, Dryden received a number of challenges and shocks and was subjected to various influences and pressures which caused him to come by slow degrees to the realisations expressed in the Killigrew Ode: that the poetic ideals which he had been following were a prostitution of his art; if he was to produce work of permanent worth he would have to learn to distinguish more clearly between fashionable novelty (and the conceit which is always involved in the production of such novelty) and lasting excellence.

The challenges and shocks seem to have begun in the mid 1670s. Throughout his life Dryden was abused and derided by minor literary rivals. But in 1675 there had appeared the most balanced and discerning of all the attacks on him, the poem 'An Allusion to Horace' by John Wilmot, Earl of Rochester. Rochester had hailed Dryden as unquestionably the greatest living poetic genius, but had also accurately pin-pointed the ways in which he had played to the gallery by filling his dramatic writing with a blend of modish intellectuality and would-be-rakish salaciousness. Dryden's plays, Rochester had noted, have 'justly pleased the town', being 'embroidered up and down / With wit and learning', but (Rochester had advised Dryden):

> 'Tis . . . not enough, when your false sense
> Hits the false judgment of an audience
> Of clapping fools, assembling a vast crowd,
> Till the thronged playhouse crack with the dull
>   load;
> Though ev'n that talent merits in some sort,
> That can direct the rabble, and the court.

Later in his poem, Rochester had noted the patronising complacency of some of Dryden's published critical judgements (and the Sin of Pride which had prompted them), and ended by advising the poet to

> Scorn all applause the vile rout can bestow,
> And be content to please those few who know.

In 1674, the year before Rochester's poem, Thomas Rymer had published his translation of the *Reflections on Aristotle's Treatise of Poesie* by the French critic René Rapin. In his Preface, Rymer had paid Dryden a generous tribute by making a favourable comparison of the description of Night from **The Indian Emperour** with treatments of the same subject by distinguished poets of the ancient and modern world. But in the best parts of the *Reflections* themselves, Rapin had presented a grander and more dignified conception of poetry and the poet's function than any which Dryden had served hitherto, or which he could have found described in such a sustained form in the existing body of English literary criticism.

Dryden was deeply impressed both by the work of Rapin and of his translator. In **'The Author's Apology for Heroick Poetry, and Poetic Licence'** of 1677 he declared the French writer to be 'alone sufficient, were all the other critics lost, to teach anew the rules of writing'. And in a letter of the same year he called Rymer's *Tragedies of the Last Age* 'the best piece of Criticism in the English tongue', and added: 'I thinke myself happy that he has not fallen upon me, as severely and wittily as he has upon Shakespeare and Fletcher, for he is the only man I know capable of finding out a poets blind sides'. Many years later, after the appearance of the *Short View of Tragedy*, in which Rymer had severely criticised *Othello* as 'a

Bloody farce, without salt or savour', Dryden remarked that, while Shakespeare's work was not touched by Rymer's strictures, 'I . . . and such as I, have reason to be afraid of him'.

Dryden had every reason to be worried by critics whose work had been inspired by the recent literary achievements in France. For, in the very same decades when his output consisted largely of the plays [written to please his audience], French audiences and readers were being offered almost yearly the major literary masterpieces of the century: the plays of Molière and Racine, the poems of La Fontaine, the poetry and critical work of Boileau, the maxims of La Rochefoucauld, the philosophical and devotional writings of Pascal and the novels of Mme de Lafayette.

If Dryden had been impressed by the criticism of Rapin, he was equally or even more enthusiastic about the work of Boileau. In his own work he was indebted both to Boileau's precept and to his example. **Mac Flecknoe,** . . . owed something to the precedent of Boileau's mock-heroic poem, *Le Lutrin.* Dryden was equally attentive to the implications of Boileau's critical work. In 1683 he made alterations and improvements to Sir William Soame's translation of *L'Art Poétique,* replacing Boileau's French examples with names from English literary history. In particular, Dryden came to value the way in which Boileau both advocated and engaged in a kind of spiritual commerce with the poets of former ages. 'What [Boileau] borrows from the Ancients', he wrote, 'he repays with Usury of his own: in Coin as good, and almost as Universally valuable'.

In the same year as the Rymer/Rapin *Reflections* and Boileau's *Le Lutrin* and *L'Art Poétique* there also appeared the final version of the most ambitious English literary masterpiece of the age. It is said that after his first reading of *Paradise Lost,* Dryden was moved to exclaim, 'This Man Cuts us All Out, and the Ancients too'. But the full magnitude of what Milton had achieved and the comprehensiveness and dignity of the Miltonic vision of Man were in fact slow to impress themselves upon him. In later life he was to confess to the critic John Dennis that at the time when he had asked Milton's permission to write **The State of Innocence** he 'knew not half the extent of his greatness'. As he grew older, Dryden drew increasingly on the phrasing and thought of *Paradise Lost* in a way that clearly reveals the depth of his preoccupation with Milton's masterpiece.

As well as these literary stimuli, there were circumstances in Dryden's personal life which helped to dislodge him from his former complacency and infatuation with worldly success. Official favour had not brought the security which he had hoped for, and his salary from the Royal Exchequer was frequently in arrears. So strongly did Dryden feel about this aspect of his career that he even included in his funeral panegyric on Charles II some splendidly double-edged lines on the poets of his former master's court:

> Tho little was their Hire, and light their Gain,
> Yet somewhat to their share he threw;
> Fled from his Hand, they sung and flew,

Like Birds of Paradise, that liv'd on Morning
  dew.
Oh never let their Lays his Name forget!
The Pension of a Prince's praise is great.
                                       (*Threnodia Augustalis*)

Dryden's first-hand experience of court life cannot have encouraged any simple-minded admiration of the institution or of the values which prevailed there. Neither can the severe beating-up which he received in December 1679 at the hands of an aristocrat's thugs for his supposed hand in some satirical verses about court personalities.

Dryden was also beginning to reflect more generally on the uncertainties of human life. It has been convincingly argued [by Paul Hammond, in his *John Oldham and the Renewal of Classical Culture,* 1983] that the death in 1683 of the promising young poet John Oldham (on whom Dryden wrote a serenely dignified elegy, and whose achievements in verse-translation in some respects anticipate Dryden's own) caused him to reflect deeply and seriously on mortality in general, and on the mortality of poets in particular. (pp. 93-7)

By the early 1680s, then, various factors were encouraging Dryden to reconsider the earlier course of his literary career. The Killigrew Ode shows that Dryden felt this reconsideration to have profound implications for his spiritual life as well. These were the years when, Sir Walter Scott noted [in *The Works of John Dryden,* Vol. I], 'reiterated disappointment, and satiety of pleasure, prompted [Dryden's] mind to retire within itself and think upon hereafter'.

In 1682, when he published ***Religio Laici: or A Laymans Faith,*** Dryden was a member of the Church of England. The impulse for this poem (unlike much of his other work of the period) seems to have come from Dryden himself. The poem's immediate occasion was the controversial translation into English of a French work, the *Histoire Critique du Vieux Testament* by the French Catholic theologian, Richard Simon. Simon had demonstrated the unreliability of the texts of the Bible and had argued for the consequent need for Christians to accept the arbitration of the Church and the authority of Church traditions on all controversial questions of scriptural interpretation.

Dryden's poem consists of a series of reflections, couched for the most part in a verse which is plain, spare, and often pointed and pithy, on the nature of authority in religious matters. He questions, in turn, the teachings of the Deists (who believed that adequate knowledge of God could be attained by the exercise of Reason alone), of the Roman Catholics (whose reliance on the authority of tradition and priestly say-so Dryden judges to be excessive), and of the Protestant sectaries (whose claims to be able to interpret Scripture by the unaided exercise of the 'inner light' he regards as deluded and dangerous). Dryden then goes on to argue for the necessity of a religious stance in which the reading of Scripture, respect for Church tradition and the exercise of Reason are all allowed to play no more or less than their proper part. Only by restraining his innate tendencies towards fruitless theological speculation (and the discord and wrangling which are their inevitable consequence), Dryden suggests, will Man attain that 'common

quiet' which it is the peculiar prerogative of religion to provide. The ideal stance, Dryden suggests in ***Religio Laici,*** can be best achieved within the Church of England.

By 1685 Dryden had been prompted to modify his position, and in that year he was received into the Roman Catholic Church. The precise circumstances of his conversion remain, and will perhaps always remain, obscure. We know, however, that Dryden became aligned with the body of moderate opinion within the small English Catholic community. He strongly dissociated himself from the extreme positions of the Jesuits (who argued that English Catholics could legitimately work for the overthrow of any heretic on the English throne—thus showing themselves, in Dryden's eyes, to be as subversive as the Protestant sectaries) and the 'Blackloists' (an English Catholic splinter group who had tried to exalt Tradition to the status of sole guide in questions of scriptural interpretation and who claimed that Faith had the status of quasi-'scientific' truth).

In 1687, in the midst of political troubles and tensions which were mounting towards the end of James II's reign, Dryden published his first and only major declaration and defence of his Catholic faith, ***The Hind and the Panther.*** Dryden's second Christian poem is an altogether larger and more ambitious piece than ***Religio Laici.*** It is cast as an extended beast-fable. Dryden found partial precedent for this form in some of the more recondite traditions of Renaissance writing. But his reasons for writing his Catholic poem as a beast-fable were not merely antiquarian or whimsical. ***The Hind and the Panther*** is, like ***Religio Laici,*** a poem directed against religious bigotry by a writer who is avowedly not claiming for his doctrinal discussions any privileged authority or divine inspiration. By setting his poem in the world of beasts and birds, Dryden gives it a lightness of touch which is not an evasive frivolity but a kind of tact—a built-in guarantee against the very kind of portentous dogmatism which the poem seeks to expose. For in Dryden's hands the depiction of the animal world was almost always touched with a humour which, among other things, directs the mind inevitably toward human foibles and pretensions.

The Hind and the Panther attempts a defence of the moderate Catholic position on questions of reason, faith and Church authority (voiced in the speeches of the 'milk white hind') against the criticisms of its Anglican detractors (represented by the 'spotted panther'), and addresses itself to the particular problems and dangers facing the English Catholics and the nation as a whole in 1687. The bird fables of the poem's Third Part treat the damage being done to the Catholic cause by the extreme policies of James II's advisers, and offer dark forebodings of the fate which might await the English Catholics under any future Protestant monarch. The delicately sympathetic yet wry wit of these fables (in which the contemporary parties and personalities are imagined as swallows, pigeons, buzzards, martins and domestic poultry) both brings home the danger and political violence of the current conflicts, and simultaneously charms the reader into a sense of the inhumane absurdity of doctrinal discord. By exploiting the humorous incongruities (and similarities) between the fables' ornithological settings and the human events to which they refer, Dryden is able to tease his readers out of complacent or fixed attitudes to the current controversies, and to tap areas of their sensibilities which would normally lie dormant when contemplating such matters.

The Hind and the Panther reveals some of the ways in which Dryden's religious thinking had shifted in emphasis during the 1680s. Most noticeably, it puts more stress than had *Religio Laici* on the vital need for a Church with sufficient authority to stifle the dangerous and potentially anarchic excesses of Protestant individualism, and insists that the Catholic Church alone has such authority.

But the two Christian poems of the 1680s also have a great deal in common. It is difficult to believe that only strategic considerations caused Dryden to stress, in *The Hind and the Panther,* the common theological ground shared by the Anglican and Catholic churches, and to avoid dwelling on what (to Anglicans) were the more offputting aspects of Catholic worship and doctrine—miracles, saints, the rôle of the Virgin Mary. A main concern of Dryden's is to stress the common core of Christian belief which men of good will from different denominations can share.

Both *Religio Laici* and *The Hind and the Panther* put a significant stress on the 'quiet' and 'rest' from 'endless anguish' which religious faith and the resistance of vain theological speculation bring to the believer. Both poems emphasise the unknowableness of ultimate truths. In *Religio Laici* the prime folly of the Deists is that they fancy themselves capable of comprehending through their own Reason truths which are by definition outside its scope:

> How can the *less* the *Greater* comprehend?
> Or *finite Reason* reach *Infinity?*
> For what cou'd *Fathom GOD* were *more* than
> He.

The same thought finds expression in Part I of *The Hind and the Panther:*

> Let reason then at Her own quarry fly,
> But how can finite grasp infinity?

In *Religio Laici* Dryden had likened religion to the light of the sun which eclipses lesser lights. In *The Hind and the Panther* Dryden returns to the image, now emphasising the dazzling mystery of God's presence:

> Thy throne is darkness in th' abyss of light,
> A blaze of glory that forbids the sight;
> O teach me to believe Thee thus conceal'd,
> And search no farther than thy self reveal'd;

In both poems, Dryden's desire for a religious certainty which involves accepting the mystery of ultimate truths (rather than trying to attain knowledge of God's secrets) does not involve the abdication of Reason, but rather a just recognition of the scope (and therefore the limitations) of that 'noble' human faculty. Reason, faith, private reflection upon Scripture and due reverence for the traditions of the Church all have their contributions to make in both the Anglican and Catholic phases of Dryden's religion.

Profoundly abhorrent to both the Anglican and Catholic Dryden are those groups (in both Protestant and Catholic camps) who claim doctrinal certainty from their own resources. Such men, Dryden suggests, think themselves entitled to stir up dissent and disorder in both Church and State on the basis of little more than an egotistical delusion. In *The Medall* Dryden had written of the sects' wilful imposition on Scripture of the meanings that they wanted to see in it:

> Happy who can this talking Trumpet seize;
> They make it speak whatever Sense they please!
> 'Twas fram'd, at first, our Oracle t'enquire;
> But, since our Sects in prophecy grow higher,
> The Text inspires not them; but they the Text inspire.

In his 'Postscript' to the translation of the *History of the League* Dryden had specifically equated the religious bigotry and violence (the two are seen as inseparable) of the Protestant sects and of the Jesuits: 'Their Tenets in Politicks are the same; both of them hate Monarchy, and love Democracy: both of them are superlatively violent; they are inveterate haters of each other in Religion, yet agree in the Principles of Government'.

But Dryden's point about the sects and the Jesuits is not a narrowly partisan one. Much of the enduring power of his writing about the religious extremists, and about the form which religious conduct should properly take, seems to stem not so much from narrow party antagonisms as from an acute and thorough awareness of the inherently fallible and self-deluding nature of Man. In *The Medall,* Dryden had included some large general reflections in his evocation of the anarchic impulses in the crowd to which he shows Shaftesbury appealing:

> Ah, what is man, when his own wish prevails!
> How rash, how swift to plunge himself in ill;
> Proud of his Pow'r, and boundless in his Will!

Dryden perceives Man's doubts and uncertainties with equal acuteness. The much-admired opening of *Religio Laici* offers us a carefully pondered evocation of the benighted course of human life:

> Dim, as the borrow'd beams of Moon and Stars
> To *lonely, weary, wandring* Travellers
> Is *Reason* to the *Soul:* And as on high,
> Those rowling fires *discover* but the Sky
> Not light us *here;* So Reason's glimmering Ray
> Was lent, not to *assure* our *doubtfull* way,
> But *guide* us upward to a *better Day.*
> And as those nightly Tapers disappear
> When Day's bright Lord ascends our Hemisphere;
> So pale grows *Reason* at *Religions* sight;
> So *dyes,* and so *dissolves* in *Supernatual Light.*

This passage alone would be enough to prevent us from taking Dryden's own description of the verse of *Religio Laici* ('unpolish'd, rugged Verse . . . / As fittest for Discourse, and nearest Prose') too literally. For while these lines might seem superficially to have the rhetorical structure of a piece of discursive prose, it is also clear that Dryden conveys his 'point' to the reader's imagination in a strikingly suggestive series of related metaphors and images, and by the steady, dignified movement of the verse rather than simply by a process of reasoning. The 'Majestick' manner described in the poem's preface is sufficiently flexible to evoke the sadly resigned course of a man's life ('To *lonely, weary, wandering* Travellers') as well as the stately grandeur of the Sun in the heavens ('When Day's bright Lord ascends our Hemisphere': where the verse moves with a vital spring in its step).

So dense is the passage with poetic thought that it is worth dwelling on a little further. Dryden's images are precise and telling. The moon and planets reflect the light of the (unseen) sun. Their light is thus 'borrow'd, 'lent' them by the sun, just as human life and the reasoning powers which accompany it are 'lent' to Man by God for a short space of time. The reflected light, like human reason, is entirely dependent for its very existence as well as for such power as it possesses on an unseen source of energy. Reason's light, like that of the planets, is 'glimmering'—genuine, but sporadic and uncertain. Its existence reveals the existence of God (as the planets reveal the existence of the sun) but does not illuminate that existence. Man's path through life will remain 'doubtful' (a word which seems to encompass the meanings 'unclear' and 'hesitating'). His reason has been given him not so that life will be any less of a trial or a mystery, but as a means whereby he might recognise the existence of the source whence it was derived in the first place. He does this by looking 'upward' to the sky, raising his sights beyond the tribulations of this world to the glories of the heavens. The images force the imagination to make complex and fruitful connections between the imagined traveller benighted on the highway and the human soul contemplating the mysteries of religion.

The train of imagery is continued into the following lines, which depict the vain attempts of the pagan philosophers Epicurus and Aristotle to discover the Summum Bonum, the happiness which it is the peculiar prerogative of religion to provide:

> Some few, whose Lamp shone brighter, have
>   been led
> From Cause to Cause, to *Natures* secret head;
> And found that *one first principle* must be:
> But *what,* or *who,* that *UNIVERSAL HE;*
> Whether some *Soul* incompassing this Ball
> *Unmade, unmov'd;* yet *making, moving All;*
> Or various *Atoms* interfering Dance
> Leapt into *Form,* (the Noble work of *Chance;*)
> Or this great *All* was from *Eternity;*
> Not ev'n the *Stagirite* himself could see;
> And *Epicurus Guess'd* as well as He:
> As *blindly grop'd* they for a *future State;*
> As *rashly Judg'd* of *Providence* and *Fate:*
> But least of all could their Endeavours find
> What most concern'd the good of Humane kind:
> For *Happiness* was never to be found;
> But vanish'd from 'em, like Enchanted ground.
> One thought *Content* the Good to be enjoy'd:
> This, every little *Accident* destroy'd:
> The *wiser Madmen* did for *Vertue* toyl:
> A Thorny, or at best a barren Soil:
> In Pleasure some their glutton Souls would
>   steep;
> But found their Line too short, the Well too
>   deep;
> And leaky Vessels which no *Bliss* cou'd keep.

Dryden does not simply view these benighted and groping pagan travellers from the confident vantage-point of one who knows. These men's lamp genuinely did shine 'brighter'. Epicurus's vision of a universe consisting of atoms colliding at random in a void was a vision of a '*Noble* work of Chance'. But the images of happiness vanishing before the philosophers like a conjurer's illusion, and of the men who, wishing to soak their bodies in the cooling depths of a well, find that they haven't enough cord to let themselves down to water level are almost comic. They serve to remind us that the world will inevitably seem cruel and frustrating to anyone, however distinguished (and the revered Aristotle is in this respect no more favoured than the reviled Epicurus), who seeks to explain its workings and ends merely by recourse to his own reasoning.

The passage ends with another telling image: the pagans' activities have resulted in a kind of crazy dance ('wilde Maze') resembling a planetary orbit with no sun at the centre, or the line drawn by a compass without a fixed foot:

> Thus, *anxious Thoughts* in *endless Circles* roul,
> Without a *Centre* where to fix the *Soul:*
> In this wilde Maze their vain Endeavours end.
> How can the *less* the *Greater* comprehend?
> Or *finite Reason* reach *Infinity?*
> For what cou'd *Fathom GOD* were *more* than
>   *He.*

In context, the rhetorical questions might seem to denote sympathetic fellow-feeling as much as admonitory exasperation. We are therefore not surprised when, later in the poem, we find Dryden siding charitably with those theologians who could not bring themselves to conceive of a God who would refuse a wise pagan like Socrates a place in heaven.

Dryden makes frequent returns in both ***Religio Laici*** and ***The Hind and the Panther*** to Man's propensity to disrupt or frustrate his own happiness by wilfully placing excessive reliance on his own judgement or on his deluded self-image. The depiction of the Protestant sectaries near the end of ***Religio Laici*** allows us to view their activity not as a freak aberration peculiar to 'the enemy' but as a natural process which, once started, develops under its own momentum. In characteristically Drydenian fashion the chain of events is depicted in the form of a miniature drama-cum-narrative. We are shown how, first, the Catholic priests jealously guarded their monopoly on interpretation of the Scriptures. Then, after the Bible had been translated at the Reformation, each Protestant extremist took it upon himself to expound the Scriptures as he wished. The fragile vulnerability of the Bible to such coarse exponents is captured in the very way they handle the book:

> The tender Page with horney fists was gaul'd;
> And he was gifted most that loudest baul'd

The sectaries seem driven to their activity by a mysterious and irresistible physical urge:

> Plain *Truths* enough for needfull *use* they found;
> But men wou'd still be itching to *expound*

John Dryden (1631-1700), around age 67. Portrait by Sir Godfrey Kneller.

Their worship is rendered as a bizarre metamorphosis which grotesquely travesties the sacrament of Holy Communion:

> While Crouds unlearn'd, with rude Devotion
>   warm,
> About the Sacred Viands buz and swarm,
> The *Fly-blown Text* creates a *crawling Brood;*
> And turns to *Maggots* what was meant for *Food.*

In our mind's eye the bustling Enthusiasts seem instantly transformed into a mass of crawling grubs. The 'warmth' (that is, 'Zeal') of their devotion is, at the same time, the warmth of a day when the flies are buzzing around a joint destined for the meal table. Our minds are directed towards the apparently inevitable process whereby Man generates the means to rob himself of his most precious possession:

> *A Thousand daily Sects rise up and dye;*
> A Thousand more the perish'd Race supply.
> So all we make of Heavens discover'd Will
> Is, not to have it, or to use it ill.
> The Danger's much the same; on several Shelves
> If *others* wreck *us,* or *we* wreck our *selves.*

Dryden employs the same technique—of charting a gener-

al human trait by means of a miniature narrative—in Part I of *The Hind and the Panther,* when writing of the evils of religious persecution. The passage moves from a specific historical situation (the persecution of the Huguenots in France) to a set of large reflections about the characteristics inherent in the nature of Man which cause persecution in the first place. Since the passage works as a single unit, it will be useful to follow it through, step by step.

Dryden begins with a specific reference to the Huguenot persecutions (couched within the terms of his beast-fable):

> From *Celtique* woods is chas'd the *wolfish* crew:

But he immediately checks himself and moves to a general reflection:

> But ah! some pity e'en to brutes is due:
> Their native walks, methinks, they might enjoy
> Curb'd of their native malice to destroy.
> Of all the tyrannies on humane kind
> The worst is that which persecutes the mind.

Persecution, Dryden continues, goes against the inherent nature of Man, against the very ingredients in humanity which differentiate Man from the animals and which reveal Man's divine origins:

> Let us but weigh at what offence we strike,
> 'Tis but because we cannot think alike.
> In punishing of this, we overthrow
> The laws of nations and of nature too.
> Beasts are the subjects of tyrannick sway,
> Where still the stronger on the weaker prey.
> Man onely of a softer mold is made;
> Not for his fellows ruine, but their aid.
> Created kind, beneficent and free,
> The noble image of the Deity.

These preliminary thoughts lead into a miniature replay of the biblical (or Miltonic) account of Creation. First the beasts are made by God in a single stroke of effortless ease (captured in the rapid run of the last line):

> One portion of informing fire was giv'n
> To Brutes, th' inferiour family of heav'n:
> The Smith divine, as with a careless beat,
> Struck out the mute creation at a heat:

The creation of Man is an altogether more carefully pondered affair:

> But, when arriv'd at last to humane race,
> The god-head took a deep consid'ring space:
> And, to distinguish man from all the rest,
> Unlock'd the sacred treasures of his breast:
> And mercy mix'd with reason did impart;
> One to his head, the other to his heart:
> Reason to rule, but mercy to forgive:
> The first is law, the last prerogative.

Dryden's first man, like Milton's, combines magisterial authority with a physical delicacy and vulnerability. His rule is that of the most clement and beneficent of monarchs, and rests on a mutual love of great beauty between lord and subjects. He is, in Dryden's account, quite literally full of the milk of human kindness:

> And like his mind his outward form appear'd;
> When issuing naked, to the wondring herd,

He charm'd their eyes, and for they lov'd, they
    fear'd.
Not arm'd with horns of arbitrary might,
Or claws to seize their furry spoils in fight,
Or with increase of feet t' o'ertake 'em in their
    flight.
Of easie shape, and pliant ev'ry way;
Confessing still the softness of his clay,
And kind as kings upon their coronation day:
With open hands, and with extended space
Of arms, to satisfie a large embrace.
Thus kneaded up with milk, the new made man
His kingdom o'er his kindred world began:

But then in just a few lines the picture is alarmingly reversed:

Till knowledge misapply'd, misunderstood,
And pride of Empire sour'd his balmy bloud.
Then, first rebelling, his own stamp he coins;
The murth'rer *Cain* was latent in his loins,
And bloud began its first and loudest cry
For diff'ring worship of the Deity.
Thus persecution rose, and father space
Produc'd the mighty hunter of his race.

The milk of human kindness has, in a disconcertingly physical image, mysteriously and suddenly curdled. Adam's begetting of his son is seen as an act of stubborn and proud defiance, transmitting genetically the wilfulness which will become the murderousness of Cain and consequently the intolerance and blood-lust of the whole human race. The momentary beauty of Man in God's original creation, has been almost immediately transformed into something more fearful. The effect is to make one wonder whether the 'cannot' in the earlier lines—

Let us but weigh at what offence we strike,
'Tis but because we cannot think alike.

should not have been italicised, to bring home the fact that what is being referred to is more a harsh law to be bitterly lamented than a trivial blindness out of which Man could be easily reasoned. The overall effect is to remind us of Man's godlike potential and then, in rapid succession, to impress upon us how totally and irremediably fallen is the present state of humanity, the only state which we will ever know.

We may surmise that a significant part of Dryden's ability to write so tellingly in both *Religio Laici* and *The Hind and the Panther* of Man's pride, vanity and capacity for self-delusion must be attributed to the acuteness of his diagnosis of these propensities in himself. 'To find in our selves the Weaknesses and Imperfections of our wretched kind', he wrote in the Epistle Dedicatory to *Don Sebastian,* 'is surely the most reasonable step we can make towards the Compassion of our Fellow-Creatures'. In Parts I and III of *The Hind and the Panther* there occur passages which have often been taken as confessions by Dryden of what he had come to think of as grievous personal sins.

The term 'confessions' must here be understood with tact. Both the passages referred to express with considerable passion and emphasis the need for humans to repent and reject certain vices. But the second passage is cast dramatically as part of a speech by the Hind. And there is no question in either case of an embarrassing *cri de cœur* from the poet disturbing the poem's overall decorum. Any personal pressure which lies behind the passages is firmly under artistic control.

But it is interesting that in both the 'confessional' passages in *The Hind and the Panther* Dryden puts a strong emphasis on the need to conquer the sin of pride. The first passage presents some striking images of the delusions which, Dryden says, had misled him from youth well into middle age:

My thoughtless youth was wing'd with vain desires,
My manhood, long misled by wandring fires,
Follow'd false lights; and when their glimps was
    gone,
My pride struck out new sparkles of her own.
Such was I, such by nature still I am,
Be thine the glory, and be mine the shame.
Good life be now my task: my doubts are done.

Long after the buoyant flights of (misplaced) youthful confidence, Dryden suggests, a man can remain deluded by the will-o'-the-wisps ('wandering fires') and (?) wreckers' beacons ('false lights') which circumstances seem to contrive to deceive him. But even when these have passed, the mind can (on its own anvil, as it were) 'strike out' equally delusive glimmerings of its own. And he knows that the attractions of self-generated delusions are never easy to shrug off: indeed, it is only by fixing the mind on something beyond or above the narrow perspective of an individual view that they can even be recognised for what they are.

The same emphasis on the need to conquer Pride is prominent in the passage in Part III on worldly fame (the Hind is speaking):

If joyes hereafter must be purchas'd here
With loss of all that mortals hold so dear,
Then welcome infamy and publick shame,
And, last, a long farwell to worldly fame.
'Tis said with ease, but oh, how hardly try'd
By haughty souls to humane honour ty'd!
O sharp convulsive pangs of agonizing pride!
Down then thou rebell, never more to rise,
And what thou didst, and do'st so dearly prize,
That fame, that darling fame, make that thy sacrifice.

The nature of the 'pride' and 'worldly fame' being referred to here is deliberately kept general. Yet the acute pain which the pursuit of such fame causes and the difficulty (or impossibility) of any human being able to extricate himself from that pursuit are tellingly captured in several phrases (*'sharp convulsive pangs', 'agonizing* pride', *'darling* fame', 'to humane honour *ty'd'*).

In the light of the other evidence it is difficult to resist the speculation that at least part of the impulse behind both these 'confessional' passages in *The Hind and the Panther* came from the reflections which Dryden had been entertaining about the course of his earlier career. There are perhaps more than accidental resemblances between the wording of the rejection of 'worldly fame' in the passage quoted above, the vehement repentance for his 'prostitution' of his Muse in his theatrical writings (voiced in the Killigrew Ode) and the thoughts uttered years before, in the *Aureng-Zebe* Dedication about 'the wretched affectation of Popularity'. This was the same piece in which Dryden had declared his weariness of writing for the stage and his hatred of certain kinds of Courtier:

> A popular man is, in truth, no better than a Prostitute to common Fame, and to the People. He lies down to every one he meets for the hire of praise; and his Humility is onely a disguis'd Ambition.

(1676 text)

If *Religio Laici* and *The Hind and the Panther* contain many passages of substantial general interest, it must be admitted that both poems, and particularly the latter, remain for long stretches closely tied to the immediate circumstances in which they were written, and densely and specifically allusive to contemporary events, debates, and political and religious dilemmas.

In poetic terms, the most sustainedly free-standing and vivid manifestation of the period of rethinking and self-scrutiny in which Dryden had been engaged during the 1680s is to be found in the verse translations which he contributed to the second of Jacob Tonson's collections of Miscellany Poems, the remarkable little volume entitled *Sylvae.*

Sylvae appeared in 1685, the same year in which Dryden was received into the Catholic Church. The composition of the poems which he contributed to the volume had clearly excited Dryden: in his preface he speaks of the 'hot fits' of activity which had brought them into being—in contrast to the 'cold prose fits' in which he had at the same time composed his version of Maimbourg's *History of the League.* Having started in a desultory fashion to translate a few poems by Theocritus and Horace, he tells us, he was surprised to find 'something that was more pleasing in them, than my ordinary productions'. So he went on to do more.

The Preface to *Sylvae* reveals the spirit of delighted discovery with which Dryden surveyed his achievement on completing the volume. His comments on the authors he had been translating and on the art of translation have a freshness, directness and confidence which tends to make the elegance of much of his earlier criticism seem rather formal, and its interest rather academic. In the 1680 preface to *Ovid's Epistles,* for example, Dryden had made a famous tripartite division of translation into Metaphrase, 'or turning an Authour word by word, and Line by Line, from one Language into another', Paraphrase, 'where the Authour is kept in view by the Translator, so as never to be lost, but his words are not so strictly follow'd as his sense, and that too is admitted to be amplyfied, but not alter'd', and Imitation, 'where the Translator (if now he has not lost the Name) assumed the liberty not only to vary from the words and sence, but to forsake them both as he sees occasion: and taking only some general hints from the Original, to run division on the ground-work, as he pleases'. But by 1685 he has, in the light of practical experience, adopted a more flexible approach. Whereas in

1680 he had been doubtful about the translator's right to add anything which cannot be directly traced to the text of his original, and had specifically disapproved of those translators who were content to depart from both the words and sense of their original in order to write 'as . . . that Authour would have done, had he liv'd in our Age, and in our Country', in the *Sylvae* preface he has moved closer to seeing translation as a kind of vigorous artistic collaboration across the ages. Wherever he has enlarged on the literal sense of his originals, Dryden says,

> I desire the false Criticks wou'd not always think that those thoughts are wholly mine, but that either they are secretly in the Poet, or may be fairly deduc'd from him: or at least, if both these considerations should fail, that my own is of a piece with his, and that if he were living, and an *Englishman,* they are such, as he wou'd probably have written.

Dryden's new-found confidence is amply justified by the quality of the poems to which his remarks refer. The translations of episodes from each of the five books of Lucretius's *De Rerum Natura* and of certain Odes of Horace contained in *Sylvae* have had many distinguished admirers. Not surprisingly, since these poems speak with a directness, urgency and compelling rhythmic assurance, and have a generality and range of imaginative implication which Dryden had never managed so sustainedly in any of his previous publications.

It is one of the most extraordinary facts about Dryden's literary career that in the very same year that he was engaged in the last stages of the religious reflections which were to lead to his assumption of Catholicism he was also composing a series of poems which are unashamedly pagan in inspiration. These poems assert, with an imaginative vibrancy and conviction which it is impossible to believe was merely assumed on Dryden's part, the belief that, since the soul is mortal and man's life is beset by a host of delusions and vain desires, the ultimate wisdom is to 'live in the present'. Man should, the poems suggest, enjoy the present hour to the full, taking no thought for the morrow, since the future is unknowable and man is subject to inexorable forces and processes over which he can have no control.

It is also an extraordinary fact that, the year before Dryden expressed vehement repentance of the impious obscenities with which he felt he had defiled some of his earlier works, he had published, in two of his Lucretian translations, poems which treat the power of sexual love with an uninhibited frankness and freedom which he had never remotely matched before.

By general consensus, one of the finest of the *Sylvae* poems is that which Dryden entitled *Translation of the Latter Part of the Third Book of Lucretius: Against the Fear of Death.* In his preface Dryden had given an excellent description of the 'noble pride and positive assertion', the 'sublime and daring Genius', the 'fiery temper' and 'perpetual torrent of Verse' which characterise the Latin poet's writing and which he had tried to emulate in his version. But he had proceeded immediately to disclaim any complicity with Lucretius's argument that, since the soul dies along with the body, it is absurd to fear the grave. Without the prospect of an afterlife of the kind offered by Christianity, Dryden had protested, there is nothing to prevent anyone from indulging in bestial excesses in this life, and nothing to reconcile one to the palpable injustices which abound in the world.

But no such inhibitions or reservations restrain the translation itself. In his version Dryden has achieved a passionate imaginative identity with the vehement mortalism on which Lucretius insists in his turbulently sweeping verse-paragraphs. The fallacy which clouds most men's thinking about death, the poem asserts, is that consciousness survives when the body dies. But, Lucretius insists, a human body is a knot intrinsicate of soul and body:

> we are only we
> While Souls and bodies in one frame agree.

When the body dies, so, inevitably, does the consciousness:

> So, when our mortal frame shall be disjoyn'd,
> The lifeless Lump, uncoupled from the mind,
> From sense of grief and pain we shall be free;
> We shall not feel, because we shall not *Be*.

To reinforce the point, we are shown the tumult of atomic activity which, in the Lucretian understanding of things, constitutes the ultimate reality in the world we inhabit. Even, the poet insists, if the atoms have combined at some time in the past to produce persons identical to us, we can have no memory of the fact, since the faculties of perception will, by definition, have perished along with the dissolution of the physical frame. Dryden's enjambment conveys a powerful sense of the hectic movement of the atoms across a void, and some striking phrases ('pause of Life', 'gaping space') capture the absoluteness of the chasm between life and nothingness:

> For backward if you look, on that long space
> Of Ages past, and view the changing face
> Of Matter, tost and variously combin'd
> In sundry shapes, 'tis easie for the mind
> From thence t' infer, that Seeds of things have
>   been
> In the same order as they now are seen:
> Which yet our dark remembrance cannot trace,
> Because a pause of Life, a gaping space
> Has come betwixt, where memory lies dead,
> And all the wandring motions from the sence are
>   fled.

Lucretius acknowledged a great debt to the Greek philosopher Epicurus. But it will already be apparent that the exhortation to live life in the present to be found in *Against the Fear of Death* is something far removed from the facile hedonism which is nowadays (as it was in Dryden's day) often popularly associated with the term 'epicurean'. Indeed, certain verbal details in his version make it quite clear that Dryden saw in Lucretius's poem an indictment of those self-styled libertines of his own day who affected to live by the motto 'Eat, drink and be merry, for tomorrow we die'. Such revellers receive a stern blast of the poet's scorn:

> Yet thus the fools, that would be thought the
>   Wits,
> Disturb their mirth with melancholy fits,
> When healths go round, and kindly brimmers
>   flow,
> Till the fresh Garlands on their foreheads glow,
> They whine, and cry, let us make haste to live,
> Short are the joys that humane Life can give.
> Eternal Preachers, that corrupt the draught,
> And pall the God that never thinks, with
>   thought;
> Ideots with all that thought, to whom the worst
> Of death, is want of drink, and endless thirst,
> Or any fond desire as vain as these.

The 'Wits'' merrymaking (and, in using the word, Dryden's mind is clearly on the Restoration libertines whom he had observed at close quarters) is shallow and anxiety-ridden. The 'kindly' brimmers and 'glowing' garlands bring them no joy because their hold on the life which they are professedly making such haste to live is so precarious. Their crime is not their revelling as such but their failure to have any real understanding of the human happiness at whose shrine they purport to worship. The criticism is reinforced and extended in Nature's great speech which stands at the centre of Dryden's translation.

Nature's tirade, like the poem as a whole, impresses us as much by its tone and spirit as by its paraphrasable argument. Her scornful contempt for the ingratitude of humans in complaining that they are about to die, is captured in the disdainful half-mimicry of human protest which forms part of her first insistent rhetorical question:

> What dost thou mean, ungrateful wretch, thou
>   vain,
> Thou mortal thing, thus idly to complain,
> And sigh and sob, that thou shalt be no more?

Man complains that he is about to die, Nature continues, and yet he has derived no more benefit from the life which has been given him than a body which has excreted its food without having first derived from it any of the nutriment or pleasure which that food offers. Nature's images are precise and earthy. Life is envisaged as something which must properly be felt and relished in every fibre of the body:

> For if thy life were pleasant heretofore,
> If all the bounteous blessings I cou'd give
> Thou hast enjoy'd, if thou hast known to live,

(where the emphasis on 'live' brings out what a paltry parody of 'living' it is that most men engage in)

> And pleasure not leak'd thro' thee like a Seive,
> Why dost thou not give thanks as at a plenteous
>   feast
> Cram'd to the throat with life, and rise and take
>   thy rest?
> But if my blessings thou hast thrown away,
> If indigested joys pass'd thro' and wou'd not
>   stay,
> Why dost thou wish for more to squander still?

Nature, she says, is not responsible if man fails to make use of her gifts. She makes her point in a triplet which, in the circular movement of its last line, seems to contain both a humorous admission of exasperated defeat and a miniature enactment of the cyclical process which it describes:

> To please thee I have empti'd all my store,
> I can invent, and can supply no more;
> But run the round again, the round I ran before.

The poet's scorn for the young 'Wits' is matched by Nature's contempt for the aged who will not resign life with equanimity when their appointed time has arrived, even though their capacity to enjoy life has long since passed. The old man's perverseness in being unwilling to die is seen as the final stage of a perverseness which has been his in different guises throughout life:

> But if an old decrepit Sot lament;
> What thou (She cryes) who hast outliv'd content!
> Dost thou complain, who has enjoy'd my store?
> But this is still th' effect of wishing more!
> Unsatisfy'd with all that Nature brings;
> Loathing the present, liking absent things;
> From hence it comes thy vain desires at strife
> Within themselves, have tantaliz'd thy Life,
> And ghastly death appear'd before thy sight
> E're thou hadst gorg'd thy Soul, and sences with
> delight.
> Now leave those joys unsuiting to thy age,
> To a fresh Comer, and resign the Stage.

Why are these tirades not merely shrugged off by the reader as callous, and the poem as a whole (for all its energy) rejected as a remorseless and merely dispiriting jeremiad? Why is the effect, in fact, quite the opposite of depressing—one, rather, of exhilaration and release? Partly because Nature's criticisms do not merely depend on her say-so. There is an irresistible tang of truth to be found in many of the poem's direct portrayals of the Vanity of Human Wishes.

In this poem, for example, Sisiphus is not a figure to be found among the mythological inhabitants of Hades, but on the hustings and in the courts of this world. In his portrait of this figure, Dryden's verse evokes in its surging, restless rhythms, the heady elation which the demagogue feels and the mysterious inner necessity which prompts his activity. Here we have an unforgettable image of the kind of subversive politician whom he had earlier characterised in the 'Achitophel' portrait:

> The *Sisiphus* is he, whom noise and strife
> Seduce from all the soft retreats of life,
> To vex the Government, disturb the Laws;
> Drunk with the Fumes of popular applause,
> He courts the giddy Crowd to make him great,
> And sweats and toils in vain, to mount the
> sovreign Seat.

The self-defeating agony which accompanies such activity is equally memorably given in the laboured trudge of the lines which follow:

> For still to aim at pow'r, and still to fail,
> Ever to strive and never to prevail,
> What is it, but in reasons true account
> To heave the Stone against the rising Mount

And the nemesis which awaits this Sisiphus is captured in the vivid rush of the final fourteener:

> Which urg'd, and labour'd, and forc'd up with
> pain,
> Recoils and rowls impetuous down, and smoaks
> along the plain.

Later, when the poet is summing up his catalogue of the vain desires which torment men's lives, the whole of mankind is seen as suffering from a mysterious unrest which constantly stimulates it to action which can never satisfy or fulfil. It is no accident, therefore, that Dryden's thoughts here turned to the scene in Shakespeare's *Macbeth* where Banquo's ghost appears to remind the hero of the horrors he has committed to attain what he thought were his own most deeply cherished wishes:

> Thus every man o're works his weary will,
> To shun himself, and to shake off his ill;
> The shaking fit returns and hangs upon him still.
> No prospect of repose, nor hope of ease;
> The Wretch is ignorant of his disease.

But it is clear that Dryden, like Lucretius, saw this poem not merely as chastising deluded humanity but as offering him consolation, and consolation, moreover, which could be effective this side of the grave. There are, Dryden wrote in the Preface to *Sylvae,* arguments in the poem 'which are strong enough to a reasonable Man, to make him less in love with Life, and consequently in less apprehensions of Death'. In the lines which immediately follow those quoted above, Dryden writes that, were 'The Wretch' to understand the disease from which he is suffering

> he wou'd know the World not worth
> his care:
> Then wou'd he search more deeply for the cause;
> And study Nature well, and Natures Laws

And in the fragment from the Second Book of Lucretius which precedes *Against the Fear of Death* in *Sylvae* and forms a preface to the longer poem, Dryden had imagined the pleasure of ascending

> To Vertues heights, with wisdom well supply'd,
> And all the *Magazins* of Learning fortifi'd;
> From thence to look below on humane kind,
> Bewilder'd in the Maze of Life, and blind:
> To see vain fools ambitiously contend
> For Wit and Pow'r; their lost endeavours bend
> T'outshine each other, waste their time and
> health,
> In search of honour, and pursuit of wealth.

The same fragment ends:

> For life is all in wandring errours led;
> And just as Children are surpriz'd with dread,
> And tremble in the dark, so riper years
> Ev'n in broad day light are possest with fears:
> And shake at shadows fanciful and vain,
> As those which in the breasts of Children reign.
> These bugbears of the mind, this inward Hell,
> No rayes of outward sunshine can dispel;
> But nature and right reason, must display
> Their beames abroad, and bring the darksome
> soul to day.

Read hastily, and out of context, these passages might suggest that the Lucretian consolation resides either in the advocacy of a quietistic retirement (where the wise man withdraws from life to regard his fellow humans with untouched detachment or *Schadenfreude*) or in the cultivation of a rational, logical, understanding of human weakness, terror, and delusion which will by itself make the human lot more tolerable.

Dryden himself seems to have interpreted the Lucretian consolation in something like the first of these two senses ten years before composing the *Sylvae* translations. In the Dedication to *Aureng-Zebe* he had, significantly, likened his own playwriting career to a Sisiphus-like torture. In the same piece, he had turned to Lucretius for thoughts about the nature of 'true greatness'. 'True greatness', Dryden had there remarked (drawing for support on the Lucretian description of the gods living undisturbed by danger and fear, oblivious of the striving and warrings of mankind), 'if it be any where on Earth, is in a private Virtue; remov'd from the notion of Pomp and Vanity, confin'd to a contemplation of it self, and centring on it self'. The Lucretian desire to 'look below on humane kind' from 'Vertues heights', however, did not much appeal to Dryden at this date, since 'The truth is, the consideration of so vain a Creature as man, is not worth our pains.'

By 1684 Dryden had come to see the Lucretian consolation as something more active and vital. For by then he had come to see Lucretius's exhortation to study nature and nature's laws not as an invitation to withdraw from life or to indulge in abstract speculation, but rather as a command to turn aside from an obsession with superficial preoccupations, anxieties and pleasures and to contemplate the magnitude and grandeur of the natural processes of which human life is merely a small part. And he had come to see that the serenity to be had from contemplating mankind 'with wisdom well supply'd / And all the *Magazins* of Learning fortifi'd' was not the kind of peace that comes from a cold detachment from man and his doings, but rather the tranquillity and content which derives from the ability to enjoy to the full the true goods of life, and to separate them from the desires which, for all their apparent attractiveness, imprison man in a hell of frustration and unfulfilment. Such a tranquillity can only be achieved, Lucretius suggests, by seeing humanity from a sufficiently large and inclusive perspective.

Behind this crucial extension of Dryden's interest in Lucretius can be seen the influence of a literary figure whose importance for Dryden's period of self-scrutiny and inner reflection in the 1680s was [great]. For some years now Dryden had been reading and reflecting on the work of the great French essayist Michel de Montaigne. It is perhaps not surprising that Dryden had come to find much congenial matter in the work of a writer who had insisted so fully on the changeability and inconsistency of the human mind and on man's infinite capacity for self-delusion and unwarranted self-aggrandisement.

Dryden did not fail to notice that, in his essay *That to Philosophise is to Learn to Die,* Montaigne had quoted and commented extensively on the closing pages of Lucretius's Third Book to support his own arguments against the fear of death. In particular, Montaigne had insisted that to fancy that one can avoid death is to suffer from a monstrous delusion, to think egotistically that the Doom of Man can be reversed for an individual. He who fears death pathetically seeks exemption from the processes which govern all nature:

> Your death is a part of the order of the universe, 'tis a part of the life of the world . . . 'Tis the condition of your creation; death is a part of you, and whilst you endeavour to evade it, you avoid your selves . . . Equality is the soul of equity. Who can complain of being comprehended in the same destiny wherein all things are involved?

Montaigne's last question can perhaps be usefully seen as a master-idea behind Dryden's translation, the thought which above all justifies the scornful harangues and denunciations and which gives them a positive purpose and effect. For man's delusions are seen in the poem not merely as a folly but a kind of blasphemy against the nature of things. The study of nature's laws which Lucretius advocates is a study of the vast natural cycles in which any individual human life is only a small ingredient:

> Is Nature to be blam'd if thus she chide?
> No sure; for 'tis her business to provide,
> Against this ever changing Frames decay,
> New things to come, and old to pass away.
> One Being worn, another Being makes;
> Chang'd but not lost; for Nature gives and takes:
> New Matter must be found for things to come,
> And these must waste like those, and follow Natures doom.
> All things, like thee, have time to rise and rot;
> And from each others ruin are begot;
> For life is not confin'd to him or thee;
> 'Tis giv'n to all for use; to none for Property.

The stately march and gravity of the verse here, with its obvious biblical echoes, gives a sense of the grandeur and dignity of the inexorable processes being described. From this perspective, the poet suggests, each individual life is to be seen not as a piece of private property which its owner has the right to squander as he pleases but as a sacred trust which, during the short time in which it is given to man, must be properly *used*.

It is therefore perhaps not surprising that, despite all the scorn at the false ideals and aspirations of man, the poet is able at one point to show a warm appreciation of some of the true goods of life. Lucretius is scornful of those who lament that when they die, they will miss the domestic pleasures of wife, children and friends: to lament thus is vain, since when one is dead one's desire for such things (as well as one's pleasure in them) will be no more. It is the survivors whose lamentation has some point.

But in the course of his tirade, Lucretius gives a telling miniature evocation of the domestic pleasures in question:

> But to be snatch'd from all thy houshold joys,
> From thy Chast Wife, and thy dear prattling boys,
> Whose little arms about thy Legs are cast
> And climbing for a Kiss prevent their Mothers hast,
> Inspiring secret pleasure thro' thy Breast,

All these shall be no more.

Perhaps the most striking feature of these lines is the conspicuous unsentimentality of the details selected. The poet does not evoke a fireside idyll, but recalls the children's (from one point of view) tiresome pestering of their parents. Dryden's mind here perhaps turned again to *Macbeth,* this time to the tender rebuke which Lady Macduff offers her little son, just before they are both murdered: 'Poor prattler, how thou talk'st.' He also stresses the 'secret' pleasure which the father feels—his open expression of joy perhaps being prevented by surface annoyance, or suppressed in deference to his wife's attempts to get on with her work.

This is a touching and telling passage, but the main emphasis in *Against the Fear of Death* is, it must be admitted, on those forces which prevent man from laying a secure hold on the good things of life, rather than on those good things themselves. Elsewhere in *Sylvae,* in his translations from Horace, Dryden offered images of that very happiness which the conditions of life so often preclude.

Horace's Second Epode had long been one of the most celebrated classical treatments of the longing of urban man for peace of mind and human satisfactions in a humble rural environment. In his version, Dryden improved on Ben Jonson's and Abraham Cowley's fine renderings of the same poem by achieving an apparently effortless mellifluousness of verse-music and harmoniousness of compositional arrangement which mirrors the content of soul which is the poem's subject. In his translation of Horace's *Odes I.9,* he conveyed a vivid sense of the joyful release to be found in convivial mirth.

In the best of his Horatian renderings, Dryden tried to capture what it might be like to speak from the stance towards life commended by Lucretius's Nature. Dryden judged that in his translation of the twenty-ninth Ode of Horace's Third Book ('Paraphras'd in Pindarique Verse; and Inscrib'd to the Right Honourable Lawrence Earl of Rochester') he had captured the 'Briskness', 'Jollity' and 'good Humour' which are especially characteristic of this Roman poet even more satisfactorily than in his other Horatian versions. The Ode is cast in the form of an invitation. Horace calls upon his patron Maecenas to leave for a while 'The smoke, and wealth, and noise of *Rome'* and to partake of the poet's hospitality in the country. As it proceeds, the poem develops into a celebration and demonstration of precisely what Horace means when, in stanza III, he exhorts his patron:

> Come, give thy Soul a loose, and taste the plea-
> sures of the poor.

The Ode begins with a series of images which prepare us for the final affirmation—the heat of the day, the bustle of Rome, the nervous anxiety of Maecenas's busy public life. Dryden renders the last in terms which have obvious application to the city life of his own day:

> Thou, what befits the new Lord May'r,
> And what the City Faction dare,
> And what the *Gallique* Arms will do,
> And what the Quiver bearing Foe,
> Art anxiously inquisitive to know:

The poet then turns to the comforts offered by the realisation that the future is unknowable. In his rendering, Dryden has made a daring blend of the wise Christian God ordering things beneficently for his chosen creatures, and an epicurean deity utterly unconcerned with the human lot:

> But God has, wisely, hid from humane sight
> The dark decrees of future fate;
> And sown their seeds in depth of night;
> He laughs at all the giddy turns of State;
> When Mortals search too soon, and fear too late.

The next stanza shows the nature of the comfort offered by such a realisation. The poet reveals his full cognizance of the destructive power of Fortune. It is likened to a river in full spate destroying the habitations and terrain of a valley. But at the same time Dryden displays in the rapid *élan* of his verse that he is in a state of mind where he is able to contemplate with equanimity, even pleasure, natural phenomena which would ordinarily seem overwhelmingly awesome:

> Enjoy the present smiling hour;
> And put it out of Fortunes pow'r:
> The tide of bus'ness, like the running stream,
> Is sometimes high, and sometimes low,
> A quiet ebb, or a tempestuous flow,
> And always in extream.
> Now with a noiseless gentle course
> It keeps within the middle Bed;
> Anon it lifts aloft the head,
> And bears down all before it, with impetuous
> force:
> And trunks of Trees come rowling down,
> Sheep and their Folds together drown:
> Both House and Homested into Seas are
> borne,
> And Rocks are from their old foundations
> torn,
> And woods made thin with winds, their scatter'd
> honours mourn.

The confidence to enjoy such destruction comes from an inner conviction, the knowledge that, unlike those rebuked by Lucretius's Nature, the poet has not let pleasure leak through him like a sieve. A similar emphasis is put on the word 'liv'd' as in the Lucretius version. The poet's defiant delight is conveyed in his vibrant rhythms:

> Happy the Man, and happy he alone,
> He, who can call to day his own:
> He, who secure within, can say
> To morrow do thy worst, for I have liv'd to
> day.
> Be fair, or foul, or rain, or shine,
> The joys I have possest, in spight of fate are
> mine.
> Not Heav'n it self upon the past has pow'r;
> But what has been, has been, and I have had my
> hour.

When Dryden makes the well-established comparison between Fortune and a fickle woman, he enjoys the freedom to evoke her amorality with a lightness of touch which shows him to be more delighted than disgusted by her perverse waywardness:

> Fortune, that with malicious joy,
> Does Man her slave oppress,

Proud of her Office to destroy,
  Is seldome pleas'd to bless.
Still various and unconstant still;
  But with an inclination to be ill;
Promotes, degrades, delights in strife,
  And makes a Lottery of life.
I can enjoy her while she's kind;
  But when she dances in the wind,
And shakes her wings, and will not stay,
  I puff the Prostitute away:
The little or the much she gave, is quietly re-
  sign'd:
Content with poverty, my Soul, I arm;
  And Vertue, tho' in rags, will keep me warm.

The version of Horace's twenty-ninth Ode makes it particularly clear that to speak of the Horatian and Lucretian translations in *Sylvae* as offering 'philosophical consolation' is misleading if it suggests that the poems offer a series of wise precepts which the reader can be expected to put easily into practice in his subsequent daily life. It would be naive to assume that, after writing *Against the Fear of Death,* Dryden would have found it much easier in his ordinary dealings to put aside the worldly desires so tellingly anatomised by Lucretius, or that, after composing the version of Horace's twenty-ninth Ode, he could have lived his subsequent life in the state of exultant insouciance embodied in the poem—or that he would have expected his readers to be able to do so.

The release and wisdom which the study of Lucretius and Horace had given Dryden was one which found expression primarily *in the exercise of his art,* in the act of finding *those particular words and rhythms.* While writing the poems, we may deduce, Dryden must have momentarily achieved something of the freedom of spirit which the poems commend. The poems embody their own precepts. They thus allow the reader to feel something of the same liberation of spirit, and the resultant release of pleasure which we imagine must have possessed the author in the act of writing.

'The mind', wrote Dr Johnson in the Preface to his edition of Shakespeare, 'can only repose on the stability of truth.' Johnson's remark accounts more than anything else for one's feeling that in reading *Against the Fear of Death* one is being exposed not to a misanthropic tirade or a moral lesson, but to something deeply exhilarating and pleasurable. The 'repose', the deep satisfaction, offered by the poem (and, in its different way, by the version of Horace's twenty-ninth Ode) derives from our consciousness of being released from our ordinary anxieties and preoccupations by being confronted with a view of human life which we recognise is truer and larger than any we could manage in the ordinary heat of living. Thus, while we are reading a work of *literature* we recognise that we are, in important senses, more fully and truly alive than is usually possible in 'real life'. And that feeling is profoundly pleasurable.

Similar thoughts account for the success of another of the *Sylvae* poems, the episode from the Fourth Book of Lucretius entitled *Concerning the Nature of Love.* On one level, this episode can be seen as a series of warnings against the torments and delusions of sexual passion. Its depiction of love, and lovers' behaviour, can be seen as an-

other instance of the Lucretian denunciation of the Vanity of Human Wishes. In the Preface to *Sylvae,* Dryden remarked wryly of the passage:

> I am not yet so secure from that passion, but that I want my Authors Antidotes against it. He has given the truest and most Philosophical account both of the Disease and Remedy, which I ever found in any Author: For which reasons I Translated him.

But Dryden's translation of the episode shows that in one sense he needed no such 'Antidotes'. For the descriptions of sexual passion in the poem are written in a manner that, though they may momentarily take our breath away by their fullness of detail and sharp explicitness, show their author to be entirely lacking in that embarrassment and coyness which comes from fear or insecurity. They are thus utterly unembarrassing to read. So intent is Dryden's focus on the facts of the case, so devoted a student of 'Nature's Laws' does he show himself to be, so thoroughgoing is his fascination with this force to which man and woman must, of necessity, submit, and which is capable of giving such pleasure and such pain, that the poem quite avoids two of the pitfalls into which it might so easily have fallen: on the one hand, a self-protective cynicism about sexuality, born of fear, disillusionment, or loathing, and, on the other, the desire to titillate or snigger.

As it is, the consolation and pleasure which the poem offers lie in its ability to allow us to concentrate, with unsalacious and unprurient (but not humourless) attentiveness, on aspects of human lovemaking which are so often evaded by the diversionary tactics of euphemism, pornography or quasi-religiosity. Dryden's descriptions of sexual intercourse combine a surging rhythmic drive with a diction which is biologically precise, but which also incorporates strokes of distancing wit. The result is that we are allowed to view the hectic activity of lovers *in flagrante* in a way that is simultaneously engaged and detached. We are imaginatively participating in the scene to a degree that prevents any danger of our interest being merely voyeuristic. But at the same time we are allowed to stand back sufficiently to enable us to take a clear look at phenomena in which we are normally too closely involved to see so steadily:

So Love with fantomes cheats our longing eyes,
Which hourly seeing never satisfies;
Our hands pull nothing from the parts they
  strain,
But wander o're the lovely limbs in vain:
Nor when the Youthful pair more clossely joyn,
When hands in hands they lock, and thighs in
  thighs they twine;
Just in the raging foam of full desire,
When both press on, both murmur, both expire,
They gripe, they squeeze, their humid tongues
  they dart,
As each wou'd force their way to t'others heart:
In vain; they only cruze about the coast,
For bodies cannot pierce, nor be in bodies lost:
As sure they strive to be, when both engage,
In that tumultuous momentary rage,
So 'tangled in the Nets of Love they lie,
Till Man dissolves in that excess of joy.

Then, when the gather'd bag has burst its way,
And ebbing tydes the slacken'd nerves betray,
A pause ensues; and Nature nods a while,
Till with recruited rage new Spirits boil;
And then the same vain violence returns,
With flames renew'd th' erected furnace burns.
Agen they in each other wou'd be lost,
But still by adamantine bars are crost;
All wayes they try, successeless all they prove,
To cure the secret sore of lingring love.

Of all the subjects which Dryden tackled, love is often thought to be the area where he had least success. Critics this century can be roughly divided into those who see his handling of the subject as jolly and robust but superficial, and those who condemn it more roundly as coarse, sniggering, salacious and even depraved. The objections are long-standing. Wordsworth, in one of his letters, referred to Dryden as having had no other notion of love except

Dryden's house (now demolished) in Fetter Lane.

as 'absolute sensuality and appetite'. And in his *History of England,* Lord Macaulay remarked that 'What was innocent contracted a taint from passing through his mind. He made the grossest satires of Juvenal more gross, interpolated loose descriptions in the tales of Boccaccio, and polluted the sweet and limpid poetry of the Georgics with filth which would have moved the loathing of Virgil.'

There is evidence in Dryden's work to support some of these strictures. As we have seen, and as he himself noted in the Killigrew Ode, he had in some of his earlier plays succumbed to the bad habits of his age. The 'fires', 'torments', 'pantings' and 'pains' of the lovers in the plays and songs are often little more than the last gasps of Petrarchan cliché. And the mixture of prurience and sentimentality in some of Dryden's earlier treatments of love and lovers reveals that love is not being taken seriously as a great *power*.

But the version from Lucretius's Fourth Book might suggest that Dr Johnson was not censuring Dryden in his famous remarks on his love poetry:

> Dryden's was not one of the 'gentle bosoms': Love, as it subsists in itself, with no tendency but to the person loved and wishing only for correspondent kindness, such love as shuts out all other interest, the Love of the Golden Age, was too soft and subtle to put his faculties in motion. He hardly conceived it but in its turbulent effervescence with some other desires: when it was inflamed by rivalry or obstructed by difficulties; when it invigorated ambition or exasperated revenge.

From *Concerning the Nature of Love* we might conclude that, so intense was Dryden's awareness, at his best, of the power of sexual passion, and of the universality of sexual love, and so fully did he respond in his imagination to both its torments and delights, that he could rarely summon up much interest in idyllic or romantic portrayals of lovers. He was all-too-conscious that, the facts of the case being as they are, such portrayals can easily lapse into cliché, sentimentality, or self-parodic solemnity.

But Dryden is also able to render with equal intensity and conviction Lucretius's passionate and delighted celebration of the creative fecundity of sexual love. In the invocation to Venus which opens the first Book of *De Rerum Natura,* the Roman goddess is seen as an embodiment and concentration of the procreative power whose influence pervades not only the human realm but also that of the animals. It is also felt in the great regenerative and cyclical processes of so-called 'inanimate' nature. In his rendering of this passage, Dryden achieves a hymn-like note which both conveys, in the large roll of its sentences and the urgency of its repeated phrases, the grandeur of the processes being described, and also (by putting the emphasis at key moments on sharp, active verbs) their vitality:

> Delight of Humane kind, and Gods above;
> Parent of *Rome;* Propitious Queen of Love;
> Whose vital pow'r, Air, Earth, and Sea supplies;
> And breeds what e'r is born beneath the rowling
>   Skies:
> For every kind, by thy prolifique might,

> Springs, and beholds the Regions of the light:
> Thee, Goddess thee, the clouds and tempests
>   fear,
> And at thy pleasing presence disappear:
> For thee the Land in fragrant Flow'rs is drest,
> For thee the Ocean smiles, and smooths her
>   wavy breast;
> And Heav'n it self with more serene, and purer
>   light is blest.

The hymn modulates into a wide survey of Venus's sphere of influence. Venus's power, the poet shows, is manifested in bright colour, sharp sensation, energetic muscular action. Again the emphasis falls, at the crucial points, on active verbs and participles ('teeming', 'bound', 'Strook,' 'Stung', 'scatter'st'):

> For when the rising Spring adorns the Mead,
> And a new Scene of Nature stands display'd,
> When teeming Budds, and chearful greens ap-
>   pear,
> And Western gales unlock the lazy year,
> The joyous Birds thy welcome first express,
> Whose native Songs thy genial fire confess:
> Then salvage Beasts bound o're their slighted
>   food,
> Strook with thy darts, and tempt the raging
>   floud:
> All Nature is thy Gift; Earth, Air, and Sea:
> Of all that breaths, the various progeny,
> Stung with delight, is goaded on by thee.
> O're barren Mountains, o're the flow'ry Plain,
> The leavy Forest, and the liquid Main
> Extends thy uncontroul'd and boundless reign.
> Through all the living Regions dost thou move,
> And scatter'st, where thou goest, the kindly
>   seeds of Love.

Lucretius's invocation to Venus ends with a passage which, like Nature's speech in Book III of *De Rerum Natura,* was a favourite of Montaigne's. Venus is imagined as a bringer of peace, since, at those moments when her lover Mars falls prey to her charms, he has no spare energies for stirring up the warfare which agitates the world. In his essay *Upon Some Verses of Virgil* (which we know Dryden had been reading while composing the *Sylvae* poems) Montaigne paid eloquent tribute to the power and immediacy of Lucretius's description which, he says, 'does not so much please, as it fills and ravishes' the mind.

Dryden's version of the passage shows him revelling in the love-play of the two gods, his enjoyment resting in part on a humorous relish of the thought that, if, in succumbing to sexual passion, man *can* be submitting to a force which dooms him to agony and frustration, he can also (looked at from another point of view) be thought of as participating in one of the great creative and beneficent processes of nature, whose hallmarks are pleasure and delight:

> To thee, Mankind their soft repose must owe,
> For thou alone that blessing canst bestow;
> Because the brutal business of the War
> Is manag'd by thy dreadful Servant's care:
> Who oft retires from fighting fields, to prove
> The pleasing pains of thy eternal Love:
> And panting on thy breast, supinely lies,
> While with thy heavenly form he feeds his fam-
>   ish'd eyes:

> Sucks in with open lips, thy balmy breath,
> By turns restor'd to life, and plung'd in pleasing
>   death.
> There while thy curling limbs about him move,
> Involv'd and fetter'd in the links of Love,
> When wishing all, he nothing can deny,
> Thy Charms in that auspicious moment try;
> With winning eloquence our peace implore,
> And quiet to the weary World restore.

The warm humour with which the seduction of Mars is imagined is worlds away from the kind of prurient salaciousness which merely degrades its subject. Such a moment, coming where it does, has the power to make us feel momentarily that it is, indeed, love which makes the world go round.

What were the lasting effects on Dryden's life and career of the period of self-scrutiny and reflection which he went through during the early and mid 1680s? On the personal level, it led to a commitment to Roman Catholicism which was sustained till the poet's death. After the Revolution of 1688, Dryden tactfully but firmly resisted offers to receive him back into government favour. One significant effect of his conversion was the decision of all three of his sons (two of whom were promising poets whose work had appeared beside their father's) to follow him into the Catholic Church and to make the journey to Rome.

But, poetically, I have suggested, the most sustainedly significant product of Dryden's spiritual transformation was the burst of vivid creative energy evidenced in the best of the poems included in the miscellany *Sylvae* of 1685. To trace the connections between the (apparently quite different) Christian and pagan effects of Dryden's spiritual metamorphosis clearly requires some considerable tact. I shall end with a few tentative suggestions.

In the 1680s Dryden seems to have gone simultaneously through two spiritual metamorphoses, one in his capacity as man and the other in his capacity as poet. The two metamorphoses came into various states of complex interconnection with one another, but never achieved absolute identity.

Dryden the man sought as an Anglican and found as a Catholic that peace of mind and spiritual reassurance which comes from belonging to a Church with sound authority and established tradition. The precise nature of that peace of mind, and the struggles which Dryden felt he had put behind him when he achieved it, remain obscure. *The Hind and the Panther* has much to say on the doctrinal and political aspects of religion, but practically nothing about the more private, spiritual dimension. What we do learn of Dryden's spiritual struggles has to be inferred from the discreetest hints in the poetry itself, and from the general doctrinal positions which the poet eventually assumed as the result of his private meditations. It does however seem safe to suggest that the comfort which Dryden derived from his Catholicism was centred on a mystery, the ineffable and inscrutable mystery of a God whose mind and purpose mortal man can never fathom. And his Catholicism seems to have given him a heightened sense of the error of some of his own former actions, and the resolve to make 'good life' his object henceforth.

The burst of new poetic energy found in *Sylvae* seems also to have derived from something which we might call a new-found spiritual confidence. But the ultimate truths on which the spiritual confidence of Dryden the poet rested are much more clearly presented in his work than are those of Dryden the man. In both the Christian poems and the *Sylvae* translations, Dryden depicted the delusions, vanities, desires and egotisms which beguile and disturb man, in both his public and private rôles, and which cause him to subvert the state, the Church and his own peace of mind. In the classical translations these delusions are firmly and clearly attributed to a failure to apprehend the workings of those laws and processes of Nature which are observable by all and from which no man can be exempt.

To divide Dryden the man from Dryden the poet in this way is clearly to oversimplify. We are dealing here with the complex movements of a subtle and sophisticated mind, not with a bizarre case of schizophrenia. As well as the obvious differences, there are important points of resemblance (noted by Dryden and exploited in his translations) between the teaching of the Gospels and the vision of life's joys and evils presented in the poems of Lucretius and Horace.

But it remains true that Dryden's new-found contact with pagan antiquity was to prove far more fruitful for his subsequent work than his Catholic faith. For whereas he wrote only one short Catholic poem after *The Hind and the Panther,* the vast bulk of his work after 1687 (and almost all the best) was to be devoted to the results of his spiritual communings with a number of congenial master-spirits from pagan Greece and Rome. (pp. 99-131)

David Hopkins, in his John Dryden, *Cambridge University Press, 1986, 216 p.*

Douglas Murray   (essay date 1987)

[*In the excerpt below, Murray discusses Dryden's effective use of musical concepts and symbols in his political verse.*]

Given Dryden's milieu, it would have been surprising had he not referred to musical subjects in his poetry. As it was, the ancient tradition of philosophizing about music and the high level of musical activity in seventeenth-century England provided him with musical images and ideas which found their way into his verse, not only into the well-known and often-researched St. Cecilia poems but also into the poems which Dryden wrote to support the Stuart cause, both in his public role as laureate and in his private role as citizen.

The first element in Dryden's musical environment was the long tradition, beginning with Plato and Pythagoras and continuing through St. Augustine and Boethius, of the symbolic meaning of music in the cosmos. *Musica mundana,* the inaudible harmony of proportion and order in the visible universe; *musica humana,* the inaudible harmony of proportion and integration which should exist within each man; and *musica instrumentalis,* the audible—and hence sensual and limited—music which should echo celestial harmonies: all these conceptions were in-

stilled into humanistically-educated minds. Commentators of a theological bent were fond of paralleling love and music, since both bind separate entities together: music harmonizes disparate sounds into concords just as love joins men and women into families, friendships, communities, and nations—and just as God's loving acts of creation joined and continue to join the universe into a coherent unity.

If this tradition of philosophizing about music was one element in Dryden's musical education, there was a second, no less important: the high level of musical knowledge and appreciation in Dryden's time. From Thomas Morley's *A Plaine and Easie Introduction to Practical Musicke* (1597) we learn that at the beginning of Dryden's century ignorance of music was accounted a severe breach of etiquette. Samuel Pepys's diary affords many examples of the sort of musical ability and appreciation common to members of his and Dryden's class in the latter half of the century. Dryden perhaps had the opportunity to take his first musical steps under the tutelage of the famous Dr. Richard Busby, headmaster of Westminster School, who, despite his fondness for corporal punishment, "was not without some feeling for music, and even kept an organ in his house" [John Sargeaunt, *Annals of Westminster School,* 1898]. At Cambridge, the young Dryden had further opportunity to grow in musical stature. Nicholas Hookes at Trinity College, Dryden's *alma mater,* wrote in "To Mr. LILLY, Musick-Master in *Cambridge*" (1653) that "We gave good *Musick* and *Musicians* here, / If not the best, as good as any where. . . . " Hookes continues to praise excellent Cambridge lutenists, harpers, violinists, and cornet players. Thus, Dryden's interest in music must have developed in his early years, not just in the decades of the St. Cecilia odes. But even without such evidence, Dryden's readers would conclude that the poet knew and loved music, simply from the musical conceptions within his poems of the 60's, 70's, and early 80's.

The musical motif which Dryden took most to heart in this poetry was the commonplace that the ideal state should be constructed upon harmonic principles. Most Renaissance commonplaces originated in the classics, and this is no exception. Both Plato and Aristotle insisted on the large role which music should play in the education of citizens of the ideal republic. Especially rulers and others in authority must possess musical knowledge. Plato compared the civil discord within an imperfect state with the failure to produce musical harmony: they may be truly called "states of discord," he says, "in which the rulers are afraid of their subjects." As Jean Bodin wrote in *The Six Bookes of a Commonweale* (1576, trans. 1606), Plato "thought the chaunges and ruines of Commonweales to ensue, when as the consent of the sweetnesse which proceedeth from the harmonie therof is interrupted and broken."

During the Renaissance, Englishmen adopted and enlarged upon such ideas. Sir Thomas Elyot, for example, suggests in *The Boke Named the Gouernour* (1531) that the tutor of a future leader

> shall commende the perfecte understandinge of
> musike, declaringe howe necessary it is for the

better attaynynge the knowledge of a publicke weale: whiche, as I before have saide, is made of an ordre of astates and degrees, and, by reason thereof, conteineth in it a perfect harmony: whiche he shall afterwarde more perfectly understande, when he shall happen to rede the bokes of Plato, and Aristotle, of publicke weales: wherin be written diuers examples of musike and geometrye. In this fourme may a wise and circumspecte tutor adapte the pleasant science of musike to a necessary and laudable purpose.

One of the most circulated instances of the musico-political metaphor occurs in Jean Bodin's aforementioned *Les six Livres de la République,* Englished by Richard Knolles in 1606. This work had great influence on English royalist thought throughout the seventeenth century and became part of the Cambridge curriculum. Bodin, in addition to the statement already quoted, includes an illuminating *exemplum* concerning the civilizing power of music: "the Cynethenses in Arcadia . . . hauing giuen over the pleasure of musique, shortly after fell into such sedition and civill warres as wherein no kind of crueltie was forgotten, or not put in execution." Every Cynethensesian had, in the former peaceful times, been

> vppon great paines bound to exercise him selfe therein [in music], vntill he was thirtie yeares old, which was the means (as saith *Polybius*) the first lawgivers of that people wisely deuised, to quiet and tame them, being by nature rough and barbarous, as commonly all the inhabitants of the mountaines and cold countries be.

Bodin continues with praise of the French who, once barbarians, have become the world's most civilized nation, largely through their practice of music.

The association between music and politics soon found its way into the poetry of Britain. In his manuscript *Basilikon Doron,* Henry Peacham instructed Henry, the future Prince of Wales, in the art of kingship. In one of his poems there, a harp, representing Ireland, addresses the king:

> Cum mea nativo squallerent sceptra cruore,
> 　　Edóque lugubres vndíque fracta modos:
> Ipse redux nervos distendis (Phoebe) rebelles,
> 　　Et stupet ad nostros Orpheus ipse sonos.

A few years later, Henry Peacham adopted this image for his published emblem book, *Minerva Brittana* (1612). The poem there accompanying the drawing of a harp amplifies the Latin original:

> WHILE I lay bathed in my natiue blood,
> And yeelded nought saue harsh, & hellish
> 　　soundes:
> And saue from Heauen, I had no hope of good,
> Thou pittiedst (Dread Soueraigne) my woundes,
> 　　Repair' dst my ruine, and with Ivorie key,
> 　　Didst tune my stringes, that slakt or broken
> 　　lay.
>
> Now since I breathed by thy Roiall hand,
> And found my concord, by so smooth a tuch,
> I giue the world abroade to Vnderstand,
> Ne're was the musick of old Orpheus such,
> 　　As that I make, by meane (Deare-Lord) of
> 　　thee,

From discord drawne, to sweetest Vnitie.

Here, foreshadowing many of Dryden's ideas, the king himself, a symbolic Orpheus, brings harmony to the Hibernian kingdom. The musical metaphor also appeared in Shakespeare's celebration of the monarchy: in *King Henry V* Exeter says that

> . . . government, though high, and low, and
> 　　lower,
> Put into parts, doth keep in one consent,
> Congreeing in a full and natural close,
> Like music. (I, ii, 180-83)

The musico-political poem which Dryden would most certainly have seen was Andrew Marvell's "The First Anniversary Of the Government under O.C.," published in 1655, the year after Dryden's graduation from Cambridge. In the following passage, Cromwell, builder of the commonwealth, becomes a modern Amphion, musician-architect of Thebes:

> So when *Amphion* did the Lute command,
> Which the God gave him, with his gentle hand,
> The rougher Stones, unto his Measures hew'd,
> Dans'd up in order from the Quarreys rude:
> This took a Lower, that an Higher place,
> As he the Treble alter'd, or the Base:
> . . . .
> Thus, ere he ceas'd, his sacred Lute creates
> Th'harmonious City of the seven Gates.
> 　　Such was that wondrous Order and Consent,
> When *Cromwell* tun'd the ruling Instrument;
> While tedious Statesmen many years did hack,
> Framing a Liberty that still went back;
> . . . .
> The our *Amphion* issues out and sings,
> And once he struck, and twice, the pow'rful
> 　　Strings.
> 　　The Commonwealth then first together came,
> And each one enter'd in the willing Frame;
> . . . .
> Yet all compos'd by his attractive Song,
> Into the Animated City throng.

With such music sounding in English political poetry, it is to be expected that the young Dryden should adopt these motifs for his own works. The early poem best exemplifying the symbolic association of music with kingship is Dryden's second celebratory piece on Charles II, **"To His Sacred Majesty, A Panegyrick on His Coronation"** (1661). Music, as before and since at English coronations, plays its significant role in the ceremony:

> Next, to the sacred Temple you are led,
> Where waites a Crown for your more sacred
> 　　Head:
> How justly from the Church that Crown is due,
> Preserv'd from ruine and restor'd by you!
> The gratefull quire their harmony employ
> Not to make greater but more solemn joy.
> Wrapt soft and warm your Name is sent on high,
> As flames do on the wings of Incense fly:
> Musique her self is lost, in vain she brings
> Her choisest notes to praise the best of Kings:
> Her melting strains in you a tombe have found,
> And lye like Bees in their own sweetnesse
> 　　drown'd.
> He that brought peace and discord could attone,

His Name is Musick of it self alone.

In this Baroque exercise in historical portraiture, Dryden insists upon the limitations of audible music: it cannot make a "greater but more solemn joy" (l. 50). Since the King, whose "Name is Musick of it self alone" (l. 58), stands receiving his rightful honor and obedience, any audible music—even that of the choristers in Westminster Abbey—is purely decorative and inconsequential. This is only appropriate, since the king, as representative of transcendent harmony, was the person under whose leadership, Dryden and the royalists hoped, harmony could take form upon the earth. The final couplet contains one of Dryden's best quibbles, in this case a musical one: with a single well-chosen word, the poet brings to mind "atone," "tune," and "tone," as well as the theological dimension.

Dryden's next important passage about music and kingship appears in **"The Epilogue Spoken to the King at the opening the Play-House at Oxford on Saturday last. Being March the Nineteenth 1681."** This work was written to be spoken before King and Parliament during the Exclusion Bill crisis. Charles, in his attempt to insure his brother James's succession, had dissolved the London Parliament, calling another to meet in Royalist Oxford on 21 March 1681. With these events in mind, Dryden addresses king and subject:

> This Place the seat of Peace, the quiet Cell
> Where Arts remov'd from noisy business dwell,
> Shou'd calm your Wills, unite the jarring parts,
> And with a kind Contagion seize your hearts:
> Oh! may its Genius, like soft Musick move,
> And tune you all to Concord and to Love.
> Our Ark that has in Tempests long been tost,
> Cou'd never land on so secure a Coast.
> From hence you may look back on Civil Rage,
> And view the ruines of the former Age.

Although Dryden here does not mention the king by name or position, his implication is strongly royalist. The magical "seat of Peace" (l. 11) is Oxford, long known for royalism. Dryden hopes that the city will provide a mount of vision from which suspicious parliamentarians can look back upon past "ruines" (l. 20) brought about by dissent. He also hopes that the spirit of Oxford will spread in the "kind Contagion" (l. 14) of Love. Here Dryden alludes to the Augustinian-Boethian notion that love is the binding force in the cosmos, though he gives the commonplace a political cast, for in these lines harmonious brotherly love is political cooperation, the basis, Dryden claims, of the real commonwealth.

On the death of Charles II, Dryden wrote the elegy *Threnodia Augustalis* (1685), in which he took stock of what his patron had done for England, especially for its artistic life:

> As when the New-born Phoenix takes his way,
> His rich Paternal Regions to Survey,
> Of airy Choristers a numerous Train
> Attend his wondrous Progress o're the Plain:
>> So, rising from his Fathers Urn,
>> So Glorious did our *Charles* return;
>> Th' officious Muses came along,
> A gay Harmonious Quire like Angels ever Young:

> (The Muse that mourns him how his happy Triumph sung)
> Even *they* cou'd thrive in his Auspicious reign;
>> And such a plenteous Crop they bore
>> Of purest and well winnow'd Grain,
>> As *Britain* never knew before.
> . . . .
> Oh never let their Lays his Name forget!
> The Pension of a Prince's Praise is great.
> Live then, thou great Encourager of Arts,
>> Live ever in our Thankful Hearts. . . .

Charles, restorer of civil harmony, had brought harmony and peace to the arts as well. England, once a waste land where no muses dwelt, had blossomed under his leadership into something like the civilized Arcadia described by Jean Bodin.

Threnodia Augustalis, while a dirge for Charles, is concurrently a celebration of his successor James II. Accordingly, to inaugurate the new reign Dryden uses the musicopolitical metaphor. We learn that

> . . . *James* the drowsy *Genius* wakes
> Of *Britain* long entranc'd in Charms,
> . . . .
> No Neighing of the Warriour Steeds,
> No Drum, or louder Trumpet, needs
> T'inspire the Coward, warm the Cold,
> His Voice, his sole Appearance makes 'em bold.
> (ll.470-71, 474-77)

Here, as in **"To His Sacred Majesty,"** Dryden compares the audible *musica instrumentalis* with the inaudible music kings bring. If Charles's "Name is Musick of it self alone," James's voice and appearance are music as well, here the kind of sound which, like the Phrygian mode in Plato, inspires men to action. Once again, as in earlier poems, the inaudible harmony produced by royalty proves to be of greater consequence and efficacy than any mundane music which the ear can register.

Dryden produced **Brittannia Rediviva** (1688) in celebration of the birth of the future Old Pretender to James II. In the poem Dryden prays, "let us know / No sweeter music than his Cryes below" (ll. 322-23). Dryden compares the voice of the prince to mundane audible music, and as we have come to expect, the earthly *musica instrumentalis* comes off second best. The babe, as future legitimate King, is the future harmonizer of the realm.

One quality which all these references to music share is their kinship with Renaissance writing about music theory. As John Hollander posits [in his *The Untuning of the Sky: Ideas of Music in English Poetry, 1500–1700,* 1970], references to music in the poetry of the middle ages and sixteenth-century Renaissance tended primarily to be symbolic. Poets then emphasized the inaudible harmony of the cosmos and the harmony within man—*musica mundana* and *musica humana.* The audible *musica instrumentalis,* when mentioned at all, was primarily intended as a reflection or imitation of the two higher sorts of music. The empirical effect of audible music should be the reharmonization of the disparate elements within man and society into their proper concordant relationships. All this—the emphasis upon the cosmic order of the universe and earthly music's role as an imitation and symbol of that order—lies behind Dryden's many musico-political metaphors. Also as a direct result of Renaissance ideas about music is Dryden's continual de-emphasis of audible music and his exaltation of the higher and more perfect national harmony which the king brings. The newer baroque treatment of music in literary works was different: baroque poets tended to treat music more realistically, often referring to audible music without implying any notion of world order; and baroque poets emphasized the expressive qualities of music, as Dryden was to do himself in the middle stanzas of the **"Song for St. Cecilia's Day"** (1687) and in the whole of **"Alexander's Feast"** (1697).

From the fact that these musical images we have been describing were based on Renaissance commonplaces, we can draw two conclusions. First, as Dryden's readers have long told us, even though Dryden and the Restoration represent a new start after the Civil War, the Laureate was [as Jay Arnold Levine wrote in "Dryden's *Song for St. Cecilia's Day, 1687*," *Philological Quarterly* 44, 1965] a "Janus-faced figure," whose poetic images and techniques often look backward. Here, in these poems concerning kingship, Dryden reveals his allegiance to the values which the old medieval-renaissance universe expressed—not, of course, allegiance to the myths of the *primum mobile* or of epicycles but to the spiritual meaning which lay behind such details: Dryden asserted his belief that the Great Harmonizer orders and proportions the cosmos, and that, if man would but unite under His royal representative, such an order could become manifest in Restoration England.

The second conclusion is that, when Dryden merely adopts learned and proper commonplaces from the Ancients and the Moderns, he fails to move us or to convince us that these poems rank among his best works. Not even the erudition of Dryden's greatest proponents has been able to convince many to read these panegyrics. In the royal poems we have just quoted—with the exception of the Oxford playhouse epilogue—the musical references seem mere props in grand historical portraits, added almost as afterthoughts to increase the sitter's majesty and importance.

It is, instead, when Dryden modifies and inverts the tradition that he achieves fine effects, something more distinctively his own. If he associated the true Stuart kingship with ordered, pleasing sound, he associated the ideas that he distrusted with harmonic chaos. Throughout his poetry, he used terms of musical opprobrium for descriptions of the inverted politics of the Whigs, the inverted religion of the Dissenters, and the inverted art of Shadwell. In the **"Prologue *to the* University *of* Oxford"** (1680), Dryden writes that "Discords, and Plots which have undone our Age / With the same ruine, have o'erwhelm'd the Stage."

The theme of *Mac Flecknoe* (1682) is inverted kingship; appropriately, Flecknoe and Shadwell, the sovereigns of dullness, bring discord in their wake just as the Stuarts bring harmony. Flecknoe describes Shadwell's royal progress up to the Thames to the coronation site, telling his "son" that

> When thou on silver *Thames* did'st cut thy way,
> With well tim'd Oars before the Royal Barge,

> Swell'd with the Pride of thy Celestial charge;
> And big with Hymn, Commander of an Host,
> The like was ne'er in *Epsom* Blankets tost.
> Methinks I see the new *Arion* Sail,
> The Lute still trembling underneath thy nail.
> At thy well sharpned thumb from Shore to Shore
> The Trebel squeaks for fear, the Bases roar:
> Echoes from *Pissing-Ally, Sh—*call,
> And *Sh—*they resound from *A-Hall.*

Music accompanies the coronation of Shadwell, just as it had that of Charles II. But the source of "harmony" is the London mob, a group whose squeaking and roaring provides no aural beauty or principle of organization. The only aspect of this coronation music which receives praise is the rhythm, but this is, of course, only the facile singsong of Shadwell's verse.

Dryden's most complex and fully developed satirical association of discord with dissent comes in the prologue to his libretto **Albion and Albanius** (1684), the masque-like allegory celebrating the Stuart House. In the Prologue Dryden urges the City to support the new King James II; the poet once again uses music to present his image of the ideal nation:

> In France, *the oldest Man is always young,*
> Sees *Opera's daily, learns the Tunes so long,*
> *Till Foot, Hand, Head, keep time with ev'ry Song.*
> *Each sings his part, echoing from Pit and Box,*
> *With his hoarse Voice, half Harmony, half Pox.*
> Le plus grand Roy du Monde, *is always ringing;*
> *They show themselves good Subjects by their singing.*
> *On that condition, set up every Throat;*
> You Whiggs *may sing, for you have chang'd your Note.*
> *Cits and Citesses, raise a joyful strain,*
> *'Tis a good Omen to begin a Reign:*
> *Voices may help your Charter to restoring;*
> *And get by singing, what you lost by roaring.*

In this passage Dryden writes with that mixture of tones which is characteristic of him at his best, that tonic mixture which here, as elsewhere, skirts toward but then skirts back away from lack of control. Of course, he is not just being satirical, for these lines present the now-familiar theme of the king as center of order. If every citizen would join in the same tune—that is, support the king—freedom would paradoxically be restored. Only in the king's service will the Whigs find their long-desired perfect freedom. Notice Dryden's praise of the French and his advocacy of the civilizing power of music, recalling the aforementioned passage in Bodin's *The Six Bookes.* But, too, here is Dryden's typically jaunty and confident satire in his sophisticated sneers at the vulgar roaring of the Whiggish *"Cits and Citesses"* as well as in his patriotic laughter at the foppish French, whom Englishmen could not, of course, take totally seriously as models.

Yet Dryden, as so often, after establishing here his duality, manages to wrest something positive out of the opposition he has set up between two undesirable groups: the last three lines quoted above conclude the prologue, and in them Dryden shies away from satire into affirmation and, with the word *"Voices"* (l. 45), introduces the patriotic opera. That word would have, first of all, reminded the audience that it was about to hear music. It must also have hinted that proper attention to the royalist poet's and composer's message would restore freedom: the political vision voiced in the opera *"may help your Charter to restoring"* (l. 45). Finally, the *"Voices"* are potentially the voices of the *"Cits and Citesses"* themselves, whom Dryden invites to *"raise* [in spirit] *a joyful strain"* (l. 43) and so join the *"singing"* (l. 46) of the royalists. Thus, instead of merely adding an ornamental overlay of a Renaissance commonplace onto his poetical structure, Dryden here fully assimilates the tradition into something powerfully and distinctly his own. (pp. 39-46)

> *Douglas Murray, "The Royal Harmony: Music and Politics in Dryden's Poetry," in* Restoration: Studies in English Literary Culture, 1660-1700, *Vol. 11, No. 1, Spring, 1987, pp. 39-47.*

Jack M. Armistead   (essay date 1987)

[*Armistead is a literary scholar whose writings include* Nathaniel Lee *(1970) and* Four Restoration Play-

Scene from All for Love, *engraving by Van der Gucht (after H.F.B. Gravelot) for the 1735 edition of* The Dramatick Works of John Dryden, Esq.

wrights *(1984). In the following excerpt, he explains the function and purpose of allusions to magic and other occult phenomena in Dryden's verse and dramatic works.*]

To learn how John Dryden makes the occult an important part of his vision is to learn a great deal about the intellectual assumptions that shaped Restoration culture. It is well to remember that for Dryden, as for many of his contemporaries, some of them staunch members of the Royal Society, the occult and visible worlds were intertwined. The existence of spiritual intelligences, the efficacy of talismans, the ancient truths buried in alchemical documents, the validity of astrology—these and related issues were being probed earnestly by thinkers already deeply committed to the inductive, materialistic, experimental frame of mind. Elsewhere I have examined some of the ways in which this curious angle of vision seems to affect the dramatic works of Dryden and his contemporaries, especially Shadwell and Lee. In this essay I shall examine Dryden's allusions to magic in the poetry, with special attention to his analyses of power. Such an enterprise clearly reveals that he belonged to what Charles Webster calls "the intellectual elite" of the later seventeenth century, who continued to find in "the conceptual infrastructure of magic" an instructive fiction [*From Paracelsus to Newton*, 1982].

From the outset Dryden's use of this fiction presumes that the reader can distinguish various types of magical art and their moral implications. At one moral extreme was the daemonic black magician, the practitioner of goety, who used forbidden ceremonies to invoke the power of evil spirits. Somewhat less objectionable, but still condemned by most orthodox Christians, was the daemonic white magician, the theurge, who ceremonially invoked and manipulated neoplatonic middle spirits, elemental beings, or angels. One variety of such "white" wizardry, cabbalistic magic, had gained some credence in the Church, because it purported to capture the influence of stars or angels by manipulating Hebrew letters and their numerical equivalents. Of all the practitioners of magic, however, the most widely accepted were the natural magicians, the alchemists and purveyors of sympathetic medicine, for they eschewed daemonic powers altogether. Instead, they worked to release and guide the hidden forces within and between all objects in the physical world.

By the time of Dryden in the later part of the century, these distinctions had become blurred by the growing interest in inductive science. Francis Bacon had popularized the notion that the scientific method would make practicable a true natural magic, and Robert Boyle and his colleagues carried this concept into the fledgling scientific establishment after the Restoration. At the same time, the influence of Paracelsus and his disciples encouraged many of the "new" philosophers to insist that much of the ancient natural magic was essentially scientific, and Henry More led the Cambridge Platonists through an effort to find buried in cabbalistic and neoplatonic thought a set of truths that would reconcile demonology with atomism, heliocentrism, and a quantitatively structured world. Only the rawest forms of daemonic magic were omitted from these respectable deliberations. The practicing conjurers either kept very quiet, as did Elias Ashmole, or found themselves consigned to the lunatic fringe, as did John Heydon and Samuel Pordage.

Dryden himself employs occult phenomena in plays of the 1660s and 1670s, and during the same period writes prose conjectures about the world of daemons, specters, half-devils, witches, magicians, prodigies, and oracles. But not until 1677 does he take a personal stand. In **"The Author's Apology for Heroic Poetry and Poetic License,"** he speaks for the first time of "things above us" as existing in realms beyond the human mind, and he approves the use of biblically authorized imagery to represent them. What is new about this train of thought is neither the interest in persistent folk beliefs about the supernatural nor the reference to demonology in classical literature. Several times in previous years Dryden had used these precedents to explain the employment of magic and prophecy in his plays. The novelty appears as he injects the scriptures into the equation. On the one hand, he seems to keep his philosophical distance, emphasizing that the Bible authorizes the "description" of "immaterial substances," rather than the belief in them, and that only the "vulgar" populace accepts such descriptions as genuine. But on the other hand, he clearly affirms the existence of "things above us" that can only be conceived by analogy with "beings more within our knowledge." In the 1680s and 1690s he further approves the imagery of spirit life found in the writings of Christian platonists.

This shift in orientation has an equivalent not only in the plays, but also in the poems about public life and the arts. In his public poetry we can see him moving from the imagery of old-style magic—with its proud, solitary operators producing effects by secret means—to that of the more communal, open experimentation with occult forces and sympathies that characterized the type of natural magic espoused by many of Dryden's contemporaries. In the 1680s, however, in keeping with his prose comments about Christian platonism, he begins to emphasize daemonic magic, theurgy, and goety, and the vocabulary of natural magic is employed to a lesser extent.

In the earliest public poems, the true magicians are the divinely ordained leaders and their chosen ministers. As the sun and other stars convey divine power to the rest of creation, so these great souls become conduits for God's energy in society. As rational beings, however, they must have techniques of communicating this power. In the case of Oliver Cromwell, as depicted in the **"Heroique Stanzas"** (1659), the technique is that of the uniquely gifted military hero who selects his generals and plots his strategies with the almost mystical skill of the consummate alchemist:

> For from all tempers he could service draw;
> The worth of each with its alloy he knew;
> And as the *Confident* of *Nature* saw
> How she Complexions did divide and brew.
> . . . .
> When such *Heroique Vertue* Heav'n sets out,
> The Starrs like *Commons* sullenly obey;
> Because it draines them when it comes about.
>
> (97-107)

Like the old-fashioned alchemist, however, Cromwell operates in isolation, founding his strategy of reform and

conquest upon "deep Secrets" (128) that are not shared with his retainers. His heroic potency is a unique gift of God, and in his absence only the blueprint of order, the *"faire Designment"* (96), remains.

After the Restoration, power is returned to its natural agent, the monarch, and political magic loses its mystery. In **Astraea Redux** (1660), Charles's return is heralded by General Monck's measured, systematic preparations (151-72), which are contrasted to the hasty and untimely efforts of "Chymists" (162) and enchanters (190). As Charles is crowned in **To His Sacred Majesty** (1661), the alchemy of conquest is displaced by the natural magic of "love," which is "destin'd to [his] Countries peace" (122):

> Now while the sacred Oyl annoints your head,
> And fragrant scents, begun from you, are spread
> Through the large Dome, the peoples joyful
> sound,
> Sent back, is still preserv'd in hallow'd ground:
> Which in one blessing mixt descends on you,
> As heightned spirits fall in richer dew.
>
> (59-64)

The public, communal nature of this process, sharply contrasting with Cromwell's personal mode, predicts the shape of things to come. Unlike his predecessor, Charles operates from the center of a natural structure, whose parts are informed and bound together by his love. In **"To My Lord Chancellor"** (1662), the king's relation to subordinates is equated with that between God and the stars (83-86), sun and moon (47-48), sun and planets (149-54), mines and streams (66). The mechanics of this system are not founded on "deep Secrets"; their basis can be discovered: "we might unwind the clue / As men do Nature" (71-72), until we come, for instance, to the Earl of Clarendon, who is spoken of in Pythagorean terms as the "Soul" of public "harmony" (116).

The peak of Dryden's interest in natural magic as a source of telling imagery comes in **Annus Mirabilis** (1667). There Charles is presented as a kind of supervising alchemist of the post-Baconian variety, and the events associated with the Dutch Wars and the Great Fire are treated as parts of a grand chemical reaction. He studies the ingredients of war "with careful eyes" and judges that they will behave "like vapours that from Limbecks rise," only to "descend again" in "richer showers" (49-52). Like the Dutch enemy, the fiendish fire is incited by an alchemical dream of material self-indulgence, "By pow'rful charms" of literal "gold and silver" (943-44). But again, Charles, the new-style Christian alchemist, loving, corporate-minded, and in touch with Providence, understands that the "Chymick flame" will produce a more enduring, utilitarian result, "a City of more precious mold" (1169-70). And while his enemies work feverishly to achieve their "proud designs" (137), he relies on what "all-maturing time" can "bring to light" as he, "like Heav'n, does each day's labour bless" (559-60).

In this providential laboratory, the monarch-magician and his assistants no longer need miracles or sorcery. Using a "scientific" knowledge of naval strategy, Albemarle saves his crippled fleet without the aid of those "flaming pillars, and . . . clouds" upon which the escaping Israelites depended (368). And the fiends, specters, and witches that seem to promote their own wicked ends through the great fire (890-92, 989-92) are finally no match for the divine alchemy that Charles has witnessed and sponsored, an alchemy whose methods he enshrines in the Royal Society:

> O truly Royal! who behold the Law,
> And rule of beings in your Maker's mind,
> And thence, like Limbecks, rich Idea's draw,
> To fit the levell'd use of humane kind.
>
> (661-64)

The fiends (545, 991), ghosts (321, 739, 889), genii (1127), and angels (62, 893) that briefly appear in *Annus Mirabilis* belong among the "separated beings" that Dryden tends to invoke, as in his heroic plays of this period, only when he needs a language to represent major changes in the natural order. In the poetry devoted to extraliterary subjects, to politics and private life, such beings do not begin to play an important role until the 1680s, when he begins to employ them in his analyses of the domestic troubles that threaten Charles's peaceable kingdom of love. Since the monarch and his deputized natural magicians have now established their providential function within the natural order, surely, says the narrator of *Absalom and Achitophel* (1681), the emerging treason must indicate diabolical intervention:

> when to Sin our byast Nature leans,
> The carefull Devil is still at hand with means;
> And providently Pimps for ill desires.
>
> (79-81)

Throughout *Absalom and Achitophel* and *The Medal* (1682), the radical Whigs, led by Shaftesbury, are spoken of as either fiends or magicians. Their arts threatened the "Form and Order" ([*Absalom and Achitophel*], 531) fostered by Charles and maintained by those "Holy Bands" of nature ([*Absalom and Achitophel*], 339) that constitute "our native Strength" ([*The Medal*], 72). In *The Medal* Shaftesbury seeks "Pow'r" (50) by "wicked means" which he, "like white Witches" (62), fools himself into considering pious. He intends to "clip" the king's "regal Rights within the Ring" (229), in effect to penetrate "the magic circle of kingship symbolized by the . . . national currency" and to substitute his own portrait for that of his monarch at the powerful center. While he sits as model for this portrait, his worshipful artists, like hermetic priests, work to draw his own spiritual potency into the image. Ironically, they succeed; the "Idol seem'd . . . alive" with his true nature, the "*Lucifer*" (21) within him, "the Fiend confess'd, without a vaile" (81). This link between Shaftesbury and the Egyptian form of diabolical magic is strengthened later in the poem where he is said to employ a false "*Mercury*" (263) in the chemistry of politics. "*Mercury*" alludes not only to Shaftesbury's slippery nature, to the Protestant newspapers (with *Mercury* in their titles) which spread the Whig propaganda, and to a dangerous remedy for syphilis, but also to one of the key elements in the alchemy supposedly invented by Mercurius Trismegistus, the ancient Egyptian magus-king. In hermetic alchemy, mercury was considered "a sharpe liquor, passable, and penetrable . . . most pure . . . quickning, and . . . the foode of life." However, when applied for Shaftes-

bury's infernal purposes, it "pass'd through every Sect, or theirs through Thee" (264-66), without rarefying the treasonous concoction.

Likewise, the Whigs of *Absalom and Achitophel* seek raw power through illegitimate means, as if there were no divine energy informing natural phenomena and hence no divinely sponsored method for tapping it. Zimri is a bumbling "Chymist" whose "peculiar Art" lies in "squandring Wealth" (550, 559). Shimei misapplies "Power" (612) gained from the London mob to "free the suffring Saint from Humane Laws" (609). Corah becomes the converse of Moses' magical brass serpent; instead of counteracting the venom of rebellion, he protects and incites the rebels (632-35). Achitophel himself employs "Impious Arts" (498, and see 289 and 402) of rhetoric and bribery to orchestrate a revolution. To recruit Absalom, he interprets the conflict between himself and King David as a competition between rival forms of magic. Absalom, he insists, has been chosen by good fortune to revive the mosaical kingdom of theurgy and miracles, visions, dreams, and sacred prophecies (230-39); David, on the other hand, is a fallen angel (273) who has been "Charm'd into Ease" (708) and now tries to "Enchant" (423) his son with "Love," which is "Nature's trick" (423-24).

The narrator, of course, insures that we see through this diabolical propaganda. It is Absalom who is the victim of infernal designs, and it is the resurgent king, invoking the divine presence, who wields "Lawfull Pow'r" (1024). The full potency of "Establish'd Pow'r" 993), we are told, is accessible only to the "faithful Band / Of Worthies" (914-15) who perform their rituals within nature's divinely ordained order. In describing Thomas, Earl of Ossory, as one of these, the narrator conflates the traditional image of perfection with the magician's conjuring circle, implying that Ossory's life had magical potency because it was centered on his faithful soul: "O Narrow Circle but of Pow'r Divine" (838).

In writing Charles's funeral ode, *Threnodia Augustalis* (1685), Dryden seems to have sensed that England was passing into a new phase of its history. Charles had weeded out rebels and cultivated the arts and sciences, leaving behind a demi-paradise. If Cromwell had been the "*Confident of Nature,*" absorbing stellar power, Charles had become the more sociable confidant of scientific virtuosi, draining, filtering, and directing their best work (341-45). Now that the "Promis'd Land [is] in view," however, the chosen flock needs no further "Miracles" (427-28). The dying king's physicians are "Sons of Art" (160), heirs of his own patronage of natural magic in its modern guise, but they cannot finally counteract fate. By acting as "second Causes" (110) with their "Charms of Art" (151), they can only briefly prevent "the Royal Soul" (150) from returning to "her Native Sphear" (150-52). As Anne Barbeau Gardiner has pointed out, these medical men are like the sorcerers in Pliny and Lucian, vainly "calling the distressed moon down from the sky to save it from [the] eclipse" that is part of God's primary magic. Meanwhile, the country's martial spirit is released from Charles's own "Charms" (471) of loving husbandry as James assumes the throne. An era of "Arts," "Science," and "soft Humanity" (348-50) is displaced by one of expanding empire.

But James is not able to move his country in the new direction. Instead, he spends his brief, tumultuous reign confronting one domestic crisis after another. In **The Hind and the Panther** (1687), as in **Absalom and Achitophel,** Dryden once again senses that "the *Daemon*" is being permitted into the garden (pt. 3, 314). The radical Whigs, those "dire Magicians" (pt. 3, 721) of the Puritan persuasion, were exposed during Charles's reign before they could thoroughly infect the Protestant cause; now the Panther / Anglican Church has been charmed again (pt. 3, 725), and without the divinely sponsored power of James and his mother faith, it is impossible to undo the enchantment. On their own, the Anglicans are outside the true magic circle: "like *Aegyptian* Sorcerers," they "vainly lift" the "magick wand," only to discover that they could, "with like infernal force / Produce the plague" of sectarian enthusiasm, "but not arrest the course" (pt. 2, 538-42).

In his last great public poem, **Britannia Rediviva** (1688), Dryden hopes that the birth of an heir to James will point the way out of the current troubles. He envisions the prince as embodying potent holy power that can resist the diabolical magic, the "fascinating Eyes," "Spells, and Sorceries" (203, 200), of the Whig "Fiends" (122). In developing this idea, he compares the prince not only to Christ, "the Godhead cloath'd in Earth" (123), but also to "the Sacred *Tetragrammaton*" (197). In this his only overt reference to cabbalistic magic, he implies that the prince is like the four-lettered name of God (in Hebrew) upon which Christian cabbalists, following Pico della Mirandola's example, would meditate. As a potent symbol for the ineffable creative Word, the Tetragrammaton gave access to both stellar and angelical forces; it became the ultimate door to magical power.

In the poem, then, this reference suggests that the prince will in some way complete the magical cycle of history begun with Charles's reign of love and continued in what this poem calls James's reign of "Justice" (355). As we have seen, Dryden symbolized the former as Christlike co-operation with natural forces through post-Baconian natural magic; justice, however, raises the magic higher, to "Heav'ns self" (355), implying more direct access to divine power. The prince will in some way "fill the *Trine*" (327), become the third part of the "*Unit*" (326), not only in the biological, astrological, and trinitarian senses, but in the sense of rounding out the age of love and justice with a monarchy of more transcendent virtue. Beyond such visions the poet cannot go, however, for he cannot expect to "read the Book which Angels cannot read" (227).

Events, of course, proved that these pious hopes could not be realized. Public life went its Whiggish way, and a dispossessed Dryden turned to safer, narrower, more private subjects. Even in the late poems, however, the imagery and vocabulary of magic contributes to the development of important themes. In **"To . . . The Duchess of Ormond"** (1700), God is seen as the ultimate alchemist, weighing and mixing the elements for the Duchess's body to fashion "so sweet a cage, / A soul might well be pleas'd

to pass an age" (118-19). Nevertheless, the elegant container is invaded by disease. When the attending physician, Christopher Morley, finds his natural magic as weak as that of the doctors who failed to save Charles II in **Threnodia Augustalis,** he is "inspir'd" by the lady's guardian "angel" to "find the remedy" (131-32), "As once the Macedon, by Jove's decree, / Was taught to dream an herb for Ptolomee" (133-34). In **"On the Death of a Very Young Gentleman"** (c. 1687-1693) the author offers the survivors an alchemical consolation. Try to think of the boy not as dead but rather as having been "rarify'd" (23); surely "His great Creator drew / His spirit, as the Sun the Morning Dew" (25-26). Although this is the true alchemy, Dryden implies, you the parents can apply the same process psychologically by treating your relationship with the other offspring as a kind of alembic:

>   divide
> That Love in many which in one was ty'd.
> . . . .
> Love him by Parts, in all your num'rous Race,
> And from those Parts form one collected Grace;
> Then, when you have refin'd to that degree,
> Imagine all in one, and think that one is He.
>   (46, 52-55)

This exhortation to "imagine" the process of alchemy leads us to another sphere of activity for the interpretation of which Dryden found the metaphor of magic particularly useful: art itself, especially literary art, music, and painting. Early in his career he speaks of artistic endeavours in the most exalted terms of Renaissance wizardry, but by the later 1660s, just as he begins to use the idiom of natural magic to describe the management of political power, he likewise begins to compare the artist's skill to the natural magician's virtuosity. Then, as his personal difficulties mount in the 1680s, his vision of the artist darkens; the times are unpropitious, and the bard becomes the inhibited craftsman.

At first, however, the enthusiastic patronage of Charles and his ministers must have given Dryden grounds for the highest expectations. In **"To My Lord Chancellor"** (1662) he rejoices that

> At length the Muses stand restor'd again
> To that great charge which Nature did ordain;
> And their lov'd Druids seem reviv'd by Fate,
> While you dispence the Laws and guide the
>   State.
>
>   (23-26)

Interest in the British druids, those ancient magician-priest-poets, had been revived earlier in the century when poets like Carew and Drayton traced the British monarchy and, by implication, their own lineage, back to an ancient world in which bards embodied political and priestly powers. The last druids, those in Wales, were considered heirs of Noah and of the magical theology of Hermes Trismegistus, Orpheus, and Pythagoras; later, the druidical union of lawgiver and wizard split into the partnership of king and magician-bard typified by Arthur and Merlin. Although less popular in the Restoration, this tradition obviously appealed to Dryden, since in his **"Life of Plutarch"** (1683) he discusses "our *Druydes,* who were nearest to the *Pythagoreans* of any Sect," and in ***King Arthur*** (1691) he gives a major role to Merlin.

During the 1660s, then, he seems to endow poets, including himself, with druidical powers. Appropriately, however, these modern druids see nature not as a living organism but rather as a mechanical structure shaped and moved by spiritual forces that realize God's law. The poems by Sir Robert Howard, writes Dryden in the epistle to his **"Honored Friend"** (1660), figure forth a "providence of wit" (34), a sub-creation whose "Atoms" (31) are so subtly controlled by Howard's "Genius" (35) that "dull souls, admire, but cannot see / What hidden springs within the Engine be" (21-22). Such artistry restores poetry's dominion over "Morall Knowledge" (45) just as "*Charls* ascends the Throne" (105) of political power. The poet, then, becomes a natural magician whose manipulation of images and language through the spiritual potency of his "genius" corresponds to God's handling of corpuscular reality and the king's governance of society.

The same analogies are implicit in Dryden's response to the critics in his "Prologue" to ***The Indian Emperour*** (1665), with the addition that here poetic force is ascribed more directly to heaven. As God's surrogate and champion against the "pow'r" that critics derive from "the Devil" (2-3), the playwright offers a little world so complex that "each man" should "take but what he understands, / And leave the rest upon the Poets hands" (28-29). The dramatist has veiled his deepest impulses and structures from all but the most adept and pious interpreters, just as "Heav'n" in ***Religio Laici*** is said to hide "from humane Sense / . . . the secret paths of *Providence*" (186-87).

By 1667 Dryden is assigning a somewhat lower status to the poetry of his own time, though he continues to use the metaphor of magic to describe it. Beginning with the "Prologue" to ***The Tempest*** (1667), he distinguishes between the poet-magus of the past, such as Shakespeare, who created virtually a second nature (8) and gave it laws (7) which his successors can only follow, and the modern poet-scientist who imitates and improves but cannot really create. Dryden reinforces this distinction with the vocabulary of daemonic magic: "*Shakespear's* Magick could not copy'd be, / Within that Circle none durst walk but he" (19-20); his "pow'r is sacred as a King's" (24) and presumably derives from the same divine source. As Charles becomes the presiding alchemist in ***Annus Mirabilis,*** Shakespeare becomes the presiding theurge in this prologue, and the bards of the Restoration become, by implication, his proteges, his Clarendons and Albemarles; only through painstaking study of his artistic works and the natural creations of his divine master can they reach the highest level of achievement possible for them, the level of natural magic. For them, as for Charles's deputies and successors, the age of miracles is over.

Thus, the best modern poetry is the product of careful study and imitation. Lesser poets are mere quacks, says the speaker of the **"Prologue . . . to the University of Oxon."** (1673); they

> build their Poems the *Lucretian* way,
> So many Huddled Atoms make a Play,
> And if they hit in Order by some Chance,

> They call that Nature, which is Ignorance.
>   (32-35)

More accomplished writers examine "with Care th' Anatomy of Man" and draw "Fame from Science, not from Fortune" (25-27). In the "Epilogue" to the **"University of Oxon."** (1673) this scientific art is distinguished from mere "Art Magique" (25), the mindless exploitation of vulgar tastes for spectacular effects on stage. Perhaps in order to remove the scenes of magic and demonology in his own plays from this category of "Art Magique," Dryden explains in some of his critical essays how daemons and sorcery can legitimately be represented both in the drama and in heroic poetry: the poet uses his well-informed fancy to combine images derived from experience, popular beliefs, philosophy, or, indeed, Shakespeare. With something like this principle in mind, Dryden can use the speaker of his prologue to ***Tyrannick Love*** (1669) to praise the "conjuring" dramatist who "Allow'd his Fancy the full scope and swing" (16-17).

It is difficult not to hear notes of regret in Dryden's espousal of a "modern" role for the poets of his day. The language used in his famous renunciation of rhyme in the "Prologue" to ***Aureng-Zebe*** (1675) implies that he felt inhibited by more than a verse form: "Nature," says the speaker, "flies him like Enchanted Ground" (10). This is the same phrase he would use a few years later in ***Religio Laici*** (1682) to describe the failure of the great ancient philosophers to achieve a unified theory of happiness: "For *Happiness* was never to be found; / But vanish'd from 'em like Enchanted ground" (27-28). Their problem, and perhaps Dryden suspected it was his own as well, was that their "*anxious Thoughts* in *endless Circles* roul, / Without a *Centre* where to fix the *Soul*" (36-37). In theology, only "*Reveal'd Religion*" (68) could provide the center. In the circle of poetry, Dryden seems to feel, "sacred" potency has been inaccessible since Shakespeare, so that now, as he puts it in the "Epilogue" to ***Aureng-Zebe,*** "a Poet must confess, / His Art's like Physick, but a happy ghess" (11-12).

When he returned to the theme of artistic magic in the 1680s, Dryden's estimation of the prospects for great achievement had dropped still further. Aware that none of the early Christian geniuses, the Shakespeares and Raphaels, had borne offspring in Restoration England, he felt that somehow the progress of art had been stymied. In **"A Song for St. Cecilia's Day, 1687,"** God's creative magic is represented in musical terms; it is a composition that unites the physical and supernal dimensions of reality in a harmony "closing full in Man" (15). Its lower range is first recreated by the pagan musician Orpheus, whose tuneful wizardry could command plants, animals, and human passions. Then, with her faith-inspired organ, St. Cecilia "rais'd the wonder high'r" (51), unwittingly conjuring "An angel" (53) from the supernal realm. A similar contrast is drawn in **"Alexander's Feast"** (1697). There Timotheus is the Orpheus figure, egotistically manipulating emotions through masterful fiction-making that is in one instance compared to necromancy (138-46). Again, St. Cecilia, adding the sacred "arts" of the organ to "nature's mother wit," enlarges the "narrow bounds" of pagan music and is able to invoke "an angel" (161-70). Of the composers in Dryden's time only Purcell could approach such musical magic. In **"An Ode, on the Death of Mr. Henry Purcell"** (1696) he is both "our *Orpheus*" (16), with power to tune the discord of hell (21-22), and the teacher of angel singers (23). Thus he might have linked nature and heaven in the full "Scale of Musick" (24); unfortunately, "the God-like Man, / . . . too soon retir'd, / As He too late began" (13-15).

On the other hand, had Purcell lived he might well have met the fate of other Restoration artists. "'Tis hard, my friend," Dryden lamented in his epistle to Motteux (1698),

> to write in such an age,
> As damns not only poets, but the stage.
> That sacred art, by heav'n itself infus'd,
> Which Moses, David, Solomon have us'd,
> Is now to be no more: the Muses' foes
> Would sink their Maker's praises into prose.
>
> (1-6)

And so with the finest Restoration painter. In the epistle **"To Sir Godfrey Kneller"** (1694) Dryden compares his own poetic subordination to Shakespeare with Kneller's relation to Raphael and Titian. They were truly creative spirits, true magicians of painting as Shakespeare was a true magician of poetry. Kneller, like Dryden himself, should be "Proud to be less; but of [their] Godlike Race" (76). "Bounded by the Times" (147), he must be content with "imitating Life" (18) rather than contending "with Heroes Memory" (119). Kneller has taken his craft as far as anyone can in "these inferior times" (118); it remains earthbound and lacks the Promethean "Fire" (25) that Dryden once expected the greatest Restoration artists to possess. But in the final analysis, it imitates life so well, exists in such complete harmony with "Nature" (8), that "Time" will "Add every Grace" that the painter could not provide (176-81).

Through the efforts of scholars like Steven Zwicker and James Garrison, we have seen that Dryden's religious conversion in the 1680s was accompanied by a gradual abandonment of his political dream, the dream of a redeemed, civilized community centering on a providentially sponsored patriarch-king. In this study I have tried to show that this dream and its loss were bound up with Dryden's understanding of power, and that the "infrastructure" of magic provided him with a language to interpret important aspects of the appropriation of power. To examine the genius of a Cromwell or a Shakespeare he found the lenses of Renaissance alchemy or theurgy most revealing, but as he moved into the early Restoration for his subjects, he turned to the kind of natural magic promoted by Bacon and the Royal Society. The poets and kings of the new age, working from the center of society, would be disciplined, sociable observers and promoters of providence at work through secondary causes. When the political scene darkened in the 1680s, Dryden found richer interpretive possibilities in the imagery of daemonic and cabbalistic magic. He began to see both artists and monarchs as victims of an evil wizardry that had been permitted to frustrate the unfolding of a higher art and a higher politics. Divinely ordained power had been withdrawn to the private soul and to time itself, the last magician of the age,

> for former things
> Are set aside, like abdicated kings;
> And every moment alters what is done,
> And innovates some act till then unknown.
>
> (pp. 381-93)

Jack M. Armistead, "Dryden's Poetry and the Language of Magic," in Studies in English Literature, 1500-1900, *Vol. 27, No. 3, Spring, 1987, pp. 381-98.*

Alastair Fowler (essay date 1987)

[*In the following excerpt, Fowler presents a concise overview of Dryden's oeuvre.*]

The Restoration brought relief for a majority of Charles II's subjects. But relief was not the only mood, nor was relaxation—nor yet overrelaxation and riot. There was also, at first, a darker mood of anxiety and tension, recrimination and score-settling. At such a time, writers who could make themselves heard by a broad range of social groups were invaluable—writers like Marvell, who said that the Parliamentary cause was 'too good to have been fought for', or George Savile, Marquis of Halifax, who wrote *The Character of a Trimmer* (1688), or Dryden, 'We have been so long together bad Englishmen'.

Although not himself well off, John Dryden (1631-1700) became used to the company of fashionable gentlemen, and eventually arrived—not without difficulties and failures—at a poise that allowed him to address men of different status with equal dignity. By his boldness in crossing lines of rank and allegiance he was enabled to mediate to middle class readers a European tradition of larger values, which had previously been accessible only to the educated and privileged. He did not achieve this by his personal qualities alone, nor by tact and tactics in selecting just the tone that would appeal—now Biblical, now polite. In large part his success was due to the special ease of his style, which took the reader more fully into account than had that of any previous English writer.

At the same time, Dryden's achievement may be seen as part of a late seventeenth-century triumph of the lucid plain style over the Senecan style with its significant darkness. The Earl of Shaftesbury's famous announcement of the new taste went so far as to describe the style of the Senecan essayists as a monotonous 'common amble'—an atomistic succession of independent short sentences, witty without variation. The new style, as Dryden came to practise it, used more variety of models, in accordance with the subject matter. For with him style followed the line of thought in a highly functional way. Only, he took the greatest care to hide the art of this; so that it appears, if at all, only in a certain hyper-natural quality. He avoids obvious patterning where he can. And where something like it is inevitable, as in parallel clauses (ISOCOLON) of comparison or contrast, he carefully mutes the effect—an effort diametrically opposite to that with which Dr Johnson, in a later period with a different taste, will underline his parallelisms. Thus Dryden's Shakespeare 'was naturally learn'd; he needed not the spectacles of books to read Nature; he looked inwards, and found her there'. The contrast finds plain and full statement; but it is not balanced out weightily, word against word. Dryden's effect has much to do with the way in which he carefully anticipates the reader, pacing him through the difficulties—and providing for these in the rhythms and proportions of the sentence structure. Yet all this is only part of an integral address towards his imagined reader, which is just as much expressed in the ease, in the tone of equal footing. And Dryden's ease is no mere imitation of breeding: he unites grace of manner with reason and robust morality in a firm, challenging way. He is perhaps the earliest critic still capable of persuading.

Dryden's criticism amounts to a substantial body of work, much of it occasional: between forty and fifty prologues, epilogues and letters, besides the formal *Essay Of Dramatic Poesy* (1668) and *A Parallel Betwixt Poetry and Painting* (1695). Yet it is not at first obvious where the importance or lasting value of these miscellaneous pieces resides. Excellent critics have valued Dryden as the first to venture at length into descriptive criticism—the *Essay* contains a long account of Jonson's *Epicoene*. But sharp descriptiveness hardly seems the main impression his work gives. There is more of that in his neglected near-contemporary John Dennis; although for description in English on the modern scale one has to wait for Addison on Milton (1712), Joseph Warton *On the Genius and Writings of Pope* (1756) and Hugh Blair's *Lectures on Rhetoric* (1762; not published until 1783).

The significance of Dryden's criticism lies in the fact that he was the first to address anything like a full range of critical topics. He displays an astonishing variety of interests, including speculations about genre or genesis; appreciations of Shakespeare's greatness; and judicial assessments—many of them thrown out casually, yet lasting to this day. His views are distinguished by breadth and soundness of taste, by intellectual acuity and independence. He set a benchmark for all subsequent criticism.

Dryden's essays reflect the multifarious concerns of a practising poet and dramatist, deeply involved in the politics of his difficult craft, and therefore prudently cautious in his pronouncements. There were precedents in French—in prefaces like Corneille's—for a writer's discussing his ideas. But Dryden's preference for particular issues derived primarily from the exploratory, sceptical cast of his own mind. His freedom is wonderfully engaging. Big names do not overawe him—'Neither am I much concerned at Mr Cowley's verses before *Gondibert* (though his authority is almost sacred to me) . . . '. Sidney and Jonson and their immediate successors had on the whole treated fixed rules, and were in any case constricted by their authorities and by the rhetorical forms they used (forms of controversy or praise like the epideictic oration). But Dryden ranged wherever his interest led, among the various questions of his time—French versus English dramatic styles; rhyme versus blank verse; and the rest—illuminating them all and adumbrating, cumulatively, a whole aggregate of literature. He was the first to express an adequate idea, in English, of what literature is. For, like his great contemporary Sir Christopher Wren, Dryden was free from slavery to theoretical rules.

Among Dryden's exploratory speculations, some of the most interesting concern the operation of rhyme as a beneficial constraint in composition, a means of generating poetic ideas. 'Imagination in a poet is a faculty so wild and lawless that like an high-ranging spaniel it must have clogs tied to it, lest it outrun the judgment': the writing process needs to be slowed, to allow time for more creative choices. A similarly interesting topic is the genesis of wit. Again the imagination is 'like a nimble spaniel' and

> beats over and ranges through the field of memory, till it springs the quarry it hunted after . . .
> the first happiness of the poet's imagination is properly invention, or finding of the thought; the second is fancy, or the variation, driving, or moulding of that thought, as the judgment represents it proper to the subject . . .
> (*An Account of the Ensuing Poem*)

The analogy of the dog was a stock one in European criticism. But it was a newer idea, characteristic of Dryden, to use it to introspect on the experience of composition. He substitutes a phase of psychological action ('the variation, driving, or moulding of that thought') for the one of rhetorical arrangement that usually followed invention in such contexts.

Some of Dryden's best writing is in his occasional works, particularly prologues and epilogues to plays. He was the unrivalled master of this genre, and he brought it to a height never approached since. Often the prologues and epilogues are panegyric; which need not at all mean that they flatter. In fact, they can be belligerent. Dryden opted for society; but he never ceased trying to bully or coax or shame it into a bit of sense. Thus the Prologue to *Oedipus* anticipates an unfavourable reception, and advises the audience that in such an event they should 'Damn it in silence, lest the world should hear'. Dryden's authority allowed him to say anything—so long as he judged his tone to perfection:

> See twice! Do not pell-mell to damning fall,
> Like true born Britons, who ne'er think at all:
> Pray be advised; and though at Mons you won,
> On pointed cannon do not always run.
> (Prologue from *Oedipus* 23-6)

Dryden's dispraises, as in his satires *The Medal* and *MacFlecknoe* (both 1682), have become more famous. And they are brilliant and funny, if not always very just. *Absalom and Achitophel* (1681), written at the request of Charles II against Shaftesbury's party, has a Biblical allegory with a useful distancing effect. In this the king is King David, who 'wide as his command / Scattered his Maker's image through the land' in the shape of natural sons (implying that Monmouth is only one of many). The meat of the satire is found by Dryden's lash in a series of characters: the best are those of Shaftesbury (Achitophel), Monmouth (Absalom) and Buckingham (Zimri). This transportation of the entire satiric prose character form into verse—as distinct from Butler's use of its materials on a different scale—set a pattern for much satire in the succeeding age. To this pattern, in fact, Edward Young's 'The Love of Fame' (1725) and Pope's 'Of the Characters of

Women' (1735) conform, as much as to the ultimate model in the Latin satirists. Dryden's Achitophel is

> For close Designs, and crooked Counsels fit;
> Sagacious, Bold, and Turbulent of wit:
> Restless, unfixt in Principles and Place;
> In Power unpleas'd, impatient of Disgrace.
> A fiery Soul, which working out its way,
> Fretted the Pigmy Body to decay:
> And o'er inform'd the Tenement of Clay.
> A daring Pilot in extremity;
> Pleas'd with the Danger, when the Waves went high
> He sought the Storms; but for a Calm unfit,
> Would Steer too nigh the Sands, to boast his Wit.
> Great Wits are sure to Madness near ally'd;
> And thin Partitions do their Bounds divide:
> Else, why should he, with Wealth and Honour blest,
> Refuse his Age the needful hours of Rest?
>   (lines 152-66)

The ambivalent epithets and concessions of positive qualities, together with the high dignified tone, combine to create a believable great figure, with a presumption of justice on the satirist's part. Respectfulness makes criticism all the more telling. We are as far as possible, here, from the style of Donne or Cleveland. Normal proportions of imagery, easy development of the natural metaphor of a pilot, judicious impersonality: such are the features in Dryden that prepare one to accept as reasonable even his later insinuations about Shaftesbury's Satanic role.

The critical *oeuvre* of a lifetime is not without its connecting themes. In Dryden's case—and indeed in the Restoration generally—perhaps the most prominent was pursuit of the heroic ideal, both in the sense of literary EPIC (grand narrative) and of social nobility. Even a metre could be chosen because it was 'more noble'. In Dryden's writing, the epic *Aeneis* (1697) . . . constitutes the *chef d'oeuvre;* while *Absalom and Achitophel* is heroic satire *par excellence.* In it, even the most adverse characterizations, such as those of Shaftesbury and Buckingham, have considerable dignity. But *Annus Mirabilis* (1667) was already a strenuously heroic poem. And, more obviously still, the aspiration to epic actuated Dryden's repeated attempts at heroic drama. Again and again he tried to emulate the grandeur of Shakespeare's heroic tragedies—to achieve a purified form that would maintain elevation in diction, character and social decorum more consistently. These attempts were never wholly successful. Nevertheless *All for Love* (1678), ostensibly a *rifacimento* or remake of *Antony and Cleopatra,* can stand as an independent achievement of real force, capable of arousing excitement on the modern stage.

Many other writers, too, were fascinated by the epic ideal. Some, such as Abraham Cowley, attempted the epic poem itself. Others translated ancient epics, or, like Clarendon, gave epic shape to works in quite other genres. The tendency may have had something to do with the heroic nature of recent history, and surely had much to do with the sovereign place of epic in Restoration literary theory. Dryden considered it 'undoubtedly the greatest work which the soul of man is capable to perform'. Yet epics of real

quality failed to materialize; the old aristocratic values of the genre had lost their cosmic validity, and new validation was wanting. This failure was not because of any indistinctness of aim. The idea of epic was all too sharply defined; only its implementation eluded the poets.—All of them, paradoxically, except the republican John Milton (1608-74). (pp. 125-30)

> *Alastair Fowler, "Restoration Literature," in his* A History of English Literature: Forms and Kinds from the Middle Ages to the Present, *Basil Blackwell, 1987, pp. 125-46.*

Leon Guilhamet   (essay date 1987)

[*In the excerpt below, Guilhamet analyzes two of Dryden's major satires—*MacFlecknoe *and* Absalom and Achitophel—*praising the poet for developing the genre into a literary form of remarkable structural, intellectual, and thematic richness.*]

Dryden's *Mac Flecknoe* is a remarkable poem. Although much of its satire is personal, i.e., directed against Thomas Shadwell, its strongest satirical thrust has more general, cultural significance. The dynamic of the poem is activated by a profound paradox: although Shadwell is an essentially comic figure in the poem, who, despite his rotund materiality, amounts to nothing, the threat he poses to culture and art in particular cannot be so easily dismissed.

The satire consists in two closely related emphases: first, the personal, comic ridicule directed at Shadwell; and second, the assessment of the impact on culture and art by Shadwell and his kind. The mock-heroic qualities of the poem thus have a double significance. Mac Flecknoe (Shadwell) is reduced in stature by implied comparison with the heroes of epic. But also the maintenance of the heroic style and manner imparts, paradoxically, some signficance to Mac Flecknoe and thus to what he represents. This requires us to take him more seriously than even Father Flecknoe himself might seem to do.

The deliberative form of the poem is apparent at the outset. The poem opens on the conclusion of a deliberation to determine Flecknoe's successor. True also to epic requirements, the poem begins in medias res, not at the beginning of the deliberation, but somewhat later at the point where the resolution of it is to be explained. This enables Flecknoe to announce his decision and present his reasons for it. Although the question has already been settled, we are to consider the evidence as if the deliberation were still in progress.

Yet the particularly judicial quality of this deliberation may lead us to the realization that *Mac Flecknoe* is the recapitulation of a sessions poem. There was, however, no real selection process. With Shadwell the obvious and necessary choice, the sessions structure is only the merest formality. But this is true as well of every genre that contributes to the poem. Each one reveals its momentary relevance to satire and promptly yields to yet another formal strategy. The ultimate structure is the sum of these diverse parts.

Unusual to a sessions poem or more general judicial and

deliberative structures is the unmistakable heroic sound of the opening six lines. The disquieting "Non-sense" in line six, however, abruptly changes our sense of the preceding five verses:

> All humane things are subject to decay,
> And, when Fate summons, Monarchs must obey:
> This *Fleckno* found, who, like Augustus, young
> Was call'd to Empire, and had govern'd long:
> In Prose and Verse, was own'd, without dispute
> Through all the Realms of *Non-sense,* absolute.
>   (1-6)

The word "Non-sense" is the axle on which the poem turns from the impression of heroic poetry to its counter-genre, mock-heroic. Thus, right at the outset, the issue of generic identity becomes important to our understanding of **Mac Flecknoe.** By line 6 we have begun to realize that one kind of literature is being played consciously against another. Also, "Non-sense" stresses a departure from sense; i.e., it is less a negative quality than the absence of any quality at all. Shadwell's peculiar kind of nonsense proceeds from his inability to achieve any generic integrity. The generic transformation to satire has begun.

If the opening lines have a heroic sound to them, they also masquerade as history. Flecknoe is compared to Augustus (3) and a rough outline of his reign is sketched (4-10). Once the setting is given, Flecknoe begins to describe his deliberations, interrupting the historical narration like one of Thucydides' movers and shakers. The words that follow are in the heightened language of panegyric; but, of course, only Flecknoe and his attendants can regard them as words of praise.

Dryden's introduction of kinds continues apace. The allusion to Augustus sets the action in classical history, but soon biblical history and dramatic history are fused:

> *Heywood* and *Shirley* were but Types of thee,
> Thou last great Prophet of Tautology:
> Even I, a dunce of more renown than they,
> Was sent before but to prepare thy way. . . .
>   (29-32)

Here begins the process of extracting Shadwell from the tradition of Ben Jonson, with which he had aligned himself, and placing him among the lightly regarded Heywoods and Shirleys. To accomplish this Dryden draws an analogy with a typological reading of biblical history. On the one hand, Shadwell is the antitype of two inferior earlier dramatists and, on the other, he is the Christ to whom Flecknoe has been John the Baptist. [In his *Typologies in England: 1650–1820,* 1982] Paul J. Korshin identifies this as "typological satire" and points out the importance of yet another structure, the prophecy, in the composition of **Mac Flecknoe.**

Already major demands are being placed on the reader to disentangle levels of style and a series of integrated literary kinds which follow one another with rapidity. But even more difficulty is to come. Flecknoe's Portuguese recital is only a prelude to Shadwell's English success:

> My warbling Lute, the Lute I whilom strung
> When to King *John* of *Portugal* I sung,

> Was but the prelude to that glorious day,
> When thou on silver *Thames* did'st cut thy way. . . .
>   (35-38)

Here we reach a central question of genre. The "warbling Lute" suggests lyrical poetry, or more precisely the popular songs that Flecknoe supposedly sang to his own accompaniment at the court of King John (Catherine of Braganza, Charles's queen, was John's daughter). The use of "whilom" suggests a medieval, perhaps gothic, quality, as though Flecknoe were a wandering minstrel or troubador, a lutanist of a more romantic and lyrical time. But although "whilom" ("whylom") appears often in Chaucer, it is to be found in Spenser as well. So the passage is by no means restricted to a medieval locus, for the "silver *Thames*" and the lines that follow, "With well tim'd Oars before the Royal Barge, / Swell'd with the Pride of thy Celestial charge . . . " (39-40), are probable echoes of panegyric by Edmund Waller, and also recall more generally the language of Spenser in his *Prothalamion* (1596) and Shakespeare in Enobarbus's great description of Cleopatra upon the river Cydnus. The Spenser and Shakespeare allusions stress the bondage of love. The insistence upon the lute in succeeding lines (44, 58, 210) underscores the ineffectual romantic lyricism with which both father and son are identified. The lute may also suggest the unripe sexual loves of Shadwell satirized later in the poem (122-25). When in book 4 of the *Dunciad* Pope imagines realms to which Dulness directs her children, he includes "Love-whisp'ring woods, and lute-resounding waves" (4:306). Pope undoubtedly follows Dryden in linking and disparaging lutany and love.

But the old poet's lute playing in Portugal is also a typological prefiguration of Shadwell's far more extensive musical career. With the lute still in his hand, the heir apparent rivals the "Morning Toast" for the attention of the "little Fishes" (49-50) and, like a thresher translated from field to podium, rises into sway over a consort of musicians:

> Sometimes as Prince of thy Harmonious band
> Thou weild'st thy Papers in thy threshing hand.
>   (51-52)

Such an assembly, Dryden suggests, is all that Shadwell can aspire to be prince of—unless he become prince of dullness as well. The crudity of his musical understanding, however, is indicated by his "threshing hand," hardly expressive of grace and indicative of a profession to which Shadwell might better have aspired. The chief point throughout this complex pattern of accusations is that Shadwell has improperly assumed the roles of playwright and satirist, for neither of which nature has fitted him. A corollary of this is that comedy and satire are genres requiring consummate artistic skill. Shadwell would do better to confine his efforts to less demanding forms.

Unfortunately, however, Flecknoe's son has not been content to play his lute and lead his band. He has, first and foremost, attempted to write plays, and such has been his success that

> All arguments, but most this Plays, perswade,
> That for anointed dullness he was made.
>   (62-63)

Next Dryden describes in some detail the milieu from which Shadwell's plays spring. Again, a sense of the past, with a Spenserian flavor, is evoked:

> An ancient fabrick, rais'd t'inform the sight,
> There stood of yore, and *Barbican* it hight. . . .
>
> (66-67)

A faint hint of the glorious Elizabethan past may have been given earlier in Flecknoe's account of Shadwell's musical success: "When thou on silver *Thames* did'st cut thy way . . . " (38). The absurdity of the immense lutanist

> Swell'd with the Pride of thy Celestial charge;
> And big with Hymn, Commander of an
> Host . . .
>
> (40-41)

is underscored in the implicit comparison with the white swans and "silver streaming Themmes" of Spenser's *Prothalamion*. Here, too, Shadwell, pregnant with pride and hymn, is seen as unnaturally bisexual. The images suggest his association with religious dissent as well, pride and hymn singing being ordinary charges in anti-Puritan satire. The introduction of Spenserian diction also provides a comparison with the vulgar "suburbian" language of Shadwell's plays. In the neighborhood around the Barbican, a place associated with low pleasures, Mac Flecknoe's plays find a good reception:

> Pure Clinches, the suburbian Muse affords;
> And *Panton* waging harmless War with words.
> Here *Fleckno*, as a place to Fame well known,
> Ambitiously design'd his *Sh*—'s Throne.
>
> (83-86)

The passage ends with a flow of Shadwellian titles and character names. But the setting is by no means complete. Shadwell's territory, from Bun-Hill to Watling Street, is evoked in all its crowded and irrelevant chaos, leading up to the parody of Vergilian majesty represented by Flecknoe and his son.

The essential dramatic quality of this coronation scene and of the poem generally has been pointed out. But it is also important to underscore how deliberately Dryden employs certain aspects of Shadwell's dramatic style for purposes of satire. Just as the title of Flecknoe's play, *Love's Kingdom* (1664), has set a precedent for his son's self-indulgence in ale and opium, and the youthful practice of sex, it has provided the inspiration to his art as well. Thus Shadwell's opera *Psyche* (1674)—and, by implication, his mind—have sprung from his loins. By these images unnatural qualities and practices are attributed to Shadwell. He can now be seen as a bit more dangerous than Flecknoe's comic account may seem to make him.

Next begins a series of events, some of which are drawn from stylistic oddities in Shadwell's plays. In *The Sullen Lovers* (1668), the term "owl" is used a number of times to denote stupidity or foolishness. Dryden introduces his owls just as the coronation is complete, when Shadwell's brains are entirely opiated:

> His Temples last with Poppies were o'erspread,
> That nodding seem'd to consecrate his head:

> Just at that point of time, if Fame not lye,
> On his left hand twelve reverend *Owls* did fly.
>
> (126-29)

In Flecknoe's panegyric on his son which follows, explicit references to *The Virtuoso* (1676), *Epsom Wells* (1673), and *Psyche* are included in unfavorable comparison with the estimable art of Etherege. But when Jonson's name is introduced, Dryden employs direct parody of Shadwell's style, utilizing language from *The Virtuoso*. What relation can we possibly have to Jonson? Flecknoe asks:

> Where sold he Bargains, Whip-stitch, kiss my
> Arse,
> Promis'd a Play and dwindled to a Farce?
>
> (181-82)

In *The Virtuoso* Sir Samuel Hearty responds to Longvil: "Prithee Longvil, hold thy peace with a whipstitch, your nose in my breech." This locution is evidently one of Hearty's favorites, for he repeats it three times in the course of the play.

The second line of this couplet is also of interest. In it Dryden sums up his objections to Shadwell: he is incapable of achieving his purposes. In attempting to be witty, he succeeds only in being dull. The insight is developed in a parody of lines from the epilogue to Shadwell's *The Humorists* (1671). Here, first, are Shadwell's lines:

> A Humor is the Byas of the Mind,
> By which with violence 'tis one way inclin'd:
> It makes our Actions lean on one side still,
> And in all Changes that way bends the Will.
>
> (15-18)

Flecknoe's praise emphasizes his son's originality or innovation, always a negative in Dryden's view:

> This is thy Province, this thy wondrous way,
> New Humours to invent for each new Play. . . .
>
> (187-88)

The invention of new humors is totally perverse, an unnatural parody of true creativity. This is followed by a direct parody of Shadwell's lines:

> This is that boasted Byas of thy mind,
> By which one way, to dullness, 'tis inclin'd;
> Which makes thy writings lean on one side still,
> And in all changes that way bends thy will.
>
> (189-92)

Shadwell, then, is condemned by his own works. Jonson promises a play and delivers one. Shadwell, on the other hand, aborts. The promise he tenders is never realized in performance. If Shadwell is portly, like Jonson, and that bulk pledges a Jonsonian performance (similar to Pope's "I cough like Horace, and, though lean, am short"), there the resemblance ends:

> Nor let thy mountain belly make pretence
> Of likeness; thine's a tympany of sense.
> A Tun of Man in thy Large bulk is writ,
> But sure thou'rt but a Kilderkin of wit.
>
> (193-96)

The word "tympany" is a brilliant choice, uniting percussion with pregnancy, tumor, and bombast. Again and again, but always in surprising variation, Flecknoe's panegyric repeats the major attack of Dryden's satire: Shadwell is never in control of his own ends. Whatever he intends, the opposite is always realized:

> Like mine thy gentle numbers feebly creep,
> Thy Tragick Muse gives smiles, thy Comick sleep.
> With whate'er gall thou sett'st thy self to write,
> Thy inoffensive Satyrs never bite.
>
> (197-200)

It is clear from all of this that Shadwell has missed his calling. His abilities do not permit him to aspire to tragedy, comedy, or satire. Instead he should turn his energies to lesser forms:

> Thy Genius calls thee not to purchase fame
> In keen Iambicks, but mild Anagram:
> Leave writing Plays, and chuse for thy command
> Some peacefull Province in Acrostick Land.
> There thou maist wings display and Altars raise,
> And torture one poor word Ten thousand ways.
>
> (203-8)

The province of anagrams and acrostics reminds Flecknoe of his son's other talent as musical director and lutanist:

> Or if thou would'st thy diff'rent tallents suit,
> Set thy own Songs, and sing them to thy lute.
>
> (209-10)

Surely anagram, acrostic, and song do not argue for much difference in talent. Shadwell's ineffectuality is mirrored in whatever form or genre he endeavors to work with. It stands to reason, then, that he should choose the least effectual genres available.

Flecknoe's oration, like his son's plays, would go on forever were it not for the introduction of a deus ex machina or some other contrivance. The contrivance in *Mac Flecknoe,* as in *The Virtuoso,* is a trap door. Shadwell's own characters work that door by which the action is brought to sudden conclusion, and the poet is left above as reigning king of dullness. Once again, Dryden effectively parodies Shadwell's dramatic technique, just as earlier in the poem, he parodies his language and dramatic theory. To a certain extent, *Mac Flecknoe* assumes the form of a Shadwell comedy.

Thus, in *Mac Flecknoe,* Dryden employs a very subtle interplay of genres, both as form and theme. The hierarchy of genres provides a basis for comic ridicule leveled against Shadwell, since he is relegated to the inferior forms for lack of poetic talent. But the form of Dryden's poem is precisely compatible with his subject matter in another important way. Just as Shadwell "Promis'd a Play and dwindled to a Farce . . . " (182), Dryden, by the heroic style of his opening lines "promises" a heroic poem. Of course, the promise was never meant to be kept, but true to its parody of a Shadwell play, *Mac Flecknoe* "dwindles" to a farce.

The poem begins like a heroic poem, but promptly establishes its dramatic affinities by use of elaborate theatrical metaphors. Within the dramatic structure, the speeches of Flecknoe can be seen as deliberative oratory first and then demonstrative oratory or panegyric. There are brief sug-

gestions of medieval and Renaissance lyricism, culminating in the advice to Shadwell to confine his efforts to insignificant forms. Tragedy, comedy, and satire reign supreme, far beyond the grasp of the prince of dullness; but even as Mac Flecknoe falls ludicrously short of artistic success in those forms, the reader glimpses real achievement on the inevitable utopian or panegyrical side of the satiric coin. Jonson, Fletcher, and Etherege stand out as model playwrights, compared with whose achievements Shadwell's failures seem even more pathetic. Indeed, *Mac Flecknoe* itself emerges as an exemplar against which the "inoffensive Satyrs" of the prince of dullness can be measured and found wanting.

But if comic ridicule as it emerges from parody unifies subject and form, the poem becomes a satire as Shadwell's perversity and the harmful impact of his failed ethics and aesthetics are recognized. He is "a scourge of Wit, and flayle of Sense" (89). Though insignificant by comparison, he is nonetheless like Hannibal "a mortal Foe to *Rome*" (113). Intemperate drinking, unripe sexuality, and papaveraceous indulgence unite with dissenter enthusiasm to create something of a monster. Shadwell is only inoffensive when he chooses to be offensive; though it cannot gain access to his pen, venom does indeed lie in his "fellonious heart" (201). What is evil about Mac Flecknoe and what makes him a proper butt of satire is his unnatural influence on everything he touches. If he were merely ineffectual, he would be a comic figure, not a satiric one. Of course, he is a comic figure and a brilliant one, but the darker hints which Dryden inserts for us edge him into a more serious context. As Harry Levin tells us [in his article "The Wages of Satire," in *Literature and Society: Selected Papers From the English Institute, 1978,* edited by Edward W. Said, 1980], "When comedy becomes more purposeful than playful, then it is satire."

But finally what makes Mac Flecknoe dangerous is not his intentions, since they, we have seen, are never realized. The poem itself does not turn from playful to purposeful at a single turning point. Rather the poem becomes a satire as Shadwell's perversity in life and art emerge in antithesis to classical and traditional values. *Mac Flecknoe* can be read largely as comedy. But as we contemplate the failure of ethical and artistic values which Shadwell represents, his accession to the throne of dullness becomes less of a laughing matter.

. . . . .

The genre of *Absalom and Achitophel* has proved controversial for generations of critics. Some regard it as satire, but they seldom do so without serious reservations. Epic or epyllion is another possibility, and Verrall in [his 1914 *Lectures on Dryden*] decided it was a combination of satire and epic. Perhaps Paul Ramsey, tongue in cheek, has expressed the problem best when, after reviewing the generic uncertainties of the poem, he writes [in his book *The Art of John Dryden,* 1969]: "Hence we can say that the poem is an occasional, polemical, historical, satirical, panegyrical, truncated, narrative, allegorical poem."

But even Ramsey has not included all the possibilities, as the following essay will show. *Absalom and Achitophel,* as is typical of complex satires, makes use of many belletristic forms. Characteristic of satire, too, it employs rhetorical forms as essential parts of its structure.

The poem begins as biblical history, but an attentive reader will promptly realize that the "pious times, e'r Priestcraft did begin" (1) are equivalent to an imagined Agapemone or Cloudcuckooland. The most notable pious time without priests was in the Garden of Eden itself. But if such a utopia existed at a later date, it was surely before the time of David.

But Dryden's purpose in alluding to such a time is to show us that it occurred mainly in David's bed, where the king, perhaps, "inspir'd by some diviner Lust" (19), begets the ill-fated Absalom. The point is that Absalom is a child of nature; i.e., a natural child or bastard and fruit of love "When Nature prompted, and no law deny'd / Promiscuous use of Concubine and Bride . . . " (5-6). As a natural man, "What e'r he did was done with so much ease, / In him alone, 'twas Natural to please . . . " (27-28). Absalom, indeed, representing nature, unites that same nature with a second key term in the poem, "grace": "His motions all accompanied with grace; / And *Paradise* was open'd in his face" (29-30). Here "grace" means merely gracefulness, but the term will come to represent a complex of meanings as the poem proceeds. It is enough to note, for the time being, that Absalom is associated with it at an early stage.

In his salad days David had indulged in love freely, prompted by nature; but it is important to note that no law had denied him his amours. For Absalom there are excesses as well; but for these the law is manipulated somewhat, even to the point of exonerating him from murder:

> Some warm excesses, which the Law forbore,
> Were constru'd Youth that purg'd by boyling
> 　o'er:
> And *Amnon's* Murther, by a specious Name,
> Was call'd a Just Revenge for injur'd Fame.
> 　　　　　　　　　　　　(37-40)

The "nature" and "grace" of Absalom, we shall see, attracts similar qualities in the Jews.

The Jews in the poem are equivalent to the English, as any modern edition of the poem makes abundantly clear. But not every Englishman is included among them. Rather they are a particularly enthusiastic breed, with marked dissenter qualities:

> The *Jews*, a Headstrong, Moody, Murmuring
> 　race,
> As ever try'd th'extent and stretch of grace;
> God's pamper'd people whom, debauch'd with
> 　ease,
> No King could govern, nor no God could
> 　please. . . .
> 　　　　　　　　　　　　(45-48)

This grace is God's and David's both. As God's, the theological concept is introduced, and a comment is made on the Calvinist position. "As ever try'd th'extent and stretch of grace" suggests that having God's grace may be contingent upon one's behavior. This, of course, was an Arminian position, rejected by the majority of dissenting Protes-

Laocoon, by Franz Cleyn; plate 38 in The Works of Virgil, *translated by Dryden.*

tants. For them grace was a free gift of God's, which placed its possessors among the elect. Dryden, as we shall see, is taking the Arminian position: grace is under God's control and its transmission contingent upon good behavior. But the populace behaves as though its behavior is not at issue.

If the people, in their passion for grace, as opposed to good works, find Absalom attractive, his natural qualities make him suitable to their ends as well. Just as Absalom had "*Paradise* . . . open'd in his face," the people are represented in an Edenic setting produced by their own wild imaginations:

> These *Adam*-wits, too fortunately free,
> Began to dream they wanted libertie;
> And when no rule, no president was found
> Of men, by Laws less circumscrib'd and bound,
> They led their wild desires to Woods and Caves,
> And thought that all but Savages were Slaves.
> 　　　　　　　　　　　　(51-56)

By choosing a natural life they become, in effect, savages, making Absalom, the natural man, their leader. Dryden will make all of this clear in due course. For the time being it is enough to identify the exponents of "the Good Old

Cause" with a kind of lawless self-indulgence. The only problem is that

> when to Sin our byast Nature leans,
> The carefull Devil is still at hand with means;
> And providently Pimps for ill desires:
> The Good Old Cause reviv'd, a Plot requires.
>
> (79-82)

It is not the plot, however, that causes concern. Dryden drops any pretense to suspense by informing us promptly: "This Plot . . . fail'd for want of common Sense . . . " (134). But the effects of the plot are much more dire, leading to a serious attack on lawful monarchy. It is this larger uprising that Dryden will dissect throughout the remainder of the poem.

At this point there is also an adjustment of form. With the introduction of the magnificent Theophrastan character of Achitophel, Dryden brings his full satiric powers to bear. Earlier, the mood of the rabble had been presented with skill, but a general assessment was the outcome. Here we get down to specifics; the characterization brings to light information pro and con; but the final result is disastrous to Shaftesbury. He is clearly on trial. Indeed, the poem has moved from what Earl Miner calls "partisan history" to a quasi-judicial setting. The judicial aspect of the portrait is made clear about halfway through:

> So easie still it proves in Factious Times,
> With publick Zeal to cancel private Crimes.
>
> (180-81)

Achitophel's late criminal behavior is contrasted with his earlier judicial temperament:

> Yet, Fame deserv'd, no Enemy can grudge;
> The Statesman we abhor, but praise the Judge,
> In *Israels* Courts ne'er sat an *Abbethdin*
> With more discerning Eyes, or Hands more
>   clean:
> Unbrib'd, unsought, the Wretched to redress;
> Swift of Dispatch, and easie of Access.
>
> (186-91)

Here also the narrator establishes his own essential fairness in presenting the evidence with restraint and exactitude.

More important, Achitophel, who before upheld the law, now violates and abuses it. His earlier dedication may be cited to prove that even the worst among us recognizes at some time the inherent value of legal probity. But now,

> *Achitophel,* grown weary to possess
> A lawfull Fame, and lazy Happiness;
> Disdain'd the Golden fruit to gather free,
> And lent the Croud his Arm to shake the Tree.
> Now, manifest of Crimes, contriv'd long since,
> He stood at bold Defiance with his Prince:
> Held up the Buckler of the Peoples Cause,
> Against the Crown; and sculk'd behind the
>   Laws.
>
> (200-207)

Legal issues become paramount as the evidence against Achitophel piles up. His arguments are presented and will be presented in greater detail as the temptation of Absalom is overheard in its entirety.

Achitophel's speech marks another stylistic shift, as Miltonic diction introduces the elaborate temptation:

> Him he attempts, with studied Arts to please,
> And sheds his Venome, in such words as
>   these. . . .
>
> (228-29)

Since Milton's language and imagery were invented to capture the grandeur of a biblical subject, the shift is by no means abrupt. Indeed in most effective satire the seams between stylistic shifts are usually not easily apparent. But the Miltonic diction here is unmistakable, and so a sense of Satanic evil on the grand scale is evoked. Mixed with biblical language (the "Young-mens Vision, and the Old mens Dream!"), the Miltonic effects set off Achitophel's rhetorical speech from the rest of the poem in a particularly striking way.

The satirist undertakes the apparently contradictory task of both separating out genres and integrating them. Since every satire is a collection of more or fewer different genres, the essential task is to integrate them into a focused satire. Nonetheless, the various generic identities contribute to meaning in diverse ways, depending on how satiric intention and related artistic purposes are to be combined.

In this case, the brilliant shift to a Satanic temptation contrasts Achitophel unfavorably with the mild David. The shift from narrative to rhetorical form also sets off this passage from the remainder of the poem. This use of rhetorical forms, specifically persuasive in their intention, also underscores the judicial theme, which will emerge as even more important as the poem proceeds. But at the same time that the speech becomes a brilliant setpiece and tour de force in its generic identity, it may be found to have a strong thematic unity with the poem as a whole.

Achitophel's temptation of Absalom, like Satan's directed to Eve, is perfectly adjusted to its object. Absalom, as we have seen, is the natural man from several points of view. As such he is also love's minion who "seem'd as he were only born for love" (26). Recognizing this attribute, Achitophel presses his argument in precisely the right direction. Barely muted sexual imagery begins the attack as the tempter calls Absalom "Thy longing Countries Darling and Desire . . . " (232). The sexuality, however, is never explicit, since the stress is more completely on vague and visionary associations. He is "The Young-mens Vision, and the Old mens Dream!" (239). And even more explicitly, Absalom is something higher than an object of sense; he is a veritable god and Christ-figure:

> Thee, *Saviour,* Thee, the Nations Vows confess;
> And, never satisfi'd with seeing, bless. . . .
>
> (240-41)

The emphasis next returns to Absalom's natural qualities as his failure to assert himself as ruler by right of nature (not natural right, except in the perverse sense of his bastardy) is seen as depriving the people of joy, sustenance, and what is rightly theirs by natural law:

> How long wilt thou the general Joy detain;
> Starve, and defraud the People of thy Reign?
>
> (244-45)

The significance of the word "starve" is brought into brilliant relief by the Miltonic imagery to follow:

> Believe me, Royal Youth, thy Fruit must be,
> Or gather'd Ripe, or rot upon the Tree.
>
> (250-51)

We see by this that what the people starve for is the forbidden fruit of Eden. If Absalom agrees to supply their needs, we understand just what they will be getting. The people do not hunger after truth and righteousness, but rather after the sweet fruits of sin.

Next, as Achitophel launches upon a catalogue of David's weaknesses, he points to another naturalistic reason for Absalom's right by nature: David is now in his declining years. Early in the temptation Absalom's "dawning day" was noted. Now Absalom is told to shun David's

> example of Declining Age:
> Behold him setting in his Western Skies,
> The Shadows lengthning as the Vapours rise.
>
> (267-69)

As Achitophel concludes the first effort at temptation, he recurs to Absalom's chief characteristic, his love of love. Here the tempter speaks of the special value of whatever rule is "Giv'n by the Love of all your Native Land . . . " (300). Thus Absalom, the love-child, is seduced by love to assert his right by nature to the throne. Of course, his natural debt to his father and the fact that he has no legal right to the kingship are conveniently ignored. Youth, vigor, and love, it would seem, entitle Absalom to rule. It is, of course, a romantic and totally fallacious assumption. In fact, Absalom's shaky answer to Achitophel's arguments stresses David's lawful and just rule: "My Father Governs with unquestion'd Right" (317). David is "Good, Gracious, Just, observant of the Laws" (319). "Who sues for Justice to his Throne in Vain?" (322) The crown "Is Justly Destin'd for a Worthier Head" (348) and "His Lawfull Issue shall the Throne ascend" (351). It is clear from all this that Absalom recognizes that law and justice are against his claim; but his natural gifts and status cry out for dominion: "Desire of Greatness is a Godlike Sin" (372).

In Achitophel's second try at a weakening Absalom, the tempter asserts his ability to manipulate money to his own political advantage. David, who is characterized as generous, is always in need of money. Achitophel will therefore be able to govern him by Parliamentary control of the royal purse strings:

> Let him give on till he can give no more,
> The Thrifty Sanhedrin shall keep him poor:
> And every Sheckle which he can receive,
> Shall cost a Limb of his Prerogative.
>
> (389-92)

The parsimony and concomitant love of money of the Parliamentary forces will become a significant point of attack for Dryden's satire as the poem continues. But here Achitophel makes one more appeal to the natural law. In trying to make Absalom suspicious and fearful of his father's motives, the tempter exhorts the young man to resort to "Self-defence [which] is Natures Eldest Law" (458).

Finally Achitophel, saving the best for last, presents an argument perfectly suited to Absalom's character:

> And who can sound the depth of *David's* Soul?
> Perhaps his fear, his kindness may Controul.
> He fears his Brother, though he loves his Son,
> For plighted Vows too late to be undone.
> If so, by Force he wishes to be gain'd,
> Like womens Leachery, to seem Constrain'd:
> Doubt not, but when he most affects the Frown,
> Commit a pleasing Rape upon the Crown.
>
> (467-74)

This is a tissue of bad suppositions, but ones carefully calculated to prevail. David's mildness does indeed suggest to his enemies that he is fearful, and so why should he not fear his brother (James) who is, after all, consistently portrayed as an ogre by Achitophel and his partisans? The simile, rightfully distressing to feminists, is nonetheless perfect to capture the hot-blooded youth. He is a would-be rapist, if not a confirmed one, and his lust after the crown would make it seem an appropriate object of his advances. The perverse sexuality of Absalom thus comes to the fore as his essential characteristic. This tainted sexuality colors even the lines that follow:

> Secure his [David's] Person to secure your Cause;
> They who possess the Prince, possess the Laws.
>
> (475-76)

Aside from the shocking suggestion that David can be susceptible to Absalom's sex appeal, these lines communicate the view that personal influence, however demeaned and demeaning, is superior to the law. That, of course, is Achitophel's perverse belief. As equivocal in sex as Absalom is lusty, Achitophel always looks to pervert whatever challenges his power. Since to him nothing is sacred and everything is manipulable, his temptation speeches embody these monstrous assumptions. The idea of possessing the crown by means of sex (Absalom identifies rape with love) "With *Absalom's* Mild nature suited best" (478). If we take the meaning of these lines seriously, fail to overlook his "warm excesses" (37), and believe that "*Amnon's* Murther" (39) refers to something in Monmouth's past as well as in Absalom's, the two lines which follow cannot be read literally:

> Unblam'd of Life, (Ambition set aside,)
> Not stain'd with Cruelty, nor puft with Pride. . . .
>
> (479-80)

Perhaps there is some irony here, but the tendency to overlook sexual transgressions in David probably extends to his son as well. Absalom has the overt sexual nature of his father, and as the son of his father likewise enjoys the indulgence of David's supporters.

After adding a further explanation of Absalom's character and a call to lament his transgression rather than accuse (486), more details of the rebels are presented. Here the buying and selling motif, mentioned earlier, is developed further. Here also the outworn anti-Semitic identification of the Jews with usury and mercantilism is used to satirize the enemies of David:

> The next for Interest sought t'embroil the State,
> To sell their Duty at a dearer rate;
> And make their *Jewish* Markets of the Throne,
> Pretending publick Good, to serve their own.
> Others thought Kings an useless heavy Load,
> Who Cost too much, and did too little Good.
> These were for laying Honest *David* by,
> On Principles of pure good Husbandry.
>
> (501-8)

Puritans and dissenters, united in their opposition to David, reduce everything to thrift. Duty, which should be freely and willingly done, is sold to the highest bidder. These are the ancestors of the contemporary weapons manufacturers who encourage wars, the better to sell their merchandise.

Anti-Puritan satire continues as the rabblement

> Resum'd their Cant, and with a Zealous Cry,
> Pursu'd their old belov'd Theocracy:
> Where Sanhedrin and Priest inslav'd the Nation,
> And justifi'd their Spoils by Inspiration;
> For who so fit for Reign as *Aaron*'s Race,
> If once Dominion they could found in Grace?
>
> (521-26)

"Cant," "Zealous cry," "Theocracy," "Inspiration," and "Grace" are all contemptuous references to the dissenter tendencies of David's opponents. The final term, "Grace," picks up a significant theme mentioned earlier. Grace, in various forms, from Absalom's grace of motion and David's kingly grace to the strictly theological concept, has thematic significance in the poem. Here the dissenters seek to rule under the aegis of their idea of grace. Already we have seen that Absalom is attracted to the kingship because of his natural qualities. It is clear at this point in the poem that Absalom seeks to rule by right of nature; the dissenting mob, by right of grace.

Dryden goes on to score a direct hit by characterizing the Puritan concept of predestination and free grace. In doing this he facetiously unites the concepts of nature and grace:

> These, out of meer instinct, they knew not why,
> Ador'd their fathers God and Property:
> And, by the same blind benefit of Fate,
> The Devil and the *Jebusite* did hate:
> Born to be sav'd, even in their own despight;
> Because they could not help believing right.
>
> (535-40)

Thus grace comes naturally to the rabble whether deserved or not. With them everything comes and goes by instinct, including grace. We may recall that "By natural Instinct they change their Lord" (219).

Interesting and effective as this part of the poem may be, it is inevitable that we think of it as a narrative transition between the remarkable temptation of Absalom and the brilliant character-portraits of Zimri, Shimei, and Corah. At this point it becomes clear just how important it is to note the generic shifts in the poem. First, there is the narrative or historical account by which the essential themes are set. This includes establishing the relationship between Absalom and David as well as limited characterizations of both. The mob is presented in historical relief so that its tendencies and character can be evaluated.

This combination of narrative and characterization leads us directly into the first of the great character-portraits: that of Achitophel himself. Once we understand his character, we are ready to see him in action, and the dialogue (consisting mainly of long rhetorical speeches) between him and Absalom, the key to Absalom's resolution to act, is presented.

The portrait of Zimri embodies its essential theme in two discrete concepts. The first is that Zimri is so mercurial that his character is in constant transition, never static, and therefore practically indescribable. A figure in perpetual movement can never focus on a single end. Although he is unlike the other plotters in his incapacity for plot, he reflects the instability of the mob. This inability to effect evil makes him essentially harmless:

> A man so various, that he seem'd to be
> Not one, but all Mankinds Epitome.
>
> (545-46)

By running through the diapason of human characteristics, Zimri retains a certain humanity which the other plotters manage to dispense with. Nonetheless, governed by the changeable moon, Zimri eludes definition as he assumes the roles of "Chymist, Fidler, States-Man, and Buffoon" (549-50). In a constant state of metamorphosis, by assuming all roles, he defines himself in none. This mercurial quality he shares with the satirist-panegyrist:

> Rayling and praising were his usual Theams;
> And both (to shew his Judgment) in
>   Extreams . . .
>
> (555-56)

This inclination toward excess (which strongly marks the plot itself, 110), however, is precisely what the judicious narrator of the poem seeks to avoid. Like Mac Flecknoe, Zimri lacks the ability to accomplish his ends. This makes him essentially a comic figure whom laughter follows everywhere:

> Begger'd by Fools, whom still he found too late:
> He had his Jest, and they had his Estate.
> He laught himself from Court . . .
>
> (561-63)

But also, like Mac Flecknoe, Zimri possesses a second trait. Contrasting with his comic ineffectuality is his felonious heart. He is "wicked but in will, of means bereft" (567). As such he remains a curiously amphibean creature who lives for evil but can never achieve it.

That Zimri is evil and therefore perverse, Dryden leaves no doubt. But his role as satiric butt arises more from his association with the plot than from any success as a plotter. As inconsequential traitor, he seems as giddy and volatile as the Jews of the poem. And he is like them in yet another respect: By his variousness he becomes a one-man crowd.

With the portrait of Shimei, Dryden focuses on a much more dangerous opponent of the king. Shimei is presented as a miser in both public life and private. He is therefore the opposite of the generous David. Much worse is his activity in the law where he perverts justice in his role as judge:

His Hand a Vare of Justice did uphold;
His Neck was loaded with a Chain of Gold.
During his Office, Treason was no Crime;
The sons of *Belial* had a glorious Time. . . .
(595-98)

His badges of justice reflect only his love of wealth and a desire to turn public office into private aggrandizement. His perversion of the legal system includes anything that will serve his "higher law":

If any durst his Factious Friends accuse,
He pact a Jury of dissenting *Jews:*
Whose fellow-feeling in the godly Cause,
Would free the suff'ring Saint from Humane
    Laws.
For Laws are only made to Punish those,
Who serve the King, and to protect his Foes.
(606-11)

Thus, in their supposed state of grace, the dissenter plotters can ignore the law. But the end they have in view is never religious; it always involves the filling of their coffers:

His business was, by Writing, to Persuade,
That Kings were Useless, and a Clog to
    Trade. . . .
(614-15)

Shimei's miserliness is further reflected in his inhospitality. The demonstration of this gives Dryden an opportunity to present a brief symposium:

And, that his noble Stile he might refine,
No *Rechabite* more shund the fumes of Wine.
Chast were his Cellars, and his Shrieval Board
The Grossness of a City Feast abhor'd:
His Cooks, with long disuse, their Trade forgot;
Cool was his Kitchen, tho his Brains were hot.
(616-21)

Thus the dinner never really comes off. The only cooking is in Shimei's brains, overheated with rebellion.

To sum up, Dryden unites the two major indictments against Shimei: his perversion of the law and his niggardliness:

And *Moses*'s Laws he held in more account,
For forty days of Fasting in the Mount.
(628-29)

In his account of Shimei Dryden stresses two major themes of the poem. As in the portrait of Zimri, Shimei epitomizes traits of the populace at large: venality and loudmouthed dissatisfaction with a lawful king.

With Corah we reach the nadir of the conspiracy and a high point of Dryden's satiric effort. The poetry communicates the paradox which Corah represents: lowborn, but "High as the Serpent of thy mettall made . . . " (634). Like the character-portrait of Shimei, the one of Corah develops two major themes: the perversion of the law and the Puritan tendencies of the plotters. Again, these two themes are united.

Corah's role as false witness is begun early and developed to a climax. He is, first, the "Arch-Attestor for the Publick

Good" (640). False testimony ironically dignifies his entire lineage:

Who ever ask'd the Witnesses high race,
Whose Oath with Martyrdom did *Stephen*
    grace?
(642-43)

The use of "grace" introduces yet another meaning of that word. It attests to the uses to which false oaths may be put and recalls with irony the theological concept of grace with which the dissenter plotters identify. This, indeed, is their achievement. No doubt the mention of the first martyr, Stephen, suggested to many a later martyr, King Charles I, whose decollation some prototypes of Oates were responsible for.

That Oates is identified with Puritans and dissenters is readily apparent. His is a "Saintlike Grace" (648), the word "Saint" referring, of course, to the dissenter opponents of the Church of England. He also speaks as a prophet (655) and is taken with visions (656). The perversion of judgment and law by lust after profit is made clear in the following lines:

Let *Israels* foes suspect his heav'nly call,
And rashly judge his writ Apocryphal;
Our Laws for such affronts have forfeits made:
He takes his life, who takes away his trade.
(664-67)

By identifying once again the Puritan vision with the perversion of law and the advancement of mercenary motives, Dryden intensifies his satire. The vulgarity and obscenity of false witness and unjust denunciation emanate directly from Corah's perverse religious principles:

His Zeal to heav'n, made him his Prince despise,
And load his person with indignities:
But Zeal peculiar priviledg affords;
Indulging latitude to deeds and words.
And *Corah* might for *Agag*'s murther call,
In terms as course as *Samuel* us'd to *Saul*.
(672-76)

Corah, then, stands erect, the monumental brass who perverts deeds and words totally. But most important, as a perjurer he stands as a living rebuke to justice itself. The stinging final line of Corah's character-portrait, "For *witness* is a Common Name to all" (681), sums up his contribution. He has transformed the name of witness, whether to an alleged crime or the truth of God's word, to a reproach. In doing so, he has erected a monument of himself to all that is evil in human affairs. He has truly become a monumental brass. Corah's judicial record, as well as that of Shimei, serves as a foil to the concluding judicial resolution of the poem.

Dryden takes us next from character-portrait to Absalom's rhetorical foray. True to his mild nature, the natural son of David speaks "with a kind compassionating look, / And sighs, bespeaking pity" (694-95). His short speech is framed to elicit sympathy, and so it does, but not entirely on its own merits:

Youth, Beauty, Graceful Action, seldom
    fail:
But Common Interest always will prevail:

99

And pity never Ceases to be shown
To him who makes the peoples wrongs his own.
                                   (723-26)

After a short account of Monmouth's success with the people, the narrator delivers a warning, followed by a closely reasoned argument denying the right of the people to decide who their king should be. The argument is that laws must have precedence over the will of the people and the arbitrary sway of any monarch:

And Laws are vain, by which we Right enjoy,
If Kings unquestioned can those laws destroy.
                                   (763-64)

If such a disregard for law is allowed, only one outcome is possible:

. . . Government it self at length must fall
To Natures state; where all have Right to all.
                                   (793-94)

Here Dryden expresses horror at a Hobbesian state of nature; but the use of the word nature also recalls the association of Absalom and the dissenting rebels with that concept. Thus the point is made that if Absalom, Achitophel, and their accomplices are successful, there will be a return to nature in the Hobbesian sense. That is, all distinctions of right and property will give way to the primitive struggle for survival. The speaker in the poem contemplates the destruction of society's fabric:

To change Foundations, cast the Frame anew,
Is work for Rebels who base Ends pursue:
At once Divine and Humane Laws controul;
And mend the Parts by ruine of the Whole.
                                   (805-8)

The important word "base" is resonant with many aspects of the evil of conspiracy. Rebellion's new foundation and frame are tempered, so to speak, with the baseness of Absalom's birth and the even baser metal of Corah. Each conspirator pursues his own base end to the destruction of the whole. At this, the lowest point of the narrative, David seems impotent and, paradoxically, ineffectually mired in his own goodness:

Now what Relief can Righteous *David* bring?
How Fatall 'tis to be too good a King!
                                   (811-12)

But at this moment there is a formal shift in the poem to a new voice, not heard clearly until now. It is the voice of panegyric which is to give an account of those who support David and the monarchical cause: "Some let me name, and Naming is to praise" (816).

The litany of praise begins with Barzillai. Since this is the only fully developed portrait of praise, Dryden might well have been tempted to establish some parallels with the earlier character-portrait of Achitophel. This would seem to be the case. Achitophel was presented in an extended maritime metaphor:

A daring Pilot in extremity;
Pleas'd with the Danger, when the Waves went
    high
He sought the Storms; but for a Calm unfit,

Would Steer too nigh the Sands, to boast his
    Wit.
                                   (159-62)

Barzillai is presented with relation to some water imagery too, but with an entirely different result:

Long since, the rising Rebells he withstood
In Regions Waste, beyond the *Jordans* Flood:
Unfortunately Brave to buoy the State;
But sinking underneath his Masters Fate. . . .
                                   (819-22)

More striking is the comparison of sons. Achitophel's son is alive, but barely so. The boy is

. . . that unfeather'd, two Leg'd thing, a Son:
Got, while his Soul did hudled Notions try;
And born a shapeless Lump, like Anarchy.
                                   (170-72)

Barzillai's son is unfortunately dead, but he lives in Dryden's elegiac offering:

His Eldest Hope, with every Grace adorn'd,
By me (so Heav'n will have it) always Mourn'd,
And always honour'd, snatcht in Manhoods
    prime
By'unequal Fates, and Providences crime:
Yet not before the Goal of Honour won,
All parts fulfill'd of Subject and of Son;
Swift was the Race, but short the Time to run.
Oh Narrow Circle, but of Pow'r Divine,
Scanted in Space, but perfect in thy Line!
                                   (831-39)

Unlike Achitophel's boy, Barzillai's son is adorned with grace, yet an additional meaning for that key word in this poem, but one that resonates with the other meanings. Unlike the shapeless lump, Barzillai's child fulfills all aspects of being subject and son. He is "perfect" in his line. Another extraordinary irony is that Achitophel's living son, who may endure the anarchy of his life for years to come, is treated in a mere three lines. Barzillai's son, on the other hand, who lived a scanted life, is immortalized in a full twenty-three lines, by which Dryden offsets, in traditional elegiac form, the "crime" of Providence:

By Sea, by Land, thy Matchless Worth was
    known;
Arms thy Delight, and War was all thy Own:
Thy force, Infus'd, the fainting *Tyrians* prop'd:
And Haughty *Pharaoh* found his Fortune
    stop'd.
Oh Ancient Honour, Oh Unconquer'd Hand,
Whom Foes unpunish'd never coud withstand!
But *Israel* was unworthy of thy Name;
Short is the date of all Immoderate Fame.
It looks as Heaven our Ruine had design'd,
And durst not trust thy Fortune and thy Mind.
Now, free from Earth, thy disencumbred Soul
Mounts up, and leaves behind the Clouds and
    Starry Pole:
From thence thy kindred legions mayst thou
    bring
To aid the guardian Angel of thy King.
                                   (840-53)

The elegant ascendance of the alexandrine (851) may suggest, with only a slight adjustment of the basic iambic pentameter, the line variation of classical elegiacs. In this part of the poem, Dryden moves easily from panegyric to elegy, and back to panegyric again.

The next panegyrical character-portraits are of Zadoc the priest and the Sagan of Jerusalem. The first parallels certain aspects of Shimei's portrait earlier in the poem. Unlike Shimei, who accepts high office as a reward for his hatred to Charles, Zadoc shuns both power and position. The Sagan of Jerusalem's "hospitable Soul" (867) may remind us of Shimei's inhospitable kitchen. The "heavenly eloquence" (869) of John Dolben, "Him of the Western dome," (868) is the antithesis of Shimei's foul curses. In general the cultural attitudes of David's supporters are the opposite of those belonging to Achitophel's followers. By such deliberate patterning, the structure of the poem is strengthened.

David's party is characterized by "Pillars of the Laws, / Who best cou'd plead and best can judge a Cause" (874-75). Jotham embodies the powers of deliberation in public assemblies (884) and Amiel ruled with reason the deliberations of the Sanhedrin (902-3). These details once again show the importance that Dryden attributes to rhetorically related skills.

The climax and conclusion of the poem comes with David's speech, which Godfrey Davies, [in "The Conclusion of Dryden's *Absalom and Achitophel*," *Huntington Library Quarterly* 10, 1946-1947], proved was based on Charles' "Declaration." Although the incorporation of some principal elements of Charles' speech in the poem had obvious political utility, the conclusion has been condemned for lack of artistry, by critics from Johnson on. These objections can be dismissed, I believe, when the relationship of David's speech to the key terms we have been examining is made clear.

In the course of the poem, we have seen a trend toward disregard for law emerge. Those who defend the rights of a lawful king have seemed to fall from power along with their master. Nature and grace, both perversely misinterpreted, have taken the place of law, and, as a result, a catastrophe impends. The deliberative efforts of the plotters have also seemed to advance their cause despite the arguments of the narrator.

But true to the tradition of satire in which speech usually counts for more than action, David delivers a declaration that changes the probable course of action and resolves the central problem of the poem.

First David displays nature, rightly understood, by expressing his feelings for his son, Absalom. Even after Absalom's pretensions David shows fatherly affection by offering his son the opportunity of a pardon:

> With how few Tears a Pardon might be won
> From Nature, pleading for a Darling Son!
> (959-60)

The king, however, makes it clear that his natural feelings are not to be mistaken for weakness. He is prepared to act with severity, and will do so if the circumstances require it. In specifying the source of Absalom's aberration, David points to the two remaining key concepts in the poem:

> Whence comes it that Religion and the Laws
> Should more be *Absalom*'s than *David*'s Cause?
> His old Instructor, e're he lost his Place,
> Was never thought indu'd with so much Grace.
> (969-72)

Absalom's attempt, under the guidance of Achitophel, to make a case for his own succession is an obvious perversion of the law. In addition, another meaning of "grace" is put forward in line 972. The significance of this is that only the grace which is properly David's is sufficient to uphold religion and law. Since Achitophel was manifestly inadequate, from the point of view of grace, to uphold religion and law, it is clear that his pupil will fare no better. The concept of insufficiency of grace refers also to the theological meaning discussesd earlier. David possesses grace of every kind, whether it be that which comes from God or that which informs his kingly bearing. The plotters, on the other hand, lack all grace, theological or social.

Finally, therefore, it is the law that comes to the fore. David puts aside his natural feelings and, like the judge he becomes in the passage, prepares to pass sentence on the criminals before him:

> Must I at length the Sword of Justice draw?
> Oh curst Effects of necessary Law!
> (1002-3)

> Law they require, let Law then shew her Face;
> They coud not be content to look on Grace,
> Her hinder parts, but with a daring Eye
> To tempt the terror of her Front, and Dye.
> (1006-10)

This passage, which most commentators have found difficult, makes sense within the thematic pattern I have been describing. The image here is of Law as a gorgon. Those who rely on David's God-given grace, that is, who obey and accept the king as mediator, will never have to suffer the penalty of Law, i.e., look it directly in the face as they suffer the supreme penalty. David's grace consisted in his generosity and moderation of the laws. Those who were not content with David's mediating role, having willed to thrust the king aside, must now confront the reality of law without the protection of that gracious mediator. Such grace as David has comes from God, of course, but it is real grace, not the false concept to which the dissenters make pretense. In David true grace is personal, social, and theological. It has a comprehensiveness extending to all aspects of human existence and far beyond the narrow ideology of the plotters.

What is important to see is that in this final speech David has emerged as judge, representing the will of God. The sword of justice is poised above the plotters' heads, and with the iteration of the word "law," the fact that we have been witnesses to a trial becomes abundantly clear. The arguments of the narrator have been those of a prosecuting attorney. The treacherous dialogue between Absalom and Achitophel has been presented to condemn them. We have been allowed to look into the motives of the plotters to assess their religious, political, and, indeed, their cultural deficiencies. As jurymen and women, we are forced to render a guilty verdict. The deliberations of the early part of the poem have become increasingly judicial as the question of law emerges into prominence. Dryden, as he has done so often, turns upside down whatever biblical pattern may be found in the narrative. Grace is found inadequate to the plotters, who make their claim to be especially entitled to grace. Saint Paul claimed that with Christ the covenant of law—the old Hebrew law—had been replaced by the new covenant of grace. But Dryden reverses the process. Finding the dissenting populace and its plotting leaders unworthy of grace, and therefore unworthy of the very Christianity they profess, Dryden, in an extraordinary tour de force, returns the covenant of law to the place of preeminence it held among the ancient Hebrews. Since the English dissenters have, like the Jews, made their own calf of gold—Monmouth—and rejected God's lawful representative—David—they are entitled to the same harsh punishment that an angry Old Testament God often meted out. In that sense, then, if in no other, the parallel between England and ancient Israel holds good. The English who have denied their king have turned themselves into Jews and as such merit the harsh penalties of Hebrew Law.

Even as the covenants are reversed, however, there remains the hope that penalties will not have to be exacted. In that hope, a retiring David transforms to the assertive Charles, a Christian king, who stresses repentance and forgiveness. Although judge and jury have returned a verdict, the sentence cannot as yet be carried out. Thus *Absalom and Achitophel* poises on the edge of final judgment, holding back, as it were, the full force of the covenant of law until all pleas for repentance have gone unheeded.

If repentance does come to the plotters, it will signal a transformation which has been an important theme in the poem from the beginning. The giddy Jews, misguided by Puritan enthusiasm, wish for a world governed by natural law. Achitophel, by means of Miltonic allusion, becomes Satan; Absalom, convinced by specious arguments from nature, abandons filial duty for treasonous intrigue; Zimri, becoming everything, remains nothing; and Oates variously assumes the shapes of "monumental brass," serpent, comet, and—quintessentially—false witness.

The multiplicity of genres, the threat of destruction to the state, and the transformations of the main characters under the influence of ridicule or panegyric are evidence for the poem's identity as a generic satire. The elaborate thematic pattern of nature, grace, and law reveals not just an immediate political purpose, but a strong cultural bias. Dryden's "panegyrical imagination" shapes a tradition as well as an apology for the Stuarts and the royalist cause. Against the background of this ancient order, the grasping, hypocritical, and perverse modernity of the dissenters is seen as a direct threat to a major value system:

> 'Gainst Form and Order they their Power employ;
> Nothing to Build and all things to Destroy.
> (531-32)

Their deforming might, bent on destruction, can only be neutralized by an even stronger commitment to tradition on the part of Charles and his retainers. *Absalom and Achitophel,* a satire of epic scope, by a demonstrated dedica-

tion to tradition, transforms instability to peace in a comprehensive interpretation of history, human nature, and the role of civilization. (pp. 71-99)

> Leon Guilhamet, "Dryden," in his Satire and the Transformation of Genre, *University of Pennsylvania Press, 1987, pp. 71-99.*

Jack M. Armistead   (essay date 1988)

[*In the following excerpt, Armistead identifies Dryden's references to occult symbols and traditions as a powerful dramatic device in his* Tyrannick Love.]

Dryden's second full-scale heroic play (or third, depending on whether you count his collaboration on *The Indian Queen*) is of special interest because of its marked employment of magic and demonology. *Tyrannick Love* was produced in June 1669 and first published in 1670; two years later a second edition contained an expanded preface to answer critics who had ridiculed, among other elements, the seemingly gratuitous display of occult lore. Until the last ten years, all important accounts of the play, following Walter Scott's [in his introduction to *The Works of John Dryden,* 1808], shared this penchant for dismissing the scenes of prophecy and conjuration as fashionable window dressing, part of the music and spectacle that were expected by the audience but were irrelevant to plot or theme.

In [his book *Dryden's Heroic Plays,* 1981], the first serious effort, though a brief one, to read the spirits back into the play, Derek Hughes has understood them as "actors" who, like Maximin, "are themselves slaves of the transient" and thus belong within his "drama within drama." More recently, [in her work *A Mirror to Nature,* 1986] Rose A. Zimbardo has interpreted the daemons and their supervising angel as a "poetic metaphor" for the play's central movement upward from mundane to spiritual heroism and love. It seems to me that each of these readings has merit: Maximin is to some extent mirrored in the occult scene, and the scene does function metaphorically within the play. Neither Hughes nor Zimbardo, however, considers that Act 4, scene 1 is part of a larger occult dimension that includes the prophecy in 1.1, the angelic intervention in 5.1, and Maximin's use of the terminology of magic throughout the play. When these elements are analyzed alongside the rest, I would argue, they suggest that Dryden was using the occult to better purpose than has yet been maintained. He was building on previous experience to make a comment on the relation between history and Providence and thus to enrich the contextual design of the play.

That it has such a design has, in fact, never been demonstrated, so that I shall have to make that case as well. Zimbardo is the first critic to operate on the assumption that the play is, indeed, well unified, though her aim is to deal only with its general movement. Before her analysis appeared, even sympathetic commentators considered it a derivative rush-job in which the various elements of plot and idea do not hang together: Dryden, after all, admitted to spending only "seven weeks" in composing it, and most of the plot can be found in previous plays or romances, if not in historical or legendary sources. But what if Dryden's haste reflected an effort to be timely? And what if, as Maximillian E. Novak suggests [in volume 10 of his edition of *The Works of John Dryden,* 1970], Dryden was consciously shaping his sources in order to editorialize about Restoration trends and events. If so, his dramatic design is more complex than we have thus far suspected; it embodies the aesthetic and intellectual wholeness that Zimbardo remarks upon, but it also becomes a paradigm for Restoration culture at a crucial moment.

I am not claiming that we fail to perceive this complex structure before we understand its occult features. On the other hand, they do provide an authoritative guide, because they constitute Dryden's most original contribution to the traditional story. Although the St. Catherine legend in both prose and dramatic versions includes the miraculous intervention of angels to destroy the instruments of torture and to carry the saint's body to heaven or Mount Sinai (or both), none of the known sources invokes necromancy and the conjuring of daemons as Dryden does. I will argue that to understand this essentially new material is to gain a clearer picture of the play's construction.

But let us begin with what can be surmised without the occult "chorus." Notwithstanding [Arthur Kirsch's assumption, in *Dryden's Heroic Drama,* 1965] that the martyrdom of St. Catherine would not have appealed to the Restoration, in fact Dryden could hardly have chosen a fitter vehicle if, as Novak suggests, one of his purposes was to compliment Catherine of Braganza in public. During 1668-69 she was twice rumored to be pregnant and twice reported to have miscarried of the heir that Charles II never was able to sire. Thus at this time, as Novak puts it, "a compliment to the Queen . . . was very much in order." Jacob Huysmans had paid such a compliment in 1664 by painting her as St. Catherine of Alexandria, and this painting may be alluded to in Placidius's account of the vision in 1.2.100-08. But Dryden need not have been thinking either of this painting or of the martyrdom of Dorothea in *The Virgin Martyr.* Since the Middle Ages, St. Catherine had been one of the most popular female saints in both England and Continental Europe, and after the Reformation she claimed both Protestant and Catholic sympathies. [As Anna Brownell Jameson wrote in her *Sacred and Legendary Art,* 1896, she] was considered "the inspirer of wisdom and good counsel in time of need," the patroness of intellect, learning, eloquence, courageous piety, and chastity. In England, where her story was told in print several times before Dryden took it up, she was celebrated in murals and panels, stained glass, ivories, and the names of churches and colleges—the latter including St. Catherine College, Cambridge.

For an alert Restoration audience, then, the symbolic value of St. Catherine's story at this time would have been great. It would have helped to counterbalance disappointment over Catherine of Braganza's miscarriages, since one of St. Catherine's chief attributes was her transcendence of sexuality: as Queen of Egypt she had refused to marry for the purpose of producing an heir and later, in a dream, she had become the bride of Christ. In another way the implicit comparison of the two Catherines was more daring. Like her namesake, the English Queen was a living

contradiction of the libertine materialism and secularism that flourished in the court. Novak, Bruce King [in his *Dryden's Major Plays,* 1966], and Anne Barbeau Gardiner [in her *The Intellectual Design of John Dryden's Heroic Plays,* 1970] have shown that St. Catherine's legendary triumph over fifty philosophers is transformed by Dryden into a series of confrontations in which Catherine, voicing a Latitudinarian fusion of reason and faith, prevails over representatives of the most fashionable philosophical systems in the Restoration: Stoicism (Apollonius), Epicureanism (Placidius), and Hobbism (Maximin).

Derek Hughes has argued, wrongly in my estimation, that Dryden's Catherine is not in any way normative, that her self-centered isolation from human suffering depicts an attitude that is as unsavory as Maximin's opposite kind of extremism. Yet as Hughes undermines Catherine's arguments for refusing succor to Berenice in 4.1, he ignores the initial and most general explanation for her decisions: "As some to witness truth Heav'ns call obey; / So some on Earth must, to confirm it, stay" (4.1.462-64). Catherine distinguishes between her own martyrdom, Providentially ordained, she believes, to promote the Christian faith, and Berenice's destiny to "stay" on earth to confirm that faith. Dryden's emphasis on this distinction is underlined by his providing for the heroic rescue of Berenice by Porphyrius after both have become Christians—an action that significantly alters the received legend, in which these two converts are cruelly executed: "I have taken from the Church two Martyrs," says Dryden in his Preface to the play, "in the persons of Porphyrius and the Empress."

The philosophical significance of Berenice and Porphyrius is well described by Barbeau: they embody the norms of religious toleration, balanced polity, controlled passion, and, finally, trust that they are helping to realize a Providential design. But both also constitute allusions to Restoration court life. Berenice suggests certain aspects of Catherine of Aragon not implicit in the portrait of St. Catherine: her tolerance for the monarch's philandering and her invulnerability to the suggestion of divorce. Of course, like both St. Catherine and Catherine of Aragon, she embraces an alien religion and fails to conceive an heir.

The contemporary significance of Porphyrius is perhaps clearer, since in his dedicatory epistle Dryden implies a comparison with James, Duke of Monmouth. By 1669, along with rumors that Charles II might divorce his barren queen, there was already talk of legitimizing Monmouth as the Protestant heir to the throne. It would have been easy for a Restoration audience to interpret the actions of Porphyrius in the final scene as an advisory to Monmouth foreshadowing the more explicit one to be offered twelve years later in ***Absalom and Achitophel.*** Urged by his army to accept the role of Roman Emperor, Porphyrius advocates allegiance to the "Two Emperours at *Rome* the Senate chose" (5.1.661) and elects for himself a life of love and service. So, implies Dryden, should Monmouth: he should resist the temptation offered by those who would overturn fate by contriving to have him declared a legitimate heir. Like Porphyrius, he should accept his divinely-ordained role of heroic servant to the state.

Within the Providential dispensation, then, Porphyrius

and Berenice join Catherine as Dryden's "patterns of piety" who are "equally removed from the extremes of Superstition and Prophaneness." Both Hughes and, before him, [Michael W. Alssid in his *Dryden's Rhymed Heroic Tragedies,* 1974] identify these extremes with Catherine and Maximin respectively, but I think they are only half correct: "Prophaneness" would immediately have been understood in the seventeenth century as a reference to the blasphemous irreverence of Maximin, but the word "superstition," as it was used in the Restoration, would have pointed not to Catherine's otherworldly faith but rather to the "false, pagan, or idolotrous religion" (*OED*) of a Placidius, perhaps even to the outmoded Pagan heroism and platonism of Charinus and Valeria respectively, both of whom are invested with a religious fervor. When Maximin himself uses the word "superstition" (1.1.162), he speaks of Catherine and the other Christians, but Dryden's contrast between Catherine and Maximin is not that between a superstitious zealot and a materialistic power-monger; it is that between the extremes of self-negating faith and of self-centered will. It can also be seen as a contrast between one who finds herself within God's drama and one who tries to impose his own scenario on reality.

The minor characters of Charinus, Valeria, Apollonius, and Felicia all seem to represent either outmoded or misplaced forms of passion; they become martyrs to "tyrannic love" of different sorts and thus help to fill out the implications of Dryden's theme. The historical son of Maximin was murdered along with his father, but Dryden's Charinus articulates the ideals of pagan heroism, which seem to die with him in battle as he competes with Porphyrius for the Emperor's favor. Maximin's daughter Valeria has no historical equivalent; as Kirsch first pointed out, she descends from the "self-sacrificing lovers of Cavalier drama." Her entire being is invested in Porphyrius, and she dies a suicide, a martyr to pure, unrequited love. The other two minor martyrs, Apollonius and Felicia, represent the love of truth and maternal love, respectively. Although both die as Christians, the one must first recognize that the truth of Stoicism has been displaced by that of the new faith, and the other struggles to conquer the tyrannical force of maternal love before being led to execution.

Beyond their formal significance, these minor characters also seem to reflect upon Restoration England. Charinus and Valeria embody forms of heroism and love that were widely felt to have been left behind along with the severed head of Charles I. Apollonius seems to suggest the unhappy fate of Christian philosophy in the increasingly libertine court of Charles II, just as Dryden laments the possible damning of his "godly out-of-fashion Play" (Epilogue, 1.22) by the wits in his audience. Perhaps Felicia is a comment on the potential loss of reverence for elders and family ties in that same atmosphere, though, of course, she also serves within the play as Catherine's greatest temptation to forego martyrdom.

Let us now try to place Maximin within these contexts. In his Preface Dryden complains that one of his sources, the anonymous *Le Martyre de Sainte Catherine* (published 1649), "betrayed" him "into an Errour . . . by mistaking

that first Maximin for a second." On the one hand, he has given his antagonist the personal background, physical stature, unflinching cruelty, and anti-patrician sentiments of the earlier Maximin (AD 235-38), the first emperor to come from barbarian stock and the first to rise from the military ranks. Likewise, in the course of the play he alludes to persons and events associated only with the earlier Maximin's reign, and he sets the play near the besieged town of Aquileia, where the first Maximin was murdered by his soldiers. Although this Maximin was widely believed to have inaugurated a new era of persecutions, the martyrdom of Catherine was always associated with "the Great Persecution" begun in Africa about AD 303 by Diocletian's co-Emperor, the later Maximin. In effect, then, whether inadvertently or not, Dryden has moved the legendary martyrdom of St. Catherine back about seventy years.

Why? He seems not to have wanted his audience to think of Maximin's death in the way that Eusebius and subsequent historians understood the fall of Diocletian's colleague: as marking the Edict of Milan and the triumph of Christianity through Constantine. Instead, he invests the death of his tyrant with something like the same significance as the death of Zempoalla in *The Indian Queen.* Both make way for a Christian order that is destined to emerge not immediately, but sometime in the future. Of course, the analogy breaks down at this point. While Montezuma and Orazia become proto-Christian rulers, and thus augur well, Porphyrius and Berenice leave political power to the co-rulers elected by the Roman Senate. Historically, these elected Augusti soon fell victim to a military revolt, and for the rest of the century the empire degenerated as one after another soldier-tyrant assumed the imperial robes, claimed divine status, and attempted to dominate.

Seen in this light, the play reads as a piece of cautionary advice. Maximin's story, says Dryden, should be ranked with those biblical examples of wickedness that are "set as Sea-marks for those who behold them to avoid." For an English Restoration audience, "Those" would surely refer to Charles II and his supporters, and they are being asked to observe what can happen if a monarch does not resist the recurrent trends toward materialism, lust, power politics, and absolute rule. In 1668 and 1669, frustrated by the inconclusive efforts to defeat the Dutch and reestablish England's empire over sea trade, distressed about the fall of Clarendon, disappointed by the barrenness of his queen, Charles increasingly found solace among his mistresses and libertine courtiers, and became increasingly cynical about the prospects of cooperation with Parliament. The logical extreme of these tendencies is exhibited in Maximin's rejection of his barren but pious queen, his lust for another woman, and his determination to impose his will on the Roman Senate.

Responding to Maximin's initiatives, the other characters act out options that were being entertained in 1668-69: the wishfulfillment dream of romantic heroism (Charinus), the absurd revival of Caroline platonism (Valeria), the vogue of pagan philosophies (Apollonius and Placidius), the temptations of materialism and hedonism (Placidius), the Whigs' desire to legitimize Monmouth (the soldiers and Porphyrius). These private scenarios, however, are shown in contrast to the less self-indulgent courses chosen by Dryden's "patterns of piety," which also have topical implications. Porphyrius and Berenice depict the kind of virtuous accommodation to Providence that Dryden perceives in Catherine of Aragon and recommends to Monmouth. If their Providential role is to survive and represent virtue in a vicious age, Saint Catherine's equally Providential role, perhaps reflecting another trait of Charles II's queen, is to complete God's drama of martyrdom, figuring forth the full power of His will.

Let us now examine the occult material to see if it sharpens our perception of the emerging design. One of the first things we notice is that, as usual, Dryden's dramatization of the invisible world is more sophisticated than what his audience might have seen in other English plays between 1667 and 1669. Only two employed the occult in an important way. John Caryl's *The English Princess, or, the Death of Richard the III*, performed in March 1667, reworks Shakespeare by returning to "plain Hollinshead and downright Stow." Several of its characters sense that they are playing a key role in the designs of Providence, and the language of magic is used metaphorically throughout, as when the king tells Catesby that he is "well read in that mysterious Art" of dissembling (1.3.6-7). At one point the Priour of Lichfield, acting a part equivalent to that of Placidius at the beginning of Dryden's play, announces that his study of prophecies by "the wise *Gildas*" indicates that the Earl of Richmond and Princess Elizabeth will start a glorious line of monarchs whose continuance is eclipsed by an infernal "Tempest" (the civil wars) and "black" deed (the execution of Charles I). Then "a Prince [Charles II] will rise" to embody the highest virtues of his dynasty and, by overcoming domestic and foreign foes, will make England the "center of his Power" (3.6.32-34). Of course, Richard is confronted in a dream by the ghosts of his former victims, and he dies professing his atheism and cursing fate on Bosworth Field. The Epilogue comments that when the play ends the audience becomes king and should avoid tyranny, for "Commonwealths of Tyrants are much worse" than Richard. In a general way, perhaps this play helped prepare the Restoration audience for **Tyrannick Love**, in that both allude to Restoration England, use prophecy and occult terminology to explore tensions between love and power, and ground the action on a belief in Providential design.

It may be, as Novak believes, that the 1668 revival of Dekker and Massinger's *Virgin Martyr* contributed little to Dryden's composition of **Tyrannick Love**. Nevertheless, the marked similarities between the two plays make it instructive for us to compare them. Both are set in the Roman Empire during a period of persecution—in the Dekker/Massinger play, the Great Persecution sponsored by Diocletian and the later Maximin (beginning AD 303)—and the main action is framed and partly interpreted by metaphysical episodes involving spirit life. Dorothea, the female martyr in the earlier play, has an unrequited lover in Antoninus, son of the Governor of Caesaria, and he in turn fails to return the love of Artemia, daughter of Diocletian. Like Catherine, Dorothea is supported by an angel as she confounds pagans, materialists, and torturers before finally being executed.

These similarities do not go very deep, however, and at the level of ideas and symbolic construction Dryden's play is easily the more interesting. Dekker and Massinger's materialists are the comic hedonists, Hircius and Spungius, a pimp and drunkard respectively, neither of whom is strongly committed to his philosophy in the way that Maximin or Placidius is. Unworthy of Dorothea's intellectual steel, they are bribed and scolded like naughty children. The philosophy of Theophilus and his daughters, unlike that of their equivalents in Dryden's play, Apollonius and Placidius, is practically without theoretical coherence, an undifferentiated mix of Mithraism and Graeco-Roman polytheism fueled by the pseudo-epicurean pursuit of pleasure. To defeat these pagans, Dorothea has only to declare the viciousness of their gods and arrange a miracle. The supernatural features in Dekker and Massinger are one-dimensional: Harpax, a devil who incites Theophilus to persecute Christians, shrinks from the presence of Angelo, an angel in the guise of Dorothea's page, who represents divine truth and care.

In contrast to Dekker and Massinger, Dryden vastly complicates the metaphysical dimension by employing not angels and devils but an angel and legions of middle spirits, elemental daemons of the sort described by Paracelsus, Agrippa, Henry More, and the Abbe de Villars. Novak has identified the chief source for these spirits in "A Discourse concerning the Nature and Substance of Devils and Spirits," appended to the third edition of Reginald Scot's *The Discovery of Witchcraft* (1665), but of course Dryden had already used similar beings in his earlier plays, so that a new source indicates only that he continued to read and think about demonology. Indeed, he implies as much in his Preface: "what I have said of Astral or Aerial Spirits . . . is . . . taken from those who have written on that Subject." Although his employment of these beings has more in common with *The Injur'd Princess* than with *The Virgin Martyr*, in that they become an indirect means of commenting on Restoration England, their true progenitors are the magicians and daemons of Dryden's own earlier plays.

Yet both the description of the invisible world and the ritual used to invoke its inhabitants are more fully described here than in the previous works. Early in the play a theatrical tableau is conjured up by the necromancer, Nigrinus, who employs "holy words" to invoke a "Scene of Fate" performed by "Ghosts" outside his "Magick Circle." Later, like Ismeron and the High Priest in **The Indian Queene** and **The Indian Emperour**, Nigrinus is charged to use the full "pow'r" of his "Art" (4.1.11, 2) to generate love in the hearts of Catherine and Valeria. He chooses the "*Venus* hour" and "wexing Moon," describes his "Chalk . . . Circle," and censes the air with a carefully formulated fumigant (4.1.28-38). The spirits are "Astral forms . . . , / Fram'd all of purest Atoms of the Air," and they are morally neutral, though "most subservient to bad Spirits will" (4.1.15-18). "Next man in ignorance and sin" (4.1.180), they have passions, live in social hierarchies, and engage in romantic and military pursuits (4.1.56-72).

One immediately notices that these third-century Roman ghosts and spirits behave very much as did their counterparts in Dryden's first heroic plays, even though the Indian versions were derived from very different sources (with the possible exception of Henry More): classical religion and myth, and histories of early America. Like Ismeron and the High Priest, Nigrinus commands an "earthy Fiend" but considers him inappropriate to consult about such "light intents" as love (4.1.14); instead, like his predecessors, he invokes aeriel spirits (4.1.15-16), only to discover that they, like their Indian cousins, have no power to generate love and only a limited ability to foretell the future of a relationship. Damilcar pronounces the fate of Maximin's love for Catherine and that of Placidius for Valeria "In double sense, and twi-light truth" (4.1.201-02). The sensuous dream that she inspires in Catherine, unlike that of Zempoalla, is not sent by God to shadow forth truth but is designed to promote the libertine version of the Epicurean pleasure principle:

> Love and Time with reverence use,
> Treat 'em like a parting friend:
> Nor the golden gifts refuse
> Which in youth sincere they send:
> For each year their price is more,
> And they less simple than before.
>
> [4.1.137-42]

The project fails for the same reason that the aerial spirits lose power in the American plays: the Christian deity sends Catherine's guardian angel, Amariel, to chase away the dream spirits with his flaming sword, just as in *The Indian Emperour* "A God more strong" overwhelms the Indian deities. As before, Dryden affirms elemental or disembodied spirits and preserves a role for them within the incipient Christian order. He endows both the ghostly prophecy in Act 1 and Damilcar's predictions in Act 4 with full validity: Charinus dies in battle; Catherine resists temptation and gains her martyr's crown; Valeria finally asks Placidius to help her and, for one moment before her suicide, gives her hand "while I have life" (5.1.560); and the multiple deaths in the final act do free Maximin from the bonds of love. Accordingly, Dryden sees to it that Amariel banishes Damilcar and her crew not to hell or oblivion but rather to continuing duties among the natural elements (4.1.163-70).

The relation between these occult phenomena and the main action is more carefully worked out in *Tyrannick Love* than it was in the earlier plays. In fact, Act 4, scene 1 serves as a kind of code for Dryden's overall design. Like Porphyrius and Berenice, Damilcar and Nakar have to reconcile their love for each other with the need "to perform what the man will have done" (4.1.73) and the need to serve a larger empire. The "man" is Nigrinus, the magician, who is like Maximin in his failed effort to manipulate earthly forces but unlike him in recognizing that "No charms prevail against the Christians God" (4.1.200). The empire that Damilcar and Nakar serve is that of the natural world, and its elemental strife not only mirrors the political and military strife within the Roman empire but suggests that both are to be understood in the same way: as a Providentially ordained pattern of change whose dynamics are driven by love in its various forms.

Intelligent beings within either "empire" can respond to the promptings of love by humbly discovering or pursuing their ordained roles (as do Catherine, Felicia, Apollonius, Berenice, and Porphyrius), by attempting to control the course of events (Maximin), or by persisting in some outmoded manner of thought or behavior (Charinus, Valeria, and Placidius). At the occult level, these conflicting options are resolved comically. The egotistical sorcerer, Nigrinus, experiences a Christian revelation, while the aerial spirits, whose powerful roles as pagan daemons have been superceded, are reprimanded and brought within the new dispensation by a superior daemon, the angel Amariel. At the mundane level, however, the various unstable elements interact tragically and move Rome into a protracted phase of violence and disorder. Under the Christian Providence, neither dictatorial strongmen nor their recruits from the invisible world control the course of change; they have been displaced by the higher magic of love.

These worlds, the comically occult and the tragically visible, are linked not only by analogy but also through language and character. Maximin's idiom expresses the exercise of sovereignty over social and political reality as a kind of magic. Like Zempoalla, he deals with life as if it were simply a game of power played on a purely natural stage; he sees himself as a dominating magician, superior to the "Christian Sorceress" (2.1.251) in his knowledge of the "Secrets of Empire" (4.1.249). At one point, he leaps beyond this vision and identifies himself as "The Spirit of the World" itself, diffused through "every mind" (4.1.303) and controlling the "little Fates" (4.1.305) of all other beings.

The concept is Platonic and Stoic, but knowledgeable members of the audience would have perceived two fallacies in Maximin's use of it. First, he invokes it to justify the lawless exercise of his will, whereas the original Platonic notion of *anima mundi* presumed that the world soul realized its intelligence in a lawful fashion, by introducing "into the time-space continuum the perfect order of the godhead's paradigm" [S. K. Heninger, Jr., *Touches of Sweet Harmony,* 1974]. Secondly, Maximin thinks of the world soul as having free will, a notion that is contradicted not only by the ancient doctrine but also by Henry More's recent advocacy of a Christianized version of it: More's spirit of nature is [according to E. A. Burtt's *The Metaphysical Foundations of Modern Physical Science,* 1932] "the immediate plastic agent of God through which his will is fulfilled in the material world. . . . it possesses life, but not . . . reason, or free will." In trying to emphasize his own self-sufficiency, then, Maximin unwittingly uses occult language that reduces his role to that of a mindless force of God. As Catherine would put it, he is controlled by a "pow'r" that he does not "see" (5.1.334).

The visible and occult worlds are also linked through an important character, Placidius. Placidius is a "power-seeker" only in the sense that he believes in the two kinds of magic that the play equates: the human power of Maximin and the occult mysteries of Nigrinus. Both types claim control over material elements of the world and, unrecognized by Placidius, both types are superseded by the magic of love. At the start, like any Restoration courtier, he is confident of his value as advisor to the Emperor and of his essentially Epicurean philosophy. He is equally confident in the power of magic. Though these perspectives were often at war in the seventeenth century, they also tended to converge in some of the important thinkers of Dryden's day—thinkers such as Henry More, who repeatedly argued for the coexistence of spiritual and mechanical aspects of the natural order; Robert Boyle, who embraced atomism even as he contemplated the "inestimable multitude of spiritual beings" in the universe; Walter Charleton, who passed through a neoplatonic phase on his way to Christianizing the Epicuran philosophy; and Elias Ashmole who, like Newton, intensely pursued occult interests while actively promoting the Royal Society.

What all of these men shared, a guiding faith in Christianity, is of course exactly what Placidius lacks. His refusal, perhaps inability, to interpret both materialism and the occult in light of the new faith makes him unable to decipher the Providential meaning of events that seem to be conspiring against him. He feels "forc'd by Fate" (5.1.27), betrayed by "Love and good Nature" (5.1.136), but like Zempoalla and Montezuma he cannot perceive these as benign influences on his civilization. Like them he dies violently, though not by his own hand. Despite his Epicurean commitment to pleasure through self-control, he is increasingly driven by the passions of jealousy and revenge, until at the last he and Maximin destroy each other in a rhetorical ecstasy of primitive emotion. Just as Maximin can be seen as a message to Charles II, so Placidius can be understood as Dryden's warning against a fashionable attitude of mind in Charles's court. Through negative example, perhaps he also affirms the Christian endeavors of the Mores, Boyles, and Charletons.

Never had Dryden so carefully integrated the occult episodes with the main plot, and never had topical issues been so widely diffused through the play's design. In *The Indian Queen* and *The Indian Emperour,* he had suggested parallels between patterns of change in early America, early Christian Europe, and Restoration England, and in doing so he had reconciled popular notions of Indian occultism with both modern and ancient European ideas. In *The Tempest,* though the sense of change through time is muted by an ahistorical setting, he had adjusted the Shakespearean paradigm to reflect the Restoration consciousness of modernity, of the displacing of absolutist rule and mystery by a more cooperative leadership and a more empirical and pragmatic understanding of issues.

Tyrannick Love takes more liberties with received history than did the American plays, as if Dryden were shaping his materials toward the tightness of structure that he had achieved in *The Tempest,* yet he wished also to invest the play with some sort of historical validity. As the newly appointed Poet Laureate, he seems to have felt some urgency about commenting on the drift of current events, which he must have seen as the first serious threats to Restoration stability: the Dutch wars, Clarendon's fall, the Queen's barrenness, Whig plans for legitimizing Monmouth, the King's libertinism and impatience with constitutional rule. He was not yet ready to draw the kind of

overt parallels that he and Lee would attempt in *The Duke of Guise* (1682), but some sort of editorializing must have seemed in order.

That he regarded the occult as an important aid in this kind of enterprise, rather than as mere entertainment or embellishment, is clearly demonstrated in the American plays and *The Tempest,* where magicians and daemons deepen and enrich meaning. Although his prose of this period indicates skepticism about the empirical reality of spirit life and the efficacy of magic, it also shows an abiding fascination with these matters. Indeed, to judge from his poetry he was at this time refining, rather than losing, his interest in occultism. Just as in *The Tempest* the prideful sorcery of Dryden's Prospero gives way to a more "scientific" approach to invisible forces, so in *Annus Mirabilis* the king is depicted as a loving natural magician instead of an isolated wizard, and in poems about art during the 1660s the Druidical bard becomes a natural magician whose artful control of words corresponds to God's handling of corpuscular reality and the king's governance of society.

In this latest variation on the theme, Dryden depicts a world that has just moved beyond the pagan phase of power and mystery without fully recognizing what has occurred. Its emperors and thinkers will for a time continue the tradition of absolutism, materialism, and sorcery without the cosmic support required for enduring success. They do not see that love, the highest magic of the Christian God, has transformed the Roman civilization, and until this dawns on them, all their efforts to restore order and prosperity, like Maximin's efforts to satisfy his personal desires, will be "vain experiments" (4.1.398). Surely, Dryden was hoping that the lesson would not be lost on the court of Charles II. (pp. 367-83)

Jack M. Armistead, "Dryden and the Occult as Dramatic Code: 'Tyrannick Love'," in Papers on Language & Literature, *Vol. 24, No. 4, Fall, 1988, pp. 367-83.*

James Engell   (essay date 1989)

[*In the following excerpt, Engell discusses Dryden's literary views, emphasizing his enduring importance and relevance as a critic, and observing that in judging works of literature "Dryden successfully uses criteria of human interest, experience, motivation, and, above all, delight and amusement."*]

Few critics in any literature have achieved the scope and suppleness, the accessibility and relevance, of Dryden. He synthesizes varied approaches: mimetic, generic, structural, linguistic, and cultural. Yet he combines these without letting any single approach—or its specific vocabulary—get in the way of others. Rarely cluttering or obscuring basic appeals of literature, he embodies a totality of immediate, informed response. His energy turns to technical issues of craft, while also reflecting problematic ideals of a living, not an academic, civilization. In this sense he stands with Dante, Chaucer, and Spenser or, following his own century, with Voltaire, Lessing, and Goethe—in recent generations with James, Eliot, Bakhtin, and Frye.

The latter end of last week, I had the honour of a visit from my Cousine your Mother, & my Cousin Dorothy, with which I very much comforted: within this Moneth, there will be playd for my profit, an old play of Fletchers, calld the pilgrim corrected by my good friend Mr Vanbrook; to which I have added A New Masque; & am to write a New prologue & Epilogue for the same tragedy, calld the Revolt of Capoua, will be playd At Betterton's House within this fortnight. I am out with that Company, & therefore if I can help it, will not read it before tis Acted; though the Authour much desires I should. do not think I will refuse a present from fair hands, for I am resolvd to save my Bacon. I beg your pardon, for this slovenly letter, but I have not health to transcribe it. My service to my Cousin your Brother who I hear is happy in your Company, which He is not, who most desires it, & who is, Madam,

         Your most obligd, Obedient
         Servant

            John Dryden.

Thursday, April the 11
     1700.

Second page of Dryden's last surviving letter, to his young cousin Mrs. Elizabeth Steward, in which he mentions The Secular Masque.

Of all European critics writing before 1700, Dryden is the most forward-looking and retains power to engage us. In one voice he is Neander—the new man—who refreshes our views more than do Boileau, Casaubon, the Scaligers, Vida, or even Corneille. Compared to contemporaries such as Rymer, who was no poet, Dryden's theoretical statements, like water, seek their own practical level. He combines his undogmatic theory with practice, wringing energy and tension from the two. He will tack and then beat to the wind. Although Dryden's practice as a critic is the subject of this [essay], it is inseparable from his practice as a poet. As Hegel notes in the *Aesthetics,* both a theoretical bent and practical execution "are bound together in the genuine artist."

Some recent studies indicate that Dryden's criticism derives from continental theory, others that his prefaces bolster English or personal traits of composition. This only reveals how dialectical and various his criticism really is. A classicist and a *comparatiste,* instrumental in bringing French criticism to English letters, he encourages selective introduction of continental theory while simultaneously confronting figures who shape English poetry: Chaucer, Shakespeare, Jonson, and Milton. Dryden also knows that much of what is good in English criticism during his own lifetime has come from France, and he acts as the transfer agent.

Yet it is misleading to see Dryden as the champion of an already established national tradition; it is better to say he conceives one—not as a manifesto—but continually over his career. As Eric Rothstein urges [in his *Restoration and Eighteenth-century Poetry,* 1981], Dryden and his contemporaries are "the inventors of 'English Literature' " and fulfill the desire of the English Renaissance for a vernacular, independent canon backed by literary principles. Envisioning a more capacious and informed tradition, Dryden draws liberally from classical authors, French and Italian critics, and the English past. His achievement is a mosaic fitted together over forty years. If he becomes a coffeehouse arbiter, it is because he spent hours at his desk in the Long Acre house and later, as Pope told Spence, on the ground floor in Gerrard Street. There is hardly one kind of literature he fails to touch and, as Johnson's epitaph says of Goldsmith, does not grace by touching it. And, as Johnson praises Dryden, "perhaps no nation ever produced a writer that enriched his language with such variety of models"—drama and dramatic criticism, translation, lyric, narrative, and meditative verse, comments on genre, and several types of discursive prose. "Variety of models" describes his critical stance, too.

Wearing Virgil's armor more comfortably than Swift pictures him in *The Battle of the Books,* Dryden expresses his love of classical literature through useful reference and translations. His awareness of the past never drags him into stale nostalgia; he remains open to the educative and formative functions of criticism, realizing that readers and writers are not like the younger Pitt, on whom Macaulay, echoing Coleridge, passed the admiring but ultimately negative verdict that Pitt did not grow but was "cast." Literature, asserts Taine, lives only through the individuals it animates and changes. Similarly, Erich Auerbach contends that "what we understand and love in a work is a human existence, a possibility of 'modifications' within ourselves." And although it may be impossible to define such changes or modifications, they are not random. Dryden never loses sight of Aristotle's first observation in the *Poetics:* humans are animals who imitate. Life and art are linked—both ways, as Wilde pointed out two centuries later—by our drive to imitate and, in the process, to fashion ourselves. Dryden speaks of a "just and lively image of human nature" and prefers to see living "character" and "life-touches" in a work. One danger now is that Dryden will be seen with a literal mind: distant in time, a figure in "the history of criticism" providing raw ideas that others refine. That view has fractional truth, but his ability to hold many approaches in solution makes him particularly appealing. He speaks of "character" in a work, and his own shines through his criticism. Johnson notes how in Dryden's prose we sense inevitable ease and timelessness. Congreve says his friend's writing seemed, like gold, incorruptible, an image Eliot echoes when he speaks of Dryden's "uncorruptible sincerity of word."

Taken singly, Dryden's observations prove insufficient for understanding his critical response. If he is inconsistent and contradicts himself, the same applies to Hazlitt or even Johnson, who changed his mind as the decades passed. Systematic consistency seems no more valid a criterion of criticism than of art. Dryden proceeds by accretion, assimilation, comparison, and re-comparison, by a friendly tug-of-war between practice and theory. He has the method of an artisan. Working with refractory materials, he realizes that "method," once mastered, must often be modified or abandoned. For him the critical precepts of the ancients were drawn first from practice. In the preface to *Aeneis* (1697), he refers to "those many rules of imitating nature which Aristotle drew from Homer's *Iliads* and *Odysseys,* and which he fitted to the drama."

My concern is with the relevant strategies Dryden uses to maneuver between theory and practice, critical and creative acts: how he retains integrity without losing pluralism. Part of his attraction is that he brings criticism out of the scholar's closet. Although Pope and others note that Dryden in person was not "conversible," and that his acquaintance and conversation were limited mostly to literary topics and figures, he lived in the world of affairs and fits his criticism for a generally educated—not a specialized—audience. He does this without sacrificing either depth of thought or delight of expression. Auden says poets wish to be read by the rich, the beautiful, and the powerful, when in fact they are more generally read by the pimply boy sitting alone in a corner of the school cafeteria. Dryden succeeds in winning an audience of wide cultural influence. His criticism still seems to talk to us, participating in a world where we do not need an expert's passport to travel.

In large part Dryden pilots English criticism out from its "dead water" to "a vast ocean." Near the end of his career, he describes the disorientation he felt at the beginning: "As I may say, before the use of the loadstone, or knowledge of the compass, I was sailing in a vast ocean, without other help, than the polestar of the Ancients, and the rules of the French stage amongst the Moderns, which are extremely different from ours, by reason of their opposite taste." Faced with a mixed, comparatively thin heritage of English criticism, little of it systematic, yet with strong English poets ranging back more than 250 years, Dryden and his contemporaries could simultaneously feel attracted to, but distanced from, the organized criticism practiced on the Continent. Ironically, the Interregnum eventually increased the impact of French thought on English culture. If Charles returned directly from Netherlands soil, his court brought French ideas. True, "the rules of the French" were "extremely different from ours," but the appeal was that such rules could exist—and could improve poetry (as they did Dryden's poems of the 1680s). English literature could then find its own principles, something, at any rate, to calm and order the growing chaos Pope would envision as a force that "buries all." The Restoration seemed an ideal time to shape a strengthened poetic practice according to systematic criteria drawn from the classics and the learned spirit of French intellectual criticism—and thus for the first time publicly to yoke critical theory with poetic (and critical) practice. Dryden remarks in his dedication of the *Aeneis* that, "Impartially speaking, the French are as much better critics than the English as they are worse poets." Could one not legitimately strive for the best of both worlds?

Dryden's "method" of discourse, the way he combines theoretical ideas and a practical eye, is a gift we are in danger of losing from lack of practice. It is tempting, though not quite accurate, to apply to him a phrase that Burke, in the *Speech on American Taxation,* uses in a different context: "consistent in theory and valuable in practice." Yet in Dryden's case it would likewise be false to say "*in*consistent in theory" and let the matter drop. The truth lies in a degree of play present between the compass of theory and the rudder of practice. Perhaps it is not far-fetched here to see Descartes as a presence. The *Discourse on Method,* and rationalist philosophy in general, helped to pressure literary criticism into a posture where it felt more eager than ever to generate and defend "method." Hence Rapin's famous reply, echoed by Pope, that critical rules "Are Nature still, but Nature methodiz'd." The perpetual drift of some critics toward a "scientific" approach reenacts this tendency. Dryden genuinely appreciates the new science, but realizes it can form no template for criticism. He quips that Hobbes's version of Homer was "bald" (it is), and said in the **"Preface to Fables"** that Hobbes studied "poetry as he did mathematics, when it was too late." But Dryden read Hobbes and Descartes carefully. Like those English critics more exposed to science than their peers—Johnson, Coleridge, Shelley, Emerson, Richards—Dryden knew science could not provide a strict pattern for literature. He sensed the temptation of it, and the irony as well. For literature and criticism do need to borrow materials and intellectual perspective from technical fields; letters must take cognizance of science. Yet too often it is a high-school understanding of science that leads to an "imitation" of it in criticism. Those who have done scientific research see up close that "method" is a fluid, exasperating, often plural set of procedures and assumptions difficult to define even for a restricted subarea. Those who read in the history and philosophy of science are unenthusiastic about something as large and diverse as "scientific method" becoming a model for criticism.

Most of Dryden's critical efforts are prefatory. They explain, defend, or comment on his poetry or translations. He writes in an easy tone of semiformal but personal address, or in the series of familiar addresses, which form the *Essay on Dramatic Poesy.* "It is all," Bonamy Dobrée notes [in his *Dryden's Mind and Art,* edited by Bruce King, 1969], "beautifully conversational . . . he is talking to, not at, the addressee of the essay." We might quibble over an exact characterization of such prose, but it is universally admired, as Mark Van Doren long ago pointed out. In addition, this use of the preface was, Johnson notes [in his *Lives of the Poets,* edited by George Birbeck Hill, 1905], "a kind of learning then almost new in the English language." Dryden is a critic who shares. He shares as he moves from one point to another, providing a reader the courtesy of making his points as clear as one would do for the sake of a friend. And in sharing he hovers between talking as a reader and responding as a writer—and so do we. In Dryden's prefaces the audience and artist, reader and critic, critic and scholar, are dissolved in dialogue. This is disciplined conversation; and in that sense it is dialogic criticism.

Reflecting on Dryden's "negligent" method of preface and personal address (to patron, friend, or fellow artist), we can see how vitally it unites theory and practice. Other examples are well known: Horace's *Ars Poetica* to Piso, Longinus' *On the Sublime,* which is addressed to a friend or group of artists, Corneille's three *Discours,* Davenant's Preface along with Hobbes's reply, and naturally the 1800 Preface to the *Lyrical Ballads.* Constantly using the modern shorter title of Johnson's *Lives,* we tend to forget they were originally *Prefaces, Biographical and Critical, to the Works of the English Poets,* first printed as introductions to separate volumes of each poet's work.

The prefatory method, often similar to the verse epistle, remains a dominant mode of critical discourse from *Joseph Andrews* and Johnson's edition of Shakespeare through Arnold's 1853 Preface, the exquisite pieces of Henry James and Conrad, and Wilde's underrated preface to *Dorian Gray.* That flawed masterpiece the *Biographia Literaria* began specifically as a preface to *Sibylline Leaves,* and Coleridge intended to defend and to correct Wordsworth's Preface to the *Lyrical Ballads.* (Coleridge even insisted that a type face identical to Wordsworth's Preface be used). Then, as Coleridge enlarged his "preface," he planned it as a companion volume to the poems; it grew into a separate work. Letters from a rich body of criticism: Voltaire, Rilke, Keats, Byron, Wilson—these are often personal, individual, one reader to another, and hence speak universally. Goethe's *Conversations with Eckermann* presents another case of method that follows the discourse found at the heart of a literate, civilized community: speaking to one another about what we read.

Discussing catachresis, but in a remark taking on greater scope, Dryden has Eugenius say, "that wit is best conveyed to us in the most easy language; and is most to be admired when a great thought comes dressed in words so commonly received that it is understood by the meanest apprehensions, as the best meat is easily digested." This is the precept under which Dryden conducts criticism, and a lesson we often miss. What he says of Cleveland [in *Of Dramatic Poesy*], in line with his bias in favor of a more natural, passionate language, could be applied to many academic styles: "we cannot read . . . without making a face at it, as if every word were a pill to swallow." We are fed "many times a hard nut to break our teeth, without a kernel for our pains." Anticipating Johnson's aversion to mere bookishness, Dryden touches on the masquerade of academic discourse when he describes Ben Jonson's Truewit as "a scholar-like kind of man, a gentleman with an allay of pedantry, a man who seems mortified to the world by too much reading. The best of his discourse is drawn not from the knowledge of the town, but books. And, in short, he would be a fine gentleman in an university." We would be less than honest if we failed to admit that Dryden voices this implicit rebuke. Of course the style of criticism is immeasurably important. Goldsmith notes in *The Bee* that Dryden's pen "formed the Congreves, the Priors, and the Addisons . . . and had it not been for Dryden, we never should have known a Pope." He goes on to add that "Dryden's excellencies, as a writer, were not confined to poetry alone. There is in his prose writings an ease and elegance that have never yet been so well united in works of taste or criticism."

Dryden's critical achievement includes the prologues and epilogues to his plays. [As Edward Pechter noted in his 1975 work *Dryden's Classical Theory of Literature,* they] run in verse "a course parallel to the essays in many ways." In these short poems we hear direct address to the audience, an utterance acutely aware of—and attempting to influence or to humor—reader response. There could be no more compact resolution of theory and practice in verse criticism. Dryden also exposes the sinews and ligaments that connect social behavior with the stage, and cultural values with literature and language at large. With the frank and open address, the lack of affectation and literary posing (things he elsewhere indulges in), the rapid jabs at—and alternatre complicities with—the reader, then the scolding of crude "popular" tastes, these poems and their varied tones might remind us of *Don Juan,* as Byron was reminded by them. Taken as a separable body of work, the prologues and epilogues form one of the finest examples in English of the conscious, articulated relation of a poet to all levels of his audience. They reveal how much Dryden felt he had to please the most uninformed taste, and how much he calculated to elevate and refine it.

A rough measure of the shift in Anglo-American criticism is that, in the 1930s, T. S. Eliot could speak explicitly of Dryden as a theorist and of his propensity "to theorise," while thirty-five years later, in his introduction for the Regents Critical Series, Arthur Kirsch stresses the pragmatic side of Dryden's prefaces and essays. In light of an increased theoretical orientation of English criticism, beginning with Wellek and Warren's *Theory of Literature* in 1949, Dryden now appears less theoretical than he once did. Unless we seek attention through discourse and opinions that are determinedly outlandish, or unless, like the Wizard of Oz, we mystify our audience more than our sub-

ject requires, no controversial reassessment of Dryden's criticism seems likely. Though many of its judgments have been questioned or rejected, the last complete revaluation of him is in Saintsbury's *English Men of Letters* volume more than a century ago (1881). Interesting views and fresh connections have been uncovered, but no revolution is likely to shake our attitude toward Dryden as a critic.

However, Dryden holds principles and interests that qualify him as a broker of theory. We may speak about his idea of the delight or pleasure of the text, of his dialogic foreshadowing of Bakhtin, especially on the subject of Menippean satire, of his interest in the nature of literary genre and structural principles. Theoretical concerns arise when we observe that Dryden is among the first English writers to understand, at least implicitly, the conditions imposed on a literature that is primarily printed and read—that is, written as well as heard—where books and writing are the main instruments of transmission. In the preface to **Annus Mirabilis** he reverts to a "School distinction" (in the way Kant would use terms coined by the schoolmen). Dryden revives the distinction between "wit written" and "wit writing." Yet his application has, I believe, connections with what is now referred to as "arche-writing." In addition, Dryden pays attention to at least two other issues of language and structure that have haunted English criticism since the Renaissance: poetic diction (the language of poetry seen in contrast to the language of prose), and especially the desire for a more "natural" language.

Of all Dryden's works in verse or prose, the most familiar are **Absalom and Achitophel** and **Mac Flecknoe,** which are anthologized with greatest frequency. As soon as historical pointers are given and a few words glossed, the poems become accessible even to a reader only vaguely aware of political and literary intrigues in Restoration England. Now it is just these two poems of his own that Dryden classifies as Varronian or Menippean satire, placing them in that genre along with Apuleius' *Golden Ass,* Erasmus' *Praise of Folly,* and Spenser's *Mother Hubbard's Tale.* In his exploration of literary "kinds," perhaps his comments on this genre or mode—the satiric, the style of which, as he is quick to point out, is multileveled and various—retain most relevance. We should include Dryden's prologues and epilogues here, for they are best seen as satiric in nature, much in the sense Dryden calls Chaucer of *The Canterbury Tales* a satirist. Dryden's own account of Menippean or varied satire bears striking resemblances to twentieth-century commentary, especially to that of Mikhail Bakhtin in *The Dialogic Imagination.*

Although Dryden contends that "an Heroic Poem is certainly the greatest work of human nature," and then compares the heroic to the epic and tragic, concluding that the heroic exceeds them because it "forms a hero," his longest essay on any genre is the **Discourse concerning the Original and Progress of Satire.** This preface, admittedly with its share of padding and flattery to the Earl of Dorset, runs about one hundred pages, longer than the famous **Essay on Dramatic Poesy** published twenty-five years earlier in 1668. It is here, in the **Discourse concerning Satire,** that Dryden explores Menippean or Varronian satire. Before examining the implications of his position in this essay, let us consider parallels with Bakhtin who, though employing a somewhat different vocabulary, covers the same territory in his essay "Epic and Novel."

In looking at the roots of the novel, Bakhtin takes up the whole nature of seriocomic writing, or what the ancients called *spoudogeloion.* Here, he says, "belong Roman satire (Lucilius, Horace, Persius, Juvenal) . . . and finally Menippean satire (as a genre) and dialogues of the Lucianic type." These are precisely the subjects and writers whom Dryden treats in his essay. The idea of the Menippean satire, according to Bakhtin, is "to put to the test and to expose ideas and ideologues," which is what occurs in a poem such as *Absalom and Achitophel.* For him, this genre grasps "the 'todayness' of the day" and emphasizes it "in all its randomness." For Dryden, in a similar vein, this genre arises from "chance and jollity," and includes characters about whom "stories . . . were told . . . in bakehouses and barbers' shops." Dryden calls it "a sort of *ex tempore* poetry" or "their clownish extemporary way of jeering" and connects it with the speaking, raillery, and verbal sparring of individuals caught up in celebrations and feasts, especially the saturnalia. For him the origin is carnivalesque. So, too, for Bakhtin, a direct connection exists with the saturnalia, and the "central hero of the genre," typified first by Socrates, is "a speaking and conversing man." Thus, both critics link the genre with the historical and social setting of the carnivalesque, and Dryden, by way of translating a paragraph from Dacier, also links Socrates with the central figure or archetype of this kind of satire.

Perhaps the closest parallel comes in an insistence that this kind of literature, which Bakhtin explicity identifies as the forerunner of the modern novel, contains a variety of styles, a series of voices, a "dialogized story" that is "full of parodies and travesties, multistyled." For Dryden, too, such variety is the key element. As Bakhtin sees "heteroglossia" as characteristic of these texts, Dryden points to the "mixture" of verses encountered in such satire: "And if variety be of absolute necessity . . . yet it may arise naturally . . . in the several subordinate branches of it [satire], all relating to the chief. It may be illustrated according with variety of examples in the subdivisions of it, and with as many precepts as there are members of it; which, altogether, may complete that *olla,* or hotchpotch, which is properly a satire."

We should not push the parallels between Dryden and Bakhtin so far that we forget, first of all, that it would be quite natural for them to come to similar conclusions when looking at the same satiric dialogues by the same writers. Second, Dryden was leaning on those Renaissance scholars who had preceded him, just as Bakhtin was immersed in literary history. And third, Dryden does not speculate about the novel or novelistic form. In many places we could find appropriate parallels to the idea of dialogue in poetry and in criticism. Plato and, more recently, Martin Buber come to mind. A suggestive statement [made by Ludwig Feuerbach in his *Grundsätze der Philosophie der Zukunft* ("Principles of a Philosophy of the Future"), 1967] connects the larger philosophical process of dialectic with that of dialogue: "The true dialectic is not

a monologue of the solitary thinker with himself, it is a dialogue between I and Thou."

Still, though Dryden does not have the terms "dialogic" and "heteroglossia" (instead, "dialogue," "mixture," and "variety" were at hand), several ideas of the two critics move together in emphasis and outlook. Even while arguing for the final, fluid irreducibility of Bakhtin's terms and concepts, two of his best English-speaking commentators [Katerina Clark and Michael Holquist, in their *Mikhail Bakhtin,* 1984] connect "heteroglossia" and "polyphony" with "his several attempts to find a single name for *variety,*" sheer variety in literary voice, language, and perspective. The spirit of mixture, of what Bakhtin calls "novelness," emerges in the *Discourse concerning Satire.* At one point Dryden is commenting on Boileau's *Lutrin.* It combines, he says, "the majesty of the heroic, finely *mixed* with the venom of *the other.*" Dryden applies the highest aesthetic and moral terms to this form of writing which is, after all, not tragic nor heroic nor epic: "This, I think, my Lord, to be the most beautiful, and most noble kind of satire." Here we might recall how Dryden, though giving the two etymologies for "satire" and Isaac Casaubon's arguments for distinguishing them, sees some value in the one from "satura," a Roman dish filled with a variety of fruit. It could be argued that in Dryden's time "variety" meant not primarily the quality of variousness but more a change or succession. However, the definition Johnson gives includes "intermixture," and I believe it is this intermixing quality that Dryden and others, especially novelists who constantly use the term "variety" to defend the genre in their prefaces, have in mind.

It is tempting to think of Dryden, writing in the last decade of his life, as turning more to the idea of dialogue, mixture, and variety typified by his theoretical view of Menippean satire and also by his own poetry. His later, more adroit and varied prologues and epilogues indicate this shift. So does *Absalom and Achitophel,* a poem affecting the last twenty years of his poetic practice and one in which Mark Van Doren [in his *Poetry of John Dryden,* 1920] says Dryden "realized at once that he had woven patches of verse which would wear like iron, and proceeded to acquaint himself with all the varieties of texture which the new weave would admit." Like Pope, he never writes the epic poem he hoped to achieve. And although he translates the *Aeneid,* his later critical work and "translations" also turn toward Chaucer and ancient fables. In this, Dryden responds to a sense that poetry and criticism are shifting to fresh scenes and an accompanying fresh investigation of the past. He may also be following his impulse for a narrative art that shows, in dramatic form, a full range of passion and the "life-touches" of action and emotion imitated with immediate directness. At any rate, Dryden orients his critical bearings more in this new direction during his last twenty years.

Bakhtin says "contemporary reality," with its direct gazes at "everyday life" and with the "living people" in their "diversity of speech and voice" before us in "a zone of crude contact, where we can grab at everything with our own hands," serves as the basis for the novelistic. We might equally turn with Dryden, in his **"Preface to Fa-**

bles," to his encounter with Chaucer's creations: "I see . . . all the Pilgrims in the *Canterbury Tales,* their humours, their features, and the very dress, as distinctly as if I had supped with them at the *Tabard* in Southwark." Dryden identifies Chaucer as "a satirical poet," though, more important, "he must have been a man of a most wonderful comprehensive nature" (as Shakespeare had a "comprehensive soul"). Dryden is recognizing in Chaucer these same qualities highlighted by Bakhtin's observations. The passage concerning the pilgrims is almost too famous to continue quoting—how Dryden praises "the matter and manner of their tales," how they "are so suited to their different educations, humours, and callings, that each of them would be improper in any other mouth." This is "heteroglossia" by an older name, but smells as sweet. "'Tis sufficient to say, according to the proverb," adds Dryden, with the right spirit for his subject, "that *here is God's plenty.*" The same impulse to admire the range of passion and voice in everyday life is behind Dryden's opinion of Shakespeare—as it is behind Johnson's of Shakespeare and Hazlitt's of Shakespeare and Chaucer.

Dryden obviously held "variety" as a conscious value throughout most of his career. Neander prefers English to French drama for several reasons; specifically, English plots "are fuller of variety." And it is no coincidence that Dryden stands near the chronological verge of the English novel. One of his young readers, who spent much time writing satires and dialogues for one party or another but in later years wrote his famous novels (or proto-novels), is Daniel Defoe. Significantly, two of the more eloquent, earlier defenses of the novel in English—the preface to *Joseph Andrews* and the apologia in *Northanger Abbey*—stress the novel's characteristic stamp of variety. Fielding's definition rests on this quality and, however familiar, is worth noting again: "Now, a comic romance is a comic epic-poem in prose; differing from comedy, as the serious epic from tragedy: its action being more extended and comprehensive; *containing a much larger circle of incidents, and introducing a greater variety of characters.*" Austen reemphasizes this hallmark in an aside that closes chapter five. Novels are works "in which the most thorough knowledge of human nature, the happiest delineation *of its varieties . . .* are conveyed to the world." From the start, the novel is associated with this quality. In his prefatory remarks Defoe assures readers of *Robinson Crusoe* that they will encounter "Wonders" of great "Variety."

Although T. S. Eliot's affinities with Dryden will be discussed later, let me interject here that *The Waste Land* may be read as the great modern Menippean satire, a poem of varied levels, of "fragments . . . shored," which Eliot originally entitled (even there borrowing from Dickens' *Our Mutual Friend*), "He do the police in different voices." The variety of styles and levels in much modernist writing casts that whole movement in a Menippean mode, for, unless we insist on a straitjacket definition, works such as *Ulysses, The Sound and the Fury,* Pound's *Cantos,* and novels such as Vonnegut's *Slaughterhouse Five* all rely on the technique of varied voices caught in juxtaposed immediacy. Faulkner originally wanted to use a variety of type faces and ink colors to capture the different voices in his

novel. Petronius, with whom Eliot finally, after Pound's editing, begins *The Waste Land,* represents an archetypal Menippean mode. And Dryden, with what Johnson calls his "variety of models," acts as a powerful center of gravity for Eliot throughout the 1920s.

In Dryden we have a critic who engages himself in dialogue with what he reads, whether Virgil, Bouhours, Chaucer, Shakespeare, or Oldham. He expresses interest in what is characteristic of an author, the "character" of a work and what he repeatedly calls an author's "turns" of thought—what makes a writer's voice distinct. The *Preface to Ovid's Epistles* outlines this attitude: "Nor must we understand the language only of the poet [to be translated], but his particular turn of thoughts and of expression, which are the characters that distinguish and, as it were, individuate him from all other writers." He sounds as if he were distinguishing characters in the dialogue of a play. This emphatically does not mean reducing a writer to anecdotes or biographical squibs, the kind of "character" Graham Greene justly deplores in the press's treatment of Evelyn Waugh. Dryden's term "character" is not what makes a celebrity, but rather features of style and thought that, taken in aggregate, uniquely establish the quality of an author's writing.

It is no accident that the scene of *Mac Flecknoe* is a stage, and that *Absalom and Achitophel* includes pronounced theatrical elements in speeches and characters. Though rarely noted, Dryden's major critical principles (imitation, pleasure, characteristic yet varied voices) are those we would expect of a practicing dramatist. His experience in the theater, his sense of audience, the critical comments in his prologues and epilogues, the fact that his first piece of criticism is in effect a small play about dramatic poetry—all these contribute to the dialogue and friendly confrontation encountered in his criticism. We find a connection with the novel here, too, for dialogue taken from the theater later sharpens the fiction of Fielding, and even Richardson explains to readers approaching *Clarissa* that his epistolary novel is actually "written in the Dialogue or Dramatic Way."

More than other English critics of his stature, early in his career Dryden is closely familiar with the theater. Eliot strives for it with success, but nearer the end of his last productive phase; Wilde earnestly achieves it in several instances, including the tone and method of *The Decay of Lying* (itself a dialogue play) and parts of *Dorian Gray.* Hazlitt loved verse tragedy above other genres and founded many of his critical bywords on it—imitation, passion, and nature. Fielding and Goldsmith exhibit the dramatic and speaking sense of criticism in brief, brilliant flashes. The criticism of these writers—Dryden first among them—reflects, in varying degrees, their sensibility and apprenticeship to the theater. They are critics in dialogue, or often capable of it, a manner essentially foreign to Johnson, Arnold, Pound, and even Coleridge. For instance, of all romantic critics who admire Edmund Burke, Hazlitt is particularly sensitive in commenting on the dramatic nature and structure of Burke's speeches and presence in the House of Commons.

It has become a commonplace—a correct one—to observe

how Dryden remains flexible within his standards and rules, how he rejects flat formulae (what Johnson in his *Life of Dryden* calls "theorems"), yet how he embraces principles by which to judge literature. One reason for this flexibility within classical bounds is his belief that poetry must be passionate, that truth to feeling—not a copy of action—but truth in the *"life-touches"* of art is not only important but fundamental, and must come first. This is what Dryden [in his **"Of Heroic Plays"**] chooses to paraphrase from Davenant on the subject of heroic poetry: *"That it ought to be dressed in a more familiar and easy shape; more fitted to the common actions and passions of human life . . . and figuring a more practicable virtue to us than was done by the Ancients or Moderns."*

Auden observes that Dryden avoids violent personal emotion except in some passages throughout the plays. The pervasive thrust, similar to Eliot's, aims at formal values and objectivity (the external, not necessarily the eternally true), a use and recasting of the past, plus a molding or shaping of emotional response into more intense and universalized expression. This has little to do with self-expression in the romantic sense, yet Dryden puts great weight on the value of feeling and emotion. This is not contrary to, but a part of his "formalism." Part of the structure—the most *necessary* part of it, in fact—is based on feeling. It is emotive.

At the end of **Heads of an Answer to Rymer,** Dryden notes that Rapin (in his *Réflexions sur la poétique d'Aristote,* 1674) "attributes more to the *dictio,* that is, to the words and discourses of a tragedy, than Aristotle had done." And Dryden closes the **Heads,** if we follow most editors' arrangement of its paragraphs, by quoting Rapin's "remarkable" words: " 'Tis not the admirable intrigue, the surprising events, the extraordinary incidents that make the beauty of a tragedy; 'tis the discourses when they are natural and passionate." But then, actually, there follows a short, final paragraph of three words referring to "natural and passionate" discourses in the tragedies of one poet: "So are Shakespeare's." In the **Heads** we hear this explicit theme many times. It is "new passions" and "all the passions in their turns" that create the excellence and individual stamp of modern, particularly English, tragedy. Dryden does not publish these observations, but they indicate, as they indicated to Johnson, who admired them, a premium on the direct and essential in feeling as a quality in poetic speech. The prime example held up is Shakespeare, who influenced English criticism more than any critic. Not plot nor "the justness of the occasion" give him his force, but "the raising of . . . passions . . . from the excellency of the words and thoughts." The extensive, published defence of passion, of a psychological depth of "anger, hatred, love, ambition, jealousy, revenge" that distinguishes characters themselves, comes in **"The Grounds of Criticism in Tragedy."** And, though Dryden begins his discussion with plot and manners, he concludes it with feeling—with Shakespeare again, if only because the essay is prefaced to an adapted **Troilus and Cressida** (1679).

Little more than sixty years after Shakespeare's death, Dryden takes a critical line that continues through the eighteenth century, strengthens in the Romantic period,

and remains emphatic: the power of expression and feeling in individual phrasing and parts of discourse. This becomes so embedded in English criticism that Arnold eventually warns against undue emphasis on it. Yet despite this warning, even Arnold's touchstones provide an emotional register of high seriousness. (It often goes unnoticed, even in sympathetic accounts, that his touchstones reverberate with sharply pitched *emotion* over life and death more than they do with any grandiose or "high"—in the sense of superior—code of ethics, philosophy, or morality.)

To some extent the New Criticism, and also Russian Formalism, the Prague Circle, French Structuralism, and deconstruction do not speak about human feelings with the direct intensity Dryden does. Modern formalism and textualism seem to harbor a certain timidity—or lack of felt acquaintance—in the face of what the eighteenth century calls the passions. At its basic level Dryden's sense of genre is the contrast between tragedy and comedy, which is in turn based on feelings of pleasure and pain—the states of consciousness—produced or elicited by actual reading. His formalism is oriented to the disciplining, sharpening, and intensifying of passion. (Is it too much to speculate that this is one origin of Eliot's stress on passion rather than on subjective, personal feeling?) But much modern formalism seems to have wrung emotion out or left it on the sidelines, a criticism sometimes more passionless than dispassionate. If a theory of literature becomes, in essence, schematic or classificatory, without regard to human feelings and values, then feeling and value, suffering and pleasure, will receive less attention in literature.

For Dryden a play is a *"just and lively image of human nature, representing its passions and humours, and the changes of fortune to which it is subject."* The emphasis falls first on passion, action second. He lauds Seneca for "the scene in the *Troades* where Ulysses is seeking Astyanax to kill him." It "bears the nearest resemblance of any thing" in Roman tragedy "to the excellent scenes of passion in Shakespeare." And in imitating the images of nature, it is not that Shakespeare makes us see them; "bare imitation" is not enough. When "he describes any thing, you *more* than see it, you feel it too." This sounds like Hazlitt on gusto: Chaucer makes us feel, not see, the atmosphere surrounding his pilgrims.

Dryden particularly emphasizes, as Johnson also will, the feeling of pleasure and delight poetry can bring. Frost, echoing Horace in his own rural voice, says a poem should begin in delight and end in wisdom. This is as good a short version of Dryden's blend of delight and didacticism as we are likely to get. [In his preface to *The Literary Criticism of John Dryden,* 1966], Arthur Kirsch shrewdly points out that of all critics whom we might call neoclassical, it is first Dryden, then Johnson, who understand that pleasure and delight, the desire to read and to continue reading, must come before any ethical or intellectual point is driven home. "The notion that classical rules and precedents ultimately derive their authority from an ability to please centuries of readers is the root assumption of all neoclassical criticism, from Sir Philip Sidney to Samuel Johnson. But with the exception of Johnson, only in Dryden does that assumption really operate; in the others it is often solely an uncompromising appeal to authority." Rymer's determined method of formalizing English dramatic literature could not work because, as Dryden points out, it is contradicted by the experience and the response of audiences.

Dryden's high valuation of pleasure in literature can be seen as early as the ***Essay on Dramatic Poesy.*** As often with the expression of his principles, it becomes more open, more direct as he grows older. Without forgetting literary form, he supplements concern for it with increased emphasis on the characteristic powers and voices of individual poets. This soon governs his ideas of form. **"The Grounds of Criticism in Tragedy"** and the ***Heads*** come at the crucial turning point of the late 1670s. Later, in the ***Discourse*** on satire (1693), Dryden uses the issue of translation to reflect on what exactly in a text is the pleasurable part—what is essential to its enjoyment (which a translator may overlook or mangle): "A noble author would not be pursued too close by a translator," he says. What exactly it is cannot be pinned down like a specimen. In this escape of Dryden's lies an affinity with Barthes' *jouissance:* like sexual pleasure it consists in a certain free play, personally felt, and would not be pursued or interpreted either microscopically or literally. We go back to variety, for at the "moment he takes his pleasure," [as Barthes wrote in *The Pleasure of the Text,* 1973, the] reader "mixes every language."

After discussing translations of Juvenal by Holyday and Stapylton, Dryden pauses to make a general reflection: "They who will not grant me, that pleasure is one of the ends of poetry, but that it is only a means of compassing the only end, which is instruction, must yet allow, that, without the means of pleasure, the instruction is but a bare and dry philosophy: a crude preparation of morals, which we may have from Aristotle and Epictetus, with more profit than from any poet." Dryden's argument in favor of tragicomedy, a century before Johnson's, leans heavily on basic psychological inclinations and on the emotional (and therefore concomitant structural) impact that tragicomedy has on the audience. So we get imitation, pleasure, structure, and "reader-response" all sheaved together. "Our variety," says Neander (again that term *variety*), "if well ordered, will afford a greater pleasure to the audience." There is more play. To express a simple passion without its natural interminglings will not appeal to "the concernment of an audience." A "bare imitation" cannot "excite the passions."

An emphasis on pleasure and suggestive, natural language at the level of phrasing cannot be overestimated. Dryden protests against words and clauses "placed unnaturally, that is, contrary to the common way of speaking," especially "without the excuse of a rhyme to cause it." He makes the same point about similar attempts to "poeticize" the obvious. Given the line *"Sir, I ask your pardon,"* some, he says, "would think it sounded more heroically to write, *Sir, I your pardon ask.*" He quickly follows this with the charge of "unnatural," even in cases where the word order must be altered to rhyme. Later, Dryden admitted that some of his own plays fell short of this developed standard. The remarks anticipate Johnson's laughter at Thomas Warton's use of Miltonic inversions: "*Gray

evening is common enough; but *evening gray* he'd think fine." In blank verse Dryden advises that "Variety of cadences is the best rule" because it helps actors and refreshes listeners. If we put aside his sometime preference for rhyme (especially in tragedy), we see that he gravitates to the advantages of English blank verse or, as he calls it by the French and Latin names, *prose mesurée* and *sermo pedestris.*

Dryden apparently had difficulty reciting his own lines in company. He seemed shy. But in an age when poetry was so often read aloud, he seems to have been one of the first English poets to realize that poetry was being read as much as heard, and that every hearing of it also constituted a new reading. Dryden knows he is writing for readers as much or more as for listeners. He underscores this awareness not only through his prefaces but by specific asides. For instance, in Chaucer's "Wife of Bath," we find this apology:

> Now wolden some men seye, paraventure,
> That for my necligence I do no cure
> To tellen yow the joye and al th'array
> That at the feeste was that ilke day.

Dryden renders it directly: "Perhaps the reader thinks I do him wrong / To pass the Marriage-Feast and Nuptial Song," which implies a written, not a spoken narrative.

In addition, the older Dryden takes increasing pains with his prologues and epilogues: he insists that folio copies of them be circulated among the audience before the play starts and before any recitation begins—so that even these poems are read before heard. The practice, though not uncommon, Dryden pursues with vigor. He intentionally turns the poems into texts for response and examination, to reinforce the effect that the prologues and epilogues have on the way the play was received, criticized, and remembered.

Religio Laici is usually considered as a statement by Dryden about his religious belief. But it also represents some of his thoughts on the interpretation of written texts. Though this is not the place for a full-scale examination of the poem, which deals with biblical hermeneutics, we see in it Dryden's recognition of interpretive communities of readers (religious sects), and of the power of writing over speech:

> *Tradition written* therefore more commends
> *Authority,* than what from *Voice* descends.

He concludes that in issues "needful" for faith the Bible is clear, but that in many other instances it is impossible to interpret with precision: not *"every where* / Free from Corruption, or intire, or clear."* He thus sees the difficulty and even impossibility of univocal interpretation, or of discerning all the authors' intentions. It is enough for him that there is sufficient agreement "In *all* things which our needfull *Faith* require." He painfully admits the influence of speculation or prejudice on interpretation, and of the importance and difficulties raised by canons and authority.

We should not place too much emphasis on this, but there are indications that Dryden thought consciously and systematically about the special circumstances of inscribing and interpreting texts. The test is the effect on reader or audience. A passage in his letter to Sir Robert Howard prefacing **Annus Mirabilis** points up the issue:

> The composition of all poems is, or ought to be, of wit, and wit in the poet, or wit writing (if you will give me leave to use a school-distinction) is no other than the faculty of imagination in the writer which, like a nimble spaniel, beats over and ranges through the field of memory, till it springs the quarry hunted after; or, without metaphor, which searches over all the memory for the species or ideas of those things which it designs to represent. Wit written is that which is well defined, the happy result of thought, or product of imagination.

The end, however, is not a particular kind of text, but a particular kind of effect on the reader:

> But to proceed from wit, in the general notion of it, to the proper wit of an heroic or historical poem, I judge it chiefly to consist in the delightful imaging of persons, actions, passions, or things. 'Tis not the jerk or sting of an epigram, nor the seeming contradiction of a poor antithesis (the delight of an ill-judging audience in a play of rhyme), nor the jingle of a more poor paronomasis; neither is it so much the morality of a grave sentence affected by Lucan, but more sparingly used by Virgil; but it is some lively and apt description, dressed in such colours of speech that it sets before your eyes the absent object as perfectly and more delightfully than nature.

Here wit means capacity of mind generally (OE *witan*). The "wit in the poet, or wit writing" is a prewriting or mental process that involves memory, conception, and invention—with the final aim being the act of inscribing itself, of "wit written," the specific inscribed words of the text, words which are a "well defined" product and belong properly to a particular species of composition, to a particular kind of text (such as heroic stanzas or the dialogue in drama). But furthermore—and here Dryden's intelligence goes beyond an otherwise common set of observations—the written wrods, the figures and tropes, the "elocution" must be "sounding and significant." (He repeats this phrase five years later in the **Defence of the Epilogue** as "more sounding, and more significant," and yet again almost thirty years later in his preface to **Aeneis**). What is written must be varied and apt, with the stipulation that no matter what kind of text is composed, the written words are "dressed in such colours of speech" that they set before the reader's "eyes" the absent object. In other words, the wheel comes full circle: readers find their own minds and senses returned, through a "lively" hint of the act of speech, to the immediacy of "nature," now presented even more delightfully, because accompanied with the greater "accuracy" only "wit written" can provide. The reader's imagination has been directed and sharpened. But in this sharpening process any "remoteness" or impression of "labor" should be avoided—the qualities that texts might exhibit if left in the realm of what is only inscribed in texts and, as a result, ignored the need to draw

upon and inscribe the liveliness of speech. We are left with the pleasure of the text, with what Barthes finally calls *Writing aloud,* the "sounding" part of composition that throws "the anonymous body of the actor into my ear."

Dryden became a great English critic, but not because he was the first. Sidney, Jonson, Henry Reynolds, and numerous others precede him. Yet Dryden is undoubtedly a seminal figure. Johnson, aware of the English lineage—and of earlier Continental critics including the younger Scaliger, Vida, and Castelvetro—pointedly calls Dryden "the father of our criticism." Eliot echoes this assessment in the 1930s: "Dryden was positively the first master of English criticism" and wrote "the first serious literary criticism in English by an English poet." And Auden, asked by Eliot's firm Faber and Faber to select and introduce a volume of Dryden's verse, avers that his critical prose retains "the highest historical and aesthetic importance."

The connection with Eliot's publishing house is more than coincidental. Dryden's considerable influence on twentieth-century poetry comes primarily through Eliot. The full influence of Dryden on Eliot, for whom in some respects he acts as a model, has yet to be recognized. Finishing the decade of his poetic transformation, Eliot begins three essays on "John Dryden: the Poet, the Dramatist, the Critic" (1932, originally five talks for the BBC in 1930) with the self-conscious proposition that Dryden might best be approached in the context of English letters precisely by tracing "his *influence.*"

Eliot then makes a personal anticipation of W. J. Bate's *The Burden of the Past and the English Poet* (1970) and Harold Bloom's *The Anxiety of Influence* (1973). He states: "For 'influence,' as Dryden had influence, a poet must not be so great as to overshadow all followers. . . . It should seem then no paradox to say that Dryden was the great influence upon English verse that he was, because he was *not* too great to have any influence at all. He was neither the consummate poet of earlier times, nor the eccentric poet of later. He was happy both in his predecessors [precursors] and in his successors." Francis Jeffrey put the situation succinctly more than a century earlier. Speaking of the hopeful poet, he said: "He is perpetually haunted and depressed by the ideal presence of those great masters, and their exacting critics. . . . Thus, the merit of his great predecessors chills, instead of encouraging his ardour" [*Contributions to the Edinburgh Review,* 1846]. Many of Eliot's aims are conscious foster children of Dryden's. ("Conscious" is a key word in Eliot's description of Dryden himself, as Pechter says Dryden was "conscious" in styling himself a modernist.) The one who went before is great enough to guide, but not so great that he smothers or stunts the imaginative space of those who follow. Goethe said he would not like to be an Englishman, because the example of Shakespeare would prove too overwhelming.

One week after Eliot died, the *Times Literary Supplement* pointed out affinities between the great Modern and a long-deceased other Modern: "Mr. Eliot resembled Dryden in the apparently casual and informal movement of his thought rather than Dr. Johnson in his orderly argumentation and combative briskness. He perhaps also re-sembled Dryden more as a person." The parallel is extended into areas of religion, cultural concern, technical crafts-manship and interest in poetic drama. During much of his career Eliot consciously paid homage to Dryden through the sincerest form of flattery. By a considerable margin he wrote more on Dryden than on any other author. . . . Dryden becomes Eliot's "complete man." The hundred-plus pages of criticism he devotes to him thus form the single largest cohesive body of criticism written about any single author by a major poet of the Modern movement. When Eliot concludes that "Dryden gives what is the soundest and most commonsense view possible for his time and place," we are in part reading Eliot's program for himself. The image of Dryden as a poet and man of letters shares in Eliot's familiar, compound ghost.

Eliot admits that his own opinion is no discovery. But while he does not "pretend that Dryden as a critic is often profound . . . the more I consider contemporary reflexion upon poetry, the more thankful I am for what we may call Dryden's critical orthodoxy," an orthodoxy which has now become an anomaly. Dryden's brand of criticism, un-extravagant yet wonderfully varied, lucid, and informed by the same pen with which he wrote poetry—some of it mediocre but much of it excellent and some of it time-less—this kind of criticism is unorthodox and rare today. Perhaps because it appears deceptively easy, like a perfect pas de deux we imagine doing if only someone would "show us the steps." Eliot praises Dryden for setting a "good example for critics by practising what he preached." In imitating him, Eliot is consciously leverag-ing the burden of the past and the anxiety of influence to advantage. (pp. 15-40)

Dryden is the first English poet consciously to confront, in an extended fashion, the ghosts of his English literary past, to wrestle with them first as a critic and then to bring them into service, particularly Shakespeare and Chaucer, though also Jonson and Milton, with whom Dryden estab-lishes his personal, critical relations. He is the first English poet to handle the anxiety of influence and the burden of the past in a self-conscious way. Eliot recognizes this.

Saintsbury notes [in his *Dryden,* 1881] that in the **Defence of an Essay of Dramatic Poesy** Dryden disparages the older dramatists. His tone is unusually flip and dismissive; he is prosperous and on familiar terms at court. He had even lent King Charles £500. "It was at this time, and at this time only," Saintsbury says, "that he spoke disre-spectfully of his great predecessors." This assertion over-simplifies Dryden's changing attitudes, and some of his later favorable remarks about Shakespeare harbored polit-ical motives. Yet if we put aside that **Defence** and perhaps, too, the **Defence of the Epilogue,** it is clear that Dryden becomes engaged not only in a give-and-take struggle of emulation with Shakespeare, Jonson, and Fletcher but also with a wider admiration of Milton and Chaucer. In effect, he selects strong poets before him, then highlights one or two things that attenuate their pressure: Chaucer is obscure and needs translating; his meter is rough (then still misunderstood); Shakespeare has faults and lacks cer-tain refinements of judgment and language; Milton is un-

like Dryden in temperament and conviction. Thus, no poet poses a crushing threat to Dryden's own sense of what he wishes to be. There is a difference to be achieved. Furthermore, there are several models (including Virgil, the Latin satirists, and French dramatists) to draw upon. So the past is not summed up in one specific poet who be-comes a single idol and therefore a more inhibiting pres-ence, as Shakespeare seems to have acted upon Coleridge.

Dryden is generally not classified as a humanist in the way More and Erasmus are. The archaeology of humanism has as many levels as the city of Troy. Dryden is not remark-ably erudite, and his view of civilization does not engage philosophical questions in a sustained fashion. He is not a seminal thinker, but he is an intellectual, a master of lan-guage and the purposes of poetry. The claims of his criti-cism appear modest, even nonchalant. But the geniality of manner should not obscure a fundamental quality: he ex-amines the value of language and literary structure in the context of human feeling and ethical value. "Qui dit lang-age," says Lévi-Strauss, "dit société." In Dryden's case this maxim is particularly apt. His criticism searches out the self-image that a culture and a civilization create through literature. In him there is always—as in Virgil, whom he loves so deeply—a wider reference. Criticism is a humane social enterprise before; after, it is a professional one.

Dryden believes "moral truth is the mistress of the poet as much as of the philosopher." This does not mean incul-cating a code; nor is it a moralistic pose. All it assumes is that the poet should consider the end and effect of writing to be important along with the means and forms by which it is carried out. Making a distinction as valuable as it sub-tle, Dryden says that "poesy must resemble natural truth, but it must *be* ethical." That is, poesy or art cannot copy or give us exact reference to life, to our ideas, to things or to experience. It simply *re-sembles* these to our minds and feelings. But in its essence it therefore presents us with a pattern analogous to experience. Furthermore, the poet must choose what to represent and how to do it. That is unavoidable unless the poet becomes a purely mechanic instrumentality. And Dryden would contend that this process could be "free" from ethics only if the imitation in no way resembled "natural truth" or experience.

Time and again Dryden successfully uses criteria of human interest, experience, motivation, and, above all, de-light and amusement. The Interregnum is summed up once this way: "we have been so long together bad En-glishmen, that we had not leisure to be good poets." The hopeful, equitable insertion here of the word "together" puts much in perspective. It is to "those milder studies of humanity" and "life-touches" of art that Dryden wishes to turn. Whom we admire at once reflects and shapes our being. Of all authors in English—questions of versifica-tion and polish aside—Dryden loves two, Chaucer and Shake-speare, and admires Milton. In his criticism and transla-tions he always seeks the particular stamp, the "charac-ter" of an author with the particular "turns" of thought and expression that combine to make an individual voice, the individually creating soul.

Dryden's achievement poses, at least implicitly, a disturbing question. Are his range, scope, ease of reference, and knowledgeable participation possible only in the relative infancy of a body of national criticism, or in a culture that, compared with ours, is small? Must specialization and refinement, the compartmentalization of university departments and the looser-knit, more pluralistic structures of politics, theater, scholarship, and "culture" (whatever we now understand by that word), necessarily drive the individual critic to attain an ever smaller stature?

Whenever we read an eighteenth-century critic, we are reading Dryden as well. His views on refinement of language, and yet his intensely ambivalent attitude toward refinement when offered the alternative of rough greatness and sublimity; his consideration of poetic diction and "natural" language, of Shakespeare and Chaucer, of a capacious sense of imitation and the end of pleasure; his thoughts on tragicomedy and the progress of arts and literature in the stream of time, on the nature of readers' psychological "assent," and the importance of passion in poetic language: all these preoccupations of 1700 through 1820, and later, Dryden first encounters and gives a varied, often modern voice. Here is a critic with whom we can still enter into dialogue, a writer whose every concern and judgment we may not wish to repeat or scrutinize, but whose method and attitude extend to us opportunities we are in danger of losing. His criticism is not a product but a process, and his readers are made to feel indispensable partners in that process. He wishes to make a tacit compact, with latitude for disagreement. In taking up any subject he is in dialogue with his several readers, with other critics and authors, and ultimately with the larger human community that our acts of reading imply. (pp. 40-3)

> *James Engell, "Practical Theorist: Dryden's 'Variety of Models'," in his* Forming the Critical Mind: Dryden to Coleridge, *Cambridge, Mass.: Harvard University Press, 1989, pp. 15-43.*

Paul Hammond   (essay date 1991)

[*In the following excerpt, Hammond interprets Dryden's translating work as a metaphor for his conception of literature. "Dryden's translations," Hammond asserts, "address the changing and unchanging nature of man, metamorphosing one text into another in order to reveal what is eternal and what is contingent in human life."*]

Much of Dryden's work was a kind of translation. His poetry often reappropriates the images through which religious and political life was currently being represented, translating individuals and causes into unexpected shapes. His literary criticism brings together writers across different times and cultures, considering one in terms of another, working out the relative characteristics of particular authors, languages and societies by a process of continual comparison. At many points in his writing Dryden appeals to classical Latin and Greek precedents, inviting us to read the present through the language of the past, and *vice versa.* That reciprocal movement through which the classics are both the standard of judgment and the object of judgment is crucial: it enables the modern writer by giving him a vocabulary of forms, tropes and *topoi,* authoris-

ing his writing by placing him in a revered tradition; at the same time it avoids disabling him by making his work merely a supplement to a structure which is already completed. Dryden's criticism moves between a sense of the eternal, fundamental stability of Nature, into which classical writers had a privileged insight, and the changing and contingent experience of human societies which gives the modern writer fresh resources and a standpoint from which to comment upon his precursors. Although this engagement with the classics always characterised his work, translation came to dominate Dryden's career after the early 1680s. In devoting himself so fully to translation, Dryden was not according to his Latin and Greek predecessors any simple and automatic authority; indeed, by the process of selection Dryden constructs his own canon from among the classics, and the very inclusion of Chaucer and Boccaccio alongside the ancients immediately refashions our sense of a classical tradition; then through the process of arrangement, by interleaving tales from Ovid and Homer with others from Chaucer and Boccaccio, he encourages us to debate the nature of authority, to ponder the play of different and often incompatible viewpoints. This extensive play between texts from different cultures raises the question of the nature of 'culture', and, indeed, the nature of 'nature'. In the Preface to *Fables Ancient and Modern* (1700) Dryden remarks (*à propos* of Chaucer's characters) that 'Mankind is ever the same, and nothing lost out of Nature, though every thing is alter'd' (ll. 448-9). Dryden's translations address the changing and unchanging nature of man, metamorphosing one text into another in order to reveal what is eternal and what is contingent in human life.

This is managed through a highly self-conscious manipulation of texts, which generally begins with a critical preface in which the modern English reader is told something about the characteristics of each classical writer. We are told about the philosophy of Lucretius and Persius, the verse forms of Horace, Ovid's obsession with witty turns of phrase and his inability to leave well alone. The translation of Juvenal and Persius is prefaced by a long *Discourse Concerning the Original and Progress of Satire,* which is not only a scholarly enquiry into the ancient origins of satire, but a critical and moral comparison of the satirical work of Juvenal, Persius and Horace. In the course of the essay Dryden moves into a discussion of heroic poetry, matching Homer and Virgil against Spenser and Milton, exploring the cultural ambitions of epic and asking whether Milton has fashioned an appropriate language. Dryden's pioneering criticism of Chaucer in the Preface to *Fables* illustrates his procedures:

> In the first place, As he is the Father of *English* Poetry, so I hold him in the same Degree of Veneration as the *Grecians* held *Homer,* or the *Romans Virgil:* He is a perpetual Fountain of good Sense; learn'd in all Sciences; and therefore speaks properly on all Subjects: As he knew what to say, so he knows also when to leave off; a Continence which is practis'd by few Writers, and scarcely by any of the Ancients, excepting *Virgil* and *Horace* . . . *Chaucer* follow'd Nature every where; but was never so bold to go beyond her . . . The Verse of *Chaucer,* I confess, is not

Harmonious to us; but 'tis like the Eloquence of one whom *Tacitus* commends, it was *auribus istius temporis accommodata:* They who liv'd with him, and some time after him, thought it Musical; and it continues so even in our Judgment, if compar'd with the Numbers of *Lidgate* and *Gower* his Contemporaries.

(ll. 307-36)

In Chaucer Dryden has found the 'original' of English poetry, our equivalent to Homer and Virgil; he can stand comparison with those two classics, and at least in his discipline exceeds many (particularly, by implication, the extravagant Ovid). His versification may be rough to our ears, but was acceptable in his day. All cultures have their own form of growth towards perfection. The manner which Dryden adopts in these critical prefaces is that of the congenial man of letters, passing his own judgment as a practising poet, selecting and debating learned opinions which he has culled from the scholarly editions, and presenting a discourse which illuminates for the ordinary reader the texts which he is about to meet. Our sense of the literary tradition, of cultural continuity and difference, is repeatedly refashioned.

Dryden's translations helped to mould a new readership, and formed an important development in Restoration publishing. They were a joint venture with Jacob Tonson, who was establishing himself as the leading publisher of his day, issuing contemporary writers alongside modern English classics such as Spenser and Milton. The series began with *Ovid's Epistles* (1680), a rendering of the *Heroides* to which Dryden contributed translations of three poems and a preface on the theory and practice of translation. Tonson's *Miscellany Poems* (1684) responded to and encouraged the new fashion for verse miscellanies, where readers could find poems of different kinds by different hands—satires, songs, prologues, translations. This miscellany included translations by various writers from Ovid's *Elegies,* Horace's *Odes* and Virgil's *Eclogues.* Tonson's second miscellany, *Sylvae* (1685), over which Dryden had some editorial influence, began with a preface in which Dryden offered a critical assessment of the four writers from whom he had translated selections: Virgil, Lucretius, Horace and Theocritus. In the third miscellany, *Examen Poeticum* (1693), Dryden printed substantial passages translated from Ovid's *Metamorphoses* and Homer's *Iliad.* The same year saw the publication of a complete translation of the satires of Juvenal and Persius; Dryden was responsible for the long prefatory essay on satire, five of Juvenal's poems and all of Persius. Just four years later, in 1697, Tonson published Dryden's complete translation of Virgil, the **Eclogues, Georgics** and **Aeneid,** and in 1700 his **Fables Ancient and Modern,** which gathered translations from Homer, Ovid, Boccaccio and Chaucer, with some original pieces.

This sustained project derives from the cultural and commercial intuitions of Dryden and Tonson. There was clearly a readership for the Latin poets in English translation, as can be seen from the earlier success of Brome's composite Horace, and Creech's complete Lucretius. The volumes would have appealed to those who knew little or no Latin but wished to share the pleasure and instruction

which these poets offered, but also to those who were concerned that English culture should match itself successfully against the classical achievement of Greece and Rome—not to mention that of France, that self-confidently classicising rival across the channel. The translation of classical poetry into English is at once an act of appropriation and humility, conquest and self-criticism. The domestication of Ovid and Virgil—with their dismemberment into anthologies—reduces their intimidating status as idols of an alien and unattainable perfection: in the idiom of Restoration translators they are given contemporary 'dress' and 'made to speak' English. At the same time they challenge English culture by forcing poets to find an English vocabulary and verse adequate to the Latin originals, and by laying English society under judgment from classical notions of culture, morality and empire. Through the domestication of classical texts, their revoicing in English, English itself acquires a different voice as images of Englishness and modernity are shaped and questioned by the models of antiquity. For Dryden it was through translation that the found a way of addressing some of the most deeply troubling issues of his life and times: human sexuality, mortality, the power and decay of empire, the place of human beings in the natural world, the role and predicament of the writer.

Dryden's translation of Virgil's *Eclogue* IX in **Miscellany Poems** speaks of the hard usage meted out to poets. Time was when Moeris had sung a song in praise of Augustus' reign:

"Why, *Daphnis,* dost thou search in old Records,
To know the seasons when the stars arise?
See *Caesars* Lamp is lighted in the Skies:
The star, whose rays the blushing grapes adorn,
And swell the kindly ripening ears of Corn.
Under this influence, graft the tender shoot;
Thy Childrens Children shall enjoy the fruit."
The rest I have forgot, for Cares and Time
Change all things, and untune my soul to rhime:
I cou'd have once sung down a Summers Sun,
But now the Chime of Poetry is done.
My voice grows hoarse; I feel the Notes decay.

(ll. 62-73, in ii 170-1)

Once the poet had urged that the old writings were superfluous, since the present was sufficiently illuminated by Caesar's star, but now that confident song of modernity is itself no more than a quoted fragment from the past. The poet's voice has grown hoarse. As the poem's headnote points out, Virgil had been in danger of being assaulted and killed, and was forced to speak in this indirect way (through a dialogue with an inset quotation) about his own harsh treatment; now Dryden uses a translation of Virgil's poem to voice, albeit through all these rhetorical disclaimers, the dangers and the lack of reward which attend his own poetic speech.

More is at issue here than Charles II's failure to pay his laureate's salary on time. Dryden had survived the crisis of the early 1680s physically unscathed (apart from the Rose Alley assault), but who knows what his public speech and its reception cost him in terms of inward spiritual and emotional anguish? We do not know, because

Dryden chose not to use the language of public utterance—inevitably now politicised and commercialised—to voice his inner dialogue. He would not respond with any *apologia* to the personal attacks on him by Shadwell and others. But somehow, in ways which we cannot trace because they never quite emerge into the world of writing, out of these years come **Religio Laici** and then Dryden's conversion to Rome. As early as the Dedication to **Aureng-Zebe** in 1676 Dryden had written about the self-betrayal involved in public writing, in this case in being the Sisyphus of the stage. In his memorial poem for John Oldham in 1684 (contemporary with *Eclogue* IX) Dryden had contemplated the premature silencing of the poet's tongue, the young hope of Augustan England now enveloped in gloomy night. In that poem he had used the Virgilian episode of Nisus and Euryalus in an unexpected way. The race in which the two friends take part ends with Nisus stumbling and falling, while Euryalus goes on to win. In a memorial poem one would expect Nisus to represent the fallen Oldham, and Euryalus the surviving Dryden, left to complete the race, to finish the poetic task. But the application is reversed: Oldham is the young victor Euryalus; Dryden is the older man, Nisus, the fallen one. It is typical of Dryden's elusive mode of representing himself that this allusion teases us into a misreading, and that even when the image has been re-read against our expectations we still do not know what kind of 'fall' Dryden means. The story haunted him, for he translated from the **Aeneid** the episode of the race and the later story of the death of the two friends, and published the fragments in **Sylvae,** with many verbal echoes of the poem on Oldham. The pieces are placed at the beginning of his contributions to that collection, thus acting as a preface to all that follows.

The imaginative confrontation of death which those poems make, dramatising Dryden's own mortality while holding it at bay through translation, avoiding the trauma of writing directly about one's own death, is continued in **Sylvae** with his extracts from Lucretius. These translations, together with the pieces from Horace which follow them, amount to an attempt to work out how man can make himself free, how one may fashion a self which is not wholly in thrall to the cravings of the physical body, nor cravenly subjected to the whims of the world's political masters. It is not accidental that this struggle with the constraints which determine one's life is conducted through a wrestling with other people's philosophies and formulations: it is by moving between these different rhetorics, now appropriating them, now questioning their adequacy, that Dryden essays a kind of self-fashioning without ever wishing to commit himself publicly to speaking himself in his own voice, singly and without contradiction. In the words of Montaigne: 'If I speake diversly of my selfe it is because I look diversly upon my selfe . . . I have nothing to say entirely, simply, and with soliditie of my selfe, without confusion, disorder, blending, mingling, and in one word.' Nor is the self which these translations fashion simply that of the poet: it is the reader who is invited to ponder, compare and select, fashioning his own values and mode of freedom through his consideration of Dryden's work. (pp. 142-47)

Paul Hammond, in his John Dryden: A Literary Life, *Macmillan, Academic and Professional Ltd., 1991, 184 p.*

FURTHER READING

Armistead, J. M. "Dryden's *King Arthur* and the Literary Tradition: A Way of Seeing." *Studies in Philology* LXXXV, No. 1 (Winter 1988): 53-72.
> Argues that, contrary to traditional scholarly views of Dryden's work, the poet develops the Arthurian legend not to glorify a particular dynasty but to proclaim "the divine mission of his country."

Bridges, Robert. "Dryden on Milton." In his *Collected Essays, Papers, & c.,* Vol. 10, pp. 271-82. London: Oxford University Press, 1932.
> Defends John Milton against unfavorable criticism by Dryden and denounces Dryden's translations of Geoffrey Chaucer's poetry.

Brower, Reuben Arthur. "Introduction: An Allusion to Europe: Dryden and Poetic Tradition." In his *Alexander Pope: The Poetry of Allusions,* pp. 1-14. Oxford: Clarendon Press, 1959.
> Affirms Dryden's influence in reviving the role of the public poet.

Bywaters, David. *Dryden in Revolutionary England.* Berkeley: University of California Press, 1991, 196 p.
> Describes "the rhetorical strategies by which John Dryden, in his published works between 1687 and 1700, sought to define contemporary politics and to formulate a defensible political stance."

Chase, Lewis Nathaniel. *The English Heroic Play: A Critical Description of the Rhymed Tragedy of the Restoration.* New York: Russell & Russell, 1965, 250 p.
> Analysis of English heroic drama, with numerous references to relevant works by Dryden.

Daiches, David. "The Establishment of a Critical Scene: Dryden." In his *Critical Approaches to Literature,* pp. 182-232. Englewood Cliffs, N.J.: Prentice-Hall, 1956.
> Examination of Dryden's critical thought, drawing primarily from his *Of Dramatic Poesie.*

Dobrée, Bonamy. "Milton and Dryden: A Comparison and Contrast in Poetic Ideas and Poetic Method." *Journal of English Literary History* 3, No. 1 (March 1936): 83-100.
> Investigation of the similarities and differences in the aesthetics and poetry of Milton and Dryden.

Donnelly, Jerome. "Fathers and Sons: The Normative Basis of Dryden's *Absalom and Achitophel.*" *Papers on Language and Literature* 17, No. 4 (Fall 1981): 363-80.
> Relates the Aristotelian conception of character to the father–son relationship of Absalom and Achitophel.

Drydeniana. (The Life and Times of Seven Major British Writers: Dryden, Pope, Swift, Richardson, Sterne, Johnson, Gibbon). New York: Garland Publishing, 1975.

Facsimile reprints of numerous early critical writings on Dryden's works.

Dyson, A. E., and Lovelock, Julian. "Beyond the Polemics: The Opening of Dryden's *Absalom and Achitophel*." In their *Masterful Images: English Poetry from Metaphysicals to Romantics*, pp. 71-96. New York: Harper & Row, 1976.
> Discusses issues raised by this question: "Is Dryden's *Absalom and Achitophel* chiefly a polemical work, with art at its service; or, beyond the polemics, is it chiefly a triumph of form?"

Ehrenpreis, Irvin. "Dryden the Playwright." In his *Acts of Implication: Suggestion and Covert Meaning in the Works of Dryden, Swift, Pope, and Austen*, pp. 20-50. Berkeley and Los Angeles: University of California Press, 1980.
> Examines several themes and techniques in Dryden's dramas.

Eliot, T. S. *John Dryden: The Poet, The Dramatist, The Critic.* New York: Terence & Elsa Holliday, 1932, 68 p.
> Emphasizes the formative influence Dryden has had on English poetry and prose.

Fujimura, Thomas H. "John Dryden and the Myth of the Golden Age." *Papers on Language and Literature* 11, No. 2 (Spring 1975): 149-67.
> Explores Dryden's utilization of myth, particularly that of the Golden Age, in his poetry.

Garrison, James D. *Dryden and the Tradition of Panegyric.* Berkeley and Los Angeles: University of California Press, 1975, 263 p.
> Traces Dryden's development of the panegyric through 1688.

Grace, Joan C. "John Dryden's Theory of Tragedy: 'They, Who Have Best Succeeded on the Stage Have Still Conform'd Their Genius to Their Age'." In her *Tragic Theory in the Critical Works of Thomas Rymer, John Dennis, and John Dryden*, pp. 89-128. London: Associated University Press, 1975.
> Discusses Dryden's theory of tragedy. Grace predicates her study on the belief that "all the central ideas in Dryden's criticism concerning probability, characterization, verisimilitude, the unities, and the use of rhyme are connected with the problem of what to imitate nature means in his age."

Hagstrum, Jean H. "John Dryden: Sensual, Heroic, and 'Pathetic' Love." In her *Sex and Sensibility: Ideal and Erotic Love from Milton to Mozart*, pp. 50-71. Chicago: University of Chicago Press, 1980.
> Examines Dryden's heroic plays and *All for Love*. Hagstrum considers Dryden to have elucidated the physical and emotional dimensions of love, writing that "he endows the theme of love with the elevation, delicacy, and tenderness that antiquity lacked, and, in quite un-Gallic fashion, his oeuvres often throb with a bold and hearty physicality."

Hall, Albert. "Charles II: Dryden's Christian Hero." *Modern Philology* LIX, No. 1. (August 1961): 25-35.
> Study of *Absalom and Achitophel* focusing on Dryden's interest in Christian epic.

Hall, James M. *John Dryden: A Reference Guide.* Boston: G. K. Hall & Co., 1984, 424 p.

Annotated bibliography of writings on Dryden from 1668 to 1981.

Harth, Phillip. *Contexts of Dryden's Thought.* Chicago: University of Chicago Press, 1968, 304 p.
> Focuses on Dryden's religious thought through an analysis of what Hart considers his "longest and most important poems," *Religio Laici* and *The Hind and the Panther.*

Hill, Geoffrey. "Dryden's Prize-Song." In his *The Enemy's Country: Words, Contexture, and Other Circumstances of Language*, pp. 63-82. Stanford, Calif.: Stanford University Press, 1991.
> Comments on Dryden's strategies of reconciling his artistic integrity with the obligation to please his readers.

Hughes, Derek. *Dryden's Heroic Plays.* Lincoln: University of Nebraska Press, 1981, 195 p.
> Study of the heroic plays, which Hughes relates to Dryden's later career.

Huxley, Aldous. "Forgotten Satirists." *The London Mercury* I, No. 5 (March 1920): 565-73.
> Discusses the Popish Plot and the various political poems which it inspired, including *Absalom and Achitophel.*

Hyman, Stanley Edgar. "English Neo-Classicism." In his *Poetry and Criticism: Four Revolutions in Literary Taste*, pp. 39-84. New York: Atheneum, 1961.
> Comparative study of *All for Love* and *Antony and Cleopatra.*

Kermode, Frank. "Dryden: A Poet's Poet." *The Listener* LVIII, No. 1470 (30 May 1957): 877-78.
> Discusses Dryden's comic-heroic works in the context of their intended audience, Dryden's literary contemporaries.

King, Bruce, ed. *Twentieth Century Interpretations of "All for Love."* Englewood Cliffs, N.J. Prentice-Hall, 1968, 120 p.
> Collection of critical writings on Dryden's most discussed drama.

———. *Dryden's Mind and Art.* Edinburgh: Oliver and Boyd, 1969, 211 p.
> Collection of essays on several topics, including "Dryden and the Heroic Ideal," "Anne Killigrew: Or the Art of Modulating," and "Dryden's Imagery."

Kinsley, James, and Kinsley, Helen, eds. *Dryden: The Critical Heritage.* London: Routledge and Kegan Paul, 1971, 414 p.
> Annotated selection of essays, from first reviews to early nineteenth-century criticism; contains a cross-section of Dryden's own criticism of his works.

Krutch, Joseph Wood. *Comedy and Conscience after the Restoration.* New York: Columbia University Press, 1924, 271 p.
> Includes numerous references to Dryden, his dramas, and dramatic theory. Krutch considers him a pioneer in Restoration Comedy.

Leavis, F. R. "*Antony and Cleopatra* and *All for Love:* A Critical Exercise." *Scrutiny* V, No. 2 (September 1936): 158-69.
> Highlights the distinguishing qualities of *Antony and Cleopatra* and Dryden's adaptation of the play, *All for Love.*

Manlove, C. N. "Dryden." In his *Literature and Reality, 1600-1800,* pp. 57-75. New York: St. Martin's Press, 1978.
> Contrasts Dryden's satire with that of Alexander Pope. There follows an assessment of Dryden's translation of Geoffrey Chaucer's "Nun's Priest's Tale."

McFadden, George. *Dryden: The Public Writer, 1660-1685.* Princeton N.J.: Princeton University Press, 1978, 305 p.
> Concentrates on Dryden as poet and public figure, emphasizing in particular his dramatic works.

Miner, Earl, ed. *John Dryden.* London: G. Bell & Sons, 1972, 363 p.
> Collection of critical essays on various aspects of Dryden's work, including "Dryden's Grotesque: An Aspect of the Baroque in His Art and Criticism," "Dryden and Satire: *Mac Flecknoe, Absalom and Achitophel, The Medall,* and *Juvenal,*" and "Dryden and Seventeenth-Century Prose Style."

Monk, Samuel Holt. "Dryden and the Beginnings of Shakespeare Criticism in the Augustan Age." In *The Persistence of Shakespeare Idolatry: Essays in Honor of Robert W. Babcock,* edited by Herbert M Schueller, pp. 49-75. Detroit: Wayne State University Press, 1964.
> Establishes Dryden as highly influential to the development of Shakespeare criticism.

Monk, Samuel Holt, and Latt, David J. *John Dryden: A Survey and Bibliography of Critical Studies, 1895-1974.* Minneapolis: University of Minnesota Press, 1976, 199 p.
> Extensive bibliography of writings on Dryden and his works.

Myers, William. *Dryden.* London: Hutchinson University Library, 1973, 200 p.
> Survey of Dryden's works.

Nicoll, Allardyce. *Dryden as an Adapter of Shakespeare.* London: Shakespeare Association, 1922, 35 p.
> Compares *The Tempest, All for Love,* and *Troilus and Cressida* with their Shakespearian antecedents.

———. *Dryden & His Poetry.* New York: Russell & Russell, 1923, 152 p.
> Survey of Dryden's life and work, with extensive quotation from his poetry.

Osborn, James M. *John Dryden: Some Biographical Facts and Problems,* revised edition. Gainesville: University of Florida Press, 1965, 316 p.
> Reviews previous studies of Dryden's life and explores several biographical issues and problems regarding the poet.

Pearcy, Lee T. "Dryden: Translation as Style" and "Dryden: Style in Translation." In *The Mediated Muse: English Translations of Ovid 1560-1700,* pp. 100-21, 121-38. Hamden, Conn.: Archon Books, 1984.
> Stylistic analyses of Dryden's translations of the works of the Roman poet Ovid.

Pechter, Edward. *Dryden's Classical Theory of Literature.* Cambridge: Cambridge University Press, 1975, 233 p.
> Analytical and comparative study of Dryden's literary theory.

Reverand, Cedric D. II. *Dryden's Final Poetic Mode: The Fables.* Philadelphia: University of Pennsylvania Press, 1988, 239 p.
> Reverand offers an exhaustive analysis of Dryden's *Fables,* deploring the relative scholarly neglect of what he judges an important work.

Smith, David Nichol. *John Dryden.* Cambridge: Cambridge University Press, 1950, 93 p.
> Contains four lectures—"Early Verse and Criticism," "Plays," "Satires and Religious Poems," and "Translations, Odes, Fables."

Sowerby, Robin. *Dryden's Aeneid.* Bristol: Bristol Classical Press, 1986, 248.
> Detailed analysis of Dryden's acclaimed translations of Vergil's epic. According to Sowerby, it is in the "art, of communicating the ancient poet's ideas with force and energy equal to his own, that Dryden has so completely exceeded all who have gone before, and all who have succeeded him."

Spingarn, J. E., ed, Introduction to *Critical Essays of the Seventeenth Century, Vol, 1, 1606-1650,* pp. ix-cvi. Oxford: Clarendon Press, 1908.
> Overview of seventeenth-century criticism that considers Dryden "the first great modern critic."

Tillyard, E. M. W. "Dryden: *Ode on Anne Killigrew,* 1686." In his *Poetry and Its Background: Illustrated by Five Poems, 1470-1870,* pp. 49-65. New York: Barnes & Noble, 1955.
> Discusses Dryden's ode in the context of its theology, manner, reverance for art, classicism, and heroic conventions.

Verall, A. W. *Lectures on Dryden.* Edited by Margaret de G. Verrall. New York: Russell & Russell, 1963, 271 p.
> Comprehensive discussion of Dryden's works.

Wallerstein, Ruth. "To Madness Near Allied: Shaftesbury and His Place in the Design and Thought of *Absalom and Achitophel.*" *The Huntington Library Quarterly* VI, No. 4 (August 1943): 445-71.
> Detailed analysis of *Absalom and Achitophel* that focuses on the portrayal of the Earl of Shaftesbury.

Ward, Charles E. *The Life of John Dryden.* Chapel Hill: University of North Carolina Press, 1961, 380 p.
> Standard biography of Dryden.

Weinbrot, Howard D. " 'Nature's Holy Bands' in *Absalom and Achitophel:* Fathers and Sons, Satire and Change." *Modern Philology* 85, No. 4 (May 1988): 373-92.
> Explores the political, ethical, and theological implications of Dryden's poem.

Winn, James Anderson. "Imitations." In his *Unsuspected Eloquence: A History of Relations between Poetry and Music,* pp. 194-286. New Haven, Conn.: Yale University Press, 1981.
> Includes a discussion of Dryden's "Song for St. Cecilia's Day, 1687." Comparing Dryden's poem to the music of J. S. Bach, Winn praises the poet's unique ability to successfully integrate a type of musical imitation into the formal structure of his work.

———. *John Dryden and His World.* New Haven, Conn.: Yale University Press, 1987, 651.
> Exhaustive, detailed, and richly documented and illustrated biography of Dryden.

Young, Kenneth. *John Dryden: A Critical Biography.* London: Sylvan Press, 1954, 240 p.

Study of Dryden's life and works. Young regards him as "a Conservative in politics and an innovator in poetry."

Zwicker, Steven N. *Politics and Language in Dryden's Poetry: The Arts of Disguise.* Princeton, N. J.: Princeton University Press, 1984, 248 p.
    Analyzes the linguistic, narrative, stylistic, and formal strategies in Dryden's political discourse.

Additional coverage of Dryden's life and career is contained in the following sources published by Gale Research: *Dictionary of Literary Biography,* Vols. 80 and 101.

George Farquhar

1678-1707

Irish-born English dramatist, novelist, essayist, and poet.

INTRODUCTION

Considered one of the most notable dramatists of the Restoration period, Farquhar was instrumental in reforming the theatrical practices of his age. His most famous plays, *The Recruiting Officer* and *The Beaux' Stratagem,* continued in the traditions of the Comedy of Manners but they demonstrate a natural humor, warmth, and fidelity to life lacking in the works of Farquhar's contemporaries. They are further acclaimed for extending the perimeters of Restoration drama by introducing country settings, manners, and characters later adopted and perfected by Oliver Goldsmith and Richard Sheridan.

Born in Londonderry, Ireland, Farquhar had a liberal education that began with attending the Londonderry Free Grammar School under the instruction of Ellis Walker, an educator who acquired local fame for having his students perform the comedies of Terence and William Shakespeare. In 1694 Farquhar entered Trinity College in Dublin as a sizar, or a student who performs menial duties for a small allowance, but his studies came to an abrupt end in 1696 when he left Trinity without a degree. Some biographers speculate that he may have been expelled from the college. He then joined Dublin's Smock Alley Theatre, where he became acquainted with stage life and began a lifelong friendship with the Irish actor Robert Wilks. Farquhar was a poor actor who had a thin voice and occasionally suffered from stage fright, and his acting career ended in 1697 after he accidentaly stabbed and seriously injured a fellow player during a duelling scene. Nonetheless, his theater experience proved invaluable in helping him to gain a firm understanding of the potential and the limitations of the stage. Encouraged by Wilks to try writing comedies, Farquhar traveled to London and contacted Christopher Rich, manager of the Theatre Royal in Drury Lane, where Farquhar's first play, *Love and a Bottle,* was successfully produced in 1698. The success of his second play, *The Constant Couple; or, A Trip to the Jubilee,* consolidated Farquhar's reputation. It featured the character of Sir Harry Wildair, played by Wilks, whose tremendous popularity inspired Farquhar to write *Sir Harry Wildair: Being the Sequel of The Trip to the Jubilee.* The play was staged in 1701 but was coldly received by audiences. An unexpected failure, it received little critical attention and was the first in a series of unsuccessful productions. In 1703, supposing her to be wealthy, Farquhar married a penniless widow and left London the following year to accept a commission to the army as a lieutenant of Grenadiers. His service on a recruiting campaign in England's west country inspired one of Farquhar's most famous

pieces, *The Recruiting Officer*—an immediate success upon its production in 1706. Despite his newly-achieved fame, the closing years of Farquhar's life were marred by poverty and failing health. Financial support from Wilks enabled him to work on his last play, *The Beaux' Stratagem;* completed in only six weeks, it is regarded by many to be Farquhar's finest work. Shortly after *The Beaux' Stratagem* was staged, Farquhar died of tuberculosis at the age of twenty nine.

Critics stress Farquhar's importance as a transitional figure in English literary history. He began his career during a time when Restoration drama was extremely popular, but when critics of the morality embodied by these plays were also gaining prominence. Jeremy Collier's *A Short View of the Profaneness and Immorality of the English Stage* (1698), which attacked the lax morality and sexual attitudes in Restoration drama, was published in the same year that Farquhar's first play, *Love and a Bottle,* was performed. Scholars have noted that Farquhar was naturally affected by these changes and that, though he is usually identified with the writers of the Comedy of Manners, he stands apart from them in several significant particulars. His early comedies, *Love and a Bottle, The Constant Couple,* and *Sir Harry Wildair,* are similar to other Restoration dramas in that they are licentious in tone and tend to focus on sexual intrigue. Yet they also contain intricate plots incorporating mistaken identities, multiple disguises, and trick marriages, providing a sharp contrast to, for example, the simple story lines of John Vanbrugh. In addition, their dialogue, though lively, lacks the witty, cynical hardness of the comedies of William Wycherley and William Congreve. Wit in Farquhar's plays, while still an important trait, is less apparent and is often subordinated to plot and character, with comedy achieved through situation and natural plot progress rather than through daring repartee. Farquhar's later plays, *The Inconstant* and *The Twin Rivals,* diverge even more from the high Comedy of Manners, for they follow Aristotle's dictum that comedies should instruct their audience by chastising vice, laughing at weakness, and rewarding virtue. *The Recruiting Officer* and *The Beaux' Stratagem,* Farquhar's most celebrated plays, also exhibit this new moral dimension, only, unlike his previous dramas, their morality is less forced and more natural as a result of Farquhar's excursion into portraying provincial life and country manners. Moreover, Farquhar's characters in these later plays differ from the heartless rakes of Restoration drama in that his country maids, inn-keepers and highwaymen are genteel and are portrayed in a sympathetic light. Their vivacity, openness, and unpredictable behavior render them more realistic than the traditional character types of Restoration drama and contribute to an atmosphere of unaffected gaiety and freshness. Even Farquhar's treatment of the common Restoration theme of marital incompatibility sets him apart from his predecessors: in *The Beaux' Stratagem,* Farquhar resolves the conflict by introducing a separation by mutual consent or divorce, a serious note that also suggests equality of the sexes. Yet critics have noted that Farquhar's lighthearted and somewhat idealistic closing marks an end to Restoration comedy and heralds the advent of sentimental drama.

Farquhar's *The Recruiting Officer* and *The Beaux' Stratagem* were tremendously popular with contemporary audiences and have been long acknowledged as Farquhar's greatest works. Eighteenth-century critics and dramatists extolled these plays for their sentiment and humanity, proposing that Farquhar was the founder of a new and possibly superior form of comedy. The Romantic critics Charles Lamb, William Hazlitt, and Leigh Hunt held Farquhar in high esteem and were the first to class him with Restoration writers, defining him in relationship to their achievements. Hazlitt praised Farquhar's heroes for their honesty, asserting that unlike the common Restoration rakes, "they are real gentlemen, and only pretended impostors." Hunt agreed with Alexander Pope, who found the natural language in Farquhar's plays "wanting in an air of good breeding" and who suggested that it lacked the polish and glitter of Restoration comedy. Nonetheless, Farquhar's depth of feeling, theatrical skill, and diverse characters prompted Hunt to pronounce him, in comparison with other Restoration dramatists, "upon the whole, the truest dramatic genius, and the most likely to be of lasting popularity." The critics of the Victorian era were generally hostile to the writers of Restoration drama because of the bitter satire, licentious wit, and hedonistic values they presented, but tended to view Farquhar favorably because he engendered greater morality in his plays. Edmund Gosse commented that "Farquhar succeeds in being always wholesome, even when he cannot persuade himself to be decent." In the twentieth century, scholars have discussed Farquhar's comedies apart from Restoration drama, and William Archer even asserted that Farquhar rebelled against Restoration comedy. Several modern critics concur with Archer, but also blame Farquhar for adultering the Comedy of Manners and ushering in sentimental comedy. They assert that his works stand between these two dramatic periods without committing to either one and therefore come across as confused and inconsistent. John Palmer has argued that, because Farquhar "never really discovered in his art a neutral territory where the values he borrowed were reconciled with the values he contributed," he helped to bring about the demise of the English comic spirit. Recent criticism is more positive, noting that Restoration drama was already in decline by the time Farquhar began writing and that he was correct to seek out a new form. Pointing out that the naturalism and simplicity of Farquhar's plays are distinctly modern, Bonamy Dobrée proposed that Farquhar is "the Shaw of his time."

Exalting humor of situation above wit and character, and emphasizing plot above dialogue, Farquhar's comedies escaped the conventional manners of Restoration drama and contributed an unsurpassed freshness, deep perception of human nature, and imaginative liveliness to the English stage of the late seventeenth and early eighteenth centuries. Comparing Farquhar to other playwrights of his time, William M. Thackeray concluded that Farquhar was "something more than a mere comic tradesman: [he] has a grand drunken diabolical fire in him."

PRINCIPAL WORKS

Love and a Bottle   (drama)   1698

The Adventures of Covent Garden in Imitation of Scarron's City Romance   (novel)   1699

The Constant Couple; or, A Trip to the Jubilee   (drama) 1699

Sir Harry Wildair: Being the Sequel of The Trip to the Jubilee   (drama)   1701

The Inconstant; or, The Way to Win Him   (drama) 1702

Love and Business in a Collection of Occasionary Verse and Epistolary Prose Not Hitherto Published. A Discourse Likewise upon Comedy in Reference to the English Stage in a Familiar Letter   (essay, poetry, and letters)   1702

The Twin Rivals   (drama)   1702

The Stage Coach [with Peter Anthony Motteux] (drama)   1704

The Recruiting Officer   (drama)   1706

The Beaux' Stratagem   (drama)   1707

The Works of the Late Ingenious Mr. George Farquhar: Containing All His Poems, Letters, Essays, and Comedies Published during His Lifetime (poetry, letters, essays, and dramas) 1711

The Complete Works of George Farquhar. 2 vols. (dramas, essays, poetry, letters) 1930

*This work is an adaption of Jean de La Chapelle's *Les Carosses d'Orléans*.

Susanna Centlivre   (poem date 1701)

[*Centlivre, a popular dramatist during the Restoration period, is responsible for writing the only piece of positive criticism about Farquhar's plays to appear during his lifetime. In the following verse epistle, entitled "Epistle XL. To Mr. Farquhar upon his Comedy Call'd A Trip to the Jubilee," originally published in 1701 in* Letters of Wit, Politics, and Morality *by Cardinal Bentivoglio, Centlivre favorably assesses the degree of morality in Farquhar's play.*]

> Sir,
> Amongst the many friends your Wit has made,
> Permit my humble Tribute may be paid;
> My Female Genius is too weakly fraught
> With learn'd Expressions to adorn my Thought.
> My Muse too blush'd, when she this task began,
> To think that she must Compliment a Man.
> She paus'd a while—At last she bid me say,
> She lik'd the Man, and I admir'd the Play.
> For since the learned *Collier* first essay'd
> To teach Religion to the Rhiming Trade,
> The *Comick* Muse in Tragick posture sat,
> And seem'd to mourn the Downfall of her State;
> Her eldest Sons she often did implore
> That they her ancient Credit would restore.
> Strait they essay'd, but quickly to their cost:
> They found that all their industry was lost.
> For since the *Double Entendre* was forbid,
> They could not get a Clap for what they did.
> At last *Thalia* call'd her youngest Son,
> The graceful and the best beloved one:
> My Son, said she, I have observ'd Thee well,
> Thou doest already all my Sons excell;
> Thy Spring does promise a large harvest crop,
> And Thou alone must keep my Glory up.
> Go, something Write, my Son, that may atone
> Thy Brother's Faults, and make thy virtues known.
> I'll teach Thee Language in a pleasant stile:
> Which, without Smut, can make an audience smile.
> Let fall no words that may offend the Fair;
> Observe Decorums, dress they Thoughts with Air;
> Go—lay the Plot, which Virtue shall adorn;
> Thus spoke the Muse; and thus disds't Thou perform
> Thy **Constant Couple** does our Fame return,
> And shews our Sex can love when yours esteem,
> And *Wild-Air's* Character does plainly shew,
> A man of sense may dress and be a Beau.
> In *Vizor* many may their picture find;

> A pious Out-side, but a poisonous Mind.
> Religious Hypocrites thou'st open laid,
> Those holy Cheats by which our Isle is sway'd,
> Oh! mayst thou live! And Dryden's Place supply,
> So long till thy best Friends shall bid thee die;
> Could I from bounteous Heav'n one wish obtain,
> I'd make thy person lasting as thy Fame.

(pp. 31-2)

Susanna Centlivre, in a poem in The Development of George Farquhar as a Comic Dramatist *by Eugene Nelson James, Mouton, 1972, pp. 31-2.*

Arthur Bedford   (essay date 1706)

[*In the following excerpt, Bedford attacks Farquhar's* The Recruiting Officer *for its immoral parodying of authority.*]

There was lately published a *Comedy* call'd **The Recruiting Officer,** to render this Employment [of abusing superiors on the stage] as odious as possible. This was acted in *London* by some who stile themselves *Her Majesties Servantts,* and also in *Bristol,* whilst others were beating up for *Volunteers.* Here one *Captain* is represented as a notorious *Lyar,* another as a Drunkard, one intreagues with Women, another is scandalously guilty of *debauching* them; and tho the *Serjeant* was married to five Women before, yet the *Captain* perswades him to marry another, as a Cloak for such Roguery, to make up his five Wives half a Dozen, and to cheat the *Queen,* by entering a Child born the Day before into the Muster-Roll, and after all he stiles these *Debaucheries an Air of Freedom, which People mistake for Lewdness, as they mistake Formality in others for Religion,* and then proceeds in commending his own Practice, and exposing the other. In this *Play* the *Officers* are represented as quarrelsom, but Cowards. The *Serjeant* makes the *Mob* drunk to list them, gives two of them two Broad Pieces of Gold, for Pictures, and finding the Mony upon them, pretends that they are listed: At another Time he is ready to swear anything for the Good of the Service; and also perswades Men to list in the Disguise of a *Conjurer,* with most profane Language in Commendation of the *Devil.* . . . In this *Play* the *Officers* confess, that they greatly abuse the new listed *Soldiers; Debauching* of the Country Wenches is represented as a main Part of the Service; All the private *Centinels* are guilty of stealing Horses, Sheep and Fowls, and the *Captain* desires, that he may have but one honest Man in the Company for the Novelty's sake. After this the *Justices of the Peace* are made the Jest of the *Stage,* for discharging their Duty in listing of Soldiers, and the *Constable* hath a Lash into the Bargain, that no one who serves his Country on this Occasion, may escape the *Play-House* Censure. (pp. 150-52)

It may be observed, That when the *Souldiers* were guilty of *Immoralities* in *Spain,* they were caress'd by the *Stage,* and there crown'd with Success; but now we hear of no such Complaints, they are censur'd and ridicul'd. When they really were debauch'd, they were never thus affronted; but since the Endeavours used to reform the Army, they are thus expos'd. The greater and more signal the Services are, which they do the Nation, the more the *Play-Houses* shew their Resentments; and whilst others justly applaud them for their Merits, the *Poets* and *Actors* are the only Persons who thus lampoon them. What Thanks are due to such Men from the *French King* I shall not determine, but I am sure, that they deserve none from the *English Government;* and if neither Mr. *Dennis* nor this *Author* [Farquhar] can render the *Stage* more useful, we are not, in the least, beholden for their Assistance. (p. 154)

> Arthur Bedford, "Superiors and Others Abused by the Stage," in The Evil and Danger of Stage-Plays, 1706. Reprint by Garland Publishing, Inc., 1974, pp. 145-76.

Elizabeth Inchbald   (essay date 1806-09)

[*A proponent of social and moral reform, Inchbald took part in London's theatrical and literary circles for nearly forty years as an actress, playwright, editor, and novelist. Although she was best known by her contemporaries for her plays, her two novels,* A Simple Story *(1791) and* Nature and Art *(1796), are her most original and important works. In the following excerpt, Inchbald disapproves of "the well-drawn characters, happy incidents, and excellent dialogue" in Farquhar's* The Beaux' Stratagem, *finding that they disguise the play's immorality.*]

It is an honour to the morality of the present age, that this most entertaining comedy is but seldom performed; and never, except some new pantomime, or other gaudy spectacle, be added, as an afterpiece, for the attraction of an audience.

The well-drawn characters, happy incidents, and excellent dialogue, in **The Beaux Stratagem,** are but poor atonement for that unrestrained contempt of principle which pervades every scene. Plays of this kind are far more mischievous than those which preserve less appearance of delicacy. Every auditor and reader shrinks from those crimes which are recommended in unseemly language, and from libertinism united with coarse manners; but in adorning vice with wit, and audacious rakes with the vivacity and elegance of men of fashion, youth, at least, will be decoyed into the snare of admiration.

Charmed with the spirit of Archer and Aimwell, the reader may not, perhaps, immediately perceive, that those two fine gentlemen are but arrant impostors; and that the lively, though pitiable Mrs Sullen, is no other than a deliberate violator of her marriage vow. Highly delighted with every character, he will not, perhaps, at first observe, that all the wise and witty persons of this comedy are knaves, and all the honest people fools. (pp. 3-4)

> Elizabeth Inchbald, "Remarks," in her Remarks for The British Theatre, Scholars' Facsimiles & Reprints, 1990, pp. 3-5.

William Hazlitt   (essay date 1819)

[*Hazlitt was an eminent English essayist and critic whose work, typically focusing on characterization, reflects the influence of Romanticism. One of the first great dramatic critics, his reviews were published in* The Examiner, The Morning Chronicle, The Champion, The London Magazine, *and* The Times. *Some of these were subsequently collected in his* The Round Table *(1817) and* A View of the English Stage *(1818). In the following excerpt from his* English Comic Writers, *originally published in 1819, Hazlitt differentiates Farquhar's comic heroes from those of his contemporaries, claiming that Farquhar "makes us laugh from pleasure oftener than from malice."*]

Farquhar's chief characters are . . . adventurers; but they are adventurers of a romantic, not a knavish stamp, and succeed no less by their honesty than their boldness. They conquer their difficulties, and effect their "hairbreadth 'scapes" by the impulse of natural enthusiasm and the confidence of high principles of gallantry and honour, as much as by their dexterity and readiness at expedients. They are real gentlemen, and only pretended impostors. Vanbrugh's upstart heroes are without "any relish of salvation," without generosity, virtue, or any pretensions to it. We have little sympathy for them, and no respect at all. But we have every sort of good-will towards Farquhar's heroes, who have as many peccadilloes to answer for, and play as many rogue's tricks, but are honest fellows at bottom. I know little other difference between these two capital writers and copyists of nature, than that Farquhar's nature is the better nature of the two. We seem to like both the author and his favourites. He has humour, character, and invention in common with the other, with a more unaffected gaiety and spirit of enjoyment, which overflows and sparkles in all he does. He makes us laugh from pleasure oftener than from malice. He somewhere prides himself in having introduced on the stage the class of comic heroes here spoken of, which has since become a standard character, and which represents the warm-hearted, rattle-brained, thoughtless, high-spirited young fellow, who floats on the back of his misfortunes without repining, who forfeits appearances, but saves his honour; and he gives us to understand that it was his own. He did not need to be ashamed of it. Indeed there is internal evidence that this sort of character is his own, for it pervades his works generally, and is the moving spirit that informs them. His comedies have on this account probably a greater appearance of truth and nature than almost any others. His incidents succeed one another with rapidity, but without premeditation; his wit is easy and spontaneous; his style animated, unembarrassed, and flowing; his characters full of life and spirit, and never overstrained so as to "o'erstep the modesty of nature," though they sometimes, from haste and carelessness, seem left in a crude, unfinished state. There is a constant ebullition of gay, laughing invention, cordial good humour, and fine animal spirits, in his writings. (pp. 111-12)

His fine gentlemen are not gentlemen of fortune and fashion, like those in Congreve; but are rather "God Almighty's gentlemen." His valets are good fellows: even his chambermaids are some of them disinterested and sincere. But his fine ladies, it must be allowed, are not so amiable, so witty, or accomplished, as those in Congreve. Perhaps they both described women in high life as they found them: Congreve took their conversation, Farquhar their conduct. In the way of fashionable vice and petrifying affectation, there is nothing to come up to his 'Lady Lurewell,' in the *Trip to the Jubilee.* She by no means makes good Mr. Burke's courtly and chivalrous observation, that the evil of vice consists principally in its want of refinement; and one benefit of the dramatic exhibition of such characters is, that they overturn false maxims of morality, and settle accounts fairly and satisfactorily between theory and practice. Her lover, Colonel Standard, is indeed an awkward incumbrance upon so fine a lady: it was a character that the poet did not like; and he has merely sketched him in, leaving him to answer for himself as well as he could, which is but badly. We have no suspicion, either from his conduct, or from any hint dropped by accident, that he is the first seducer and the possessor of the virgin affections of Lady Lurewell. The double transformation of this virago from vice to virtue, and from virtue to vice again, her plausible pretensions and artful wiles, her violent temper and dissolute passions, show a thorough knowledge of the effects both of nature and habit in making up human character. Farquhar's own heedless turn for gallantry would be likely to throw him upon such a character; and his goodness of heart and sincerity of disposition would teach him to expose its wanton duplicity and gilded rottenness. Lurewell is almost as abandoned a character as Olivia in [Wycherley's] the *Plain Dealer;* but the indignation excited against her is of a less serious and tragic cast. Her peevish disgust and affected horror at everything that comes near her, form a very edifying picture. Her dissatisfaction and *ennui* are not mere airs and graces worn for fashion's sake; but are real and tormenting inmates of her breast, arising from a surfeit of pleasure and the consciousness of guilt. All that is hateful in the caprice, ill humour, spite, *hauteur,* folly, impudence, and affectation of the complete woman of quality, is contained in the scene between her and her servants in the first act. The depravity would be intolerable, even in imagination, if the weakness were not ludicrous in the extreme. It shows, in the highest degree, the power of circumstances and example to pervert the understanding, the imagination, and even the senses. The manner in which the character of the gay, wild, free-hearted, but not altogether profligate or unfeeling Sir Harry Wildair, is played off against the designing, vindictive, imperious, uncontrollable, and unreasonable humours of Lurewell, in the scene where she tries to convince him of his wife's infidelity, while he stops his ears to her pretended proofs, is not surpassed in modern comedy. (pp. 112-14)

The *Beaux' Stratagem* is the best of his plays, as a whole; infinitely lively, bustling, and full of point and interest. The assumed disguise of the two principal characters, Archer and Aimwell, is a perpetual amusement to the mind. Scrub is an indispensable appendage to a country gentleman's kitchen, and an exquisite confidant for the secrets of young ladies. The *Recruiting Officer* is not one of Farquhar's best comedies, though it is light and entertaining. It contains chiefly sketches and hints of characters, and the conclusion of the plot is rather lame. He informs us, in the dedication to the published play, that it was founded on some local and personal circumstances that happened in Shropshire, where he was himself a recruiting officer;

and it seems not unlikely that most of the scenes actually took place at the foot of the Wrekin. The *Inconstant* is much superior to it. The romantic interest and impressive catastrophe of this play I thought had been borrowed from the more poetical and tragedy-practised muse of Beaumont and Fletcher; but I find they are taken from an actual circumstance which took place, in the author's knowledge, at Paris. His other pieces, *Love and a Bottle,* and the *Twin Rivals,* are not on a par with these; and are no longer in possession of the stage. The public are, after all, not the worst judges. Farquhar's *Letters* prefixed to the collection of his plays, are lively, good-humoured, and sensible; and contain, among other things, an admirable exposition of the futility of the dramatic unities of time and place. (p. 117)

William Hazlitt, "On Wycherley, Congreve, Vanbrugh, and Farquhar," in his Lectures on the English Poets, and the English Comic Writers, *edited by William Carew Hazlitt, George Bell and Sons, 1876, pp. 91-120.*

Leigh Hunt (essay date 1840)

[*An English poet and essayist, Hunt is remembered as a literary critic who encouraged and influenced several Romantic poets, especially John Keats and Percy Bysshe Shelley. Hunt produced volumes of poetry and critical essays and, with his brother John, established* The Examiner, *a weekly liberal newspaper. In his criticism, Hunt articulated the principles of Romanticism, emphasizing imaginative freedom and the expression of a personal, emotional, or spiritual state. In the following excerpt, Hunt offers an assessment of Farquhar's works, criticizing the "gratuitous" dialogue and loose morality of his earlier plays, but finding* The Recruiting Officer *and* The Beaux' Stratagem *admirable for their natural liveliness and originality.*]

In looking critically at Farquhar's plays in succession, nothing need be added to what has been said respecting the earliest one, *Love and a Bottle,* except that much of the talk is gratuitous, and that in this play, perhaps more than in any of the rest, is to be seen the "pert low dialogue" which Pope accused him of writing; that is to say, brisk only, with a pretence of something better, and on that account wanting in an air of good breeding. Nor is *Sir Harry Wildair* without it in the *Constant Couple,* nor even *Archer* in his last play, the *Beaux-Stratagem.* It was probably owing to the conflict between the author's habits of personal reserve, and his sympathy in spirit with all that was the reverse. Goldsmith, who was a very diffident man, carried the same error into his *Young Marlow* in *She Stoops to Conquer;* or rather would have carried it, had not the very intensity of his consciousness of the danger ingeniously converted it into a part of his comic intention. And *Marlow,* who in one of his situations is a copy of *Archer,* is, after all, really pert, and gives himself airs, to the supposed chambermaid, beyond what a thorough-bred gentleman would have done. *Sir Harry Wildair,* nevertheless, as Steele said, is very entertaining in spite of what that good-natured critic himself thought "low;" and will always interest, as a kind of epitome of youthful spirits and freedom from care, let loose upon the world. The plot of the play is as lively as the character, and, like most of Farquhar's plots, is the author's own; and, considering the manners of the times, almost everything is natural in it, with the exception of the outrageously farcical notion of the swimming-girdle, which was to carry Clincher to Civita Vecchia.

Farquhar, who had been so modest in his preface to the **Constant Couple** as to describe himself "below the envy of great wits and above the malice of little ones," had either got so warmed into a better opinion of himself by the time he wrote the **Inconstant,** or perhaps was really so unaware of the superiority of a great *poetical* genius, as to brand those who accused him of spoiling Fletcher's *Wildgoose Chace* with wishing them no other injury than that they "would say it again!" *Spoiling,* it certainly could not be called; any more than it could be called spoiling an eagle's wing to pluck a feather from it, and turn it into a toy. But the wording of the taunt implies something contemptuous of a reverence towards the eagle; and this becomes a blindness to the height to which the eagle soared. Farquhar's **Inconstant** is a pleasant play (as far as the chief characters as well as the plot are pleasant; which we cannot, we own, very well think they are, either in the copy or the original); but compared with the *Wild Goose Chace,* it is not a whit livelier, nor indeed so lively, nor has it anything of the other's robust and masterly expression or imagination. It is, in truth, with the exception of the highly interesting adventure that is taken from a fact in the history of a French gentleman, neither more nor less than Fletcher's play with all the poetry taken out of it;—the age of the demi-gods of Elizabeth, brought down to the standard of the sprightly parade officers of the times of Captains Vanbrugh and Farquhar. We are not to suppose that Apollo could have been less of a "gay fellow about town," if he chose it, than the wittiest gallant that stuck a bay-leaf in his peruke: only, without question, (if that be "spoiling,") his language would have had ten ideas in it to the other's one.

The **Twin Rivals** was an attempt to write a comedy in a fit of critical instead of playful inspiration. Critics have spoken well of it accordingly, and thought it the completest of his productions; but the town did not like it, nor did the author repeat the experiment. Collier, it seems, by Farquhar's own account, had piqued him into an endeavour to show how moral and profoundly satirical he could be. It is the story of a Hunchback, . . . who in a most impudent manner, as a retaliation upon fortune, tries to deprive his elder brother of a title and estate. Upon looking through it again, while writing this paragraph, we find we have not marked in it a dozen lines.

In the **Recruiting Officer** he took his revenge; threw himself entirely upon his animal spirits, and produced accordingly one of his very best plays. In everything connected with it he was fortunate; for he went only upon grounds of truth and observation, and his own impulses. . . . Every character in the piece, of any prominence, is thought to be a genuine transcript from nature; and there is a charm of gaiety and good-humour throughout it, that enables us to put the best and least tragical construction

Farquhar had the highest animal spirits, with fits of the deepest sympathy, the greatest wish to please rather than to strike, the most agreeable diversity of character, the best instinct in avoiding revolting extravagances of the time, and the happiest invention in plot and situation; and, therefore, is to be pronounced, upon the whole, the truest dramatic genius, and the most likely to be of lasting popularity; as indeed he has hitherto been.

—Leigh Hunt

upon certain anti-sentimentalities, which Steele perhaps was too much out of his customary good-humour to choose to consider in any light but one. We seem to breathe the clear, fresh, ruddy-making air of a remote country town, neighboured by hospitable elegances. The sturdy male peasants will find their legs in life somehow, as the *Serjeant* has done; and the females will be taken more care of by the *Captain* himself, and by the good-natured *Sylvia* too, than the censor at first sight might suppose. The morals are not the best, we allow; and especially in the matter of *lying* (which always gives us a pang), they may be infinitely improved, as we doubt not they will, though not from the austerest quarters. When the best morals arrive, everybody will be as happily taken care of as the "ladies" themselves;—not the case certainly at present, nor provided for even by the prospective ethics of dear, excellent Richard Steele.

The sprightly success of the **Recruiting Officer** had probably the happiest effect upon the composition of our author's best and most successful production, the **Beaux Stratagem;** an excellent play, which, like the one just mentioned, and the **Inconstant,** is always acted whenever actors can be found. Its plot is new, simple, and interesting; the characters various, without confusing it; the dialogue sprightly and characteristic; the moral bold, healthy, admirable, and doubly needed in those times, when sottishness was a fashion. *Archer* and *Aimwell,* who set out as mere intriguers, prove in the end true gentlemen, candid, conscientious, and generous. *Scrub* and *Boniface,* though but a servant and an innkeeper, are quotable fellows both, and have made themselves prominent in theatrical recollection,—the former especially, for his quaint ignorance and sordid cunning. And *Mrs. Sullen* is the more touching in her distress, from the cheerfulness with which she wipes away her tears. *Sullen* is an awful brute, yet not thoroughly inhuman; for he feels after all that he has no right to such a wife. The only fault in the termination, is what Mrs. Oldfield objected to,—that the law had provided no sanction for it; so that it became but a higher kind of sale by halter. But what a lesson did not this very want imply? The footsteps of the gravest ultimate reforms are often found in places where they are least looked for. But Nature speaks there, and there they come. (pp. lxxii-lxxv)

Of the four dramatists of whom we have thus endeavoured to give some account . . . Farquhar had the highest animal spirits, with fits of the deepest sympathy, the greatest wish to please rather than to strike, the most agreeable diversity of character, the best instinct in avoiding revolting extravagances of the time, and the happiest invention in plot and situation; and, therefore, is to be pronounced, upon the whole, the truest dramatic genius, and the most likely to be of lasting popularity; as indeed he has hitherto been. (pp. lxxviii-lxxix)

> *Leigh Hunt, in an introduction to* The Dramatic Works of Wycherley, Congreve, Vanbrugh, and Farquhar, *Edward Moxon, 1840, pp. ix-ci.*

Edmund Gosse (essay date 1891)

[*A distinguished English literary historian, critic, and biographer, Gosse wrote extensively on seventeenth- and eighteenth-century English literature. His commentary in* Seventeenth-Century Studies *(1883),* A History of Eighteenth Century Literature *(1889),* Questions at Issue *(1893), and other works is generally regarded as sound and suggestive, and he is also credited with introducing the works of the Norwegian dramatist Henrik Ibsen and other Scandinavian writers to English readers. In the following excerpt, he briefly examines the style and narrative persona of Farquhar's* Love and Business.]

There are some books, like some people, of whom we form an indulgent opinion without finding it easy to justify our liking. . . . Some times we like a book, not for any special merit, but just because it is what it is. The rare, and yet not celebrated, miscellany of which I am about to write has this character. It is not instructive, or very high-toned, or exceptionally clever, but if it were a man, all people that are not prigs would say that it was a very good sort of fellow. If it be, as it certainly is, a literary advantage for a nondescript collection of trifles to reproduce minutely the personality of its writer, then *Love and Business* has one definite merit. (pp. 147-48)

In order to bring down a few brace of golden game, [Farquhar] shovels into Lintott's hands his stray verses of all kinds, a bundle of letters he wrote from Holland, a dignified essay or discourse upon Comedy, and, with questionable taste perhaps, a set of copies of the love-letters he had addressed to the lady who became his wife. All this is not very praiseworthy, and as a contribution to literature it is slight indeed; but, then, how genuine and sincere, how guileless and picturesque is the self-revelation of it! There is no attempt to make things better than they are, nor any pandering to a cynical taste by making them worse. Why should he conceal or falsify? The town knows what sort of a fellow George Farquhar is. Here are some letters and some verses; the beaux at White's may read them if they will, and then throw them away.

As we turn the desultory pages, the figure of the author rises before us, good-natured, easy-going, high-coloured,

not bad-looking, with an air of a gentleman in spite of his misfortunes. We do not know the exact details of his military honours. We may think of him as swaggering in scarlet regimentals, but we have his own word for it that he was often in *mufti.* His mind is generally dressed, he says, like his body, in black; for though he is so brisk a spark in company, he suffers sadly from the spleen when he is alone. We can follow him pretty closely through his day. He is a queer mixture of profanity and piety, of coarseness and loyalty, of cleverness and density; we do not breed this kind of beau nowadays, and yet we might do worse, for this specimen is, with all his faults, a man. (pp. 149-50)

> *Edmund Gosse, "Love and Business," in his* Gossip in a Library, *William Heinemann, 1891, pp. 145-57.*

Alex Charles Ewald (essay date 1892)

[*In the following excerpt, Ewald presents a brief overview of Farquhar's plays, excusing his amorality because, unlike his contemporaries, Farquhar was "never cruel or savage in his satire."*]

Of all the elements which enter into the composition of pure comedy, Farquhar was a consummate master. His plots were invariably carefully thought out, the incidents skilfully developed, and every scene naturally arose from the environment of the story. His dialogue, if never supremely witty, is always lively and entertaining, yet seldom, as is the case with Congreve, arresting the progress of the play for the mere sake of introducing sparkling conversation. A keen observer of life and manners, his characters possess a marked individuality of their own, each being the typical representation of some passing fashion or creature of the hour. In the dramatic gallery of Farquhar we see the fashionable gallant of the day, anxious as to the conduct of a campaign or a coquette, ever busy with the wiles of intrigue, preaching his loose morality, and seldom failing to confound sensuality with love. Heartless, dissolute, and indifferent to everything save his own interests and pleasures, the one redeeming point of this gay rake is, that he is never brutal or inhuman in his sentiments or actions. There, too, we see limned in that gallery the Irish adventurer, with his schemes for self-advancement, a common and conspicuous personage of his time, the Jesuit priest plotting and unscrupulous, the bravo captain, the recruiting officer with his blarney and alluring offers, the stupid squire, the women modest and immodest, the airy and flippant fop, the rollicking landlord, and the rest of the portraits which, though often painted with a broad and coarse touch, yet show that a true and keen artist was at work on the canvas. Though now banished from the stage, the characters of Roebuck, Mockmode, Sir Harry Wildair, Lady Lurewell, Young Mirabel, Serjeant Kite, Boniface, Cherry, Scrub, and Squire Sullen will always continue to live in the library, and be as much objects of interest to the reader of the nineteenth century as they were to the spectator of the eighteenth. In face of the plays given to us by Farquhar, it is absurd to place him upon a pedestal of purity from which the most superficial perusal of his works must at once depose him. All that can be said of him—and the admission is no slight compliment—is that living at the time he did, when the atmosphere of the Restoration was still heavy upon both the stage and the dramatist, his comedies compare most favourably with those of his contemporaries. He occupies a middle position between the vicious writers of the close of the seventeenth century and the comparatively purer writers of the beginning of the eighteenth century. He deals with vicious subjects, and seldom goes outside their circle for the mechanism of his plots; but he does not, as did Wycherley, prefer vice to virtue, and render the latter always dull and despicable. His dames of fashion are as lax and faithless as women not wholly lost to all social restrictions can well be, yet on the same canvas he can depict a modest, graceful, and attractive maiden. If he represents a gallant as ever bent on intrigue and a scoffer at all the regularities of life, he is no less able to portray manhood in its nobler and more honest aspect. In the comedies of Farquhar, as is so often the case with the other dramatists of the Restoration, wit is not always allied with profanity, humour with indecency, modesty with stupidity, and rectitude with timidity or lack of opportunity. The shady scenes, it is true, predominate in his pages; but the author is not so completely enamoured of darkness as to refuse to admit the light. Whatever his faults may be, Farquhar, unlike Swift or Voltaire, is never cruel or savage in his satire. He studies human nature always from a genial and kindly standpoint. The failings of the creatures of his imagination never spring from a bitter and relentless source—his *dramatis personæ* sin and fall because their humanity works too strongly within them to tolerate restraint; they love and drink and gamble because they are so essentially human that they cannot prevent their frailties from assuming the supremacy. Yet they are always men and never yahoos. Throughout the whole of the comedies of Farquhar we never meet with a sentiment or an incident in which the author places his characters beyond the reach of our sympathy, or outside the region of humanity. He frequently errs against good taste in the scenes he depicts; we recognise his indelicacy, his often low tone of morality, his occasional ribaldry; but throughout there is nothing of the venom and savage hate of the man who loves to hurl foul scorn and degradation upon his kind. We rise from a study of his plays regretting much that might with advantage be omitted; but still shining clear above all defects we see the genius, the cheery humour, the kindly heart, the skilful manipulation of the true master of comedy. (pp. xii-xv)

> *Alex Charles Ewald, in an introduction to* The Dramatic Works of George Farquhar, *Vol. 1, John C. Nimmo, 1892, pp. v-xv.*

Louise Imogen Guiney   (essay date 1894)

[*In the following excerpt, Guiney focuses on the sympathetic and charitable nature of Farquhar's plays, contrasting them favorably with those of other Restoration dramatists.*]

Farquhar's name is usually mentioned with those of Congreve, Wycherley, and Vanbrugh, although in spirit, as well as in point of time, he was relatively removed from the influences which formed them. Many critics of our ar-

Robert Wilks, Irish actor and close friend of Farquhar.

tificial comedy, notably Hazlitt, Macaulay, and Thackeray, have allowed him least mention of the four; but he is, in reality, the best playwright among them, and it is greatly to the credit of a discreditable period if he be taken as its representative. (p. 406)

Pope, and Steele as well, a much gentler observer, found Farquhar's dialogue "low"; and so may it have sounded between the brave extravagancies of the Jacobean buskin, and the modulated utterances of *Cato* and *The Revenge.* But it is not "low" to modern tastes; it has, in general, a simple, natural gusto infinitely preferable to the Persian apparatus of the eighteenth century. More plainly in Farquhar's work than in that of any contemporary, we mark the glamour of the Caroline æsthetics fading, and the breath of life blowing in. . . . He reports, from the beginning, what he himself apprehends; his plays are shorthand notes, albeit somewhat timid in character, upon his transitional and commonplace time. His company is made up of individuals he had seen in a thousand lights at the Spread Eagle and the Rummer; in the Inner Temple, Spring Gardens, and Saint James's Park; in barracks domestic and foreign; and in his native north, where adventurers, eloquent in purest Londonderry, stumbled along full of whiskey and ideas. He anticipates certain moods and phrases of Private Ortheris's thorough-going love of London, and pictures his exiled Dicky as "just dead of a consumption, till the sweet smoke of Cheapside and the dear perfume of Fleet Ditch" made him a man again. In this laughing, affectionate mastery of the local and the temporal lay Farquhar's whole strength and weakness. What was ably said by Hazlitt of Hogarth, the great exemplar, covers all practicians of his school: "He had an intense feeling for, and command over the impressions of senses and habit, of character and passion, the serious and the comic; in a word, of nature as it fell in with his own observation, or came into the sphere of his actual experience. But he had little power beyond that sphere, or sympathy with that which existed only in idea. He was 'conformed to this world, not transformed.'" Or, as Leigh Hunt, in his beautiful Memoir, adds, with equal acuteness, of Farquhar himself: "He could turn what he had experienced in common life to the best account, but he required in all cases the support of ordinary associations, and could not project his spirit beyond them." His homely materialism is a drop, or a rise, from Congreve and his aristocratic abstractions. Farquhar, who in his youth had modelled himself upon Congreve, never attained, nor could attain, Congreve's scholarly elegance of proportion and his consummate English. But he had the happiness of being no merely literary dramatist; he had technical knowledge and skill; he brought the existing heroes with their conniving valets, the laughing, masking, conscienceless fine ladies with their buxom, equivocal maids, out of their disreputable moonlight into healthful comic air; and he added to them, in the transfer, a leaven of lovableness which will forever keep his masterpieces upon the boards. Farquhar lacked imagination; but he had insight of another order, which is his praise, and which distinguishes him from all his fellows: he had sympathy and charity.

The major blot on the dramatic literature of the period was not its impurity, but rather its concomitant utter heartlessness, which Erasmus and his ascetic friend Dean Colet would have proclaimed to be the much more evil thing. The slight sporadic touches of tenderness, of pity, of disinterested generosity, which are to be found by patient search in Congreve, come in boldly with Farquhar, and boldly overrun all his pages. Vanbrugh's scenes stand on nothing but their nervous animation and their biting extravagant sarcasm. His women in high life have no individuality; they wear stings of one pattern. Etherege's typical Man of Mode is a tissue of untruth, hardness, and scorn, all in impeccable attire: not a diverting, but a most mournful spectacle. Thinking of such dainty monsters, Macaulay let fly his famous invective against their creators: "Foreheads of bronze, hearts like the nether millstone, and tongues set on fire of hell!" George Farquhar may be exempted altogether from this too-deserved compliment. There is honest mirth in his world of fiction, there is dutifulness, there is true love, there are good women. There is genuine friendship between Lovewell and Roebuck, between Trueman and Hermes Wouldbe, between Archer and Aimwell, and between the good Tummas of *The Recruiting Officer* and his Costar, whom he cannot leave behind. Sylvia, Angelica, Constance, Leanthe, Oriana, Dorinda, free-spoken as they are, how they shine, and with what morning freshness, among the tiger-lilies of that gross garden of the Restoration! These heroines are an innovation, inasmuch as they are free maids, not wedded wives. As to the immortal periwigged young bloods their suitors, they are "real gentlemen," as Hazlitt, who loved Farquhar, called them, "and only pretended impostors."

In their conversations, glistening with epigram and irony, malevolence has no part; they sneer at no virtue, they tamper with none; and at every turn of a selfish campaign they find opportunity for honorable behavior. From the mouths of these worldlings comes satire hot and piping against worldliness; for Farquhar is as moralizing, if not as moral, as he dares be. Some of the least attractive among them, the most greedy and contriving, have moments of sweetly whimsical and optimistic speech. Thus Benjamin, the hunchbacked plotter against his elder brother in *The Twin Rivals,* makes his adieu after the fashion of a true gallant: "I scorn your beggarly benevolence! Had my designs succeeded, I would not have allowed you the weight of a wafer, and therefore will accept none." Or again, the same person soars into a fine Aurelian speculation: "Show me that proud stoic that can bear success and champagne! Philosophy can support us in hard fortune; but who can have patience in prosperity?" Over his men and women in middle life Farquhar lingers with complacence entirely foreign to his colleagues, to whom mothers, guardians, husbands, and other apple-guarding dragons were uniformly ridiculous and odious. Justice Balance is as attractive as a hearth-fire on a December night; so is Lady Bountiful. Over Fairbank, the good goldsmith, Farquhar gets fairly sentimental, and permits him to drop unaware into decasyllabics, like the pastoral author of *Lorna Doone.* His rogues are merely roguish, in the softened acceptation of the word; in his panorama, though black villains come and go, it is only for an instant, and to further some one dramatic effect. He has eulogy for his heroes when they deserve it, and when they do not, you may trust him to find a compassionate excuse, as when poor Leanthe feelingly says of her lover that "his follies are weakly founded upon the principles of honor, where the very foundation helps to undermine the structure." Even Squire Sullen, for his lumpishness, is divorced without derision, and in a peal of harmless laughter.

Farquhar, indeed, is all gentleness, all kindness. He had the pensive attitude of the true humorist toward the world he laughed at; his characters let slip words too deep for their living auditors. It is curious that to a Restoration dramatist, a "nether millstone," we should owe the most perfect brief description in the language of ideal married life. In the great scene in the fourth act of *Sir Harry Wildair,* where Lady Lurewell, with her "petrifying affectation," is trying to tease Sir Harry out of all endurance on the subject of his wife (supposed to be dead), and the degree of affection he had for her, he makes reply: "My own heart whispered me her desires, 'cause she herself was there: no contention ever rose but the dear strife of who should most oblige, no noise about authority; for neither would stoop to command, where both thought it glory to obey." This is meant to be spoken rapidly, and not without its tantalizing lack of emphasis; but what a pearl it is, set in the superlatively caustic dialogue! English chivalry and English literature have no such other golden paragraph in their rubrics, unless it be the famous tribute to the Lady Elizabeth Hastings that "to love her was a liberal education," or Lovelace's unforgetable song:—

I could not love thee, dear, so much,
Loved I not Honour more.

The passage takes on a double beauty when we remember that it required some courage, in its time and place, to have written it. It is not uncharacteristic of George Farquhar that it should be introduced as it is, on the top wave of a vivacious and strong conversation which immediately sweeps it under. The conjugal tie, among the leaders of fashion, was still something to laugh at and toy with. Vanbrugh, from whom nobody need expect much moral illumination, had put in the mouth of Constant in a play which was a favorite with Garrick, a bit of sincerity quoted, as it deserved to be, by Leigh Hunt: "Though marriage be a lottery, in which there are a wondrous many blanks, yet there is one inestimable lot, on which the only heaven on earth is written." And again: "To be capable of loving one is better than to possess a thousand." This was in 1698; and Farquhar, therefore, was not first, nor alone, in daring to speak for the derided ideal of wedlock. Steele, soon after, in the *Spectator,* arose as the very champion of domestic life, nor has English wit ever subsisted since by its mockery of the conditions which foster

> Home-keeping days and household reverences.

But it was Farquhar who uttered in their behalf the most memorable word of his generation. That one circumstance is lofty autobiographical evidence in his favor, which is more than borne out by what we know of his beautiful behavior in relation to his own early and extraordinary marriage.

There were in him a mellowness and unction which have their freest play in professedly subjective writing, and had he lived longer, or a little later, we should have found him also, with his skirmishing turn for psychology, among the novelists and the essayists. As it is, the analytic portrait of himself, which figures in one of the letters in his miscellaneous publication of 1702, *Love and Business,* might have come bodily, and with charming melancholy grace, from the *Spectator*. His *Discourse upon Comedy* is a pioneer exposition of the theory, long ago adopted by the English world, that the observance or breach of the dramatic unities may safely be left to the discretion of the wise, and that in all such matters it is better to be guided by Shakespeare than by Aristotle; the whole little thesis is excellent throughout in Farquhar's clear, sunny, forceful style. He had so correct a perception of all the laws which govern his art and the considerations which bear upon it, that it is somewhat surprising he should have lacked not the capacity, but the will, to help powerfully in regenerating public taste. He was young, he was of provincial nurture, he was carried away by the theatrical tradition. Yet his mind was a Medea's kettle out of which everything issued cleaner and more wholesome. Despite the bad old maintained conditions, and the prodigious animal spirits of his characters, they conduct their mad concerns with sense and moderation; they manage tacitly to proclaim themselves as likely to lead sober citizen lives from to-morrow on. They are to be classed as neutrals and nondescripts, for they have all the swagger of their libertine predecessors, and none of their deviltry. Some uneasiness, some misgiving in Farquhar himself, lends them that air of compromise and condoning which is their endearing blemish. It does not, however, affect the action of his two incompa-

rable last comedies, *The Recruiting Officer* and *The Beaux' Stratagem.* Using, in a manner entirely original, the conventional types back of him, he adopted the claim to approbation which the originators of those types never dreamed of. In fine, the fear of the Reverend Jeremy Collier was heavy upon his soul, and led him into divers vagaries. In a capital preface, he once set up for a castigator of vice and folly, and offered to appease "the ladies and the clergy," as, no doubt, in some measure apparent to the more metaphysical among them, he may have done. It is enough for an immature genius born under Charles the Second to have foreshadowed an imperative reform; and Farquhar everywhere foreshadows it, albeit with what theologians might call absence of the necessary intention. One cannot help begrudging him to the period he adorned, for he was worthy to flourish on the manlier morrow, and to hold a historic position with the men to whom we owe the tone and trend of English letters. (pp. 407-13)

> *Louise Imogen Guiney, "Gentle George Farquhar," in* Poet Lore, *Vol. VI, Nos. 8 & 9, August-September, 1894, pp. 406-13.*

H. Macaulay Fitzgibbon   (essay date 1898)

[*In the following excerpt from his preface to Farquhar's* The Beaux' Stratagem, *Fitzgibbon praises the play's brisk action and distinct cast of original characters, pronouncing* The Beaux' Stratagem *Farquhar's best work.*]

Each play that Farquhar produced was an improvement on its predecessors, and all critics have been unanimous in pronouncing *The Beaux-Stratagem* his best, both in the study and on the stage, of which it retained possession much the longest. Except *The Recruiting Officer* and *The Inconstant,* revived at Covent Garden in 1825, and also by Daly in America in 1885, none of Farquhar's other plays has been put on the stage for upwards of a century. Hallam says: 'Never has Congreve equalled *The Beaux-Stratagem* in vivacity, in originality of contrivance, or in clear and rapid development of intrigue'; and Hazlitt considers it 'sprightly, lively, bustling, and full of point and interest: the assumed disguise of Archer and Aimwell is a perpetual amusement to the mind.' The action—which commences, remarkably briskly, in the evening and ends about midnight the next day—never flags for an instant. The well-contrived plot is original and simple (all Farquhar's plots are excellent), giving rise to a rapid succession of amusing and sensational incidents; though by no means extravagant or improbable, save possibly the mutual separation of Squire Sullen and his wife in the last scene—the weak point of the whole. Farquhar was a master in stage-effect. Aimwell's stratagem of passing himself off as the wealthy nobleman, his brother (a device previously adopted by Vanbrugh in *The Relapse* and subsequently by Sheridan in his *Trip to Scarborough*), may perhaps be a covert allusion to the romantic story of the dramatist's own deception by the penniless lady who gave herself out to be possessed of a large fortune, and who thus induced him to marry her.

The style adopted is highly dramatic, the dialogue being natural and flowing; trenchant and sprightly, but not too witty for a truthful reflex of actual conversation. The humour is genial and unforced; there is no smell of the lamp about it, no premeditated effort at dragging in jests, as in Congreve. As typical examples of Farquhar's *vis comica* I would cite the description of Squire Sullen's homecoming, and his 'pot of ale' speech, Aimwell's speech respecting conduct at church, the scene between Cherry and Archer about the £2000, and the final separation scene—which affords a curious view of the marriage tie and on which Leigh Hunt has founded an argument for divorce. This play contains several examples of Farquhar's curious habit of breaking out into a kind of broken blank verse occasionally for a few lines in the more serious passages. Partaking as it does of the elements of both comedy and farce, it is the prototype of Goldsmith's *She Stoops to Conquer,* which it resembles in many respects. It will be remembered that Miss Hardcastle compares herself to Cherry (Act III.), and young Marlow and Hastings much resemble Archer and Aimwell. Goldsmith was a great admirer of the works of his fellow-countryman, especially *The Beaux-Stratagem,* and refers to them several times. . . . Unlike Goldsmith, unhappily, Farquhar's moral tone is not high; sensuality is confounded with love, ribaldry mistaken for wit. The best that can be said of him is that he contrasts favourably with his contemporary dramatists; Virtue is not *always* uninteresting in his pages. He is free from their heartlessness, malignity, and cruelty. The plot of *The Beaux-Stratagem* is comparatively inoffensive, and the moral of the whole is healthy. Although a wit rather than a thinker, Farquhar in this play shows himself capable of serious feelings. It is remarkable how much Farquhar repeats himself. Hardly an allusion or idea occurs in this play that is not to be found elsewhere in his works. (pp. vi-viii)

This play has added several distinct original personages to our stock of comedy characters, and it affords an excellent and lifelike picture of a peculiar and perishing phase of the manners of the time, especially those obtaining in the country house, and the village inn frequented by highwaymen. The sly, rascally landlord, Boniface (who has given his name to the class), is said to have been drawn from life, and his portrait, we are told, was still to be seen at Lichfield in 1775. The inimitable 'brother Scrub,' that 'indispensable appendage to a country gentleman's kitchen' (Hazlitt), with his ignorance and shrewd eye to the main chance, is likewise said to have been a well-known personage who survived till 1759, one Thomas Bond, servant to Sir Theophilus Biddulph; others say he died at Salisbury in 1744. Although Farquhar, like Goldsmith, undoubtedly drew his incidents and personages from his own daily associations, there is probably no more truth in these surmises than in the assertion (repeatedly made, though denied in his preface to *The Inconstant*) that Farquhar depicts himself in his young heroes, his rollicking 'men about town,' Roebuck, Mirabel, Wildair, Plume, Archer. Archer (copied by Hoadley in his character of Ranger in *The Suspicious Husband*) is a decided improvement on his predecessors, and is the best of all Farquhar's creations; he is assuredly the most brilliant footman that ever was, eminently sociable and, with all his easy, rattling volubility, never forgetful of his self-respect and never indifferent to the wishes or welfare of others. As Hunt has pointed out,

the characters of Archer and Aimwell improve as the play progresses; they set out as mere intriguers, but prove in the end true gentlemen. They are sad rogues, no doubt, but they have no bitter cynicism, no meanness; Aimwell refuses to marry Dorinda under any deception. They are thoroughly good fellows at bottom, manly, accomplished, high-spirited, eloquent, generous—the forerunners of Charles Surface. Marriage retrieves them and turns them into respectable and adoring husbands. Though rattle-brained, much given to gallantry, and somewhat lax in morality, they are not knaves or monsters; they do not inspire disgust. Even the lumpish blockhead, Squire Sullen—according to Macaulay a type of the main strength of the Tory party for half a century after the Revolution—contrasts favourably with his prototype Sir John Brute in Vanbrugh's *Provoked Wife.* He is a sodden sot, who always goes to bed drunk, but he is not a demon; he does not beat his wife in public; he observes common decency somewhat. His wife is a witty, attractive, warm-hearted woman, whose faults are transparent; the chief one being that she has made the fatal mistake of marrying for fortune and position instead of for love. There is something pathetic in her position which claims our sympathy. She is well contrasted with her sister-in-law, the sincere, though somewhat weakly drawn, Dorinda; whilst their mother-in-law, Lady Bountiful, famed for her charity, is an amusing and gracious figure, which has often been copied. Cherry, with her honest heart and her quickness of perception, is also a distinct creation. Strange to say, the only badly drawn character is Foigard, the unscrupulous Irish Jesuit priest. Farquhar is fond of introducing an Irishman into each of his plays, but I cannot say that I think he is generally successful; certainly not in this instance. They are mostly broad caricatures, and speak an outlandish jargon, more like Welsh than Irish, supposed to be the Ulster dialect: anything more unlike it would be difficult to conceive. (pp. ix-x)

> H. Macaulay Fitzgibbon, in a preface to The
> Beaux-Stratagem by George Farquhar, n. p.,
> 1898, pp. v-xvi.

Adolphus William Ward   (essay date 1899)

[*In the following excerpt, Ward surveys Farquhar's plays, finding in them elements of moral degradation but concluding that the dramatic invention of his* The Recruiting Officer *and* The Beaux' Stratagem *entitles Farquhar to "mention among the more distinguished authors of our later comic drama."*]

Were it not, perhaps, for one of his plays, George Farquhar . . . would hardly deserve to be ranked by the side—not of Congreve and Wycherley, but even of Vanbrugh. Farquhar, an Irishman by birth and early in life an actor on the Dublin stage (he afterwards served in the army), seems to have bestowed some attention upon the theory as well as the practice of the comic drama, and to have had a keen eye towards finding new expedients with which to supplement the familiar methods of gratifying the public palate. He is happy in the description of a wider range of manners than that commanded by Vanbrugh; but his dialogue is in general less gay and sparkling, and while his morality is no better than that of the most reckless of his contemporaries, he has a coarseness of fibre which renders him more offensive to a refined ear. The vivacity of his dramatic invention is however indisputable; and the freshness of mind which enabled him to widen the range of popular comedy in his last two plays entitles him to mention among the more distinguished authors of our later comic drama.

His earliest play, *Love and a Bottle* (1698), while in parts extremely gross in tone, and altogether coarse in treatment, is fluent rather than sparkling in its dialogue. In some degree this comedy recalls [Wycherley's] *The Plain-Dealer;* but the brutality of its principal personage is of a less complex kind. Farquhar's idea of a hero, indicated already in this play, is more fully developed in his *The Constant Couple, or A Trip to the Jubilee* (1700) and its sequel *Sir Harry Wildair* (1701). So much of plot as the former of these plays possesses, Farquhar seems to have taken from a kind of scandalous novel, imitated from Scarron [*The Adventures of Covent Garden,* 1699], in the authorship or concoction of which he had been himself concerned. It is, however, unnecessary to trace the adventures of Lady Lurewell either to their literary or to their probable historical source. Both plays doubtless derived their popularity from the figure of Sir Harry Wildair, for which Farquhar with a kind of mock modesty takes credit. In this character, whatever scope it may have provided for lively acting, the element of utter impudence reigns paramount; nor is the manner of the impudence, to my mind, especially agreeable. But what fascinates one generation is not necessarily irresistible to another. On the whole, *Sir Harry Wildair* is perhaps happier than the earlier play; but the design—which is to exhibit the hero as all but absolutely incorrigibile—can hardly be borne with, and is moreover in its essence the reverse of comic. Parts of this play are, however, decidedly entertaining. Sir Harry's supposed brother (really his wife in disguise) makes an amusing figure, which once more illustrates the not very edifying views held by the world of fashion and its mirror, the comic stage, as to the university education of the age. But though the dialogue of this comedy is vivacious and occasionally witty, it must as a whole, notwithstanding its termination, be described as utterly bad in spirit, and as furnishing a signal example of the degradation which the English comic drama had by this time reached. For *The Inconstant, or The Way to Win Him* (1703) Farquhar 'took the hint from Fletcher's *Wild-Goose-Chase,* and to those who say, that I have spoiled the original, I wish no other injury, but that they would say it again.' Fletcher's play was theatrically one of the most brilliantly successful of its author's comedies; but Farquhar's version cannot be denied the praise of being both brisk and entertaining; and the fifth act (founded on fact) adds an ingenious contrivance of the author's own. There was moreover some boldness in laying the scene in Paris; although the manners, such as they are, differ in no wise from those of the English comedy of this age in general; and Young Mirabel is a mere reproduction of Sir Harry Wildair. It is striking, that even an idea like that of *The Wild-Goose-Chase* should suffice to give, so to speak, more body to this play than most contemporary comedies possess.

In the Preface to *The Twin-Rivals* (1705) the author announces his intention of taking advantage of the success of Collier's attack upon the theatre, so as to 'make the stage flourish by virtue of that satire by which' its assailant 'thought to suppress it.' Farquhar can however hardly be said to move very easily in his moral enterprise. This comedy is, to say the least, quite as coarse as anything he had previously written, while the virtuous characters are not very interesting. The notion of making the villain of the action a humpback is presumably meant as a tribute to morality. Teague, the Irish servant, is fairly amusing. In *The Recruiting Officer* (1706) the author sought to break fresh ground. The comedy, dedicated 'to all friends round the Wrekin,' was intended as a sketch of country (Shropshire) manners, as well as of the humours of the recruiting system. From both points of view the attempt was legitimate and novel, and attaches a certain historical interest to the picture in which it resulted. But the colours are in this comedy laid on as coarsely as in the lowest scenes of our eighteenth-century novels; there is little to choose between Captain Plume and Sergeant Kite, and hardly more between the young ladies and the country wenches of Shropshire. In *The Beaux' Stratagem* (1707) Farquhar achieved his master-piece. This comedy, justly the most celebrated of his plays and destined to an enduring life on the stage, deserved its success in the first instance by the cleverness of the plot, which is ingenious without being improbable. Some of the incidents, indeed, are of dubious import, including one at the close,—a separation by mutual consent,—which throws a glaring light on the view taken by the author and his age of the sanctity of the marriage-tie. But the comedy is also an excellent picture of manners. The inn with its rascally landlord and highwaymen-guests and the country-house into which the Beau is carried in a fainting-fit, stand before us as scenes from real life; and some of the characters are drawn with much humour and spirit. The most successful conception is that of Archer, who pretends to be the valet of his friend the Beau, but carries on adventures on his own account. This became one of Garrick's most famous parts; and indeed the easy volubility of the pretended servant furnishes an admirable opportunity for a fine actor of light comedy. Altogether this play is written in the happiest of veins; and may be regarded as the prototype of Goldsmith's *She Stoops to Conquer,* like which it hovers rather doubtfully on the borders—not always easy to determine—of comedy and farce. (pp. 481-85)

Adolphus William Ward, "The Later Stuart Drama," in his A History of English Dramatic Literature to the Death of Queen Anne, *Vol. III, revised edition, 1899. Reprint by Octagon Books, Inc., 1966, pp. 277-518.*

John Palmer   (essay date 1913)

[*An English diplomat, drama critic, editor, and author of numerous detective novels, Palmer wrote several books on drama including* Moliere: His Life and Works *(1930). In the following excerpt, he offers a general overview of Farquhar's plays, suggesting that their moral and artistic inconsistencies significantly contributed to the decline of English comedy.*]

Farquhar is the last of the five principal figures in the half century of English comedy that began with Etherege. Facts continue to be kind. We have found in the lives and works of the four conspicuous predecessors of Farquhar an uninterrupted story of the development of a definite type of comedy. In Farquhar the story continues without a break. The comedy of manners, reaching perfection in Congreve, perceptibly droops in Vanbrugh, and in Farquhar is extinguished. It was no accident of history that Farquhar had no successor. Farquhar killed the comedy to which he contributed the last brilliant examples.

Farquhar's position in English comedy has not yet been historically considered. Critics have approached Farquhar from many points of view; never as the heir of Congreve. That Farquhar was the last of the comic dramatists, that he really succeeded Etherege and Wycherley, is one of those too obvious facts which invariably escape. Between the lines of most criticisms of the plays of Farquhar, more especially those which were written in the late nineteenth century—we detect an indulgence, a determination to make the most of his good, and the least of his bad qualities, which contrasts remarkably with the treatment usually bestowed upon his predecessors. The explanation of this is that Farquhar is invariably approached as a late nineteenth-century author, who, from youth, inexperience, hot blood, and high spirits, did not quite come off either morally or artistically. His heart is felt to be in the right place. He introduced, it is said, fresh air into the theatre. He took a serious interest in moral problems. The nauseous comedy of Wycherley; the heartless comedy of Congreve, is abandoned. Farquhar, in fact, has been treated as a reformer of the old theatre; and as the possible founder of a better type of play.

This is history inverted. When we come to consider his plays in detail we shall find in Farquhar precisely that acceptance of an outgrown convention which mars the comedy of Vanbrugh. Where the critics find in Farquhar humanity and fresh air we shall detect an emotional and romantic treatment of sex stifling the parent stem of a comedy whose appeal depended upon an entirely different system of moral and imaginative values. Farquhar's comedies are the direct result of an author, whose temperament and environment were not much unlike those of his nineteenth-century critics, trying to write comedies like Congreve. The consequent inconsistencies, often resulting in serious moral and artistic offence, are more patent than in Vanbrugh's case; for Farquhar was more careless a writer than his predecessor, and never really discovered in his art a neutral territory where the values he borrowed were reconciled with the values he contributed. (pp. 242-44)

Etherege and Farquhar are antithetical. For the one playwriting, or diplomacy—life itself—was an agreeable diversion. All was accepted in the sanguine faith that the ready and present sensation, idea, or adventure, would in its passing be justified. For the other life was rather a pilgrimage than a play; fortune was suspected; the present was marred with gaingiving. The contrast between the temperaments of these two men is fundamental to an understanding of Farquhar's position as an English comic writer.

Farquhar accepted the tradition of Etherege. He is expressing himself in a foreign language, an attempt which was equally disastrous for his message and for his idiom. (pp. 256-57)

Farquhar's first play, *Love and a Bottle,* clearly pointed the characteristics of his comedy. Roebuck, the gallant hero of the tale, is the predecessor of Sir Harry Wildair, Captain Plume and Mr. Archer. He is the Restoration gentleman at point of being redeemed to a reluctant and uncertain belief in the virtues of monogamy. He is Farquhar's attempt to realise and consistently to deal with a figure which he had mechanically accepted from the theatre of his predecessors. In Roebuck the insincerity of Farquhar's effort to project himself into the comic world of Congreve glares obviously through the lines of his pert cynicism. His author's brutality is forced. Roebuck is a tedious hypocrite, feigning harder to be bad than Alderman Gripe feigned to be good. Farquhar himself feels the contradiction between his personal instincts and the conduct of his heroes. Every now and then he pauses vaguely to justify himself and smooth out the inconsistencies of his comedy. Leanthe says of Roebuck: "Wild as wind and unconfined as air! Yet I may reclaim him. His follies are weakly founded upon the principles of honour, where the very foundation helps to undermine the structure. How charming would virtue look in him whose behaviour can add a grace to the unseemliness of vice." This passage has been quoted as putting Farquhar morally above his predecessors. Merely it is an attempt to justify in his conscience the motives of a stage-figure he had picked up from Congreve and Wycherley at second-hand. Roebuck corresponds to nothing truthful or real in Farquhar. Seen through these words of Leanthe he is a dishonest attempt to graft on to the unimpassioned comedy of the Restoration, based upon the morality of Charles II., the emotional comedy of the Revolution, based upon the immorality of William III. Sexual irregularity is now explained as an amiable excess of the qualities which make a devoted husband. Moreover, concomitant with this confusion of moral values, there proceeds that other degradation of comedy which we noted in the plays of Vanbrugh—a "passionate and luscious" treatment of sex. In *Love and a Bottle* we meet the stock phrases of the theatre of Aphrodite—"Soft, melting, white and yielding waist"; "folded fast"; "broken sighs"; "heat of love," and so forth—the whole being intended to convey a correct and Victorian impression that nothing more nor less than an interchange of souls is in question.

Farquhar had but one avenue of escape from the perplexities of a comic world whose laws were in revolution. His style was light and rapid as a bird's wing. His best scenes are those in which ease and rapidity of motion defeat the critical eye. They are sleight-of-hand. *Sir Harry Wildair* completely sums the qualities of Farquhar. The confusion of values, noted in the character of Roebuck, is in Wildair worse confounded. But Sir Harry is ever so "brisk and airy," that to offer a serious indictment would seem like taxing the air. He bustles happily through two consecutive plays—*The Constant Couple* and *Sir Harry Wildair.* He is never out of spirits or countenance. Impudence is his most engaging quality. In Sir Harry, Farquhar almost escapes the rocks on which his comedy is invariably wrecked. Sir Harry is rarely a victim of Farquhar's moral and artistic inconsistency. He avoids exhibiting himself as a contradiction in terms by refusing to be anything whatever explicitly, save an incarnation of irresponsible high spirits.

Sir Harry is introduced in a passage not altogether innocent of an uneasy preliminary attempt to justify, or, at any rate, to remove the sting of his irregularity: "He's a gentleman of most happy circumstances, born to a plentiful estate, has had a genteel and easy education, free from the rigidness of teachers and pedantry of schools. His florid constitution being never ruffled by misfortune, nor stinted in its pleasures, has rendered him entertaining to others, and easy to himself:—turning all passion into gaiety of humour, by which he chooses rather to rejoice his friends than be hated by any."

His virtue is never to be serious, never to be abashed, rarely to disturb the reader. Even a challenge he refuses to accept, save as an opportunity to be gay:

> STANDARD. I hope you're no coward, sir.
>
> SIR HAR. Coward, sir! I have eight thousand pounds a year, sir.
>
> STAND. You fought in Flanders to my knowledge.
>
> SIR HAR. Ay, for the same reason that I wore a red coat, because 'twas fashionable.
>
> STAND. Sir, you fought a French count in Paris.
>
> SIR HAR. True, sir; he was a beau like myself. Now you're a soldier, Colonel, and fighting's your trade; and I think it downright madness to contend with any man in his profession.
>
> STAND. Come, sir, no more dallying: I shall take very unseemly methods if you don't show yourself a gentleman.
>
> SIR HAR. A gentleman! why there again now? A gentleman! I tell you once more, Colonel, that I am a baronet, and have eight thousand pounds a year. I can dance, sing, ride, fence, understand the languages. Now, I can't conceive how running you through the body should contribute one jot more to my gentility. But pray, Colonel, I had forgot to ask you: what's the quarrel?
>
> STAND. A woman, sir.
>
> SIR HAR. Then I put up my sword.—Take her.
>
> STAND. Sir, my honour's concerned.
>
> SIR HAR. Nay, if your honour be concerned with a woman, get it out of her hands as soon as you can.

In a passage like this Sir Harry carries himself off successfully. He keeps the reader at arm's length, pleased with his pleasant and dazzling exterior. Even his marriage is credible in the rush of high spirits and happy speech in which it is celebrated:

> SIR HAR. Canst thou not guess, my friend?

Whence flows all earthly joy? What is the life of man and soul of pleasure?—woman! What fires the heart with transport, and the soul with raptures?—lovely woman! What is the masterstroke and smile of the creation, but charming, virtuous woman? When nature, in the general composition, first brought woman forth, like a flushed poet ravished with his fancy, with ecstasy she blessed the fair production!

Nevertheless Sir Harry is not entirely proof. In the scenes between Wildair and Angelica, we are often conscious of the insincerity and make-believe of a comedy where all the postulates are at issue. We have no right to insist that Farquhar's moral values should square with our own, but we have every right to insist that, in one and the same artistic presentment of life, the values should not be slurred, confused, or inter-destructive. Farquhar has cleverly minimised the peril into which his comedy necessarily falls whenever Sir Harry encounters Angelica. He has allowed Sir Harry to believe that Angelica is a daughter of Paphos. Primed with Burgundy, and believing Angelica to be within compass of his purse, he jests with her virtue without losing the sympathy of his nineteenth-century critics:

> ANGEL. What madness, Sir Harry, what wild dream of loose desire could prompt you to attempt this baseness? View me well. The brightness of my mind, methinks, should lighten outwards, and let you see your mistake in my behaviour. I think it shines with so much innocence in my face,
>
> That it should dazzle all your vicious thoughts.
> Think not I am defenceless 'cause alone.
> Your very self is guard against yourself:
> I'm sure, there's something generous in your soul;
> My words shall search it out,
> And eyes shall fire it for my own defence.

Sir Harry's retort, in liquor and under a false impression as to Angelica's social position, is a telling commentary upon the next two centuries of English comedy. "This is the first whore in heroics," said Sir Harry, "that I have met with." Sir Harry had to be drunk to be so perspicacious and so honest. Had he said anything so true to the morality of his immediate ancestors when sober, he would not have married Angelica. It would then have been too painfully clear that Angelica and Sir Harry belonged to two different worlds. Presenting Sir Harry in this scene as drunk and deceived is Farquhar's ingenious device to make a gentleman, of whom Dick Steele might approve, behave like the friend of Etherege and Rochester.

Farquhar's next original comedy—we may safely omit *The Inconstant,* Farquhar's adaptation of Fletcher's *The Wild Goose Chase*—was *The Twin Rivals,* produced in 1702. Nemesis has definitely overtaken him. Farquhar is here revealed in a deliberate attempt to reconcile the theatre of Congreve with the preaching of Jeremy Collier. The general result is a wavering of his comedy between two irreconcilable conventions, and in the end a pitiful descent into scenes where the feeling is utterly false, and where the expression sinks below the level of anything we have yet read. (pp. 258-64)

Farquhar in his next play, *The Recruiting Officer,* sets off his comedy with the humours of country life and manners. Here definitely was Farquhar's opportunity to shake off the influences that thwarted him, and to find for himself a new convention. But the change of scene is all. Captain Plume is again Sir Harry Wildair—Congreve's libertine playing, in the teeth of his character, for the sympathy of Collier's parishioners. Having for a while consistently lived up to his reputation as the successor of Mr. Horner, he suddenly asserts for the comfort of his audience: "I'm not that rake that the world imagines; I have got an air of freedom, which people mistake for lewdness in me, as they mistake formality in others for religion. The world is all a cheat; only I take mine, which is undesigned, to be more excusable than theirs, which is hypocritical. I hurt nobody but myself, and they abuse all mankind."

Farquhar's last and best play, *The Beaux' Stratagem,* shows at their highest power all the qualities that make and mar his comedy. To pick holes is an ungrateful enterprise. This play is an act of splendid courage—a conspicuous triumph of the author over the man. Farquhar was dying, haunted with fears for his family left without provision. He was looking back upon a life of which the leitmotiv was hope unsatisfied:

> AIM. But did you observe poor Jack Generous in the Park last week?
>
> ARCH. Yes, with his autumnal periwig, shading his melancholy face, his coat older than anything but its fashion, with one hand idle in his pocket, and with the other picking his useless teeth; and, though the Mall was crowded with company, yet was poor Jack as single and solitary as a lion in the desert.
>
> AIM. And as much avoided, for no crime upon earth but the want of money.

Jack Generous is the only spot of gloom in *The Beaux' Stratagem.* It is the sunniest of his plays. For the circumstances of its writing alone it deserves a high place in our regard. But we must not, therefore, falter in our analysis. The play shows no development upon any one of its predecessors. Archer is again Sir Harry Wildair, straight out of Congreve or Etherege. Archer delivers himself in a speech upon the five senses in the absolute manner of Sir Frederick Frollick:

> Give me a man that keeps his five senses keen and bright as his sword; that has 'em always drawn out in their just order and strength, with his reason as commander at the head of 'em; that detaches 'em by turns upon whatever party of pleasure agreeably offers, and commands 'em to retreat upon the least appearance of disadvantage or danger! For my part, I can stick to my bottle while my wine, my company, and my reason, holds good; I can be charmed with Sappho's singing without falling in love with her face; I love hunting, but would not, like Actæon, be eaten up by my own dogs; I love a fine house, but let another keep it; and just so I love a fine woman.

This single speech is a perfect expression of the attitude which determined the half-century of life and literature which preceded its delivery. Nevertheless, in the same play are collected sentiments and motives which are directly contrary. Consider the root question of marriage. Farquhar has been commended for his insistence in marriage upon an alliance of spirit:

> DOR. But how can you shake off the yoke? Your divisions don't come within the reach of the law for a divorce.
>
> MRS. SUL. Law! what law can search into the remote abyss of nature? What evidence can prove the unaccountable disaffections of wedlock? Can a jury sum up the endless aversions that are rooted in our souls, or can a bench give judgment upon antipathies?

Farquhar here restores to English comedy the normal English idea of sex-relationship. Restoration Society, as we have seen, dissociated the act of sex from sentiments of friendship or the transports of romantic exaltation. Farquhar has outlived the influences which determined the Restoration attitude. His comedy unhappily divides itself into scenes where the Restoration attitude is for the form's sake accepted, and scenes where for the moral's sake it is condemned. It is significant that, unconsciously torn between two irreconcilable alternatives, he finally resorts, in his happiest manner, for refuge to his old device of lightly skimming the surface of his theme for fear of tumbling into a pitfall. . . . (pp. 266-68)

As with Vanbrugh we have been forced in reading the plays of Farquhar to dwell unduly upon the darker side. It has been necessary to insist that these two authors, accepting a comedy which expressed the society of the Restoration, were unable consistently to present life from the point of view of the men who served as their models. Their plays are pitted with inconsistencies. They never succeeded in bridging the gulf that separated their personal convictions from the moral and artistic conventions of the theatre into which they intruded. Nevertheless their positive merits must not be neglected. Vanbrugh reaches his height in scenes where humour and insight play tolerantly between two worlds. Farquhar is able to blind us to the worst of his faults in the happy running of his speech and fancy. He is perhaps the lightest of foot of all our comic authors. Farquhar was born too late. He should have come from Ireland in the 'sixties or 'seventies and have been accepted into the company of Etherege and Sedley. He might then have had for his share a more brilliant glory—to assist the rise of English comedy; actually he assisted the fall. It must be at the charge of Farquhar himself that no successor was found to continue the tradition. (p. 274)

John Palmer, "George Farquhar," in his The Comedy of Manners, *G. Bell & Sons, Ltd., 1913, pp. 242-74.*

Louis A. Strauss   (essay date 1914)

[In the following excerpt, Strauss discusses Farquhar's works, asserting that Farquhar's plays mark a decisive and meaningful turning point in English drama, for

they recombined the elements of Restoration comedy into a new and more perfect form of comedy.]

Farquhar's position in English comedy is, historically, of far greater significance than is generally acknowledged. His work marks a turning-point in the drama so decided and meaningful that, without seeking to magnify his importance, I am disposed to mention him with such innovators as Lyly, Shakespeare, Jonson, and Etherege. As author of one of the last perfect specimens of comedy of manners and of the first two splendid examples of comedy of the balanced modern type, he emerges from the ranks of the Orange and Augustan comedians as the prophet of a new order. For while he introduced no comic principle hitherto unknown, he blended the essentials of character, plot, and situation in juster proportions than any previous writer of realistic comedy, lifting their interest to an equality with that of the dialogue, to which they had been subordinated in the wit-ridden comedy of manners. The result was a form of comedy unsurpassed for naturalness and fidelity to life: the form adopted and perfected by Sheridan and Goldsmith.

Mr. William Archer [in *George Farquhar*], with a fine appreciation of Farquhar's genius, has lamented his early death as a great blow to the English drama—one of its many instances of unfulfilled promise. I would emphasize, on the other hand, the richness and completeness of Farquhar's personal achievement, and the unlikelihood of further achievement had his life been prolonged. . . . I am bound to express my conviction that Farquhar had done his life-work. He had shown the way to a new order of comedy; an order, to be sure, in which imagination and invention played a far greater part than in the old. But it does not follow that, had he lived, he would have occupied the new field—in fact, all signs point to the contrary. The world was not ready for the new comedy even if Farquhar was able to furnish it. (pp. xiii-xv)

Farquhar came at precisely the right moment to invent a new comedy. He was young enough to learn from his more mature contemporaries the best they had to teach; from Congreve the art of crisp, clever dialogue, from Wycherley the value of odd but strikingly human characters, from Vanbrugh the trick of telling situation and the humour of incident; besides these, he caught from Etherege the spirit of nonchalance and irresponsibility which are at once the life and death of comedy of manners. He added nothing new: he had no theory of a regenerated drama. And yet, by virtue of his healthy nature, he responded to the changing ideals of the life about him; and with a touch he recombined the elements into a new comedy, a comedy as fresh and natural as that just preceding had been artificial.

Despite the shortness of his career, Farquhar's work divides itself obviously and logically into three periods. In the first, which includes *Love and a Bottle, The Constant Couple,* and *Sir Harry Wildair,* he continued in the tradition of the times and wrote comedy of manners. In the second, he cast about and experimented in the endeavor to rescue comedy from the censure of the Puritans. The result was *The Inconstant* and *The Twin Rivals,* both failures, significant of his inability at that time to reform comedy and yet please the public. In his last year of life, consti-

tuting the third period, he produced two comedies, utterly unlike each other as to plot, situations, and characters, but far more unlike his previous efforts and those of his contemporaries. That the complete success of *The Recruiting Officer* and *The Beaux' Stratagem* did not work an immediate revolution in comedy and open another brilliant period of creation merely shows that the drama was, for the nonce, dead. The long devotion to the stage of such genius as that of Steele and of Fielding, with such incommensurate results, enforces this conclusion beyond reasonable doubt.

Farquhar's first play, *Love and a Bottle,* is plainly a very young man's effort to out-manner the mannerists. His conception, unfortunately, lays its main stress upon the reckless profligacy of the hero, and Farquhar's youth and natural redundancy of spirits were not conductive to moderation in the portraiture. At no time in his career was he profoundly troubled with the moral problems that occasionally force themselves upon the artist and make him reflect seriously on the wherefore of his art. Despite his experiments and his *Discourse,* we cannot believe that he ever went beyond the conviction that what the public wants must be good. At this time, in particular, he was entirely free from moral concern. A newcomer in London, he seems most anxious to prove that he has fully steeped himself in the city's vice and is therefore capable of producing a comedy complete as to all the fashionable forms of debauchery. We may, with Mr. Archer, forgive him a part of his sin on the strength of his youth and inexperience: but it is here, rather than in *Sir Harry Wildair,* that Farquhar reaches his lowest moral level.

The play, such as it is, is a genuine comedy of manners. The hero, Roebuck, is too much a swashbuckler to be a perfect rake, but Leanthe's description of him, beginning "Wild as winds and unconfin'd as air," shows that Farquhar was aiming at the creation of such a character as he afterwards happily achieved in the hero of *The Constant Couple.* The unsubdued Wild-Irishman in the author comes out in Roebuck and prevents that delicate pose of diablerie that is the charm of the true manners-hero. Farquhar was "catched young," as Foigard says, but not young enough to help this play. Pope's charge of "pert, low dialogue" against Farquhar finds its chief justification in this first comedy. He strains after wit, and while he achieves an occasional bright effect, the usual result is mere cracking smartness that must have been offensive to ears attuned to the silken subtleties of Congreve. But Mr. Archer is again right in protesting against the unfair comparison of Farquhar with Congreve on the score of wit. After his first play Farquhar rarely went out of his way to be witty, while Congreve lets dialogue run on at the expense of plot, character, incident, and all. We may readily admit that Farquhar could never have attained the high perfection of Congreve in this particular; but as the exponent of a more natural style of comedy this should not be held against him.

Love and a Bottle, despite its adherence to the comic conventions of the day, is especially characteristic in the dash and breeziness of its action. The leading characters are little better than the hero; Lovewell, the good young man, is hopelessly unreal, while the heroines, Lucinda and Leanthe, are neither attractive nor convincing. On the other hand, the female rake, so familiar in the comedy of the period, is conspicuous by her absence in this as in all of Farquhar's plays, unless Lady Lurewell, at her second appearance, can be so denominated. Mockmode, the country squire, is dimly suggestive of the Sullen to come, but the combination of bumpkin and university fool is not effective. Lyrick is the conventional poet, and Brush and Pindress the familiar clever servants borrowed by English from French comedy. The happiest stroke in the play is Farquhar's adaptation of Rigadoon the dancing-master and Nimblewrist the fencing-teacher from Molière's *Bourgeois.*

On the whole, in spite of its rawness, *Love and a Bottle* is a promising first venture and at several points significant of the author's individuality.

Farquhar attains the full perfection of the comedy of manners in his second play, *The Constant Couple, or a Trip to the Jubilee.* It follows from this that the leading character, Sir Harry Wildair, is not so much a new creation, as a re-creation under new conditions, of the familiar Frollicks, Bellmours, and Dorimants, any of whom might readily be substituted for another without materially altering the play affected. Sir Harry is an air rather than a character. He carries with him an atmosphere of buoyancy and gaiety, an apparent unmorality, which hits off the frivolity of the age in its most attractive guise, and is the all-in-all of comedy of manners. Unmorality is hinted at by Farquhar in the preface to the play: "I have not," he says, "displeased the ladies, nor offended the clergy; both which are now pleased to say that a comedy may be diverting without smut and profaneness." As to the ladies we may believe him; among the other class of judges I venture to surmise some difference of opinion. But certain it is that many, like Farquhar, made the mistake of associating the wickedness of comedy with mere smut, overt cynicism, or downright profaneness: whereas, in reality, it lies in the core of the thing, the most perfect comedy of manners being really the worst, in point of morals, regardless of mere external decency.

In all respects, as compared with *Love and a Bottle,* the second play marks a great advance in dramatic art. The earlier work ended in an absurdly farcical tangle of disguises and cross-purposes: here the plot is simple and coherent, the several threads being admirably interwoven and mutually helpful. The dialogue shows a surer and easier touch, though Farquhar's dramatic prose never attains the distinction of that of Etherege or Congreve. His worst fault is a tendency to break into bastard blank verse disguised as prose. But though the dialogue is weaker than should be in comedy of manners, the characterization is more than sufficiently strong. In Col. Standard, a debrutalized Manly, we have a really striking study of a brave disbanded officer—the model for Lessing's Tellheim in *Minna von Barnhelm.* Vizard, the villain, is drawn with remarkable dignity and restraint, while Smuggler, Clincher, and Dicky are genre studies of impressive vitality. Lady Lurewell is a convincing portrait of a coquette with a history. Of course Sir Harry is the life of the play, and

his breezy, graceful, irresponsible presence casts a spell over the others sufficient to preserve the true tone of comedy of manners, to which strong characterization is not essential, if, indeed, it is not hostile.

Of the moral tone we need not say much; in classifying the play we have said enough. To treat it seriously in detail is to break a butterfly upon the wheel. Farquhar, a true child of nature, is no more personally accountable for the morals of his hero or play than is a young Fijian for his anthropophagous appetite or a young Turk for practicing polygamy. He gave form to the accepted ideals of his age, not because he had seriously questioned them, and approved, but because he had the gift of expression and it was the obvious thing to do. Without the easy-going conscience that allowed him to slip into the common ways of his generation, Farquhar could never have accomplished the work he was reserved for. The disposition to revolt would have led him into sentimental comedy, or into an ugly moralism, like that of *The Twin Rivals. The Constant Couple,* with its lightness of spirits combined with sureness of touch in portraiture, is an earnest of his fitness to introduce a new comedy worthy of the name.

Sir Harry Wildair is a weak sequel to *The Constant Couple.* The popularity of the preceding play, which owed much to the acting of Wilks, induced Farquhar to reassemble the leading characters in a new setting. Without exception they lose by the process, and though the new play enjoyed a moderate success, thanks to the popularity of its forerunner, Farquhar undoubtedly cheapened himself by this commercial venture. The plot is absurdly trumped-up, depending upon the feigned death of Angelica: and the appearing of her ghost is glaringly out of place and stupidly flat. Lady Lurewell becomes a pitiful intrigante, and Standard has completely lost his manhood. Sir Harry himself is shorn of his glory; the impalpable charm of his freshness could scarcely endure through another five acts. The traveling humour of Jubilee Clincher is miraculously changed to a political one, doubtless suggested by Jonson's Sir Politick Wouldbe. Fireball, the sea-captain, is violent rather than strong; and the French sharper adds nothing to the ensemble. This is easily the poorest of Farquhar's plays.

The two plays of Farquhar's middle period, both produced in 1702, are sharply distinguished from his earlier works. The turn given to *The Inconstant,* adapted from Fletcher's *Wild-Goose Chase,* by the realistic, semi-tragic incident of the last act, completely transforms the play from a light comedy of manners to something like modern melodrama, and must have suggested to the author the thorough-going moralism that characterizes *The Twin Rivals.* In *The Inconstant* Farquhar attempted, in young Mirabel, to create another sprightly traveled gentleman like Wildair. His unwillingness to fulfill his betrothal contract with Oriana furnishes the motive of a succession of intrigues against him by his and her friends, from each of which he squirms triumphantly. In the end he is entrapped by a false courtezan, and, on the point of being murdered by her bravoes, is rescued by Oriana disguised as a page. The unexpected seriousness and dramatic intensity of this final situation is a complete surprise, and may possibly have displeased the public, for it certainly ruins the play as comedy of manners. From a moral standpoint the play is an improvement upon its forerunners. The rake is given a wholesome lesson—a cold plunge that sobers him. "The Way to Win Him," we must understand, is for the heroine to show devotion to the rake she loves instead of matching her wit against his. The donning of male attire, always a favorite comedy device of Farquhar, is here made a matter of moral principle.

The Twin Rivals begins where *The Inconstant* left off—it is moralistic through and through, and avowedly so. It is Farquhar's direct answer to Jeremy Collier's onslaught upon the stage, being designed to prove that "an English comedy may answer the strictness of poetical justice" (Preface). Various reasons have been assigned for the failure of the play: the competition of strong plays by Steele and Cibber; the offensive realism of the character of Mrs. Mandrake; the impersonation of this part by a male comedian; and so on. Farquhar himself protests that the play suffered from the absence of lewdness: the public "stand up for the old poetick license. A play without a beau, cully, cuckold, or coquette is . . . poor . . . entertainment." Turning to the critics he hits a stumbling block upon which criticism is forever breaking its shins, viz., as to what is fit subject-matter for comedy. "'Tis said, I must own, that the business of comedy is chiefly to ridicule folly, and that the punishment of vice falls rather into the province of tragedy; but if there be a middle sort of wickedness, too high for the sock and too low for the buskin, is there any reason that it shou'd go unpunish'd?" In other words, the present play is tragi-comedy. But the question is hardly one of classification. Plays are not condemned because they do not precisely fit their pigeonhole. The wise critic no longer dogmatizes as to the limits of this or that art, for he knows that it is the prerogative of genius to overleap boundaries. Farquhar's point as to the material is well taken: the question is, what use does he make of it?

And the answer is that he has jumped from the extreme of reckless immorality to its opposite, unpleasant moralism. The play has the stark ugliness of a modern problem play. Admirably conceived and constructed, the interest skillfully suspended and enhanced by a rising series of climaxes, the comedy is yet devoid of pleasing quality and awakens only disgust. It is true that we are spared the beau and the cuckold; but with them we lose also the brightness that is of their train. In its place we have a sermon, which might well have been taken to heart by the public of that day. But, to apply Farquhar's favorite formula in the *Discourse upon Comedy*, it is the *utile* without the *dulci;* in other words, however good the purpose of the play, it fails to please artistically, and this is a fatal fault in comedy, as in all art.

The skeleton of Farquhar's moralism shows painfully through the thin shell of his characterization. Almost his first stroke shows the over-zealousness of the untrained preacher. The younger Wouldbe is no rake, but what our melodrama calls a deep-dyed villain. And so, forsooth, Farquhar gives him a hump to help out the allegory. The other characters lose likewise in strength and humanity through their subserviency to a thesis. The elder Wouldbe

and Truman are conventional pictures of manly virtue, as are Constance and Aurelia of womanly. Mandrake is an inconceivably monstrous hellcat, and Subtleman an equally villainous shyster. His device, by the way, of inserting a paper into a dead man's mouth, and drawing it out to obtain the last words of the deceased, is almost ingenious enough to excuse his stupidity in making Teague a witness to the forged will. And the hero's denunciation of him, "Thou art the worm and maggot of the law," &c. is superb invective, surprising, in its intensity, from so good-natured an author as Farquhar.

In general, *The Twin Rivals* plainly shows the poet out of his element. It is the attempt of an amiable, easygoing author to be serious upon a subject he has hitherto played with lightly. In his anxiety to moralize he sees no mean between attractive frivolity and an earnestness that is repulsively realistic. He honestly endeavored, contrary to the practice of the time, to render virtue attractive and vice ugly, and he overdid with a vengeance. This abortive attempt to be truly moral, designed to refute Collier's contention that the stage was hopelessly steeped in immorality, is the best vindication of the preacher's position that could possibly have been written. But Farquhar presently gave proof that he could, without conscious effort, assist the cause which his good intentions signally injured.

Scene from Farquhar's The Twin Rivals.

The same year that brought forth the two plays just considered also saw the publication of the *Discourse upon Comedy*. It would look as if Farquhar wrote this essay to pad out the very slender little volume of letters and verse entitled *Love and Business;* and certainly they required something substantial to justify their publication, for, saving two or three letters, a more empty mass of composition has scarcely emanated from a writer of repute. I cannot find in the *Discourse* itself either a trace of an outward occasion or such uniqueness or intensity of critical conviction as would compel its composition. So I infer that Farquhar took his little careless fling at an attractive subject because his publisher requested something of the sort. Nevertheless, its appearance so near to (in fact, probably between) *The Inconstant* and *The Twin Rivals* might easily be considered significant. Farquhar doubtless was aware that the conditions obtaining in the theater called for serious reflection. The moralistic tone of the two comedies suggests that he foresaw the doom of comedy of manners. But there is no indication in the *Discourse* that this idea took form in his consciousness: if it did, he felt it the part of wisdom to suppress it. I should certainly disclaim for Farquhar anything like profound reflection upon this subject. There is a brief defense of comedy against the Puritan attacks, and a couple of jibes at Collier and his tribe: but mainly the *Discourse* has to do with the technical side of drama and dramatic criticism rather than with its moral side.

The treatise takes the form of a familiar letter to a friend, a device permitting the greatest latitude of treatment and freedom of style, of which Farquhar takes full advantage. The *Discourse* is characteristic of the author throughout: it has the airy assurance of the practical young man of letters, flushed with the success of his *Constant Couple.* The prose is too facile to call for high commendation; but the affectation of scholarship, combined with arrogance toward scholars, is delicious. There is an abundance of good critical common sense in the *Discourse,* and if we cannot call it a distinct contribution to æsthetic, it is nevertheless an important document in the history of classicism.

In brief, the work is a protest against rigidly classical standards of judgment as regards comedy and against the opposite extreme of utter laxity of construction. It vigorously assails the three unities and repudiates the authority of Aristotle; holding that the taste of Athenian critic and public cannot possibly be valid for English theater and audience. While the method of reasoning is grotesquely uncritical, the main point being that Aristotle was no poet and therefore no judge of poetry, the conclusions are sound enough and reveal the healthy instinct of a true artist. The end of comedy, he tells us, is pleasant satire, *utile dulci:* he defines comedy as a "well-fram'd tale, handsomely told, as an agreeable vehicle for counsel or reproof." And its father, Farquhar believes (with sublime disregard for Bentley), is Aesop.

It is thus apparent that Farquhar's theory of comedy is quite in accord with the prevailing views of his contemporaries, and, as is the case with them, widely removed from the spirit of his own practice. We search the *Discourse* in vain for light upon the comedy of manners. In a broad philosophical sense this comedy is satirical, but not in the sense that Farquhar has in mind. The only comedy in which he truly aimed to realize his theory is *The Twin Rivals,* and we have seen the unfortunate result. The *Discourse* admirably illustrates the blindness of the age as to its own character.

Farquhar seems to have been unconscious, in his last two plays, of any departure from the prevailing type of comedy. There is no syllable, in dedication, prologue, or epilogue, to show that they pretended to be different from his early comedies. On the surface they seem to go back to the same style: his heroes have the free-and-easy bearing of rakes; Melinda and Mrs. Sullen are sophisticated women of fashion; and matters are lightly played with that *The Twin Rivals* treated seriously. The intrigue of Archer and Aimwell is of the kind on which comedy of manners flourished. And yet we are in sympathy with the men and their schemes, because we feel that at bottom they are good men and that their success can lead to no harm. Farquhar's rakes, it is commonly admitted, have at no time been so thoroughly bad as those of his teachers in art: but there is a world of difference between Roebuck and Wildair, on the one hand, and Plume and Aimwell on the other. Not that the latter have attained to the angelic goodness of the modern leading juvenile: but that, thanks to the assertion of Farquhar's kindly and wholesome nature, as against the fashionable conventions of playwriting, we find a deeper humanity beneath the rakish exterior. What influences produced this change, and with what force each operated, are of course impossible of discovery. Doubtless his marriage and the struggle for a livelihood, his artistic growth, nourished by reflection upon the failure of his intermediate plays, his illness, with, perhaps, a mellowing and refining of his nature attendant thereon, all were contributory.

Dr. Schmid has called attention to the fact that in these two comedies Farquhar for the first time quits the purlieus of London and sets his action in provincial towns. Mr. Archer enlarges upon this theme, pointing out its bracing effect upon the tone and atmosphere of the plays, and the opportunity it afforded for fresh observation and invention. In fact, though it were easy to leap to rash conclusions and postulate romantic tendencies that do not exist, it is almost impossible to overstate the effect of the change of environment in these particulars. Farquhar brings much of London manners into the country, in the train of his captains and beaux. But he finds so much there that is new and fresh that comedy of manners is completely sunk into a new something that, by contrast, might well be called comedy of life. The stimulus it furnishes his invention and spirits is astonishing; and the more so when we reflect that this piece of good luck came to the English stage through the happy accident of his recruiting visit to Shropshire. Without this I believe he would have written no more, or at best a bad comedy or two in his early manner.

For another thing we must give Farquhar credit at the outset. I believe he felt as keenly as Steele or Cibber the impossible and revolting state of court life and city morals, though, having no liking for comédie larmoyante, he was less hopeful of a comedy emancipated from them. He did, however, strongly resent the evil tendency that his older contemporaries gleefully exploited. To my mind, the lowest, though one of the cleverest comedies of the age, is Vanbrugh's *Confederacy.* It shows the morals of the time at their worst, for here the fashionable vices have grown common, descended from the beaux and belles of the court to be the property of flunkeys and tradesmen's wives. In other words fashionable vice is vulgarized; but what is worse, it reveals corruption where virtue ought to persist. Farquhar satirizes this tendency again and again. In *The Beaux' Stratagem* Archer, the pretended valet, affects the spleen, which, "like all other fashions wears out and descends to their (gentlefolk's) servants." Farquhar alludes to "the nice morality of the footmen" in the prologue to Sir Harry Wildair and again in the *Discourse.* The last two plays strike off sparks of satire now and again, sometimes hinting that the bitterness of poverty has won into the sweetness of Farquhar's temper, but oftener revealing a growing habit of thoughtfulness regarding manners and institutions. So here again, though much of the air of comedy of manners is preserved, we find the moral tone perceptibly altered.

The Recruiting Officer has its backbone in the recruiting scenes. If the play had no other merits it should live for these scenes alone, which opened a new field of legitimate comedy of the sprightliest kind. The two volunteers, Appletree and Pearmain, are notable creations, true to their kind, "apprehensive, sturdy, brave blockheads"; in fact, the country characters of the play, Rose, Bullock, the justices, the butcher, and the smith, are a gallery of worthies hard to match, free from the traits of caricature that invariably accompanied the rustic in comedy. Justice Balance, in particular, is a fine, full-blooded picture of the country gentleman, anticipating the best work of Addison and Steele. The major characters, as more complex, are harder to deal with. Kite, a delightful relief from the clever valet of comedy of manners, is one of the most resourceful rascals in the English drama. He combines the shrewdness and wit of a confidential servant with the bluntness and authority of a petty officer, and is throughout faithful to his military character. He is the center of most of the striking passages of the play—the recruiting, astrologer, and court scenes—in each of which he surprises us afresh with his ingenious and spontaneous devices. Perhaps the part is somewhat overloaded; and it must be admitted that occasionally his cleverness is overdone. The same fault may be found with Lucy, Melinda's maid. Her stealing Melinda's signature to deceive Captain Brazen is an instance of over-elaboration that hurts the plausibility of the play.

The character of Captain Plume shows the undefined nature of the comedy in Farquhar's own mind. Plume is a rake and no rake. He is introduced to us at the outset as a Don Juan among bar-maids: witness Molly of the Castle and Kite's array of other wives. Yet he assures Silvia (Mr. Easy), in a tone of unquestionable sincerity, that he is not the rake the world believes him. He will "give up a woman for a man at any time," and he does so in the case of Rose. At one moment he tells Worthy of his attempts to make Silvia his mistress: at the next he is furious at the gossips of the town for suspecting that he may have been successful. In short, he has not the petty virtue of consistency; but

he has in abundance that quality of goodness of nature that Fielding so lovingly dwells upon. Altogether he is a likeable hero, brave, generous, and jovial, and not too profligate for redemption. He has magnetism for man and maid, gentleman and bumpkin, and is more nearly our notion of Farquhar himself than any other character of his creation. It is the very unsettled state of Plume's morals that gives the play at once its racy brightness and its ultimate wholesomeness.

Silvia, though a child of nature in the honesty of her love and her freedom from city affectation, is nothing of the coquettish ingenue which the comedy of the time invariably made the country girl. Her unflagging devotion to Plume, and his frank admiration of her sterling qualities, which he declares manly rather than womanish, give the play its firmest moral ground. Though her disguise takes her a step farther than masquerading heroines usually go, resulting in complications that are unfortunately free and suggestive, she remains the most healthful young woman of spirit in all the comedy of that period. Melinda is a vaporish creature, owing to her sudden accession of wealth, and an excellent foil to Silvia; but again, beneath all her caprice, there is an honest love, which asserts itself at the proper moment. For sheer originality of conception and faultless execution, Brazen is undoubtedly the cleverest creation in the play. To derive him from Vanbrugh's Captain Bluff and Congreve's Tattle is distinctly unjust unless we are to identify all foolish captains with one another. His refreshing audacity, mendacity, and self-conceit, his wonderfully inventive memory, above all his brisk sanguineness of success in his amours, make him the most engaging of rattle-pates. The supposed similarity to Bluff rests, I believe, in the employment of the common old masking trick to cheat him into marriage.

The characters in **The Beaux' Stratagem,** though not more vivid and original, are more finished than those of **The Recruiting Officer.** The minor persons are invested with a distinction almost Shakespearean. Bonniface is become the accepted type of English innkeeper, and his name is a part of our everyday language. Of Scrub, the factotum, it is sufficient to say that it was a favorite part with Garrick, who frequently exchanged for it the more important rôle of Archer. Cherry, the pert bar-maid, was voted adorable by eighteenth-century audiences. In Lady Bountiful, the medicine-dispensing old country lady, Farquhar has exalted a humour into a character. Her matter-of-fact common sense completely redeems her from the conventional. The unconscious humour of her diagnosis of Aimwell's malady furnishes one of the richest bits of Farquhar's comedy. "Wind, nothing but wind!" she interjects, after each grandiose flight of his description of the symptoms of love. Sullen, the impossible country husband, is the middle-step between Jerry Blackacre and Tony Lumpkin, while Gibbet, Foigard, and Gipsey all have more than a touch of individuality. In Dorinda, Farquhar has given us something better than the lay figures of his earlier plays; she is genuine and charming. While Mrs. Sullen, albeit somewhat oversensuous, is probably his best drawn and most highly-colored heroine. Aimwell is an admirable lover: his confession of the cheat in the moment of victory is a capital stroke, and saves him the true gentleman.

But Archer is Farquhar's most masterly creation. Some one has well said that in Mercutio Shakespeare anticipated all the wit and gaiety of the seventeenth-century cavalier. In Archer Farquhar has perfectly drawn the same cavalier of a later generation, when devotion had given place to pleasure-loving egoism, wit grown hard and brilliant, and poetry vanished to make way for showy prose. In place of Mercutio's free-flowing poetic fancy, we have the art of compliment in high-sounding rhetorical outburst, an echo of the heroic play at the only point where that type of drama really touched courtlife. We find all the dashing adventuresomeness of the seventeenth-century rake combined with the circumspect worldliness of his eighteenth-century successor. "Look ye, madam, I'm none of your romantick fools that fight giants and monsters for nothing; my valour is downright Swiss; I'm a soldier of fortune, and must be paid." And so fixed is his determination to get what he wants, that the modern reader is fairly aghast at the lengths of realism to which he leads his author. Thwarted in his design upon Mrs. Sullen, he fights and captures the house-breakers—then coolly asks her for her garter to bind the rogues! "The devil's in this fellow," she ejaculates. "He fights, loves, and banters, all in a breath!" And so it is: courage, sensuality, and wit are his leading qualities, and one is perpetually crowding another out of the fore. When he engages in a project, it is to the bitter end. Had he been in Aimwell's position, no such lover-like compunction would have caused him to reveal the "stratagem" that was to gain a wife for one and funds for both. "I can't stop," says Aimwell, before matters were critical, "for I love her to distraction." "'Sdeath," Archer retorts, "if you love her a hair's-breadth beyond discretion, you must go no farther." So much for love leading to matrimony; but in the pursuit of an illicit amour, Archer's intensity knows no bounds. It is a pity that the best-rounded comedy since Fletcher should be hurt by finding its climax in a scene too salacious for modern representation; and especially since that scene is so logically the outgrowth of the plot and characters that to excise or change it is to kill the play. But it is indeed so. Archer is true to himself in this scene; fortunately, in a better sense of the phrase, Mrs. Sullen is also true to herself. But this scarcely mends the matter, for Farquhar has gone as far as he could and much further than he should.

This brings the question of morals once more to the front. I have said that Farquhar wrote his last plays more or less in the same light mood of comedy of manners that characterized his early work. This means that he wrote them merely to entertain, and if the result, morally, is better than in his earlier plays, it is because the changing taste of the times and the growth of his own character have made themselves felt. Of serious moral or satirical purpose there is (I am tempted to say "fortunately" when I think of *The Twin Rivals*) not a trace. Of satire there is abundance, and of excellent quality, but it comes in occasional flashes and strikes at all sorts of things—the dishonesty of constables, the confederacy between innkeepers and highwaymen, the pensioning of army officers' illegitimate offspring, and ever and again the heartlessness of fashionable society. On the whole, the tone of *The Recruiting Officer* is anything but vicious; careless it certainly is. *The Beaux' Stratagem* is freer from indecency, but is, as we have ob-

served, deplorably voluptuous in one vital scene. On the other hand, to find fault with the close of the play as seriously countenancing divorce by mutual consent is really basing grave conclusions upon very trifling grounds. Farquhar was thinking only of the case before him—of a beautiful, clever woman mismated with a sottish and surly clown—and he certainly presents a sound argument for that particular case. He was not addicted to the envisagement of broad social questions or to attacking legal institutions; accordingly criticism has no business to generalize this case and praise or blame him for his views. It is a mistake to judge so light-hearted an author on so serious grounds. It is equally wrong to blame Farquhar for the little grief shown by Ballance, Silvia, and Aimwell, for the death of their near relations. A near relation, in the comedy of that age, was a mere conventional barrier between a hero or heroine and a fortune. The removal of that barrier was no occasion for tears and hysterics, and to introduce them would have been far worse than the apparent indifference shown. This sort of criticism, and it is very common, really deserves no answer, but if answer must be made I would point to the scene in the last act of *The Constant Couple* in which young Clincher tells of his brother's death. Here Farquhar himself pays his respects to a convention that was none of his making.

That "manners" remain an important ingredient in these plays is apparent from both the dialogue and the characters. Wit is still a strong factor—as it must be in all comedy: and Farquhar is not entirely above sacrificing even his characters at the altar of the seventeenth-century goddess. Thus Kite and Lucy, to say nothing of those to the manner born, are much too clever. Sullen spars with his wife in the last act with the finished ease of a habitué of Covent Garden. Scrub goes so far out of his own character as to quote Latin. The dialogues between Archer and Aimwell, as well as the picture scene, are unduly protracted to permit the exchange of clever broadsides. In the case of Love's Catechism, by having Cherry speak her part by rote Farquhar escapes sacrificing the character; a clever device but one that could not be used again. However, in general Farquhar makes his persons speak in character and the well contrived plots are allowed to work themselves out without delays.

Again, as regards plot, these two plays, by the care and skill employed in their construction, depart radically from the loose habits of comedy of manners. Internally they are totally unlike. *The Recruiting Officer* has the more elaborate and intricate plot, crowded with incident and striking situations, and with business enough for several comedies. That of *The Beaux' Stratagem,* while simpler and more open, loses nothing, by contrast, in point of strength and effectiveness. The impressive fact in this connection is that however Farquhar may yield to tradition, he never goes so far as to allow dialogue to destroy our interest in the developing action. It is this that enables him to produce an admirably balanced and truly natural comedy.

Accordingly, we may well say that, despite the impress that comedy of manners left upon all his work, Farquhar has in these plays left that form of art far behind him. Exalting both plot and character above dialogue, and humour of situation above wit, escaping largely the conventional and typical of manners and humours, he gave the world two comedies of unsurpassed freshness, deriving their interest from no passing fashion of the day but from their deep-grounded perception of human nature, their liveliness from the ingenious invention of a really creative imagination, and their charm from the playfulness of a buoyant, happy spirit at large in a new, untrodden field. Farquhar is at heart neither Cavalier nor Puritan, neither rake nor ascetic. He entered joyously into the game the former were playing without insight into its meaning or care as to its consequences. Troubled by the obviously just reproaches of the latter, he reacted upon this stimulus with little appreciation of its value. He was neither Cavalier nor Puritan, but a happy-go-lucky Celt who entered the world of warring conventions without prejudice as to forms of discipline, but with a mighty propensity for free living and the enjoyment of life. That is why he, of all the dramatists, could for a brief space bring comedy into the mood of a joyous representation of life, unhampered by the chronic English pretensions to moralism or satire. He could not reform comedy, for in him there was nothing of the reformer; but by giving his healthy nature free play he allowed comedy to re-form itself, rid of its tyrant, hu-

mours, and its mistress, manners, true to the larger life of the English people for the first time in a century. Emulating the playful buoyancy of Farquhar's spirits and preserving his balance of the comic elements, two other light-hearted Irishmen, Goldsmith and Sheridan, gave us all we have of distinguished excellence in later English comedy to 1880. (pp. xxxiii-lvi)

> *Louis A. Strauss, in an introduction to* A Discourse upon Comedy, The Recruiting Officer, and The Beaux Strategem *by George Farquhar, edited by Louis A. Strauss, D. C. Heath & Co., 1914, pp. xiii-lvi.*

George Henry Nettleton   (essay date 1914)

[*In the following excerpt, Nettleton offers a positive assessment of Farquhar's plays, praising their "ingenious" plot construction and original dialect.*]

George Farquhar . . . brought to English comedy an endowment of native Irish wit, good-humour, and originality. (p. 136)

The Beaux' Stratagem . . . shows both the traditions of Restoration comedy and the advent of new tendencies. Here are present in full force the familiar flings of the *beau monde* at the country, and yet something of real country atmosphere; French characters and phrases, and yet a hearty English element; much of the immorality of earlier comedy, with some of the later improvement in moral tone. Though Squire and Mrs. Sullen separate at the end with scant regard for the marriage tie, Farquhar does not scoff at virtue and exalt vice in Wycherley's fashion. The seeming intrigue between Mrs. Sullen and Count Bellair is only her scheme to solve her matrimonial troubles. Instead of trying to deceive her husband, she has him brought to her rendezvous with the Count. As the Count says, when Mrs. Sullen shows him that she has not taken his advances seriously: 'Begar, madam, your virtue be vera great, but garzoon, your honeste be vera little' (III, 3).

The dialogue is bright, witty, and vigorous. . . . Though Mrs. Sullen's long speeches (II, 1) voice the usual contempt of the town for the country, the play has genuine country atmosphere. The countrywoman who comes to Lady Bountiful to have her husband's leg cured is given, in fact, some dialectic forms of speech—'mail' for 'mile,' and 'graips' for 'gripes' (IV, 1). Scenes with the landlord, the tavern maid, and the highwaymen come as a relief from the ceaseless intrigues of fashionable London.

The plot construction is highly ingenious, especially in the very effective last act. Archer—whose name is sufficiently explained by Boniface's words (II, 3), 'You're very arch'— justifies his name by replacing the French Count at the rendezvous, and obtains entrance to Mrs. Sullen's chamber. This leads to a situation familiar in Restoration comedy in such scenes as Vanbrugh's, where Loveless carries off Berinthia (*The Relapse*, IV, 3), and Farquhar's own scene in his ***Love and a Bottle,*** where Roebuck invades Lucinda's chamber. But the ingenuity with which a stock situation is rescued from the relentless issue in Vanbrugh is Farquhar's own. The attempted robbery not merely interrupts the amour at the critical point, but offers an effec-

---

From an anonymous verse satire accusing Farquhar of plagiarism:

Is it so then, said Farquhar? My matters are safe,
  By Saint Patrick, my business is done;
For 'tis known, I have made Pit and Gallery
  laugh,
  Without anyone's help but my own.

My *Jubilee Dicky,* and airy Sir *Harry*
  Will vindicate what I have said;
And none, but myself, has a title to carry
  The laurels away on my head.

By your leave, Brother *Teague,* reply'd *Mac
  Flecknoe's* ghost
  Our countrymen are better known;
The *Beauties* are borrow'd, Of which you thus
  boast,
  But the Faults, I dare swear, are your own.

Tho', the town may allow, what you'd have 'em
  all take
  For granted, with no one you joyn;
Since none, but a man of your judgment, could
  make
  Such language, to such a design.

And I can't but applaud the resolve you have
  taken
  In the present employ which you chuse;
For it's nobler in red, to make a campaign,
  Than to butcher an innocent Muse.

> *Author unknown,* The Trial of Skill: or, A New Session of the Poets; calculated for the Meridian of Parnassus, etc., *1704.*

tive chance for Archer to display his bravery and to merit Mrs. Sullen's regard. Mrs. Sullen herself well describes him: 'The devil's in this fellow! he fights, loves, and banters, all in a breath' (V, 4). The next scene is full of rapid movement of plot and shift of situation. The whole act, handled with vigorous assurance, is of sustained interest.

Farquhar is to some extent a forerunner of Goldsmith. The opening conversation between Boniface, the innkeeper, and Aimwell and Archer about the menu is quite like that of Mr. Hardcastle, the supposed innkeeper, with Marlow and Hastings in *She Stoops to Conquer.* There is something, too, in the freshness of atmosphere, in the group of country and inn folk, and in the Irish good-humour, which is akin to the spirit of Goldsmith. Whatever Farquhar's lapses in point of morality, he has none of Wycherley's vindictive and brutal cynicism. Most of his characters, with all their faults, are companionable. They are not so clever as Congreve's, but fertile brains and facile manners make them attractive, despite some heartless traits.

While Wycherley adapted Molière and Vanbrugh followed a variety of models, Farquhar's ready brain was responsible for most of his effectiveness in plot and characters. Farquhar usually suggests to others. Highwaymen in league with the landlord may be as old as the *First Part of Henry IV,* but both Goldsmith's *She Stoops to Conquer* and Gay's *Beggar's Opera* may have found a nearer model in *The Beaux' Stratagem.* Farquhar imparts to his characters individuality. He presents a whole gallery of full-length portraits—the country squire, the Irish adventurer, the fop, the landlord, the tavern maid, the recruiting officer. He sets them in scenes vivid in their portrayal of eighteenth-century life. The inn, the country house, the gatherings of soldiers and highwaymen, enlarge a canvas which has usually represented only the fashionable world of courtier and intriguante. Effective in plot, varied in scenes and characters, Farquhar's last and best comedy brings Restoration comedy to a brilliant close, and points to the healthier humour of Goldsmith. (pp. 137-40)

> *George Henry Nettleton, "Congreve, Vanbrugh, and Farquhar," in his* English Drama of the Restoration and Eighteenth Century (1642-1780), *1914. Reprint by Cooper Square Publishers, Inc., 1968, pp. 120-40.*

Ernest Bernbaum   (essay date 1915)

[*In the following excerpt, Bernbaum comments on the development of sentimentalism in Farquhar's plays.*]

Farquhar, whose style is sprightlier than Vanbrugh's, and whose plots, though less well built, are livelier, had artistic gifts which might have enabled him to support the highest traditions in comedy. He was acquainted with that tradition, and could in his brilliant but shallow *Essay on Comedy* chat about "schooling mankind into better manners" being "the *utile,*" "the primary design of comedy"; yet he was ever ready to sacrifice the ethical to the entertaining. His observation of life was as superficial as quick, and he was too much a creature of moods to cultivate singleness of purpose. The standards of comedy were . . . flexible;

but he bent them so far that at times he distorted them. His first three plays,—*Love and a Bottle* (1698), *The Constant Couple* (1699), and *Sir Harry Wildair* (1701),— admitted characters that came near being lovable, and situations that hovered on the verge of the emotional, with a freedom that transcended the most liberal practices of his predecessors. These plays were nevertheless, in general intention and effect, true comedies, their frequent vacillations toward the sentimental being invariably checked.

Farquhar's young gentlemen are too sincerely eloquent and passionate lovers to be the rakes of Restoration comedy, and are too joyously abandoned to dissipation to be the exculpated prodigals of sentimental comedy. Their creator loved them without diminishing or wholly excusing their offenses. In *Love and a Bottle,* Leanthe apostrophises one of them:

> Wild as winds, and unconfined as air! Yet I may reclaim him. His follies are weakly founded, upon the principles of honor, where the very foundation helps to undermine the structure. How charming would virtue look in him, whose behavior can add a grace to the unseemliness of vice!

Yet neither she nor the other young ladies in these three plays, reclaim such youths by a touching appeal to "the principles of honor." Leanthe wins her scapegrace by a stratagem of no little impropriety. The modest Angelica in *The Constant Couple* is rendered very unhappy by Sir Harry Wildair's profligacy; but the notable scene between them, which might easily have been made sentimental, is kept comic (and very far from "genteel") by the drunken Sir Harry's mistaken belief that she is a lady of pleasure and that her virtuous protestations are mock-heroics. He is quite unabashed by her innocence, and finally marries her not out of pity or respect but out of reluctance to fight a duel.

In the same play, Lady Lurewell and Colonel Standard, lovers who were separated for many years, find each other again and are joyfully reunited,—a theme of inexhaustible interest to sentimentalists, who interpreted such reunions as a reward for the virtue of the characters. That is not, however, Farquhar's conception. Colonel Standard has distinctly attractive qualities, but he does not even pretend that his proposals to Lady Lurewell (before the recognition) are honorable. He and Lady Lurewell are "constant" to one another's memories only in the somewhat esoteric sense that neither will engage in love-affairs with the intention of matrimony. Lady Lurewell, though she weeps when thinking of the lover of her youth, is during most of the play spitefully occupied in entrapping and plaguing all the suitors she can attract. In these instances and many similar ones, Farquhar with some effort saves himself from a surrender to the sentimental mood; but so often he nearly submits to it that these three comedies suffer a lamentable impairment in unity of tone and in consistency of ethical principle.

Such being Farquhar's tendency, it is not surprising that he was the first to follow Cibber in writing sentimental comedy. In *The Twin Rivals* (1702) he bestowed upon the appropriately named Constance a fidelity which was not dubious like Lady Lurewell's but as true as that of Cibber's Amanda. During the long absence of Constance's fiancé Wouldbe, his rascally twin brother tries, by intrigues which occupy the greater portion of the play, to gain both her and the estate of Wouldbe. All his machinations are in vain against her faithful love. She is led to believe Wouldbe dead, and mourns him in the following words, which he, concealed, overhears:

> I have . . . no pomp of black and darkened rooms, no formal month for visits on my bed; I am content with the slight mourning of a broken heart, and all my form is tears. . . . [*Gazing on his portrait*] With this I'll sigh, with this converse, gaze on his image, till I grow blind with weeping . . .
>
> WOULDBE [*rushing forward*]
>
> Here let me worship that perfection whose virtue might attract the listening angels, and make 'em smile to see such purity, so like themselves in human shape!

Before their troubles are at an end, there is another tearful scene, in which Wouldbe, having been thrown into prison, is visited and consoled by Constance. To the sympathetically drawn portrait of these lovers, Farquhar added that of the generous merchant Fairbank, a kind-hearted citizen who, on relieving Wouldbe from poverty, is justly praised by him as follows:

> Gramercy, citizen! surely if Justice were an herald she would give this tradesman a nobler coat of arms than my brother.

Even more sentimentally treated than the story of Wouldbe and Constance is that of Richmore and Clelia. She is his forsaken mistress. In Restoration comedy she might have inveigled him into marriage by tricks of comic effect. But Richmore is induced to atone for his conduct by an appeal to his feelings. The man upon whom he tries to pass off Clelia discovers her plight, takes pity on her, and determines to see justice done. After sparing Richmore's life in a duel, he nobly pleads for the wronged girl. Richmore, exclaiming "your virtue warms my breast and melts it into tenderness," is moved to repentance and agrees to marry Clelia. This reformation Farquhar, with characteristic flightiness, sneered at in his preface, remarking that Richmore "was no sooner off the stage but he changed his mind, and the poor lady is still *in statu quo*"; in the play itself, however, the sentimental tone of the episode is sustained to the end. The preface admitted that though "the persons are too mean for the heroic," *The Twin Rivals* had "sentiments too grave for diversion." This departure from the rules Farquhar defended on the ground that "exposing vice is the business of the drama." The real issue,— whether comedy should not confine itself to exposing vice by ridicule,—he evaded. (pp. 83-7)

Hesitant resort to sentimentalism is observable in Farquhar's *The Beaux' Stratagem* (8 March, 1707). There are slight sentimental touches in the love-affair between Archer and Mrs. Sullen. She suffers under a boorish and hateful husband, and weeps when she contrasts her misery with the happiness of others. The violent wooing of her bold lover provides a very emotional scene. But these are merely such inconsequential aberrations as are found in Farquhar's true comedies. The emotional scene is interrupted by a farcical burglary, and the divorce of Mrs. Sullen takes place in the gayest possible manner. It is the other plot of *The Beaux' Stratagem* that Farquhar motivated and concluded sentimentally.

This begins, to be sure, merrily enough: Aimwell, a gentleman of broken fortunes, seeks to entrap the wealthy Dorinda into marriage by pretending to be a lord. Feigning to fall dangerously ill at her gates, he gains admission to her house. Dorinda is enchanted with the idea of becoming Lady Aimwell; and after he has rescued the household from burglary, the success of his scheme seems assured. Touched by the evident sincerity of her love, however, his sense of honor is aroused.

> AIMWELL (*Aside*) Such goodness who could injure! I find myself unequal to the task of villain; she has gained my soul and made it honest like her own. I cannot, cannot hurt her. . . . (*To Dorinda*) Madam, behold your lover and your proselyte, and judge of my passion by my conversion! I'm all a lie, nor dare I give a fiction to your arms; I'm all counterfeit except my passion. . . . I am no lord, but a poor, needy man, come with a mean, a scandalous design to prey upon your fortune. But the beauties of your mind and person have so won me from myself that, like a trusty servant, I prefer the interest of my mistress to my own. . . .
>
> DORINDA Matchless honesty! Once I was proud, sir, of your wealth and title, but now am prouder that you want it; now I can show my love was justly levelled, and had no aim but love.

Aimwell and Dorinda are thus raised above the unscrupulous lovers in most of Farquhar's plays, and attain the moral level of Wouldbe and Constance in his *The Twin Rivals. The Beaux Stratagem,* like Mrs. Centlivre's *The Gamester* and Steele's *The Tender Husband,*—which it far surpasses in delightful originality of action and briskness of dialogue,—is a sentimental comedy, but one which marks no progress in the essential characteristics of the type. (pp. 102-03)

> *Ernest Bernbaum, "The Rise of Sentimental Comedy: 1696-1704" and "The Drama of Sensibility, The Moral Essay, and Sentimental Philosophy: 1704-1709," in his* The Drama of Sensibility: A Sketch of the History of English Sentimental Comedy and Domestic Tragedy, 1696-1780, *1915. Reprint by Peter Smith, 1958, pp. 72-95, 96-118.*

Henry Ten Eyck Perry   (essay date 1925)

[*An American scholar and drama critic, Perry is the author of* The First Duchess of Newcastle and Her Husband *(1918),* The Comic Spirit in Restoration Drama *(1925), and* Masters of Dramatic Comedy *(1939). In the following excerpt, Perry offers a general assessment of Farquhar's dramas, arguing that they are neither artistic nor realistic because they never fully achieve a bal-*

ance between sentimentalism and "the true comic spirit of moral detachment and unbiased laughter."]

[Farquhar lifted] English Comedy from the Centre of Indifference in which it had been languishing under Vanbrugh's aegis and, for good or ill, . . . set it down in the freer aether of eighteenth-century sentiment. He is the connecting link between the older generation of the Restoration and the rising tide of Cibbers and Steeles, Kellys and Cumberlands, Goldsmiths and Sheridans. If to have one foot in each of two camps is a successful compromise, Farquhar is an outstanding success in his chosen field; if not to be wholeheartedly devoted to some one cause is cowardly and craven, Farquhar ignobly falls between two stools. He was an Irishman, and consistency is not to be expected of him, any more than it is to be found in his first important self-portraiture, Roebuck in *Love and a Bottle.* Roebuck is himself from Ireland, "of a wild roving temper," a gorgeous mixture of hard head and soft heart. (p. 108)

Selfish and delightful as he appears in the first act, he is a very different person by the end of the play. At the beginning of it he is a comic figure, to be laughed at but not actively censured; later he is found to have a heart of gold and to be the very personification of honor. An attempt to reconcile these opposing tendencies of the comic and sentimental spirits is made in Leanthe's often quoted words about Roebuck: "Wild as winds, and unconfined as air!—Yet I may reclaim him. His follies are weakly founded, upon the principles of honour, where the very foundation helps to undermine the structure. How charming would virtue look in him, whose behaviour can add a grace to the unseemliness of vice!" (p. 109)

Roebuck is Farquhar himself, or, at least, he is Farquhar's ideal type in its crudest form. Never again did the dramatist draw such an obviously inconsistent picture, although the contrast between honesty and knavery is present in most of his leading male figures. The most popular of them, perhaps because of Wilks's acting in the part, was the Sir Harry Wildair of Farquhar's second and third plays. Sir Harry, "the joy of the playhouse, and the life of the Park," has newly come from Paris at the opening of *The Constant Couple.* He is described before his entrance as a happy combination of bravery and gaiety, the latter a result of his free and easy education far removed from the pedantry of schools. He has in his make-up just a touch of the French beau's affectation, but, on the whole, he is an attractive figure, well-calculated to delight a pleasure-loving audience. Constancy is not one of his virtues, for at his first appearance he is in love with a dangerous lady whom he has encountered in Paris, but in the fifth act he is joined in matrimony to the insipid Angelica. (p. 110)

In the sequel he is reduced to the rôle of a devoted husband. Angelica is supposed to be dead, and though Sir Harry is engaged in an intrigue with a former love, he will hear no word against his wife's reputation. He wishes to fight a French marquis who asserts that she was unfaithful, and he terminates his affair with the woman who has repeated this slander. In a word, Sir Harry's morality has triumphed over his gaiety, so that it is no wonder that the piece failed to repeat its predecessor's success. When Angelica reappears in male disguise, as a ghost, and finally in the flesh, a neat dénouement has been achieved and a worthy lesson inculcated, but honest laughter has long since flown out of the window. That Sir Harry has become a model and is no longer a humorous type, is made very clear by his renunciation of French foppery and also by a strange scene between him and a Lord Bellamy, which is injected into the play without any apparent connection with the rest of the plot. Lord Bellamy, it seems, owes Sir Harry two hundred guineas, lost by his wife at cards, but he is unwilling to pay them. He excuses himself on the grounds of being a "man of honour," a phrase that throws Sir Harry into a fury. "Honour! that's such an impertinence!" he screams, "Pray, my lord, hear me. What does your honour think of murdering your friend's reputation? making a jest of his misfortunes? cheating him at cards, debauching his bed, or the like? . . . Come, come, my lord; no more on't, for shame; your honour is safe enough, for I have the key of its back-door in my pocket." The fact that Farquhar could put such a violent denunciation of conventional "honour" into the mouth of his hero and idol, Sir Harry Wildair, shows how very far he had got from the true Comic Spirit of moral detachment and unbiased laughter.

"Honour is a circumstance absolutely unnecessary in a natural correspondence between male and female," he wrote in his next play, *The Inconstant,* and similarly of "morals": "I tell thee, child, there is not the least occasion for morals in any business between you and I. Don't you know that of all commerce in the world there is no such cozenage and deceit as in the traffic between man and woman?" These words are put into the mouth of Young Mirabel, the inconstant hero, who is trying so hard to escape from his engagement with the lovelorn Oriana. "In a world where all is for the worst," he seems to say, "I myself will not alone be virtuous," which is one way of building a comic superstructure upon a basic discontent with the world. Many devices are used by Farquhar to reconcile his feeling for morality with his ability to entertain, since he was not able with the genius of a Molière to hold the two in suspended solution even for the two hours' traffic of the stage. The ability to draw human characters would make such a happy consummation as Molière's possible; the advantage of mannered types is that they may be tortured and twisted out of all consistency by the ingenuity of their creator. So without a thought of duplicity, Mirabel condemns society and then uses this condemnation to justify his own selfishness. For four acts he tells his father that he will not fulfill his promise to marry Oriana, and indeed he does everything in his power to escape her wiles. She, in turn, pursues him with all the ingenuity she can command: she produces a supposed lover to be his rival; she pretends to have become a nun; she feigns insanity; and finally she disguises herself as a page and follows the object of her devotion. The fifth act situation, in which she saves her lover from an adventuress and four bravoes, is an addition to Fletcher's comedy, founded, it is said, on an actual occurrence of the time. At any rate, it forms a most effective outcome for the play, even if it does change the general atmosphere from a leisurely picture of manners and customs to bustling intrigue and melodramatic action. (pp. 111-13)

Farquhar's next play, *The Twin-Rivals,* is chiefly serious drama and very little, one regrets, true comedy. The author's moral sense is in the ascendant, as is shown at once by the "Preface." Virtue must be rewarded and vice punished, even if the characters are not of a heroic cast, a dictum which means the lowering of tragedy and the elevation of comedy to the no-man's land of heavy sentiment. *Comédie larmoyante* and bourgeois tragedy are closely connected, and *The Twin-Rivals* is a good example of the fact. Instead of a principal character obviously divided between high ideals and human weaknesses, like Roebuck, Wildair, or Mirabel, in this play we have divided persons also. The twin Wouldbes are the personifications of Good and Evil—even Benjamin's body is deformed as a symbol of his character—and, as a result, neither of them really interests us. It is clear from the first that the honest Hermes is to return and oust the dishonest Benjamin, that he will marry the heroine and conserve the paternal estate. One is not even surprised at the completeness of Benjamin's dismissal to poverty and contempt or at the consignment of his accomplices to prison and the pillory. Justice is seen done with a thoroughness that belongs to morality but not to life, and consequently not to the most perfect art. (pp. 114-15)

[Farquhar's] works look forward to the complete triumph of sentimentalism upon the stage. They mark, at one and the same time, the last stand and—temporarily at least—the dying hope of the English Comic Spirit.

—*Henry Ten Eyck Perry*

The Recruiting Officer is not by any means a complete *volte-face* to the type of Congreve's comedy, but it definitely eschews the sermonizing of *The Twin-Rivals.* It is rather an attempt to return to Farquhar's own earlier successes with Roebuck and Wildair, to elaborate the figure of a well-meaning rake, and to set him in an environment giving more variety and scope for action. This milieu the dramatist found in the provincial town of Shrewsbury, where he had himself been in 1705 to get recruits for Marlborough's army. He justly dedicates his play "To all Friends round the Wrekin," for among them he had hit upon material which was to insure him a permanent place in the history of English comedy. Farquhar's early plays show a certain brilliant promise, but not till he forewent a criticism of town life and followed Vanbrugh's lead out into the freer air of the English countryside did he achieve his most solid and most genuine success. The hero of *The Recruiting Officer* (the Wilks part again) is Captain Plume, who like Roebuck and Richmore is introduced to us embarrassed with a castoff mistress. "Molly at the Castle" has just borne a son to Plume but has been comforted

in her misfortune by Plume's broad-minded sweetheart, the charming Silvia.

Silvia is the most delightful heroine in all Farquhar. Like so many of his ladies—Leanthe, Angelica, and Oriana— she has resisted her lover's desire for "consummation before the wedding," and like them she disguises herself as a boy, in order to subjugate the unwilling hero. While masquerading, she finds her lover flirting with Rose, a country girl, but neither angry nor discouraged she enters the lists as his rival. Under a threat of enlisting with another recruiting officer, she gets Rose away from Plume, enlists with him herself, and has firmly wormed her way into his heart by the time that the imposture is discovered. Also she has given her father an opportunity to find out that Plume had no designs against his daughter's honor, as a forged letter coupled with Plume's own disposition had quite naturally led him to believe. "I have got an air of freedom, which people mistake for lewdness in me," Plume himself says, and considering his past as represented by "Molly at the Castle" and his pre-nuptial proposition to Silvia, one can hardly be surprised at the misconception. Still, of all Farquhar's hero-rakes Plume is the most convincing, and we are ready to forgive his shortcomings as outbursts of excess vitality and to believe that he really means it when in the last act he tells Silvia that to her love he resigns his freedom. Before Farquhar's time the question of a gentleman's honor had scarcely entered into English comedy, though Vanbrugh had rung the changes on woman's good name in Amanda, Berinthia, and most compactly of all in the character of Lady Brute. Etherege's heroes are rascals, it is true, and they ultimately bow their necks to the yoke of wedlock, but there is no indication that the idea of reformation ever entered their creator's head. For all we know the Comic Spirit will continue to play over Sir Frederick Frollick and Dorimant long after they are married; in the case of Roebuck, Mirabel, and Plume such an outcome is absolutely incompatible with the melting mood in which we leave them. This new type of wild young man, ultimately to be domesticated by a lovely girl had been overshadowed by Vanbrugh in the subordinate figure of Worthy in *The Relapse,* but Farquhar gave him such vitality and distinction that he became a well-recognized and often repeated character in drama and in fiction. Charles Surface is no more than a weakened imitation of the same individual (as Lady Teazle is of the female of the species); Tom Jones only a well-rounded presentation of a similar figure in a more diffuse and complicated genre.

The Beaux-Stratagem, Farquhar's last comedy, furnished him with an opportunity to do the two sides of his usual picture in separate and distinct parts, just as Jacinto Benavente in a modern play, *The Bonds of Interest,* has created an idealistic master and a selfish servant to represent together the average human being. Aimwell and Archer, although contrasting figures, are not such extremely opposed types as the Wouldbe brothers in *The Twin-Rivals,* for they are both fortune-hunters and both travelling under false pretensions. Aimwell has the softer heart of the two, and just when he is on the point of successfully winning Dorinda, a rich heiress, his conscience asserts itself and he declares his true estate. Fortunately the high-minded Dorinda will allow his poverty to make no difference, and more fortunately still his elder brother, whom he was counterfeiting, has died in the nick of time, so he is now the true Viscount Aimwell. This stroke of luck brings the impecunious gentleman a fortune, large enough to support a wife in comfort, and enables him to give over Dorinda's own £10,000 to his practical-minded companion, Archer. Archer, who is no philanthropist, could not see any reason in the world for Aimwell's ultra-honesty, and when the affair is satisfactorily compounded, he has no intention at all of giving up his share in the booty. Archer is, in fact, a thorough rogue, and yet withal the most high-spirited and completely hilarious figure that Farquhar ever created. (pp. 116-19)

It is idle to speculate on what Farquhar might have added to English drama had his life been spared, though it seems likely that he might have again equalled, if not surpassed, his now extant work. Certainly in his last illness his creative faculty was operating at fever heat. Even as it is, the author of **The Recruiting Officer** and **The Beaux-Stratagem** need have no fear for his place in literature; the originality and fertility of his imagination had destined him to be a superlative creator of comic figures. From Mockmode and Lyric in his earliest play to Sullen and Scrub in his latest, his pages are peopled with clearly defined persons, sure of provoking laughter whenever and wherever they are bodied forth upon the stage. Unhappily most of his works also contain a pseudoromantic plot of cruel ladies and unhappy lovers, which seriously interferes with the end and aim of comedy. Lucinda, Aurelia, and Melinda are the airy names which betray the comic dramatist as being also a man of sentiment. "Lady Lurewell" is a more explicit epithet because her character is more realistically developed and hence more palpably absurd.

The real conflict in Farquhar's soul is most clearly visible in his treatment of his wild, young heroes. Roebuck, Wildair, Mirabel, and Plume, with their deserted whores and faithful mistresses, represent his constant attempt to paint the laughable and, at the same time, the admirable. Now this cannot be done, for as Aristotle well said in the *Poetics,* laughter implies some defect or ugliness contrary to the ideal. The two elements of license and honor are so contrasted in Roebuck's nature that he does not seem to be a credible human being. Wildair is better in reconciling the paradox, and Plume most successful of all. Yet there is always at bottom the feeling that these care-free, dashing young men are true neither to real life nor to the world of art. They are not human beings like Mercutio nor intellectual creations like Alceste; they are struggling between two worlds and will not commit themselves to either one. Occasionally an Archer steps completely into the comic picture, but then by his side there is always an Aimwell to spout high morality or a Gibbet to interfere with the impulses of nature. Archer is the last effort of the Comedy of Manners to maintain its position in the teeth of Jeremy Collier and eighteenth-century propriety. It was a losing fight though, as Farquhar must himself have realized. Try to follow his humorous impulses as he would, he always ended by throwing a sop to his morality-loving audiences. His works look forward to the complete triumph of sentimentalism upon the stage. They mark, at one and the same time, the last stand and—temporarily at least—the dying hope of the English Comic Spirit. (pp. 126-28)

Henry Ten Eyck Perry, "George Farquhar," in his The Comic Spirit in Restoration Drama: Studies in the Comedy of Etherege, Wycherley, Congreve, Vanbrugh, and Farquhar, *Yale University Press, 1925, pp. 107-28.*

Allardyce Nicoll   (essay date 1925)

[*Called "one of the masters of dramatic research," Nicoll is best known as a theater historian whose works have proven invaluable to students and educators. Nicoll's* World Drama from Aeschylus to Anouilh *(1949) is considered one of his most important works, and his six-volume* History of English Drama, 1660-1900 *(1952-59) has been highly praised for its perceptive commentaries on drama from the Restoration to the close of the nineteenth century. In the following excerpt, Nicoll discusses the "elements of disintegration" and "incipient sentimentalism" he believes to be evident in Farquhar's early plays, concluding that Farquhar's last two comedies,* The Recruiting Officer *and* The Beaux' Stratagem, *are better works because they are more similar to Restoration comedy.*]

Farquhar's work had started in the last years of the seventeenth century. **Love and a Bottle** and **The Constant Couple** had appeared at Drury Lane in 1699, and in these two plays he showed the tendencies of his art. **The Constant Couple** had evidently been a brilliant success, and it is not surprising to find that its author speedily planned for it a sequel, **Sir Harry Wildair: Being the Sequel of the Trip to the Jubilee.** This, unlike most sequels, was a success on its first production, but we, reading it in the light of other dramas of the time, can trace in it elements of disintegration. The pure spirit of the comedy of manners is still present in it, but foreign tones are entering in to spoil the brilliance of its wit. . . . [A passage] from the fifth act, and the final tag,

So, spite of Satyr 'gainst a marry'd Life,
A Man is truly blest with such a Wife,

show clearly the traces in it of incipient sentimentalism. In the midst of its greatest gaiety intrudes an element of thought.

The Inconstant: or, The Way to Win Him followed at Drury Lane about February 1702. This comedy, based on Fletcher's *The Wild-Goose Chase,* itself an early type of a comedy of manners, has less of the sentimental note, but that note appears nevertheless in those scenes where Oriana, dressing as a boy, follows her wayward lover to the house of the courtesan Lamorce and saves him there from an ignominious death. A comparison with the original Fletcherian play will show how much the spirit of the original has been altered.

The Twin Rivals was likewise a failure, for what reason does not seem perfectly clear. The influence of the newer school is here once more to be seen in the preface with its long comments on Jeremy Collier and its profession of moral aim accomplished by means of a true poetic justice.

This profession is probably cynical and satiric, for **The Twin Rivals** is not a comedy of which the author of *A Short View* would have approved, and there is more than a touch of sarcasm in the words of the Elder Wouldbee at the close: "And now I hope all Parties have receiv'd their due Rewards and Punishments." Whether these words are scornful and satiric or not, however, we can easily see how the influence of Collier and the kindred influence of the sentimental drama were operating on the minds of playwrights such as Farquhar to destroy the unity of their work.

It was probably the uncertainty concerning their aims, or the confusion between the spirit in which they had been reared and the newer atmosphere of the time that led both Farquhar and Vanbrugh, and, along with them, Congreve, to turn to farce. Farquhar's next work, in any case, was but an expansion of La Chapelle's *Les Carosses d'Orléans* as **The Stage Coach.** Although this piece has but three acts, Farquhar appears to have called in the assistance of Motteux to aid him in the rendering. There is little brilliance in the farce, but it was long popular as an afterpiece.

In **The Recruiting Officer,** a brilliantly successful comedy, Farquhar returned to pure comedy. This play is full of an exuberance of wit, and succeeds in recapturing not a little of that Restoration spirit which the eighteenth century authors seemed to be losing. At the same time, even in it there are signs of change. The atmosphere is no longer the atmosphere of the town. We are out in the countryside, and, if the principal characters are city characters, we may still feel the alteration in spirit from the politer drama of Congreve. There is, too, to be noted the greater realism of this comedy, in marked contradistinction to the element of artificiality traceable in the best plays of the preceding half-century. The immorality, which before had been often graceful and debonair, has here developed into a coarse licentiousness, and that callousness which will be marked as a characteristic of eighteenth century dramatic art is to be seen only too clearly in the abandonment of poor Rose, who, because of the reality of the play, seizes upon our sympathies. Even though she disappears amid the rioting of drunken laughter, we cannot forget her in her night of tears. That the audience felt no abhorrence at the crudity of the sentiments may be realised in a moment by a reference to the repertoires of 1706 and the succeeding years.

With **The Beaux Stratagem** we reach the end of Farquhar's career as a dramatist. As with an effort he has turned back to the spirit of his masters, and has produced a comedy more purely of manners than even his first seventeenth century works. Brilliance is in this comedy, and artificiality once more takes the place of realism. The mutual parting of Mr and Mrs Sullen, to which Mrs Oldfield, no doubt thinking of current hypocrisy and Societies for the Reformation of Manners, objected strongly, is quite in the Restoration style. Farquhar's life closed with his greatest literary triumph.

As a dramatist, Farquhar falls far short of Congreve, nor has he the strange virulence and strength of Wycherley. He is airier, more foppish, more, it may be said, of the

newer age of Anne than of the Restoration. He is in a way a link between these two periods, standing between Congreve and Cibber, just as Cibber stands between the period of Anne and that of the early Georges. (pp. 147-50)

Allardyce Nicoll, "Comedy: Comedies of Manners," in his A History of Early Eighteenth Century Drama 1700-1750, *Cambridge at the University Press, 1925, 147-64.*

William Archer (essay date 1949)

[*A Scottish dramatist and critic, Archer is best known as one of the earliest and most important translators of Henrik Ibsen's plays and as a drama critic of the London stage during the late nineteenth and early twentieth centuries. Archer valued drama as an intellectual product and not as simple entertainment. For that reason he did a great deal to promote the "new drama" of the 1890s, including the work of Ibsen and Bernard Shaw. In the following excerpt, Archer reviews Farquhar's plays, condemning his early comedies but extolling his later works and claiming that "Farquhar widened the range of comedy" by adding dignity and humor to his characters and breaking with the "irresponsible licentiousness of his school."*]

Farquhar has been, if not damned, at any rate gravely depreciated, by a single line of Pope's: "What pert, low dialogue has Farquhar writ!" This casual remark has struck the keynote of criticism for more than a century and a half. It echoes in Professor Ward's assertion that "He is happy in the description of manners in a wider range than that commanded by Vanbrugh; but his dialogue is in general less gay and sparkling, and while his morality is no better than that of the most reckless of his contemporaries, he has a coarseness of fibre which renders him less endurable than some of these are to a refined taste." We have here an indictment in three counts, which I shall attempt to meet one by one, but in inverse order. I submit, first, that Farquhar was much less nauseous in his coarseness than Wycherley, Congreve, or Vanbrugh; second, that he showed clear traces of an advance in moral sensibility, nowhere discernible in the other three; third, that the alleged lack of "sparkle" in his dialogue in reality means a return to nature, an instinctive revolt against the sterilising convention of "wit." "Gaiety" Professor Ward must surely have denied him by inadvertence. His severest critics have contested the merit of his gaiety, but not the fact.

If there is any play of Farquhar's which lends colour to the accusation of exceptional grossness, it is his earliest comedy, **Love and a Bottle,** written when he was about twenty. This is, indeed, an unfortunate effort, in which we see a raw provincial youth, without any real knowledge either of the town or of the world, simply aping the cynical licentiousness of his elders, and thinking himself a mighty fine fellow in so doing. Life, movement, and gaiety do something to redeem the play. It may even be called remarkable that an Irish hobbledehoy, within the first few months of his stay in London, could produce so spirited an imitation of the current type of comedy. But the character of Roebuck admits of no defence. It is a sheer monstrosity, a boyish fanfaronade of vice. And here, indeed,

Farquhar does descend to a grossness almost as vile as that of his contemporaries. Not quite as vile in my judgment—but that, I own, is a matter of opinion. On the other hand, however severely we may condemn this play, it is manifestly unjust to let its sins taint the whole of Farquhar's theatre, and treat as one of his general characteristics an excess into which he fell in his 'prentice work alone. In short, while I cannot admit that even *Love and a Bottle* bears out the charge of *exceptional* "coarseness of fibre," I hold it merely just to put aside this crude and boyish effort, and judge Farquhar by the plays, from *The Constant Couple* onwards, which display his talent and his character in some approach to maturity.

This sin of youth, then, being struck out of the record, we may inquire whether there are in Farquhar many, or any, of those passages of sheer nastiness at which the gorge rises in Wycherley, in Vanbrugh, and even in Congreve. Quotation being out of the question, one can only appeal to the experience of the unprejudiced reader. Morality, be it noted, is not the point at issue. So far as this particular argument is concerned, Farquhar may be as immoral as any of his fellows; and I freely admit that in point of sensuality, of what was in those days called "lusciousness" of language, he was no whit behind them. . . . Amid all the lewdness that doubtless disfigures Farquhar's plays (especially *The Constant Couple* and its sequel) one is conscious, I think, of a sweeter, cleaner, healthier mind than can be claimed for Wycherley, Congreve, or Vanbrugh, to say nothing of Otway, or D'Urfey, or (alas!) Dryden. He never, like so many of his contemporaries, showed a love for the merely malodorous. His muse stands sadly in need of chastening, but not of disinfecting.

We come now to the second count of the indictment—that "his morality is no better than that of the most reckless of his contemporaries." Here a plain distinction strikes us of once. There is certainly one point of difference between Farquhar and the three contemporaries with whom he is usually bracketed: namely, that they do not, while he very distinctly does, rise from a lower to a higher moral plane. "Manly" Wycherley is as "beastly" in his last as in his first play. Congreve's cynicism is as inhuman in *The Way of the World* as in *The Old Bachelor*. If *The Confederacy* is a little less brutal than *The Relapse* and *The Provoked Wife,* it is only because it is translated from the French. It gives no proof of moral progress on Vanburgh's part. But Farquhar, from play to play, becomes more decent and more humane. The criticism is summary indeed which lumps together *Love and a Bottle* and *The Beaux' Stratagem,* and speaks as though Farquhar's morality or immorality remained constant throughout his career. The fact is far otherwise; and unless it can be proved that Farquhar started below the level of his fellows (which is scarcely possible) it follows that he must ultimately have risen above it.

The character which made Farquhar famous shows him at his lowest moral level. Sir Harry Wildair is undeniably a reprobate, a son of chaos, inadmissible in any moral order. But at the same time there is a grace, a humanity, a lightness of touch in his portraiture which distinguishes him for the better from the ferocious, cast-iron libertines of Wycherley and Congreve. The type is not an invention of Farquhar's. It is sketched in Etherege's Sir Frederick Frollick, and other precedents could be quoted. But Farquhar breathed into it a new and enduring vitality. He gave it a touch of bravery, a touch of race, above all, a touch of humour, which still appeals to us. We feel that Sir Harry's faults arise from thoughtlessness, not from wickedness in the grain. Here is a character which does indeed lend some colour to Lamb's defence of Restoration Comedy. In a non-moral fairyland, Sir Harry would be an agreeable sprite; whereas no abrogation of moral law could render Wycherley's or Congreve's heroes other than detestable. It may be said that Farquhar, in this case, does more harm than his contemporaries, by making vice attractive. That would be true if comedy produced its effect solely or chiefly by inciting to direct imitation of particular characters. But its main effect proceeds rather from the subtle influence of its general atmosphere; and the atmosphere in which Sir Harry Wildair moves is one of harum-scarum levity rather than of deliberate turpitude. Wycherley and Congreve were no doubt as desirous as Farquhar was to render their heroes attractive, and thought that they had done so. The difference of effect shows that in Farquhar's case we have to deal with a better and saner nature, one that had taken on the taint of the time, but was not fundamentally corrupt.

And Sir Harry, I repeat, shows Farquhar at his worst. Even in the two plays in which he figures, we have another character of a much higher type—a type for which we may search Wycherley and Congreve in vain. Colonel Standard is a man with some approach to the instincts of a gentleman as we now conceive them. He is a bluff, honest soldier, not a saint, but still less a blackguard. The character is not very vividly drawn, and the incredible romance of his relation to Lady Lurewell impairs his claim to psychological consistency. But the question here at issue is not Farquhar's artistry, but the tone of his mind; and Standard, I think, gives clear evidence of an innate decency of feeling (to rank it no higher) denied to the other playwrights of the time. In *The Twin-Rivals,* again, Hermes Wouldbe and Trueman are both good fellows enough, wholly different from the Congreve-Vanbrugh type of hero. The callousness with which Wouldbe receives the news of his father's death has been censured, with apparent reason. But it is to be observed, first, that the dramatic situation made it very difficult for him to give way to feeling; second, that when he has time to reflect, he chides himself for his lack of "filial duty"; third, that the people of that day took mortality more, and family affection less, as a matter of course than we do. In Farquhar's next play, *The Recruiting Officer,* the conduct of Justice Balance and Silvia, on learning of the death of his son and her brother, seems incredibly unfeeling. To say that it belonged to the manners of the day is not, of course, to justify it; but another age may be as critical of our sensibility as we of the insensibility of the early eighteenth century. After all, there is nothing to show that the relation of Silvia to her brother had been at all intimate or tender. Perhaps they had seen very little of each other; perhaps they had been wholly unsympathetic. Mr Bernard Shaw's favourite thesis that near relatives always tend to hate each other, is flagrantly false; but the opposite belief, that they always and necessarily love each other dearly, is a superstition of modern sentimentality. The fact that Farquhar does not interrupt the course of his comedies with scenes of lamentation cannot fairly be taken as a proof that he was deficient in natural feeling.

The ethical standards of *The Recruiting Officer* and of *The Beaux' Stratagem* cannot, certainly, be called high; but there is in both a general tone of humanity which is far above the level of the age, and even above that of Farquhar's early plays, down to and including *Sir Harry Wildair.* Captain Plume, though a loose-living soldier, belongs rather to the company of Fielding's Tom Jones than to that of Wycherley's Horner or Manly, Congreve's Bellmour or Vainlove, Vanbrugh's Loveless or Worthy. As for Aimwell and Archer, adventurers though they be, they are neither brutal nor wholly unscrupulous. Aimwell, indeed, voluntarily foregoes the fruits of his intrigue, and confesses his personation, in the moment of its success—a trait of conscience inconceivable in the typical hero of the period. But it is not in definite and positive acts that the moral advance is chiefly to be noted. It is in the substitution of wholesome fresh air for the black, bitter, cruel atmosphere that weighs on us in the works of the three other playwrights. I shall try to show later that there are traces in *The Beaux' Stratagem* of an actual interest in moral problems, wholly different from the downright contempt for the very idea of morality which pervades the Restoration Comedy as a whole. In the meantime, it is sufficient to say that in all his plays, from *The Constant Couple* onwards, and especially in the last three, Farquhar gives a general preponderance to kindness over cruelty and good over evil, which reverses the order of things prevailing in his contemporaries. Where shall we look in them for a sentiment like the following (*The Twin-Rivals,* Act ii. SC. I):—

> CONSTANCE. Are you sure he's well-bred?
>
> AURELIA. I tell you he's good-natured, and I take good manners to be nothing but a natural desire to be easy and agreeable to whatever conversation we fall into; and a porter with this is mannerly in his way, and a duke without it has but the breeding of a dancing-master.

Such an utterance points forward to the nineteenth century rather than backward to the seventeenth. In the third act of the same play, the scene between Hermes Wouldbe and Fairbank is conceived in a spirit of rectitude and kindliness quite unknown to Farquhar's compeers and rivals.

That Farquhar's nature was humane seems to me beyond question; but he also moved with a general current setting towards humanity. To say that he was "reformed" by Jeremy Collier would be inexact, for the famous *Short View of the Immorality and Profaneness of the English Stage* appeared many months before Farquhar made his first essay as a dramatist. Collier's attack was nearly two years old when Farquhar scored his greatest success with the *The Constant Couple,* on which "the parson" had certainly no influence whatever. Nevertheless, there can be little doubt that Farquhar felt and welcomed the reaction in favour of decency, if not of speech, at any rate of feeling. One would like to think that he headed the reaction, but here the dates are unaccommodating. That distinction belongs to Steele. *The Funeral,* produced towards the end of

1701 . . . , marked a long step on a path which Farquhar did not clearly begin to follow until a year later in *The Twin-Rivals.* Had he been minded to relapse into the old rut, the failure of that play would have afforded him an excuse. But he was not weary in better-doing, and may fairly share with Steele the credit of having set earnestly about the ventilation of English comedy.

We come now to the question of dialogue, which we shall find shading off into another and larger question. It may be admitted at once that Farquhar's dialogue has not the dry, hard polish—the "sparkle," as Professor Ward justly calls it—of Congreve, or of Vanbrugh at his best. He is not, like Congreve, a virtuoso in style. There is perhaps no part in his plays so well written, in the literary sense, as that of Lord Foppington in Vanbrugh's *Relapse.* He was not, in fact, specifically a literary man. His verse is uniformly execrable, and his non-dramatic prose has far more ease than distinction. But we must note that if, in his dialogue, he did not achieve the glitter of Congreve, it is partly, at least, because he did not aim at it. Farquhar had plenty of wit; but he did not make with the beginning and end of his endeavour. . . . It is Farquhar's great merit to have released comedy from this circle of malign enchantment. Even in *The Constant Couple* and *Sir Harry Wildair* his characters have not quite the coterie stamp. We feel, at any rate, that they are studied from an outside point of view, by one who does not mistake the conventions of the coterie for laws of nature. In *The Twin-Rivals* the coterie tone is scarcely heard at all. With the return to a recognition (rather too formal to be artistic) of the difference between right and wrong, we have something like a return to nature in the tone of conversation. In the excellent little scene (Act i. SC. I) between Benjamin Wouldbe and the innkeeper Balderdash, there is nothing that can be called wit, but a great deal of humour; while Mrs Mandrake is a realistic life-study of extraordinary power. Finally, in *The Recruiting Officer* and *The Beaux' Stratagem,* Farquhar broke away altogether from the purlieus of Covent Garden, and took comedy out into the highways and the byways. When Congreve strayed into the country, it was only to present to us that amazing "house party" of *The Double Dealer*—Lord and Lady Touchwood, Lord and Lady Froth, Sir Paul and Lady Plyant, Mellefont, Maskwell, Careless and Brisk—in a word, the coterie at its narrowest. When Vanbrugh went down to the shires, it was only to show Tom Fashion stealing away the daughter of Sir Tunbelly Clumsey. But Farquhar introduced us to the life of the inn, the market-place, and the manor house. He showed us the squire, the justice, the innkeeper, the highwayman, the recruiting sergeant, the charitable lady, the country belle, the chambermaid, and half a score of excellent rustic types. He introduced the picaresque element into English comedy, along with a note of sincere and original observation. To have made the good folk of Shrewsbury and Lichfield express themselves with the modish, stereotyped wit of the London chocolate-house and boudoir would have been the height of absurdity. Farquhar reduced wit within something like the limits of nature, subordinating it to humour, and giving it, at the same time, an accent, all his own, of unforced, buoyant gaiety. And he had for his reward the line: "What pert, low dialogue has Farquhar writ!"

That Farquhar widened the range of comedy is obvious and generally admitted. But critics have, so far as I know, overlooked a subtler distinction between his work and that of his contemporaries, which seems to me real and important. If he was not specifically a literary man in the sense in which they were, he was specifically a dramatist in a sense in which they were not. That is to say, he was a dramatist and nothing else, whereas in Wycherley, Congreve and Vanbrugh the dramatist was as yet imperfectly differentiated from the social essayist. How often in their plays does the action stand still while the characters expatiate in reflection, generalisation, description and criticism of other characters; in short, in essays or leading articles broken up into dialogue! Comedy, as they conceived it, meant *the introspection of the coterie.* The business of the comic poet was to show the little circle, with which alone he was conversant, in the act of observing, analysing, and discussing its own manners and customs, humours and foibles. His characters were always intensely self-conscious, always perfectly aware that they were playing parts, under the critical eyes of their friends and acquaintances, upon the coterie-stage of "the town." There is scarcely a comedy of Wycherley, Congreve, or Vanbrugh from which long scenes of sheer generalisation or episodic portraiture could not be wholly excised, without leaving any sensible gap either in the action of the play or in the characterisation necessary to justify the action. . . . (pp. 16-25)

The dramatist, in fact, was not merely a dramatist but a journalist as well. He suffered his characters not only to reveal themselves in action, but to explain and satirise themselves and each other, in undramatised or imperfectly dramatised disquisition. Even his valets and lady's-maids would not infrequently deliver themselves of neat little essays, wholly unnecessary to the progress of the plot.

When we come to Farquhar, we find the differentiation between the dramatist and the essayist rapidly completing itself. In *Love and a Bottle* it is still very imperfect, but from *The Constant Couple* onwards it is much more clearly marked than in any of the other three. His characters are not for ever feeling their own pulses, taking the social temperature, or noting the readings of the wit-barometer. It is impossible to prove a negative by quotation; I can but state what I think is the fact and leave the reader to verify it. Farquhar's plots are as conventional as those of his contemporaries, his technical devices as crude; but he confines his characters within the action, and keeps the action moving, better than they do. He is much less given to the elaborate portrayal of a Jonsonian "humour" for its own sake. We do not find in his comedies that characters are minutely described before they appear, and then do nothing throughout the rest of the play but, as it were, copy their own portrait. I remember but one exception to this rule: Captain Brazen, in *The Recruiting Officer,* who is heralded by his full-length portrait, drawn by Worthy and Balance. The few lines of introduction which precede Sir Harry Wildair's entrance are scarcely a case in point; for Wildair is certainly a rounded character, not, like Dapperwit or Sparkish, or Tattle or Brisk, a mere incarnate "humour." This departure from the Jonsonian method is an

additional evidence of the fact that the dramatist, properly so-called, was more highly developed in Farquhar than in his contemporaries. (pp. 25-6)

Even as it was, in his brief literary life of eight or nine years, cut short before he can be supposed to have reached full maturity, he contrived to do work which makes him, far more than any other of his group, an influential precursor of Fielding. In humour and humanity the two are distinctly congenial; and, if we allow for difference of scale, Farquhar's power of character-drawing may quite well be measured with that of the "Great Harry." He had extraordinary ease in giving his personages individuality without caricature, or mechanical insistence or "humours." But what chiefly justifies us in regarding his too early death as one of the most notable of the many mischances that have befallen the English drama, is the steady growth we can perceive in him, not only of moral feeling, but of sober criticism of life. His first three comedies, as I have admitted, are entirely irresponsible; but in the last act of the last of them we come upon a passage which, in ironic form, strikes a note of sincere indignation. So, at least, I read the short scene in *Sir Harry Wildair* (Act V. sc. 4) between Sir Harry and Lord Bellamy. The almost savage scorn with which Sir Harry here spits in the face of "smart" society—of what I have called the coterie—is not in his normal character. It reminds one of a tirade by one of the debauchee moralists of the younger Dumas. Farquhar is here uttering the bitterness of his own spirit; and from this time onward he is no longer irresponsible, not even in the semi-Elizabethan *Inconstant* which he borrowed from Fletcher. Especially noteworthy is the growth of his sympathy with the finer aspects of womanhood. Leanthe in *Love and a Bottle* is a romantic impossibility, Lucinda a very vulgar personage. Angelica in *The Constant Couple* is a lay-figure, and in *Sir Harry Wildair* a convention; while Lady Lurewell is, in *The Constant Couple,* a melodramatic man-hater, not unlike Dumas's *Etrangère,* and has become, in *Sir Harry Wildair,* a vapourish, corrupt fine-lady. But in the later plays the heroines are always natural, agreeable women, with as much refinement as the atmosphere of the age would permit. I have already quoted an admirable saying of Aurelia's in *The Twin-Rivals.* Silvia, in *The Recruiting Officer,* in spite of the absurdity of her disguise and the coarseness of some of the episodes that spring from it, seems to me to have more than a touch of the free, generous, self-reliant womanhood of Shakespeare's heroines in the past and Mr Meredith's in the future. Dorinda, in *The Beaux' Stratagem,* is a pleasant figure, and even Mrs Sullen is not the ordinary female rake of Restoration Comedy. Professor Ward writes of this play: "Some of the incidents are dubious, including one at the close—a separation by mutual consent, which throws a glaring light on the view taken by the author and his age on the sanctity of the marriage tie." I venture to suggest that what is here set down to Farquhar's discredit is, in fact, a remarkable proof of the increasing earnestness of his outlook upon life. We have in this comedy (especially in the scenes between Mrs Sullen and Dorinda at the end of Act iii., and between Squire Sullen and Sir Charles Freeman at the beginning of Act v.) a serious and very damaging criticism of the conventional view that there can be no immorality in marriage save breach of the marriage vow. These scenes are, in fact, a plea for what Farquhar regarded, rightly or wrongly, as a more rational law of divorce. We may or may not think the plea a sound one; but it is certain that a serious discussion of the ethics of divorce was a homage to the idea of marriage which Wycherley, Congreve, or Vanbrugh would never have dreamt of paying. To them marriage meant nothing but a legal convention governing the transmission of property from (reputed) father to son. For the rest, it merely added a relish to libertinism. Where marriage constitutes no bond, divorce can have no function. When Farquhar seriously (and wittily) set himself to show that a certain type of marriage was loathsome and immoral, he broke once for all with the irresponsible licentiousness of his school. He admitted a moral standard, and subjected social convention, not to mere cynical persiflage, but to the criticism of reason. Having reached this point at twenty-nine, how far might he not have advanced if another twenty years had been vouchsafed him? (pp. 27-9)

> *William Archer, in an introduction to* George Farquhar, *edited by William Archer, A. A. Wyn, Inc., 1949, pp. 3-29.*

Louis Kronenberger   (essay date 1952)

[*A drama critic for* Time *magazine from 1938 to 1961, Kronenberger was a distinguished historian, literary critic, and author highly regarded for his expertise in eighteenth-century English history and literature. Among his best known writings are the nonfiction accounts* Kings and Desperate Men: Life in Eighteenth-Century England *(1942), which examines British culture of that century, and* Marlborough's Duchess: A Study in Worldliness *(1969), a biography of the first duke of Marlborough. His critical works include* The Thread of Laughter: Chapters on English Stage Comedy from Jonson to Maugham *(1952) and* The Republic of Letters *(1955). In the following excerpt, Kronenberger comments on the transitional character of Farquhar's plays, tracing their departure from the Comedy of Manners and accusing Farquhar of killing Restoration comedy "without creating anything better or even counter-balancing."*]

George Farquhar brings us to the last of the Restoration playwrights; and it is quickly evident that he *is* the last. It is less, with Farquhar, that the tradition has thinned out than that it has been mingled—we cannot call it blended—with something new. . . .

Right off, in *The Constant Couple,* we feel something new, something individual; a release of air, a certain brightening of the theatrical landscape. Taking each man at his characteristic best, we are inclined to call Etherege airy, Wycherley lusty, Congreve witty, Vanbrugh lively. Farquhar might well be called exuberant, but is perhaps best called gay. Gaiety is, in either case, something one does not merely possess, but communicates; something that creates an atmosphere, that evokes a contrast: we know that life is ordinarily not like this, and that this is too enchanting to last. (p. 167)

[The] Farquhar of *The Constant Couple* . . . is indeed not

very good. But already he has gaiety, already he can make a scene a little better or brighter than the thing itself strictly is, a character rather less typical or trite than his behavior stamps him. *The Constant Couple,* on the whole, is a pretty perfunctory and mechanical job: Farquhar has plainly gone to the Restoration for his material and his methods. And yet he has come back with something that the Restoration does not have; he offers, certainly, a bad play, yet not too bad an evening in the theater. Or we might better compare it to a party—a party where the guests were commonplace, and the games were silly, and the food was rather bad, but the hosts had a knack for making it all seem rather pleasant.

Some of the characters in *The Constant Couple* are sheer stereotypes. Vizard is the outwardly pious, well-behaved young man with an incessant eye to the main chance and a black unscrupulous nature. Who knows today in what primitive piece of fiction he first appeared, or in what work of interstellar television he will expire? The Restoration knew him; the eighteenth century will know him best as Blifil in *Tom Jones,* as Joseph Surface in *The School for Scandal.* His uncle, Smuggler, equally pious and sanctimonious on the surface, equally grasping and heartless underneath, though even more familiar in Restoration and later comedy, has been less so since Victorian times: he gradually passed out of comedy into melodrama, and was repudiated even there when, after Victorian times, melodrama cleaned house. There is nothing new, either, about Farquhar's Colonel Standard or his Clincher brothers.

Lady Lurewell, however, is more convincing because a crossbreed. As a woman whose lover betrayed her and who thereupon vowed revenge upon all his sex, she is a rather tiresome type. But as a woman whose methods of revenge have a certain cruel ingenuity, a touch of Volpone, about them, Lady Lurewell is not without interest. Our enjoyment springs from the number of aspirants to her favors and her fortune, and from her ability to disappoint them one and all. The ending, to be sure—where her betrayer-beau doesn't so much turn up again as prove to have been there all the time—is in the silliest traditions of romantic comedy. But we have now reached that point in the theater's history where the characters will more and more wind up in each other's arms, having been less and less in each other's arms at earlier and more illicit stages of the play.

It is Sir Henry Wildair who fans *The Constant Couple* into life and gives it, fitfully, its exhilaration. He is in no sense an exceptional character: he does nothing very new, says nothing very witty, suggests nothing very piquant. But that is in some sense what is good about him: he is a young rake who, though his principal adventure is farcical, is in all his motivations and reactions perfectly realistic. His point of view and his philosophy of life are completely convincing. He indulges in neither hypocrisies nor heroics; he has no need to. When Colonel Standard challenges him to a duel, and he refuses, Standard cries, "I hope you're no coward, sir." And Sir Harry answers: "Coward, sir?—I have eight thousand pounds a year, sir." This is as profoundly honest and sensible as can be: why should a young man with everything in the world to make him happy, duel with a man he doesn't dislike over a woman he isn't deceived by? "Coward, sir?—I have eight thousand pounds a year." It clears the air. It has the force and thrust of "Dost thou think because thou art virtuous there shall be no more cakes and ale?" And everywhere we have the sense of a young man who does what he pleases as politely as he can but as forcibly as he has to, without embarrassment or concealment, of a young man who can enjoy every luxury, even that of being honest. And on no one can Farquhar better bestow his own gift of gaiety than on a Sir Harry, for whom life is indeed a charming thing, and living an uncomplicated business.

Sir Harry's relations with Lady Lurewell have a good seventeenth-century comedy-of-manners air about them; his encounters with Angelica are merely in the vein of farce, half romantic and half rowdy. His being led to understand that Angelica is a courtesan full of genteel pretensions, and that her mother is a procuress with the manner of a grande dame, opens one of those classic situations in which, once the situation is sprung, the rest is up to the individual author. It is the author's resourcefulness, imaginativeness, humor that will count. Farquhar, on the whole, does an entertaining job, and Sir Harry helps him. For Sir Harry, with presumably better knowledge of demimondaines than of great ladies, takes all this fine talk for a way of commanding the highest price from him; and Farquhar, too, has the sense to make Sir Harry arrive at the climactic interview all befuddled with burgundy. And, befuddled with burgundy, he is free of tongue and of purse alike; and when, after he offers Angelica a hundred guineas for a single night's hospitality, she draws herself up in outraged virtue, he himself becomes a little irritated:

> SIR HAR.: [Aside.] This is the first whore in heroics that I have met with.—[Aloud.] Look ye, madam, as to that slender particular of your virtue, we sha'n't quarrel about it; you may be as virtuous as any woman in England, if you please; you may say your prayers all the time.—But pray, madam, be pleased to consider what is this same virtue that you make such a mighty noise about? Can your virtue bespeak you a front row in the boxes? No; for the players can't live upon virtue. Can your virtue keep you a coach and six? No, no, your virtuous women walk a-foot. Can your virtue hire you a pew in a church? Why, the very sexton will tell you, no. Can your virtue stake for you at picquet? No. Then what business has a woman with virtue? Come, come, madam, I offered you fifty guineas: there's a hundred.—The devil! Virtuous still! Why, 'tis a hundred, five score, a hundred guineas.

> . . . .

> SIR HAR.: Affront! 'Sdeath, madam! a hundred guineas will set you up at basset, a hundred guineas will furnish out your lodgings with china; a hundred guineas will give you an air of quality; a hundred guineas will buy you a rich escritoir for your billets-doux, or a fine Common-Prayerbook for your virtue. A hundred guineas will buy a hundred fine things, and fine things are for fine ladies; and fine ladies are for fine gentlemen; and fine gentlemen are—egad, this burgundy, makes a man speak like an angel.—

Come, come, madam, take it and put it to what use you please.

This final speech is what is characteristic of Farquhar, and pleasant about him: what it has is not sparkle, but spin. It is also, in its way, very much to the point. In Farquhar a certain sense of reality is always conjoined or contrasted with the romantic plots and trappings; there is always something down to earth as well as up in the air. And Farquhar can not only challenge the increasingly fashionable trappings with a pinch of the old realism, he can enliven them with a pinch of the old raciness. Farquhar can have Sir Harry mistake a private house for a bordello; seventy years later Goldsmith will only have his young men mistake a private house for an inn. It is to Goldsmith's credit that he makes a far better play of it, partly because he *does* make a play of it, where Farquhar merely exploits it for two or three scenes. Indeed, Farquhar's whole play is jumbled: a halfway house between the seventeenth and eighteenth century that is a rooming-house to boot, where a variety of people lead aimless and unrelated lives. The author himself still lives in lodgings, has not yet found his artistic home.

What comes out in Farquhar's next play, *The Twin-Rivals,* is how naturally gifted a man of the theater he was. Here, again, is a kind of gaiety or exuberance; and here, in the treatment of scenes and the handling of stories, is a kind of flow. This, however, is to emphasize something in the author rather than praise very much in the play, for what Farquhar possesses here he has also very sadly misused. He was bound to misuse it perhaps, he was bound to burst the mold of Restoration comedy; it was all too dry for him, and foppish, and enameled. (pp. 168-72)

For an act or two *The Twin-Rivals* might well be a Restoration vintage, because the plot is nondescript enough to fit any age and because all the evil characters engross the action. Benjamin Wouldbe, besides being hunchbacked, is the younger twin, the one who will not inherit either the title or the estate; and he is disgruntled enough to stop at nothing in his efforts to beat out his brother. Although touched with Elizabethan vigor, he has sufficient Restoration coldheartedness to fit the familiar Restoration frame. And Richmore, callous about all obligations—he will abandon a mistress, trap a nephew, walk out on a friend—fits the Restoration pattern to a *t*. So, too, does Mrs. Mandrake, who having presumably started as a midwife and moved on to become a procuress and go-between, literally knows about everybody from birth, and can put what she knows to excellent use. And so long as these villains hold the limelight, the play moves forward with real dash and go, only stopping now and then for a cynical delineation of the way of the world. A scene like that between Ben Wouldbe and the tavern-keeper Balderdash, in which Balderdash forsakes the man who has been his most liberal patron because he can no longer give him patronage, has a truly brutal frankness about it, all the directness of a glass of water thrown in one's face. And when Ben has installed himself in his father's house and has assumed his brother's title, the crowd of hangers-on have the old Restoration smack. And every so often there is something in the writing—of sheer humor or curiously modern irony—that without being in the familiar Restoration manner perfectly consorts with it. Consider Richmore refusing to do anything about the girl he has got with child:

> MRS. MAN.: And won't you marry her, Mr. Richmore?
>
> RICH.: My conscience won't allow it; for I have sworn since to marry another.
>
> MRS. MAN.: And will you break your vows to Clelia?
>
> RICH.: Why not, when she has broke hers to me?
>
> MRS. MAN.: How's that, sir?
>
> RICH.: Why, she swore a hundred times never to grant me the favour; and yet you know she broke her word.
>
> MRS. MAN.: But she loved, Mr. Richmore, and that was the reason she forgot her oath.
>
> RICH.: And I love Mr. Richmore, and that is the reason I forgot mine. Why should she be angry that I follow her own example, by doing the very same thing from the very same motive?
>
> . . . .
>
> MRS. MAN.: But won't you provide for poor Clelia?
>
> RICH.: Provide! why, ha'n't I taught her a trade? Let her set up when she will, I'll engage her customers enough, because I can answer for the goodness of the ware.

The reaction is familiar Restoration, but there is an odd, almost whimsical, touch of humor involved in the callousness. Much of the time, too, there is a decided recognition of the way of the world—though this, in Farquhar, smacks of one who has rubbed elbows with hardship and even felt the whip of insolence, where in Wycherley or Congreve there is rather the sense of drawing-room hypocrisies and the cold treachery of one's own friends. Not that Farquhar scamps the treachery: Ben can dispose of whatever qualms he has for cheating his brother by remarking, with a shrug, that even the first two brothers were enemies.

Up to the second scene of the third act we can, I think, enjoy ourselves. In many ways it is the same old Restoration story, only without the brittleness. If there is not so much wit, there is a good deal more humor. And though sex plays its part in the proceedings, the main part is allotted to money. Mrs. Mandrake, we feel, is not just an old bawd, but a very accomplished businesswoman; Ben Wouldbe's grudge against life may have started, we feel, with his hump, but the hump, like Richard III's, is as much a pretext for being a villain as it is a cause; and after so much amorous thieving, it is enjoyable to see some one set about cheating his brother out of a fortune. In all this, we have a vague sense of heading all the way back to Jacobean times, but there is a good, spanking breeze to carry us backward.

Still, we cannot but feel that the sky is clouding over. We cannot help knowing that with so many things amiss—usurpers in power, damsels in distress, betrayers at large—the forces of Virtue and Vengeance must be marshalling themselves backstage. When clouds form in circumstances like these, we can be sure that every cloud has a silver lining. Act III, Scene 1, closes with Benjamin Wouldbe uttering words of fashionable cynicism about a rogue. Act III, Scene 2, opens with the return of his brother, the true heir and the virtuous one, mouthing blank verse. The fact that the blank verse is intolerably bad, and that the sentiment it clothes is moth-eaten and stagy, is hardly the worst of it; the worst is what a portent these things are. And not of a return to bloodstained, highbooted Elizabethan times, but of that long trek forward, through mile after mile of painted cardboard scenery, into the Victorian future. With that one blank-verse speech we have crossed a frontier; we are in the realms of tiresome romantic comedy, even in the foothills of tawdry melodrama; and Mrs. Mandrake at her worst—as when she descants on which twin was born first—carries us clean across the mountain range, past melodrama to burlesque: she sounds like practically any nurse in any opera by Gilbert & Sullivan.

Simply as playwriting, *The Twin-Rivals* does not collapse; Farquhar keeps it going with this device or that; the plot thickens along with the language; the villains are still far from undone, the damsels remain in distress; and now and then, there is even a return to form, a certain humor and briskness, even sharpness. This humor never quite deserts Farquhar, any more than the romantic conventions of the story ever quite destroy his realistic sense of values. But there is no use pleading this or that small extenuation; it would be like summoning character witnesses who, with the defendant on trial for murder, would depose that he always brushed his teeth before going to bed. The plain fact is that in the last half of *The Twin-Rivals* Morality so brazenly triumphs that Comedy is pushed clean over the precipice.

The triumph is pervasive. That the good brother should oust the bad brother is not the crux of it; commonsense almost insists that he should, and comedy never balks at seeing justice done. The trouble goes far deeper, in the way virtue everywhere wins out, in the way that vice itself bolts to virtue's side. The rake is reformed: Richmore takes Clelia in matrimony. Romantic comedy sits enthroned, with Restoration comedy dead at its feet. The pity is that comedy should be rushing from one undesirable extreme to another; that something too brutal should give way to something so bogus.

In *The Recruiting Officer,* we find Farquhar even further removed from the traditional atmosphere of Restoration comedy. The scene is not simply Shrewsbury rather than London; there is a sense of the countryside and the out-of-doors, of military stir and almost plebeian bustle. This may suggest anything from the Mermaid dramatists to outright musical comedy, but in climate or coloration at any rate, it does not suggest Etherege or Congreve. A little later we may question whether Farquhar harmonized all these new and undomiciled elements, but we can certainly say right off that he had broken the Restoration mold, that by now something had quite vanished in terms of manners as well as morality. Tucker Brooke has said that, compared with Wycherley, Etherege, and Congreve, Farquhar seems more a man of the world and less a man about town, and the distinction is weightier than at first may appear, for it distinguishes not simply Farquhar's performance from the others', but his potentialities. Although Farquhar died at twenty-nine, we already are conscious of some one who lived a more varied and, so to speak, more absorbent life than his predecessors. It's not just that he is putting his own military adventures to use in *The Recruiting Officer,* but that he was moving in all kinds of directions at once—and not just backward into the bucolic byways of the Elizabethans, not just forward into the tara-diddles of romantic comedy, but directly outward, to provide touches and glimpses of early eighteenth-century *country* manners, of recruits and bumpkins side by side with rakish captains and pretty heiresses. Farquhar was, finally, moving inward, into the wistful, humorous gaiety of his own nature, and the *sense of the truth* of his mind. Here and there we shall find a scene we have nowhere found earlier, one that instead of having a Restoration cynicism or a Wycherley-like violence, has a harsh satirical humor—a humor that is harsh because it is humane. Farquhar, whose own personal life was full of struggle and whose own social life was not spent among the highborn, knew something about what life itself, the world rather than the great world, was made of.

It cannot be said, however, that in his playwriting the world was too much with him. It was often far too little.

THE

Recruiting Officer.

A

COMEDY.

As it is Acted at the

THEATRE ROYAL

IN

DRURY-LANE,

By Her MAJESTY's Servants.

Written by Mr. FARQUHAR.

—— *Captique Æolis, donifque coacti.*
Virg. Lib. II. Æneid.

LONDON:

Printed for BERNARD LINTOTT at the *Crofs Keys* next
Nando's Coffee-Houfe near *Temple-Bar.*

Price 1 *s.* 6 *d.*

Title page of the first edition, 1706.

If in *The Recruiting Officer* we escape from the town into the country, we shift equally from an artificial world of masks to a romantic one of disguises. We pass from a milieu where friends cannot be sure of each other's hearts to where a father does not recognize his daughter's voice, from a world where people are deceived by character to one where they are misled by plot. Silvia, in *The Recruiting Officer,* dresses up like a man; Kite dresses up like a fortune-teller; Worthy is led to believe that Melinda cares about Brazen; Brazen, for that matter, is led to believe it too. Palpably, the play might have been written a hundred years earlier.

In its own day, and for generations after, *The Recruiting Officer* was a great success—thanks, no doubt, to the variety of its scenes and characters, to its facile mingling of realism and romance, thanks also to its humor and verve. But if such a mélange was refreshing to Farquhar's contemporaries, it is not at all satisfying to us. The plot, as it proceeds, grows rather tiresome and exceedingly cut-and-dried. What one finds dullest about romantic comedy isn't the idea that people will live together happily ever after, but that for so very long they aren't allowed to live together at all, that we must watch the author inventing or appropriating ruses that will keep them apart—the letter that doesn't arrive, the message that isn't delivered, the words that are overheard and can be taken two ways, the lover who is carried off to a tavern when he has promised to call on the girl—not to speak of those sudden quarrels that blow up over nothing at all, in which the hero stomps and the heroine flounces out of the room. And in the next scene, he sullenly watches her trip arm-in-arm across the stage with Lord Poodle; or she bites her lip—or tosses her head—as he exits laughing like mad with Miss Wick. In *The Recruiting Officer,* the complications that separate both romantic couples are at once too pat and too protracted. With one of the pairs it is no great matter, but the relations between Silvia and Plume could prove much more rewarding, as they are people of spirit: and the idea of an attractive girl who is also not so much tomboy as a forthright, no-foolishness toughie, is fairly novel. But once Silvia dresses up like a man, all individuality vanishes. Nor does Farquhar provide any great fun by way of compensation.

Storywise, the play is loose and ungartered, and lacking, too, in tone and point of view. Farquhar is groping for something that will channel his talents in the very act of liberating them, that will be expressive as well as creative. But beyond the fact that he is still young and a little green and living sorely from hand to mouth, clearly the voice of Jeremy Collier has been heard in the land. There is finally the fact that this is an Irishman with the quick bright humor of his race, but also with its sense of hurry and want of control. He is facile: he writes with a pen that need never slow down, and that frequently ought to. When we think of his next achievement, of *The Beaux Stratagem,* as the work of a dying man, we can even better grasp how gifted Farquhar was. But it is hardly a blessing to be thus gifted; some one has said that good writing consists of natural facility and acquired difficulty.

So here, too, in *The Recruiting Officer,* there is much less to be said of its achievement as a play than of the incidental accomplishments of the author. He has only to speak—the play has only to open—for us to feel what swing and freshness he has:

> KITE: [Making a speech.] If any gentlemen soldiers, or others, have a mind to serve her Majesty, and pull down the French king: if any prentices have severe masters, any children have undutiful parents: if any servants have too little wages, or any husband too much wife: let them repair to the noble Serjeant Kite, at the sign of the Raven in this good town of Shrewsbury, and they shall receive present relief and entertainment.—Gentlemen, I don't beat my drums here to ensnare or inveigle any man; for you must know, gentlemen, that I am a man of honour. Besides, I don't beat up for common soldiers; no, I list only grenadiers—grenadiers, gentlemen. Pray, gentlemen, observe this cap. This is the cap of honour, it dubs a man a gentleman in the drawing of a trigger; and he that has the good fortune to be born six foot high, was born to be a great man.

There is little of the elegance of earlier Restoration comedy: but there is a new sort of verve.

> SILVIA: What do you expect from this captain, child?
>
> ROSE: I expect, sir—I expect—but he ordered me to tell nobody. But suppose that he should promise to marry me?
>
> SILVIA: Have a care, my dear, men will promise anything beforehand.
>
> ROSE: I know: but he promised to marry me afterwards.

Even here, where the dialogue follows a charted enough course, there is something a trifle gayer, a trifle more humorous, than we find in Etherege or even Vanbrugh. And it is sheer humor when Melinda tells Lucy that the fortune-teller informed her she should die a maid. "Die a maid!" Lucy answers—"Dear madam, if you should believe him it might come to pass, for the bare thought of it might kill one." It is his humor, not his wit, that distinguishes Farquhar from his predecessors. He is greater in germ, because richer in humanity and sheer creative fancy, than they are. But it is true that, as John Palmer says, he killed Restoration comedy as it had existed. And he killed it without creating anything better or even counter-balancing.

Certainly his wit is not up to his predecessors': but like his humor his satire introduces something new. In the trial scene, the judges are indignant that a man with a wife and five children should have been impressed into the army. It is not so much that Farquhar, here, shows feeling for the poor as that in a sense he shows feeling at all. The very words, during the scene, that carry us to a humane level of writing carry us, almost for the first time, to a human one. This is the harshness of a writer capable of indignation, and when, a moment later, the next culprit is brought to trial, Farquhar achieves more irony with a single play

on words than did any other Restoration playwright with his finest epigram:

> BALANCE: What are you, friend?
>
> MOB: A collier; I work in the coal-pits.
>
> SCRUPLE: Look'ee, gentlemen, this fellow has a trade, and the act of parliament here expresses, that we are to impress no man that has any visible means of a livelihood.
>
> KITE: May it please your worships, this man has no visible means of livelihood, for he works underground.

One is reminded not of Farquhar's fellow-countryman Congreve but of his fellow-countryman Swift, or one jumps a couple of centuries to the domains of Farquhar's fellow-countryman Shaw.

Farquhar's last play, *The Beaux Stratagem,* is almost certainly his best; but only for reaching a more brightly sustained level of entertainment than his earlier works do. It fails to resolve the discord sounding through all his works. No more than his first play does it achieve a settled point of view. Or rather, just at the very end, after retreating to the frontier of Restoration comedy without crossing it, and after plunging off the cliffs of romantic tutti-frutti, it does sound—in the dissolving of the marriage of the Sullens—a refrain that seems to clarify Farquhar's feeling toward sex and society. This marital break-up is singularly sane and down-to-earth and modern; it simply argues that incompatible marriages shall not be made bearable—and also farcical—by outside attachments; or very hard to bear, and as we should say full of frustration and neurosis, by the parties resigning themselves to an unhappy life together. It suggests—at least where there are no children involved—that husband and wife amicably part. Thus it retorts equally upon Restoration sin and romantic suffering; thus it makes an end of marriage as a mere game, but equally of marriage as a form of servitude. And the scene between Mrs. Sullen and her countryfied toper of a husband is managed with a proper lightness and banter, driving in no moral spike with heavy blows, only, as it were, throwing up a window-blind to let in the light of day upon the dim seduction chambers and garish romantic corridors of the rest of *The Beaux Stratagem.*

The rest of the play, in terms of attitudes and ingredients, is the merest gallimaufry. There are familiar elements in it of Elizabethan comedy, of Restoration comedy, of the horseplay of the Goldsmith school, of romantic comedy tinged with melodrama, of romantic comedy garnished with music, of mild swashbuckle and of momentary realism. There is also the matter of setting—the fact that so much of the play is laid at an inn, as so much of eighteenth-century fiction rides in and out of innyards; the fact that the plot thickens through the presence of highwaymen, as so much of eighteenth-century fiction lumbers along till accosted by the gentlemen of the road. The inn here is by no means the first one to play a great role in stage comedy—even the inns where Falstaff roistered were not the first—but Farquhar enjoys the honor of having, in the character of Boniface, given to common speech a generic name for an innkeeper—or is it for an innkeeper who is also a robber? Of course an inn as the setting for a play is an extraordinarily good one: nowhere can people meet and mingle so quickly and easily, nowhere come from such differing worlds or be of such different kinds.

Despite the stratagem advertised in the play's title, the plot offers nothing very vivid or new. That two gallants should make a last try at marrying a fortune by alternatively posing as master and servant, is not startling; that one of them should be rather dashing and worldly, the other more romantic and susceptible, is not startling either; Dorinda and her sister-in-law Mrs. Sullen are both continuators of a type; the presence of highwaymen may have then seemed less pat, but seems all too routine now. The story fails to be enriched by either outlaws or in-laws. And though Lady Bountiful, even more than Boniface, has given a name to the language, her chief importance is perhaps historical, marking the arrival of a truly benevolent character on the comedy stage—for which only brief congratulations are in order, as Lady Bountiful's successors will tend to drive comedy off it. Virtue, clearly, is mounting her steed, and Romance is already in the saddle. In the culminating episodes of the romance between Dorinda and Aimwell, we are witnessing—incident by incident—the finale of every piece of twaddle that is said to be loved by servant girls and known to be by finer folk. First Aimwell, having won Dorinda's love and being about to succeed in marrying her, must break down and confess that he has been an impostor. And Dorinda can but answer:

> Matchless honesty!—Once I was proud, sir, of your wealth and title, but now am prouder that you want it.

She then exits, to create a little suspense; when she returns, she too—after flying to his arms—must make confession. And what a pleasing confession it is: she has learned that Aimwell's brother is dead, and that Aimwell is now a viscount with a fine estate.

Doubtless this element of highflown tosh—brightened with Farquhar's gaiety of spirit and rather lusty use of sex—doubtless this blend of the romantic, the comic and the spicy, has kept *The Beaux Stratagem* alive all these two centuries. The play does have variety, and variety, at no matter what expense of tone or style or lifelikeness, is welcome to most playgoers. What makes *The Beaux Stratagem* an artistic muddle makes it equally a popular success. We, at least, can prize the small special things that are evidence of how good Farquhar might have become. He cannot touch the level of Congreve (though he scarcely tries to), but at a reasonably high level, where the writing is starched with at least a pinch of style, he can be perhaps the most satisfying, or at any rate enjoyable, of all the Restoration writers. The gaiety that benefits from the Queen Anne prose is more welcome than more-wit-with-less-spirit would be. But the satiric, the ironic note is fitfully present also. "How can you be merry," Lady Bountiful asks her daughter-in-law, "with the misfortunes of other people?" "Because," the girl answers, "my own make me sad." And there is that excellent retort that Mr. Dobrée noted ahead of me. When Archer has caught one of the highwaymen and, on the point of killing him, says:

"Come, rogue, if you have a short prayer say it." "I have no prayer," the man answers: "the government has provided a chaplain to say prayers *for* us on these occasions."

Farquhar is rather hard to sum up. None of his plays is really satisfactory. He used too much of the old to be regarded as having produced anything truly new—used, and in many cases, misused it. It is hard to see how, twenty years after the death of Charles II, Farquhar or any one else could have written in the old spirit; and once Jeremy Collier mounted the moral barricades and Queen Anne sat stolidly on the throne, it was impossible. Farquhar had, besides, the soul of an Irishman and the spirit of a humorist, and they soon drove him out-of-doors and to provincial towns for his settings. Unfortunately, he was also—as it were—driven out-of-doors for his plots, and the romantic, the bucolic, one must almost say the archaic, insisted on being part of the proceedings. Farquhar is perhaps not so individually culpable as he at first may seem: the novel during the century just beginning was to be stuffed with scraps and bits of the same sort. Moreover, a man dead at twenty-nine, working—if not indeed potboiling—in a medium that is not only the most rigid in form but perhaps the least truly adventurous in spirit, and at just the moment when social and sexual morality were under indictment and changing course—how could he be expected to shake the heavy seaweed of convention and popular taste from him, and to strike out, with clean strokes, toward what his talents really craved? Unless, to be sure, he was altogether an artist.

Instead, he was the child (and the rather lost child) of a transition, and all the more lost because it was a transition from something artistically better than himself to something artistically worse. He gains by contrast with what went before, but he also, and very heavily, loses by comparison. Whatever the reputation, or popularity, or fitful merit of *The Beaux Stratagem,* it simply cannot find a place in the company of Etherege's best, or Wycherley's, or Congreve's, or even Vanbrugh's. Farquhar's place is really with Shelley's inheritors of unfulfilled renown. But amid so much that is uninteresting and unabsorbed and meretricious in his work, so much that the best comic tradition must deprecate and even find hateful, there are an exuberance and a flow of spirits that are very engaging, and a sharp sense of life and a sudden ability to blow the gaff clean off it that are very impressive. That, out of deference to conventional morality, he often blew it right back on, and sometimes blew back even more than had been there before, is what we must most regret. As the child of a transition, he was caught between two sets of antagonistic values; he necessarily formulated no harmonious values of his own. (pp. 172-83)

Louis Kronenberger, "Farquhar: 'The Constant Couple,' 'The Twin Rivals,' 'The Recruiting Officer,' 'The Beaux Stratagem'," in his The Thread of Laughter: Chapters on English Stage Comedy from Jonson to Maugham, *Alfred A. Knopf, 1952, pp. 167-83.*

Bonamy Dobrée   (essay date 1959)

[*An English historian and critic, Dobrée distinguished himself both as a leading authority on Restoration drama and as a biographer who sought, through vivid depiction and style, to establish biography as a legitimate creative form. Dobrée is also known for his editing of* The Oxford History of English Literature *and the* Writers and their Work *series. In all his writings, Dobrée's foremost concern was to communicate to the reader his aesthetic response to the work under discussion. In the following excerpt, he suggests that Farquhar infused "a new spirit into the old form" of comedy by augmenting his plays with humanity and satire.*]

Farquhar was the only dramatic writer of any comic power at the beginning of the century who managed to infuse a new spirit into the old form, partly by setting side by side with it a spirit critical of matters which had hitherto lain outside its view. Had he not died at the age of twenty-nine it is possible that he might have discovered some way of expressing the ethos of the century—its domestic sense, its sentimentality, its notion of social morality—in comic form. By his last two plays, he stands out from among his contemporaries for sheer originality, for zest, for acute criticism of social assumptions, and a sense of the stage that transcends tricks. He was brilliantly alert to the ridiculous, while at the same time wielding the Meredithian sword of common sense, and was aware that the method of art is indirect—that comedy must primarily amuse, though it may incidentally teach: it is no mere 'agreeable vehicle for counsel and reproof'. Incidental, certainly, must have been any teaching on the plane of sexual morality of his first play, *Love and a Bottle* (1699), where the love exhibited is redolent rather of a late lascivious reign than of the decorum of William III's; there is, however, a touch of romantic comedy of the girl masquerading as a page (though Wycherley also made use of that Elizabethan trick), common enough in the plays of the next twenty years. In so far as Farquhar shows any originality here it is in his satire of the young fop up from Oxford, learning to dance and push (fence) and sing, an originality not so much in the theme as in Farquhar's zestful enjoyment of it all. He rejoices in the fool as much as he enjoys mocking at the folly. But his next few plays, *The Constant Couple* (1699), *Sir Harry Wildair* (1701) and its sequel, *The Inconstant* (1702), together with *The Twin Rivals* acted at the end of the same year, are dreary rehashes of the theme of *Love's Last Shift*. In them the hero, pursuing his unselective amours through four acts, suddenly vows fidelity to some heroine whom he has approached in the belief that she is a prostitute, or who has—with an interlude as a page—returned from a supposed grave, all being of an unreality both of fact and of sentiment redeemed only by a certain inventiveness of plot and liveliness of conventional dialogue. 'What low pert comedy e'en Farquhar writ' is an understandable comment in the context of these plays. Here and there, it is true, there is a telling phrase, something revealing a mind at work; and in the last we are conscious of a growling discomfort somewhere in the background; but on the whole this Farquhar is merely the able hack playwright earning his sparse living by turning out the expected machine-made goods.

Then after some four years' interval (apart from an adaptation from the French) there appeared *The Recruiting Officer,* the scene laid well outside the tedious precincts of fashionable London, the characters on the whole free of the deadening eroticism of those in Farquhar's previous plays, the themes the live ones of the day—chiefly the recruitment of men for the War of Spanish Succession—the subsidiary figures freshly observed, and a great sense of fun pervading the whole wholesome atmosphere; then in 1707 *The Beaux's Stratagem,* the best of all his work. It is, of course, absurd to say that he in any way approaches Congreve in excellence—except possibly in contrivance of plot, where Congreve was clumsy; there is no modulation of phrasing, no pondered sentiment, no values above the commonplace. But Farquhar brought to English society that cool, appraising glance, that sense of the falsity of assumptions, that mocking critical spirit which is so often the gift of the Irishman. He is, in a sense, the Shaw of his time. He had no very subtle sense of comedy, as is shown by his *Discourse upon Comedy,* which is chiefly devoted to scourging academic critics; but he had an eye for the comic and the incongruous, and a feel for what would go on the stage, including the unexpected. His people in his last two plays are no longer puppets; they are flesh and blood filled with vitality, sometimes a stage vitality (and that is a good deal) but more often that of real life. For the highwayman, when told on his capture 'if you have a short prayer, say it' to retort, 'Sir, I have no Prayer at all; the Government has provided a Chaplain to say Prayers for us on these Occasions', is as far-reaching as it is delightfully surprising, and needs no gloss. The people in both these plays are likeable where they are meant to be, and we feel that Farquhar was possessed of a real humanity lacking in most of his contemporaries. (pp. 233-34)

Bonamy Dobrée, "Drama," in his English Literature in the Early Eighteenth Century, 1700-1740, *Oxford at the Clarendon Press, 1959, pp. 223-56.*

Eric Rothstein   (essay date 1964)

[*An American educator, Rothstein has established himself as an authority on Restoration drama through his two books,* George Farquhar *(1967) and* Restoration Tragedy: Form and the Process of Change *(1967). In the following excerpt, he examines the satire, structure, and themes of Farquhar's early works, asserting that Farquhar's* Discourse *and* The Twin Rivals *redefined the moral development of the stage.*]

Although the years 1701 through 1703 saw the number of Collierite publications markedly diminish, the zeal of the reformers and the consequent distress of the theatres seems hardly to have abated. It was in this perilous atmosphere that Farquhar attempted perhaps the most ambitious and potentially telling attack upon Collier's abolitionist demands: the publications, in February and December 1702 respectively, of the *Discourse upon Comedy* and *The Twin-Rivals.* The relativism of the *Discourse* strikes at Collier's *aesthetic* position both by denying the validity of his classical authorities and by affirming that of popular consensus. *The Twin-Rivals* rebuts the force of

Collier's *moral* invective by presenting, concretely, the kind of moral comedy that Collier himself claimed to favor and that the various apologies for comedy had presented, verbally, as a justifying ideal. In demonstrating the value of comedy, Farquhar meant to confound the abolitionists and make the stage flourish. *The Twin-Rivals* failed and thus accomplished neither. I would suggest, however, that its ethos and its structure make it an extremely interesting document as well as a skillful play. I should like to discuss its purposeful novelty and its relationship both to Farquhar's canon and to the development of the stage at the beginning of the eighteenth century, drawing an eventual moral.

Since, as I shall point out, *The Twin-Rivals* was honed on its direct predecessors, it will be worthwhile to scrutinize them in slight detail. One may choose as typical enough Farquhar's first play, *Love and a Bottle* (1699), which deftly incorporated most of the "Liberties" that Collier defines early in *A Short View*. . . . Mockery of the clergy comes within the first fifty lines, as a beggar derides their keenness in knowing where charity begins and ends: "A Captain will say Dam'me, and give me Six-pence; and a Parson shall whine out God bless me, and give me not a farthing." And a summary of the plot will indicate its libertine freedom.

More disturbing than these particularities, as Collier knew, are the assumptions made by *Love and a Bottle,* assumptions largely shared by wit-comedy in general, about human nature. Like [John Vanbrugh's] *Love's Last Shift, Love and a Bottle* demonstrates the compatibility of fifth-act reclamation with a "naturalistic" attitude: throughout the play the rake does what he likes, while the women and Lovewell "wou'd if they cou'd." The women, significantly like Wycherley's, are prudes only by hypocritic principle; when Pindress is reproached for a *double-entendre,* she can respond:

> Ay Madam, and your Ladyship wou'd seem to blush in the Box, when the redness of your face proceeded from nothing but the constraint of holding your Laughter. Didn't you chide me for not putting a stronger Lace in your Stays, when you had broke one as strong as a Hempen Cord, with containing a violent Tihee at a smutty Jest in the last Play?

Furthermore, the women are directly, physically, passionate. Roebuck's vocation to a chaste life comes immediately from Leanthe's superior erotic achievements, and the prelude to his rapturous repentance evokes her, violently aroused, in the most sensuous physical terms:

> ROEB. I'm on the Rack of Pleasure, and must confess all.
> When her soft, melting, white, and yielding Waste,
> Within my pressing Arms was folded fast,
> Our Lips were melted down by heat of Love,
> And lay incorporate in liquid kisses,
> Whilst in soft broken sighs, we catch'd each other's Souls.

The evocation—it is more than a description—has been made vivid enough so that Roebuck's conversion, to a per-

petuity of such legitimate delights, can be plausible to the audience. Further, passion is ratified by using its sensations as metaphors for that conversion: Roebuck and Leanthe are fused, "incorporate," interinanimated physically just as they are soon to be united, because of the physical relationship, morally and spiritually. Libertine roving is disavowed not because it is immoral but because its superiority is empirically disproved.

Finally, Farquhar was aware, like Collier, that the modish "courtly love" practiced by virtuous men is as secular, as pagan, as asocial as the rakes' libertine abandon:

> ROEB. An honorable Mistress! what's that?
>
> LOV[EWELL]. A vertuous Lady, whom you must Love and Court; the surest method of reclaiming you.—As thus.—Those superfluous Pieces you throw away in Wine may be laid out—
>
> ROEB. To the Poor?
>
> LOV. No, no. In Sweet Powder, Cravats, Garters, Snuff-boxes, Ribbons, Coach-hire, and Chair-hire. Those idle hours which you mispend with lewd sophisticated Wenches, must be dedicated—
>
> ROEB. To the Church?
>
> LOV. No, To the innocent and charming Conversation of your vertuous Mistress; by which means, the two most exorbitant Debaucheries, Drinking and Whoring will be retrench'd.
>
> ROEB. A very fine Retrenchment truly!

The Restoration cynic and the reactionary highflying Anglican divine understood, as the benevolists and sentimentalists did not, the nature and effect of even the most virtuous surrender to passion. The terms in which plays like *Love and a Bottle* encompass both virtuous and rakish characters depend, in fact, on a recognition of the twinship between rakery and amorous decorum. Love and Honour can be mocked as "romantick" ideals, while they are simultaneously accepted as values sufficient to sustain the Lovewells and Leanthes and to resolve the plots in bourgeois harmony. Similarly, this recognized identity between the two varieties of sexual pursuit, of libido and impetuosity, permits the audience to accept "decent" characters who are willing to befriend and embrace the Roebucks. Since rutting is the way of the world, only the mode of the chase differentiates the pure from the sinful; and one knows that for the sinful the change of mode will be easy. It will involve neither sacrifice nor change of direction, and, therefore, introduction into social propriety, through a marriage and perhaps a repentance, can be quite near, even in the most profligate moments.

Love and a Bottle is the simplest of the Farquhar plays preceding *The Twin-Rivals,* but as wit-comedy it is exemplary of all three. Sir Harry Wildair can take his Angelica for a whore without making amends other than marriage; while, after her presumed death in the next play, he can play a "piping hot warm Heretick" to at least six nuns in five days without at all impairing his position in the eyes of virtue. The women, Angelica and Lurewell, are both warmly passionate. Like *Love and a Bottle,* the Wildair plays end with the satisfaction of physical desire in marriage, the coincidence of the social with naturalistically conceived private desires. All three of these comedies, then, *Love and a Bottle, The Constant Couple,* and *Sir Harry Wildair,* present a world highly desirable to the individual male: (a) women, being chaste, can be possessed and held, but (b) this chastity does not preclude an intense and steamy physical passion; meanwhile (c) the man can possess, before the pleasures grow climactic in marriage, large numbers of (equally) sexually greedy women, including particularly the conventionally inaccessible, nuns or other men's wives.

Together with the love plots in each of the plays are two kinds of satire. One attacks those people who try to deny the wits' world, or to falsify its credentials either by parodying them or by succeeding without them: the prude and the hypocrite; the fop and the "wou'd be" wit; the dolt and the man without prowess or virility. This is protective satire, validating the wits' world by seeing things from its point of view. There is also a second body of satire, what might be called "supporting satire." In each of these three plays, Farquhar picks matters extraneous to the plays themselves to mock. In *Love and a Bottle,* he chooses a conventional butt, the poor poet (Lyrick); in *Sir Harry Wildair,* he takes advantage of the contemporary War of the Spanish Succession to sneer at the French. Supporting satire, as the name I have given it suggests, is not *merely* a means of varying fare and keeping the audience laughing, although the uncontroversial good humor it creates does incline them toward accepting more tendentious jibes. Its support comes more significantly in its possibilities of creating guilt by association: if the prude and the French are satirized together and if everyone opposes the French, the prude can be tainted by juxtaposition.

The linear structure of these Farquhar plays, then, is tripartite: first, the love plot(s); secondly, the defense of the lovers in the satiric attack on their enemies: and thirdly, the supporting satire, only incidentally necessary to the narratives but rhetorically advantageous. Of course there is blurring and merging of these three modes, but insofar as they work out separately it follows, both logically and empirically, that the satiric plots be farcical (because ridiculous, pretentious, and therefore light in tone; but not witty), and the love plots peripatetic. Since Farquhar's early plots characteristically deal with the lovers' reaching proper rapport (rather than, say, with the defeat of blocking characters), and since, as suggested above, the supposed extremes of rakery and decorous virtue are actually quite close together, the peripeteias never become very serious. At the expository beginnings of the plays, the love scenes are most often carried through by wit, a wit that effervesces through the introduction of characters and themes, marking proper allegiances; while, as one draws nearer the resolution of the action, wit tends to become subsidiary to *lazzi,* close to farce or the chase. The lightness, or even flimsiness, of the plot throws the emphasis on the scene and its individual effect, and often on still more local matters, on the stunt, the quip, the brisk exchange. The satiric plots, still less continuous as narrative, and denied wit, are far more thoroughly dominated by

lazzi: the farther from the love plot one gets, the more the buffoon is called for. . . . The texts of the plays, unfortunately, can hardly make clear the pervasiveness of farce, because they give no idea of how much time was taken up with it and because many effects depend on being seen. A reader of *The Constant Couple* can imagine Johnson's (Smugler's) being dressed in woman's clothing and beaten, but can hardly reconstitute the effect of having the same superbly elegant suit worn in turn by the different-sized Pinkethman, Haynes, and Bullock, or that of having the towering Bullock tour the scenes of the play with the diminutive "Dicky" Norris. So as not to distort Farquhar's intention, one must picture the farce indicated and hypothesize the possibilities for improvisation. If one adds this farce to the principles of theme, of structure, and of dramatic device already outlined, the peculiarities of *The Twin-Rivals* should become apparent.

Farquhar, constructing a prefatory apologia for his "damn'd" comedy at the end of its meager run in late December 1702 tried to explain why he had written what he did:

> The Success and Countenance that Debauchery has met with in Plays, was the most Severe and Reasonable Charge against their Authors in Mr. *Collier's Short View;* and indeed this Gentleman has done the *Drama* considerable Service, had he Arrign'd the Stage only to Punish it's Misdemeanours, and not to take away it's Life; but there is an Advantage to be made sometimes of the Advice of an Enemy, and the only way to disappoint his Designs, is to improve upon his invective, and to make the Stage flourish by vertue of that Satyr, by which he thought to suppress it.

It is useless to speculate upon the possible disingenuousness of the opening admissions. What is far more significant is that, if Farquhar is to be taken literally, and I do not see why he should not be, *The Twin-Rivals* was to be written as an extension of Collier's "Satyr." Collier, arraigning the stage with great vigor and persistence, had denounced lewdness, lavished satirical invective upon the ideals behind it, and used decency (the plays of Terence, Jonson, Molière, et al.) only as a counterweight. Farquhar, vindicating the stage by showing its moral potentialities, wrote *The Twin-Rivals* on precisely those principles of organization, and, as I shall suggest, attacked not only "Immorality, and Profaneness" but also, by parody, the conventions of the offending immoral plays he was leaving behind.

The Twin-Rivals opens with a familiar scene: *"The Curtain drawn up, discovers* Young Wou'dbe *a Dressing, and his* Valet *Buckling his Shooes."* Scenes of the rake being dressed are among the most expressive gambits of witcomedy: in them, the rake can preen his aspect and his intellect before the play itself begins, so that the audience can experience his soon-to-be-employed aplomb, his carefully groomed predatory skills, his naturally artful elegance. In opening scenes like this, for instance, Dorimant or Sir Humphrey Scattergood (Shadwell's *The Woman-Captain*) are given their proper places, and their preparation and anticipation are meant to be vicariously echoed by the public's. But unlike Sir Humphrey and Dorimant, Young Wou'dbe has been contrived to inspire no "identification" or sympathy. He is a hunchback. Other than that, he has the conventional appanage of the rake, the qualities which conventionally appealed for support: he is an indigent, a sensualist and debauché, a clever manipulator, and, most important, a younger brother. The younger brother is, again, a stock character in wit-comedy because he is a sympathetic underdog: if society respects primogeniture, wit-comedy erects a hierarchy of merit. Shadwell's *Squire of Alsatia,* Cibber's *Love's Last Shift,* Mrs. Pix's *The Beau Defeated,* Vanbrugh's *The Relapse* all present examples of the stereotype from the fifteen years preceding *The Twin-Rivals. The Relapse* is perhaps directly relevant. In both plays, the exploits begin after unsuccessful attempts at borrowing money, and both plays turn on an exchange of brothers; *The Relapse* was a familiar play—it had been revived at Drury Lane the month before—and it was one of those particularly attacked by Collier. The relationship is obviously tenuous, but less so than it might be if there were no hint that *The Twin-Rivals* was using the conventions of other plays to make its point. I would further speculate that the hunchback, played as he was by Colley Cibber, might well have been meant to call to mind another ambitious younger brother in another Drury Lane play, Cibber's Richard III.

Young Wou'dbe is a rake manqué (or augmenté), his character extruded into a hump. The actual rake in the play is the dashingly promiscuous Richmore, who has attained a certain libertine grace:

> Y.W. Have you forgot, *Richmore,* how I found you one Morning, with the *Flying Post* in your hand, hunting for Physical Advertisements?
>
> RICH. That was in the Days of *Dad,* my Friend, in the days of dirty Linnen, Pit-Masks, Hedge-Taverns, and Beef-Stakes; but now I fly at nobler Game; the Ring, the Court, *Pawlet's* and the *Park:* I despise all Women that I apprehend any danger from, less than the having my Throat cut; and shou'd scruple to Converse even with a Lady of Fortune, unless her Virtue were loud enough to give me Pride in exposing it.

The delight in exposing virtue as hypocrisy, the supposition that virtue *is* hypocrisy, marks Richmore as the Dorimant, or the Sir Harry Wildair, of *The Twin-Rivals.* All the rake's ingenuities are in his mouth:

> MAN[DRAKE]. And will you break your Vows to *Clelia?*
>
> RICH. Why not, when she has broke her's to me?
>
> MAN. How's that, Sir?
>
> RICH. Why; She Swore a Hundred times never to grant me the Favour, and yet you know she broke her Word.
>
> MAN. But she lov'd Mr. *Richmore,* and that was the Reason she forgot her Oath.
>
> RICH. And I love Mr. *Richmore,* and that is the reason I forgot mine—Why shou'd she be Angry

that I follow her own Example, by doing the very same thing from the very same Motive?

This is not only clever evasion; it also indicates Richmore's actual attitude, that love is self-interest. Clelia's love and his own are, to him, very legitimately paralleled. He and Benjamin Wou'dbe—Benjamin, the beloved youngest—are differentiated from the good characters not specifically by lack of scruple but by lack of realization that the New Order no longer permits one to be naturalistic. Like such Shakespearean villains as Iago, Edmund, or Richard III, they reason quite coherently and consistently from assumptions about nature different from those of the good characters. *The Twin-Rivals* is one of the first comedies to distinguish such assumptions, although pathetic tragedy had for some time begun to insist on doing so. Both heroic tragedy and wit-comedy, however, had supported an ethic of self-aggrandizement for all characters, an ethic of *gloire,* and thus Young Wou'dbe and Richmore, surprised by four post-Collier lovers, are merely Old Comedy figures in a new setting. Their ideas of Love and Honour are surprisingly like Roebuck's:

> LEAN [THE]. I don't believe it, Sir; you cou'd not be so hard-hearted sure: Her honourable Passion, I think, shou'd please you best.
>
> ROEB. O Child! Boys of your age are continually reading Romances, filling your Heads with all that old bombast of Love and Honour: But when you come to my years, you'll understand better things.

They are also strikingly like Sir Harry Wildair's:

> STAND[ARD]. Sir, my Honour's concern'd.
>
> WILD. Nay, if your Honour be concern'd with a Woman, get it out of her Hands as soon as you can. An honourable Lover is the greatest Slave in Nature; some will say, the greatest Fool.

Both Roebuck and Sir Harry are free to beget their bastards without being forced into marriage: they are heroes; Richmore, a villain.

The differences between the earlier comedies and *The Twin-Rivals* in tone and in the view of the rake may be symbolized by two comparisons with Shakespearean passages, two naturalistic, hedonistic rationalizations for vice. The first is Sir Harry Wildair's [in *The Constant Couple*]:

> . . . but pray, Madam, be pleas'd to consider what is this same Vertue that you make such a mighty Noise about—Can your Vertue bespeak you a Front Row in the Boxes? No. . . . Can your Vertue keep you a Coach [sic] and Six? no, no. . . . Can your Vertue hire you a Pue in a Church? Why the very Sexton will tell you, no. Can your Vertue stake for you at Picquet? no. Then what business has a Woman with Vertue?

The original of this is obviously Falstaff's honor speech, and Falstaff, like Sir Harry, was conceived as waggish, droll, and salacious, although superior to a mere clown. The other speech from Farquhar is that with which Young Wou'dbe concludes Act II of *The Twin-Rivals:*

Y. W.[*Solus.*] The Pride of Birth, the Heats of Appetite, and Fears of Want, are strong Temptation to Injustice—But why Injustice?—The World has broke all Civilities with me; and left me in the Eldest State of Nature, Wild, where Force, or Cunning first created Right. . . . My Brother! What is Brother? We are all so; and the first two were Enemies—He stands before me in the Road of Life to Rob me of my Pleasures—My Senses, form'd by Nature for Delight, are all alarm'd—My Sight, my Hearing, Taste, and Touch, call loudly on me for their Objects, and they shall be satisfy'd.

The reference to the "State of Nature" is probably meant to allude to Hobbes, with whom direct association was part of the iconography of Restoration villainy. The speech itself, a fine speech to end an act, is rather in the manner of Edmund in *King Lear,* especially the Edmund of Tate's version, who has become considerably more sensually motivated than was Shakespeare's, an Edmund who titles himself "a born Libertine" and who gloats, "to my hand thy [Gloster's] vast Revenues fall, / To glut my pleasure that till now has starved." The use of Edmund, especially a rakish Edmund, to give parallel tone to Young Wou'dbe is justified, for the first crime of each is to substitute a competitive and individualistic world for the proper and normative world of social order. Such a competitive world was the assumption of wit-comedy, and its resolution [according to Arthur C. Kirsch in *"The Significance of Dryden's 'Aureng-Zebe',"* ELH, XXIX, 1962] "the union of public and private pride." But *moral* satire cannot thrive in a competitive world: it defends not certain types of people but a certain type of social order. Its favored characters are deduced from, are exemplary of, that order; whereas those of wit-comedy must be far more independent if their eventual union with social order is to be celebrated.

If the bad characters were really to be bad, comic analogues of Richards and Edmunds, the tone of the play had to be deepened. Effective and serious satire required vices which were more than diverting follies—Farquhar remarks on this in his preface—and virtuous characters who could serve as bright contrasts. Thus, by a kind of dramatic Manicheeism, this love plot had to be dignified from the earlier libidinous frolics. And because Restoration comedy had evolved no means for dealing with dignified virtue, techniques of representation had to be imported from tragedy. Love took on that true-hearted frenzy which was associated with tragic virtue, and frequently the characters of comedies in which such love appears explicitly refer it to contemporary tragedy. The level of decorum curiously changes too, and noble characters, like the Elder Wou'dbe, may at times be lent the dignity of blank verse. The wit's aphorism is replaced by its tragic counterpart, the "sentiment." Hermes, the Elder Wou'dbe, never approaches wit, even where wit was traditionally most approachable, in the making of similitudes. His resource is invective, or, euphemistically, righteous indignation:

E. W. Thou art the Worm and Maggot of the Law, bred in the bruis'd and rotten parts, and now art nourish'd on the same Corruption that produc'd thee—The *English* Law as planted

first, was like the *English* Oak, shooting its spreading Arms around to shelter all that dwelt beneath its shade—but now whole Swarms of Caterpillars, like you, hang in such Clusters upon every Branch, that the once thriving Tree now sheds infectious Vermin on our Heads.

These images are forceful, obvious, and concrete without calling attention to themselves; their impact, unlike the impact of wit, is little more than their paraphrasable content; form is no longer an important criterion. And indeed, the whole movement from the Old Comedy to the New at the end of the seventeenth century was, like the movement from the heroic play to the pathetic tragedy twenty-five years before, an insistence on the dominance of content and a consequent rejection of the pleasing distractions of form, a shifting of interest from the way one did things to the things one did. Such a shifting of interest is plain in *The Twin-Rivals:* not only the righteousness of Hermes Wou'dbe but also the affection lavished on a faithful "Cit," the goldsmith Fairbank, and, in a more tempered way, the faithful Irish valet Teague, gives evidence of it.

But, having testified to his hero's wholesomeness by making him a prig, Farquhar found himself in difficulties. Wit, in most of the comedies his audiences had seen, was more than itself a value; it was also a badge, an indication of value, a communicative as well as a self-contained convention. Thus he was faced with the serious danger of making Richmore and Young Wou'dbe admirably witty or their moral adversaries contemptibly dull. His solution came from Steele, who, in *The Funeral* (1701), "founded a two-couple pattern which was followed in a whole tradition of subsequent plays" [John Harrington, *The Gay Couple in Restoration Comedy*, 1948]. Farquhar set up two complementary couples, both pairs true and sensible lovers, but one rather gayer and wittier than the other. The hope is for a kind of charm by attraction. Relationships are kept uncomplicated: there are no love-chases or amatory joustings, such as Roebuck and Lovewell or Wildair and Standard engage in. They are also kept generous. Little flashes of individuality can be set off and paid for by the sweetly social. Thus Aurelia, talking with Constance about the seduced Clelia, is permitted one sally at Clelia's expense—falling from virtue, after all, must not be encouraged:

CON. I'm glad you mention'd her [Clelia]; Don't you observe her Gayety to be much more forc'd than formerly, her Humour don't sit so easily upon her.

AUR. No, nor her Stays neither, I can assure you.

But neither must ill nature, and Aurelia cannot joke a second time without a reprimand from Constance: "That's cruel, *Aurelia,* How can you make merry with her Misfortunes? I am positive she was no easy Conquest." Trueman, Aurelia's suitor, has slightly less rein: he never ventures past one flurry of stale courtly lover's wit, save when he believes (falsely, of course) that Aurelia has been unchaste. Even then his imagination suffers from a sad poverty. As a result, most of the vicarious feeling in favor of the lovers depends on convention and on their energetic opposition to Richmore and Benjamin Wou'dbe. The main action of the play is their maintaining a little quadrangle of decency which the indecent assault, and the four are less significant in themselves as lovers than as agents of the satire, blocking the progress of villainy.

Indeed, the love-relationships themselves are almost extraneous to the main action. If wit-comedy, the comedy of the individual, takes its force from the consolidation of a new society about the lovers (which is the lighter side of the general comic theme of the creation of such a new society), moral satire, the comedy of the public, takes its force from the purging of the old society by the lovers, by the agencies of social decency. *The Twin-Rivals* can not and does not assume the "highly desirable world" of the earlier Farquhar comedies; romantic passion remains inobtrusive and love respectably Platonic; and universal naturalism or hedonism is confined to the villains' minds. Thus the first two kinds of action common to the four plays with which I have been dealing—the love plots and the attack upon love's enemies—differ radically in *The Twin-Rivals* from the corresponding movements in the other plays. The relative unity of the two plots and the presence of real conflict in *The Twin-Rivals* also make its structure far more single-minded and focussed than had earlier been true. (pp. 33-40)

Professor Nicoll remarks [in his *History of English Drama*, 1955] that *The Twin-Rivals* is not a comedy of which the author of *A Short View* would have approved." Perhaps not; the author of *A Short View* was disinclined to approve. But *The Twin-Rivals* is written on Collier's principles, insofar as any consistent principles can be extracted from Collier's harangues. . . . *The Twin-Rivals* not only puts vice in the stocks but also, openly, mirrors Providence in distributing eventual rewards and punishments. The failure of the play was more than a judgment on an individual piece; it was an indication that Collier's principles were not really to be those of the New Comedy. (p. 41)

Eric Rothstein, "Farquhar's 'Twin-Rivals' and the Reform of Comedy," in PMLA, Vol. LXXIX, No. 1, March, 1964, pp. 33-41.

Michael Shugrue (essay date 1965)

[*Shugrue is an educator and the editor of* George Farquhar: The Recruiting Officer *(1966), the author of* English in a Decade of Change *(1969), and a contributor to several scholarly journals. In the following excerpt from his introduction to Farquhar's* The Recruiting Officer, *Shugrue contrasts the intellectual humor of Restoration comedy with the natural humor of Farquhar's play, arguing that Farquhar's characters are more credible and human.*]

The Recruiting Officer, which re-established Farquhar's reputation as a successful dramatist after the relative unpopularity of his plays between 1701 and 1706, was . . . highly topical. It continues to be an amusing, informative, first-hand account of the recruitment of soldiers for Queen Anne's army in the War of the Spanish Succession under the Mutiny and Impressment Acts of 1703, 1704, and 1705. Those Acts provided that debtors and even convicted felons might be released from prison if they would

agree to serve in the army or navy. More relevant to *The Recruiting Officer,* justices of the peace were empowered to raise and levy able-bodied men who had no lawful calling, employment, or visible means for their maintenance and livelihood to serve as soldiers. Farquhar demonstrates, in the machinations of Sergeant Kite, Captain Plume, and Squire Balance, that the Acts could easily be used to ensnare innocent men into forced service. When Kite gains a collier for Captain Plume's company by reminding Justice Balance that the coal miner "has no visible means of livelihood, for he works underground," Farquhar humorously and yet realistically reports on a social injustice of his day. But Farquhar exposes, too, the woman brought to court with her "husband": "We agreed," she explains, "that I should call him husband to avoid passing for a whore, and that he should call me wife to shun going for a soldier." If Farquhar pictures his society accurately, his wit and good humor transform a potentially unpleasant situation into comedy.

Farquhar did not intend to focus on the social ills of impressment; he was not concerned with social reform. He wrote to entertain his audience, to delight rather than to instruct. And he chose in large part to reach his goal by using themes and devices which had proved successful either in his earlier plays or in the plays of such brilliant predecessors as Wycherley, Etherege, Vanbrugh, and Congreve—plays which as a former actor he knew well. (p. xiv)

The clever, intellectual, often brittle wit of Restoration comedy, however, gives way in *The Recruiting Officer* to a more natural and an easier kind of humor. If Farquhar's characters less frequently speak in epigrams, if they less often discuss the world of fashion and society, they seem more human, more natural, more credible than the glittering conversationalists of the Restoration drawing room. Farquhar did not reject *in toto* Restoration conventions of characterization and turn to tender sentiments, but he nonetheless took a step toward the sentimental drama of the eighteenth century by modifying the hardness of the dramatic characters of Wycherley and his kind, a hardness that fascinates the viewer and reader of Restoration plays even as it puts him off.

The sparkle of Restoration wit has not entirely disappeared. Silvia's sauciness before her father in the trial scene and her braggadacio as Captain Pinch and Jack Wilful, as well as Plume's cocksure gallantries early in the play, give it many breezy, witty moments, although these scenes are charged with an affability that is often missing in previous comedy. Silvia's attempts to trick her father into giving his permission for her marriage and Melinda's proud disdain of Worthy approximate the prudential attitudes of Restoration drama, in which men and women are marriageable commodities. Perhaps the country atmosphere gives wider scope to Farquhar's characters. Certainly such episodes as Plume's revelation to Silvia that he is not so much the coxcomb in fact as in appearance mellow the play: "I'm not that rake that the world imagines. I have got an air of freedom which people mistake for lewdness in me as they mistake formality in others for religion." Through Plume the audience sees, too, that Silvia does not suffer from "the ingratitude, dissimulation, envy, pride, avarice, and vanity of her sister females." Melinda and Worthy also come to a genuine understanding of one another because they recognize and admit their faults to each other. These people have their faults; some, in fact, like Brazen, who is a walking folly, exemplify Restoration caricature. But most of Farquhar's major characters have a real concern for one another, a respect and affection that add dimension to them. Even loutish, foolish Bullock *does* care about his sister, Rose. The play owes much in its tone and manner of characterization to Restoration comedy, but it possesses a humanity and charm in its people and situations that are not typical of Wycherley and Etherege.

Structurally, Farquhar's play is an extraordinarily busy one. Three plots are interwoven to make its fabric. The first traces Captain Plume's efforts to enlist men for the army, efforts mightily aided by the crafty Sergeant Kite, whose tricks, including his personification of an astrologer, charm and cajole the Shropshire lads into the Queen's Grenadiers. The enlistment practices, indeed, provide much of the humor in the play. Plume's and Kite's successes in recruitment are wittily measured against the empty boasts of Captain Brazen, who has failed to recruit a single man, much less meet his quota. The other two threads of the plot are romantic. Plume courts Silvia, who,

in turn, disguises herself as a rakish young recruit to test his affection for her and to win her father's permission to marry him, a difficult task since Plume has no fortune to match hers. The third plot line concerns Melinda, the country heiress. Worthy tries to win her despite the obstacles which her inheritance of twenty thousand pounds has put in his way. He fears that the young heiress, blinded by a pride induced by her new wealth, will succumb to the foolish advances of Captain Brazen. Lucy, Melinda's maid, complicates matters when she attempts to win Brazen by pretending to be her mistress. Farquhar handles the complicated threads of these three plots with dexterity and good humor. Mistaken identities, disguises assumed not only by Silvia but also by Kite and Lucy, forged letters—all complicate the play and leave many knots to be unraveled before the final curtain falls.

Farquhar's greatest contribution to the early eighteenth-century theater, however, was not his adaptation of familiar dramatic techniques nor his skillful plotting, but his use of a country setting and his appreciation of rural life. William Archer [in his *George Farquhar,* 1906] succinctly described his innovation in his two great plays, *The Recruiting Officer* and *The Beaux' Stratagem:*

Farquhar broke away altogether from the pur-

Engraving of a scene from Farquhar's The Recruiting Officer.

lieus of Covent Garden, and took comedy out into the highways and byways. . . . Farquhar introduced us to the life of the inn, the market-place, and the manor house. He showed us the squire, the justice, the innkeeper, the highway-man, the recruiting sergeant, the charitable lady, the country belle, the chambermaid, and half a score of excellent rustic types.

Removing the setting of the play from London to Shrews-bury and dealing sympathetically with rural characters like Silvia, Balance, Worthy, Melinda, and even Rose gave a new dimension to Farquhar's comedy. As John Loftis states [in his *Comedy and Society from Congreve to Fielding,* 1959], "Farquhar's last two plays provide the single instance of appreciative treatment of rusticity; there is in fact no parallel to them until Charles Johnson's work of the second decade of the century." Farquhar's experiences as a recruiting officer in Lichfield and Shrewsbury encour-aged him to let new air into the theater by way of an accu-rate representation of a society not confined to the draw-ing rooms of fashionable London. His portrayal of coun-try life, based on personal observation, adds a charm and freshness to *The Recruiting Officer* that account in no small part for its continuing popularity. His dedication of the play to "All Friends round the Wrekin [a hill near Shrewsbury]" testifies to the affection with which he viewed the country folk he had known in 1705 and 1706: "The entertainment I found in Shropshire," he wrote, "commands me to be grateful, and that's all I intend." He may have duped and bribed rustics, in the manner of the wily Kite and Plume, into joining the Grenadiers, but he retained respect and admiration for the people of Shrews-bury. He invites them to laugh at his comedy, to see them-selves portrayed sympathetically and not merely as fools and louts on exhibition before civilized society.

Particularly in its use of country setting, *The Recruiting Officer* anticipates Farquhar's comic masterpiece, *The Beaux' Stratagem.* In the latter play Farquhar shifts the scene from London to the country, this time to Lichfield, where he had first served as a recruiting officer. The inns, the market place, and the country houses again provide backdrops for the good-humored pursuit of love and posi-tion in marriage. And from Plume, who respects Silvia's mind and virtue, develops Aimwell, who reveals his deceit to Dorinda out of admiration for her goodness. The cari-catures are still evident: Foigard, the priest with a heavy Irish accent, and Squire Sullen, the sot. But again the country principals, Dorinda and Mrs. Sullen, are depicted with sympathy and understanding. Even echoes of recruit-ing and impressment run through *The Beaux' Stratagem* and remind one of Farquhar's earlier triumph. (pp. xv-xviii)

> *Michael Shugrue, in an introduction to* The Recruiting Officer *by George Farquhar, Uni-versity of Nebraska Press, 1965, pp. ix-xxi.*

A. J. Farmer　(essay date 1966)

[*Farmer was a critic and professor of English whose writ-ings include* Walter Pater as a Critic of English Litera-ture *(1931) and* George Farquhar *(1966). In the follow-*

ing excerpt, Farmer illustrates the moral evolution of Farquhar's plays, suggesting that their new moral di-mension is directly linked to his presentation of provin-cial life and society.]

Farquhar's career is a short one—some eight or nine years in all—but it shows a distinct evolution. His early plays, close to the Restoration model, are licentious in tone, and it is largely because of them that his morality has been brought into question. But, even in these works, the licen-tiousness is in the language rather than in the thought. The time was not over-nice in expression, as is evident in the work of his fellow-playwrights, Vanbrugh in particu-lar, who is his direct contemporary. The later plays show a gradual improvement, due in part, no doubt, to the new standards which, in the opening eighteenth century, make for more refinement and decency in speech. If, in *The Re-cruiting Officer,* the dialogue has still that 'pert, low' touch which Pope stigmatized, there is little to offend, and much to please, the taste of the modern reader or playgoer in the verbal exchanges of *The Beaux' Stratagem.* It is true that, down to the end, Farquhar keeps a certain liberty of expression: but the frank outspokenness does not cover, as with so many of his predecessors, a fundamental indiffer-ence to morality. 'Farquhar,' writes Edmund Gosse, 'suc-ceeds in being wholesome, even when he cannot persuade himself to be decent.'

More important, the characters themselves have moved away from their prototypes of the older theatre. Out of the Restoration rake, the fickle and heartless libertine of Eth-erege and Wycherley, he has made a new type. Roebuck and Wildair, gay, vivacious, open, if wild and unpredict-able in their behaviour, have a good deal in common with Fielding's Tom Jones: together with his heedless flighti-ness, they have his warm heart. More restrained, Mirabel the inconstant and Captain Plume are of the same com-plexion; they can be moved by a sincere sentiment and hasten to repair any wrong their thoughtlessness may have caused. Aimwell and Archer, young and easy-going, show themselves bold in the cause of their love; they are adven-turers, like all Farquhar's heroes, and practise deception, but it never goes very far. Comparing them with Van-brugh's creations, Hazlitt observes:

> Farquhar's chief characters are also adventur-ers, but they are of a romantic, not a knavish stamp, and succeed no less by their honesty than by their boldness . . . They are real gentlemen and only pretended imposters. Vanbrugh's up-start heroes are 'without any relish of salvation', without generosity, virtue, or any pretensions to it. We have little sympathy for them, and no re-spect at all. But we have every sort of goodwill towards Farquhar's heroes, who have as many peccadilloes to answer for, and play as many rogue's tricks, but are honest fellows at bottom.

In a well-known essay, Lamb affirmed that the characters of Wycherley and Congreve inspire no particular senti-ment in us because they belong to a world which has no connection with reality. Allowing for the paradox innate in the critic's conception of the 'artificial comedy', we can admit that we feel we have little in common with such cre-ations. If they were translated into real life, we should be repelled by the inhumanity of a Horner or even of Congreve's Mirabel. About Farquhar's heroes there is an absence of calculating cynicism and a fundamental generosity that appeal to us.

The same applies to Farquhar's heroines. Some are merely stage *ingénues* innocent and trusting, and destined to be rescued by their lovers from dishonour or from undesired marriages; such are Isabella in **The Stage Coach,** Constance and Aurelia in **The Twin Rivals.** Others, more characteristic, are determined and resourceful; Leanthe, Oriana and Silvia are ready to affront difficulties and danger, if necessary, in order to remain by their lover's side; witty and audacious, they have been compared to the Rosalinds and Violas of Shakespearian comedy. Like their predecessors, they gain a new charm disguised as young men. In them, there is a kind of naturalistic philosophy: men are not considered as enemies, as is the case in so many Restoration plays. Lurewell represents an exceptional case: if she sets out to use her beauty to entrap men, it is to revenge her sex for the unjust treatment she herself has received, or believes she has received, at men's hands. But nowhere, among Farquhar's women, do we find a character like the lying, licentious and vindictive Olivia of Wycherley's *Plain Dealer.* His conception of womanhood is best illustrated in his last play, with Dorinda, charming, unaffected, direct in thought and speech, and with Mrs Sullen, a woman who has not been embittered by her unhappy experience and can still believe in happiness.

Precisely because these characters are closer to humanity than most creations of Restoration comedy, we are the more ready to take into serious account the author's presentation of the problem which more than any other preoccupied the writers of the time: that of the relations of men and women in the contemporary social structures. It was seen by Farquhar's predecessors essentially from the man's point of view, with his age-old right to pleasure, and Farquhar's first plays reproduce this conception, illustrated by Roebuck and Wildair. But, as he proceeds, he moves towards the woman's standpoint. It is expressed directly by Oriana, in **The Inconstant;** and Silvia, in **The Recruiting Officer,** rises against the conventional attitude which allows men a privileged position in the pursuit of love. Already there is a sense of the equality of the sexes and, in the concluding scene of **The Beaux' Stratagem,** we see Squire Sullen and his wife discussing calmly and as admitted equals a situation which they agree is due to faults on both sides. One might imagine such a dialogue in Shaw, and it is no doubt with this in mind that Bonamy Dobrée thinks that, had Farquhar lived to continue his development, he might have been the Shaw of his time. As it is, we are with him on the way to the new 'sentimental' comedy of Steele and Cibber, which was to insist on a view of the relationship of the sexes more acceptable to us than that pictured in the Restoration theatre.

The new moral dimension in Farquhar's plays is directly linked to his incursion into provincial life and society. Here, too, a significant change is to be noted. One remembers the ridiculous figure cut by the country gentry in the plays of his predecessors. Vanbrugh, in *The Relapse,* had poured scorn on country life, showing us the grotesque Sir Tunbelly Clumsey, his boisterous daughter Hoyden and their uncouth household. In Farquhar's portrait of Squire Mockmode, and that of young Clincher, some traces of this attitude remain. But, in **The Recruiting Officer,** the Shropshire worthies appear in a completely different light: Balance, Simple and Worthy are men of culture and good breeding, and Balance's daughter, Silvia, unconventional and unspoken as she is, has nothing in common with Hoyden. Squire Sullen is a reversion to the Restoration type, but without the ridicule attached to him in Wycherley or Congreve; his shortcomings result from temperament rather than from his rural upbringing. In a general way, provincial life is portrayed agreeably; the characters are seen in a sympathetic light. Lady Bountiful is a pleasing figure, for whom Restoration comedy offers no equal. Farquhar thus breaks the link binding comedy to fashionable London life, with its narrow outlook; he takes us into a pleasanter world, where life is simpler. In **The Beaux' Stratagem,** the young gentlemen from London seem like intruders; finally, they are conquered by the charm of country existence. Farquhar thus takes us back to the joyous, open-air atmosphere of Elizabethan comedy, and he opens the way to Goldsmith whose inspiration, in *She Stoops to Conquer,* owes not a little to Farquhar.

Farquhar's plays have not the robust construction we admire in Wycherley, nor the intricacy which makes Congreve's comedies an intellectual delight. This indifference to a highly mechanized plot Farquhar shares with Vanbrugh. In both cases, the story told is full of unexpected turns, but it is rarely complicated. The effects Farquhar seeks are often obtained by the use of all the current, often hackneyed devices of the stage: disguises, hidden identities, unexpected encounters. But he shows great skill in his timing. Cherry, for instance, has been pressed by Boniface to employ all her wiles to persuade the pseudo-footman Archer to reveal his real identity and that of his master; left alone, she indignantly soliloquizes: 'This landlord of mine . . . would betray his guest, and debauch his daughter into the bargain—and by a footman, too.' And, as she ends, Archer enters. Or Scrub, anxious to deceive Foigard in whom he detects a rival for Gipsy's favour, tells him: 'Gipsy . . . she's dead two months ago.' Whereupon Gipsy makes her appearance.

His dialogue lacks, no doubt, the glitter and polish of Etherege or Congreve, and the power of Wycherley, but it has an unaffected ease and naturalness often lacking in the work of these writers. It has vivacity and a colloquial ring. The constant straining after wit is replaced by an engaging humour, presented with zest, as Mrs Sullen's description to Dorinda of life with the squire shows:

> He came home this morning at his usual hour of four, wakened me out of a sweet dream of something else, by tumbling over the tea-table, which he broke all to pieces; after his man and he had rolled about the room, like sick passengers in a storm, he comes flounce into bed, dead as a salmon into a fishmonger's basket; his feet cold as ice, his breath hot as a furnace, and his hands and face as greasy as his flannel nightcap. O matrimony! He tosses up the clothes with a barbarous swing over his shoulders, disorders the whole economy of my bed, leaves me half-naked,

and my whole night's comfort is the tuneable
serenade of that wakeful nightingale, his nose.
O, the pleasure of counting the melancholy
clock by a snoring husband!

(*The Beaux' Stratagem*, II,i)

All the plays, even the earliest ones, are full of such passages, and their cheerful spontaneity more than makes up
for the lack of dazzling repartee. (pp. 29-34)

A. J. Farmer, in his George Farquhar, *Longmans, Green & Co., 1966, 40 p.*

Kenneth Muir   (essay date 1970)

[*An English scholar, Muir specializes in Shakespearean
criticism but is also an expert in seventeenth-century
drama and the author of several books including* The
Comedy of Manners *(1970). In the following excerpt
from that work, Muir offers a detailed assessment of
Farquhar's plays, noting that Farquhar sought out a new
and more idealistic comic form because the formula for
Restoration drama had worn thin.*]

Love and a Bottle, Farquhar's first and feeblest comedy,
was performed in 1698. There is nothing of interest in either the plot or the characters; and the Irish hero, Roebuck, fornicator and drunkard, is apparently regarded by
the author as a man whose virtues, which are not very apparent, outweigh his vices, and not as an object of satire.
The only sign that Farquhar might develop into a tolerable dramatist is an occasional liveliness in the dialogue.

The Constant Couple, Farquhar's second play, is a very
great improvement. It has some brisk scenes and one well-
drawn character, Sir Harry Wildair. This was a favourite
acting part, sometimes played by women, and the chief
reason for the continued popularity of the play. But in
other respects the play is seriously defective. The main
plot, which does not concern Sir Harry, depends on a double impossibility: that Lady Lurewell should not recognise
the man who had seduced her some years before, and that
Colonel Standard should not realise that the woman he
now loves is the girl he once seduced. Nor does Lady
Lurewell's conduct in the course of the play, avenging the
wrongs of her sex on her would-be lovers, make a happy
ending either plausible or satisfying. The other plot is also
badly constructed. In the second scene of Act II Sir Harry
meets Clincher Junior at Angelica's house. In the third
scene of Act III, after he has talked with Standard, visited
Lady Lurewell's, and met Clincher's elder brother, Sir
Harry returns to Angelica's house to find that time has
stood still during his absence: Clincher Junior is still in
process of being introduced to Angelica.

The other great defect of the play is that at moments Farquhar adopts an inflated diction and falls into the rhythms
of blank verse, as in Angelica's speech in the first scene of
Act V:

What madness, *Sir Harry,* what wild Dream of
loose Desire could prompt you to attempt this
Baseness? View me well.—The Brightness of my
Mind, methinks, should lighten outwards, and
let you see your Mistake in my Behaviour. I
think it shines with so much Innocence in my

Face, that it should dazzle all your vicious
Thoughts. Think not I am defenceless 'cause
alone. Your very self is Guard against yourself:
I'm sure there's something generous in your
Soul; My Words shall search it out, and Eyes
shall fire it for my own Defence.

Sir Harry accuses her of having come from reading Nat
Lee and says she is the first whore in heroics he has met
with. But she is not the only heroine of the period who
protests too much. One of the faults of sentimental comedy is that its characters are apt to be self-conscious about
their virtues, as though they were spiritual *nouveaux riches.* Farquhar suffered also from the fact that he was a very
poor poet. Yet the scenes between Sir Harry and Angelica
are the best in the play. They embody a genuinely comic
situation. Vizard, who has been repulsed by Angelica, has
his revenge by telling Sir Harry she is a prostitute, and (in
his letter of introduction) telling her mother Sir Harry is
a suitor for Angelica's hand. Sir Harry and Angelica are
therefore talking all the time at cross-purposes, Sir Harry
supposing that she is offended when he offers her money
only because he has not offered her enough.

The play has plenty of bustling action, some of it farcical.
The elder Clincher's gaiety is explained by the fact that he
is in mourning for his father and, later in the play, the
younger Clincher is delighted to hear of his brother's
death and even gets Tom Errand to swear that he has
killed him. This sort of insensibility is proper to farce, but
not to comedy. Yet Farquhar is not without touches of
wit. He has some neat satire of the reformation of the stage
by Jeremy Collier:

We are all so reformed that gallantry is taken for
vice, and hypocrisy for religion.

In the last act, Alderman Smuggler, who is a swindler and
a hypocrite, says:

Lord! Lord! What Business has a Prentice at a
Playhouse, unless it be to hear his Master made
a Cuckold, and his Mistriss a Whore! 'Tis ten to
one now, but some malicious Poet has my Character upon the Stage within this *Month:* 'Tis a
hard matter now, that an honest sober *Man*
can't Sin in private for this Plaguy Stage. I gave
an honest Gentleman Five Guineas myself towards Writing a Book against it: And it has done
no good, we see.

Sometimes, however, the satire is turned, not against the
citizen, but against the gentleman. When Mrs Errand discovers Clincher in her husband's clothes, she accuses him:
'Oh, Mr. Constable, here's a rogue that has murdered my
husband, and robbed him of his clothes'. At which the
Constable exclaims: 'Murder and robbery! then he must
be a gentleman'.

Farquhar's next play, *Sir Harry Wildair,* was a sequel to
The Constant Couple, and generally inferior to it. It has
a wretched plot—Sir Harry's wife, supposed dead, disguises herself as a ghost, and Colonel Standard's wife
nearly commits adultery—but there are some amusing
passages of dialogue. (p. 142)

Farquhar's next play, *The Twin Rivals* (1702), is not really a comedy of manners. In the preface he claims that he has learnt from Collier's strictures on the immorality of contemporary drama and that he has 'endeavoured to show, that an English comedy may answer the strictness of poetical justice' by punishing the immoral characters at the end of the play. But, he says, the audience were disappointed; for, as one of them said: 'however pious we may appear at home, yet we never go to that end of the town but with an intention to be lewd'.

Farquhar thought that the most material objection to the play was that the vices of some of the characters were examples of wickedness—'a middle sort of wickedness'—rather than folly; but he argued that, as the characters were too mean for tragedy, 'they must of necessity drop into comedy'. This is true enough; but the trouble about the play is that it contains hardly any wit or humour, and very little satire. The situations, and much of the language, belong to sentimental comedy. The chief interest—the only interest, indeed—is to see what happens next, in particular to see how the plots of the villains will be frustrated. Benjamin Wouldbe plots with a midwife and a scoundrelly lawyer to succeed to his father's estate and so disinherit his virtuous elder brother, Hermes; and Richmore plots to marry his pregnant mistress to his unsuspecting nephew, Trueman, and to rape Aurelia. The plots are linked by the fact that Aurelia is a friend of Constance, beloved by the twin brothers, and also by the fact that Mandrake is a bawd as well as a midwife. Aurelia is rescued in the nick of time by Trueman; Richmore promises to marry the woman he has seduced—though in the preface Farquhar declares that after the fall of the curtain he changes his mind; Benjamin is foiled when Mrs Mandrake is compelled to confess, and Hermes marries Constance.

The sentimentality may be seen at its worst in the scene (III.3) where Hermes enters Constance's room unperceived to find her in tears, because she thinks he is dead.

> HERMES. In Tears! perhaps for me! I'll try.[*Drops a Picture, and goes back to the entrance, and listens.*]
>
> AURELIA. If there be aught in Grief delightful, don't grudge me a share.
>
> CONSTANCE. No, my dear *Aurelia,* I'll ingross it all. I lov'd him so, methinks I should be jealous if any mourned his death besides myself. What's here?—[*Takes up the Picture.*] Ha! see, Cousin—the very Face and Features of the Man! Sure, some officious Angel had brought me this for a Companion in my Solitude! Now I'm fitted out for Sorrow! With this I'll sigh, with this converse, gaze on his Image till I grow blind with weeping!
>
> AURELIA. I'm amazed! how came it here?
>
> CONSTANCE. Whether by Miracle or humane Chance, 'tis all alike; I have it here. Nor shall it ever separate from my Breast. It is the only thing cou'd give me joy; because it will increase my Grief.
>
> HERMES. [*Coming forward*] Most Glorious Woman! Now I am fond of life.

The mawkishness of the sentiments, the tendency to drop into poetic diction and verse rhythms, show Farquhar at his worst. The play deserved to fail; and its failure proved salutary to the dramatist for it led him to seek for a new form of comedy which would avoid both the sentimentality of his last play and the 'manners' formula which was already wearing thin. Vanbrugh in *The Relapse* had already set some scenes outside London; and Farquhar's experiences as a recruiting officer in Lichfield and Shrewsbury suggested the theme of one of his remaining plays and the settings of both.

Farquhar has been praised by some critics, notably Archer [in his introduction to *George Farquhar*, 1906] and Strauss [in his introduction to *A Discourse Upon Comedy: The Recruiting Officer and The Beaux' Stratagem,* 1914], for breaking away from London and showing us

> the life of the inn, the market-place, and the manor house. He showed us the squire, the justice, the innkeeper, the highwayman, the recruiting sergeant, the charitable lady, the country belle, the chambermaid, and half a score of excellent rustic types . . . Farquhar reduced wit within something like the limits of nature, subordinating it to humour, and giving it, at the same time, an accent, all his own, of unforced, buoyant gaiety.

Other critics, who lament the decline of the comedy of manners, are inclined to blame Farquhar for substituting sentiment and humour for wit and satire. *The Twin Rivals* may justly be deplored; but Farquhar deserves the credit of learning from his mistake and of discovering a new vein of comedy after the old one was exhausted. Not only was there a changed climate of opinion, but also a move by the Lord Chamberlain against profanity and indecency. Farquhar himself, or his publisher, deleted from the second edition of *The Recruiting Officer* two passages which had appeared in the first. In Act IV Silvia had asked Plume—in French—if he had slept with Rose; and Act V had begun with a scene in which Rose sulked because she had not been seduced, as she had hoped.

The Recruiting Officer and *The Beaux' Stratagem* are Farquhar's most original plays and greatly superior to anything he had written before. They both have excellent plots, amusing characters, and lively dialogue; and they both kept their popularity on the boards during the whole of the eighteenth century and after. (pp. 145-47)

The Recruiting Officer was first performed on 8 April 1706 and it was an immediate success. It had been written so hastily that there are several inconsistencies. Lucy forges Melinda's name and yet, later, steals her signature. Silvia calls herself Jack Wilful and Captain Pinch in different scenes without anyone commenting on the discrepancy. In III.2 Plume quotes two couplets previously used by Brazen though Plume had not overheard him. But it is unlikely that these points would be noticed during a performance of the play. (p. 147)

Plume, the nominal hero of the play, is an amiable rake, who will presumably turn over a new leaf when he is married to Silvia. This, at least, is the implication of Balance's speech to Worthy (III.1):

I was just such another Fellow at his Age. I never set my Heart upon any Woman so much as to make my self uneasie at the Disappointment. But what was very surprizing both to myself and Friends, I chang'd o' th' sudden from the most fickle Lover to be the most constant Husband in the World.

There is, of course, an element of sentimentality in this attitude; and elsewhere Farquhar feels it necessary to explain that, despite his bastards, Plume is not as bad as his reputation. He tells the disguised Silvia:

> No, Faith, I'm not that Rake that the World imagines; I have got an Air of Freedom, which People mistake for Lewdness in me, as they mistake Formality in others for Religion.—The World is all a Cheat; only I take mine, which is undesign'd, to be more excusable than theirs, which is hypocritical. I hurt no body but my self, and they abuse all Mankind—Will you lye with me?

The last five words of this speech are presumably not intended by Plume in a sexual sense; but as he has already kissed 'Jack Wilfull' and admitted 'his' charm, the spectator is bound to regard the words as equivocal.

Melinda tells Silvia that if she had been a man she would have 'been the greatest Rake in *Christendom*'; and Silvia confesses:

> I should have endeavour'd to know the World, which a Man can never do thoroughly without half a hundred Friendships, and as many Amours.

In accordance with this view, she agrees to be godfather to Plume's bastard, and she arranges to sleep with Rose, to protect her from Plume, rather than out of jealousy. In her masculine attire, she apes the manners and language of rakes, so that through her Farquhar is able to satirise what he partly admires.

More interesting than either hero or heroine are the comic rogues, Sergeant Kite and Captain Brazen. Some of Kite's illegal methods of recruiting are reminiscent of those used by Falstaff in *Henry IV*. But, in addition, he gets some of his recruits by disguising himself as a fortune-teller; he goes through a form of marriage with Plume's cast-off mistresses; and, despite his roguery, he endears himself to the audience by his ingenuity and by the effrontery of his autobiography:

> You must know, Sir, I was born a Gypsie, and bred among that Crew till I was ten Year old; there I learn'd Canting and Lying. I was brought from my Mother, *Cleopatra*, by a certain Nobleman for three Pistols, who, liking my Beauty, made me his Page; there I learned Impudence and Pimping; I was turn'd off for wearing my Lord's Linen, and drinking my Lady's Brandy, and then turn'd Bailiff's Follower. There I learn'd Bullying and Swearing. I at last got into the Army, and there I learn'd Whoring and Drinking—So that if you Worship pleases to cast up the whole Sum, *viz.*, Canting, Lying, Impudence, Pimping, Bullying, Swearing, Whor-

ing, Drinking and a Halbard, you will find the Sum Total will amount to a Recruiting Sergeant.

Brazen is an equally effective stage character—and a favourite rôle of actors—but his lies and affectations and the exaggeration with which Farquhar depicts them make him a figure of farce. Rose and the recruits are nicely sketched in and the only unsatisfactory characters in the play are Worthy and Melinda. Worthy is dull and acts only as a foil to Plume; Melinda is likewise a foil to Silvia and her actions are determined by the necessities of the plot.

There is very little wit in the dialogue—perhaps Farquhar felt that the comedy of wit had reached its apotheosis in Congreve—but there is plenty of humour, which British audiences have always found more to their taste. When, for example, Kite translates 'Carolus' on a coin as Queen Anne; or when the Constable introduces the three Justices and himself as 'four very honest gentlemen'; or when the Justices enlist a man because his wife has a child each year and the wife says, 'Look'e Mr Captain, the parish shall get nothing by sending him away; for I won't lose my teeming time if there be a man left in the parish'; or when Rose, disappointed with her bedfellow, complains to Silvia, 'I wonder you could have the conscience to ruin a poor girl for nothing'—such remarks reveal Farquhar as an admirable writer of comedy, but of a comedy far removed from that of the fashionable drawing-room. *The Recruiting Officer* is completely free from the sentimentality of the previous plays. This may be due to the fact that Farquhar knew more about recruiting than he did about fashionable society.

The laughter which the play provokes as M. Hamard says [in *Le Ruse des Galants,* 1965], is 'based on tolerance and the joyous acceptance of the world as it is—good in the eyes of the rational, sensible man'. Wit combats would be out of place in such a comedy.

The last of Farquhar's plays, written when he was dying, is also his best. *The Beaux' Stratagem* (1707) has a more original plot, a wittier dialogue, and a livelier group of characters than any of his previous plays. Some critics have complained that the comic Irish Jesuit, Foigard, is a comparative failure and that Count Bellair could be cut without great loss. As to Foigard, we may well agree; and the Bellair episode is a clumsy way of trying to arouse Sullen's jealousy. Another complaint which many critics have levelled against Farquhar is that the 'divorce' by mutual consent at the end of the play is too fantastic and farcical. To which one could argue that it is not intended to be realistic. The pretty ceremony is clearly Utopian. Farquhar had been studying Milton's plea for divorce on grounds other than adultery and he echoes several phrases from *The Doctrine and Discipline of Divorce*. When Sullen tells his wife that they are 'two Carcasses join'd unnaturally together' and she retorts 'Or rather a living Soul coupled to a dead Body'; or when she asks if a bench can 'give Judgement upon Antipathies' and tells Dorinda that 'casual Violation is a transient Injury, and may possibly be repair'd' and that when there is a natural antipathy, 'not all the golden Links of Wedlock nor Iron Manacles of Law can keep 'em fast', Farquhar is paraphrasing or literally quoting from Milton's treatise. And when Mrs Sullen concludes Act III with some rhymed couplets—

> Must Man, the chiefest Work of Art Divine,
> Be doom'd in endless Discord to Repine?

we may be sure that the last word was suggested by Milton's account of the disappointed husband who 'sits repining'. It is reasonable to assume that the divorce scene, far from being farcical, was the thing with which Farquhar was deeply concerned. Mrs Sullen's predicament is pathetic and it could have been treated tragically. Married to a drunken boor, she has no escape under the actual laws at the beginning of the eighteenth century, and she is unwilling to adopt the usual recourse of ill-treated wives. She is allowed a number of complaints about the conduct of her husband, and in one or two places—e.g. the end of Act III or the beginning of Act IV—the comic muse is put to flight. But, in general, Farquhar makes her use her misfortunes as a subject for her wit, as in her splendid account of the pleasures of matrimony:

> O Sister, Sister! if ever you marry, beware of a sullen, silent Sot, one that's always musing, but never thinks:—There's some Diversion in a talking Blockhead; and since a Woman must wear Chains; I wou'd have the Pleasure of hearing 'em rattle a little. Now you shall see; but take this by the way:—He came home this morning at his usual Hour of Four, waken'd me out of a sweet Dream of something else, by tumbling over the Tea-table, which he broke all to pieces; after his Man and he had rowl'd about the Room, like sick Passengers in a Storm, he comes flounce into Bed, dead as a Salmon into a Fishmonger's basket; his Feet cold as Ice, his Breath hot as a Furnace, and his Hands and his Face as greasy as his Flannel Night-cap.—Oh Matrimony! He tosses up the Clothes with a barbarous swing over his Shoulders, disorders the whole Œconomy of my Bed, leaves me half naked, and my whole Night's Comfort is the tuneable Serenade of that wakeful Nightingale, his Nose! O, the Pleasure of counting the melancholly Clock by a snoring Husband!

Even if Squire Sullen had been a more amicable husband, it is doubtful whether his wife would have been happy, for she shares the opinions of most heroines of the comedy of manners about the superiority of London life to that of the country. When Dorinda tells her she shares in all the pleasures that the country affords, she retorts:

> Country Pleasures! Racks and Torments! Dost think, Child, that my Limbs were made for leaping of Ditches, and clambring over Stiles? or that my Parents, wisely foreseeing my future Happiness in Country Pleasures, had early instructed me in the rural Accomplishments of drinking fat Ale, playing at Whisk, and smoaking Tobacco with my Husband?

Dorinda, Sullen's sister, is a rather colourless foil to his wife, and she obtains as a husband the less interesting of the two adventurers. Aimwell's conversion has been condemned as the intrusion of sentimentality; but it is not so much the conversion as the language in which it is expressed that is at fault:

Such goodness who cou'd injure! I find myself unequal to the Task of Villain; she has gain'd my Soul, and made it honest like her own: I cannot, cannot hurt her.

His confession that he is not Viscount Aimwell hardly deserves Dorinda's exclamation: 'Matchless honesty!'

Archer, despite his unscrupulousness, is a gay and attractive figure, whether he is making love to Cherry, making friends with Scrub, trying to seduce Mrs Sullen, or fighting the robbers. Because he is posing as Aimwell's servant, he is able to move up and down the social scale and, being on the verge of penury, his conduct is treated by the author with leniency: for Farquhar himself, as he was writing the play, was dying in a garret.

A number of the minor characters are equally successful. Boniface, with his catch-phrase 'as the saying is', became the generic term for a country inn-keeper throughout the eighteenth century; Cherry, his daughter, has always been a favourite with audiences; Scrub, is a nice mixture of clown and simple-minded country servant; and Gibbet is an amusing rogue.

The dialogue of all these characters is sprightly and humorous. When Gibbet is asked to say a prayer before he is killed, he retorts: 'the government has provided a chaplain to say prayers for us on these occasions'. When Cherry says she is young and doesn't understand wheedling, Boniface exclaims:

> Young! why you Jade, as the saying is, can any Woman wheedle that is not young? Your Mother was useless at five and twenty. Not wheedle! would you make your Mother a Whore, and me a Cuckold, as the saying is?

Occasionally the play drops into farce as in the scene where Mrs Sullen, pretending to be her mother-in-law, advises a country-woman how to cure her husband's sore leg:

> Well, good Woman, I'll tell you what you must do. You must lay your Husband's Leg upon a table, and with a Chopping-knife you must lay it open as broad as you can; then you must take out the Bone and beat the Flesh soundly with a rowling-pin; then take Salt, Pepper, Cloves, Mace and Ginger, some sweet Herbs, and season it very well; then rowl it up like Brawn, and put it into the Oven for two Hours.

This is justified by its success. But, when Aimwell awakens from his bogus fit to declaim fustian, audiences tend to be embarrassed:

> Where am I?
> Sure I pass'd the Gulph of silent Death,
> And now I land on the *Elisian* Shore—
> Behold the Goddess of those happy Plains,
> Fair *Proserpine*—Let me adore thy bright Divinity.

In some respects the play looks forward to the novels of Fielding and Smollet; and in other respects it leads on to the comedies of Goldsmith. Farquhar is sometimes blamed for adulterating the comedy of manners; but he was writing for a different audience than the one which had witnessed *The Country Wife* a generation earlier. The old form of comedy was in decline and Farquhar was right to seek for a new form as well as a different subject-matter.

But Farquhar's most staunch admirer, William Archer, praises him for largely irrelevant reasons; that he has a 'sweeter, cleaner, healthier mind' than Congreve or Wycherley; that his characters are less repulsive; that he is more humane than his contemporaries; that his dialogue is more natural because he is not, like Congreve, always striving to be witty; that he gets on with the plot and does not engage in irrelevant discussions; and that he admitted a moral standard.

To all this one may retort that, from the moral point of view, Aimwell's desire to marry a wealthy heiress by pretending to be a lord is worse than any action of Valentine or Mirabell; and the actions of Aimwell and Archer are not rendered more moral by the former's repentance or the latter's failure. Some of Farquhar's dialogue is natural enough; but in many passages he is guilty of pseudo-poetic rant, much further from natural speech than anything in Congreve. Dialogue should not be a mere reproduction of everyday speech and, of course, characters in a play should not be assessed by their virtuousness or wickedness, or we should be in danger of supposing that Falstaff and Volpone were inferior to the Good-Natured Man. (pp. 147-53)

> *Kenneth Muir, "George Farquhar," in his* The Comedy of Manners, *Hutchinson University Library, 1970, pp. 142-53.*

Oldmixon on Farquhar's comedies:

All that love Comedy will be sorry to hear of the Death of Mr. *Farquhar,* whose two last Plays had something in them that was truly *humorous* and *diverting.* 'Tis true the Criticks will not allow any Part of them to be regular; but Mr. *Farquhar* had a Genius for Comedy, of which one may say that it was rather above Rules than below them. His *Conduct,* tho not *Artful,* was *surprizing:* His *Characters,* tho not Great, were Just: His Humour, tho *low, diverting:* His *Dialogue,* tho *loose* and *incorrect, gay* and *agreeable;* and his *Wit,* tho not *super-abundant, pleasant.* In a word, his Plays have in the *toute ensemble,* as the Painters phrase it, a certain Air of *Novelty* and *Mirth,* which pleas'd the Audience every time they were represented: And such as love to laugh at the *Theater,* will probably miss him more than they now imagine.

> *John Oldmixon, in* The Muses Mercury, *May, 1707.*

Alan Roper   (essay date 1971)

[*In the following excerpt, Roper provides a detailed examination of Farquhar's use of image and action to create metaphors in* The Beaux' Stratagem.]

To complete the patterns of literary history, it sometimes seems that if Farquhar had not existed, it would be necessary to invent him. In the customary division of neoclassic comedy into forty years of wit and sex and some eighty years of sentiment and love, Farquhar is that necessary thing, a transitional writer. He began his dramatic career in 1698, at a time that was [according to Dale Underwood in *Etherege and the Seventeenth-Century Comedy of Manners,* 1957] "in many profound respects a period of transition." By the laws of sociological determinism it is, then, not surprising to find [according to Ernest Bernbaum in his *The Drama of Sensibility,* 1915] that his heroes are "too sincerely eloquent and passionate lovers to be the rakes of Restoration comedy, and are too joyously abandoned to dissipation to be the exculpated prodigals of sentimental comedy." Farquhar, we learn [in Henry Ten Eyck Perry's *The Comic Spirit in Restoration Drama,* 1925], is "the connecting link between the older generation of the Restoration and the rising tide of Cibbers and Steeles" (both of whom, incidentally, were older than Farquhar). Therein lies his sorrow. [Louis Kronenberger states in his *The Thread of Laughter,* 1952], "As the child of a transition, he was caught between two sets of antagonistic values; he necessarily formulated no harmonious values of his own." Poor Farquhar! It was a cross fate that visited upon such a child of his age the combined sins of Rochester and Jeremy Collier.

These formulas of literary history depend customarily upon what may be called a principle of moral extrapolation. Values and attitudes that are, at least potentially, contributions to a total structure of words are detached from that structure, scrutinized in themselves, and allocated a position in a pattern composed of similarly detached pieces from other plays. These pieces may be scenes, statements about the nature of fool, rake, or gentleman, or something to be ranged beneath the awful banner of themes. Such an activity is not especially perverse when it confines itself to descriptive classification, but it rarely does confine itself thus. Moral values are intoxicating things to critics, and soon lead to the loud confrontation of ethical preferences. We are all familiar with the cries in this ethicocritical war: cynical, immoral, maudlin, mature, immature, responsible, frivolous, aware, myopic.

Critical reaction to one scene may serve to illustrate the possible consequences of such combat. In the fifth act of ***The Beaux' Stratagem,*** Archer, the unregenerate beau, gains entry into the bedchamber of Mrs. Sullen, a provoked wife of developed sensuality and enfeebled virtue. Archer woos Mrs. Sullen in a mixture of mock-heroic rant, impatient exhortation to hurry on to the right, true end of love, and a nervous reminder to Mrs. Sullen to keep her voice down. He kneels before her in randy excitement, and she, weak, womanly vessel that she is, knows the imminent capitulation of her virtue. "Rise," she explains, "rise thou prostrate Ingineer, not all thy undermining Skill shall reach my Heart." Rarely has the trope of chastity's besieged fortress been put to more pointed comic use. Archer's erotic tunneling is not, after all, directed to her heart. Abandoning the soft sell of persuasion by mythological tropes, Archer lays hold of Mrs. Sullen. "Thieves, Thieves, Murther," she cries. Enter Scrub, the butler, calling "Thieves, Thieves, Murther, Popery," and bringing news that a band of robbers has broken in. With seduction interrupted, Archer's attention is given to apprehending the burglars. To one critic [Ernest Bernbaum], Archer's "violent wooing" of Mrs. Sullen "provides a very emotional scene," one of the "slight sentimental touches in the love-affair" between them. But, fortunately for comedy, this sentimental moment is "interrupted by a farcical burglary." To another critic [Henry Ten Eyck Perry], the scene exemplifies Farquhar's consistent failure to be either artistic or realistic, because his heroes, torn between "license and honor,"

> will not commit themselves to either one. Occasionally an Archer steps completely into the comic picture, but then by his side there is always an Aimwell to spout high morality or a Gibbet [the chief burglar] to interfere with the impulses of nature. Archer is the last effort of the Comedy of Manners to maintain its position in the teeth of Jeremy Collier and eighteenth-century propriety.

To the first critic the wooing is sentimental and the interruption a welcome return to the business of comedy, even if at the level of farce. To the second critic the wooing is comic apparently because it exhibits [according to Eric Rothstein in *George Farquhar,* 1967] "the impulses of nature," and the intrusive Gibbet is the rather startling avatar of Jeremy Collier. Their disagreement partly results, I suspect, from an examination of the scene in itself and a measuring of it against some external standard of the comic. But what is important is the demonstrable fact that the scene is a necessary contribution to the total statement of the play, the sum of its doings and sayings. And the fact is important, critically important, just because it is demonstrable.

It was William Archer who pointed somewhere in the direction we should look. He drew a distinction between the dramatist as dramatist and the dramatist as social essayist. In the plays of Wycherley, Congreve, and Vanbrugh he found that the action frequently stands still "while the characters expatiate in reflection, generalisation, description, and criticism of other characters; in short, in essays or leading articles broken up into dialogue." Farquhar, by a contrast all in his favor, "confines his characters within the action, and keeps the action moving. . . . He is much less given to the elaborate portrayal of a Jonsonian 'humour' for its own sake." For William Archer, [Wycherley's] *The Country Wife* and [Congreve's]*The Way of the World* were *The Spectator* struggling to come into being. Archer certainly underestimated both the dramatic effectiveness and the significance of the conversational mode in the best Restoration comedies. But he was right to distinguish it at least from Farquhar's final dramatic mode, in which the means of social definition are a combination of saying and doing, of significant action as a source of verbal analogy.

Such a dramatic mode differs from what we find in a play like *The Old Bachelor* where, instead of action as a source of verbal analogy, we have speech, proper and improper, as the effective action. Congreve's first play exhibits various acceptable and unacceptable life styles, styles that reveal themselves in the way characters use language. These uses of language require for their proper exposition an analysis more detailed than the limits of the present essay permit. But part of the use of language is the use of metaphor, and the use of metaphor in *The Old Bachelor* is not only interesting in itself; it also provides us with some of the terms with which to define, if disjunctively, the use of metaphor in ***The Beaux' Stratagem.*** (pp. 169-72)

The proposition can be illustrated by comparing the way in which a character in *The Old Bachelor* and a character in ***The Beaux' Stratagem*** ridicule the reliance of another upon the clichés of précieuses exclamations. Here is Congreve:

> VAINLOVE. Did I dream? Or do I dream? Shall I believe my Eyes, or Ears? The Vision is here still.—Your Passion, Madam, will admit of no farther reasoning.—But here is a silent Witness of your acquaintance.—*Takes out the Letter, and offers it: She snatches it, and throws it away.*
>
> ARAMINTA. There's poison in every thing you touch.—Blisters will follow—
>
> VAINLOVE. That Tongue which denies what the Hands have done.
>
> ARAMINTA. Still mystically senceless and impudent.—I find I must leave the place. (IV,iii)

Nothing, indeed, can exceed the elegance of that "mystically," superficially a mere intensifying adverb, amusing by its hyperbolic incongruity, but actually justifying itself by its pointed reference to Vainlove's "visionary" exclamations and by the weight and appropriateness it gives to "senceless." The wit writing here, as so often in Congreve, produces in what is wit written an intelligent pressure on the words. Now Farquhar:

> ARCHER. Well, but heark'ee, *Aimwell.*
>
> AIMWELL. *Aimwell!* call me *Oroondates, Cesario, Amadis,* all that Romance can in a Lover paint, and then I'll answer. O *Archer,* I read her thousands in her Looks, she look'd like *Ceres* in her Harvest, Corn, Wine and Oil, Milk and Honey, Gardens, Groves and Purling Streams play'd on her plenteous Face.
>
> ARCHER. Her Face! her Pocket, you mean; the Corn, Wine and Oil lies there. In short, she has ten thousand Pound, that's the English on't. (III,ii)

Archer is ridiculing less a lapse of style, a loss of poise, than what he takes to be a loss of candor, a self-deceiving cant. The jeering explicitness of "Her Face! her Pocket, you mean" and "that's the English on't" is remote from the sensibility responsible for Araminta's "still mystically senceless and impudent." It is very close to Rymer's brusque *Short View of* [and shortest way with] *Tragedy,* or Fielding's bluff English response to epic simile and heroic hyperbole in *Tom Jones,* or to Dr. Johnson, that *Jean Bull philosophe,* kicking the stone and thus refuting Berkeley. With such a passage as this between Archer and Aimwell before us, and with the memory of Araminta's snub of Vainlove, it is not hard to see how Pope, in his imitation of Horace's epistle to Augustus, came by his opinion of Farquhar's "pert low Dialogue."

If there were nothing more to say about this exchange between Archer and Aimwell, there would be no reason to see or read *The Beaux' Stratagem* with a greater expectation of pleasure than we might bring to Cibber's *The Careless Husband* or Susanna Centlivre's adaptation of *The Gamester*. But the exchange, whatever its inadequacy as humor, is also one of the many moments in *The Beaux' Stratagem* in which a concern with motive in matters of love finds expression in terms of metaphors drawn from the play's continuous movement, physical and ideological, between two places, the inn and the house. What Farquhar gives us in *The Beaux' Stratagem,* and to a lesser extent in *The Recruiting Officer,* is a play notable for a conspicuous (if at times forcibly imposed) integrity of action, character, dialogue, and setting. By making the moral world of his play commensurate with fully realized places, he is closer, for all the lesser comprehensiveness and intensity of his imagination, to Shakespeare and Jonson than he is to Congreve and Etherege. (pp. 176-78)

It was not so at the beginning of Farquhar's career. *Love and a Bottle,* his first play, offers an intrigue plot with a complex and farcical life of its own. As a vehicle for socially satiric conversations on love, friendship, soldiers, wine, seduction, foppery, snuff, dancing, poetry, theaters, fencing, Oxford, it is distracting in its robust complications. The protagonist is no self-aware honest man, but a randy Irishman just arrived in London, ready to chase offstage with a priapic bellow in adolescent pursuit of a passing woman (IV, iii). As the most lustful example of lusty *juventus,* he prompts not a set of analogies based upon clothes and cards, fruit and mirrors, but a series of quasi-theological references to paradise, forbidden fruit and forbidden knowledge, serpents, devils, flesh, and fall. Driven out of Ireland, that venomless paradise, by fleshly indulgence in forbidden fruit with his whore, he comes to London to enter into sin (I, i), to be a rakehelly rascal (III, i). He seeks in the back door to his mistress's house "the narrow Gate to the Lovers Paradise" (IV, iv). Reclaimed at the end by the love of a good woman, he pensions off his whore, rejecting her as a stale iniquity, and is ready to pronounce the moral: *"Paradice was lost by Woman's Fall; / But Vertuous Woman thus restores it all."* The theology is, obviously, confused by the indiscriminate use of paradise as a source both of moral definition and double entendre. In addition, the physical activity implied by the paradise references has only a tenuous likeness to the physical activity of the intrigues. Paradise organizes a set of quasi-theological glosses upon an action to which it is only superficially analogous.

In subsequent plays Farquhar several times took up a favorite topic of some of his predecessors: the social falsity of travel in providing, not a broadening of a gentleman's understanding, but matter for his folly or iniquity to feed upon. Both *The Constant Couple* and *Sir Harry Wildair* are dominated by the past or future travels of a number of the main characters. But the kind of character definition the travels provide has, once again, little reference to the details of what these busy characters actually do. The drift of the plays is to the working out of relationships by a reclamation from folly or incontinence or by the removal of misapprehension over identity or personality. Travel certainly contributes to misapprehension and redeemable

incontinence, and it is to some extent a unifying motif since so many of the characters are affected by it. But there is no necessary connection, no true analogy. Incontinence and misapprehension can originate elsewhere, as they do in *The Constant Couple* when the vallain revenges himself on the hero by persuading him that the heroine is a whore, her mother a bawd, and their house a brothel.

It was in *The Recruiting Officer* and, less clearly, in *The Twin Rivals* that Farquhar found his way to uniting the busy activity of his intrigue plots and the social definitions implied by the occurrence of related metaphors in conversation. The very title of *The Recruiting Officer* suggests those twin concerns with enlisting soldiers and getting wives which serve not only as a means to revitalize such aging literary preoccupations as love and honor and the trope of the love battle; they also provide parallel actions that are mutually revelatory because they are analogies for each other. Especially do they share a concern with financial trickery in the purchase of recruits or mistresses and the monetary disposition of daughters in marriage. The two activities are united by the heroine's disguising herself as a young man in order to be "enlisted" by the hero so that she might test his love and worth and prove to her father the falsity of disposing of her only to a high bidder. The enlistment intrigues are both a source of metaphor for the love intrigues and the means by which the complications of the love plot are resolved. The chief weakness of *The Recruiting Officer* is that the important subplot of the civilian second lovers expresses its analogy with the main plot wholly in terms of the conventional tropes of the love battle, in contrast with the metaphorical density of the main plot itself—with its paralleling, often identification, of wenching and enlisting, fighting for money and marrying for money, false honor on the battlefield and false love at home. Consequently, the revitalized analogy emerges as true of a recruiting officer's situation, but lacking full relevance for more general social concerns as they affect sex relations and marriage. The Petrarchan tropes of the subplot insist upon an analogy with the main plot which exists only tenuously. If *The Recruiting Officer* is not completely satisfactory, however, it does point clearly to the grounds of success in Farquhar's last and best play, *The Beaux' Stratagem.*

The Beaux' Stratagem chiefly establishes its meanings by a fruitful juxtaposition of its two, alternating scenes of action, the inn of Boniface and the house of Lady Bountiful, and by an interrelation of hospitality and sexual emotion—love or appetite. In each place and activity it is chiefly the attitude toward money which distinguishes the right from the wrong way. Such a movement and such attitudes are reminiscent of [Shakespeare's] *The Merchant of Venice,* with its alternation between Venetian streets and the walks of Belmont.

Boniface's hospitality is, as his name promises, only superficially good. He bustles about, providing food and drink to distract from his chief concern with tricking guests out of their money. He overcharges the French prisoners of war, and when he thinks Aimwell and Archer are highwaymen, he plans to betray them and thus gain the £200 they deposit with him (I,i). To prove his suspicions and gain the means for betrayal he is willing that his daughter Cherry be debauched by Archer, who is disguised as Aimwell's servant. He will harbor no rogues but his own Gibbet, Hounslow, and Bagshot, highwaymen and housebreakers based at his inn. But when they are caught he absconds with all the money he can lay hands on, leaving the highwaymen to swing (V,iv). This false, financially motivated hospitality contrasts with the true hospitality of Lady Bountiful, who lays out half of her income "in charitable Uses for the Good of her Neighbours" (I,i). Lady Bountiful's care for the poor is given dramatic, if negative, realization in the scene between Mrs. Sullen and the country-woman with a sick husband (IV,i). Mrs. Sullen's reaction to the countrywoman, her issuing of maliciously false advice, is so deliberately overstated as to effect a comic neutralization of any outrage at her careless cruelty. Her advice, reminiscent of Medea's instructions to the daughters of Pelias for the "rejuvenation" of their father, has something of the inventive hyperbole of Lady Wishfort's ritual commination of Foible in [Congreve's] *The Way of the World*. Mrs. Sullen's response is, of course, that of the townee bored with the simple pieties of the country.

These contrasting attitudes to hospitality parallel in the main intrigue of courtship and marriage the distinction between those who approach marriage for love and those who approach it for money. Charity is the social counterpart of the private virtue of love. At the beginning of the play both Aimwell and Archer are fortune hunters, and marriage to them would be more tolerable than marriage to Squire Sullen, Lady Bountiful's son, with his similar financial motivation, only because they are more witty and agreeable. Sullen assures his wife's brother when he comes to take her away from an unhappy marriage that he has no quarrel with his wife's fortune, he only hates his wife (V,i). In the final scene of separation by mutual consent, Sullen readily parts with his wife, but has to be forced to part with her portion by Archer's handing over the husband's papers to Mrs. Sullen's brother. Aimwell is intent upon marrying the fortune of Dorinda, Lady Bountiful's daughter, although his final reclamation to selfless love is prepared for in the opening scene by Archer's characterization of him as "an amorous Puppy . . . [who] can't counterfeit the Passion without feeling it." Archer can, and he demonstrates his sexual virtuosity by busying himself with minor speculations in sex and money with Cherry at the inn and an amour with the susceptible Mrs. Sullen at the house as incidental relief from intriguing on Aimwell's behalf. His appetite for Cherry is sharpened when she tells him she has £2,000, but he rejects her suggestion of marriage: "what need you make me Master of your self and Money, when you may have the same Pleasure out of me, and still keep your Fortune in your Hands" (II,ii).

In one of the early conflations of women and property, Archer remarks, "I love a fine House, but let another keep it; and just so I love a fine Woman" (I,i). Like the beaux, Mrs. Sullen, understandably embittered, thinks in terms of money. Her thoughts run on her dowry, and she observes shortly afterward that "Women are like Pictures of no Value in the Hands of a Fool, till he hears Men of Sense bid high for the Purchase" (II,i). Immediately, Mrs. Sullen is concerned with the property approach to women, but her simile prepares for the wooing of herself and Dorinda by the beaux in terms of the pictures in the house. When the women compare notes afterward, it emerges that Archer "thought" Mrs. Sullen the original of a Venus, while Aimwell took Dorinda "for *Venus* her self" (IV,i). The mythological eroticism of the paintings recurs in the trope Archer indulges in when he first enters Mrs. Sullen's bedchamber (V,ii), thus completing the circle of pictures, property, mythology, and eroticism.

Even the innocent Dorinda has to lose her social and financial taint, her wish to marry a title. "Why," she says to Mrs. Sullen, "my Ten thousand Pounds may lie brooding here this seven Years, and hatch nothing at last but some ill natur'd Clown like yours:—Whereas, If I marry my Lord *Aimwell*, there will be Title, Place and Precedence, the Park, the Play, and the drawing-Room, Splendor, Equipage, Noise and Flambeaux" (IV,i). When Aimwell's love for Dorinda has brought him to "prefer the Interest of my Mistress to my own" and to confess that he has pretended to the title of his brother to trick her, she, in return, finds herself prouder that he is without title and fortune than she was when he apparently possessed them: "Now I can shew my Love was justly levell'd, and had no Aim but Love" (V,iv). Shortly afterward, Sir Charles Freeman, who has come to take away his sister Mrs. Sullen, gives the news of Lord Aimwell's death. Although Freeman and his news are usually and with some justice taken as a facile deus ex machina allowing virtue to live happily ever after, Lord Aimwell's death accomplishes two things, one quasi-symbolic, the other morally realistic. When Aimwell's conscience works on him and makes him declare to Dorinda "I'm all Counterfeit except my Passion" (V,iv), he not only echoes Archer's early marking of his inability to counterfeit a passion without feeling it and the later discussion of imperfect imitation in paintings, he has also, morally speaking, ceased to be counterfeit at all. He is accordingly rewarded by becoming the veritable Lord Aimwell. Dorinda and Aimwell do not need his title and wealth, for they would still have £5,000, half her portion, the other half going, in accordance with the beaux' agreement, to Archer. They "earn" the title and fortune as soon as they renounce them. Aimwell's access of wealth also enables him to propose a Solomonic test of motivation by offering Archer not half of Dorinda's portion, but a choice between Dorinda and her whole fortune. Archer takes the £10,000.

Love and hospitality are, then, paralleled in a manner richly productive of incidental metaphor. The principal form of these metaphors is to compare love with a dwelling or property, as in Aimwell's rapture over Dorinda's cornucopian beauty and Archer's jeering response to it. When Mrs. Sullen asks Archer how he got into her bedchamber, he replies, "I flew in at the Window, Madam, your Cozen *Cupid* lent me his Wings, and your Sister *Venus* open'd the Casement" (V,ii). The visitation of Cupid is also implied in Archer's catechism of Cherry: "Where does Love enter?" (II,ii), and it recurs in Mrs. Sullen's exclamation to Dorinda, "I own my self a Woman, full of my Sex, a gentle, generous Soul,—easie and yielding to soft Desires; a spacious Heart, where Love and all his Train might lodge. And must the fair Apartment of my Breast be made a Stable for a Brute to lie in?" (IV,i). When, earlier, Dorinda endeavors to console Mrs. Sullen with the recollection that her husband makes her an allowance, she retorts, "A Maintenance! do you take me, Madam, for an hospital Child, that I must sit down, and bless my Benefactors for Meat, Drink and Clothes?" And with such a low view of charity, she naturally goes on to express contempt for Lady Bountiful's benevolence: "spreading of Plaisters, brewing of Diet-drinks, and stilling Rosemary-Water with the good old Gentlewoman, my Mother-in-Law" (II,i).

In addition to producing incidental metaphors, the paralleling of love and hospitality is accompanied by a conventional discrimination of their values into selfishness and selflessness which is fully implicated into character, action, and setting. The schemes of the beaux involve Aimwell's pretending a fit calculated to play upon Lady Bountiful's hospitality and so bring them within the house. Because such an entry is devious and is designed to gain money, or sexual gratification, or both, it may properly be associated with the sexual and financial atmosphere of the inn. The beaux are intent upon carrying the values of the inn to the house. The infiltration, in fact, has already begun. Mrs. Sullen is involved in a liaison with Count Bellair, a captured French officer who lodges at the inn, by which she hopes to put a jealous edge on Sullen's dull appetite for her. But Sullen himself is also occupied in carrying the values of the inn to the house, for he spends long hours at the inn, returning to the house with an aching head to call for food and drink as if he were still at the inn, or, as Mrs. Sullen puts it, returning late at night to come "flounce into Bed, dead as a Salmon into a Fishmonger's Basket; his Feet cold as Ice, his Breath hot as a Furnace, and his Hands and his Face as greasy as his Flanel Nightcap.—Oh Matrimony!" (II,i). The nature of matrimony at the inn is further revealed in the exchange between Boniface and Sir Charles Freeman. Boniface asks, "Are not Man and Wife one Flesh?" and Freeman replies, "You and your Wife, Mr. Guts, may be one Flesh, because ye are nothing else—but rational Creatures have minds that must be united" (V,i). The inn's values are flesh and money.

Lest there be any doubt about the nature of the values and social distinctions involved in character, action, and verbal analogy, there is in the activities of the highwaymen a superficially inconsequential subplot which is, in fact, integral with the total meaning and action of the play. The highwaymen, principally Gibbet, their leader and spokesman, are the most conspicuously predatory representatives of the inn at which they are based. Their attempted robbery of the house at the instigation of Boniface parallels the beaux' attempt to gain money from the house by pretended love. Just as the analogies in *The Recruiting Officer* depend in part upon the trope of the love battle, so the importance of Gibbet and his gang depends in part upon the convention that highwaymen are "gentlemen of the road," a convention, of course, which Gay later put to good use in *The Beggar's Opera*. The parallel between the beaux' stratagem and Gibbet's housebreaking is present in his insistence that "there's a great deal of Address

and good Manners in robbing a Lady, I am the most a Gentleman that way that ever travell'd the Road" (IV,i). We should not forget that Aimwell and Archer are also gentlemen who travel the roads of England in search of a lady's fortune. When they first put up at Boniface's inn, he mistakes them for highwaymen because, like Gibbet, they have a box of money and keep their horses saddled. Gibbet laments that he is "only a younger Brother" (V,ii), a condition of notorious financial consequences which he shares with Archer (II,ii) and also with Aimwell, of course. The analogy between Archer's sexual housebreaking and Gibbet's monetary housebreaking is further prepared for by Bellair's remark that if Sullen "but knew the Value of the Jewel he is Master of, he wou'd always wear it next his Heart, and sleep with it in his Arms" (III,iii). When Mrs. Sullen, her husband's neglected jewel, rallies her virtue to cry "Thieves, Thieves, Murther" at Archer's offered familiarity, the echo of Scrub's "Thieves, Thieves, Murther, Popery," inspired not by her plight but by the presence of robbers, serves to identify the activities of Archer and Gibbet. Lest the point should still prove elusive, Scrub proceeds to mistake Archer for one of the housebreakers, and Archer cheerfully admits that he too has come to rob Mrs. Sullen, but of a different jewel.

In addition to making even clearer the moral status of the beaux' stratagem, the highwaymen's adventure contributes largely to the comic resolution of the play. In the last act the inn and its values make a bodily assault upon the house and its values. Gibbet's housebreaking not only interrupts Archer at a crucial moment, it moves Cherry to rouse Aimwell to the rescue because Lady Bountiful is her godmother and she loves Dorinda. With the collapse of the burglary, Boniface absconds, robbing his own inn. It is, moreover, during the burglary that Sullen's papers are confiscated by Archer and handed over to Mrs. Sullen's brother to force the restitution of her portion. At the end of the play the forces of the inn are scattered, although none will be too severely punished, for even Gibbet has £200 in reserve to buy his life at the sessions. Gibbet and his gang may appear to operate, inconsequentially, within a buffo subplot, may be permitted a few rough jests from time to time, and may be ready, at authorial fiat, to dissolve sentiment into comedy or, perhaps, comedy into sentiment. But the presence of Gibbet, what he says and does, confirms the propriety of reading *The Beaux' Stratagem* as a play in which image and action are mutually enriching: what one character does provides others and himself with metaphors for conversation. I confess to a great fondness for Gibbet, and am reluctant to sacrifice him to those who would find him Jeremy Collier in disguise or the Comic Spirit made flesh. I think him an ineluctable highwayman, a gentleman of the road, and not the less interesting for that. (pp. 178-86)

Alan Roper, " 'The Beaux' Strategem': Image and Action," in Seventeenth-Century Imagery: Essays on Uses of Figurative Language from Donne to Farquhar, *edited by Earl Miner, University of California Press, 1971, pp. 169-86.*

John Ross (essay date 1977)

[*In the following excerpt from his introduction to* The Recruiting Officer, *Ross claims that while Farquhar's basic themes in this play are drawn from other works, their "air of naturalness" is an original contribution to Restoration drama.*]

The Recruiting Officer, and its successor **The Beaux' Stratagem,** are acknowledged as the latest masterpieces of Restoration comedy, with a difference indeed, yet still native to the world of Congreve's *Love for Love* or Vanbrugh's *Relapse.* If, after 1700, the Restoration comic spirit had been in retreat, there is nothing decadent in **The Recruiting Officer,** rather, in Leigh Hunt's words, 'a charm of gaiety and good humour throughout . . . We seem to breathe the clear, fresh, ruddy-making air of a remote country town, neighboured by hospitable elegance'.

The play is most original in its combining of the modes of Restoration comedy with a sympathetic and relatively realistic treatment of a country-town society. In the comedies of the time, country people had almost always been measured against the standards of London gentility and caricatured either as boorish clodpates or absurdly inept pretenders to town sophistication. Here 'all the variety and sense of real life that enhanced the traditional London scene are transferred to Shrewsbury; and Shrewsbury values become the normative values of the play' [Eric Rothstein, *George Farquhar*]. Farquhar's country town Justice is declared to be true to life, 'a worthy, honest, generous gentleman . . . of as good an understanding as I could give him', implicitly as an answer to the most elaborate example of the booby squire stereotype, Sir Wilfull Witwoud of Shropshire in *The Way of the World.* Justice Balance nonetheless is shown as sometimes fallible, both as a father and a judge. By shifting his milieu, Farquhar has gained the added advantage of independence from the contemporary polarizing of stances about human nature between cynics and sentimentalists, allowing him to express an unusually genial though clearsighted view of men's frailties.

The author's own enjoyment of his experiences in Shrewsbury pervades the play. The impression of 'fresh air' Hunt speaks of has a firm basis in that for more than half its length the action is set out of doors, in the marketplace or on the walks beside the Severn. In the part of the play preceding Act IV, scene ii the outdoor-indoor ratio is five-to-one. Even the indoor scenes are permeated with references to 'the sharp air from the Welsh mountains', galloping 'after the hunting-horn', the activity of the poacher, who 'kills all the hares and partridges within five mile round', or to the wider vista of continental campaigning.

In presenting the life of Shrewsbury sympathetically Farquhar was taking further a trend in some earlier relatively minor plays of the period. He allows, however, for the dominant comic attitude of scorn for provincial characters by focusing it on his lower-class characters, the peasants Tummas and Costar, Rose and Bullock, though even they are made likeable and at times surprisingly shrewd. Conventional complaints about the noise, dirt, and scandal of the Town are incongruously advanced by Melinda against Shrewsbury. Allowed a rich mixture of human types, and of civilized values with healthy rusticity, Shrewsbury is made an analogue rather than a foil to the London world, and a microcosm of civilian society. The primary duality is rather between this world and the alien world of the army and of the continental war rumbling away offstage, which initiates the action by its intrusion into Shrewsbury to demand its 'complement of men'.

The key motif of the play is the interrelation of loving and fighting. Usually the merest commonplace of Restoration imagery, it has here provided Farquhar with the means of resolving with unusual grace the artistic problem of endowing an entertaining variety of comic material with a satisfying degree of coherence. As the two wooing plot-strands concerning Plume and Silvia, Worthy and Melinda, wear the guise of warfare, so do Plume's recruiting ploys take on to one degree or another the forms of seduction. Structurally, one of the favourite patterns of Restoration comedy, the combination of two love actions with a topic action (cf. Etherege's *The Man of Mode*), has been integrated primarily through the activities of the central figure, Captain Plume, who is at once the rakish lover-hero and the soldier engaged in the occupation of recruiting. Even his love-making takes on 'a businesslike importance as he woos country girls' like Rose or Molly, 'to lure their brothers and sweethearts into the army'. He also takes over the running of Worthy's campaign to win the

Scene from Farquhar's **The Beaux' Stratagem.**

hand of Melinda. As James observes, 'Plume is perhaps Farquhar's best hero in the sense that he sets plots in motion', and the forms they take derive from his breezy personality.

Silvia likewise links two plot-strands and initiates action. When the accident of her brother's death has suddenly made her the next inheritor of her father's estate, the latter adopts a blocking role in relation to her match with Plume, making her promise not to dispose of herself to any man without his consent (II. ii). Plume is too preoccupied with his duties and Worthy's affairs, too realistic about the disproportion in social status that has arisen between them, and too little aware of the real nature of the block, to respond actively to news of her departure into the country. Silvia then assumes a 'pursuing heroine' role and seizes upon the device of disguising herself in breeches as a prospective gentleman-volunteer, 'Jack Wilful'. This not only enables her to engineer a situation in which her father will 'consent' through legally impressing her to serve as a soldier under Plume's command; it also gives her the power to eliminate Rose as a short-term rival in love, and to learn more about her lover before committing herself. In this fashion she successfully recruits Plume into her world through the very means by which he believes he is recruiting 'Jack Wilful' into his. From the time of her entry in disguise in Act III, scene ii, this wooing action is woven into the recruiting action to the extent that the two gain a measure of ironic identity.

Even in the introduction of the well-worn breeches device, an air of naturalness is preserved in the working of the plot. . . . Silvia's sprightly, enterprising personality and healthy sentiments, and her understanding of the rake she loves, evidenced in Act I, scene ii, make the male disguise seem far more natural to her than to most comic heroines who have used it; and her later appearance as 'Jack Wilful' is prepared for here 'by having Melinda mention four times . . . that Silvia would make a good man' [James]. Indeed the last of these ('You begin to fancy yourself in breeches in good earnest . . .') might be taken to have suggested the scheme. (pp. xviii-xxi)

A brief survey of the design of the play and the development of its themes will provide further evidence of skilful craftsmanship. A light-heartedly equivocal attitude to recruiting, and the military world it serves, emerges in the epigraph and prologue, which mock-heroically invest them with the dimensions of the Trojan War. The 'arts' by which Ulysses entices Achilles to go off to fight play an essential role in ensuring the Greek victory, yet the baits offered here, instead of undying fame, are 'plunder, fine laced coats and glitt'ring arms'. The allusion to the Wooden Horse in the epigraph likewise emphasizes the slyness of the means by which even the most glorious wars are won. (pp. xxiii-xxiv)

Here and there Farquhar has planted indictments of the army system and its officers for their vicious inefficiency and corruption. And the obligatory reading of the Articles of War against mutiny and desertion, in which every conceivable offence is punishable by death, cannot but produce a dark shadow in the hitherto amusing court-room scene. Warfare itself is seen as grim rather than glorious.

Even so, in the immediate past is set Marlborough's famous victory at Blenheim, England's first great victory on land since Agincourt. Plume is entitled to exploit its warm afterglow; and to mouth a few platitudes about glory yielding full return for life, once he can afford to resign his commission.

Arthur Bedford in *The Evil and Danger of Stage Plays* (Bristol, 1706) ferociously assailed **The Recruiting Officer** as destructive of patriotism and slanderous about the average character of the nation's military officers. He wildly overstates his case, and shows no sensitivity to the genial tone of the play, so that he takes as deliberate defamation much that is simply humorous realism. Some of the satirical touches he notices are unquestionably intended. . . . They are, however, given relatively little dramatic emphasis, beside that given to humorous situation, and are balanced against expressions of cheerfully affirmed patriotism ('Huzza for the Queen!'). The effect of each satiric attack upon the army world is modified ironically by its immediate context, and by the pervading atmosphere of good humour. Farquhar's view of human nature was orthodox for his time. 'It was a dual entity; its baser passions were constantly at war with its nobler, and too frequently victorious. In this world, moral perfection was quite unattainable' [Ernest Bernbaum, *The Drama of Sensibility*, 1958]. Nonetheless, Silvia provides a positive example of what can be achieved in this world through bravery and generous love, and the comic dramatist may ameliorate the condition of man in society by corrective satire. (p. xxviii)

Farquhar's dialogue has been described by Pope [in 'Imitation of "The First Epistle of the Second Book of Horace"'] as 'low' and 'pert', by [John] Oldmixon [in *The Muses Mercury*, May, 1707] as 'loose and incorrect' yet 'gay and agreeable'. In many cases 'lowness' and, grammatically, 'looseness' and 'incorrectness', are entirely proper to the speaker, and Farquhar must be regarded as one of the pioneers in the development of life-like, naturalistic stage speech. He has discovered that the juxtapositional modes of normal speech differ from those of formal grammar, and developed a means of presenting them, particularly effective in the mouths of Kite and Brazen. The pleasant characters, Pearmain, Appletree, Rose, and Bullock, are given a slight but adequately distinguishing dialect and turn of phrase, that have nothing to do with stage-bumpkinery.

The speech modes given to the gentlemen and ladies preserve, usually in relaxed, unobtrusive form, the patterns of Restoration wit: antithesis, paradox, simile. In Act III, scene ii, when Plume declares he is drunk enough to fancy himself 'mighty witty', he produces at once a semi-personifying antithesis ('Reason still keeps its throne, but it nods a little') and a dreadful punning simile ('As fit [for a frolic] as close pinners for a punk in the pit'), extends Worthy's metaphor of Melinda as ship, then goes on to out-banter Brazen.

There is relatively little dialogue that is not dramatically active: even Brazen and Plume's topical chat in V. iv about the theatre and privateer as rival investments serves to lead up to the disclosure of Brazen's expectation of marrying Melinda. There is little general reflection and only two 'characters' to briefly halt the action. 'The comedy . . . rests on its characters . . . and its intrigues . . . Although there are flashes of wit . . . the characters are too busy intriguing to carry on much witty talk and are really outside the pale of high society' [James].

The tone even of Plume's or Silvia's speeches is in Pope's sense 'pert', yet the limitations in their sensibilities are fitting to their situations, and their voices, like those of every other character from highest to lowest, are human and alive. The presiding sensibility is the author's: it does not receive direct expression through the mouth of any one character; instead, meaning is created through characters in interaction.

William Archer in his preface to the first Mermaid edition of Farquhar's plays rightly drew attention to the degree to which, in his sense, Farquhar was a pure dramatist, and not, as many of his Restoration predecessors were, a mixture of dramatist and essayist. In **The Recruiting Officer** Farquhar has created a masterpiece of theatre in which human resourcefulness triumphs over chance and social restriction, and good-natured satire is mixed with humour. Critical discussion of comedies of this era has taken rather far the retrospective creation of genre pigeon-holes, and valued over-exclusively the comedy of wit. In talking about this play some comparisons with other comedies of the time are needful, yet it deserves to be experienced and enjoyed for itself as 'a comedy of life' [Louis A. Strauss]. (pp. xxx-xxxi)

> *John Ross, in an introduction to* The Recruiting Officer *by George Farquhar, edited by John Ross, Ernest Benn Limited, 1977, pp. xiii-xxxiii.*

Peter Dixon   (essay date 1986)

[*In the following excerpt from his introduction to Farquhar's* The Recruiting Officer, *Dixon compares the "good-humored satire" of Farquhar's play with Ben Jonson's* Bartholomew Fair, *praising Farquhar's skill for creating a "whole community" with a wide variety of characters.*]

In the frontispiece to the 1708 volume [of Farquhar's collected plays] Jonson identifies himself by carrying a copy of *Bartholomew Fair.* That play has a special kinship with **The Recruiting Officer,** notably in its tolerant attitude towards human frailty and its relatively good-humoured satire. Phrases which have recently been applied to Farquhar's comedy [by Robert D. Hume in *The Development of English Drama in the Late Seventeenth Century,* 1976]—'an affectionate but tartly realistic picture of the army and recruiting', 'almost a comic documentary'—aptly describe, *mutatis mutandis,* Jonson's re-creation of the fair. And *Bartholomew Fair,* like **The Recruiting Officer,** is its author's most intensely localised play. As Jonson's characters converge on the fairground, so do Farquhar's on Shrewsbury—and from significantly different directions. In the opening scene Plume is welcomed there by Kite; he has travelled by way of London, bringing with him the values and attitudes of a man-about-town. In the following scene Melinda welcomes Silvia back to Shrews-

bury from her father's estate. Silvia brings from the country a directness and outspokenness, even a cheerful vulgarity, that contrast refreshingly with Melinda's airs and graces. Later, as 'Captain Pinch', her imitation of a London rakehell, Silvia pretends to have journeyed like Plume from the capital, to prey on the unsuspecting provincials. A busy market-town is fertile ground for both tricksters and recruiters (they are sometimes the same thing), and Plume's is not the only recruiting party to advance upon Shrewsbury. Like Bartholomew Fair the town allures with baits of profit and pleasure.

In some ways Shrewsbury mirrors London. It has its counterpart of St James's Park in the walk by the Severn; both are fine places for assignations. And it has its 'season'. Having spent the summer months on their estate Justice Balance and his daughter return to their town house for the social round of the winter months. But Farquhar brings Shrewsbury to vigorous life on its own terms, and so demonstrates—the demonstration having considerable historical importance—that a provincial town could furnish a viable setting for comedy. His success is not simply a matter of topographical details (references to churches, inns, the Severn) nor even of incidental dabs of local colour, though he is aware of the popular Shropshire pastime of 'prison-bars' (II. i. 6) as well as of the regional dialect. He creates the sense of a whole community, with its range of occupations, its hierarchy of classes, and its network of social, economic and legal relationships. Rose's father is a farm-tenant of Justice Scale; her mother was Silvia's nurse. Rose herself has often seen Justice Balance 'ride through our grounds a-hunting' (III. i. 284), which as a man of property he is entitled to do. The local ne'er-do-well who maintains his family by shooting hares and partridge, and by his 'hunting' contravenes the Game Laws, is conscripted into the army as a felon. For all the dedication's compliments to Shrewsbury and its polite inhabitants, the play gives a rounded picture, not a rosy one. Mr Worthy (admittedly a partial witness) complains of a puritanical streak: 'we live in such a precise, dull place, that we can have no balls, no lampoons . . .' (I. i. 224-6). It is a place in which the constable preserves and uses his right to break into premises in order to hunt out fornication (V. i). But outward staidness does not inhibit gossip and back-biting, and Worthy acknowledges that unpleasant rumours about Plume and Silvia have begun to circulate (I. i. 253).

The county town setting and the plot, with its confrontation of the military and the civilian, afford very natural opportunities to display a wide variety of characters, only some of whom are related to the comic types of earlier Restoration drama. The coquette and her pert, intriguing, eavesdropping confidante are familiar enough. The military men, Plume, Brazen and Kite, offer interesting variations on the standard Restoration trio of rake, fop and witty resourceful servant, while the inhabitants of Shropshire, both high and low, are genuinely new departures. Farquhar is right in claiming that his country gentleman, Justice Balance, is far from being the uncultivated booby of Restoration comic tradition, and that his farmer's son is no mere clodpate. Bullock, despite his clumsiness and impatience, has a touching sense of responsibility for his sister's welfare, and a sturdy, if rather misguided, spirit of independence.

Farquhar has endowed his characters with remarkably lifelike language, expressive of a wide range of personalities from the reticent butcher, Mr Pluck, to the garrulous Brazen, loose in thought and syntax. The 'natural Air of free Conversation' which Farquhar demanded of good comedy [in his ***Discourse upon Comedy***] is much assisted by a generous use of colloquialisms, proverbs, dialect words, military jargon and rogues' slang. These ingredients also make for energy, a vivacity of language which contributes to the play's buoyancy and to our sense of Jonsonian affinities. Bonamy Dobrée [in his *Restoration Comedy*] has commented on an 'atmosphere of exaggeration' in Farquhar that is akin to Jonson and is well exemplified by Kite's vivid autobiography (III.i.117ff.) and his 'recruiting strain'. It equally characterises the speech of such a minor character as Kite's first would-be victim. Kite and his cunning meet their match as this individual catches up the sergeant's wheedlingly intimate 'brother':

> Brother! Hold there friend, I'm no kindred to you that I know of, as yet. . . . Therefore take your cap and your brothership back again, for I an't disposed at this present writing. No coaxing, no brothering me, faith.
>
> (I.i.38ff.)

The *O.E.D.* cites precedents for 'brothership' and 'brothering', but they are remote enough for us to accept these words as examples of Farquhar's linguistic inventiveness. The vigorous language endows this anonymous member of the Shrewsbury crowd with a real personality. He is truculent, suspicious, standing on his dignity even when mollified by Kite's offer of drinks at the Raven Inn:

> Nay, for that matter, I'll spend my penny with the best he that wears a head—that is, begging your pardon sir, and in a fair way.

Liveliness, as in all Farquhar's plays, is also more crudely manifested in an abundance of noise—the beating drum and huzzas of the first scene, the rowdy singing in II.iii, Kite's mimicked trumpet-call amid the clashing of swords (III.ii), Brazen's pistol shot (V.vi)—and physical action. There is much quarrelling and expostulation, several hasty exits, and two impetuous entrances, as the constable and his followers burst into Silvia's antechamber (V.i), and as Worthy parts Brazen and Lucy (V.vi). Characters are seized, cuffed, slapped on the shoulder, struck over the head.

Such bustling activity requires the full width of the stage. Plume and Brazen *'fight a traverse or two'* back and forth across the stage (III.ii.246.1). Bullock *'whistles about the stage'* as he waits for Rose to complete her bargain (III.i.75-6). It also demands the full use of the very considerable depth possessed by the Drury Lane theatre. Scenes of intimate conversation would occupy the forestage or platform; there the actors would be flanked by spectators in the stage-boxes and would be close to those in the pit. Large properties, such as Kite's conjuring table with its astrological apparatus, and the judicial bench in the courtroom scene, would be sited in the rear stage area and 'discovered' by sliding apart the painted flats or shutters which formed the backcloths for the preceding scenes. During the fortune-telling episode the projecting wings or sidescenes would also be utilised, to provide hiding-places for Worthy and Plume, and in III.i Brazen would enter well upstage ('yonder he comes . . . that bluff fellow in the sash') meandering in and out of the sidescenes before he approaches Worthy and Balance downstage.

Large stage properties can inhibit grouping and movement. Farquhar skilfully creates an impression of flexibility in the fortune-telling and courtroom scenes by developing the dramatic action in an apparently free-wheeling way. For most of IV.ii Kite is seated at his table; variety and interest are secured through the arrival of successive clients, the farcical business of the 'devil' under the table-cloth, and the sense of a military operation whose success depends on Kite's alert adjustment to the challenge of each moment. Similarly in the courtroom scene. The bench itself clearly sets the three Justices and Plume apart from the prisoners and their hangers-on, and from the two 'staff officers', Kite and the constable. Again, the rigidity of the setting is counteracted by the succession of prisoners, by the rapid exchange of pleas and accusations, and by Silvia's raking attack on the assembled agents of law and order.

Not that Farquhar's scenes, for all their seeming unpredictability, are ever less than carefully moulded, with a very sure and practised eye for theatrical effect. There is patterning in the two scenes just considered, as well as in those which are less anchored to stage properties, for the fortune-seekers fall into two distinct sets—the tradesmen fed with military promises, the ladies and Brazen with romantic ones—while the courtroom proceedings are framed by Kite's opening and concluding business with the constable and his staff. This combination of shapely scene-structure with liveliness and spontaneity is one of the happiest achievements of Farquhar's comic art. (pp. 10-13)

> *Peter Dixon, in an introduction to* The Recruiting Officer *by George Farquhar, edited by Peter Dixon, Manchester University Press, 1986, pp. 1-51.*

FURTHER READING

Archer, William. "The *Short View* and After." In his *The Old Drama and the New: An Essay in Re-Valuation,* pp. 203-27. Boston: Small, Maynard and Company, 1923.

> Suggests that the moral tone and general humanity of Farquhar's plays make them superior to the Restoration comedies of the preceding age.

Brown, Ivor. "Sweet Sullen." *The Saturday Review* (London) 143, No. 3718 (29 January 1927): 153-54.

> Analysis of Farquhar's *The Beaux' Stratagem* which praises the character of Mrs. Sullen for her rebellion against the "disgusting hypocrisy" of Restoration conventions.

Burns, Edward. "The Last Restoration Comedies— Farquhar, Centlivre, and Steele." In his *Restoration Comedy: Crises of Desire and Identity,* pp. 212-36. London: The Macmillan Press, 1987.

> Evaluates the development of Farquhar's plays from the artificial style of Etherege to the "realist comedy of broader social scope and robustly moral intention."

Flynn, Carol Houlihan. " 'A Softer Man': Pope's, Swift's, and Farquhar's Feminine Ideal." *The South Atlantic Quarterly* 84, No. 1 (Winter 1985): 51-62.

> Explores Farquhar's treatment of women in his comedies, suggesting that he stripped women of their sexuality, both literally and metaphorically, for the purpose of correcting their flaws.

Larson, Martin A. "The Influence of Milton's Divorce Tracts on Farquhar's *Beaux' Stratagem.*" *Publications of the Modern Language Association of America* XXXIX, No. 1 (March 1924): 174-78.

> Argues that the "separation by mutual consent" at the close of Farquhar's *The Beaux' Stratagem* was borrowed directly from John Milton's *Doctrine and Discipline of Divorce.*

Loftis, John. "The Survival of the Restoration Stereotypes, 1693-1710." In his *Comedy and Society from Congreve to Fielding,* pp. 43-76. Stanford, Calif.: Stanford University Press, 1959.

> Suggests that Farquhar's oversimplification of social fact in his plays is actually "an artistic gain in that [his] plays have a consistency of tone based upon settled opinion."

Robertson, J. G. "Lessing and Farquhar." *Modern Language Review* II, No. 1 (October 1906): 56-9.

> Examines the influence of Farquhar's comedies on the German dramatist Gotthold Ephraim Lessing, stating that "there has hitherto been a tendency to overestimate the extent of that influence."

Rothstein, Eric. *George Farquhar.* New York: Twayne Publishers, 1967, 206 p.

> Critical overview of Farquhar's life and work.

Stonehill, Charles. Introduction to *The Complete Works of George Farquhar,* edited by Charles Stonehill, pp. xi-xxxiii. New York: Gordian Press, 1930.

> Highly regarded biographical and critical overview ranking Farquhar as "one of the foremost of English dramatists."

Additional coverage of Farquhar's life and career is contained in the following source published by Gale Research: *Dictionary of Literary Biography, Vol. 84.*

Restoration Drama

INTRODUCTION

The term Restoration Drama refers to the dramatic styles practiced by English playwrights in the years following the reestablishment of the monarchy in 1660. Having been barred from staging plays for nearly two decades under Puritan Parliamentary rule, Restoration dramatists were interested in perfecting two distinct yet closely related dramatic types, the comedy of manners and the heroic tragedy, both of which probably derived from seventeenth-century French models of classical drama. Foremost among the comedies of manners, the works of William Wycherley, William Congreve, Sir John Vanbrugh, Sir George Etherege, and George Farquhar are generally characterized by the witty repartee of fashionable London rakes in pursuit of sizable dowries and sexual intrigues. Scholars agree that the cynical, bawdy nature of these plays was a reaction to social and artistic repression enforced by the ban on all theatrical performances during the eighteen-year Interregnum. In contrast to the comedies of manners stand the heroic dramas of Nathaniel Lee, Thomas Otway, and, most notably, John Dryden. Generally set in distant, exotic lands, these works often represented the conflict between a great hero's passion for a lady and his duty to his country. These two dramatic types became the object of a critical attack in Jeremy Collier's *A Short View of the Profaneness and Immorality of the English Stage* (1698), a lengthy pamphlet condemning Restoration drama as immoral and blasphemous. Collier's remarks engendered a controversy surrounding the question of morality in the plays which has continued to this day.

The monarchy was reestablished in 1660 following a period of civil war and Parliamentary rule known as the Commonwealth and Protectorate (1642-60). Immediately before this, Charles I, who claimed to rule by divine right, and Parliament, which claimed the right to govern the nation independent of the crown, were engaged in a struggle for power. Tensions erupted into civil war in 1642, with the statesman Oliver Cromwell leading the Parliamentarian forces to victory three years later. Under Puritan influence, Parliament issued a ban on public stage productions, hoping to suppress what was viewed as an immoral practice and to eliminate the theatrical companies whose Royalist tendencies derived from their largely aristocratic patronage. After Charles was beheaded for treason in 1649, England continued under Parliamentary rule until 1660, when Charles II was crowned King of England. One of his first actions, lifting the ban on performances, led to the reopening of theaters and a resurgence of dramatic composition and productions.

Scholars have found the boundaries of Restoration comedy of manners hard to define, though Etherege is often considered the originator of the form, mainly for the wit and satire of his *The Man of Mode; or, Sir Fopling Flutter* (1676). The final dates given to mark the close of the era for this dramatic style generally span a wide range of years, though Congreve's masterpiece *The Way of the World* (1700) is frequently cited, as is Farquhar's *The Beaux' Strategem* (1707), with its comparatively genteel, morally exemplary tone presaging eighteenth-century Sentimental comedy. These and other Restoration comedies portray young London aristocrats involved in duels of wits with sexually voracious widows and society ladies while in pursuit of love intrigues and large dowries. The fashionable, witty courtiers who appear as main characters in Etherege's plays and others such as Wycherley's *The Country Wife* (1675), reflect the largely aristocratic audience of the time, while other typical characters, including fops, bawds, scheming valets, and country squires, are portrayed as dim-witted by comparison. Often, multiple plots exist within individual plays with little or no relation between them and little indication of their relative significance. Critics have noted that the main interest of the works lies in the characters' witty dialogue, involving discussions of marital behavior, relations between the sexes, and fashionable, aristocratic manners. Scholars have found the origins of this type of comedy difficult to trace due to the turbulent climate of pre- and post-Restoration England and the eighteen-year ban on performances. Possible sources of influence include the Elizabethan comedy of humors, especially the plays of Ben Jonson and the classical French theater, particularly the works of Molière. The latter had begun to gain prominence as a comic dramatist in the French court of Louis XIV several years before the Restoration, writing plays which inspired numerous translations and adaptations by other dramatists of the day.

Heroic drama, another product of the Restoration theater, found expression in such works as Nathaniel Lee's *The Rival Queens* (1677) and Thomas Otway's *Venice Preserved* (1682), but its greatest exponent was John Dryden, whose *Conquest of Granada* (1670-71) typifies the excessive spectacle and violent emotional conflict in this dramatic form. The major themes of heroic drama involve the honor, fate, and illicit or exotic love of a great hero whose individual will clashes with civilized society. As in the comedies, central love plots are often complicated by intrigue, but a code of valor and heroic argumentation in these dramas replaces the social code of "sensible behavior" and repartee of Restoration comedy. These dramas also differ from their lighter counterparts in their use of elaborate scenery and exotic settings; forsaking London for Mexico, Morocco, and India, they shift the focus of Restoration drama from the social or sexual conquests of urban rakes to the epic conquering of empires. Integral to these dramas was the heroic couplet, a poetic form featuring rhymed pairs of lines in iambic pentameter. This technique was immensely popular in the mid-seventeenth century, and though it was used widely by the playwrights of heroic drama, Dryden became best known for the form, especially in his *The Conquest of Granada, Tyrannick Love* (1669), and *Aurenge-Zebe* (1675).

Works written for the Restoration stage were performed for several decades before critics began to question their propriety. In 1698 Collier, an English clergyman, published *A Short View of the Immorality and Profaneness of the English Stage,* an attack on what he saw as the immorality, frivolity, and blasphemy of Restoration drama. This work led to what has been called the Jeremy Collier Stage Controversy, a debate lasting for many years and involving a furious exchange of pamphlets and essays from proponents of either side of the issue. Ironically, both sides argued from the same critical standpoint: that literature is meant to instruct its audience and, thus, that its merits can be defined by its effects on the general public. Collier's supporters considered Restoration plays dangerous in their symbolic representation of aristocratic social indifference and contempt for the merchant class, values which threatened to undermine the peace and social cohesion of a country still recovering from the Civil War. They also perceived the dramas as morally intolerable in their advocation of sexual permissiveness and lax values. The critics who opposed Collier insisted that the intent of comedy was to expose vice rather than to represent virtue. By presenting immorality on stage, Collier's opponents contended, dramatists believed that they could simultaneously amuse audiences and provide moral instruction.

The controversy surrounding the morality of Restoration comedy continued into the nineteenth century; some commentators echoed Collier's attack on the plays while others defended them, insisting that the question of a play's morality was irrelevant to its success or failure as literature. In his essay "On the Artificial Comedy of the Last Century" (1823), Charles Lamb defended Restoration playwrights by positing that the dramas take place in the autonomous world of the theater, a realm in possession of its own value system not transferrable to real life. Some twentieth-century commentators have followed Lamb in praising Restoration comedies as lighthearted romps, while others claim that the literary merit of the works lies in their serious portrayal of the consequences of certain moral actions.

Despite widespread affirmation of the plays' worth, the attack on Restoration drama has not ended. Critical contention over the morality of the dramas continues, as well as the assertion that the plays do not reflect actual lives in seventeenth-century England, but merely a utopia of fashion and manners. In addition, L. C. Knights's essay "Restoration Comedy: The Reality and the Myth" (1937) took a new approach by condemning the works on the basis of their aesthetic elements, calling the plays "trivial, gross, and dull." Knights's essay initiated its own avenue of ongoing critical debate. Nevertheless, as John Wain writes, Restoration plays have survived because their writers "had the comedian's gift of not pressing for a logical solution, but accepting the muddle and making it seem, for all their artificiality, genuinely human."

REPRESENTATIVE WORKS

Behn, Aphra
   The Rover; or, The Banished Cavaliers   1677
   The Emperor of the Moon   1687
Centlivre, Susanna
   The Busie Body   1709
   A Bold Stroke for a Wife   1718
Cibber, Colley
   Love's Last Shift; or, The Fool in Fashion   1696
   The Careless Husband   1704
Congreve, William
   Love for Love   1695
   The Way of the World   1700
Dryden, John
   Tyrannick Love; or, The Royal Martyr   (1669)
   The Conquest of Granada by the Spaniards, I and II
      1670-71
   Marriage A-la-Mode   1673
   Aureng-Zebe   1675
   All for Love; or, The World Well Lost   1677
Etherege, George
   The Comical Revenge; or, Love in a Tub   1644
   The Man of Mode; or, Sir Fopling Flutter   1676
Farquhar, George
   The Recruiting Officer   1706
   The Beaux' Stratagem   1707
Lee, Nathaniel
   *The Rival Queens; or, The Death of Alexander the
      Great*   1677
   The Princess of Cleve   1681
Otway, Thomas
   The Orphan; or, The Unhappy Marriage   1680
   Venice Preserved; or, A Plot Discovered   1682
Vanbrugh, John
   The Relapse; or, Virtue in Danger   1696
   The Provoked Wife   1697
Wycherley, William
   The Country Wife   1675
   The Plain Dealer   1676

GENERAL OVERVIEWS

Earl Miner

[*Miner is an American educator and critic and the author of numerous scholarly works on the English poet John Dryden. In the excerpt below, he provides a general description of Restoration comedy and heroic drama, concluding that though the period produced no equivalent to Shakespeare, "it did achieve the second great harvest of English drama."*]

The fact that Restoration drama has long been the problem child of English literature has not prevented people from making up their minds about it. The history of its criticism from its own day to ours shows that the effort to evaluate it has raised fundamental questions about the conventions, techniques, range, sociology, and morality of literature. Much of its fascination has indeed been extra-literary, and settled judgments have often been made upon very little literary evidence. If only a lively literary period could arouse such personal responses, only the combination of real literary merit and a relevance to our day can account for the remarkable rise in the quality as well as quantity of criticism of Restoration drama in the past twenty years. The subject has proved to be quite difficult, but numerous writers have combined historical knowledge and critical acumen to advance our understanding. Most of the best work . . . has earned the right to evaluate by accepting the discipline of historical or critical analysis. Although the reinterpretation is far from complete, the result, to paraphrase Dryden, has been to reveal to us almost a whole new drama. My purpose in this [essay] is the more modest one of description, both of Restoration drama and of fruitful approaches to it.

Restoration drama must be described as three groups of works. For most people it is still limited, unfortunately, to Wycherley's *Country Wife,* Etherege's *Man of Mode,* and Congreve's *Way of the World.* A rough division of interpretations and of responses might in fact be made purely upon the basis of preferences among the three, often with an accompanying insouciance for the rest of the achievement of four or five prolific decades of theatre. It must be confessed that many professional students of Restoration drama have not cast their nets much more widely. At least he who addresses himself to the dull task of combing bibliographies will discover that the twentieth century critical view of Restoration drama is confined, with but few exceptions, to Dryden, Wycherley, Etherege, Congreve, and Otway. . . . There are signs of change, but the common reader may rejoice to concur with the professional critic.

A second description of Restoration drama must, however, take a larger province into view. If we accept the usual dates of inclusion, from about 1660 to about 1700, there are to consider about two hundred dramatists and almost one hundred plays of unknown authorship. The bouncy Shadwell alone wrote twenty, his satiric commentator Dryden nearly thirty. It cannot be said that this vast wood has been wholly uncharted, much less that it is all enchanted forest. But neither can it be measured by the three familiar landmarks. A full description of what Restoration drama means would have to include the sum of the productions appearing, for short runs of three days or so, during those same four decades. That is what Pepys and the other theatregoers saw, applauded, hissed, described in their diaries and letters, or criticized in the coffeehouses. In this larger sense, it includes the dramatists of "the former age"—Shakespeare, Jonson, Beaumont and Fletcher, Webster, and others—whether in pristine form or in adaptation. It includes translations and adaptations of foreign plays, the beginnings of English opera, puppet shows, variety theatre, pageants, masques, and cantatas, in addition to the staples of comedy, tragedy, and heroic play in their numerous mutations and combinations.

From time to time the general public has had the opportunity of seeing revivals. The early and basically mindless play by Newcastle and Dryden, *Sir Martin Mar-all,* keeps an audience in constant laughter. A late play like Farquhar's *Recruiting-Officer* moves by the naturalness of its

language and feeling. The Tate-Purcell *Dido and Aeneas* and the cantatas based upon Dryden's St. Cecilia Day odes evoke admiration whenever they are heard. What we so easily term Restoration drama is extremely varied and very much in need of careful discriminations. It not only includes many types of theatrical experience but also changes markedly in a normal literary evolution from those first days when the theatres were reopened under Charles II to the time when a softer eighteenth century taste led to a preference for moral tears over the bracing laughter of comedy and to a rejection of tragedy darkened by fate or illicit love and of the high astounding terms of the heroic play. The real problem of Restoration drama is that it is too little known.

There is, however, a more familiar problem, sexual morality. So fascinating has the problem been to the moralists and the prurient that consideration of Restoration comedy, with which the problem has been associated, has directed attention away from the other forms. Although the comedy has attracted consistent moral criticism, the nature of the censure has varied. Restoration criticism charged it with profanity in the strict sense; eighteenth and nineteenth century critics found it guilty of sexual license. Aware that neither of these censures is quite suited to the twentieth century, modern traducers of Restoration comedy have sophisticated the charge into one of sterile preoccupation with sex. Undoubtedly the comedy is openly occupied with sexual behavior. Worse still, to the moralists of all periods, the characters persist in talking about their sexual notions and ideas, in overturning received notions of social behavior. Some people find it annoying to have moral problems constantly discussed, especially in the seemingly topsy-turvy Restoration terms. The adverse critics—including those among our contemporaries—are annoyed by the sexual chatter, and it would be difficult to say whether the ingenuity of some of our defenders of Restoration comedy responds more to the plays or their critics.

So much critical smoke must arise from some degree of literary fire; at least it is generally conceded that in the next century comedy turned moral and dull (not that these qualities were, or are, inseparable). One might wish that the moral problem had been treated by critics in the larger terms of personal exploitation of others or of economic morality, but one must take history as one finds it and say that the critics' discussion in fact revolves about sex, which the dramatists treat by no means uniformly. Wycherley is largely satiric, though possessed of some ambiguity about sexual freedom. Etherege condones license within the limits of a reasoned code. Dryden usually allows his characters to reach for, but not to grasp, forbidden fruits. Congreve likes to place the license in the past and to adapt attitudes found in his predecessors. Other writers bring other variations, but with Farquhar and Vanbrugh sex approaches the melodramatic and so admits a degree of growing hysteria or uncertainty about the subject. It was clearly an age when marriage customs and relations between the sexes occupied men's thoughts and conversation. Conventional notions were often ridiculed as writers groped for more satisfactory norms. Two short, not very attractive stories published together early in the Restoration as *The Ephesian and Cimmerian Matrons* illustrate the complexity of attitude. The first tells how a widow mourns her dead husband only to yield to a passing soldier in a charnel-house atmosphere. The other is even less edifying. Each is, however, interlarded with disquisitions on love—the first in a neo-Epicurean vein justifying the woman and denying the validity of the "Platonicks" of the century, the second (despite its sordid tale) justifying an idealistic code of love. The two plots of these stories and the two attitudes toward them give four versions of love which, along with the numerous contemporary treatises on marriage and polygamy, show that the age was like our own in possessing an irresistible urge to talk about matters that frightened and fascinated it. The persistency of the concern and the seeming cynicism in which it is cast are what continue to upset people.

We may dismiss from consideration the foolish old lechers, the cuckolds, and the willing widows, all of whom are comic types inherited from sources as distant as Chaucer and Elizabethan drama. But we cannot ignore the prudes, the rakish men of sense, or the witty virgin ladies seeking husbands. The prudes and the virgin ladies are foils to the witty rakes, either in revealing that the openness of the men entitles them to sexual freedom or by affirming, in whatever modified fashion, conventional moral standards. The prudes become stock comic types, and their frequent sober equivalents, the seriously virtuous characters, are usually rarefied to the point of becoming symbols. It is the virgin, witty young women who determine the end of the action, namely marriage. The normal movement of English comedy from disorder to order is confirmed by reinstatement of the characters after numerous trials into the most basic social unit, the family, and is strengthened by persuasive economic settlements. The threats to such movement come not so much from outside pressures as from rebellious impulses within, giving characters a more complex motivation than in earlier comic drama. The movement of a Restoration comedy is, therefore, perversely like that of romantic drama. Only the virgin woman is permitted her choice of husband; and the man's code, though freer, is nonetheless a code. How strong the final reconciliation is can be judged by the ritual dance that concludes so many of the comedies.

In other words, the Restoration discovered in the freedom of action of the young men and the freedom of speech of the young women a way of testing and even mocking the social values centering on marriage. Youth challenged the forms and conventions inherited from age, wittily mocking those elders who like Congreve's Lady Wishfort sought youth's freedom, or heartlessly dismissing the women who did not wait till marriage. Yet male Youth had to yield finally and become Age. The fact that marriage was the basis of the society economically as well as personally and that it repeatedly involves estates, lawyers, priests, and parents suggests the extent to which sex is commonly a shorthand for social freedom and convention throughout a wide range of subjects. The realism of detail and the witty questioning of social standards should not blind us to the romantic and socially affirmative conclusions. Plays as far separated in time and nature as Dryden's *Marriage a-la-mode* (1672) and Farquhar's *Beaux'*

Stratagem (1707) concern the nature of marriage and finally support either normal Restoration or very modern views of it. Ultimately, the strongest adverse criticism that can be made of Restoration comedy is that both its questioning and affirmation are too often conventional and mechanical. The many plays, however, that make these elements fresh yet again, or which are as profoundly ironic as *The Country Wife,* show that the concern with sex was a powerful, positive motive force. When that force diminished, when youthful disorder disappeared, comedy became sentiment, and morality became dull.

What is of greater significance than the use of sexual subjects is the playwrights' attitudes toward them. Our proper literary and sociological concern is with the way the plays mirror or distort the social reality on the one hand and the moral ideal on the other. Because the question of the relation between literature and morality is so difficult and because (it must be insisted again) Restoration comedy is so various, no one critical answer holds. The traditional explanations are (1) that the dramatists, themselves depraved, enjoyed picturing immoral actions; (2) that they created a fanciful never-never land which no one should take seriously; and (3) that they were only describing their age.

The first charge originated with the latter-day puritanical attackers of the stage, of whom the liveliest was the Jacobite Anglican cleric, Jeremy Collier [in his *A Short View of the Immorality and Profaneness of the English Stage,* Ch. 4].

> To sum up the Evidence. A fine Gentleman is a fine Whoring, Swearing, Smutty, Atheistical Man . . . a Man of Breeding and Figure that burlesques the *Bible,* Swears, and talks Smut to Ladies, speaks ill of his Friend behind his Back, and betraies his Interest: A fine Gentleman . . . Fine only in the Insignificancy of Life, the Abuse of Religion, and the Scandals of Conversation. These worshipful Things are the *Poets* Favourites.

Collier notoriously took offense at the comic representation of priests and was, as Dryden observed, obscene where the dramatists were wanton. He is of the kind given to moral outrage at literature in any age. Yet there is a germ of truth in what he says. To some extent the dramatists did delight in depicting behavior immoral or profane by the standards of the day. The lives of Etherege, Sedley, Buckingham, and Rochester are notorious, in Dryden's words on Buckingham in *Absolom and Achitophel,* "all for Women, Painting, Rhiming, Drinking; / Besides ten thousand freaks that dy'd in thinking." But the fact is that the plays use their sexual concerns to raise other serious matters and that their bawdry is at least of an open, healthy kind.

The second view, propounded by Charles Lamb [in his "On the Artificial Comedy of the Last Century"], sees in Restoration comedy a pleasant fantasy, a cloud-cuckoo land in which nothing is meant seriously and nothing therefore should give offense. It is difficult to believe that he had read the plays seriously or that, if he had, he was not ironically glossing them over with a fanciful pre-

Victorian prudery. Yet his view, too, has a certain validity if taken rightly. To some extent Restoration comedy does enact a fairy tale in which the improvident, brilliant young rascal of essentially sound principles ultimately gets wife and fortune and settles down. Regarded in these terms Restoration comedy has a plot movement like the novels of Jane Austen or, even more, like Fanny Burney's *Evelina,* with the romantic roles of men and women reversed. In a strange way there is something of romance and fairy tale in this drama. Although no one nowadays would be likely to consider it dominant, the romantic element is significant, as the combination of comic with heroic strains in many plays shows.

The third view, that Restoration comedy merely holds up a mirror to society, has been most cogently expressed by H. F. B. Brett-Smith [in *The Dramatic Works of Sir George Etherege*]: we "must adopt the point of view of the age, and not blame the author for picturing what he saw." The trouble with this view is both literary and sociological. It fails to account for most of what is in the plays and is refuted by the lives of the dramatists' contemporaries, great and small, which differed morally very little from our own. Yet this view, too, is a useful reminder of the accuracy of the dramatists in picturing London with the Mulberry Garden, the Mall, the New Exchange, or Locket's, with the dress and occupations of the time, and with the felt sense of life in the national metropolis. Such fidelity to actual life counters the wish-fulfilment in the movement of the plot and gives Restoration comedy a firm basis in social realities.

None of the interpretations just described has wide currency today. . . . The two prevailing views treat Restoration comedy either as expressive of a coherent philosophy shared by the heroes and dramatists or as fundamentally satiric in a criticism of social institutions and individual behavior.

The philosophy attributed to the dramatists is variously characterized as naturalism, libertinism, or neo-Epicureanism. Drawing, it is said, upon classical naturalism, Renaissance scepticism, and French libertinism, the dramatists exhibit "the naturalistic, skeptical, and libertine temper of the times" [Thomas H. Fujimura, *The Restoration Comedy of Wit*]. It is said that the dramatists who hold such views express them in the ambiguously good and bad versions of reality and appearance, art and nature which will be discussed subsequently. The philosophy offered a dignified, although almost despairing, comic vision into the nature of human experience and was a late humanist offshoot at once inimical to rational humanism and yet part of it. The contention that this philosophy is at work is most persuasive with respect to Etherege. For other writers it is not so much wrong as partial. For Dryden, it is almost wholly inadequate, for Congreve somewhat more relevant. It suits what is often called "the comedy of manners" far better than "the comedy of humours" practiced by Shadwell and others. But without question it has materially advanced our understanding of Restoration comedy. . . . (pp. 1-7)

At first sight the belief that Restoration comedy is satiric seems merely to confirm the obvious. Everyone knows

that in it the wits dismiss fools, fops, cuckolds, bumpkins, prudes, and other enemies of good sense. But not all critics have agreed that satire is the decisive element, that the truewits are themselves judged and found wanting. The view that the comedy is often dark because it shows the triumph of experience over hope has not been widely held. Yet it is the repeated tribute to Wycherley by writers as diverse as Dryden, Lansdowne, and Farquhar that the direction of his genius was satiric. Moreover when Dryden, in one of his many such passages, wrote of "The satire, wit, and strength of manly Wycherley" in his poem to Congreve, he explicitly claimed the same for Congreve. He might have done the same for himself, for Etherege (although *The Man of Mode* is somewhat ambiguous), and for others. The most explicit evidence that Restoration comedy is to be understood satirically, or at least ironically, is found in the banter of the prologues and epilogues, of which Dryden and Sir Car Scroop are masters, and in the Latin tags and the prefaces attached to the plays. The sociological evidence is yet more formidable. Restoration audiences often protested what they thought had gone too far (Congreve's characterization of Maskwell and Lady Touchwood in *The Old Bachelor,* for example), and it is impossible to believe that the "Cits" and other sober persons who heard themselves attacked would have continued to attend if they did not believe that the fine wits and ladies also smarted under the lash. The most elementary fact to be understood about Restoration comedy is one which the critics have had most difficulty in setting forth: that to it we must bring normal human assumptions to be shared with the dramatists and, at a distance of three centuries, with the original audiences; and that the judgment shared is based upon ethical and even social norms common to us and the Restoration. Once we understand this, we are in the theatre again as it has been known in every period and place where it has thrived. Living theatre, and pre-eminently comedy, is impossible without the assumption that we are seeing a play, a representation of reality to be judged by the shared experiences of normal human beings.

All of these interpretations of Restoration comedy are partial and, in varying degrees, conflicting. The conflict is no cause for surprise, for the comedy is not a simple or single thing; it is complex in every major instance and various in its decades of development. To understand that diversity and complexity it shares with other major periods of stage comedy, it is necessary to introduce further considerations. We may begin with the simple fact that the audience was by no means exclusively the court audience it is often claimed to be. The highly romantic assumptions about its differences from Shakespeare's are not verified by evidence. Like the Elizabethan, the Restoration theatre brought in many kinds of people. Pepys is respectable to those who know him well. Evelyn is respectable even to those who do not. More significantly, the Dorset Garden theatre of the Duke's Company had the reputation of drawing a bourgeois city audience, yet the plays performed there differ not at all from those performed by the other company. Throughout the Restoration, Tory plays were hooted at by Whig claques, whose vitality came from people antagonistic to the court. The audience included the mercantile "Cits," members of the country gentry on annual visits to London, lawyers and doctors, fine ladies and prostitutes, booby lords and wits. It is true that city and country found themselves laughed at in the plays, but the satiric compass of the plays included the wits and ladies as well, and the audience judged what were after all comedies and not documentaries by normal human standards. The mixed character of the audience is particularly involved in the resolution of the plays. The courtly wits certainly get their virgin brides and fortunes, but they get them by marrying into country or city families. The broad-based audience had the repeated satisfaction of seeing the young wits yield to the society they had spent so much of the play in rejecting and bow before forces from which they had claimed to be farthest removed. The profitable marriages they managed brought them under the control of, indeed reconciled them to, the familiar bonds of marriage and family, so uniting them with the normal human concerns of the diverse audience and affirming the vitality of the nation it represented. The cynics might yield with witty protest, but they yielded. No matter how witty and bold, the Harriets and Millamants retained their virginity, and their final triumph affirmed not only the wishes of the audience but also the realities and hopes of human life.

So regarded, Restoration comedy can be understood to resemble the comedy of other periods and languages, and this is probably the point most in need of understanding. Once that is accepted, we are entitled to ask how the comedy of these decades may be characterized so as to differentiate it from other English comedy. The most common term for it is of course "comedy of manners," a phrase which, like most other literary characterizations, is useful if not taken too seriously. It has been sharply questioned in recent years, some critics wishing to ban it altogether and others seeking to substitute such alternatives as "comedy of wit." What the objectors have in mind is the function of "wit" in attacking the society of the day. Manners, they argue, are precisely what is under attack, and the comedy deals with far more fundamental individual and social issues than can possibly be implied by that term. Such objections are well founded. Whether through satire, wit, libertinism, or humours, the dramatists are in search of truth, especially that true source of personal happiness and integrity which social forms may obscure or imperil. The proviso scene in *The Way of the World* is but one of many in which this effort is explicitly enacted on the stage. Less explicit enactments mark the plays from Dryden to Vanbrugh. The sense of anger, of danger, of despair, and sometimes almost of terror only half-concealed shows that the best of these plays are far more serious than a phrase like "comedy of manners" can imply.

Yet the idea of manners has some value. The plays *are* concerned with good form, do depict the social life of London, and do seek to formulate a meaningful role for the individual in society. Such concerns are better expressed by Miss Kathleen Lynch's phrase, "the social mode of Restoration comedy" [in her book by the same name], which defines "manners" more meaningfully. It must, after all, be admitted that whatever the essences involved, the surface of Restoration comedy is far more social than any earlier English comedy except Jonson's. If the risk of

Elizabethan "romantic comedy" lay in an effort to free human nature from the accidents of time and place that might go too far and take the plays out of touch with reality, the risk of Restoration comedy is that the effort to secure individual integrity and happiness in the face of society has little room for maneuver. Women may still disguise themselves as young men, but fairies with their magic potions, aerial spirits, and enchanters are as dead as Pan. The sea captain who could tell a Viola, "This is Illyria, Lady," is replaced by the servant announcing a guest or taking Lady Wishfort her ratafia. Only by traversing that narrow isthmus between foppery and boorishness and by defining his individuality in social terms could a character qualify for dignity and sympathy. We observe that Wycherley's Manly in *The Plain Dealer* wishes to leave London society for the New World, but also that Aphra Behn's play *The Widow Ranter* shows Virginia to be a social copy of England, and that Thomas Southerne's *Oroonoko* (though a tragedy of a kind) presents a blackamoor hero with manners yet more polished than those of the transplanted English, who themselves behave as if London had been transported with them to Surinam. The fact that Restoration comedy is almost always located in a real historical place, and that place London, and set in a historical time, the present, means that existing society sets the backdrop for the plays. The characters may challenge or alter it, but they cannot evade it. Whether or not their actions can be said to make up a comedy of manners, the arena in which they must act is the public, social one that is known, for all its comic distortions, to be a valid image of London. No one could quarrel with the description of this drama as social comedy.

In these plays the polarity of the individual and society is related to a thematic polarity commonly referred to as art and nature. Both terms are ambiguously positive and negative. Art is positive in suggesting that which human beings can add to life to make it more bearable and attractive; it is a positive symbol of what is good in society and civilization. It is also negative in suggesting the artfulness, artifice, sham, cant, and hypocrisy created by human beings to deceive others and themselves; it is a negative symbol of what is wrong in society and civilization. Nature is positive in suggesting what the individual feels and knows to be true in himself and others; it is a vital, unsullied norm within. But it is also negative in suggesting the selfishness, brutality, and anarchy that Thomas Hobbes saw in "a state of nature"; it represents that which would bring human decencies to ruin. My description is schematic in the interest of brevity. The comedies, which are not schematic, show how thoroughly the values and dangers represented by the terms mingle. Their complex implications are sorted out only with the utmost difficulty, and the characters are driven to adjust their conduct to ambiguous standards. In fact, the plays often suggest that man is caught in the dilemma of his inability to take the positive without the negative, to adjust his own drives to social needs, or the world to himself. If it turns out that marriage is the only solution advanced, that is only partly because marriage is the conventional ending of comedy. More importantly it brings order to individual lives within an orderly society and affords, in its promise of generation, man's deep hopes for a meaningful future.

The dilemma just described appears in different guises in other forms of Restoration drama. If the problem is posed "seriously" rather than "comically," we are in the world of the heroic plays and tragedies. Since these are relatively less known, I shall deal with them more briefly. Heroic plays are an acquired taste. Dryden, the undoubted master of the form, wrote that a heroic play "ought to be an imitation, in little, of an heroic poem [i.e., epic]; and, consequently, that Love and Valour ought to be the subject of it" [in his Preface to *The Conquest of Granada*]. He went on to justify spectacle and other imaginative effects, saying that they were necessary to convince spectators of the reality represented, and to say that he would refuse to weigh "love and honour . . . by drams and scruples." Yet in his heroic plays "Love and Valour" are usually found defined as "love and honour" and weighed carefully, if not as minutely as in contemporary French drama. Moreover what Dryden speaks of as a single subject ("Love and Valour") is closely related to the "nature" and "art" of the comedies. Instead of treating society in terms of contemporary London, however, the heroic play seeks liberation in another time and place, thereby slackening the hold of contemporary society over individuals, taking man closer to the "state of nature," and allowing for grander conflict between natural individualism and civilized society. Nature and art are, then, magnified in special ways by heroic drama, and it is not surprising that it should be Dryden who introduced into the language (in Part One of *The Conquest of Granada*) the phrase, "the noble savage." His "heroic" rather than sentimental definition of the conflict of individualism with society produced those operatic flights of tough-minded rhodomontade that have been hard for many critics to accept.

The heroic play is related to comedy in another major respect, growing from the rhetorical conception of poetry. Both are distortions in the artist's mirror of the norm of nature, the comic in the lower direction of satire, the heroic in the higher of panegyric and heroic. No doubt the departure seems greater for heroic drama, but it is nonetheless a departure from the same normative standard. Dryden explains the matter well in his "Account" prefixed to *Annus Mirabilis:*

> Such descriptions or images . . . are, as I have said, the adequate delight of heroic poesy; for they beget admiration, which is its proper object; as the images of the burlesque, which is contrary to this, by the same reason beget laughter: for the one shows nature beautified, as in the picture of a fair woman, which we all admire; the other shows her deformed, as in that of a lazar, or of a fool with distorted face and antic gestures, at which we cannot forbear to laugh, because it is a deviation from nature.

It is not true, therefore, that the heroic plays represent a norm and the comedies divergence from it. There are ideal norms in some of the comedies and real villains in the heroic plays. More than that, the "admiration" or wonder evoked by the heroic plays involves its own distortions; they are closer to the comedies than is usually acknowledged. In *Marriage a-la-mode* or *The Spanish Friar*, comic scenes alternate or are integrated with heroic, and in both

Southerne's *Oroonoko* and Aphra Behn's *Widow Ranter,* to name but two of many examples, scenes of comedy sandwich the heroic plot. Both comedy and heroic drama further employ a central love plot complicated by intrigue; heroic argument is the counterpart of comic repartee; and the code of valor is a heroic equivalent of comic canons of sensible behavior. Both forms involve artistic distortions, but what is heightened is recognizable human life.

There is a further respect in which, despite the differences, the heroic play and comedy share common ground. Viewed in seventeenth century terms, their wit and much of their metaphor are not those of imagination (or "fancy"), which discerns resemblances in things unlike, but of reason (or judgment), which discerns the differences between things that seem alike. Whatever the purely imagistic strands of the plays, far-fetched comparisons are repeatedly given to the fops to reveal their false wit. The close discrimination of fops from wits, of permissible self-interest from exploitation, and of art from nature provides a major occupation for the comedy. Similarly, the heroic play discriminates (with more minuteness than Dryden chose to admit) between rival claims of love pressed upon a man or woman, between the cross-purposes of honour, and between the claims of love and honour themselves. At root both forms are arts of discrimination and judgment, although their imaginative configurations, selections of experience, and rhetorical heightenings of course differ.

In the Restoration, the prevailing comic language is prose, the heroic, rhymed verse, and the tragic, rhymed or blank verse. Yet the cadence and tone are again remarkably alike, as in these passages treating the agonies of love.

> Why, whither in the devil's name am I a-going now? Hum—let me think—is not this Silvia's house, the cave of that enchantress, and which consequently I ought to shun as I would infection? To enter here, is to put on the envenomed shirt, to run into the embraces of a fever, and in some raving fit be led to plunge myself into that more consuming fire, a woman's arms. Ha! well recollected, I will recover my reason, and begone. (Congreve, *The Old Bachelor,* III, ii).

> O heav'ns! is there not punishment enough
> In loving well, if you will have't a crime,
> But you must add fresh torment daily to't,
> And punish us like peevish rivals still,
> Because we fain would find a heaven here?
> But did there never any love like me,
> That, untried tortures, you must find me out?
> Others, at worst, you force to kill themselves;
> But I must be self-murdress of my love,
> Yet will not grant me pow'r to end my life,
> My cruel life; for when a lover's hopes
> Are dead and gone, life is unmerciful. [. . .
> *weeps*]
> (Wycherley, *The Plain Dealer,* IV, ii)

> I'm pleased and pained, since first her eyes I saw,
> As I were stung with some tarantula.
> Arms, and the dusty field, I less admire,
> And soften strangely in some new desire;
> Honor burns in me not so fiercely bright,
> But pale as fires when mastered by the light . . .
> I fear it is the lethargy of love!

'Tis he; I feel him now in every part:
Like a new lord he vaunts about my heart;
Surveys, in state, each corner of my breast,
While poor fierce I, that was, am dispossessed.
I'm bound; but I will rouse my rage again;
And, though no hope of liberty remain,
I'll fright my keeper when I shake my chain.
(Dryden, 1 *The Conquest of Granada,* III, i)

For all their obvious differences, the three passages share a common ethos and similarity in imagery. What is most interesting, however, is the tone. Congreve's Heartwell is foolish but psychologically just. Wycherley's Fidelia (who, disguised as a man, must woo the faithless mistress of the man she loves) is less psychological than sentimental and tragic. Dryden's Almanzor is the best self-analyst of the three. But how does the tone of his speech compare with those of Heartwell and Fidelia? I think that the concluding triplet is crucial. It shows that we are intended to smile—a little. He is no poor dove like Fidelia, and in fact his predicament is very close to Heartwell's. Whether he knows it or not, his speech mingles the admirable with the excessive. Proof that this modern response was shared by Dryden's contemporaries can be found in Colley Cibber's recollections of the faults of the able actor Booth in playing Morat, a Herculean villain in Dryden's heroic play, *Aureng-Zebe.*

> There are in this fierce Character so many Sentiments of avow'd Barbarity, Insolence, and Vainglory, that they blaze even to a ludicrous Lustre, and doubtless the Poet included those to make his Spectators laugh while they admir'd them; but *Booth* thought it depreciated the Dignity of Tragedy to raise a Smile in any part of it, and therefore cover'd these kind of Sentiments with a scrupulous Coldness and unmov'd Delivery.

The mingling of laughter with admiration in the heroic play, like that of unsullied feminine fidelity with depravity in Wycherley's comedy, shows how much alive contemporary audiences were to shades of tone, and how mature were sensibilities that could accept contradictory emotions in a single experience. The audiences and playwrights had an interest in, and a literary language for, psychological shades of meaning and responses to them. More fundamentally, their rhetorical conceptions of art enabled them to glide easily from the admirable to the ludicrous or to mix them finely, as is shown not only by Dryden's heroic plays but also by much of his nondramatic poetry.

I have chosen to speak in the main of elements common to the comedies and the heroic plays, hoping to make intelligible a form of serious drama which is little known and less understood by comparing it with the relatively more familiar comedies. But a few words must be said about their differences, which are those of atmosphere, subject, and theme. The comedies take place in St. James's Park or the Mall, from which the heavens are visible but are seldom looked at. The heroic plays take place in a celestial realm, and their characters are brilliant comets burning fiercely through the sky and not seldom crashing to earth. What they were like on the stage can best be represented by quoting Colley Cibber again, this time on the heroic actor Kynaston.

> He had a piercing Eye, and in Characters of heroick Life a quick imperious Vivacity in his Tone of Voice that painted the Tyrant truly terrible. There were two plays of *Dryden* in which he shone with uncommon Lustre; in *Aurenge-Zebe* he play'd *Morat,* and in *Don Sebastian, Muley Moloch;* in both these Parts he had a fierce, Lion-like Majesty in his Port and Utterance that gave the Spectator a kind of trembling Admiration!

Restoration tragedy is less easily defined, because it varies so much more. The "heroic" variation is best represented by Dryden's *All for Love,* the "fatalistic" variation by his *Don Sebastian,* and the "emotional" variation by Otway's *Venice Preserv'd* and *The Orphan.* In all these, emotion as it is usually understood in tragedy plays a larger role than it does in the heroic play. It is felt more directly, is subjected to less rational analysis. In writing tragedy, the dramatists usually held to the same distance in time and space from the English present that marked heroic tragedy, although the tragic scene showed man in a European or classical state rather than in a state of nature. The tragedies did, however, tend to touch upon the more domestic elements that are closer to comedy. They are chiefly concerned with love, whose domesticity the tragic dramatists seek to transcend by treating it as illicit, exotic, or fated. Apart from Dryden, the public mode of Restoration literature is surprisingly absent from tragedy, and even in his tragedies, the center is most often love or fate, rather than power, justice, or kingship such as are typical of Shakespeare. Whether the proper word for this aspect of the love tragedy is domestic or romantic may be open to question, but the experience is brought closer to the conditions of the audience than it had been in the earlier period. As Rowe said in his Prologue to *The Fair Penitent,* "We ne'er can pity what we ne'er can share." The tragedy of fate in Dryden and Lee's *Oedipus* and in Dryden's later plays raises metaphysical concerns commonly harmonized with love.

If pity and fear are the emotions aroused and purged by classical tragedy, it was pity and admiration which most Restoration tragedy emphasized. Cibber's tribute to Mrs. Barry, though confined to one actress, suggests the character of the tragic as distinguished from the heroic drama.

> Mrs. *Barry,* in Characters of Greatness, had a Presence of elevated Dignity, her Mien and Motion superb and gracefully majestick; her Voice full, clear, and strong, so that no Violence of Passion could be too much for her: And when Distress or Tenderness possess'd her, she subsided into the most affecting Melody and Softness. In the Art of exciting Pity she had a Power beyond all the Actresses I have yet seen, or what your imagination can conceive. Of the former of these two great Excellencies [i.e., Dignity] she gave the most delightful Proofs in almost all the Heroic Plays of *Dryden* and *Lee;* and of the latter [Pity] in the softer Passions of *Otway's Monimia* and *Belvidera.*

Tragedy maintained the pressure of society upon the individual felt in comedy and heroic plays but dealt with a thwarted passion rather than with reason or volition, evoking pity rather than terror. Although in some respects the least sentimental period in our literature, with Otway and also at times with Lee the age found full scope for tears.

A second important emotion aroused by Restoration tragedy was admiration, and it is perhaps this response which most distinguishes the tragic drama of the age from that in other periods. Its introduction as a dramatic ideal came immediately from the epic impulse of the age and through the heroic drama. Its earlier antecedents lie in the addition of *admiratio* to the *dulce et utile* set by Horace as the ends of poetry and in the heroic or "Herculean" drama that had continued since antiquity as an important but rather minor strain. We have already observed how the admirable in the heroic plays admitted the comic, but it also admitted the softer emotion of pity by combining "Love and Valour" into a single dramatic subject. Cibber's comments on Booth, Kynaston, and Mrs. Barry may be recalled. Admiration (with its Restoration sense inclusive of wonder), pity, and laughter are not responses we have lost. But since the Romantics, perhaps since the eighteenth century, we have forgotten how to experience the three together. Dryden is the last to create characters in the tradition of heroic admiration, and *Don Sebastian* is the last of his great plays to show that element in strength. What seems to have happened after him is that a growing tendency of moralism gradually supplanted the heroic with a moral form of the admirable. The tendency is evident in Dryden himself, although never to the point of dominant moral sentiment. For him, the sublimity of the heroic provided that element of exaggerated scope which admitted something of tragic fear, even while absorbing it in admiration. Significantly, the fear lasts longer in his villains than in his tragic heroes, who achieve greater, less comic credibility by the encounters with fate and love.

Instead of fear or admiration, Otway and Lee supplied melodrama, and they had their lesser imitators. The development of this element is often laid to the disturbed personalities of the two men. But in fact, the plays exhibit an element of hysteria related to passion that was found to be highly effective on the stage, even if we may agree that it lacks the dignity of the highest tragedy. There are some signs of comic forms of hysteria in the later Restoration comic writers as well, and in both genres it is due partly to sensationalism and partly to a diminishing of theatrical nerve in the face of the audience's growing appetite for moral and tearful sentiment. No dramatist after Dryden writes convincingly as if fate or its equivalent in metaphysical terms were a reality. Having left behind these larger forces, the other dramatists had to content themselves with conflicts within and between individuals, working them up to pitches of passion that provoked pity. To turn again to faculty psychology, the role of the will is the crucial factor in accounting for changes in the forms of Restoration drama. In the libertine code of the comedies and in the glorious posings of the heroic plays, the will determined the action of the heroes and heroines. They exulted in their freedom—at least till the end, when reason or society or both brought the will under control. Dryden's trag-

edies show the will in a dilemma, struggling with or against reason or passion, pitted against larger forces such as fate. With Otway the passions rather than the will are the center of things, challenging will and reason alike, as if a suppressed sexuality lay at the root of it all. Theatrically, all forms of Restoration drama are high-pitched, far different from the mood of all passion spent in Milton's *Samson Agonistes,* the greatest closet drama published in the age.

Since this essay is [introductory in nature], its emphasis has been upon the common elements and resemblances that make a general charcterization possible. A proper historical or critical reading of the plays themselves would of course reveal many differences between playwrights, numerous mixed forms, and steady change. Plays like *The Rehearsal* (written by Buckingham and others) do not fit into any of the forms discussed, except possibly as parody. More important, my account has left out the sheer delight the comedies gave their audiences and the moving images of tragic dignity seen on those candlelit stages. In the following century people were not quite sure what to do with Restoration plays, but they went on cutting and applauding them, emerging with the remarkable judgment that Otway was second only to Shakespeare. That judgment, like the loss in popularity of the heroic play, tells us more about the new century than the old. For the Restoration, it is more significant that Dryden should do what no one else has been able to do, seek to draw, as he said, the bow of Ulysses and in *All for Love* attempt to rival Shakespeare on his highest ground. The result was not *Antony and Cleopatra,* but it was a fine play and gave evidence both of the continuity of English drama and of the vitality of the dramatic impulse in the age. It was an age of great theatre, for though the plays ran for short runs they were acted by some of the greatest players in English theatrical history, and in a physical theatre of very considerable ingenuity and flexibility. The Restoration produced no Shakespeare, and has thereby something in common with all other periods save Shakespeare's own. But it did achieve the second great harvest of English drama and was the last for many generations in which the theatre lived as a creative force. (pp. 7-17)

Earl Miner, in an introduction to Restoration Dramatists: A Collection of Critical Essays, *edited by Earl Miner, Prentice-Hall, Inc., 1966, pp. 1-18.*

William Hazlitt

[One of the most important commentators of the Romantic age, Hazlitt was an English critic and journalist. He is best known for his descriptive criticism in which he stressed that no motives beyond judgment and analysis are necessary on the part of the critic. In the following excerpt, which originally appeared in his Lectures on the English Comic Writers *(1819), Hazlitt comments on those figures he considers the four principal Restoration comic dramatists: William Congreve, William Wycherley, John Vanbrugh, and George Farquhar.]*

Comedy is a "graceful ornament to the civil order; the Corinthian capital of polished society." Like the mirrors which have been added to the sides of one of our theatres, it reflects the images of grace, of gaiety, and pleasure double, and completes the perspective of human life. To read a good comedy is to keep the best company in the world, where the best things are said, and the most amusing happen. The wittiest remarks are always ready on the tongue, and the luckiest occasions are always at hand to give birth to the happiest conceptions. Sense makes strange havoc of nonsense. Refinement acts as a foil to affectation, and affectation to ignorance. Sentence after sentence tells. We don't know which to admire most, the observation or the answer to it. We would give our fingers to be able to talk so ourselves, or to hear others talk so. In turning over the pages of the best comedies, we are almost transported to another world, and escape from this dull age to one that was all life, and whim, and mirth, and humour. The curtain rises, and a gayer scene presents itself, as on the canvas of Watteau. We are admitted behind the scenes like spectators at court, on a levee or birthday; but it is the court, the gala day of wit and pleasure, of gallantry and Charles II! What an air breathes from the name! what a rustling of silks and waving of plumes! what a sparkling of diamond earrings and shoe-buckles! What bright eyes (Ah, those were Waller's Sacharissa's as she passed.)! what killing looks and graceful motions! How the faces of the whole ring are dressed in smiles! how the repartee goes round! how wit and folly, elegance and awkward imitation of it, set one another off! Happy, thoughtless age, when kings and nobles led purely ornamental lives; when the utmost stretch of a morning's study went no farther than the choice of a sword-knot, or the adjustment of a side-curl; when the soul spoke out in all the pleasing eloquence of dress; and beaux and belles, enamoured of themselves in one another's follies, fluttered like gilded butterflies, in giddy mazes, through the walks of St. James's Park!

The four principal writers of this style of comedy (which I think the best) are undoubtedly Wycherley, Congreve, Vanbrugh, and Farquhar. The dawn was in Etherege, as its latest close was in Sheridan.—It is hard to say which of these four is best, or in what each of them excels, they had so many and such great excellences.

Congreve is the most distinct from the others, and the most easily defined, both from what he possessed and from what he wanted. He had by far the most wit and elegance, with less of other things, of humour, character, incident, &c. His style is inimitable, nay perfect. It is the highest model of comic dialogue. Every sentence is replete with sense and satire, conveyed in the most polished and pointed terms. Every page presents a shower of brilliant conceits, is a tissue of epigrams in prose, is a new triumph of wit, a new conquest over dulness. The fire of artful raillery is nowhere else so well kept up. This style, which he was almost the first to introduce, and which he carried to the utmost pitch of classical refinement, reminds one exactly of Collins's description of wit as opposed to humour,

> Whose jewels in his crisped hair
> Are placed each other's light to share.

Sheridan will not bear a comparison with him in the regular antithetical construction of his sentences, and in the mechanical artifices of his style, though so much later, and

though style in general has been so much studied, and in the mechanical part so much improved since then. It bears every mark of being what he himself in the dedication of one of his plays tells us that it was, a spirited copy taken off and carefully revised from the most select society of his time, exhibiting all the sprightliness, ease, and animation of familiar conversation, with the correctness and delicacy of the most finished composition. His works are a singular treat to those who have cultivated a taste for the niceties of English style: there is a peculiar flavour in the very words, which is to be found in hardly any other writer. To the mere reader his writings would be an irreparable loss: to the stage they are already become a dead letter, with the exception of one of them, *Love for Love*. This play is as full of character, incident, and stage-effect, as almost any of those of his contemporaries, and fuller of wit than any of his own, except perhaps the *Way of the World*. It still acts, and is still acted well. The effect of it is prodigious on the well-informed spectator. . . . The gay, unconcerned opening of this play, and the romantic generosity of the conclusion, where Valentine, when about to resign his mistress, declares—"I never valued fortune, but as it was subservient to my pleasure; and my only pleasure was to please this lady,"—are alike admirable. The peremptory bluntness and exaggerated descriptions of Sir Sampson Legend are in a vein truly oriental, with a Shakespearian cast of language, and form a striking contrast to the quaint credulity and senseless superstitions of Foresight. The remonstrance of his son to him, "to divest him, along with his inheritance, of his reason, thoughts, passions, inclinations, affections, appetites, senses, and the huge train of attendants which he brought into the world with him," with his valet's accompanying comments, is one of the most eloquent and spirited specimens of wit, pathos, and morality, that is to be found. The short scene with Trapland, the money-broker, is of the first water. What a picture is here drawn of Tattle! "More misfortunes, Sir!" says Jeremy. "*Valentine*. What, another dun? "*Jeremy*. No, Sir, but Mr. Tattle is come to wait upon you." What an introduction to give of an honest gentleman in the shape of a misfortune! The scenes between him, Miss Prue, and Ben, are of a highly coloured description. Mrs. Frail and Mrs. Foresight are "sisters every way;" and the bodkin which Mrs. Foresight brings as a proof of her sister's levity of conduct, and which is so convincingly turned against her as a demonstration of her own—"Nay, if you come to that, where did you find that bodkin?"—is one of the trophies of the moral justice of the comic drama. The *Old Bachelor* and *Double Dealer* are inferior to *Love for Love*, but one is never tired of reading them. The fault of the last is, that Lady Touchwood approaches, in the turbulent impetuosity of her character, and measured tone of her declamation, too near to the tragedy-queen; and that Maskwell's plots puzzle the brain by their intricacy, as they stagger our belief by their gratuitous villany. Sir Paul and Lady Pliant, and my Lord and Lady Froth, are also scarcely credible in the extravagant insipidity and romantic vein of their follies, in which they are notably seconded by the lively Mr. Brisk and "dying Ned Careless."

The *Way of the World* was the author's last and most carefully finished performance. It is an essence almost too fine; and the sense of pleasure evaporates in an aspiration after something that seems too exquisite ever to have been realised. After inhaling the spirit of Congreve's wit, and tasting "love's thrice reputed nectar" in his works, the head grows giddy in turning from the highest point of rapture to the ordinary business of life; and we can with difficulty recall the truant fancy to those objects which we are fain to take up with here, *for better, for worse.* What can be more enchanting than Millamant and her morning thoughts, her *doux sommeils?* What more provoking than her reproach to her lover, who proposes to rise early, "Ah! idle creature!" The meeting of these two lovers after the abrupt dismissal of Sir Wilful, is the height of careless and voluptuous elegance, as if they moved in air, and drank a finer spirit of humanity.

> *Millamant.* Like Phœbus sung the no less amo-
>   rous boy.
> *Mirabell.* Like Daphne she, as lovely and as coy.

Millamant is the perfect model of the accomplished fine lady:

> Come, then, the colours and the ground prepare,
> Dip in the rainbow, trick her off in air;
> Choose a firm cloud, before it falls, and in it
> Catch, ere she change, the Cynthia of a minute.

She is the ideal heroine of the comedy of high life, who arrives at the height of indifference to everything from the height of satisfaction; to whom pleasure is as familiar as the air she draws; elegance worn as a part of her dress; wit the habitual language which she hears and speaks; love, a matter of course; and who has nothing to hope or to fear, her own caprice being the only law to herself and rule to those about her. Her words seem composed of amorous sighs; her looks are glanced at prostrate admirers or envious rivals.

> If there's delight in love, 'tis when I see
> That heart that others bleed for, bleed for me.

She refines on her pleasures to satiety; and is almost stifled in the incense that is offered to her person, her wit, her beauty, and her fortune. Secure of triumph, her slaves tremble at her frown: her charms are so irresistible, that her conquests give her neither surprise nor concern. "Beauty the lover's gift?" she exclaims, in answer to Mirabell—"Dear me, what is a lover that it can give? Why one makes lovers as fast as one pleases, and they live as long as one pleases, and they die as soon as one pleases; and then if one pleases, one makes more." We are not sorry to see her tamed down at last, from her pride of love and beauty, into a wife. She is good-natured and generous, with all her temptations to the contrary; and her behaviour to Mirabell reconciles us to her treatment of Witwoud and Petulant, and of her country admirer, Sir Wilful.

Congreve has described all this in his character of Millamant, but he has done no more; and if he had, he would have done wrong. He has given us the finest idea of an artificial character of this kind; but it is still the reflection of an artificial character. The springs of nature, passion, or imagination are but feebly touched. The impressions appealed to, and with masterly address, are habitual, external, and conventional advantages; the ideas of birth, of fortune, of connexions, of dress, accomplishment, fashion, the opinion of the world, of crowds of admirers, continually come into play, flatter our vanity, bribe our interest, soothe our indolence, fall in with our prejudices;—it is these that support the goddess of our idolatry, with which she is everything, and without which she would be nothing. The mere fine lady of comedy, compared with the heroine of romance or poetry, when stripped of her adventitious ornaments and advantages, is too much like the doll stripped of its finery. In thinking of Millamant, we think almost as much of her dress as of her person: it is not so with respect to Rosalind or Perdita. The poet has painted them differently; in colours which "nature's own sweet and cunning hand laid on," with health, with innocence, with gaiety, "wild wit, invention ever new;" with pure red and white, like the wilding's blossoms; with warbled wood-notes, like the feathered choir's; with thoughts fluttering on the wings of imagination, and hearts panting and breathless with eager delight. The interest we feel is in themselves; the admiration they excite is for themselves. They do not depend upon the drapery of circumstances. It is nature that "blazons herself" in them. Imogen is the same in a lonely cave as in a court; nay more, for she there seems something heavenly—a spirit or a vision; and, as it were, shames her destiny, brighter for the foil of circumstances. Millamant is nothing but a fine lady; and all her airs and affectation would be blown away with the first breath of misfortune. Enviable in drawing-rooms, adorable at her toilette, fashion, like a witch, has thrown its spell around her; but if that spell were broken, her power of fascination would be gone. For that reason I think the character better adapted for the stage: it is more artificial, more theatrical, more meretricious. . . . Somehow, this sort of acquired elegance is more a thing of costume, of air and manner; and in comedy, or on the comic stage, the light and familiar, the trifling, superficial and agreeable, bears, perhaps, rightful sway over that which touches the affections, or exhausts the fancy. There is a callousness in the worst characters in the *Way of the World,* in Fainall, and his wife and Mrs. Marwood, not very pleasant; and a grossness in the absurd ones, such as Lady Wishfort and Sir Wilful, which is not a little amusing. Witwoud wishes to disclaim, as far as he can, his relationship to this last character, and says, "he's but his half brother;" to which Mirabell makes answer—"Then, perhaps, he's but half a fool." Peg is an admirable caricature of rustic awkwardness and simplicity, which is carried to excess without any offence, from a sense of contrast to the refinement of the chief characters in the play. The description of Lady Wishfort's face is a perfect piece of painting. The force of style in this author at times amounts to poetry. Waitwell, who personates Sir Rowland, and Foible, his accomplice in the matrimonial scheme upon her mistress, hang as a dead weight upon the plot. They are mere tools in the hands of Mirabell, and want life and interest. Congreve's characters can all of them speak well, they are mere machines when they come to act. Our author's superiority deserted him almost entirely with his wit. His serious and tragic poetry is frigid and jejune to an unaccountable degree. His *forte* was the description of actual manners, whether elegant or absurd; and when he could not deride the one or embellish the other, his attempts at romantic passion or imaginary enthusiasm are forced, abortive, and ridiculous, or commonplace. The description of the ruins of a temple in the beginning of the *Mourning Bride,* was a great stretch of his poetic genius. It has, however, been over-rated, particularly by Dr. Johnson, who could have done nearly as well himself for a single passage in the same style of moralising and sentimental description. To justify this general censure, and to show how the lightest and most graceful wit degenerates into the heaviest and most bombastic poetry, I will give one description out of his tragedy, which will be enough. It is the speech which Gonsalez addresses to Almeria:

> Be every day of your long life like this.
> The sun, bright conquest, and your brighter eyes
> Have all conspired to blaze promiscuous light,
> And bless this day with most unequal lustre.
> Your royal father, my victorious lord,
> Loaden with spoils, and ever-living laurel,
> Is entering now, in martial pomp, the palace.
> Five hundred miles precede his solemn march,
> Which groan beneath the weight of Moorish
>   wealth.
> Chariots of war, adorn'd with glittering gems,
> Succeed; and next, a hundred neighing steeds,
> White as the fleecy rain on Alpine hills;
> That bound, and foam, and champ the golden
>   bit,
> As they disdain'd the victory they grace.
> Prisoners of war in shining fetters follow:
> And captains of the noblest blood of Afrie
> Sweat by his chariot-wheels, and lick and grind,
> With gnashing teeth, the dust his triumphs raise.
> The swarming populace spread every wall,
> And cling, as if with claws they did enforce
> Their hold, through clifted stones stretching and
>   staring
> As if they were all eyes, and every limb
> Would feed its faculty of admiration,
> While you alone retire, and shun this sight;
> This sight, which is indeed not seen (though
>   twice
> The multitude should gaze) in absence of your
>   eyes.

This passage seems, in part, an imitation of Bolingbroke's entry into London. The style is as different from Shakespeare as it is from that of Witwoud and Petulant. It is plain that the imagination of the author could not raise itself above the burlesque. His 'Mask of Semele,' 'Judgment of Paris,' and other occasional poems, are even worse. I would not advise any one to read them, or if I did, they would not.

Wycherley was before Congreve; and his *Country Wife* will last longer than anything of Congreve's as a popular acting play. It is only a pity that it is not entirely his own [the plot was partly borrowed from Molière]; but it is enough so to do him never-ceasing honour, for the best things are his own. His humour is, in general, broader, his characters more natural, and his incidents more striking than Congreve's. It may be said of Congreve, that the workmanship overlays the materials: in Wycherley, the casting of the parts and the fable are alone sufficient to ensure success. We forget Congreve's characters, and only remember what they say: we remember Wycherley's char-

acters, and the incidents they meet with, just as if they were real, and forget what they say, comparatively speaking. Miss Peggy (or Mrs. Margery Pinchwife) is a character that will last for ever, I should hope; and even when the original is no more, if that should ever be, while self-will, curiosity, art, and ignorance are to be found in the same person, it will be just as good and as intelligible as ever in the description, because it is built on first principles, and brought out in the fullest and broadest manner. Agnes, in Molière's play, has a great deal of the same unconscious impulse and heedless *naïveté,* but hers is sentimentalised and varnished over (in the French fashion) with long-winded apologies and analytical distinctions. It wants the same simple force and *home* truth. It is not so direct and downright. Miss Peggy is not even a novice in casuistry: she blurts out her meaning before she knows what she is saying, and she speaks her mind by her actions oftener than by her words. The outline of the plot is the same; but the point-blank hits and master-strokes, the sudden thoughts and delightful expedients—such as her changing the letters, the meeting her husband plump in the Park as she is running away from him as fast as her heels can carry her, her being turned out of doors by her jealous booby of a husband, and sent by him to her lover disguised as Alicia, her sister-in-law—occur first in the modern play. There are scarcely any incidents or situations on the stage which tell like these for pantomimic effect, which give such a tingling to the blood, or so completely take away the breath with expectation and surprise. Miss Prue, in *Love for Love* is a lively reflection of Miss Peggy, but without the bottom and weight of metal. Hoyden is a match for her in constitution and complete effect, as Corinna, in the *Confederacy,* is in mischief: but without the wit. . . . Pinchwife, or Moody (as he is at present called), is, like others of Wycherley's moral characters, too rustic, abrupt, and cynical. He is a more disagreeable, but less tedious character, than the husband of Agnes, and both seem, by all accounts, to have been rightly served. The character of Sparkish is quite new, and admirably hit off. He is an exquisite and suffocating coxcomb; a pretender to wit and letters, without common understanding, or the use of his senses. The class of character is thoroughly exposed and understood; but he persists in his absurd conduct so far, that it becomes extravagant and disgusting, if not incredible, from mere weakness and foppery. Yet there is something in him that we are inclined to tolerate at first, as his professing that "with him a wit is the first title to respect;" and we regard his unwillingness to be pushed out of the room, and coming back, in spite of their teeth, to keep the company of wits and raillers, as a favourable omen. But he utterly disgraces his pretensions before he has done. With all his faults and absurdities, he is, however, a much less offensive character than Tattle. Horner is a stretch of probability in the first concoction of that ambiguous character (for he does not appear at present on the stage as Wycherley made him); but notwithstanding the indecency and indirectness of the means he employs to carry his plans into effect, he deserves every sort of consideration and forgiveness, both for the display of his own ingenuity, and the deep insight he discovers into human nature—such as it was in the time of Wycherley. The author has commented on this character, and the double meaning of the name, in his *Plain Dealer,* borrowing the remarks, and almost the very words, of Molière, who has brought forward and defended his own work against the objections of the precise part of his audience in his *Critique de l'Ecole des Femmes.* There is no great harm in these occasional plagiarisms, except that they make one uncomfortable at other times, and distrustful of the originality of the whole. The *Plain Dealer* is Wycherley's next best work, and is a most severe and poignant moral satire. There is a heaviness about it indeed, an extravagance, an overdoing both in the style, the plot, and characters; but the truth of feeling and the force of interest prevail over every objection. The character of Manly, the Plain Dealer, is violent, repulsive and uncouth, which is a fault, though one that seems to have been intended for the sake of contrast; for the portrait of consummate, artful hypocrisy in Olivia is perhaps rendered more striking by it. The indignation excited against this odious and pernicious quality by the masterly exposure to which it is here subjected, is "a discipline of humanity." No one can read this play attentively without being the better for it as long as he lives. It penetrates to the core; it shows the immorality and hateful effects of duplicity, by showing it fixing its harpy fangs in the heart of an honest and worthy man. It is worth ten volumes of sermons. The scenes between Manly after his return, Olivia, Plausible, and Novel, are instructive examples of unblushing impudence, of shallow pretensions to principle, and of the most mortifying reflections on his own situation, and bitter sense of female injustice and ingratitude on the part of Manly. The devil of hypocrisy and hardened assurance seems worked up to the highest pitch of conceivable effrontery in Olivia, when, after confiding to her cousin the story of her infamy, she in a moment turns round upon her for some sudden purpose, and affecting not to know the meaning of the other's allusions to what she has just told her, reproaches her with forging insinuations to the prejudice of her character and in violation of their friendship. "Go! you're a censorious ill woman." This is more trying to the patience than anything in the *Tartuffe.* The name of this heroine, and her overtures to Fidelia as the page, seem to have been suggested by *Twelfth Night.* It is curious to see how the same subject is treated by two such different authors as Shakespeare and Wycherley. The widow Blackacre and her son are like her lawsuit—everlasting. A more lively, palpable, bustling, ridiculous picture cannot be drawn. Jerry is a hopeful lad, though undutiful, and gets out of bad hands into worse. Goldsmith evidently had an eye to these two precious characters in *She Stoops to Conquer.* Tony Lumpkin and his mother are of the same family, and the incident of the theft of the casket of jewels and the bag of parchments is nearly the same in both authors. Wycherley's other plays are not so good. The *Gentleman Dancing Master* is a long, foolish farce, in the exaggerated manner of Molière, but without his spirit or whimsical invention. *Love in a Wood,* though not what one would wish it to be for the author's sake or our own, is much better, and abounds in several rich and highly-coloured scenes, particularly those in which Miss Lucy, her mother Crossbite, Dapperwit, and Alderman Gripe are concerned. Some of the subordinate characters and intrigues in this comedy are grievously spun out. Wycherley, when he got hold of

a good thing, or sometimes even of a bad one, was determined to make the most of it, and might have said with Dogberry truly enough, "Had I the tediousness of a king, I could find in my heart to bestow it all upon your worships." In reading this author's best works—those which one reads most frequently over, and knows almost by heart, one cannot help thinking of the treatment he received from Pope about his verses. It was hardly excusable in a boy of sixteen to an old man of seventy.

Vanbrugh comes next, and holds his own fully with the best. He is no writer at all as to mere authorship; but he makes up for it by a prodigious fund of comic invention and ludicrous description, bordering somewhat on caricature. Though he did not borrow from him, he was much more like Molière in genius than Wycherley was, who professedly imitated him. He has none of Congreve's graceful refinement, and as little of Wycherley's serious manner and studied insight into the springs of character; but his exhibition of [w]it in dramatic contrast and unlooked-for situations, where the different parties play upon one another's failings, and into one another's hands, keeping up the jest like a game at battledore-and-shuttlecock, and urging it to the utmost verge of breathless extravagance, in the mere eagerness of the fray, is beyond that of any other of our writers. His fable is not so profoundly laid, nor his characters so well digested, as Wycherley's (who, in these respects, bore some resemblance to Fielding). Vanbrugh does not lay the same deliberate train from the outset to the conclusion, so that the whole may hang together, and tend inevitably from the combination of different agents and circumstances to the same decisive point; but he works out scene after scene, on the spur of the occasion, and from the immediate hold they take of his imagination at the moment, without any previous bias or ultimate purpose, much more powerfully, with more *verve,* and in a richer vein of original invention. His fancy warms and burnishes out as if he were engaged in the real scene of action, and felt all his faculties suddenly called forth to meet the emergency. He has more nature than art: what he does best, he does because he cannot help it. He has a masterly eye to the advantages which certain accidental situations of character present to him on the spot, and he executes the most difficult and rapid theatrical movements at a moment's warning. Of this kind are the inimitable scenes in the *Provoked Wife,* between Razor and Mademoiselle, where they repeat and act over again the rencontre in the Mulberry-walk between Constant and his mistress, than which nothing was ever more happily conceived, or done to more absolute perfection. That again in the *Relapse,* where Loveless pushes Berinthia into the closet; the sudden meeting in the *Confederacy* between Dick and Mrs. Amlet; the altercation about the letter between Flippanta and Corinna, in the same play, and that again where Brass, at the house of Gripe the money-scrivener, threatens to discover his friend and accomplice, and by talking louder and louder to him, as he tries to evade his demands, extorts a grudging submission from him. This last scene is as follows:—

> DICK. I wish my old hobbling mother han't been blabbing something here she should not do.
>
> BRASS. Fear nothing, all's safe on that side yet.

But how speaks young mistress's epistle? soft and tender?

DICK. As pen can write.

BRASS. So you think all goes well there?

DICK. As my heart can wish.

BRASS. You are sure on't!

DICK. Sure on't!

BRASS. Why then, ceremony aside—[*Putting on his hat*]—you and I must have a little talk, Mr. Amlet.

DICK. Ah, Brass, what art thou going to do? wo't ruin me?

BRASS. Look you, Dick, few words; you are in a smooth way of making your fortune; I hope all will roll on. But how do you intend matters shall pass 'twixt you and me in this business?

DICK. Death and furies! What a time dost take to talk on't?

BRASS. Good words, or I betray you; they have already heard of one Mr. Amlet in the house.

DICK. Here's a son of a whore. [*Aside.*]

BRASS. In short, look smooth, and be a good prince. I am your valet, 'tis true: your footman, sometimes, which I'm enraged at; but you have always had the ascendant I confess: when we were schoolfellows, you made me carry your books, make your exercise, own your rogueries, and sometimes take a whipping for you. When we were fellow-'prentices, though I was your senior, you made me open the shop, clean my master's shoes, cut last at dinner, and eat all the crust. In our sins too, I must own you still kept me under; you soar'd up to adultery with the mistress, while I was at humble fornication with the maid. Nay, in our punishments you still made good your post; for when once upon a time I was sentenced but to be shipp'd, I cannot deny but you were condemn'd to be hang'd. So that in all times, I must confess, your inclinations have been greater and nobler than mine; however, I cannot consent that you should at once fix fortune for life, and I dwell in my humilities for the rest of my days.

DICK. Hark thee, Brass, if I do not most nobly by thee, I'm a dog.

BRASS. And when?

DICK. As soon as ever I am married.

BRASS. Ay, the plague take thee.

DICK. Then you mistrust me?

BRASS. I do, by my faith. Look you, Sir, some folks we mistrust, because we don't know them: others we mistrust, because we do know them: and for one of these reasons I desire there may be a bargain beforehand: if not [*raising his voice*] look ye, Dick Amlet—

DICK. Soft, my dear friend and companion. The

dog will ruin me [*Aside*]. Say, what is't will content thee?

BRASS. O ho!

DICK. But how canst thou be such a barbarian?

BRASS. I learnt it at Algiers.

DICK. Come, make thy Turkish demand then.

BRASS. You know you gave me a bank-bill this morning to receive for you.

DICK. I did so, of fifty pounds; 'tis thine. So, now thou art satisfied; all is fixed.

BRASS. It is not indeed. There's a diamond necklace you robb'd your mother of e'en now.

DICK. Ah, you Jew!

BRASS. No words.

DICK. My dear Brass!

BRASS. I insist.

DICK. My old friend!

BRASS. Dick Amlet [*raising his voice*] I insist.

DICK. Ah, the cormorant [*Aside*].—Well, 'tis thine: thou'lt never thrive with it.

BRASS. When I find it begins to do me mischief, I'll give it you again. But I must have a wedding suit.

DICK. Well.

BRASS. A stock of linen.

DICK. Enough.

BRASS. Not yet—a silver-hilted sword.

DICK. Well, thou shalt have that too. Now thou hast everything.

BRASS. Heav'n forgive me, I forgot a ring of remembrance. I would not forget all these favours for the world: a sparkling diamond will be always playing in my eye, and put me in mind of them.

DICK. This unconscionable rogue! [*Aside*]— Well, I'll bespeak one for thee.

BRASS. Brilliant.

DICK. It shall. But if the thing don't succeed after all—

BRASS. I am a man of honour and restore: and so, the treaty being finish'd, I strike my flag of defiance, and fall into my respects again. [*Takes off his hat.*]

The *Confederacy* is a comedy of infinite contrivance and intrigue, with a matchless spirit of impudence. It is a fine careless *exposé* of heartless want of principle; for there is no anger or severity against vice expressed in it, as in Wycherley. The author's morality in all cases (except his *Provoked Wife*, which was undertaken as a penance for past peccadilloes) sits very loose upon him. It is a little upon the turn; "it does somewhat smack." Old Palmer, as Dick Amlet, asking his mother's blessing on his knee, was the very idea of a graceless son.—His sweetheart Corinna is a Miss Prue, but nature works in her more powerfully.—Lord Foppington, in the *Relapse,* is a most splendid caricature: he is a personification of the foppery and folly of dress and external appearance in full feather. He blazes out and dazzles sober reason with ridiculous ostentation. Still I think this character is a copy from Etherege's *Sir Fopling Flutter,* and upon the whole, perhaps, Sir Fopling is the more natural grotesque of the two. His soul is more in his dress; he is a more disinterested coxcomb. The lord is an ostentatious, strutting, vain-glorious blockhead; the knight is an unaffected, self-complacent, serious admirer of his equipage and person. For instance, what they severally say on the subject of contemplating themselves in the glass, is a proof of this. Sir Fopling thinks a looking-glass in the room "the best company in the world;" it is another self to him: Lord Foppington merely considers it as necessary to adjust his appearance, that he may make a figure in company. The finery of the one has an imposing air of grandeur about it, and is studied for effect: the other is really in love with a laced suit, and is hand and glove with the newest-cut fashion. He really thinks his tailor or peruke-maker the greatest man in the world, while his lordship treats them familiarly as necessary appendages of his person. Still this coxcomb-nobleman's effeminacy and mock-heroic vanity are admirably depicted, and held up to unrivalled ridicule; and his courtship of Miss Hoyden is excellent in all its stages, and ends oracularly.

> LORD FOPPINGTON.—Now, for my part, I think the wisest thing a man can do with an aching heart, is to put on a serene countenance; for a philosophical air is the most becoming thing in the world to the face of a person of quality: I will therefore bear my disgrace like a great man, and let the people see I am above an affront. [*then turning to his brother*] Dear Tam, since things are thus fallen out, pr'ythee give me leave to wish thee joy, I do it *de bon cœur,* strike me dumb: you have married a woman beautiful in her person, charming in her airs, prudent in her conduct, constant in her inclinations, and of a nice morality—slap my vitals!

Poor Hoyden fares ill in his lordship's description of her, though she could expect no better at his hands for her desertion of him. She wants sentiment, to be sure, but she has other qualifications—she is a fine bouncing piece of flesh and blood. Her first announcement is decisive—"Let loose the greyhound, and lock up Hoyden." Her declaration, "It's well they've got me a husband, or ecod, I'd marry the baker," comes from her mouth like a shot from a culverin, and leaves no doubt, by its effect upon the ear, that she would have made it good in the sequel, if she had not been provided for. Her indifference to the man she is to marry, and her attachment to the finery and the title, are justified by an attentive observation of nature in its simplest guise. There is, however, no harm in Hoyden; she merely wishes to consult her own inclination: she is by no means like Corinna in the *Confederacy,* "a devilish girl at the bottom," nor is it her great delight to plague other people.— Sir Tunbelly Clumsy is the right worshipful and worthy father of so delicate an offspring. He is a coarse, substantial contrast to the flippant and flimsy Lord Foppington. If the one is not without reason "proud to be at the head of so prevailing a party" as that of coxcombs, the other may look big and console himself (under some affronts) with being a very competent representative, a knight of the shire, of the once formidable, though now obsolete class of country squires, who had no idea beyond the boundaries of their own estates, or the circumference of their own persons. His unwieldy dulness gives, by the rule of contraries, a lively sense of lightness and grace: his stupidity answers all the purposes of wit. His portly paunch repels a jest like a wool-sack: a sarcasm rebounds from him like a ball. His presence is a cure for gravity; and he is a standing satire upon himself and the class in natural history to which he belonged. Sir John Brute, in the *Provoked Wife,* is an animal of the same English growth, but of a cross-grained breed. He has a spice of the demon mixed up with the brute; is mischievous as well as stupid; has improved his natural parts by a town education and example; opposes the fine-lady airs and graces of his wife by brawling oaths, impenetrable surliness, and pothouse valour; overpowers any tendency she might have to vapours or hysterics by the fumes of tobacco and strong beer, and thinks to be master in his own house by roaring in taverns, reeling home drunk every night, breaking lamps, and beating the watch. He does not, however, find this lordly method answer. He turns out to be a coward as well as a bully, and dares not resent the injuries he has provoked by his unmanly behaviour. . . . The ironical conversations in this play between Belinda and Lady Brute, as well as those in the *Relapse* between Amanda and her cousin Berinthia, will do to compare with Congreve in the way of wit and studied raillery, but they will not stand the comparison. Araminta and Clarissa keep up the ball between them with more spirit, for their conversation is very like that of kept-mistresses; and the mixture of fashionable *slang* and professed want of principle gives a sort of zest and high seasoning to their confidential communications, which Vanbrugh could supply as well as anybody. But he could not do without the taint of grossness and licentiousness. Lady Townly is not the really vicious character, nor quite the fine lady, which the author would have her to be. Lady Grace is so far better; she is what she pretends to be, merely *sober* and insipid. Vanbrugh's *forte* was not the sentimental or didactic; his genius flags and grows dull when it is not put into action, and wants the stimulus of sudden emergency, or the fortuitous collision of different motives, to call out all its force and vivacity. His antitheses are happy and brilliant contrasts of character; his *double entendres* equivocal situations; his best jokes are practical devices, not epigrammatic conceits. His wit is that which is emphatically called *mother-wit.* It brings those who possess it, or to whom he lends it, into scrapes by its restlessness, and brings them out of them by its alacrity. Several of his favourite characters are knavish, adroit adventurers, who have all the gipsy jargon, the cunning impudence, cool presence of mind, selfishness, and indefatigable industry; all the excuses, lying dexterity, the intellectual juggling and legerdemain tricks, necessary to fit them for this sort of predatory warfare on the simplicity, follies, or vices of mankind. He discovers the utmost dramatic generalship in bringing off his characters at a pinch, and by an instantaneous *ruse de guerre,* when the case seems hopeless in any other hands. The train of his associations, to express the same thing in metaphysical language, lies in following the suggestions of his fancy into every possible connexion of cause and effect, rather than into every possible combination of likeness or difference. His ablest characters show that they are so by displaying their ingenuity, address, and presence of mind in critical junctures, and in their own affairs, rather than their wisdom or their wit "in intellectual gladiatorship," or in speculating on the affairs and characters of other people.

Farquhar's chief characters are also adventurers; but they are adventurers of a romantic, not a knavish stamp, and succeed no less by their honesty than their boldness. They conquer their difficulties, and effect their "hairbreadth 'scapes" by the impulse of natural enthusiasm and the confidence of high principles of gallantry and honour, as much as by their dexterity and readiness at expedients. They are real gentlemen, and only pretended impostors. Vanbrugh's upstart heroes are without "any relish of salvation," without generosity, virtue, or any pretensions to it. We have little sympathy for them, and no respect at all. But we have every sort of good-will towards Farquhar's heroes, who have as many peccadilloes to answer for, and play as many rogue's tricks, but are honest fellows at bottom. I know little other difference between these two capital writers and copyists of nature, than that Farquhar's nature is the better nature of the two. We seem to like both the author and his favourites. He has humour, character, and invention in common with the other, with a more unaffected gaiety and spirit of enjoyment, which overflows and sparkles in all he does. He makes us laugh from pleasure oftener than from malice. He somewhere prides himself in having introduced on the stage the class of comic heroes here spoken of, which has since become a standard character, and which represents the warm-hearted, rattle-brained, thoughtless, high-spirited young fellow, who floats on the back of his misfortunes without repining, who forfeits appearances, but saves his honour; and he gives us to understand that it was his own. He did not need to be ashamed of it. Indeed there is internal evidence that this sort of character is his own, for it pervades his works generally, and is the moving spirit that informs them. His comedies have on this account probably a greater appearance of truth and nature than almost any others. His incidents succeed one another with rapidity, but without premeditation; his wit is easy and spontaneous; his style animated, unembarrassed, and flowing; his characters full of life and spirit, and never overstrained so as to "o'erstop the modesty of nature," though they sometimes, from haste and carelessness, seem left in a crude, unfinished state. There is a constant ebullition of gay, laughing invention, cordial good humour, and fine animal spirits, in his writings.

Of the four writers here classed together, we should perhaps have courted Congreve's acquaintance most, for his wit and the elegance of his manners; Wycherley's, for his sense and observation on human nature; Vanbrugh's, for his power of farcical description and telling a story; Farquhar's, for the pleasure of his society, and the love of good fellowship. His fine gentlemen are not gentlemen of fortune and fashion, like those in Congreve; but are rather "God Almighty's gentlemen." His valets are good fellows: even his chambermaids are some of them disinterested and sincere. But his fine ladies, it must be allowed, are not so amiable, so witty, or accomplished, as those in Congreve. Perhaps they both described women in high life as they found them: Congreve took their conversation, Farquhar their conduct. In the way of fashionable vice and petrifying affectation, there is nothing to come up to his *Lady Lurewell,* in the *Trip to the Jubilee.* She by no means makes good Mr. Burke's courtly and chivalrous observation, that the evil of vice consists principally in its want of refinement; and one benefit of the dramatic exhibition of such characters is, that they overturn false maxims of morality, and settle accounts fairly and satisfactorily between theory and practice. Her lover, Colonel Standard, is indeed an awkward incumbrance upon so fine a lady: it was a character that the poet did not like; and he has merely sketched him in, leaving him to answer for himself as well as he could, which is but badly. We have no suspicion, either from his conduct, or from any hint dropped by accident, that he is the first seducer and the possessor of the virgin affections of Lady Lurewell. The double transformation of this virago from vice to virtue, and from virtue to vice again, her plausible pretensions and artful wiles, her violent temper and dissolute passions, show a thorough knowledge of the effects both of nature and habit in making up human character. Farquhar's own heedless turn for gallantry would be likely to throw him upon such a character; and his goodness of heart and sincerity of disposition would teach him to expose its wanton duplicity and gilded rottenness. Lurewell is almost as abandoned a character as Olivia in the *Plain Dealer;* but the indignation excited against her is of a less serious and tragic cast. Her peevish disgust and affected horror at everything that comes near her, form a very edifying picture. Her dissatisfaction and *ennui* are not mere airs and graces worn for fashion's sake; but are real and tormenting inmates of her breast, arising from a surfeit of pleasure and the consciousness of guilt. All that is hateful in the caprice, ill humour, spite, *hauteur,* folly, impudence, and affectation of the complete woman of quality, is contained in the scene between her and her servants in the first act. The depravity would be intolerable, even in imagination, if the weakness were not ludicrous in the extreme. It shows, in the highest degree, the power of circumstances and example to pervert the understanding, the imagination, and even the senses. The manner in which the character of the gay, wild, free-hearted, but not altogether profligate or unfeeling Sir Harry Wildair, is played off against the designing, vindictive, imperious, uncontrollable, and unreasonable humours of Lurewell, in the scene where she tries to convince him of his wife's infidelity, while he stops his ears to her pretended proofs, is not surpassed in modern comedy. (pp. 91-114)

The dialogue between Cherry and Archer, in the *Beaux' Stratagem,* in which she repeats her well-conned love catechism, is as good as [Wildair and Lurewell's dialogue, just mentioned], but not so fit to be repeated anywhere but on the stage. The *Beaux' Stratagem* is the best of his plays, as a whole; infinitely lively, bustling, and full of point and interest. The assumed disguise of the two principal characters, Archer and Aimwell, is a perpetual amusement to the mind. Scrub is an indispensable appendage to a country gentleman's kitchen, and an exquisite confidant for the secrets of young ladies. The *Recruiting Officer* is not one of Farquhar's best comedies, though it is light and entertaining. It contains chiefly sketches and hints of characters, and the conclusion of the plot is rather lame. He informs us, in the dedication to the published play, that it was founded on some local and personal circumstances that happened in Shropshire, where he was himself a recruiting officer; and it seems not unlikely that most of the scenes actually took place at the foot of the Wrekin. The *Inconstant* is much superior to it. The romantic interest and impressive catastrophe of this play I thought had been borrowed from the more poetical and tragedy-practised muse of Beaumont and Fletcher; but I find they are taken from an actual circumstance which took place, in the author's knowledge, at Paris. His other pieces, *Love and a Bottle,* and the *Twin Rivals,* are not on a par with these; and are no longer in possession of the stage. The public are, after all, not the worst judges. Farquhar's 'Letters,' prefixed to the collection of his plays, are lively, good-humoured, and sensible; and contain, among other things, an admirable exposition of the futility of the dramatic unities of time and place. This criticism preceded Dennis's remarks on that subject, in his 'Strictures on Mr. Addison's *Cato;*' and completely anticipates all that Dr. Johnson has urged so unanswerably on the subject, in his preface to 'Shakespeare.'

We may date the decline of English comedy from the time of Farquhar. For this several causes might be assigned in the political and moral changes of the times; but among other minor ones, Jeremy Collier, in his *View of the English Stage,* frightened the poets, and did all he could to spoil the stage, by pretending to reform it: that is, by making it an echo of the pulpit, instead of a reflection of the manners of the world. He complains bitterly of the profaneness of the stage; and is for fining the actors for every oath they utter, to put an end to the practice; as if common swearing had been an invention of the poets and stage-players. He cannot endure that the fine gentlemen drink, and the fine ladies intrigue, in the scenes of Congreve and Wycherley, when things so contrary to law and gospel happened nowhere else. He is vehement against duelling, as a barbarous custom of which the example is suffered with impunity nowhere but on the stage. He is shocked at the number of fortunes that are irreparably ruined by the vice of gaming on the boards of the theatres. He seems to think that every breach of the ten commandments begins and ends there. He complains that the tame husbands of his time are laughed at on the stage, and that the successful gallants triumph, which was without precedent either in the city or the court. He does not think it enough that the stage "shows vice its own image, scorn its own feature," unless they are damned at the same instant, and carried off (like Don Juan) by real devils to the infernal regions, before the faces of the spectators. It seems that the author would have been contented to be present at a comedy or a farce, like a Father Inquisitor, if there was to be an *auto da fé* at the end, to burn both the actors and the poet. This sour, nonjuring critic has a great horror and repugnance at poor human nature, in nearly all its shapes; of the existence of which he appears only to be aware through the stage: and this he considers as the only exception to the practice of piety, and the performance of the whole duty of man; and seems fully convinced, that if this nuisance were abated, the whole world would be regulated according to the creed and the catechism. This is a strange blindness and infatuation! He forgets, in his overheated zeal, two things: First, That the stage must be copied from real life, that the manners represented there must exist elsewhere, and "denote a foregone conclusion," to satisfy common sense. Secondly, that the stage cannot shock common decency, according to the notions that prevail of it in any age or country, because the exhibition is public. If the pulpit, for instance, had banished all vice and imperfection from the world, as our critic would suppose, we should not have seen the offensive reflection of them on the stage, which he resents as an affront to the cloth, and an outrage on religion. On the contrary, with such a sweeping reformation as this theory implies, the office of the preacher, as well as of the player, would be gone; and if the common peccadilloes of lying, swearing, intriguing, fighting, drinking, gaming, and other such obnoxious dramatic common-places, were once fairly got rid of in reality, neither the comic poet would be able to laugh at them on the stage, nor our good-natured author to consign them over to damnation elsewhere. The work is, however, written with ability, and did much mischief: it produced those *do-me-good,* lack-a-daisical, whining, make-believe comedies in the next age (such as Steele's *Conscious Lovers,* and others), which are enough to set one to sleep, and where the author tries in vain to be merry and wise in the same breath; in which the utmost stretch of licentiousness goes no farther than the gallant's being suspected of keeping a mistress, and the highest proof of courage is given in his refusing to accept a challenge. (pp. 116-19)

> *William Hazlitt, "On Wycherley, Congreve, Vanbrugh, and Farquhar," in his* Lectures on the English Poets, and the English Comic Writers, *edited by William Carew Hazlitt, Bell & Daldy, 1870, pp. 91-120.*

Edmund Gosse

[*A distinguished English literary historian, critic, and biographer, Gosse wrote extensively on seventeenth- and eighteenth-century English literature. In the essay below, he examines how the preeminence of French theater during the Commonwealth period served to influence English dramatists of the Restoration.*]

The tragedies and comedies of the Restoration constitute a body of writing which is apt to suffer from comparison with an earlier school of English drama. But there was no continuity between the plays written under Charles I. and those written under Charles II., and the first thing to be done, in appreciating the latter, is to dismiss all consideration of the former. If the founder of the Restoration stage, William Davenant, was a relic of pre-Commonwealth times; if the earliest comic playwright of the new age, John Wilson, was a close disciple of Ben Jonson; if much of the richness of Jacobean language clung about the tragedies of Dryden; if Fletcher was still acted and Shakespeare sedulously adapted; these were accidental and not essential facts. What was essential was that for nearly twenty years stage-plays had not been represented in England, and that the tradition of acting—which is a very fragile thing, and needs to be handed down week by week and almost night by night—was broken and completely lost. In consequence, when there arose an irresistible public demand for the performance of drama in England, the revival could not come from memories of a stage, which had been already in decay a quarter of a century earlier, which none but elderly people had seen, and the character of which no one any longer recollected or cared to recollect.

There was, however, a stage with which all the politest Englishmen of the day were exactly familiar, on which indeed they had, until the moment of the restoration of their monarchy, seen acted the most moving and civilising spectacles. In considering the drama of England from 1665 to 1700, we waste time and lose our way if we try to connect what we see with the productions of the Elizabethan age. The first necessity of critical appreciation is to perceive that this drama is an offshoot of "classical" drama as developed in France, and as witnessed in Paris up to the moment of the king's return. The theatre in France had begun to dominate society in the second quarter of the seventeenth century, and it had moved in sympathy with the general craving for increased social refinement. The Hôtel de Bourgogne, with its long tradition from so far back as 1548, had "marked time," as we say now, until the personal taste of Louis XIV. had given a new and strong social prominence to the stage. The success of Corneille's *Mélite* in 1629 began the fashion for stately and ceremonious tragedy. The poet and the actor, Corneille and Mondory, the one inactive without the other, now played into one another's hands, and a crisis in the art of the world was marked by the great polite success of *Le Cid* in 1636.

It was soon after this that the exodus of English Royalists began, and in the main it was to Paris that they ultimately gravitated. Those of them who loved the theatre—and it must be recollected that every one whose tastes were in any measure theatrical was an adherent to the monarchy—all infatuated English playgoers arrived in Paris to find flourishing there a drama of a class entirely different from what they had left behind them languishing in London. They had left a stage that was rapidly fading into incoherence and folly; they found one which bore all the signs of youth and strength and logic. They watched such finished actors as Bellerose and Montfleury performing at the Bourgogne. In the very year in which the English Parliament published the sternly insolent ordinance forbidding all acting of stage-plays, the aristocratic English exiles had the exquisite pleasure of seeing Richelieu's theatre in the Palais Royal opened for spectacles of the highest refinement, where for the first time the impudence of audiences was kept in check and an air of good breeding made obligatory on the pit itself.

No wonder, then, that the civilising influence of the stage, as a beautiful instrument in the work of social refinement, should attract and interest the English emigrants in Paris.

Small blame to them if this, indeed, became their chief solicitude in the thought of introducing at home—should they ever return to their Roundhead-ridden island—a drama built on the same lines as the French and possessing the same educational character. The poet had hitherto been a negligible citizen, the actor a mountebank and a vagabond, in English esteem. Here in Paris they found actors permitted to appear at court, and poets associating on equal terms with "the best people." They noticed, no doubt with ecstatic approval, the tragic dignity of Bellerose, and if they stayed long enough in France, they saw a genuine nobleman, the Sieur de Prine Fosse, become the darling of playgoers under the delicate pseudonym of Floridor.

In examining any period of literary art, it is imperative that we should ask ourselves, not, what do we ourselves like best, but what did the purveyors of all this elaborate entertainment design? We have formed a modern notion of "refinement" very different from that which was current in Europe in 1660. The simplicity of demeanour, the reduced emphasis, the moral severity, which we now regard as necessary for good behaviour, were not valued at our rate in the courts of the seventeenth century. To be "polite" was largely a matter of parade, of demeanour, even of clothes and ornaments. The fault of English society at the Restoration was its grossness, by which we must not be too ready to understand its immorality, nor even its indelicacy. It was slovenly in deportment, in thought, blunt in language. The rude manners of an earlier generation had been reflected in the plays of Charles I.'s reign, and the revival of these pieces was resisted. Evelyn plainly puts it, that, in 1661, "the old plays began to disgust this refined age." The wit and polish of the French were set forward by the playwrights as the new objects of English imitation. Some one has said of the ideal theatre that it should be "the Corinthian capital of polished society," and that is what the founders of Restoration drama designed the stage of Davenant and Killigrew to be. There was little appeal made in it to the higher elements of spiritual life; "the springs of nature, passion, or imagination are but feebly touched," as Hazlitt notes. What was mainly attempted was to put the public in close contact with all that was attractive in the pomp of life, in its relation with birth and fashion. Tragedy was to represent, in superhuman dignity, the solemn pageant of society; comedy was to paint, in more or less ridiculous colours, its elegancies and affectations. The object of the playwright, odd as it may sound to us, was, as Dryden says in his preface to *The Maiden Queen* (1668), "to show one great and absolute pattern of honour," and to avoid anything in language or manners which should approach to indecorum.

The literature which was produced in these conditions is not lightly to be dismissed as in its nature absurd because we are now wholly out of sympathy with the moral causes which inspired it. The London audiences, like the English dramatists, of the Restoration, looked upon the theatre as something quite distinct from nature. We can best appreciate their feeling if we regard tragedy, as they conceived it, as being an art halfway towards opera. We may be quite sure that sensible persons in the reign of Charles II. were as conscious as we are of the fact that even emperors and princes, under the influence of violent passion, do not spout and shout, nor stride across their palaces with measured gestures and emphatic declamation. But the noble convention of verse itself is already far upon the road of the non-natural, and if we admit the blank iambics of *Hamlet* we go very little further in admitting the rhymed couplets of *The Indian Emperor.* If the latter had been in their own class as good, or even half so good, as the former, there is little doubt that rhyme would have attached itself to tragedy in England as it did in France. No one complains because *Phèdre* is written in rhymed couplets.

But the misfortune was that the English playwrights of the Restoration, active and enthusiastic as they were, did not rise in technical merit to the level of classic tragedy. They missed altogether the harmonious beauty of the ideal Greek play; but they comprehended scarcely better what the finest French tragedians had revealed in the movement of the passions. To say the worst at once, what all the Restoration dramatists suffer from is a tendency to produce common and inadequate poetry. Their inefficiency lies upon them like a blight—dulness in Dryden, flatness in Otway, bombast in Lee. They aimed at subduing emotion to a level of pompous grandeur, but they lacked the splendour of the Greeks, the purity and elasticity of the French. Flat, bombastic, dull—so they are lamentably apt to appear to us when we read them, and in order to endure them we have to remind ourselves of a number of circumstances which justice demands that we should recognise. In particular, the effect of the rhymed verse, which modern critics almost always ridicule, should be judged on the stage itself. The rarity with which Restoration tragedies are given nowadays makes this difficult to do. But some years ago, a careful performance of Dryden's *Maiden Queen* on a London stage revealed to the surprise of the present writer the fact that the repercussion of the rhymes aided rather than impeded his intelligence of the evolution of the plot.

It must be remembered that, whether in rhymed or blank verse, tragedy under Charles II. was delivered in a kind of undulating sing-song. Some idea of its effect may perhaps be gained from Mr. Yeats' experiments in the delivery of verse in his Irish theatre. This was pleasing to the noble amateurs who patronised the stage, and it gave the audience, eager for self-improvement, an impression of being present in the best of company. The tradition of Elizabethan acting, as we have seen, was entirely lost, and when the theatres were opened again, it was necessary for Betterton (1635-1710), who was already without a rival the most capable actor in England, to go over to Paris to study, not merely his Dryden, but his Shakespeare parts. He is supposed to have visited the theatre of Molière, and perhaps in *Don Garcie de Navarre* he received impressions of the best way to represent tragi-comedy. But probably what pleased him best were not such French tragedies as we admire to-day, but those of Quinault and Thomas Corneille, with their languishing ardours of love and romantic travesties of history. These seem, at all events, to have inspired the founder of English "heroic" tragedy, Roger Boyle, first Earl of Orrery (1621-79), who had spent his youth in France, and whose *Henry V.,* in 1664, offered

Betterton that part of Owen Tudor in which he is said to have laid the basis of his boundless reputation.

These plays are hardly comprehensible by us to-day, unless we understand them to represent, as we have said, a semi-operatic convention which had its civilising influence on manners. When Diderot asked his terrible questions: "Has any one ever spoken as we declaim? Do kings walk otherwise than does every man who walks well? Do princesses always hiss between their teeth when they talk?" he laid the axe to the root of the whole practice of classical histrionics. There was a radical absence of simplicity about the convention of tragedy, and a determined abuse of all the tricks of rhetoric, and these faults were more obvious in England than in France. But we must take the Restoration plays for what they had to give to a double English audience, composed of men of taste, nurtured in the principles of the French stage, and of coarse citizens, ready to be improved in mind and manners by representations which sacrificed everything to pomp, decorum, and refinement. The slow deaths of magnificent tyrants, queens nobly canorous on the rack, the sacrifice of royal infants upon pagan altars, no longer seem to us moving or interesting subjects, but under Charles II., as under Louis XIV., they took the large aspect of scenes inspiring, to the sound of verbal music, the most exquisite sentiments of loyalty and pity. The tragedy of the Restoration was really a species of historical oratorio, and to this rule the tender domestic plays of Otway, in which there is no melody and no pomp, but a striving after the humility of nature, offer almost the solitary exception.

Comedy after the Restoration was a slower growth than tragedy. The Royalists came home with their pockets full of tragedies, but Paris had not supplied them with many pieces of diversion before 1660. It may be the habit to insist, too peremptorily, that comedy did not exist in France before Molière, but it is perfectly correct to say that it held no position of importance or respect. Comedy was not what polite people went to the theatre to see, nor was it what English noblemen and their pleasant monarch dreamed of introducing for the improvement of manners on to the new London stage. It was by a very curious accident, which may have definitely affected the history of the English stage, that the return of the Royalists occurred at the moment of the settlement of Molière in Paris, and the development of a classic comedy among the French. The opening of the splendid list of Molière's comedies with *Les Précieuses Ridicules* (1659) coincided with the retirement of Richard Cromwell and the formation of Lambert's Committee of Safety, events which drew all hearts and thoughts of Englishmen in Paris towards their home; while Molière's next triumph, in *Sganarelle,* was lost to the exiles in the blaze and excitement of restoration. Paris, therefore, became to them once more a foreign city exactly at the moment when it was becoming the scene of the creation of comedy.

Doubtless for that reason, although the influence and imitation of Molière are felt in the early English comedies to an extent to which critical justice has never been done, yet that imitation and influence are blunter and less intelligent than would have been the case had English-speaking playgoers seen them in the original. When Molière was ejected from the Petit Bourbon and went to the Palais Royal, a thing new to Europe was revealed on the comic stage, and it is a great pity that the English poets and actors were not any longer on the spot to observe it. Perhaps Orrery and Betterton were, but their thoughts were habituated to tragedy and the tragic formulas. Hence, while Molière positively lifted France into moral light, the English comic writers who followed him failed to civilise the roughness of their audiences. On the contrary, they sank towards the level of their coarse auditors; they flattered and cajoled the impudent *petits-maîtres,* the gross citizens, whom they professed to satirise. The French comic stage fought for the respect of the audience, and we see in *Les Fâcheux* the courage with which Molière took up the battle against impudence.

However, although there is much to regret in the low level of comedy between 1665 and 1700, there is much to applaud. To Molière was due the increasing naturalness of the action in the plays of Shadwell and Dryden, to say nothing of those of Wycherley and Congreve. If we eliminate Shakespeare and the purely poetic parts of the Elizabethans, there is nothing in earlier English comedy to compare with the best pieces of the Restoration stage, whether in structure, language, or humour. What is to be regretted is the absence of grace. If we compare what is perhaps the most uniformly diverting of Dryden's comedies, *Sir Martin Mar-all* (in which both Molière and Quinault are heavily laid under contribution)—if we compare this boisterous composition with *Les Plaideurs,* which was produced at Paris almost exactly at the same time, we may see what English comedy lacked in comparison with French. There are liveliness, a romping, dare-devil exhibition of character, much dramatic high spirits, but a total absence of that extraordinary elegance of mind and intellectual high breeding which mark the no less gay and entertaining comedy of Racine.

No English writer dared to rise in company with Molière to the high flights of character-painting in comic verse. Sir George Etheredge (1634-93) came first, and tried with insufficient energy to raise his audiences to the Parisian level. His *Comical Revenge, or Love in a Tub* (1664), is the earliest specimen we possess in English of classic comedy. It is curious to read the contemporary comment on Etheredge's plays; they "were esteemed by men of sense for the trueness of some of their characters, and the purity, freeness, and easy grace of their dialogue, but on their first appearance they were barbarously treated by the audience." It is a strange notion to us that Dorimant and Sir Fopling Flutter should be distasteful, on account of their refinement and the delicacy of the poet's treatment of them, to spectators at the Duke's Theatre in the reign of Charles and James. But we may conceive this first attempt at a Molièresque analysis of character to be as shocking to admirers of the old rough comedy as Ibsen and Madame Duse were fifteen years ago to lovers of the conventional play and of the stereotyped actor. Towards anything new in the theatrical world audiences are habitually "barbarous." Increased naturalness in writing or performing is always bitterly resisted at first.

There followed Wycherley (1640?-1716), a dramatic artist of more skill and weight than Etheredge, and more intelligently awake to the paramount merits of Molière. He set himself to create scenes of current social life as he cynically saw it, in a state of decomposition. His diagnosis of vice was scandalously farcical, and his picture of society under Charles II. was too heartless and too violent to be anything but a caricature. Nevertheless, Wycherley has vitality, and while we cross his vociferous stage, the curious and unholy men and women who hurtle against us seem living beings. His plays were closely adapted to the temper of the times, and their coarseness, which is offensive to our taste, was not apparent to his immediate contemporaries. Dryden praises "the satire, wit, and strength of manly Wycherley," and describes *The Plain Dealer* as "one of the most bold, most general, and most useful satires which has ever been presented in the English theatre." Thirty years later, one of the most austere of our moralists spoke of *The Country Wife* as "that very pleasant and instructive satire." This appreciation of the comedies of Wycherley continued to exist, without much abatement, until Macaulay made his celebrated attack on them, denying every species of value to the stage of this playwright. Macaulay went much too far in his diatribe. It is true that Wycherley sacrifices nature to artifice, and that he misses the variety, the depth, and the logic of Molière. Nevertheless, he deserves commendation for escaping from the kind of farcical comedy which consisted in dragging mere absurdities, "humours," across the footlights, and in an incessant rattle of extravagant language. He had studied the French with care, and he knew how to build up a comedy. His chief faults arose from his violence, his want of decorum.

His immediate contemporary, Thomas Shadwell (1640?-92), had less art than Wycherley, and he was strikingly less modern. Like all the rest of the comic playwrights of the Restoration, Shadwell studied Molière according to his lights, and he had travelled in France when the earliest of the new comedies were being produced in Paris. But his attitude towards French drama differs from that of Wycherley, who completely accepted the new classic form of comedy, while Shadwell was always reflecting how to plant buds of Molière on to the old worn stock of Ben Jonson. In his first play, *The Sullen Lovers* (1668), Shadwell says that he had already written most of his piece when he received "the report of a play of Molière's of three acts, called *Les Fascheux,*" and that he stole two short scenes out of it. The date of *Les Fâcheux* is 1661, but these poets of the Restoration had a curious wish to have it supposed that they wrote their works in extreme youth. Wycherley o'ervaulted his own ambition in this respect so far as to pretend to have written *The Plain Dealer,* which is founded on *Le Misanthrope,* several years before 1666, when that play was produced in Paris. The attitude of all the English playwrights to Molière was so ungenerous that it is difficult to be patient with them. Shadwell has the impudence to say, in the preface to *The Miser* (1672), while admitting his debt to *L'Avare* (1668), "I think I may say without vanity, that Molière's part of it has not suffer'd in my hands, nor did I ever know a French Comedy made use of by the worst of our Poets, that was not better'd by 'em. 'Tis not barrenness of wit or invention that makes us borrow from the French, but laziness." In the face of such fatuity it is almost annoying to have to admit that Shadwell's bustling comedies have excellent qualities of humour.

But Congreve (1670-1729) was the one man who brought intellect to bear on the comic stage of the Restoration. His first merit resides in his style, in the extreme beauty of the language that he uses. This quality was first insisted upon by Hazlitt, who says, very happily, that *The Double Dealer* and *The Way of the World* "are a singular treat to those who have cultivated a taste for the niceties of English style; there is a peculiar flavour in the very words, which is hardly to be found in any other writer." In Congreve's first play, *The Old Bachelor* (1693), this beauty of language is already ripe, and illuminates the exuberant wit which sparkles from one artificial scene to another. In this play the working of a powerful mind is far more apparent than that of an observant eye or a sympathetic heart. The last Congreve never possessed, but his eye became exquisitely trained. In *The Double Dealer* (1694), where there is a still more scintillating, cruel, and prodigal display of wit, the observation of life is more apparent, but this reaches its highest point in *Love for Love* (1695), the most interesting comedy, and therefore the most interesting play, produced in England between the Commonwealth and the reign of George III. Congreve wrote but one other comedy, *The Way of the World* (1700), which had the unaccountable bad fortune to be damned, although it was a work of consummate wit and stage-craft. The fashion of the public, however, was changing, and Congreve, disgusted at what he called "that general taste which seems now to be predominant in the palates of our audience," withdrew in great dudgeon from the theatre, and would write no more plays, though he was still under the age of thirty.

This retirement, in the last year of the century, really marks the close of our period, but there were several dramatists who endeavoured, during the first decade of the eighteenth century, to carry on the tradition of the Restoration stage, while reconciling it to the altered taste which had driven Congreve from the boards. By examining the successes of these latest playwrights we may discover what it was which the shifting fashion of the age desired. Purely intellectual amusement, a direct appeal to the mind of the spectator, was no longer desired. Perhaps it never had been genuinely desired, and it is difficult to believe that Congreve's pyrotechnics were not always high over the heads of his audience. But with the opening of a new century playgoers began more and more to crave the humbler kind of amusement which was ultimately to be found in the novel of domestic manners. The great successes of the period were those of Sir John Vanbrugh (1672-1726), where the language is negligent, but where passages of everyday life are presented with marvellous fidelity; the rattling story is here the great matter, and not the delicate poise of wit or vanity of stage effect. In Congreve's plays we are always thinking of Congreve; in Vanbrugh's we do not ask who it is who presents the exciting adventures of Dick and Brass. Colley Cibber (1671-1757) was a lighter, more innocent, more insipid Vanbrugh, but in George Farquhar (1678-1707) the line of seventeenth-century dramatists closes in a figure of a very pleasing originality. Farquhar was what was then called "a pretty

fellow"—a new type, a sentimental soldier, garrulous and tender, contrasting in a good-natured way with the hard and cynical types of satirist who had preceded him. He lies even further from literature than Vanbrugh, but he has great knowledge of life, and a brisk delivery. In him the step between the play and the novel was finally taken, and he himself perceived this. "Comedy," he says in 1702, "is no more at present than a well-framed tale handsomely told as an agreeable vehicle for counsel and reproof." (pp. vii-xvii)

> *Edmund Gosse, in an introduction to* Restoration Plays from Dryden to Farquhar, *J. M. Dent & Sons Ltd., 1912, pp. vii-xvii.*

Joseph Wood Krutch on the setting and characters of Restoration comedy (1920):

The Restoration Comedies belong almost exclusively to one type—what we call "society comedy" or the "comedy of manners." The scene is usually London, and the chief persons, with few exceptions, members of high society. If the country or any city besides London is introduced, it is only for the purpose of ridicule. "The country is as terrible, I find, to our English ladies, as a monastery to those abroad; and on my virginity, I think they would rather marry a London gaoler, than a high sheriff of a county, since neither can stir from his employment," says one of the characters in [Wycherley's] *The Country Wife,* and the attitude is typical. The scene moves usually in a restricted circle: the drawing room, the park, the bed chamber, the tavern, then the drawing room again, through which scenes move a set of ever recurring types—the graceful young rake, the faithless wife, the deceived husband, and, perhaps, a charming young heroine who is to be bestowed in the end on the rake. Shadwell (who himself sometimes wrote very much the kind of thing he complained against) described the type in a preface to *The Sullen Lovers.* "In the plays which have been wrote of late," he says, "there is no such thing as a perfect character, but the two chief persons are commonly a swearing, drinking, whoring ruffian for a lover, and an impudent ill-bred tomrig for a mistress—and there is that latitude in this, that almost anything is proper for them to say; but their chief subject is bawdy and profaneness."

Joseph Wood Krutch, in his Comedy and Conscience after the Restoration, *Columbia University Press, 1924.*

Harley Granville-Barker

[*An English dramatist, actor, producer, and critic, Granville-Barker was noted for his contributions to the New Drama movement, signalling his break from the stereotypical social comedy and melodrama of London theater. In the excerpt below, he considers the wit and social relevance of Restoration drama, claiming that "the plays no more reflect the morality of the time than a Palais Royal farce reflects home life in France."*]

Great dramatic movements seem for some reason—it would be instructive to determine it—to be exceptionally short-lived. All that was vital in Elizabethan and Jacobean drama had burned out in fifty years. Its public, like our own—but like every public, I suppose, anywhen and any-where—had been more remarkable for appetite than taste. Shakespeare's genius and Jonson's power shine among much magnificent rubbish and much more, probably (if what has perished may be judged by what remains), that was rubbish unqualified. Yet at the worst, in its youth certainly, it had amazing vigour; and this, in the theatre, will compensate for the lack of many loftier virtues.

Why its vitality should have slackened when it did I do not know. The vogue of the indoor theatres may have been partly responsible. Their more sophisticated patrons would be after something new and the old methods would in any case be less effective in the straitened surroundings. The history of these theatres from 1610 to their closing by the Puritans and of their influence upon playwriting has still to be worked out. One now expects it to show that their technical resources developed to a very close kinship indeed with the theatres of the Restoration. But it may well be that the playwrights who were working for the old theatres as well never reconciled themselves very fruitfully to the new condition of things.

There has been of late much re-editing and re-valuing of Restoration drama. For the industry of the re-editing one can have nothing but gratitude. But the re-valuing leaves me, for the most part, blankly amazed. As to the comedy, I was trained in the doctrine (a compromise between Lamb and Macaulay) that, its indecency forgiven, we should find in the best of it—in Wycherley at his best, for instance—brilliancy and wit incomparable. About the tragedy little was said. But now it appears that Wycherley is not only a brilliant wit and a great playwright, but a stern moralist besides. Shadwell stands with the best, and Buckingham's *Rehearsal* is a masterpiece of humour. Dryden's pot-boilers are polished gems of art; his tragedies rank with Racine's, and Lee and Otway are his peers.

One must make some allowance for the editor, who, plunged into a year or so's hard labour upon Shadwell or Lee, suddenly asks himself: Why on earth, if this fellow is no good, am I spending my time on him? The likely answer will be: As I *am* spending my time on him he *must* be some good. And the next step is to prove him so. I, in my turn, make bold to say that this talk about the moral purpose of Restoration comedy is all stuff and nonsense, and the present claims made for the 'art' of it are not much better. As to the tragedy, it was a respectable effort to do the wrong thing, which lapsed into extravagance, impotence, and absurdity.

With one or two of these latter editors the obscenity of the comedy is apparently to its credit, though they just avoid telling us this in so many words. Instead, they praise it as a revealing picture of the manners and morals of the time. It is nothing of the sort, as anyone who will read such uncalculating documents as the Verney papers, or Dorothy Osborne's letters, or Evelyn's Diary, or even Pepys' (read as a whole), may discover. It is no more a picture of the time than are Mr. Aldous Huxley's satirical novels of the life of the average England of to-day.

It was, in this respect, a flattering of the little Court clique and their snobbish disciples, upon whose patronage the theatre now depended. A strange sort of flattery? Not at all! When men like Charles and Rochester and Sedley, women like Castlemaine and the Duchess of Buckingham, cast aside all decency and restraint, nothing so flatters them as such witness to their achievement. Doubtless there were such 'goings on' as Wycherley depicts in *The Country Wife* and *The Plain Dealer,* less intensified in fact than in the fiction (doubtless there are in some smutty little corners to-day); and it may be that the laughter and applause spread the taste for them a little. But the plays no more reflect the average morality of the time than a Palais Royal farce reflects home life in France.

Wycherley, deliberately or instinctively, was certainly the most skilful of the flatterers; since his moral attitude—for which M. Perromat praises him as he might a Savonarola—accorded quite perfectly with the rakes' conceit of themselves. Poor Dryden did his best to provide the fashionable stuff. But it was in his nature to take both life and literature seriously. And of all literary commodities, calculated immorality, a tribute paid by virtue to vice, is most swift to mortality. It stinks betimes. He must, in his heart, have sighed over the mechanical obscenities of *Limberham or the Kind Keeper* as wearily as ever we do.

But putting such questions aside, what purely dramatic claims can Restoration comedy make? It introduced women to the stage. That was a fairly inevitable revolution, which had far-reaching consequences. But to what account did Etherege and Wycherley and Shadwell turn it? The Elizabethan dramatist had set his boys a hard task, and the setting of it could tax his own skill. These gentlemen just asked the women to exploit their sex. 'Natural' conversation in comedy dates from now? Perhaps; though I fancy Shirley's conversation is as natural when he chooses to make it so. As to the pure craft of the playwright, the Elizabethans had developed a technique of construction to suit their semi-localized stage. Localization now becomes complete, but this is turned to no account, the Elizabethan licence continues—blunderingly exhibited too! There is a stage direction in Wycherley's *Love in a Wood* ('prentice work truly, but it has earned from its latest editor glowing praise), *They all go off in a huddle, hastily.* The play's stagecraft is summed up in that—young men and their mistresses chattering their bawdry and chasing each other through scene after scene, till one asks: How could an audience both be clever enough to understand the story and stupid enough to be interested by it when they did? (pp. 113-17)

[Dramatic wit] is a rare flower, which springs from deep thought, and from something deeper; great wits have ever been the most serious of men. You cannot fill five acts of a play with it, and if you could the result would be intolerable. Three hours' continuous lightning will suffice to blind a man. Quote to the contrary plays which are feasts of wit, and it will be found to be harmless, tricky, fantastic stuff—summer lightning, in fact. Even so, the never-ceasing flicker will weary us.

But wit, with King Charles come home again, was the order of the day. The cynical impudence that the fashionable dramatists had to offer was not much of a substitute, but in the glamorous excitement of a theatre it could be counted on—it still can!—to take most people in. And Restoration audiences, emerging from the shadow of Puritanism, were probably very ready to laugh. But mark the candid Pepys, who on Saturday, May 2nd, 1668, sees the first performance of Shadwell's *Sullen Lovers,* and finds it to have "many good humours in it, but the play tedious and no design at all in it." He goes again on the Monday and sees it "with less pleasure than before, it being but a very contemptible play, though there are many little witty expressions in it, and the pit did generally say that of it." Nevertheless the very next day he and Creed go again; this time "up to the balcony box where we find my lady Castlemayne and several great ladies: and there we sat and I saw the *Impertinents* [its second title] once more. . . . And to see the folly how the house do this day cry up the play more than yesterday, *and I for that reason like it, I find, the better too."* The italics, as one says, are mine.

No doubt there was in Restoration comedy a certain vitality, which the theatres, before the Puritans came to close them, may have largely lost. And it was topical in a distorted fashion and within its narrow range; and the smart chatter of the best of it is given a literary turn. But what other virtues has it? The plundering of plots and even characters from the French and the Elizabethans is no matter. Shakespeare and Molière had been plunderers too. But they turned their booty to better account, gave likelihood to the stories and life to the characters. Wycherley and his fellows do neither. Their plots are clock-work and their characters are puppets. To the art of the theatre they bring nothing. There is no single sign in these comedies of the artist's enquiring love for his work, few enough of the mere craftsman's pleasure in it. For these gentlemen the stage and its actors are just a gaudy means to the exhibiting of their precious wit. (pp. 128-30)

> Harley Granville-Barker, "Wycherley and Dryden," in his On Dramatic Method: Being the Clark Lectures for 1930, *Sidgwick & Jackson, Ltd., 1931, pp. 113-55.*

Thomas H. Fujimura

[*In the following excerpt, Fujimura explores the effects and structure of Restoration or wit comedy, noting that the "Truewits" of these plays made the dramatic form palatable "by the beauty of the language and the standard of decorum which governs their speech and conduct."*]

[In studying the aesthetics of wit comedy, one must consider] first, its effect, and second, its structure. Some readers may feel that the "manners" critics have dealt adequately with the aesthetic problem, in rejecting the moral test and in setting up "manners" as the criterion. Critics like Dobrée, Palmer, and Perry have ably presented the view that the plays are dispassionate in treatment and intellectual in their appeal, and consequently amoral, and that style, both literary and social, is the chief concern. They have also stressed the sincerity of the writers to vindicate the comedies morally.

However, this whole point of view, though no doubt aesthetic by comparison with the moralistic approach, is not adequate. To describe the plays as wholly intellectual in appeal is really to deny their aesthetic nature, for, as Kant pointed out, there is considerable difference between "a judgement of cognition" and "a judgment of taste." In reading wit comedy, we are also never quite dispassionate, since we are involved in the action insofar as we side with the Truewits against the Witwouds and Witlesses. There is always a judgment of value involved which, though basically aesthetic, embraces other values. Thus, the circumscription of interest to the style represents a serious neglect of these other values. There is little doubt that moral valuations are often involved in the aesthetic experience, and this is true of wit comedy. Finally, to use the sincerity of the writer as a moral argument in defense of wit comedy is to confuse an ethical with an aesthetic argument. What is apparent from these facts is that the "manners" critics have taken too narrow a view of Restoration comedy, and that consequently they have not only devitalized it but have failed to show how other valuations enrich the "judgement of taste."

"The live question with regard to Restoration comedy is still . . . whether the code which it expresses can be brought into accord with any reasonably respectable modern one" [John Harrington Smith, *The Gay Couple in Restoration Comedy*]. This is the ethical question recently raised by John Harrington Smith, and the fact that it still rises in the mind of a modern critic seems to indicate that the "manners" interpretation has never been quite convincing or adequate. I am therefore suggesting a naturalistic and hedonic theory of art as the proper approach, to do away with the moral obstacle and also to get to the heart of wit comedy. Particularly important in such an approach is the role of wit, for wit is playful and hedonic in character, and hence serves to palliate the naturalism and the freedom of speech and conduct. Wit comedy necessarily deals with morality insofar as it touches on human relations, but since it is witty, it approaches morality from an aesthetic rather than a practical point of view. This whole problem can be clarified, I think, if we consider the nature of aesthetic experience, with particular regard to wit.

The aesthetic experience, according to Stephen C. Pepper [*The Basis of Criticism in the Arts*], must be vivid in quality, highly organized, and pleasurable. Of particular importance is the high degree of organization, or unity (of the work as well as of the experience), for this alone makes possible the exclusion of practical considerations. The work of art is like a house within whose walls we are content to remain, because we are, at the moment, fully engrossed in the pleasurable activity within. From this point of view, Horace's familiar juxtaposition of *utile* and *dulce* is not valid (though it is understandable in view of the practical orientation of the Roman mind), and the stress on *utile* by critics like Collier is questionable. The function of a work of art is not to teach, but to facilitate an experience that is at once vivid, complete, and pleasant. For this reason, the choice of subject matter is not of such primary importance as Collier believed: the artist may deal with devils and libertines as well as with saints. On the other hand, it is not sound to assert, with the "manners" critics, that content is completely unimportant. The sounder position, I think, is to reject content (and morality) as the primary criterion of the aesthetic experience, but, at the same time, to recognize the fact that we cannot disregard it completely and be satisfied with a simple theory of art for art's sake.

First of all, moral judgments may enter negatively and make an aesthetic experience impossible because the content is morally displeasing. For readers to whom the content of wit comedy is distasteful, I have suggested the importance of seeing the comedies in the light of philosophical naturalism; and this should not be difficult today, since most readers are already familiar with the naturalistic writings of Dreiser, Farrell, Faulkner, Cain, and Caldwell. The characters in naturalistic works are presented as egoistic, malicious, and libertine, in accordance with the writers' conception of human nature; and if this fact is recognized, the moral obstacle will become less formidable.

Second, the moral sense is undoubtedly aroused by most literary works, because they deal with human character and action. But our moral faculty is exercised within the aesthetic framework, and is subordinated to the aesthetic experience. For example, our hatred of Iago's villainy must be a contemplative one: the moment that a person is impelled to clamber on the stage to punish Iago, the aesthetic experience is nullified. The moral standard in the work of art may be puritanical, prudential, or libertine; it does not constitute a separate part to be judged by itself. In wit comedy, the moral standard is naturalistic; but the realistic depiction of libertine and egoistic conduct is assimilated into the aesthetic experience by the witty treatment and the beauty of the language, and our moral judgment is necessarily affected by the aesthetic framework in which it is exercised.

Third, when a work of art is said to satisfy our moral faculty, it is only in a very general sense. The work of art introduces us to an orderly and meaningful world, and a world which is meaningful because the values in it (both *utile* and *dulce*) are the values that we ourselves prize. There is no need for a point for point correspondence between the mores of the society portrayed and our own mores; all that is required, from the negative point of view, is that there be no serious endorsement of practices that would be abhorrent to a normal civilized person, such as cannibalism or incest. In wit comedy, the diffused sense of a meaningful world is not destroyed by the sexual irregularity of some of the characters, particularly since the libertine conduct is confined to the masculine Truewits and to the less reputable figures. We are also satisfied that the hypocritical, the stupid and boorish, and the affected are punished, and that the Truewit, with whom we identify ourselves, is rewarded. We agree with the dramatist's valuation, in the degradation of Witless and Witwoud, and in the elevation of Truewit, who represents taste, common sense, decorum, wit, and youth. The values in *The Way of the World* differ from those in *Oedipus Rex,* but they both create in us the impression of a meaningful world in which there are values that we cherish.

Finally, in the aesthetic experience, there is a willing suspension of our moral judgment to a considerable degree, so that we momentarily accept the values of the author, even though they are not in complete accord with our own. If a reader could enjoy only the writer whose standards he accepted completely, none but a reader who was morally anesthetized could find pleasure in such disparate authors as Bunyan, Dante, Ovid, and Petronius. Obviously, there is considerable flexibility in our moral sense, as long as our primary concern is not the morality of the work. In the aesthetic experience, there is no conversion to a particular doctrine; and whatever dogmas or creeds are presented, we view them contemplatively. Thus, in reading Dante, we need not become Catholics; but, for the sake of the aesthetic experience, we must accept imaginatively the assumptions of the Catholic faith. Similarly, in reading wit comedy, we are not called upon to become libertines, skeptics, or egoists. But during the reading, we must willingly suspend our disbelief so far as not to reject the naturalistic assumptions of the play.

The primary purpose of aesthetic activity is hedonic, and not practical; and the idea of persuasion, which is so important in neoclassical criticism (principally because of rhetorical influences), must be relegated to a very minor position. The authors of wit comedy were interested principally in the pleasure to be derived from aesthetic activity; and in the evaluation of their work, the standard one must use is the quality and degree of pleasure they afford. The importance of pleasure in the aesthetic experience and the nature of that pleasure cannot be overemphasized, since this is the crucial point in the disagreement over the merits of wit comedy. If one begins with the assumptions of a Collier, that pleasure is evil, one cannot appreciate wit comedy.

In the plays, there is the pleasure arising from the vicarious satisfaction of our malice, egoism, sexuality, and cynicism, when we identify ourselves with the Truewits. Our pleasure is aroused also by the beauty of the language, in the fine balance of ideas, the rhythm of the speech, and the pointedness of the expression. There is pleasure, too, in perceiving the fine sense of proportion, of moderation, good taste, and naturalness implicit in the ideal of decorum. There is the pleasure to be derived from the cleverness of the Truewits, their intellectual superiority, vivacity, acuteness, and originality, and the fine felicity of their similitudes.

Finally, fusing all this is the satisfaction one feels in the successful synthesis achieved through the witty apprehension of life. The witty muse dances gaily over the surface of life, thrusting a sharp lance now and then at the heavy torso of mundane existence; its eyes sparkle with gaiety, and there is a radiance in its features at once intellectual and malicious and playful. We are carried away by it, and we join in the dance of the witty muse, content for the moment with its gay whirling. We do not forget the larger issues of life, nor do we flee them, as Lamb suggested; rather we are so affected by the magic touch of the witty muse that we see such issues in a shimmer of beauty, as when the first sun-drenched day of spring sets the dewdrops glistening on the flower tips. Our vision is transformed—and perhaps constricted—but such a narrowing of our vision is conducive to a more unified vision, so that we see more clearly and directly and wholly, if not more largely. Life is seen consistently from one point of view; and seen thus, life falls into an integrated pattern without loose ends. Such is the gift of the aesthetic vision.

Of these various sources of pleasure in wit comedy, the one which requires special consideration is the vicarious satisfaction of our egoism, malice, sexuality, and skepticism. The moralistic critics have always been most severe on these seemingly negative elements in wit comedy, and perhaps there may be some dubiety as to their salutary effect.

The best statement of the point of view I am suggesting is the theory of catharsis, formulated by Aristotle in the *Poetics,* and applied to comedy in the *Tractatus Coislinianus.* A modern restatement is that of Freud in his *Wit and Its Relation to the Unconscious,* in which he develops the thesis that since society does not sanction the direct expression in public of such primitive tendencies as sex and hostility, the individual finds vicarious satisfaction through wit. There is pleasure in skeptical, malicious, and sexual wit because our repressed tendencies are satisfied by the short cut provided by wit; and such relief from restraint is conducive to mental health. According to this theory, the vicarious satisfaction of our sexual, malicious, and cynical tendencies through wit comedy will make us less likely to express these tendencies directly, and perhaps dangerously, among our fellow men.

Such a purgative theory, however, is not to be taken as a complete explanation of how wit comedy affects us: in its cruder form, as psychic and emotional purgation, it merely indicates the biological function of art. It is not this medicinal theory but the theory of catharsis as purification which is much sounder as a description of the aesthetic effect.

A work of art produces in us a feeling of purification and well-being: there is, at once, a sense of the immediacy and intensity and novelty of a pleasurable experience, as well as the absence of any practical demands or consequences. In the aesthetic experience, the nexus between us and the practical world is weakened, and we live for a moment more abundantly, vigorously, and intensely than we normally do.

Wit comedy produces this sense of well-being because it presents to us a meaningful world where a definite order prevails and definite values exist. The world of wit comedy is not a simple fairyland where the laws of cuckoldry have replaced those of matrimony; it is not quite so topsy-turvy, nor so simple. It is rather a world reduced to harmony through the dramatist's witty apprehension of life. The great issues of life, the great sorrows and noble gestures of tragedy, do not interfere here with our single, harmonious vision of life; nor is there room for involvements of a strongly emotional nature, or for the practical interests of the actual world. Rather, life is seen as a witty enterprise, where the illusions of the world are pricked by the pin of wit, and the bubble of dogmatism and conventional morality is treated as mercilessly as the bubble of vice and hypocrisy. The witty muse flits over the surface of things, hitting those who take life too seriously—or too frivolously.

Where, one might well ask, is the principle by which the witty muse lives? Is it manners, decorum, license, or is it the *élan vital* of Bergson? But the witty muse answers not; it only mocks at such impertinent questions. If we try to label it the fanciful spirit, it retreats to the realm of decorum. If we seek to identify it with pure reason, it answers with fanciful sophistry. If we seek to brand it as immoral, it points out its services to morality in its exposure of hypocrisy and bigotry. If we call it the civilizing spirit of laughter, it mocks us with its cynical and sexual rejoinders. The witty muse is mercurial and elusive and indefinable; it pretends to no practical purpose, for it is concerned chiefly with pleasure. But beneath the constantly changing surface, it is always playful (though often with a mixture of seriousness in its levity). It sits gracefully in the company of sophisticated men and women, with its head cocked to one side, and over its features plays a sprightly and malicious smile like a bright flame. It is the soul of irreverence, and respects no man and no thing. But to those who keep it company, it is kind indeed, for it bestows on them both freedom and pleasure. This perhaps suggests something of the effect of wit comedy.

Structure is the second point to consider in the aesthetics of wit comedy. The organization of the plays is very simple: the plot consists of an outwitting situation involving Truewits, Witwouds, and Witlesses. This is the basic *comic* situation, and by *comic* I mean principally the interaction of people on the stage which produces laughter in the audience. The elaboration of this situation takes some of these forms: the Truewit and his mistress outwit those who stand in their way (such as parents, guardians, and foolish rivals); they expose and ridicule those who are less witty than they (Witwoud and Witless); and they often try to outwit each other. A play may contain all of these outwitting situations. In *The Way of the World,* for example, Mirabell and Millamant outwit Lady Wishfort, Fainall, and Marwood, who stand in their way; they expose Witless and Witwoud in the persons of Petulant, Sir Wilfull Witwoud, and Witwoud; and at the same time, they carry on a wit contest between themselves.

In addition to the comic outwitting situation, there is considerable *wit play*—in fanciful similitudes, raillery scenes, and expressions of skeptical, sexual, and sophistical wit. This wit play is not always related to the comic situation and may exist for its own sake, but the exploitation of nondramatic wit provides considerable pleasure and is an important feature of wit comedy.

The sources of comic-witty pleasure in the plays, then, are principally two: (1) the outwitting situation (embracing plot and character), and (2) the nondramatic wit (*dianoia* and diction). To this we might add *comic wit,* which is a synthesis of the two mentioned above: this occurs most often in courtship and "proviso" scenes, such as those between Dorimant and Harriet, or Mirabell and Millamant, when the couple thrust and parry with the weapon of wit in order to outwit each other. An understanding of these two elements in the structure of wit comedy involves, first, a consideration of the comic and the role of laughter, and second, a consideration of wit.

In wit comedy, when we laugh at those involved in a comic situation, we identify ourselves with the Truewit and glory in his triumph over the inferior person (Witless,

(1)

THE
Man of Mode,
O R,
S^R Fopling Flutter.

ACT I. SCENE I.

*A Dreſſing Room, a Table Covered with a Toilet,
Cloaths laid ready.*

Enter Dorimant *in his Gown and Slippers, with a Note in
his hand made up, repeating Verſes.*

Dor. **N**OW *for ſome Ages had the pride of* Spain,
Made the Sun ſhine on half the World in vain.
[*Then looking on the Note.*

For Mrs. Loveit.
What a dull inſipid thing is a Billet doux written in
Cold blood, after the heat of the buſineſs is over?
It is a Tax upon good nature which I have
Here been labouring to pay, and have done it,
Put with as much regret, as ever Fanatick paid
The Royal Aid, or Church Duties ; 'Twill
Have the ſame fate I know that all my notes
To her have had of late, 'Twill not be thought
Kind enough. Faith Women are i'the right
When they jealouſly examine our Letters, for in them
B   We

First page of the 1676 quarto edition of Etherege's third play.

Witwoud, parents, and rivals). Such laughter is best explained by the "malicious" theory, particularly in the form in which Hobbes expounded it; for it was the most widely accepted among the writers of the period. The classical definition of the comic is likewise the most relevant for wit comedy.

The comic, according to Aristotle, is to be found in some human defect, either physical or moral, which is not so extreme as to be painful. The *Tractatus Coislinianus* names the buffoon, the impostor, and the ironical man as the chief types in comedy, and these figures from classical comedy suggest, though they do not actually correspond to, Witless, Witwoud, and Truewit.

Witless and Witwoud are ridiculous because of a defect, intellectual, social, and aesthetic; and in laughing at them, we feel a sense of superiority, or what Hobbes described more picturesquely as a sense of "sudden glory." There is little didactic value to such laughter, since we are seldom persuaded to see our own defects; and James Sully is quite right in his observation [in—*An Essay on Laughter*] that when we laugh at moral deformities, it is not because we see them as *moral* defects: the comic situation itself excites our risibility, and we derive pleasure from the triumph of

> The Wit suffers, then, from accusations of cynicism, frivolity, and immorality. The essential character of the Wit, however, is his freedom, for he refuses to be committed to a dogmatic position, and he believes in the free exercise of the human intelligence.
>
> —*Thomas H. Fujimura*

the superior person over the inferior, whether it be in the moral, physical, or intellectual realm.

The nonutilitarian and malicious character of the laughter in wit comedy is especially clear from the ridicule of the fool. The Truewits in the plays confess as much, and in *The Man of Mode,* Lady Townley is quite explicit on this point:

> L. TOWN: 'Tis good to have an universal taste; we should love Wit, but for Variety be able to divert our selves with the Extravagancies of those who want it.
>
> MEDLEY: Fools will make you laugh.
>
> EMILIA: For once or twice! but the repetition of their Folly after a visit or two grows tedious and unsufferable.
>
> L. TOWN: You are a little too delicate, *Emilia.*
>
> (*Enter a Page.*)
>
> PAGE: Sir *Fopling Flutter,* Madam, desires to know if you are to be seen.
>
> L. TOWN: Here's the freshest Fool in Town, and one who has not cloy'd you yet. Page!
>
> PAGE: Madam!
>
> L. TOWN: Desire him to walk up.
>
> DORIMANT: Do not you fall on him, *Medley,* and snub him. Sooth him up in his extravagance! he will shew the better.
>
> MEDLEY: You know I have a natural indulgence for Fools and need not this caution, Sir! (III, ii)

So the incorrigible Sir Fopling Flutter walks into the trap, to be exposed to the malicious laughter of the Truewits— and of the audience. In *The Country Wife,* Horner voices the sentiments of his fellow Wits toward fools when he says, "In short, I converse with 'em, as you do with rich fools, to laugh at 'em and use 'em ill" (III, ii); and Mrs. Joyner, in *Love in a Wood,* observes that "every wit has his cully"—to serve as a foil (I, i). Addison agreed with Hobbes, in the *Spectator* #47, that men laughed out of a sense of superiority, and consequently found fools a satisfying object of ridicule.

The fool is ludicrous because of a defect, usually that of ignorance. In the *Philebus,* Plato suggested that the ridiculous arises from ignorance—from "the vain conceit of beauty, of wisdom, and of wealth." Of these three forms of conceit, the most common in wit comedy are "conceit of beauty," as in Sir Fopling and Monsieur Paris, and the "conceit of wisdom," as in Witwoud and Dapperwit. This defect of ignorance characterizes the five orders of fools enumerated by the Marquess of Halifax: blockhead, coxcomb, vain blockhead, grave coxcomb, and the half-witted fellow. These types are not mutually exclusive, of course, and in wit comedy the basic distinction is between Witless (the stupid blockhead or boor) and Witwoud (the pretender to wit). Coxcomb is a generic term applicable to any silly, conceited person; and the fop is a fool who manifests his ignorance by excessive addiction to senseless fashions. Our laughter at such fools is malicious, but at the same time, it preserves its aesthetic character insofar as we are not practically concerned with them.

The second element in the structure is the wit-play, as distinguished from the comic situation. Wit differs from the comic in two ways: objectively, in the content; and subjectively, in the effect. Wit has to do with ideas and words rather than with people and action. Further, it titillates the mind without arousing real laughter, and often it leads us by a short cut to a destination which we had not expected at all. . . . (pp. 58-69)

Finally, in comic wit, we have a fusion of the comic (involving character and action) and the witty (involving words and ideas). Wit becomes "an attitude or manner of behaviour" [Sully, *An Essay on Laughter*], as the Truewits utilize the whole arsenal of wit to outwit others and to cope effectively with the world about them. Comic wit results from the collision of a witty mind with people and circumstances which it can treat playfully. It is not merely the result of a critical and dispassionate observation of life, since wit, in this sense, implies the ability, not only to perceive the incongruities of human action and thought, but to be master of them in a playful manner. Hence the Wit is usually an ironic person who treats life with a mixture of "levity and seriousness."

As the central figure in wit comedy, the Truewit is the master of the comic situation, the artist of verbal wit, and the source of comic wit. His witty temper is grounded in skepticism, and he is usually a man critical of dogmatism or "enthusiasm." He is against the idealist who considers man divine, and consequently he lays himself open to the charge of cynicism. However, he is equally the enemy of the practical man whose only ideal is prudence and worldly success; and thus, as an enemy of the prudential view, he is charged with frivolity. Likewise, the Wit is opposed to the moralist who condemns pleasure, and consequently he exposes himself to the charge of immorality. The Wit suffers, then, from accusations of cynicism, frivolity, and immorality. The essential character of the Wit, however, is his freedom, for he refuses to be committed to a dogmatic position, and he believes in the free exercise of the human intelligence.

In this spirit, the Wits of the Restoration attacked what they considered dogmatic and false: they criticized what they thought the pretenses of religion and morality, and they warred against what they believed to be hypocritical

and unnatural. The motive for such witty attacks was sincere: it was a desire for truth and honesty. The Wit who indulged in skeptical, cynical, and sexual wit did so from a feeling that the moral and religious conventions observed by the majority of men were artificial (and unnatural), and that in refusing to recognize the sexual, malicious, and selfish nature of man, society was hypocritical. The Wits believed in being true to nature, and they poked witty fun at artificiality wherever they found it, whether in religious and moral observances or in social conventions. It is indeed ironic that these enemies of artificiality should today be considered the authors of an artificial comedy and the proponents of an artificial code of manners.

As to whether such witty criticism is dangerous, there is no real argument. Wit is playful in its criticism, and since it is more concerned with mockery than persuasion, it can affect only those who are already predisposed to such criticism. The enemies of wit were answered pretty effectively, I think, by the Earl of Shaftesbury. Wit, he declared [in "A Letter concerning Enthusiasm" (1708), in *Characteristicks*, I], is an enemy of "enthusiasm" and dogmatism; it is a critical weapon in the service of reason ["Advice to an Author" (1710), *Characteristicks*, II]; and it is a means of freeing the human mind of error and pretension ["Sensus Communis," *Characteristicks*]. He was also of the opinion that there is less to be feared from the Wits than from the bigots, who would smother truth. And, indeed, the greatest enemies of truth are the dogmatists and fanatics, who are so convinced that they possess the truth that they will suppress all beliefs but their own. But truth is a woman with a thousand beautiful faces, and wit, with its skepticism, keeps us from being seduced by one fair face.

The point brought up by John Harrington Smith has been answered, I think. On the ethical side, the standard in wit comedy is naturalistic; and the sexuality and malice of the characters are not offensive if we remember that the witty authors tried to present people as true to life, in accordance with their bias. At the same time, we have no reason to reject their constant criticism of pretension, artificiality, hypocrisy, vanity, avarice, exaggeration, boorishness, and folly, nor the implicit praise of naturalness, reason, moderation, sincerity, and truth. Furthermore, the naturalistic depiction of the Truewits is rendered palatable for most readers, I think, by the beauty of the language and the standard of decorum which governs their speech and conduct. Above all, wit comedy introduces us to a harmonious, graceful, and free world where the playful judgment can be exercised, and it provides a satisfying experience, at once vivid, complete, and pleasurable. There can be no question, therefore, of the sanity and value of wit comedy. . . . (pp. 69-72)

Thomas H. Fujimura, "The Aesthetics of Wit Comedy," in his The Restoration Comedy of Wit, *Princeton University Press, 1952, pp. 58-72.*

Brice Harris

[In the following essay, Harris discusses five representative Restoration comedies.]

Not infrequently these days *Restoration Drama* has come erroneously to denote those comedies of manners which flourished between the appearance of George Etherege's *Comical Revenge* (1664) and William Congreve's *Way of the World* (1700). This popular error, easy to make and to perpetrate, is almost justifiable. Indeed, no plays in Restoration England came anywhere so near reflecting certain aspects of social London and the Court of Westminster as did those of Wycherley, Farquhar, Vanbrugh, Etherege, and Congreve. Other plays on the billboards reflected the current scene hardly at all except perhaps in indicating the taste of its audiences.

Thus Shakespeare, Ben Jonson, and Beaumont and Fletcher were popular during this forty-year period, but their plays, revived, adapted, or transmuted to satisfy the requirements of French classicism, were scarcely localized or timely. The blank-verse tragedies of Dryden, Otway, Nat Lee, and lesser writers were historical, or romantic, or "Elizabethan," and only occasionally topical. Despite its overwhelming popularity with London audiences, the *heroic drama* of Dryden and Orrery, and less exactly of Davenant and Howard, featured faraway places and remote times. *The Rehearsal* (1671), that delightful extravaganza which helped to terminate the rage of *heroic drama,* and the Jonsonian plays of Thomas Shadwell were, to be sure, closer to the London scene. Hence, it is understandable when twentieth-century readers think first of the Lord Foppingtons, the Dorimants, the Millamants, and the Miss Hoydens, their wit and their foibles and their indiscretions, as the sole constituents of Restoration drama. Actually, Restoration drama must be regarded as beginning with the formal reopening of the theaters shortly after the return of Charles II in 1660 and continuing to some vague date centering, say, around 1700.

Of these various types, none was more popular for a decade after 1664 than the heroic plays of John Dryden, written alone or in collaboration with Sir Robert Howard, his brother-in-law. Sometimes inappropriately called heroic tragedies, these plays were reminiscent of the French prose romances of Calprenède and Mlle. de Scudéry. Male and female characters were dominated almost completely by the passions of love and honor, characteristics that were evident in the decadent drama before 1642. In Dryden's *Conquest of Granada* (1670), the warrior Almanzor found himself defending his chivalric honor at every turn while the heroine Almahide wept fervent, faithful tears at his feet. The dialogue was bombastic and unreal; the action was noisy and confusing, digressing frequently into songs and dances; the scenery fanciful and operatic. The line was the rhymed couplet, which Dryden defended vigorously as most appropriate for plays until eventually his cause was lost. *Tyrannic Love* (1669), *The Conquest of Granada* (1670), and *Aureng-Zebe* (1675) were the best known of Dryden's heroic plays.

The Rehearsal is best understood and appreciated after one has read an heroic drama, preferably *The Conquest of Granada.* Conceived as early as 1663 by Villiers, Second Duke of Buckingham, and his witty friends, Thomas Sprat of the Royal Society and the clergy, Martin Clifford, and perhaps even Samuel Butler, *The Rehearsal* shifted its target twice before selecting Dryden for the bull's-eye. It was aimed first at William Davenant, whose flattened nose still bobs up twice in the play, and then at Sir Robert Howard. Finally Dryden became the Mr. Bayes, poet of mode, who invited Smith and Johnson to witness the rehearsal of his new play. As Bayes screams directions and simpers foolishly to his guests, the poor players stumble through their parts: Thunder, whispering and restrained, and Lightning, slow and halting, render a burlesque prologue; four soldiers advance and give the countersign, are at once killed by four other soldiers whom they in turn kill, and all eight are revived at the sound of a musical note; Prince Prettyman, rapturously and impatiently awaiting the arrival of his love, Cloris, lies down and falls asleep as she approaches; Drawcansir, obviously Dryden's Almanzor, huffs and puffs across the stage in burlesque heroics that conclude with a monstrous carnival of murder in which his mere appearance frightens to death two armies, one of foot soldiers, one of cavalry riding hobby-horses. Long ere this, Johnson and Smith have sneaked away, and the players are ready for mutiny. Thus, with ridiculous actions and scenes and abundant parody of actual lines from *The Conquest of Granada* and other heroic plays, Buckingham and his fellow wits helped to drive heroic drama from the stage. Read with imagination today, *The Rehearsal* can be almost as rollicking, merry, clever, sharp, and unforgettable as it was in 1671.

Dryden had fought valiantly for rhymed drama by providing several examples of it as well as by defending it in critical essays. Toward the end of his *Essay of Dramatic Poesy* (1668) he stated at length his preference for rhyme, and for a period of years argued the point with his brother-in-law, Sir Robert Howard, a controversy which he himself summarized at the conclusion of his *Defence of an Essay.* But steadily his convictions in the matter were changing. By 1675 in the prologue to *Aureng-Zebe* he confessed a truth: he was growing "weary of his long-lov'd mistress, Rhyme." He was ready for Shakespeare's medium, blank verse, and for Shakespeare's tragic subjects, for example, the story of Antony and Cleopatra.

All for Love (1678) was not Dryden's first adaptation of Shakespeare, but it was his best as well as his greatest tragedy. Here he eschewed rhetoric as well as rhyme and confined himself to the neo-classical principles of the unities, which Crites had so carefully explained in the *Essay of Dramatic Poesy.* Where Shakespeare's Antony took twelve years to fret his way across the stage, Dryden's appeared for one day only, his last. Thus, the unity of time. In *Antony and Cleopatra,* action shifted at will between Alexandria, Rome, Athens, Messina, Actium, and various other parts of the Roman Empire, whereas in *All for Love,* the setting was solely Alexandria. Thus the unity of place. Dryden cut the cast of characters from thirty-odd to a round dozen, and restricting the narrative closely to the last affairs of Antony and Cleopatra, emphasized the unity of action. For Enobarbus, clownish and human and realistic, he found no place, but for Ventidius he created a place second only to the protagonists. Dryden's Cleopatra, too, lacked the "infinite variety" of Shakespeare's Cleopatra. She and Antony played the game of Love and Honor with the simple emotions of Almahide and Almanzor. The story itself needs no summarizing, but the first scene between Ventidius and Antony, Dryden's favorite, and the dramatic meeting of Octavia and Cleopatra in Act III are memorable.

Venice Preserved (1682), Thomas Otway's masterpiece and the outstanding blank-verse tragedy of the Restoration, relates the poignant story of a sensitive but irresolute young Venetian named Jaffeir, his courageous friend, Pierre, and his tender and devoted wife, Belvidera. Mistreated by his father-in-law, the senator Priuli, Jaffeir listens readily to Pierre's plot to destroy the state. During a series of night scenes he moves for a time in the sordid world of anxious conspirators and an attractive harlot, Aquilina. Then Jaffeir tells Belvidera of the plot. She encourages him to tell the Senate all that he knows and request a pardon for the conspirators. Instead, the conspirators are condemned, and though Belvidera secures a belated pardon for them through Priuli, Jaffeir stabs himself and Pierre at the scaffold. As the ghosts of Pierre and Jaffeir rise and sink before her, Belvidera goes mad and dies of a broken heart.

The comic underplot of the tragedy, variously admired and despised by readers, ridicules Anthony Ashley Cooper, Earl of Shaftesbury, as the Venetian senator Antonio. In name, appearance, age (each is sixty-one), and ambitions the comparison is exact. The conspiracy in Venice clearly reminds Otway of the recent "Popish Plot" in England. Belvidera, not present in St. Réal's *La Conjuration,* Otway's source, is his greatest character—tender, sensitive, Shakespearean. *Venice Preserved,* in fact, is Elizabethan rather than classical despite the fact that the unities of time and place are not forgotten. Romantic poetry is here, pity and sympathy and compassion are here, and so are those personal conflicts of love and friendship so peculiar to Shakespeare. Finally, this play is close to being a tragedy of the hearth, a domestic tragedy, of the type which Nicholas Rowe composed so successfully a generation later.

Otway, Dryden, and Nat Lee dominated blank-verse tragedy of the Restoration although Lee's plays have seldom become anthology pieces in the twentieth century. *The Rival Queens* (1677), his most popular play in his time and for a century after, is still the best known today. It recounts the story of Roxana and Statira, the two wives of Alexander the Great, who vie with each other to retain or regain his favor. Characterized by rant, melodrama, and artifice, *The Rival Queens* has bequeathed a much-used phrase to posterity: "When Greeks joined Greeks, then was the tug of war" (IV, ii, 419), although posterity seldom knows the source of the quotation and almost universally misquotes it. A more impressive blank-verse tragedy than any of Lee's was Otway's *The Orphan* (1680), the absorbing and emotional story of Polydore and Castalio, twin brothers who were in love with the same girl, the orphaned Monimia. With the exception of *All for Love,* Dry-

den's tragedies were not in the same class with Otway's two well-known tragedies.

The comedies of manners obviously did not encompass all of Restoration drama nor did they spring full grown from Restoration soil. Their rise was not independent or spontaneous, flaring up overnight after Restoration society discovered that it liked to see its image on the stage. The comedies of Molière influenced the English comedies of manners materially, but certain native tendencies and directions were more important. A courtly mode of conduct had found favor in Cavalier society before the Puritan ascendancy. Quite naturally it had become conventionalized and by the time Etherege began to write, its comic aspects were obvious. This social mode of life, where gallantry, wit, and artificiality were dominant, provided the chief materials of Restoration comedy. Indeed, the gay couples in these plays, the Harriets and the Dorimants who amused themselves with the game of love, have been successfully traced from Shakespeare through Fletcher and Suckling and Killigrew down to Etherege.

The conventionalized pattern which the social mode of Restoration life demanded of its followers was not basically different in intent from that of many other manners groups. It was simply more rigid. Its code was drawn with hair lines. Its fashionable gentlemen and ladies must meet the requirements if they wished to avoid the scorn and the ridicule that would inevitably follow if they erred or fell short. Those who professed the code and did not abide by it were even more amusing than the unfortunates who made no attempt to follow it. Thus country people, clergymen, scholars and poets, merchants and tradesmen, in fact anybody who worked for his living, had no time to engage in such activities. But dancing across the stage was an entire generation of fops and dunces, coquettes and mistresses, pseudo-wits and social enthusiasts of various orders that rocked the theater audiences with laughter. It is supremely easy for a modern reader to fall into step with this sophisticated and artificial brilliance and to enjoy it thoroughly. The steady barrage of wit, the cruelty of youth to crabbed age, the emptiness of an artificial social world, the sadistic abandonment to limbo of those who do not live as someone else thinks they should—all these may grow wearisome, may surfeit a reader at a distance of nearly three hundred years. However that may be, let us hope that he will not weary of [these] five representative plays . . . : two from the early period by Etherege and Wycherley, three from the later period by Congreve, Vanbrugh, and Farquhar. These plays . . . span the thirty-two years from 1675 to 1707.

The Man of Mode (1676) was the last in point of time of three plays by Sir George Etherege, the other two being *The Comical Revenge* (1664) and *She Would if She Could* (1668). The story is negligible. One may not be chided for forgetting what happens in this play, but one can scarcely forget the animated scenes: Dorimant and Foggy Nan, the Orange-Woman; or Sir Fopling fresh from Paris, perfumed and overdressed and lisping, laughed at and mimicked by the wits; or Old Bellair shouting his pet expression "A-dod," paying suit to his son's lover, and otherwise amusing youth at the expense of crabbed age; or Dorimant passing himself off to Lady Woodvill as plain Mr. Courtage and affecting to love things old fashioned; or Bellinda paying an unexpected visit to Dorimant's mistress because the chairman assumed that she was the usual woman retreating from Dorimant's backstairs. Nor can one forget the duel of wits between the gay lovers, Harriet and Dorimant. Each is determined not to appear unfashionably in love, not to be the first to admit his love. From the moment that Dorimant first appears, repeating Edmund Waller's verses, to the concluding scene where Harriet is telling Dorimant about her melancholy country life, the dialogue abounds with epigram and simile, cleverness and innuendo. It was supposed in that day that Dorimant was a likeness of Lord Rochester, Medley was Sir Charles Sedley, Sir Fopling was Beau Hewitt. Enjoyment of the play does not turn on such topical interpretation. Dorimant shared his typical qualities with many of the courtiers of Charles II.

The Country Wife (1675), the third of William Wycherley's four plays, is a true comedy of manners, relatively free from the scorn, disillusion, and pessimism of *The Plain-Dealer*, his last play. By the very nature of his trickery Horner exhibits a certain scorn of mankind, but it is hardly noticeable compared to Manly's, which, combined with the sarcastic dedication to Madam B., places him well within the ranks of Butler and Swift. But Horner is still the courtier, the ideal gentleman of the social mode. Borrowing an idea from Terence's eunuch, he announces his impotency and thus unsuspected enjoys the favors of the Lady Fidget while the fops and pseudo-wits ridicule him. When Pinchwife, worn-out beau and jealous benedict, brings his wife Margery to London, Horner sees her at a play and pays his suit to her. Disguising her as a boy only aids and abets Horner's schemes. Now Pinchwife dictates a strong letter for her to sign and is duped by Margery into carrying a substitute letter to Horner in which she declares her regards. Conveyed by her own husband, who thinks the disguised girl is his sister Alithea, to Horner's apartment, Margery returns denying the reports about Horner. Pinchwife is assured by his sister and his erstwhile friend, Horner, that Margery is innocent, and apparently believes them. Pinchwife's jealousy is cleverly contrasted with the quite different attitudes of two other men on the same subject. The fop Sparkish poses as completely free from jealousy, so free that he encourages Harcourt to make love to Alithea before his very eyes. Sir Jasper Fidget, on the other hand, is so convinced of Horner's impotency that he laughs himself sick in one room while Lady Fidget and Horner close the door in the next room to examine china—the famous china scene.

The Relapse (1696), first of a sizable number of plays by Sir John Vanbrugh, was a sequel to a play which is almost forgotten except by the learned—Colley Cibber's *Love's Last Shift*, produced early in 1696. Cibber at the time was a hanger-on at the Theatre Royal, an occasional actor who aspired to write. Either he was lucky or he recognized keenly the straws in the winds of public taste, for his *Love's Last Shift* was the first of the sentimental comedies that were to absorb the minds of early eighteenth-century audiences. The story of Cibber's play can be told in one sentence: Loveless, who deserted Amanda eight years ago,

comes back to London, so completely fails to recognize her that he chooses her for his mistress, and then turns into a tender and repentant spouse when she convinces him of her identity. But John Vanbrugh saw the play and was not convinced by Loveless's repentance. *The Relapse* was his answer. Cibber himself was apparently not overcome by the dignity and seriousness of his play, in which he had taken the part of Sir Novelty Fashion, the coxcomb. He was delighted to act the part of Lord Foppington in Vanbrugh's play.

Loveless and Amanda are transferred to the cast of characters in *The Relapse*, and Sir Novelty is dubbed with a title, Lord Foppington. Vanbrugh changes the rest of the cast, it must be confessed, much to the improvement of personalities and of narrative. Sir Tunbelly Clumsey, country gentleman, and his flippant and irresponsible daughter, Miss Hoyden, both of whom break the social code at every turn, are as amusing a pair of characters as one could find in any comedy of the day. To revert to the main plot, Loveless assures Amanda that he will suffer no *relapse* into past indiscretions when he returns to London. But becoming enamored of a young widow named Berinthia, Loveless proceeds to disprove to Vanbrugh's entire satisfaction those qualities of repentance with which Cibber had endowed him in *Love's Last Shift*.

Two years after Vanbrugh's *Relapse* and two years before Congreve's *Way of the World*, Jeremy Collier blasted plays, players, and playgoers with his *Short View of the Immorality and Profaneness of the English Stage*. Various societies for reforming manners had sprung up during the 1690's, Dryden had earlier declaimed against the "steaming ordures of the stage" in those "lubric and adult'rate" times, and Cibber had wittingly or unwittingly hit upon a formula for writing clean plays. But it remained for Collier to supply the blow that actually destroyed them. The divine had read and digested a great many more plays than one would expect from the cloth. Furthermore, he had copiously extracted passages which he published, some of them proving his point, some of them proving nothing. But public opinion was largely on his side, and in the pamphlet warfare that followed, the controversy that bears his name, he won most of the battles.

The Way of the World (1700) was the last of four deservedly famous comedies which Congreve wrote, the other three being *The Old Batchelor* (1693), *The Double Dealer* (1693), and *Love for Love* (1695). Congreve, like Vanbrugh, was accused in Collier's *Short View*. It would seem that *The Way of the World* was his best answer to Collier, despite the fact that the public only mildly approved it. Here again the story is of small moment. The importance lies in the brilliance, the sparkle of the dialogue, the ridicule of false wit of which Witwoud and Petulant were guilty, and the exhibition of true wit in the word combats of Millamant and Mirabell. Here in one closely woven fabric are the ideal gentleman and lady who live scrupulously by the code, and here are the numerous defaulters. Lady Wishfort is the antiquated coquette who uses too much rouge and flutters painfully at middle age over the appearance of a budding love—Restoration dramatists and poets chronicled her type as gleefully as Horace did. Sir Wilfull is a drunkard and a rustic, therefore amusing. Mrs. Marwood and Mrs. Fainall have fallen unfashionably in love. Thus every character is pegged into a rigid position, and his character is carefully defined in the code of the day. The brilliance and the cruelty of the play are overwhelming and somewhat wearisome. But few readers will deny that *The Way of the World* is the ultimate in the Restoration comedy of manners. Whether they find it greater than more recent comedies of manners, say those of Oscar Wilde or Noel Coward, will depend on their own critical taste.

The Beaux' Stratagem (1707), George Farquhar's last play, has always been included with the best of the Restoration comedies of manners, despite the fact that in point of time it is out of line. It may be called a transition piece. Like Farquhar's early plays, which began to appear in 1698, it has some though not so much of the Restoration temper. But it also adheres to many of the principles of sentimental comedy. Aimwell, whose very name connotes the moral change, falls unfashionably in love with Dorinda and, romantically repentant, approaches the altar. The story of the stratagem of the two penniless beaus is also important and well told, an ingredient seldom found in the strict comedy of manners. Escaping to the country in search of adventures that will fill their flat purses, Aimwell and Archer meet Lady Bountiful's daughter, Dorinda, and her son's wife, Mrs. Sullen. After several mad and merry episodes, Aimwell receives his reward and Archer is well on the way to fortune and a wife, albeit a divorcée. Farquhar successfully fuses plot, situation, and character. He connects dialogue with plot and character, largely eschewing mere verbal brilliance. He leaves the refined circles in London rendezvous—their walks, their parks, their drawingrooms—and hastens to Lichfield where he introduces one to real bourgeois life. Cherry and Boniface from the local inn are there, and Bagshot, the highwayman, and his companions are there. These people breathe. Blood flows in their veins. They remind one of characters in Fielding's or Smollett's novels. There is naturalness and fidelity to life. The comedy of manners is well on its way to the superb art form best expressed by Goldsmith and Sheridan in their comedies of the 1760's and 1770's. (pp. vi-xvii)

> Brice Harris, in an introduction to Restoration Plays, *edited by Brice Harris, The Modern Library, 1953, pp. vi-xvii.*

John Loftis

[*Loftis is an American educator and critic whose studies include* Comedy and Society from Congreve to Fielding *(1959). In the following excerpt from that work, he examines the use of stereotypical urban and country characters in the works of William Congreve, George Farquhar, and John Vanbrugh.*]

George Farquhar, in a defensive preface to *The Twin Rivals* (1702), commented on the rigid pattern of expectation against which he and his fellow dramatists wrote. The audience, he complained,

> take all Innovations for Grievances; and, let a Project be never so well laid for their Advantage,

yet the Undertaker is very likely to suffer by't. A Play without a Beau, Cully, Cuckold, or Coquete, is as Poor an Entertainment to some Pallats, as their Sundays Dinner wou'd be without Beef and Pudding.

"A Play without a Beau, Cully, Cuckold, or Coquete"—or without a knavish citizen or a booby squire—was uncommon at the turn of the century, and was unusual even among Farquhar's own comedies. Just as the dramatic tradition responsible for these character types was pervasive, so was it conservative, inhibiting the readjustment of comedy to the social facts of life. Playwrights were working with stereotypes, most of which were already established—and some long established—in the first decade after the Restoration.

Congreve, Vanbrugh, and Farquhar, the three ablest dramatists writing at the end of the seventeenth century, make little acknowledgment of social changes in their plays, all of which bear the strong impress of dramatic tradition. Their moral judgments sometimes waver, but their social judgments, in comedies intensely preoccupied with social relations, are firm; and the judgments are those of a stratified society. Yet their oversimplification of social fact can be interpreted as an artistic gain in that their plays have a consistency of tone based upon settled opinion. At any rate, the writers of their time who recorded social relationships more faithfully wrote poorer plays.

Congreve, Vanbrugh, and Farquhar were Whigs; but they were Whigs at a time when the party affiliation did not imply sympathy for the business community; they base their plays on social assumptions quite like those expressed later by Swift in the *Examiner,* writing as an authorized spokesman of the Tory ministry led by Harley and St. John.

Even before 1710 several writers—Burnaby, Baker, Steele, and Mrs. Centlivre, among others—wrote plays in which there is a perceptible modification of social judgment: not a decisive shift of sympathy from the gentry to the merchants (as there was in certain plays of a decade or so later), but still a departure from the unyielding assumption that in the antagonism between merchants and gentry the merchants were in an indefensible position. Yet there was not in the years just before and after 1700 a general alteration in the dramatic treatment of social themes. When we come to the undistinguished comedies which then as always formed the larger number of those produced we find a deep and, for the most part, unquestioning conservatism. The obscure dramatists, in their lame and halting comedies, did little more than play variations on a set of conventions, giving no direct attention to the society that was their ostensible subject. Compared with the distinguished comedies of Congreve, Vanbrugh, and Farquhar, most of the comedies of the period 1690-1710 seem poor copies cut to a common pattern by semiskilled artisans.

Except for Farquhar, the dramatists, though they wrote less about rural-urban than about merchant-gentry antagonism, are as conventionally contemptuous of rustics (of country squires and of their families and dependents) as of members of the business community. The dramatic character of the booby squire is formalized (as it was even in Shakespeare's time), and exemplars of the character appear with some regularity. Farquhar's last two plays provide the single instance of appreciative treatment of rusticity; there is in fact no parallel to them until Charles Johnson's work of the second decade of the century.

The seventeen or so plays that Congreve, Vanbrugh, and Farquhar wrote reveal a treatment of class relationships based on a consistent body of social opinion.

In the society these dramatists present, if not in the historical reality, the only "honest" way to an estate open to a gentleman without expectations lies in matrimony. (There are dishonest means, such as those attempted by Maskwell in Congreve's *Double Dealer* and Young Wouldbe in Farquhar's *Twin Rivals.*) The concentration on courtship, traditional though it is in comedy, can be seen in these particular comedies as concentration on the decisive episode in life. For marriage is the only event the outcome of which is likely to alter in any substantial way a person's permanent status in a society in which status is immensely important. Social status and happiness or unhappiness in marriage are by no means the only things in life that matter, but they do matter. These plays can end in marriage with a finality impossible in an age of acknowledged economic individualism.

Nearly all of the comedies treat problems of love—they are constructed in terms of a love chase culminating in marriage. Only a few, and those usually sequels to other plays, treat the affairs of couples already married. But without significant exception, the love affairs are entangled with economic considerations, very often with the terms of strict marriage settlements. In this respect the comedies seem to reflect contemporary conditions in a very distinct manner. In the words of [H. J. Habakkuk, "Marriage Settlements in the Eighteenth Century," *Transactions of the Royal Historical Society,* XXII (1950)]:

> Calculations of material interest have played an important part in marriages between propertied families in almost all periods. But there is evidence that in the early eighteenth century they were more important than for the early seventeenth century and for most of the sixteenth century, and that the material interests involved were more exclusively a matter of wealth.

In the comedies, as in contemporary life, there were well-established patterns of reciprocity in the financial terms of marriage settlements, and the dramatic characters are forthright in talking about them. When deciding whether or not to marry, the principals in the love affairs, as well as their older and more prudent friends and relatives, are acutely conscious of their prospective mate's fortune or lack of it. A young woman in Vanbrugh's *Provoked Wife,* in talking to her aunt about the young man she loves, expresses a common attitude about wealth and marriage (III): "But if I cou'd make a Conquest of this Son of *Bacchus,* and rival his Bottle; What shou'd I do with him, he has no Fortune: I can't marry him; and sure you wou'd not have me commit Fornication?" She does at last marry him, since she herself possesses £10,000, enough to enable them to live modestly. Without the money, presumably,

she would not have married him. In the comedies of Congreve, Vanbrugh, and Farquhar, grossly imprudent marriages do not occur among gentlefolk except where there is trickery. Mrs. Frail in Congreve's *Love for Love* explains to Ben that (III) "marrying without an Estate, is like sailing in a Ship without Ballast."

Wealth is only slightly less important than love as a motivating force in these comedies, and the amount of wealth, which is often in the form of a landed estate, is described as precisely as is the condition of the heroine's affections. Millamant in *The Way of the World* has £12,000 if she marries with her aunt's approval, £6,000 if without; Miss Hoyden in *The Relapse* is heiress to £1,500 a year; Silvia in *The Recruiting Officer* has £1,500 before her brother dies, whereupon she becomes heiress to £1,200 a year; Mrs. Sullen in *The Beaux' Stratagem* had £10,000 at the time of her marriage; Lady Lurewell in *The Constant Couple* has £3,000 a year. The gentlemen who pursue these ladies make no pretense of indifference to their fortunes, which in case of marriage often provide the couple with their sole support, since the gentlemen frequently are younger sons.

Younger sons, in fact, are conspicuous in these plays, having sufficient breeding to be taken seriously, and having the incentive of economic necessity to drive them to lively escapades. A character in Vanbrugh's *Journey to London* describes their plight (I):

> What prudent Cares does this deep foreseeing Nation take, for the Support of its worshipful Families! In order to which, and that they may not fail to be always Significant and useful in their Country, it is a settled Foundation-Point that every Child that is born, shall be a Beggar—Except one; and that he—shall be a Fool.

Young Fashion in *The Relapse* courts Miss Hoyden, using his older brother's title, only to encounter awkward situations when his brother appears; and Aimwell in *The Beaux' Stratagem* assumes his brother's title in his effort to capture a lady with a fortune, learning at the end of the play that he has inherited the title in earnest. The action of *The Twin Rivals* turns on the efforts of a son, younger than his brother by only a few minutes, to replace his brother as heir. Colonel Standard in *The Constant Couple* is in financial straits because his regiment has been disbanded, though he is the younger son of a lord. The hardships occasioned by the principle of primogeniture (a common topic in these plays) are suggested by Young Fashion's remark to his brother Lord Foppington in *The Relapse* (III): "Oons, if you can't live upon Five Thousand a Year, how do you think I shou'd do't upon Two Hundred?"

The heads of families in these plays have very large incomes, the size of which is often stated. Lord Foppington, we have just noted, has £5,000 a year; and the elder Wouldbe in *The Twin Rivals* inherits a peerage and £7,000 a year; Sir Harry Wildair in *The Constant Couple* and in its sequel of his own name has £8,000. Sir Paul Plyant in *The Double Dealer,* though he does not cite figures, describes the components of his "plentiful" estate (III): "Why, I have, I thank Heaven, a very plentiful Fortune, a good Estate in the Country, some Houses in Town, and some Mony, a pretty tolerable personal Estate." Presumably, however, he is not immensely rich, as are the lords in other plays, and as is Sir Harry Wildair, who has a lordly fortune. The country squires have smaller, though still large, incomes: Mr. Balance in *The Recruiting Officer* has £1,200 a year; Sir Tunbelly Clumsey in *The Relapse* has £1,500 a year; the father of Lady Lurewell in *The Constant Couple* had £3,000 a year, which she inherited; Mockmode in *Love and a Bottle* has 5,000 acres, from which he derives an abundant income, the precise amount not specified.

We may compare these incomes of characters portrayed or referred to in the comedies with the estimates of incomes made by Gregory King of persons in similar social positions. Temporal lords, according to King, had incomes averaging £2,800 a year, baronets had £880, knights had £650, esquires had £450, and gentlemen had £280 [*Two Tracts,* Barnett (ed.)]. These sober estimates of *average* income, it is apparent, are much below the incomes of characters in parallel positions in the plays: the dramatists obviously exercised their privilege of endowing their characters munificently. Even so it would appear that the dramatists used some rough scale of what constituted a fit income for a given rank. The only character whose income seems totally disproportionate is Sir Harry Wildair—and he is presented as exceptional in every way.

The social rank of the important characters is most frequently that of the lower levels of the nobility and the upper levels of the squirearchy: no comedy contains a character of rank higher than an earl and only *The Confederacy* contains major characters of rank inferior to the gentry. The barrier between the nobility and the squirearchy is not impassable in these comedies: there is some movement, and some attempted movement, from one group to another, and members of the two groups mingle socially. Lord Foppington of *The Relapse,* formerly Sir Novelty Fashion of Cibber's *Love's Last Shift,* has by means of a £10,000 bribe been made a baron. Sir Tunbelly Clumsey with his £1,500 a year hopes to marry his daughter to Foppington and thus ennoble his grandchildren. Mr. Balance of *The Recruiting Officer* also has ambitions for his daughter (II): "The Death of your Brother makes you sole Heiress to my Estate, which three or four Years hence will amount to twelve hundred Pound per *annum;* this Fortune gives you a fair Claim to Quality and a Title; you must set a just Value upon your self, and, in plain Terms think no more of Captain *Plume.*" But if lords appear in a number of the comedies, only in *The Twin Rivals* and *The Relapse* do they appear as main characters, if we leave out of account Aimwell in *The Beaux' Stratagem,* who discovers at the end of the play that he has inherited his brother's peerage.

Only Vanbrugh's *Confederacy* has major characters of rank inferior to the gentry (though a number of the plays have such characters who appear incidentally). The social milieu of *The Confederacy* is entirely that of the City, and not even of its highest ranks: it is that of Gripe and Moneytrap, "Two rich money Scriveners," of a station distinctly inferior to that of the aldermen and international traders who appear incidentally in other plays. Far-

quhar gives most attention to the society of the wealthier squires, precisely as do the other dramatists, and he has no play in which the chief characters are not gentlefolk, even though he presents some minor characters from humble life more vividly and sympathetically than do the others. Sergeant Kite of *The Recruiting Officer* and Scrub and Cherry of *The Beaux' Stratagem* are among the most memorable figures in comedy of the Restoration tradition: they are fully realized as attractive individuals—Cherry, especially, who offers herself in marriage to Archer with a dowry of £2,000 accumulated by her putative father in his dealings with highwaymen. But characters from humble life always have minor, even if attractive, roles in Farquhar's plays. His important innovation lay not in his treatment of humble characters but in his treatment of rural life—of which more later.

The antimercantile bias of Congreve, Vanbrugh, and Farquhar was such that no attractive merchant character appears in any of their plays (except for one introduced briefly in *The Twin Rivals*). In some plays the merchants are ignored; in others they are the butt of casual but derisive jokes; and in still others they are ridiculed in dramatic caricatures, sometimes very harsh ones. At no time is there an implied acknowledgment of the importance of the merchant and of trade to the nation; on the contrary, there is a tone of contempt for the business community and for the prudential virtues associated with it, which is only occasionally lightened by irony. Even the wit in which the plays abound has a social bias. Wit, as these dramatists understood and esteemed it, was a gentleman's accomplishment, which a citizen could neither practice nor appreciate; and in their comedies they persisted in thinking of merchants as citizens.

Of the three dramatists, Congreve is the wittiest, and the carefully disciplined though metaphorical volubility of his characters makes them by all odds the sprightliest conversationalists of the Restoration stage. In fact, Congreve's sympathetic characters are among the most accomplished conversationalists in English literature; and their conversation is emphatically that of the *beau monde.* In his dedication of *The Way of the World* to the Earl of Mountague, Congreve alludes to his standard for dramatic dialogue:

> If it has happen'd in any Part of this Comedy, that I have gain'd a Turn of Stile, or Expression more Correct, or at least more Corrigible than in those which I have formerly written, I must, with equal Pride and Gratitude, ascribe it to the Honour of Your Lordship's admitting me into Your Conversation, and that of a Society where every body else was so well worthy of You, in Your Retirement last Summer from the Town: For it was immediately after, that this Comedy was written.

Congreve overstates the debt, of course; poets are not on their honor in dedications. But the standard of aristocratic elegance in conversation here described seems indeed to be the regulating one in his plays, in all of which the most favored characters are urbane gentlemen or noblemen who either possess or gain through marriage a landed estate.

Of Congreve's four comedies, *The Old Bachelor* (1693) is the most clearly shaped by social assumptions. The comedy has three separate actions, each concerned with a distinct social group; there is some correlation between the characters' social position and the degree of sympathy or contempt that Congreve shows for them. The admirable characters, the "Truewits" in Congreve's terminology, are Bellmour and Vainlove and their female counterparts Araminta and Belinda—all members of the gentry, devoted to wit and fun, foes to piety, settled industry, and rusticity. It is they who dominate the intrigues and with whom members of the audience are intended to identify themselves; and it is they who are rewarded—by matrimony—at the conclusion. There are two principal characters who are treated satirically, the one a booby squire, Sir Joseph Wittol, and the other a City banker, Alderman Fondlewife, both of whom suffer indignities. Fondlewife, a hypocritical, Nonconformist banker, is the most harshly treated of the major characters. Within the satiric framework of the play his offenses (which are made to seem his class's offenses) of hypocrisy, jealousy, and uxoriousness are more harshly regarded than is the adultery of Bellmour, which seems even to be condoned.

Vanbrugh's *Confederacy* (1705), a play about Court-City rivalry, is an adaptation of a French play (Florent Carton Dancourt's *Les Bourgeoises à la Mode*) first produced in Paris in 1692. Vanbrugh followed his original closely, even to many details of the dialogue, changing the locale, however, to London and making the characters English. His play can be considered a commentary on English society even though it is an adaptation, because he obviously chose his original for its relevance to the English scene and further reworked it in English terms.

The Confederacy abounds in comic situations; it has a vivacity that saves it from mere sordidness; but the world of vice it portrays precludes lightness of tone. The confederacy of the title is that of the wives of Gripe and Moneytrap to entice each other's husband, with mutual consent, as a means of getting money to support their social pretensions, which include the fashionable vice of gambling. With its central situation of City women aping the gentry, the play resembles many written by earlier dramatists: in its socio-economic values it is not far removed from Jonson and Massinger. Always in the background of the intrigues, determining the direction they take, is the jealousy and envy felt by characters of the merchant class for the nobility and gentry. The City wives desire money for the social opportunities it brings; love and lust for them are but secondary motivations. Court-City rivalry appears steadily, in the incidental conversation as well as in the absurd situations to which the two wives, Clarissa and Araminta, are driven by their social ambitions; and Vanbrugh's judgment, delivered through satire, is emphatically that citizens should keep their places. The drift of his satire is suggested in a conversation between an old peddler and her neighbor (I):

> MRS. CLOGGIT: . . . how do you speed amongst your City Customers?

> MRS. AMLET: My City Customers! Now by my truth, Neighbour, between the City and the Court (with Reverence be it spoken) there's not a — to chuse. My Ladies in the City, in Times past, were as full of Gold as they were of Religion, and as punctual in their Payments as they were in their Prayers; but since they have set their Minds upon Quality, adieu one, adieu t'other, their Money and their Consciences are gone, Heav'n knows where.

Here is suggested the theme of the action to follow.

Farquhar's *Constant Couple* (1699) . . . presents in Alderman Smuggler as bitter a caricature of the miserly, lecherous, and hypocritical merchant as can be found in the whole range of seventeenth-century comedy. But the caricature differs from earlier ones only in its greater harshness and more explicit insistence on hypocrisy. There are the usual two love intrigues in *The Constant Couple,* one culminating in the marriage of Sir Harry Wildair, a baronet with £8,000 a year, and Angelica, the daughter of a titled lady of unspecified rank; and the other in the marriage of Colonel Standard, the younger son of a lord, and Lady Lurewell, the heiress of a baronet, in possession of £3,000 a year. These are the principal characters, all of whom are treated sympathetically. The several prominent characters who are not members of the small circle of wealth, fashion, and quality (of whom Smuggler is but the most conspicuous) are without exception the subjects of satire.

These three plays—*The Old Bachelor, The Confederacy,* and *The Constant Couple*—contain the dramatists' most extended and most severe satirical attacks on the merchants; but their other plays contain evidence, even if not such unambiguous evidence, of the same hostility.

No other of Congreve's comedies includes important merchant characters nor detailed treatment of Court-City rivalry. *The Double Dealer* (1693) has only a single intrigue, one dominated by the machinations of an Iago-like villain. The social and economic assumptions upon which the action of the play turns, however, are the traditional ones; and both the prologue and the epilogue contain conventional hits at citizen-cuckolds. Yet Congreve shows himself to be no uncritical lover of quality by his inclusion in the play of telling satire directed at aristocratic snobbery. Mercantile life touches the action of *Love for Love* (1695) and *The Way of the World* (1700) only tangentially. In the earlier play, Trapland, a scrivener who is Valentine's principal creditor, appears briefly to dun him and to be made a fool of—though not to be duped out of his money. Valentine's—and it seems fair to say Congreve's—latent contempt for the merchants comes out in his feigned lunatic ravings when he replies to a question about what will happen in the City on the morrow (IV):

> Oh, Prayers will be said in empty Churches, at the usual Hours. Yet you will see such zealous Faces behind Counters, as if Religion were to be sold in every Shop. Oh things will go methodically in the City, the Clocks will strike twelve at Noon, and the horn'd Herd Buz in the Exchange at Two.

In short, just enough is said about the City to establish the traditional attitude of amused contempt. In *The Way of the World* (1700) merchants and mercantile life are all but ignored—there are no merchant characters, and I find only one direct allusion to their class (a conventional one to citizen-cuckolds [III]). The social milieu is that of the wealthier gentry, and it is a milieu inimical to the business community in the premium placed upon wit. The characters, as in Congreve's other plays, are much concerned about money: not about earning it, for that cannot be done in the society in which they live, but in possessing it in the form of an estate.

So too the characters in Vanbrugh's plays. Those of *The Provoked Wife* (1697), to illustrate, belong to the gentry: no prominent character of an inferior rank appears. Sir John Brute, the husband of the "provoked wife," is a gentleman of ample fortune, whose wife married him, he explains (I), for his money; his sottish overindulgence is limited neither by scarcity of funds nor by responsibilities. The other two prominent male characters, Constant and Heartfree, are both "Gentlemen of the Town." Since Constant is involved in an intrigue with Sir John Brute's wife, in which adultery and not matrimony is the object, his economic position has no relevance to the action and does not become apparent except in general terms; but Heartfree wishes to marry Belinda, and the chief obstacle to his doing so is his poverty. He does ultimately marry her, as we have seen, since she has a fortune sufficient to enable them to live modestly. Belinda speaks of her acquiescence with a social realism altogether typical of the play (V):

> I can't help being fond of this Rogue; and yet it go's to my Heart to think I must never Whisk to *Hide-Park,* with above a Pair of Horses; Have no Coronet upon my Coach, nor a Page to carry up my Train. But above all—that business of Place—Well; Taking Place, is a Noble Prerogative.

Farquhar's comedies are far more topical than Congreve's and Vanbrugh's. Himself an army officer (as indeed was Vanbrugh), he includes military characters in nearly all of his plays and through them provides comment, always from the soldier's point of view, of England's changing diplomatic and military position. He makes a soldier's matter-of-fact evaluations of international affairs, and only rarely is he chauvinistic. The topicality of his plays—of *Sir Harry Wildair,* for example, which chronicles the first reaction in London to the news of the Spanish King's death, or of *The Recruiting Officer,* which treats with at least poetic truth the problems of impressment in county towns—makes a strong claim on the historical imagination and is, I believe, pure gain. But it frequently crowds out extended treatment of social issues. In *The Constant Couple* only is there concentrated attention to social rivalry. Yet all of his comedies portray a society in which land is assumed to be the proper basis for social pretentions; and in all of them the central characters belong to the nobility or to the gentry.

The comedies of these dramatists satirize absurdities in behavior wherever they are found. Congreve's Lord Froth, Vanbrugh's Sir John Brute, and Farquhar's Young Wouldbe remind us that the dramatists had an eye to folly and wickedness in fashionable life. They were, after all,

critics of social behavior rather than of the social structure, which they took largely for granted. (pp. 43-54)

In the London of Congreve, Vanbrugh, and Farquhar there must have been hundreds, even thousands, of country squires who had come to the metropolis, having invested in joint stock companies, "to be at hand to take the advantage of buying and selling, as the sudden rise or fall of the price directs." The clash between these rustics and their more sophisticated London acquaintances, together with the corollary issues of the rival advantages of country and town, provides one of the major themes of late-seventeenth-and early-eighteenth-century comedy.

The treatment of rural-urban relations in the drama is inextricably associated with the distinction, by no means a clear one, between the aristocracy and the squirearchy. Most of the aristocrats of the seventeenth and eighteenth centuries had country houses and derived a large part of their income from the land. But as a group they were, and indeed still are, as Sir Lewis Namier puts it, "amphibious," having allegiance to both town and country [*England in the Age of Revolution*]. In the upper classes there were, of course, infinite gradations of rank, prestige, and affluence; and it is impossible to distinguish firmly between the families who could view a season in London as a normal perquisite of their rank and those for whom London was strange and alien. In actual life personal accomplishments, independent of social rank, were no doubt decisive in determining whether or not a man was regarded as a rustic. But in the plays there is an inverse correlation between a character's rank and his rusticity, provided he is not a permanent resident of London. The lords and sons of lords who appear in the plays are never rustics, even though presumably they would live most of the year in the country, but gentlemen of lower rank very often are.

The rusticity of dramatic characters is, then, entangled with considerations of rank. Rusticity itself, implying social maladroitness, is always portrayed as a liability, though it is not always treated with the same severity. Of the three most prominent dramatists writing at this time Farquhar is most tolerant of it, and Vanbrugh perhaps least. Congreve several times caricatures country squires in London; and yet he acknowledges dramatically that sophistication may occasionally be less desirable than rusticity.

Apart from *The Double Dealer,* Congreve includes a country squire in each of his comedies: Sir Joseph Wittol in *The Old Bachelor,* Sir Sampson Legend in *Love for Love,* and Sir Wilfull Witwoud in *The Way of the World,* all three contemptible in varying measure. Sir Joseph is the worst: a dim-witted coward and an easy target for town parasites. Raillery at the expense of the squirearchy appears in the play even in episodes in which Sir Joseph does not figure—as in Belinda's description to her friend Araminta of a meeting with a country family (IV):

> BELINDA: Oh; a most comical Sight: A Country Squire, with the Equipage of a Wife and two Daughters, came to Mrs. *Snipwel's* Shop while I was there—But, oh Gad! Two such unlick'd Cubs!

ARAMINTA: I warrant, plump, Cherry-cheek'd Country Girls.

The tone of these remarks, and of those that follow, provide an ironical reflection upon the "Truewits" themselves. Yet within the total context of the play, a contempt for rusticity is unmistakable. Sir Joseph Wittol is, appropriately it would seem, ingloriously married to the tarnished Sylvia.

In *Love for Love,* apart from the maladroit squire Sir Sampson Legend, who is Valentine's father, a memorable rustic appears in Miss Prue, "a silly awkward Country Girl." Yet Sir Sampson and Miss Prue, though they are duped by town-bred friends and relatives, have a redeeming bucolic charm about them, even if they appear at a disadvantage in repartee. Congreve's preference for town over country appears in his treatment of wit as the accomplishment of an urbane gentleman, an accomplishment resented by merchant and squire alike. "I hate a Wit," comments Sir Sampson Legend about Valentine (V). "I had a Son that was spoil'd among 'em; a good hopeful Lad, 'till he learn'd to be a Wit—And might have risen in the State—But, a pox on't, his Wit run him out of his Mony, and now his Poverty has run him out of his Wits."

In *The Way of the World* Congreve makes sport of rusticity, and as usual he presents his "Truewits," notably Millamant and Mirabell, as urbane and witty. But he is far from uncritical of the effects of town life. In the Witwouds he introduces a pair of brothers, the elder a country squire and the younger a town-bred lawyer, who illustrate respectively the results of country and town life; and the squire, booby though he is, comes off the better. He has independence, common sense, and courage, though he lacks social finesse; whereas his brother (for whom the family name was apparently chosen) has sacrificed the integrity of his personality to a desire to keep pace with town fashion. However, *The Way of the World,* in its splendid embodiment of wit, must be viewed as one of the most brilliant tributes to urbanity produced by the Augustan age; for wit, as Congreve understood it, is dependent for its existence on a crowded social life such as only a city or a richly endowed estate could make possible. It is inconsistent with prolonged rural retirement.

Vanbrugh is harsher with his squires than Congreve, though he has left a more memorable group of them: Sir Tunbelly Clumsey of *The Relapse,* Polidorus Hogstye of *Aesop,* Sir Francis Headpiece of *A Journey to London*—exemplars of a literary tradition that culminates in Addison's Tory fox hunter of the *Freeholder* essays and in Fielding's Squire Western of *Tom Jones.* These characters are, in their vigorous absurdities, among Vanbrugh's most notable achievements. They lack subtlety, as do all of Vanbrugh's characters, and they do not seem to be the result of considered thought; town and country in fact are frequently opposed in contrasting characters in such a way that the country represents dull virtue and London attractive sin. Fielding, who later saw the antithesis in much the same terms, preferred dull virtue. Not so Vanbrugh; he satirizes both extremes, but his sympathies rest firmly with the Town.

Moved apparently by the emotional dishonesty of the con-

clusion of Cibber's *Love's Last Shift,* Vanbrugh explores in *The Relapse* (1696) the probable future domestic affairs of a man and wife with utterly different personalities. A source of strain between Amanda and Loveless appears at once, even in the too perfect bliss they enjoy at the opening of the play, in their differing attitudes toward a life of retirement in the country. Loveless's overprotestations of contentment do not prevent Amanda from expressing apprehension at his forthcoming visit to London (I):

> Forgive the Weakness of a Woman,
> I am uneasie at your going to stay so long in Town,
> I know its false insinuating Pleasures;
> I know the Force of its Delusions;
> I know the Strength of its Attacks;
> I know the weak Defence of Nature;
> I know you are a Man—and I . . . a Wife.

Loveless's subsequent behavior when exposed to the temptations of London justifies Amanda's fear.

In the second intrigue of *The Relapse,* in which Young Fashion accomplishes a deceitful marriage to Miss Hoyden, Vanbrugh confronts country and town in the persons of two extreme exemplars of rural and urban vices, respectively: Sir Tunbelly Clumsey and Lord Foppington. Sir Tunbelly, whose personal qualities are fairly indicated by his name, has £1,500 a year, is a justice of the peace, and is deputy lieutenant of his county. Although socially ambitious, desiring his daughter's marriage to a lord (even such a new one as Lord Foppington), he is laughably deficient in the very social accomplishments in which Lord Foppington, the stage fop, is proficient to the point of absurdity—hence the result is the same. In the juxtaposition of the two caricatures, Vanbrugh exploits to its full humorous potential the mutual reaction of town and country.

The same rural-urban antagonism is exploited in Vanbrugh's *Aesop* (1697), *The Country House* (1698), and *A Journey to London,* a fragment about half the length of a complete play, first published by Cibber in 1728 after Vanbrugh's death. *A Journey to London* presents a particularly choice description of a foolish squire. Sir Francis Headpiece, "a Country Gentleman" having the foolish hope that he can secure a lucrative place at court and thus repair his fortune, has through extravagant expenditure gained election to Parliament. His uncle describes him (I):

> Forty years and two is the Age of him; in which it is computed by his Butler, his own person has drank two and thirty Ton of Ale. The rest of his Time has been employ'd in persecuting all the poor four-legg'd Creatures round, that wou'd but run away fast enough from him, to give him the high-mettled pleasure of running after them.
>
> . . . His Estate being left him with two Joyntures, and three weighty Mortgages upon it; He, to make all easy, and pay his Brother's and Sister's portions, marry'd a profuse young Housewife for Love, with never a Penny of Money.

In this play as in his others, Vanbrugh is critical of the sophisticated vice of fashionable London; but he shows no inclination to prefer rural simplicity.

Farquhar's last two comedies, *The Recruiting Officer* (1706) and *The Beaux' Stratagem* (1701), the comedies by which he is best known, both have settings in country towns: the one in Shrewsbury and the other in Lichfield. And these semirural settings contribute to the distinctive tone of the plays, the tone of healthy vitality and of easy accommodation to evil that in considerable measure is responsible for their attractiveness. The gang of highwaymen who are associated with Boniface in *The Beaux' Stratagem* are as amiable a lot as Gay's thieves in *The Beggar's Opera* twenty years later.

Farquhar's earlier rustics, however—Mockmode in *Love and a Bottle* (1698) and Clincher, Jr., in *The Constant Couple* (1699)—are less agreeable. Mockmode, the more fully developed character of the two, differs from the dramatic stereotype of the squire only to the extent that he has had a university education. He is an obtuse, yet not unappealing, character come to London to learn to be a wit, who in his determination to acquire the urbane graces must mirror many of Farquhar's contemporaries. "You Country Gentlemen, newly come to *London*," remarks his landlady (II), "like your own Spaniels out of a Pond, must be shaking the Water off, and bespatter every body about you." And his dancing master explains to him (*ibid.*) that " 'Squire and Fool are the same thing here," a judgment in which Farquhar, in his early plays at least, seems to concur.

His last two plays, then, represent a major shift in attitude, a shift away from the traditional contempt for the squirearchy. In his dedication of *The Recruiting Officer* "To All Friends round the Rekin" Farquhar tells of the circumstances that led to his choice of locale:

> 'Twas my good fortune to be order'd some time ago into the Place which is made the Scene of this Comedy; I was a perfect Stranger to everything in *Salop,* but its Character of Loyalty, the Number of its Inhabitants, the Alacrity of the Gentlemen in recruiting the Army, with their generous and hospitable Reception of Strangers.

> This Character I found so amply verify'd in every Particular, that you made Recruiting, which is the greatest Fatigue upon Earth to others, to be the greatest Pleasure in the World to me. . . .

> Some little Turns of Humour that I met with almost within the Shade of that famous Hill, gave the rise to this Comedy; and people were apprehensive, that, by the Example of some others, I would make the Town merry at the expense of the Country-Gentlemen: But they forgot that I was to write a Comedy, not a Libel; and that whilst I held to Nature, no Person of any Character in your Country could suffer by being expos'd.

Farquhar distinguishes between stage tradition and contemporary life—in *The Recruiting Officer* and in *The Beaux' Stratagem* as well as in this dedication. If he does not refrain from portraying in Mr. Sullen of the later play a memorable example of the brutish degeneration to which a retired country life can lead, he treats country gentlemen as a class respectfully.

He was too witty a man, and too clever a playwright, to treat rural-urban rivalry soberly, despite his resolution to avoid the caricatures of country types. In *The Beaux' Stratagem* he includes much gay conversation about the rival claims of town and country. When early in the play Aimwell and Archer assess their situation, Archer apostrophizes London (I): "So much Pleasure for so much Money, we have had our Penyworths, and had I Millions, I wou'd go to the same Market again." Town and country provide Dorinda and Mrs. Sullen, too, with a recurrent subject of conversation. "But pray, Madam," Dorinda asks her sister-in-law (II), "how came the Poets and Philosophers that labour'd so much in hunting after Pleasure, to place it at last in a Country Life?" Mrs. Sullen replies: "Because they wanted Money, Child, to find out the Pleasures of the Town: Did you ever see a Poet or a Philosopher worth Ten thousand Pound? If you can shew me such a Man, I'll lay you Fifty Pound you'll find him somewhere within the weekly Bills." Mrs. Sullen is wittier than Dorinda, and her points are more telling; but the argument cannot be won. It is, of course, not the words of any character that establish the dramatist's attitude toward the subject, but rather the total impression created by the play; and in evaluating this impression much must be made of the exuberance of the people who inhabit the countryside. Farquhar surely had some sympathy with the objection expressed by Mr. Balance of *The Recruiting Officer* (II) to the drift of people and wealth to London and its environs.

Farquhar's admiration for the country, as we have seen, was not widely shared at the time he was writing. Other dramatists, including the obscure ones, were customarily as contemptuous of rustics as they were of merchants, and as traditional in portraying them. Thomas Wright in *The Female Virtuosos* (1693) presents a typical pair of rustics in Sir Timothy Witless, "A Country Gentlemen," and his son Witless, "A *Cambridge* Scholar," a father and son who bear some resemblance to Steele's later Sir Harry Gubbin and Humphry Gubbin of *The Tender Husband* (1705). Young Witless's rusticity is overlaid but not concealed by a university-acquired pedantry. "A Country Knight that affects to speak Proverbs," Sir Barnaby Buffler of Edward Ravenscroft's *The Canterbury Guests* (1694) is an arrogant and self-centered squire of fifty-five whose £1,500 a year has induced Alderman Furr of London to offer him his daughter in marriage. In George Powell's *Cornish Comedy* (1696), the traditional rustic appears in Swash, "A true Country Squire that makes Recreations his business." Mary Pix's *Beau Defeated* (1700) includes "a Country Squire" in the elder Clerimont "Whose sole delight," according to another character (II), "lay in his Kindred Hounds, who for his Hunting Companions, entertain'd all the Lubbers of the four adjacent Parishes, till the Country was going to Petition the Parliament for Labourers." The anonymous *Intriguing Widow* (1705) portrays in Clodhopper, "A Country Squire," an extreme exemplar of the rustic, one whose speech is countrified almost to the point of unintelligibility. William Taverner's *The Maid the Mistress* (1708) includes Squire Empty of Essex, whose name conveys an adequate impression of his shortcomings.

Steele's Humphry Gubbin of *The Tender Husband* (1705), the most attractive of the stage bumpkins of the time, is a character exhibiting at once strong individuality and generic resemblances to the stereotype of the booby. Steele seems to have taken suggestions for him from earlier comedies, just as Goldsmith in turn took suggestions from Humphry for Tony Lumpkin. Sir Harry Gubbin, who is the brother-in-law of Mr. Tipkin, the merchant, has brought his son Humphry to London to have him marry his cousin Biddy Tipkin. Humphry, although twenty-three and not without spirit, has been maltreated by his father to the point that he is oafish in his manners and all but illiterate. His trip to London comes to him as a sudden revelation of his deprivation; and he is ridiculous but at the same time appealing as, for the first time possessed of independence, he pursues the pleasures of the town. Finding his cousin unappealing, he marries a tarnished woman, though one of some personal integrity. In depicting Humphry's vulnerability to town sharpers and his naïve delight in London, Steele plays variations on a familiar dramatic theme; but he gives it a remarkable vigor by expending more sympathy than was usual on his rustic.

The Tender Husband is set in London, as are all Steele's other comedies, all of Cibber's that are about English life, all of Burnaby's, and all but two of Mrs. Centlivre's. Baker shows somewhat more variety, choosing as locales such fashionable resorts and suburbs as Tunbridge Wells, Oxford, and Hampstead Heath. Late-seventeenth- and early-eighteenth-century comedy must in fact be viewed as intensely urban; apart from the last two plays of Farquhar's, even in the few ostensible exceptions the rural locales serves primarily as pretexts for sniping at rural life. In addition to *The Recruiting Officer* and *The Beaux' Stratagem,* only Ravenscroft's *Canterbury Guests* (1694), Motteux's *Love's a Jest* (1696), Powell's *Cornish Comedy* (1696), Doggett's *The Country Wake* (1696), Walker's *Marry, or, Do Worse* (1703), Mrs. Centlivre's *The Man's Bewitched* (1709), and a few others have provincial settings.

The immense growth of London gave a certain timeliness to the jokes about country manners. "Why, the City stands where it did," remarks a character in Motteux's *Love's a Jest* (I), "but the Suburbs are like to overtake you in *Hertfordshire.*" (pp. 68-76)

> John Loftis, *"The Survival of the Restoration Stereotypes, 1693-1710,"* in his Comedy and Society from Congreve to Fielding, *Stanford University Press, 1959, pp. 43-76.*

Geoffrey Marshall

[*In the excerpt below, Marshall compares Restoration comedy with the serious drama of the period, noting similarities in language, characterization, form, and theme.*]

In the Restoration, theatrical fare changed quickly, with the companies changing their offerings every few days. Comedies followed tragedies on sequential evenings as the repertory companies competed for a very small audience. The audience was so small that it failed to support the two

theaters which were chartered at the Restoration, and the companies were forced to merge. The United Company was the only theater for more than twelve years (1682-1695). Under these circumstances of audience size and theatrical variety, it is puzzling, even baffling, to compare Restoration comedy and tragedy. The bombast and posturing of the serious plays seem to belong in a different universe from that of the sexual Darwinism of the comedies. Rant and wit seem contrasting poles of rhetorical effect.

Alan Downer, in [*The British Drama*] (1950), describes the Restoration split: "The serious counterpart of Restoration comedy is so utterly different that it is difficult to believe they were intended for the same theatre and audiences." Obviously the same theater and audience are involved, however, and Downer wonders at the phenomenon of "the same actor, the same audience, each apparently accepting and believing in a totally different concept of virtue, a totally different set of ethical values," as they change from comedy to tragedy and back again. More recently, Anne Righter, in a survey of heroic tragedy [*Restoration Theatre*], has said much the same thing: "In their attitudes and values, in all of their basic presuppositions, comedy like Etherege's *She Wou'd if She Cou'd* (1668) and a tragedy like Dryden's *Tyrannic Love* (1669) exist quite simply at opposite poles." Both Downer and Righter go on to attempt to explain the coexistence of apparently irreconcilable genres in this era, as have other historians of the drama.

In a quick and visceral response to this split between comedy and tragedy, one might immediately suspect that the dichotomy is false. It does not seem likely that an audience, especially a homogeneous audience like that of most of the Restoration period, when so few people attended, would change its ethical standards from night to night—even if only two standards were involved, one for each genre. While not impossible, it seems untrue to our experience that the audience would, for example, systematically accept libertinism one night and piety and chastity the next. Certainly hypocrisy is possible for any audience, and so is intellectual and moral inconsistency. Imlac, in Dr. Johnson's *Rasselas,* wisely notes, "Inconsistencies cannot both be right; but, imputed to man they may both be true" (Chapter 8). Nevertheless, allowing for the profound differences in convention between comedy and tragedy, and allowing for hypocrisy and fuzzy thinking, and allowing for the human willingness to be entertained at the expense of coherence, it remains unlikely that two antithetical forms would exist simultaneously. If they are like other human products, the genres in this era should show similarities, together with their differences. This is, I think, the case. In what follows, I will assume the existence of considerable differences between the genres, differences which are superficial and differences which are subtly profound. But these differences have received due attention, and I would like to show some of the similarities which exist. The similarities exist together with the differences, and not rather than the differences.

[Some evidence has shown] that there is fundamental similarity between the nonmetaphoric language of comedy and the language of tragedy in this period. Once one begins to explore similarities of language, moreover, many begin to appear. The prose spoken by the comic protagonists is often, for instance, rhythmical and structurally balanced. Our ear picks up the rhythms created by parison and isocolon, which create effects similar to those achieved by balanced heroic couplets.

> She's the most passionate in her love and the most extravagant in her jealousy of any woman I ever heard of. (*The Man of Mode,* I. 172-73)

> It is our mutual interest to be so. It makes the women think the better of his understanding and judge more favorably of my reputation; it makes him pass upon some for a man of very good sense, and I upon others for a very civil person. (*The Man of Mode,* I. 399-402)

> Come, madam, in short, you see I am resolved to have a share in the estate, yours or your son's. If I cannot get you, I'll keep him, who is less coy you find. But if you would have your son again, you must take me too. Peace or war? Love or law? (*The Plain Dealer,* IV.i.323-27)

> Then let 'em show their innocence by not understanding what they hear, or else show their discretion by not hearing what they would not be thought to understand. (*The Way of the World,* I.i. 475-78)

The verbal wit represented in these speeches is everywhere in the comedies and tragedies alike. The Restoration playwright and audience delighted in the neatly balanced or antithetical phrase, the rhythmical open and close of a sentence. We can find these wonderful, highly crafted sentences everywhere—in letters, in dispatches, in essays, in courtesy books, in prose fiction.

In comedy and tragedy alike, the language is marked by extensive use of simile. The simile is the most explicit of rhetorical figures; it calls attention to itself with *like* and *as* and, as it were, protects the artist from any accusation of distorting reality. The simile stops short of identifying A and B, which, according to some theories, would be a distortion of reality. The simile appears in the serious plays, perhaps as a conscious echo of the epic simile, in those moments when vividness is sought:

> My hearts so plain,
> That men on every passing thought may look,
> Like fishes gliding in a Chrystal brook:
> When troubled most, it does the bottom show,
> 'Tis weedless all above; and rockless all below.
> (*The Conquest of Granada,* Part I, Act IV,
> p. 35)

> I stand
> Like one that in a Desart seeks his way,
> Sees several Paths, yet doubting of the right,
> Stands in a maze, and fears to venture upon any.
> (Banks, *The Island Queens,* III, p. 33)

> Then like the Monarch o' the Winds, I'le go
> And loose my stormy Squadrons on the Foe,
> And when the mighty vapour's spent and done,
> The wasting *Roman* inundation gone,
> And not a Cloud in all the Heav'ns we see,

> I'le come a hot and pleasant Calm to thee.
> (*The Destruction of Jerusalem,* Part II,
> Act III, p. 34)

In comedy, simile appears as the foundation of one form of wit, most famously exemplified by Witwoud, in *The Way of The World:*

> MIR. You seem to be unattended, madam. You used to have the beau monde throng after you, and a flock of gay fine perukes hovering round you.

> WIT. Like moths about a candle. I had like to have lost my comparison for want of breath.

> MILL. Oh, I have denied myself airs today. I have walked as fast through the crowd—

> WIT. As a favorite in disgrace, and with as few followers.

> MILL. Dear Mr. Witwoud, truce with your similitudes; for I am sick of 'em—

> WIT. As a physician of a good air. I cannot help it, madam, though 'tis against myself. (II. i. 296-307)

From everything we can read, we gain the impression that comedy and tragedy alike catered to the pleasure which comes from hearing an apt, pointed, or poignant comparison.

The characters of comedy and tragedy are similar in a surprising number of ways. Most important, they are alike *flawed* characters. The tragic protagonist is by definition flawed, whether the definition comes from Aristotle, some intervening French or Italian critic, or French or English dramatic practice. All agree, also, that comic characters are imperfect creatures whose limitations, follies, and affectations make them fit objects for laughter. Dryden describes the comic-tragic parallel clearly [in "Parallel in Poetry and Painting," *Critical Essays,* II]: "The characters of comedy and tragedy . . . are never to be made perfect, but always to be drawn with some specks of frailty and deficience."

The theoretical position is familiar to students of literary history, but its critical implications are not always obvious. If the playwrights consistently followed this precept and displayed flawed characters, then some specific plays may need to be reinterpreted. If Etherege followed the precept, then Dorimant cannot be understood to be a "hero" in the sense that his behavior was designed to be a model for sophistication and wit. If Wycherley followed it, then Manly must be flawed in some fashion. If Congreve followed it, then Mirabell is flawed (or not comic). If Dryden followed it, then Almanzor is flawed. And so, perhaps, are St. Catherine in *Tyrannick Love,* and Aureng-Zebe, and Jaffeir in *Venice Preserv'd,* and Mustapha. There are other alternatives, of course, including the possibility that some of these plays are not tragedies—for example, *Tyrannick Love.*

I have tried to avoid defining these plays according to their genre in the belief that definition requires a different approach from that which I wish to take, and I have used the term "serious" to indicate those plays which are not primarily designed to provoke laughter. Nevertheless, even within the capacious category of "serious drama," it seems fair to say that most characters are flawed—St. Catherine, in this instance, excluded—at least to the extent that they are unable to bring about external or internal harmony. Even good men like Aureng-Zebe are marred by weaknesses and indecision. Jaffeir's intentions are obviously good, but that is not enough in the ambiguous universe Otway has constructed. Mustapha's selflessness is admirable, but it is not sufficient to heal the suffering of his brother and rival.

In comedy, as well, the flaws are present in most cases, minor characters and some women excepted. I believe the case has been made that Dorimant is a "deficient" man in the sense that he sometimes loses control of the situation ("I never was at such a loss before!" [V. i. 299]), and in the sense that his libertinism, his pursuit of the "heat of the business," is defeated, apparently, by Harriet. Dorimant's "flaws" are nothing, of course, when compared to Sir Fopling Flutter's, and there are obviously degrees of deficiency in various characters. Manly, too, has been convincingly shown to be a man of often blind moral vigor. Manly is able to see and witheringly condemn the "spaniels of the world" with their "decorums, supercilious forms, and slavish ceremonies," but he is himself willing to be something less than a man: "I rather choose to go where honest, downright barbarity is professed, where men devour one another like generous hungry lions and tigers, not like crocodiles" (*The Plain Dealer,* I. 616-19). Manly's statement of preference is certainly downright and honest, but those qualities do not make the preference attractive. Manly is blind to his own misjudgment of character and his own extremism, though it may be that he would believe extremism in the pursuit of virtue is no vice. In any case, Manly's flaws appear in his paradoxes—"generous tigers"—which may be ironic, but which nevertheless express an extreme, not an ideal.

Mirabell is uncomic, I think. Our laughter is never directed toward him in a sustained way, and the only mildly satiric moment involving him comes when Millamant calls him "sententious Mirabell" and accuses him of looking like Solomon at the dividing of the child (II. i. 523). Mirabell is too stuffy to be amusing, and most of the play's comedy takes place apart from him.

Whatever the degree of flaw in comic and serious character, there is an important implication about the audience and its response when a play is constructed with flawed characters. The audience to such a play is assumed to be educable, alert, critical, distanced, vain, and itself flawed. Each of these characteristics is necessary for a play with flawed characters to succeed in delighting and instructing its audience. They must be educable because otherwise instruction could not take place. They must be alert because judgment is constantly required in order to distinguish fools from knaves. The audience must be critical rather than forgiving because forgiveness erases flaws or renders them impotent. They must be distanced from the play because otherwise flaws are not comic. Intimacy, sympathy, empathy—all change laughter from a corrective to a loving acknowledgment of the human community. To laugh *with* someone is to acknowledge shared flaws of no permanent significance. No one laughs in shame. Moreover, the audience is assumed to be vain, because if they were not—if they were humble or perhaps indifferent to their fellow man—then no laughter could act upon them as a moral force. The humble man is not shamed by laughter directed at him—see, for example, Christian in *Pilgrim's Progress*—only the vain man is. Lastly, and perhaps most obviously, the audience must be assumed to be flawed, for otherwise there is no point in revealing the ridiculousness of folly. A play that does so might delight a perfect audience, but it could not instruct them.

This outline speaks only of comedy, but a parallel justification could be developed for tragedy. The tragic audience also must be assumed to be flawed, critical, and so on, in order for pity and fear to work upon them. A perfect audience would destroy a tragedy as quickly as a perfect protagonist would. A perfectly good audience would feel no fear, though they might feel pity, and a perfectly evil audience might feel fear, but no pity. Beneath the bantering tone of many prologues to serious plays, is the expectation that the audience is going to watch the play sharply, critically, and with reason as well as emotion. The audience is self-possessed and well informed. The bantering tone says, in effect, "We all know what is good, just, cruel, and so on, and tonight a playwright, very much like yourselves, is going to show these emotions in action." The rhetorical gambit is obvious, but if there were no shared values, the assumption of them in the prologue would not save the play. Here are the opening lines of the Prologue to *Venice Preserv'd:*

> In these distracted times, when each man dreads
> The bloudy stratagems of busie heads;
> When we have fear'd three years we know not
>   what,
> Till Witnesses begin to die o' th' rot,
> What made our Poet meddle with a Plot?
> Was't that he fansy'd, for the very sake
> And name of Plot, his trifling Play might take?
> For there's not in't one Inch-board Evidence,
> But 'tis, he says, to reason plain and sense,
> And that he thinks a plausible defence.

Otway gathers up the audience in a casual "we" and assumes that everyone is aware of the Popish Plot and that everyone, in addition, has a slightly Tory bias. He traps the audience into critical approval by suggesting that the play is acceptable to reason and therefore every reasonable man will find it pleases him. This leaves the audience, presumably, without recourse except to applaud or be thought irrational. Nevertheless, all this badinage and warm-up before the play assumes an audience literate, well informed, familiar with the conventions of the form they are about to see, and prejudiced in favor of reasonableness as a value.

All of this changes as the eighteenth century begins and progresses. The definitions of comedy and tragedy change and so, radically, does the assumed nature of the audience. The nature of the audience and the play are so intimately connected that cause-effect relationships are difficult to determine. The change which takes place about the turn of the century may be due to a change in audience, or it may be due to a change in dramatic literature, or it may be due to some combination of these. All three possibilities have been suggested. In any case, the Restoration audience for comedy and for tragedy is assumed to be the same. The audience had expectations for comedy which differed from their expectations for tragedy, but their attitude toward their role as audience would seem to have been constant.

The admirable characters of comedy and tragedy alike—characters to whom we give our general approval, even though they are flawed to one degree or another—are predominantly characterized by self-possession, *sprezzatura,* or what the period called "ease." Almanzor has given the catch phrase to the heroic protagonists with his bold assertion, "I alone am king of me" (I. i. 206). The remark indicates an unwillingness to accept superior moral authority and also a blunt confidence in his own standards. Almanzor's frequent changes in allegiance are superficial in the sense that his fundamental allegiance to his word and to his sense of honor never changes. He shifts allegiance as he must in a world where most men are not true to their word and are not motivated by honor. As men break their word to him, violate the standards of honor which he cherishes, Almanzor feels that his ties to them are broken and he is free to make other arrangements. No matter whom he serves at the moment, Almanzor is typically self-possessed and confident. He knows his impulses, he knows his strength, and he knows what he believes. This gives him the "freedom" of which he boasts (I. i. 206-209).

Dorimant possesses the same conviction, the same sense of self-confidence, the same bold assertiveness of manner which comes from self-confidence and moral superiority. The last may seem an odd quality to attribute to Dorimant, but Restoration rakes typically act from what they feel to be a moral stance more honest and thorough than those of their contemporaries. It is only with slight irony that Medley tells young Bellair, in *The Man of Mode,* that Bellair's fiancée will not approve his friendship with Medley and Dorimant: " 'Tis not her interest you should keep company with men of sense, who will be talking reason" (I. 298-99). Dorimant could say, with Almanzor, "I alone am king of me." His more likely phrasing of the same idea, however, would be, "I am honest in my inclinations" (II. ii. 188). The libertine and the epic hero pride themselves on honesty, on courage, on self-control. They differ drastically, on the other hand, in the degree of their willingness to use dissimulation, in their sexual mores, in their social sophistication, in their political significance, and in many other ways. At the same time, the general appearance of the Restoration protagonist is remarkably the same, no matter what the genre.

The serious and the comic protagonist are similarly affected by women with whom they fall in love. The admirable women in Restoration drama are the chief means of socialization of their men. We can again parallel *The Conquest of Granada* and *The Man of Mode.* Almahide and Harriet both bring their lovers into line with social modes, or, more accurately, into line with custom. Almanzor is brought, though not very smoothly, into an awareness of the necessity for art in his manner, and into an awareness of the limitations inherent in his fellow men, who are nevertheless of hitherto unsuspected importance to him. Dorimant, too, is brought into line with custom—specifically, marriage—and brought to the modification of his otherwise wholly self-interested behavior.

That women typically redeem the protagonists may reveal the existence of two different kinds of plays: there are serious and comic plays of the sort just described, in which admirable, self-possessed protagonists are brought to custom by love; and there are plays in which the protagonists are not admirable because, or partly because, they lack self-possession—such plays as *All for Love,* or *Venice Preserv'd,* or *The Plain Dealer.* Plays like the last three are ambiguous in their moral meaning and have been the subjects of considerable critical discussion. Our response to each of these plays is different, but we can be aware that, in all the plays, the protagonists are acted upon as much as acting—they lack the powerful self-assurance which marks the rake and the hero alike. Nor do they exhibit the arrogance, boastfulness, smugness, and contempt which are shabby imitations of *sprezzatura* sometimes found in would-be rakes.

Antony is the shadow of an emperor as *All for Love* begins, and Cleopatra's role does not bring him to heroism, but to defeat, at least in public, social, and customary terms. Belvidera, in *Venice Preserv'd,* at first appears to act redemptively, to bring Jaffeir back from the brink of treason and murder, but her good intentions are inadequate for dealing with the ambiguities and confusions of their world. The act to save Venice is the same act that makes Jaffeir a traitor to his friend. Belvidera preserves a state controlled by faithless and weak men, "Where all agree to spoil the Publick Good, / And Villains fatten with the brave man's Labours" (I. 208-209). The women of *The Plain Dealer* play no redemptive role. Manly learns something about himself by overhearing how easily he has been deceived by Olivia, and at the end of the play he turns away from misanthropy and exile with the help of Fidelia, a figure from the green world of romance and altogether unsuited, in language, morality, and faithfulness, for the world of the play. Olivia prompts him to revenge, not to socially acceptable patterns, and Fidelia is a *deus ex machina* and a cause of change only in the same sense that lightning is a cause of fire—unpredictably and incoherently.

Generally, and significantly, the characters in Restoration drama can be measured against a spectrum of inner strengths and weaknesses. The weakest characters are "naturals," individuals unable to control themselves and suitable only for farce and sentimentality. At the other extreme are saints or near saints, such as St. Catherine or Cato, and absolute villains, such as the Empress of Morocco or Abdelazer. This spectrum is carefully calibrated, and characters exist along its whole length. Dorimant and Horner and Fainall are all rakes, but they are easily distinguished personalities. Aureng-Zebe, Mustapha, Alexander, and Brutus also can be distinguished one from another. The spectrum of strengths and weaknesses is the same for comedy and tragedy, and the man of courage and action is of chief importance to both.

Formally, comic and serious drama are also similar. Both are extremely episodic. The emotionally serial tragedy is matched by comedies with notoriously complex plots. The difficulty that generations have experienced with *The Way of the World* is exemplary, and we have evidence that the audience of the Restoration preferred plays with elaborate intrigue and skillfully timed plots and counterplots. The most famous example is Sir Samuel Tuke's adaptation of a Spanish play, *The Adventures of Five Hours.* Tuke's play was a large success, and Pepys, in 1663, described it as "the best, for the variety and the most excellent continuance of the plot to the very end, that I ever saw, or think I ever shall" [quoted in Helen McAfee's *Pepys on the Restoration Stage*]. In countless comedies, the rake-hero has so many irons in the fire that he must exercise perfect control of the world around him or else all will collapse in damaging discoveries and revelations.

Thematically, Restoration drama treats every major theme which appears in other literature of the period; moreover, most themes appear in both comedy and tragedy—with different emphasis, to be sure. The themes of the Restoration have been isolated in terms of dichotomies, and the dichotomies are useful so long as we do not confuse them with choices. When art and nature, for instance, appear as contrasts, they do not appear necessarily as choices; one need not choose *either* art *or* nature. In fact, Restoration drama insists repeatedly that only a combination of the two makes a full man in a whole universe.

The clash of art and nature appears in Dryden's drama almost from the start—which is to say, in Restoration serious drama almost from the start. In *The Indian Emperour,* first acted in 1665, Dryden draws the contrast between Montezuma, the native ruler, and Cortez. Cortez, as the play opens, sees the difference between the Indian manners and his own. "All their Customs," he says, "are by Nature wrought, / But we, by Art, unteach what Nature taught" (I. i. 13-14). Almanzor, the noble savage, is thus not the first figure to contrast spontaneous morality with civilized dissimulation. Almanzor does form something of a parallel to Manly, in *The Plain Dealer,* however, in that both learn the necessity for art in life, and the need sometimes to call a spade a garden implement.

The heroic protagonists are often transparent men, whose feelings, loyalties, and ideologies lie out in the open for all to see. They are either naive about the use of appearance or morally unwilling to dissimulate. Zanger, in *Mustapha,* woos by proclaiming, "I for sacrifice bring such a heart / As Nature offers in disdain of Art" (III. iii. 380). Villains, on the other hand, are consummate manipulators of appearance. In Otway's *Don Carlos,* for instance, two villains plan to deceive the king and inflame his jealousy:

> Watch every look, each quick, and subtle glance,
> Then we'l from all produce such Circumstance
> As shall the King's new Jealousie advance.
> (I. 202-204)

This sounds something like *Othello,* and it is. In both plays, the issue is manipulation of appearances. Villains live by deception, and in every play which has a villain, dissimulation, artifice, and pretense of all sorts are present.

Comic villains, like Fainall, are also dissimulators, but comic protagonists can be distinguished from tragic often by the protagonist's skill with dissimulation. In heroic and tragic drama the protagonist is often without any experience with or inclination toward art. Dorimant, Mirabell, and Horner are masters of deception, and the native comic protagonist, like Parson Adams or Tom Jones, is a development of the eighteenth century.

The use of art—that is, any form of skilled manipulation of nature—does not distinguish good from evil. Nature also fails to provide an automatic measure of a man. Almanzor is "as free as Nature first made man" (I, p. 7). This freedom enables him to follow his standard of honor with single-mindedness and sets him apart from the vacillation and compromise of those around him. But what happens when that freedom is applied to the moral realm, or, more specifically, to sexuality? Here is Don John of Otway's *Don Carlos:*

> How vainly would dull Moralists Impose
> Limits on Love, whose Nature brooks no Laws:
> Love is a God, and like a God should be
> Inconstant: with unbounded liberty
> Rove as he list.
> (III. 1-5)

Or here is Dorimant, the man of mode, turning to nature for the analogy to his infidelity: "Constancy at my years? 'Tis not a virtue in season; you might as well expect the fruit the autumn ripens i' the spring" (II. ii. 179-81). Dorimant and Almanzor are perhaps being selective about what part of nature they refer to, but the term *nature,* at any rate, appears in the mouth of hero and villain alike as justification for his behavior.

Neither art nor nature is itself good or evil. Both are ambiguous, and the ambiguity of these central terms can produce exciting dialogue as the terms appear and reappear like Proteus in varied shapes. If there is a consensus in the period, it may be represented by the proviso scene in *The Way of the World.* There Mirabell and Millamant work out an arrangement which contains both art and nature—an arrangement in which he insists on giving nature its place in such matters as breeding: "I denounce against all strait-lacing, squeezing for a shape, till you mold my boy's head like a sugar loaf "; and she insists that art shall have its place before she will "by degrees dwindle into a wife." To avoid the "flusomely familiar," she goes to the opposite extreme: "Let us never visit together, nor go to a play together. But let us be very strange and well-bred; let us be as strange as if we had been married a great while, and as well-bred as if we were not married at all." (IV. 235-36, 184-87.) In each play, when this theme appears significantly, the characters must make their own amalgam without a prescribed formula; each compromise and combination of nature and art is made afresh.

Compromise is also necessary in the conflict of the individual and society which appears in Restoration drama. The weight of custom, law, convenience, and lethargy is sometimes felt in bizarre ways. For example, in *Aureng-Zebe* the Mogul laws prescribe the death of all sons who rival the firstborn. Sometimes the signs of social pressure are more familiar as exemplified by the sexual double standard. In comedy and in tragedy, the aspirations and inclinations of the central figures must clash with the demands of society sooner or later because, fundamental to all of the major philosophic views of the period, is the notion that men are flawed and therefore unable to work together smoothly. Sometimes social responsibility is expressed as duty, to parent, to state, or to friend. Sometimes it is expressed as law or custom. Sometimes it is expressed in abstractions which embody social values: law, order, peace, right, calm, social status. Against all of these responsibilities the individual, comic or serious, attempts to realize his will in the world.

Unlike the contrast of art and nature, however, the Restoration plays suggest that when the individual and society clash, there is, and should be, a winner—society. Sometimes the cost of society's victory is great, as in *All for Love,* and sometimes it is small, as in *The Man of Mode,* when Dorimant moves to the country for a trial period before marriage. But, so far as I am aware, no Restoration play unequivocally asserts the right of the individual against that of society. The nation had just undergone a period of individual freedom—represented by parliamentary secular government and antiepiscopal church governments—which had led, in the judgment of those in control when the Restoration was accomplished, to anarchy. Society exacts its price for order, harmony, and peace, but the alternatives to order, harmony, and peace are worse. This lesson from experience was dramatized in comedy and in tragedy.

The complex relationships of reason and the irrational in man form another theme which appears in both genres, sometimes tentatively and sometimes with an aphoristic clarity which suggests that to know the truth is to live by it. There is no handy and accurate way to summarize this set of relationships. There was no universal formula for the application of reason or the release of passion, and although the claims of reason are stated repeatedly and aggressively, the claims are more often battle cries than statements of fact. For example, in Rowe's *Tamerlane,* the protagonist loses his temper with the Sultan Bazajet and is about to kill him, when another character pleads for Bazajet's life on grounds of honor. Tamerlane relents, saying, "Sultan be safe. Reason resumes her Empire" (IV. p. 53). Tamerlane's statement is at once a periphrastic way of saying, "I have agreed not to kill you"; an assertion of a widely held belief, that reason should rule; and wishful thinking. No one in the audience then or now would believe that this momentary victory over passion, coupled with exclamatory assertion of reason's pre-eminence, is a description of future behavior. Tamerlane is saying that he wishes he could live by reason at all times; almost everyone in the Restoration would have echoed the sentiment.

The comic and the serious drama are like fun-house mirrors—stretching, compressing, and bending the image of man as he passes between and before them. We can recognize the creature in the mirror, despite the distortion, and

that part which we recognize, those significant clues to identity, are found in both comic and serious reflections. As has already been mentioned, there is an amusing parallel between some comic ladies and the tragic heroines. These comic ladies are characterized by passionate impatience and lack of self-control. They are quickly driven to extremes and out of the empire of reason. Lady Wishfort, in *The Way of the World,* is "panting ripe" and forever impatient, forever in a haste to "marry anything that resembled a man." In a brilliant moment in the play, Wishfort has been in a passion and "frowned a little too rashly" for her makeup. "There are some cracks discernible in the white varnish," Foible tells her. "Cracks, say'st thou? Why I am arrantly flayed; I look like an old peeled wall." (III. i. 129-33.) The circumstances are wonderfully comic, but the image has *Dorian Grey* connotations which can echo in serious plays as well. The cracks which appear in the facade under strains of passion are often the fragmentations of madness—madness provoked by despair, loss, and anger. Phraartes sees Clarona die, in *The Destruction of Jerusalem,* Part II, and erupts in a great cry:

> Aloft!—I see her mounting to the Sun!—
> The flaming Satyr towards her does roul,
> His scorching Lust makes Summer at the Pole.
> Let the hot Planet touch her if he dares!—
> Touch her, and I will cut him into Stars,
> And the bright chips into the Ocean throw!—
> —Oh! my sick brain!—where is *Phraartes* now?
> Gone from himself!—who shall his sense restore?
> None, none, for his *Clarona* is no more!—
> (V. pp. 54-55)

Phraartes approaches schizophrenia ("where is *Phraartes* now?"), and Lady Wishfort exemplifies the follies of artful appearance as a substitute for reality, but there is a common ground between them. Both show versions of what it is to lose the art—and it is art, not nature—which is control. The characters and their situations are so obviously different that this small common ground is all the more revealing of the substantial links joining the dramatic genres.

It does not matter which of the traditional pairs we employ in examining the drama—thought and feeling, reason and passion, mind and matter—all Restoration plays reveal the same fear of uncontrolled feeling. All of them reveal a fear of madness. All of them imagine the human creature as delicately balanced, easily swayed, easily deceived, easily hurt, and much too often corruptible. "When we come to particulars," Southerne has a character say in *The Fate of Capua,* " 'tis only to find fault: / Men are but men" (I, p. 15).

If we examine the drama for its positive values, we find the same unanimity—allowing always for differences in emphasis. Ben Ross Schneider, Jr., conducted a methodical analysis of Restoration comedy [in *The Ethos of Restoration Comedy*] to find quantitative evidence for the values in the plays. The result of his analysis was the isolation of four points of ethical emphasis in comedy: liberality, courage, plain dealing, and love. In terms of volume of emphasis, these four values receive the most attention. As we might expect, these four appear also in the serious plays.

I will not pretend to the systematic and voluminous methods employed by Schneider; but I am confident that the employment of such methods in the study of the serious drama would certify these four as prominent values, although liberality might be relatively insignificant compared to the others, and reasonableness, that is, the ability to act upon the recommendations of reason, would take the fourth prominent position.

Love has always been recognized as essential to serious drama, and that fact does not need elaboration. Courage is an obvious necessity for heroic figures, and therefore provides us with further evidence for the ambiguity of certain Restoration plays—for instances, *All for Love* and *Venice Preserv'd*—in which the central characters seem to accept some value, such as love, as superior to courage, or perhaps seem to lack courage. On the other hand, even in those instances, the characters have a clearly established background of courage and manliness, which unambiguously affirms the playwright's assumption of courage as a great virtue.

Plain speaking is perhaps less obvious as a value in the serious drama, but plain dealing, plain speaking, and honesty in all forms are obvious virtues in plays in which villainy is characterized by deception and all other forms of manipulation of appearance and reality. In some serious plays, such as Otway's *The Orphan*, plain speaking is the thematic core; in others, it appears as a virtue exemplified in the hero and lacking in the villain, without ever becoming the focus of the play, or even receiving particular attention. Pulcheria, in Lee's *Theodosius* (1680), gives an exemplary innocent heroine's point of view: "I thought the meaning of all rational men / Should still be gather'd out of their Discourse" (II. 204-205). One example is perhaps sufficient to illustrate the general context of plain dealing in the serious plays. Orrery's *Mustapha* contains advice to a virtuous but naive Christian queen on the art of policy:

> Love does but change the weather of your Brow;
> Which should no more a constant meaning bear
> Than th' outward face of Heav'n should still be
>   clear.
> The Great should in their Thrones mysterious
>   be;
> Dissembling is no worse than mystery.
> Obscurity is that which terrour moves;
> The gods most awful seem'd in shady Groves.
> And our wise Prophet's Text a rev'rence bears
> Where it is hard and needs Interpreters.
> QUEEN. I ever was without dissembling bred,
> And in my open Brow my thoughts were read:
> None but the guilty keep themselves unknown.
>   (IV. i. 152-63)

The last line, "None but the guilty keep themselves unknown," is analogous to Tamerlane's exclamatory assertion of reason's empire. It is a value unquestioned in most plays, yet almost impossible to practice.

Virginia Birdsall has examined the Restoration comedies from a different perspective [in *Wild Civility: The English Comic Spirit on the Restoration Stage*] to discover in the plays elements of hostility, aggression, and manipulation of power in the sexual relationships, together with a consistent appreciation and acceptance of "animal vigor" in the admirable characters. The characters who delight us and whose triumphs we actively support, says Birdsall, "are on the side of the instincts and of freedom, life, and health." Certainly these matters receive distinctive treatment in comedy, but they are present in serious drama as well.

In a way, the serious plays provide the other half of the comedies. By that I mean that the animal spirits which are appreciated in the comedy are matched in serious drama by an element of control. The tragedies do not deny vigor; they say instead that vigor is not enough to give life meaning or coherence. Libertine values and unchecked libido characterize the villains of serious drama. Villains possess the sexual hostility and aggression which Professor Birdsall has described in the protagonists of comedy. But in both genres, I believe, the sexual aggressiveness is evil if unchecked. Dorimant is, of course, seen as an evil man by representatives of the older generation in *The Man of Mode* and by all of the women in the play. The only characters who find his sexual athletics admirable are his male peers—and not all of them, but only his rivals. Part of Dorimant's excitement for us and for the characters in the play is his antisocial threat. He is, if allowed to pursue his "flesh and blood," a threat to the order of society; and the witty exchanges, as the play opens, between Dorimant, Medley, and the Shoemaker are reverberant as well as amusing. The Shoemaker is able—and Etherege is able—to criticize Dorimant by being ironic and therefore indirect: " 'Zbud, I think you men of quality will grow as unreasonable as the women: you would engross the sins o' the nation. Poor folks can no sooner be wicked but th' are railed at by their betters" (I. 253-56). A man of quality is defined in this speech as a man who is jealous of his vices, and no perceptive audience would miss the point.

The raging lust of Maximin, in *Tyrannick Love*, is nothing like Dorimant's urbane lechery, except that both men are obeying vital instincts. That core in both of them is identical, while the manner of artistic development of character and the context in which they appear are the difference. Neither one at this core is less antisocial than the other. Dorimant is brought into line by Harriet. Maximin is killed. Almanzor, in *The Conquest of Granada,* is brought into line by Almahide. His attempted rape of her, in Part II, is barbaric and instinctive. It illustrates the moral ambiguity of nature. We see the appetite brought under control in another important instance with Morat, in *Aureng-Zebe.* Indamora acts the redemptive woman to Morat's libertinism. Morat is a serious version of the comic figure whom Professor Birdsall describes. He is anxious for "Renown, and Fame, / And Pow'r, as uncontrol'd as is my will" (V, p. 68). He is a dangerous and destructive man throughout the play until Indamora has had an opportunity to argue with him and to bring him to see that his is a "Soul irregularly Great" and that *regularity* (pattern, order, harmony) comes through the imposition of law upon appetite. Morat does not abandon his love for her, but he does cease his villainy and dies asking his wife's forgiveness.

The contrast of Dorimant and Maximin is a false one. They are not comparable characters *in toto,* whatever their initial similarities. Maximin attempts to live by unchecked will. Dorimant may attempt it, but he fails. Morat is a better parallel to Dorimant, and their stories are, in some measure, similar. Certainly we can understand how the same audience could watch both plays and comprehend the characterization without a dislocation of its ethical system. This is not to ignore the considerable differences between *The Man of Mode* and *Aureng-Zebe* in terms of intention, scale, social and political significance, and language. It is, rather, to assert that there is a substratum which is similar if not identical in the two plays.

Finally, comic and serious drama seem to share one unattractive feature—neither seems to have been exploratory or even curious about moral possibilities beyond the stylized and limited problems permitted by their conventions. Both comic and serious plays are affirmative and defensive of established values. They have been described as catering to a clique by means of the manners and fashions which they exhibit, but there is, in addition, a moral cliquishness about the plays. The audience is not provoked by these plays, but reassured. The audience leaves having been reinforced in its beliefs, beliefs which it brought to the theater. There is nothing unsettling.

This is not to say that instruction does not take place, but it takes place by affirmation. Instruction comes primarily through satire in the comedies, which is to say, through shame. Shame cannot be experienced unless one understands and feels that he has violated a standard, and normally playwrights assume that the audience knows the standards and that the playwright's task is to illustrate the violation. In serious drama, instruction comes through similar illustration and through fear—the serious analogue to shame.

D. R. M. Wilkinson [in *The Comedy of Habit*] and others in recent years have been very critical of the ethical values of Restoration comedy. Unlike nineteenth-century criticism, with its sexual hysteria, recent studies have faulted the comedy for its poverty of imagination, its repetitiousness, its class arrogance, and its insularity. Perhaps the faults can be found in the serious plays as well. But Wilkinson mentions one especially provocative idea: "Societies in which Reason provides the first court of appeal tend to recognize Folly as the chief crime and to make Ridicule the commonest form of punishment." Ridicule is not the mode of the serious plays, even though reason is the first court of appeal. In fact, serious drama focuses upon vice, the product of corrupted will, and not upon folly, the product of corrupted reason. Reason, then, is a weak or even helpless remedy for the disease in serious drama, and yet reason is the faculty which is emphasized repeatedly. If reason is a means to happiness or peace, then, theoretically, only a fool is unhappy. Theoretically, discursive argument can serve as a major means of correction. Theoretically, logic is the rhetoric of moral imperative. Yet, quite obviously, in reality and in the plays, none of these theoretical assertions hold. *De facto*, reason is not sufficient, and only theory holds that it is. The fact is that a man in love is not necessarily affected by ridicule, though theory says he should be. The fact is that a prince who is his father's rival has no rational solution to his problem, though theory ignores or denies such Gordian knots.

Restoration serious drama trips over its own feet by offering an explicit moral premise which it denies by the action. Such plays as *Aureng-Zebe, Don Sebastian, Venice Preserv'd, The Orphan, All for Love, Lucius Junius Brutus, Theodosius, Tamerlane, The Mourning Bride, The Empress of Morocco,* and *Mustapha* do not concern themselves with folly—a lack of good sense, understanding, or foresight. Sometimes villains are fools in these plays, but the protagonists rarely are. The protagonists are courageous, and they are men and women of intelligence, and at times of even excessive thoughtfulness. Their ability to reason with their problems is legendary. While they are not fools, the emphasis upon reason would suggest that failure to follow its dictates is necessarily the radical source of human misfortune.

Serious and comic drama, then, shared an emphasis on reason and its crucial role in man's health and welfare. At that point the two forms part company, however, with comedy touching only lightly upon man's passionate nature and with serious plays giving passion all the attention they can manage. It may appear perverse to accuse the comedies of ignoring man's passionate nature, but I mean that while they rather flippantly picture man as a creature driven by sexual self-interest, which he either satisfies, sublimates, or represses, they have nothing much of interest to say about pity, benevolence, anxiety, hatred, friendship, loyalty, filial affection, and on and on. They draw man with one passion or at most two, the second usually being fear. The serious plays come much closer to illustrating the variety of human passions.

The analogies which I have suggested between comedy and serious plays end with the Restoration—I do not mean 1685 or 1700 or any fixed date, but that traditional place, that continuum, in which one set of isolatable patterns is replaced by another near the end of the seventeenth century. In their place appears a new set of analogies to accompany the new comedy and the new serious drama. Every element can again be paralleled, but the drama from 1700 to 1800 is not the present concern. A few illustrations may reveal something of the nature of the change from one era to the next, however, and give extra emphasis to the nature of Restoration thought and practice.

In the generalizations which follow, I do not mean to describe a wholesale, absolute change in manner. Plays similar to those of the Restoration continued to be written and performed throughout the eighteenth century. But there were notable changes. The protagonists of the new plays are not significantly flawed. Instead, they are essentially good men and women caught in misfortune. Their flaws, such as they are, are underplayed, or appear as temporary aberrations. Addison, in *Spectator* No. 39, cites approvingly Seneca's statement that a well-written tragedy is one which describes "a virtuous man struggling with misfortunes." This very non-Aristotelian definition can apply equally well to comedy or to tragedy. For instance, it applies to Addison's own tragedy, *Cato,* which shows "A brave man struggling in the storms of fate" (Prologue, 1.

21) or to Steele's *The Conscious Lovers,* which hopes to "please by wit that scorns the aids of vice" (Prologue, 1. 19).

In comic and serious plays in the new manner, the protagonists act as models for emulation rather than as patterns of behavior to be shunned. The prologue to *Cato,* contributed by Pope, begins:

> To wake the Soul by Tender Strokes of Art,
> To raise the Genius, and to mend the Heart,
> To make Mankind in conscious Virtue bold,
> Live o'er each Scene, and Be what they behold:
> For this the Tragic-Muse first trod the Stage.

Here is an amazing and genuinely radical statement couched in tactful heroic couplets. The key phrase is "*Be what they behold.*" Catharsis is gone, or at least diminished. The audience might have pity, but not fear. *Hamartia* is gone. Emulation has apparently replaced admiration, the emotion of respectful awe which had been emphasized as one effect of tragedy by the seventeenth-century aestheticians in both England and France. One might aspire to act like Cato, or his son Portius, but one would not aspire to act like Oedipus or Macbeth or Achilles or Antigone. Neither Achilles nor Almanzor is a paradigm of virtuous social behavior.

If the central figure in comedy is no longer significantly flawed, then he is no longer foolish, and if he is not foolish then he cannot be satirized or ridiculed, and without ridicule the opportunities for laughter are severely curtailed. Steele recognized this chain of thought and faced it squarely. In the Preface to *The Conscious Lovers,* he raises the question whether there can be laughter if the characters are not ridiculous. His answer is no. Rather than satire and exposure, Steele's play will operate by "example and precept." "Anything that has its foundation in happiness and success must be allowed to be the object of comedy," Steele says, "and sure it must be an improvement of it to introduce a joy too exquisite for laughter."

The eighteenth-century audience changed with, or was changed by, the new fashion. The new audience was almost the converse of the Restoration audience, which I described as educatable, alert, critical, distanced, vain, and flawed. The eighteenth-century audience is assumed to be educated, alert, sympathetic, benevolent, emotional, sensitive, and good at heart. Delight and instruction are still part of the transaction between drama and audience, but in an altogether new manner.

Steele acknowledged that some people cried at performances of *The Conscious Lovers,* and he argued that this reaction ought not to be blamed until we better understand the relationship between head and heart. Moreover, "to be apt to give way to the impressions of humanity is the excellence of a right disposition and the natural working of a well-turned spirit." Tears thus become the outward sign of an inward condition which the audience is presumed already to possess. The older comedy had hoped to inspire or promote reason and good sense in the audience, not to tap funds of it already there. The new audience is already good, or very nearly so, and the new plays are expected to reinforce or excite that goodness.

Prose became the language of both comedy and tragedy in the eighteenth century, while thematically most of the earlier issues remained. Perhaps the most significant thematic change involves attitudes toward the country. In Restoration comedy, the country was a purgatory, desolate and barren of entertainment, fashion, and conversation. The country was lethargic, rude, tedious. In Restoration serious plays, the country appears only in the guise of the pastoral conventions or the country retreat of the Happy Man, both guises being direct descendants of classical models.

Country folk remain bumpkins in the eighteenth century, but their rustic manners often only cover a sharp edge of honesty and spontaneous benevolence. Characters like Sir Willful Witwoud, in *The Way of the World,* are satiric naifs as well as clumsy churls. Belcour, in *The West Indian* (1771), is a man of feeling and a naif from an uncivilized world. The country family, the Hardcastles, in *She Stoops to Conquer* (1773), are out of date, unsophisticated, socially embarrassing, and considerably more attractive in the honest forthrightness of their emotions than the polished city folk. Eighteenth-century tragedies, on the other hand, remain primarily in the Restoration mode developed by Otway, Banks, and Southerne; and the country remains a pastoral ideal, impossible for a political man, and something to be spoken of wistfully as a place of paradisiacal loveliness and peace. In the Gothic and melodramatic plays, like John Home's *Douglas* (1756) and George Colman's *The Iron Chest* (1796), the country has little thematic importance and is primarily a backdrop—isolated, ancient, vaguely sinister.

The clash of passion and reason remains the life of eighteenth-century drama, comic and serious alike. George Barnwell, in *The London Merchant,* is seduced "when every passion with lawless anarchy prevailed and reason was in the raging tempest lost" (III. iv. 51-52). He gives clear expression to the entire era's understanding of the agony of a man who knows his flaw and is helpless nevertheless. "Oh, conscience," Barnwell exclaims, "feeble guide to virtue, who only shows us when we go astray but wants the power to stop us in our course!" (III. v. 27-29).

We find the comic analogue, as in Restoration comedy, in the hysterical, middle-aged women. Forty-five lines into George Colman's *The Jealous Wife* (1761), Major Oakly says to his wife: "I beg, my dear, that you would moderate your passion! Shew me the letter and I'll convince you of my innocence."

> MRS. OAKLY. Innocence! abominable! innocence! But I am not to be made such a fool: I am convinced of your perfidy, and very sure that—
>
> OAKLY. 'Sdeath and fire! your passion hurries you out of your senses.

There seems to have been little change here in one hundred years. The ethical predisposition of the eighteenth century is profoundly different in its emphasis upon feeling and benevolence, but the tendency is still to treat passion in much the same way as in the Restoration. (pp. 186-211)

Geoffrey Marshall, "Comedy and Tragedy, the

Sentimental, and a Critical Crux," in his Restoration Serious Drama, *University of Oklahoma Press, 1975, pp. 186-225.*

JEREMY COLLIER STAGE CONTROVERSY

John Dryden

[*Regarded by many scholars as the father of modern English poetry and criticism, Dryden dominated literary life in England during the last four decades of the seventeenth century. Through deliberately and comprehensively refining the language of Elizabethan England in all his works, he developed an expressive, universal diction which has had immense impact on the development of speech and writing in Great Britain and North America. Although recognized as a prolific and accomplished Restoration dramatist, Dryden wrote a number of satirical poems and critical pieces which are acknowledged as his greatest literary achievements. In the former, notably* Absalom and Achitophel *(1681),* Religio Laici *(1682), and* The Hind and the Panther *(1687), he displayed an irrepressible wit and forceful line of argument which later satirists adopted as their model. In the latter, particularly* Of Dramatic Poesy *(1668), Dryden originated the extended form of objective, practical analysis that has come to characterize most modern criticism. In the following excerpt from the preface to his play* An Evening's Love: or, The Mock Astrologer *(1671), Dryden discusses his understanding of wit and comedy, claiming that their chief end is "divertisement and delight." Jeremy Collier centered a large portion of his attack on Restoration drama,* A Short View of the Immorality and Profaneness of the English Stage *(1698), upon this essay.*]

I had thought, Reader, in this preface to have written somewhat concerning the difference betwixt the plays of our age and those of our predecessors on the English stage: to have shown in what parts of dramatic poesy we were excelled by Ben Jonson, I mean humour and contrivance of comedy; and in what we may justly claim precedence of Shakespeare and Fletcher, namely in heroic plays. But this design I have waived on second considerations; at least deferred it till I publish the *Conquest of Granada,* where the discourse will be more proper. I have also prepared to treat of the improvement of our language since Fletcher's and Jonson's days, and consequently of our refining the courtship, raillery, and conversation of plays: but as I am willing to decline that envy which I should draw on myself from some old opiniatre [stubborn] judges of the stage; so likewise I am pressed in time so much that I have not leisure, at present, to go through with it.

Neither, indeed, do I value a reputation gained from comedy so far as to concern myself about it any more than I needs must in my own defense: for I think it, in its own nature, inferior to all sorts of dramatic writing. Low comedy especially requires, on the writer's part, much of con-

versation with the vulgar: and much of ill nature in the observation of their follies. But let all men please themselves according to their several tastes: that which is not pleasant to me may be to others who judge better; and, to prevent an accusation from my enemies, I am sometimes ready to imagine that my disgust of low comedy proceeds not so much from my judgment as from my temper; which is the reason why I so seldom write it; and that when I succeed in it (I mean so far as to please the audience), yet I am nothing satisfied with what I have done; but am often vexed to hear the people laugh, and clap, as they perpetually do, where I intended 'em no jest; while they let pass the better things without taking notice of them. Yet even this confirms me in my opinion of slighting popular applause, and of condemning that approbation which those very people give, equally with me, to the zany of a mountebank; or to the appearance of an antic on the theater, without wit on the poet's part, or any occasion of laughter from the actor besides the ridiculousness of his habit and his grimaces.

But I have descended, before I was aware, from comedy to farce; which consists principally of grimaces. That I admire not any comedy equally with tragedy is, perhaps, from the sullenness of my humour; but that I detest those farces which are now the most frequent entertainments of the stage, I am sure I have reason on my side. Comedy consists, though of low persons, yet of natural actions and characters; I mean such humours, adventures, and designs as are to be found and met with in the world. Farce, on the other side, consists of forced humours and unnatural events. Comedy presents us with the imperfections of human nature. Farce entertains us with what is monstrous and chimerical: the one causes laughter in those who can judge of men and manners, by the lively representation of their folly or corruption; the other produces the same effect in those who can judge of neither, and that only by its extravagances. The first works on the judgment and fancy; the latter on the fancy only: there is more of satisfaction in the former kind of laughter, and in the latter more of scorn. But how it happens that an impossible adventure should cause our mirth, I cannot so easily imagine. Something there may be in the oddness of it, because on the stage it is the common effect of things unexpected to surprise us into a delight: and that is to be ascribed to the strange appetite, as I may call it, of the fancy; which, like that of a longing woman, often runs out into the most extravagant desires; and is better satisfied sometimes with loam, or with the rinds of trees, than with the wholesome nourishments of life. In short, there is the same difference betwixt farce and comedy as betwixt an empiric [quack] and a true physician: both of them may attain their ends; but what the one performs by hazard, the other does by skill. And as the artist is often unsuccessful while the mountebank succeeds; so farces more commonly take the people than comedies. For to write unnatural things is the most probable way of pleasing them, who understand not nature. And a true poet often misses of applause because he cannot debase himself to write so ill as to please his audience. . . .

Ben Jonson is to be admired for many excellencies; and can be taxed with fewer failings than any English poet. I know I have been accused as an enemy of his writings; but without any other reason than that I do not admire him blindly, and without looking into his imperfections. For why should he only be exempted from those frailties from which Homer and Virgil are not free? Or why should there be any *ipse dixit* in our poetry, any more than there is in our philosophy? I admire and applaud him where I ought: those who do more do but value themselves in their admiration of him; and, by telling you they extol Ben Jonson's way, would insinuate to you that they can practice it. For my part, I declare that I want judgment to imitate him; and should think it a great impudence in myself to attempt it. To make men appear pleasantly ridiculous on the stage was, as I have said, his talent; and in this he needed not the acumen of wit, but that of judgment. For the characters and representations of folly are only the effects of observation; and observation is an effect of judgment. Some ingenious men, for whom I have a particular esteem, have thought I have much injured Ben Jonson when I have not allowed his wit to be extraordinary: but they confound the notion of what is witty with what is pleasant. That Ben Jonson's plays were pleasant, he must want reason who denies: but that pleasantness was not properly wit, or the sharpness of conceit, but the natural imitation of folly: which I confess to be excellent in its kind, but not to be of that kind which they pretend. Yet if we will believe Quintilian in his chapter *De movendo risu,* he gives his opinion of both in these following words: *stulta reprehendere facillimum est; nam per se sunt ridicula: et a derisu non procul abest risus: sed rem urbanum facit aliqua ex nobis adjectio* [*Institutio Oratoria,* VI. iii. 71: "It is easy to make fun of folly, for folly is itself ridiculous, and our response always verges on laughter; but the joke improves when we add something of our own"].

And some perhaps would be apt to say of Jonson as it was said of Demosthenes: *non displicuisse illi jocos, sed non contigisse* [*Ibid.,* VI. iii. 2: "Not that he disliked jokes, but that he lacked the power to make them"].

I will not deny but that I approve most the mixed way of comedy; that which is neither all wit, nor all humour, but the result of both. Neither so little of humour as Fletcher shows, nor so little of love and wit as Jonson; neither all cheat, with which the best plays of the one are filled, nor all adventure, which is the common practice of the other. I would have the characters well chosen, and kept distant from interfering with each other; which is more than Fletcher or Shakespeare did: but I would have more of the *urbana, venusta, salsa, faceta* [the four terms describe kinds of wit: *urbanitas,* urbanity and learning; *venustus,* grace and charm; *salsus,* the salt of wit; *facetus,* polished elegance] and the rest which Quintilian reckons up as the ornaments of wit; and these are extremely wanting in Ben Jonson. As for repartee in particular; as it is the very soul of conversation, so it is the greatest grace of comedy, where it is proper to the characters. There may be much of acuteness in a thing well said; but there is more in a quick reply: *sunt enim longe venustiora omnia in respondendo quam in provocando* ["For wit always appears more successful in reply than in attack"]. Of one thing I am sure, that no man ever will decry wit but he who despairs of it himself; and who has no other quarrel to it but that

which the fox had to the grapes. Yet, as Mr Cowley (who had a greater portion of it than any man I know) tells us in his character of wit, rather than all wit let there be none [Cowley's "Ode: Of Wit," lines 35-36]. I think there's no folly so great in any poet of our age as the superfluity and waste of wit was in some of our predecessors: particularly we may say of Fletcher and of Shakespeare what was said of Ovid, *in omni ejus ingenio, facilius quod rejici, quam quod adjici potest, invenies* [*Institutio Oratoria,* VI. iii. 5: "In all his wit you will find it easier to remove than to add"]. The contrary of which was true in Virgil, and our incomparable Jonson.

Some enemies of repartee have observed to us that there is a great latitude in their characters which are made to speak it: and that it is easier to write wit than humour; because, in the characters of humour, the poet is confined to make the person speak what is only proper to it. Whereas all kind of wit is proper in the character of a witty person. But, by their favor, there are as different characters in with as in folly. Neither is all kind of wit proper in the mouth of every ingenious person. A witty coward and a witty brave must speak differently. Falstaff and the Liar speak not like Don John in the *Chances,* and Valentine in *Wit without Money* [comedies by John Fletcher]. And Jonson's Truewit in the *Silent Woman* is a character different from all of them. Yet it appears that this one character of wit was more difficult to the author than all his images of humour in the play: for those he could describe and manage from his observations of men; this he has taken, at least a part of it, from books: witness the speeches in the first act, translated *verbatim* out of Ovid *De arte amandi;* to omit what afterwards he borrowed from the sixth satire of Juvenal against women.

However, if I should grant that there were a greater latitude in characters of wit than in those of humour; yet that latitude would be of small advantage to such poets who have too narrow an imagination to write it. And to entertain an audience perpetually with humour is to carry them from the conversation of gentlemen, and treat them with the follies and extravagances of Bedlam.

I find I have launched out farther than I intended in the beginning of this preface. And that, in the heat of writing, I have touched at something which I thought to have avoided. 'Tis time now to draw homeward: and to think rather of defending myself than assaulting others. I have already acknowledged that this play is far from perfect: but I do not think myself obliged to discover the imperfections of it to my adversaries, any more than a guilty person is bound to accuse himself before his judges. 'Tis charged upon me that I make debauched persons (such as, they say, my Astrologer and Gamester are) my protagonists, or the chief persons of the drama; and that I make them happy in the conclusion of my play; against the law of comedy, which is to reward virtue and punish vice. I answer first, that I know no such law to have been constantly observed in comedy, either by the ancient or modern poets. Chaerea is made happy in the *Eunuch,* after having deflowered a virgin; and Terence generally does the same through all his plays, where you perpetually see not only debauched young men enjoy their mistresses, but even the courtesans themselves rewarded and honored in the catastrophe. The same may be observed in Plautus almost everywhere. Ben Jonson himself, after whom I may be proud to err, has given me more than once the example of it. That in the *Alchemist* is notorious, where Face, after having contrived and carried on the great cozenage of the play, and continued in it without repentance to the last, is not only forgiven by his master, but enriched by his consent with the spoils of those whom he had cheated. And, which is more, his master himself, a grave man and a widower, is introduced taking his man's counsel, debauching the widow first, in hope to marry her afterward. In the *Silent Woman,* Dauphine (who, with the other two gentlemen, is of the same character with my Celadon in the *Maiden Queen,* and with Wildblood in this) professes himself in love with all the Collegiate Ladies: and they likewise are all of the same character with each other, excepting only Madam Otter, who has something singular: yet this naughty Dauphine is crowned in the end with the possession of his uncle's estate, and with the hopes of enjoying all his mistresses; and his friend Mr Truewit (the best character of a gentleman which Ben Jonson ever made) is not ashamed to pimp for him. As for Beaumont and Fletcher, I need not allege examples out of them; for that were to quote almost all their comedies.

But now it will be objected that I patronize vice by the authority of former poets, and extenuate my own faults by recrimination. I answer that, as I defend myself by their example, so that example I defend by reason, and by the end of all dramatic poesy. In the first place, therefore, give me leave to show you their mistake who have accused me. They have not distinguished, as they ought, betwixt the rules of tragedy and comedy. In tragedy, where the actions and persons are great, and the crimes horrid, the laws of justice are more strictly to be observed; and examples of punishment to be made to deter mankind from the pursuit of vice. Faults of this kind have been rare amongst the ancient poets: for they have punished in Oedipus, and in his posterity, the sin which he knew not he had committed. Medea is the only example I remember at present who escapes from punishment after murder. Thus tragedy fulfils one great part of its institution: which is, by example, to instruct. But in comedy it is not so; for the chief end of it is divertisement and delight: and that so much, that it is disputed, I think, by Heinsius, before Horace his *Art of Poetry,* whether instruction be any part of its employment. [McMillin adds in a footnote: Daniel Heinsius was a Dutch scholar who edited Horace in 1610. Dryden is wrong to suggest that he urged delight more than teaching as the purpose of comedy.] At least I am sure it can be but its secondary end: for the business of the poet is to make you laugh: when he writes humour, he makes folly ridiculous; when wit, he moves you, if not always to laughter, yet to a pleasure that is more noble. And if he works a cure on folly, and the small imperfections in mankind, by exposing them to public view, that cure is not performed by an immediate operation. For it works first on the ill nature of the audience; they are moved to laugh by the representation of deformity; and the shame of that laughter teaches us to amend what is ridiculous in our manners. This being, then, established, that the first end of comedy is delight, and instruction only the second, it may reasonably be in-

ferred that comedy is not so much obliged to the punishment of faults which it represents, as tragedy. For the persons in comedy are of a lower quality, the action is little, and the faults and vices are but the sallies of youth, and the frailties of human nature, and not premeditated crimes: such to which all men are obnoxious, not such as are attempted only by few, and those abandoned to all sense of virtue: such as move pity and commiseration, not detestation and horror; such, in short, as may be forgiven, not such as must of necessity be punished. But, lest any man should think that I write this to make libertinism amiable, or that I cared not to debase the end and institution of comedy so I might thereby maintain my own errors, and those of better poets, I must further declare, both for them and for myself, that we make not vicious persons happy, but only as Heaven makes sinners so; that is, by reclaiming them first from vice. For so 'tis to be supposed they are, when they resolve to marry; for then enjoying what they desire in one, they cease to pursue the love of many. So Chaerea is made happy by Terence, in marrying her whom he had deflowered: and so are Wildblood and the Astrologer in this play. (pp. 352-57)

But I have said more of this than I intended; and more, perhaps, than I needed to have done. I shall but laugh at them hereafter who accuse me with so little reason; and withal condemn their dullness who, if they could ruin that little reputation I have got, and which I value not, yet would want both wit and learning to establish their own; or to be remembered in after ages for any thing but only that which makes them ridiculous in this. (p. 360)

> *John Dryden, in an excerpt in* Restoration and Eighteenth-Century Comedy, *edited by Scott McMillin, W. W. Norton & Company, Inc., 1973, pp. 352-60.*

Jeremy Collier

[An English clergyman, Collier is most remembered for his attack on Restoration comedy in A Short View of the Immorality and Profaneness of the English Stage *(1698). In the following excerpt from that work, he derides the dramatists of his day for their use of profane language and disregard for religion and holy scripture.]*

An . . . Instance of the Disorders of the *Stage* is their *Profaness:* This Charge may come under these two particulars.

1st. Their Cursing and Swearing.

2dly. Their Abuse of Religion and Holy Scripture.

1st Their Cursing and Swearing. What is more frequent then their wishes of Hell, and Confusion, Devils and Diseases, all the Plagues of this World, and the next, to each other? And as for Swearing; 'tis used by all Persons, and upon all Occasions: By Heroes, and Paltroons; by Gentlemen, and Clowns: Love, and Quarrels, Success, and Disappointment, Temper, and Passion, must be varnish'd, and set off with *Oaths.* At some times, and with some *Poets* Swearing is no ordinary Releif. It stands up in the room of Sense, gives Spirit to a flat Expression, and makes a Period Musical and Round: In short, 'tis almost all the Rhetorick, and Reason some People are Masters of: The manner of performance is different. Some times they mince the matter; change the Letter, and keep the Sense, as if they had a mind to steal a Swearing, and break the Commandement without Sin. At another time the Oaths are clipt, but not so much within the Ring, but that the *Image and Superscription* are visible. These expedients, I conceive are more for variety, then Conscience: For when the fit comes on them, they make no difficulty of Swearing at Length. Instances of all these kinds may be met with in the *Old Batchelour, Double Dealer,* and *Love for Love.* And to mention no more, *Don Quixot,* the *Provok'd Wife,* and the *Relapse,* are particularly rampant and scandalous. The *English Stage* exceed their predecessors in this, as well as other Branches of immorality. *Shakespear* is comparatively sober, *Ben Jonson* is still more regular; And as for *Beaument* and *Fletcher,* In their *Plays* they are commonly Profligate Persons that Swear, and even those are reprov'd for't. Besides, the Oaths are not so full of Hell and Defiance, as in the Moderns. (pp. 56-7)

A *Second* Branch of the Profaness of the *Stage* is their Abuse of Religion, and *Holy Scripture.* And here sometimes they don't stop short of Blasphemy. To cite all that might be Collected of this kind would be tedious. I shall give the *Reader* enough to justifie the Charge, and I hope to abhor the Practice.

To begin with the *Mock-Astrologer.* In the First *Act* the Scene is a *Chappel;* And that the Use of such Consecrated places may be the better understood, the time is taken up in Courtship, Raillery, and ridiculing Devotion. *Facinta* takes her turn among the rest. She Interrupts *Theodosia,* and cries out: *why Sister, Sister—will you pray? what injury have I ever done you that you pray in my Company?* *Wildblood* Swears by *Mahomet,* rallies smuttily upon the other World, and gives the preference to the Turkish Paradise! This Gentleman to incourage *Jacinta* to a Complyance in Debauchery, tells her *Heaven is all Eyes and no Tongue.* That is, it sees Wickedness but conceals it. He Courts much at the same rate a little before. *When a Man comes to a great Lady, he is fain to approach her with Fear, and Reverence, methinks there's something of Godliness in't.* Here you have the Scripture burlesqu'd, and the Pulpit Admonition apply'd to Whoring. Afterwards *Facinta* out of her great Breeding and Christianity, swears by *Alla,* and *Mahomet,* and makes a Jest upon Hell. *Wildblood* tells his Man that *such undesigning Rogues as he, make a Drudge of poor Providence.* And *Maskall* to show his proficiency under his Masters, replies to *Bellamy,* who would have had him told a Lie. *Sir upon the Faith of a Sinner you have had my last Lie already. I have not one more to do me Credit, as I hope to be saved Sir.*

In the close of the *Play,* They make sport with Apparitions and Fiends. One of the Devils sneezes, upon this they give him the Blessing of the Occasion, and conclude *he has got cold by being too long out of the Fire.*

The *Orphan* lays the Scene in Christendom, and takes the same care of Religion. *Castalio* Complements his Mistress to Adoration.

No Tongue my Pleasure and my Pain can tell:
'Tis Heaven to have thee, and without thee Hell.

Polydor when upon the attempt to debauch *Monimia* puts up this ejaculation.

Blessed Heaven assist me but in this dear Hour:

Thus the *Stage* worships the true God in Blasphemy, as the *Lindians* did *Hercules* by Cursing and throwing stones. This *Polydor* has another Flight of Profaness, but that has got a certain *Protection,* and therefore must not be disturb'd.

In the *Old Batchelour, Vain-love* asks *Belmour, could you be content to go to Heaven?*

Bell. Hum, not immediately in my Conscence, not heartily.—

This is playing I take it with Edge-Tools. To go to Heaven in jeast, is the way to go to Hell in earnest. In the Fourth *Act,* Lewdness is represented with that Gaity, as if the Crime was purely imaginary, and lay only in ignorance and preciseness. *Have you throughly consider'd (says Fondlewife) how detestable, how Heinous, and how crying a Sin the Sin of Adultery is? have you weighed I say? For it is a very weighty Sin: and altho' it may lie—yet thy Husband must also bear his part; For thy iniquity will fall on his Head.* I suppose this fit of Buffoonry and profaness, was to settle the Conscience of young Beginners, and to make the Terrors of Religion insignificant. *Bellmour* desires *Latitia to give him leave to swear by her Eyes and her Lips:* He kisses the Strumpet, and tells her, *Eternity was in that Moment. Latitia* is horibly profane in her Apology to her Husband; but having the *Stage-Protection* of Smut for her Guard, we must let her alone. *Fondlewife* stalks under the same shelter, and abuses a plain Text of Scripture to an impudent Meaning. A little before, *Latitia* when her Intrigue with *Bellmour* was almost discover'd, supports her self with this Consideration. *All my comfort lies in his impudence, and Heaven be prais'd, he has a Considerable Portion.* This is the *Play-house* Grace, and thus Lewdness is made a part of Devotion! Ther's another Instance still behind: 'Tis that of *Sharper* to *Vain-Love,* and lies thus.

I have been a kind of God Father to you, yonder: I have promis'd and vow'd something in your Name, which I think you are bound to Perform. For Christians to droll upon their Baptism is somewhat extraordinary; But since the *Bible* can't escape, 'tis the less wonder to make bold with the *Catechisme.*

In the *Double Dealer,* Lady *Plyant* cries out *Jesu* and talks Smut in the same Sentence. Sr. *Paul Plyant* whom the Poet dub'd a Fool when he made him a Knight, talks very Piously! *Blessed be Providence, a Poor unworthy Sinner, I am mightily beholden to Providence:* And the same word is thrice repeated upon an odd occasion. The meaning must be that *Providence* is a ridiculous supposition, and that none but Blockheads pretend to Religion. But the Poet can discover himself farther if need be. Lady *Froth* is pleas'd to call *Jesu a Hackney Coachman.* Upon this, *Brisk* replies, *If Jehu was a Hackney Coachman, I am answer'd—you may put that into the Marginal Notes tho', to prevent Criticisms—only mark it with a small Asterisme and say,—Jehu was formerly a Hackney Coachman.* This for a heavy Piece of Profaness, is no doubt thought a lucky one, because it burlesques the Text, and the Comment, all under one. I could go on with the *Double Dealer* but he'll come in my way afterwards, and so I shall part with him at present. Let us now take a view of *Don Sebastian*. And here the *Reader* can't be long unfurnish'd. *Dorax* shall speak first.

> *Shall I trust Heaven*
> *With my revenge? then where's my satis-*
>   *faction?*
> *No, it must be my own, I scorn a Proxy.*

But *Dorax* was a Renegado, what then? He had renounc'd Christianity, but not Providence. Besides; such hideous Sentences ought not to be put in the Mouth of the Devil. For that which is not fit to be heard, is not fit to be spoken. But to some People an Atheistical Rant is as good as a Flourish of Trumpets. To proceed. *Antonio* tho' a profess'd Christian, mends the matter very little. He is looking on a Lot which he had drawn for his Life: This proving unlucky, after the preamble of a Curse or two, he calls it,

> *As black as Hell, an other lucky saying!*
> *I think the Devils in me:—good again,*
> *I cannot speak one syllable but tends*
> *To Death or to Damnation.*

Thus the Poet prepares his Bullies for the other World! Hell and Damnation are strange entertaining words upon the *Stage!* Were it otherwise, the Sense in these Lines, would be almost as bad as the Conscience. The *Poem*

> **Augustus William Schlegel on the indecency of Restoration comedy (1808):**
>
> The last, and not the least defect of the English comedies is their offensiveness. I may sum up the whole in one word by saying, that after all we know of the licentiousness of manners under Charles II., we are still lost in astonishment at the audacious ribaldry of Wycherley and Congreve. Decency is not merely violated in the grossest manner in single speeches, and frequently in the whole plot; but in the character of the rake, the fashionable debauchee, a moral scepticism is directly preached up, and marriage is the constant subject of their ridicule. . . . [In] the series of English comic poets, Wycherley, Congreve, Farquhar, Vanbrugh, Steele, Cibber, &c., we may perceive something like a gradation from the most unblushing indecency to a tolerable degree of modesty. However, the example of the predecessors has had more than a due influence on the successors. From prescriptive fame pieces keep possession of the stage such as no man in the present day durst venture to bring out. It is a remarkable phenomenon, the causes of which are deserving of inquiry, that the English nation, in the last half of the eighteenth century, passed all at once from the most opposite way of thinking, to an almost over-scrupulous strictness of manners in social conversation, in romances and plays, and in the plastic arts.
>
> *Augustus William Schlegel, in his* Course of Lectures on Dramatic Art and Literature, *translated by John Black, AMS Press, 1973.*

---

warms and rises in the working: And the next Flight is extreamly remarkable:

> *Not the last sounding could surprize me more,*
> *That summons drowsy Mortals to their doom,*
> *When call'd in hast they fumble for their Limbs.*

(pp. 60-6)

To conclude. Profaness tho' never so well corrected is not to be endured. It ought to be Banish'd without *Proviso,* or Limitation. No pretence of *Character* or Punishment, can excuse it; or any *Stage-Discipline* make it tolerable. 'Tis grating to *Christian* Ears, dishonourable to the Majesty of God, and dangerous in the Example. And in a Word, It tends to no point, unless it be to wear off the horrour of the Practise, to weaken the force of Conscience, and teach the Language of the Damn'd. (p. 96)

> *Jeremy Collier, "The Profaneness of the Stage," in his* A Short View of the Immorality and Profaneness of the English Stage, *1698. Reprint by Garland Publishing, Inc., 1972, pp. 57-96.*

William Congreve

[Congreve is widely considered one of the greatest English writers of the Restoration comedy of manners. The author of many plays, he is best remembered for The Old Bachelor *(1693),* The Double Dealer *(1694),* Love for Love *(1695), and* The Way of the World *(1700). His comedies are remarkable for wit and sparkling dialogue, but their alleged profanity and licentiousness brought them under Jeremy Collier's lash in* A Short View of the Immorality and Profaneness of the English Stage *(1698). Here, in an excerpt from his* Amendments of Mr. Collier's False and Imperfect Citations *(1698), Congreve defends his comedies, basing his argument on Aristotle's theory of comedy and noting that "as vicious people are made ashamed of their follies or faults by seeing them exposed in a ridiculous manner, so are good people at once both warned and diverted at their expense."]*

I have been told by some that they should think me very idle if I threw away any time in taking notice even of so much of Mr. Collier's late treatise of the Immorality, *etc.* of the English stage as related to myself, in respect of some plays written by me; for that his malicious and strained interpretations of my words were so gross and palpable that any indifferent and unprejudiced reader would immediately condemn him upon his own evidence and acquit me before I could make any defense.

On the other hand, I have been taxed of laziness, and too much security, in neglecting thus long to do my self a necessary right, which might be effected with so very little pains; since very little more is requisite in my vindication than to represent truly and at length those passages which Mr. Collier has shown imperfectly and for the most part by halves. I would rather be thought idle than lazy; and so the last advice prevailed with me.

I have no intention to examine all the absurdities and falsehoods in Mr. Collier's book; to use the gentleman's own metaphor in his preface, *an inventory of such a ware-*

house would be a large work. My detection of his malice and ignorance, of his sophistry and vast assurance, will lie within a narrow compass, and only bear a proportion to so much of his book as concerns myself.

Least of all would I undertake to defend the corruptions of the stage; indeed if I were so inclined, Mr. Collier has given me no occasion, for the greater part of those examples which he has produced are only demonstrations of his own impurity, they only savor of his utterance, and were sweet enough till tainted by his breath.

I will not justify any of my own errors; I am sensible of many, and if Mr. Collier has by any accident stumbled on one or two, I will freely give them up to him, *nullum unquam ingenium placuit sine venia* [from Seneca, *Epistles,* CXIV. 12: "No without pardon of something"]. But I hope I have done nothing that can deprive me of the benefit of my clergy; and though Mr. Collier himself were the ordinary, I may hope to be acquitted.

My intention, therefore, is to do little else but to restore those passages to their primitive station which have suffered so much in being transplanted by him. I will remove 'em from his dunghill and replant 'em in the field of nature; and when I have washed 'em of that filth which they have contracted in passing through his very dirty hands, let their own innocence protect them.

Mr. Collier, in the high vigor of his obscenity, first commits a rape upon my words, and then arraigns 'em of immodesty; he has barbarity enough to accuse the very virgins that he has deflowered, and to make sure of their condemnation he has himself made 'em guilty. But he forgets that while he publishes their shame he divulges his own.

His artifice to make words guilty of profaneness is of the same nature; for where the expression is unblameable in its own clear and genuine signification, he enters into it himself like the evil spirit; he possesses the innocent phrase and makes it bellow forth his own blasphemies; so *that one would think the muse was legion.*

To reprimand him a little in his own words, if these passages produced by Mr. Collier are obscene and profane, *why were they raked in and disturbed unless it were to conjure up vice and revive impurities? Indeed Mr. Collier has a very untoward way with him; his pen has such a libertine stroke that 'tis a question whether the practice or the reproof be the more licentious.*

He teaches those vices he would correct and writes more like a pimp than a p——. Since the business must be undertaken, why was not the thought blanched, the expression made remote, and the ill features cast into shadows? So far from this, which is his own instruction in his own words, is Mr. Collier's way of proceeding, that he has blackened the thoughts with his own smut; the expression that was remote, he has brought nearer; and lest by being brought near its native innocence might be more invisible, he has frequently varied it, he has new-molded it, and stamped his own image on it; so that it at length is become current deformity and fit to be paid into the devil's exchequer.

I will therefore take the liberty to exorcise this evil spirit and whip him out of my plays wherever I can meet with him. Mr. Collier has reversed the story which he relates from Tertullian; and after his visitation of the playhouse, returns, having left the devil behind him. [McMillin adds in a footnote: Collier had cited Tertullian's story (*De Spectaculis,* XXVI) about a woman who brought the devil home with her from the theater.]

If I do not return his civilities in calling him names, it is because I am not very well versed in his nomenclatures; therefore, for his *foot pads,* which he calls us in his preface, and for his *buffoons* and *slaves in the Saturnalia,* which he frequently bestows on us in the rest of his book, I will only call him Mr. Collier, and that I will call him as often as I think he shall deserve it.

Before I proceed, for method's sake, I must premise some few things to the reader, which if he thinks in his conscience are too much to be granted me, I desire he would proceed no further in his perusal of these animadversions, but return to Mr. Collier's *Short View,* etc.

First, I desire that I may lay down Aristotle's definition of comedy, which has been the compass by which all the comic poets since his time have steered their course. I mean them whom Mr. Collier so very frequently calls *comedians;* for the distinction between *comicus* and *comoedus* and *tragicus* and *tragoedus* is what he has not met with in the long progress of his reading.

Comedy (says Aristotle) is an imitation of the worse sort of people. Μιμησισ φαυλοτερων, *imitatio pejorum.* He does not mean the worse sort of people in respect to their quality, but in respect to their manners. This is plain from his telling you immediately after, that he does not mean κατα πασαν κακιαν, relating to all kinds of vice; there are crimes too daring and too horrid for comedy. But the vices most frequent, and which are the common practice of the looser sort of livers, are the subject matter of comedy. He tells us farther, that they must be exposed after a ridiculous manner. For men are to be laughed out of their vices in comedy; the business of comedy is to delight as well as to instruct; and as vicious people are made ashamed of their follies or faults by seeing them exposed in a ridiculous manner, so are good people at once both warned and diverted at their expense.

Thus much I though necessary to premise, that by showing the nature and end of comedy we may be prepared to expect characters agreeable to it.

Secondly, since comic poets are obliged by the laws of comedy, and to the intent that comedy may answer its true end and purpose above-mentioned, to represent vicious and foolish characters—in consideration of this, I desire that it may not be imputed to the persuasion or private sentiments of the author if at any time one of these vicious characters in any of his plays shall behave himself foolishly or immorally in word or deed. I hope I am not yet unreasonable; it were very hard that a painter should be believed to resemble all the ugly faces that he draws.

Thirdly, I must desire the impartial reader not to consider any expression or passage cited from any play as it appears in Mr. Collier's book, nor to pass any sentence or censure upon it out of its proper scene, or alienated from the character by which it is spoken; for in that place alone, and in his mouth alone, can it have its proper and true signification.

I cannot think it reasonable, because Mr. Collier is pleased to write one chapter of *Immodesty* and another of *Profaneness,* that therefore every expression traduced by him under those heads shall be condemned as obscene and profane immediately, and without any further inquiry. Perhaps Mr. Collier is acquainted with the *deceptio visus,* and presents objects to the view through a stained glass; things may appear seemingly profane, when in reality they are only seen through a profane medium, and the true color is dissembled by the help of a sophistical varnish. Therefore, I demand the privilege of the *habeas corpus* act, that the prisoners may have liberty to remove and to appear before a just judge in an open and an uncounterfeit light.

Fourthly, because Mr. Collier in his chapter of the profaneness of the stage has founded great part of his accusation upon the liberty which poets take of using some words in their plays which have been sometimes employed by the translators of the Holy Scriptures, I desire that the following distinction may be admitted, *viz.* that when words are applied to sacred things and with a purpose to treat of sacred things, they ought to be understood accordingly; but when they are otherwise applied, the diversity of the subject gives a diversity of signification. And in truth he might as well except against the common use of the alphabet in poetry because the same letters are necessary to the spelling of words which are mentioned in sacred writ.

Though I have thought it requisite and but reasonable to premise these few things, to which, as to so many *postulata,* I may when occasion offers refer myself, yet if the reader should have any objection to the latitude which at first sight they may seem to comprehend, I dare venture to assure him that it shall be removed by the caution which I shall use, and those limits by which I shall restrain myself, when I shall judge it proper for me to refer to them.

It may not be impertinent in this place to remind the reader of a very common expedient which is made use of to recommend the instruction of our plays, which is this. After the action of the play is over and the delight of the representation at an end, there is generally care taken that the moral of the whole shall be summed up and delivered to the audience in the very last and concluding lines of the poem. The intention of this is that the delight of the representation may not so strongly possess the minds of the audience as to make them forget or oversee the instruction. It is the last thing said, that it may make the last impression; and it is always comprehended in a few lines and put into rhyme, that it may be easy and engaging to the memory. . . . (pp. 415-19)

> *William Congreve, in an excerpt in* Restoration and Eighteenth-Century Comedy, *edited by Scott McMillin, W. W. Norton & Company, Inc., 1973, pp. 415-19.*

Samuel Johnson

[*Johnson is one of the outstanding figures in English literature and a leader in the history of textual and aesthetic criticism. He was a prolific lexicographer, essayist, poet, and critic whose lucid and extensively illustrated* Dictionary of the English Language *(1755) and* Prefaces, Biographical and Critical, to the Works of the English Poets *(10 vols., 1779-81; reissued in 1783 as* The Lives of the Most Eminent English Poets)*were new departures in lexicography and biographical criticism. In the following excerpt from his* Lives, *Johnson provides a generally neutral overview of the controversy ignited by Jeremy Collier's polemic against immorality on the English stage.*]

About this time [i.e., after the appearance of Congreve's *The Mourning Bride* (1697)] began the long-continued controversy between Collier and the poets. In the reign of Charles the First the Puritans had raised a violent clamour against the drama, which they considered as an entertainment not lawful to Christians, an opinion held by them in common with the church of Rome; and Prynne published *Histrio-mastix,* a huge volume, in which stageplays were censured. The outrages and crimes of the Puritans brought afterwards their whole system of doctrine into disrepute, and from the Restoration the poets and players were left at quiet; for to have molested them would have had the appearance of tendency to puritanical malignity.

This danger, however, was worn away by time; and Collier, a fierce and implacable Nonjuror, knew that an attack upon the theatre would never make him suspected for a Puritan; he therefore (1698) published *A Short View of the Immorality and Profaneness of the English Stage,* I believe with no other motive than religious zeal and honest indignation. He was formed for a controvertist; with sufficient learning; with diction vehement and pointed, though often vulgar and incorrect; with unconquerable pertinacity; with wit in the highest degree keen and sarcastick; and with all those powers exalted and invigorated by just confidence in his cause.

Thus qualified, and thus incited, he walked out to battle, and assailed at once most of the living writers, from Dryden to Durfey. His onset was violent: those passages, which while they stood single had passed with little notice, when they were accumulated and exposed together, excited horror; the wise and the pious caught the alarm, and the nation wondered why it had so long suffered irreligion and licentiousness to be openly taught at the publick charge.

Nothing now remained for the poets but to resist or fly. Dryden's conscience, or his prudence, angry as he was, withheld him from the conflict; Congreve and Vanbrugh attempted answers. Congreve, a very young man, elated with success, and impatient of censure, assumed an air of confidence and security. His chief artifice of controversy is to retort upon his adversary his own words: he is very angry, and, hoping to conquer Collier with his own weapons, allows himself in the use of every term of contumely and contempt; but he has the sword without the arm of Scanderbeg; he has his antagonist's coarseness, but not his strength. Collier replied; for contest was his delight, he was not to be frighted from his purpose or his prey.

The cause of Congreve was not tenable: whatever glosses he might use for the defence or palliation of single passages, the general tenour and tendency of his plays must always be condemned. It is acknowledged, with universal conviction, that the perusal of his works will make no man better; and that their ultimate effect is to represent pleasure in alliance with vice, and to relax those obligations by which life ought to be regulated.

The stage found other advocates, and the dispute was protracted through ten years; but at last Comedy grew more modest, and Collier lived to see the reward of his labour in the reformation of the theatre.

Of the powers by which this important victory was achieved, a quotation from *Love for Love,* and the remark upon it, may afford a specimen.

> SIR SAMPS. *Sampson's a very good name; for your Sampsons were strong dogs from the beginning.*
>
> ANGEL. *Have a care—If you remember, the strongest Sampson of your name pull'd an old house over his head at last.*

'Here you have the Sacred History burlesqued, and Sampson once more brought into the house of Dagon, to make sport for the Philistines!' (pp. 26-8)

> *Samuel Johnson, "Congreve," in his* Lives of the English Poets, *Vol. II, Oxford University Press, 1906, pp. 22-34.*

John Palmer

[*In the following excerpt, Palmer defends Restoration drama from Jeremy Collier's famous attack, claiming that the dramatists' works expressed the manners of the age so faithfully and artistically that their morality does not come into question.*]

It is a recognised principle of English law that the worst criminal should have counsel. It has been sensibly felt that innocence is a frail barricade against a really vigorous and alert prosecution, and that it would be grossly unjust to leave a prisoner to fend for himself against the practised onslaught of a specialist. The comic dramatists of the Restoration are in the position of criminals tried for their reputation without counsel. Surely it is grossly against even the coarse sense of justice typified in the ordinary procedure of the courts to condemn them for having failed in these circumstances to establish their innocence.

"Art for morality's sake," said Jeremy Collier; and Congreve accepted it. It is easy for a modern critic to say that Congreve should have refused. We have thought a good deal about art since 1698, and written even more than we have thought. We have tested formulæ at the opposite extreme to Collier's. It is possible to understand how Collier was wrong and how difficult it was for Congreve to perceive exactly why and where.

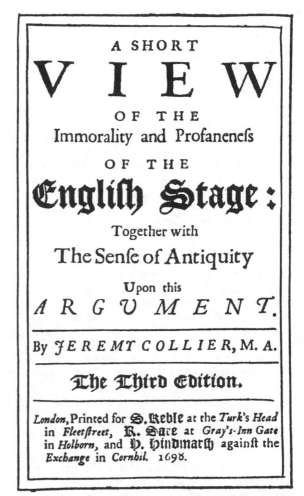

Title page of the third edition of Jeremy Collier's attack on Restoration drama, A Short View of the Immorality and Profaness of the English Stage *(1698).*

Art is not primarily concerned with morality. It is not the aim or business of comedy to improve the world. Good morality is not necessarily good art, else every good man would of necessity be a great artist. / We are not committing ourselves to any nonsense about "art for art's sake"— really a pleonasm. When we say that art is not primarily concerned with morality, we mean that in most cases (the exceptions prove the rule) an artist is first concerned with beautifully expressing something he has felt or seen. He endeavours to give local habitation and a name to a piece of life imaginatively realised. His art is fashioned in the heat of a desire to see life in shape and form. His impulse is not the impulse of a moralist to improve the world: it is the impulse of an artist to express it.

Here, in the art of a poet or dramatist, enters a paradox and stumbling-block. Art is not primarily concerned with morality, but morality is the stuff of the poet's art. The artist is dealing with emotions and conduct which in the world whence he draws his material are determined by a positive morality. Morality is his subject, though it is not his object. The critics of Collier's generation, and incompetent critics of every generation, invariably confuse the subject with the object—worse, they mistake the subject of a picture or a poem for the work itself.

The problem is further confused by the continuous inter-influence of subject and object. The artist's purpose is to give form and imaginative reality to a piece of life—beauty is his object. But just as the beauty which a worker in marble and bronze aims at expressing is conditioned by his material, so is the poet's work conditioned by the period in which he lives, the moral laws which his moods and characters unconsciously obey. He does not aim at enforcing or weakening the moral code; but in the result he necessarily does so. The moralist, Jeremy Collier for instance, perceives the result; and mistakes it for the intention. The artist himself, working intuitively, if he is not also a critic, is equally liable to mistake it.

The most difficult question remains. Can good art be bad morality? If Collier has proved that the result of Congreve's impulse to express beautifully the life of his time is morally vicious, has he also proved that it is bad art? First we must be quite clear as to what morality means. If it means the definite system of moral values from which Collier attacked the plays of Congreve, then it is immediately obvious that bad morality as Collier understood it is quite consistent with good art as any artist understands it. It is not necessarily bad art—nor ever was—to suggest that man and wife though they be made one flesh will often remain two fools. If by morality is understood the minutiæ of the contemporary code, then obviously bad morality may be not only good art but better manners.

But there is a higher morality than that of Jeremy Collier—a plane upon which Plato and S. Francis, Confucius and Elijah may meet. Without being a Manichee one may reasonably see in the history of mankind an angel of darkness in conflict with an angel of light; and without in the least circumscribing the sphere of the artist one may confidently assert that the highest art has invariably expressed the highest morality. A great artist does not consciously intend to be a great prophet. His prophesying comes by the way. His impulse is to create imaginatively in the likeness of things felt and seen; but precisely in proportion to the strength of his artistic impulse he sees clearer and feels deeper into life than common folk. He aims at winning from the chaos of life one more province for the imagination of man; but the province when put upon the map is perceived to be in the loftiest sense a moral as well as an imaginative triumph. "Art for art's sake" is in the event, "Art for morality's sake." The greatest artists are also those who have contributed most to the morality of the Commonwealth. Morality is an accident of the artist's accomplishment, though it is not the intention. It is required of the artist that he should sincerely live for his art alone. These other things are, thereafter, added unto him.

This is the heart of the matter. The artist must himself be sincere. Only so long as he obeys an impulse to express the thing he sees, reaching into the unconquered spaces of life, is he protected against falsehood. Responding to a genuine inspiration he will leave the moral result of his endeavours to look after itself. But if he is, as an artist, immoral; if he repeats a message which he has not himself realised imagi-

natively, he is then at the mercy of mischance. Congreve, though not one of the very great artists of the world, was within his limits sincere. He is therefore saved not only artistically but morally. Vanbrugh, who accepted without examination artistic conventions which had no real relation to the truth he might otherwise have expressed, is, both ways, as inevitably damned.

How shall we at last decide the critical and moral questions raised in the course of this study? The evidence is before us; and some liberty of dogmatism may, after so long an argument, be permitted. What is the position of Etherege, Wycherley, Congreve, Vanbrugh and Farquhar in the light of all we have been able to see and hear?

We have looked into a period of our social history unlike any that preceded it or followed. We found in Etherege a man who in temperament and mind accurately reflected this period in his personal character, and received a sincere impulse to reflect it artistically in his comedies. His sincerity as an artist has met the inevitable reward. His plays are morally as well as artistically sound. He felt and saw the comedy of contemporary life; and he honestly sought and found the means to express it. The result of his honesty and purity of motive as an artist is that, as soon as we enter the imaginative regions of his comedy, we are sensible that the laws are harmonious and just; they will bear inspection. We are sensible of a strange land; but it does not occur to us to question the finality of its laws so long as we remain within its bounds. They are not laws with which we are familiar to-day in the homes of Kensington or Mayfair; but having submitted our imagination to the author in the act of consenting to read his comedy, that suggestion can only intrude when the comedy is put away. Moreover, when the comedy is put away, we are aware that the morality of this strange country, just because Etherege was as an artist sincerely endeavouring to see life and express it, has a positive value of its own. We have contemplated a phase of human experience; realised it imaginatively. We have explored a mood of the human spirit which is in every age, though in this particular age it was more conspicuous. Etherege, aiming at beauty, has brought down truth as well; and, if from the standpoint of the narrow morality of this or that generation, truth may often seem an angel of darkness, from the standpoint of the higher morality of all time it is seen as an angel of light.

Wycherley followed. The truth of Wycherley is in the main the truth of Etherege. He was sufficiently the man of his period to enter and possess as his artistic right the comic world which Etherege had opened up before him. His comedies admirably illustrate the main point of our argument, that in art he who would save his moral shall lose it, and he that would lose his moral for art's sake shall find it. So long as Wycherley obeys a simple impulse to express the attitude towards life of his time, the reader who enters his comedy from another world instinctively accepts the picture and is not offended. But when the singleness of Wycherley's artistic purpose is confused by a malignant puritanism, inconsistent with the temper of his comedy, then we are immediately arrested. Wycherley's whole fabric tumbles about us.

Wycherley's lapses are the exception. His plays are masterpieces of sustained comedy, broken only very rarely by the intrusions of the shorter catechist. *The Country Wife,* for example, is almost perfect. With the exception of the tea-drinking scene between Mr. Horner and the Fidgets it answers the severest test of imaginative sincerity; and, in proportion as it does so, it equally satisfies the severest test of morality. So long as the laws of Mr. Horner's comic kingdom are faithfully observed, Mr. Horner is quite immune from the attacks of Collier and his successors. Mr. Horner is in another world, whence there is no treaty of extradition for his attachment. When, for instance, he is accused of indecent gallantry, those of us who are seised of his imaginative kingdom already know that gallantry cannot here be indecent. It is a first law of the cloud-cuckoo-land of *The Country Wife* that the act of sex has no more suggestion of the indecently amorous than tumbling upstairs or losing one's hat in a gale. Wycherley has already created an atmosphere where passion is unable to breathe. Mr. Horner goes after his friend's wife precisely as boys go after their neighbour's apples. Either you have accepted this convention, and without further thought of the proprieties, enter with zest into the collection of Mr. Horner's china, or the comedy is worse than nonsense. Lamb was entirely accurate in this regard when he virtually describes Mr. Horner as a fairy. He was wrong when, and if, he assumed that Mr. Horner never had a prototype in real life. Mr. Horner, in fact, is a perfect fairy for the very reason that he is also a faithful portrait. It is because Mr. Horner imaginatively expresses his period so well that he is morally immune from the censure of any other period.

Wycherley, on the other hand, is fairly open to criticism when he breaks the laws of his own comedy—when the passionate satire of *The Plain Dealer* intrudes into the dispassionate comedy of *The Country Wife.* The illusion of fairyland is lost. Everyday values intrude into our thoughts. Mr. Horner as a comic figure is spiritually lost, in whose place we seem to see an ineligible guest for a modern house-party.

Vanbrugh and Farquhar inevitably come in here. What was accidental in Wycherley was fundamental in them. They took over the comic kingdom of Mr. Horner; but administered it according to the laws of Queen Anne. They accepted as the figures of their comedy characters which had no relation to their own imaginative vision of life, or their attitude towards society. They did not obey a simple artistic impulse to express something clearly seen and vividly felt. They accepted a formula whose significance was outworn, writing entertainingly within its bounds, and slurring where [there were] possible inconsistencies of which they were only half aware. The result of their artistic insincerity is, as ever, a moral as well as an imaginative degeneration. So long as Mr. Horner borrows the wives of his friends in the same spirit as he would borrow their books, he may proceed unchallenged and unashamed. But when Mr. Horner seduces one particular wife of one particular friend with every circumstance of suggestive ar-

dour the case is different. Vanbrugh and Farquhar read romantic love into Mr. Horner's affairs. They are trying to reconcile two inconsistent attitudes. Romantic love cannot be reconciled with a comic treatment of adultery. The result upon the reader is that, driven from one convention to another, he finally retires for refuge to the conventions of his own well-regulated life of every day. He then sees Vanbrugh's Loveless and Farquhar's Mr. Archer forcibly seducing a pretty woman in his immediate presence.

Congreve, like Etherege and Wycherley at his best, is immune from any such criticism. His comedies are the perfect expression of an attitude. They are as consistent in art as in morality. All we have found in the Comedy of Etherege is expressed in Congreve upon a higher imaginative level. Congreve saw more clearly what he had to express and drew with a firmer hand.

Congreve is the summit of our theme. He produced the most perfect specimens of the comedy we have studied. Nevertheless we must end upon a statute of limitations. A critic could no more put Congreve upon a level with Shakespeare than he could put Catullus upon a level with Homer, or Scarlatti upon a level with Beethoven. But if Congreve attained the extreme limit of beauty in the artistic expression of the life of his time, whence comes this sense of his inferiority to the greatest? The obvious answer is that Shakespeare's subjects are bigger than those of Congreve; that whereas Shakespeare expressed Falstaff and Othello, Congreve expressed Mirabell and Witwoud. But this difference of subject is not the root of the matter. It is a visible token of the contrast; not the contrast itself. The contrast itself is in the creative energy of the two men. Whereas Shakespeare was ardently impelled to look quite through the shows of things, to penetrate into the depths of himself and of the life he saw, to body forth in imagination secrets he was furiously urged to discover, Congreve was mildly driven to fashion an image of existence observed at ease, incuriously, with no ambition to pursue the spirit of truth into the dark. That almost invisible curl of the lip with which he seems to follow the movements of his creatures is not of a man who could be stirred in imagination to the depths. He is not less than Shakespeare because his subjects are less; for an artist's subjects, be they what they may, are never by one jot less or greater than the artist. Congreve is less than Shakespeare, because the mood in which he wrote is not that of a man whose imagination is, like Shakespeare's, working at the limit of pressure. If after-generations had lost his work entirely, they would have lost a perfect artistic reflexion of English Society at a particular period. Had they entirely lost the work of Shakespeare, they would have lost an embattled fortress upon boundaries which part the waters of chaos from the solid earth redeemed by great artists for the habitation of man. (pp. 288-97)

John Palmer, "Critical Conclusions," in his The Comedy of Manners, *G. Bell & Sons, Ltd., 1913, pp. 275-97.*

OTHER CRITICAL INTERPRETATIONS

Charles Lamb

[An essayist, critic, and poet, Lamb is credited with initiating the revival of interest in Elizabethan and Restoration drama in nineteenth-century England. He is chiefly remembered for his Elia *(1823), a series of essays admired for their breadth, quaint style, and intimate tone. In the following excerpt from that collection, Lamb claims that though the characters of Restoration comedy are morally reprehensible, it is inappropriate to judge them on those terms, as they exist only in the "passing pageant" of drama.]*

The artificial Comedy, or Comedy of manners, is quite extinct on our stage. Congreve and Farquhar show their heads once in seven years only, to be exploded and put down instantly. The times cannot bear them. Is it for a few wild speeches, an occasional license of dialogue? I think not altogether. The business of their dramatic characters will not stand the moral test. We screw every thing up to that. Idle gallantry in a fiction, a dream, the passing pageant of an evening, startles us in the same way as the alarming indications of profligacy in a son or ward in real life should startle a parent or guardian. We have no such middle emotions as dramatic interests left. We see a stage libertine playing his loose pranks of two hours' duration, and of no after consequence, with the severe eyes which inspect real vices with their bearings upon two worlds. We are spectators to a plot or intrigue (not reducible in life to the point of strict morality) and take it all for truth. We substitute a real for a dramatic person, and judge him accordingly. We try him in our courts, from which there is no appeal to the *dramatis personæ,* his peers. We have been spoiled with—not sentimental comedy—but a tyrant far more pernicious to our pleasures which has succeeded to it, the exclusive and all devouring drama of common life; where the moral point is every thing; where, instead of the fictitious half-believed personages of the stage (the phantoms of old comedy) we recognise ourselves, our brothers, aunts, kinsfolk, allies, patrons, enemies,—the same as in life,—with an interest in what is going on so hearty and substantial, that we cannot afford our moral judgment, in its deepest and most vital results, to compromise or slumber for a moment. What is *there* transacting, by no modification is made to affect us in any other manner than the same events or characters would do in our relationships of life. We carry our fire-side concerns to the theatre with us. We do not go thither, like our ancestors, to escape from the pressure of reality, so much as to confirm our experience of it; to make assurance double, and take a bond of fate. We must live our toilsome lives twice over, as it was the mournful privilege of Ulysses to descend twice to the shades. All that neutral ground of character, which stood between vice and virtue; or which in fact was indifferent to neither, where neither properly was called in question; that happy breathing-place from the burthen of a perpetual moral questioning—the sanctuary and quiet Alsatia of hunted casuistry—is broken up and disfranchised, as injurious to the interests of society. The privileges of the place are taken away by law. We dare not dally with images, or names, of wrong. We bark like foolish dogs at shadows. We dread infection from the scenic representation of disorder; and fear a painted pustule. In our anxiety that our morality should not take cold, we wrap it up in a great blanket surtout of precaution against the breeze and sunshine.

I confess for myself that (with no great delinquencies to answer for) I am glad for a season to take an airing beyond the diocese of the strict conscience,—not to live always in the precincts of the law-courts,—but now and then, for a dream-while or so, to imagine a world with no meddling restrictions—to get into recesses, whither the hunter cannot follow me—

> —Secret shades
> Of woody Ida's inmost grove,
> While yet there was no fear of Jove—

I come back to my cage and my restraint the fresher and more healthy for it. I wear my shackles more contentedly for having respired the breath of an imaginary freedom. I do not know how it is with others, but I feel the better always for the perusal of one of Congreve's—nay, why should I not add even of Wycherley's—comedies. I am the gayer at least for it; and I could never connect those sports of a witty fancy in any shape with any result to be drawn from them to imitation in real life. They are a world of themselves almost as much as fairyland. Take one of their characters, male or female (with few exceptions they are alike), and place it in a modern play, and my virtuous indignation shall rise against the profligate wretch as warmly as the Catos of the pit could desire; because in a modern play I am to judge of the right and the wrong. The standard of *police* is the measure of *political justice.* The atmosphere will blight it, it cannot live here. It has got into a moral world, where it has no business, from which it must needs fall headlong; as dizzy, and incapable of making a stand, as a Swedenborgian bad spirit that has wandered unawares into the sphere of one of his Good Men, or Angels. But in its own world do we feel the creature is so very bad?—The Fainalls and the Mirabels, the Dorimants and the Lady Touchwoods, in their own sphere, do not offend my moral sense; in fact they do not appeal to it at all. They seem engaged in their proper element. They break through no laws, or conscientious restraints. They know of none. They have got out of Christendom into the land—what shall I call it?—of cuckoldry—the Utopia of gallantry, where pleasure is duty, and the manners perfect freedom. It is altogether a speculative scene of things, which has no reference whatever to the world that is. No good person can be justly offended as a spectator, because no good person suffers on the stage. Judged morally, every character in these plays—the few exceptions only are *mistakes*—is alike essentially vain and worthless. The great art of Congreve is especially shown in this, that he has entirely excluded from his scenes,—some little generosities in the part of Angelica perhaps excepted,—not only any thing like a faultless character, but any pretensions to goodness or good feelings whatsoever. Whether he did this designedly, or instinctively, the effect is as happy, as the design (if design) was bold. I used to wonder at the strange power which his *Way of the World* in particular possesses of interesting you all along in the pursuits of characters, for whom you absolutely care nothing—for you neither hate nor love his personages—and I think it is owing to this very indifference for any, that you endure the whole. He has spread a privation of moral light, I will call it, rather than by the ugly name of palpable darkness, over his creations; and his shadows flit before you without distinction or preference. Had he introduced a good character, a single gush of moral feeling, a revulsion of the judgment to actual life and actual duties, the impertinent Goshen would have only lighted to the discovery of deformities, which now are none, because we think them none.

. . . I feel the better always for the perusal of one of Congreve's—nay, why should I not add even of Wycherley's—comedies. I am the gayer at least for it; and I could never connect those sports of a witty fancy in any shape with any result to be drawn from them to imitation in real life. They are a world of themselves almost as much as fairyland.

—Charles Lamb

Translated into real life, the characters of his, and his friend Wycherley's dramas, are profligates and strumpets,—the business of their brief existence, the undivided pursuit of lawless gallantry. No other spring of action, or possible motive of conduct, is recognised; principles which, universally acted upon, must reduce this frame of things to a chaos. But we do them wrong in so translating them. No such effects are produced in *their* world. When we are among them, we are amongst a chaotic people. We are not to judge them by our usages. No reverend institutions are insulted by their proceedings,—for they have none among them. No peace of families is violated,—for no family ties exist among them. No purity of the marriage bed is stained,—for none is supposed to have a being. No deep affections are disquieted,—no holy wedlock bands are snapped asunder,—for affection's depth and wedded faith are not of the growth of that soil. There is neither right nor wrong,—gratitude or its opposite,—claim or duty,—paternity or sonship. Of what consequence is it to virtue, or how is she at all concerned about it, whether Sir Simon, or Dapperwit, steal away Miss Martha; or who is the father of Lord Froth's, or Sir Paul Pliant's children.

The whole is a passing pageant, where we should sit as unconcerned at the issues, for life or death, as at a battle of the frogs and mice. But, like Don Quixote, we take part against the puppets, and quite as impertinently. We dare not contemplate an Atlantis, a scheme, out of which our coxcomical moral sense is for a little transitory ease excluded. We have not the courage to imagine a state of things for which there is neither reward nor punishment. We cling to the painful necessities of shame and blame. We would indict our very dreams. (pp. 323-30)

Charles Lamb, "On the Artifical Comedy of

the Last Century," in his Elia, *1823. Reprint by Woodstock Books, 1991, pp. 323-37.*

Thomas Babington Macaulay

[*Macaulay was a distinguished historian, essayist, and politician of mid-nineteenth-century England. For many years he was a major contributor of erudite, highly opinionated articles to the* Edinburgh Review. *Besides these essays, collected in* Critical and Historical Essays *(1843), his most enduring work is his five-volume* History of England from the Accession of James II *(1849-61), which, despite criticism of its strong bias toward the Whig political party, is revered for its consummate rhetorical and narrative prose. In the following excerpt from Macaulay's review of Leigh Hunt's edition of* The Dramatic Works of Wycherley, Congreve, Vanbrugh, and Farquhar *(1840), he disagrees with Charles Lamb's defence of Restoration comedy as a "Utopia of gallantry," declaring instead "that the world of Restoration] dramatists is a world into which no moral enters."*]

In some respects, Mr Leigh Hunt is excellently qualified for the task which he has now undertaken [in editing *The Dramatic Works of Wycherley, Congreve, Vanbrugh, and Farquhar,* 1840]. His style, in spite of its mannerism—nay, partly by reason of its mannerism—is well suited for light, garrulous, desultory *ana,* half critical half biographical. We do not always agree with his literary judgments; but we find in him what is very rare in our time—the power of justly appreciating and heartily enjoying good things of very different kinds. He can adore Shakspeare and Spenser without denying poetical genius to the author of 'Alexander's Feast;' or fine observation, rich fancy, and exquisite humour to him who imagined 'Will Honeycomb' and 'Sir Roger de Coverley.' He has paid particular attention to the history of the English drama, from the age of Elizabeth down to our own time, and has every right to be heard with respect on that subject.

The plays to which he now acts as introducer are, with few exceptions, such as, in the opinion of many very respectable people, ought not to be reprinted. In this opinion we can by no means concur. We cannot wish that any work or class of works which has exercised a great influence on the human mind, and which illustrates the character of an important epoch in letters, politics, and morals, should disappear from the world. If we err in this matter, we err with the gravest men and bodies of men in the empire, and especially with the Church of England, and with the great schools of learning which are connected with her. The whole liberal education of our countrymen is conducted on the principle, that no book which is valuable, either by reason of the excellence of its style, or by reason of the light which it throws on the history, polity, and manners of nations, should be withheld from the student on account of its impurity. The Athenian Comedies, in which there are scarcely a hundred lines together without some passage of which Rochester would have been ashamed, have been reprinted at the Pitt Press and the Clarendon Press, under the direction of syndics and delegates appointed by the Universities; and have been illustrated with notes by reverend, very reverend, and right reverend commentators. Every year the most distinguished young men in the kingdom are examined by bishops and professors of divinity in the *Lysistrata* of Aristophanes, and the Sixth Satire of Juvenal. There is certainly something a little ludicrous in the idea of a conclave of venerable fathers of the church rewarding a lad for his intimate acquaintance with writings, compared with which the loosest tale in Prior is modest. But for our own part we have no doubt that the great societies which direct the education of the English gentry, have herein judged wisely. It is unquestionable that an extensive acquaintance with ancient literature enlarges and enriches the mind. It is unquestionable that a man whose mind has been thus enlarged and enriched, is likely to be far more useful to the state and to the church, than one who is unskilled, or little skilled in classical learning. On the other hand, we find it difficult to believe that, in a world so full of temptation as this, any gentleman, whose life would have been virtuous if he had not read Aristophanes and Juvenal, will be made vicious by reading them. A man who, exposed to all the influences of such a state of society as that in which we live, is yet afraid of exposing himself to the influences of a few Greek or Latin verses, acts, we think, much like the felon who begged the sheriffs to let him have an umbrella held over his head from the door of Newgate to the gallows, because it was a drizzling morning, and he was apt to take cold. (pp. 490-91)

But we should be justly chargeable with gross inconsistency, if, while we defend the policy which invites the youth of our country to study such writers as Theocritus and Catullus, we were to set up a cry against a new edition of the *Country Wife,* or the *Way of the World.* The immoral English writers of the seventeenth century, are indeed much less excusable than those of Greece and Rome. But the worst English writings of the seventeenth century are decent, compared with much that has been bequeathed to us by Greece and Rome. Plato, we have little doubt, was a much better man than Sir George Etherege. But Plato has written things at which Sir George Etherege would have shuddered. Buckhurst and Sedley, even in those wild orgies at the Cock in Bow Street, for which they were pelted by the rabble and fined by the Court of King's Bench, would never have dared to hold such discourse as passed between Socrates and Phædrus on that fine summer day, under the plane-tree, while the fountain warbled at their feet, and the cicadas chirped overhead. If it be, as we think it is, desirable that an English gentleman should be well informed touching the government and the manners of little commonwealths, which both in place and time are far removed from us—whose independence has been more than two thousand years extinguished, whose language has not been spoken for ages, and whose ancient magnificence is attested only by a few broken columns and friezes—much more must it be desirable that he should be intimately acquainted with the history of the public mind of his own country; and with the causes, the nature, and the extent of those revolutions of opinion and feeling, which, during the last two centuries, have alternately raised and depressed the standard of our national morality. And knowledge of this sort is to be very sparingly gleaned from Parliamentary debates, from state papers, and from the works of grave historians. It must either not

be acquired at all, or it must be acquired by the perusal of the light literature which has at various periods been fashionable. We are therefore by no means disposed to condemn this publication, though we certainly cannot recommend the handsome volume before us as an appropriate Christmas present for young ladies.

We have said that we think the present publication perfectly justifiable. But we can by no means agree with Mr Leigh Hunt, who seems to hold that there is little or no ground for the charge of immorality so often brought against the literature of the Restoration. We do not blame him for not bringing to the judgment-seat the merciless rigour of Lord Angelo; but we really think that such flagitious and impudent offenders as those who are now at the bar, deserved at least the gentle rebuke of Escalus. Mr Leigh Hunt treats the whole matter a little too much in the easy style of Lucio, and perhaps his exceeding lenity disposes us to be somewhat too severe.

And yet, it is not easy to be too severe. For, in truth, this part of our literature is a disgrace to our language and our national character. It is clever, indeed, and very entertaining; but it is, in the most emphatic sense of the words, 'earthly, sen'sual, devilish.' Its indecency, though perpetually such as is condemned, not less by the rules of good taste than by those of morality, is not, in our opinion, so disgraceful a fault as its singularly inhuman spirit. We have here Belial, not as when he inspired Ovid and Ariosto, 'graceful and humane,' but with the iron eye and cruel sneer of Mephistopheles. We find ourselves in a world, in which the ladies are like very profligate, impudent, and unfeeling men, and in which the men are too bad for any place but Pandæmonium or Norfolk Island. We are surrounded by foreheads of bronze, hearts like the nether millstone, and tongues set on fire of hell.

Dryden defended or excused his own offences, and those of his contemporaries, by pleading the example of the earlier English dramatists; and Mr Leigh Hunt seems to think that there is force in the plea. We altogether differ from this opinion. The crime charged is not mere coarseness of expression. The terms which are delicate in one age, become gross in the next. The diction of the English version of the Pentateuch, is sometimes such as Addison would not have ventured to imitate; and Addison, the standard of purity in his own age, used many phrases which are now proscribed. Whether a thing shall be designated by a plain noun-substantive, or by a circumlocution, is mere matter of fashion. Morality is not at all interested in the question. But morality is deeply interested in this—that what is immoral shall not be presented to the imagination of the young and susceptible in constant connexion with what is attractive. For every person who has observed the operation of the law of association in his own mind, and in the minds of others, knows, that whatever is constantly presented to the imagination in connexion with what is attractive, will commonly itself become attractive. There is undoubtedly a great deal of indelicate writing in Fletcher and Massinger; and more than might be wished even in Ben Jonson and Shakspeare, who are comparatively pure. But it is impossible to trace in their plays any systematic attempt to associate vice with those things which men value most and desire most, and virtue with every thing ridiculous and degrading. And such a systematic attempt we find in the whole dramatic literature of the generation which followed the return of Charles the Second. We will take, as an instance of what we mean, a single subject of the highest importance to the happiness of mankind—conjugal fidelity. We can at present hardly call to mind a single English play, written before the civil war, in which the character of a seducer of married women is represented in a favourable light. We remember many plays in which such persons are baffled, exposed, covered with derision, and insulted by triumphant husbands. Such is the fate of Falstaff, with all his wit and knowledge of the world. Such is the fate of Brisac in Fletcher's *Elder Brother*—and of Ricardo and Ubaldo, in Massinger's *Picture*. Sometimes, as in the *Fatal Dowery,* and *Love's Cruelty,* the outraged honour of families is repaired by a bloody revenge. If now and then the lover is represented as an accomplished man, and the husband as a person of weak or odious character, this only makes the triumph of female virtue the more signal; as in Jonson's Celia and Mrs Fitzdottrel, and in Fletcher's Maria. In general, we will venture to say, that the dramatists of the age of Elizabeth and James the First, either treat the breach of the marriage-vow as a serious crime—or, if they treat it as matter for laughter, turn the laugh against the gallant.

On the contrary, during the forty years which followed the Restoration, the whole body of the dramatists invariably represent adultery—we do not say as a peccadillo—we do not say as an error which the violence of passion may excuse—but as the calling of a fine gentleman—as a grace without which his character would be imperfect. It is as essential to his breeding and to his place in society that he should make love to the wives of his neighbours, as that he should know French, or that he should have a sword at his side. In all this there is no passion, and scarcely any thing that can be called preference. The hero intrigues, just as he wears a wig; because if he did not, he would be a queer fellow, a city prig, perhaps a Puritan. All the agreeable qualities are always given to the gallant. All the contempt and aversion are the portion of the unfortunate husband. Take Dryden for example; and compare Woodall with Brainsick, or Lorenzo with Gomez. Take Wycherley, and compare Horner with Pinchwife. Take Vanbrugh, and compare Constant with Sir John Brute. Take Farquhar, and compare Archer with Squire Sullen. Take Congreve, and compare Bellmour with Fondlewife, Careless with Sir Paul Plyant, or Scandal with Foresight. In all these cases, and in many more which might be named, the dramatist evidently does his best to make the person who commits the injury graceful, sensible, and spirited; and the person who suffers it a fool or a tyrant, or both.

Mr Charles Lamb, indeed, attempted to set up a defence for this way of writing [in his essay "On the Artificial Comedy of the Last Century," 1823]. The dramatists of the latter part of the seventeenth century are not, according to him, to be tried by the standard of morality which exists, and ought to exist in real life. Their world is a conventional world. Their heroes and heroines belong, not to England, not to Christendom, but to an Utopia of gallantry, to a Fairyland, where the Bible and Burns's Justice are unknown—where a prank which on this earth would be rewarded with the pillory, is merely matter for a peal of elvish laughter. A real Horner, a real Careless would, it is admitted, be exceedingly bad men. But to predicate morality or immorality of the Horner of Wycherley, and the Careless of Congreve, is as absurd as it would be to arraign a sleeper for his dreams. They belong 'to the regions of pure comedy, where no cold moral reigns—when we are amongst them we are amongst a chaotic people. We are not to judge them by our usages. No reverend institutions are insulted by their proceedings, for they have none among them. No peace of families is violated, for no family ties exist among them. There is neither right nor wrong—gratitude or its opposite—claim or duty—paternity or sonship.

This is, we believe, a fair summary of Mr Lamb's doctrine. We are sure that we do not wish to represent him unfairly. For we admire his genius; we love the kind nature which appears in all his writings; and we cherish his memory as much as if we had known him personally. But we must plainly say that his argument, though ingenious, is altogether sophistical.

Of course we perfectly understand that it is possible for a writer to create a conventional world in which things forbidden by the Decalogue and the Statute Book shall be lawful, and yet that the exhibition may be harmless, or even edifying. For example, we suppose that the most austere critics would not accuse Fenelon of impiety and immorality, on account of his *Telemachus* and his *Dialogues of the Dead*. In *Telemachus* and the *Dialogues of the Dead*, we have a false religion, and consequently a morality which is in some points incorrect. We have a right and a wrong, differing from the right and the wrong of real life. It is represented as the first duty of men to pay honour to Jove and Minerva. Philocles, who employs his leisure in making graven images of these deities, is extolled for his piety in a way which contrasts singularly with the expressions of Isaiah on the same subject. The dead are judged by Minos, and rewarded with lasting happiness for actions which Fenelon would have been the first to pronounce splendid sins. The same may be said of Mr Southey's Mahommedan and Hindoo heroes and heroines. In *Thalaba*, to speak in derogation of the Arabian imposter is blasphemy—to drink wine is a crime—to perform ablutions, and to pay honour to the holy cities, are works of merit. In the *Curse of Kehama*, Kailyal is commended for her devotion to the statue of Mariataly, the goddess of the poor. But certainly no person will accuse Mr Southey of having promoted or intended to promote either Islamism or Brahminism.

It is easy to see why the conventional worlds of Fenelon and Mr Southey are unobjectionable. In the first place, they are utterly unlike the real world in which we live. The state of society, the laws even of the physical world, are so different from those with which we are familiar, that we cannot be shocked at finding the morality also very different. But in truth, the morality of these conventional worlds differs from the morality of the real world, only in points where there is no danger that the real world will ever go wrong. The generosity and docility of Telemachus, the fortitude, the modesty, the filial tenderness of Kailyal, are virtues of all ages and nations. And there was very little danger that the Dauphin would worship Minerva, or that an English damsel would dance with a bucket on her head before the statue of Mariataly.

The case is widely different with what Mr Charles Lamb calls the conventional world of Wycherley and Congreve. Here the costume, the manners, the topics of conversation are those of the real town, and of the passing day. The hero is in all superficial accomplishments exactly the fine gentleman, whom every youth in the pit would gladly resemble. The heroine is the fine lady, whom every youth in the pit would gladly marry. The scene is laid in some place which is as well known to the audience as their own houses, in St James's Park, or Hyde Park, or Westminister Hall. The lawyer bustles about with his bag, between the Common Pleas and the Exchequer. The Peer calls for his carriage to go to the House of Lords on a private bill. A hundred little touches are employed to make the fictitious world appear like the actual world. And the immorality is of a sort which never can be out of date, and which all the force of religion, law, and public opinion united can but imperfectly restrain.

In the name of art, as well as in the name of virtue, we protest against the principle that the world of pure comedy is one into which no moral enters. If comedy be an imitation, under whatever conventions, or real life, how is it possible that it can have no reference to the great rule which directs life, and to feelings which are called forth by every incident of life? If what Mr Charles Lamb says were correct, the inference would be, that these dramatists did not in the least understand the very first principles of their craft. Pure landscape painting into which no light or shade enters, pure portrait painting into which no expression enters, are phrases less at variance with sound criticism, than pure comedy into which no moral enters.

But it is not the fact, that the world of these dramatists is a world into which no moral enters. Morality constantly enters into that world, a sound morality, and an unsound morality; the sound morality to be insulted, derided, associated with every thing mean and hateful; the unsound morality to be set off to every advantage, and inculcated by all methods, direct and indirect. It is not the fact, that none of the inhabitants of this conventional world feel reverence for sacred institutions, and family ties. Fondlewife, Pinchwife, every person in short of narrow understanding, and disgusting manners, expresses that reverence strongly. The heroes and heroines too, have a moral code of their own, an exceedingly bad one; but not, as Mr Charles Lamb seems to think, a code existing only in the imagination of dramatists. It is, on the contrary, a code actually received, and obeyed by great numbers of people. We need not go to Utopia or Fairyland to find them. They are near at hand. Every night some of them play at the 'hells' in the Quadrant, and others pace the Piazza in Covent-Garden. Without flying to Nephelococcygia, or to the Court of Queen Mab, we can meet with sharpers, bullies, hard-hearted impudent debauchees, and women worthy of such paramours. The morality of the *Country Wife* and the *Old Bachelor,* is the morality, not, as Mr Charles

Lamb maintains, of an unreal world, but of a world which is a great deal too real. It is the morality, not of a chaotic people, but of low town-rakes, and of those ladies whom the newspapers call 'dashing Cyprians.' And the question is simply, whether a man of genius, who constantly and systematically endeavours to make this sort of character attractive, by uniting it with beauty, grace, dignity, spirit, a high social position, popularity, literature, wit, taste, knowledge of the world, brilliant success in every undertaking, does or does not make an ill use of his powers. We own that we are unable to understand how this question can be answered in any way but one.

It must, indeed, be acknowledged, in justice to the writers of whom we have spoken thus severely, that they were, to a great extent, the creatures of their age. And if it be asked why that age encouraged immorality which no other age would have tolerated, we have no hesitation in answering that this great depravation of the national taste was the effect of the prevalence of Puritanism under the Commonwealth.

To punish public outrages on morals and religion is unquestionably within the competence of rulers. But when a government, not content with requiring decency, requires sanctity, it oversteps the bounds which mark its proper functions. And it may be laid down as a universal rule, that a government which attempts more than it ought will perform less. A law-giver who, in order to protect distressed borrowers, limits the rate of interest, either makes it impossible for the objects of his care to borrow at all, or places them at the mercy of the worst class of usurers. A lawgiver who, from tenderness for labouring men, fixes the hours of their work and the amount of their wages, is certain to make them far more wretched than he found them. And so a government which, not content with repressing scandalous excesses, demands from its subjects fervent and austere piety, will soon discover that, while attempting to render an impossible service to the cause of virtue, it has in truth only promoted vice. (pp. 491-98)

It was the same with our fathers in the time of the Great Civil War. We are by no means unmindful of the great debt which mankind owes to the Puritans of that time, the deliverers of England, the founders of the great American Commonwealths. But in the day of their power they committed one great fault, which left deep and lasting traces in the national character and manners. They mistook the end and overrated the force of government. They determined not merely to protect religion and public morals from insult—an object for which the civil sword, in discreet hands, may be beneficially employed—but to make the people committed to their rule truly devout. Yet if they had only reflected on events which they had themselves witnessed, and in which they had themselves borne a great part, they would have seen what was likely to be the result of their enterprise. They had lived under a government which, during a long course of years, did all that could be done, by lavish bounty and by rigorous punishment, to enforce conformity to the doctrine and discipline of the Church of England. No person suspected of hostility to that church had the smallest chance of obtaining favour at the court of Charles. Avowed dissent was punished by imprisonment, by ignominious exposure, by cruel mutilations, and by ruinous fines. And the event had been, that the Church had fallen, and had, in its fall, dragged down with it a monarchy which had stood six hundred years. The Puritan might have learned, if from nothing else, yet from his own recent victory, that governments which attempt things beyond their reach are likely not merely to fail, but to produce an effect directly the opposite of that which they contemplate as desirable.

All this was overlooked. The saints were to inherit the earth. The theatres were closed. The fine arts were placed under absurd restraints. Vices which had never before been even misdemeanors were made capital felonies. And it was solemnly resolved by Parliament, 'that no person shall be employed but such as the House shall be satisfied of his real godliness.' The pious assembly had a Bible lying on the table for reference. If they had consulted it they might have learned that the wheat and the tares grow together inseparably, and must either be spared together, or rooted up together. To know whether a man was really godly was impossible. But it was easy to know whether he had a plain dress, lank hair, no starch in his linen, no gay furniture in his house; whether he talked through his nose, and showed the whites of his eyes; whether he named his children Assurance, Tribulation, or Maher-shalal-hash-baz—whether he avoided Spring Garden when in town, and abstained from hunting and hawking when in the country—whether he expounded hard scriptures to his troop of dragoons, and talked in a committee of ways and means about seeking the Lord. These were tests which could easily be applied. The misfortune was, that they were tests which proved nothing. Such as they were, they were employed by the dominant party. And the consequence was, that a crowd of impostors, in every walk of life, began to mimic and to caricature what were then regarded as the outward signs of sanctity. The nation was not duped. The restraints of that gloomy time were such as would have been impatiently borne, if imposed by men who were universally believed to be saints. Those restraints became altogether insupportable when they were known to be kept up for the profit of hypocrites. It is quite certain that, even if the Royal Family had never returned—even if Richard Cromwell or Henry Cromwell had been at the head of the administration—there would have been a great relaxation of manners. Before the Revolution many signs indicated that a period of license was at hand. The Restoration crushed for a time the Puritan party, and placed supreme power in the hands of a libertine. The political counterrevolution assisted the moral counter-revolution, and was in turn assisted by it. A period of wild and desperate dissoluteness followed. Even in remote manor-houses and hamlets the change was in some degree felt; but in London the outbreak of debauchery was appalling. And in London the places most deeply infected were the Palace, the quarters inhabited by the aristocracy, and the Inns of Court. It was on the support of these parts of the town that the playhouses depended. The character of the drama became conformed to the character of its patrons. The comic poet was the mouthpiece of the most deeply corrupted part of a corrupted society. And in the plays before us, we find distilled and condensed, the essential spirit of the fashionable world during the Anti-puritan reaction.

The Puritan had affected formality; the comic poet laughed at decorum. The Puritan had frowned at innocent diversions; the comic poet took under his patronage the most flagitious excesses. The Puritan had canted; the comic poet blasphemed. The Puritan had made an affair of gallantry felony, without benefit of clergy; the comic poet represented it as an honourable distinction. The Puritan spoke with disdain of the low standard of popular morality; his life was regulated by a far more rigid code; his virtue was sustained by motives unknown to men of the world. Unhappily it had been amply proved in many cases, and might well be suspected in many more, that these high pretensions were unfounded. Accordingly, the fashionable circles, and the comic poets who were the spokesmen of those circles, took up the notion that all professions of piety and integrity were to be construed by the rule of contrary; that it might well be doubted whether there was such a thing as virtue in the world; but that, at all events, a person who affected to be better than his neighbors was sure to be a knave.

In the old drama there had been much that was reprehensible. But whoever compares even the least decorous plays of Fletcher with those contained in the volume before us, will see how much the profligacy which follows a period of overstrained austerity, goes beyond the profligacy which precedes such a period. The nation resembled the demoniac in the New Testament. The Puritans boasted that the unclean spirit was cast out. The house was empty, swept, and garnished, and for a time the expelled tenant wandered through dry places seeking rest and finding none. But the force of the exorcism was spent. The fiend returned to his abode; and returned not alone. He took to him seven other spirits more wicked than himself. They entered in, and dwelt together: and the second possession was worse than the first. (pp. 499-501)

Thomas Babington Macaulay, in a review of "The Dramatic Works of Wycherley, Congreve, Vanbrugh, and Farquhar," in The Edinburgh Review, *Vol. LXXII, No. CXLVI, January, 1841, pp. 490-528.*

William Archer

[*A Scottish dramatist and critic, Archer is best known as one of the earliest and most important translators of Henrik Ibsen's plays and as a drama critic of the London stage during the late nineteenth and early twentieth centuries. Archer valued drama as an intellectual product and not as simple entertainment. For that reason he did a great deal to promote the "new drama" of the 1890s, including the work of Ibsen and Bernard Shaw. Throughout his career he protested critical overvaluation of Elizabethan and Restoration drama, claiming that modern works were in many respects equal to or better than their centuries-old predecessors. In the excerpt below, Archer attacks Restoration comedy, calling it immoral, lacking in substantive wit, and structurally flawed.*]

In dealing with the Comedy of the Restoration, it is necessary, but extremely difficult, to avoid mixing up two lines of enquiry which ought to be kept distinct. We have to ask ourselves two questions: First, is this body of literature defensible from the moral point of view? Second, is it admirable from the technical or purely artistic point of view? Let me at once confess that my answer to the first question is so emphatically in the negative that I cannot quite trust myself to form an unbiassed judgment on the second question. But I will try to give reasons for whatever criticisms I may advance.

It is the fashion of the day to deny that we have any right to regard the dramatists of the Restoration as moral agents, as responsible human beings, at all. "Others abide our question, they are free." Charles Lamb's delightful paradox on "The Artificial Comedy of the Last Century" is taken seriously as the corner-stone of a whole critical system. Lamb, as we all know, would have had us see in these comedies "a world in themselves almost as much as fairyland," or (in a juster image) an Alsatia where the writs of decency do not run. Leigh Hunt and Hazlitt took up the tale; Macaulay broke the butterfly of paradox on the wheel of his logic; and now that Macaulay's commonsense has become the derision and the scoff of even "Macaulay's schoolboy," we are confronted by a clique of enthusiasts who so love the atmosphere of this fetid fairyland, this insanitary Alsatia, that they (in my judgment) ridiculously over-estimate the intellectual and technical merits of the literature in which its fragrance is preserved. In the fulness of time comes Mr. John Palmer with an ingenious and brilliantly written book, *The Comedy of Manners,* in which he shifts the ground of the defence, and adopts what he calls the "historical" standpoint. The "historical" argument is that because Etherege and Wycherley would not have understood our objections to their outlook upon life, therefore these objections are irrelevant and futile. The plain answer is, I think, that historical understanding is one thing, æsthetic appreciation another, and that we are not bound to consider a thing delightful and desirable merely because we can (more or less) picture to ourselves the mental attitude of men who were so unfortunate as to take a pleasure in it. To understand an attitude is one thing, to imitate it is another; and attitudinizing æsthetics are the negation and the bane of sound criticism.

Another of Mr. Palmer's arguments (he will scarcely call it "historical") is this: "It is perfectly true that rape and adultery are part of the action of the majority of the plays of our comic dramatists. But the treatment being purely comic, these actions cease to be morally significant." "Thus men may grow wiser every day!" says Touchstone. "It is the first time that ever I heard breaking of ribs was sport for ladies." So to Mr. Palmer I reply, "It is the first time that ever I heard that rape was legitimate matter for 'comic treatment'." We shall hear next of comic cannibalism.

All this special pleading must, I think, be brushed aside. Let us get rid, if you like, of the terms "moral" and "immoral," and put the matter thus: *The very essence of social comedy is to present a certain criticism of life. Restoration comedy acutely realises this: it is full to overflowing of sen-* *tentious generalisations, of a sort of perverted, would-be morality. And its criticism of life, whether explicit or implied in action, is stupid, nauseous and abominable beyond anything else that can be found in the world's dramatic literature.* If this be thought too sweeping, let me say: *beyond anything of which the rumour has reached me.*

I do not think it has ever been noticed how unique is this phenomenon. For better or worse, Restoration Comedy certainly stands alone. Its brutality, its bestiality, are unrivalled. The coarseness of Aristophanes is of a wholly different quality, and immeasurably less offensive. Plautus and Terence are refinement itself in comparison with Wycherley and Dryden, Otway, Southerne and Aphra Behn. In the classic drama of France and Spain there is, to my knowledge, nothing at all comparable to the works of these writers and their contemporaries. It may be possible, here or there, to discover some obscure play that may be likened to *Love in a Tub,* or *The Country Wife,* or *The Soldier's Fortune;* but it is quite certain that there is no body of dramatic literature which calls for such defences as those at which we have just been glancing, and which can be acquitted only on the plea that comedy has no concern with decency or good manners. If we are to find any parallel to this literature, it must be, I think, in a certain type of modern French farce, and in its British adaptations. But though the tone of these pieces is often sickening, their cynicism is not so aggressive and self-complacent as that of the Restoration. No—there is no denying that England holds what is now called a record in the matter of boastful, brazen, foul-mouthed lewdness; and it is surely a very perverted form of literary patriotism that undertakes to glory in her shame.

Putting all considerations of morality aside, who can possibly deny that the writers of this period have a morbid passion for all that is malodorous and unsavoury? Where else shall we find a body of literature in which sexual disease is a constant and succulent subject of jest? Foul linen, foul breath, physical misfortunes and deformities of all sorts are the most favourite of topics. We hold our noses as we read. It is all very interesting from a "historical" point of view, as illustrating the coarse insensitiveness of our ancestors' nerves. But, æsthetically, a stench is a stench, even if it is wafted to us from the seventeenth century.

Drunkenness is an accomplishment in which the fine gentlemen of this literature glory scarcely less than in unbridled licentiousness. The very least of their foibles is a raffish rowdyism which delights in nocturnal "rambling," as they call it, and window-smashing. In the very first scene of the very first play in which the true Restoration spirit is shown, Etherege's *Love in a Tub,* we find that the hero, Sir Frederick Frollick, has been drunk overnight, and being denied admission to a disreputable house, has raised a riot which has alarmed the whole neighbourhood. We are told that he

> marched bravely at the rear of an army of link-boys; upon the sudden gave defiance, and then waged a bloody war with the constable; and having vanquished that dreadful enemy, committed a general massacre on the glass-windows.

To talk of a fantastic fairyland in such a connection is manifestly absurd. This is a passage of sheer realism, only too justly representing the manners of the author and his crew. "Well, then," say the enthusiasts, shifting their ground from fairyland to Alsatia, "is it not the business of comedy to mirror life?" Yes, but not to demand admiration for drunken blackguardism. The whole case for Restoration comedy as a purely non-moral product breaks down the moment we look into it. It is insistent in its criticism of life; it is constantly calling upon us for admiration of one line of conduct and condemnation, or at all events ridicule, of another. And the line of conduct it despises is relatively good, while that which it admires is consistently infamous.

Even if all these charges were baseless—even if Restoration comedy were sanitary and civilised—we should still have to set it down as one of the narrowest and pettiest of literary phenomena. It is concerned with one topic alone—what we may mildly term gallantry. Everything else—foppery, affectation, rusticity, jealousy, miserliness, superstition, rascality—it makes subsidiary to that one great theme. It is an encyclopedia of loose living. Marriage is mentioned only to be jeered at. Old age is never treated otherwise than as an occasion for some gloating study of senile lust. It is a positive relief when, in some of the minor playwrights, such as Crowne and Shadwell, we find an undercurrent of political allusion—as, for instance, in the satire upon Titus Oates and the Popish Plot in Crowne's *City Politicks*. Such plays remind us that there was actually a real world around this mimic Alsatia—a world which did not give its undivided attention to debauchery. Had the theatre fairly represented its age, the British nation could never have emerged from such a morass of levity, cynicism, corruption and disease. It would have gone down in the quicksand, like the last laird of Ravenswood; and on the surface would have floated only the feather from Sir Fopling Flutter's hat. But the theatre did not fairly represent the age: it grossly and abominably libelled it. Was it not the age of Locke and Newton, of Tillotson and Barrow, of Baxter and Bunyan, of Penn and Petty, of Marvell and Walton, of Sir William Temple and Dorothy Osborne, of Evelyn and Pepys? I do not hesitate to add Pepys to this list; for, though he was no Puritan, he showed that a man of that age could have his weaknesses and yet be a useful and reputable member of society; and his diary paints a very different picture, even of the Court end of the town, from that which we gather from the dramatists. Mr. Palmer makes a great deal of the fact that neither Pepys nor Evelyn utters any emphatic protest against the villainies of the stage. This is scarcely true of Evelyn. On February 9, 1665, before the scandal was at its height, he wrote to Viscount Cornbury: "Plays are now with us become a licentious excess and a vice." But it may be admitted that it is remarkable how slow the decent men of the period were in raising any public protest. No doubt they shared that insensitiveness to foul odours which was a characteristic of their time, and which we can recapture only by a foolish effort of "historical" affectation. But the main explanation, I suggest, is that they stood too near the phenomenon to see it in its true perspective. Only to very exceptional men does evil become more intolerable through familiarity. Most of us, when it is thrust every day upon

our observation, accept it with a sort of fatalism, as a thing inevitable and beyond our power to change.

Mr. Palmer, however, is incautious when he says, "All the evidence agrees as to the blindness of the period to the enormous sinfulness of the theatre." In occasional speeches in the plays themselves, and in many lines of prologues and epilogues, we find frank confession of the corrupt state of affairs. Several dramatists seem to have been quite alive to the mote in their neighbour's eye. But the notablest—one may almost say the noblest—confession comes from the greatest man, and is to be found in a poem published in 1686, twelve years before Jeremy Collier "trumpeted a revolution," and heralded a slow re-awakening of conscience and common-sense. The writer is John Dryden, in his ode *To the Pious Memory of Mrs. Anne Killigrew;* and this is what he says:

> O gracious God! how far have we
> Prophaned Thy heavenly gift of poesy!
> Made prostitute and profligate the muse,
> Debased to each obscene and impious use. . . .
> O wretched we! why were we hurried down
> This lubrique and adulterate age
> (Nay, added fat pollutions of our own)
> T' increase the steaming ordures of the stage?
> What can we say t' excuse our second fall?

Mr. Palmer does not quote these lines: they do not figure in the manifestoes of the Phœnix Society. Nor were they only the ejaculation of a lucid interval. Even under the sting of Collier's attack, the poet, then nearing his end, had the manliness and good sense to admit that, though "perhaps the parson stretched a point too far," his strictures were substantially just. I am content to take my stand with Dryden, even as against Mr. Palmer and the learned editor of the works of Mrs. Aphra Behn.

Mr. Palmer, in a notable passage [of his *Comedy of Manners*], admits that the sheer ugliness of much of the language of these plays mars the æsthetic enjoyment of the modern reader. He says:

> The just critic has simply to overlook the offensiveness of words which today are æsthetically—we are not now upon a question of morals—offensive. Words which jar upon the ear of a modern reader, and spoil his pleasure, passed unnoticed in the Theatres of Fletcher and Congreve. The just critic must simply ignore them. *Indeed, to recover the true flavour of passages where they occur, they must be omitted.*

We have here a direct condemnation of the painful pedantry of the latter-day Societies which insist on thrusting seventeenth century plays, entirely unexpurgated, upon mixed audiences of modern men and women. Mr. Palmer hits the nail accurately on the head—the policy is finally condemned by the plain fact that this language does not and cannot produce upon modern hearers the effect that the author intended. But Mr. Palmer does not tell us how "the just critic," even in reading, is to ignore what offends his senses. As well exhort him to "ignore" the dissonances of an untuned piano. And, finally, if we are permitted to find ugly words æsthetically offensive, it is hard to see why we should be forbidden, in the name of "history," to express the same judgment of still uglier thoughts and actions. Mr. Palmer's whole argument suffers from an inextricable confusion between historic interest and æsthetic pleasure. He is for ever, and quite unconsciously, shifting from the one standpoint to the other.

Let us now try, so far as possible, to put aside all ethical considerations, and regard this literature from the purely æsthetic and technical point of view. Here we are at once confronted with the little word—I had almost said the baneful little word—"wit," and the questions to which it gives rise.

The English word "wit" is roughly equivalent to the French *esprit,* the German *Geist;* but it will scarcely be denied, I think, that English "wit" is more closely associated with all sorts of verbal facetiousness, from the epigram down to the pun, than is the corresponding word in either of those languages. Now from the Restoration down to our own day, from Etherege to H. J. Byron, it has been assumed as a matter of course that verbal wit is the first concern of comedy; and that assumption has, I believe, more than anything else, artificialized and sterilised the English drama. Whence did it arise? A full answer to that question would demand a lecture to itself. There can be no doubt, however, that the Restoration took it over from the Elizabethans. About the time of Shakespeare's birth, men began to notice and reflect upon the language they spoke and wrote; and they took a childish delight in the discovery of verbal coincidences, double meanings and the like. We know how Shakespeare himself was attacked by these linguistic measles; how such a play as *Love's Labour's Lost* shows the fever at its height; and how he did not, even to the end, quite shake off its effects. Beaumont and Fletcher and Ben Jonson, the idols of the Restoration, were specially valued for their "wit," and this was the quality which their disciples of the new generation specially set themselves to imitate. Doubtless, however, the conversational habits of the age did, in some measure, excuse this pre-occupation. The self-conscious straining after verbal wit which, in Elizabeth's day, had been confined to comparatively narrow circles of courtiers and men-about-town, had now extended, one may say, to the whole of that society to which the playhouses looked for their support. Dryden, in one of his prologues, says that, in his own polished age, one heard as much wit in ordinary conversation as was to be found in the best pages of the pre-war dramatists; and we may be sure that he meant what he said. Taking Mr. Palmer's "historic" point of view, then, we must admit that the "wit" of the Restoration comedy was probably, in a measure, realistic—it was but a legitimate exaggeration of a straining after verbal smartness which did in fact characterise the conversation of the people whose manners it set forth to portray.

None the less must we regard this constant strain, this incorrigible artificiality, as a disease which fastened upon English comedy in the seventeenth century, and endured, as a pure convention, for something like a hundred and fifty years after it had ceased to have any excuse in the prevailing fashion of society. That the dialogue of comedy should be aërated by humour no one would deny. Even epigram and repartee are welcome in due time and place. But

in the great masters of comedy—in Molière and Holberg—we find none of that constant chasing after verbal wit which, to English comedy-writers, seems the first essential of their craft. In some hands it degenerated into sheer inanity, in others into the boorish rudeness which earned for a certain class of plays the designation of "the comedy of no-manners."

Now as to the quality of this wit to which, in the Restoration Comedy, nature, verisimilitude and decency are so constantly sacrificed. It has, I think, been too much taken for granted. True wit, it seems to me, may be defined as humour with a barb to it; and a barbed saying ought surely to stick in the memory. But I find, after assiduous reading of Etherege, Wycherley, Congreve and Vanbrugh, that my memory retains scarcely any of their boasted similes and epigrams. The reason is, perhaps, not that they lack barb but that they lack substance. There is no permanent significance, no weight of thought, behind them. Here are two barbed sayings from Oscar Wilde's comedies which have stuck in my memory since the moment I first heard them: "Vulgarity is the behaviour of other people" and "There are only two tragedies in life: not getting what you want—and getting it." I try in vain to remember anything in Restoration Comedy in the least comparable to these two sayings—the one incisively satirical, the other pregnant and profound. Yet Macaulay, who was certainly not prejudiced in favour of this literature, could write of "the gorgeous blaze [of wit] which dazzles us almost to blindness in *Love for Love* and *The Way of the World.*"

Etherege, to be sure, is not Congreve, but is held to have been Congreve's great precursor and tutor in the art of sparkling dialogue. Let us, then, take Etherege at his best and see what we can make of him; and to be sure of getting him at his best I turn to one of the passages selected for special praise by Mr. Edmund Gosse [in his *Seventeenth-Century Studies*], who may almost be called his real discoverer.

> The great merit of *The Man of Mode* . . . rests in the brilliance of the writing and the force of the characterisation; and the characterisation culminated in "Sir Fopling Flutter," the monarch of all beaux and dandies, the froth of Parisian affectation—a delightful personage, almost as alive to us today as to the enchanted audience of 1676. During two acts, the great creature was spoken of, but never seen. . . . At last, in the third act, when curiosity has been raised to a fever, the fop appears. He is introduced to a group of ladies and gentlemen of quality, and when the first civilities are over he begins at once to criticise their dress. . . .

> (pp. 172-81)

Mr. Gosse's comment on this passage is: "The hand that throws in these light touches, in a key of rose-colour on pale grey, no longer reminds us of Molière, but exceedingly of Congreve"; and he goes on: "The brightest scenes in *The Man of Mode* show the original direction taken by Etherege in that line which was more specially to mark the triumph of English Comedy."

Now one can perfectly understand that the scene [commented on] by Mr. Gosse may have been very effective on the stage. The farcical self-anatomy of a fop, beau, exquisite, dandy, swell—whatever you choose to call him—has from time immemorial been an unfailing stimulus to laughter in the theatre. But where, one cannot but ask, is the wit in this passage? Is there a single word in it that is beyond the compass of the most ordinary intelligence? We may, indeed, find a certain modish grace in the phrasing, which is perhaps not entirely due to the beautifying touch of time; but elegance of style is a quite different thing from wit. Considering the assiduity with which Etherege's fine gentlemen aimed at wit, it seems to me remarkable that they so seldom attained it; and this, I think, may be said, not of Etherege's characters alone. Viewing this body of literature as a whole, we cannot but feel that, in the matter of wit, criticism has, in the most good-natured way, taken the will for the deed. Is there any dramatist of today, who, in reading his predecessors of the Restoration—the best pages of Congreve apart—has not said to himself, "Heavens! how cheaply the men of that age acquired the reputation of wits!"

Wycherley's wit is confessed on all hands to be inferior to Congreve's, to be, indeed, somewhat lacking in grace; but it is supposed to possess a compensating vigour and pungency. His admirers take their stand upon Dryden's Alexandrine: "The satire, wit and strength of manly Wycherley." It would, no doubt, be rash to maintain that there is nothing in this judgment. Indeed, one sees readily enough, in contrasting him with Etherege on the one hand and Congreve on the other, how robustness came to be reckoned his leading characteristic. His cynicism lays about it with a weapon comparable to the cutlass of Manly in *The Plain Dealer,* that "ferocious sensualist" (as Leigh Hunt puts it) into whom he has transmogrified the exquisite Alceste of Molière. But what his contemporaries called strength very often seems to us moderns little better than laborious verbosity. Extracts are apt to do him a certain injustice, for if ever he wrote with ease and gusto it was in passages so gross as utterly to defy quotation. Furthermore, it is only fair to remember that his professional wits, such as Dapperwit, Sparkish and Novel, are satirically presented—they are fools, and sometimes gulls. But a fool may be lightly or may be heavily handled; and Wycherley's touch is of the heaviest. Here is a short passage from *Love in a Wood* (Act II, Sc. 1), where Lydia meets Dapperwit during a moonlight "ramble" in St. James's Park:

> LYDIA. (*Aside.*) Now do I guess I know my coxcomb. (*To Dapperwit.*) Sir, I am extremely glad I am fallen into the hands of a gentleman that can speak soft things; and this is so fine a night to hear soft things in—morning I should have said.
>
> DAPPERWIT. It will not be morning, dear madam, till you pull off your mask. (*Aside.*) That, I think, was brisk.
>
> LYDIA. Indeed, dear sir, my face would frighten back the sun.
>
> DAPPERWIT. With glories more radiant than his own. (*Aside.*) I keep up with her I think.
>
> LYDIA. But why would you put me to the trou-

ble of lighting the world, when I thought to have gone to sleep?

> DAPPERWIT. You only can do it, dear madam, let me perish!
>
> LYDIA. But why would you (of all men) practice treason against your friend Phœbus, and depose him for a mere stranger?
>
> DAPPERWIT. (*Aside.*) I think she knows me.
>
> LYDIA. But he does not do you justice, I believe; and you are so positively cock-sure of your wit, you would refer to a mere stranger your plea to the bay-tree.
>
> DAPPERWIT. (*Aside.*) She jeers me, let me perish!

One is inclined to say with the hero of a Victorian farce, "What badinage! What persiflage!" Is this, under any convention, to be called good writing?

But *Love in a Wood,* it may be said, was Wycherley's 'prentice piece, and (if he told the truth) was written when he was only nineteen. A more favorable specimen of his wit may be found in his latest, and some say greatest, work, *The Plain Dealer*—in the scene of detraction in Act II, Sc. 1, from which Sheridan no doubt took the idea of his Scandalous College. It is too long for quotation, and is easily accessible. You will recognise in it the touch of the true dramatist, but very little that can rightly be called wit. There is humour rather than wit in the character of Novel, and in the way in which Olivia prevents him from getting a word in edgewise. Such a phrase as "most splendidly, gallantly ugly" is, at a pinch, worth remembering. So is a line of Lord Plausible's, a little further on:

> OLIVIA. Can anyone be called beautiful that squints?
>
> LORD PLAUSIBLE. Her eyes languish a little, I own.

But, after making the best case we can for it, must we not allow that, in the corresponding passages in *The School for Scandal,* Sheridan immeasurably improves upon his model? There is in his wit an invention, a fantasy, a poise and a polish which Wycherley never approaches.

With regard to Congreve, I have already quoted Macaulay's famous hyperbole. Are we to set it down simply as a peculiarly flagrant example of his vice of over-statement? Or is there indeed something that "dazzles us almost to blindness" in the writing of this periwig'd Olympian? If Macaulay had not bracketed *Love for Love* with *The Way of the World,* one might almost have subscribed to his raptures; for there is, in fact, something dazzling in the character of Millamant. She is the one great creation of this whole literature: a creature as living as Rosalind or Imogen, as Emma Woodhouse or Beatrix Esmond. She is the Lady in this rout of Comus, not unbesmirched by her environment, but imparting a sort of wayward beauty even to her blemishes. How splendid is her entrance, as Mirabell pictures it.

> Here she comes, i' faith, full sail, with her fan

spread and her streamers out, and a shoal of fools for tenders.

How all the real ghosts, so to speak, of St. James's Park are eclipsed by this ghost of a woman who never existed! She has first a little skirmish with Witwoud, and then the scene goes on:

> MRS. FAINWALL. But, dear Millamant, why were you so long? . . . You were dressed before I came abroad.
>
> MILLAMANT. Aye, that's true.—Oh, but then I had—Mincing, what had I? Why was I so long?
>
> MINCING. O mem, your la'ship stayed to peruse a packet of letters.
>
> MILLAMANT. Oh, aye, letters—I had letters—I am persecuted with letters—I hate letters.—Nobody knows how to write letters, and yet one has 'em, and one does not know why. They serve to pin up one's hair.
>
> WITWOUD. Is that the way? Pray, madam, do you pin up your hair with all your letters? I find I must keep copies.
>
> MILLAMANT. Only with those in verse, Mr. Witwoud; I never pin up my hair with prose.—I think I tried once, Mincing?
>
> MINCING. O mem, I shall never forget it.
>
> MILLAMANT. Aye, poor Mincing tift and tift all the morning.
>
> MINCING. Till I had the cramp in my fingers, I'll vow, mem; and all to no purpose. But when your la'ship pins it up with poetry, it sets so pleasant the next day as anything, and is so pure and so crisp. . . .
>
> MILLAMANT. Mirabell, did you take exceptions last night? Oh aye, and went away.—Now I think on 't I'm angry—no, now I think on 't I'm pleased—for I believe I gave you some pain.
>
> MIRABELL. Does that please you?
>
> MILLAMANT. Infinitely; I love to give pain.
>
> MIRABELL. You would affect a cruelty which is not in your nature; your true vanity is in the power of pleasing.
>
> MILLAMANT. Oh, I ask your pardon for that—one's cruelty is one's power; and when one has parted with that, I fancy one's old and ugly.
>
> MIRABELL. Aye, aye, suffer your cruelty to ruin the object of your power, to destroy your lover—and then how vain, how lost a thing you'll be! Nay, 'tis true: you are no longer handsome when you've lost your lover; your beauty dies upon the instant; for beauty is the lover's gift. . . .
>
> MILLAMANT. Oh, the vanity of these men!—Fainall, d'ye hear him? If they did not commend us, we were not handsome! Now you must know they could not commend one, if one were not handsome. Beauty the lover's gift!—Lord, what is a lover, that it can give? Why, one makes lovers as fast as one pleases, and they live as long

as one pleases; and they die as soon as one pleases; and then, if one pleases, one makes more.

This is something better than wit: this is fantasy expressing itself in exquisite style. When we come to the famous scene of the covenant between Mirabell and Millamant (Act IV, Sc. 1) we are in presence of one of the summits of English prose. It is a gem of many shining facets: a thing as perfect in its way as Hamlet's "What a piece of work is man."

But Millamant is unique in Congreve's theatre—nay in the world's theatre—and, as I have said, something much greater than wit went to her creation. For the rest, Congreve's wit, though incontestable, is not at all miraculous. It is a heresy to say it, but it seems to me a plain fact that he is not as witty as Sheridan. Here is a characteristic little passage from the first act of *Love for Love*. Valentine's servant, Jeremy, has been warning him against the hopeless scheme of making his living as a poet, when the professed wit, Scandal, enters:

> SCANDAL. What, Jeremy holding forth?
>
> VALENTINE. The rogue has (with all the wit he could muster up) been declaiming against wit.
>
> SCANDAL. Aye? Why then, I'm afraid Jeremy has wit; for wherever it is, it's always contriving its own ruin.
>
> JEREMY. Why, so I have been telling my master, sir; Mr. Scandal, for Heaven's sake, sir, try if you can dissuade him from turning poet.
>
> SCANDAL. Poet! he shall turn soldier first, and rather depend upon the outside of his head than the lining. Why, what the devil, has not your poverty made you enemies enough? Must you needs show your wit to get more?
>
> JEREMY. Aye, more indeed; for who cares for anybody that has more wit than himself?
>
> SCANDAL. Jeremy speaks like an oracle. Don't you see how worthless great men, and dull rich rogues, avoid a witty man of small fortune? Why, he looks like a writ of inquiry into their titles and estates; and seems commissioned by Heaven to seize the better half.

How flat, how laboured this is! How hard it is to force a smile at it! Read the whole scene, from the rise of the curtain to Jeremy's exit, and you will feel as though the two wits and the valet had laid their heads together to compose a social essay, and had not, after all, produced a very sprightly one.

Let us turn, now, to the question of what may be called structural technique, and see how the comic poets of the Restoration, developed their subjects, or, in plainer terms, told their stories. We may note at the outset that the modern conception of a play as the working-out of a given theme, or the presentation of a single adventure, was foreign to the ideas of the time. In those days the dramatist's problem was, not to give his action organic unity, but to fill a predetermined mould, so large that one action seldom or never sufficed for it. Therefore the underplot, now almost banished from the stage, was an established institution; and a play would often consist of two or three almost unconnected actions, so nearly equal in extent and importance that it was hard to say which was the main plot and which the underplots. I do not, however claim for the modern formula any inherent superiority. It might even be argued that a play with two or three deftly interwoven actions might give a broader and essentially truer picture of life than one in which a single theme is, so to speak, lifted out of its context and subjected to intensive study. Unfortunately, the deft interweaving seldom or never occurred.

In the very first of Restoration comedies, Etherege's *Love in a Tub,* we have three distinct actions: (a) the sentimental romance (written in "heroic" couplets) of the rivalry of Bruce and Beaufort for the love of Graciana; (b) the "coney-catching" intrigue of Wheedle, Palmer and Sir Nicholas Cully, a piece of sheer Elizabethanism; (c) the amours of Sir Frederick Frollick and the Widow Rich. These three actions touch at several points, but can never be said to intermingle. The author seems, indeed, to have felt that some sort of unity was desirable, and to have tried to secure it by making Frollick the cousin of Beaufort and the Widow Rich the aunt of Graciana. But these relationships lead to nothing of the slightest moment; all mention of them might be suppressed without in the least affecting the movement of the play. In the three actions taken severally there is no inventive or manipulative skill. The sentimental plot is pure rodomontade; the comic plots consist of sheer buffoonery, helped out by disguises, drunkenness and all the stock expedients of farce. The comedy takes its name from a piece of outrageous horseplay of which Sir Frederick Frollick's French valet is the victim. This might almost be called a fourth plot, but, more accurately, it is an interpolated incident, unattached to any of the three actions. There is, in short, no trace of anything that can be called artistry either in the invention or in the ordering of the incidents. The conception and organisation of the play demanded no talent whatsoever. What talent it possesses lies in the spirited portrayal of dissolute and knavish character.

The plot of Etherege's second comedy, *She Wou'd if She Cou'd* (1668), shows a certain advance on that of *Love in a Tub.* The situation in the third act, where Sir Oliver Cockwood and his martinet of a spouse, each out on a clandestine frolic, are brought face to face with each other at the Bear Tavern, has been repeated scores of times in modern French farces; it is not here elaborated with any ingenuity. Sir Joslin Jolly in this play fixes the type of the Silenus-like, libidinous old man (repeated and outdone by Otway in his Sir Jolly Jumble), who became a stock figure in the comedy of the period, and sometimes reappears to this day, expurgated but unchastened, in the baser sort of musical farces.

The intrigue of *The Man of Mode* (1676), from which I have already quoted a scene, is heavy, flat and devoid of ingenuity. The piece is, however, less brutal than its predecessors. The worst passage in it is the opening scene, where Dorimant (supposed to represent Lord Rochester) addresses the orange-woman with gratuitous and foul-mouthed ruffianism. There is a clever scene of comedy in the third act, where Young Bellair and Harriet go through the motions of love-making, in order to deceive Old Bellair and Lady Woodvil, who are watching them:

> HARRIET. Peace! Here they come. I will lean against this wall, and look bashfully down upon my fan, while you, like an amorous spark, modishly entertain me. . . .
>
> Y. B.ELLAIR. Now for a look and gestures that may persuade 'em I am saying all the passionate things imaginable.
>
> HARRIET. Your head a little more on one side, ease yourself on your left leg, and play with your right hand. . . .
>
> Y. BELLAIR. A little exercising will make me perfect.
>
> HARRIET. Smile, and turn to me again, very sparkish.
>
> Y. BELLAIR. Will you take your turn and be instructed?
>
> HARRIET. With all my heart.
>
> Y. BELLAIR. At one motion play your fan, roll your eyes, and then settle a kind look upon me.

So the scene goes on. There is more of the true dramatist in it, I venture to think, than in all the babble of Sir Fopling Flutter. If it is really original—if it is not borrowed from some French comedy—it is the best thing Etherege ever did.

We now come to Wycherley, whose career interlocks with that of Etherege, his first play having been produced some four years before Etherege's last. Though in technique he is in no way in advance of his contemporaries, we sometimes feel in his work, as I have said, the touch of a real dramatist—of a man who might have done excellent work had he not been so entirely content with the facile expedients of his age.

In his first play, *Love in a Wood,* there are three plots, not interwoven, but simply running parallel with one another.

The characters of the first intrigue are Sir Simon Addleplot, Dapperwit and Mrs. Martha. It is without interest or ingenuity, and Sir Simon's disguise is merely preposterous.

The second intrigue is that of Gripe and Lucy, with those exemplary matrons, Mrs. Joyner and Mrs. Crossbite pulling the strings. This plot is practically worked out in the one very vigorous, though disgusting scene, of the entrapping and blackmailing of Gripe. (Act III, Sc. 3)

In the third intrigue, that of Ranger and Lydia, Valentine and Christina, there is a certain ingenuity; but it turns (a) on improbable mistakes of persons in the dark; (b) on the improbable circumstance that Ranger plans to meet the pseudo-Christina at Vincent's lodging instead of his own; (c) on the coincidence which brings the real Christina there at the same moment.

Lady Flippant, the widow who is constantly denouncing

marriage while hunting for a husband or a lover, wanders through all three intrigues without belonging to any of them.

The Gentleman Dancing Master is by far the least offensive, and certainly not the least able of Wycherley's plays. There is something really rather charming in the character of Hippolita; Gerrard is quite decent for a Wycherley hero; the contrast between the Francophil and the Hispanophil monomaniacs must have been really comic; and the idea of helping out the audacious attempt to pass Gerrard off as a dancing-master by making Formal resent his sister's pretension to greater perspicacity than his own, is a real dramatic invention. This is Wycherley's own idea: his debt to Calderón's *Maestro de Danzar* is, on the whole, very slight.

In spite of its merits, however, the play failed, and the reason is not far to seek. Matters began to go wrong, I conceive, when Hippolita, in the fourth act, suddenly refuses to run away with Gerrard—with no possible motive except that of furnishing the playwright with a fifth act. Then in the fifth act, the behaviour of Monsieur becomes too imbecile for tolerance; and the irruption of Flirt and Flounce, with the long and utterly preposterous negotiation between Monsieur and Flirt (a sort of topsy-turvy social essay) must have decided the failure.

In fear, perhaps, lest the play should be considered too refined, Wycherley introduced in Act IV an episode of irrelevant indecency in Prue's attempted seduction of Monsieur. Nothing leads up to it, and nothing ensues from it. Cut it out, and you would leave no perceptible gap. Like Etherege's scene at the Bear Tavern, it has reappeared in many modern French and Anglo-French farces.

Macaulay has been much derided for saying that "Wycherley's indecency is protected against the critics as a skunk is protected against the hunters. It is safe because it is too filthy to handle and too noisome even to approach." But of *The Country Wife* this is literally true. There is one side of it, at any rate, which one cannot even investigate technically, since its technical merits depend upon the answer to questions which it is impossible to discuss.

The intrigue, however, from which the play takes its name, is not exempt from examination; and its technical merits must be pronounced very slight. The action depends entirely on Pinchwife's incredible maladroitness and stupidity; while there is no psychological coherence or consistency in Margery's state of mind. She is now densely ignorant, and again preternaturally knowing, just as the needs of a given situation happen to dictate. Pinchwife's leaving her alone at the Exchange (Act III, Sc. 2), in order to see "if the coach be at the door," and again in the letter-scene (Act IV, Sc. 2), "whilst he goes to fetch wax and a candle," are technical ineptitudes far more indefensible than Joseph Surface's much-criticised exit during the Screen Scene; and the passage (Act IV, Sc. 1) in which Margery imposes herself upon him as Alithea, and induces him to take her to Horner's, is simply an elaborate and clumsy impossibility. The coxcomb, Sparkish, is a very coarse caricature, and the scene in which Harcourt, dressed as a "Levite," passes himself off, in spite of Ali-

thea's protests, as his own twin-brother, is extravagant to the point of puerility. The women's drinking-bout in the last scene adds a finishing touch to the loathsomeness of what is surely the most bestial play in all literature.

Beside it *The Plain Dealer* seems almost sweet and clean; but it is technically misshapen beyond the rest of its kindred. Its first two acts consist of laboured, verbose talk, serving only to show that Olivia has (not inexcusably) betrayed her surly brute of a lover. In the third act the action stands absolutely still, while we are treated to a panorama of Westminister Hall, centring around the Jonsonian "humour" of the Widow Blackacre and her hopeful son—an episode wholly irrelevant to the main plot. In the fourth and fifth acts we have a conventional intrigue turning upon a woman dressed up as a man and a substitution of persons in the dark—the sort of intrigue which it is easy to elaborate to any extent, if you can get your audience to swallow the fundamental impossibilities. The satire of the play is sometimes coarsely effective, but dramatically I regard it as Wycherley's feeblest.

The history of Congreve's plays and their varying fortunes proves, I think, that technique is not a matter of temporary convention, but is, rightly understood, a fundamental factor in the dramatist's art. This is, indeed, apparent the moment we agree upon a rational definition of the term. The critics who profess to disparage technique are usually confounding it with some system of artifice which has a local and temporary vogue. Rightly understood, technique means simply the handling of dramatic material in such a way as to seize and hold the attention of an audience and to give it a high degree of that pleasure which the theatre is specially fitted to impart. A good technician is one who thoroughly understands the psychology of his audience; and though audiences obviously differ from age to age and from place to place, there are certain basic principles which are universally valid. No one pretends, of course, that technique is everything. Many plays have, in virtue of other merits, lived down great technical defects. But initial success or failure is very apt to be determined almost entirely on grounds of technique; and that, I think, is the reason why *The Old Bachelor* and *Love for Love*, comparatively trivial plays, were brilliant successes, while *The Double Dealer* and *The Way of the World*, far abler and more ambitious works, were failures on their first production.

I am far from implying that *The Old Bachelor* and *Love for Love* were technical masterpieces. The truth is that Congreve never showed the smallest skill in the handling of his material; but in his first and third comedies he hit upon themes so simple that little or no art was required for their effective presentation, while in his second and fourth plays his themes were so complex that only the finest constructive art could have kept them clear and comprehensible.

It would take far too long to justify this criticism in detail. But I must indicate in a few words what I conceive to be the crucial differences between the plays.

In *The Old Bachelor* (1693) we have two farces and three comedies running side by side, with scarcely any intermingling. The Bellmour-Fondlewife-Lœtitia plot and the Wittol-Bluffe-Sharper plot are mere commonplaces of the Jacobean stage: the citizen befooled by the courtier, and the rustic simpleton (Etherege's Cully over again) robbed by bandits of the city. Then we have episodes of comedy in the relations of Heartwell and Sylvia, Vainlove and Araminta, Bellmour and Belinda. In all these there is no complexity, nothing that puts any strain on the attention of the audiences. For ten minutes at the end the different streams flow together in the mock marriage of Heartwell and Sylvia, the masked marriages of Sylvia and Lucy to Wittol and Bluffe. Here a certain tax was put, not only on the credulity of the audience, but on its power of keeping clear the threads of an intricate series of deceptions. But the whole business lasted only a few minutes; and it is recorded that the successive unmasking of four beautiful women (Mrs. Leigh, Mrs. Bracegirdle, Mrs. Monfort and Mrs. Bowman) gave the audience such delight that they burst into a thunder of applause.

The plot of *Love for Love* (1695), while incredible enough in all conscience, is comparatively well-knit and clear. It can be comprehensibly narrated in about a page of print—I have made the experiment. This is a very good test of a workable plot. I would say to any beginner in playwriting: "Your story ought to be what the Greeks called *eusynopton*. See if you can relate it clearly in about two hundred and fifty words; and if that proves impossible, either simplify and clarify it, or (better, perhaps) scrap it."

This test, applied to *The Double Dealer* (1693), at once explains its initial failure. It takes pages on pages to narrate the plot, and a whole volume could not render it clear. Congreve started with a clever idea—that of depicting a new type of villain whose method should be to deceive people by telling them the truth. But to have succeeded in this attempt would have demanded the technical dexterity of a Scribe; and, from the technical point of view, Congreve's fingers were all thumbs. Maskwell's plots soon become so intricate as to defy, not only belief, but comprehension. Well may Lord Touchwood say in the last act: "I am confounded when I look back, and want a clue to guide me through the various mazes of unheard-of treachery." Macaulay ascribes the failure to the melodramatic horrors of the plot. "The audience," he says, "was shocked by the characters of Maskwell and Lady Touchwood. And, indeed, there is something strangely revolting in the way in which a group that seems to belong to the house of Laius or of Pelops is introduced into the midst of the Brisks, Froths, Carelesses and Plyants." Unless Macaulay was founding on evidence unknown to me, I take leave to doubt this account of the matter. I do not believe that the audiences of that day were capable of being shocked, but I am sure that they were capable of being bored and bewildered by an intrigue of such insane overcomplexity.

It is well-known that Congreve's undoubted masterpiece, *The Way of the World* (1700), was almost as great a failure as *The Double Dealer;* and the reason, I think, was the same—clumsy over-elaboration of plot. We have in the first place to master a very complex set of relationships, licit and illicit, between the persons of the play; and that done, we find it extremely difficult to bear in mind, from moment to moment, the motives of all concerned. That this obscurity was the real cause of failure, in the case both of *The Double Dealer* and *The Way of the World,* is, I think, apparent from the fact that both plays lived down their inauspicious start and were popular throughout the eighteenth century. When a play has any qualities which invite revival, and especially when its author has attained the position of a classic, people no longer trouble much about its technical merits or defects, for which they are, indeed, more or less prepared in advance. A well-constructed play, however, has not only a better chance of initial acceptance, but continues to give more unmixed pleasure. Bad technique, even if not necessarily fatal, is always an Achilles-heel which tends to the shortening of life.

Etherege, Wycherley and Congreve are, to my thinking, the typical dramatists of the Restoration; for though Congreve's last play appeared forty years after that event, he belongs characteristically to the seventeenth, not to the eighteenth, century. He marks the end of an old order, not the beginning of a new; whereas Farquhar and Steele . . . show the efforts of a new humanity to release itself from the brazen cynicism of what may be called the Stuart period. But there is one notable figure—Sir John Vanbrugh—whom it is difficult to allot definitively to either group. His only entirely original plays, however, belong in date to the seventeenth century, *The Relapse* having been produced in 1696, *The Provok'd Wife* in 1697; and though some glimmerings of a new spirit appear in them, they are not sufficiently distinct to mark him off in any decisive way from the men of the Restoration. He had less wit and more humour than his three predecessors; his work is not quite so dry and hard as theirs; but Jeremy Collier certainly did him no wrong in calling him up for judgment along with them.

The two plots of *The Relapse,* though wholly unconnected, are absolutely clear, and one of them—the Tom Fashion and Miss Hoyden plot—is ingenious and amusing. The dialogue, except for the execrable blank-verse in which Amanda and Loveless choose to express themselves, is easier and less self-conscious than that of Congreve. The word "wit," though mentioned in both prologue and epilogue, does not, I think, occur once in the body of the play; yet a good deal of the dialogue is really witty. There are some very nauseous passages, but the nastiness is not so ingrained as in Wycherley and Congreve. Young Fashion even shows some trace of moral scruple, and Amanda does actually resist the assault of Worthy—in whose name, be it noted, there is no suspicion of irony. As for Lord Foppington—an elaboration of Cibber's Sir Novelty Fashion—he is far the best fop of the whole period. There is even a touch of race in him; at all events, he is more credible and less loathsome than most of his kindred. The scene of his toilet, in which he ignores his newly-returned brother, while he gives himself over into the hands of his tailor, his shoemaker, his hosier and his perruquier, shows the fop in action, whereas the scene from Etherege, so highly praised by Mr. Gosse, merely shows the fop in highly improbable speech. One passage from

Vanbrugh's scene is delightfully humorous and at the same time true to nature:

> FOPPINGTON. Hark thee, shoemaker, these shoes a'n't ugly, but they don't fit me.
>
> SHOEMAKER. My lord, methinks they fit you very well.
>
> FOPPINGTON. They hurt me just below the instep.
>
> SHOEMAKER. (*Feeling his foot.*) My lord, they don't hurt you there.
>
> FOPPINGTON. I tell thee, they pinch me execrably.
>
> SHOEMAKER. My lord, if they pinch you, I'll be bound to be hang'd, that's all.
>
> FOPPINGTON. Why, wilt thou undertake to persuade me I cannot feel?
>
> SHOEMAKER. Your lordship may please to feel what you think fit; but that shoe does not hurt you—I think I understand my trade—
>
> FOPPINGTON. Now, by all that's great and powerful, thou art an incomprehensible coxcomb; but thou makest good shoes, and so I'll bear with thee.
>
> SHOEMAKER. My lord, I have worked for half the people of quality in town these twenty years; and 'tis very hard I should not know when a shoe hurts, and when it don't.

[*The Provok'd Wife*] is one of the most malodorous plays of the time, which is saying a great deal, and it has no special merit either of conception or of manipulation. *The Confederacy* is a spirited play, but a mere adaptation from the French. *A Journey to London,* which Vanbrugh left unfinished, might have proved his best play. Two years after his death (that is to say in 1728) Cibber worked it up into *The Provok'd Husband,* one of the most popular, and certainly one of the best, comedies of its period. Though Cibber was only seven years younger than Vanbrugh, and had actually begun to write in 1696, before Collier took the field, the mere process of time had effected such a change in manners that *The Provok'd Husband* shows scarcely a trace of Restoration brutality. Vanbrugh's fragment was cleaner and humaner than most of his other work, and Cibber still further cleansed and humanised it—thereby earning the scorn of Leigh Hunt, who reproached him with "dull vanity and time-serving self-love," because he introduced a couple of gentlemen and a lady into his play. Where he did, perhaps, merit reproach was in abandoning Vanbrugh's attempt to interweave the two plots, and leaving them to run side by side without ever really touching.

It is, on the whole, a just discrimination which has set Etherege, Wycherley, Congreve and Vanbrugh apart from the other comic dramatists of their period. They had all a certain literary gift which was denied to such writers as Shadwell and Crowne. Yet there are times, as I have already said, when the lesser writers afford us a momentary refreshment, by getting into touch with something like real life as distinct from the artificial, self-conscious world of wits, fops and drabs from which the more pretentious playwrights scarcely ever emerged. Their realism was crude, coarse and brutal enough, and their technique was, as a rule, conspicuous by its absence; but their plays are sometimes historical or sociological documents of considerable value. They are nearer to the Elizabethans than their better-known contemporaries. Shadwell's *Squire of Alsatia,* for example, is pure Ben Jonson. The theme of this play is that of the *Adelphi* of Terence. Chapman had used it in *All Fools* and Cumberland was to use it again, eighty years later in *The Cholerick Man.* It is curious to compare these four versions of the story, and interesting, though far from surprising, to find that Shadwell's is immeasurably the coarsest and most brutal.

Crowne was, I think, a man of more innate ability than Shadwell. His *Sir Courtly Nice,* founded on a Spanish original, is by no means a bad piece of extravagant foolery. It is interesting to note that he read the first three acts to Charles II just before his death, and that the Merry Monarch thought them "not merry enough. Sir Courtly Nice, though he gives the play its name, has, in fact, quite a small part. Though held up to ridicule for his extravagant fastidiousness, he has in reality a touch of refinement in his composition. When, in the third act, he is made sick by the sheer beastliness of the drunken Surly, one can only say, "Small blame to him!"

An enthusiastic admirer of the genius of Mrs. Aphra Behn has lately edited, with much erudition, an *édition de luxe* of her works. "In her own day," he says, "probably for reasons purely political, a noisy clique assailed her on the score of impropriety"; which is as much as though one were to say that, for reasons purely political, Mistress Eleanor Gwynn was suspected of being no better than she should be. After referring to what he calls a "jaded couplet" from Pope, this champion of slandered innocence proceeds: "The pinchbeck sobriety of later times was unable to tolerate her freedom. She was condemned in no still small voice as immoral, loose, scandalous; and writer after writer, leaving her unread, reiterated the charge." I have not left her unread—I have read her plays, which alone concern me—and I do not hesitate to call them the most worthless stuff that ever pretended to take rank as dramatic literature. Mrs. Centlivre is a genius by comparison.

Before concluding let me revert for a moment to my initial theory of the two elements in drama, which I defined as "faithful or would-be faithful imitation and wilful, sometimes hysterical, exaggeration." We have seen that in Restoration tragedy the latter element prevailed to the exclusion of almost everything else: it was "bombast, bombast all the way," rising at frequent intervals to sheer hysteria. In comedy, then, did the element of imitation assert itself more effectively? A little more, no doubt,—that was inevitable. It professed to put on the stage, not Almanzors, Alexanders and Belvideras, but contemporary men and women, like those who thronged the streets, the parks, the coffee-houses and the theatre itself. And it did, here and there, make some approach to sober imitation—but only here and there. Over-emphasis, over-colouring, gross and palpable exaggeration was the law of its being; and it attained its effects by the use of a sort of rhetoric almost as far from the truth of human speech as the rants of the tragedians. Even its masterpiece, Millamant, is a lyrical creation, by many degrees removed from reality. She stands out from her surroundings because the exaggeration, in her case, happens to take the direction of exquisiteness: she is the one thing of beauty in a realm of repulsiveness. It is characteristic that Charles II should have found *Sir Courtly Nice* not sufficiently "merry." Continuous merriment, ranging from the giggle to the guffaw, was the one thing aimed at—the effect, in a word, which we of today demand, not from comedy, but from farce. The smile of intellectual recognition was systematically postponed to the laughter evoked by gross absurdity. There was, no doubt, a certain appeal to nature, but it was to nature deliberately and systematically denaturalised. How much delicacy of observation went to the making of a "merry" comedy we may judge from the fact that Wycherley, Congreve and Farquhar all scored their first successes with plays written almost or quite in their teens, before they could possibly have any competent and first-hand knowledge of the manners they professed to depict.

Here again, as in the case of tragedy, we may appeal for corroboration to contemporary accounts of the triumphs of acting. Listen to Colley Cibber's description of James Nokes, the great comedian of his young days, the original of Sir Nicholas Cully in *Love in a Tub* and Sir Oliver Cockwood in *She Wou'd if she Cou'd:*

> In the Ludicrous Distresses, which by the Laws of Comedy, Folly is often involv'd in, he sunk into such a mixture of piteous Pusillanimity, and a Consternation so ruefully ridiculous and inconsolable, that when he had shook you to a Fatigue of Laughter, it became a moot point whether you ought not to have pity'd him. When he debated any matter by himself, he would shut up his Mouth with a dumb studious Powt, and roll his full Eye into such a vacant Amazement, such a palpable Ignorance of what to think of it, that his silent Perplexity (which would sometimes hold him several Minutes) gave your Imagination as full Content as the most absurd thing he could say upon it. . . . What Tragedy ever shew'd us such a Tumult of Passions rising at once in one Bosom! or what buskin'd Heroe standing under the Load of them could have more effectually mov'd his Spectators by the most pathetick Speech, than poor miserable *Nokes* did, by this silent Eloquence and piteous Plight of his Features?

Who does not feel that such acting as this, no doubt admirable in its way, would be utterly out of place in any modern comedy? Imagine it in *Lady Windermere's Fan,* in *His House in Order,* in *Candida,* in *The Voysey Inheritance* or in *A Bill of Divorcement*! Or take, again, Cibber's picture of a coquette of the period—Mrs. Monfort as Melantha in Dryden's *Marriage à la Mode:*

> The first ridiculous Airs that break from her are upon a Gallant never seen before, who delivers her a Letter from her Father recommending him to her good Graces as an honourable

> Lover. . . . She crumbles it at once into her Palm and pours upon him her whole Artillery of Airs, Eyes and Motion; down goes her dainty, diving Body, to the the Ground, as if she were sinking under the conscious Load of her own Attractions; then launches into a Flood of fine Language, and Compliment, still playing her Chest forward in fifty Falls and Risings, like a Swan upon waving Water; and, to complete her Impertinence, she is so rapidly fond of her own Wit, that she will not give her Lover Leave to praise it.

That such a performance might be very delightful, no one who remembers that greatest of comic actresses, Ada Rehan, can doubt; but clearly it does not represent any character observed in nature. Its coquetry is amplified, distended, immeasurably bombasted out, like heroism in Dryden's Almanzor or passion in Lee's Alexander. (pp. 183-202)

William Archer, "Restoration Comedy," in his The Old Drama and the New: An Essay in Re-Valuation, *Small, Maynard and Company, 1923 pp. 172-202.*

Bonamy Dobrée

[*An English historian and critic, Dobrée distinguished himself both as a leading authority on Restoration drama and as a biographer who sought, through vivid depiction and style, to establish biography as a legitimate creative form. In the following excerpt, he argues that Restoration comedy is based upon late seventeenth-century sexual and social realities and not, as Charles Lamb has claimed, on a fairyland "of cuckoldry—the Utopia of gallantry, where pleasure is duty, and the manners perfect freedom."*]

'I could never connect these sports of a witty fancy', Lamb wrote in his famous essay upon [Restoration] comedy,

> in any shape with any result to be drawn from them to imitation in real life. They are a world of themselves—almost as much as fairyland. . . . They break through no laws of conscientious restraints. They know of none. They have got out of Christendom into the land of—what shall I call it?—of cuckoldry—the Utopia of gallantry, where pleasure is duty, and the manners perfect freedom. It is altogether a speculative scene of things, which has no reference whatever to the world that is.

But that this is untrue, even his admiring contemporaries had to admit. 'Perhaps', Leigh Hunt commented, 'he thought that he could even play his readers a child's trick, and persuade them that Congreve's fine ladies and gentlemen were doing nothing but "making as if."' Most assuredly he was mistaken.' Lamb's trick, indeed, was innocent enough; he was trying to persuade his readers to become Congreve's also, in spite of their prudish horror. For Leigh Hunt was right; and Macaulay, though his moral judgement was irrelevant, was not wrong in his facts: 'A hundred little tricks are employed to make the fictitious world appear like the actual world.' And Hazlitt in a brilliant passage showed that although this comedy might have no reference whatever to the world that is, it was very like a society that had been; 'we are almost transported to another world, and escape from this dull age. . . . '

Lamb's delightful argument does of course contain a useful truth; we must not confuse moral and aesthetic values. But it would not be of great importance at the present day in connexion with Restoration comedy were it not that many critics accept his dicta blindly; it is constantly assumed that to appreciate Restoration comedy we must accept Elia's attitude [Lamb wrote under this pseudonym]. Yet if we read this comedy in Lamb's spirit, we shall certainly find it very refreshing, but we shall miss seeing what it really was.

It is admittedly tiresome, but it seems unavoidable, to have to approach this work through Collier and Swift, Johnson, Macaulay, and Taine, and excuse its 'impurity.' For 'impurity' was its most important subject. How could it avoid dealing with sex when the distinguishing characteristic of Restoration comedy down to Congreve is that it is concerned with the attempt to rationalize sexual relationships? It is this that makes it different from any other comedy that has ever been written; but if we regard it as creating a wholly fantastic world we shall not see this. It said in effect, 'Here is life lived upon certain assumptions; see what it becomes.' It also dealt, as no other comedy has ever done, with a subject that arose directly out of this, namely, sex-antagonism, a consequence of the experimental freedom allowed to women, which gave matter for some of its most brilliant scenes.

'Sex in Congreve,' Mr. Palmer says, 'is a battle of the wits. It is not a battlefield of the emotions'; but this was so in real life as well as in the plays of Congreve. 'When sex laws remain rigid . . . ', writes Mr. Heape [in *Sex Antagonism*], 'while society becomes more and more complicated and the life led by its members more purely artificial, the probability of the growth of drastic sex-antagonism is vastly increased, becomes indeed, a certainty.' But although men recognized with Hobbes that in the political world liberty and security are incompatible, and that a compromise has to be made, they did not see the necessity of applying the maxim in the social world. Men may not want the bonds of marriage, but once married they want to keep their wives to themselves. Women may be inconstant, but they want to be secure. Thus 'virtue' retains its social prestige. This was perfectly understood in those days, and was exquisitely phrased by Ariana speaking to Courtal (Etherege, *She Would if She Could*, v.i): 'I know you would think it as great a scandal to be thought to have an inclination for marriage, as we should be believed willing to take our freedom without it.' Indeed, a woman's virtue was of great importance, unless she was one of the king's mistresses. Says Lady Fidget to Horner (Wycherley, *The Country Wife*, iv. iii): 'But first, my dear sir, you must promise to have a care of my dear honour', because (v. iv) 'Our reputation! Lord, why should you not think that we women make use of our reputation, as you men of yours, only to deceive the world with less suspicion?'

But if sex did indeed become a battle of the wits rather than a question of the emotions, it must not be assumed that the figures represented on the stage were any less flesh

and blood than their human types. Certainly, and here is the importance for us, the audiences did not regard the actors as puppets playing at a life of their own, but as men living an existence which they were almost invited to share.

But let us repeat that the object of the bawdry in these plays was not to tickle the desires of the audience. The motto of Restoration comedy was not 'Thrive, lechery, thrive', nor its subject the successful pursuit of the town coquette by the town gallant, though this provided many scenes. Its great joke was not 'and swearing she would not consent, consented.' It had a profounder philosophy. Its joke, indeed, is rather a grim one; it is more accurate to say that it is

> How nature doth compel us to lament
> Our most persisted deeds,

for having consented, she regretted; he, having instituted liberty, repented of it.

But apart from these considerations, and apart from Lamb, does not the whole question of impurity, and any attempt to justify it, seem a little absurd? For even if we abhor the idea of sexual looseness in real life, this does not preclude the possibility of turning the common facts of life into art. No one objects to 'adultery being part of the action' in *Agamemnon, The Rape of Lucrece,* or *Anna Karenina.* And just as in these works something definite is made of the theme, so in our period the writers of comedy who were also artists, crystallized sex excitement into a comic appearance. Therefore the only questions arising are these: If we are disgusted at the 'impurities' which are the material of much of this comedy, are they handled with sufficient skill to make us indifferent to the subject-matter? Or is there, in spite of much that disgusts us, enough beauty and intelligence to overbalance our revulsion in favour of delight? Or can we simply accept the life of the time, and without associating it with ourselves, derive interest and pleasure from the observation and understanding of men whose outlook on life died with their erring bodies some two centuries ago? Surely this seems the reasonable attitude. Indeed, condemnation at this distance, emotion at two hundred years, itself provides a target for the comic imps. (pp. 22-6)

If we were to try to sum up what the comedy of this period as a whole achieved, it would be to say that it gave a brilliant picture of its time rather than a new insight into man. [Hippolyte Taine in his *History of English Literature*] has wondered why, with all its mastery of vivid description, racy idiom, and polished phrase, this English comedy did not come to a fuller perfection, did not reach the level of Molière, and, we would add, of Jonson. Apart from the fact that astonishing genius of every kind is not to be met with in every decade, the explanation perhaps lies in this: these writers never came to the condition of seeing life whole, though what they saw they perceived very clearly. They loved it with Etherege, or, like Wycherley, snatched from it a fearful joy, or, like Congreve, tried in their dissatisfaction to distil from it something exquisite: they hardly ever related it, as Molière nearly always did, to a larger world; they did not try to construct something terrific out of it as Jonson was able to do.

Their time forced them to be too critical, though it is hardly fair to blame a time for the very peculiarities that gave them their best material. But they were forced to be too moral, that is, too engaged with the immediate application of their ideas. It is in this sense that the word moral has been used throughout: nothing so foolish is suggested as that art and morality are incompatible, any more than that they are necessary to one another. Without a moral vision there would have been no *Divine Comedy,* no *War and Peace.* Without the notions of good and evil and divine justice there would have been no Greek tragedy and no *Paradise Lost.* But the morality of the Restoration dramatists, taken as a whole, was not a universal vision; it could not be. For the medieval view was dead, had died in the iron verse of Milton; eighteenth-century scepticism was being born, had made its appearance in the shattering syllogisms of Hobbes and the trenchant strokes of Shaftesbury. Modern curiosity was awakening, and the old moral order lay in ruins about the scaffold of a king. The dramatists of that day were almost necessarily forced to be content with morality as conceived by the *honnête homme.* Wycherley could never imagine, as did Goethe's *Faust,* that all experience whatsoever might be good: Congreve would never see that the art of graceful living might, by its very fineness, miss something fundamental in life, and destroy the directness he was eager to preserve.

These are limitations; but the want of an inspiring, comprehensive philosophy such as was Dante's to use, the absence of a feeling of revolt such as urged Shelley to his most sustained flights, has its advantages. For then the creative impulse is bent inwards upon the thing, it will not be satisfied until the object made has complete validity within itself: it cannot afford to slip into life. Thus lapses into realism which scarcely injure the structure of much Elizabethan comedy are ruinous here, and it is because this kind of perfection requires a more consummate and conscious artistry that so few comedies of this period are satisfactory. Even when complete in themselves they do not always include enough 'spiritual nourishment,' to use Synge's analytic phrase, and Etherege's perfect creation, *The Man of Mode,* compared with great comedy, is Sèvreschina painting to a canvas of El Greco. Dryden, more comprehensive, was, except in one great tragedy, always a little too swayed by his experimental curiosity to attain that unity which alone can make such work close-sealed.

But *The Country Wife* and *The Way of the World* are beyond Taine's criticism, and the former can take its place among the great masterpieces of the ages, to stand beside *Volpone. The Way of the World* will always remain a trifle isolated, not because it came to so little, but because, working within such severe limits Congreve succeeded in concentrating in it matter for which others have found larger, easier mediums more convenient. It is unique—even if the comedies of Corneille may claim affinity—and likely to remain so, yet it belongs inalienably to its period: it is built upon its contemporaries, and it is by it and *The Country Wife* that the achievement of the period may be measured. It is hard to imagine that in any civilized age they will not be regarded as glories of our literature, gems of our theatrical inheritance. (pp. 171-73)

Bonamy Dobrée, "The Framework" and "Conclusion," in his Restoration Comedy, 1660-1720, *1924. Reprint by Oxford University Press, 1958, pp. 17-30, 171-73.*

Kathleen M. Lynch on the continued appeal of Restoration comedy:

Beyond the art of Congreve, Restoration comedy of manners could not advance. Its essential excellences and its essential limitations were completely realized in his work. In brilliant dialogue, in vivid contrasts of social types, in the expression of that eager, yet formal urbanity of temper which characterized Restoration society at its best, Congreve triumphed over all other comic dramatists of his age. It was his further distinction to reveal clearly how inexpressive such comedy must be of the realities of character, how profound must be its silences concerning human passions, how restrained and stereotyped must remain its rule of life. It is not strange that this drama broke down in conflict with the reactionary forces of eighteenth century sentimentalism. It is not strange that its fashions have been regarded with hostility by large groups of people sympathetic with other habits of thought. To certain limited audiences, however, Restoration comedy of manners will continue to appeal. It will appeal to them not only as a picturesque literary phenomenon of a special era, but also as an interpretation of a type of comic predicament perpetually recurring in civilized society, whenever the lives of men and women become dominated by artificial standards of social discipline.

Kathleen M. Lynch, in her The Social Mode of Restoration Comedy, *Macmillan, 1926.*

L. C. Knights

[*Knights is a renowned English Shakespearean scholar and critic. In the excerpt below, he discards the notion of Restoration comedy as lacking in good values and cynical in its portrayal of sexual relations, declaring that "the criticism that defenders of Restoration comedy need to answer is not that the comedies are 'immoral,' but that they are trivial, gross and dull."*]

Apart from the presentation of incidental and unrelated "wit" (which soon becomes as tiring as the epigrams of the "good talker"), Restoration comedy has two main interests—the behaviour of the polite and of pretenders to politeness, and some aspects of sexual relationships. Critics have made out a case for finding in one or other of these themes a unifying principle and a serious base for the comedy of manners. According to [Kathleen M. Lynch in her *The Social Mode of Restoration Comedy*], the "thoroughly conventionalized social mode" of the courtly circle "was discovered to have manifestly comic aspects, both when awkwardly misinterpreted, and when completely fulfilled through personalities to which, however, it could not give complete expression," and both these discrepancies were exploited by Etherege and his successors. Bonamy Dobrée [in *Restoration Comedy*], attributing to the comic dramatists "a deep curiosity, and a desire to try new ways of living," finds that the distinguishing characteristic of Restoration comedy down to Congreve is that it is concerned with the attempt to rationalize sexual relationships. It is this that makes it different from any other comedy that has ever been written. . . . It said in effect, "Here is life lived upon certain assumptions; see what it becomes." It also dealt, as no other comedy has ever done, with a subject that arose directly out of this, namely sex-antagonism, a consequence of the experimental freedom allowed to women, which gave matter for some of its most brilliant scenes.

These accounts, as developed, certainly look impressive, and if Restoration comedy really answered to them—if it had something fresh and penetrating to say on sex and social relations—there would be no need to complain, even if one found the "solutions" distasteful. But Miss Lynch's case, at all events, depends on a vigorous reading into the plays of values which are not there, values which could not possibly be expressed, in fact, in the prose of any of the dramatists. (The candid reader can turn up the passages selected by Miss Lynch in support of her argument, and see if they are not all in the factitious, superficial mode that I have described.)

We may consider, by way of illustration, Etherege's *The Man of Mode*. When the play opens, Dorimant ("the finest of all fine gentlemen in Restoration comedy") is trying to rid himself of an old mistress, Mrs. Loveit, before taking up with a new, Bellinda, whilst Young Bellair, in love with Emilia, is trying to find some way out of marrying Harriet, an heiress whom his father has brought to town for him. The entertainment is made up of these two sets of complications, together with an exhibition of the would-be modishness of Sir Fopling Flutter. Events move fast. After a night spent in various sociabilities Dorimant keeps an appointment with Bellinda at 5 a.m. Letting her out of his lodgings an hour or so later, and swearing to be discreet "By all the Joys I have had, and those you keep in store," he is surprised by his companions, and in the resulting confusion Bellinda finds herself paying an unwilling visit to Mrs. Loveit. Dorimant appears and is rated by the women before he "flings off." Meanwhile Young Bellair and Emilia have secretly married. Dorimant, his equanimity recovered, turns up for the exposure, followed by his mistresses. The lovers are forgiven, the mistresses are huddled off the stage, and it is decided that Dorimant, who, the previous day, had ingratiated himself with Harriet's mother, and whose "soul has quite given up her liberty," shall be allowed to pay court to the heiress.

It seems to me that what the play provides—apart from the briskly handled intrigue—is a demonstration of the physical stamina of Dorimant. But Miss Lynch sees further. For her, Dorimant is "the fine flowering of Restoration culture." Illustrating her theory of the double standard, she remarks: "We laugh at Sir Fopling Flutter because he so clumsily parodies social fashions which Dorimant interprets with unfailing grace and distinction. We laugh at Dorimant because his assumed affectation admits of so poor and incomplete an expression of an attractive and vigorous personality." The "unfailing grace and distinction" are perhaps not much in evidence in Dorimant's spiteful treatment of Mrs. Loveit; but even if we ignore

those brutish scenes we are forced to ask, How do we know that there *is* this "attractive and vigorous personality" beneath the conventional forms? Dorimant's intrigues are of no more human significance than those of a barnyard cock, and as for what Miss Lynch calls "his really serious affair with Harriet" (I feel this deserves a *sic*), it is purely theatrical, and the "pangs of love" are expressed in nothing but the conventional formulae: "She's gone, but she has left a pleasing Image of herself behind that wanders in my Soul." The answer to the question posed is that Miss Lynch's account is a mere assumption. Nothing that Dorimant actually *says* will warrant it—and nothing in the whole of Restoration comedy—in the words actually spoken—allows us a glimpse of those other "personalities" to which the conventional social modes "could not give complete expression." The "real values" simply are not there.

A minor point can be made in passing. It is just possible to claim that Restoration comedy contains "social criticism" in its handling of "the vulgar." "Come Mr. Sharper," says Congreve's Belinda, "you and I will take a turn, and laugh at the vulgar; both the great vulgar and the small," and Etherege's Lady Townley expresses the common attitude of the polite towards the social nuisances: "We should love wit, but for variety be able to divert ourselves with the extravagancies of those who want it." The butts, unfortunately, are only shown as fools by the discrepancy between their ambitions and their achievements, not because their ambitions are puerile. The subject is hardly worth discussing, since it is obviously nothing but an easily satisfied sense of superiority that is diverted by the "variety" of a constant succession of Dapperwits, Froths and Fopling Flutters. "When a humour takes in London," Tom Brown remarked [in his *Works*, Vol. III], "they ride it to death ere they leave it. The primitive Christians were not persecuted with half that variety as the poor unthinking beaus are tormented with upon the theatre . . . A huge great muff, and a gaudy ribbon hanging at a bully's backside, is an excellent jest, and new-invented curses, as, Stap my vitals, damn my diaphragm, slit my wind pipe, sink me ten thousand fathom deep, rig up a new beau, though in the main 'tis but the same everlasting coxcomb."

In the matter of sexual relations Restoration comedy is entirely dominated by a narrow set of conventions. The objection that it is only certain characters, not the dramatists themselves, who accept them can be more freely encountered when the assumptions that are expressed most frequently have been briefly illustrated.

The first convention is, of course, that constancy in love, especially in marriage, is a bore. Vanbrugh, who was the most uneasy if not the most honest of the comic dramatists (I think that in *The Provok'd Wife* he shows as unusually honest), unambiguously attributes this attitude to Sir John Brute:

> What cloying meat is love—when matrimony's the sauce to it! Two years marriage has debauch'd my five senses. . . . No boy was ever so weary of his tutor, no girl of her bib, no nun of doing penance, or old maid of being chaste, as

I am of being married. Sure there's a secret curse
entail'd upon the very name of wife!

The woman's well enough; she has no vice that
I know of, but she's a wife, and—damn a wife!

What Vanbrugh saw as a fit sentiment for Sir John had by
that time (1697) served the Restoration stage—without
change—for thirty years. In *She Wou'd if She Cou'd* Etherege had exhibited Sir Oliver Cockwood in an identical
vein: "A pox of this tying man and woman together, for
better, for worse." "To have a mistress love thee entirely"
is "a damn'd trouble." "There are sots that would think
themselves happy in such a Lady; but to a true bred Gentleman all lawful solace is abomination." If Sir Oliver is
a fool it is only because he is a trifle gross in his expression.
"If you did but know, Madam," says the polite Freeman,
"what an odious thing it is to be thought to love a Wife
in good Company." And the convention is constantly
turning up in Congreve. "There is no creature perfectly
civil but a husband," explains Mrs. Frail [in *Love for
Love*], "for in a little time he grows only rude to his wife,
and that is the highest good breeding, for it begets his civility to other people." "Marry her! Marry her!" Fainall advises Mirabell [in *The Way of the World*], "Be half as well
acquainted with her charms, as you are with her defects,
and my life on't, you are your own man again." And Witwoud: "A wit should no more be sincere than a woman
constant; one argues a decay of parts, as t'other of beauty." Appetite, it seems (and this is the second assumption),
needs perpetually fresh stimulus. This is the faith of Rhodophil in *Marriage à la Mode* and of Constant in *The
Provok'd Wife,* as well as of Wycherley's old procuress,
Mrs. Joyner. "If our wives would suffer us but now and
then to make excursions," Rhodophil explains to
Palamede, "the benefit of our variety would be theirs; instead of one continued, lazy, tired love, they would, in
their turns, have twenty vigorous, fresh, and active lovers." "Would anything but a madman complain of uncertainty?" asks Congreve's Angelica [in *Love for Love*], for
"security is an insipid thing, and the overtaking and possessing of a wish, discovers the folly of the chase." And
Fainall, in *The Way of the World,* speaks for a large class
when he hints at a liking for sauce—a little gentleman's
relish—to his seductions: "I'd no more play with a man
that slighted his ill fortune than I'd make love to a woman
who under-valued the loss of her reputation." Fainall, of
course, is what he is, but the attitude that makes sexual
pleasure "the bliss," that makes woman "delicious"—
something to be savoured—as well as "damned" and "destructive," demands, for its support, "the pleasure of a
chase."

Would you long preserve your lover?
    Would you still his goddess reign?
Never let him all discover,
    Never let him much obtain.
                                [*The Old Bachelor*]

Restoration comedy used to be considered outrageously
outspoken, but such stuff as this, far from being "outspoken," hovers on the outskirts of sexual relations, and sees
nothing but the titillation of appetite (" 'Tis not the success," Collier observed [in *A Short View of the Profaneness
and Immorality of the English Stage*], "but the manner of

gaining it which is all in all"). Sex is a hook baited with
tempting morsels; it is a thirst quencher; it is a cordial; it
is a dish to feed on; it is a bunch of grapes; it is anything
but sex. (This, of course, explains why some people can
combine a delighted approval of Restoration comedy with
an unbalanced repugnance for such modern literature as
deals sincerely and realistically with sexual relationships.)

Now the objection referred to above was that sentiments
such as these are not offered for straightforward acceptance. Many of them are attributed to characters plainly
marked as Wicked (Maskwell, for example, is the black-a-
vised villain of melodrama), or, more frequently, as trivial,
and the dramatist can therefore dissociate himself. He
may even be engaged in showing his audience the explicit,
logical consequences of the half-unconscious premises on
which they base their own lives, saying, as Mr. Dobrée has
it, "Here is life lived upon certain assumptions; see what
it becomes." To this there are several answers. The first
is that reflexions of the kind that I have quoted are indistinguishable in tone and style from the general epigrammatic stock-in-trade (the audience was not altogether to
be blamed if, as Congreve complained, they could not at
first "distinguish betwixt the character of a Witwoud and
a Lovewit"); and they are largely "exhibited," just as all
the self-conscious witticisms are exhibited, for the sake of
their immediate "comic" effect. One has only to note the
laughter of a contemporary audience at a revival, and the
places where the splutters occur, to realize how much of
the fun provides a rather gross example of tendency wit.
The same attitudes, moreover, are manipulated again and
again, turning up with the stale monotony of jokes on
postcards, and the play that is made with them demands
only the easiest, the most superficial, response.

**The criticism that defenders of
Restoration comedy need to answer is not
that the comedies are "immoral," but that
they are trivial, gross and dull.**

—*L. C. Knights*

But it is, after all, useless to argue about the degree of detachment, the angle at which these attitudes and assumptions are presented. As soon as one selects a particular
comedy for that exercise one realizes that all is equally
grist to the mill and that the dramatist (there is no need,
here, to make distinctions) has no coherent attitude of his
own. A consistent artistic purpose would not be content
to express itself in a style that allows so limited, so local
an effect.

But it is the triviality that one comes back to. In Dryden's
Marriage à la Mode the characters accept the usual conventions: constancy is dull, and love only thrives on variety.

PALAMEDE. O, now I have found it! you dislike

her for no other reason but because she's your wife.

RHODOPHIL. And is not that enough? All that I know of her perfections now, is only by memory . . . At last we arrived at that point, that there was nothing left in us to make us new to one another . . .

PALAMEDE. The truth is, your disease is very desperate; but, though you cannot be cured, you may be patched up a little: you must get you a mistress, Rhodophil. That, indeed, is living upon cordials; but, as fast as one fails, you must supply it with another.

The mistress that Rhodophil selects is Melantha, whom Palamede is to marry; Palamede falls in love with Doralice, Rhodophil's wife, and the ensuing complications provide sufficient entertainment (the grotto scene, III, ii, is really funny). Mr. Dobrée, however, regards the play as a witty exposure of the impossibility of rationalizing sex relations, as Palamede and Rhodophil attempt to rationalize them. Dryden "laughs morality back into its rightful place, as the scheme which ultimately makes life most comfortable." But what Dryden actually does is to *use* the conventions for the amusement they afford, not to examine them. The level at which the play works is fairly indicated by the opening song:

Why should a foolish marriage vow,
    Which long ago was made,
Oblige us to each other now,
    When passion is decayed?
We loved, and we loved, as long as we could,
    'Till our love was loved out in us both;
But our marriage is dead, when the pleasure is fled:
    'Twas pleasure first made it an oath.

If I have pleasures for a friend,
    And further love in store,
What wrong has he, whose joys did end,
    And who could give no more?
'Tis a madness that he should be jealous of me,
    Or that I should bar him of another:
For all we can gain, is to give ourselves pain,
    When neither can hinder the other.

The lovers make no attempt to "rationalize sex" for the simple reason that genuine sexual feelings no more enter into the play as a whole than feelings of any kind enter into the song. (The obviously faked emotions of the heroic plot are, after all, relevant—and betraying.) And according to Mr. Dobrée, "In one sense the whole idea of Restoration comedy is summed up in the opening song of *Marriage à la Mode.*"

In a sense, too, Mr. Dobrée is right. Restoration comedy nowhere provides us with much more of the essential stuff of human experience than we have there. Even Congreve, by common account the best of the comic writers, is no exception. I have said that his verbal pattern often seems to be quite unrelated to an individual mode of perceiving. At best it registers a very limited mode. Restoration prose is all "social" in its tone, implications and general tenor, but Congreve's observation is *merely* of the public surface. And Congreve, too, relies on the conventional assump-

tions. In *The Way of the World,* it is true, they are mainly given to the bad and the foolish to express: it is Fainall who discourses on the pleasures of disliking one's wife, and Witwoud who maintains that only old age and ugliness ensure constancy. And Mirabell, who is explicitly opposed to some aspects of contemporary manners, goes through the common forms in a tone of rather weary aloofness: "I wonder, Fainall, that you who are married, and of consequence should be discreet, will suffer your wife to be of such a party." But Congreve himself is not above raising a cheap snigger; and, above all, the characters with some life in them have nothing to fall back on—nothing, that is, except the conventional, and conventionally limited, pleasures of sex. Millamant, who says she loathes the country and hates the town, expects to draw vitality from the excitement of incessant solicitation:

I'll be solicited to the very last, nay, and afterwards . . . I should think I was poor and had nothing to bestow, if I were reduced to an inglorious ease, and freed from the agreeable fatigues of solicitation. . . . Oh, I hate a lover than can dare to think he draws a moment's air, independent of the bounty of his mistress. There is not so impudent a thing in nature, as the saucy look of an assured man, confident of success. The pedantic arrogance of a very husband has not so pragmatical an air.

Everyone seems to have found Millamant intelligent and attractive, but her attitude is not far removed from that expressed in

Would you long preserve your lover?
    Would you still his goddess reign?

and she shares with characters who are decidedly not attractive a disproportionate belief in "the pleasure of a chase." Which is not surprising in view of her other occupations and resources; visiting, writing and receiving letters, tea-parties and small talk make up a round that is never for a moment enlivened by the play of genuine intelligence. And although Congreve recognizes, at times, the triviality of his characters, it is to the world whose confines were the Court, the drawing-room, the play-house and the park—a world completely lacking the real sophistication and self-knowledge that might, in some measure, have redeemed it—that he limits his appeal.

It is, indeed, hard to resist the conclusion that "society"—the smart town society that sought entertainment at the theatres—was fundamentally bored. In *The Man of Mode* Emilia remarks of Medley, "I love to hear him talk o' the intrigues, let 'em be never so dull in themselves, he'll make 'em pleasant i' the relation," and the idiotic conversation that follows (II, i), affording us a glimpse of what Miss Lynch calls "the most brilliant society which Restoration comedy has to offer," suggests in more than one way how badly society *needed* to be entertained. It is the boredom—the constant need for titillation—that helps to explain not only the heroic "heightening" of emotion, but the various scenic effects, the devices of staging and costume that became popular at this period. (Charles II "almost died of laughing" at Nell Gwynn's enormous hat.) The conventions—of sexual pursuit, and so on—were an attempt to make life interesting—an impossible job for those who were aware of so limited a range of human potentialities.

The dominating mood of Restoration comedy is, by common account, a cynical one. But one cannot even say that there is here, in contrast to naïve Romantic fervours, the tough strength of disillusion. If—recognizing that there is a place in the educational process for, say, La Rochefoucauld—one finds the "cynicism" of the plays distasteful, it is because it is easy and superficial; the attitudes that we are presented with are based on so meagre an amount of observation and experience. Thus, "Elle retrouvait dans l'adultère toutes les platitudes du mariage" has, superficially, much the same meaning as, "I find now, by sad experience, that a mistress is much more chargeable than a wife, and after a little time too, grows full as dull and insignificant." But whereas the first sentence has behind it the whole of *Madame Bovary*, the second comes from *Sir Martin Mar-all*, which (although Dryden shares the honours with the Duke of Newcastle) is perhaps the stupidest play I have ever read, and the context is imbecility.

But the superficiality is betrayed at every turn—by the obvious rhythms of the interspersed songs, as well as by the artificial elegance of the prose. And the cynicism is closely allied with—merges into—sentimentality. One thinks of the sentimentally conceived Fidelia in the resolutely "tough" *Plain Dealer;* and there is no doubt that the audi-

Nathaniel Lee (1653?-1692). From a nineteenth-century engraving.

ence was meant to respond sympathetically when, at the end of *Love for Love,* Angelica declared her love for Valentine: "Had I the world to give you, it could not make me worthy of so generous a passion; here's my hand, my heart was always yours, and struggled very hard to make this utmost trial of your virtue." There is, of course, a good deal of loose emotion in the heroic plays, written—it is useful to remember—for the same audience:

> I'm numbed, and fixed, and scarce my eyeballs
>   move;
> I fear it is the lethargy of love!
> 'Tis he; I feel him now in every part:
> Like a new lord he vaunts about my heart;
> Surveys, in state, each corner of my breast,
> While poor fierce I, that was, am dispossessed.
>   [*The Conquest of Granada*]

> A secret pleasure trickles through my veins:
> It works about the inlets of my soul,
> To feel thy touch, and pity tempts the pass:
> But the tough metal of my heart resists;
> 'Tis warmed with the soft fire, not melted down.
>   [*Don Sebastian*]

"Feeling," in Dryden's serious plays, is fairly represented by such passages as these, and Dryden, we know, was not alone in admiring the Fletcherian "pathos." But it is the lyric verse of the period that provides the strongest confirmatory evidence of the kind of bad taste that is in question. It is not merely that in Etherege, Sedley and Dorset the feeling comes from much nearer the surface than in the Metaphysicals and the Caroline poets, intellectual "wit" no longer strengthens and controls the feeling. Conventional attitudes are rigged out in a conventional vocabulary and conventional images. (The stock outfit—the "fair eyes" that "wound," the "pleasing pains," the "sighs and tears," the "bleeding hearts" and "flaming darts"—can be studied in any anthology.) There is, in consequence, a pervasive strain of sentimental vulgarity.

> Farewell, ungrateful traitor!
>   Farewell, my perjured swain!
> Let never injured creature
>   Believe a man again.
> The pleasure of possessing
> Surpasses all expressing,
> But 'tis too short a blessing,
>   And love too long a pain.
>   . . . . . .
> The passion you pretended,
>   Was only to obtain;
> But when the charm is ended,
>   The charmer you disdain.
> Your love by ours we measure
> Till we have lost our treasure,
> But dying is a pleasure
>   When living is a pain.

This piece of music-hall sentiment comes from Dryden's *The Spanish Friar,* and it does not stand alone. The mode that was to produce, among other things of equal merit, "When lovely woman stoops to folly," had its origin in the lyrics of the Restoration period. Most of these were written by the group connected with the theatres, and they serve to underline the essential criticism of the plays. The criticism that defenders of Restoration comedy need to answer is not that the comedies are "immoral," but that they are trivial, gross and dull. (pp. 9-19)

> *L. C. Knights, "Restoration Comedy: The Reality and the Myth," in* Restoration Drama: Modern Essays in Criticism, *edited by John Loftis, Oxford University Press, 1966, pp. 3-21.*

Marvin Mudrick

[*Mudrick is an American educator and critic. In the following excerpt, he evaluates the reputation and effectiveness of Restoration comedy, noting that though they appear to treat only trivial matters, the plays do involve serious issues, namely "the cult of manners that grandly offers to regulate a whole society."*]

The high reputation of Restoration comedy has been sustained on surprisingly slight critical authority. It is true that the squeamishness of the two centuries following *The Way of the World* prevented more than an occasional outraged dismissal, or defensive impressionistic survey, of what was taken (except, disingenuously, by Lamb) for the accurate reflection of a debauched society. Critics during the past several decades have had no such excuse. The inhibition removed, we expect due and favorable examination of the age of Wycherley and Congreve. The most persuasive recent examination, however, is an attack, by L. C. Knights [in *Explorations*]; and Mr. Knights is not squeamish, but bored: "The criticism . . . [their] defenders . . . need to answer is not that the comedies are 'immoral,' but that they are trivial, gross and dull."

It may be said for the defenders that they, at least, are not bored with this "finely polished art of the intellect that gives us amply in return for the vulgarity" [A. Nicoll, *Restoration Drama*]. They find the novel virtue of the Restoration comic dramatist in his "desire to try new ways of living" [Bonamy Dobrée, *Restoration Drama*]; they explore his preoccupation with "life . . . accepted and observed—not as a problem, but a pageant" [John Palmer, *The Comedy of Manners*]; they single out his invention of "personalities" of "unfailing grace and distinction," to which the "thoroughly conventionalized social mode" of the court of Charles II "could not give complete expression [Kathleen M. Lynch, *The Social Mode of Restoration Comedy*]; they confide that in the contemplation of his plays "we become for the moment pagan, without a thought of the morrow, existing solely for the joy of the hour" [Nicoll, *Restoration Drama*]. They can also penetrate, through a modish generalization by Congreve's Angelica on the pleasures of the sex-chase ("Uncertainty and expectation are the joys of life," etc.), to the heart and *Weltschmerz* of Restoration comedy:

> This is not the observation of a jilt, of a baggage without sensibility, but of a woman who has known and suffered, who has been disappointed in her early estimate of things. It is the weary cry of the knower who realizes that happiness may not be sought for or grasped, and that joy must be snatched as it flies. These were not mere puppets, but breathing, living, desiring men and women. [Dobrée, *Restoration Comedy*]

From such throbbing appreciation it is salutary to turn back to the plays themselves and to agree with Mr. Knights. Certainly Restoration comedy lacks the "quality and variety," the vigor and scope, of interest and idiom that the Elizabethan playwrights, for example, could draw upon. In Restoration wit "the verbal pattern appears at times to be completely unrelated to a mode of perceiving," the words "have an air of preening themselves on their acute discriminations," though "the antitheses are mechanical, and the pattern is monotonously repeated." "In the matter of sexual relations Restoration comedy is entirely dominated by a narrow set of conventions," and even these conventions the dramatist does not, characteristically, examine in order to trace and predict the directions they may give to human impulses. Rather, he exploits them in order to gratify "the constant need for titillation" of an inanely artificial society "lacking the real sophistication and self-knowledge that might, in some measure, have redeemed it" [Knights, *Explorations*].

Still, the indictment may not be so damaging as it seems. Mr. Knights's least disputable charge, concerning the inferiority of Restoration to Elizabethan drama, reminds us that, whatever their relative merits, each of them was authoritative enough to define its age as an age of drama— the rarest kind of literary age—during which a number of playwrights, united by a community of conventions and interests and identifiable by common qualities of idiom and style, not only hold the stage but dominate the writing of their time. Aside from the century of Shakespeare and Congreve, there is indeed no English literary period with a surviving, not to mention dominating, drama. Mr. Knights's comparison may imply, then, more odium than it should: the fact that the Restoration theater is, by the standard of the Elizabethan, unresourceful and limited must be seen in the light of the equally unarguable fact that, though the English stage has had other names and other entertainments, it has had no other theater at all.

As for the superiority of Elizabethan *comedy* to Wycherley and Congreve, that is altogether arguable. "The fault . . . of Shakespeare's comic Muse," remarked Hazlitt, "is . . . that it is too good-natured and magnanimous." It is scarcely unorthodox to suggest that Shakespeare's comic figures are for the most part either casually witty observers or the merest butts, and that his "comedies" are good-natured mélanges always ready to sacrifice any dramatic pattern—including the comic patterns of mechanism and vitality, plausibility and substance, deceit and exposure—in order to examine the margin of humanness, the strong (and at times dramatically fatal) pathos discoverable by Shakespeare in Malvolio and Shylock as well as in Shallow and Falstaff. The so-called "problem comedies"—*Measure for Measure* and *Troilus and Cressida*, especially—are in fact Shakespeare's solution of his comic problem: they are irreducible tragicomedies, in which Shakespeare creates a form hospitable to the pathos and self-exhausting complexity of motive that he constantly discovers in protagonists not quite grand or lucky enough to be tragic.

The claim of Elizabethan comedy must rest, eventually, with Jonson, who lacked Shakespeare's talent for pathos and Fletcher's weakness for it and was therefore unimpelled to make new genres or to corrupt old ones. The contribution of Jonson's audience was the Elizabethan delight in roguery—we have the testimony of the pamphleteers and "true-history" writers as well as the dramatists—and nothing is more susceptible to the logic of comedy than the cycle of deception and self-deception, exposure and mortification between rogue and gull or between rogue and rogue, the innocent dishonest dream of something for nothing, the most enduring symbol of which is Jonson's own Alchemist. What Jonson himself contributed was the virtue of his defect: incapable of pathos, he is supremely capable of reducing motive to monomania and so diverting attention from the players to the gusto and intricate strategy of the game itself—the game, that is, of comedy, in which there are the manipulated and the manipulators, dupedom and the triumphant or foiled ingenuity of conscious appetite.

Jonson's power is dramatic; it affirms itself primarily, not in scene-shifting or stage-business, but in language. Even the live precision and tension of his plot grow out of the sardonic precision of his verse, as if everything—in *this* comic world at least—can be said directly, as if every purpose proclaims itself. It is a language of perfect transparency in which self-recognition is offered to all, as when Mosca flatters the lawyer, one of Volpone's would-be heirs:

> I oft have heard him say how he admir'd
> Men of your large profession, that could speak
> To every cause, and things mere contraries,
> Till they were hoarse again, yet all be law;
> That, with most quick agility, could turn
> And return; make knots, and undo them;
> Give forked counsel; take provoking gold
> On either hand, and put it up; these men,
> He knew, would thrive with their humility.
> And, for his part, he though he should be blest
> To have his heir of such a suffering spirit,
> So wise, so grave, of so perplex'd a tongue,
> And loud withal, that would not wag, nor scarce
> Lie still, without a fee. . . .

It is a language in which man can even take the measure of his own desires, as when Sir Epicure, awaiting from the Alchemist the promised philosopher's stone, prophesies his own creatable paradise:

> I will have all my beds blown up, not stuff'd:
> Down is too hard; and then, mine oval room
> Fill'd with such pictures as Tiberius took
> From Elephantis, and dull Aretine
> But coldly imitated. Then, my glasses
> Cut in more subtle angles, to disperse
> And multiply the figures, as I walk
> Naked between my succubae. My mists
> I'll have of perfume, vapour'd 'bout the room,
> To lose our selves in; and my baths, like pits
> To fall into; from whence we will come forth,
> And roll us dry in gossamer and roses. . . .

It is a language, like Chaucer's or Swift's, rooted in an idiom rich with particular moral values—the ground of agreement between author and audience—and freely expressive of any moral deviations that human impulse contrives. It may be, indeed, the very freedom and particularity of the idiom that tempt Jonson—even in *Volpone* and *The Alchemist*—to scatter his shots with conversational exuberance, to indulge at times a strenuous self-righteousness (as through the straw figures of purity that he sets up against his energetic Vices), to stray out of comedy into topical satire, to aim at easy irrelevant targets like Sir Politic Would-Be. The Elizabethan tendency to this sort of logorrhea (so feelingly pointed out in Shakespeare by Jonson himself) is a tendency that makes even the best of Jonson's comedies blur at the edges. Wycherley—in *The Country Wife* at least—attending to similar comic deceits and disclosures, taking off from a device very similar to the initiatory device in *Volpone,* and working for the most part with characters obviously conceived as Jonsonian humours, manages to achieve a tough precision comparable to Jonson's; the achievement is on a smaller scale doubtless, but without Jonson's waste and misfire; and the conventions, however narrow, of the Restoration theater and the Restoration audience may be in part responsible.

In *Volpone* and *The Alchemist,* the two principal themes are avarice and lust, which are for Jonson—and his audience—moral deviations not only grave but almost inseparable, as though one inevitably implies the other; and if this mingling of sins seems to draw on the strength of the Christian-ethical tradition (which after all concerns itself with men and not comic figures), it also divides the attention and weakens Jonson's central comic effect: the clutter of single obsessions maneuvering and colliding. Like many other Elizabethan dramatists, Jonson suffers from a surplus of themes, a superabundance of interests that he shares with his audience.

By the time of the Restoration, however, the popular audience of Jonson (and Shakespeare), already dwindling with the spread of Puritan sympathies during the Caroline period, had vanished entirely. Wycherley's spectators were "the courtiers and their satellites" [Nicoll, *Restoration Drama*], and for such an idle and fashionable group, certain of Jonson's themes would have appeared barbarous and dull. For the Restoration audience, lust was, fashionably, little more than a casuistical Puritan distinction; and avarice was a tiresome trait hardly worth discussing among gentlemen or representing on a civilized stage—a trait of shopkeepers. (The latter, regarding the theaters as no better than brothels, never paid the price of admission and so did not have to be appeased.) For such an audience—without occupation, consciously straining toward an ideal of heroically casual debauchery, setting out to make up for the lost years under the Commonwealth—perhaps the only possible theme and motive was sex, that neutral stuff which the Elizabethans had graded into love and lust but which might now subside into unity again.

A dramatist is far more likely, in any case, to be numbed than invigorated by the prescriptions of theme and motive that his audience imposes and anticipates. Certainly, just as Elizabethan tragedy is in its mass a hodgepodge of butchery and tattered passions, so Restoration comedy is, in its overwhelming mass, a hodgepodge of premature sophistications, of inert, self-admiring wit and resolutely impertinent reversals of established sexual morality. We need look for verification no further than the comedies of Dryden, that most illustrious of hack playwrights, whose characters, as Mr. Knights remarks [in *Explorations*] of Etherege's Dorimant, are engaged in "intrigues of no more human significance than those of a barn-yard cock." There are, nevertheless, exceptions in both periods; and an age—of drama or of any other genre—is to be judged, ultimately, by its masterpieces. *The Country Wife* is, as Mr. Knights says of Restoration comedy generally, "in the matter of sexual relations . . . entirely dominated by a narrow set of conventions." We have in it the fixed focus on the sex-pursuit, the wits and would-be wits exercising themselves on the pleasures of variety and the pains of marriage, the neglected and yearning wives, the jealous husband fearing cuckoldry and the foolish one inviting it, but no marriage—in this view of wives as damageable possessions—proof against it. The question whether Wycherley yields to and exploits these conventions, or examines and substantiates them, is left to be considered.

Volpone's pretense of mortal illness, which alerts every acquaintance persuaded of being his sole heir, is Jonson's device for drawing out and illuminating the unity of avarice, the reduction and dehumanizing of appetite, in the specious diversity of a society for which money has become its own justification. Wycherley's device, within the conventions of his own stage and society, is equally brilliant: the rake Horner, to lull the suspicion of husbands and to secure in time the devotion of wives whose only coyness is for reputation's sake, pretends to have been made a eunuch and to be therefore no longer dangerous to either. Jonson's speaking rapacities, drawn out by his device, are obsessed by money, Wycherley's by sex; and Wycherley is no more the defender or dupe of the obsession he treats than is Jonson of his. As in Jonson, everything is expressed directly, in a transparent idiom, through which communication is both easy and impossible: Horner and Harcourt—the two manipulators—say what they mean and take care, when necessary, to be misunderstood; their dupes—Sparkish, Sir Jasper and his "ladies"—give themselves away in every phrase with no such intention at all; Alithea, saying what she means and intending to be taken at her word, is not believed especially when she is most earnest; Pinchwife, the cuckold in spite of himself, says what he means and, since his words mean more than he guesses, is understood in ways that must at last confirm his ferocious cynicism; only the country wife, like a judgment on this murk of rutting deceptions, says what she means with such country candor and naïveté as to clear the air from time to time, until she learns, having lost her lover, to lie habitually and for the sake of comfort with her husband: "And I must be a country wife still too, I find; for I can't, like a city one, be rid of my husband, and do what I list."

Standards become private and narcissistic, masquerading behind words once susceptible to public definition: honor, for example. For Pinchwife, honor is the patrolling of his "freehold," the banner of anticuckoldism. For Sparkish, it is the modish reflex against such insults as he is competent to unriddle. For Lady Fidget, it is a vacuum, the absence of scandal—" 'tis not an injury to a husband, till it be an injury to our honours; so that a woman of honour loses no honour with a private person." For her husband

it is the proper filling of social rôles in savorless private lives, as when he tells his wife to "go to your business, I say, pleasure, whilst I go to my pleasure, business," and sends her off to play games with that unscandalous shadow of a man, Horner. For Alithea, honor is stubbornness of fidelity to a detestable commitment, the sort of honor that sentimental comedy will take in dead earnest during Wycherley's own lifetime. Only for Horner, the sardonic, privileged observer, like Shakespeare's Diomede making his opportunities in a corrupt age without giving up a certain hard clarity of vision, is honor significantly honorable, the saving (for his own honorless aims) of his mistresses' reputations, which is all they wish saved, until, forced to choose between the "honor" of a concealed mistress and harmless Alithea's, he chooses his pleasure and must submit to Alithea's wistful reproach: "I always took you for a man of honour."

The dialogue is, throughout, a great web of ambiguities and unexpected, symbolic relevances: firecracker strings of *double-entendre* as in the china scene, intentions and words at cross-purposes and exposing each other, unconscious prophecies by gulls of their inevitable gulling, the insidious slipperiness of language in a society alerted to sex only. And the ambiguities are never merely stock comic devices in set-piece scenes and episodes, they are the confusions to which mind makes itself liable by reducing itself to caricature, by converting language into an unintentionally rich symbolism of aborted single impulse, such as flows over in the grotesque drinking scene between Horner and the ladies: "The filthy toads," says Mrs. Dainty—she is talking about men—"choose mistresses now as they do stuffs, for having been fancied and worn by others"; "For being common and cheap," adds Mrs. Squeamish; "Whilst women of quality," concludes Lady Fidget, "like the richest stuffs, lie untumbled, and unasked for."

This is the age of Nell Gwyn and the Duchess of Cleveland. "Is it not a frank age?" Sparkish the ape of fashion asks rhetorically, having just misinterpreted to his own satisfaction—as civility, as wit, as up-to-dateness or upside-downness—a rival's insults to him and declarations of love, over her protest, to the girl he is to marry. "Blame 'em not, they must follow their copy, the age," says one of Horner's friends about poets who create fashionable fools. Frankness, somehow, is not enough. Nor is monomaniacal vigilance: "What a swarm of cuckolds and cuckold-makers!" cries Pinchwife, preparing to assist with tenacious (if unintended) complaisance at his own cuckolding; and, having dictated to his wife her letter of disavowal for which she substitutes her own breathless solicitation, directs her to "write on the backside, 'For Mr. Horner,' " and delivers it up—wife and all—himself. Heroism is not enough: "I will not be a cuckold," says Pinchwife, "there will be danger in making me a cuckold"; and Horner punctures that bubble, "Why, wert thou not well cured of thy last clap?"

Wycherley's toughmindedness, like Jonson's, is likely to repel tender critics. "There can be no question," remarks one of the recent admirers of Restoration comedy [Nicoll, *British Drama*], "but that Wycherley is indescribably vulgar." Another will not admit him to the suave and truly comic company of Etherege and Congreve because

> Social folly and hypocrisy are much closer realities to . . . [him] than the social poise and integrity which make amends. . . . When other writers of Restoration comedy ridicule folly and vice, it is more lightheartedly and rarely with corrective emphasis. . . . On some occasions, Wycherley assails some of the most cherished ideals of the age. . . . At such times . . . [he] is playing false to the tradition of Restoration comedy of manners; he confirms our suspicion that he was not 'born' a Restoration gentleman.

[Lynch, *The Social Mode*]

The view that comedy is necessarily "lighthearted," gentlemanly, and careful of the "ideals of the age" would of course have startled comic dramatists from Aristophanes to Jonson; chiefly responsible, perhaps, for a view so vapidly genteel and, since Meredith, so nearly axiomatic are the false example of Shakespeare and the sentimental comedy that has dominated the English stage since 1700. Nor does the term "comedy of manners" brighten and rarefy the comic atmosphere so much as all that. A comic dramatist must use the materials his audience affords him: the period during which the surface and finish of life, wit and social adeptness monopolized the audience's image of life produced as its characteristic genre the comedy of manners; just as in a period of more diversified interests Jonson, concentrating on a single possible Elizabethan image of life—life as energy and appetite—produced the comedy of humors. But to treat an image of life is not necessarily to defend or suppress its defects. Wycherley merely had less faith than his audience in the durability of manners and in their power to withstand the pressure of impulse or self-interest. The author has his rights also.

Still, to wince at Wycherley is more reasonable than to find in Congreve a prevailing "joyousness" and the portrait of a "*beau monde . . . indulgently idealized*" [Lynch, *The Social Mode*]; and this traditional view of *The Way of the World* particularly, as the prop and casual glory of Restoration society (or rather of its ghost), as an elegantly falsified testament dedicated by the age to itself, has long served both addicts and detractors of Restoration comedy, who unite in affirming that the comedy of manners can breathe only in an "air of modish triviality" [Nicoll, *British Drama*].

Congreve, it is true, presents a society of superficies, in which manners are second nature and, therefore, distinctions of a primary nature—moral and psychological—are difficult to make. In the great world Fainall is scarcely distinguishable from Mirabell, and the false wits—snappers-up of considered trifles—scarcely distinguishable from the true ones. Both Fainall and Mirabell are witty and languidly polite, and the false wits can learn patterns of politeness and patterns of wit from such formal and artificial instructors. Manners are, or appear to be, opaque and durable, a common film of plausibility over the variety of impulse and motive.

Taken by itself, the entire first act of *The Way of the World* is a surface of ease and plausibility, barely ruffled even by the need to appear witty and detached. One is untempted, for example, to penetrate, so long as it occupies the stage, the rehearsed, serpentine elegance with which Fainall and Mirabell discuss women, courtship and marriage:

> She once used me with that insolence [says Mirabell, remembering Millamant] that in revenge I took her to pieces, sifted her, and separated her failings; I studied 'em, and got 'em by rote. The catalogue was so large that I was not without hopes one day or other to hate her heartily; to which end I so used myself to think of 'em at length, contrary to my design and expectation, they gave me every hour less and less disturbance; till in a few days it became habitual to me to remember 'em without being displeased. They are now grown as familiar to me as my own frailties; and in all probability, in a little time longer I shall like 'em as well.

"Marry her, marry her!" says Fainall. "Be half as well acquainted with her charms as you are with her defects, and my life on't, you are your own man again. . . . I have experience; I have a wife, and so forth." Later, Witwould stumbles into these verbal dexterities with a compliment: "No man in town lives well with a wife but Fainall. Your judgment, Mirabell?" And Mirabell replies: "You had better step and ask his wife, if you would be credibly informed."

Manners—assembling themselves in the phrases so neatly pieced and developed, seeming to repel attention except to themselves—will very shortly, however, clear into a disquieting transparency: Mirabell *is* anxiously in love and incapable of rationalizing his way out of it; Fainall *has* learned from his own calculatedly loveless marriage and his secret affair that experience is a murderer of illusions; Mrs. Fainall, when she is asked, offers a great deal of personal information, if only later the fact that her lover, as well as the pander for her hateful marriage, was Mirabell himself.

> Men are ever in extremes, either doting or averse. While they are lovers, if they have fire and sense, their jealousies are insupportable. And when they cease to love, (we ought to think at least) they loathe; they look upon us with horror and distaste, they meet us like the ghosts of what we were, and as from such, fly from us.

"You hate mankind?" asks Mrs. Marwood. "Heartily, inveterately." "Your husband?" asks Mrs. Marwood. "Most transcendently; aye, though I say it, meritoriously." Mrs. Marwood, loving Mirabell without hope, trapped by Fainall in an affair from which she has long since withdrawn any love of her own, can at least amuse herself while she awaits the next occasion to cripple Mirabell's hope of love and dowry both—inventing this bitter catechism for rejected ladies to live by.

The astonishing fact about the dialogue of *The Way of the World* is not that it gives an immortal voice to the transience of manners—as indeed it does—but that it expresses, with its own imperturbable logic, a pervasive sophistication stifling all vitality except fury, jealousy, cunning, affectation, contempt, and perhaps the dignified uneasiness that occasionally breaks through Mirabell's façade. Manners have tortured the characters, and their language, into the substance as well as the style of self-baffling intricacy. There is never even the sense—as there always is in *The Country Wife*—of imminent sexual explosion: impulse and motive have suffered alchemical changes; personality has been, for the aims of the drawing-room, subtilized into a sleek, complacent uniformity; sex and self-interest and the need to sustain a perilous façade are all dissolved into one another. Charm at its best is the carefully poised, self-protective affectation of Millamant, scoring off Mrs. Marwood who has just insisted that she hates Mirabell:

> O madam, why so do I. And yet the creature loves me, ha! ha! ha! How can one forbear laughing to think of it! I am a sibyl if I am not amazed to think what he can see in me. I'll take my death, I think you are handsomer and, within a year or two as young; if you could but stay for me, I should overtake you, but that cannot be. . . .

In such a world, affectation may be the only armor. Cuckoldry and cozening, and the rigors of labyrinthine intrigue, are the way of this world, which is Fainall's world and Mrs. Marwood's; and Fainall is ultimately privileged to describe himself, in a corrosive shower of wit, as the blindest and most emblematic dupe of all:

> And I, it seems, am a husband, a rank husband; and my wife a very errant, rank wife, all in *the way of the world*. 'Sdeath, to be a cuckold by anticipation, a cuckold in embryo! Sure I was born with budding antlers, like a young satyr, or a citizen's child. 'Sdeath! to be out-witted, to be out-jilted, out-matrimonied! If I had kept my speed like a stag, 'twere somewhat; but to crawl after, with my horns, like a snail, and be outstripped by my wife, 'tis scurvy wedlock.

The comedy of manners does not necessarily trifle; it is hospitable to serious issues. It has for its subject, after all, the cult of manners that grandly offers to regulate a whole society, and the Arnoldian predisposition of Mr. Knights ought to have led him to scrutinize more patiently that cultivated appearance of triviality which Congreve, for one, accepts from his audience, and which he polishes into an ironic gloss not quite dazzling enough to conceal the moral turbulence beneath. (pp. 98-115)

> *Marvin Mudrick, "Restoration Comedy and Later," in* English Stage Comedy, *edited by W. K. Wimsatt, Jr., Columbia University Press, 1955, pp. 98-125.*

John Wain

[*Wain is one of the most prolific English authors of contemporary fiction and poetry. As a critic, he centers his writings on the belief that, in order to judge the quality of a piece of literature, the critic must make moral as well as imaginative judgements. In the excerpt below from a 1955 essay, he posits that, despite isolated examples of brilliance, Restoration dramatists fail as a group because of their confused morals: "they make fun of marriage for instance, for five long acts and then meekly lead the hero to the altar in the last scene."*]

One of the main checks on one's natural wish to take Restoration comedy seriously is, of course, the frightful confusion it exhibits whenever a moral attitude is to be taken up. Critics who enthusiastically recommend its fearless questioning of fundamental social questions, or indignantly deny that it is 'immoral', seldom argue their case with any plausibility. In so far as the charge of 'immorality' is put in Victorian terms—anything that mentions the unmentionable is immoral—it is easy to brush aside; but in fact we do expect an artist to have *artistic* morality; to take up a consistent attitude towards problems of conduct, and not merely to trifle with them. Trifling is exactly what these dramatists are doing, and their defenders on this score are often driven to produce desperate arguments. Mr. J. W. Krutch, for instance, in his *Comedy and Conscience after the Restoration* (1949), has much to say of comedy but rather less about conscience; he points out (chap. 2) that there was a lot of corruption in real life at that time, so the audiences were hardened to it, and adds: 'Nor is there anything in this which need damn the dramatists as men. They had no deliberate intention of encouraging vice, which, being men of sense, they no doubt hated.' This will hardly do. Indeed, Mr. Krutch evidently feels unhappy with it himself, because, after quoting a few statements by dramatists on the topic—notably Dryden's Preface to *An Evening's Love* and Mrs. Behn's Preface to *The Dutch Lover*—he just lets the whole thing go: 'The truth of the matter seems to be that the poets were not interested in morality either one way or the other.' A bunch of footlers, in other words. Mr. J. H. Wilson in his *The Court Wits of the Restoration* (1948) even takes the view that, since these writers had no problems to face in their own lives, they had no need to thrash anything out in their work. 'Since their own society was obviously well-ordered, they discussed no problems.' It is true that Mr. Wilson—whose book, by the way, is in the main an excellent one—is talking not about Restoration dramatists as a whole, but about a group within them, namely Rochester, Scroope, Etherege, Wycherley, Dorset, Mulgrave, and Buckingham. But he shows no impulse to differentiate between these writers and their socially humbler colleagues. Was the society of Rochester, of Wycherley, of Etherege, so 'obviously well-ordered'? Did not these men, in fact, get their lives into a corresponding mess, matching the mess they made of their work?

This talk of getting one's life into a mess reminds me that Rochester, who made one of the most determined of the various efforts to act out these fantasies, and died of it in his thirties, is generally said to be the model for Dorimant in Etherege's *The Man of Mode, or, Sir Fopling Flutter*, and I ought to pause here to say that I except this play from all these remarks about incoherence and indecision. In fact, it is the one play I should feel able to point to, as an example of a Restoration comedy with the courage of its author's convictions. The trouble with the others is that they are simply not facing the real issue, which I take to be a fairly clear-cut one. If a man makes a deliberate choice of a certain way of life, he must know beforehand—or, if he does not, he will very soon find out—that it will bring with it certain special problems. If he decides to play for certain rewards, he will have to encounter certain dangers and penalties. The rakes in Restoration comedy have chosen to live the life of pleasure; they are putting every-thing into subordination to the satisfaction of their immediate appetites. Now this *could* be the material for a very interesting kind of comedy, one that would include, and make comic play with, the miseries of such a man as well as his delights. But in fact no Restoration comedian took his subject-matter seriously enough to make the attempt: except, as I say, for Etherege in this one play. Quite apart from its brilliance, *The Man of Mode* is head and shoulders above the other plays of this kind because it is *about* something; Professor Knights's quip, that the play demonstrates nothing 'except the physical stamina of Dorimant', is a mere flippant evasion; its subject is the life-style of a man like Rochester, and its human consequences. Suppose we decide to behave like this, *what will happen*?

Dorimant, in his relationships with women, has the fighter-pilot's mentality; he wants to get them before they get him. He is at war with the sex, and they immediately feel it and feel a very real wish to injure him (which doesn't prevent their feeling attracted to him). When introduced to Harriet, for instance, he begins at once to spar with her in a way that, while superficially it is a mere Beatrice-and-Benedick act to conceal the fact that they have genuine feelings for one another, has within it an element of real malice:

> DORIMANT. You were talking of Play, Madam; Pray what may be your stint?
>
> HARRIET. A little harmless discourse in publick walks, or at most an appointment in a Box bare-fac'd at the Play-House; you are for Masks, and private meetings, where Women engage for all they are worth, I hear.
>
> DOR. I have been us'd to deep Play, but I can make one at small Game, when I like my Gamester well.
>
> HAR. And be so unconcern'd you'l ha' no pleasure in't.
>
> DOR. Where there is a considerable sum to be won, the hope of drawing people in, makes every trifle considerable.
>
> HAR. The sordidness of mens natures, I know, makes 'em willing to flatter and comply with the Rich, though they are sure never to be the better for 'em.
>
> DOR. 'Tis in their power to do us good, and we despair not but at some time or other they may be willing.
>
> HAR. To men who have far'd in this Town like you, 'twould be a great Mortification to live on hope; could you keep a Lent for a Mistriss?
>
> DOR. In expectation of a happy Easter, and though time be very precious, think forty daies well lost, to gain your favour.
>
> HAR. Mr. Bellair! let us walk, 'tis time to leave him, men grow dull when they begin to be particular.
>
> DOR. Y'are mistaken, flattery will not ensue,

though I know y'are greedy of the praises of the whole Mail.

> HAR. You do me wrong.
>
> DOR. I do not; as I follow'd you, I observ'd how you were pleased when the *Fops* cry'd *She's handsome, very handsome, by God she is,* and whisper'd aloud your name; the thousand several forms you put your face into; then, to make your self more agreeable, how wantonly you play'd with your head, flung back your locks, and look'd smilingly over your shoulder at 'em.
>
> HAR. I do not go begging the mens as you do the Ladies Good liking, with a sly softness in your looks, and a gentle slowness in your bows, as you pass by 'em—as thus, Sir—(*Acts him*) Is not this like you?

After another bout of sparring, later on, Dorimant remarks aside, 'I love her, and dare not let her know it, I fear sh'as an ascendant o're me and may revenge the wrongs I have done her sex.' To make the documentation complete we are shown, earlier on, a typical specimen of these 'wrongs', the truly frightening scene of Dorimant's visit to Mrs. Loveit, the mistress he wishes to be rid of, while she is in the company of Bellinda, whom he has his eye on at the moment; one gets the impression—as, no doubt, one is meant to—that his extreme brutality to Mrs. Loveit is itself a form of sexual display for Bellinda's benefit. Mrs. Loveit, in a fit of agony which has nothing comic about it, tears her fan to pieces:

> DOR. Spare your Fan, Madam, you are growing hot, and will want it to cool you.
>
> LOV. Horrour and distraction seize you. Sorrow and Remorse gnaw your Soul, and punish all your Perjuries to me—(*Weeps.*)
>
> DOR. *So Thunder breaks the Cloud in Twain, And makes a passage for the Rain.* (*Turning to* Bellinda.) Bellinda, you are the Devil that have rais'd this storm; (*To* Bellinda.) you were at the Play yesterday, and have been making discoveries to your Dear.
>
> BELL. Y'are the most mistaken Man i' the World.
>
> DOR. It must be so, and here I vow revenge; resolve to pursue, and persecute you more impertinently than ever any Loving Fop did his Mistress, hunt you i' the *Park,* trace you i' the *Mail,* dog you in every visit you make, haunt you at the Plays, and i' the Drawing Room, hang my nose in your neck, and talk to you whether you will or no, and ever look upon you with such dying Eyes, till your Friends grow Jealous of me, send you out of Town, and the World suspect your reputation. (*In a lower voice*) At my Lady *Townley's* when we go from hence. (*He looks kindly on* Bellinda.)
>
> BELL. I'le meet you there.

Goaded by this, Mrs. Loveit launches herself across the room and tries to push him away, crying, 'Stand off, you sha'not stare upon her so.' On Dorimant's retorting (significantly), 'Good! There's one made jealous already,' the poor creature is reduced to playing a card that she knows will be useless, but cannot help producing:

> LOVEIT. Is this the constancy you vow'd?
>
> DOR. Constancy at my years! 'tis not a Virtue in season, you might as well expect the Fruit the Autumn ripens i' the Spring . . . Youth has a long Journey to go, Madam; should I have set up my rest at the first Inn I lodg'd at, I should never have arriv'd at the happiness I now enjoy.

The old commonplace of Restoration comedy is trotted out, but this time it rings true because we are shown the consequences, among them the uneasiness that preys on Dorimant. Throughout the play he is shown as barely managing to hold his own, and in one scene the women definitely get the better of him and humiliate him without mercy (Act V, Sc. i). All in all, the reader or spectator of the play is left in no doubt as to the nature of the sexual relationship that is its main subject-matter; each side is lusting for the other's downfall and suffering. Dorimant is seriously annoyed when Mrs. Loveit manages to regain her composure and draw some sort of a veil over her feelings for him; savagely he promises himself to put an end to all that: 'had it not been for some powerful Considerations which will be removed tomorrow morning, I had made her pluck off the mask, and shew the passion that lyes panting under'.

One can, in fact, comfortably discuss this play without mentioning its eponym, though a complete account would have, of course, to make due mention of Sir Fopling as a satisfactory 'brilliant' piece of satiric portraiture. But the centre of the play is Dorimant's warfare against women, whom he takes on in the persons of Mrs. Loveit, Harriet, and Bellinda. The ruthlessness of Etherege's logic makes the play harrowing, but at least it is never false and unsatisfactory; it is literature, where most other Restoration comedy is mere diversion, on however high a level. The ending, whereby Harriet is left in (temporary?) possession of Dorimant's affections, is free of the usual sentimentality; he is going down to the country to court her, in what she describes as:

> a great rambling lone house, that looks as it were not inhabited, the family's so small; there you'l find my Mother, an old lame Aunt, and my self, Sir, perch'd up on Chairs at a distance in a large parlour; sitting moping like three or four Melancholy Birds in a spacious vollary—Does not this stagger your Resolution?

Harriet can trade badinage with Dorimant amiably enough, considering the ferocity with which she has got rid of all competition. A moment before uttering these lines, for instance, she has turned to the grief-stricken Loveit with: 'Mr. *Dorimant* has been your God Almighty long enough, 'tis time to think of another.'

The ruthlessness of all these people, though unpleasant to read about, has at least the harsh ring of truth; when men like Dorimant are tamed, it is generally by pert baggages like Harriet who have the necessary savagery. But, though I cannot claim to have read the whole corpus, I am fairly sure there is nothing else in Restoration comedy that carries this kind of conviction.

Wycherley, at any rate, never achieved clarity on any basic moral issue. The whole plot of the *Plain Dealer* is simply a piece of crude misanthropy and getting one's own back. No doubt it is rather a neat trick, when a mistress has deceived and deserted you, to enjoy her in a darkened room when she thinks you are somebody else; and if, at the end of the play, you can get the love of a good woman and a handsome lump sum in addition, surely that *proves* you are the hero of the piece. If Wycherley's mind really worked like this, he must have been little better than an idiot, and a nasty idiot into the bargain. *The Country Wife* is even worse, because more tangled. Horner is meant to be admired for his clever trick, but Harcourt is equally so for his persistent attempt to marry Alithea honourably. It is the same with Congreve. Most of *Love for Love* is in fact pretty direct propaganda *for* good sexual morality; one notes the conversion of Scandal, and the punishment of Tattle, which is rather like that of Lucio in *Measure for Measure*. At first sight it looks as if Congreve were in favour of a simple 'wild oats' outlook, where the characters settle down to marriage after a period on the tiles. But there is a harshness that goes uncomfortably with any such genial tolerance. What about Valentine's illegitimate son? Is he to get any share in the warmth and affection that is being slopped about in the last scene? Admittedly it is trying to be dunned for money, but Valentine's reaction to being told of the arrival of 'the Nurse with one of your Children from *Twitnam*' is a little harsh, even in the circumstances:

> Pox on her, cou'd she find no other time to fling my Sins in my Face: Here, give her this [*Gives Mony.*] and bid her trouble me no more; a thoughtless two handed Whore, she knows my Condition well enough, and might have overlaid the Child a Fortnight ago, if she had had any forecast in her.

No doubt we are to think he does not mean this seriously, as his friend Scandal refers to the boy as 'my Godson'; but, considering that the whole thing is only brought in by way of stage patter, it seems an odd way of getting a laugh.

Mirabell is another case. In *The Way of the World*, Congreve brought Restoration comedy up to the very frontiers of respectability; except for his much greater brilliance, he all but joins hands with Goldsmith and Sheridan. But in their haste to approve of Mirabell as much as they do of Charles Surface, some critics have simply not noticed what a cad he is. Hear Professor Fujimura giving him a character:

> Mrs. Fainall, we gather, was an attachment of the past, before he fell in love; and since she was a widow at the time, and hence, according to the naturalistic conception of widows, highly inflammable, he could hardly be blamed for satisfying her sexual appetite as well as his own. When the play opens, Mirabell has apparently broken off all relations with her, and he is pursuing matrimony with a serious purpose.

Not a word about the fact that he has pushed Mrs. Fainall

into a marriage of hell, to suit his own convenience; indeed he tells her in so many words that it was in case she became pregnant: when she rounds on him with, 'Why did you make me marry this Man?' he answers airily, 'Why do we daily commit disagreeable and dangerous Actions? To save that Idol Reputation. If the Familiarities of our Loves had produc'd that Consequence, of which you were apprehensive, where cou'd you have fix'd a Father's Name with Credit, but on a Husband?' Admirable realism, no doubt, but this man is the *hero;* we are supposed to care whether he is happy or not; no wonder Lamb could only defend these plays by saying that they were simply aesthetic patterns with no humanity involved at all.

These strictures could perhaps be met by the counter-accusation that I am asking for a neat black-and-white pattern, with the good people rewarded and the bad ones punished. If Manly behaves like a cad, and still comes out on top, why not? That's life, isn't it? I see this objection, yet the whole nature of these plays forbids my admitting it. Quite apart from the fact that in comedy, the good people *are* usually rewarded and the bad ones discomfited—it is this, more than any other single feature, that stamps it as comedy—these plays are not comedies merely but satiric comedies; their writers are always claiming that they are out to pillory vice and folly 'with an armed and resolved hand'. Manly is not a portrait of a cad who exploits his caddishness and gets away with it; he is meant to be a pat-

Thomas Otway (1652-1685).

tern of surly virtue, and his tiresome parade of moral superiority, though cant, is unconscious cant. There have been, it is true, examples of writers who broke clear of the conventions they set out to observe; Wycherley might be defended as an author who goes beyond the usual scope of moralistic comedy and produces a new kind, a problem-play made out of comic ingredients. But though I can imagine such an argument, I cannot make this claim; I must leave it for someone else to do; the notion of the Restoration comedians as writers of Shavian debates on moral and social issues—in my opinion, it simply does not hold water. I should prefer to rest the defence mainly on a humbler argument; that these dramatists are saved by their incidental excellences, notably their spirited drawing of grotesques. If, on mature consideration, we decided that their works were deformed wholes, rendered to tolerable by the brilliance of isolated parts, should we be surprised? Would it be the first time we had come across such works?

What, after all—to put the question another way—are the most *enjoyable* passages in Wycherley and Congreve?—the passages we should point to if we wanted to convince a doubter that he would find some pleasure in their plays if he read them over, or went to see them? To my mind, the answer is clear; not the smart-Alec 'combats of wit', not the vaunted 'social criticism', but the passages which have some richness of language; and this means, in practice, their passages of broad comedy, when the buffoons take the stage. The only time when these dramatists write like poets, when any kind of colour and life radiate from the words on the page, is when they are writing speeches for their grotesques to utter. In these scenes they are the heirs of Shakespeare. It hardly needs to be argued that these writers were conscious of Shakespeare; his achievement was tangibly present to their minds, so that they were forever introducing random scraps of his material into their work; what I am arguing here is that their best moments nearly always come when they are imitating Shakespeare's trick of getting a grotesque, but rich, comic effect by means of language alone. One of the ways in which Shakespeare proved himself a great poet was by his gift of spinning out yards of material from an empty top-hat; some of his best comic writing is based on the flimsiest and stalest of jokes, and the result is a virtuoso exercise, as if he had been challenged to write well on third-rate music-hall material. Take, for example, Bardolph's red nose, which, as Dr. Jonson severely remarked, 'seems to have taken more hold on Shakespeare's imagination than any other'. This is true; Shakespeare was the only one who thought it funny; yet he lavishes resources on it that boost the subject up to many times its natural power. Most of us, I take it, would sacrifice any ten pages of the 'serious' writing in *Henry IV, Part I,* rather than let go a passage like this one:

> BARD. Why, Sir *Iohn,* my Face does you no harme.
>
> FALST. No, Ile be sworne: I make as good vse of it, as many a man doth of a Deaths-Head, or a *Memento Mori.* I neuer see thy Face, but I thinke vpon Hell fire, and *Diues* that liued in Purple; for there he is in his Robes burning, burning. If thou wert any way giuen to vertue,

I would sweare by thy Face; my Oath should bee, *By this Fire,* that's God's Angel. But thou art altogether giuen ouer; and wert indeede, but for the Light in thy Face, the Sunne of vtter Darkenesse. When thou ran'st vp Gads-Hill in the Night, to catch my Horse, if I did not thinke that thou hadst beene an *Ignis fatuus,* or a Ball of Wild-fire, there's no Purchase in Money. O thou art a perpetuall Triumph, an euerlasting Bone-fire-Light: thou hast saued me a thousand Markes in Linkes and Torches, walking with thee in the Night betwixt Tauerne and Tauerne: but the Sack that thou hast drunke me, would haue bought me Lights as good cheape, as the dearest chandlers in Europe. I haue maintain'd that Salamander of yours with fire, any time this two and thirtie yeeres, Heauen reward me for it.

BARD. I would my Face were in your Belly.

FALST. So should I be sure to be heart-burn'd.

The trick is to keep the thing going without anything to back it up except language. Congreve and Wycherley can both do this, and if we want proof that these men were poets, we shall find it here much more readily than in their 'official' versifications. (The only Restoration 'wit' who was a genuine poet *in verse* was Rochester, to my mind.) When I say that Wycherley and Congreve 'imitated' Shakespeare in this respect, I may be putting it too specifically; but at all events they showed, when they attempted this kind of thing, that they had inherited a splinter of Shakespeare's sensibility. Congreve has the best examples, and the most frequent; the reason being, obviously, that he is on the whole the best stylist. So there is no need for quotation to establish the point about *him.* But Wycherley has it too. Take the sort of lines he writes for the Widow Blackacre. She has been approached (*The Plain Dealer,* II, i) by two suitors, an old man and a young one. I will not copy out the interruptions, cries of 'How, lady!' and 'Hey, brave mother', etc., but just give her lines.

'First, I say, for you, Major, my walking Hospital of an ancient Foundation, thou Bag of Mummy, that wouldst fall asunder, if 'twere not for thy Cere-cloaths—

'Thou wither'd hobling, distorted Cripple; nay, thou art a Cripple all over; wou'dst thou make me the Staff of thy Age, the Crutch of thy Decrepidness? Me—

'Thou senseless, impertinent, quibling, driveling, feeble, paralytick, impotent, fumbling, frigid Nincompoop!

'Wou'dst thou make a Caudlemaker, a Nurse of me? Can't you be Bed-rid without a Bed-fellow? Won't your Swan-skins, Furrs, Flannels, and the scorch'd Trencher keep you warm there? Wou'd you have me your Scotch Warming-pan, with a pox to you? Me!—

'If I wou'd have marry'd an old Man, 'tis well known I might have marry'd an Earl; nay, what's more, a Judge, and been covered the Winter-nights with the Lamb-skins, which I prefer to the Ermins of Nobles: And durst thou think I wou'd wrong my poor Minor, there, for you?'

The young suitor, for his part, gets, among other things, this broadside:

FREEMAN. Nay, prythee, Widow hear me.

WIDOW. No, Sir, I'd have you to know, thou pitiful, paltry, lathback'd Fellow, if I wou'd have marry'd a young Man, 'tis well known, I cou'd have had any young Heir in *Norfolk;* nay, the hopefull'st young Man this day at the *King's-Bench Bar;* I, that am a Relict and Executrix of known plentiful assets and parts, who understand my self and the Law: And wou'd you have me under Covert-Baron again? No, Sir, no Covert Baron for me.

Some readers will exclaim, Jonson! But although this passage, with its smattering of law-terms, is Jonsonian in its method—Jonson liked to read up bits of specialist information and then throw them into his comic tirades, as in *The Alchemist*—I fancy the real impulse towards this kind of thing is Shakespearean, so far as it derived from a literary source at all. After all, Shakespeare played this game better than anyone else, and they would naturally follow the most conspicuous leader, however much they talked of 'humours'. Dryden is on my side here; his famous verse compliment to Congreve, on *The Old Batchelor,* says he is like Shakespeare, and I do not believe this is just large and meaningless talk.

It would take too long to list all, or most, of the Shakespearean echoes in Wycherley and Congreve, but I believe anyone who knows his Shakespeare fairly thoroughly will be pulled up every two or three pages by something that is unmistakably lifted. Sometimes it will be a verbal echo, sometimes a situation. Fidelia, in *The Plain Dealer,* might be paralleled in many Elizabethan plays, but one feels that the model for any beautiful and virtuous girl masquerading as a boy, in English drama, is basically Shakespearean. Elsewhere in the play, fragments of Shakespeare come through in a distorted way; the widow Blackacre's comic grief about 'my child and my writings' gets a laugh by the same device as Shylock's 'my daughter and my ducats'; Vernish, the false friend, says of Manly, 'I'll lead the easy, honest fool by the nose', which is a direct verbal reminiscence of one of Iago's speeches; Manly, invited to 'dine with my lord', retorts 'No, no; the ordinary is too dear for me, where flattery must pay for my dinner,' which has the ring of Enobarbus's account of Antony at Cleopatra's dinner-party—'And for his ordinary, paies his heart, For what his eyes eate onely.'

Othello and *Hamlet* were, on the whole, the two plays that obsessed these dramatists; one never reads far without coming across something that recalls one or the other. Wycherley, though a clumsy writer and unable even to imitate another man's rhythms successfully (in some respects this is to his credit, of course), even gives Manly's lines a breath, now and then, of the bitter melancholy of Hamlet's prose speeches.

In Congreve's case it is the same; I shall give no details, since it is so obvious as to be boring. The reader who wants to see what I mean in a hurry, without bothering to work through the plays, might turn to the scenes in *The Double*

> I think we should give over all attempt to build up the Restoration dramatists as inquiring minds, keenly watching the social seismograph, and think of them rather as minor but genuine artists whose great merit is that they were sensitive to the dominant confusions of their epoch, and able to render them in all their richness.
>
> —*John Wain*

Dealer where Maskwell is working up Lord Touchwood's suspicions of his wife (the reminiscence of *Othello* even extends to making the victim cry out 'give me the Occular Proof !'), and, of course, Valentine's ravings when he is feigning madness, in *Love for Love*. Charles Whibley presumably thought he was praising Congreve when he said that Valentine 'speaks in the very accent of Hamlet', but I am afraid it is more to the point to say, simply, that Congreve's writing in these scenes is embarrassingly tied to Shakespeare's, in spite of his efforts to break free. Nor is it, of course, only Congreve and Wycherley who are under this compulsion; all the Restoration dramatists share it, so that in reading their work we soon learn to watch for the lumps of undigested Bard; merely sighing wearily as we note, for instance, that the Nurse in Vanbrugh's *The Relapse* is a tenth-rate copy of the Nurse in *Romeo and Juliet*.

But if these dramatists are obsessed by Shakespeare, there is one important respect in which they take a pride in not resembling him or any other Elizabethan. In the comedies of Shakespeare's age it was customary to have two relatively simple plots; in Restoration comedy it is *de rigueur* to bind everything up into a single very complicated one. The motive is, in each case, clear enough; the Elizabethan double plot helped the play to deal with a wider sweep of life; Restoration dramatists thought it vulgar to deal with a wide sweep of life, and in any case were hampered by a notion of elegance which, inexplicably, forbade multiple plots while countenancing absurd constrictions and convolutions within the single plot.

In fact, the plots of Restoration comedies are usually the worst thing about them. To recount, baldly, the action of half a dozen of these plays is to be left with an appalling sense of futility. Even Shakespeare's comic structures have more interest—and, in any case, the merit of Shakespearean comedy is, like that of the Dickensian novel, slightly to one side of the actual plot; it consists in the creation of a world. In Restoration comedy the plot is placed rather centrally; it is one of the things we are meant to admire; it also makes a show of dealing directly with the material of daily life—a heightened and smoothed-out version of the daily life of the fashionable set in the audience. Money, for instance, is a constant theme, whereas Shakespeare hardly ever mentions it in his 'golden' comedies (I don't mean things like Shylock's five thousand ducats). These plots make a show of realism, which they at once destroy by turning into fantastic arabesques: it is one more symptom of the narrowing process that can be seen going on all through the seventeenth century. They withdrew their sympathies into a limited area, and then proceeded to weave intricate patterns within that area. It is something to do with the civilization they were living in, of course; it is like the difference between Byrd and Purcell; but if we trace the process through music alone we get too flattering a view of it. This stately formality, which delights in patterns, is not really well served by fribbling ingenuity. Compare the dances which Purcell wrote for *The Old Batchelor* with the play itself ! Or, if I seemed a moment ago to be over-kind to Shakespeare's comic plots, compare the most outrageous of them with the plot of *The Way of the World*, which, since I cannot sort it out myself, I give in the words of Mr. Crane Taylor:

> Mirabell is in love with Millamant, niece and ward of Lady Wishfort, who intends that she shall marry her nephew Sir Wilfull Witwoud, a country squire. In order to disguise his love for Millamant, Mirabell affects a fondness for Lady Wishfort, who discovers his duplicity and is highly incensed. When cajolery fails to win her favour, Mirabell plays a prank on her which, if publicly known, would make her the laughing-stock of the town. To secure complete secrecy and safeguard Lady Wishfort, he has his man Waitwell marry her maid Foible, and then court Lady Wishfort in the guise of Sir Rowland. Mrs. Marwood, jealous of Mirabell's love for Millamant, had previously disclosed his false pretences to Lady Wishfort, and now informs her of this trick also. Fainall, a rakish acquaintance of Mirabell, married Lady Wishfort's daughter, formerly a mistress of Mirabell, in order to secure her fortune. Mrs. Marwood, Fainall's mistress, advises him that he may secure all of Lady Wishfort's fortune, including the amount held in trust for Millamant, by threatening to expose her daughter, his wife, as an immoral character. As he is making his accusation before the assembled characters, Mincing and Foible, maids to Millamant and Lady Wishfort, give evidence of the relation between Mrs. Marwood and Fainall. He is enraged, and swears to publish his wife's scandal if her fortune is not assigned to him. Mirabell offers to help Lady Wishfort out of this dilemma, and she promises him her niece Millamant. Thereupon, he produces a will, sworn to by Witwoud and Petulant, two fops who could write their names but read little; this will was made by Lady Wishfort's daughter before she married Fainall, and conveys all of her property in trust to her friend Mirabell. Thus, she and lady Wishfort are safeguarded, Fainall and Mrs. Marwood are thwarted, and Mirabel and Millamant are to be married.

One can only say, faced with this kind of thing, that there seems to be a kind of cross-word puzzle pleasure for which most people have a streak of hankering, and that this pleasure wanders about, so to speak, and attaches itself, in a parasitic way, to this or that 'host' among the arts. In our time, complicated plots have gone out (except on the pictures, where they baffle highbrows much more than the rest of the audience), and puzzle-interest has attached it-self to poetry. This is, at any rate, the only defence of such a plot that occurs to me.

It is, to repeat the word, a *narrowing*. Shakespeare could see that his 'low-life' characters were funny, but at the same time he was able to identify with them to some extent; Dogberry is a butt, no doubt, and yet he is still an officer of the watch, and he is given an important part in the action. This, as well as being true to life ('odd people, whom you would normally laugh at, can sometimes put you in their debt'), gives the play a richness of effect that comes through as a kind of glow. It is like holding a glass of wine up to the light; if you hold Restoration comedy up to the light, you see no glow; the glass is simply lined with paper of the right colour. To take a familiar example— everything in Shakespeare is familiar, by this time—we might select Dogberry's gobbling with outraged dignity as he arrests the villains.

> Dost thou not suspect my place? does thou not suspect my yeeres? O that hee were heere to write mee downe an asse! but masters, remember that I am an asse: though it be not written down, yet forget not that I am an asse: No thou villaine, thou are full of piety as shall be prou'd vpon thee by good witnesse, I am a wise fellow, and which is more, an officer, and which is more, a houshoulder, and which is more, as pretty a peece of flesh as any in Messina, and one that knowes the Law, goe to, and a rich fellow enough, goe to, and a fellow that hath had losses, and one that hath two gownes, and euery thing handsome about him: bring him away: O that I had been writ downe an asse!

What were the *losses*, we wonder? Did he get fleeced of some of his money, or is it an intimate, personal loss? The mere fact that we can speculate is the important point; Shakespeare has drawn in a dimension behind Dogberry, giving him, in that one phrase, a history and an identity. The reason why this kind of thing is so rare in Restoration comedy is not because they were incapable of it; it is not a very uncommon achievement, though naturally Shake-speare is better at it than everyone else (he is better at *any-thing* than everyone else). It is because of the narrowing, the withdrawal of sympathies. Everything is seen from the point of view of one class, and of one type of person within that class. There are passages in Wycherley and Congreve where the comic character becomes a real person, but they stick out more obviously as exceptions; they are like tapers which barely get alight before they flicker out in the har-sher atmosphere. Wycherley's chief example, I suppose, is the Country Wife herself, and particularly the one quo-tation that everyone knows—the half-pathetic little post-script to one of her letters to Horner: 'Be sure you love me, whatever my husband says to the contrary, and let him not see this, lest he should come home and pinch me, or kill my squirrel.'

Congreve, a more perceptive and, on the whole, better-hearted man than Wycherley, has more of this quality. I find a distinct flavour of it in the scene where Sir Sampson Legend is momentarily fooled into thinking that Angelica will really marry him (*Love for Love*, V, ii). She, in the ap-proved heartless manner, has her own motives for leading him by the nose. The result might have been something like the terrible 'Nacky, Nacky' scene in *Venice Preserv'd;* indeed Congreve cannot be accused of failing to pour ap-propriate scorn on that favourite butt of the time, the lust-ful dotard; but Sir Sampson comes out of it, after all, not wholly disgraced. Of course he was the right social class, which must have been a help.

It is clear, in any case, that Sir Sampson is one of the char-acters whose lines Congreve most enjoyed writing; in the priggish letter to Dennis in which he tried to express the *rationale* of his work, he harked back to the Jonsonian 'hu-mour', and no doubt the old man is a prime specimen: but the real motive for creating him was to use up some of the fund of exuberantly comic language that Congreve was so good at spouting. The exchange between him and Fore-sight (II, v) is very lovingly written, and shall be quoted.

> SIR SAMP. . . . Pox o'th' time; there's no time but the time present, there's no more to be said of what's past, and all that is to come will hap-pen. If the Sun shine by Day, and the Stars by Night, why, we shall know one another's Faces without the help of a Candle, and that's all the Stars are good for.
>
> FORE. How, how? Sir *Sampson,* that all? Give me leave to contradict you, and tell you, you are ignorant.
>
> SIR SAMP. I tell you, I am wise; and *sapiens dominabitur astris;* there's Latin for you to prove it, and an Argument to confound your *Ephemer-is*—Ignorant!—I tell you, I have travell'd old *Fircu,* and know the Globe. I have seen the *An-tipodes,* where the Sun rises at Midnight, and sets at Noon-Day.
>
> FORE. But I tell you, I have travell'd, and tra-vell'd in the Coelestial *Spheres,* known the *Signs* and the *Planets,* and their Houses. Can judge of Motions Direct and Retrograde, of *Sextiles, Quadrates, Trines* and *Oppositions,* Fiery *Trigons* and Aquatical *Trigons.* Know whether Life shall be long or short, Happy or Unhappy, whether Diseases are Curable or Incurable. If Journeys shall be prosperous, Undertakings successful; or Goods Stoll'n recover'd, I know—
>
> SIR SAMP. I know the length of the Emperor of *China's* Foot; have kiss'd the *Great Mogul's* Slip-per, and rid a Hunting upon an Elephant with the Cham of *Tartary,*—Body o'me, I have made a Cuckold of a King, and the present Majesty of *Bantam* is the Issue of these Loins.
>
> FORE. I know when Travellers lye or speak Truth, when they don't know it themselves.
>
> SIR SAMP. I have known an Astrologer made a Cuckold in the Twinkling of a Star; and seen a Conjuror that cou'd not keep the Devil out of his Wife's Circle.
>
> FORE. What, does he twit me with my Wife too? I must be better inform'd of them,—*Aside.*—Do you mean my Wife, Sir *Sampson?* Tho' you made a Cuckold of the King of *Bantam,* yet by the Body of the Sun—

SIR SAMP. By the Horns of the Moon, you wou'd say, Brother *Capricorn.*

FORE. *Capricorn* in your Teeth, thou Modern *Mandevil; Ferdinand Mendez Pinto* was but a Type of thee, thou Liar of the first Magnitude. Take back your Paper of Inheritance; send your Son to Sea again. I'll wed my Daughter to an *Egyptian* Mummy, e'er she shall Incorporate with a Contemner of Sciences, and a Defamer of Virtue.

SIR SAMP. Body o'me, I have gone too far;—I must not provoke honest *Albumazar,*—an *Egyptian* Mummy is an Illustrious Creature, my trusty Hieroglyphick; and may have Significations of Futurity about him; Odsbud, I would my Son were an *Egyptian* Mummy for thy sake. What, thou are not angry for a Jest, my good *Haly*—I reverence the Sun, Moon and Stars with all my Heart.—What, I'll make thee a Present of a Mummy: Now I think on't, Body o'me, I have a Shoulder of an *Egyptian* King, that I purloin'd from one of the Pyramids, powder'd with Hieroglyphicks, thou shalt have it brought home to thy House, and make an Entertainment for all the *Philomaths,* and Students in Physick and Astrology in and about *London.*

FORE. But what do you know of my Wife, Sir *Sampson?*

SIR SAMP. Thy Wife is a Constellation of Virtues; she's the Moon, and thou art the Man in the Moon: Nay, she is more Illustrious than the Moon; for she has her Chastity without her Inconstancy, s'bud I was but in Jest.

The vaunted 'social criticism', then, is nothing; the vaunted 'wit', not much; the broad comedy is what mainly carries these plays along; this puts these writers in alignment with, let us say, Fielding and the early Dickens, rather than with the fine discriminators and the delicate ironists. If I have made this point clearly enough, it is almost time for me to stop: but there is one more point still to make. Wycherley and Congreve ought to be given their due. If the false praise is finally disposed of, let us not empty away the true praise with it. In fact I want to end with something not far off a *volte-face.*

Throughout this essay I have been talking as if confusion were always and everywhere a bad thing, by comparison with clarity. I have denied these dramatists the status of acute social commentators, even the status of serious artists, because their work is riddled with inconsistencies; because they make fun of marriage, for instance, for five long acts and then meekly lead the hero to the altar in the last scene. Why (I have been asking) should we be asked to admire both Horner and Harcourt in the same play? If Fidelia Grey is a 'good' character, why is not Manly a bad one?

Up to a point, I think this argument holds. A writer cannot very well obtain our assent, intellectual or emotional, if he is in an utter muddle over the fundamentals of what he is talking about. On the other hand, it is something if he succeeds in documenting, in a convincing and memorable way, a confusion that exists in the society he lives in.

He might even be said to make it his aim, whether consciously or not, to demonstrate and exploit this confusion. I think we should give over all attempt to build up the Restoration dramatists as inquiring minds, keenly watching the social seismograph, and think of them rather as minor but genuine artists whose great merit is that they were sensitive to the dominant confusions of their epoch, and able to render them in all their richness. Most of these confusions existed around the topic of sexual morality, and marriage in particular. And here we may notice a clue; marital infidelity is taken almost for granted—as it has to be if the comic plot is to get started at all—but *marriage is regarded as indissoluble.* Two or three times in the mass of Restoration comedy one might come across a mention of divorce, but generally speaking it is simply not taken into account. It follows that the attitude to marriage that we find in these plays is the same, broadly speaking—and allowing for comic exaggeration—as that taken in any society where marriage is indissoluble. Today, if we want jokes in the comic papers about cuckoldry, the place to look for them is in the Latin countries, where divorce is either not allowed for by the law, or purposely made difficult and expensive. The Nordic, Protestant kind of society, which is trying to proceed on the assumption that an unhappy marriage is better washed out, tends not to see anything funny in the 'hand-your-hat-on-his-horns' *motif.*

It is a matter of common sense that once divorce is socially recognized there will be a falling-off in trench humour about marriage. Only people who regard marriage as a once-and-for-all plunge, and hence as a desperately dangerous adventure, will be able to joke about it in this way. Their attitude is in itself illogical; it is illogical to take something so seriously that you leave yourself no way of commenting on it except by ribaldry; but it happens to be the attitude that most human beings, even now, adopt. If we look at Restoration comedy as literature, rather than as a narrowly social document, we shall see that what it really demonstrates is the invincible strength of the institution of marriage. The comic resentment ('Why should a foolish marriage vow That long ago was made', etc.) is the nearest they dare get to a radical criticism of it; their most destructive comment on marriage is to point out that people are sometimes unfaithful to one another, which is about the same as saying that glass is unsuitable for making windows with because it sometimes gets broken. It is significant that the real onslaught on marriage, in the lifetime of these men, was made by someone who had less sense of humour, and less belief in the therapeutic value of a good laugh, than they had; Milton, who was the diametric opposite of a man like Wycherley, spent years campaigning vehemently for divorce on the grounds of incompatibility; the Restoration dramatists would be no more likely to do this than they would be to write religious epic poems. They were, like all jokers, men of compromise; their theme was the moulding of human nature to fit in with 'the armies of unalterable law', where Milton's attitude was that these things should be met head-on; Samson pulling down the temple of Dagon was his ideal of behaviour, and it is not a comic one.

I do not think, then, that the Restoration comedians should be dismissed on the grounds that they were inconsistent and muddled, though earlier on I had to argue as if I did think so, if only to dispel the clouds of incense. Realistic writers have to reflect what actually goes on, and it is a fact that most people not only never achieve, but never try for, the kind of clarity that makes them take up a consistent attitude towards the bedrock facts of their lives. Restoration comedy shows us a world in which people put up with—on the whole, gladly enough—a set of confusions remarkably like our own; they managed, as we manage, to rub along with them somehow; they had no very effective way of dealing with serious problems, except to laugh at them, but in this again they were much like ourselves. Congreve and Wycherley were not great writers, and the rest (setting aside Etherege as the author of one remarkable play) are not even worth considering as artists; but their work has lived, and I suspect that the reason for this is that they had the comedian's gift of not pressing for a logical solution, but accepting the muddle and making it seem, for all their artificiality, genuinely human. (pp. 14-35)

John Wain, "Restoration Comedy and Its Modern Critics," in his Preliminary Essays, *Macmillan & Co. Ltd., 1957, pp. 1-35.*

FURTHER READING

Anthony, Rose. *The Jeremy Collier Stage Controversy: 1698-1726.* Milwaukee, Wis.: Marquette University Press, 1937, 328 p.

Provides an analysis of Jeremy Collier's *Short View of the Immorality and Profaneness of the English Stage* (1698) and discusses replies to this pamphlet and other related criticism.

Bevis, Richard W. *English Drama: Restoration and Eighteenth Century—1660-1789.* London: Longman, 1988, 341 p.

Surveys Restoration drama from its first appearance after the Commonwealth to the late eighteenth century, noting its historical, intellectual, and theatrical context.

Brown, John Russel and Harris, Bernard, eds. *Restoration Theatre.* Stratford-Upon-Avon Studies 6. London: Edward Arnold, 1965, 240 p.

Collection of nine essays on Restoration drama discussing elements of dramatic language and focusing on three of its comic masters: Etherege, Wycherley, and Congreve.

Brown, Laura. "The Defenseless Woman and the Development of English Tragedy." *Studies in English Literature 1500-1900* 22, No. 3 (Summer 1982): 429-43.

Study of the defenseless woman as a character in Restoration tragedy, emphasizing "the sources of her passivity, the consequences of her prominence, [and] the nature of her role in dramatic history."

Burns, Edward. *Restoration Comedy: Crises of Desire and Identity.* London: Macmillan, 1987, 283 p.

Traces the development of Restoration comedy through selected interpretations of individual plays and accounts of writers' careers in an attempt to reevaluate its dramatic form and larger historical context.

Gosse, Edmund. "Sir George Etheredge" and "Thomas Otway." In his *Seventeenth-Century Studies,* pp. 259-342. London: William Heinemann, 1914.

Biographical and critical sketches of two Restoration dramatists.

Holland, Norman N. *The First Modern Comedies.* Cambridge, Mass.: Harvard University Press, 1959, 274 p.

Treats plays by Etherege, Wycherley, and Congreve in an attempt to show that Restoration comedies contain intellectual substance that "comes supprisingly close to our twentieth-century world-view."

Hume, Robert D. *The Development of English Drama in the Late Seventeenth Century.* Oxford: Clarendon Press, 1976, 525 p.

Analysis of the Restoration theater which shows that "plays from this period closely reflect fads and fashion in a small, highly competitive theatrical world which is constantly being buffeted by political and social change."

———. *The Rakish Stage.* Carbondale: Southern Illinois University Press, 1983, 382 p.

Collection of essays by Hume presenting "an overview of the drama of this [the Restoration] period (concentrating on comedy), focusing on matters of content, ideology and values, impact, and genre."

Hunt, Leigh. "Biographical and Critical Notices." In *The Dramatic Works of Wycherley, Congreve, Vanbrugh, and Farquhar, with Biographical and Critical Notices,* edited by Leigh Hunt, pp. ix-xxxviii. London: George Routledge and Sons, 1875.

Insightful discussion of four Restoration dramatists.

Loftis, John, ed. *Restoration Drama: Modern Essays in Criticism.* New York: Oxford University Press, 1966, 371 p.

Collection of historical, explicative, and evaluative essays representative of the variety of approaches taken and conclusions reached in modern criticism of Restoration drama. Essayists include Loftis, L. C. Knights, F. W. Bateson, and Bonamy Dobrée, among many others.

Love, Harold, ed. *Restoration Literature: Critical Approaches.* London: Methuen & Co., 1972, 318 p.

Collection of essays on Restoration comedy, tragedy, and the writers of the period, including studies by Love, Michael Wilding, Harold F. Brooks, and others.

McDonald, Charles O. "Restoration Comedy as Drama of Satire: An Investigation into Seventeenth Century Aesthetics." *Studies in Philology* LXI, No. 3 (July 1964): 522-44.

Considers Restoration comedy in terms of its success as "a fully adult form of satiric and comic art." McDonald maintains that the essentially moral intentions of the dramatists "were stifled by the Sunday-school sort of pietism demanded by Collier and other 'moralists' and supplied obligingly by the sentimental playwrights."

Miles, Dudley Howe. *The Influence of Molière on Restoration Comedy.* New York: Octogon Books, 1971, 272 p.

Attempt to determine "the nature and extent of the influence exerted by Molière on English comedy from 1660 to 1700."

Muir, Kenneth. *The Comedy of Manners.* London: Hutchinson University Library, 1970, 173 p.

Offers individual chapters on nine Restoration comic dramatists.

Nettleton, George Henry. *English Drama of the Restoration and Eighteenth Century: (1642-1780).* New York: Macmillan Co., 1921, 366 p.

Study of Restoration drama tracing its development from Elizabethan drama to the works of Sheridan.

Paxman, David B. "The Burden of the Immediate Past: The Early Eighteenth Century and the Shadow of Restoration Comedy." *Essays in Literature* 17, No. 1 (Spring 1990): 15-29.

Examines the "burden of the past" felt by writers of dramatic comedy during the first three decades of the eighteenth century. Paxman asserts that these playwrights "viewed their immediate predecessors as having cultivated (though sometimes with morally noxious varieties) the few remaining patches of comic terrain."

Perry, Henry Ten Eyck. *The Comic Spirit in Restoration Drama.* New York: Russell & Russell, 1962, 148 p.

Analyzes the comic theory and practice of five major Restoration dramatists: Etherege, Wycherley, Congreve, Vanbrugh, and Farquhar.

Rodway, Allan. "Restoration Comedy Re-Examined." *Renaissance and Modern Studies* XVI (1972): 37-60.

Maintains that Restoration comedies were not libertine enough: they failed to explore the possibilities of a "rational" morality as opposed to the stern Puritan doctrines of the Commonwealth and Protectorate.

Schneider, Ben Ross, Jr. *The Ethos of Restoration Comedy.* Urbana: University of Illinois Press, 1971, 201 p.

Studies four pairs of elements in the ethical structure of Restoration plot and character: generosity vs. meanness, liberality vs. avarice, courage vs. cowardice, and plain-dealing vs. double-dealing.

Simon, Irene. "Restoration Comedy and the Critics." *Revue des Langues Vivantes* XXIX, No. 5 (1963): 397-430.

Overview of critical reaction to Restoration comedy, from Collier's *Short View of the Immorality and Profaneness of the English Stage* (1698) to twentieth-century interpretations. This is followed by a brief study of what Simon calls the three best comedies of the Restoration—Etherege's *The Man of Mode,* Wycherley's *The Country Wife,* and Congreve's *The Way of the World.* The essayist uses Norman Holland's *The First Modern Comedies* (1959) as a basis for argumentation.

Smith, John Harrington. *The Gay Couple in Restoration Comedy.* Cambridge, Mass.: Harvard University Press, 1948, 252 p.

Traces "the rise, prosperity, and decline of the 'gay couple'," the hero and heroine, in an attempt to understand Restoration comedic theory.

Wilcox, John. *The Relation of Molière to Restoration Comedy.* New York: Columbia University Press, 1938, 240 p.

Undertakes "to find which Restoration plays contain borrowings from Molière, to tell the nature and the extent of these borrowings, and then to arrive at a just estimate of his influence of Restoration writers individually and on their comedy as a type."

Zimbardo, Rose A. *A Mirror to Nature: Transformations in Drama and Aesthetics—1660-1732.* Lexington: University Press of Kentucky, 1986, 248 p.

Explores the "transition in dramatic imitation of nature from the imitation of ideas," or the intellectual understanding of the universe as an interconnected whole, "to the imitation of human nature," or focus on the individual psyche, as reflected in Restoration drama.

Sir John Vanbrugh

1664-1726

English dramatist and essayist.

INTRODUCTION

An accomplished dramatist, John Vanbrugh wrote satirical comedies that are praised by scholars for their brilliant wit and invention. His best known plays, *The Relapse* and *The Provok'd Wife,* have attracted critical attention for extending the boundaries of the Comedy of Manners by appealing to both the intellect and the emotions, thus creating a new type of comedy that was neither didactic nor sentimental. Vanbrugh's dramas were also the subject of a significant controversy which generated much debate that gradually reformed and elevated the moral standards of the Restoration stage.

Little is known about Vanbrugh's early life. He was born in London to a wealthy family and may have been educated at the King's School, Chester, which was then a seminary of the highest repute. At age nineteen, Vanbrugh was sent to France, perhaps to complete his education; while there, he gained an appreciation for the works of Jean Baptiste Poquelin Molière, Edmé Boursault, and others who greatly influenced the thematic content of his later dramas. Vanbrugh returned to England and in 1686 was commissioned to the Earl of Huntington's foot regiment as an ensign, eventually rising to the rank of captain. Four years later, Vanbrugh resigned from the army and returned to France where he was arrested in Calais and imprisoned for espionage. During his eighteen months in prison, he began writing sketches for a comedy which would later become *The Provok'd Wife.* Vanbrugh was eventually paroled and returned to England in 1692.

Through a close friendship with Sir Thomas Skipwith, a theatrical proprietor and manager of the Theatre Royal in Drury Lane, Vanbrugh became acquainted with London theater life. After attending a performance of Colley Cibber's *Love's Last Shift* (1695) at the Theatre Royal, Vanbrugh was struck by the situation with which the piece closed. Finding *Love's Last Shift* incomplete and too idealistic, Vanbrugh immediately wrote a sequel entitled *The Relapse.* Completed in only six weeks, the piece proved to be a great success in the following season, winning Vanbrugh immediate fame. While Vanbrugh's second production, *Aesop, Part I,* failed, *The Provok'd Wife,* which opened in 1697 and is usually regarded as his masterpiece, became tremendously popular. Both *The Relapse* and *The Provok'd Wife* attracted much critical attention for their candid treatment of lax morality and sexual attitudes and were attacked by Jeremy Collier in his *A Short View of the Profaneness and Immorality of the English Stage* (1698). Vanbrugh immediately responded in *A Short Vindication of "The Relapse" and "The Provok'd Wife" from Immo-*

rality and Profaneness, arguing that Collier did not understand that the purpose of comedy is to uphold virtue by representing its opposite on the stage. Collier's criticism fuelled an outspoken debate among playwrights, reviewers, and theatergoers that eventually induced James I to enforce an act against profane swearing on the English stage. However, the controversy engendered by Collier's denunciation of Vanbrugh's plays only increased their popularity.

Early in the eighteenth century, Vanbrugh collaborated with dramatist William Congreve in the establishment of a new theater, the Queen's Theatre in Haymarket, which was both designed and built by Vanbrugh in 1703. The project was supported by the Kit-Kat Club, a liberal political society whose members included such renowned literary figures as Congreve, Joseph Addison, and Sir Richard Steele. Although the theater failed, Vanbrugh's association with the members of the Kit-Kat Club, especially the Earl of Carlisle, proved profitable, enabling him to receive an appointment to serve as Clarenceux King of Arms in 1705. It was Carlisle who promoted Vanbrugh as an architect; Vanbrugh's first notable achievement was Carlisle's country home, Castle Howard. His most famous work,

Blenheim Palace, the home of the first Duke of Marlborough, is regarded by many as the culminating monument to English baroque architecture. For his accomplishments, Vanbrugh was knighted by George I in 1714. In the final years of his life, Vanbrugh continued to design country homes and write plays, primarily adaptations of French works; his most commercially and artistically successful adaptation, *The Confederacy,* is based on Florent Carton Dancourt's *Les Bourgeoises à la mode* (1692). Vanbrugh's final piece, *A Journey to London,* remained unfinished at the time of his death but was completed two years later by Colley Cibber, who retitled it *The Provok'd Husband.*

The plots of Vanbrugh's plays are simple and feature everyday domestic realism. Although their structure is often described as weak, the dramas are replete with wit and an astuteness of perception which enabled Vanbrugh to relate seemingly disparate things, inducing Alexander Pope to assert, "How Van wants grace who seldom wants for art." Most often Vanbrugh's plays concentrate on two social themes—the predicament imposed upon the younger brother as a result of the law of primogeniture, and the issue of marital incompatibility. The first theme frequently deals with a cynical, fortunehunting younger brother, as in the subplot of *The Relapse,* and dominates many of Vanbrugh's later works. The latter theme is a preeminent feature in *The Relapse* and *The Provok'd Wife,* where Vanbrugh examines the consequences of a loveless marriage. In *The Relapse,* particularly, Vanbrugh's realism is so harsh that the central characters, Loveless and Amanda, are finally incapable of arriving at any form of resolution, an ending which significantly darkens Vanbrugh's comedy.

Many critics have noted that Vanbrugh's dramas form a vital link between the cynical comedy of the Restoration and the sentimental drama of the late eighteenth century because his plays contain elements of both. His two original works, *The Relapse* and *The Provok'd Wife,* in particular, closely follow the conventions of Restoration drama where hedonistic values, bitter satire, and licentious wit converge to expose the vices of the age. However, Vanbrugh's works also exhibit a marked departure from Restoration comedy. In addition to portraying how one should not live, Vanbrugh's plays instruct the audience on how to enjoy a virtuous life. Several of his characters, such as Worth in *The Relapse,* defy traditional morality yet always return to respectability in a struggle to regain their human dignity, thus distinguishing themselves from the many conceited fops and falsely pious hypocrites also presented in Vanbrugh's work. Moreover, while characterization in much of Restoration drama is highly impersonal and indifferent, Vanbrugh's characters tend to evoke emotion and sympathy from the audience. Scholars note that Vanbrugh's dramas are not sentimental; *The Relapse* was written as a direct indictment of what Vanbrugh judged as false sentimentality in Colley Cibber's *Love's Last Shift.* His plays are characterized by a more realistic treatment of love, encompassing both its passion and pathos.

Vanbrugh's *The Relapse* and *The Provok'd Wife* were enormously popular with contemporary audiences but also received extensive criticism which began with Collier and continued throughout the eighteenth, nineteenth, and twentieth centuries. Collier asserted that Vanbrugh's dramas encouraged immorality, thus violating the neoclassical critical belief that the function of drama is to uphold morality. Echoing Vanbrugh's own response to Collier, Alan Roper has recently suggested that *The Relapse* is innately moral because it is, above all, "both true and honest." Thus, Roper finds that the integrity of Vanbrugh's viewpoint contributes to the ethical design of his plays. Other critics disagree, claiming that discussion of the degree of morality in Vanbrugh's plays is irrelevant because his primary concern, despite his assertion in *A Short Vindication,* was to entertain. There is universal agreement that Vanbrugh is less graceful than Congreve and less serious than Wycherley, but that he surpasses them both in natural humor and originality. Leigh Hunt found Vanbrugh's complex characters and witty dialogue admirable, and pronounced that he did not view Vanbrugh's adaptations as problematic, since "What he borrows, he seems to change at one blow into something better." Modern critics have emphasized the view that Vanbrugh's plays stray from the conventions of Restoration drama through their presentation of the theme of social decadence. Gerald Berkowitz has written that Vanbrugh's characters "become lower in our estimation as they rise closer to the social ideal," and Roper has noted that in *The Relapse* "it is impossible to identify and follow a decent private life while still engaging fully in the pleasures of public living." According to these commentators, Vanbrugh's comedies are tinged with the tragic, an aspect which later influenced the dramatist George Farquhar.

Although they have undergone various adaptations over the last two centuries, Vanbrugh's best plays survive and remain powerfully effective because their themes appeal to the common sense, their humor transcends time, and their note of despair renders them modern. While critical discussion of his drama continues, Vanbrugh maintains a prominent place among the comic dramatists of the Restoration and is perhaps best remembered, in the words of Jonathan Swift and Alexander Pope, as "a Man of Wit, and of Honour."

PRINCIPAL WORKS

Aesop, Part I (drama) 1696
The Relapse; or, Virtue in Danger (drama) 1696
Aesop, Part II (drama) 1697
The Provok'd Wife (drama) 1697
The Country House (drama) 1698
A Short Vindication of "The Relapse" and "The Provok'd Wife," from Immorality and Prophaneness (essay) 1698
The Pilgrim (drama) 1700
The False Friend (drama) 1702
Squire Trelooby (drama) 1704
The Confederacy (drama) 1705
The Mistake (drama) 1705
The Cuckold in Conceit (drama) 1707

The Plays of Sir John Vanbrugh. 2 vols. (dramas)
  1719
*A Journey to London; or, The Provok'd Husband
  (drama) 1728

*This work was completed by Colley Cibber.

John Vanbrugh   (essay date 1697)

[*In the following Prologue to* The Provok'd Wife, *Vanbrugh outlines his intention, jokingly referring to his past and future critics.*]

> Since 'tis th' intent and business of the stage,
> To copy out the follies of the age;
> To hold to every man a faithful glass,
> And shew him of what species he's an ass:
> I hope the next that teaches in the school,
> Will shew our author he's a scribbling fool.
> And that the satire may be sure to bite,
> Kind Heav'n! inspire some venom'd priest to
>   write,
> And grant some ugly lady may indite.
> For I wou'd have him lash'd, by heavens! I
>   wou'd,
> Till his presumption swam away in blood.
> Three plays at once proclaim a face of brass,
> No matter what they are; that's not the case—
> To write three plays, e'en that's to be an ass.
> But what I least forgive, he knows it too,
> For to his cost he lately has known you—
> Experience shews, to many a writer's smart,
> You hold a court where mercy ne'er had part;
> So much of the old serpent's sting you have,
> You love to damn, as heaven delights to save.
> In foreign parts, let a bold volunteer,
> For public good, upon the stage appear,
> He meets ten thousand smiles to dissipate his
>   fear.
> All tickle on th' adventuring young beginner,
> And only scourge th' incorrigible sinner;
> They touch indeed his faults, but with a hand
> So gentle, that his merit still may stand;
> Kindly they buoy the follies of his pen,
> That he may shun 'em when he writes again.
> But 'tis not so in this good-natur'd town,
> All's one, an ox, a poet, or a crown;
> Old *England's* play was always knocking down.
>
>   (pp. 203-04)

> *Sir John Vanbrugh, in a prologue to his* Sir
> John Vanbrugh, *edited by A. E. H. Swaen,
> Charles Scribner's Sons, 1896, pp. 203-05.*

Jeremy Collier   (essay date 1698)

[*An English clergyman, Collier is most remembered for his astringent study* A Short View of the Immortality and Profaneness of the English Stage. *In the following excerpt from that work, he charges Vanbrugh's* The Relapse *and* The Provok'd Wife *with "immorality" and "profaneness," also criticizing the structure, plot, and treatment of women in* The Relapse.]

The ***Provok'd Wife*** furnishes' the Audience with a Drunken Atheistical Catch: 'Tis true this Song is afterwards said to be *Full of Sin and Impudence.* But why then was it made? This Confession is a miserable *Salvo;* And the Antidote is much weaker than the Poyson: 'Tis just as if a Man should set a House in a Flame, and think to make amends by crying *Fire* in the Streets. In the last *Act Rasor* makes his Discovery of the Plot against *Belinda* in *Scripture* phrase. I'le give it the *Reader* in the Authors Dialogue.

> BELIND. *I must know who put you upon all this Mischief.*
>
> RASOR. *Sathan and his Equipage. Woman tempted me, Lust weaken'd,—And so the Devil overcame me: As fell* Adam *so fell I.*
>
> BELIND. *Then pray Mr.* Adam *will you make us acquainted with your* Eve?
>
> RASOR unmasks *Madamoselle* and says, *This is the Woman that tempted me: But this is the Serpent* (meaning Lady *Fanciful) that tempted the Woman; And if my Prayers might be heard, her punishment for so doing should be like the Serpents of old, uc.*

This *Rasor* in what we hear of him before, is all Roguery, and Debauch: But now he enters in *Sackcloth,* and talks like *Tribulation* in the *Alchemist.* His Character is chang'd to make him the more profane; And his Habit, as well as Discourse, is a Jest upon Religion. I am forced to omit one Line of his Confession. The Design of it is to make the *Bible* deliver an obscene Thought: And because the Text would not bend into a Lewd Application; He alters the words for his purpose, but passes it for Scripture still. This sort of Entertainment is frequent in the ***Relapse.*** Lord *Foplington* laughs at the publick Solemnities of Religion, as if 'twas a ridiculous piece of Ignorance, to pretend to the Worship of a God. He discourses with *Berinthia* and *Amanda* in this manner: *Why Faith Madam,—Sunday is a vile Day, I must confess. A man must have very little to do at Church that can give an account of the Sermon.* And a little after: *To Mind the Prayers or the Sermon, is to mind what one should not do. Lory* tells young *Fashion, I have been in a lamentable Fright ever since that Conscience had the Impudence to intrude into your Company.* His Master makes him this Comfortable Answer. *Be at peace, it will come no more:—I have kick'd it down stairs.* A little before he breaks out into this Rapture. Now Conscience I defie thee! By the way we may observe, that this young *Fashion* is the *Poets* Favorite. *Berinthia* and *Worthy,* two *Characters* of Figure, determine the point thus in defence of Pimping.

> BERINTH. *Well, I would be glad to have no Bodies Sins to answer for but my own. But where there is a necessity—*
>
> WORTH. *Right as you say, where there is a Necessity, a Christian is bound to help his Neighbour.*

Nurse, after a great deal of Profane Stuff concludes her expostulation in these words: *But his Worship:* (Young Fashion) *over-flows with his Mercy and his Bounty; He is not only pleas'd to forgive us our Sins—but which is more than all, has prevail'd with me to become the Wife of thy Bosom:*

This is very heavy, and ill dress'd. And an Atheist must be sharp set to relish it. The Vertuous *Amanda* makes no scruple to charge the Bible with untruths.

> ——*What Slippery stuff are Men compos'd of? Sure the Account of their Creation's false, And 'twas the Womans Rib that they were form'd of.*

Thus this Lady abuses her self, together with the Scripture, and shews her Sense, and her Religion, to be much of a Size.

Berinthia, after she has given in a Scheme for the debauching *Amanda,* is thus accosted by *Worthy: Thou Angel of Light, let me fall down and adore thee!* A most Seraphick Compliment to a Procuress! And 'tis possible some Angel or other, may thank him for't in due time.

I am quite tired with these wretched Sentences. The sight indeed is horrible, and I am almost unwilling to shew it. However they shall be Produced like Malefactors, not for Pomp, but Execution. Snakes and Vipers, must sometimes be look'd on, to destroy them. (pp. 77-80)

From the Form and Constitution of the *Fable* [in **The Relapse**], I observe

Ist. That there is a *Misnommer* in the Title. The *Play* should not have been call'd the **Relapse, or Virtue in Danger.** *Lovelace,* and *Amanda,* from whose *Characters* these Names are drawn, are Persons of Inferiour Consideration. *Lovelace* sinks in the middle of the *Fourth* Act, and we hear no more of him till towards the End of the *Fifth,* where he enters once more, but then 'tis as *Cato* did the Senate house, only to go out again. And as for *Amanda* she has nothing to do but to stand a shock of Courtship, and carry off her Virtue. This I confess is a great task in the *Play-house,* but no main matter in the *Play.*

The *Intrigue,* and the *Discovery,* the great Revolution and success, turns upon *Young Fashion.* He without Competition, is the Principal Person in the *Comedy.* And therefore the *Younger Brother,* or the *Fortunate Cheat,* had been much a more proper Name. Now when a *Poet* can't rig out a *Title Page,* 'tis but a bad sign of his holding out to the *Epilogue.*

2ly. I observe the *Moral* is vitious: It points the wrong way, and puts the *Prize* into the wrong Hand. It seems to make *Lewdness* the reason of *Desert,* and gives *Young Fashion* a second Fortune, only for Debauching away his First. A short view of his *Character,* will make good this Reflection. To begin with him: He confesses himself a *Rake,* swears, and Blasphemes, Curses, and Challenges his Elder Brother, cheats him of his Mistress, and gets him laid by the Heels in a Dog-Kennel. And what was the ground of all this unnatural quarrelling and outrage? Why the main of it was only because Lord *Foplington* refused to supply his Luxury, and make good his Extravagance. This *Young Fashion* after all, is the *Poets* Man of Merit. He provides, a *Plot* and a Fortune, on purpose for him. To speak freely, a Lewd Character seldom wants good Luck in *Comedy.* So that when ever you see a thorough Libertine, you may almost swear he is in a rising way, and that the *Poet* intends to make him a great Man. In short; This *Play* per-

verts the End of *Comedy:* Which as Monsieur [René] *Rapin* observes ought to regard Reformation, and publick Improvement. But the **Relapser** had a more fashionable Fancy in his Head. His *Moral* holds forth this notable Instruction.

Ist. That all *Younger Brothers* should be careful to run out their Circumstances as Fast, and as Ill as they can. And when they have put their Affairs in this posture of Advantage, they may conclude themselves in the high Road to Wealth, and Success. For as *Fashion* Blasphemously applies it, *Providence takes care of Men of Merit.*

2ly. That when a Man is press'd, his business is not to be govern'd by Scruples, or formalize upon Conscience and Honesty. The quickest Expedients are the best; For in such cafes the Occasion justifies the Means, and a Knight of the *Post,* is as good as one of the *Garter.* (pp. 209-12)

The *Manners* in the Language of the *Stage* have a signification somewhat particular. *Aristotle* and *Rapin* call them the Causes and Principles of Action. They are formed upon the Diversities of Age, and Sex, of Fortune, Capacity, and Education. The propriety of *Manners* consists in a Conformity of Practise, and Principle; of Nature, and Behaviour. For the purpose. An old Man must not appear with the Profuseness and Levity of Youth; A Gentleman must not talk like a Clown, nor a Country Girl like a Town Jilt. And when the *Characters* are feign'd 'tis *Horace's* Rule to keep them Uniform, and consistent, and agreeable to their first setting out. The *Poet* must be careful to hold his *Persons* tight to their *Calling* and pretentions. He must not shift, and shuffle their Understandings; Let them skip from Wits to Blockheads, nor from Courtiers to Pedants. On the other hand. If their business is playing the Fool, keep them strictly to their Duty, and never indulge them in fine Sentences. To manage otherwise, is to desert *Nature,* and makes the *Play* appear monstrous, and Chimerical. So that instead of an *Image of Life,* 'tis rather an Image of Impossibility. To apply some of these remarks to the **Relapser.**

The fine *Berinthia,* one of the Top-Characters, is impudent and Profane. *Lovelace* would engage her Secrecy, and bids her Swear. She answers *I do.*

> Lov. By what?
>
> Berinth. *By Woman.*
>
> Lov. *That's Swearing by my Deity, do it by your own, or I shan't believe you.*
>
> Berinth. *By Man then.*

This Lady promises *Worthy* her Endeavours to corrupt *Amanda;* and then They make a Profane jest upon the Office. In the progress of the *Play* after a great deal of Lewd Discourse with *Lovelace,* *Berinthia* is carried off into a Closet, and Lodged in a *Scene* of Debauch. Here is Decency, and Reservedness, to a great exactness! Monsieur *Rapin* blames *Ariosto,* and *Taffo,* for representing two of their Women over free, and airy. These *Poets* says he, *rob Women of their Character, which is Modesty.* Mr. *Rymer* is of the same Opinion: His words are these. *Nature knows nothing in the Manners which so properly, and particularly distinguish a Woman, as her Modesty.—An impudent Woman is fit only to be kicked, and expos'd in Comedy.*

Now *Berinthia* appears in *Comedy* 'tis true; but neither to be *kick'd*, nor *expos'd*. She makes a Considerable Figure, has good Usage, keeps the best Company, and goes off without Censure, or Disadvantage. Let us now take a Turn or two with Sir *Tun-belly's* Heiress of 1500 pounds a year. This Young Lady swears, talks smut, and is upon the matter just as ragmanner'd as *Mary the Buxsome*. 'Tis plain the **Relapser** copied Mr. *Durfey's* Original, which is a sign he was somewhat Pinch'd. Now this *Character* was no great Beauty in *Buxsome;* But it becomes the Knights Daughter much worse. *Buxsome* was a poor Pesant, which made her Rudeness more natural, and expected. But *Deputy Lieutenants* Children don't use to appear with the Behaviour of Beggars. To breed all People alike, and make no distinction between a *Seat,* and a *Cottage,* is not over artful, nor very ceremonious to the Country Gentlemen. The **Relapser** gives *Miss* a pretty Soliloquy, I'll transcribe it for the *Reader.*

She swears by her Maker, *'tis well I have a Husband a coming, or I'de Marry the Baker I would so. No body can knock at the Gate, but presently I must be lock'd up, and here's the Young Gray-hound—can run loose about the House all day long, she can, 'tis very well!* Afterwards her Language is too Lewd to be quoted. Here is a Compound of Ill Manners, and Contradiction! Is this a good Resemblance of Quality, a Description of a great Heiress, and the effect of a Cautious Education? By her Coarsness you would think her Bred upon a Common, and by her Confidence, in the Nursery of the *Play-house.* I suppose the **Relapser** Fancies the calling her *Miss Hoyden* is enough to justifie her Ill Manners. By his favour, this is a Mistake. To represent her thus unhewn, the should have suited her Condition to her Name, a little better. For there is no Charm in *Words* as to matters of Breeding, An unfashionable Name won't make a Man a Clown. Education is not form'd upon Sounds, and Syllables, but upon Circumstances, and Quality. So that if he was resolv'd to have shown her thus unpolish'd, he should have made her keep *Sheep,* or brought her up at the *Wash-Boul.* (pp. 218-22)

[Next] I shall consider his *Play* with respect to the

Three Unities of Time, Place, and Action.

And here the *Reader* may please to take notice, that the Design of these Rules, is to conceal the Fiction of the *Stage,* to make the *Play* appear Natural, and to give it an Air of Reality, and *Conversation.*

The largest compass for the first *Unity* is Twenty Four Hours: But a lesser proportion is more regular. To be exact, the Time of the History, or *Fable,* should not exceed that of the *Representation:* Or in other words, the whole Business of the *Play,* should not be much longer than the Time it takes up in *Playing.*

The Second *Unity* is that of *Place.* To observe it, the *Scene* must not wander from one Town, or Country to another. It must continue in the same House, Street, or at farthest in the same City, where it was first laid. The Reason of this Rule depends upon the *First.* Now the Compass of *Time*

being strait, that of *Space* must bear a Correspondent Proportion. Long journeys in *Plays* are impracticable. The Distances of *Place* must be suited to Leisure, and Possibility, otherwise the supposition will appear unnatural and absurd.

[The] Third *Unity* is that of *Action;* It consists in contriving the chief Business of the *Play* single, and making the contents of one Person distinguishably great above the rest. All the Forces of the *Stage* must as it were serve Under one *General:* And the lesser Intrigues or Underplots, have some Relation to the Main. The very Oppositions must be useful, and appear only to be Conquer'd, and Countermin'd. To represent Two considerable Actions independent of each other, Destroys the beauty of Subordination, weakens the Contrivance, and dilutes the pleasure. It splits the *Play,* and makes the *Poem* double. He that would see more upon this subject may consult *Corneille.* To bring these Remarks to the Case in hand. And here we may observe how the **Relapser** fails in all the *Rules* above mention'd.

Ift. His *Play* by modest Computation takes up a weeks Work, but five days you must allow it at the lowest. One day must be spent in the First, Second, and part of the Third *Act,* before Lord *Foplington* sets forward to Sir *Tunbelly.* Now the Length of the Distance, the Pomp of the Retinue, and the Niceness of the Person being consider'd; the journey down, and up again, cannot be laid under four days. To put this out of doubt, Lord, *Foplington* is particularly careful to tell *Coupler,* how concern'd he was not to overdrive, *for fear of disordering his Coach-Horses.* The Laws of *Place,* are no better observ'd than those of *Time.* In the Third *Act* the *Play* is in *Town,* in the Fourth *Act* 'tis stroll'd Fifty Miles off, and in the Fifth *Act* in *London* again. Here *Pegasus* stretches it to purpose! This *Poet* is fit to ride a Match with Witches. *Juliana Cox* never Switched a Broom stock with more Expedition! This is exactly

Titus at *Walton Town,* and *Titus* at *Islington.*

One would think by the probability of matters, the *Plot* had been stolen from Dr. O—s.

The *Poet's* Success in the last *Unity* of *Action* is much the same with the former. *Lovelace, Amanda,* and *Berinthia,* have no share in the main Business. These Second rate *Characters* are a detached Body: Their Interest is perfectly Foreign, and they are neither Friends, nor Enemies to the *Plot. Young Fashion* does not so much as see them till the Close of the Fifth *Act,* and then they meet only to fill the *Stage:* And yet these *Persons* are in the *Poets* account very considerable; Insomuch that he has misnamed his *Play* from the Figure of two of them. This strangness of *Persons,* distinct Company, and inconnexion of Affairs, destroys the Unity of the *Poem.* The contrivance is just as wise as it would be to cut a Diamond in two. There is a loss of Lustre in the Division. Increasing the Number, abates the Value, and by making it more, you make it less.

Thus far I have examin'd the *Dramatick* Merits of the *Play.* And upon enquiry, it appears a Heap of Irregularities. There is neither Propriety in the *Name,* nor Contrivance in the *Plot,* nor Decorum in the *Characters.* 'Tis a thorough Contradiction to Nature, and impossible in *Time,* and *Place.* Its *Shining Graces* as the Author calls them, are *Blasphemy* and *Baudy,* together with a mixture of *Oaths,* and *Cursing.* Upon the whole; the **Relapser's** Judgment, and his Morals, are pretty well adjusted. The *Poet,* is not much better than the *Man.* As for the *Profane* part, 'tis hideous and superlative. . . .

[The author's] defence in his *Preface* is most wretched: He pretends to know nothing of the Matter, and that *'tis all Printed;* Which only proves his Confidence equal to the rest of his Virtues. To out-face Evidence in this manner, is next to the affirming there's no such Sin as *Blasphemy,* which is the greatest Blasphemy of all. His Apology consists in railing at the *Clergy;* a certain sign of ill Principles, and ill Manners. This He does at an unusual rate of Rudeness and Spite. He calls them the Saints with Screw'd *Faces, and wry Mouths.* And after a great deal of scurrilous Abufe too gross to be mention'd, he adds; *If any Man happens to be offended at a story of a Cock and a Bull, and a Priest and a Bull-dog, I beg his Pardon,* &c. This is brave *BearGarden* Language! The **Relapser** would do well to transport his Muse to *Samourgan* [a school for training bears] There 'tis likely he might find Leisure to lick his *Abortive Brat* into shape; And meet with proper Business for his Temper, and encouragement for his Talent. (pp. 228-32)

> *Jeremy Collier, in his* A Short View of the Immorality and Profaneness of the English Stage, *1698. Reprint by Garland Publishing, Inc., 1972, 288 p.*

John Vanbrugh   (essay date 1698)

[*In the following excerpt from his* A Short Vindication of the "Relapse" and the "Provok'd Wife," *from* Immorality and Prophaneness, *Vanbrugh defends* The Relapse *and* The Provok'd Wife *from Jeremy Collier's critical attack (see excerpt above), claiming that it is the nature of comedy to encourage morality by representing its opposite on the stage.*]

When first I saw Mr. *Collier's* Performance upon the Irregularities of the Stage [in *A Short View of the Immorality and Prophaneness of the English Stage*] (in which amongst the rest of the Gentlemen, he's pleas'd to afford me some particular Favours), I was far from designing to trouble either my self or the Town with a Vindication; I thought his Charges against me for Immorality and Prophaneness were grounded upon so much Mistake, that every one (who had had the curiosity to see the Plays, or on this Occasion should take the trouble to read 'em) would easily discover the Root of the Invective, and that 'twas the Quarrel of his Gown, and not of his God, that made him take Arms against me. (pp. 1-2)

I may be blind in what relates to my self; 'tis more than possible, for most People are so: But if I judge right, what I have done is in general a Discouragement to Vice and Folly; I am sure I intended it, and I hope I have performed it. Perhaps I have not gone the common Road, nor observed the strictest Prescriptions: But I believe those who know this Town, will agree, That the Rules of a College

of Divines will in an Infinity of Cases, fall as short of the Disorders of the Mind, as those of the Physicians do in the Diseases of the Body; and I think a man may vary from 'em both, without being a Quack in either.

The real Query is, Whether the Way I have varied, be likely to have a good Effect, or a bad one? That's the true State of the Case; which if I am cast in, I don't question however to gain at least thus much of my Cause, That it shall be allow'd I aim'd at the Mark, whether I hit it or not. This, if it won't vindicate my Sense, will justify my Morals; and shew the World, That this Honest Gentleman, in stretching his Malice, and curtailing his Charity, has play'd a Part which wou'd have much better become a Licentious Poet, than a Reverend Divine. (pp. 3-5)

The First Chapter in his Book is upon the Immodesty of the Stage; where he tells you how valuable a Qualification Modesty is in a Woman: For my part I am wholly of his mind; I think 'tis almost as valuable in a Woman as in a Clergyman; and had I the ruling of the Roast, the one shou'd neither have a Husband, nor the t'other a Benefice without it. If this Declaration won't serve to shew I'm a Friend to't, let us see what Proof this Gentleman can give of the contrary.

I don't find him over-stock'd with Quotations in this Chapter: He's forc'd, rather than say nothing, to fall upon poor Miss *Hoyden* [of **The Relapse**]. He does not come to Particulars, but only mentions her with others, for an immodest Character. What kind of Immodesty he means, I can't tell: But I suppose he means Lewdness, because he generally means wrong. For my part, I know of no Bawdy she talks: If the Strength of his Imagination gives any of her Discourse that Turn, I suppose it may be owing to the Number of Bawdy Plays he has read, which have debauch'd his Taste, and made every thing seem Salt, that comes in his way.

He has but one Quotation more in this long Chapter, that I am concern'd in: And there he points at the **Provok'd Wife,** as if there were something in . . . that Play, to discountenance Modesty in Women. But since he did not think fit to acquaint the Reader what it was, I will.

Lady *Brute* and *Bellinda* speaking of the Smuttiness of some Plays, *Bellinda* says,

> *Why don't some Reformer or other beat the Poet for it?*
>
> L. B. *Because he is not so sure of our Private Approbation, as of our Publick Thanks: Well, sure there is not upon Earth so impertinent a Thing as Womens Modesty.*
>
> B. *Yes, Mens Fantasque, that obliges us to it: If we quit our Modesty, they say we lose our Charms; and yet they know That very Modesty is Affection, and rail at our Hypocrisy.*

Now which way this Gentleman will extract any thing from hence, to the Discouragement of Modesty, is beyond my Chymistry: 'Tis plainly and directly the contrary. Here are two Women (not over Virtuous, as their whole Character shews), who being alone, and upon the rallying Pin, let fall a Word between Jest and Earnest, as if now and then they found themselves cramp'd by their Modesty. But lest this shou'd possibly be mistaken by some part of the Audience, less apprehensive of Right and Wrong than the rest, they are put in mind at the same Instant, That (with the Men) if they quit their Modesty, they lose their Charms: Now I thought 'twas impossible to put the Ladies in mind of any thing more likely to make 'em preserve it. I have nothing more laid to my Charge in the First Chapter.

The Second [chapter of Collier's book] is entituled, *The Prophaneness of the Stage;* which he ranges under Two Heads.

> *Their Cursing and Swearing.* And *Their Abuse of Religion and the Holy Scriptures.*

As to *Swearing,* I agree with him in what he says of it in general, That 'tis contrary both to Religion and Good Manners, especially before Women: But I say, what he calls *Swearing* in the Playhouse, (at least where I have to answer for it) is a Breach upon neither.

And here I must desire the Reader to observe, His Accusations against me run almost always in general Terms, he scarce ever comes to Particulars: I hope 'twill be allow'd a good sign on my side, that it always falls to my turn to quote the thing at length in my Defence, which he huddles together in my Charge. What follows will be an Instance of it.

He says . . . (where the Business of Swearing is upon the *Tapis*) with a great deal of Honesty and Charity, That in this respect the **Relapse** and the **Provok'd Wife** are particularly rampant and scandalous.

Wou'd not any body imagine from hence, that the Oaths that were used there, were no less than those of a Losing Bully at *Baggammon,* or a Bilk'd Hackney-Coachman? Yet after all, the stretch of the Prophaneness lies in Lord *Foppington's Gad,* and Miss *Hoyden's I-Cod.* This is all this Gentleman's Zeal is in such a Ferment about.

Now whether such Words are entirely justifiable or not, there's this at least to be said for 'em; That People of the Nicest Rank both in their Religion and their Manners throughout *Christendom* use 'em.

In *France* you meet with *Par Die, Par Bleu, Ma Foy, uc.* in the constant Conversation of the Ladies and the Clergy, I mean those who are Religious even up to Bigotry it self; and accordingly we see they are always allow'd in their Plays: And in *England,* we meet with an Infinity of People, Clergy as well as Laity, and of the best Lives and Conversations, who use the Words *I-gad, I-faith, Codsfish, Cot's my Life,* and many more, which all lye liable to the same Objection.

Now whether they are right or wrong in doing it, I think at least their Example is Authority enough for the Stage; and shou'd have been enough to have kept so good a Christian as Mr. *Collier* from loading his Neighbour with so foul a Charge as Blasphemy and Prophaneness, unless he had been better provided to make it good.

The next thing he takes to task in this Chapter, is the Abuse of Religion and Holy Scripture. Now here I think

he shou'd first clearly have prov'd, That no Story, Phrase, or Expression whatsoever in the Scripture, whether in the Divine, Moral, or Historical part of it, shou'd be either repeated, or so much as alluded to, upon the Stage, to how useful an End soever it might be applied: This I say he shou'd have first put past a dispute, before he fell upon me for an Abuser of the Holy Scripture; for unless that be to abuse it, I am innocent.

The Scripture is made up of History, Prophecy, and Precept; which are things in their Nature capable of no other Burlesque than what calls in question either their Reality or their Sense: Now if any Allusion I have made, be found even to glance at either of them, I shall be ready to ask Pardon both of God and the Church. But to the Trial.

The first Accusation lies upon the **Provok'd Wife,** where *Rasor* is highly blam'd by Mr. *Collier;* for . . . pleading the same Excuse to an untoward Prank he had newly play'd, which *Adam* did heretofore upon a more unfortunate Occasion: *That Woman having tempted him, the Devil overcame him.* How the Scripture is affronted by this, I can't tell; here's nothing that reflects upon the Truth of the Story: It may indeed put the Audience in mind of their Forefather's Crime, and his Folly, which in my Opinion, like *Gunpowder-Treason,* ought never to be forgot.

The Line in *Rasor's* Confession, which Mr. *Collier's* Modesty ties him from repeating, makes the Close of this Sentence: *And if my Prayers were to be heard, her punishment for so doing shou'd be like the Serpent's of old, she shou'd lye upon her face all the days of her life.*

All I shall say to this, is, That an Obscene Thought must be buried deep indeed, if he don't smell it out; and that I find he has a much greater Veneration for the Serpent than I have, who shall always make a very great distinction between my Respects to God and the Devil. (pp. 6-15)

I cou'd . . . say a great deal against the too exact observance of what's call'd the Rules of the Stage, and the crowding a Comedy with a great deal of Intricate Plot. I believe I cou'd shew, that the chief entertainment, as well as the Moral, lies much more in the Characters and the Dialogue, than in the Business and the Event. And I can assure Mr. *Collier,* if I wou'd have weakned the Diversion, I cou'd have avoided all his Objections, and have been at the expence of much less pains than I have: And this is all the Answer I shall make to 'em, except what tumbles in my way, as I'm observing the foul play he shews me, in setting the **Relapse** in so wrong a Light as he does, at his opening of the Fable on't.

In the first Page of his Remarks upon this Play, he says I have given it a wrong Title; The **Relapse,** or **Vertue in Danger,** relating only to *Loveless* and *Amanda,* who are Characters of an Inferior Consideration; and that the *Younger Brother,* or the *Fortunate Cheat* had been much more proper; because *Young Fashion* is, without competition, the principal Person in the Comedy.

In reading this Gentleman's Book, I have been often at loss to know when he's playing the Knave, and when he's playing the Fool; nor can I decide which he's at now. But this I'm sure, *Young Fashion* is no more the Principal Person of the Play, than He's the best Character in the Church; nor has he any reason to suppose him so, but because he brings up the Rear of the most insignificant part of the Play, and happens to be the Bridegroom in the close on't.

I won't say any thing here irreverently of Matrimony, because *à la Francoise* Bigottry runs high, and by all I see, we are in a fair way to make a Sacrament on't again. But this I may say, That I had full as much respect for *Young Fashion,* while he was a Batchellor, and yet I think while he was so, *Loveless* had a part, that from People who desire to be the better for Plays, might draw a little more Attention. In short; My Lord *Fopington,* and the *Bridegroom,* and the *Bride,* and the *Justice,* and the *Matchmaker,* and the *Nurse,* and the *Parson* at the rear of 'em, are the Inferior Persons of the Play (I mean as to their business) and what they do, is more to divert the Audience, by something particular and whimsical in their Humours, than to instruct 'em in any thing that may be drawn from their Morals; though several useful things may in passing be pickt up from 'em too.

This is as distinct from the main intention of the Play, as the business of *Gomez* is in the *Spanish Fryar.* I shan't here enter into the Contest, whether it be right to have two distinct Designs in one Play; I'll only say, I think when there are so, if they are both entertaining, then 'tis right; if they are not, 'tis wrong. But the Dispute here is, Where lies the principal business in the **Relapse**? (pp. 57-60)

[I designed Loveless] for a natural Instance of the Frailty of Mankind, even in his most fixt Determinations; and for a mark upon the defect of the most steady Resolve, without that necessary Guard, of keeping out of Temptation. But I had still a farther end in *Loveless's* **Relapse,** and indeed much the fame with that in the **Provok'd Wife,** though in different kind of Characters; these latter being a little more refin'd, which places the Moral in a more reasonable, and I think a more agreeable View. There; The Provocation is from a *Brute,* and by consequence cannot be suppos'd to sting a Woman so much, as if it had come from a more Reasonable Creature; the Lady therefore that gives her self a Loose upon it, cou'd not naturally be represented the best of her Sex. Virtuous (upon some ground or other) there was a Necessity of making her; but it appears by a Strain of Levity that runs through her Discourse, she ow'd it more to Form, or Apprehension, or at best to some few Notions of Gratitude to her Husband, for taking her with an Inferior Fortune, than to any Principle of Religion, or an extraordinary Modesty. 'Twas therefore not extremely to be wondred at, that when her Husband made her House uneasy to her at home, she shou'd be prevail'd with to accept of some Diversions abroad. However, since she was Regular while he was kind, the Fable may be a useful Admonition to Men who have Wives, and wou'd keep 'em to themselves, not to build their Security so entirely upon their Ladies Principles, as to venture to pull from under her all the Political Props of her Virtue.

But in the Adventures of *Loveless* and *Amanda,* the Caution is carri'd farther. Here's a Woman whose Virtue is rais'd upon the utmost Strength of Foundation: Religion, Modesty, and Love, defend it. It looks so Sacred, one wou'd think no Mortal durst approach it; and seems so fix'd, one wou'd believe no Engine cou'd shake it: Yet loosen one Stone, the Weather works in, and the Structure molders apace to decay. She discovers her Husband's return to his Inconstancy. The unsteadiness of his Love gives her a Contempt of his Person; and what lessens her Opinion, declines her Inclination. As her Passion for him is abated, that against him's inflam'd; and as her Anger increases, her Reason's confus'd: Her Judgment in disorder, her Religion's unhing'd; and that Fence being broken, she lies widely expos'd: *Worthy's* too sensible of the Advantage, to let slip the Occasion: He has Intelligence of the Vacancy, and puts in for the Place.

Poor *Amanda's* persuaded he's only to be her Friend, and that all he asks, is to be admitted as a Comforter in her Afflictions. But when People are sick, they are so fond of a Cordial, that when they get it to their Nose, they are apt to take too much on't.

She finds in his Company such a Relief to her Pain, she desires the Physician may be always in her sight. She grows pleas'd with his Person as well as his Advice, yet she's sure he can never put her Virtue in Danger. But she might have remembred her Husband was once of the same Opinion; and have taken warning from him, as the Audience, I intended, shou'd do from 'em both.

This was the Design of the Play; which I think is something of so much greater Importance than *Young Fashion's* marrying Miss *Hoyden,* that if I had call'd it the *Younger Brother,* or the *Fortunate Cheat,* instead of **the Relapse,** or **Virtue in danger,** I had been just as much in the wrong, as Mr. *Collier* is now. (pp. 67-71)

> *John Vanbrugh, in his* A Short Vindication of the "Relapse" and the "Provok'd Wife," *1698. Reprint by Garland Publishing, Inc., 1972, 79 p.*

Giles Jacob (essay date 1719)

[*In the following excerpt, Jacob offers a favorable assessment of Vanbrugh's plays, praising their originality and ethical design.*]

This Gentleman is descended from a very good Family in *Cheshire,* and had bestow'd on him a liberal Education. He was early inclin'd to Writing, and tho' his Plays are all universally applauded, yet his Modesty would not permit him to affix his Name to any. He has a great deal of Wit in all his Performances, and shews a very great sprightliness of Conversation. His Characters are justly drawn, appear more like Originals than Copies, and shew the Lineaments of Nature without the Stiffness of Art. His Men of Wit are really so, and, as another Author has observ'd, he puts Folly into such a Light, that it is as diverting to the Reader as Spectator; and his Fools are so pleasing, that you are not weary of their Company before they leave you. His Dialogue is extremely easy, and well turn'd, and I may venture to say, that this Gentleman and Mr. *Congreve* have justly gain'd the Preference of all our Modern Writers of Comedy. His Plays are as follow,

I. *The Relapse* or *Virtue in Danger,* being the Sequel to *Love's last Shift,* or *The Fool in Fashion;* a Comedy, acted at the Theatre Royal, 1697. This Play was acted with great Applause; and the Character of my Lord *Foppington* falls very little short of Sir *George Etherege's* Sir *Fopling Flutter,* which is allow'd to be a Master-piece; but the broken Scenes are judg'd an Irregularity. This Play was writ in Six Weeks.

II. *The Provok'd Wife;* a Comedy, acted at the Theatre in *Lincolns-Inn-Fields* with great Applause: But some of our Criticks objected against it as a loose Performance, tho' I think the Design of it is very just; for it teaches Husbands how they ought to expect their Wives should shew a Resentment, if they use them as *Sir John Brute* did his: Such Husbands may learn, by fatal Experiene, that neglected and abus'd Virtue and Beauty may be provok'd to yield to the Motives and Revenue, and that the forcible Solicitations of an agreeable Person, who not only demonsstrates a Value, but a Passion for what the Possessor flights, may be sufficiently prevalent with an ill-us'd Wife to forfeit her Honour.

III. *Æsop,* a Comedy, acted at the Theatre Royal, with Applause. This play was originally writ in *French* by Mr. *Boursaut,* but the scenes of Sir *Polydorus Hogstye,* the *Players,* the *Senator* and the *Beau* are added by the Author. This Play contains a great deal of general Satire, and very useful Morality, yet it had not the Success it merited, especially in the first two Nights Representation: It was admir'd that this Play, which very much excels the *French* one, should not hold out above a Week, when that was acted for near a Month together; but these Things are easily accounted for, when we consider that at *Paris* there is no Prejudice against the Stage, and, in this City, all publick Entertainments are determin'd by Patty Censures. (pp. 262-63)

> Giles Jacob, "Sir John Vanbrugh," in his *The Poetical Register; or, The Lives and Characters of the English Dramatic Poets, 1719. Reprint by Garland Publishing, Inc., 1970, pp. 262-64.*

Colley Cibber   (essay date 1740)

[*Cibber was a well-known Restoration dramatist whose* An Apology for His Life *(1740) provides a valuable history of the English stage from the time of Shakespeare to his own. Other works of Cibber include:* Love's Last Shift; or, The Fool in Fashion *(1696),* The Careless Husband *(1705), and* The Provok'd Husband *(1728), written with Vanbrugh. In the following excerpt, Cibber praises the natural style, wit, and humor of Vanbrugh's plays, noting the superiority of* The Relapse *to his own* Love's Last Shift.]

Though to write much, in a little time, is no excuse for writing ill; yet Sir John Vanburgh's pen is not to be a little admir'd for its spirit, ease, and readiness, in producing plays so fast, upon the neck of one another; for, notwithstanding this quick dispatch, there is a clear and lively simplicity in his wit, that neither wants the ornament of learning, nor has the least smell of the lamp in it. As the

face of a fine woman, with only her locks loose about her, may be then in its greatest beauty; such were his productions, only adorn'd by nature. There is something so catching to the ear, so easy to the memory, in all he writ, that it has been observ'd by all the actors of my time, that the style of no author whatsoever gave their memory less trouble than that of Sir John Vanbrugh; which I myself, who have been charg'd with several of his strongest characters, can confirm by a pleasing experience. And indeed his wit and humour was so little laboured, that his most entertaining scenes seem'd to be no more than his common conversation committed to paper. Here I confess my judgment at a loss, whether, in this, I give him more, or less, than his due praise? For may it not be more laudable to raise an estate (whether in wealth or fame) by pains, and honest industry, than to be born to it? Yet, if his scenes really were, as to me they always seem'd, delightful, are they not, thus, expiditiously written, the more surprising? Let the wit and merit of them, then, be weigh'd by wiser criticks than I pretend to be. But no wonder, while his conceptions were so full of life and humour, his must should be sometimes too warm to wait the slow pace of judgment, or to endure the drudgery of forming a regular fable to them. Yet we see the *Relapse,* however imperfect, in the conduct, by the mere force of its agreeable wit, ran away with the hearts of its hearers; while *Love's Last Shift,* which (as Mr. Congreve justly said of it) had only in it a great many things that were *like* wit, that in reality were *not* wit; and what is still less pardonable (as I say of it myself) has a great deal of puerility and frothy stage-language in it, yet by the mere moral delight receiv'd from its fable, it has been, with the other, in a continued and equal possession of the stage for more than forty years. (pp. 114-15)

> Colley Cibber, in a chapter in his An Apology for His Life, *J. M. Dent & Sons, Ltd., 1740, pp. 96-115.*

The London Chronicle   (essay date 1758)

[*In the following excerpt from a review first published in 1758, the anonymous critic praises Vanbrugh's comic wit, but attacks* The Provok'd Wife *for its deficiency in grace.*]

At Drury-Lane last Saturday evening was presented the *Provoked Wife,* a comedy, written by Sir John Vanbrugh.

How Van wants grace who seldom wants for art

is a line of Mr. Pope, in his *Imitation of Horace's Epistle to Augustus:* and it is verified in this comedy, where Sir John has displayed a most enchanting vein of wit and humour, but is so horridly deficient in what, I imagine, Mr. Pope means by the word *grace* that one can hardly help being angry with oneself for being so excessively pleased with him.

It is generally thought that Mrs. Cibber wants spirit in the character of Lady Brute; but if she does, it is in my opinion rather an advantage to it, which would otherwise appear too licentious: and, when all is said and done, her ladyship, and my cousin Belinda (which part is performed with a great deal of life by Miss Haughton) are at best a couple of as willing tits as a man would desire to meet with: but as I do not apprehend characters of this kind are likely to do much mischief, I cannot help thinking that the author was wholly in the right rather to draw his women as he has done, than by giving them opposite manners, to have made them such unmeaning things as half our modern comedies are filled with. For instance, can any one think that Lady Brute would give half so much pleasure to the audience if instead of being a wanton, intriguing, witty wag (as Razor calls her) the author had copied her from Patient Grizel.

It is amazing to me that Mr. Garrick will *attempt* the part of Sir John Brute; a part which he not only apparently *mistakes,* but in which he is absolutely prejudicial to the morals of his countrymen.

[James Quin] made him a Brute indeed, an ill-natured, surly swine of a fellow; and I dare swear every body most heartily despised and detested him: But with Garrick it is quite a different case; the knight is the greatest favourite in the play; such a joyous agreeable wicked dog, that we never think we can have enough of his company; and when he drinks confusion to all order, there is scarce a man in the house, I believe, who is not for that moment a reprobate in his heart. In truth he is so very much the entertainment of the audience, that, to speak in a phrase which Sir John Brute might be supposed to make use of himself, whenever he goes off the stage, we are like so many people sitting round a table after the wine and glasses are removed, till he comes on again.

The celebrated scene in which Sir John is brought before the Justice in his wife's cloaths, was at the first representation of this comedy quite different. He then came on in the habit of a Clergyman: but so indecent a freedom taken with that sacred order was very justly decried; upon which the author altered it as it now stands, much for the better in every respect: and though I have borne a *little hard* upon Mr. Garrick in *other parts* of the character, in this scene it must be allowed that he is the finest caricatura of a fine lady that ever was represented.

Constant and Heartfree are very natural and spirited characters. But, without a joke, I do not think Mr. Havard well calculated to appear to advantage in either of them. The inimitable Mrs. Clive, though her person is greatly against her in this part, gives perfect satisfaction in the affected and impertinent Lady Fanciful, the hint of which character the author has taken from the French; and it is the very same from whence Dryden had before translated his Melantha in *Marriage-à-la-mode;* which has since been frittered into an execrable farce, called *The Frenchified Lady never in Paris.* (pp. 30-1)

"On 'The Provoked Wife' and 'The Millers'," in The English Dramatic Critics: An Anthology, 1660-1932, *edited by James Agate, Arthur Barker Limited, 1932, pp. 30-2.*

William Hazlitt   (lecture date 1819)

[*Hazlitt was an eminent English essayist and critic whose work, typically focusing on characterization, reflects the influence of Romanticism. He was also one of the first great dramatic critics whose reviews were published in the* Examiner, *the* Morning Chronicle, *the* Champion, *the* London Magazine, *and the* Times. *Some of these pieces were subsequently collected in his* The Round Table *(1817) and* A View of the English Stage *(1818). In the following exerpt taken from an 1819 lecture, Hazlitt discusses Vanbrugh's dramatic skill, pointing out that "what he does best, he does because he cannot help it."*]

[Vanbrugh] holds his own fully with the best. He is no writer at all as to mere authorship; but he makes up for it by a prodigious fund of comic invention and ludicrous description, bordering somewhat on caricature. Though he did not borrow from him, he was much more like Molière in genius than Wycherley was, who professedly imitated him. He has none of Congreve's graceful refinement, and as little of Wycherley's serious manner and studied insight into the springs of character; but his exhibition of [w]it in dramatic contrast and unlooked-for situations, where the different parties play upon one another's failings, and into one another's hands, keeping up the jest like a game at battledore-and-shuttlecock, and urging it to the utmost verge of breathless extravagance, in the mere eagerness of the fray, is beyond that of any other of our writers. His fable is not so profoundly laid, nor his characters so well digested, as Wycherley's (who, in these respects, bore some resemblance to Fielding). Vanbrugh does not lay the same deliberate train from the outset to the conclusion, so that the whole may hang together, and tend inevitably from the combination of different agents and circumstances to the same decisive point; but he works out scene after scene, on the spur of the occasion, and from the immediate hold they take of his imagination at the moment, without any previous bias or ultimate purpose, much more powerfully, with more *verve,* and in a richer vein of original invention. His fancy warms and burnishes out as if he were engaged in the real scene of action, and felt all his faculties suddenly called forth to meet the emergency. He has more nature than art: what he does best, he does because he cannot help it. He has a masterly eye to the advantages which certain accidental situations of character present to him on the spot, and he executes the most difficult and rapid theatrical movements at a moment's warning. (pp. 104-05)

[Vanbrugh] works out scene after scene, on the spur of the occasion, and from the immediate hold they take of his imagination at the moment, without any previous bias or ultimate purpose, much more powerfully, with more *verve,* and in a richer vein of original invention.

—*William Hazlitt*

Vanbrugh's *forte* was not the sentimental or didactic; his genius flags and grows dull when it is not put into action, and wants the stimulus of sudden emergency, or the fortuitous collision of different motives to call out all its force and vivacity. His antitheses are happy and brilliant contrasts of character; his *double entendres* equivocal situations; his best jokes are practical devices, not epigrammatic conceits. His wit is that which is emphatically called *mother-wit.* It brings those who possess it, or to whom he lends it, into scrapes by its restlessness, and brings them out of them by its alacrity. Several of his favourite characters are knavish, adroit adventurers, who have all the gipsy jargon, the cunning impudence, cool presence of mind, selfishness, and indefatigable industry; all the excuses, lying dexterity, the intellectual juggling and legerdemain tricks, necessary to fit them for this sort of predatory warfare on the simplicity, follies, or vices of mankind. He discovers the utmost dramatic generalship in bringing off his characters at a pinch, and by an instantaneous *ruse de guerre,* when the case seems hopeless in any other hands. The train of his associations, to express the same thing in metaphysical language, lies in following the suggestions of his fancy into every possible connexion of cause and effect, rather than into every possible combination of likeness or difference. His ablest characters show that they are so by displaying their ingenuity, address, and presence of mind in critical junctures, and in their own affairs, rather than their wisdom or their wit "in intellectual gladiatorship," or in speculating on the affairs and characters of other people. (pp. 110-11)

> *William Hazlitt, "On Wycherley, Congreve, Vanbrugh, and Farquhar," in his* Lectures on the English Poets, and the English Comic Writers, *edited by William Carew Hazlitt, revised edition, George Bell and Sons, 1876, pp. 91-120.*

A Short Vindication of "The Relapse" and "The Provok'd Wife" from Immorality and Profaneness (1698)

The Stage is a Glass for the World to view it self in; People ought therefore to see themselves as they are; if it makes their Faces too Fair, they won't know they are Dirty, and by consequence will neglect to wash 'em: If therefore I have shew'd *Constant* upon the Stage, what generally the Thing call'd a Fine Gentleman is off on't, I think I have done what I shou'd do. I have laid open his Vices as well as his Virtues: 'Tis the Business of the Audience to observe where his Flaws lessen his Value; and by considering the Deformity of his Blemishes, become sensible how much a Finer Thing he wou'd be without 'em.

> *John Vanbrugh, in his* A Short Vindication of "The Relapse" and "The Provok'd Wife" from Immorality and Prophaneness, *edited by Arthur Freeman, Garland Publishing, 1972.*

Leigh Hunt (essay date 1849)

[*An English poet and essayist, Hunt is remembered as*

a literary critic who encouraged and influenced several Romantic poets, especially John Keats and Percy Bysshe Shelley. Hunt produced volumes of poetry and critical essays and, with his brother John, established the Examiner, *a weekly liberal newspaper. In his criticism, Hunt articulated the principles of Romanticism, emphasizing imaginative freedom and the expression of personal emotions or spirituality. In the following excerpt from an essay written in 1849, Hunt differentiates Vanbrugh from his contemporaries, claiming that Vanbrugh's plays defend virtue "by unmasking the pretenders to it."*]

[Vanbrugh's] character as a comic writer is clear and obvious. It is straightforward, cheerful, confident, and robust; something between Flemish and French; not over-nice in its decorums, not giving too much credit to conventional virtues, nor yet disbelieving in the virtues that will always remain such, and that are healthy and hearty; but as his jovial and sincere temperament gave him a thorough dislike of hypocrisy, the licence of the times allowed him to be plain-spoken to an extent which was perilous to his animal spirits; and an editor in these days is startled, not to say frightened, at sallies of audacity and exposure, which, however loath to call affrontery, he is forced to think such, and is only prevented by belief in the goodness of his heart from concluding to be want of feeling. Of feeling indeed, in the sentimental sense, Vanbrugh shows little or none. He seems to have thought it foreign to the satire and mirth of comedy. His plots are interesting, without having the teasing perplexity of Congreve's; and he is more uniformly strong than Farquhar, and cheerful than Wycherley. What he borrows, he seems to change at one blow into something better, by sleight, or rather force, of hand. He is easy in invention, and true and various in character. His style is so natural and straightforward, that [Colley] Cibber says the actors preferred it to every other, it was so easy to learn by rote. What he wants (except at the bottom of his heart) is every species of refinement, but that of a freedom from all cant and nonsense. He has no more poetry in him, in a sense apart from what is common to everything artistic, than a sailor who would see nothing in Shakespeare's "Bermoothes," except the turtle. But in a superiority to circumstances sophisticate, the best-bred of gallants could not beat him, whether from absence of veneration, or presence of good health. His *Lord Foppington* is the quintessence of nullification, and of the scorn of things which he does not care for; while *Miss Hoyden,* without delay or "mistake," is for consolidating everything into the tangible and plentitudinous, for which she does care. (pp. 34-5)

It was complained of, with regard to Vanbrugh's first comedy **The Relapse,** that he had taken the penitent of Cibber's play (*Love's Last Shift*), and made him fall into his old ways again; which hurt the moral. But Vanbrugh laughed at the morals of Cibber. He knew that so flimsy and canting a teacher could only teach pretences; and in undoing his work he left society to find out something better. On the other hand, when Cibber took up the author's unfinished play, the **Journey to London,** and fancied that he had improved it with his *Lord Townly* and *Lady Grace,* and his insipid perfect gentleman, *Mr. Manly,* he made a blunder of such dull vanity and time-serving self-love, as it is melancholy to think of in the sprightly Colley, but much more to read, after reading Vanbrugh's three acts! It is worth the reader's while to refer to Cibber's play, and compare them. What a poor, pick-thank set of common-place usurpers of attention,—of pretenders to a "clear stage and no favour,"—after the heartier moral fair-play of Vanbrugh! What a half-sided lesson, taking it at its best, and a servile playing into the hands of the stronger sex, as if nothing could be more exemplary or further-sighted! The very name of Lord "Loverule," instead of "Townly," shows that the "reciprocity" was not to be all on one side in Vanbrugh's play. But everything is miserably washed down in Cibber, even to poor John Moody and the foot-men.

Dick Amlet, Mrs. Amlet, and *Brass,* in **The Confederacy,** are all perfection, after their kind,—the unfeeling son, whose legs are doted on by his mother; the peddling moth-er, hobbling about, with fine ladies in her debt; and *Brass,* exquisite *Brass,* whom one can hardly help fancying made of the metal that christens him, and with a voice that rings accordingly. We know of no better comic writing in the world than the earlier scenes of *Lord Foppington* in **The Relapse,** and those between *Dick Amlet* and his mother, and of *Brass* securing his bargain with *Dick,* in the play before us.

We find we have passed over **The Provoked Wife,** which, to say the truth, is a play more true than pleasant; and it is not so much needed as it was in Vanbrugh's day, when sottishness had not become infamous among decent peo-ple. So long do the vices of the stronger sex contrive to have themselves taken, if not for virtues, at least for some-thing like manly privilege!

One reason has been given why *Æsop* did not succeed. An-other we take to be that the French, in their old levity, used to think themselves bound to sit out any gravity that appealed to their good sense; while the English never pre-tended to be able to dispense with something strong and stirring. Besides, morality of so very obvious and didactic a sort was too great a contradiction to the taste of the times, and to Vanbrugh's own previous indulgence of it. Rakes scouring the streets at night, and ladies carried off swooning with love from antechambers, had ill prepared the sons and daughters of Charles II. for the lessons of the sage Grecian, adapting his "wise saws" to modern in-stances.

"How Van wants grace, who never wanted wit!"

says Pope: and it is true. Yet this graceless wit, often far less so than he appears, and covertly implying virtues su-perior to their common forms, has a passage in one of the coarsest of his plays, that preaches a love truer than any to be found in Pope:—

> "CONSTANT. Though marriage be a lottery, in which there are a wondrous many blanks, yet there is one inestimable lot, *in which the only heaven on earth is written.* Would your kind fate but guide your hand to that, though I were wrapt in all that luxury itself could clothe me with, I should still envy you.
>
> HEARTFREE. And justly too: for to be CAPABLE

of loving one, is better than to possess a thou-sand."

> **Provok'd Wife,** Act V., Scene 4.

But the old question may here be asked, "What signify one or two passages of this sort, when all the rest is so differ-ent?" To which it should long ago have been answered, *ev-erything;* when the difference is more in appearance than reality, and fighting the battles of virtue itself by unmask-ing the pretenders to it. (pp. 35-7)

> *Leigh Hunt, "John Vanbrugh," in* Sir John Vanbrugh, *edited by A. E. H. Swaen, Charles Scribner's Sons, 1896, pp. 19-52.*

John Palmer   (essay date 1913)

[*An English diplomat, drama critic, editor, and author of numerous detective novels, Palmer has written several books on drama including* Moliere: His Life and Works *(1930). In the following excerpt, Palmer asserts that Vanbrugh was the "perfect translator," whose adapta-tions of other playwrights' works are better than the orig-inals, but greatly criticizes the apparent disregard for so-cial and moral standards in Vanbrugh's plays.*]

The dialogue between Constant and Heartfree of **The Pro-voked Wife** upon the topic of a happy marriage could have appeared in no comedy of any one of Sir John Vanbrugh's predecessors. We rub our eyes suddenly to discover moral-ity of the Victorian fireside intruding into the morality of Spring Garden:

> CONSTANT. Though marriage be a lottery, in which there are a wondrous many blanks, yet there is one inestimable lot, in which the only heaven on earth is written. Would your kind fate but guide your hand to that, though I were lapped in all that luxury itself could clothe me with I should still envy you.
>
> HEARTFREE. And justly too: for to be capable of loving one, is better than to possess a thou-sand.

But for the most part, Vanbrugh, as a witness that times are about to change, is revealed in a wilful reaction against the new morality—a reaction which testifies that he has fallen beneath its influence. Vanbrugh is an *immoral* au-thor. He was sufficiently [Jeremy] Collier's contemporary to disagree with him, to dislike him, to contradict him in precept and example. He understands Collier. He knows how Collier may be shocked and exasperated. Congreve and Wycherley were unable even to see what Collier was driving at. When Congreve is wicked, his wickedness *ex-presses* the morality of his period. When Vanbrugh is wicked, his wickedness *outrages* the morality of his. (pp. 202-03)

Vanbrugh wrote but two complete original plays, and part of a third. The rest were closely adapted or translated from the French. Vanbrugh was the perfect translator. He was easily fired with the dramatic possibilities of a situation. In every case his adaptations from Dancourt, Boursault, even Molière, are better than their originals. Moreover, one of his two original and complete comedies was suggested by the conclusion of another play. These facts are a key to the quality of Vanbrugh's work. Vanbrugh drew his inspiration more from the theatre than from life. His best original creations, like Foresight and Ben Legend of *Love for Love,* are cleverly sketched, effective stage figures; and one of his best-known characters, Lord Foppington of *The Relapse* is Cibber's Sir Novelty Fashion theatrically improved precisely in the same way in which *The Confederacy* is improved from *Les Bourgeoises à la Mode.* Vanbrugh's spirit of authorship is hereby admirably illustrated. He accepted the material of his comedy with little care for its moral or social significance; his one aim was to amuse honest gentlemen of the town—"to divert (if possible) some part of their spleen in spite of their wives and their taxes"—a task for which his agreeable style, his gift of wise humour, his instinct for the theatre excellently qualified him. (pp. 225-26)

The Relapse was Vanbrugh's continuation of *Love's Last Shift* by Colley Cibber. The play falls into two plots or sections—one presenting the moral adventures of Loveless and Amanda; the other introducing Sir Tunbelly Clumsey and his daughter Hoyden. The two plots are to the last moment almost entirely disconnected, but when Collier, in this regard, attacked Vanbrugh's construction he missed the really serious blemish. Vanbrugh answered Collier quite reasonably that "whether it be right to have two distinct designs in one play, I'll only say I think when there are, if they're both entertaining, then they're right, if they are not, 'tis wrong."

"Entertaining" requires a commentary. If we are first entertained with a scene in which the moral struggles of a wedded pair to preserve their virtue are presented with an assumption that virtue is from heaven, and should certainly prevail in the best of possible worlds; and, immediately upon this, are asked to be equally well entertained with scenes imitated from the theatre of Congreve and Wycherley, where wedded virtue is, at most, the better part of discretion—then we may be allowed to inquire whether the entertainment is not a little too freely mixed. (pp. 226-27)

Note that the wheel is almost full circle here. Etherege delivered his first comedy in mixed prose and verse, and with an equally disastrous confusion of romantic and comic threads. The rise of English comedy was determined when, in his second play, Etherege discarded the pretences of verse. The decline of English comedy is determined when in his first play Vanbrugh restored confusion. The mischief of this confusion is the pause it gives to the reader, breaking his illusion of an ordered comic world, wherein it would be impertinent for his private sense of moral values to intrude. The reader is in the plays of Vanbrugh frequently arrested and compelled to ask himself, what is the law and the prophets of this curious tribe? Inconsistency in the artist sends the spectator for a standard rudely back to his own experience—a test which the plays of Vanbrugh are not able to sustain. Nor would they be required to sustain it, but for their own lack of coherence.

Vanbrugh's true character appears most clearly in touches of humorous observation equally independent of the two hemispheres of his comedy. When neither the moral standards of his home-life at Greenwich, nor the moral standards of the comedy of Congreve are at issue, Vanbrugh falls back upon a vein of native humour in which he quite easily excels everyone of his predecessors. These touches, as all Vanbrugh's happiest effects, are usually suggested by the flow of the scene:

> WOR. What! she runs, I'll warrant you, into that common mistake of fond wives, who conclude themselves virtuous, because they can refuse a man they don't like, when they have got one they do.
>
> BER. True, and there I think 'tis a presumptuous thing in a woman to assume the name of virtuous, till she has heartily hated her husband, and been soundly in love with somebody else. Whom if she has withstood—then—much good may it do her!

The Relapse, in the majority of its scenes, is the product of these three suggested elements: Loveless's soliloquy is Vanbrugh, the husband-to-be of Harriet Yarborough, the contemporary of Jeremy Collier; the passage between Worthy and Berinthia is Vanbrugh, shrewd, fluent, and witty, as the poets loved him; then there is Vanbrugh, the successor of Congreve and Wycherley, who accepted the convention of Restoration comedy without being of the Restoration world. (pp. 228-29)

[There] intrudes into his comedy an element which was to kill it. He hesitates between two kingdoms. Society was in revolution, and Vanbrugh belonged to the new period. But he accepted for his models a comedy based upon the old. His theatre no longer reflects the moral values of life. The connexion is broken, and confusion has ensued. But we must not dwell upon this aspect of the plays of Vanbrugh to the exclusion of his undoubted merits. Vanbrugh had so shrewd a penetration into motive and character, so level a judgment, so embracing a humour, that had he taken the theatre more seriously than he did, he might have founded a new school of English comedy in strict relation with the new social period that was setting in. He might, in a word, have started English comedy upon a fresh career. But he idly chose to continue an exhausted vein. He accepted a convention that he could not honestly employ. He was content to be inspired by the old theatre rather than by the new life to which he belonged. (p. 236)

> *John Palmer, "Sir John Vanbrugh," in his* The Comedy of Manners, *G. Bell & Sons, Ltd., 1913, pp. 201-41.*

Bonamy Dobrée   (essay date 1924)

[*An English historian and critic, Dobrée distinguished himself both as a leading authority on Restoration drama and as a biographer who sought to establish biography as a legitimate creative form. Dobrée is also known for his editing of* The Oxford History of English Literature *and* Writers and Their Work *series. In all his writings, Dobrée's foremost concern was to communicate to the reader his aesthetic response to the work under discussion. In the following excerpt, Dobrée offers a general assessment of Vanbrugh's plays. He argues that Vanbrugh had no individual vision to convey, and that as a result, his comedies lack both realism and wit.*]

Vanbrugh had one valuable requisite of the writer of critical comedy, a contempt for all cant and humbug; but he failed to be anything of a poet because he had no peculiar vision, and thus his plays can add nothing either to our knowledge of life, or to our aesthetic experience. He presented life as he saw it, but he saw it no differently from the hundred and one other people with whom he daily mingled. Thus if there is no vinegar in his comedies, neither is there any salt. He never for a moment took his audiences away from the life they saw around them (except in a few passages, especially in his first comedy, that approach burlesque), nor did he show it from any particular angle. He probably took his comedies no more seriously or strenuously than he took life; both for him were a matter of easy adaptation, a little rough and tumble, and a great deal of good luck. He put down naturally what occurred to him easily, with the result that his comedy, as Congreve remarked of Cibber's *Love's Last Shift,* 'had only a great many things that were like wit, that in reality were not wit'.

But he had more than a little sense of the stage. He knew what would be effective, and we follow his plays with the amusement we feel at all evasions, and at revelations of the cunning in humanity. In all his works it is the plot that matters, and he put the moral second. . . .[He] confessed fondness for a moral when driven to make some statement [in his **Short Vindication**] . . . and this is further shown by his adaptation of Boursault's *Esope.* Yet in **The Relapse,** the interest is clearly not in the 'problem' play of Loveless, Amanda, and Berinthia, as the title would imply, nor even in the character of Lord Foppington, but in the story of Tom Fashion outwitting his brother, and carrying off the heiress Hoyden. Collier was quite right when he said the play should have been called *The Younger Brother or The Fortunate Cheat.* Indeed, his only idea in writing the play, and not a bad one either, was to divert the gentlemen of the town, if possible, 'and make them forget their spleen in spite of their wives and taxes'.

His originality consisted in breathing the spirit of Middleton or Massinger into the works of his French and English contemporaries. He accepted their plays and the conventions of his time, but altered, and it must be confessed, spoiled them. He never saw what the others were at, nor knew what he was doing, and he was genuinely surprised when accused of profaneness and immorality. Where he was frankly late Elizabethan, as in the scene between Sir John Brute and the justice, or when he shows us Sir Tunbelly Clumsey, he is full of vitality, and blows a breezy atmosphere into life. But this is the end of his originality. As the list of his plays shows, he found it more pleasant to adapt than to create, and even in his original productions he is derivative. Continually, in little sentences, we catch a reminiscence of an older writer, not only despoiled but ruined. Again and again we are reminded of other characters or incidents; the parson in **The Relapse** reminds us of the parson in *The Cheats,* or of Busy in *Bartholomew Fair.* Lady Fanciful in **The Provok'd Wife** is a revival of Dryden's Melantha; while in **The Confederacy,** Dick's surrender of his ring reminds us forcibly of Alderman Gripe's relinquishment of his in Wycherley's *Love in a Wood.*

These borrowings would not matter, had he, like Congreve who borrowed freely, improved upon his originals; but he had not the lightness of touch, the sureness of point, the racy descriptiveness of his predecessors. We may take a few instances of his pilferings, not of course to convict him, but to make a critical comparison. We have quoted a passage from *The Old Bachelor,* showing Heartwell in front of Silvia's door. This is Heartfree, Vanbrugh's version of the misogynist, in **The Provok'd Wife:**

> What the plague ails me?—Love? No, I thank you for that, my heart's rock still.—Yet 'tis Belinda that disturbs me; that's positive—Well, what of all that? Must I love her for being troublesome?

and so on for some lines. Belinda, again, now and then takes a hint from her sister in Congreve:

> For when a man is really in love, he looks so insufferably silly, that tho' a woman liked him well enough before, she has then much ado to endure the sight of him.

Congreve's young woman has said:

> Could you but see with my eyes, the buffoonery of one scene of address, a lover, set out with all his equipages and appurtenances; O gad!

The latter is vivid, the former commonplace. Thus **The Confederacy** is full of reminiscences of Congreve, but the delight, the exquisite touch, is lacking. In **The Confederacy** we read of Brass giving a letter to Flippanta for her mistress, and a turn is provided, not by the French author, but by the creator of *The Way of the World.* When she receives the missive, Flippanta asks, 'Are there any verses in it?' and Brass assures her that there is 'not one word in prose, it's dated in rhyme'. This might be amusing if there were no higher standard to make it seem flat, but we cannot help remembering Millamant:

> MILLAMANT. I am persecuted with letters—I hate letters—Nobody knows how to write letters; and yet one has 'em, one does not know why. They serve one to pin up one's hair.
>
> WITWOUD. Is that the way? Pray, madam, do you pin up your hair with all your letters? I find I must keep copies.
>
> MIL. Only with those in verse, Mr. Witwoud. I never pin up my hair with prose—I think I tried once, Mincing.
>
> MIN. O Mem, I shall never forget it.
>
> MIL. Ay, poor Mincing tift and tift all the morning.

And if all the joy is gone, so is all the philosophy, all the poetry if you will. We may remember Angelica's wistful remark quoted in the last chapter and compare it with a like utterance by Clarissa:

> I always know what I lack, but I am never pleased with what I have. The want of a thing is perplexing enough, but the possession of it is intolerable.

Vanbrugh is full of high spirits, fun, and frolic; but his

plays express no desire, the light of the intellect does not illuminate them; in a word, he lacked creative capacity.

It is claimed for him that his dialogue is brisk and easy. 'There is something', Cibber said, 'so catching to the ear, so easy to the memory, in all he writ, that it has been observed by all the actors of my time, that the style of no author whatsoever gave their memory less trouble.' A little consideration shows this to be something of a left-handed compliment, for what is so easy to learn may not be worth the learning. Dialogue, 'so easy to the memory' often degenerates into stuff like this passage from *The Relapse:*

> AMANDA. Why, do you then resolve you'll never marry?
>
> BERINTHIA. O no; I resolve I will.
>
> AMAN. How so?
>
> BER. That I never may.
>
> AMAN. You banter me.
>
> BER. Indeed I don't. But I consider I'm a woman, and form my resolutions accordingly.
>
> AMAN. Well, my opinion is, form what resolution you will, matrimony will be the end on't.
>
> BER. Faith, it won't.
>
> AMAN. How d'you know?
>
> BER. I'm sure on't.
>
> AMAN. Why, do you think 'tis impossible for you to fall in love?
>
> BER. No.
>
> AMAN. Nay, but to grow so passionately fond, that nothing but the man you love can give you rest?
>
> BER. Well, what then?
>
> AMAN. Why, then you'll marry him.
>
> BER. How do you know that?
>
> AMAN. Why, what can you do else?
>
> BER. Nothing, but sit and cry.
>
> AMAN. Psha!

This is wretched either as life or as art, yet it is not the worst passage deliberately selected. His repartee seldom gets home: if we say that Wycherley used a bludgeon, and Congreve a rapier, we may continue the metaphor and say that Vanbrugh gives us many a lively bout at singlesticks; his personages even come to actual blows on more occasions than one. But he has happy passages, and can claim to have created one character, Lord Foppington. If not quite delicate enough for fantasy, erring too much on the side of exaggeration, yet Lord Foppington succeeds in convincing by consistency with himself. Neither Leigh Hunt who called him 'the quintessence of nullification', nor Hazlitt who wrote of him as 'the personification of the foppery and folly of dress and appearance in full feather', quite do him justice. For at bottom he is a very sound man of business, and it is this that makes him a creation of Van-

brugh's and not a mere imitation of Sir Fopling, Sir Courtly, and Sir Novelty. He deliberately aims at absurdity because it pays, and he is proud to be the leader of the coxcombs because they form 'so prevailing a party'. All this is well carried out. One never knows what he is going to say, but once spoken, one realizes it is the only thing he could have said. His argument against reading has cogency; 'Far to my mind the inside of a book, is to entertain one's self with the forc'd product of another man's brain. Naw I think a man of quality and breeding may be much diverted with the natural sprauts of his own.' His behaviour when he finds himself cheated of his heiress is exemplary:

> Naw, for my part, I think the wisest thing a man can do with an aching heart, is to put on a serene countenance; for a philosaphical air is the most becoming thing in the warld to the face of a person of quality; I will therefore bear my disgrace like a great man, and let the people see I am above an affrant.

The motives may not be of the highest, but they will serve for a 'nice marality'.

Now and again, as in Lord Foppington's presence, we feel that had Vanbrugh taken the trouble, he might have written good comedy. But on the one hand he was too good-natured for critical comedy, and on the other he lacked the depth of perception to write any other. He confused his values even too much for what he was doing. For instance, he thought he was treating sex exactly as Congreve did, but with him love is no longer a battle of the wits, but a struggle of desire against conscience. The persons of his plays commit adultery with the full knowledge that they are acting contrary to their own morality, and in consequence there is sometimes an atmosphere of lasciviousness which destroys the comic.

Berinthia's surrender to Loveless is a sufficient example. His plays abound in platitudes on sexual morality, and he has been praised for his line, 'To be capable of loving one, is better than to possess a thousand'. But this is not the comic way of inculcating a moral, and thus on the whole his plays make for cuckoldry rather than for continence. The question does not arise with Congreve, but with Vanbrugh it is important, for it shows that he was not sure enough of his attitude to write comedy, which needs at least clarity of outlook.

Indeed there are passages in *The Provok'd Wife* that might without incongruity have fitted into Lillo's *The London Merchant.* One is even led to think that Vanbrugh's real gift was for domestic drama. Cibber was right when he said 'that his most entertaining scenes seem'd to be no more than his common conversation committed to paper', and his husband and wife quarrel scenes have a realism which gives the whole atmosphere of dull hopelessness of such scenes in real life:

> LADY BRUTE. Do you dine at home to-day, Sir John?
>
> SIR JOHN. Why, do you expect I should tell you what I don't know myself?

LADY BRUTE. I thought there was no harm in asking you.

SIR JOHN. If thinking wrong were an excuse for impertinence, women might be justified in most things they say or do.

LADY BRUTE. I'm sorry I have said anything to displease you.

SIR JOHN. Sorrow for things past is of as little importance to me, as my dining at home or abroad ought to be to you.

It is all a little vulgar as compared with Dryden or Congreve, and the scene ends with a cheap cliché:

LADY BRUTE. What is it disturbs you?

SIR JOHN. A parson.

LADY BRUTE. Why, what has he done to you?

SIR JOHN. He has married me.

But after all, this was his first attempt at that kind of scene, and there is a much better one in *A Journey to London,* which if finished, would have given him a much higher place in our literature than he actually holds.

LADY ARABELLA. Well, look you, my Lord, I can bear it no longer; nothing still but about my faults, my faults! an agreeable subject truly!

LORD LOVERULE. But Madam, if you won't hear of your faults, how is it likely you would ever mend 'em?

LADY A. Why, I don't intend to mend 'em. I can't mend 'em, I have told you so a hundred times; you know I have tried to do it, over and over, and it hurts me so, I can't bear it. Why, don't you know, my Lord, that whenever (just to please you only) I have gone about to wean myself from a fault (one of my faults I mean, that I love dearly) han't it put me so out of humour, you could scarce endure the house with me?

LORD L. Look you, my dear, it is very true that in weaning one's self from—

LADY A. Weaning? why ay, don't you see, that ev'n in weaning poor children from the nurse, it's almost the death of 'em? and don't you see your true religious people, when they go about to wean themselves, and have solemn days of fasting and praying, on purpose to help them, does it not so disorder them, there's no coming near 'em; are they not as cross as the devil? and then they don't do the business neither; for next day their faults are just where they were the day before.

LORD L. But Madam, can you think it a reasonable thing, to be abroad till two a clock in the morning, when you know I go to bed at eleven?

LADY A. And can you think it is a wise thing (to talk your own way now) to go to bed at eleven, when you know I'm likely to disturb you by coming these at three?

Lady Arabella goes on to point out with much spirit that

hers is by far the more civilized way of life, and when Lord Loverule suggests that 'to go to bed early and rise so, was ever esteemed a right practice for all people', she retorts disgustedly that beasts do it. The quarrel becomes increasingly acerb, until:

LADY A. I won't come home till four to-morrow morning.

LORD L. I'll order the doors to be locked at twelve.

LADY A. Then I won't come home till to-morrow night.

LORD L. Then you shall never come home again, Madam.

We can see there is no subtlety or originality in all this, but there is a certain zest, and the fun is heightened when Lady Arabella recounts her version of the quarrel to her friend Clarinda.

CLAR. Good-morrow, Madam; how do you do to-day? you seem to be in a little fluster.

LADY A. My Lord has been in one, and as I am the most complaisant poor creature in the world, I put myself into one too, purely to be suitable company to him.

CLAR. You are prodigious good; but surely it must be mighty agreeable when a man and his wife can give themselves the same turn of conversation.

LADY A. O, the prettiest thing in the world.

CLAR. But yet, tho' I believe there's no life so happy as a married one, in the main; yet I fancy, where two people are so very much together, they must often be in want of something to talk upon.

LADY A. Clarinda, you are the most mistaken in the world; married people have things to talk of, child, that never enter into the imagination of others. Why now, here's my Lord and I, we han't been married above two short years you know, and we have already eight or ten things constantly in bank, that whenever we want company, we can talk of any one of them for two hours together, and the subject never the flatter. It will be as fresh next day, if we have occasion for it, as it was the first day it entertained us.

CLAR. Why, that must be wonderful pretty.

LADY A. O, there's no life like it. This very day now, for example, my lord and I, after a pretty cheerful *tête-à-tête* dinner, sat down by the fire-side, in an idle, indolent, pick-tooth way for a while, as if we had not thought of one another's being in the room. At last, stretching himself, and yawning twice, my dear, says he, you came home very late last night. 'Twas but two in the morning, says I. I was in bed (*yawning*) by eleven, says he. So you are every night, says I. Well, says he, I am amazed how you can sit up so late. How can you be amazed, says I, at a thing that happens so often? Upon which we entered into conversation. And tho' this is a point has entertained us above fifty times already, we always find so many new pretty things to say upon't, that I believe in my soul it will last as long as we live.

Here, as everywhere, his women are admirably cool, and get the better of the altercations. Their reasonable unreasonableness is well pictured, and there is great gusto in their portrayal.

For when all is said, if Vanbrugh cannot interest us much in his characters or in his view, his sense of fun, and his broad humour, which he had in abundance, carry him through. *The Confederacy* is full of good and amusing, if superficial characterization, and we get a slightly whimsical sense of the bustling atmosphere of London life. Moreover, we are all agog in all his plays to see how the situation will turn, and it was by cunning devices Vanbrugh held his audiences. He is in his way good fun, but it is rather like that of a pillow fight on a greasy pole above a pool of water. After his domestic scenes, for which he had a real turn, he is at his best in his pseudo-Elizabethan portrayals; in Sir Tunbelly Clumsey who appears armed and attended at his gates; or in Sir John Brute in his cups, disguised as a parson or a woman according to the pre- or post-Collier version. But his comedies are not all of a piece. They are always robust, in burlesque, common morality, or common sense, but he lacked that 'little twist of brain' which makes the comic writer or the satirist, or the literary artist in any sense. He took the writings of others and made what he could of them; he took life as he found it, and left it there. (pp. 151-61)

> Bonamy Dobrée, "Vanbrugh and Farquhar," in his Restoration Comedy: 1660-1720, *1924. Reprint by Greenwood Press, Publishers, 1981, pp. 151-70.*

René Hague   (essay date 1928)

[*In the following excerpt, Hague discusses the style and intent of Vanbrugh's plays, noting that Vanbrugh was responsible for creating a new type of comedy which is neither didactic nor sentimental.*]

Concerning some of the Restoration dramatists there is an annoying remark of Horace Walpole's: "Etherege, Congreve, Vanbrugh and Cibber, wrote genteel comedy because they lived in the best company." It is annoying not only by reason of the assumption that the manners of "the best company" are the only fit material for genteel comedy but also because it implies that the virtue of the Comedy of Manners lay in its being an accurate portraiture of a certain class of society. It elevates what was merely a necessary condition for the writing of a certain sort of comedy to the position of chief cause of dramatic artistry. It is, nevertheless, an interesting remark, for it may stand for a whole school of criticism, not only of the Restoration drama, but of every sort of literary work. It was at one time a very popular pastime among the learned laboriously to hunt out from the work of a great artist what would be called a picture of the age in which he lived. Perhaps no writer has suffered so much from this type of criticism as has Shakespeare—witness the mass of literature which

is concerned with every aspect of him except the dramatic, and which will find in him never a mirror of the entertainment required by the Elizabethan playgoer, but always an index to his philosophical and moral standards. The greater the artist the greater is the injustice done to him when the critic refuses to consider his work as a piece of literature, and insists on treating it as a social document. From what one can gather of Shakespeare's dramatic theory there is little that can be held to excuse this view. There is, however, this difference between the great Elizabethans and their successors, that the latter were far more conscious of what they wished to do, even if they did not always read their intentions correctly. Thus Vanbrugh will say (in the Prologue to the *Provok'd Wife*) that it is for the dramatist to "copy out the Follies of the Age." If he was pressed into a corner, as by Collier's attack, he would go even further and claim a moral purpose, the inculcation of virtue by the representation of the absurdity of its contrary. This was, of course, a very lame excuse for what he actually did, and what every second-rate writer always has done, that is, to provide just the dramatic recreation which would fill the theatre and cause general satisfaction and good humour. In a sense critical comedy is a sort of social corrective. That was the defence of the dramatists against Puritan attacks, and it was thus that Vanbrugh answered. It was a very unfortunate rejoinder to the savage attack that had singled him out in particular, and it is an indication both of his innocence and of the folly of the line that he took up, that he was quite taken by surprise. His surprise showed that he was not concerned in his work with any moral purpose; while the *Vindication of the Relapse and the Provok'd Wife from Immorality and Prophaness* declared

> If I judge right, what I have done is in general a Discouragement to Vice and Folly; I am sure I intended it and I hope I have performed it. Perhaps I have not gone the common Road, nor observed the strictest Prescriptions;

and again,

> The real Query is, Whether the Way I have varied, be likely to have a good Effect, or a bad one?

To argue in this manner was to accept Collier's premise—that the dramatist consciously takes into consideration the effect of his work as an incentive to good or bad. Vanbrugh was so astounded when the huge uproar arose that he was surprised into admitting that he had a purpose that had never entered his head. It is quite apparent from the way in which he speaks of providing recreation for men who are tired of taxes and their wives that he was really concerned with the production of a good show for the Tired Business Man or his eighteenth-century equivalent. The whole question of the so-called immorality of Vanbrugh and his contemporaries is one of very great interest, as the freedom of their speech and the quality of many of their jokes has sometimes been too glibly taken to indicate a corresponding instability in the moral standards of the day. A recent writer of Shakespearean studies, Mr. Elmer Stoll, has spoken very forcibly of the fallacy of thus arguing from literature to life. It was an argument dragged out by Collier, and one which will probably never be killed.

When Mr. Palmer wrote in his *Comedy of Manners* that "when Congreve is wicked, his wickedness *expresses* the morality of his period. When Vanbrugh is wicked, his wickedness *outrages* the morality of his" he was doing just what Collier did, he was confusing a joke with a sermon, he was taking Vanbrugh seriously. We cannot argue from his plays to his ideas about morality; all that we can do is to appreciate his idea of a joke, and to understand just what sort of amusement was preferred by the average man of the day. For this purpose Vanbrugh is the very man to read. He was so typical, so ordinary, one might say, a man about town, that one may gather more of that nature from him than from a greater satirist, such as Wycherley, or a greater artist, such as Congreve. (pp. 395-96)

A superficial examination of his literary work might lead one to the conclusion that Vanbrugh was possessed of little originality. Of the nine plays (ten, if one includes Cibber's version of the *Journey to London, The Provok'd Husband*) there are only three that are not adapted or translated from the work of another writer. And of these three, one is incomplete (*The Journey to London*) and one (*the Relapse*) was suggested by and written as a sequel to Cibber's *Love's Last Shift*. This leaves only one entire play which was all Vanbrugh's from conception to production, *The Provok'd Wife*. The question of originality is one to which we may return, but the mention of his habit of adapting and translating suggests two observations. In the first place the circumstances in which the *Relapse* was produced are typical of the man and of his work, and to understand them is useful for an appreciation of both. Vanbrugh sees and is amused by a play of Cibber's, in which a wife succeeds in winning back her husband from the delights of the town. Vanbrugh picks up the story, and in six weeks has the answer ready. Of course the husband and wife come back to town, and the reformation is no more lasting than one could expect it to be. The whole thing is done very quickly, almost carelessly. It was no more than an amusing exercise, not worth, in the author's opinion, the labour of excessive care, and first acted only as a convenient way of repaying an obligation to a friend who happened to own a theatre. Such was his entry into dramatic creation, and his work has, in consequence, just those qualities which one would expect from the frame of mind which produced it. Cibber, speaking as an actor, praised Vanbrugh on the ground that his dialogue was so natural and true to life that it was exceptionally easy to learn. His characters said just what an ordinary person in their position would have said. This, of course, is partly the trouble of which we complain. Generally speaking, he had but two manners of writing. Either he wrote down hastily the sort of conversation that was accepted as amusing in the clubs and drawing rooms of the day, or he gave way to frank burlesque. The former has naturally lost much of its savour by now, for it has none of the real poetry with which the wit of, for example, *The Way of the World* is clothed. When he wrote burlesque as in the Sir Tunbelly Clumsey scenes of the *Relapse* he had sufficient native vigour and love of a rather crude joke to make it effective, but hardly sufficient idea of real humour for it to raise that delicious inward amusement which is so much more pleasant than the guffaw. When Sir Tunbelly arms himself with his ridiculous old weapons and comes

out to beat off the man to whom his daughter should be married, one has to make a considerable effort to accept the situation. It is the more difficult as the rest of the play is supposed to be the usual critical comedy, which cannot be written unless the characters conform to the conventions of the society that is being criticised. This mixing of the two styles is another point which is apparent in the adaptations. Vanbrugh seldom followed his original at all closely. Except in the *Mistake* (from Molière's *Le Dépit Amoureux*) in which his changes were slight, he either altered, added, or omitted, or did all three, according to his inclination. When he was successful, he was sufficiently so to merit at all events a good claim to the title of "the perfect translator" which one of his editors has applied to him. Unfortunately he was not often so happy. The only occasion, on which he really succeeded in taking a French play and moulding it into an English equivalent, was when he made Dancourt's *La Maison de Campagne* into *The Country House*. Leigh Hunt says of this: "We know not on what occasion he was induced to translate a farce from the French of Dancourt, not worth the trouble": an unfortunate judgment, for one does not by preference disagree with Leigh Hunt. If you are not amused by its absurdities, you may, of course, dismiss it as a silly farce, not worth the trouble of translation: but it has this merit, that it was not written in quite the usual style of critical comedy (though with a vague basis of satire) and that its very looseness gave Vanbrugh his chance. *The Country House* is as amusing to read as a good farce can be to see, for the plot is carried out to its logical and ridiculous conclusion with a gaiety and disregard for probability that are frivolous or amusing according to one's mood. I think it was wrong of Leigh Hunt not to be amused by the uninvited guest who bounces in and says:

> Treat us without ceremony: good wine and Poultry you have of your own. Wild-Fowl and Fish are brought to your Door. You need not send abroad for anything but a Piece of Butcher's Meat, or so.—Let us have no Extraordinaries.

And this is the infuriated host turned inn-keeper:

> MR. BARNARD. Gentlemen, do you call? Will you please to see a Room, Gentlemen? Here, somebody. Take off the Gentlemen's Boots there!
>
> DORANT. Father! Unkle! What is the meaning of this?
>
> MR. BAR. Here, shew a Room—Or will you please to walk into the Kitchen first, and see what you like for Dinner!
>
> 1 GEN. Make no Preparations, Sir, your own Dinner will suffice.
>
> MR. BAR. Very well, I understand ye; let's see, how many are there of ye, 1, 2, 3, 4; well, Gentlemen, it is but half a crown a piece for your selves, and six pence a head for your servants; your Dinner shall be ready in half an Hour; here, shew the Gentlemen into the *Apollo*.
>
> 2 GEN. What, Sir, does your Father keep an Inn?

Colley Cibber as Lord Foppington in the first production of The Relapse *(1696).*

MR. BAR. The Sword Royal, at your Service, Sir.

In selecting as his theme the story of the man who took a house in the country to save himself expense and was so inundated by visitors that in the end he got rid of them by announcing that his house was now an inn, Vanbrugh chose a task that he was capable of executing. That his talents lay in this direction is shown again by contrast in his version of Boursaulte's *Aesop.* Such elegance as redeemed the dull moralising of the French is altogether lost in the English. Both parts are quite intolerably boring. For the reader, who, if he is ingenious, can "skip" what he wills without losing the thread, it is bad enough. To be forced to witness it on the stage would be too much.

Some time ago Mr. Dobrée wrote of Vanbrugh (in his *Restoration Comedy*) that

> His originality consisted in breathing the spirit of Middleton or Massinger into the works of his French and English contemporaries. He accepted their plays and the conventions of the time but altered, and, it must be confessed, spoiled them. He never saw what the others were at, nor knew what he was doing.

This is that confusion of style which has been mentioned, and it is this ignorance of the direction in which his talents should be employed that lays Vanbrugh, at first reading, open to the charge of lack of originality. That, however,

he did not generally choose to use his powers as they should have been used did not, at times, prevent him from finding his proper level. Leaving aside the translations, and the adaptation of Fletcher's *The Pilgrim,* there are three plays worth considering—***The Relapse, The Provok'd Wife,*** and ***The Journey to London.*** If Vanbrugh is to hold his position in literature it is on these three that his reputation will rest. It should be assured, for—one is glad to say it—these original works are all far superior to anything he wrote which was derived from another author. The circumstances in which ***The Relapse*** was written have already been mentioned. In the very beginning of his career, he did a thing that was evidence of true dramatic power, he took a weak and ill-sketched character, Cibber's Sir Novelty Fashion, elevated him to the peerage and in doing so made him a stronger and more convincing figure. Cibber's Fashion was simply a fool. Vanbrugh's Lord Foppington is more than that. He is a business man who sees that it pays to side with the coxcombs. He is heartily, wilfully, a Fop; a Fop by conviction, and not by mere lack of sense; and he knows how to deal with younger brothers who want to borrow money. It was no easy task, said Virgil, to steal the club from Hercules. Cibber was no Hercules; but to steal the cudgel from the pigmy and make it into a club was a very creditable feat.

The very beginning of ***The Provok'd Wife*** provides an example of a little domain in which Vanbrugh was quite supreme. There is some splendid quarrelling, too, in the

Confederacy, where Clarissa has quite the most exasperating power of teasing that can ever have goaded an angry man to fury. No one can write such good quarrels between husband and wife. He manages to capture the ridiculous silliness of these wrangles, and has the knack of starting them off in the pig-headed contradictory tone of the quarrelsome:

> LADY BRUTE. Do you dine at home to-day, Sir John?
>
> SIR JOHN. Why, do you expect I should tell you, when I don't know myself?
>
> LADY BRUTE. I thought there was no harm in asking you.

In Lady Brute's rejoinder you get all that sense of hopelessness, which, if taken seriously to heart, gives you the dreariness of Strindberg (the *Dance of Death* occurs as an example). Vanbrugh preferred to laugh. There is a swing and riotousness through the whole play, an utter carelessness of everything except dramatic effect that brought down upon his unfortunate and innocent head the most virulent attacks of Collier's powerful gang of purity-mongers. Fineness in the delineation of character was not among his virtues; but he made up for the lack by an ability to draw a really strong and downright picture. When he was working upon another man's play he had no chance to practise this gift of caricature. It is only in the three plays mentioned that he is free to exercise it. You find it, for example, in Sir John Brute, who can hardly speak except in extremes. For example.

> CONSTANT. Fie, fie; you have one of the best Wives in the world, and yet you seem the most uneasie Husband.
>
> SIR JOHN. Best Wives!—the woman's well enough, she has no vice that I know of, but she's a Wife and—damn a wife. If I were married to a Hogshead of Claret, Matrimony would make me hate it.

It is passages such as that which illustrate the absurdity of many of the attacks on the morality of the stage at that period, and many, too, of the excuses that have been put up for it. The whole thing was, to Vanbrugh, simply a huge joke.

That he never lived to finish *The Journey to London* was one of the most unfortunate tricks of fate. His last play, written after he had had to struggle with very many difficulties and disappointments, it is also his most vigorous. It is the one, too, which most indicates his power as the caricaturist. Exaggeration is his weapon. Mr. Dobrée speaks of Wycherley using a bludgeon, Congreve a rapier, while Vanbrugh "gives us many a lively bout at single-sticks." The liveliest comes in *The Journey to London,* between Lord Loverule and his lady. Even better than the quarrel is Lady Arabella's account of it:

> O there's no life like it. This very day, now for example, my Lord and I, after a pretty cheerful *tête-à-tête* dinner, sat down by the fire-side, in an idle, indolent, pick-tooth way for a while, as if we had not thought of one another's being in the room. At last (stretching himself and yawning

twice): "My dear," says he, "you came home very late last night." " 'Twas but two in the morning," says I. "I was in bed (yawning) by eleven," says he. "So you are every night," says I. "Well," says he, "I am amazed, how you can sit up so late." "How can you be amazed," says I, "at a thing that happens so often?" Upon which, we entered into conversation. And though this is a point that has entertained us above fifty times already, we always find so many pretty new things to say upon it, that I believe in my soul it will last as long as we live.

You may find two quite distinct writers in Vanbrugh. There was the man who made jokes that will raise as good a laugh now as they did two hundred years ago and the man who, for want of energy and care, was simply content to plod along the path that had been marked out already by the pioneers of the drama after the Civil War. It is not merely that at times Vanbrugh was more successful than at others, his manner being the same both in his failures and in his successes. It was more than that—an actual difference of kind. You cannot accurately class *The Journey to London* in the same category as *Aesop, The False Friend,* or *The Mistake.* Mr. Palmer wrote that Vanbrugh might have started a new vein of comedy instead of exhausting the old. That he did squeeze almost the last dregs out of the old is indeed a fact; but he did also begin, though only just begin, a new. . . . Vanbrugh pointed the road, and it is a little unfair to him not to give him credit for that; still more unfair is it to blame him as some have blamed him too severely for the death of English Comedy. (pp. 397-402)

René Hague, "Sir John Vanbrugh," in The London Mercury, *Vol. XVIII, No. 106, August, 1928, pp. 395-402.*

Paul Mueschke and Jeannette Fleisher   (essay date 1934)

[*In the following excerpt, Mueschke and Fleisher offer a reevaluation of Vanbrugh's plays, arguing that Vanbrugh's chief contribution to drama is his plays's appeal to emotion and the intellect, while maintaining a Comedy of Manners framework.*]

Vanbrugh's position in the history of drama has never been adequately defined. He and his successor, Farquhar, have suffered more than any other dramatists of their period from the ill effects of biased criticism, which has viewed their work solely in the light of a particular tradition, the Comedy of Manners; and the resulting deformity, caused by the failure of their work to fit the mould, is condemned by the very critics who have produced it. They have recognized that the work of Vanbrugh is no longer typically of the Comedy of Manners genre, but they have neglected to analyze the difference in an individual study, and have contented themselves with regarding as inferior any divergences or deviations from the accepted Comedy of Manners norm. These deviations, moreover, have been taken to point toward sentimental comedy, and Vanbrugh, having been dubbed a "transition" figure, has suffered the penalty of "not belonging." (pp. 848)

[It is necessary] to reconsider the frequent application of the term sentimental to Vanbrugh, and to make the attempt to distinguish clearly between elements of common sense and of emotional falsification. Sentimentalism in comedy is essentially an optimistic falsification of human nature by exalting a standard of impeccable but conventional morality which the audience, moved to tears by the contemplation of virtue in distress, rendered "sensible" through the emotions of pity and admiration, is to emulate. The classic early example of sentimentalism in the heyday of the Comedy of Manners is the concluding act of Colley Cibber's *Love's Last Shift* (1696). Vanbrugh's general attitude was certainly antagonistic to this absurd portrayal of the reformative power of virtue in reclaiming a confirmed rake, and **The Relapse** was his answer to it. But while there is agreement concerning Vanbrugh's adherence in the main to true comedy (the comedy of laughter), those critics, who view the expression of any hearty common sense attitude toward the more serious aspects of life as an intrusion of emotion into the divinely unemotional realm of the Comedy of Manners, apply "sentimental" indiscriminately to Cibber, Steele, and Vanbrugh.

Certain fundamental attitudes of Vanbrugh must be clearly comprehended before the essential distinctions between a common-sense, an idealistic, and a sentimental point of view can be legitimately made. Vanbrugh's attitude toward women, for example, once understood, will afford a clue to the interpretation of many passages which have been the subject of endless debate on their alleged sentimentalism.

As Bernbaum pointed out, the so-called reformation of Worthy in **The Relapse** is immediately followed by a typical Restoration proviso: "How long this influence may last, Heaven knows; but in this moment of my purity, I could on her own terms accept her heart" (v,4). Any man, we feel, may be allowed his "moment of purity." The soliloquy, as a whole, however, is an important indication of the nature of Vanbrugh's attitude toward women:

> WORTHY (SOLUS). Sure there's divinity about her! And sh' as dispensed some portion on't to me. For what but now was the wild flame of love, or (to dissect that specious term) the vile, the gross desires of flesh and blood, is in a moment turned to adoration. The coarser appetite of nature's gone, and 'tis, methinks, the food of angels I require. How long this influence may last, heaven knows; but in this moment of my purity, I could on her own terms accept her heart. Yes, lovely woman! I can accept it. For now 'tis doubly worth my care. Your charms are much increased, since thus adorned. When truth's extorted from us, then we own the robe of virtue is a graceful habit (v,4).

The language, it must be admitted, is more than a little tainted with the emotional extravagance which we associate with sentimentalism, but the code Worthy is enunciating, and to which Vanbrugh himself no doubt subscribed, is a common-sense and not a false idealization of a particular woman. In other words, though the enjoyment of wenching and the seduction of ladies who thus far had retained their reputations was a gentlemanly amusement and a necessary initiation to the state of manhood, yet to the woman who retained her chastity in the face of his ardent attack, the most licentious rake paid tribute. And above this, Vanbrugh was capable of conceiving of an ideal in love (an ideal which his own late and satisfied marriage seems to indicate his having waited for and attained). His most disillusioned rakes, who are more aware of the faults of women than they are of their own, who perceive clearly the rarity of a happy marriage or of a woman capable of making one, can still say of one particular woman, as Vanbrugh did of his wife [in his Letter to Tonson, 18 June 1722, in *The Complete Works of Sir John Vanbrugh*], "She's special good."

To Heartfree's despairing plea for advice, in **The Provok'd Wife:** "Shall I marry—or die a maid?" (v,5), Constant first retorts the usual Restoration formula, but his final judgment is an expression of that idealism which would have been utterly foreign to the nature of a Horner or a Dorimant, but which, handled by Vanbrugh, seems perfectly consonant with the nature of his brand of rake.

> CONST. Why faith, Heartfree, matrimony is like an army going to engage. Love's the forlorn hope, which is soon cut off; the marriage-knot is the main body, which may stand buff a long time; and repentance is the rear-guard, which rarely gives ground as long as the main battle has a being.
>
> HEART. Conclusion then; you advise me to whore on, as you do.
>
> CONST. That's not concluded yet. For tho' marriage be a lottery in which there are a wondrous many blanks; yet there is one inestimable lot, in which the only heaven on earth is written. Would your kind fate but guide your hand to that, tho' I were wrapt in all that luxury itself could clothe me with, I still should envy you.
>
> HEART. And justly too: for to be capable of loving one, doubtless is better than to possess a thousand. But how far that capacity's in me, alas I know not (v,4).

That last sceptical touch is Heartfree's almost intuitive defence against the charges of undue sentimentalism which have been leveled at him.

The most direct description of the ideal mate—temperate, reasonable, sensible, possessing chiefly those virtues the lack of which had been the cause of domestic infelicity as Vanbrugh had observed it—is placed in the mouth of Sir Charles, in **A Journey to London.** He is a man of wide experience with women and with the rest of the world, convinced that most women, including his friend's wife, Lady Arabella, are not worth the expense of a sigh or a sleepless night, and intelligently aware that technical chastity is a vastly over-emphasized commodity, but he too has met the one woman whose sober intelligence and good sense might conceivably make the state of matrimony more than endurable:

> SIR CHARLES (to Lord Loverule) . . . know at least, I have so much of my early folly left, to think, there's yet one woman fit to make a wife of: How far such a one can answer the charms

of a mistress, marry'd men are silent in, . . . for that, I'd take my chance; but could she make a home easy to her partner, by letting him find there a cheerful companion, an agreeable intimate, a useful assistant, a faithful friend, and (in its time, perhaps) a tender mother, such change of life from what I lead seems not unwise to think of (II,1).

Recognizing this basic fact, that Vanbrugh repeatedly visualizes an ideal woman, one may formulate a more reliable criterion for the application or rejection of the term sentimental to those passages which relate to this conception. Tom Fashion, for example, has been accused of sentimentalism for enunciating what we have come to recognize as a fairly sound observation: "I think no woman is worth money that will take money," (**Relapse,** III,1), upon which the following conversation ensues between himself and Lord Foppington:

> FASHION. Why, is it possible you can value a woman that's to be bought?
>
> LORD FOP. Prithee, why not as well as a padnag?
>
> FASHION. Because a woman has a heart to dispose of; a horse has none (III,1).

When one accepts the fact that Vanbrugh takes his women more seriously than Congreve, for all the wit with which he endowed Millamant, took her; that such women as Lady Brute possess intelligence, common sense, and emotion; that Vanbrugh, though painting realistically the follies and foibles of most women, frequently conceives of one ideal woman—why, then, should we doubt that Tom is speaking sincerely, and Vanbrugh through him, in asserting that a "woman has a heart to dispose of?" So long as there is no falsity in the characterization of the person speaking, and the sentiment expressed is not ridiculously ennobled beyond human approach, but is instead recognizably legitimate, there can be no charge of sentimentalism. It is a grave mistake to set up as a norm a flippantly witty attitude toward life and to condemn as sentimental anything which deviates from it. Vanbrugh's atmosphere is admittedly different from Congreve's. He did not set out to present sex-antagonism at its wittiest and in the "driest" light, removed from the emotion which conceivably accompanied sex in life. He permitted his heroes to use the word "heart" without apology because they were beginning to think in different terms from those of Horner. This is different from the Comedy of Manners, as Palmer defines it, but that it is necessarily inferior does not follow. Vanbrugh was not falsifying the picture; both Tom and Lord Foppington are thoroughly in character. Though Tom is capable of conceiving a woman's possessing a heart, Foppington is as typically Restoration in outlook:

> LORD FOP. Look you, Tam, of all things that belang to a woman, I have an aversion to her heart. Far when once a woman has given you her heart, you can never get rid of the rest of her bady (III,1).

Again, Tom experiences a "qualm of conscience" in bringing himself to accede to Coupler's proposed method of tricking his brother. That he has a conscience at all distinguishes him immediately from the ordinary Restoration rake. Lory's attitude is far the more usual of the two, and, if Palmer's criterion be right—and the impersonal, unfeeling spirit of the Comedy of Manners is the perfection of comedy—then Lory is superior dramatically to Tom Fashion. In his way, Lory is an exceedingly effective creation, a worthy addition to the long line of clever Restoration servants, who can pimp for their masters and dress them with equal facility, but Tom's divergences from the Restoration type do not lessen the effectiveness of his character portrayal. A conscience need not damn a man— particularly when it is so easily cast overboard to save the plot! The intrusion of feeling, common sense, and human compassion do not destroy comic effectiveness. An appeal to the emotions as well as to the intellect of an audience is not destructive of the comic spirit. The success of the achievement depends on the consistency and degree of effectiveness of the presentation. (pp. 850-54)

Vanbrugh's purpose in comedy, despite his assertion to the contrary in the **Vindication,** was no doubt primarily to entertain; in his first two plays at least, he was in no sense a moral crusader, upholding either the conventional Christian code or championing a radical system of new social values; but his attitude toward the life of his time, reflected in his plays, nevertheless presents a distinct difference from that of Etherege and Congreve, on the one hand, or Cibber and Steele, on the other. In Vanbrugh, and later in Farquhar, we begin to find a new approach toward comedy. The completely impersonal aloofness of the typical Comedy of Manners school, which exploits every situation to the utmost solely for its comic possibilities, has been transmuted by a generous-hearted personality into a more rational and sympathetic treatment of certain aspects of the life which Vanbrugh knew. In particular, Vanbrugh's plays reveal a persistent interest in two social problems with which his intimate knowledge of upper-class society must have rendered him thoroughly familiar: the predicament of the younger brother, due to the operation of the law of primogeniture, and the problem of marital incompatibility, which seems to have had especial fascination for him. Vanbrugh's presentation is sympathetic, rational, and sustained, rather than indifferent, impersonal, and incidental, as is the case with the typical dramatists of the Comedy of Manners. (p. 855)

In *Love's Last Shift,* the brothers are allies; they are the conventional wooers of two cousins, aiding and abetting each other in their design (a typical Restoration situation in plot, if not in treatment throughout). In **The Relapse,** the situation has become quite different. The brothers are rivals for the same girl; the younger tricks and outwits the elder, after having made every effort to win his help by reasonable means, to no avail; and the final plot victory is awarded the younger. Vanbrugh has created in Foppington just the sort of person who is incapable of sympathy with any one but himself or of appreciating the predicament of his younger brother—a character the antithesis of the Elder Worthy. Vanbrugh has not attempted, however, to present Tom in contrast to Foppington as an epitome of virtue, to win for him the shallow sympathy of sentimentalism, but has kept him as consistently realistic as Foppington himself, depicting him as a young spend-thrift rake-hell, product of his education and environment, which have bred him up with expensive appetites and then made it impossible for him to satisfy them, while his elder brother, even more improvident and extravagant in his methods of spending money, is free to squander as much as he pleases, because he was thrust forth into the world first. In other words, Vanbrugh is not engaged in making a case for the abolition of primogeniture, but his critical presentation of a familiar situation is colored by a decidedly sympathetic appreciation of the predicament of the younger brother. The superior dramatic effectiveness of the portrait of Lord Foppington does not vitiate this interpretation of the dramatist's purpose. Unquestionably, Vanbrugh, though delighting in the presentation of his superb affectation, meant nevertheless to show the insurmountable difficulty which just such a character offered to the needs of a younger brother, however legitimate they might be. It is this sympathy with the younger brother rather than with Foppington as a *person* which makes Vanbrugh award the bride and her fortune to young Fashion. His reply to Collier that he didn't think Hoyden was much of a prize is evasive—and quite all right for Collier—but we are justified in concluding that there was forethought in the award. One must not forget that Hoyden's money went with her—sufficient reward in itself to cap the success of a younger brother's fortune-hunt. Vanbrugh's significant changes in the Cibber plot support the conviction that his perception of social values was different from that of his predecessors, and that his treatment of the younger brother is a realistic, critical portrayal of the problem occasioned by the law of primogeniture. He has achieved complete success in his presentation without sacrificing comic effect—for comic effect is not destroyed by giving the audience an occasional more serious thought than, as Bernard Shaw puts it, which man is to get which woman at the end of five acts.

Even more important in Vanbrugh is the persistent commentary running through all three plays on the theme of marital incompatibility, on which his dramatic inventiveness rings all the variations which keen observation, a good sense of humor, and genuine human sympathy, can produce. The individuality of Vanbrugh's treatment of the marital relationship has been overlooked or misunderstood largely because of a failure to distinguish clearly between four distinct attitudes toward marriage in the literature of the period: the romantic, sentimental, common sense, and cynical Restoration points of view. The romantic idealizes pre-marital love and regards marriage itself as the most exalted state of happiness. The sentimentalist holds basically the same attitude as the romanticist, but falsification is substituted for genuineness of emotion through exaggeration. The distinction is chiefly one of degree. The hedonistic cynicism typical of the Comedy of Manners does sometimes include in its general philosophy of disdain incidental criticism of the marital relationship, but its approach is primarily comic exploitation of the disaffected couple. The common sense approach is primarily rational and critical; the possibilities of attaining romantic love are not denied, but the limitations of husband and wife in an actual marital relationship are clearly recognized.

> If indeed *The Relapse* is a play concerned with the frality of man, whose hold upon happiness and virtue is tenuous to the extreme, then it would appear that Vanbrugh conceived this play in a spirit more akin to that of tragedy than of comedy.
>
> —*Lincoln B. Faller*

The latter attitude, which colors and determines the nature of Vanbrugh's presentation of the problem, marks a great advance over the treatment which had prevailed in the comedies of Etherege, Wycherley, Congreve, and the lesser Restoration dramatists. [There, the] characters concerned are invariably minor and unintelligent, and the causes of the quarrel are usually external. In Vanbrugh, the treatment of marital incompatibility is basic; plot and character hinge upon it; and incompatibility is analyzed as the clash of personal temperaments. The difference is one of spirit and tone, as well as of the degree of interest devoted to it. (pp. 863-65)

The causes of incompatibility are dwelt on at length; the contributing faults of both husband and wife are clearly presented, particularly in *The Provok'd Wife,* where the problem is most fully handled, but the dramatist's and the audience's sympathies are enlisted in behalf of the more reasonable spouse, by the use of exaggeration and the deliberate caricature of the less reasonable, especially in the case of Sir John Brute.

For his presentation of marital incompatibility, Vanbrugh employed certain character types which recur with slight variations in *The Relapse* and *The Provok'd Wife,* in both of which it is the wife who has the more reasonable grievance; the situation is reversed in *A Journey to London,* in which it is the husband whose sensible mode of living is outraged by his wife's extravagant intemperance, and the character types consequently vary somewhat more greatly. The recurrent character types in *The Relapse* and *The Provok'd Wife* are: (1) a woman of considerable intelligence, who questions her husband's right to neglect her for another, or for boorish amusements, and who would like to seek either revenge or satisfaction with a gallant, but is prevented from so doing by a recollection of her virtue (e.g., Amanda); (2) a gallant, who is not a typical rake, but a gentleman of charm and "respectability," the sort of man who would be capable of attracting a fairly intelligent and not too flippant woman, who is looking for companionship as well as physical satisfaction (e.g., Constant); (3) a husband, who has either philandered inexcusably—in his wife's eyes—(e.g., Loveless), or who is wholly out of sympathy with her in everything which constitutes daily living (e.g., Sir John Brute); and (4) a confidante of the wife, who is the willing recipient of her tale of woe (e.g., Belinda). In *A Journey to London,* the aggrieved husband is substituted for the wife, the would-be seducer is eliminated, and the confidantes are doubled.

Vanbrugh, before beginning *The Relapse,* had already practically completed *The Provok'd Wife,* a sustained and rational treatment of marital incompatibility, which exploits to the full both the comic and the critical aspects of his theme. In the former play, however, the first to be presented on the stage, the treatment of the problem is less competently handled; the issues involved are less securely grasped; and Vanbrugh's dramatic limitations become more obvious in his attempt to reconcile a serious treatment of the marital problem with a Comedy of Manners framework plot.

It has been recognized that Vanbrugh revolted against Cibber's absurd presentation in *Love's Last Shift* of Loveless' sentimental reformation, accomplished through the contemplation of prostrate virtue in the form of a kneeling feminine apotheosis of chastity, and that he had written *The Relapse* in a spirit of protest against its falsity, exerting his ingenuity in raising the final curtain once more to peep at reunited wedded bliss in the next act, and in constructing a conclusion in harmony with the logic and truth of human nature. Vanbrugh's version of the story of Loveless and Amanda avoids the false perspective through which Cibber's blind optimism viewed life; rather Vanbrugh regards the problem from a realistic, common sense point of view, which neither wholly excludes feeling nor exalts the falsity of high-sounding sentiment which passes current for genuine emotion; but his limitations as a dramatist are unfortunately responsible for the blurred ineffectiveness of his handling of the theme at certain vital points in its development. (pp. 866-67)

By the time Vanbrugh came to the stage, the range of situation possibilities in sexual intrigue must have been well-nigh exhausted. He might have gone on in the same tradition, focussing his attention primarily on the courtship—chase stage of the sex game, but his interests seem to have been somewhat broader and more varied. He was, no doubt, as capable of enjoying a wench with soldierly unconcern as the coolest rake of them all, but he brought to his work a conception of values which set him apart from Etherege or Congreve—a set of values, however, which is not radical in the sense that it reveals far-reaching vision or deliberate planning on the part of Vanbrugh. What it does reveal is that Vanbrugh had parted company with the Comedy of Manners tradition to the extent of approaching rationally and more critically those social problems, the perception of which had aroused his thoughtful sympathy. He wrote plays not primarily as vehicles of instruction, but with the intent of pleasing. Where, however, a problem affected the lives of the classes he knew—the position of the younger brother in society, for example—Vanbrugh was capable of being touched by his predicament as his generous nature was capable of being touched by the needs of a friend. He envisioned no drastic changes in the established social system; he was a good monarchist, a loyal Whig, a Church of Englander, and a respectable gentleman; but he was also humane, generous, and capable of a sympathetic comprehension of the difficulties of others.

In the light of this analysis, Vanbrugh's relation to the comedy which precedes him may be more accurately defined. His divergences from Restoration comedy embrace the spirit of his treatment, the substance of his material, and the nature of his dramatic devices. The familiar elements of the Comedy of Manners which had held the stage for the past forty years, are no longer preëminent. First, returning to the method of Etherege, he tends to minimize the element of sheer plot intrigue. Notably more simple than those of Congreve or Wycherley, his plots cease to derive their comic interest so much from intricate complications as do those of his predecessors. He is content with simple situations, humanized by his interest in a new code of social values. Second, he discards the habitual contrast of true and false wits, and with it disappears also, unfortunately, much of the epigrammatic brilliance of Congreve and Etherege. The breakdown of the conventional contrasting juxtaposition of true and false wits results in a significant modification of the fop. Lord Foppington is intellectually the superior of all his predecessors, endowed with a superb philosophy of imperturbable nonchalance, supported by never-failing wit in repartee. A further modification in his character is the result of his participation in the younger brother plot—a situation from which Vanbrugh derives a type of comedy hitherto unexploited on the Restoration stage. Third, his emphasis no longer falls on sexantagonism between a rake and a witty woman of equal intelligence, indulging in sharp repartee for its own sake, in which some of the finest effects of the Comedy of Manners had been achieved. His witty dialogues occur more frequently between his heroine and her confidante (e.g., Lady Brute and Belinda) or between two men (e.g., Constant and Heartfree), but even here the nature of the conversations is notably modified by the interest of the character in the social problem on which the plot hinges. The change in the character of the rake is obvious and significant, though, as has been noted in the case of Worthy, not always happy or dramatically successful.

Vanbrugh has relegated these well-worn devices to the background or eliminated them entirely, and the expression of typical Restoration cynicism has been consigned to the type of character for whom the dramatist has obviously no sympathy. The comic method which he developed in their stead, essentially different in quality from that which had preceded, constitutes his positive contribution to the drama. His plays, no longer the vehicle solely for superficial ridicule, derive their distinctive comic vitality from a central corpus of persistent ideas, intimately related to the social life of his time, which determines not only his choice of characters but also the extent and nature of his emphasis on particular aspects of their individuality. Hence, it to this central interest of Vanbrugh that both his strength of originality and his most glaring weaknesses are traceable. (pp. 886-87)

The real nature of Vanbrugh's originality has been overlooked or misapprehended chiefly for two reasons: first, he has been judged exclusively by the standards of the Comedy of Manners; and second, he failed to establish a direct living tradition in English comedy. He and Farquhar stand, as it were, between two dramatic antitheses. Vanbrugh's work in some respects leaves much to be desired; where the comic spirit of Restoration comedy has been obscured by propagandism, as in the Loverule plot in *A Journey to London,* he is distinctly inferior to the earlier tradition; but, for the most part, his divergences are a happy contribution to what might have developed into a new type of critical comedy in English drama, had not the forces of sentimentalism prevailed. His perception of social values in situations which had formerly been exploited solely for their comic possibilities resulted in a more human approach toward the social life of his time. His comedy still sparkles with the old wit, but his people and his situations are closer to life. Farquhar, the exponent of natural comedy, is his only successor, and it is to be deplored that their departure in the direction of a richer comedy of life and of laughter developed no tradition which could flourish against the oncoming avalanche of the comedy of tears. (p. 889)

> *Paul Mueschke and Jeannette Fleisher, "A Re-evaluation of Vanbrugh," in* PMLA, *Vol. XLIX, 1934, pp. 848-89.*

Louis Kronenberger   (essay date 1952)

[*A drama critic for* Time *magazine from 1938 to 1961, Kronenberger was a distinguished historian, literary critic, and author highly regarded for his expertise in eighteenth-century English history and literature. Among his best known writings are the nonfiction accounts* Kings and Desperate Men: Life in Eighteenth-Century England *(1942), which examines British culture of that century, and* Marlborough's Duchess: A Study in Worldliness *(1969), a biography of the wife of the first Duke of Marlborough. His critical works include* The Thread of Laughter: Chapters on English Stage Comedy from Jonson to Maugham *(1952) and* The Republic of Letters *(1955). In the following excerpt, Kronenberger claims that* The Relapse, The Provok'd Wife, *and* The Confederacy *are not true Restoration comedies, noting that in* The Relapse, *especially, the unresolved moral dilemma of the play detracts both from the play's significance and its sense of fun.*]

At first sight, **The Relapse** is genuine Restoration comedy. And yet something has been left out; something that on Vanbrugh's part shows not incompetence but incompatibility. In the most characteristic Restoration comedy there is a kind of artifice that controls the entire action. (p. 154)

In **The Relapse,** however, the artifice that ought to condition the whole ensuing activity never quite does so. We miss a certain tone, a certain traditional voice-level: Vanbrugh, like his Amanda, *wants* to take the worldly fashionable view, to treat love and sex as a game, to give a hard enameled surface to life. But he rarely does so. Or rather, he never does for long; he can contrive but not sustain the sort of hard frivolity he is after. He lacks the right mixture of urbanity and brutality; he cannot, as it were, delicately crisp and starch his characters with vice. Indeed, he cannot treat the situation of Amanda and Berinthia as either a confederacy of women against men or an alliance of reciprocal deception. Amanda not only remains virtuous, she becomes in time almost Victorian, first resisting the tempter's advances, then receiving his remorseful idolatry. (Nor is this because she is inherited from Cibber.) Berinthia, on the other hand, not only sins with Loveless, but

proves utterly treacherous to Amanda, and serves as procuress for Worthy. She becomes one of the basest of Restoration characters—far *too* base for the situation Vanbrugh has contrived. The two women are set against each other like characters in sentimental drama, but the story they are part of is not sufficiently weighted for such a contrast. The whole thing is personal in tone where it should be social, and ends by substituting staginess for artifice. The whole thing misses, goes flat, turns a little dull, and, in Berinthia's case, offers a really hateful character whom we never care enough about to hate.

It is in the other plot, involving Tom Fashion, Lord Foppington, and Miss Hoyden, that Vanbrugh comes to life. Here, where the action is so largely farcical, the treatment can be brisk. Here we are in a world of mischievousness rather than malice; here deception has more the air of a prank than of a betrayal, here are no tender feelings to consider nor highbred sensibilities to display: the characters bear not names but labels—Miss Hoyden, Lord Foppington, Sir Tunbelly Clumsy. Only Tom Fashion, the younger brother who decides to make his fortune by courting Miss Hoyden in Lord Foppington's name, could fit equally well into either plot. He could remain a rakish man-about-town, part of Amanda's set, or go forth, as he does, an impostor into the country.

His imposture is high-spirited and amusing. Except for a few shots at Foppington's expense, the fun in **The Relapse** is reasonably primitive, with a smack of the eighteenth century about it—of that side of the eighteenth century that tends to be forgotten. No century could show more elegance and finesse, but none either, had a beerier or rowdier sense of fun. (pp. 155-56)

We are suddenly thrust into an eighteenth-century world of foxhunts and draughty country houses, where men may be brutes but aren't villains, and ways will be gross but never venomous. There is a quite new sort of bustle and joviality. And yet there is something a little wrong about the way in which **The Relapse** winds up: in proper farce, when a Tom Fashion bests a Lord Foppington, when brother outwits brother, there must be a real contrast of character or a sufficient rough justice or wild luck to the outcome to make it all go down. Here there is too much the suggestion of a swindle; here, though Foppington has given Tom cause enough—by refusing him help—to attempt his prank, he hasn't given him quite cause enough to succeed at it. We feel a moral scruple, as we do more strongly about Berinthia's baseness. It may be that Tom seems the worse swindler and Berinthia the greater villainess just because the tone is otherwise so good-natured; but whatever the reason, we do feel a little jarred. Even though he attacked the play chiefly on other grounds, we can understand how Jeremy Collier should have chosen **The Relapse** as a chief target. In one way, it is among the least offensive or, at any rate least heartless, of Restoration comedies; but for just that reason, where it does seem immoral it seems glaringly so. And if we are to be blunt, we must find something wonderful in Collier's—and virtually every one else's—silence concerning the quite pointless homosexual fooling between Tom and Old Coupler. It, too, mars the tone of the play. Two traditions, the one dying, the one coming to birth, meet here but fail to harmonize; even in the matter of whether to use prose or a kind of verse, Vanbrugh still shilly-shallies. But for all that, *The Relapse* is a decidedly promising first play.

Perhaps the chief superiority of Vanbrugh's second play, *The Provoked Wife,* is that, unlike *The Relapse,* it is just one play rather than two. It is better ordered, indeed very compactly ordered. The situation is made clear at once, with an opening soliloquy by the husband, a passage-at-arms between husband and wife, and a soliloquy by the wife. . . . (pp. 158-59)

The story follows out of prevailing Restoration attitudes, but is actually given a more farcical and at the same time more realistic turn. The realism—which is merely relative—lies in the characters' reasonably "normal" behavior. We feel that Constant is really in love with Lady Brute, that he is also a typical young man-about-town, neither heartless nor sentimental. We feel that Lady Brute is a slightly—but only slightly—better-than-average young society woman, who got a worse husband than might be expected by marrying for position, but who did marry for position. And so on. (p. 160)

The situations, on the other hand, the general swing and movement, smack of the farcical. One reason for this is their having a typical Vanbrugh breeziness; but another is that the situations matter more than the characters in them; we care more about the plot for the fun it brings than for the light it sheds. From inhabiting London during a particular age, Vanbrugh wrote a certain kind of play, just as he must have worn a certain kind of coat. If he was not very original, there was yet much that he could report at first hand, much that came out of personal experience or observation. And yet if one were pinned down to say what point of view Vanbrugh expresses here, in terms of Restoration life or of all life, one would find it very hard to answer. Perhaps the nearest to a sound answer is to say that Vanbrugh wrote from the point of view of the *playwright*—with the desire, that is, to be more than anything else, theatrically effective. His is simply the psychology of the entertainer; even where we feel the touch of the satirist, it is not the nature of his target that seems to interest Vanbrugh, but only the accuracy of his marksmanship. This raises, though it does not quite resolve, the question whether Vanbrugh was a hack. We should need to know whether he was, at bottom, stage-minded or audience-minded, whether what interested him was the stage itself, or the box office.

Either way, he has a good enough plot in *The Provoked Wife,* but little by way of theme—only a moral dilemma as to whether, because her boorish husband *is* her husband, Lady Brute shall remain faithful to him. Moreover, this dilemma is never really resolved. The story fades out with nothing really resolved, with Sir John and Lady Brute hardly even reunited; they are merely still married and in the same room. But intentional or not, that perhaps is the most lifelike touch of all; we are back, as we might be in life, exactly where we began, with nothing accomplished. But in a play where nothing of the sort has been accomplished, we may wonder how much has been essayed.

The moral dilemma not only fails to add significance: it actually takes off from the fun. Once Lady Brute begins to have scruples, once she becomes a conscious judge of her own behavior, she forces us to become conscious judges of it too. She intrudes a sense of guilt and a sense of honor into a situation where, if they are not to carry real weight, they are better off ignored. (pp. 160-61)

It is worth noticing that no one sins in the play—and that we have reached the stage where it is referred to as sinning. And neither here nor in *The Relapse* is any husband cuckolded; nor are the gallants either so heartless or so rakish as they once were. The language, to be sure, is still so free that one might easily infer that the morals still are loose, but free language is from this time on pretty much a thing in itself, which persists throughout most of the ever more moral eighteenth century. (pp. 161-62)

The play contains its snatches of agreeable enough wit. "You know," says Belinda to Lady Brute, "we must return good for evil." "Oh," Lady Brute replies "that may be a mistake in the translation." But Vanbrugh is seldom witty for long: indeed the instinctive playwright in him is better at ideas than is the writer of comedy at execution. When Lady Brute and Belinda agree to be frank with each other about what they want and like, the scene (Act III, Scene 3) is ready-made for the stage. No doubt it rattles along, but consider what Congreve or Etherege would have made of it. Consider, again, Lady Fanciful. Mr. [Bonamy] Dobrée compares her—for her affectations—to Melantha in Dryden's *Marriage à la Mode;* but the women are otherwise so unlike that the comparison seems pointless. It seems more to the point to compare her—for her conceit over her non-existent charms—with Lady Pliant in Congreve's *Double Dealer.* Here, at any rate, we need not speculate on how Congreve would have gone at such a woman; we know how he did. Congreve's is a special talent, but in Restoration comedy generally we find a more precise treatment of character, a more specific delineation of manners than we do here. Everything seems a little brisker now, and a little more blurred.

All this does not leave us with a great deal to say about Vanbrugh's *The Confederacy,* though it seems to me Vanbrugh's best piece of work. Despite how much of it is borrowed, *The Confederacy* reflects credit on Vanbrugh the playwright. It makes plain, once more, in how great a degree he just *was* a playwright rather than a social critic or student of manners. *The Confederacy* strikes me as easier to read—and perhaps easier to act—than any other of Vanbrugh's plays. It is well formed and well knit, having a plot that happily embraces two separate intrigues and that concisely involves *all* the characters. We are very far from the plotting of *The Relapse,* with its two intrigues that never really meet at all.

Also the play is as satisfactory in one sense as it may be limited in another. In terms of sexual morality, we have moved still farther away from the Restoration. Dick Amlet, posing as Colonel Sprightly, ventures on nothing even faintly illicit in his courtship of young Corinna: he is all scamp and no rake. And though Gripe and Moneytrap are infatuated with each other's wives and doubtless would sin if they could, the wives themselves have no thoughts of sinning with them or with any one else. Even Brass, posing as Dick Amlet's valet, has no sexual designs on Clarissa Gripe's pert maid, Flippanta. We are out of the tunnel at last: this is a play in which sex plays only the most perfunctory part. And what is so satisfactory about *The Confederacy* is that sex has simply been put to one side—it has not been discarded in favor of sentiment. Hearts that used to be made of stone are not turning into hearts made of pudding; we have not exchanged the betrayed husband for the repentant rake. And Vanbrugh has come far closer than in his earlier plays to creating a classic comedy pattern. Here he was helped, of course, by the particular French play he was borrowing from, a play that regards deception as a conscious *game*. The two wives, with the help of Brass and Flippanta, deliberately form a conspiracy, and one that is based on a good comic point: namely, that men will give to other men's wives what they refuse to give to their own. We are back again in a world of fraud, where the young gallant is an impostor, with designs on rather the young lady's fortune than her virtue, and where wives seek to make, not cuckolds of their husbands, but benefactors of their swains. (pp. 162-63)

[William] Hazlitt complains of a "heartless want in principle" in the play, and of its showing "no anger or severity against vice." He is, strictly speaking, right, for Vanbrugh is quite as easy-going about morality here as he is about everything else. He lets the wives bilk each other's husbands; he lets Dick Amlet turn impostor with impunity. Nor are the ladies otherwise very charming; nor is Amlet very much of a friend, or even a son. But as no one is particularly virtuous, so no one is particularly vile, while those who are wronged are themselves up to mischief. There is nothing comparable here to Tom Fashion's successful cheat or Berinthia's genuine baseness in *The Relapse,* and the whole thing is saved by being treated as a game. "We have been more lucky than wise," says Flippanta at the end—a phrase that doesn't so much sum up this comedy as it does all light comedy, for the characters cannot be wise, or they will never get into trouble, and they must be lucky, or they will never get out. Hazlitt's objection seems dubious in terms of the play, but rather valid in terms of the playwright. Through caring very little about morals, Vanbrugh fails to calculate certain of his effects; that is why a Berinthia emerges as so much worse than she was probably meant to be. In his rather flabby good-naturedness, Vanbrugh stands at the opposite pole from a moral extremist like Wycherley. (pp. 163-64)

> *Louis Kronenberger, "Cibber and Vanbrugh: 'Love's Last Shift', 'The Relapse', 'The Provoked Wife', 'The Confederacy',' in his* The Thread of Laughter: Chapters on English Stage Comedy from Jonson to Maugham, *Alfred A. Knopf, 1952, pp. 147-65.*

Eugene Waith   (essay date 1968)

[*Waith is an English scholar and critic who has established himself as an authority on Restoration drama through his compiling and editing of* Restoration Drama *(1968),* Ideas of Greatness: Heroic Drama in

England *(1971), and* French and English Drama of the Seventeenth Century *(1972). In the following excerpt, he discusses* The Relapse, *criticizing certain aspects of the play's structure, but concluding that Vanbrugh's comic scenes are superior to Cibber's in* Love's Last Shift.]

The play which inspired *The Relapse* was *Love's Last Shift* by Colley Cibber, actor, playwright, and ultimately Poet Laureate, who sufficiently aroused the scorn of Alexander Pope to become the chief satirical butt of the last version of *The Dunciad.* But despite Cibber's appearance there as the king of dullness, *Love's Last Shift* is not a dull play. The fop, Sir Novelty Fashion, is one of the most entertaining representatives of his tribe, and Cibber himself acted the part with great acclaim. The more serious plot, in which Loveless is seduced by the wife he deserted ten years earlier, has won a niche in literary history as a perfect indication of the new morality which was overtaking comedy in the last decade of the century. There are sound reasons for looking at the play in this light. Cibber boasts in his epilogue that "There's not one cuckold made in all this play," while also pointing out that, to please the men, he is "lewd for above four acts." One is apt to be repelled by the strategy of presenting a bawdy situation which is nevertheless technically quite moral, and *The Relapse* may seem like a healthy return to the greater license of the earlier comedies.

It is dangerous, however, to pigeonhole the two plays in this way. *Love's Last Shift* is by no means ruined by its moral ending, though it clearly anticipates the increasingly didactic element in sentimental comedy. *The Relapse,* while making fun of the moral ending, by no means rejects the entire play; it is only in part a return to the earlier comic mode.

In one important respect Vanbrugh was following directly in Cibber's footsteps, for, as the alternative title proclaims, he carried on the satire of Sir Novelty Fashion, now Lord Foppington, and Cibber again acted the part. It is fairer to see Vanbrugh as building on Cibber's play than as seriously attacking it or trying to turn back the clock. While both plays are typical of the last decade of the century, the most significant difference between them is one of quality: *The Relapse* is far better.

According to Vanbrugh's prologue, he wrote his sequel in six weeks. Brilliant as it is, it has faults of style and structure which may be attributable to this remarkable speed. Three scenes are written in a strange combination of verse and prose. . . . In all of them Vanbrugh probably sought the emotional intensification which greater metrical regularity is capable of producing. It was, of course, common from Elizabethan times onward to use verse in such scenes, leaving prose for scenes of lower emotional key. Vanbrugh's alternations of verse and prose within a single scene, however, seem more accidental than planned. No editor has been able to be sure which lines were intended as verse, and some of the passages where the metrical pattern breaks down are probably rough drafts which were never corrected. The resulting style of these scenes, in any case, is an interesting example of the sort of flexibility which in our time T. S. Eliot has deliberately cultivated in some of his plays, where blank verse is at times indistinguishable from prose, at other times more insistently rhythmical.

The structure of the play is lumpy. Not only are the scenes which develop each of the two plots bunched together in such a way that one almost forgets one plot for considerable periods of time, but also the scenes in which Lord Foppington appears tend to break down into independent skits: Lord Foppington on books, Lord Foppington's day, Lord Foppington and the doctor. These scenes are excellent fun, but all are demonstrations of his "humor"—separate bits which do little to advance the plot.

In spite of these strictures, *The Relapse* is continuously appealing because it does abound in good comic scenes. In addition to the Lord Foppington scenes, excellent vehicles for an actor, there are fine scenes of clowning at the country house of Sir Tunbelly Clumsey, where good-natured oafishness is contrasted to the clever refinement of the city. Finally, there is the splendid scene in which Berinthia is carried off crying "very softly" (so as not to arouse her maid): "Help, help, I'm ravished, ruined, undone."

The comic perspective in these scenes is a mixture of the "hard view" and the "soft view" of human nature. . . . If heartless hedonism is represented in the rather attractive guise of witty banter in some of Young Fashion's scenes and in the libertine dialogue of Berinthia and Worthy (III,2), the latter's conversion by Amanda strikes a very moral note, and suggests that despite the relapse of Loveless, it is, after all, possible to appeal to a rake's better nature. Similarly, if in the early scenes Lord Foppington is made despicable for his triviality and selfishness, he is shown to have some semblance of human dignity in the midst of his comic misfortunes at Sir Tunbelly's house. Both the conversion of Worthy and the partial rehabilitation of Lord Foppington take us into a world quite distinct from that of *The Man of Mode*. Etherege's Sir Fopling may show to advantage in the latter part of the play when his good nature is compared to the malice of Dorimant, but to the end he remains a fluttery fool, worrying about the angle of his periwig at his last appearance, and informing his friends that he is conserving his vigor so that he can make his court "to the whole sex in a ballet." One cannot imagine his speaking the lines of Lord Foppington's penultimate speech: "Now, for my part, I think the wisest thing a man can do with an aching heart is to put on a serene countenance, for a philosophical air is the most becoming thing in the world to the face of a person of quality; I will therefore bear my disgrace like a great man and let the people see I am above an affront."

As for Dorimant, no doubt he is committed to marriage with Harriet and, worse yet, a visit to the country, but he gives no indication of feeling, like Worthy, that "the coarser appetite of nature's gone." His last words to Belinda suggest the contrary.

The Relapse . . . seems to have no one comic view of the world. Libertinism and reform are left to interact endlessly as in a reversible chemical equation, when the whole problem of Loveless's relapse is put aside to give final emphasis to the success of Young Fashion's trick on his brother. In the light-hearted masque which precedes the denouement, Cupid and Hymen agree that change is what everyone wants, whether from bondage to freedom or freedom to bondage. Perhaps, after all, this is Vanbrugh's comic view. (pp. 398-401)

Eugene Waith, in an introduction to Restoration Drama, *edited by Eugene Waith, Bantam Books, 1968, pp. 398-401.*

Perry on Vanbrugh's dramatic innovation:

Country folk seem to have had an especial attraction for our author, for even in his first play, *The Relapse,* some of the best scenes are those laid at the country-house of Sir Tunbelly Clumsey—the first time in an important Restoration Comedy that the painter of contemporary manners had been willing to turn his attention from the foibles of fashionable society and fasten it upon the life of the provinces. Vanbrugh himself did not perhaps realize the far-reaching significance of his innovation. As the range of comedy widened and its narrow boundaries were pushed back, it became harder and harder for the dramatist to maintain the clarity of vision and the fixity of purpose with which he had been wont to regard his material. Vanbrugh is, no doubt, more human in his outlook than Congreve, his atmosphere is fresher and more natural, but by the same token his feelings sometimes interfere with the comic sense of detachment necessary to his art. He has probed beneath the surface of things, as Congreve never did, but in so doing he has forfeited many an honest laugh for the sake of a kindly and sympathetic, and sometimes even an emotionally false, touch of nature.

Henry Ten Eyck Perry, in his The Comic Spirit in Restoration Drama, *Yale University Press, 1925.*

Pieter Jan Van Niel   (essay date 1969)

[*In the following excerpt, Van Niel explores Vanbrugh's treatment of the relationship between sexual gratification and morality in* The Relapse.]

Restoration comedy is undergoing a gradual reappraisal in terms of its meaning. Close study of the verbal structure of the plays is revealing far more than witty word-play. Indeed, the complex language is seen as the means of a profound exploration of human experience within a comic form. Close attention to the meaning of the words leads to an apprehension of the play's central action, and it is this action that holds the meaning of the play.

The literal movement of John Vanbrugh's *The Relapse* is simply from country to town. But it is how this movement is delineated in relation to particular characters, and how it ties together the metaphors and imagery of the play, that clarifies the metaphysic which informs the play. Concurrent with the structural design is an assumption of town attitudes by the characters of both the primary and secondary plots—with the notable exceptions of one character from each plot (Amanda and Tunbelly). But the primary tension in the play is between the country, supposedly free of the affectation, clandestine affairs, and sex games of the town, and the Restoration town to which the characters go. This metaphorical opposition is set up immediately.

Loveless, in the country, apparently enjoying a faithful and loving marriage, seems to have forsworn the town and its artificial ethic as he "opens" the play:

> Through all the roving pleasures of my youth
> (Where nights and days seem'd all consum'd in joy,
> Where the false face of luxury display'd such charms
> As might have shaken the most holy hermit,
> And made him totter at his altar),
> I never knew one moment's peace like this.
> Here—in this little soft retreat,
> My thoughts unbent from all the cares of life,
> Content with fortune,
> Eas'd from the grating duties of dependence,
> From envy free, ambition under foot,
> The raging flame of wild destructive lust
> Reduc'd to a warm pleasing fire of lawful love,
> My life glides on, and all is well within.

This revealing speech, which sets up the main tension of the play, certainly functions on several levels. Comically it seems to mock in its over-sentimentality the sweet-satiated posture of Colly Cibber's *Love's Last Shift*—indeed some have gone so far as to see this réposte as the main purpose of *The Relapse.* But, examined in relation to the central action, the speech's luxuriant verbosity also hints that Loveless might be attempting to convince himself that he likes the "country" way of life better than that which he has forsworn. The speech makes us aware that the faithfulness of which Loveless speaks might disappear at the least provocation. The obvious charm of the town to Loveless is revealed by the defensive tone of the words: the "raging flame of wild destructive lust"—a powerful attraction such as might sway even "the most holy hermit" and cause him to "totter at his altar"—burns still in Loveless. Already he is making excuses for what may (as he instinctively senses) come! The immediate dissimilarity of the "flame of wild destructive lust" and the "well within" of "lawful love" (note the alignment of "holy hermit" with "lawful love" and the contrasting coupling of "lust" with "destructive") is defined metaphysically as the play develops as a tension between a libertine assertion on one hand and a Christian posture on the other.

Loveless by nature is incapable of constancy. His identity is defined as essentially libertine both by the unraveling of the play and by his representative change—both physical and mental—from country to town. Amanda's nature, in direct, poignant, and ironic contrast, is not libertine, but is that of one searching for a meaningful and ordered existence. The conflict in her own consciousness between her moral posture—part of her identity—and the imposing assertions of the town in both her husband and confidante ultimately drives her out of the society in a curious manner.

But it is not only in the primary plot that the informing tension of the play develops. The secondary plot also works to delineate the nature of love, contrasting and in-

terplaying characters with those of the primary plot. Lord Foppington, by nature a rustic, comically attempts to emulate the ways of the town. We do not laugh at Loveless, for his wit is more refined and a part of his identity; we do laugh at Foppington both because he is ridiculous in his bourgeois manner and because the nature of his desire for the sophistication of the town points up the folly of that desire itself. The irony of Loveless' or Foppington's actions is compounded in the realization that beneath the latter's comic assertions exists the same "flame" of lust— an ultimately identical bestiality which reduces all persons in the play to a common denominator. The comedy of the secondary plot is also ironic in the rendering of Miss Hoyden who exudes blatant libidinal energy. Her desire to live in the "town manner" is amusing within the bounds of the buffoonery surrounding her desire for constant sexual stimulation (through either intercourse or intrigue); yet the insistent presence of that libidinal energy moves us to condemn her actions. The true nature of the town— unordered, subject to a chaos inflicted by a tide of irrational energy—is thus projected comically by the secondary characters, who function finally in a manner similar to those of the "sophisticated" primary characters once the latter's disguisings, role-playings, and cloaks of manners are removed. In *The Relapse* role-playings are part of the sexual game, as are "manners"; and the "removal" of the "wit" as the play progresses defines the nature of that energy which informs the characters' actions. That is, the sexual ethnic of the town functions to disguise the irrationality which the characters do not wish to confront. Thus the ever-present irony of either a "low" or "high" character attempting to assume a way of life defined negatively by the play's action, tolls continuously, and somewhat ominously, as the play progresses.

The brilliant development of the primary plot of Amanda-Loveless-Berinthia-Worthy revolves around several metaphoric complexes which tie together both plots and define the nature of the tension and its ethical ramifications. Love as a "raging flame" functions integrally with other carefully established images in the first scene, images which permeate the play and make Loveless' speech and Amanda's response to it primary to an understanding of the play. Loveless employs strong imagery in describing his love to Amanda, saying:

> The utmost blessing that my thought can reach,
> *(taking her in his arms)*
> Is folded in my arms, and rooted in my heart.

In an almost pastoral scene the Christian commonplace of a blessed state is suggested, a state which is supposedly "rooted" in Loveless' heart. The abounding irony of the play is Loveless' rejection of Amanda—and a love which implies a state of grace—for something else which is far from blessed.

Amanda's immediate response to Loveless' declaration shows revealing insight on her part and contains a concept which continually informs the rest of the play. She replies to his image with a plea for constancy:

> AMAN. There let it grow for ever.
>
> LOV. Well said, Amanda—let it be for ever—

Would heaven grant that—

AMAN. 'Twere all the heaven I'd ask.
But we are clad in black mortality,
And the dark curtain of eternal night
At last must drop between us.

Amanda knows her plea is hopeless. She is uncomfortably aware that their love cannot be eternal, for death must finally claim both of them. Heaven to her would be a state of eternal love, but Amanda recognizes the fact that their finiteness denies them "heaven" or eternal grace. This tension between "heaven" and "mortality" ranges further in importance however, both in Amanda's own realizations and in the inter-relatedness of the images which she calls into play with other images in **The Relapse.** Darkness, blackness, night—images of death—are equated by Amanda with the death of something else in her marriage, which possibility frightens her and makes her instinctively jealous. Faithlessness by Loveless holds a special terror for her:

AMAN. 'Twere all the heaven I'd ask.
But we are clad in black mortality,
And the dark curtain of eternal night
At last must drop between us.

LOV. It must: that mournful separation we must see. A bitter pill it is to all; but doubles its ungrateful taste, when lovers are to swallow it.

AMAN. Perhaps that pain may only be my lot;
You possibly may be exempted from it.
Men find out softer ways to quench their fires.

LOV. Can you then doubt my constancy, Amanda?
You'll find 'tis built upon a steady basis—

The sudden, almost jolting, turn of the discussion from death to the subject of inconstancy implies a relationship most important to the concept of the whole play, a relationship between physical death and the death of love by faithlessness. Amanda's "softer ways to quench their fires" reveals her equating of Loveless' sexual desire to fire (an image which Loveless' speech has set up, and which continues to inform the play typically): inconstancy would be "the softer way" for Loveless than death in losing his partner in love. Amanda seems to express an instinct in understanding that the very presence of desire in man implies mortality, death, darkness, either by the less obvious "death-assertion" of inconstancy or by death itself. The working out of **The Relapse** revolves around this central metaphysic.

The paradigm of Time, change, inconstancy, and death must be carefully clarified, as it is in **The Relapse.** Man by his very nature is the agent of and subject to desire; the presence of sexual desire implies change and finally, as Time the "great changer" progresses, mortality. The apprehension of a partner as merely a sexual object, as the satisfier of desire, as having value given by the desire and not by an appreciation of qualities of character, subjects the relationship of the law of Time. For as soon as the appetite for the object (partner) is satisfied, the object changes, lessens in value (value which is determined by appetite). Finally, when the desire wanes to nothing, the re-

lationship dies. In this way, each sexual encounter can be seen as an assertion of man's ultimate vulnerability, and as a moment in a growing discovery of an innately mortal identity determined by Time and the corresponding irrevocability of death.

Shakespeare's frequent and profound examinations of sexual desire echo in Amanda's conclusions. Troilus' passionate plea for Cressida's fidelity is doomed from the outset because of the sexual definition of their relationship. For their basic perception of each other is in terms of sexual gratification, thus *assigning* the partner value rather than appreciating those aspects of character which make the partner an individual human being. In *Troilus and Cressida* it is very clear that the law of Time and change affects the relationship of the lovers, for that relationship is based on no lasting interaction. However, Bassanio's love for Portia and the quality of her boundless response (developed in *The Merchant of Venice* through the use of such imagery as the metaphoric casket scene, and through the blossoming rather than the restricting of Portia's womanhood and individuality through marriage) suggests a conquering of Time's law, for such love as they share attains a certain permanency through the knowledge of the innate value which they sense in each other. Certainly they feel desire for one another, but that desire is not stimulated merely by physical demand; the values which they define in marrying, and will continue to apprehend in their union, are timeless—in a sense, divine. Amanda wants the kind of relationship which Portia has with Bassanio, but she senses the impossibility of such a relationship. For the universe in which she lives is similar to that in which Troilus finds himself enmeshed; the miracle of love which Portia and Bassanio define is not to be found in the world of **The Relapse.**

Thus the relationship based only on sexual gratification is subject to change, and therefore to Time; and as Time implies death, so a relationship between the presence of desire in man, and death, is seen. It is interesting that in the world of **The Relapse** desire seems assuaged only momentarily, appetite appears to be the law of existence; partners are viewed as sexual objects; integral identity, with one notable exception, is non-existent. These points should be remembered as one examines the image of "fire" in relation to the desire-death complex.

Fire loses its energy—ceases being fire—when it is extinguished; love if based on desire ceases, in a sense, when its consummation assuages an appetite. Life grows finally to be extinguished by the act of death just as fire is extinguished by its own process. Time changes man's life through death, as well as through the change of the sexual relationship. Loveless expresses an awareness of Time in his opening speech:

Perhaps, *when time shall be no more,*
When the aspiring soul shall take its flight,
And drop this pond'rous lump of clay behind it,
It may have appetites we know not of,
And pleasures as refin'd as its desires—
But till that day of knowledge shall instruct me,
The utmost blessing that my thought can reach. . . .

[italics mine]

As the "pond'rous lump of clay"—man's mortality—is left, and pleasures become more "refined" in a situation imaginatively projected by Loveless in words implying Christian salvation ("that day of knowledge"), Time would be overcome. Thus the tension between the law of Time, related to the presence of sexual energy in man, and a projected state of grace through blessed love again occurs. Amanda is painfully aware that this tension does exist. Her own response to this ambiguity—between the order of her marriage and the underlying presence of irrevocable sexuality in Loveless and in the world of the town—is developed carefully as the sexual deed is analyzed progressively through *The Relapse.* A metaphysical position of some import finally appears, further defined by the presence of images of disease as well as death.

As Loveless returns to the town and reassumes his libertine identity, he immediately feels strongly attracted to Berinthia. He cannot withstand the magnitude of his want, and so he confesses it to Berinthia in hopes of consummating an affair. He describes his desire as the presence of a disease, and the consuming nature of the sexual deed begins to be clarified as he enumerates the symptoms of a sickness in declaring his love:

> My heart began to pant, my limbs to tremble,
> My blood grew thin, my pulse beat quick,
> My eyes grew hot and dim. . . .
> So left the field,
> And fled for shelter to Amanda's arms.
> What think you of these symptoms, pray?

Berinthia responds, already assuming the role of the "doctor" which becomes pointedly ironic if the doctor is to be a "healer":

> BER. Feverish, every one of 'em.
> But what relief, pray, did your wife afford you?
>
> LOV. Why, instantly she let me blood,
> Which for the present much assuag'd my flame.
> But when I saw you, out it burst again,
> And rag'd with greater fury than before.
> Nay, since you now appear, 'tis so encreas'd
> That in a moment, if you do not help me,
> I shall, whilst you look on, *consume to ashes.*
> [Italics mine.]

Time consumes life, and the sexual deed is pictured in the play as consuming in a similar sense. The "flame" of his desire has made Loveless "feverish," *sick* with passion, and although he has had intercourse with his wife, the flame's "fury" is unabated. Sickness and tempestuousness are inherent in his desire, a desire clearly irrational, painted in imagery similar to that employed by Racine in *Phèdre* (fire, passion, fury, storms, rage). The words "consume to ashes" are pointed, for the sexual act implies a metaphoric death; the fire of passion when it burns out leaves "ashes." The interdependence of the sexual deed and death thus becomes increasingly clear.

The implication of this interdependence is worked out carefully in the play. Man asserts his identity within this play by the sexual deed, for it is plain that desire is the ultimate basis of self (even a Foppington and a Loveless are *ultimately* the same). Yet a great irony exists in the fact that as man asserts his identity, he is constantly asserting his mortality and approaching death. And as man becomes more and more subject to the "sickness" of an assertion of object-self and object-partner, he becomes more and more subject to the law of Time and finally, Death. An ironic *abrogation* of self in the final result is thus suggested by its precursor, the sexual deed.

The life-sustainer, blood, is equated in Loveless' confession to Berinthia (and throughout the play) with sperm ("she let me blood"). Again a working irony appears, for blood flows until death; similarly, the sexual act dies upon ejaculation by the male. Furthermore, while one is alive blood must always flow, and the ever-present need for sexual rejuvenation defined in the play assumes interesting connotations. In each union one attempts to attain revitalization, to keep "the blood" running, and yet almost pathetically asserts more and more the irrevocability of death: man dies, in one sense, many deaths before the final climax which ends his blood flow in every sense. In *The Relapse* the minute concern on the part of the town people to keep up affairs even vicariously points up the presence of this need for constant stimulation and rejuvenation and reinforces the irony of their existence.

Berinthia extends the imagery of the play, both by being a "town" member and by using words which are tantamount to those spoken by Loveless and Worthy. In counseling Amanda to have an affair, she describes the sexual act as to "let blood in the fond vein." The female desire needs to be extinguished by "blood," just as the male desire is answered in the letting of "blood" in the woman's "fond vein."

The diseased, consuming nature of the sexual deed relates constantly to the tension set up by Amanda at the play's outset, between the "blessedness" of lawful love ordered by marriage and consuming desire. The "black mortality" of which she speaks is first seen as death, but later is clarified as the presence of inconstancy in man; the play defines desire as a sickness which subjects man to the law of change (inconstancy) and thus the law of Time. The infected state of man, his "mortality," is projected carefully in the affair of Berinthia and Loveless. As Loveless attempts to consummate his desire, Berinthia speaks in most interesting terms:

> BER. (breaking from him) O Lard, let me go:
> 'Tis the plague, and we shall all be infected.
>
> LOV. (catching her in his arms, and kissing her)
> Then we'll die together, my charming angel.
>
> BER. O Ged—the devil's in you.

The lovers will "die together" from "the plague." Note the subtle relationship of these words to Amanda's original realization of the presence of death or inconstancy as the destruction of her marriage to Loveless. The law of change is informing Amanda's marriage to its death, as well as functioning in the projected "death" of the sexual act within the Berinthia-Loveless union.

Of paramount importance, too, is Loveless' reference to Berinthia as his "angel," and her response as she laughingly replies that "the devil's" in Loveless. Disease, death, mortality, infection, all associate typically with the presence of the Devil in man's life. That "blessed state" of "lawful love" which Loveless enjoyed with Amanda is replaced by an unlawful relationship which is demonic in nature: Berinthia is anything but an "angel" and the "devil" exists in Loveless as the presence of irrational desire. The perversion of Berinthia's "angelic" self further complicates the central irony of the play: Berinthia is as much consumed by the irrationality of desire as is Loveless; but of more importance is the fact that she appears to read as a persona of the Devil. Indeed, a pointed inversion of the whole Christian ethic occurs within the play, illustrated by careful development of the imagery and the central motif of movement from country to town (from lawful love to irrational promiscuity).

Loveless and Berinthia both worship the opposite sex, and sex itself. Consummation of desire is their "raison d'être":

> Lov. Will you then keep my secret?
>
> Ber. I will, if it don't burst me.
>
> Lov. Swear.
>
> Ber. I do.
>
> Lov. By what?
>
> Ber. By woman.
>
> Lov. That's swearing by my diety. Do it by your own, or I shan't believe you.
>
> Ber. By man, then.

Berinthia and Loveless swear their vows in a suggestion of a ritual marriage, but in an inversion—a perversion—of the normal marriage rite. Their deity is sexual consummation, and their bond is criminal, sealed with unfaithfulness. Berinthia paints the expected assignation in words fraught with double-entendre, and in images far-reaching in their irony:

> O Ged—Now do I pray to heaven, with all my heart and soul, that the devil in hell may take me, if ever—I was better pleased in my life—this man has bewitch'd me, that's certain. (sighing) Well, I am condemn'd, but, thanks to heaven, I feel myself each moment more and more prepar'd for my execution—nay, to that degree, I don't perceive I have the least fear of dying. No, I find, let the—executioner be but a man, and there's nothing will suffer with more resolution than a woman. Well, I never had but one intrigue yet: but I confess I long to have another. Pray heaven it end as the first did, though, that we may both grow weary at a time; for 'tis a melancholy thing for lovers to outlive one another.

With all her "heart and soul," Berinthia, having subjected herself to "the devil in hell," incongruously prays "to heaven"! In the consummation of the sexual act—the "execution"—the parties involved are "condemned" not only to the "death" of the sexual act, but in the underlying metaphysic of the play, to the inevitable hell of mortality. Of course Berinthia employs the words in a "witty" manner, to speak of the expected assignation; but the words function far beyond her use as they relate to the whole play.

The melancholy which Berinthia would feel if lovers were to "outlive one another" contrasts sharply with that malaise Amanda instinctively experiences in her distrust and awareness of the irrationality of desire as the play begins. To Berinthia, for one partner to outlive the other would be the maintenance of desire by one when the other's appetite had expired; to Amanda, "all the heaven" of letting love "grow forever"—within the bounds of an *ordered* sexual consummation—is an uncertainty because of the law of Time and change, and the thought of separation arouses melancholy in her as she unconsciously apprehends the impossibility of lasting love. Amanda appears to want a relationship which might extend beyond the immediacy of sexual gratification, whereas Berinthia entertains no such delusions as to the human condition. Berinthia subjects herself willingly to the law of "black mortality" which Amanda so fears—the assertion of self through sexual acts, and the corresponding growth of self unto death—whereas Amanda seems unable to accept directly an overtly sexual definition of existence. Berinthia's concerns are wholly sexual, and in the final analysis somewhat grotesque.

Berinthia assumes a more obviously demonic identity as she is consumed by appetite's irrationality even more than Loveless and Worthy. The planning of an affair becomes as titillating to her as actual participation—Berinthia assumes the role of instigator, of planner, and is delighted with herself in the process:

> So, here's fine work. What a business have I undertaken! I'm a very pretty gentlewoman, truly; but there was no avoiding it: he'd have ruined me if I had refused him. Besides, faith; I begin to fancy there may be as much pleasure in carrying on another body's intrigue as one's own. This at least is certain, it exercises almost all the entertaining faculties of a woman: for there's employment for hypocrisy, invention, deceit, flattery, mischief, and lying.

The perversion of Berinthia's rationality is apparent in her use of Worthy's demands as an excuse to comply in arranging his desired affair with Amanda; her obvious fascination with the process of the "intrigue" replaces even this moment of feigned rationality with a strange qualification to her character. Indeed, a listing of what appear to be the "town-defined" seven deadly sins seems to occur at the end of the speech—and these sins are those to which Berinthia is subject and of which, in promulgating, she is also agent. Her damnation and that which she induces in others, while treated lightly within the character of her own moral insouciance, seriously informs the metaphysic defined by the whole action of the play. Berinthia's nature furthers, and does not heal, the disease which consumes Loveless, Worthy, herself, and the others from both town and country.

Interestingly, Worthy appears more ideally suited to Berinthia than does Loveless, for both she and Worthy are painted in colors of the dark world. In praise of Berinthia's scheme to help seduce Amanda, Worthy says:

> Wor. (kneeling) Thou angel of light, let me fall down and adore thee!

BER. Thou minister of darkness, get up again, for *I hate to see the devil at his devotions.*

WOR. Well, my incomparable Berinthia—how shall I requite you?

BER. Oh, ne'er trouble yourself about that: Virtue is its own reward: there's a pleasure in doing good, which sufficiently pays itself. Adieu. [Italics mine.]

The Christian myth—typically realized in drama as the ordering process of love and man's attainment of grace through the union of marriage—is inverted in *The Relapse,* and the inversion becomes more apparent at this moment. To "fall down and adore" the "angel of light" is to worship Christ Jesus; yet Berinthia's Devil persona exudes other connotations, and to refer to her as "angel" as do Loveless and Worthy, calls into play a paradigm of irony. Loveless rejects a state of grace for damnation in following a "false" angel—Berinthia; Worthy's words reinforce this inversion, an inversion which proves to be the play's structure. Furthering the focus of the inversion, Berinthia claims Worthy as a member of the demonic world, calling him the "minister of darkness." Ironically she continues, playing the role of the Saviour (as does the Biblical anti-Christ) by defining her tempting and scheming within the traditional Christian commonplace of "virtue is its own reward." Again the words function both on the level of meaning the characters give them (of wit, jousting, and playing the sexual game) as well as on the various metaphysical levels contained in the play.

The inversion of the Christian ethic and the association of Berinthia with the devil is underlined by Loveless' plans to surprise Berinthia in her bedroom. He hides in her closet, saying:

> I'll e'en in there, and attack her just when she comes to her prayers: that's the most likely to prove her critical minute, for then the devil will be there to assist me.

Worthy's wooing of Amanda further defines the negation of the Christian ethic. In pleading for her acquiescence, Worthy compares his begging to the cry of the suppliant for mercy. In the realm of his inverted state of being, an act of grace would correspond to the assuagement of his glowing, feverish, "burning," consuming desire:

> Behold a burning lover at your feet,
> His fever raging in his veins.
> See how he trembles, how he pants!
> See how he glows, how he consumes!
> Extend the arms of mercy to his aid. . . .

The fusing of typical images in this speech reveals much of the ironic overthrow of normative Christian action. As with Loveless, the "fever" of desire rages in Worthy's "veins," in the ducts which carry his infected "blood." His blood needs answering, his fire must be extinguished, and yet fire put out is *dead;* sex the life-giver is also sex the life-consumer, and man asserts his mortality even as he asserts his sexuality. Salvation is not possible in the context of the world of *The Relapse,* for man's identity is limited by his mortality, and his mortality is proved by his essential sexuality. Thus the act of grace is transformed from a life-giving, redeeming action of love's miraculous transcendence over death into an assertion of self-abrogation.

Worthy clarifies further the nature of the irony of the play as he attempts to seduce Amanda and is (at least to his knowledge) rebuffed:

> Sure there's divinity about her;
> And sh'as dispens'd some portion on't to me.
> For what but now was the wild flame of love,
> Or (to dissect that specious term)
> The vile, the gross desires of flesh and blood,
> Is in a moment turned to adoration.
> The coarser appetite of nature's gone,
> And 'tis, methinks, the food of angels I require. . . .

This speech, because of its versification one would suppose, has often been read as part of a witty reply to the sentimentality of a Cibber, but such reading directly defies the most important part of any play—its structure. The movement, integrity, and metaphysical content of *The Relapse* clearly suggest the presence of a far more viable creative assertion—the examination of one part of man's humanity (his basic energy) with all its ramifications.

In a rather pessimistic rendering of the nature of man, *The Relapse* projects a sense of the impossibility of constancy and the all-power of change. Worthy dreams momentarily of constancy which he sees possible only if lovers are to reach into the "deep reserves" of each other, beyond the presence of sexuality. He sees constancy as a product of the more sensitive nature of woman. Thus he responds to Amanda as truly angelic, in opposition to the sexual spirit he apprehends in Berinthia. He reflects for a moment that indeed something greater is to be desired than a life of assignations. It is the quality of this reflection which makes Worthy, potentially a highly sensitive individual, the most "worthy" character in the play. He says:

> Could women but our secret counsels scan,
> Could they but reach the deep reserves of man,
> They'd wear it on, that that of love might last;
> For when they throw off one, we soon the other cast.
> Their sympathy is such—

But women are unable to "scan" the "secret counsels" of men, are unable to provide salvation through helping, that "love might last": Berinthia is of another world than that in which constancy is possible; Amanda, strangely confused and fascinated by the town "ethic," is not one who can inspire faithfulness even if it were approachable in the play's world. Indeed, the relapse into damnation includes both men and women, for both are mere embodiments of sexual energy, an energy which implies and proves mortality. In lines which resound the melancholic toll of Amanda's first-scene trepidations, Worthy concludes:

> The fate of one the other scarce can fly;
> They live together, and together die.

Worthy apprehends the likeness of feminine and masculine identity—Amanda's "black mortality" he sees as an irrevocable fact. This couplet suggests Worthy's great self-awareness, which separates him from the other characters in the play. Unlike the others, he confronts existence, sees its nature of irrevocability, and faced head-on with a savage conclusion chooses to play the "game" of living until death. So he phrases his discovery in game-like couplets, making light of the situation as much as he can (even then, that death knoll still rings in the lines). Worthy is far more honest than Loveless who puzzles not over life's situation but merely subjects himself to its forces, or Berinthia whose perversion of affair-arranging qualifies whatever self-awareness she may express, or Amanda who seems finally unable to come to terms with the world as it is in any meaningful fashion.

Indeed, while Amanda's instinctive fear of inconstancy reveals some sensitivity in her character, her actions qualify her person constantly. Amanda would seem to abhor the ways of the town, and yet she is fascinated by the very undercurrents to which she ultimately responds. Note the highly revealing scene with Berinthia during which time Amanda poorly feigns refusal of a projected affair with Worthy and reveals a curious response to sexuality:

> AMAN. Alas! Berinthia, did I incline to a gallant (which you know I do not), do you think a man so nice as he could have the least concern for such a plain unpolished thing as I am? It is impossible!
>
> BER. Now have you a great mind to put me upon commending you.
>
> AMAN. Indeed that was not my design.
>
> BER. Nay, if it were, it's all one, for I won't do't; I'll leave that to your looking-glass. But to show you I have some good-nature left, I'll commend him, and maybe that may do as well.
>
> AMAN. You have a great mind to persuade me I am in love with him.
>
> BER. I have a great mind to persuade you you don't know what you are in love with.
>
> AMAN. I am sure I am not in love with him, nor never shall be; so let that pass: but you were saying something you would commend him for.

Berinthia praises Worthy and asks Amanda how she likes the "doctrine" of the man. Amanda answers:

> So well that, since I never intend to have a gallant for myself, if I were to recommend one to a friend, he should be the man.

Amanda weaves around the issue at hand, searching for compliments, and going out of her way to let Berinthia know she does indeed feel attraction for Worthy. This circumvention which seems to be Amanda's particular aberration permeates the later seduction scene with Worthy as she almost leads him on, at once enjoying the roles of both "abstainer" and "desired woman." But Amanda would prefer, in her inability to confront her own sexuality, to play with the undercurrents of energy she senses within and without her being, rather than let those energies force her into a direct response or action.

Thus even the typically "virtuous" Amanda is revealed to have a strangeness about her, a perversion if you will, and one sees finally in *The Relapse* a world of strange grotes-

queries and nonconfrontations. The obvious homosexuality of Coupler is another manifestation of the same black ugliness which hides beneath the town veneer of each individual; human motivation in one way or another emanates from a basis of barely controlled, sinister energy. Indeed, Coupler's actions, in their similarity to Berinthia's, illuminate the basis of the latter's identity. For both are panderers, and both are ultimately grotesque. And Coupler's overt homosexuality has its more hidden counterpart in Berinthia's delight in pandering.

In this play, relationships not only are defined as lacking in sexually transcendent qualities, but are projected in terms of a particular aberration according to the make-up of the individual character; yet each unique perversion is rooted in the same all-informing blackness of the irrational. Loveless is libertine; Berinthia, voyeuristic; Amanda, sexually uneasy and very probably frigid (is it significant that when she "let" Loveless "bleed" she did not "abate" his "fury"?). Worthy seems the least perverted of the primary characters, though he too is plainly affected—"infected"—by the germs of mortality.

The Relapse, then, appears to be a realization of the powers of darkness, a ritual of damnation, a painting of a very present hell. As Christian hope is extinguished, even the institution of the church is abrogated, overrun by the demands of the sexual appetite. Hoyden is already married, but the chaplain can rationalize another marriage. He is easily convinced to conclude that:

> To take two husbands for the satisfaction of the flesh is to commit the sin of exorbitancy, but to do it for the peace of the spirit is no more than to be drunk by way of physic: besides, to prevent a parent's wrath is to avoid the sin of disobedience; for when the parent's angry the child is froward. So that upon the whole matter, I do think, though Miss should marry again, she may be saved.

It is of course quite obvious that Hoyden wishes to "take two husbands" precisely "for the satisfaction of the flesh." Beneath the comedy of the scene lies a cynical rendering of a powerless, unethical church, bound by irrationality, emptied of any meaning either functional or metaphysical, and tributary to the all-consuming chaos.

In a curious victory of the powers of the irrational over the order of the Christian miracle of love, the ritual of the normative comic gamos—usually a celebration of the ordering power of love—is inverted into a grotesque revel, a feast of the black world. Fashion "wins" Miss Hoyden back in what would appear to be some assertion of order, but their union has been presented negatively from their first meeting. Fashion has made it obvious that not only will the financial gain Hoyden brings him ease the cuckoldry he will undoubtedly experience, but that her role in the sex games of the town will cause him some delight and titillation:

> I'm much mistaken if she don't prove a March hare all the year round. What a scamp'ring chase will she make on't, when she finds the whole kennel of beaux at her tail! hey to the park, and the play, and the church, and *the devil;*

she'll show 'em sport, I'll warrant 'em. But no matter: she brings an estate will afford me a separate maintenance. [Italics mine.]

Fashion's appraisal of the situation precludes any sense of mutual valuation in their relationship, as does Hoyden's nature. The value of the love union is abrogated as it is by the primary plot characters, and the union of artifice is once again projected as the norm in *The Relapse.*

We smile at least at the antics of the secondary characters, yet beneath the lightness of the language, which is filled with stock Restoration comic devices, flows a river of discontent, a pessimistic evaluation of the nature of man and the universe. We appreciate the clever comedy of Berinthia's words as she is carried off by Loveless, but as we respond to the creative force of the play as defined by its structure, irony has its day:

> BER. (very softly) Help, help, I'm ravished, ruined, undone! O Lord, I shall never be able to bear it.

The fact is unavoidable that the casual, sexually defined affair in which Berinthia and Loveless indulge serves to further the abrogation of marriage as an ordering institution. And their affair is a result of the apparent irrevocability of the forces of evil; forces destructive to agent and subject alike. A feeling of onrushing doom underlies the game-playing of *The Relapse*'s town and defines especially the psychically demonic Berinthia. The forces of the dark world are not to be overcome in the world of *The Relapse.*

The malediction of human existence which *The Relapse* examines explodes disparagingly in the song of the Mask and the ritual (demonic) gamos. Hymen claims the support of the "Throne" of Cupid, and proclaims himself as the supporter of change and inconstancy:

> I therefore advise thee to let me go on,
> Thou'lt find I'm the strength and support
>   of thy throne;
> For hadst thou but eyes, thou would'st
>   quickly perceive it,
> How smoothly thy dart
> Slips into the heart
> Of a woman that's wed;
> Whilst the shivering maid
> Stands trembling, and wishing, but dare not
>   receive it.

And the chorus echoes a song of change:

> For change, w'are for change, to whatever it be,
> We are neither contented with freedom nor thee.
> Constancy's an empty sound.
> Heaven and earth and all go round;
> All the works of nature move,
> And the joys of life and love
> Are in variety.

Marriage is synonymous with inconstancy; sexuality is the law of existence by desire of all, including the "shivering maid" who "dare not receive it." Only change obtains, implying the passage of time, and mortality.

The world's damnation "celebrated" in the feast is reinforced by the sudden departure of Tunbelly, a departure which, while comic in manner, is savage in implication.

Tunbelly stalks off to the comparative sanity of the country, leaving the rest of the characters to "be damned":

> Art thou brother to that noble peer? Why then, that noble peer, and thee, and thy wife, and the nurse and the priest—may *all go and be damned together.* [Italics mine.]

Tunbelly's anger reaches beyond the fact that he has been made a fool; he leaves a society of game-playing, perverted individuals. The damnation which he senses—if only momentarily—includes all segments of the society (the church, a wife, a peer, a nurse, etc.). Buffoon or sophisticate, the envelopment of blackness excuses no one.

In production it is imperative to paint a canvas of frantic involvement by the town characters, of desperate searching for affairs, of using even an affair's arrangement as a means of avoiding a confrontation with the values of the world in relation to their own identities. The world should be seen as out of focus, beyond control, consuming the species man. The inevitability and nature of the demonic in man should be drawn as Vanbrugh drew it—with the implication of a self-created hell.

A metaphysic of profound import abounds in *The Relapse,* even as a definite apprehension projects in Congreve's *Way of the World;* in both, the nature of man is closely examined, and in each, a different conclusion is clarified. In *Way of the World,* an apprehension of possible order, meaningfulness, and mutual evaluation projects in a highly normative comic structure; Vanbrugh's play, however, views existence pessimistically, carefully defining a heart of darkness beating blood to the human race, and leaving no room for goodness.

The Relapse is profoundly contemporary in theme. Its despair is modern. Within the comic form of this Restoration comedy lies a metaphysic which deals with a problem common to all men. (pp. 318-32)

> *Pieter Jan Van Niel, " 'The Relapse'—Into Death and Damnation," in* Educational Theatre Journal, *Vol. XXI, No. 3, October, 1969, pp. 318-32.*

Alan Roper   (essay date 1973)

[*In the following excerpt, Roper examines Vanbrugh's commentary on morality in* The Relapse *as expressed through the characters' use of language in the play.*]

Love's Last Shift is a quite skillfully plotted play, distributing its attention duly between its three plots, and connecting the plots by employing the principals of one as subordinates in another. But, among its several deficiencies, perhaps the most crucial is its total failure to reconcile the pleasures of the town and single life with the mutual happiness of marriage. It was not for nothing that Vanbrugh began *The Relapse,* the "sequel" to [Cibber's] *Love's Last Shift,* with the reunited Loveless and Amanda withdrawn from the pleasures and temptations of the town into a seemingly safe rural virtue. Such a withdrawal is a necessary consequence, not only of Loveless' manifestly unstable character—his former extravagance in vice becomes at the end an equal extravagance in virtue—but also of Cibber's tacit insistence that the speech and activities of the town are not only distinct from, but decidedly inimical to the virtuous happiness of marriage.

The last act of *Love's Last Shift* marks the effective silencing of the language of wit. There is nothing more to be said which is both witty and apropos. And so the play ends with a fatuous masque in which various allegorical personages conduct a muddled debate over the relative eminence of love, reason, marriage, and so forth. So, too, perhaps, Vanbrugh began *The Relapse, or Virtue in Danger* with Loveless and Amanda withdrawn from the town, and sententiously exchanging some well-thumbed texts from conventional morality, as a depressing prelude to Vanbrugh's noble attempt to rescue the language of wit from the condition in which Cibber left it.

The Relapse is about the bankruptcy of a traditional morality and the language in which it has been conventionally expressed. Vanbrugh restores the credit of the language by selling off the few remaining assets of the morality.

Consider a typical exchange from the last act. Cibber's Loveless and Amanda have returned from the untaxing virtue of country retirement to the dangerous temptations of London, Loveless having donned the helmet of virtue for the occasion. But the helmet is soon doffed so that he may get closer to Berinthia, Amanda's lovely cousin, who has come to stay with them at Amanda's invitation. Berinthia has recently been the mistress of Worthy, Cibber's Young Worthy, that honest intriguer, who schemed as much for others as for himself. Vanbrugh's Worthy schemes for himself, and, discovering Berinthia's weakness for Loveless, urbanely blackmails her into forwarding his own adulterous suit to Amanda. By the last act, Loveless and Berinthia have consummated their affair, and it remains only to drive Amanda into Worthy's arms. Berinthia has a stratagem. This is how she describes it to Worthy, and this is how he responds. She will herself meet Loveless by appointment, and will first tell Amanda

> that to my certain Knowledge, her Husband has a Rendez-vous with his Mistress this Afternoon; and that if she'll give me her word, she'll be satisfied with the discovery, without making any violent Inquiry after the Woman, I'll direct her to a place, where she shall see 'em meet.

> Now, Friend; this I fancy may help you to a Critical Minute. For Home she must go again to dress. You (with your good breeding) come to wait upon us to the Ball. Find her all alone: Her Spirit enflam'd against her Husband for his Treason; and her Flesh in a heat from some Contemplations upon the Treachery: Her Blood on a Fire; her Conscience in Ice; a Lover to draw, and the Devil to drive—Ah poor *Amanda*.

> WORTHY. *kneeling.* Thou Angel of Light, let me fall down and adore thee?

> BERINTHIA. Thou Minister of darkness, get up again, for I hate to see the Devil at his Devotions.

> WORTHY. Well, my incomparable *Berinthia*— How shall I requite you—

> BERINTHIA. O ne'er trouble your self about that: Virtue is its own Reward: There's a pleasure in doing good, which sufficiently pays it self. Adieu.

> WORTHY. Farewell, thou best of Women.

The exchange between Worthy and Berinthia is typical of the play's wit because it achieves its effects by confounding heaven and hell. Where traditional morality had clearly distinguished the paths of damnation and salvation, *The Relapse* consistently confuses them by setting the signposts to heaven along the path to damnation. Such a transfer of pious formulas from their normal context of ethical injunction to a context of vicious practices is properly metaphorical.

Metaphors like Berinthia's "Virtue is its own Reward" are not merely witty through the outrageousness of their transfer, they are also satiric in their implication that the current language of virtue glosses an actual viciousness. Such a satiric point is even more evident in the sub-plot, which is concerned with the rival efforts of Cibber's Sir Novelty Fashion, now created Lord Foppington, and his younger brother, Tom Fashion, to marry the country fortune of Miss Hoyden. Each brother "marries" Hoyden in turn, the marriages being performed by Bull, chaplain to Hoyden's father, Sir Tunbelly Clumsey. The resolution of the rival claims of the brothers in favor of Tom Fashion involves settling the consciences of Hoyden, Bull, and Hoyden's Nurse, who connives at both matches. In this settling of consciences, the methods of casuistry are cynically applied to the justification of self-interest, with the evident satiric point that casuistry is typically used to make vice look with the face of virtue.

Berinthia's "Virtue is its own Reward" is also strictly ironic in its use of a cliché of moral congratulation as a means to self-deprecation. As such, it is defensive. The metaphor enables Berinthia to talk about the fact without, as it were, referring to it. The metaphor places a shield of language between her and the actuality of her deeds and motives. Berinthia's description of Amanda—"Her Blood on a Fire; her Conscience in Ice; a Lover to draw, and the Devil to drive"—is an elegant figure of climax and antithesis which enables Berinthia to talk about a projected betrayal of Amanda—her cousin, her friend, her hostess—without contemplating the iniquity. Until, it seems, she allows her attention to stray from the words themselves to the thing signified, and adds "Ah poor *Amanda*," a momentary loss of poise, perhaps, from which she is rescued by Worthy's outrageous "Thou Angel of Light, let me fall down and adore thee." Such a language of wit permits the user to maintain a perilous balance between what the appetites will have and what the conscience insists should be. It settles the conscience by ridiculing it, and by ridiculing the conscience justifies the appetites which contradict it. It takes the dead metaphors of piety—those rocks of reason, helmets of salvation, and fortresses of virtue displayed for us in the opening scene—and galvanizes them into unholy life. It provides a vital language for expressing a social decadence.

The life, the liveliness, of this wit language may be felt by contrast with the first scene of the play, in which conventional morality is conventionally expressed. The play opens with Loveless first soliloquizing and then exchanging congratulations with Amanda upon their retired felicity, as they, two steadfast Christian souls, march on to glory. Loveless enters "reading," and the language both of them use is evidently literary and secondhand. The tired tropes of salvation perform their exhausted dance, fluttering uncertainly, now to the rhythms of verse, now of prose, swelling with sententious complacency, then shrinking to a nervous exchange of antitheses:

> LOVELESS. That for my Temperance, Then for my Constancy.—
>
> AMANDA. Ay, there take heed.
>
> LOVELESS. Indeed the Danger's small,
>
> AMANDA. And yet my Fears are great,
>
> LOVELESS. Why are you so timerous?
>
> AMANDA. Because you are so bold,
>
> LOVELESS. My Courage shou'd disperse your apprehensions.
>
> AMANDA. My Apprehensions shou'd allarm your Courage.
>
> LOVELESS. Fy, Fy, *Amanda* it is not kind thus to distrust me.
>
> AMANDA. And yet my Fears are founded on my Love.

What Amanda evidently and justly fears is that Loveless is using language to hide from himself the actuality of his inclinations, much as Worthy and Berinthia, we may say, use wit language to distract themselves from the actuality of their deeds and motives. Loveless talks temperance, but Amanda knows very well, as he should too, that his is no settled inclination to virtue. Such a character is rare in this world, where the more usual possibility of virtue consists in continence, in restraining the appetites from what they would have.

With Loveless, that hopeless recidivist, speedily relapsed into incontinence, the main plot can focus on its main interest, the endangered virtue of Amanda. Amanda becomes the isolated Christian soldier, beset by devils urbanely citing scripture, conscious of an enemy within in her early inclination to Worthy, an enemy later seconded by her exasperation with Loveless.

These resonances of the morality play find their comic, almost farcical, echo in the sub-plot, when the brothers Fashion lay siege to Miss Hoyden's doubtful virtue. Sir Tunbelly Clumsey's country house is not only, what Tom Fashion's servant sees it to be, the dread castle of romance kept by a grim churl, it is also the fortress of the old moral allegory, a castle of imperseverance, with clownish guards, a lubricious duenna, and a perverted voice of conscience. Tom Fashion slips easily by these befuddled sentries to that inner chamber in which is locked up the precious jewel of Miss Hoyden's virtue, wrapped in a dirty tucker. The subplot, indeed, is rather like what might be produced by crossing a morality play with a jest book.

The scenes at Sir Tunbelly's house parallel, through character and action, the effect produced in language by Worthy and Berinthia when they illustrate their vicious homilies with the texts of piety. With this presentation of how fallible and absurd the old fortress of virtue can be, there is an extra point to the plotting of Worthy and Berinthia when they dextrously exchange tropes for the besieging, the storming, the undermining, and the blowing up of Amanda's virtue. These, or others like them, are the very tropes with which Amanda must defend herself when, inclined toward Worthy, betrayed by her husband, tutored by Berinthia, and then, quite alone, possessed of a morality which can only be expressed in words that vice has already arrogated to itself, she comes to renew that ancient encounter between good and evil. "Ah poor *Amanda*," indeed.

The scene of Worthy's attempted seduction of Amanda must be difficult to stage plausibly. The language, at least at the scene's climax, might well strike as strained or forced. During the first half of the scene, Worthy and Amanda trade analogies, Worthy using the language of urband dissimulation, Amanda trying unsuccessfully to use the same language to express sincerity. "With just such honest words as these," she exclaims, "the worst of Men deceiv'd me." Worthy wins, or seems to win, the battle of words when Amanda admits there is an action of his which might gain for him part of her heart, that action is never "to ask whatever is unfit for me to grant." Since in Worthy's world women are supposed to deny with their tongues what they desire with their bodies, he is emboldened to physical action. Worthy attempts, that is, to repeat the earlier action of Loveless when he entered Berinthia's bed-chamber, wooed her, and carried her off to the couch in the closet as she cried out, "Help, help, I'm Ravish'd, ruin'd, undone. O Lord, I shall never be able to bear it"; but she cried out, as that most witty of stage directions has it, *"Very softly."* Worthy almost repeats the success of Loveless. He pulls Amanda down onto a couch and exclaims "My Life, my Soul, my Goddess—O forgive me?" Amanda: "O whither am I going? Help, Heaven, or I am lost." Amanda staggers in the path of virtue because she acknowledges both her appetites and the difficulty of continence. The language, here, of imminent sexual climax will always seem absurd to the disengaged, for the words it uses have no meaning in themselves; they are merely vehicles for expressive groans. What gives a special hysteria to the scene between Amanda and Worthy is that Amanda insists on reading off the literal sense of these vehicles for groans, even though she knows the sense has been perverted into its opposite. If men consistently use heaven as a metaphor for hell, they will soon be unable to communicate with each other about heaven itself. Something like this almost happens to Amanda. She wins because Worthy's linguistic dilemma proves more acute than hers. Worthy, like Berinthia, has set thick the road to hell with heavenly signposts. But, in this moment of physical action and exquisite randy excitement, he can no longer read off his signposts with the proper aware irony. And so he stumbles back into the road to heaven, succumbing as much to the language as to the virtue of Amanda.

Amanda leaves Worthy with some nicely cadenced propositions about the sovereignty of the mind over the appetites, leaves him, indeed, with the language of Cibber's Amanda, assured, relaxed, and somewhat complacent. As a resourceful man, Worthy quickly rallies, and the sometime voluptuary of vice finds new titillation for his jaded palate in the smooth syrups of virtue. "The Coarser Appetite of Nature's gone, and 'tis methinks the Food of Angels I require, how long this influence may last, Heaven knows. But in this moment of my purity, I cou'd on her own terms, accept her Heart." Worthy commences a voluptuary of virtue, and with that beginning, the main plot ends, quite unresolved, although another scene is needed to settle the rivalries of the sub-plot.

It's quite proper, of course, that in a play as honest as *The Relapse* the main plot should be left unresolved. The play endorses again and again, in both its plots, that, as Berinthia puts it, "no Man worth having is true to his Wife, or can be true to his Wife, or ever was, or ever will be so." To put it another way, the play accepts that it is impossible to identify and follow a decent private life while still engaging fully in the pleasures of public living. This sense of an unresolvable discrepancy between public and private life is properly tragic. And if the wish is to write a comedy which uses language as honestly and intelligently as Vanbrugh uses it, there is nothing to be done with the action but let it trail off indecisively.

Vanbrugh's honesty and intelligence are exercised in his witty inversion of a traditional language and morality which are principally those of homiletic literature. No one who has read even cursorily in the large seventeenth-century corpus of injunctions to piety and virtue can fail to note the presence of its characteristic texts and tropes in *The Relapse,* especially in the opening scene between Loveless and Amanda. Indeed, it would be easy to gather extracts from a variety of pious works to serve as a source of annotations upon the play.

But there are at least two ways in which such an activity can be distracting. It can be distracting by implying that the play alludes precisely to this literature, instead of, as seems to be the case, drawing upon those of its formulas and rhythms disseminated in the popular consciousness. Another possible distraction is more serious. The presence of the annotations, putting, we may say, the straightforward, positive case for the homilies and their morality, might betray an unwary reader into assuming that the moral purpose of *The Relapse* is to recommend the very texts it so wittily ridicules, and quite clearly, if implicitly, to condemn Worthy, Berinthia, and Tom Fashion for their impiety.

Support for such a strained reading can be quickly found in Vanbrugh's own vindication of *The Relapse*'s language and morality, when he endeavored to defend himself from Jeremy Collier's charge that, in effect, he had not only neglected to recommend piety in his play, he had openly advocated impiety. Vanbrugh's intellectual contortions in this exchange with Collier are now sad to contemplate. He quite failed to see that in any debate between a man of ironic and intelligent scepticism and a man of humorless and impercipient dogmatism, the dogmatist will almost always win, because he is interested in submission, not communication, while the sceptic, trying to communicate in order to avoid submission, is forced into arguing on his opponent's terms, and so is lost. Collier, for instance, attacked Vanbrugh's blasphemy in making Worthy exclaim to Berinthia "Thou Angel of Light, let me fall down and adore thee." Absurdly, Vanbrugh's defense was that Berinthia's retort, "Thou Minister of darkness, get up again, for I hate to see the Devil at his Devotions," provided the correct moral placing and reproof of Worthy's blasphemy, and it was therefore disingenuous of Collier not to quote Berinthia's retort as well as Worthy's exclamation. But, plainly enough, both remarks are very funny, and in much the same way: through their outrageously flippant hyperbole. Collier, rather like Amanda, refused to see, or at least to tolerate, the wit of the first remark, and Vanbrugh, unable to defend it as wit, was forced into a defense on Collier's terms of absurd solemnity.

Collier, indeed, played Amanda to Vanbrugh's Worthy, and with much the same success. It's unsurprising, therefore, that Vanbrugh adduced Worthy's "conversion" by Amanda as prime evidence of his play's virtuousness, arguing that Worthy's soliloquy after Amanda has left shows where the moral emphasis lies. But Worthy's "virtue" is believable because he acknowledges the uncertainty of its duration, just as Amanda's undoubted virtue is believable because she recognizes, but just manages to cover up, its vulnerability. We are far indeed from the unquestioning steadfastness and easy, absolute conversion of Cibber's Amanda and Loveless. Vanbrugh the apologist equivocates, blurring the sharp honesty of the dramatist into the shiftiness of a Cibber.

The Relapse is undoubtedly a moral play, but not because it recommends and shows the practicality of virtue. It is moral because, without recommending vice, it shows the ubiquitousness of vice, its virtuous pretenses and defenses; shows, too, the general inefficacy of conventional injunctions to piety when they are applied to the actuality of man's nature. Above all, the play is moral because it is both true and honest. Such a morality is intimate with the play's wit, requiring no apology from dramatist and critic that this is a very funny play.

The danger of a thorough homiletic annotation of the play is that it may, quite simply, attempt to defend the play against Collier, even if tacitly, in just the way that Vanbrugh himself attempted to defend it, and with the same disastrous results. If the texts that are ridiculed in the interests of wit are held to contain, unwittily, the moral positive of the play, then the wit becomes an embarrassment to the morality, as it was to Vanbrugh in his labored vindication. But if the wit is properly seen as the primary vehicle of the play's morality, because it is the appropriate expression of those undoubted virtues, truth and honesty, then the wit is not the play's embarrassment, but its glory.

Thorough homiletic annotation is, in any case, unnecessary to a proper appreciation of the play. We are not yet so secularized as to have quite lost touch with the terms and injunctions of Christian homiletics. A small reminder at most can put us in touch with ancestral, if not childhood memories. Vanbrugh himself suggests what form that reminder should take. The last scene of the play opens with Hoyden discussing with her Nurse which of the brothers Fashion she should take. She leans towards Foppington, because, among other things, the elder brother will have more money than the younger. Nurse sagely points out that wealthy lords are given to squandering their money on "their Sluts and their Trulls" and do not allow a wife even "a spare half Crown, to buy her a Practice of Piety."

The Practice of Piety: Directing a Christian how to walk that he may please God, by Lewis Bayly, Bishop of Bangor, had gone through some fifty editions in the seventeenth century by the time **The Relapse** was written and performed. We may take Vanbrugh's hint to treat it as a representative popular work. As its sub-title indicates, *The Practice of Piety* makes intermittent use of the old metaphor of spiritual journey which was to serve Bunyan so well. The metaphor is operative in **The Relapse,** both straightforwardly in the opening scene and the scene of Amanda's attempted seduction by Worthy, and ironically inverted in some of the exchanges between Worthy and Berinthia. The metaphor also glosses the primary significance of the two actions. Loveless, having assured himself of his piety in the country, journeys to London in order to prove, in combat with vice, his cloistered virtue. Tom Fashion, having dispensed with his conscience in London as a result of his reception by his brother, journeys to the country in order to prove, in combat with seeming virtue, how warmly the world smiles on the man unhampered by conscience. Loveless loses in London the conscience he thought he had in the country. Tom Fashion succeeds in the country because he lost his conscience in London. If we need to be reminded that man's doings in the world are and often have been cast as a spiritual journey, then Bayly or almost any Christian apologist will serve our purpose.

When Loveless announces his plan to launch into London temptation, he assures Amanda that he will prove his virtue by surrounding himself with topers and declining to join in their revelry. We really don't need Bishop Bayly to tell us that Loveless is foolhardy, but he does, of course:

> The *first* sign of God's favour to a sinner, is, to give him *grace* to forsake *evil companions.* . . . Many a time is poor *Christ* (offering to be new born in thee) thrust into the *Stable;* when these lewd companions by their *drinking, plays,* and *jests,* take up all the best room in the *Inn* of thy heart.

But there is one matter in which the Bishop may help. When Worthy speaks, after his "conversion" to virtue, of "the Food of Angels," or when Loveless, at the outset, ponders upon the possibility that after death the soul "may have Appetites we know not of, / And Pleasures as refin'd as its Desires," we may easily assume that the characters alone are in error, using language which pulls down heaven to the hedonistic delights of the world. Bayly reminds us that, in between warning against indulgence, conventional morality could give voluptuous rewards to virtue. To the elect in heaven, God himself will be *"beauty to our eyes, musick to our ears, honey to our mouths, perfume to our nostrils, meat to our bellies."* These are dangerous metaphors with which to console a hedonist, who may well be distracted from a voluptuous and uncertain future

to those more certain present pleasures which have served to define the future. **The Relapse** demonstrates fully just how dangerous it is to talk in this way, to use language so carelessly.

At one point Bayly identifies quite closely the basis of Vanbrugh's wit—that ironic application of the terms of virtue to the practices of vice:

> The last, and not the least block whereat *Piety* stumbleth in the course of Religion, is by adorning *vices* with the names of Virtues, as to call drunken *carousing,* drinking of *healths* . . . *Whoredom,* loving a *Mistress* . . . Children of *Belial, good Fellows.* . . So on the other side, to call *Sobriety* in words and actions, *Hypocrisie.* . . *Devotion, Superstition.* . . scruple of *Concience, Precisness,* &c. And whilst thus we call *evil good,* and *good evil,* true Piety is much hindered in her *progress.*

The good Bishop is right. The progress of true piety is much hindered by such inversions. But, with **The Relapse** before us, we must agree that the course of honest wit lies fair and clear.

Vanbrugh's is a bright, bleak world. Its people have inherited an old cloak of language, patched with clichés and snagged on the thorns of scepticism. The best they can do is turn the cloak inside out, present the lining to the world, and hope to stay snug and smart for a winter or so, until the century drags itself off into oblivion. The east wind nips shrewdly, so that virtue's steely bones look bleak there. But Worthy and Berinthia draw their turned cloak about them, and jest against the cold. (pp. 53-64)

> *Alan Roper, "Language and Action in 'The Way of the World', 'Love's Last Shift', and 'The Relapse'," in ELH, Vol. 40, No. 1, Spring, 1973, pp. 44-69.*

Gerald M. Berkowitz   (essay date 1973)

[*In the following excerpt, Berkowitz suggests that Vanbrugh manipulated the conventions of Restoration comedy to build complexity and realism in his plays, and to create a new comic style distinct from the high Comedy of Manners of Etherege and Wycherley.*]

Sir John Vanbrugh (1664-1726) is the author of nine dramatic comedies, of which two—**The Relapse** (1696) and **The Provok'd Wife** (1697)—and a fragment of a third—*A Journey to London* (1728)—are original, and the rest free translations and adaptations, primarily of contemporary French comedies. Despite his limited output, Vanbrugh is generally classed along with Etherege, Wycherley, Congreve and Farquhar as one of the most talented writers of the Restoration comedy of manners. Of the five, however, he has received the least critical attention, with only one significant article in the last century dealing with the characteristics and merits of his plays [Mueschke and Fleisher in *PMLA* 49 (1934)].

Part of this neglect may be attributed to Vanbrugh's dual career. By many he is better remembered as an architect than as an author, and there have been more extended studies of his buildings than of his plays. A more significant factor is Vanbrugh's historical position: writing primarily in the ten years surrounding the turn of the century, he comes between the high comedy of manners of Wycherley and the fullblown sentimentality of Richard Steele. Inevitably he is labeled as a transitional figure, and thus easily dismissed as an imperfect adherent of one or the other school. But to dismiss Vanbrugh (or, indeed, Farquhar, about whom the same judgment is frequently made) as transitional is to accuse him of not being capable of doing what he wanted to, without even realizing, perhaps, that he was producing something other than the imitation Etherege or incipient Steele he was supposedly attempting.

It is the purpose of this study to offer an alternative definition of Vanbrugh's work and of his contribution to the course of British comic drama. I will limit myself for now to Vanbrugh's treatment of the conventions inherited from Etherege and Wycherley—the rather limited number of character types, stock scenes, and comic devices which define the world of the comedy of manners. Implicit, however, in such an account are changes in the depth and scope of the plays: more complex characters can bear more complex dramatic burdens, and a new comic style will produce or presuppose a new comic perspective. The plays of Vanbrugh are different in significant ways from those of Etherege and Wycherley, and also from those of Steele and Cumberland, and intentionally so. It was his role to expose the limitations of the conventional comedy he inherited and to prove that successful comedy could be created outside these limitations. It would be an overstatement to assert that he caused the transition, but it is important to see that he helped to shape it and, indeed, to make it possible.

Vanbrugh began to write at a time when, for various reasons, the established form of dramatic comedy had lost its viability but not its predominance. The combination of religious, social and economic forces acting on the theatre in the last decade of the century is familiar, and has been well summarized by John Loftis [in his *Comedy and Society from Congreve to Fielding,* 1959] and others. But it is very likely that change would have come to comedy in the 1690's even without outside influences for a reason inherent in the nature of Restoration comedy. The very artificial comedy of manners, with its very few character types and potential plots, eventually had to run dry; there were only a limited number of permutations that could be made on the stock elements. And when the theatre at Lincoln's Inn Fields opened in 1695 and ended Drury Lane's thirteen-year monopoly, the need for new plays doubled. It must have become imperative for dramatists to expand the comic universe to find new material.

Vanbrugh's basic method for enlarging the dramatic vocabulary is subversion and modification rather than direct attack or innovation. He accepts the conventions of the comedy of manners, but works subtle variations on their context or application so that they are turned against themselves. He thereby exposes their limitations, demonstrating that they are barely able to do what they set out to, and certainly cannot withstand even the slightest pres-

sure. Conventions thus treated are not necessarily destroyed, but are either transformed into essentially new devices with new applications or robbed of their absolute authority, so that alternative values and devices can be proposed without automatically being rejected.

Vanbrugh's treatment of the wit-duel formula is a good example of his method. One of the most delightful scenes in any comedy of manners is the almost obligatory encounter between the hero and heroine in which they spar through a balanced and clever repartee, and thus prove themselves well matched and superior in manners and wit to the rest of the world. These scenes are frequently the closest approach that the Etherege-Wycherley comedy makes to courtship and lovemaking between such characters, and are thus central to the development of plot and character, as well as to the humor of the play.

Typical of such wit-encounters is this portion of a scene between Vanbrugh's Constant and Lady Brute in *The Provok'd Wife:*

> LADY BRUTE. Sure you think me scandalously free, Mr. *Constant.* I'm afraid I shall lose your good Opinion of me.
>
> CONST. My good Opinion, Madam, is like your Cruelty, never to be remov'd.
>
> LADY BRUTE. But if I shou'd remove my Cruelty, then there's an end of your good Opinion.
>
> CONST. There is not so strict an Alliance between 'em neither. 'Tis certain I shou'd love you then better (if that be possible) than I do now; and where I love, I always esteem.

Notice the form that this dialogue takes. Each speech is simultaneously defensive parry and offensive thrust, a response to the preceding speech that twists its image or argument (often by repeating a key word) in order to score a point for the opposite side. There are no jokes with obvious laughter points in the exchange; we do not respond to any specific lines, but delight in the symmetry of the statements and counterstatements and in the ability of the participants to keep this verbal one-upmanship going so suc-

A scene from a 1763 production of The Provoked Wife.

cessfully. Clearly form is more important than content in such encounters; it would probably be possible to enjoy the theatrical moment without even understanding English, since the rhythms and repetitions, and not the meaning of the words, are what really carry the scene. Indeed, wit and euphemism are frequently employed specifically to cover meaning; this encounter between Constant and Lady Brute is a seduction scene, and their verbal ability is meant to disguise the sexual reality of the favors Lady Brute's "Cruelty" withholds.

Vanbrugh, however, does not lose sight of that reality, and he will not allow us to. Unlike his predecessors in the game of seduction, Constant is unable to maintain his appeal on the level of wit and euphemism; and the verbal sallies soon give way to physical liberties and ultimately to attempted rape:

> CONST. Forgive me, therefore, since my Hunger rages, if I at last grow Wild, and in my frenzy force at least, This from you. [*Kissing her Hand.*] Or if you'd have my Flame soar higher still, then grant me this, and this, and Thousands more; [*Kissing first her Hand, then her Neck. Aside.*] For now's the time She melts into Compassion.
>
> LADY BRUTE. [*Aside.*] Poor Coward Virtue, how it shuns the Battle. O heavens! let me go.
>
> CONST. Ay, go, ay: Where shall we go, my Charming Angel,—into this private Arbour.— Nay, let's lose no time—Moments are precious.
>
> LADY BRUTE. And Lovers wild. Pray let us stop here; at least for this time.
>
> CONST. 'Tis impossible; he that has Power over you, can have none over himself. (IV.iv)

This physical element has been in Constant's mind from the start—indeed, it has been lurking beneath these wit-duels since Etherege—but Vanbrugh is the first to let it overcome the artificial restraint of the repartee, thus demonstrating how very tenuous that restraint was and how very hypocritical was the masking of lust by language.

It is clear, in addition, that this effect is intentional, and not a matter of Vanbrugh's inability to control the convention. The scene progresses, step by step, from euphemism to statement to overt action to rape, from carefully controlled language to uncontrolled passion. The breakdown of the convention is made a logical and inevitable result of the situation. It is also made comic, exposing the absurdity of the pretense and lowering Constant and Lady Brute to the level of those fools and witwouds who cannot control reality through language. In fact the scene descends even further, to the level of physical farce, as the lovers are interrupted and frightened off by the eavesdropping Lady Fancyfull. Vanbrugh's point is implicit: the only difference between witty gallant and lustful fool is language, and language is no longer an effective distinction.

Vanbrugh had turned the wit-seduction convention against itself in a similar way a year earlier in the corresponding scene in *The Relapse* (V.iv), where Worthy's attempt at lovemaking slipped rapidly from the verbal level to the physical. The same pattern held in an exchange between Loveless and Berinthia (III.ii), while another set of wit-seduction encounters in *The Relapse* also served to expose the inherent lechery and hypocrisy of the situation:

> A. I'm at leisure to hear what 'twas you had to say to me.
>
> B. What I had to say, was only to Eccho the Sighs and Groans of a dying Lover.
>
> A. Phu, will you never learn to talk in earnest of any thing?
>
> B. Why this shall be in earnest, if you please; for my part, I only tell you matter of fact, you may take it which way you like best; but if you'll follow the Women of the Town, you'll take it both ways; for when a Man offers himself to one of them, first she takes him in jest, and then she takes him in earnest.
>
> A. I'm sure there's so much jest and earnest in what you say to me, I scarce know how to take it. (IV.ii)

The scene is typical enough, except that "A" and "B" are not lady and gallant; they are lady and confidante, Amanda and Berinthia. Berinthia is seducing Amanda for Worthy, her own former lover, in order to cover up her developing affair with Amanda's husband. This duel, and the others between Amanda and Berinthia (e.g., V.ii), must be meant to be disturbing, because they are Vanbrugh's chief means of discrediting his villainess. Significantly, it is the meaning of the words, and their implications, that we are most aware of, not just their music or cleverness. Reality is exposed through the wit-duel instead of being masked by it, and both the hypocrisy of the situation and the limitations of the device are exposed as well.

It is noteworthy that the wit-duel, even in its weakened form, disappears in Vanbrugh's later plays, to be replaced by other devices or by exchanges which have progressed in implications and dramatic power far beyond the limits of the convention. The debate between Loverule and Arabella in *A Journey to London* begins with the familiar rhythms and repetitions, but exposes more than the verbal abilities of the speakers:

> LORD LOVE. But Madam, can you think it a Reasonable thing, to be abroad till Two a Clock in the Morning, when you know I go to bed at Eleven?
>
> LADY ARA. And can you think it a Wise thing (to talk your own way now) to go to Bed at Eleven, when you know I am likely to disturb you by coming there at Three? . . . I'll have you to know I keep Company with the politest People in the Town, and the Assemblies I frequent are full of such.
>
> LORD LOVE. So are the Churches now and then.
>
> LADY ARA. My Friends frequent them often, as well as the Assemblies.
>
> LORD LOVE. They wou'd do it oftener, if a Groom of the Chamber there were allow'd to furnish Cards and Dice to the Company.

LADY ARA. You'd make a Woman mad.

LORD LOVE. You'd make a Man a Fool.

LADY ARA. If Heaven has made you otherwise, that won't be in my Power.

LORD LOVE. I'll try if I can prevent your making me a Beggar at least.

LADY ARA. A Beggar! Croesus! I'm out of Patience—I won't come home 'till four tomorrow Morning.

LORD LOVE. I'll order the Doors to be lock'd at Twelve.

LADY ARA. Then I won't come home till tomorrow Night.

LORD LOVE. Then you shall never come home again, Madam. (II.i)

The purpose of this scene is not to show how clever and well-matched Loverule and Arabella are, but to reveal how perilously close to dissolution their marriage is. The exchange is not static, but moves toward a climax. Truth is not buried beneath euphemism, but brought clearly to the surface. Matter dominates the scene, not form; and the similarities to the traditional wit-duel merely make us more aware of the differences in tone and import—what we learn about the couple is especially shocking because it comes through a convention established to hide such things. After weakening the convention, Vanbrugh was able to modify it; by modifying it, he can use it in situations for which it was inappropriate before; and by introducing such new combinations of form and matter, he not only makes a satirical comment, but also significantly enlarges the dramatic vocabulary.

A world that judges behavior and language purely in terms of style judges physical appearance the same way, and the characters of the Etherege-Wycherley comedy are very concerned with the modes and rituals of dressing. Etherege's plays, in fact, all begin in the morning, as the hero-gallant dresses and plans his day. Thus, in a real sense, we are introduced to his character as we are introduced to his appearance; he puts on his attitudes with his clothes. The foolishness and lack of grace that characterize the fop are also dramatised through a study of his dress. Typically, Vanbrugh's Lord Foppington is introduced in a scene that calls attention to his fashions:

LORD FOP. Death and Eternal Tartures, Sir, I say the Packet's too high by a Foot.

TAYL. My Lord, if it had been an Inch lower, it would not have held your Lordship's Pocket-Handkerchief.

LORD FOP. Rat my Pocket-Handkerchief! Have not I a Page to carry it? You may make him a Packet up to his Chin a purpose for it: But I will not have mine come so near my Face. . . . Mr. *Foretop*, you don't intend to put this upon me for a full Periwig?

FORE. Not a full one, my Lord? I don't know what your Lordship may please to call a full one, but I have cram'd 20 Ounces of Hair into it.

LORD FOP. What it may be by Weight, Sir, I shall not dispute; but by Tale, there are not 9 Hairs of a side. (I.iii)

There is, however, an added element in this scene (which actually goes on in this manner quite a bit longer), which makes our first impression of Lord Foppington different from our reactions to his predecessors. In the room with Foppington and his lackeys is his impoverished younger brother, who has come to beg for a loan, and whose plea is ignored in deference to the more "important" business at hand:

Y. FASH. But let's accost him—*To Lord Fop.*] Brother, I'm your Humble Servant.

LORD FOP. O Lard, *Tam,* I did not expect you in *England;* Brother, I am glad to see you— *Turning to his Taylor.*] Look you Sir, I shall never be reconcil'd to this nauseous Packet.

Young Fashion is on stage throughout Lord Foppington's dressing scene, and at the same time that we laugh at the elder brother's foppishness we are not allowed to lose sight of his concurrent heartlessness. Foppington's concern with style is not seen in a vacuum, but in a realistic context; it is thus not merely a foolish eccentricity, but rather a serious distortion of values. Vanbrugh has changed the situation from that of enacting an important ritual ineptly to that of attaching undue importance to an insignificant act. The scene is still comic, but darkly comic; as with the wit-duels, the assumption that style is the most important concern in any situation is now open to question.

Vanbrugh's subversive modifications thus extend to the conventional character types as well. Lord Foppington is generally considered the greatest of the long line of fops in the comedy of manners, but our response to him is a new and complex one. In addition to the new moral concerns, Foppington does not share the conventional fops' stupidity. They had always placed very low on the wit scale in their plays, proving themselves completely inept in their attempts to control or manipulate language with their betters. Lord Foppington, however, has an unmistakable way with a phrase, as he demonstrates in the play's final scene, when he rationalizes the loss of his intended bride to his brother:

Dear *Tam,* since Things are thus fallen aut, prithee give me leave to wish thee Jay. I do it *de bon Coeur,* strike me dumb; you have Marry'd a Woman Beautiful in her Person, Charming in her Ayrs, Prudent in her Canduct, Canstant in her Inclanations, and of a nice Marality, split my Wind-pipe. (V.v)

The balanced syntax, the successfully controlled irony, and particularly the ability to say something other than what he actually means set Foppington above and apart from his brother fops. Unprecedentedly, he is not trapped by his language, but it able to use it to extricate himself with some grace from an unpleasant situation.

Lord Foppington is clearly not only wittier but also more perceptive and intelligent than any of his predecessors. While he can be as foolish as the conventional fop, he is not a fool by nature. Amanda and Loveless tell us as much:

> AMAN. Now it moves my Pity more than my Mirth, to see a Man whom Nature has made no Fool, be so very industrious to pass for an Ass.
>
> LOV. No, there you are wrong, *Amanda;* you shou'd never bestow your pity upon those who take pains for your Contempt. Pity those whom Nature abuses, but never those who abuse Nature. (II.i)

Loveless' words point to the object of Vanbrugh's attention: not one foolish individual, but his affectations, the way he has chosen to "abuse Nature." We cannot just laugh at Foppington and dismiss him from serious consideration, but must question the reasons why he is "so very industrious to pass for an Ass."

Foppington offers part of the answer himself, when his exasperated brother attempts a supreme insult:

> Y. FASH. Now, by all that's Great and Powerful, thou art the Prince of Coxcombs.
>
> LORD FOP. Sir—I am proud of being at the Head of so prevailing a Party. (III.i)

Far from being socially inept, Lord Foppington has had the insight to see exactly what the values of his society are, and the ability to mold himself into their ultimate fulfillment. In this light, it is important to note that the supposedly rational and superior characters in *The Relapse* are also affected by the "prevailing party," even if at the same time they are more aware than Foppington of its vanity and affectation. Amanda and Loveless admit on coming to London that they are attracted to the social follies they profess to reject (II,i); Amanda later betrays an unseemly delight in flirting (II,i); and Tom Fashion acknowledges that clothes do make a man (I,iii).

The change from the view of society presented by Etherege and Wycherley is a vital one. Their fop was a social failure. Measured against successful figures presented as the social standard—Horner, Dorimant, Courtall—he was ridiculous because he couldn't play the social games as well as the others. *The Relapse* has no Dorimant. Lord Foppington is the standard of this society; his extreme affectation meets all its requirements. He is ridiculous not because he is inept at the social game but because he is so supremely successful at it. Vanbrugh has turned the convention on its head; the characters in this play become lower in our estimation as they rise closer to the social ideal. From here it is but a short step to the obverse conclusion, that those who least approach the social ideal should take on a positive value in their rejection of society's norms. It is a step that Vanbrugh doesn't quite take in this play, although he emphasizes that his hero Tom Fashion is not a part of this world ("Your education has been a little at large," Foppington reminds him in the dressing scene), but he does show a growing appreciation for alternative social values in his later plays. And Farquhar, obviously influenced by Vanbrugh, will take that step when he moves into the country in *The Recruiting Officer* and *The Beaux' Stratagem* and finds the country ethos to be a valid and even superior alternative to that of London society. Vanbrugh will have prepared the audience for such a discovery, by weakening the convention's claim to exclusiveness.

Lady Fancyfull, in *The Provok'd Wife,* is another example of this kind of reversal of norms through manipulation of a stock character. A typical lustful lady, she is quickly established as vain and affected. As in *The Relapse,* however, Vanbrugh makes it clear that Lady Fancyfull lives in a world that inspires foolish affectation in everyone—even the essentially level-headed Bellinda and Lady Brute confess to playing games of coquetry (III.iii). When everyone in the play is a slave to society's foibles, Lady Fancyfull's foolishness becomes a matter of quantity, not quality. She merely thinks and acts as the others do, but with too much gusto. Heartfree, whose opinions and taste we are led to respect, has been attracted to her; he sees that her flaws, like Foppington's, are the result of abusing Nature:

> LADY FAN. Why, what has Nature done for me?
>
> HEART. What you have undone by Art. It made you handsom; it gave you Beauty to a Miracle, a Shape without a fault, Wit enough to make 'em relish, and so turn'd you loose to your own Discretion; which has made such Work with you, that you are become the Pity of our Sex, and the Jest of your own. (II.i)

Like Foppington she has chosen deliberately to play the fool, evidently because society has convinced her that it is the proper way to act. And like Foppington, she raises questions that subvert the entire structure and morality of the Restoration comic world. When Etherege or Wycherley satirized a fop or vain lady for being unable to play the social game, he was actually affirming the standards and ethics of the society. Laughter at Lady Fancyfull reflects on Bellinda and Lady Brute, and must be tempered with doubts about the society whose demands inspire one "that Heaven had taken such wondrous pains about [to] be so very industrious, to make herself the *Jack Pudding* of the Creation" (II.i).

Vanbrugh's manipulation of conventional character types extends beyond their moral or satiric implications to the basic definitions of these stock figures. His plays are peopled with men and women who only partially resemble their counterparts in earlier plays. By giving them characteristics that are not part of the formula, or by combining elements from two or more stock types to create an original blend, or by introducing new creations, he considerably enlarges the restricted *dramatis personae* of the comedy of manners. The result, in addition to new variety and comic material, is further implied criticism of the old limitations in terms of both breadth and depth. Vanbrugh's plays not only have room for a larger and more varied population, but that population is made up to a great extent of characters who are more complex, more individualized and more realistic than those inhabiting the world of Etherege and Wycherley.

A few striking examples should be sufficient to establish the pattern. Lord Foppington, as I have noted, combines all the characteristics of the traditional fop with an intelligence and wit that make him a significant variant. His younger brother fills the plot function of the truewit-gallant, but has so little verbal ability that his encounters with Foppington leave him virtually speechless and not at all in control. Moreover, Vanbrugh emphasizes that Young Fashion is not the typical town gallant; he is not only impoverished but unattuned to the demands of society—his servant has to teach him how to flatter and how to deal with his brother, he has unprecedented attacks of scruples, and Foppington remarks that his education has been "a little at large." A hero relatively inept in the ways of the world and unable to outquip the Prince of Coxcombs is certainly an innovation in the comedy of manners. In *The Provok'd Wife,* Sir John Brute combines aspects of the conventional cuckold-fool with the grossness of a country squire, the morality of an unmarried rake, a large helping of farcical buffoonery, and occasional moments of wit and insight. And Mr. Barnard in *The Country House* (one of the adaptations) and both Loverule and Sir Francis Headpiece in *A Journey to London* are potential cuckolds with enough intelligence or sense to retain our sympathy and respect.

Another variation on formula characterizations that Vanbrugh evidently liked, since he repeated it in three plays, is the untutored young girl who, despite a general naïveté, instinctively possesses the feminine wiles, sexual inclinations and social ambitions of a town lady. Hoyden in *The Relapse,* Corinna in *The Confederacy* and, in a smaller way, Betty Headpiece in *A Journey to London* all combine the previously separate qualities of childlike innocence (e.g., Margery in *The Country House*) and precocious sexuality and sophistication (e.g., Hippolita in *The Gentleman Dancing-Master*). Hoyden is capable within the same scene of defining a terrible sin—"I never disobey my Father in any thing but eating of green Gooseberries."—and a terrible punishment—"And if I don't shew my Breeding from the head to the foot of me, may I be twice Married, and die a Maid" (IV.i). Betty is able to turn from childish squabbles with her brother to the town pastimes of gaming and flirting, with a speed and ease that astonish her London-bred uncle. Corinna is enough of a child to keep careful count of her age—"sixteen, two months, and odd days"—and to run to the maid for comfort and protection. But, in contrast to her model, the Marianne of Dancourt's *Bourgeoises à la Mode,* she also displays an awareness of the way of the world far beyond her tender years:

> I protest to you (lest you should think me too forward now) he's the only Man that wears a Beard, I'd Ink my Fingers for. May be if I marry him, in a Year or two's Time I mayn't be so nice. (II.i)

Vanbrugh's servants are also significant variations on the conventions. While servants in the comedy of manners, almost never amount to more than door-openers and message-carriers, Vanbrugh's not only play major roles in the action, but frequently surpass their masters in cleverness and wit; consider Lory in *The Relapse,* Rasor and Madamoiselle in *The Provok'd Wife,* Brass and Flippanta in *The Confederacy,* and Sancho and Jacinta in *The Mistake.* Vanbrugh is also the first to introduce representatives of the City's merchant class into significant roles, most notably in *The Confederacy,* and to make them more

than objects of social ridicule. And his first and final comedies break with convention by allowing representatives of London society (Amanda in *The Relapse* and Loverule, Uncle Richard and Clarinda in *A Journey to London*) to criticise its manners and even to suggest that the country life and virtues might be valid alternatives. The immediate effect of introducing such characters and of using aspects of the old stock figures in new combinations is to provide new comic material, but complexity and originality also produce a certain amount of depth and realism that were missing from the earlier comedy of manners.

In a further break with conventions of characterization and judgment, many of Vanbrugh's major figures violate what was, according to Elizabeth Mignon [in *Crabbed Age and Youth,* 1947] a universal law of human existence in the Etherege-Wycherley comedy:

> The ages of man or woman in Restoration comedy are neither seven nor four, but two. . . . For gallant and Belle alike, the period of decay is as rapid as their maturity. There seems to be no middle or transition stage. They are young; then suddenly they are old.

Characters over a certain age (which seems to have been about twenty) or already in the state of matrimony lose all claim to our admiration or serious consideration; almost automatically they become fools, fops, cuckolds, prudes or absurd lechers (of both sexes). In Vanbrugh's plays, however, this rule is repeatedly broken. The central figures in each of his original plays, as well as *The Confederacy* and *The Country House,* are married, and yet none is merely and automatically ridiculous. If Amanda and Loveless are assumed to be the same couple that appeared in Cibber's *Love's Last Shift* (to which *The Relapse* is a sequel), they have been married at least ten years at the start of Vanbrugh's play, yet Amanda is still attractive to Worthy, and her moral problem merits our attention. In *The Provok'd Wife* the Brutes have been married at least two years, which would seem to put Lady Brute in the class of Wycherley's Lady Fidget. Instead, Vanbrugh treats her scenes with Constant much more like those between an unmarried belle and her suitor. Lady Arabella in *A Journey to London* leads a life that degrades her, but this degradation is considered seriously, not dismissed with ridicule, and her husband's situation is very much a sympathetic one. Lady Fancyfull is Vanbrugh's counterpart to Etherege's Lady Cockwood and other lustful female fops, but she is young enough for Heartfree to have been attracted to her. Aesop (in the two plays that bear his name) is both old and wise, as are Uncle Richard and Sir Charles in *A Journey to London,* Griffard in *The Country House,* Don Alvarez and Don Felix in *The Mistake,* and the Don Felix in *The False Friend.*

It should be noted that the structure of Vanbrugh's plays demonstrates the results, as well as the process, of weakening and discrediting Restoration comic conventions. Etherege and Wycherley had one important artistic advantage: since the world of their plays was a highly artificial one, their characters and plots could be manipulated with little regard for realism or probability. By demonstrating the unnaturalness of the conventions that supported this comic world, Vanbrugh not only made room for a new realism, but also made it impossible for his plots to follow the neat pattern of his predecessors. His comedies characteristically end without resolving all the issues. Amanda in **The Relapse** successfully resists temptation, but the expected fifth act repentance and re-reformation (or exposure and dismissal) of Loveless never come, and we cannot assume that the couple will live happily ever after. Tom Fashion gets the girl and the inheritance, but we are virtually assured that his marriage will be an unsuccessful one. Sir John Brute is left at the end of **The Provok'd Wife** unsure of whether he has been cuckolded; and, while we know he hasn't, the event seems imminent. **The Confederacy** resolves all of its plot complications but not its underlying problems; the two marriages at its center are still unsatisfactory, and none of the characters has been affected sufficiently to avoid a continuing conflict.

Judged purely by the neat and artificial standards of the comedy of manners, Vanbrugh's treatment of his plot material is weak and confused. Bonamy Dobrée [in his Introduction to *The Complete Works of Sir John Vanbrugh,* 1927] sees the distinction clearly, though his definition of great art is open to question:

> What to us seems to distinguish the people of Wycherley and Congreve from those of Vanbrugh is . . . that the first two groups seem to be acting under the sway of some compelling internal mechanism, which is replaced by free will in the characters of **The Relapse** and **The Provok'd Wife.** Wycherley and Congreve were greater artists than Vanbrugh because a sense of fatality runs through their plays; their characters are in the grip of destiny; they must behave as they do. Vanbrugh did, indeed, further the decay of the art.

But Vanbrugh does not accept the standards of Etherege and Wycherley; he has rejected the logic of their comic world, and with it the "sense of fatality" of an artificially constructed plot. On his terms and in the world of his plays, to provide any simple but unrealistic conclusions would be to falsify the issue—indeed, on those occasions that he does attempt a simple and mechanical conclusion, most notably the *deus ex machina* of **The Confederacy,** it rings unmistakably false. By modifying and breaking with the conventions of the comedy of manners, Vanbrugh frees his plays and his characters from the "compelling internal mechanism" that limited the depth and scope of Restoration comedy. His plays, and those of his one major artistic heir, Farquhar, are marked by an unmistakable vitality and expansiveness, as well as a new ability to deal with serious issues, which had been missing before and which would soon disappear into the new artificialities of sentimentality. (pp. 346-61)

> *Gerald M. Berkowitz, "Sir John Vanbrugh and the Conventions of Restoration Comedy," in* Genre, *Vol. VI, No. 3, September, 1973, pp. 346-61.*

Peter Dixon (essay date 1973)

[*In the following excerpt from his introduction to* The

Provok'd Husband, *Dixon describes Cibber's role in the creation of that play, noting that Cibber subdued Vanbrugh's impulsive wit in the play to comply with his own conception of exemplary comedy.*]

For our knowledge of the genesis of **The Provoked Husband** we are almost entirely dependent on Cibber's Preface and Prologue to the play. From these we learn that during the last years of his life Vanbrugh was working on a new comedy entitled **A Journey to London.** Shortly before his death in 1726 he discussed its plan and structure with Cibber, into whose hands the unfinished manuscript subsequently passed, and from whose hands it emerged two years later as a "regular" five-act play. Its new title looks back to Vanbrugh's youthful success, **The Provoked Wife,** even while it affirms that Cibber has set his own stamp on the work, characteristically giving prominence to the scenes of domestic strife in high society. **The Provoked Husband; or, a Journey to London** opened at Drury Lane on January 10, 1728. It was published three weeks later, on January 31, simultaneously with Vanbrugh's fragment. (p. xiii)

Cibber's Prologue implies that **A Journey to London** was the product of Vanbrugh's mature years, a moral atonement for past licentiousness. But the Prologue . . . is not altogether trustworthy, and its tendentious suggestions, like those of the Preface, cannot be relied upon as evidence for the dating of Vanbrugh's fragment. The text of the fragment—assuming that Cibber published a faithful transcript of Vanbrugh's papers—yields some small clues: an allusion to the Septennial Act points to a date sometime after 1716, while references to the game of quadrille and to "toupees" suggest the early 1720s. It is therefore tempting to connect the play with Vanbrugh's letter to Jacob Tonson of June 18, 1722: the actors, he writes, are "forc'd to Act round and round upon the Old Stock, though Cibber tells me, 'tis not to be conceiv'd, how many and how bad Plays, are brought to them." Perhaps it was in this mood of dissatisfaction with the sorry state of the London theater that **A Journey to London** was conceived; or perhaps Cibber flatteringly encouraged Vanbrugh to take up again a project he had begun some years before.

All this is largely conjecture. What is certain is that the unfinished **Journey to London** is a short sketch of three and a half acts, rather less than half the length of **The Relapse.** Yet of the completed play only about a third derives from Vanbrugh, for Cibber did not simply expand and amplify; he dropped some lively, farcical material (the misadventures in the coach when the ladies go to the theater, and the hazard-playing scene) as well as whole passages of dialogue and several incidental touches of satire. These omissions allowed Cibber to develop and give prominence to the scenes between Lord and Lady Townly (Vanbrugh's Lord and Lady Loverule). It was in their quarrels and final reconciliation that his chief interest lay, whereas Vanbrugh's imagination had been stimulated by the arrival of his rustic fools in the metropolis of knaves. His provincial family, the Headpieces, occupies the center of the stage: Cibber's Wrongheads are relegated to a subordinate position (and to the subtitle of the new play), though in reorganizing the action Cibber was careful to make one of his principal characters, Manly, intimately concerned in the fortunes of both the Wrongheads and the Townlys. There is some truth in Cibber's complaint that Vanbrugh's scenes were "undigested" or "irregular," a succession of brief, vigorous, but not always very clearly interrelated episodes. Cibber has given shape and form to the play by working up three major quarrels between the Townlys, each more intense and threatening than the last, interwoven with Manly's courtship of Lady Grace—two compatible temperaments whose domestic future seems bright— and the schemings of Lady Wronghead and Count Basset. Cibber has thus imposed regularity and symmetry, and has tied up the dramatic threads. He has also skilfully exploited the resources of the theater and the abilities of the Drury Lane company. His actors, himself included, are given opportunities for virtuoso display, as in the long speeches of Lord and Lady Townly and Sir Francis. And he has created a distinct theatrical tone for each act. The bustle of Act II contrasts with the duologues of Act III, while Act IV (like the fourth act of his *Careless Husband*) is full of conspiratorial whisperings and asides, with characters grouping and regrouping as the intrigue gathers momentum. The fifth act is distinguished by its use of scene-changes and spectacle; it affords a masquerade and a dance, as well as all the distress and suspense of the dènouement.

The contrast with Vanbrugh's *Journey to London* is very marked. His rapid scenes are full of activity, and of energy threatening to erupt. The fragment breaks off at the moment when Sir Francis interrupts the rakes and ladies in their hazard-playing; violence is imminent. In a sense it is only fitting that Vanbrugh's last play should be tantalizingly unfinished. It was the unreal sense of finality in Cibber's *Love's Last Shift*, the cheerful, even smug suggestion that nothing remains to be said, which irritated and amused him, and which prompted its "sequel," *The Relapse.* Now Cibber has the last word, substituting order and tidiness for Vanbrugh's explosiveness, imposing on the plot those dramatic qualities that Vanbrugh scorned. In 1698 Vanbrugh [in *A Short Vindication of the "Relapse" and the "Provok'd Wife" from Immorality and Prophaneness*] had entered an emphatic protest against "the too exact observance of what's call'd the Rules of the Stage, and the crowding a Comedy with a great deal of Intricate Plot." In his opinion, "the chief entertainment, as well as the Moral, lies much more in the Characters and the Dialogue, than in the Business and the Event." Cibber is very much concerned with the plot and the moral lesson to be drawn from its resolution. Vanbrugh is preoccupied with the interaction of characters, especially in situations of potential or actual friction and hostility.

Throughout, Cibber has softened the rigors of the original. Vanbrugh is at pains to emphasize the nastier and harsher sides of London life, at the level both of the street and of the drawing room. The goose-pie, which has traveled with the Headpieces from Yorkshire, is violently seized by two hungry rogues who are not afraid to set on their rustic pursuers. The rakish Captain Toupee, whom Cibber dispenses with entirely, indulges in rude familiarity with Lady Loverule. And Vanbrugh's Mrs. Motherly is "an errant Bawd," her lodgings no better than a brothel—so that the Headpieces may find themselves unawares in the same em-

barrassment that John Moody experienced on his earlier visit to London, when it appears he was kidnapped into a house of ill repute. Cibber has not a word of John Moody's escapades; the author of *Love's Last Shift* would not have scrupled to joke about them, but times and audiences have changed. Of Mrs. Motherly's profession only the merest hint remains in the name itself (Mother being the common title for a bawd), and in the phrase with which she leaves Myrtilla and the Squire to their tête-à-tête: "I'll even turn you together." Time and again Cibber takes the edge off Vanbrugh's forcefulness. It is a small but significant detail that Lady Loverule responds to Clarinda's account of an unfashionably sober way of spending one's life by remarking: "Well, Clarinda, thou art a most contemptible Creature." Lady Townly's reaction is: "Well, my dear, thou art an astonishing creature." This is not to say that Lady Townly lacks spirit, but that she is spirited in a more polite and amiable way. She has a teasing, playful tone in many of her altercations with her husband, and takes an amused delight in seeing herself come off best. She is still the same coquette as in her youth; for just as a coquette values her chastity only for the bargaining power it gives her, so Lady Townly is conscious that she can make capital out of her fidelity to her husband. Lady Loverule is altogether tougher, more aggressive, more caustic of tongue. The depths of her nature are uncovered in a brief, harsh scene which Cibber omits, an interview with her mercer in which the sardonic lady merrily taunts the poor fellow into a passion. It is, however, typical of Vanbrugh's complex attitude that the mercer, Mr. Shortyard, is not simply an innocent victim of upper-class callousness; his very name passes judgment on him (unlike Cibber's neutral "Mr. Lutestring"). Again, Vanbrugh's principal villain, Colonel Courtly, has about him some of the cynicism and audacity of his Restoration forebears, whereas Count Basset, for all his sprightly metaphors from the card-table, is merely the smooth insinuating sharper. He cringes in defeat as the Colonel would never have done.

In the Prologue [to *The Provoked Husband*] Cibber alleges that Vanbrugh, as he grew older, rejected his earlier views about morality and comedy. A play, he came to believe, should explicitly punish vice, and hold up to the spectators images not only of what they are but also of what they ought to be. This certainly runs quite counter to Vanbrugh's sturdy self-defense in the *Short Vindication:* "The Business of Comedy is to shew People what they shou'd do, by representing them upon the Stage, doing what they shou'd not." That doctrine is in fact restated by one of the characters in *A Journey to London*— "Bad Examples (if they are but bad enough) give us as useful Reflections as good ones do"—and there is no evidence in the play itself, or in what Cibber discloses of Vanbrugh's intentions, to suggest a change of heart. Cibber is falsely ascribing to Vanbrugh his own faith in exemplary comedy, a faith for which he was to be tellingly rebuked by Fielding [in *Tom Jones*] in connection with this very play. The Prologue is quite misleading, suggesting a nonexistent affinity between the two dramatists. For from what Cibber says in his introductory remarks it is clear that the *Journey to London* was heading in a different direction from that taken by *The Provoked Husband*. Vanbrugh apparently planned to bring the Loverule quarrel to a climax (and in all probability to allow Lady Loverule to "make the House ring with Reprisals," as her husband predicts), before having him actually "turn her out of his doors." Their antagonism was to issue in an angry separation, without hope of reconciliation, but also without the possibility of divorce, since although the lady lives dangerously among familiar coxcombs and sharpers, she has not been unfaithful. Had Vanbrugh finished the play the high-life plot would have been a bleak study of marital incompatibility and disillusionment, a case of what Cibber calls "adultery of the mind." And no doubt the successful Sir Charles / Clarinda relationship would have stood over against the misery of the Loverules much as the two pairs in *The Provoked Wife* are contrasted with one another. In Cibber's hands the play has become a triumph of conventional morality, and of the marriage vow. Lady Townly at last begins to love her husband; more important, she learns to honor and obey him. The difference between the two endings was nicely put by the anonymous author of the first serious critique of the play, *Reflections on the Principal Characters in . . . "The Provoked Husband"*: Vanbrugh's solution to the dilemma "would have answer'd to our judgments, the other sooth[e]s our good Nature."

Cibber was quite explicit about his reasons for so drastically altering the projected course of the plot. He thought that "such violent measures" as Lord Loverule would have taken, "however just they might be in real life, were too severe for comedy, and would want the proper surprise which is due to the end of a play." Surprise of this kind was not a quality that much interested Vanbrugh, who found material rather in the impulses and obstinacies of "real life." Cibber prefers the less painful way of an eleventh-hour reformation, though in order to excite our emotions he brings us to the brink of catastrophe. The anonymous essayist observed that Cibber had "carried the severe part so far, as with the Help of the Action [i.e., acting] to draw Tears from the Eyes of his Audience, which surely can never be the natural Business of Comedy"; he might therefore "have safely ventured one Step farther." But Cibber had by now a whole series of reconciliation scenes behind him—in *Love's Last Shift, The Careless Husband, The Lady's Last Stake;* the formula was well-tried and successful. He clearly enjoyed working up these scenes, with their emotionalism and religiose language. "Save me, hide me from the world!" exclaims Lady Townly; and again: "How odious does this goodness make me!" Her reformation is scarcely prepared for (the twinges of remorse and regret she experiences in Act III are too slight to be of much consequence), and is to that extent a sentimental simplification. But in fairness to Cibber it must be said that he is not inviting the audience to wallow in the merely distressful; tears are shed over a sinner's moral reformation, not over undeserved misfortune.

Meanwhile the "scenes of the lower humor" are running their largely separate course, demanding a very different set of responses from the audience. It is true that some parallels are established between the spendthrift wives and their overindulgent, and finally provoked, husbands: Lady Wronghead's preference for wax candles is neatly matched by Lady Townly's extravagant demand for white flambeaux, and neither lady chooses to have a head for figures. But whereas Lady Townly can be brought, after some emotional bullying, to a sorrowful sense of her follies, Lady Wronghead can only be blackmailed into a temporary docility. So the Wronghead family is left in a state of uneasy truce, having learnt only the first half of the play's moral lesson: "Let husbands govern, gentle wives obey." Nor is there much hope that Lady Wronghead will come to appreciate the charm of that domestic "sobriety" which Lady Grace champions in her dialogue with Lady Townly (Act III), and which runs as a subdued theme throughout the play. The Epilogue too reminds us of the merit of Lady Grace's "comfortable scheme of life": six months of sober living in the country, followed by a sober six months in London. It is characteristic of Cibber that the play should end on a note of moderate compromise, and perhaps this is one reason for its success during the eighteenth century. The manners and persons of the main plot are ostensibly upper class, yet the sobriety which is advocated is essentially a middle-class virtue, the virtue of the citizen and the merchant who frown on extravagance. Like Richardson, Cibber has a horror of the frivolities and irresponsibilities of high life (especially when they are concentrated in the treacherous inanities of the masquerade), even while he admires the glamor of polite society. As in *Pamela* we can enjoy the best of both social worlds; we can contentedly endorse the middle-class values which the plot upholds, while at the same time we breathe the more rarefied air in which the other, genteeler half lives.

The play has something for many, if not all, tastes: plot intrigue and strongly contrasted characters; wit without bawdy and virtuous sentiment without excessive mawkishness. And it has enough "low" humor for us to suppose that Goldsmith had it particularly in mind when he commended that kind of "Laughing and even Low Comedy, which seems to have been last exhibited by Vanbrugh and Cibber." Hugh Blair went even further [in his *Lectures on Rhetoric and Belles Lettres* (1783)]; he thought *The Provoked Husband* "perhaps, on the whole, the best Comedy in the English Language." (pp. xviii-xxv)

> *Peter Dixon, in an introduction to* The Provoked Husband *by Sir John Vanbrugh and Colley Cibber, edited by Peter Dixon, University of Nebraska Press, 1973, pp. xiii-xxvii.*

Lincoln B. Faller   (essay date 1974)

[*In the following excerpt, Faller addresses Vanbrugh's depiction of marriage in* The Relapse *and* The Provok'd Wife. *He suggests that Vanbrugh's dramas are more tragic than comic since his characters are incapable of arriving at any form of conflict resolution.*]

The soft stones of Blenheim by now need constant care, but Vanbrugh's plays—happily the word is more durable—have weathered unharmed more than forty years of rare and sporadic attention. Perhaps *The Relapse* (1696) and *The Provoked Wife* (1697) would be better left as they stand, unencumbered by the scaffolding of busy critics. But the conclusion reached by Bonamy Dobrée in 1928 [in his introduction to *The Complete Works of Sir John Vanbrugh*], after he had edited not only Vanbrugh's original plays but also his translations, has not yet, it seems, been adequately shaken. "Since his work is not very difficult or subtle, and conveys no unique outlook, there does not seem to be very much to say about it," said Dobrée; and whether successive students of the plays turning to the four volumes from the Nonesuch Press have been cowed by this pronouncement or not, only a few of them have ventured into print. Writing for the most part in the additional shadow of John Palmer, they have tended, like him, to see Vanbrugh as a transitional figure between, as Palmer had put it [in *The Comedy of Manners,* 1962], "two kingdoms" of comedy. While they have been kinder than Palmer in judging the plays, dropping, for instance, his accusation that Vanbrugh is "immoral," still, I believe, they have failed to do him justice. For, judging from the two original plays he completed, Vanbrugh had, if not a "unique outlook," then one that for its subtlety and seriousness of purpose deserves a better reputation.

"Easy" Vanbrugh he was called. The reference was not to his virtue (*pace* Palmer), but to the grace of his writing, for his dialogue seemed so natural that the actors could learn his lines with scarcely any trouble at all. But Vanbrugh's ease, and ours as we experience his work, should be reckoned as hardly more than superficial. His fine ladies and gentlemen, for all their fluency of wit, lead lives that are at base far from easy, lives that, however sometimes deadening to them, are fraught for us with rich complexities. To be sure, the difficulties that confront them are frequently farcical: thus, for instance, the indignities that heap upon Lord Foppington in *The Relapse* when he goes to claim his country wife, or, in *The Provoked Wife,* the attentions that Lady Brute is made to suffer when her husband, amorous and filthy, comes home from a night of drunken riot. Yet beyond such farce there is often something to complicate and contain, even to embarrass our laughter.

Foppington, who is Vanbrugh's version of a character appearing in an earlier play by Colley Cibber, is not simply a comic butt. Cibber's character, a witless beau who makes himself ludicrous by his affectations in both dress and love, is one more incarnation of Sir Fopling Flutter. In Foppington, however, there is something attractive, even sympathetic, and this derives not only from his capacity for genuine wit, his real sense of humor, his almost imperturbable cool. "Now it moves my pity more than my mirth," says Amanda while others are criticizing his lordship, "to see a man whom nature has made no fool be so very industrious to pass for an ass" (2.151-53). We are brought almost to agree by the episode that immediately follows, in which Vanbrugh allows him a dignity that is more than comic, that lifts him above contempt. Convinced that his new peerage has made him even more irresistibly charming, obliged him even more greatly to play gallant to the ladies, Foppington offers Amanda somewhat too avid a compliment. She boxes his ear, there is some swordplay with her husband, and Foppington (no doubt his ear still ringing) falls wounded to the floor. Encouraged by a quack to believe the wound may be fatal, Foppington, as he is carried off, generously forgives his as-

sailant. This parting gesture is both comic and eminently decent, the first because Foppington has only been pinked in the side, and the second because, as the play suggests, Amanda's reproof was more than adequate. Loveless, whose fidelity to his wife has lately been strained, has been much too ready to avenge her honor. Later on, as we see Foppington trussed up and tossed about by clumsy country boobs, we cannot help laughing; and yet, for we have come to feel almost fond of him, our laughter may be tinged with some slight distress.

More complex and less easily digested than his antecedents in late seventeenth-century comedy, Foppington may perhaps be said to anticipate the amiable fools of Goldsmith and Sheridan. But there is nothing in the comedy of manners, or in that which followed upon it, quite to compare with Sir John Brute. The more we dwell upon his character, the less easily we can laugh at the trouble he brings his wife. A blustering bully with women, a coward among men, Sir John is, for the egregious vulgarity of his temper, his downright coarseness, an especially difficult character to stomach. Thus in a rare moment of affability he toasts the mistress of an acquaintance, not knowing the lady in question is his wife. Swallowing, he coughs back into the cup, a portent which would make him jealous, he says, did he love Lady Brute, "for I never drank my wife's health in my life but I puked in the glass" (3.1.98-99). In the same scene he had complained that his wife is "grown so dainty of late she finds fault even with a dirty shirt" (2.73-74), and so perhaps it is to vex her specially then, that later, returning home "all dirt and bloody" (as the stage direction specifies), he demands a kiss. Delighted by her obvious aversion to him—"I see it goes damnably against your stomach"—he demands another, and then grabs and "tumbles" her, besmearing her with his own filth. "So," he says, paying no attention to the presence of her confidante, "now you being as dirty and as nasty as myself, we may go pig together" (5.2.47, 59-60)—a foul proposition in more ways than one. As two gallants are hiding in an adjoining closet all during this scene, the action building to the inevitable discovery, it would be more than a bit obtuse to suggest that what happens here is not primarily funny. But a good deal of the laughter Sir John provokes in this, and in other scenes with his wife, is of a peculiarly embarrassed sort. We laugh at his lines not only because we find them humorous—our sympathy for Lady Brute cannot let us think him simply funny—but perhaps also because we are at a loss to respond in any other way. It is almost as if someone had told too dirty a joke.

Even in the several scenes where he appears without his wife, Sir John remains something of an obscenity. With Lord Rake and Colonel Bully he prowls the night streets, abusing the citizenry, breaking their windows, and beating the watch. When the occasion offers, he would do all this in a clergyman's gown. Such profanity, such a "sacrilege" upon the cloth (this eventually proved intolerable for the theater of Vanbrugh's day), is not, however, the fullest measure of his obscenity. Sir John acquires his clerical garb from a "dissenting journeyman taylor," whom he and his friends waylay and molest for no good reason (4.1.18). There is not very much that is funny in the tailor's predicament, for we are given no reason to believe that he is not, as he tells his tormentors, "an honest man and a good workman," and that he will not be, as he tells them, "quite undone" if they take his gown (2.24, 37-38). Even less funny is the way in which the scene has opened. It would appear that the tailor, who is glad to get away with no worse harm, has had good reason to be afraid. As Rake and Bully come rushing onstage, we realize that they have just run a man through, more or less for fun. "Is the dog dead?" asks Rake. "No, damn him," replies the Colonel. "I heard him wheeze." To which Rake, with obvious relish, adds, "How the witch his wife howled!" (2.1-3). For his part in such sport, and the way in which he treats his wife, to say nothing of his general coarseness and profanity, Sir John eventually is punished, of course. But even were he the cuckold he only thinks himself to be, so conventionally comic a punishment could hardly seem enough. After all, as Lord Rake so simply spells it out, "there's a man murdered" (4.1.6).

In his treatment of Foppington and Brute we can see with especial clarity, I should think, an essential quality of Vanbrugh's comedy, perhaps its most important. He writes as the fine ladies in *The Provoked Wife* speak, somewhere, as he tells us [in *A Short Vindication of the "Relapse" and the "Provok'd Wife," from Immorality and Prophaneness*], "between Jest and Earnest." Thus his delight in Foppington's ripe folly is mellowed with a certain sympathy, and his pleasure in Brute is tainted with disgust. In the case of Sir John especially Vanbrugh displays a sensibility exceptional among the comic writers of his age. Perhaps this is so because he very nearly is not a comic writer, or to put it differently, his plays are comedies by default. How else are we to respond to Sir John, we might ask, how else can we respond to him, but with laughter? To suggest that Vanbrugh in some marvelous way foreshadows the modern sensibility would be fatuous; still, to an audience acquainted with "black" comedy, the darkness that penumbrates jolly Sir John should not seem unfamiliar.

Disgusted with the depravity of human nature, yet tolerant of its failings, and above all bemused by both, Vanbrugh is preeminently a comedian of the human condition. It is this that sets him apart even from Wycherley, whose comedy, if not as deeply, is more consistently and so more corrosively "black." For unlike Wycherley, Vanbrugh is interested in characters who are conscious of their malaise. A concern with consciousness was of course to be a distinctive characteristic of the sentimentalists, but, unlike them, Vanbrugh is no optimist. He trusts neither in human nature nor in providence. What goes wrong is more significant than what goes right; what does not happen is more important than what does. Though both his plays end as comedies generally do, with marriages or people agreeing to marry, it can hardly be overlooked that both are more centrally concerned with marriages in the process of collapse. As one of his characters says, "Fortune, thou art a bitch" (*Relapse,* 1.2.87), and in his plays, true to its character, Fortune smiles either uncertainly, or in a way that one would do better not to examine.

The marriage of Tom Fashion, whose sentiment I have just quoted, illustrates the latter point. It would seem at the close of *The Relapse* that Tom has achieved the peak of felicity, having firmly in hand not only Miss Hoyden, but also her sizable fortune. Not so, said Vanbrugh [in *Short Vindication,* 1], when criticized for having given so great a reward to a character who "kick'd his Conscience down Stairs," for there is "no other proof of his being [the author's] Favourite, than that he has help'd him to a Wife, who's likely to make his Heart ake." While no such thought occurs to us as we watch the play, it is interesting that Vanbrugh, when forced to justify himself, would say such a thing. We do not bother to think about Tom Fashion and his bride (though if we did we would certainly agree with Vanbrugh), because we are not meant to. Their purpose, along with the other "Inferior Persons of the Play," is "to divert the Audience, by something particular and whimsical in their Humours." For, as we in the audience come quickly to appreciate, there is very little that is funny in the main business of the play, the falling apart of what once was, briefly, an ideal marriage.

The marriage that closes *The Provoked Wife* gives us something more to think about. It would seem that Heartfree and Bellinda have come to as satisfactory a relationship as one could hope for between a well-bred man and woman in late seventeenth-century society; had Lady Brute not married Sir John, she and Constant might have hoped for something similar. It is important, then, to note how closely Vanbrugh qualifies the good fortune of those who marry as well as they can. Before meeting Bellinda, Heartfree long has resisted romantic involvement, adopting a posture of detached cynicism. When, in their first scene together, Constant assures Heartfree that, despite his lack of success with Lady Brute, he intends nonetheless to love on, Heartfree's ironic reply borders on the sarcastic. "Perhaps," he says, "you have found out some new philosophy, that love's like virtue, its own reward" (2.1.188-90). But despite its easy phrasing, Heartfree's cynicism is forced, and possibly even desperate. As Constant has just assured him, "love is the devil" (1.123), and Heartfree, for all his talk, is not proof against its temptation. The truth is, as he later tells the ladies, he fears being in love only "because I always had an aversion to being used like a dog" (3.1.178). Though Bellinda ultimately collars him—making him feel that "to be capable of loving one, doubtless is better than to possess a thousand" (5.4.73-74)—even as he decides to marry, he fears that he is taking "a great leap in the dark" (5.5.27).

Bellinda, who at first had dismissed the idea of marrying Heartfree because he has no fortune, is no more certain than he that marriage can offer any lasting happiness. Though finally she decides to be more romantic than worldly, she retains a due sense of proportion. "I can't say I would live with him in a cell upon love and bread and butter," she admits to Lady Brute, "but I had rather have the man I love, and a middle state of life, than that gentleman in the chair there"—and here Bellinda points to the drunken, snoring Sir John—"and twice your ladyship's splendour" (5.2.121-24). Even this is not so romantic as it sounds. Why should Bellinda hope for happiness in marriage when her friend Lady Brute has found none? "If a man has the least spark either of honor or good nature," she believes, "he can never use a woman ill that loves him and makes his fortune both" (2.128-30). This last qualification is rich. Knowing that the gratitude of men is tickled by more than love, Bellinda can expect a modest sort of happiness; her hopes are grounded on a practical sense of human nature and how it operates in a less than ideal world.

It is such a world that traps Lady Brute, for by marrying badly she has lost her one chance at what Constant calls "the only heaven on earth" (5.4.69). If she is to find any happiness, then she must be satisfied to play in a rather earthy garden of delights. Constant, despite his capacity to conceive of the sublimely lucky marriage, the "one inestimable lot" among "a wondrous many blanks" (5.4.69-70), is more than willing to play along. But he, though of two minds, is more at home in the world than Lady Brute. She feels sharply the contradictions around and within her, as well she might, for her head is a tangle of values where the permissive code of the world of fashion, the imperatives of orthodox morality, and the demands of her own self-interest are inextricably knotted together.

Most simply, she wants a liaison with Constant, believing that he can supply the love and respect so sorely lacking in her marriage. As she says to Bellinda, "pretend what we will, . . . 'tis a hard matter to live without the man we love" (5.2.146-47). But Lady Brute's inclination to live with the man she loves, or at least to offer him the satisfaction that he craves, is powerfully inhibited by two considerations. The first of these, conventional enough, is a fear of being impolitic; she is concerned not only for her reputation, but with keeping her power over Constant. But more than this—and here we begin to touch on what makes Lady Brute so extraordinary—though she can say, "Virtue's an ass, and a gallant's worth forty on't" (1.1.77-78), still she is deterred from seeking, through intrigue, the emotional satisfaction she so sorely craves by the attractiveness of a moral ideal: "O," she says when Constant presses, "but a faithful wife is a beautiful character" (4.4.163).

Lady Brute never does manage to untangle her values. The closest she comes to the necessary moral crisis occurs when Constant nearly succeeds in forcing her, not quite against her will, into a secluded arbor in the park. What he has in mind we can guess, but at the deciding moment, some other people breaking in upon them, we are prevented from ever knowing whether Lady Brute, for all that she "would," indeed ever "could," even with Constant. Her last outcry, before they are interrupted, is typically equivocal: "Pray let us stop here, at least for this time" (4.4.205). Vanbrugh might just as well have said the same thing in his own voice to mark the end of his play. For insofar as Lady Brute is concerned, very little happens in the fifth act. Her husband, it is true, finally does get his comeuppance. Too much the coward to stand upon his honor when he finds Constant and Heartfree hiding in the closet, Sir John gets his lumps (sadly, in a figurative sense only) and is made to like them. But otherwise Lady Brute remains in the same perplexed situation. Vanbrugh gives us no indication of how she will act in the future, whether she will take refuge in the beautiful character of a virtuous wife, or whether she will take what pleasures she can by

making her husband a cuckold in fact. (Perhaps it was to divert us from so unresolved a situation that Vanbrugh devised, in the last scene, an eleventh-hour crisis in the marriage plans of Bellinda and Heartfree.)

In Lady Brute, Vanbrugh presents us with a character whose psychology is remarkably complex, and whose situation admits of no single interpretation. Indeed, though we may value richness of characterization in and of itself, it must be recognized that she, like her husband, fits uneasily into the comic mold. She escapes, and even threatens, whatever comic intentions Vanbrugh may originally have had for her. Apparently, he could not bring her to a final composition, and the play's consequent lack of resolution could be accounted a flaw. But one may also argue that the openendedness of *The Provoked Wife* is an attractive and valuable quality; it gives us something to think about. Would the possession of Constant, even in marriage, assure the happiness of Lady Brute? In any case, does she merit happiness? She has married Brute, as she tells us, out of "vanity" and "ambition" (1.1.50-51). She encourages Constant's attentions with no apparent guilt; despite her sense of morality, her greatest fear remains the loss of reputation. (This, as when she and Constant are discovered together in the park, can drop her into the vulgarest sort of cliché: "O heavens," she cries, "if they knew me, I'm ruined" [4.4.212-13].) Yet Lady Brute remains sympathetic, if only by virtue of a psychology sufficiently com-

AT THE

QUEEN'S THEATRE,
In the HAY-MARKET.

To morrow being Tuesday, the Sixth Day of November, 1705, will be presented, A New Comedy call'd,

The CONFEDERACY.

With several Entertainments of DANCING by the Famous Monsieur DESBARQUES and others, Newly Arriv'd from PARIS.

Boxes Five Shillings, Pit Three Shillings, First Gallery Two Shilings.

No Money to be Return'd after the Curtain is Drawn up. Beginning exactly at Five of the Clock.

By Her Majesty's Servants. VIVAT REGINA.

[From the original Play-bill, in the Possession of JOHN NIXON, Esq.]

Vanbrugh's Confederacy *Play Bill.*

plex to frustrate disapproval. "That you may more easily forgive me," she says to Bellinda when reproached for concealing her attachment to Constant, "remember, . . . that when our nature prompts us to a thing our honor and religion have forbid us, we would (were't possible) conceal even from the soul itself the knowledge of the body's weakness" (1.1.146-50). On the moral grounds that she herself has introduced, we can find no excuse for Lady Brute's wanting to hoodwink her soul. Still, though she may not be "the best of her sex" (as Vanbrugh was more than ready to allow), the sense of shame that prompts such an effort at self-deception, and the moral acuity that is sufficient at least to make that effort fail, makes it more easy for us as well to forgive her. (pp. 17-23)

After we are done laughing at the wit and the satire, and once we turn our attention away from the happiness promised (albeit conditionally) to Heartfree and Bellinda, *The Provoked Wife* makes us ponder a good deal more than merely the problem of "marital incompatibility." Vanbrugh seems to feel, not unreasonably, that the only real happiness that men and women can find is in each other, and if not in love, then at least in friendship. But how treacherous a footing does the world provide for either of these! "Let us do what we will," says Lady Brute to Bellinda, "most of [the men of the town] think there is no such thing as virtue considered in the strictest notions of it. . . . For they consider, we have no more religion than they have, nor so much morality; and between you and I, Bellinda, I'm afraid the want of inclination seldom protects any of us." When Bellinda, seeking some comfort, replies, "But sure we are not so wicked as they are, after all," Lady Brute allows her scant consolation: "We are as wicked, child, but our vice lies another way. Men have more courage than we, so they commit more bold, impudent sins. They quarrel, fight, swear, drink, blaspheme, and the like. Whereas we, being cowards, only backbite, tell lies, cheat at cards, and so forth" (5.2.151-58, 166-71). With these, very nearly her last lines, Lady Brute retires and the farce resumes. In its closing moments, the play wants only to entertain.

There is not so smooth an integration of farce and serious matter in *The Relapse,* perhaps because Vanbrugh, in treating the "upper" plot of this play, felt his moral sensibilities more radically engaged. *The Relapse* began, at least, as a sequel to the first of Colley Cibber's plays, *Love's Last Shift* (1696), the title of which refers to the means by which Amanda tricks Loveless back into bed, and marriage, eight years after he had abandoned her to penury and, as he thought, eventual death by smallpox. Brought to repentance by the sheer force of her love, he promises to reform, upon which Amanda, having received a convenient legacy, brings him another fortune to replace the one he had squandered. As the curtain falls they propose to live happily ever after. This romantic concoction brought tears, or so we are told, to a heretofore cynical audience, and the play is generally taken to mark a watershed in the history of sensibility. Vanbrugh, no sentimentalist, continued the story of Amanda and Loveless only to give it a more plausible conclusion.

Yet, as he points out in his *Short Vindication,* his motives

were sympathetic. Vanbrugh did not start with the intention of destroying Cibber's happy ending; this was just how things turned out. Loveless, he says,

> appear'd to me to be got into so agreeable a Tract of Life, that I often took a pleasure to indulge a musing Fancy, and suppose myself in his place. The Happiness I saw him possest of, I lookt upon as a Jewel of a very great worth, which naturally lead me to the fear of losing it; I therefore consider'd by what Enemies 'twas most likely to be attack'd, and that directed me in the Plan of the Works that were most probable to defend it. I saw but one danger in Solitude and Retirement, and I saw a thousand in the bustle of the World; I therefore in a moment determin'd for the Countrey, and suppos'd *Loveless* and *Amanda* gone out of town.

But why, once having imagined them safely out of town, did he then choose to risk their return? Judging from what he says is "the principal business in the *Relapse*"—that is, to show "the Disorders that are slipt into Loveless's House, by his being too positive in his own strength"—he sought to illustrate a moral. Of the collapse of Loveless's virtuous resolve, Vanbrugh writes [in his *Short Vindication*]:

> This I design'd for a natural Instance of the Frailty of Mankind, even in his most fixt Determinations: and for a mark upon the defect of the most steady Resolve, without that necessary Guard, of keeping out of Temptation. But I had still a farther end in *Loveless's Relapse.* . . . Here's a Woman whose Virtue is rais'd upon the utmost Strength of Foundation: Religion, Modesty, and Love, defend it. It looks so Sacred, one wou'd think no Mortal durst approach it; and seems so fix'd, one wou'd believe no Engine cou'd shake it: Yet loosen one Stone, the Weather works in, and the Structure molders apace to decay.

Certainly these are remarkable utterances. If indeed *The Relapse* is a play concerned with the frailty of man, whose hold upon happiness and virtue is tenuous to the extreme, then it would appear that Vanbrugh conceived this play in a spirit more akin to that of tragedy than of comedy. I suppose that previous writers on Vanbrugh have overlooked these passages because they seem such blatant concessions to Jeremy Collier's attack. Nonetheless, despite Vanbrugh's obvious delight in the lubriciousness of certain of his characters, despite the elegance and grace with which he endows the politest of them, despite even the blasphemy he gives them so wittily to speak, both his original plays are shaped—if not by Collier's religiosity—by a point of view quite close to Christian pessimism. Indeed, it is Vanbrugh's blasphemy, or rather that of his characters, which is most instructive in this regard.

The blasphemy is everywhere in both plays, very funny, but tending inevitably to color our sense of those who speak it and the society in which they move—a society aware of higher values, but not very serious about them. Of the two, *The Relapse*—which engaged Collier's wrath more than any other play—uses blasphemy to better effect, if only because it adds so significantly to our sense of what Amanda and Loveless have come up against in the persons of Worthy and Berinthia. "Well," says Berinthia, when Worthy persuades her to join forces with him against Amanda and Loveless, "I could be glad to have nobody's sins to answer for but my own. But where there is a necessity——." "Right as you say," Worthy interrupts, "where there is a necessity, a Christian is bound to help his neighbor" (3.2.200-203). Collier, [in *A Short View of the Immorality and Profaneness of the English Stage*], missing the point, was outraged that "Two Characters of Figure" should "determine the point thus in defence of Pimping." Nor, unsurprisingly, did he fail to note the way in which the conspirators salute each other when they feel near to gaining their complete purpose, the seduction of Amanda as well as Loveless. As Berinthia outlines her plan for bringing Amanda to the point of consent, Worthy kneels down before her and cries in mock gratitude: "Thou angel of light, let me fall down and adore thee!" To which Berinthia replies, "Thou minister of darkness, get up again, for I hate to see the devil at his devotions" (5.2.61-63).

Such language, beyond its humor, brings us to see Vanbrugh's "fine" characters—characters very nearly as "fine," surely, as Congreve's best—for what indeed they are. Worthy and Berinthia, surely not amoral, transcend mere immorality; they are libertines, in active revolt against the values they know to be virtuous, and the badge of this is (as it is with Sir John Brute) their apostasy. Having encountered them in these two scenes where they plot to destroy Amanda and Loveless's marriage so that, as Worthy says, "we may all four pass the winter very pleasantly" (3.2.199), we cannot help but observe that Vanbrugh's two most elegant characters, those most adept in the ways of the world, those the most attractively polished and charming, are as well the most fallen, and, perhaps, the most sinister.

Vanbrugh's intention in Worthy and Berinthia, he tells us himself in the *Short Vindication,* was "to shew the world how much the Trade [of Pimping] was improved." Yet here we may certainly suspect, if not his sincerity, at least the adequacy of his insight into his own work. For however much he may claim [in *Short Vindication*] that the characters in *The Relapse,* compared to those in *The Provoked Wife,* are "a little more refin'd, which places the Moral in a more reasonable, and I think more agreeable View" (refined can mean not only less coarse, but also less complicated and therefore more lucid), the fact remains that the characterization of Worthy, to say nothing of Berinthia, is still sufficiently complex to make him, and the play, a good deal more than merely a moral instrument. If we close our minds upon his libertinism, our experience of Worthy cannot be at all complete. Nor can we then appreciate Amanda's dilemma, the implications of which are among the richest that Vanbrugh leaves us to consider.

Worthy—it hardly needs saying—is an especially attractive figure, and Vanbrugh, for all he says to his discredit in the *Short Vindication,* appears to have thought so too. Of all Collier's criticisms, the one that irritated Vanbrugh the most, apparently, was Collier's ridicule of Worthy for

suddenly becoming "an Insipid *Platonick*" when he fails to seduce Amanda. Quoting the whole of Worthy's soliloquy on the occasion (the only time in the *Short Vindication* that he quotes himself), Vanbrugh suggests that Collier, in this one instance at least, ought rather to have commended these sentiments, for "there never was a homer Check given to the Lewdness of Women in any Play whatsoever." Such may accurately describe the immediate intention of Worthy's soliloquy, or not, but as rebuttal of Collier it is beside the point. For despite all that his soliloquy might do in the cause of virtue, Worthy as he speaks it is become neither insipid nor a sudden convert to platonic love. Though he may feel that "the vile, the gross desires of flesh and blood" have been "in a moment turn'd to adoration," though he declares, "The coarser appetite of nature's gone, / And 'tis methinks the food of angels I require," before he gets down to delivering his moral message to the ladies, he pauses a moment to be honest with himself, wondering, "How long this influence may last, heaven knows" (5.4.172-76). The "Poet's Fine Gentleman," as Collier sneeringly called him, remains just that; there is something fine indeed, if only from an aesthetic point of view, in Worthy's obdurate disinclination to think that, for him, tomorrow will be any different. He may be a fallen creature, but he rather smugly enjoys it; he is attractive not despite his consistent immorality, but because of it. And it would be foolish to think that he is done with Amanda.

Quite understandably, Amanda feels drawn to Worthy even as she denies him her body, and, as the structure of the plot makes clear, it is upon Amanda's temptation by Worthy, and not the relapse of Loveless, that the moral concern of the play is brought most prominently to bear. Even before she begins to mistrust her husband, Amanda has been flattered and warmed by Worthy's regard. Berinthia's propaganda for the permissive mores of the town— "I have led so private and recluse a life, my ignorance is scarce conceivable," says Amanda, all ears (2.488-89)— has had some effect. Still, though no longer so straitly laced, her virtue proves firm beneath Worthy's quite literal grasp. When, following Berinthia's lead, he urges her to revenge her husband's infidelity in kind, he understands not at all her need to keep faith, if not with Loveless, then with an ideal that Loveless himself once espoused. "How true is that philosophy which says / Our heaven is seated in our minds!" Loveless had cried in the very first words of the play, and as Amanda turns away from Worthy's embrace she recalls those words. Though "the soul . . . / Is usually . . . careless of its charge, / . . . soft, and . . . indulgent to desire," she tells her would-be seducer, "Yet still the sovereignty is in the mind" (5.4.154-56, 160). And yet—and this is another instance of Vanbrugh's large sense of character, his implicit pessimism— Amanda's mind seems not entirely clear on Worthy. Perhaps in love with him, and not unwilling to be loved, she leaves open for them the possibility of that most unstable of human relationships, the platonic affair. Poised at the brink of an elegant and dissolute world, Amanda is disinclined to step safely back. Like that other provoked wife, like her own husband, Amanda seems caught in the decaying orbit of those irremediably fallen from grace.

All this may seem to miss the point of a play that gives its largest energies to farce, after all, and which ends with a scene of festive comedy. Indeed, I have said very little of just how funny Vanbrugh can be. Doubtless his most important quality is his power to make us laugh, which we do, as Lord Foppington's wedding party turns out to be rather his brother's, quite satisfyingly enough. But even the easy comedy of this last scene, so agreeable a close to the farcical underplot, does not allow us to forget, as Vanbrugh called it [in his preface to *The Relapse*], "the barrenness of the conclusion." Amidst laughter and good humor and with exquisite subtlety, it reminds us of the fate that has befallen not only Amanda but Loveless.

Along with their undoers they have come to Foppington's party, where, with one notable exception, they remain as silent observers. The exception occurs when Foppington, as a kind of reparation for his earlier insult to Amanda, casually invites Loveless to flirt with Miss Hoyden, whom he thinks he has just married. "I'm too fond of my own wife," Loveless assures him, "to have the least inclination to yours" (5.5.75-76). Loveless may well be speaking more than mere courtesy, for, ironically, there is nothing in the play to make us feel that he no longer loves his wife. His attraction for Berinthia has been all on the level of appetite, and so, though he besmirches the high-minded values he had expressed at the beginning of the first act, we have no reason to believe that he has discarded them. "The largest boons that heaven thinks fit to grant / To things it has decreed shall crawl on earth," he had told Amanda then, "Are in the gift of women formed like you" (1.1.28-30). But now his wife, irrevocably hurt, will deny that gift, will leave him to crawl on his own.

And so at its conclusion *The Relapse,* like *The Provoked Wife,* projects beyond its merriment a sense of barrenness. The fate of Amanda and Loveless is of course the more touching, for we remember the richness of their beginning. Upon a stage filled with joking celebrants, we see them for the last time. They are standing apart with Worthy and Berinthia, avoiding each other's eyes perhaps: apparently there is nothing at all that either can say to the other.

We can only speculate on why so promising a writer never pursued more than a desultory career in the theater. Perhaps like Congreve, as some have suggested, he lost his heart for the drama as a result of Collier's attack. Perhaps, and this would seem more likely, he found that he could make more money in the more gentlemanly profession of architecture. But perhaps, too, he felt his imagination had backed him into a corner. When he died in 1726, Vanbrugh left among his papers the incomplete manuscript of *A Journey to London.* The ending he had in mind for this play may well explain why it never was finished—a husband, having all he could stand of his wife's uncontrollable gambling, was to "turn her out of doors." Cibber, who went on to complete the play, calling it *The Provoked Husband,* rejected this ending, and rightfully no doubt from the standpoint of pleasing the popular taste. The man and his wife were allowed to patch up their differences, and *A Journey to London* was brought more comfortably into line with most other memorable eighteenth-century comedies of married life, where no problems are ever so serious that they cannot be solved by the final curtain, or at least glossed over. It was away from such conventional comedy, even more in this last play than in the two he completed, that Vanbrugh felt pulled by the special tug of his imagination—a tug to which, apparently, he was uninclined to give in. Nor could he have felt much encouraged by the spirit of the age; despite some stirrings in the direction of domestic tragedy, the eighteenth century seems to have been attuned not very much, if at all, to the understatement of his somber and yet untragic view of private life.

On the surface, then, so much at one with his age, Vanbrugh seems in a private corner of his mind to have stood apart from it—apart not only from Etherege, Wycherley, and Congreve, whose moral sensibilities, where they operate, are rarely so sympathetic as his, but apart also from Cibber and Farquhar, who like Steele, Goldsmith, and Sheridan after them, along with a host of less-remembered eighteenth-century playwrights, were happy enough to overlook all that can potentially go wrong in a modest way, in a way that makes life neither sad nor ultimately joyful, just somehow tarnished and dull. It was about just this that Vanbrugh wrote, preserving his ability to tolerate easily, but not unfeelingly, what he knew of human folly. (pp. 24-9)

> *Lincoln B. Faller, "Between Jest and Earnest: The Comedy of Sir John Vanbrugh," in* Modern Philology, *Vol. 72, No. 1, August, 1974, pp. 17-29.*

Frank McCormick   (essay date 1985)

[*In the following excerpt, McCormick discusses the romantic and realistic characters of Vanbrugh's* The Relapse, *arguing that both illustrate "alternative 'right' ways of behaving."*]

"The true objection" to Vanbrugh, writes Virginia Ogden Birdsall in her recent study of Restoration comedy [*Wild Civility,* 1970], is that he is "basically dishonest", wishing to be "at one and the same time unrealistically romantic and unromantically realistic". Birdsall's criticism expresses concisely and emphatically a response which most readers of Vanbrugh's *Relapse* in particular will have felt at one time or another. How, the reader of *The Relapse* is likely to inquire, is he to account for the disjunction which he finds between Vanbrugh's apparently sympathetic treatment of his "romantically" conceived Amanda on the one hand, and his "realistic" (and again apparently sympathetic) treatment of such inveterate opportunists as Berinthia and Young Fashion on the other? (p. 53)

I will argue that *The Relapse* dramatizes in the careers of Amanda and Young Fashion alternative "right" ways of behaving, each successful in its own terms, each incompatible with the other.

Consider the main plot first. It juxtaposes a "romantically" conceived married couple, Amanda and her reformed husband Loveless, against a pair of "realistically" conceived sexual adventurers, Amanda's niece Berinthia and her former lover Worthy. Let the following fifth-act exchange between Berinthia and Worthy illustrate the moral temper of the two realists. Here they discuss Worthy's assault on the virtue of Berinthia's resolutely chaste Aunt Amanda:

> WORTHY: . . . She is not yet fully satisfied her husband has got another mistress, which unless I can convince her of, I have opened the trenches in vain; for the breach must be wider before I dare storm the town.
>
> BERINTHIA: And so I'm to be your engineer?
>
> WORTHY: I'm sure you know best how to manage the battery.
>
> BERINTHIA: What think you of springing a mine? I have a thought now come into my head, how to blow her up at once . . . [At this point Berinthia proposes her plan of inflaming Amanda's passions, and thereby weakening her resistance to Worthy's assault, by inviting her aunt to observe from a distance her husband's rendezvous with his mistress, who is none other than Berinthia herself, whereupon Worthy genuflects in tribute to her ingenuity.] (V.ii.30-63)

It is the complexity with which the motives of Berinthia and Worthy are rendered that I wish to call attention to here. That Loveless' mistress is Berinthia herself, whom the guileless Amanda has invited to live in her house as a friend and confidante, gives to Berinthia's material banter an aspect as much malicious as comic, as is manifest in the violent exuberance of her determination "to blow her up at once". But it is not so much malice as a perplexing mixture of beneficence and self-interest which inspires Berinthia's deceit: beneficence because, as we learn elsewhere, she seems genuinely persuaded that she does her aunt a favor in introducing her to the pleasures of adultery (II.i.433-645); and self-interest—how selfish are the roots of beneficence—because Berinthia agrees to serve as Worthy's advocate only after he has discovered and threatened to expose her relationship with Loveless if she refuses. Nor should we dismiss as mere persiflage the parting exchange between Berinthia and Worthy:

> WORTHY: (kneeling) Thou angel of light, let me fall down and adore thee.
>
> BERINTHIA: Thou minister of darkness, get up again, for I hate to see the devil at his devotions. (V.ii.61-63)

The exchange mocks but at the same time it pays inadvertent tribute to the persistence of those traditional standards of morality against which both are all too consciously in revolt. The Edenic temptation, the perennial struggle between the forces of darkness and light, the demonic and the angelic—these Christian themes and images continue to shape the discourse of these two Machiavellians even in its most cynical moments, and continue to demand, from Berinthia at least, a modicum of reverence, however wittily expressed.

Now let us place beside these complexly "realistic" utterances of the main plot's principal exemplars of cynicism the no less complexly "romantic" utterances of one of the play's chief exponents of idealism. "How true", observes Loveless in the soliloquy which opens *The Relapse,* "is that philosophy which says / Our heaven is seated in our minds!" And how sharp, we are likely to reply, is the contrast between Berinthia's witty cynicism and Loveless' smug affirmation of the commonplace. Loveless speaks the language of contentment. He is content with his fortune, content with his wife, content most of all with himself. But his is also a language of self-deception. Observe as he proceeds how easily apparent obstacles to his happiness—whether "luxury", "ambition", or "lust"—are made to yield to purely metaphorical solution:

> Through all the roving pleasures of my youth,
> Where nights and days seemed all consumed in joy,
> Where the false face of luxury
> Displayed such charms
> As might have shaken the most holy hermit
> And made him totter at his altar,
> I never knew one moment's peace like this.
> Here, in this little soft retreat,
> My thoughts unbent from all the cares of life,
> Content with fortune,
> Eased from the grating duties of dependence,
> From envy free, ambition under foot,
> The raging flame of wild destructive lust
> Reduced to a warm pleasing fire of lawful love,
> My life glides on, and all is well within.
>   (Enter Amanda, Loveless meeting her kindly.)
> How does the happy cause of my content,
> My dear Amanda?
>   (I.i.1-19)

The ease with which Loveless here dismisses his past debaucheries (they were but "the roving pleasures of my youth"), the vague prettiness with which he invests what he and so many minor pastoralists before him have termed their "little soft retreat", the unwittingly diffident periphrasis ("happy cause of my content") which he substitutes for the more sobering term "wife"—all is calculated to cast a pleasant glow of contentment over his wedded life. And yet, because so persistently his observations seem both hackneyed and unfelt, Loveless does not convince. He speaks, for one thing, in that blank verse in which [Colley] Cibber had couched Loveless' all-too-sudden conversion at the conclusion of *Love's Last Shift.* It is moreover (and perhaps in parody of Cibber's halting meter) a blank verse remarkably unstable both in rhythm and in length. Indeed the very instability of the verse calls attention to the precariousness of Loveless' "ideal" marriage, a marriage which, like his verse, we shall find lapsing into something more nearly resembling prose upon its first contact with the streets of London.

A recent critic [Lincoln B. Faller in "Between Jest and Earnest: The Comedy of Sir John Vanbrugh", *Modern Philology,* 72 (August 1974)] has maintained that the "main business" of *The Relapse* is the "falling apart of what once was, briefly, an ideal marriage". We might, I think, more accurately describe the marriage as one which is doomed from the outset to "fall apart" precisely because for Loveless marital bliss remains from first to last no more than a vague ideal, an artificial, "unrealistically romantic" construct compounded not of experience but of inherited metaphors and blithely unexamined assumptions drawn from the "retirement" poems in which he appears to have steeped himself in the interval between the last act of Cibber's play and the first act of Vanbrugh's.

In London on "business" we find him turning once again to metaphor to describe what he imagines to be his feelings of friendship for Berinthia, Amanda's charming young niece whose beauty so intrigues him at the theater (II.i.39-103) and whom he soon finds residing at his wife's request in his own lodgings:

> Now friendship's said to be a plant of tedious growth, its root composed of tender fibers, nice in their taste, cautious in spreading, checked with the least corruption in the soil, long ere it take and longer still ere it appear to do so; whilst mine is in a moment shot so high and fixed so fast, it seems beyond the power of storms to shake it. (III.ii.41-47)

Observe that in his labors to define the nature of his feelings for Berinthia, Loveless' metaphor of organic growth becomes increasingly, and perhaps not altogether unconsciously, phallic. It is in fact neither "love" nor "friendship" which moves him, but the "raging flame of wild destructive lust", whose promptings are the more powerful because he so obstinately refuses to acknowledge them. And given his reluctance to face the issue squarely, we should not be surprised to find those promptings drawing him, not many hours hence, into the closet of Berinthia's bedchamber, there to "attack her just when she comes to her prayers" (IV.iii.8-9). The playful mockery of the Christian pieties—"that's the most likely to prove her critical minute, for then the devil will be there to assist me"—emphasizes the fullness of Loveless' relapse by reminding us of its Christian dimensions. More than that, in anticipating as it does the similarly playful irreverence of the scheming Berinthia and Worthy, it signalizes what in a few moments his seduction of the willing Berinthia will symbolically enact, Loveless' full entry into the cynical or "realistic" ambit of the plot. We shall hear from him only once more in the play, and there it is only to seal his relapse with the glue of hypocrisy. To Lord Fopington's facetious suggestion that Loveless try his "fartune" with Hoyden, Loveless will reply with mendacious urbanity, "I'm too fond of my own wife to have the least inclination to yours" (V.v.75-76).

So much for the "fiery trial" of the husband's virtue. How will the wife, given the severe provocation of her husband's infidelity, respond to a similar test of her virtue? The first thing to be said about Amanda is that, like her husband, she is an idealist. Discussing with Berinthia the recent attentions she has received from Worthy, for instance, she insists that not "all the merit of mankind combined could shake the tender love I bear my husband. No, he sits triumphant in my heart, and nothing can dethrone him" (II.i.548-49).

And yet, although she is absolutely unshakable in what she conceives to be her duty as a wife, Amanda is not so prudishly virtuous as to be entirely indifferent to the attention she has recently been receiving from her admirers. Indeed she cannot resist telling her niece the "secret" that she has not one but two new wooers. For it is not only Worthy who "has been tampering" but Lord Fopington as well. And though she has put off Lord Fopington with a well-deserved "box o'the ear" (II.i.313), Worthy's "charms" and "art", as her rather too vehement denial of their "power to shake" her attests, seem to have hit their mark. Thus when she indignantly tells Berinthia that "no revenge should ever be taken against a husband", and that "to wrong his bed is a vengeance" which of all vengeances is the most unthinkable, she is both chanting for her own benefit the litany which had preserved her virtue during the eight long years of her husband's "abdication", and at the same time unwittingly advising both her niece and the audience that the "unthinkable" idea of wronging a husband's bed does in fact occasionally intrude into the imagination of even the most virtuous of women (II.i.559-60).

As for Berinthia, she perceives her aunt's struggle, and though she has other and more selfish reasons for doing so, she is proceeding on the basis of what she perceives to be her aunt's nascent interest in sexual intrigue when she concocts with Worthy that scheme at which we have already briefly glanced (V.ii.29-60). The plan will proceed as follows: She will arrange to have Amanda witness her husband's assignation with his mistress—the mistress being of course Berinthia herself, her identity masked by darkness. Worthy will then rush to the distressed Amanda's side, and, finding "her spirit enflamed against her husband's treason", will offer to soothe her pain with the balm of his love. It is a disagreeable scheme which Vanbrugh wisely chose not to enact on stage. What we do see dramatized is its consequences, and it is necessary that we examine these consequences in some detail. In Act V, Scene iv, Amanda enters, her "eyes" having just become "testimonies" of her husband's "falsehood". Alone on stage, she bewails her misfortune, resolves that her husband cannot be forgiven for the offense, but rejects the option of retaliating by engaging in an intrigue of her own (V.iv.12-41).

When Worthy enters, hoping to find Amanda receptive to his advances, he finds himself transformed instead from that "minister of darkness" who moments earlier had facetiously worshipped at the feet of his former mistress Berinthia ("thou Angel of light, let me fall down and adore thee") into a penitent who, "kneeling and holding [Amanda] by her clothes", finds "divinity about her", "the vile, the gross desires of flesh and blood" being "in a moment turned to adoration" (V.iv.168-73). "What must I do to be forgiven by you?" asks Worthy. Amanda's reply echoes Christ's: "Repent, and never more offend" (V.iv.144-45). In the speech which follows this exchange, with its gracefully disparaging allusion to Phaeton and the impulsive and pagan values which he represents, Amanda gives noble expression to what has been the sustaining creed of her trouble-ridden but for her part exemplary married life: ". . . still the sovereignty is in the mind, / Whene'er it pleases to exert its force" (V.iv.160-61).

I would not, of course, deny either this scene or the main plot as a whole its ironies. It begins with the pitting of two precariously conjoined romantics (Loveless and Amanda) against two opportunistically united realists (Worthy and Berinthia). It concludes not with the expected triumph of one party over the other, but with a curiously unstable re-alignment of allegiances, the two male members of each party simply exchanging roles—and in the process adopting at once new lovers and new ethics. Such labefaction of principle on the men's part must raise questions concerning the durability of their new commitments. As for the ladies, Berinthia is on record as being of the opinion that new lovers, like new lodgings, are to be had with a "quarter's warning" (II.i.644-45). (Let Loveless take note.) And though Amanda, alone of Vanbrugh's major characters, is allowed to survive her trial with her virtue and her principles intact, the traditional reward for such estimable conduct, the fifth-act repentance of the estranged husband, is denied her. What she and the audience are given instead is the quite unexpected repentance of her would-be seducer Worthy, and the effect of that repentance, so tellingly juxtaposed against the relapse of the feckless Loveless, is simply to underscore one of Vanbrugh's most persistent themes: the fickleness of human nature; the imperiousness of Hobbesian man's desire "for change, . . . for change, to whatever it be" (V.v.114).

Amanda alone resists change. Strangely compelling in her monumental intransigence (as Worthy discovers in his "moment" of "purity"), she is nevertheless clearly at odds with the society into which she finds herself cast. Vanbrugh, sensitive to her isolation in the closing moments of the play, and choosing not to attempt the Cibberian folly of reconciling her values with those of the joyfully inveterate sinners who surround her, subjects Amanda to a kind of apotheosis in her final scene. In the noble and soaring sentiments to which she gives voice in her last speech (V.iv.153-67), she is allowed to ascend rhetorically as if into another and better world—"leaving to you", to Worthy, that is, and to the audience as well, the task of deciding whether they wish to submit to the "mighty pains" which must be undergone by those who would win her Christ-like "esteem" (163-64). (pp. 53-7)

> *Frank McCormick, "Vanbrugh's 'Relapse' Reconsidered," in* Studia Neophilologica, *Vol. LVII, 1985, pp. 53-61.*

Derek Hughes   (essay date 1987)

[*In the following excerpt, Hughes examines Vanbrugh's use of the symbol of "geographic displacement" or "homelessness" to portray the moral and social condition of characters in* The Relapse.]

In an earlier article [*Cibber and Vanbrugh: Language, Place, and Social Order in "Love's Last Shift," Comparative Drama* 20 (Winter 1986-87)], I argued that the moral certitudes and simplicities of *Love's Last Shift* (1696) are reflected in Cibber's use of two linked and traditional *topoi:* Loveless' recovery of moral identity is a recovery of linguistic rectitude (and of his name) and is also, both literally and figuratively, a homecoming, initiating the recurrent appearance in Cibber's plays of the home as a symbol of moral order. In each case, the rectification of the objective, external systems of speech and place suggests that moral error is a deviation from an unambiguously defined and entirely attainable order of life. Vanbrugh, of course,

was not fond of unambiguously ordered endings, and his characters often remain in a moral maze, denied the homecoming which Cibber so repeatedly celebrates. As I have argued, imagery of the home is as common and central in Vanbrugh as in Cibber, but the imagery is usually self-negating, and the homes he portrays are centers of incurable familial and moral disorder. Naturally, Vanbrugh's differences from Cibber are most clearly defined in *The Relapse* (1696), where pessimism about the moral value of homecoming acquires particular explicitness and intricacy and is combined with considerable scepticism about the moral force of language.

One of the dominant motifs of *The Relapse* is the irremediable dislocation of its characters, the celebration of homebound marital joy being perhaps most explicitly inverted in Young Fashion's first glimpse of Sir Tunbelly's house:

> FASHION. But methinks the seat of our family looks like Noah's ark, as if the chief part on't were designed for the fowls of the air and the beasts of the field.
>
> LORY. Pray, sir, don't let your head run upon the orders of building here; get but the heiress, let the devil take the house.
>
> FASHION. Get but the house, let the devil sake [*sic*] the heiress, I say.

The first scene of the play is, however, dominated by metaphors of moral and domestic stability, as Loveless deludedly sees his transient reform as a homecoming to virtue and the knowledge of self:

> How true is that philosophy which says
> Our heaven is seated in our minds!
> Through all the roving pleasures of my
>   youth. . . .
> I never knew one moment's peace like this. . . .
> The rock of reason now supports my love,
> On which it stands so fixed. . . . (I.i.1-3, 9, 53-
>   54)

His decision to leave the stasis of his "little soft retreat" (I.i.10) is the first dislocation of many.

Loveless' first words on reaching London are nevertheless to promise Amanda that they have found another fixed home: "How do you like these lodgings, my dear? For my part, I am so well pleased with 'em, I shall hardly remove whilst we stay in town, if you are satisfied" (II.i.1-3). He keeps the letter of his promise well enough, since he manages to betray his marriage in the temporary marital home, and his progress to renewed infidelity is marked by repeated and ironic play upon the idea of home. Amanda unknowingly persuades her rival "to come and live with me" (II.i.434). Loveless makes his first approach to Berinthia after learning that Amanda is away from home (III.ii.1-2), though on this occasion he is prevented from pursuing his ardor to extremes by the announcement that "my lady's come home" (III.ii.115). Nevertheless, it does turn out that the home is the best place to lodge an unsuspected mistress, as Worthy points out to Berinthia in a speech that transforms the home from a locus of fixed marriage to that of a transient *ménage à quatre:* "the most easy, safe, and pleasant situation for your own amour is the house in which you now are . . . we may all four pass the winter very pleasantly" (III.ii.190-92, 199). In *Love's Last Shift,* Amanda's trust in Loveless had turned out to be not after all a building of "Castles in the Air" (V.ii.38). In undermining Amanda's faith in Loveless, Berinthia uses the same image, this time with irrevocable appositeness, emphasizing once again the impending disintegration of the home and place whose recovery Cibber had hymned: "Look you, Amanda, you may build castles in the air . . . if you please. But I tell you, no man worth having is true to his wife" (III.ii.277, 279-80).

When Loveless finally accomplishes his adultery with Berinthia, he gains the opportunity by pretending—significantly—that he is away from home: a pretence whose literal falsity is outweighed by its symbolic accuracy. Amanda believes that "it can't be late, for Mr. Loveless is not come home yet, and he usually keeps good hours," to which Worthy replies that Loveless will "transgress a little tonight" by being out until three or four in the morning (IV.ii.111-16), and when Loveless creeps into Berinthia's bedchamber it is in the confidence that he is thought to be elsewhere: "I think nobody has perceived me steal into the house; my wife don't expect me home till four o'clock, so if Berinthia comes to bed by eleven I shall have a chase of five hours" (IV.iii.1-4). Loveless' destruction of the meaning of his home exemplifies the condition later described by Berinthia when she talks of men wandering "from mistress to mistress, like a pilgrim from town to town, who every night must have a fresh lodging and's in haste to be gone in the morning" (V.ii.128-30), and unfixity is elevated to a cosmic principle in the dialogue between Cupid and Hymen at Lord Foppington's frustrated wedding:

> Heaven and earth and all go round,
> All the works of nature move,
> And the joys of life and love
>   Are in variety. (V.v.117-20)

The stress on sexual and moral homelessness in the Loveless plot is complemented in the underplot by a social disorientation, the combined result of these parallel preoccupations being to negate the moral and cosmic connotations of place that survive in Cibber and dominate much pre-Restoration drama—ideas which are most eloquently and memorably summed up by Shakespeare's Ulysses:

> The heavens themselves, the planets, and this
>   centre,
> Observe degree, priority, and *place*. . . .
>   How could communities,
> Degrees in schools, and brotherhoods in cities,
> Peaceful commerce from dividable shores,
> The primogenity and due of birth,
> Prerogative of age, crowns, sceptres, laurels,
> But by degree, stand in authentic *place*?

There is an obvious contrast between the stability of Ulysses' heavens and the mobility asserted in Vanbrugh's "Heaven and earth and all go round"; and, though Vanbrugh's analogy between cosmic law and social conduct is obviously not a statement of ideal principle, it is one of pragmatic observation. We do, however, find authorial

principle in Vanbrugh's un-Ulyssean treatment of "primogenity." When Lord Foppington tells his younger brother that "Nature has made some difference 'twixt you and I," we are undoubtedly to agree with Young Fashion's retort: "Yes, she has made you older.—(*Aside.*) Pox take her" (III.i.106-07). There is no hierarchy of Nature whereby primogenity confers "authentic place" on Lord Foppington, as is confirmed by the subsequent confounding of the brothers' social, marital, and personal roles. How different is the quarrel between older and younger brother that opens a famous comedy of a century earlier, *As You Like It*. There Orlando complains that he is denied the honor and education due to his "place" (I.i.15): "you have train'd me like a peasant, obscuring and hiding from me all gentleman-like qualities" (I.i.62-64). Nevertheless, he concedes the priority due to his brother's seniority: "The courtesy of nations allows you my better in that you are the first-born; but the same tradition takes not away my blood, were there twenty brothers betwixt us. I have as much of my father in me as you, albeit I confess your coming before me is nearer to his reverence" (I.i.42-46).

The point of drawing attention to this sharp but no doubt fortuitous contrast is not, of course, to suggest that Vanbrugh was specifically thinking of what in the late seventeenth century was an unfashionable and unperformed play, but to suggest that accidental but precise antitheses between *As You Like It* and **The Relapse** emerge because the former is extensively affirming an attainable correlation between moral and social order that Vanbrugh is extensively denying in the face of its continuing endorsement by Cibber. Both *As You Like It* and **The Relapse** are dominated by the idea of geographic displacement as a symbol of the characters' moral and social condition. In the earlier play, the pattern of movement is symmetrical and consistent: the universal flight to Arden culminates in restoration of order expressed in a series of appropriate placings or relocations. In **The Relapse** the displacements rather form an unresolved and criss-cross pattern, as Loveless and Amanda leave the country for the town, Fashion and Foppington leave the town for the country, Tunbelly and Hoyden leave the country for the town, and Tunbelly storms out of the town in the play's closing moments.

Immediately after the first displacement in the play—Loveless' departure from his rural security—we witness a return from abroad: Young Fashion's arrival from Europe. His return, however, is quite clearly not a homecoming, since he is indigent, does not know where to go, and pays a brief and unwelcome visit to his family only as an obviously futile last resort. The stress on Young Fashion's own displacement is amplified by the at first sight gratuitous reference to his Jacobitism—i.e., to his support for the cause of the rightly displaced hereditary monarch (I.ii.55). (Again, a fortuitous but revealing contrast with *As You Like It* presents itself: Orlando's association with his exiled hereditary ruler affirms a correlation of natural, familial, and political place that is disrupted but ultimately restored). The next scene presents another species of dislocation, as Lord Foppington exults in his newly elevated place in society, to purchase which he has endangered his estate: his home, and the land which is the traditional basis and justification of a gentleman's social position.

After two unwelcome and acrimonious visits to his brother's lodgings, the second dominated by sharp controversy about the primogeniture issue—about the brothers' relative place in the scheme of nature—Young Fashion departs for Sir Tunbelly's estate, revealing as soon as he arrives that (like Loveless) he divorces possession of a house from creation of a home: "Get but the house, let the devil take the heiress" (III.iii.8).

Arriving in turn at Sir Tunbelly's house, Lord Foppington has the mortification not only of being unrecognized but of being mistaken for a displaced vagabond:

> SIR TUNBELLY. I'm a justice of the peace and know how to deal with strollers.
>
> LORD FOPPINGTON. Strollers!
>
> SIR TUNBELLY. Ay, strollers, (IV.vi.5-8)

And Lord Foppington responds with his own sense of displacement, feeling that this is all a dream that he is in reality elsewhere: "Now do I begin to believe I am abed and asleep and that all this is but a dream. If it be, 'twill be an agreeable surprise enough to waken by and by, and instead of the impertinent company of a nasty country justice, find myself, perhaps, in the arms of a woman of quality" (IV.vi.26-31). With Young Fashion again dislodged, Foppington plans a nuptial homecoming, "not being willing to consummate in any other bed but my own" (V.i.48-49). But this never very promising institution of a marital home dissolves in the final assault on domesticity, when Young Fashion gatecrashes his brother's home and marriage feast and lays claim to his bride.

Of course, in persistently portraying ugly and unharmonious homes, Vanbrugh implies the desirability of a happy home life. But the happy and harmonious home is not a natural "norm" which the disintegrating homes are perverting. The discordant homes are the norms, and the happy home is a rarity achieved as much by chance as intelligent design: in Constant's famous words in *The Provoked Wife* (1697), "though marriage be a lottery in which there are a wondrous many blanks, yet there is one inestimable lot in which the only heaven on earth is written." Indeed, what Vanbrugh does in *The Relapse* is to deprive home and place of all symbolic and moral connotations, as can be seen in the one (cynically jocular) attempt to attach symbolic significance to a place of dwelling:

> COUPLER. Why the plague canst not thou lodge upon the ground floor?
>
> FASHION. Because I love to lie as near heaven as I can.
>
> COUPLER. Prithee let heaven alone. Ne'er affect tending that way; thy center's downwards. (V.iii.16-20)

Interestingly, this dialogue immediately precedes another act of placement with celestial connotations: the location of Parson Bull and the Nurse in the living of Fatgoose parish. This is accompanied by an image which, with a change of pronoun gender, would be appropriate to Loveless' homecoming in *Love's Last Shift*: "let us go help this poor pigeon to his *wandering* mate again" (V.iii.147-48;

italics mine). This is the most conclusive and complete establishment of a home in the whole play.

Vanbrugh's diminution of the symbolic value of local and social place appears with particular clarity when we compare him with that great exponent of traditional order, Ben Jonson, for several key images of *The Relapse* have equal prominence, but very different force, in many of Jonson's plays. For example, a number of them—most notably *Volpone, Epicoene,* and *The Alchemist*—use the corrupted home as a central dramatic symbol, and in particular the itinerant feast and dissolved marriage of *Epicoene* are comparable with the misplaced marriage feast and dissolved marriage of *The Relapse.* And, of course, the fiction of Lord Foppington's bought baronage recalls the repeated jibes of Jonson (and many others) about James I's sale of honors. The difference, of course, is that in Jonson the disruptions of domestic and social place threaten original and natural forms of order whose potency is still felt, whereas in Vanbrugh the original order (if any) rarely has a felt presence. For Jonson, the institution of home was a consummation of man's rational and sociable nature: witness "To Penshurst," where the celebration of place is also a celebration of a harmoniously hierarchical social and natural world. The poem concludes with one of the most famous affirmations of the home as a moral ideal: "Those proud, ambitious heaps, and nothing else, / May say, their lords haue built, but thy lord dwells." Sir Amorous La Foole's feast in *Epicoene,* in which he squanders his tenants' rents on strangers far from his estate, and which is so untied to place that its location changes during the course of the play, is an inversion of the hospitality and cultivation of place celebrated in "To Penshurst" and still celebrated in late seventeenth-century courtesy literature. Thomas, Lord Fairfax, for example, urged his son to "imitate your Ancestors, and love Hospitality; and to this purpose keep constantly *at home,* except urgent and necessary Occasions call you thence." "Live at home among your Neighbours," he urged elsewhere [*Advice to a Young Lord*]. Similarly, Philip Ayres [in *An Essay for the Honour, Happiness and Prosperity of the English Gentry*] urged the gentry not "to expend your Estates . . . obscurely in hugger mugger, in private and streight Lodgings in the City," and he additionally linked the maintenance of geographic place with that of social and moral place: "if within your proper orbs and stations in the Country, you would doubtless appear with greater magnificence and splendour, not only to your Tenants and Dependants, but to the whole Country round about you." In *The Relapse,* however, Sir Tunbelly's country estate provides no normative alternative to the London lodgings of Loveless and Lord Foppington, and when Sir Tunbelly presides away from home over the wrong display of hospitality, there is a sense of irremediable disorder which his irate return to his country estate does nothing to repair.

Just as Jonson's repeated portrayal of disintegrated homes derives from his belief that the home embodies a moral and natural order, so his repeated satire against degenerate or upstart gentlemen, and his insistence that honor lies in virtue and not in ancestral title, derive their force from his conviction [in *The New Inne*] that rank and virtue were originally inseparable: "goodnesse gaue the greatnesse, /

And greatnesse worship." Just such a correlation of place and nature is celebrated in the Epithalamion for Jerome Weston and Lady Frances Stuart, where the bride steps forth "in Virgin-white, / *Like what she is,* the Daughter of a Duke." Conversely, when in *Poetaster* Caesar terminates the Saturnalian disorder—moral, social, and linguistic—of Ovid's masque, he confronts the theatrically costumed social climbers Albius and Chloe with the same question that the Herald was to address to Edgar:

> CAESA. Say, sir, what are you?
>
> ALBI. I play *Vulcan,* sir,
>
> CAESA. But, what are you, sir?
>
> ALBI. Your citizen, and ieweller, sir.
>
> CAESA. And what are you, dame?
>
> CHLO. I play *Venus,* forsooth.
>
> CAESA. I aske not, what you play? but, what you are?
>
> CHLO. Your citizen, and iewellers wife, sir.

And, forthwith, the pair are returned to the place appropriate to what they "are": "they are rid *home* i' the coach, as fast as the wheeles can runne" (IV.vii.3-4; italics mine).

The belief that a man's social degree is part of what he "is" is quite absent from *The Relapse.* Lord Foppington is certainly a fatuous intruder in an exalted social sphere, and the emptiness of his ennoblement is illustrated in the problems which his associates have in remembering or recognizing his new name and title (contrast the indissoluble bond between Edgar's baptismal name and his social place). But Vanbrugh does not supply the fixed norms against which Jonson measures the subversive ambitions of his social climbers. In contrast to the case of Albius and Chloe, Foppington's moral and cultural vacancy is not allied to any threat to traditional social order (elevation from knighthood to the peerage is neither a new nor an outrageous form of social mobility), and there is no indication that the title of lord has a surviving significance and dignity of which he is unworthy. His bought barony is not a mercenary corruption of natural hierarchy but a foolish extravagance, an offence against monetary prudence rather than social order. Indeed, unlike earlier upstarts such as Sir Petronell Flash and Sir John Daw, he is not even marked by nature for inferiority, since his folly is an acquired mannerism rather than a congenital disability. One symptom of how fixed socio-moral bearings have been removed lies in the language of social disapprobation. In Cibber, the key word is "extravagant," and its literal meaning underlines Cibber's repeated designation of folly or immorality as a departure from due place; social disapprobation is semantically identical with moral disapprobation. In *The Relapse,* the words which replace "extravagant" are "impudent" and "impertinent," which of course denote departure only from decorum, so that Cibber's linkage of social and moral standards is severed. Moreover, these words are almost exclusively the property of Lord Foppington and are only emphatically used by others when he is briefly stripped of his title at Sir Tunbelly's and accused of impudence and impertinence in claiming

to be himself (IV.vi.105, 139). The vocabulary of social judgement, therefore, is weakened in meaning and debased in origin, since its arbiter is faulty in conduct (and, indeed, in pronunciation). Further disorientation is provided by the figure of Sir John Friendly. His name suggests that he is to be a normative or fundamentally good-natured gentleman, like Friendly in *Wary Widdow,* his namesake in *The Sham-Lawyer,* Frank Friendly in *The Country Wake,* or Bellamy in *Bury Fair,* and indeed Sir John conducts himself like a gentleman of sense. Yet his sole dramatic function is to validate Lord Foppington's identity and status.

One of Collier's objections to comedy [in *A Short View of the Immorality, and Profaneness of the English Stage*] was that it did not honor the relationship between social and moral excellence, and he attacked dramatists for inverting the natural basis of social order: "Is their *Charter* inlarg'd, and are they on the same Foot of Freedom with the *Slaves* in the *Saturnalia?*" Comedy, he complained, treated noblemen with a disrespect that was out of keeping with their place, and portrayed gentlemen, such as Constant in **The Provoked Wife,** who in no way embodied the moral pattern implicit in their rank. Vanbrugh's reply to the attack on Constant [in **Short Vindication**] cheerfully detached the observed facts of human existence from the framework of idealizing theory: "here *Constant* is fallen upon, for pretending to be a Fine Gentleman, without living up to the Exact Rules of Religion. If Mr. *Collier* excludes every one from that Character, that does not, I doubt he'll have a more general Quarrel to make up with the Gentlemen of *England,* than I have with the Lords, tho' he tells 'em I have highly affronted 'em."

The episode of Quaint the genealogist in *Æsop* (1697)—considerably altered from Boursault's original [Les Fables d'Esope]—provides a less polemically simplified view of the nobility and gentry. Boursault's genealogist, M. Doucet, is chiefly condemned for the fraudulent infiltration of tradesmen into the nobility, but Vanbrugh omits this stress on subverted hierarchy and instead satirizes the Welsh passion for genealogies stretching back to the Ark. He also adds a character sketch of an empty-headed young Lord, thereby turning the satire against the established rather than the upstart nobility. Boursault does condemn M. Doucet for encouraging the nobility to devote themselves to hunting rather than the service of the state, but Vanbrugh portrays the indolence of the young nobility more sweepingly and comprehensively. Though remediable in theory, it is universal in present fact: "Wer't not for such vile fawning Things as thou art, young Nobles wou'd not long be what they are: They'd grow asham'd of Luxury and Ease, and rouse up the old Spirit of their Fathers; leave the pursuit of a poor frightned Hare, and make their Foes to tremble in her stead" (III, p.34). Past greatness is acknowledged, and is acknowledged to be recoverable, but it has no present embodiment in the rising generation. Lord and fop are becoming synonymous, and Lord Foppington is not unworthy of the world into which he intrudes.

The social and moral dislocation of the characters in **The Relapse** is reflected in an obliquity and disorder of language. For example, when Loveless complacently tells Amanda of his reaction to the unidentified beauty in the theater, his language betrays his latent attraction, and he realizes, "I have talked too much, but I must turn it off another way" (II.88-89). When Berinthia and Worthy probe to uncover each other's illicit passions, they shelter behind a pretence of verbal meaninglessness:

> BERINTHIA. What do you mean by that?
>
> WORTHY. Nothing. . . .
>
> BERINTHIA. . . . . Pray tell me what you mean?
>
> WORTHY. Do you tell me, it's the same thing.
>
> BERINTHIA. I can't. (III.ii.148-49, 154-57)

In his disorder at discovering that he has welcomed the wrong Lord Foppington and abused the true, Sir Tunbelly exclaims: "I'm struck dumb; I can only beg pardon by signs" (IV.vi.213-14). And when Young Fashion hears that his brother has cuckolded him, there is another moment of linguistic collapse:

> FASHION. My brother! Which way?
>
> COUPLER. The old way; he has lain with your wife.
>
> FASHION. Hell and furies, what dost thou mean?
>
> COUPLER. I mean plainly; I speak no parable.
>
> FASHION. Plainly! Thou dost not speak common sense; I cannot understand one word thou say'st. (V.i.11-16)

The famous moment at which Berinthia is carried off to bed while protesting *"very softly"* (IV.iii.79*sd*) belongs to a pattern of incidents showing the disruption or defeat of language by illicit sexual desire. Lust causes the disruption in most of the above examples, and the power of sexual desire to erode language is most clearly illustrated when Loveless' kisses reduce Berinthia's speech to an "Um—" (III.ii.123).

Like many dramatists of the previous generation, Vanbrugh sees human nature as naturally divided: bound to society, gifted with speech, and yet possessed by desires that cannot be accommodated within the forms of social existence and which are inimical to the language which is the currency of society. (Such is the view of human nature conveyed by the bedroom tricks in *The Plain-Dealer* and *The Orphan*). For this reason (as in Carolean plays such as *The Orphan*), the word "secret" is repeatedly associated with lust. Lord Foppington confides to Amanda the "secret" (II.307) of his passion for her; Amanda asks Berinthia about her "secrets," the word here being a synonym for "Lovers" (II.443-45), and she confesses the "secret" (II.525) of her own attraction to Worthy. Later, Loveless communicates to Berinthia the "secret" (III.ii.74) of his lust for her, and Worthy and Berinthia exchange the "secrets" (III.ii.164-65) of their adulterous passions. Finally, Hoyden too flies to secrecy as the shield of sexual indiscretion, though the word itself is too ambitious for her vocabulary. Deciding to marry Lord Foppington despite her marriage to Young Fashion, she enjoins the Nurse and Chaplain "to hold your tongues and not say a word of

what's past" (IV.vi.255-56). Secrecy in lust is more than a mere practical necessity: it manifests the indomitable persistence of forces that cannot be accommodated within the forms of rational and social discourse.

In *Love's Last Shift* Amanda had reformed Loveless with eloquence inspired by heaven: human language was an echo of the divine, its degree of excellence depending on its degree of conformity to its divine original. By contrast, leading playwrights of the 1670's had implicitly denied any possibility of referring human linguistic practice to a celestial word or book: language was an externally formulated social convention, having no origin in any sphere beyond the human and little natural relationship even to the minds and characters of men. Vanbrugh adopts an interesting intermediate position between the traditionalism of Cibber and the scepticism of, say, Etherege. He does persistently judge the equivocations and obliquities of human speech against a normative idea of sacred language, but it is a sacred language that is itself spoken and devised by men. In **The Provoked Wife,** when Bellinda urges that "we must return good for evil," Lady Brute replies, "That may be a mistake in the translation" (I.i.100-01). Here the authority of Holy Writ stands in judgment on the sophistries with which Lady Brute seeks to justify infidelity to an intolerable husband; but the authority is nevertheless transmitted by indirect and human agency, and the semantic and textual problems of the Bible were of course widely discussed in the seventeenth century. As a judge of Lady Brute's arguments, its authority is beyond question, but it is not an unmediated act of divine writing on a par with Posthumus' inscribed heavenly tablet [in *Cymbeline*] or even of the apparently ghostly warning that dissuades Farquhar's Lurewell from adultery:

> Thy Matrimonial Vow is registr'd above,
> And all the Breaches of that solemn Faith
> Are register'd below.

But even here the apparently direct contact with the language of heaven is deceptive, since Angelica's "ghost" turns out to be the living Angelica.

Two normative standards of Christian discourse—the prayer and the sermon—figure prominently in **The Relapse.** Foppington, unlike Amanda, does not heed the sermons at church (II.279-93), and he regards reading without thinking as being as natural as praying without devotion (II.193-94). When Berinthia tells Amanda of Worthy's interest in her, she frivolously likens his paeans of praise to a sermon: "He used you like a text, he took you all to pieces, but spoke so learnedly upon every point, one might see the spirit of the church was in him" (IV.ii.52-55). And, immediately before Loveless enters unexpectedly to seduce her, Berinthia muses on a choice of bedtime reading, significantly rejecting a sermon for a seventies sex comedy: "What's this book? I think I had best go read. O *splénétique!* It's a sermon. Well, I'll go into my closet and read *The Plotting Sisters*. (*She opens the closet, sees Loveless, and shrieks out.*)" (IV.iii.23-26). At this point, Loveless' conduct equally violates the values of religious discourse: his reason for hiding in the closet was that it would enable him to catch Berinthia at her prayers, "for then the devil will be there to assist me" (IV.iii.10). In preferring the reading (and enactment) of sex comedy to the study of sermons, Berinthia of course contrasts with Amanda, who is uncomfortable even about treating Lord Foppington's affectations as "diversions" (II.148-63).

In anything but a play, a thematic contrast between love of devotional literature and a taste for amoral theatricals could be unambiguous enough; just such a contrast is drawn between Clarissa and Lovelace. But in a play it is harder to give wholehearted acceptance to the idea that the sermon is the normative mode of statement, especially when the form of statement with which it is being compared is that of drama itself. And, of course, Amanda herself does not live up to her rejection of the *dulce* in favor of the *utile.* Despite her reluctance to gain diversion from Lord Foppington's antics, she takes a leading part in the subsequent dialogue with him, even to the point of asking him about his "intrigues" (II.247)—an enquiry which gives him quite the wrong idea. An actress could interpret her question variously: as anything from a piece of unthinking chit-chat to an expression of latent fascination with a morally alien style of life—but there is no doubt that fascination with the morally alien predominates in a parallel conversation shortly afterwards, when she questions Berinthia about her lovers and reveals that the rejection of Worthy's advances is far more difficult than that of Foppington's: "You were always very *entertaining* company," she says, "but I find since marriage and widowhood have shown you the world a little, you are very much improved" (II.566-68; italics mine). And, by a grim logic, her fascination with Berinthia's intrigues, and consequent desire for her company, bring into existence the intrigue between Berinthia and her husband. In Cibber, pleasure and instruction are in complete harmony, and when the characters create dramatic diversions—the deceptions of Loveless and Sir Novelty—they further the ends of moral reform and satirical exposure. This is one aspect of the integration and co-operation which Cibber assumes between the signs and realities of moral existence. In Vanbrugh, the appetite for diversion is less adaptable to the calls of moral duty: Loveless actually attends a performance of *The Relapse* (II.40-46), but the play's moral warning is far less potent than the carnal temptation which is synchronized with it, with the result that the play's action proves more diverting and imitable than its lesson.

The division between Amanda's principles and inclinations—between a love of sermons and a taste for less edifying discourse, between a commitment to chastity and an increasingly painful attraction to its opposite—clearly reveals the limitations which attach to the sermon as a regulating norm of human discourse. It is not a direct fusion of the human word and the divine, as Cibber represents Amanda's rhetoric to be, and it has imperfect power to direct the mental and linguistic habits of even the most virtuously inclined. With the authority of St. Paul, divines repeatedly speak of the moral law being written by God in the human heart, and the belief in the divine writing in the heart is one basis for the belief that linguistic order can symbolize a moral and celestial order. In Vanbrugh, the word remains the vehicle of moral rectitude, but it lacks

a palpably direct bond with the language of heaven or the writing in the heart. Sermons may win theoretical assent, but there are parts of even the most virtuously inclined constitution that are impervious to their eloquence. The rules are clear and unquestionable (and *The Provoked Wife* makes clear the degradation that would follow adultery), but there is a painful discrepancy between the nature of the rules and the nature of humanity. At the end of *Love's Last Shift,* there is a parallel restoration of moral, social, and linguistic order: language, used for its natural moral purpose, recalls Loveless to his natural moral character, which is a natural concomitant of his social place. In *The Relapse,* the division or downright viciousness of human nature forbid such perfect accommodation of the patterns of social and personal life to the language of moral principle.

The denial of the traditional analogy between the composition of society and of the individual person had been implicit in many plays of the 1670's, with their stress on the insolubly perplexed relationship between man's instinct for lawless egocentricity and his need for social existence. The split between social and instinctual is often expressed in the splitting of a character into two distinct roles, as when Lady Cockwood appears to her husband in the guise of a prostitute, Manly copulates with Olivia while Fidelia talks love to her, or Bellinda tells Loveit of her own intrigues with Dorimant while seemingly describing those of a third and unnamed person. Less outrageously, Harcourt poses as his own twin brother in order to further his love for Alithea at the expense of her contractual obligation to Sparkish. In her dealings with Amanda, of course, Berinthia exactly repeats Bellinda's deception of Loveit, narrating a nameless woman's adultery with Loveless as though she herself were an innocent by-stander narrating the sins of a stranger, and doubling of identity is also apparent in the contest between the two Lord Foppingtons as well as in Hoyden's duplication of marital roles. But Vanbrugh's portrayal of the dividing self springs from a set of assumptions rather different from those which govern the most sceptical 1670's comedies in that Vanbrugh gives greater status to the moral claims of society. In Dryden and Wycherley in particular, the preoccupation with the divisions of man's nature reflects a paradox most forcefully stated by Hobbes: that man forms societies not because he is an Aristotelian political animal but for the very opposite reason—i.e., that he is a naturally antisocial being who forms societies to escape from the consequences of his own nature. Concessions to social co-existence are inescapable—even Horner's anarchic exploits lead to the foundation of a society of libertines—but the claims of society are pragmatic and empirical necessities rather than transcendent imperatives: like *The Relapse,* the comic plot of *Marriage à la Mode* presents the possibility of a *ménage à quatre,* but in the earlier play the possibility is dismissed solely because of the practical and psychological difficulties that it creates. For Vanbrugh, the prohibition of adultery has clear religious force; the divisions of man's nature proceed from the faintness with which the laws pronounced in sermons are inscribed in the human heart. In *Love's Last Shift,* by contrast, Amanda and Loveless move from division towards reintegration of self. When Loveless is first led to Amanda's house, he assumes—and is subsequently told—that he has been mistaken for someone else, and the progress from the illusion of mistaken identity to the realization that he is a husband in his marital home represents the healing of the unnatural discrepancy between his moral conduct and his social and familial role. Similarly, Amanda splits herself into wife and mistress, and in the preliminaries to disclosure speaks of Loveless' injured wife as though she were an entirely separate person. The technique of self-splitting is the same as Berinthia's, but Berinthia's division of her public and her sexual nature is unresolved and indeed irremediable. The continuing tension between public forms and private identity is indicated by the imperfect grasp of names that persists throughout the play: witness the repeated difficulties with Lord Foppington's title, Amanda's failure to discover her rival's name, and (most remarkable) Sir Tunbelly's departure for the country in continuing ignorance of his new son-in-law's name.

In Cibber, the close correspondence between man's internal moral condition and the forms of his social existence is reflected in a correspondence between his character and the outward signs which form the basis of communication and interpretation; Amanda can "read" the characters of those with whom she associates. Vanbrugh's Amanda retains the confidence that external form mirrors moral nature, believing that her rival's ugliness of character must be analogically reflected in ugliness of appearance. But she is mistaken, and there is once again a rift between the intimacies of the human constitution and the outward categories which seem to define and place it. The outward, public world is not one in which man is fully revealed, or in which his whole self is capable of dwelling; this is one aspect of Vanbrugh's stress on his characters' displacement, on the way in which the forms and patterns of society, necessary though they are, can only provide an imperfect analogy, framework, and place for the intrinsic person. Nor can the patterns of public life provide a perfect image of a moral or natural order. Critics engaged in the time-honored task of quantifying the relative sentimentality and cynicism of Cibber and Vanbrugh have noted that Amanda's reformation of Worthy differs little from the reformation of Loveless in *Love's Last Shift,* which Vanbrugh has so painstakingly reversed. Unlike Loveless, of course, Worthy does express doubts about the durability of his reform (V.iv.176), so that the tension between moral formula and human capacity remains incompletely resolved. But a more important difference is that in Cibber the reformation brings immediate restoration of familial, moral, and social harmony, whereas in Vanbrugh Amanda and Worthy remain isolated and unsatisfied. Virtue itself is homeless and displaced, and there is no system of correspondences which guarantees that a virtuous mind will receive a harmoniously ordered life. (pp. 62-78)

Derek Hughes, "Vanbrugh and Cibber: Language, Place, and Social Order in 'The Relapse'," in Comparative Drama, *Vol. 21, No. 1, Spring, 1987, pp. 62-83.*

FURTHER READING

Berkowitz, Gerald M. "Sir John Vanbrugh and the End of Restoration Comedy." *Costerus* n.s. XXXI (1981): 1-222.
    Suggests that Vanbrugh encouraged the transition from Restoration comedy to sentimental comedy by exposing the limitations of Restoration conventions and proving "that successful comedy could be created outside the bounds of those limitations."

Birrell, Augustine. "Sir John Vanbrugh." In *The Collected Essays and Addresses of the Rt. Hon. Augustine Birrell,* Vol. I, pp. 107-12. New York: Charles Scribner's Sons, 1923.
    Biographical and critical overview of Vanbrugh's works, written in 1894. Birrell remarks that "Sir John has a great deal of wit of that genuine kind which is free from modishness."

Dobrée, Bonamy. "Its Descent." In his *Restoration Comedy: 1660-1720,* pp. 39-57. Westport, Conn.: Greenwood Press, 1924.
    Argues that the French plots utilized by Vanbrugh in his adaptations "maintain the standpoint, the form, and the atmosphere, of English comedy."

————. Introduction to *The Complete Works of Sir John Vanbrugh,* edited by Bonamy Dobrée and Geoffrey Webb, pp. xi-xxxiii. London: Nonesuch Press, 1927.
    Highly regarded biographical and critical overview.

Hughes, Derek. "Cibber and Vanbrugh: Language, Place, and Social Order in *Love's Last Shift.*" *Comparative Drama* 20, No. 4 (Winter 1986-87): 287-304.
    Compares Cibber's and Vanbrugh's handling of the relationship between linguistic order and social place in their comedies.

Huseboe, Arthur R. *Sir John Vanbrugh.* Boston: Twayne Publishers, 1976, 178 p.
    Introductory biographical and critical evaluation of Vanbrugh with special emphasis on the morality in his plays.

Loftis, John. "The Survival of the Restoration Stereotypes, 1693-1710." In his *Comedy and Society from Congreve to Fielding,* pp. 43-76. Stanford, Calif.: Stanford University Press, 1959.
    Analysis of the "oversimplification of social fact" in the plays of William Congreve, George Farquhar, and Vanbrugh.

Malek, James S. "Comic Irony in Vanbrugh's *The Relapse:* Worthy's Repentance." *CLA Journal* XXVI, No. 3 (March 1983): 353-61.
    Focuses on Worthy's repentance in *The Relapse.* Malek suggests that the character's conversion adds to the comedy of the play by recognizing the absurdity of last-minute repentances.

Mignon, Elisabeth. "Vanbrugh." In her *Crabbed Age and Youth: The Old Men and Women in the Restoration Comedy of Manners,* pp. 132-59. Durham, N.C.: Duke University Press, 1947.
    Explores Vanbrugh's treatment of elderly characters in his comedies, suggesting that the aged men and women of his plays never achieve dignity.

Perry, Henry Ten Eyck. "Sir John Vanbrugh." In his *The*

*Comic Spirit in Restoration Drama: Studies in the Comedy of
Etherege, Wycherley, Congreve, Vanbrugh, and Farquhar,* pp.
82-106. New Haven, Conn.: Yale University Press, 1925.
Evaluates Vanbrugh's skills as a playwright and adapter,
arguing that he compromised his comic wit because of
public opinion and created "a great deal of very mediocre work, strongly tinged with the taint of sentimentality."

Whistler, Laurence. *Sir John Vanbrugh: Architect and Dramatist, 1664-1726.* New York: Macmillan Co., 1939, 327 p.
Overview of Vanbrugh's life and work.

Zimansky, Curt A., ed. Introduction to *The Provoked Wife,*
by Sir John Vanbrugh, pp. xiii-xxii. Lincoln: University of
Nebraska Press, 1969.
Discussion of *The Provok'd Wife* in which Zimansky argues that Vanbrugh's witty language compensates for
his weak plot.

———, ed. Introduction to *The Relapse,* by Sir John Vanbrugh, pp. xiii-xxiii. Lincoln: University of Nebraska Press,
1970.
Examines the influence of earlier dramatists on the writing of *The Relapse,* claiming that Vanbrugh "has a way
of making material peculiarly his own."

**Additional coverage of Vanbrugh's life and career is contained in the following sources
published by Gale Research:** *Dictionary of Literary Biography,* **Vol. 80:** *Restoration and
Eighteenth-Century Dramatists.*

William Wycherley

1640?-1716

English dramatist, poet, and aphorist.

The following entry presents a selection of Wycherley criticism from the last decade. For additional information on Wycherley's life and works, see *Literature Criticism from 1400 to 1800,* Vol. 8.

INTRODUCTION

One of the foremost dramatists of the Restoration, Wycherley combined irreverent social satire and complex verbal wit to create comedies of lasting interest and appeal. His plays have attracted much controversy over the years for their candid treatment of moral—particularly sexual—attitudes and behavior, with the result that Wycherley has been alternately hailed as a force for moral regeneration and denounced as a purveyor of moral indecency. Nowhere is this controversy more apparent than with regard to the play considered Wycherley's masterpiece, *The Country-Wife,* which has garnered critical superlatives from William Archer's rejection of it as "the most bestial play in all literature" to John Palmer's praise of it as "the most perfect farce in English dramatic literature."

Wycherley was born in Shropshire and was tutored by his father until the age of fifteen. At that time the elder Wycherley (an ardent Royalist who disapproved of the strict Puritan educational system which prevailed during Oliver Cromwell's Protectorate) sent his son to France that he might continue his education and learn the graces of a gentleman in a cultured, aristocratic society. While abroad, Wycherley converted to Roman Catholicism. In 1660, with the Restoration imminent, he returned to England, undertaking a brief stint of legal studies in London before entering Queen's College, Oxford. Here he studied philosophy and reverted to Protestantism. Wycherley returned to the study of law at the Inner Temple, one of the Inns of Court in London, but his interest soon palled, though the fascination he developed for London society did not. Although little is known of Wycherley's activities during the next several years, it is surmised that after abandoning his law studies, he fulfilled various minor duties in governmental and military service and may have participated in a naval battle against the Dutch.

Although the composition dates of Wycherley's plays are conjectural, it is known that his first, *Love in a Wood; or, St. James's Park,* was performed in 1671 at the Theatre Royal in London. The play was immediately successful, and Wycherley attracted the notice and approbation of London society, including that of Barbara Villiers Palmer, Charles II's mistress and soon Wycherley's own. Through her influence and his own talent and personal charm, Wycherley quickly became a favorite at court and in fash-

ionable literary circles, his popularity continuing unabated during the next few years as his remaining plays were produced. But in 1678 Wycherley contracted a debilitating disease (the nature of which is unknown); its effects plagued him for the rest of his life, perhaps accounting for the meagerness of his subsequent literary production and probably contributing to the memory lapses from which he suffered in later years. The king provided Wycherley with the means to journey to France to aid his recovery and upon his return the following year he was offered the post of tutor to the king's son, the Duke of Richmond. Before Wycherley began his duties, however, he met and secretly married the widowed Lady Laetitia-Isabella, Countess of Drogheda. It was a short marriage, but one that had disastrous effects on Wycherley's life. Both the marriage and the surreptitious manner in which it was executed displeased Charles, who withdrew his favor from Wycherley; the countess's death soon afterwards left Wycherley embroiled in endless and ruinously expensive litigation concerning the disposal of his wife's considerable fortune. Reduced finally to destitution, Wycherley was incarcerated in debtors' prison. He was released in 1686 by James II, who had succeeded to the throne following Charles's death the previous year. According to an oft-repeated anecdote, James, pleased by a court performance of *The Plain-Dealer,* had inquired after the author. Upon being informed of Wycherley's predicament, James immediately settled the dramatist's debts and bestowed a pension on him, which unfortunately came to an abrupt end a few years later when James was forced to abdicate.

Continually beset by financial difficulties, Wycherley henceforth divided his time between Shropshire and London. When he was in his sixties he befriended Alexander Pope, then a fledgling poet in his teens. At this time Wycherley began to write again, and he requested that Pope, whose genius he already recognized, aid him in polishing and, where necessary, revising his verses. Pope obliged, but at length the friendship cooled as Wycherley, whose poetry never matched the ease and wit of his plays, came to resent Pope's revisions and frequently supercilious comments. Nevertheless, Pope's 1729 edition of Wycherley's posthumous works indicates his continuing interest in the revision, as many of the poems included in the volume are in a different form from the versions published in Lewis Theobald's 1728 edition.

Just days before his death Wycherley remarried under circumstances never adequately explained. Wycherley was as usual in financial trouble, so it is possible that he willingly entered into a reciprocal agreement with the young woman whereby he could gain the immediate funds necessary to pay his debts, with the understanding that she would be repaid upon his death with a jointure on his father's estate. This scheme had the added attraction of thwarting Wycherley's nephew, whom he disliked, but to whom he was required to bequeath the estate proper by the dictates of his father's will. There is some evidence to suggest that Wycherley, who in his old age suffered from a failing memory and intermittent periods of confusion, may have actually been trapped or intimidated into the marriage, but the truth of the matter remains unknown. Wycherley died a Catholic, having reconverted, and was buried at St. Paul's, Covent Garden, in London.

Wycherley was both a product and an exponent of the Restoration, a period of social license which, following the stifling atmosphere of the Puritan interregnum, resulted in a literature renowned for its sophisticated urbanity and licentious wit. In his own comedies, Wycherley both celebrated the hedonistic cynicism of aristocratic London society and satirized its hypocrisies and follies. His dramatic canon consists of only four plays: *Love in a Wood, The Gentleman Dancing-Master, The Country-Wife,* and *The Plain-Dealer.* In subject and incident, these plays conform to the standard conventions of the Restoration comedy of manners, with the emphasis on sexual intrigue and mistaken identity. Licentiousness, a dominant feature of all Restoration literature, is particularly evident in Wycherley's work. He dealt with sexual topics candidly—indeed, delightedly—so that the bawdiness of his plays has become nearly legendary. Amply represented in Wycherley's work are such stock Restoration characters as the roguish wit; the deceived cuckold; the conceited, ineffectual fop; and the falsely pious hypocrite. Wycherley's plays are replete with wit, a quality very highly prized during the Restoration, by which was meant not just humor

or irony, but a keenness of perception that recognized the relationship between seemingly dissimilar things, a discernment of and penetration to the heart of a matter—all often expressed in elaborately fanciful similes. Such linguistic dexterity is a preeminent feature of Wycherley's work. His dialogue is invariably clever and fluent; his characters dazzle with their adroit style and verbal poise. Indeed, Wycherley has sometimes been faulted for being too clever, for occasionally sacrificing consistency of characterization for the sake of witty repartee. Wycherley's work is also characterized by pithy social satire—his most common targets hypocrisy and pretense, his most severe condemnation reserved for those who purport to be what they are not.

Critics disagree as to whether it is more accurate to identify the dramas as satire or farce. Although undoubtedly they contain elements of both, the issue leads to the question of authorial intent and the degree to which the plays should be taken as serious literature. Wycherley's work has frequently been deemed the most thematically serious of Restoration comedies; some twentieth-century scholars have argued that the plays cannot properly be categorized as typical Restoration comedies of manners, which are generally construed as clever and amusing but of negligible import. Such critics hold that beyond the witty banter and sexual innuendo of Wycherley's work lies the eternal theme of the individual in conflict with society, a theme expressed most successfully and cogently through Horner of *The Country-Wife* and Manly of *The Plain-Dealer,* characters who struggle for sexual and personal freedom. While much recent criticism has been devoted to the exploration of this theme, particularly with regard to its implications in determining Wycherley's view of morality, many other commentators believe that such a critical approach is invalid because it is unwarranted by the evidence of the plays themselves. This debate is neatly embodied in twentieth-century critical discussion of *The Country-Wife.*

A prominent issue concerning *The Country Wife* is its sexual licentiousness. The principal plot concerns the successful scheme of the protagonist Horner to convince the men of London that he is impotent in order that he may more easily gain access to their wives. The play abounds with sexual innuendo; Wycherley's bawdiest scenes, those which have caused him to be denounced as "indecent," achieve their effect not through objectionable language or particularly suggestive action, but through witty double entendres. *The Country-Wife* was very popular during the seventeenth century as an uproarious comedy. Such serious intent as was recognized revolved around the play's satiric jabs at the hypocrisy of those who publicly profess chastity but privately enjoy extramarital affairs, and to a lesser extent around Wycherley's implicit condemnation of men who abuse or neglect their wives. Although *The Country-Wife* is deemed the bawdiest play in an age notorious for its licentiousness, it was not generally considered offensive until the latter part of the eighteenth century, when changing social and sexual mores rendered it unacceptable to the public. The last performance of the play as Wycherley had written it, until the twentieth century, was in 1753. A decade later, actor and dramatist David Garrick produced an adaptation of the play called *The*

Country Girl (1766)—a considerably tamer version that deleted any mention of adultery—and it was this adaptation that was performed in the remainder of the eighteenth and throughout the nineteenth centuries. In the latter century such critics as Charles Lamb attempted to defend *The Country-Wife* by asserting that, though the world of the play is undoubtedly an immoral one, it is also a patently unrealistic one, and as such should not be subjected to the usual moral criteria. This defense was not on the whole considered valid; the prevailing nineteenth-century critical view of the unexpurgated *Country-Wife* is summed up in Lord Macaulay's contemptuous words: "In truth, Wycherley's indecency is protected against the critics as a skunk is protected against the hunters. It is safe, because it is too filthy to handle, and too noisome to even approach."

Although sporadic condemnation of *The Country-Wife*'s lewdness has lasted well into the twentieth century, in general such objections have lost their force. However, modern criticism is still concerned with the play's morality, though the nature of that concern has shifted focus. In the world of the play, which Louis Kronenberger has described as "a society almost wholly lacking in either conscience or heart," what view of morality did Wycherley endorse? Against what, or whom, is the satire directed, the individual Horner or the society against which he rebels? To what extent, if at all, is Horner representative of his creator? Critical opinion diverges widely on these issues. Many scholars view Horner as a hero, a natural man who strikes a blow for social and sexual freedom through his rejection of narrow-minded hypocrisy and restrictive social mores. Others believe that Horner is the chief villain in what Rose A. Zimbardo has called a "world of inverted moral values," and that Wycherley intended him as a selfish, offensive example of such in a play that is essentially a satire on lust. The debate has extended to question Wycherley's moralistic intent with other characters in the play: Pinchwife has been variously interpreted as a buffoon and as an active force for evil; Margery Pinchwife as a rustic innocent, a deceiving schemer, and a "true pagan"; Alithea as a fool and as the play's "moral standard." Robert D. Hume, in dismissing the moral controversy, has argued that the play is closer to farce than to satire, and as such contains no moral message: "Delightfully bawdy and funny *The Country-Wife* is, profound it is not, and only a prude, a hypocrite, or a stuffy academician would have it otherwise." The very nature of the play thus remains unresolved, as the issue of Wycherley's morality is still as much a critical stumbling block, though for different reasons, as it was in the eighteenth and nineteenth centuries.

Wycherley's *The Plain-Dealer* is considered a "problem play." Ostensibly a comedy, this play's harsh satire and omnipresent sense of bitterness have disturbed many scholars. *The Plain-Dealer* is derived from Molière's *Le misanthrope* (1666), but conspicuously lacks the note of hope and idealism present in the French play. The plain dealer of the title is Manly, whose aversion to hypocrisy and pretense is extreme to the point of monomania. Manly's intense misanthropy is unrelieved by any sense of hope or possibility of betterment, the satire of the play seeming to proceed less from a desire to instruct or ameliorate than from a pervading atmosphere of pessimism and despair. Seventeenth-century critics, after an initial period of surprise at the unconventionality of the play, preferred *The Plain-Dealer* to all of Wycherley's other plays. It was primarily on this play that Wycherley's early reputation as a moral satirist rested. The bluntness of the principal character and the savagery of his condemnation of his society were seen as a proper and courageous way to "lash this crying age," as William Congreve phrased it in his prologue to *Love for Love* (1695). Wycherley himself became known admiringly as the Plain Dealer or as "Manly Wycherley." Contemporaries lauded the fierce, straightforward satire of the play: John Dryden called it "one of the most bold, most general, and most useful Satyres which has ever been presented on the English Theatre," and John Dennis referred to it as "that excellent Play, which is a most instructive, and a most noble satire upon the Hypocrisy and Villainy of Mankind."

Later critics, not matching this early enthusiasm, have found *The Plain-Dealer* admirable on many counts, but have stopped short of wholehearted approbation, a hesitation attributable to what many have viewed as the play's nihilism. Much of the action of the play is motivated by heartless betrayal and the desire for revenge, perpetrated not only by "wicked" characters but by the protagonist Manly as well. Thus, just as Horner of *The Country-Wife* admits of conflicting interpretations, so *The Plain-Dealer*'s Manly has been found ambiguous. In his cynicism and anger, Manly has been seen—as the seventeenth century saw him—as the one honest, upright individual in a world of corruption and deceit. Alternatively, he has been regarded as a raging, irrational misanthrope whose own cruelty and inhumanity are no different from those of the world he despises. As with *The Country-Wife,* Wycherley's authorial intent has been called into question. Is the satire of the play directed against society, Manly, or both? How can what Derek Hughes has described as Manly's simultaneous "heroic magnanimity and anarchic brutality" be reconciled? Many critics suspect that the real misanthrope of the play is not Manly but Wycherley himself. *The Plain-Dealer* lacks the detachment of *The Country-Wife,* the sense that the dramatist was able to maintain his distance even while he knew and deplored his characters' follies. It has thus been suggested that, as Wycherley's loss of perspective resulted in bitter invective rather than wit or satire, the play fails as a work of dramatic art. As Bonamy Dobrée has expressed it, Wycherley's "laughter affords no release, for it is too deeply cynical." Even with these faults—perhaps in part because of the ambiguity they create—*The Plain-Dealer* continues to fascinate. The bitterness of the work, though possibly too extreme for comedy, is both sincere and compelling; as Dobrée has written, "The play reads like a cry of despair."

Wycherley's other two plays are considered decidedly less proficient than *The Country-Wife* and *The Plain-Dealer,* though they are often studied for the light they shed on

Wycherley's dramatic development. The most notable quality of *Love in a Wood* is the multiplicity of its action. Plot and subplot, intrigue and counter intrigue, combine to make *Love in a Wood* a lively—if confusing—play. The main plot turns on the fairly standard devices of mistaken identities and misunderstandings in love, while the numerous minor characters in the subplots afford much opportunity for satire against some of Wycherley's favorite targets—particularly the hypocrite and the would-be wit. Seventeenth-century critics responded favorably to the play's exuberance, but subsequent commentators have rendered a more reserved judgment. Although it is generally agreed that *Love in a Wood* shows promise of the wit and verbal dexterity that came to fruition in *The Country-Wife,* most critics believe that the play lacks structural unity, for the many plot lines and characters are insufficiently integrated. *The Gentleman Dancing-Master* met with a tepid reception initially and is still considered Wycherley's weakest play. This is principally due to its paucity of dramatic action; unlike Wycherley's other plays, which are crowded with movement and suspense, *The Gentleman Dancing-Master* has a single, simple plot, the outcome of which is never in doubt. The play also lacks the high–spirited energy of Wycherley's others, leading critics to note that while *The Gentleman Dancing-Master* is his least "indecent" play, it is also his least inspired.

Wycherley's work is a unique blend of farce and satire, sexual licentiousness and moral intent, encompassing the light-hearted irony of *The Country-Wife* and the trenchant savagery of *The Plain-Dealer,* the whole capped with adroit repartee and verbal wit. Perhaps then it is Wycherley's own conflicting characteristics that inspire such divergent critical responses and that account for the fact that so few critics remain indifferent to his work. H. A. Taine and John Dennis reflect this in their respective assessments of "William Wycherley, the coarsest writer who ever polluted the stage," and of William Wycherley, "the greatest Comick Wit that ever *England* bred."

PRINCIPAL WORKS

Hero and Leander in Burlesque (poetry) 1669
Love in a Wood; or, St. James's Park (drama) 1671
The Gentleman Dancing-Master (drama) 1672
The Country-Wife (drama) 1675
The Plain-Dealer (drama) 1676
Miscellany Poems (poetry) 1704
The Posthumous Works of William Wycherley, Esq., in Prose and Verse (poetry and aphorisms) 1728
* *The Posthumous Works of William Wycherley, Esq., in Prose and Verse, Vol. II* (poetry, aphorisms, and letters) 1729
The Complete Works of William Wycherley. 4 vols. (dramas, poetry, aphorisms, and letters) 1924

---

* This work contains revisions of some poems included in the earlier *Posthumous Works of William Wycherley, Esq., in Prose and Verse* which were undertaken by the editor.

W. Gerald Marshall (essay date 1982)

[*In the following excerpt, Marshall traces the theme of "human theatricality" in Wycherley's comedy,* The Gentleman Dancing-Master.]

The essence of *The Gentleman Dancing-Master* is not to be found in . . . surface themes or suggestions of dramatic failure. Rather, the informing ideas for the play derive from perhaps the single most important *topos* in all of Restoration comedy—the idea of man as actor, as player on the world stage. To be sure, Wycherley, himself, was haunted by this idea, as countless references in his plays and poems indicate. For instance, in his poem, **"To a Vain Young Courtier . . . ,"** Wycherley writes:

> Why are harsh statutes 'gainst poor Players made,
> When Acting is the Universal trade?
> The World's but one wide Scene,
> Our Life the Play
> And every Man an Actor *in his way.*

And in another poem, he writes, "Well might the various World be call'd a *Stage,*/And life a Play in every Turn of Age . . . [A Man] May a *Spectator* from an *Actor* grow: / May so himself, not others, entertain" (IV, 212). Given Wycherley's interest in the idea of man as player and given the fact that the court society for which he was writing was, itself, so theatrical and flamboyant, we should not be surprised to find that *The Gentleman Dancing-Master* explores this theme in very interesting, even provocative, fashion; and the treatment of the notion of man as player goes much deeper than the idea of mere social "pretense" so often discussed in relation to Restoration drama. More specifically, the play explores two types of human theatricality, one positive and the other quite negative. First, the play delineates the dramatic aspects of formal rites of passage, a type of drama that allows for personal growth and expanded social awareness. On the other hand, Wycherley presents some characters in dramas of madness, in play-worlds which reflect contemporary Restoration notions of insanity. This type of drama greatly constricts personal development and perception, and it ultimately leads to the characters' attempts to make everyone and everything around them conform to their own private "scripts." As we shall see, the convergence of these two types of theatricality in *The Gentleman Dancing-Master* provides the essence of the play's comedy as well as some very serious statements about the idea of theatre—the human potential for creating various types of play-worlds.

We will begin our discussion with Hippolita whose role is directly linked through metaphor, language, and allusion to the stage and dramatic history. First of all, Hippolita's role is associated with the commedia dell'arte tradition. In the skeleton plot outlines of the *scenari*, there is a commonplace situation in which a father, "usually a rich lord . . . his name dignified by the title 'don,' " is "fooled into marrying his daughter to her lover in spite of other matches he makes for her." In Wycherley's play, of course, Hippolita's father, who is called "Don Diego," attempts to match his daughter with Paris, and he does this after years of keeping Hippolita totally isolated from men. But Hippolita is able to outwit her father and marry another man by creating a play-world in which Gerrard appears to be her dance instructor and in which she is free to act like a more mature woman and to be with a man of her choosing. By identifying Hippolita's role with the Italian comedy, Wycherley wishes his audience to see that she is creating her own "plays"-within-the-play, for the essential defining characteristic of the commedia dell'arte is that the players must constantly improvise their own roles upon the stage. Hippolita continually improvises scenes with Gerrard in order to sustain the fiction that he is her dancing-master. For instance, when Don Diego and Caution unexpectedly enter her room and find her holding hands with Gerrard, Hippolita thinks, "What shall I do?," and she immediately improvises a little scene by whispering to Gerrard, "lead me about, as if you lead me a Corant," and she instructs him to "dance on . . . dance and sing on," even though he is obviously a poor dancer. She and Gerrard then dance a courante, a dance which "is said to have begun as a pantomime play without words." The theatrical metaphor in this scene is intensified when Caution *Puts on her Spectacles* to get a better view of Hippolita's performance; here, Caution becomes "audience" to the improvised play before her.

Such theatrics continue. In a similar scene, Don Diego demands that Gerrard teach Hippolita to dance while in his presence, and again Hippolita improvises. She immediately suggests that Don Diego and Caution leave the room, and she then tells Gerrard that she will create for him a "Dancing-School" which "in half an hour will furnish [him] with terms of the Art" of dancing. Gerrard will then be able to properly "act a Dancing-master." In another representative scene, Paris unexpectedly demands that Gerrard play the violin while he dances with Hippolita, and Don Diego is shocked to discover that a dancing-master cannot play the instrument:

> MONSIEUR [DE PARIS]: . . . if you'll play, I'le dance with her.
>
> GERRARD: I can't play neither.
>
> DON DIEGO: What a Dancing-master, and not play!

Even in such a critical situation as this, Hippolita is able to improvise a small play-within-the-play, for like a playwright-director, she instructs Gerrard, "stay then, seem to tune it, and break the strings." Gerrard then acts out a fiction by pretending that the strings accidentally break and that he is so angry over this that he must throw *"the Violin on the ground."* In this scene, Don Diego, Paris, and Caution again become audience to an improvised play. Further, in the play-world she creates, Hippolita is capable of wearing different masks in order to test Gerrard's love for her. She says to herself, "tis harder playing the Hypocrite with him, I see . . . but the mask of simplicity and innocency is as useful to an intriguing Woman, as the mask of Religion to a States-man." Little wonder, then, that Hippolita, the improviser of her own play-world, should imagine herself in a stage play: "I am thinking if some little filching inquisitive Poet shou'd get my story, and represent it on the Stage".

Hippolita's use of drama, however, is not *just* for decep-

tion; in fact, the theatricality she displays has mythic and primitive undertones. John S. Bowman [in *Drama Survey,* 1963] has briefly noted that **The Gentleman Dancing-Master** contains primitive dramatic elements, including dancing, chanting, and masking. But there is a further "primitive" element which is directly associated with Hippolita's use of drama, for her theatricality enables her to make a formal rite of passage from adolescence into womanhood. Don Diego never allows his daughter to so much as see a man; yet, the fourteen-year-old Hippolita is at that critical age of transition, tired of her "Shock-dog" bedmate and experiencing "naughty" yet pleasing dreams of men. In her play-world, Hippolita is able to move beyond adolescence and to "act" the role of a woman for the first time: she dances with a man; flirts with him; tests his true feelings for her by seeing if he would marry her if she had no inheritance; experiences love; and, most importantly, assumes a definite degree of self-assertion and forms a mature self-image, for she is able to defy her father's rigid control and marry a man of her choosing. Moreover, Hippolita's theatricality, as we have seen, allows her to establish "audiences" to her improvised scenes. These audiences usually consist of Caution and Don Diego, but Gerrard also is part of her audience, for he not only plays the dancing-master role she assigns, but also witnesses all of Hippolita's improvisations and sees her as a woman who is shrewd and in control of a difficult situation. Hippolita's dramatizations thus *condition* her audience to see her as a woman, not as an adolescent, once she abandons her use of theatricality. For instance, by the end of the play, Gerrard, who originally saw Hippolita as an "innocent" child, is quite prepared to listen to her as an equal concerning attitudes they should foster in their marriage. When Hippolita says that jealousy on the part of her husband would be "arrant sawciness" and "cowardise," Gerrard, who once held the opposite view, responds with the rather timid, "I stand corrected gracious Miss," thus submitting to her opinions. Don Diego has seen his daughter with a man throughout the play (something he had never witnessed before), and he has been constantly reminded by Caution that his daughter is having an affair with Gerrard and breaking away from his authoritative control. By the end of the play, he, too, must accept his daughter as a woman, and he humbly accepts both her scolding and blessing, just as a child might receive these things from a father:

> So, so, now I cou'd give you my blessing, Father,
> now you are a good complaisant Father, indeed.
> When Children marry, Parents shou'd obey.

Hippolita's theatricality directly conforms to the dramatic elements universally found in formal rites of passage. In his recent study of initiation ceremonies, Frank Wilbur Young [in his *Initiation Ceremonies: A Cross-Cultural Study of Status Dramatization,* 1965] correlates the essential ideas of anthropologists and sociologists regarding cross-cultural elements found in rites of passage, and he stresses the *dramatic* aspects of such initiations. First of all, he notes that all rites of passage have three "submeanings—separation, transition, and incorporation." Hippolita, of course, separates from her father, undergoes a transition stage in her play-world, and finally is incorporated into adult society. Young goes on to say that in all cultures, from primitive to modern times, there must be a "staging" or "play-acting" of the new role one is about to assume before the new social or religious identity is actually assumed; thus, the "initiate" attains an understanding of the new role and gains confidence in it. In primitive cultures, for instance, a boy might be expected to "play-act" the hunt before actually killing an animal and becoming a man. In Hippolita's case, her use of theatricality allows her to play the role of a woman before actually assuming it in everyday life. Finally, Young asserts the importance of "audience" to rites of passage. During the ceremony, it is important that the initiate "project a particular impression to an audience," for "if the audience can be led to imagine the new situation with the help of a little staging, it will find it easier to continue doing so and will then finally be so taken in by the whole thing that it comes to accept the change as permanent, real, and legitimate." As we have seen, this is precisely what is accomplished in Hippolita's use of drama, as she so conditions her audience to see her in a more mature role that they must acknowledge her new social status when her play-world dissolves. Drama thus enables Hippolita to make a smooth transition from one phase of life into another, to be accepted as a married woman who has abandoned the little-girl world in which her father held her prisoner. Drama is here a means for personal growth and natural development—potentials it has held throughout the course of human history.

Besides this positive use of drama, the play deals with a very negative type of theatricality, a type of drama which is the antithesis of that employed by Hippolita. There are indications that Wycherley envisioned around him a completely mad society, as suggested in his poem, **"To Nath. Lee, in Bethlem":**

> Heroes and Lovers, stark mad are
> ....
> Mad likewise is each Crack'd brain'd Prodigal
> ....
> Each Heroe, like a *Tom* of *Bedlam* too
> ....
> Each antic Courtier, mad for pride, we hold
> ....
> The Men of Bus'ness should for Mad-men go
> ....
> The Roaring Churchmen, seem but Mad-men too
> ....
> In fine, the whole World's giddy, running round
> So Light-Heads in it only can be found.

In *The Gentleman Dancing-Master*, Wycherley greatly develops this notion, for Don Diego and Paris function in their own dramas of madness, play-worlds of illusory perception in which they are able to make of themselves and everything about them mere fiction or play. Unlike Hippolita's dramatizations, their theatricality is highly limiting and unnatural, for it causes them to perceive everything about them in only one way and to force others to conform to their personal "scripts." In order to grasp this sense of theatre, we must look briefly at contemporary Restoration notions of madness, notions which help create this important sense of the dramatic in *The Gentleman Dancing-Master.*

As Michael V. DePorte explains [in his *Nightmares and Hobbyhorses: Swift, Sterne, and Augustan Ideas of Madness,* 1974] there begins in the Restoration a general shift away from humors psychology to an attitude which locates madness solely in the imagination. This is not to say that writers of the period cease to identify certain types of madness and personality aberrations with an imbalance of the humors; however, the Restoration develops the idea that madness can be, in many cases, the *direct* result of an obsessed imagination. With this new emphasis upon the imagination there develops a concomitant concern with perceptual aberrations involved in madness—a criterion for insanity greatly emphasized in the Restoration. As DePorte notes, the idea develops that as the imagination gains greater and greater control—the result of thinking about some matter intensely and over a long period of time—one is likely to become mad "as to one particular thing, having . . . judgment concerning other matters for the most part right." In this "hobbyhorse" situation, the dominant and obsessive idea may govern perception (understanding or definition) of the external world. For instance, Henry More [in his *Enthusiasmus Triumphatus*] writes that madness may involve obsession with one idea—"an enormous lapse of the Phansy and Judgment in some *one* thing, yet the Party should be of sound mind in *all other.*" Since no other idea "enervates the perception," the obsessed imagination will "bear itself against all the occursions and impulses of *outward* objects. . . . " And Dr. Meric Casaubon [in his *A Treatise Concerning Enthusiasme*] insists that by "continual and vehement intention" upon the same subject, "a person may crack his brain" and become mad as to "one particular object." In addition, the sick imagination may force "assent from the understanding" and determine the perception of "things outward." The period thus develops an important attitude concerning madness: one is mad if he is completely obsessed with a single idea of the fancy which, through the power of the sick imagination, totally shapes his perception of the outer world.

Don Diego and Paris clearly reflect these emerging notions of madness, and their obsessions and concomitant perceptual aberrations lead them into bizarre play-worlds in which the external and "real" world is imaginatively reconstructed in terms of their own obsessive and mad view of it. Don Diego, who is referred to as being "mad" is obsessed with Spain and Spanish culture, an obsession which results from his travels to Spain as a merchant; in practically every line of the play, he refers to Spanish values. For instance, in his initial lines he says to Caution, "Have you had a *Spanish* care of the Honour of my Family. . . . I am no Fool. . . . I have been fifteen years in *Spain* . . . Now in *Spain* he is wise enough that is grave". And he keeps his daughter totally isolated from men because he believes this is standard for a stern Spanish father.

This Spanish hobbyhorse leads Don Diego into a play-world of illusory perception: he perceives himself as being truly Spanish, but this is merely a dramatic role, for he is really British. Don Diego asserts, "I am a *Spanish* Positivo," and "I will be a *Spaniard* in every thing." Accordingly, he costumes himself in a "*Spanish* Habit," adopts the Spanish language, and takes on a "stage name," as he replaces his English name, "Sir James Formal," with the Spanish name, "Don Diego." Such dramatic improvisation is further intensified, as we have already noted, by the fact that Don Diego's entire role echoes the stock character of the foolish father in the commedia dell'arte *scenari*. Thus, Don Diego can no longer distinguish illusion from reality, and he is, indeed, the actor of a grand fiction.

In similar fashion, Don Diego falsely perceives those around him as being Spanish, thus perceiving them in fictive roles—as "characters" in his own mad play! In other words, like an audience observing a play, Don Diego does not see reality, but illusion and fiction. For instance, Don Diego, who is outraged at Gerrard for being alone with Hippolita, perceives him from a purely Spanish frame of reference, as being a Spaniard who has betrayed his trust: "I'le shew you, Trayidor Ladron, demi honra, thou dy'st". Here, Don Diego is not merely using the Spanish language; rather, his language is quite indicative of a severe perceptual aberration. For Gerrard, himself, immediately acknowledges that he has been falsely perceived as being a Spaniard: "but by the names you give me, I find you mistake your man, I suppose some *Spaniard* has affronted you." As he gazes upon Hippolita, Don Diego defines her first through an English point of view which quickly gives way to his irrational perspective in which he perceives her as a Spanish daughter who is causing her Spanish father death-like grief: "My Daughter, mi mal, mi muertè." Hippolita replies that her real identity is certainly not Spanish: "My name's *Hippolita*, Sir, I don't owne your *Spanish* names." Don Diego thus sees his daughter as a Spanish girl, and this is what causes his harsh discipline of her, since he believes that Spanish fathers are very strict concerning the upbringing of their daughters. This tendency to make "play" of reality is epitomized in the scene in which Don Diego is presented as a director of his own Spanish drama. He tells Paris that he must "wear the *Spanish* Habit" or never be allowed to marry Hippolita. Paris then appears in the full costume of a Spaniard, "*with a Spanish Hat, a Spanish Doublet, Stockins, and Shooes.*" At Don Diego's direction, his servant, the black "dancing-master," carefully explains to Paris how to play the role of a "perfect *Spaniard.*" Don Diego tells the dancing-master to "teach him to walk with the verdadero gesto, gracia, and Gravidad of a true *Castilian.*" This dramatic scene is highly representative of Don Diego's actions throughout the play, for he would direct everyone about him in a Spanish role, and then, as spectator, see before him a Spanish "play." Don Diego's obsession thus leads him into a drama of madness in which he acts a fictive role and perceives around him not reality but "drama."

Paris, who is persistently referred to as a "fool" or "idiot," is completely obsessed with the single idea of French culture, though, of course, he is British. His obsession is so great that he transcends the ridiculous mannerisms of the typical fop, even those of a Sir Fopling Flutter, since his obsession leads him into intense perceptual illusions in which practically everything around him is believed to be French! Paris' very name indicates his obsession, and in almost every line he speaks only of "*Franch* Beautes, Graces, and Embellisemènts." he loves to brag about French civility, to rave about the French coffeehouses and French waiters, to extol the value of French fashions, and to attempt to speak the French language. In fact, Paris' obsession with French culture is so intense that he actually comes to believe that he is French, thus defining himself through his paramount obsession and distorting reality. He asserts, "I am no *Anglois*," and throughout the play, he uses the second person plural when referring to Englishmen and English characteristics, thus suggesting that he is a Frenchman observing the English. For instance, he says, "you *English*, you use the debauch so much, it cannot have with you the *French* operation, you are never enjoyeè"; he then adds, "all your *English* Complaisance is pledging Complaisance."

Indeed, a heavy theatrical metaphor makes it clear that Paris is in an illusory play-world in which he acts a role which he believes is real. Of particular importance is his association with the commedia dell'arte, which would suggest that Paris is improvising some sort of drama. Paris says that he has taken acting lessons at the "*Italian* Academy at *Paris*" in order to learn to "play de Fool of Signior *Scaramouche*"—a reference to Tiberio Fiorillo, perhaps the most famous Scaramuccia, who was then acting with the Comédie Italienne in Paris. Paris does this, he says, because knowing how to "play the Fool is the Science in *France.*" Such a foolish drama is emblematic of Paris' activity throughout the play. As an actor, Paris improvises for himself the ridiculous role of a Frenchman. Gerrard notes that after only three months in France, Paris has become "so perfect a *French*-man." Indeed, Paris costumes himself in French fashions and wears French trousers which make him "look and waddle (with all those gew-gaw Ribbons) like a great old Fat, slovenly Water-dog". In his French role, Paris improvises a theatrical name by transforming his English name, "Mr. Nathanial Parris," into "Monsieur de Paris." And he improvises a language through his blundering attempts at French. His hobby-horse idea thus causes him to distort self-perception, to transform himself into a "character" in his own play!

In addition to being presented as an actor, Paris is presented as spectator of the great drama of life, and as spectator, he perceives Englishmen around him as being French; he thus sees people not as they really are, but as "characters" who are part of his mad play-world. Paris has enough traces of sanity left to realize that he is in England and not France, but the play indicates that he is in the *process* of imaginatively transforming the Englishmen around him into "Frenchmen." Paris' hobbyhorse obsession can thus, in the words of Robert South [in his *Sermons Preached Upon Several Occasions*, 1842], "cast its own colour and tincture" upon all that he perceives. When Paris strolls through downtown London, he sees the wits and courtiers not as Englishmen but as their French counterparts, the "beaux monde" of Paris. In a more specific instance of such perceptual aberrations, Paris imaginatively transforms the two Englishmen, "Mr. *Taylor*, Mr. *Smith*," into the Frenchmen "Monsieur Taileur! Monsieur *Esmit*"; and Gerrard becomes the Frenchman "Monsieur *Gerrard*." Of course, a real Frenchman visiting London would not use the French form of address for an Englishman, and he would not transform an Englishman's name into its French counterpart, if such exists. These references thus imply that Paris is so deranged that he sees these Englishmen as actual Frenchmen, just as Don Diego's language so clearly indicates his distorted perceptions. Indeed, this is the way Hippolita interprets his words, for she immediately replies that the men he has just mentioned are "Frenchmen," but she had wanted him to mention Englishmen to her. Apparently, then, for a character who truly believes that he, himself, is French, it is only a small leap to see others in the same role! Finally, Wycherley speculates as to what Paris would do if he saw an *actual* Frenchman in downtown London. While dining with Flirt and Flounce, Paris says that he hates the English waiter and demands that a French waiter be called. In Paris' highly romanticized view of French culture, anything French must be the best, but the person who enters to replace the English waiter turns out to be a mere French scullion. Paris' hobbyhorse obsession is so aroused by the presence of a Frenchman, however, that it allows him to create a grand perceptual illusion in which the scullion is imaginatively transformed into a theatrical role that conforms to Paris' idealized notions: the scullion is perceived as the "Quisinier for a King, nay for a Cardinal or *French Abbot*." Unlike Hippolita, who uses theatricality for personal growth and development, Paris creates a play-world that is limiting and constricting, one that is most unnatural and, indeed, mad. Paris' obsession leads him to see everything in one way, to make of reality mere drama or play.

The Gentleman Dancing-Master thus delineates the theme of human theatricality. But why has Wycherley chosen such widely divergent types of play-worlds to be included in this work? First of all, the presentation of dramas of madness allows Wycherley to satirize a Restoration society gone mad with eccentricities and hobbyhorse thoughts. He suggests, through the theatricality-madness motif, that over-indulgence in a particular hobbyhorse idea may cause one to slip into a purely fictive, dramatic world in which reality can no longer be distinguished from play. Though Wycherley wants to ridicule such situations, he does not rule out more positive potentials for human theatricality, and this is why Hippolita represents an alternative type of dramatization. Her role suggests that drama can be a means to personal growth and social development, a means to change one's self-identity in a positive manner. Even though Hippolita finds herself surrounded by madness, she is able to utilize theatricality for a rite of passage, to tap a very ancient source that may still allow one a new identity and a sense of personal creativity.

But *The Gentleman Dancing-Master* is, after all, a comedy, and it is here that the most interesting implications of the theatrical theme are to be found. The mad dramas of Don Diego and Paris are so absurd that they are fit material for laughter. First of all, Don Diego and Paris represent an interesting departure from the traditional "humors" character so often found in comedy. The humorist figure is essentially examined for "an idiosyncratic trait constantly exhibited" [Madeline Doran in her *The Endeavors of Art: A Study of Form in Elizabethan Drama,* 1954]. But

in reflecting Restoration concepts of insanity, Wycherley's characters are satirized primarily for an "idiosyncratic" imagination which totally distorts sense data and makes "play" of reality. In other words, Don Diego and Paris do not appear comical essentially because of an eccentric personality trait, but because of an obsessed mind which projects itself upon everything it perceives. Whereas the humors character is involved in eccentric *action,* Wycherley's characters are involved in eccentric *perception* of self and others, a perception which makes all they perceive part of their own play-worlds. Comedy, in this case, at least, has thus moved from an essential concern with aberrant action to a paramount interest in the aberrant imagination, just as the informing psychological context of the play departs from humors psychology and focuses purely on the obsessed imagination. Keeping these ideas in mind, we can further analyze the comic aspects of the play by developing Bergson's well-known idea [in his *Laughter: An Essay on the Meaning of the Comic,* 1928] that comedy is found in characters whose actions are "mechanized" or "rigid." For the essential comedy of Don Diego and Paris is found in their "rigid" *perceptions,* not so much in mechanical actions. They fictionalize reality and function in play-worlds which are shaped by a single, rigid perception. Hippolita is, however, *flexible* in and through her use of drama, for it enables her to create a much different, more natural role for herself than Don Diego would ever have permitted her. Drama thus allows her possibilities—new social identity, freedom to choose a husband, a chance to act like an adult. In Bergson's terms, Hippolita thus becomes the play's "norm," for her use of drama allows her acceptable, normal socialization which serves as a foil to the purely comic characters. The "tension" between these two types of drama thus provides the essence of the play's comedy and makes *The Gentleman Dancing-Master* a much richer play than critics have heretofore perceived. (pp. 1-8)

W. Gerald Marshall, "The Idea of Theatre in Wycherley's 'The Gentleman Dancing-Master'," in Restoration: Studies in English Literary Culture, 1660-1700, *Vol. 6, No. 1, Spring, 1982, pp. 1-10.*

Ronald Berman   (essay date 1984)

[*Berman is an American educator and critic. In the essay that follows, he examines Wycherley's last drama,* The Plain-Dealer, *as a satire which deviates from the conventions of the Restoration drama. He asserts that in the play the dramatist struggles to comprehend the nature of passion and exposes his distrust of humankind.*]

The last works of certain authors give us a good deal of trouble. Like *Amelia* or *Daniel Deronda* or *Finnegans Wake*—or Wycherley's *The Plain Dealer*—they tend to confuse feelings and even genres. They often retreat into reticence, voicing themselves through impenetrable symbols or figures. We are hardly sure whether *The Plain Dealer* is satire, so hidden are its standards. And we wonder whether it is comedy.

The general characteristics of this play are like those of the late work of Rochester. *The Plain Dealer* was produced in 1676 and printed the following year; *Poems on Several Occasions* appeared in 1680. The poems were widely circulated in the preceding decade, and I will assume that Wycherley was as conscious of Rochester as Rochester was of him:

> Of all our modern wits, none seems to me
> Once to have touched upon true comedy
> But hasty Shadwell and slow Wycherley.
> Shadwell's unfinished works do yet impart
> Great proofs of force of nature, none of art:
> With just, bold strokes he dashes here and there,
> Showing great mastery, with little care,
> And scorns to varnish his good touches o'er
> To make the fools and women praise 'em more.
> But Wycherley earns hard whate'er he gains:
> He wants no judgment, nor he spares no pains.
> He frequently excels, and at the least
> Makes fewer faults than any of the best.

Like the late Rochester, Wycherley in his last play turns against many things which had previously been Restoration standards. We recall that in Rochester's last poems (David Vieth, editor of the standard edition, calls them the poems of his "tragic maturity") there is very little pleasure taken in either the display of wit or the conquest of love. This is the period of Rochester's "Upon Nothing," dated by Vieth in 1679. The characteristics of the poetry, like those of *The Plain Dealer,* are a fascination with nihilism, obsessive treatment of the pains and wounds of love, and a rage against the social order. In fact, Rochester explicitly accuses himself of "rage" in these poems.

Like the mature Rochester, Wycherley in this play seems more interested in breaking mirrors than in exposing vices. He accepts that the Restoration has succeeded in making old morals dull and unacceptable—but, like Rochester, he now attacks the style that has displaced them. We know from Shadwell's *Virtuoso,* in which the debate between Cavalier and contemporary becomes conscious, that the Restoration recognized it had given up courtesy, idealism and morality in exchange for style, wit and pleasure. The new values were taste, grace, ease and the libertine capacity to distance emotional experience. But it is the new values that both Rochester and Wycherley attack in their late work. They attack those things that have sustained their own early work, and that are the values not of the blockhead citizens but of their own group. Betrayal is the theme of the poetry and of this play.

In *The Plain Dealer* more than any other comedy of the period we find the sense of Restoration style having broken down. It is not the fop who is a fool, but the man of wit. Wit itself has become something else, transformed into rage. And style has become the great mode of hypocrisy; not the expression of self but its concealment. It is the adversaries of Manly who show well to society, and who have the gift of speech. Manly's own language contains comparatively little epigram or argument: it is constituted largely of declamation. He is not the best reasoner in the scene, the man equipped with a taste for philosophy. Unlike Horner in *The Country Wife,* he has no Machiavelli to guide him.

Wit is useless to Manly for it cannot mediate the passionate intensity of things. He cannot reason himself out of

feeling. He cannot even use language: "I cou'd out-rail a bilk'd Whore, or a kick'd Coward . . . I must not talk, for something I must do" (Act 2). I don't want to be overliteral in my interpretation, because the last phrase expresses Manly's attitude, not his practice. The text of the play is a record of his discourse, not his silence. But his statement is strikingly unlike the incarnation of Restoration wit in other Wycherley plays. *The Country Wife* proceeds by epigram, allusion, deduction, analogy; it is rhetorically reasoned. The hero is a master of language as well as of circumstance. And indeed in Restoration comedy until long after Wycherley, the hero is a kind of cultural figure who, in contrast to his adversaries, is interested in language and ideas—even in particular books. Although deeply flawed morally, he practices what Rochester in "A Satyr Against Reason and Mankind" called

> That reason which distinguishes by sense
> And gives us rules of good and ill from thence.

The wit or rake gives us an intellectual standard against which to judge the fops, bullies, fools and victims of passion.

But Manly is not associated with sacred texts or with good sense or with right reason. His language is not philosophical. It is composed of outbursts, curses, expostulations, complaints, insults, and other indicators of all-too personal involvement in the scene. Like the butts and villains of Restoration comedy, he speaks the language of feeling.

Passion in both Restoration comedy and social life is conventionally understood to be a failure of style. Nothing is more scorned than the obsessive power of feeling, or those figures who like Olivia or Loveit or Termagant display it. But in this play the distinction between the ordinarily cool and detached hero and his passionate adversary has been discarded. The protagonist not only fails to uphold the standards of wit, he participates in the failings of sensibility. He is something of a failure as a libertine.

It is interesting to consider passion and incoherence, both so largely displayed by the central figure, as ideas in themselves. Sometimes the playwright can be very explicit—like Shaw in his enormous introductions, he can tell us more than the text can. The Restoration narrator does not have this recourse. He does have the Prologue and Epilogue, and the Epistle Dedicatory. The last of these is used with enormous effect in *The Plain Dealer.* He can make allusions to social actuality, as in the mention in *The Plain Dealer* of the reception of the earlier *Country Wife.* And he can make the language express more than it denotes. Wycherley is admired by Rochester for his "judgment" and "pains" and by others for his ease, grace and clarity. But in this play he seems not to display the linguistic equivalent of these qualities.

Manly is often irrational. And his discourse, above all, is unplanned. He is not thinking ahead a line or two, or formulating ideas. His language is a form of unconscious reaction to events. Manly says that he must either "rail" or keep silence. In describing him, Olivia tells Fidelia that "He rails at all Mankind" (Act 4). We recall that the witness invoked by Rochester in his "Satyr" asks the satirist,

What rage ferments in your degenerate mind
To make you rail at reason and mankind?

The verbal echo helps us to recognize some resemblances. The protagonist of the play, like that of the poem, is beyond the insincerity of language. Those who witness the protagonist cannot understand that, nor that incoherence is a form of statement. Manly's "rage," like that of Rochester, is not only against the enemies of good sense. It is against the idea that certain conditions can be borne. It is against the limits of language. More precisely, it is against the particular assumption that language has a necessarily diplomatic relationship between mind and object. But Wycherley does not wish to "communicate" with the objects of his satire. He wants to hate them. Possibly the incoherence of Manly, his rage and railing, is a kind of paradigm of the writer's own situation. There is now too much to satirize, and judgment cannot be contained by rhetoric.

Manly curses women, money, fools, friends and himself. Specific meanings dissolve in these curses. In some sense he is "using language as a magical instrument" in these denunciations [Robert C. Elliott, *The Power of Satire*, 1966]. But he is doing something more, implying that analysis or the making of distinctions is useless in the late Restoration world. The suggestion is that the objects of satire will never be reformed, so that they do not have to be addressed as if they would. And of course Manly is a special kind of character who does not want to argue because he does not want to hear counter-argument. The weight of discourse in this play is all on one side. There are reasonable and meliorative voices in Fidelia and Freeman, but they do not *answer* the satirical rage of Manly. His is indeed a rage against "reason" as well as "mankind."

In this play, as in the late poetry of Rochester, society is understood to be really beyond improvement, hence beyond distinctions: the knaves are everywhere and everyone is a knave. But the play goes significantly beyond Rochester in its view of society. It has what might be called a public as well as a social theme.

The distinction between *public* and *social* is important. The *OED* states that *public* refers to the national or common good. And, as Hannah Arendt pointed out in *The Human Condition,* it used to be unthinkable to view the private self as the repository of full citizenship. Each free man is free precisely because of public activity, not because he is left alone. When we talk of Restoration comedy and Restoration satire there is too often an assumption that this kind of writing is about social deviations from norms, about manners alone. But in the comedy and in the satire with a higher specific gravity—in the work of Dryden, for example—we see the powerful and indeed tragic theme of public responsibility betrayed. A fool may be a source of amusement but not those fools who affect the common good: the fools of politics or commerce. Part of Manly's rage is against these objects of satire—or, it might be said, part of Wycherley's rage is directed against them.

"The inimitable Dedication to the ***Plain-Dealer,***" said *The Spectator* in 1712, "is a Master-piece of Raillery." Addressed to Mother Bennett, a London procuress, it conveys the writer's satisfaction in finding a patron sufficient to his story. She will preside over this story; she will do what other patrons are normally supposed to do, which is represent the values of the art. Why the choice of a notorious madam for patron? Possibly because prostitution is an accurate metaphor of civic life:

> But, now I mention Publick Persons, I can no longer defer doing you the justice of a Dedication, and telling you your own; who are, of all publick-spirited people, the most necessary, most communicative, most generous and hospitable; your house has been the house of the People, your sleep still disturb'd for the Publick, and when you arose 'twas that others might lye down, and you waked that others might rest.

It is a burlesque of patronage and of something more. The Epistle continues with some lines that make plain a political resemblance:

> In fine, Madam, like a faithful Dedicator, I hope I have done my self right in the first place, then you, and your Profession, which in the wisest and most religious Government of the World, is honour'd with the publick allowance; and in those that are thought the most unciviliz'd and barbarous, is protected, and supported by the Ministers of Justice.

Two things are being said: that art can be a form of prostitution, defining the relationship of poet and public as it was seen by Dryden, Wycherley and others; and that the public realm itself, the realm of government and ministries, of courtly, mercantile and parliamentary power, is a realm of prostitution.

The first of these themes is not uncommon. Dryden, Wycherley and others expressed it. They even practiced it: Bernard Harris writes that Dryden's view of comedy "was low, and he prostituted his art because he was realistic enough to see that the art itself in his day depended upon prostitutes." This would seem to be borne out by the Prologues to *The Wild Gallant* and *An Evening's Love* and the Epilogue to *The Conquest of Granada,* all of which use images of casual or commercial venery to imply the author's relationship to his work. Just about the time that ***The Plain Dealer*** appeared (1677), John Leanerd in *The Country Innocence* wrote,

> As a young Girl that's newly come to Town,
> And in her Russet wanders up and down,
> Ventures her Maiden-head for half a Crown,
> So our young Poet with his first Design
> Hazards his credit for a Pint of Wine.

The second of these themes is possibly more interesting. It has to do with civic character. The great house of the past, perhaps even the House of Parliament, is suggested by the house of Mother Bennett. And the *"Publick Persons"* mentioned in the Epistle appear either as characters or as figures invoked by the text. This was not the only time when Wycherley drew a resemblance between social forms and prostitution: one of his poems is titled **"To the Honour of Pimps and Pimping; dedicated to the Court; and written at a Time when such were most considerable there."** And he had written that the best chance for public success at court was to "pimp, cheat, forswear thyself, and lie."

The play begins with what is literally an "image" of fakery. The Prologue tells the audience that they will dislike this play, and for a particular reason:

> Plain-dealing is, you'll say, quite out of fashion;
> You'll hate it here, as in a Dedication.
> And your fair Neighbors, in a Limning Poet,
> No more than in a Painter will allow it:
> Pictures too like, the Ladies will not please:
> They must be drawn too here, like Goddesses.
> You, as at Lely's too, wou'd Truncheon wield,
> And look like Heroes, in a painted Field;
> But the course Dauber of the coming Scenes,
> To follow Life, and Nature only means;
> Displays you as you are. . . .

There are some special connections here. Manly is one of the few comic heroes on the Restoration stage: he comes from the Dutch Wars and intrudes that fact upon London society. And the pictures that Wycherley has so carefully identified have a special function: they are about aristocrats and public figures.

The Restoration portrait is full of *gravitas*. With few nuances, it tries to sum up the power, rank and cosmetic appearance of its subject. The Gascars portrait of James II at the National Maritime Museum is exactly that of a Roman godling against a *"painted Field"* of a battle at sea. This and other pieces in the heroic vein attempt to fulfill the dictum that "the gestures of *Maiestie* are agreeable to those of honor, nobility, magnanimity, liberality, and excellency, all of which united together, would be represented . . . especially, as they sit on their thrones and tribunals" [Giovanni Paolo Lomazzo quoted by Oliver Miller in his *The Tudor, Stuart and Early Georgian Pictures in the Collection of her Majesty the Queen*, 1963]. The Huysmans portrait of Rochester is itself a criticism of such flattery. As for the Lely goddesses, the Royal Collection shows the decline of baroque portraiture into the rendition of attitudes and complexions. Lely's Anne Hyde, Lady Byron and Catherine of Braganza languish eternally in poses which imply their manner, and his Frances Brooke and Louise De Kéroualle are at the height of their powers. The politicoes and prostitutes of the Restoration are frozen into dignity, and become an aristocracy, or the image of one, impervious to vicissitudes. The rakes have the eternal power to impress, and the whores to charm.

Painting, as an art of falsification, evidently interested Wycherley. It provides him with the entry into the play. From the beginning there is an equivocal relationship between form and actuality. Throughout we are made conscious of the distinction stated by Manly between "man" and "title," which is a distinction like that between model and pose. Perhaps we should take *"Scenes"* to mean more than dramatic sequences: they will actually offer us perspectives on public selves.

Everyone in the Prologue audience evidently wishes to *"look like Heroes."* But there is only one real hero in the play: Manly, who has returned from the Dutch Wars to a society which is alarming in its decadence. One of the key words in the play, often repeated, is "Ceremony," and that word suggests the emptiness of public life. Public life

has only manner, not substance. And "Ceremony," like style, is a kind of concealment. The central act of the play, stripping off disguises—literally finding the heart of the mystery—occurs on two levels. One is penetrating the disguise of Vernish; the other is doing the same for the public order.

Ceremony of course is a version—the formal and public version—of manners. We might recall that Ben Jonson thought manners a kind of "mystery" and assumed that the readers of "To Penshurst" would understand their relationship to the *historical* virtues of aristocracy. Castiglione thought manners absolutely substantive—it is not until Lord Chesterfield that we begin to understand them as modes of politeness. Possibly their best definition for the seventeenth century comes from the Restoration's central philosophical figure, Thomas Hobbes, who said ["of the Difference of Manners"], "By manners, I mean not here, decency of behaviour; as how one should salute another, or how a man should wash his mouth, or pick his teeth before company, and such other points of the *small morals;* but those qualities of mankind, that concern their living together in peace, and unity." This is, I think, a memorable definition. One could refer to many conduct books in support of its seriousness, and many splendid examples from Sir Philip Sidney on, but perhaps the most useful example derives from Wycherley's own image of *"Heroes, in a painted Field."* In the preceding generation Velazquez had painted his *Surrender at Breda*, a canvas which profoundly expressed the ideal form for the acceptance of pain, suffering and defeat. As one art historian has put it, this canvas represents the "type" of aristocratic amenity in Spinola and is a "supreme lesson in good breeding and humanity" for its time [Enrique Lafuente Ferrari, *Velazquez*, 1960]. This picture is in fact about a ceremony which shows not only greatness in victory and in defeat, but the idea of aristocracy in action. The ceremonies in ***The Plain Dealer*** show this idea in decline. And they are viewed particularly in relation to moral and actual heroism.

The play literally begins with the idea of ceremony. Here is Manly's first speech:

> Tell not me (my good Lord *Plausible*) of your *Decorums,* supercilious Forms, and slavish Ceremonies; your little Tricks, which you the Spaniels of the World, do daily over and over. . . .

But Plausible gives as good as he gets, noting first in response that Manly is "too passionate" and that these things are "the Arts, and Rules, the prudent of the World walk by." The first exchange is the play itself: Manly's rage opposed to "Ceremony," "Courtesie," "Arts" and "Rules." The word "Ceremony" is constantly reiterated in the first act and with each repetition the contrast between form and actuality is more deeply felt. The word is invoked to imply the slavery of conventions, the mannerisms of a fop, the falsity of friendship, the impotence of civil office and the concealed hostility of social life. There are two important extended passages which confirm the Epistle and the Prologue. One has to do with the world of the Court, the second with the play's other symbolic locations, Westminster Hall and the Exchange; that is, with the two kinds of civic influence displayed by aristocracy and bourgeoisie. In the first passage we see confirmed not only Manly's sense of the way things are, but the author's allusions to government as a kind of prostitution. Freeman is admitting that the *manners* of prostitution are essential to political and social influence:

> Hah, hah, hah—What, you observ'd me, I warrant, in the Galleries at *Whitehall,* doing the business of the place! Pshaw, Court Professions, like Court Promises, go for nothing, man. But, faith, cou'd you think I was a Friend to all those I hugg'd, kiss'd, flatter'd, bow'd too? Hah, ha—
>
> (Act 1)

The resemblance between Mother Bennett's and the Court is not confined to a stroke of wit in the Prologue: Wycherley intends it to be structural. One gathers that both places have their profitable liaisons.

Manly is, so to speak, himself watching a comedy of manners. He sums up Westminster and Whitehall, the centers of commercial and legal power, with an allusion to the quintessence of fakery, Buckingham's *Rehearsal:*

> There they seem to rehearse *Bays's* grand Dance: here you see a *Bishop* bowing low to a gaudy *Atheist;* a Judge, to a Doorkeeper; a great Lord, to a Fishmonger, or a Scrivener with a Jack-chain about his neck; a Lawyer, to a Serjeant at Arms; a velvet *Physician,* to a threadbare *Chymist:* and a supple Gentleman Usher, to a surly Beef-eater; and so tread round in a preposterous huddle of Ceremony. . . .

These marionettes have no function: the lord does not rule, the bishop does not minister, the judge does not advise. This "dance" replaces other social analogies: of hierarchy and order. It is all intermixed, suggesting that social mobility is more important than stability—and that money is virtually the sole connection between these badly assorted types.

The world of "Ceremony" is far from another world, and is in the text of the play poised against it. Plausible, who is not only the incarnation of "Ceremony" but of a dessicated aristocracy, walks by Manly's guard of sailors, who make this observation:

> 1 Sailor. Here's a finical Fellow *Jack!* What a brave fair weather Captain of a Ship he wou'd make!
>
> 2 Sailor. He a Captain of a Ship! it must be when she's in the Dock then; for he looks like one of those that get the King's Commissions for Hulls to sell a Kings Ship, when a brave Fellow has fought her almost to a Longboat.
>
> 1 Sailor. On my conscience then, *Jack,* that's the reason our Bully *Tar* sunk our Ship: not only that the *Dutch* might not have her, but that the Courtiers, who laugh at wooden Legs, might not make her Prize.

Wycherley's tactic, as old as drama itself, is to have a kind of objective witness stated by this miniature chorus. The sailors express two of the major themes: that fake aristoc-

racy and heroism are opposed, and that there is violence of feeling between them.

There is literally a battle between what Manly calls "intrinsick worth" and "counterfeit Honour." Nearly every scene has inverted heroic values, images and situations. The court, we know from the beginning, laughs at wooden legs. And when Manly describes an insufferable courtier "at the head of his Sycophants" the parody of a military formation is plain. That is as close as he will get to the King's Commission. When the scene moves to Westminster the Civil War is fought again, but in a much diminished way. It now takes place in lawsuits. Heroic values are mocked by "bluster" and "sputter" and "wrangling"—the belligerence of language alone. Oldfox would like to be thought of as a Cromwellian hero, but Manly points out that his scars have been won in London's apprentice war. And the great assault upon entrenched values comes when Manly commits mayhem on the Alderman's obtrusive nose. When the real war comes to consciousness it is in terms of the following rather ugly display of City self-interest:

> ALDERMAN. No, to keep the Cripples you make this War; this War spoils our Trade.
>
> MANLY. Dam your Trade, 'tis the better for't.
>
> (Act 3)

Two of the most important settings for the war between the "intrinsick" and the "counterfeit" are drawing-room and boudoir. The manners of love in this play are consistently portrayed as if they were the manners not only of prostitution but of politics: as Eliza says in an aside to the audience, "I find kissing and railing succeed each other with the angry Men, as well as with the angry Women; and their quarrels are like Love-quarrels. . . ." (Act 2). Actual warfare may be sometimes in Manly's term "generous" but in these locations it is conducted *a l'outrance.* For one thing, in London the motif of treason is everywhere. The enemy is much less dangerous than a treacherous friend or lover. A mistress may be "like a Pyrat" who "takes you by spreading false Colours" (Act 2).

The "enemy" of course is Olivia, whose figure seems to sum up a number of issues deeply concerning Wycherley. The issues are not only of sex or money but of mind. Olivia is a kind of portrait or representative figure for polite society. And yet, this beautiful, even charming woman seems to display two qualities out of all proportion to her assumed character: a spirit of hatred and detraction that at times dwarfs the railing of Manly and a vocabulary impregnated with images of barbarism and mutilation. Olivia seems instinctively to turn to those inverted military locutions and ideas which provide so large a part of Wycherley's context. And she plays with the idea of heroism:

> NOVEL. I have an Ambition, I must confess, of losing my heart, before such a fair Enemy as your self, Madam; but that silly Rogues shou'd be ambitious of losing their Arms, and—
>
> OLIVIA. Looking like a pair of Compasses.
>
> (Act 2)

We recall the courtiers laughing at wooden legs. A dialogue like this, with its motifs repeated, is out of the ordinary. It is implicitly a symptom of some kind of cultural or moral breakdown. There is too much of a disproportion between the mode of wit and the object envisioned. This "compass" imagery of Olivia might be thought of as being as much representative of this cultural moment as John Donne's was of his.

Manners are, as Hobbes suggested, substantive. They really do have to do with "living together" in unity. At once savage and instructive, this passage and others like it tell us about a kind of decadence in wit and style and, perhaps more important, of a certain kind of psychology. For Olivia's language is connected to her sexuality. The idea of sexual warfare had for centuries been a valued and possibly indispensable trope; here it becomes literal. Olivia is not only a "fair Enemy" to Novel and a "Pyrat" to Manly; she seems to express universal aggressiveness. When associated with Olivia—as it often is—the idea of the crippled hero suggests more than one kind of mutilation:

> We Women adore a Martial Man, and you have nothing wanting to make you more one, or more agreeable, but a wooden Leg.
>
> (Act 2)

But she herself is martial:

> FIDELIA. I fenced with her eager Arms, as you did with the grapples of the Enemy's Fireship, and nothing but cutting 'em off, cou'd have freed me. . . .
>
> (Act 4)

> OLIVIA. Right, right: where are thy lips? here, take the dumb, and best Welcomes, Kisses and Embraces; 'tis not a time for idle words. In a Duel of Love, as in others, Parlying shews basely. Come, we are alone; and now the Word is only Satisfaction, and defend not thy self.
>
> (Act 4)

If there are heroic energies in this society they seem to have gone into sexuality. But that sexuality is not especially pleasurable as a relationship. It does not conform to earlier libertine expectations, which assumed the distancing of passion. One of the reasons why the play is so dark is that while Manly is a misanthrope the objects of his rage are correctly perceived. The appetites for sex and for money seem, even given the range of Restoration sophistication, to be excessive. Sexuality, which hovers on several occasions on the act of rape, is a matter of aggression. It is connected to the anality of money; expressed by imagery of assault and mutilation; represented by the prostituted embraces of false friendship and false feeling. Perhaps the most important summary point is that the public realm is indicated by empty ceremony—by kissing, embracing, hugging and assurance—while the private realm is perceived morally and psychologically in terms of militant aggressiveness. One realm is unworthy of the satirist's respect and the other baffles his ethical understanding.

Perhaps these things allow us to understand the depth of Wycherley's response to social facts. He seems, like the late Rochester and the late Swift, to have gone beyond a moral or logical barrier. Rochester's "Upon Nothing" suggests that the "gratitude" of friends, the "promises" of court and the "vows" of lovers all "Flow swiftly into thee, and in thee ever end." If that is true then the harshness and misanthropy of Rochester, Wycherley and the Swift of the last book of *Gulliver's Travels* become understandable. At some point the satirist is overwhelmed by two realizations: the extent of depravity, and the degree to which he shares it. And at some point satire gives up. It is baffled by a public realm which seems impervious to reform, and by a private realm of human character where passions are mysterious, unredeemed. It is natural for such satire to be either incoherent or incommunicative, for it to end with bellows of rage or in the whinnying of a horse. (pp. 465-77)

> Ronald Berman, "Wycherley's Unheroic Society," in *ELH*, Vol. 51, No. 3, Fall, 1984, pp. 465-78.

James Thompson   (essay date 1984)

[*In the following excerpt, Thompson analyzes dramatic language in Wycherley's comedy,* The Gentleman Dancing-Master, *arguing that the primary concern of the drama is to explore the limitations of language and the human need to be understood.*]

Since it opened in 1672, Wycherley's second play has never been popular, either with audiences or critics. *The Gentleman Dancing-Master* does not appear ever to have been revived after its first, short run, and scholars have afforded the play correspondingly slight attention: most often the play is dismissed as farce. Certainly *The Gentleman Dancing-Master* is Wycherley's least memorable play, and yet . . . the play is extremely interesting, perhaps more so than *Love in a Wood,* which is, by most measures, a better play. At any rate, Wycherley's first two productions are strikingly different; where *Love in a Wood* is all-encompassing, *The Gentleman Dancing-Master* is much more constrained. Of the five marriages in the first play, Wycherley chose but one to concentrate on in his next work. The main courtship of this second play corresponds best to the elopement of Dapperwit and Martha in *Love in a Wood,* though these lovers, transformed into Gerrard and Hippolita, are elevated and made both more sensible and more romantic than their foolish and grasping originals. This courtship expands to fill five acts, and there is but one, minor subplot, concerning Flirt, Flounce, and Monsieur, which takes up less attention or space than even Gripe's and Lucy's affair in *Love in a Wood.* The obvious question is what Wycherley has done to fill out the play, having, by comparison, reduced the action by sixty percent. This play does seem thin enough to justify Courtall's complaint in *She Would if She Could:* "A single intrigue in love is as dull as a single plot in a play, and will tire a lover worse than t'other does an audience." Wycherley has fleshed out this present play in two ways: borrowing the plot complications of the titular disguise from a play by Calderón, and the comic theme of Gallomania from plays by the Duke of Newcastle and James Howard. For our purposes, the latter is most significant, for the humor derived from the contrast of French, Spanish, and English customs, clothing, and language yields a great deal of discussion about language and its proper use. Indeed, for the first time in Wycherley's work, the right use of words becomes a central concern, as the playwright begins to explore the limits of language, its elasticity, how far Monsieur can try to debase English until his discourse tumbles into the chasm of total meaninglessness. Representative of such concerns is this exchange about the desire to speak poorly:

> MONSIEUR. But have I the Eyrè Francèz?
>
> GERRARD. As much as any *French*-Footman of 'em all.
>
> MONSIEUR. And do I speak agreeable ill *Englis'* enough?
>
> GERRARD. Very ill.
>
> MONSIEUR. Veritablemènt:
>
> GERRARD. Veritablemènt:
>
> MONSIEUR. For you must know, 'tis as ill breeding now to speak good *Englis'*, as to write good *Englis'*, good sense, or a good hand.

(I, ii, 118-26)

Throughout this play (and in the rest of his drama), Wycherley toys with the question of just how far Monsieur can go in his attempt to annihilate sense. But, as I have suggested above, language proves to be uncorruptible: even Monsieur is unable to maintain his vacuity for the whole play, and is forced, when threatened with financial loss, to lapse back into sense.

Even the farcical elements concerning French and Spanish costume can be seen to contribute to these larger concerns about meaning, for here, what one wears, what one says, and what one is are all of a piece. As in ***Love in a Wood***, clothes and words do not make, but rather reveal the man: words, clothes, and man are seen to form a whole. And it is with the whole man, outside and in, speech and self, what he is, what he thinks he is, and what he wants to be, that Wycherley is always concerned: how all of these parts fit together, whether they can be changed or altered in any way; can people make themselves into what they want to be, or are they ineluctably what they are. In this play, these questions focus on the subject of gentility and class consciousness, as in the title, which paradoxically unites gentleman and imitation gentleman. An anatomy of gentility begins in the first scene, where the heroine, Hippolita, asks of the titular gentleman, "What kind of a man is that Mr. *Gerrard*," and of her cousin Monsieur, to whom she is promised, "Is he no man" (I, i, 32, 102). These questions continue throughout the play, as the word "honour" is used and abused forty-four times and "gentleman" twenty-four times. The two prostitutes, Flirt and Flounce, loudly proclaim their "honour" (I, ii, 246), while Monsieur, the play's fool and clearly no gentleman, describes himself as "a person of Honour, a brave Gentleman" (I, ii, 29); Gerrard even refers to a waiter at a French house as "a man of Honour!" (I, ii, 180). Constant questioning of these words forces us to consider whether gen-

tility resides in innate character, breeding, education, manners, conduct in general, appearance, or speech. This central definitional problem is part of the question of language in this play, in that certain characters behave as if honor, gentility, and character are merely verbal constructs. Monsieur, the son of an English brewer, and his uncle, an English merchant, have chosen to become, respectively, French and Spanish, and in the following exchange, both behave as if the change of names produces a change of nature or at least reputation:

> DON DIEGO. Do'st thou call me Monsieur (voto a St. *Jago.*)
>
> MONSIEUR. No, I did not call you Monsieur voto a St. *Jago,* Sir, I know you are my Uncle Mr. *James Formal*-da-
>
> DON DIEGO. But I can hardly know you are my Cousin, Mr. *Nathaniel Paris;* but call me Sir *Don Diego* henceforward, look you, and no Monsieur, call me Monsieur *Guarda.*
>
> MONSIEUR. I confess my errour, Sir; for none but a blind man wou'd call you Monsieur, ha, ha, ha————But pray do not call me neder *Paris,* but de *Paris,* (si vou plai'st) Monseur de *Paris*! Call me Monsieur and welcome.

(III, i, 145-54)

The two protagonists, Hippolita and Gerrard, on the contrary, learn that gentility, honor, and character are more a matter of nature than words. Hippolita argues that Monsieur's folly is innate: "Father, you wash the Black-a-more white, in endeavouring to make a *Spaniard* of a *Monsieur,* nay an *English Monsieur* too, consider that, Father; for when they once have taken the *French* plie (as they call it) they are never to be made so much as *English* men again" (IV, i, 52-56). To Gerrard and Hippolita, character is fixed, but reputation is earned, just as in English courtesy literature gentility is not bestowed by birth, but earned through gentle conduct.

In the best tradition of intrigue comedy, it is the very confusion surrounding these questions of character and language which answers them. Pretense and disguise provide a paradoxical perspective that juxtaposes what characters are and what they are not; by their pretense to what they are not can we see what they truly are. Disguise, in the case of Gerrard, is a kind of glass which eventually reveals true character. Characters become what they imitate, and the best emblem of this process is the "*Punk* in Vizor" mentioned in the prologue: wearing a mask to disguise identity only identifies the wearer as a prostitute.

Language in ***The Gentleman Dancing-Master*** is consistently entangled in clothing, for throughout the play Wycherley toys with the familiar metaphor of language clothing thought in words. This metaphor is realized when Don Diego demands that his prospective son-in-law, Monsieur, "leave off your *French* Dress, Stammering, and Tricks" (III, i, 227-28), connecting Monsieur's affected dress with his affected language. As a condition of marriage to Hippolita, Monsieur must exchange his French dress for Spanish, a "metamorphosis" (IV, i, 316) which is concluded in act four when Monsieur puts on a Golilia, what Don Diego calls "the Ornamento principal of the *Spanish* habit":

> MONSIEUR. Will you have no mercy, no pity, alas, alas, alas, Oh I had rather put on the *English* Pillory than this *Spanish* Golilia, for 'twill be all a case I'm sure; for when I go abroad, I shall have a Crowd of Boys about me, peppering me with rotten Eggs and Turneps, helas, helas.
>
> DON DIEGO. Helas again?
>
> MONSIEUR. Alas, alas, alas.

> (IV, i, 114-23)

Monsieur's removal of his French *cravate* parallels his suppression of the hypercorrect aspiration in "helas," underscoring the identity of dress and speech. He had earlier pointed to the similarity, asking "must I leave off all *French* Beautes, Graces, and Embellisements, bote of my Person and Language?" (III, i, 250-51). The various implications of the words as clothing metaphor reveal the ways in which both clothes and words make or reveal men. In his examination of this metaphor in Restoration comedy, Holland [in his *First Modern Comedies,* 1959] mistakenly describes language as cover, disguise, or deceit: "Language was itself regarded as an outside—clothing, ornament, or, in general, a shell of accidents—within which the real substance, thought, lay hidden." Holland fails to realize that the metaphor has both positive and negative connotations, for if speech should be thought to advantage dressed, it can, like dress, be elegant or vulgar, appropriate or mismatched, as in this version from Quintilian: "Again, a tasteful and magnificent dress, as the Greek poet tells us, lends added dignity to its wearer: but effeminate and luxurious apparel fails to adorn the body and merely reveals the foulness of the mind. Similarly, a translucent and iridescent style merely serves to emasculate the subject which it arrays with such pomp of words." In **"An Epistle to Mr. Dryden,"** Wycherley compliments Dryden on the propriety of his language:

> Such is your Sense, which you so well express,
> Each Thought is brilliant in its proper Dress.

Far from hiding or disguising thought, words can be said to realize or give life to thought; as Rosemond Tuve demonstrates [in her *Elizabethan and Metaphysical Imagery,* 1947], the garment of style often indicates the ideal fusion of word and thought, "in the sense that the flesh is the soul's garment, its bodying forth or manifestation."

Like clothing, then, language both reveals and conceals; speech can give form or shape or body or life, making thoughts communicable or visible, or it can be used to hide, disguise, or deceive. We might say that Gerrard uses language to reveal his thought and character, while Monsieur uses it to conceal or at least change his thought and character, to become French instead of English. This is oversimple, however, because Gerrard and Monsieur have different conceptions of the nature and function of discourse, almost as if they speak different languages. Furthermore, nothing is finally concealed, for dress, mask, disguise, or speech always reveals the man himself.

Gerrard's and Monsieur's speech provide an extreme con-trast of translucent and opaque styles, for Gerrard's speech is unobtrusive, while Monsieur's is as conspicuous as he can make it. Gerrard's speech is normative in that his words harmoniously or decorously fit thought and speaker and culture. Monsieur's speech, like clothing in the worst taste, is completely inappropriate to the body dressed. Unlike Sir Fopling Flutter's correct French, Monsieur's is a bastardization of two languages, for he debases English sentences with French forms. His discourse thereby offends according to all four of the classical criteria of style, the Theophrastan virtues of correctness, clarity, propriety, and ornament, for his speech is not grammatically correct, but broken; not perspicuous, but confused; not brief, but prolix; not decorous, but unseemly for a native English speaker. In the Tavern scene, where Gerrard is introduced, his speech contrasts sharply with Monsieur's:

> MONSIEUR. Auh-his son (for he had but one) was making de Toure of *France, Espaigne, Italy,* an' *Germany* in a Coach and six, or rader now I think on't, gone of an Embassy hidèr to dere Master *Cromwell,* whom dey did love and fear, because he was some-thingè de greater Rebel butè now I talk of de Rebellè, none but de Rebel can love de Rebellè, and so mush for you and your Friend de *Dushe* I'le say no more, and pray you say no more of my friend de *Franch,* not so mush as of my Friend the *Franch*-Foot-man-da—
>
> GERRARD. No, no; but, Monsieur, now give me leave to admire thee, that in three months at *Paris* you could renounce your Language, Drinking and your Country (for which we are not angry with you as I said) and come home so perfect a *French*-man, that the Drey-men of your Fathers own Brew-house wou'd be ready to knock thee in the head.

> (I, iii, 101-15)

Monsieur's speech is very confused; the eleven clauses, progressing only through non sequitur, seem to parody the rambling, associative parataxis of Senecan style, while Gerrard's speech, on the other hand, is a model of logic and clarity. The suspended hypotaxis of evenly spaced members separates admiration and insult at either end of the sentence, balanced neatly with a parenthetical expression. The contrast implies, of course, that only Gerrard has the intelligence to construct a complicated or even coherent sentence.

Monsieur and Don Diego expect the very opacity of their language to mask their middle-class, English origins. In their faith in the power of words to transform them into Frenchman and Spaniard, Monsieur and Don Diego assert the primacy of the signifier: the word or sign is given priority over its referent, the signified. It will not do to say that a change of name or dress will no more change a man than a change of word will transform whatever it was thought to signify, for there are clearly two opposing systems at work here. While French accent is clearly intended to call up its signified, French culture, that object is lost in the thickness of the language itself. Monsieur apparently believes that his new name transforms him; Gerrard, on

LITERATURE CRITICISM FROM 1400 TO 1800, Vol. 21

the other hand, suggests that Monsieur was a fool before and after his trip to Paris. Don Diego, with typical myopia, quotes the appropriate proverb, but only for Monsieur: "The Ass was an Ass still, though he had the Lyons Skin on" (IV, i, 147-48). Uncle and nephew are so concerned with externals that they take care of words and dress, but let the thought and man shift for themselves. If asides conventionally represent a character's thought, it is telling that Monsieur employs normal English in his asides; his French accent is then a duplicitous facade (like Lady Flippant's shop sign in *Love in a Wood*), for Monsieur's audible speech does not emanate from the soul, and so there is no consistency or correspondence between the inner and outer man. In this respect, Monsieur differs from Wycherley's "witty" fools, Dapperwit, Sparkish, and Novel, who all exhibit a correspondence between exterior, linguistic folly, and interior, inherent folly. Monsieur's speech, on the other hand, produces a comic suggestion of emptiness; having rejected his country, his language, and his nature, it is as if there is nothing at all behind his words and dress: style is truly all there is to such a vacuous character. He is a characterless character, well suited to the farcical role he plays. Dapperwit's dull similitudes always make some obvious, clichéd sense, but Monsieur's macaronic utterances are very difficult to follow. Like the impenetrable Norman French legal language of *The Plain-Dealer,* Monsieur's is a language which, at the very least, resists interpretation, and, at the most, denies signification itself.

Monsieur's and Don Diego's attitude toward language is the same as their attitude toward clothing. To Monsieur, who will "Live and die for de *Pantaloon* against de *Spanish* Hose" (III, i, 183-84), clothing becomes an end in itself. He and his uncle are no longer concerned with Hippolita, marriage, family honor, or religion: Monsieur "cou'd kneel down and varship a pair of jenti *Pantaloons*" (III, i, 165-66). As dress becomes an end rather than a means to social grace or to comfort, so too words become ends in themselves; "jernis" and "votos" lose referents, and so are rendered meaningless out of their proper cultural and linguistic context. When Don Diego refuses him "one little *Franch* Oate" (III, i, 269), Monsieur produces a word heap, full of sound and fury but signifying nothing: "Helas, helas, den I shall take my leave, morte teste, ventre, Jernie, teste-bleu, ventre-bleu, ma foy, certes" (III, i, 272-73); language here has relapsed into primal chaos, or perhaps more appropriately we might say that their linguistic social-climbing has re-created the tower of Babel. We witness a process of reification, as Monsieur's and Don Diego's words become things; their words are like physical souvenirs brought back from a grand tour, objects of status rather than means of communication. Words to Monsieur are like Mallarmé's radiant jewels, valuable, not simply as marks for something signified, but valuable in and of themselves, an attitude woefully out of accord with prevailing theories of language in the Restoration.

Uncle and nephew value words for their social or national status, rather than common meaning, imposing a private or idiomatic value on words that accords, not with any communal sense of what words ought to mean, but with their own vanity. In consequence, they not only misuse

words, but they misconstrue everyone else's, for everyone says exactly what these two would like to hear. Hippolita observes that Monsieur "is as apt as an ill Poet to mistake the contempt and scorn of people for applause and admiration" (III, i, 32-33). Don Diego's self-deception is even more brazen: "Be a *Spaniard* like me, and ne're think people laugh at you: there was never a *Spaniard* that thought any one laugh'd at him" (IV, i, 130-31). The false Spaniard's and Frenchman's devotion to words allows them to be manipulated, not by meaning, but by sound and association:

> GERRARD. But indeed, methinks, you are not slovenly enough for a *French*-man.
>
> MONSIEUR. Slovenly! You mean negligent?
>
> GERRARD. No, I mean slovenly.
>
> MONSIEUR. Then I will be more slovenly.
>
> (I, ii, 128-32)

Because Gerrard associates "French" and "slovenly," Monsieur will endeavor to be more slovenly, no matter what the word means; he is similarly victimized by the accent rather than the substance of the French scullion's words (I, ii, 294-311). (One is reminded of Hobbes's remark that words are the money of fools if these words are valued by their association with any individual authority.)

He who controls words in this play in turn controls people, and Virginia Birdsall has observed [in her *A Wild Civility,* 1970] that Hippolita "manipulates words, artistically playing with their variable meanings and deceiving all those incapable of recognizing a double entendre either in word or action when they are faced with one." Even so, in the dancing scenes, which are as full of double meanings as the more famous scenes involving Harcourt, Alithea, and Sparkish, these double meanings do not originate with either Gerrard or Hippolita. It is rather Caution who reads sexual innuendo into the action, as here in Caution's running commentary on Hippolita's and Gerrard's dancing:

> CAUTION. See, See, she squeezes his hand now, O the debauch'd Harletry!
>
> DON DIEGO. So, so, mind her not, she moves forward pretty well; but you move as well backward as forward, or you'll never do anything to purpose.
>
> CAUTION. Do you know what you say, Brother, your self now? Are you at your beastliness before your young Daughter?
>
> (III, i, 410-16)
>
> CAUTION. de' see how she pants?
>
> DON DIEGO. She has not been us'd to motion.
>
> CAUTION. Motion, motion, motion de' call it? no indeed, I kept her from motion till now, motion with a vengenance.
>
> (III, i, 537-40)

These dancing scenes are like textbook cases of dissembling; far from actively deceiving, Hippolita and Gerrard merely allow first Don Diego and then Caution to deceive themselves, by giving them ample opportunity to assert their folly and blindness. It is not that the elders are unable to penetrate Gerrard's disguise, for Caution does and then Don Diego. Yet, neither Don Diego nor Caution is able to act because of his pride: each will "ha' no body wiser than [him] self" (IV, i, 720). In effect, father and aunt never speak directly with Gerrard and Hippolita, but only argue with themselves and end up deceiving themselves:

CAUTION. How came you hither?

GERRARD. There I am puzl'd indeed (*aside*).

CAUTION. How came you hither, I say? how———

DON DIEGO. Ay, how shou'd he come hither? upon his Legs.

CAUTION. So, So, now you have put an Excuse in his head too, that you have, so you have, but stay———

DON DIEGO. Nay, with your favour, Mistress, I'le ask him now.

CAUTION. Y Facks; but you shan't, I'le ask him, and ask you no favour that I will.

DON DIEGO. Y fackins; but you shan't ask him, if you go there to look you, you Prattle-box you, I'le ask him.

CAUTION. I will ask him, I say, come.

DON DIEGO. Where.

CAUTION. What.

DON DIEGO. Mine's a shrewd question.

CAUTION. Mine's as shrewd as yours.

(II, i, 320-36)

The business at hand, interrogation of Gerrard, is forgotten, as these two get lost in their desire to abuse and triumph over one another. Don Diego's all-consuming need to know more than anyone else and see more than anyone else results in an inability to believe that he can be wrong, a pattern which is repeated in ***The Country Wife*** in Sparkish, Sir Jasper, and Pinchwife: the fool doth think he is wise, but the wise man knows he is a fool. In ***The Gentleman Dancing-Master,*** Don Diego's passion for superiority culminates in his predictable insistence that he deceived everyone; in the untenable position of having been misled, Don Diego can only extricate himself by brazenly asserting that he knew all along Gerrard was no dancing-master, that he has himself deceived everyone else; "have a care of saying I have not deceiv'd you, lest I deceive you another way; guarda—pray, Gentlemen, do not think any man cou'd deceive me look you" (V, i, 698-700).

Though I have implied that Gerrard and Hippolita are honest, honorable, and good intentioned, asserting the "proper" concept of language, the primacy of the signified, weighing reality and not just appearance, they too exploit the dual nature of language, indeed, better than anyone else, manipulating and misleading not just the others,

but each other at first. At their first meeting, Hippolita confesses of Gerrard, "tis harder playing the Hypocrite with him, I see, than with my Aunt or Father; and if dissimulation were not very natural to a Woman, I'm sure I cou'd not use it at this time; but the mask of simplicity and innocency is as useful to an intriguing Woman, as the mask of Religion to a States-man, they say" (II, i, 90-95). Gerrard, too, uses this tactic of masking, for he is no more a dancing-master than Monsieur is a Frenchman. But, while Monsieur disguises himself as a gentleman, revealing that he has no claim to the title, Gerrard disguises himself as an imitation gentleman, revealing that he is, in fact, a gentleman. Usually "better dress'd and prouder than many a good Gentleman" (II, i, 407-8), dancing-masters represent only the appearance of gentility, as is clear from this exchange:

CAUTION. Is he a Dancing-master? He does not look like a Dancing-master.

HIPPOLITA. Pish—you don't know a Dancing-master, you have not seen one these threescore years, I warrant.

CAUTION. No matter; but he does not look like a Dancing-master.

DON DIEGO. Nay, nay, Dancing-masters look like Gentlemen, enough, Sister; but he's no Dancing-master by drawing his Sword so briskly: those tripping outsides of Gentlemen are like Gentlemen enough in every thing but in drawing a Sword.

(II, i, 281-89)

The problem with dancing-masters is that they look exactly like gentlemen, and are indeed gentlemen except in substance. This is also the construct Monsieur represents, whom Prue and Hippolita construe as a type of dancing-master: he is an "apish Kind of Gentleman" who "debases . . . Civility and good Breeding more than a City Dancing-master" (I, i, 42, 48). C. J. Rawson explores [in *Henry Fielding and the Augustan Ideal Under Stress,* 1972] the troublesome figure of the dancing-master:

Dancing-masters were a special and embarrassing case, because they were a necessary part of a 'genteel education.' Not only did one therefore see them a good deal, but they were professionals who taught gentlemen some of the marks of gentility. . . . The gentleman thus had a painful obligation to the dancing-master, and the dancing-master must have acquired pretensions of gentility which exacerbated the situation; the gentleman had to learn from a laboured specialist the graceful ease which was supposed to be his birthright, and the dancing-master could feel that he did things better than his pupils. Hence part of the particular insistence that a gentleman should learn to dance well, yet not like a dancing-master, and, more generally, the obsessional frequency with which writers of the period keep mentioning dancing-masters, often with edgily ambiguous or over-aggressive contempt. The title of Wycherley's ***Gentleman Dancing-Master*** must have derived much piquancy from this whole situation.

Such class consciousness lies at the heart of this play: can gentility or honor itself be taught or successfully pretended? The play is based on an aristocratic ideology that insists that the condition of being a gentleman is not to be achieved by wealth, clothing, language, or any form of action: rather, gentility is internal and inherent. Wycherley indicates that anyone who can confuse the French *bon ton* for true English gentility can have no pretense either to taste or to gentility. The relative fixity of social station and even nature is made abundantly clear in this exchange between Don Diego and Monsieur, who tries to remind his uncle of origins, which no accent, costume, or cash can disguise:

> DON DIEGO. We are descended look you———
>
> MONSIEUR. Nay, pray Uncle hear me.
>
> DON DIEGO. I say, we are descended.
>
> MONSIEUR. 'Tis no matter for that.
>
> DON DIEGO. And my great, great, great Grandfather was.
>
> MONSIEUR. Well, well, I have something to say more to the purpose.
>
> DON DIEGO. My great, great, great, Grandfather, I say, was———
>
> MONSIEUR. Well, a Pin-maker in———
>
> DON DIEGO. But he was a Gentleman for all that Fop, for he was a Serjeant to a Company of Train-bands, and my great, great, great Grandfather was.
>
> MONSIEUR. Was his Son, what then? won't you let me clear this Gentleman?
>
> DON DIEGO. He was, he was- - -
>
> MONSIEUR. He was a Felt-maker, his Son a Winecooper, your Father a Vintner, and so you came to be a Canary-Merchant.
>
> DON DIEGO. But we were still Gentlemen, for our Coat was as the Heralds say—was—
>
> MONSIEUR. Was, your sign was the Three Tuns, and the Field Canary; now let me tell you this honest Gentleman—
>
> DON DIEGO. Now that you shou'd dare to dishonour this Family; by the Graves of my Ancestors in Great Saint *Ellens* Church-
>
> MONSIEUR. Yard.
>
> (V, i, 370-93)

Though he gradually gives way to Monsieur's revelations, Don Diego seems little affected by it all, perhaps because his gentility is a condition of his imagination more than anything else. And yet the fragility of Don Diego's claim to illustrious ancestry is indicated by the fact that Monsieur can puncture those pretensions with a word, "yard," where the relatives are really buried. To use a distinction of Fielding's, Wycherley may not mock the bourgeois origin of this family, but only their affectation of something more. Paradoxically, the only true gentleman in the play affects something less.

The oxymoronic title, **The Gentleman Dancing-Master,** describes a paradoxical protagonist who demeans himself in order to prove himself. As Rosalie Colie has observed [in her *Paradoxica Epidemica*, 1966], oxymoron is the central trope of paradox, and both the language and plot of this play are paradoxical. Though Pope was referring to Wycherley's verse when he told Spence that Wycherley "loved paradoxes," the plays also reveal a love of paradox, and this one in particular may be seen, in part, as a type of *Encomium Moriae*, or Praise of Folly. The word "fool" is used eighty-six times in the play, mostly of Gerrard and Monsieur. But while Monsieur and Don Diego are anxious to deny their folly—"I am no Fool, Look you" (II, i, 30)—Gerrard willingly and deliberately "plays the fool"; "to be caught in a Fool's Trap—I'le venture it" (I, ii, 47), as he is "Fooled and abused" (IV, i, 620) and "made a Fool" (V, i, 37) by Hippolita. It is only when he would "be such a Fool as to steal a Woman with nothing" (IV, i, 550-51) that he wins her, "a Fools Paradise" (V, i, 32). Gerrard plays the fool by playing a dancing-master: where Monsieur tries to appear better by imitating his betters, Gerrard imitates his inferiors.

Such a paradoxical rise by falling or fall by rising is always suggested in the ironic reversal of wisdom and folly; as Touchstone of *As You Like It* says, "the fool doth think he is wise, but the wise man knows himself to be a fool" (V, i, 33). Wycherley's familiarity with this topos is clear from his poems **"Upon the Impertinence of Knowledge"** and **"In Praise of Ignorance"**; in **"Upon the Discretion of Folly,"** he writes that "the greatest Folly sure, is to be Wise," and "Folly Proves Wisdom" (III, 28). These paradoxes explore and finally assert the limitations of knowledge, while they urge acknowledgment and acceptance of these limitations. And yet, Colie argues, paradox is "often designed to assert some fundamental and absolute truth." Though *Encomium Moriae* is, on the surface, destructive and negative in its denial of our ability to know all things, yet it does promote a fundamental truth all the while, which is the importance of humility.

The significance of humility in the play before us is best represented in Hippolita's explanation of Gerrard's jealousy. Unlike the excessive jealousy of Valentine in *Love in a Wood* or Pinchwife in *The Country Wife,* here jealousy serves as proof of love, as Hippolia tells Gerrard: "jealousie in a Gallant is humble true Love, and the height of respect, and only an undervaluing of himself to overvalue" his mistress (V, i, 210-12). While Gerrard plays the fool and adopts the humiliating pose of a dancing-master, his rival overvalues himself; Monsieur remarks that "he that loves must seem a little jealous," but it is typical of Monsieur to say "seem" rather than "be," and he goes on to disclaim all jealousy because it is not "French" (I, i, 189-90): "Cousin, I doubt not your amourè for me, because I doubt not your judgment" (I, i, 172-73). Like Sparkish, Monsieur's indifference indicates that he is too self-centered to care about another's affection. In one of his better poems, Wycherley argues that jealousy elevates the mistress and humbles the lover, because it witnesses that she is worthy to be loved by many, while he is unworthy to monopolize her affections. Further, his assurance of her love would be impertinent and proud (III, 178-80). As he was later to write Pope, there could be no love without jealousy, a paradox Wycherley appears to have realized in his marriage to the Countess of Drogheda, whose "outrageous Jealousy," writes John Dennis, "proceeded from the excess of her Passion."

Gerrard's jealousy serves to reveal his love for Hippolita, while it also threatens to reveal him as no dancing-master: Don Diego "wou'd have discover'd our false Dancing-master (for passion unmasks every man)" (V, i, 163-64). However much he conceals his emotions, his affections will out, which is true of his gentility as well; despite his disguise as a dancing-master, Gerrard is recognized as a gentleman by his ready use of that emblem of gentility and honor, his sword. Don Diego observes of Gerrard: "Nay, nay, Dancing-masters look like Gentlemen, enough, Sister; but he's no Dancing-master by his drawing his Sword so briskly: those tripping out-sides of Gentlemen are like Gentlemen enough in everything but in drawing a Sword" (II, i, 286-89). (By the same token, Monsieur, like Sparkish in *The Country Wife,* will only draw when there are women around to stop the fight.) Gerrard is forced into his undignified disguise, and yet, through his willingness to lower himself, he proves to be a gentleman and worthy of Hippolita. Monsieur sums up Gerrard best: "Well, thou art a generous man, I vow and swear, to come and take upon you this trouble, danger, and shame, to be thought a paltry Dancing-master, and all this to preserve a Ladies honour and life" (IV, i, 340-44). Monsieur, too, is "disguised" (III, i, 8) as a Frenchman, but his cover only reveals his unworthiness; he tells Hippolita that he went to France "to learn to play de Fool" (III, i, 41-42), and all his affectations accomplish is the revelation of his folly. Monsieur's French facade and Don Diego's Spanish front reveal their folly, and Gerrard's disguise uncovers his gentility, just as the mask reveals the punk. In each case, the mask brings out what is already there, making character or nature manifest. The effect is similar with speech; though words would seem to conceal, Monsieur's and Don Diego's false accents only serve to illustrate their inherent folly.

For all the major characters in this play, disguise functions as a kind of trial by which they prove themselves, especially for Gerrard and Hippolita. When these two first meet, they disguise their true feelings in language that, ironically, is as opaque as Monsieur's: "My Soul, my Life, 'tis you have Charms powerful as numberless, especially those of your innocency irresistable, and do surprise the wary'st Heart; such mine was, while I cou'd call it mine, but now 'tis yours for ever" (II, i, 217-20). Though their asides in this scene reveal "love at first sight," this elaborate style, complete with Miltonic inversion, is a long way from the "Plain dealing" (V, i, 199) they achieve in the end. The lovers must purify their language before it can be used as an appropriately sincere vehicle to express love. Their oaths in particular want attention, for when the mutual distrust between Hippolita and Gerrard is at its height, she calls attention to the misuse of "faith":

GERRARD. Cou'd all that so natural Innocency be dissembl'd? faith it cou'd not, dearest miss.

HIPPOLITA. Faith it was, dear Master.

GERRARD. Was it, faith?

HIPPOLITA. Me thinks you might believe me without an Oath.

(IV, i, 524-28)

Hippolita reintroduces the word "faith" once again, only when she and Gerrard reach their understanding: "faith, here's my hand now in earnest, to lead me a Dance as long as I live" (V, i, 181-82). The word has been validated, for the concept has been realized between them. Their linguistic reform follows a pattern predictable in Wycherley: a more precise use of words leads to a more honest correspondence between speech and thought; the more exposed their true thought, the more dependent upon trust they become, reaching eventually the "language of the heart." They must purify their language, for it is only when they mean what they say that Hippolita can give her "self and fortune away franckly" (V, i, 261-62). This frankness or plain dealing is the goal of all of Wycherley's protagonists, a simple honesty purged of Ranger's duplicity and Manly's brutality, a gentle, gentlemanly honesty.

Their courtship, complicated as it is by intrigue and distrust, is a mutual trial. When Hippolita first reveals her fortune to Gerrard, he can only repeat, "Twelve hundred pound a Year" (II, i, 203-07), just as she can only repeat later, "A Coach and Six" (III, i, 506-18). Both are swayed by the promise of wealth, and so Hippolita tests Gerrard, as she later admits: "I confess I had a mind to try whether your interest did not sway you more than your love; whether the twelve hundred pounds a year I told you of, had not made a greater impression in your heart than *Hippolita*" (V, i, 236-39). Gerrard is acquitted of fortune hunting when he agrees to "be such a Fool as to steal a Woman for nothing" (IV, i, 550-51). At the same time as he is tried, Gerrard, in turn, claims to "try" Hippolita (III, i, 500). Though Hippolita's trial is less obvious, the way in which she proves her worthiness can be seen in the progress of modesty. Because Hippolita is always in danger of seeming to be "a confident coming piece" (V, i, 260), Wycherley provides a tempering counter example to Hippolita's forwardness, in the characters of the two prostitutes, whose exaggerated aggression qualifies Hippolita's appearance of immodesty. Gerrard, however, remarks that modesty is only important for the lady, claiming that "modesty in a man is as ill as the want of it in a Woman" (III, i, 461-62), and that "Modesty between Lovers is as impertinent as Ceremony between Friends" (IV, i, 475-76). He is shown to be mistaken, because some diffidence is necessary to both; moreover, the forwardness of both is dissembled; when they first meet, he says, "Love and Modesty come together like Money and Covetousness, and the more we have, the less we can shew it" (II, i, 127-28). When they put aside dissembling, modesty reasserts itself, as if they elicit the best in each other: "Well, though you are so modest a Gentleman as to suffer a Wife to be put upon you with nothing, I have more conscience than to do it: I have the twelve hundred pounds a year out of my Father's power, which is yours, and I am sorry it is not the *Indies* to mend your bargain" (V, i, 249-53). I stress modesty because it has been particularly troublesome; Dobrée believes that Wycherley had an underlying "hatred" for Hippolita [in *Restoration Comedy,* 1924], and Weales concludes [in his *The Complete Plays of William Wycherley,* 1966] that "after watching Hippolita for five acts, one wants to congratulate Monsieur on escaping marriage with her." These harsh judgments may result from a disregard for the "trial" plot common to so many Restoration comedies; because her future and fortune will lie completely in her husband's hands, Hippolita's testing of Gerrard before accepting him is only prudent. While avoiding the aggressiveness of Flirt and Flounce, she must actively "try" her choice while she has the opportunity. Ironically, Hippolita must imitate her "precise" aunt Caution, as she is described in the dramatis personae. The epithet "precise" is used again twice; before meeting her, Gerrard refers to Hippolita as "a new City-Mistress, and you know they are as inquisitive as precise in the City" (I, ii, 236-37); and Hippolita is a city mistress, even though she herself says that they "are never precise but at a Play" (V, i, 259). Wycherley plays upon the two concurrent meanings of the word, scrupulous and overscrupulous (see the *Oxford English Dictionary*); Hippolita must modulate between the two meanings, acting neither too easily like her maid Prue, nor too strictly like her aunt Caution, following the positive, correct meaning of the word, exercising true judgment.

Just as the proper conduct for a woman lies in between strictness and leniency, the proper conduct for a gentleman lies in between strictness and leniency in honor. Honor is a jest to the pseudo-French Monsieur and all too serious to the pseudo-Spanish Don Diego. Honor is obsessional to the latter (and his first and only concern), whose first words in the play are, "Have you had a *Spanish* care of the Honour of my Family" (II, i, 1). Monsieur's "honor," on the other hand, is so confused as to show that he has no understanding of the word. In act one, we see him begging a prostitute, "But will you promise then to have the care of my honour, pray, good Madam, have de care of my honèur" (I, ii, 341-42). In act five, Monsieur shows little concern that Gerrard may have seduced Hippolita, whom Monsieur still expects to marry: "I say suppose he had [seduced Hippolita], for I do but suppose it; well, I am ready to marry her however; now Marriage is as good a Solder for crack'd female-honour, as blood, and can't you suffer the shame but for a quarter of an hour, till the Parson has marry'd us, and then if there be any shame, it becomes mine" (V, i, 419-23). In Gerrard we see a model of the aristocracy: on the one hand, he is not like Don Diego, who always reaches for his sword, nor, on the other hand, is he like Monsieur, who never draws. Like a true gentleman, Gerrard wears a sword and will use it, but only when seriously provoked. Again, Gerrard's is a gentleman's sword, and Monsieur's is a dancing-master's, that is, mere decoration.

The structure of the language and the action of the play reflect this interplay between extremes, a design which Hippolita summarizes when she contrasts French levity and Spanish gravity: "We shall have sport anon, betwixt these two Contraries" (III, i, 144). The play dramatizes a series of contrasts, parallel to levity and gravity, including folly and wisdom, innocence and experience, and passivity and aggression. In scene after scene, pairs of characters play out these contrasts, often switching roles, in the way that Don Diego and Caution exchange their antithetical trust and suspicion of Gerrard. Though characters switch sides, the categories are immutable; Hippolita successfully oscillates between innocence and experience, or between activity and passivity, but without moderation or compromise. Similarly, Gerrard, the English gentleman, cannot be construed as a compromise between French levity and Spanish gravity; he is at times frivolous and other times serious. Protean and adaptable, the lovers are the only characters capable of navigating deftly between the contrasts: though a gentleman, Gerrard, when necessary, becomes a dancing-master. Following Gripe, Wycherley's first model of imbecility, Monsieur is unable to adapt his speech even momentarily to gain Hippolita's fortune; Gerrard, however, is willing to learn: "A Dancing-School in half an hour will furnish you with terms of the Art" (II, i, 484-85). Gerrard and Hippolita embody a spirit of resilience because they are not rigidly bound to any extreme. Transcending the constrictions of contradiction, they understand that it is at times wise to be foolish, and at times foolish to be wise. In so doing, they become models of correct conduct for gentleman and gentlewoman.

This play ends in the way that all of Wycherley's comedies end: with a range of marriages inviting, if not forcing, the audience to compare. Here, the two unions, between Gerrard and Hippolita and between Monsieur and Flirt, are contrasted through two parallel proviso scenes. Monsieur's and Flirt's articles of keeping are the longest, because their distrust is the greatest. Indeed, the whole scene serves to show how ill-suited Monsieur and Flirt are, reminding us of Monsieur's "incongruous Match of *Spanish* Doublet and *French* Pantaloons" (IV, i, 26-27). Flirt and Monsieur doubtless stand at opposite sides of the stage, for all of their articles deal with some type of separation:

> MONSIEUR. There's no difference betwixt a Wife and a Wench.
>
> FLIRT. Only in Cohabitation, for the first Article shall be against Cohabitation; we Mistresses suffer no Cohabitation.
>
> MONSIEUR. Nor Wives neither now.
>
> FLIRT. Then a separate Maintenance, in case you shou'd take a Wife, or I a new Friend.
>
> MONSIEUR. How! that too? then you are every whit as bad as a Wife.
>
> FLIRT. Then my House in Town, and yours in the Country if you will.
>
> MONSIEUR. A meer Wife.
>
> FLIRT. Then my Coach apart, as well as my Bed apart.
>
> (V, i, 569-81)

Gerrard's and Hippolita's proviso scene is contrastingly brief; beginning, "Let us have a good understanding betwixt one another" (V, i, 203-4); it need not be long, because they have a good understanding between them. Contrasting sharply with the incongruity of words, clothes, and people throughout this play, these two fit each other well, and as we expect in comedy, their union is celebrated by their dance. Dance is burlesqued and frustrated for four acts, until Gerrard and Hippolita reach an understanding: "faith here's my hand now in earnest, to lead me a Dance as long as I live" (V, i, 181-82). Dance has long been an emblem of harmony and marriage, as may be seen in the words of Sir Thomas Elyot: "the association of a man and a woman in dauncing may be signified matrimonie . . . which betokeneth concorde." Whether this match be imaged in terms of clothes, words, dance, or music, it represents one moment of harmony in a play dominated by discord.

In the end, it is difficult to deny that *The Gentleman Dancing-Master* is Wycherley's least successful play, having neither the good humor of *Love in a Wood,* nor the power of the later plays, and so it is discussed only in the context of the greater plays and then superficially. *The Gentleman Dancing-Master,* however, can be seen as a bridge between the earlier, lesser plays and the later ones for which we read Wycherley in the first place. This play gives the first suggestion of Wycherley's brilliant combination of the serious and the frivolous, for while it is fair to say this play is primarily a farce, larger issues are mixed into it. (For one thing, this play more than any of the others exploits national, racial, sexual, and class stereotypes.) *The Gentleman Dancing-Master* also stands out for its treatment of language, even though the possibilities are not made to seem very serious here. In the two plays that follow [*The Country Wife* and *The Plain-Dealer*], Wycherley is able to fuse the best of these early plays: high comedy and high seriousness, making the action at once funny and disturbing, which is what we have come to identify as Wycherley's particular genius. (pp. 54-70)

> *James Thompson, in his* Language in Wycherley's Plays: Seventeenth-Century Language Theory and Drama, *The University of Alabama Press, 1984, 151 p.*

Harden Jay (essay date 1984)

[*In the essay below, Jay discusses the concept of innocence as embodied in Wycherley's female characters, focusing particularly on Mrs. Pinchwife in the comedy,* A Country Wife.]

Speaking of Wycherley's *The Country Wife,* Macauley remarked on it as 'one of the most profligate and heartless of human compositions' containing 'not one truly virtuous character'. This judgement is generally cited as yet another example of the outraged, and not yet outdated, moralistic criticism which has dogged Restoration Comedy from the Rev Jeremy Collier's *Short View* onwards. Yet, on reflection, Macaulay's blunt comment seems curiously closer to the sardonic actualities of Wycherley's play than the view it was attacking—Lamb's 'cloud-cuckoo land of the imagination', 'the Utopia of Gallantry.' The influential school of criticism in which Macauley is such a prominent

figure has its even more extreme representatives—all celebrating Wycherley as the most depraved writer in a particularly depraved genre. William Archer [in his *Collected Works of George Farquhar,* 1949] finds 'deliberate turpitude' in the 'irresponsible licentiousness' and the 'inhumanly vile' scenes which predominate in the last two comedies. 'The gorge rises', he suggests, at Wycherley's 'sheer nastiness', 'absolute loathsomeness' and 'fetid brutality'. ' "Manly Wycherley" ', he concludes, 'is as "beastly" in his last as in his first play.' W. C. Ward in his Critical Introduction to Wycherley's collected plays is forced to admit that with Wycherley 'the license of his own writings is a standing witness against him.' Here *The Country Wife* demands the severest strictures; 'The immorality . . . in this play is more offensive and pronounced than in any of Wycherley's other dramas . . .' The would-be reader is also reminded of the basically 'unwholesome nature of these comedies' and of their characters, 'these stage criminals.' Such enthusiasm apart, it must be admitted that whatever conclusions this censorious school of critics may eventually arrive at as to Wycherley's intention and achievement, it starts by working from facts. There is no doubt that Wycherley's comedies do dwell on the vicious, the violent and the obscene.

There can also be little doubt that Wycherley, despite his reputation for presenting rampant immorality on stage, was by far the most morally concerned dramatist in the early era of Restoration comedy. He need only be compared with his finest contemporary, 'Easy Etherege', whose almost complete amorality slips by, practically unremarked, shrugged off in the graceful, lethal aphorism and understatement of *The Man of Mode* (1675). Where Etherege's comedies ironically, even cheerfully, accept his society and its Hobbist-libertine concept of human nature, Wycherley's, belonging to that same society, question and protest trenchantly; a protest that culminates in the *saeva indignatio* of his indictment of 'the World' as he knows it in *The Country Wife* (1675) and *The Plain Dealer* (1676). This first paradox is echoed in a second. Wycherley is famous, or infamous, as a misogynist; any audience which has seen one of the plays, any reader of the comedies will back this up. The final two acts of his gentlest, or as some would put it, his 'least offensive' play *The Gentleman Dancing Master* (1672) still reiterates one of his favourite themes, the concept of women as virtually satanic forces:

> They'll no more want an excuse to cheat a Father with than the opportunity to abuse a husband . . . Next to the Devils is the Invention of Women . . . There is hardly a Man alive but has been made a Fool of by some Woman . . . Women first fool their Fathers, then their Gallants, and then their Husbands . . . and when they come to Widows they would fool the Devil.
> (IV i; V ii)

From first to last play a variation on this theme turns up in one or more of the important characters, Mrs Joyner, the omnipresent bawd in *Love in a Wood,* Mrs Caution the envious prude in *The Gentleman Dancing Master,* the 'ladies of quality' who infest *The Country Wife,* and finally, their sum total, Olivia, the 'devil incarnate' (IV i) of *The Plain Dealer.* At the same time, no other Restoration dramatist is so concerned with the question of female innocence. Wycherley's variations on this other theme form a constant, less strident, counterpoint to his obsession with feminine depravity and duplicity. Again, each of his plays from *Love in a Wood* to *The Plain Dealer* contains a study of innocence embodied in a major female character. It is in *The Country Wife* however that this study, as his title suggests, provides the focal point of the comedy.

Innocence in Restoration comedy is a quality notable mainly by its absence. In these most worldly and sceptical of plays, which demonstrate, in Dryden's 'heightened terms' of the stage, Hobbes's axiom that 'nothing exists but body,' nothing but calculable fact, innocence, in its dual nature as a spiritual as well as an actual quality, is not admitted. The very basis of the plays is concerned with disproving ideals, 'nebulous' speculative value, by hard practical fact. In Restoration comedy there is no innocence, only ignorance. The most eloquent witness to this occurs in Dryden's lamentable rewriting of *The Tempest* where Shakespeare's 'admir'd Miranda' dwindles into a figure of fun, a grown girl unaware of the sexual facts of life:

> What a goodly Creature a Man is, I would willingly bear that nine month Pain of which our Father spoke to meet him.
>
>   (I ii)

When confronted with 'reality' the ideal, the metaphysical and the magical are exploded; nothing survives but the factual in one of its grosser forms: the bawdy joke. Wycherley's one apparent attempt at a 'symbolic' representation of innocence runs into trouble for precisely this reason. Fidelia in *The Plain Dealer* is incongruous; lacking any kind of social reality, she does not fit into the rational fabric of the play. Indeed she is not meant to. Patently, laughably, unconvincing, she is a 'breeches part' as is Mrs Pinchwife (III ii); but Fidelia retains this rôle throughout the entire action. An escapee from the absolutist-idealistic improbabilities of the heroic play which early Restoration comedy mocks so efficiently and so deliberately, Fidelia does not belong to Restoration comedy proper, she is a deliberately imported aberration. As opposed to her the audience is presented with the standard gallery of 'real' women who make up the *dramatis personae* of these plays: the whore, the envious prude, the affected hypocrite, the bored promiscuous wife, and, at the top of the scale, the brilliant, brittle, defensive she-wit. There is however one apparent exception, one oasis in an arid waste of dissimulation, depravity and acerbic repartee, an innocent despite herself, fresh, frank, impulsive and, at the same time utterly convincing—Mrs Margery Pinchwife, the country wife.

The charms of Wycherley's ingénue has been admitted by almost every critic. Even the sternest of the moralists for whom Restoration comedy seems to exercise such an unfortunate attraction, go out of their way to excuse her, and the excuse is always the same. Steele, writing in *The Tatler* of 16 April 1709, voices what was to become the generally accepted view:

> Her husband . . . is represented to be one of those debauchees who run through the vices of the town, and believe, when they think fit, they

can marry and settle at their ease. His own knowledge of the iniquity of the age makes him choose a wife wholly ignorant of it, and place his security in her want of skill to abuse him. The Poet . . . has, in the natural ideas of an untainted innocent, shown the gradual steps to ruin and destruction which persons of condition run into, without the help of a good education to form their conduct.

More recently, Mrs Pinchwife has been championed from a strangely dissimilar quarter. Here she is ranked high as a 'for life' character 'on the side of the instincts and of freedom, life and health' she represents the 'ritual theme of the triumph of life and love over the wasteland' [Virginia Ogden Birdsall in her *A Wild Civility: the English Comic Spirit on the Restoration Stage,* 1970], a sort of fertility figure instinctively breaking through moribund conventions, holding true to her deepest natural instincts.

Both approaches have a basis in fact. Certainly Mrs Pinchwife, like Congreve's Miss Prue later, is presented as *tabula rasa* at the beginning of the play, and Pinchwife gets exactly what he deserves, pulling his own marriage down around his ears. It is equally certain that she stands 'for life' in the sense that she represents instinct and impulse, a truthful iconoclast in a mannered dissimulating society. The question as regards Wycherley's intentions remains: were they as simple as either of these explanations suggests? Other, later writers may excuse, sentimentalize or celebrate adultery, but in his 'Strict Dissection of Human Nature' in what he himself and contemporaries such as Dryden saw as his 'virtuous satire', Wycherley never does. It is arguable that Mrs Pinchwife is not merely an innocent perverted by evil communications or a triumphant fertility figure, and that something much more original, disturbing and savagely comic is being presented— something much more closely related to Restoration thinking, Restoration comedy and to Wycherley's comedy in particular.

Mrs Pinchwife immediately 'took'; she rapidly became a generic comic figure travelling through numerous repetitions, ranging in scope from Ravencroft's crude parody in *The London Cuckolds* (1681) to Congreve's delicate variation with Miss Prue in *Love for Love* (1695). In Wycherley's play however she is of central importance, not, as with most of her stage descendants, a secondary character, an innocent abroad, sister to Restoration comedy's extrasocial squires and seamen, a foil for the wit of the play's sophisticates. Structurally, every Restoration comedy centres on a love affair, a courtship. This is true of *The Country Wife,* but here Wycherley does not focus on the courtship of the play's obligatory witty couple, Harcourt and Alithea. (In his next play sophisticated lovers are dispensed with altogether. The sceptical she-wit Eliza and her male counterpart Freeman never meet on stage throughout the entire action). Instead, drawn more and more strongly, to use Pope's perceptive comment by his 'love of an antithesis', structural, verbal and moral, Wycherley centres on the affair or 'courtship' between the play's opposites, wit and wittol, Horner, rake-hero and archsophisticate and Mrs Pinchwife the 'natural'. It is not the duelling debates of the witty couple but Horner's and Mrs

Pinchwife's literally criminal conversations which form the focus of the comedy and the play as a whole. The fact that these two apparent opposites converge in perfect harmony is the bleakly ironic focus of the play's comedy and its 'morality'. The very point that Horner, the wit, rake-hero, the 'Machiavel in Love', makes in one way, the guile-less Mrs Pinchwife makes even more plainly in another. The nature of the country wife's innocence as portrayed in her relationship with Horner represents the 'message' of this most nihilistic of Restoration comedies, and it is central to an understanding not only of the structure and intentions of *The Country Wife,* but to Wycherley's comic vision as a whole.

In each preceding comedy, Wycherley had shown a particular interest in the state of innocence. With the peculiar, almost scientific approach, which he shares with so many of his immediate contemporaries, his plays examine it systematically from every angle. His first heroine Christina 'the faithful Shepherdess' deliberately opts out of society 'in a dark room' (I ii) freeing herself from the practices of a circle of sophisticates and libertines. The result is disaster. Like Manly in the last play she is seen as virtually insane, referred to as 'a Mad-Woman' (I iii). Her idealistic impracticalities endanger her own love affair and help to embroil everyone in the mishaps and misunderstandings, the 'love in a wood' which gives the play its name. Hippolita, the heroine of *The Gentleman Dancing Master* (1672) is another experiment in innocence and antithesis, Christina's diametric opposite. She decides to opt into society to innoculate herself against its evils, she is

> All for going into a throng of temptations and making myself so familiar with them, that I would not be concerned for 'em a whit.
>
> (I ii)

Like Christina she fails, though for the opposite reason. The means corrupt the end. Hippolita regrets her own 'necessary' dissimulation, her 'playing the hypocrite' with her witty lover (II ii). She gains her marriage *à la mode* to the rake-hero by cheating father, duenna and suitor, but the final prophecy of the play's Cassandra, Mrs Caution—

> You have danced a fair dance . . . Now you may go jig it together till you are both weary, and though you were so eager to have him Mrs Minx, you'll soon have your belly full of him let me tell you Mistress . . .
>
> (V i)

questions the future of the marriage even in this best-humoured of Wycherley's comedies.

Mrs. Pinchwife, doubly a captive, as she is already married and under continual supervision, manages (without any apparent choice) to go further in liberating herself and her innocence than either of her predecessors. A true primitive in every sense of the word, she is literally 'in a state of nature.' If she is a fool she is the kind of fool who, as Congreve points out [in his *The Way of the World*], 'shou'd rather disturb than divert the well-natur'd and reflecting part of an Audience.' Her naive chatter seduces almost every critic, and every audience:

> Pray, Sister, where are the best Fields and Woods to walk in London . . . London Ladies . . . I warrant you, play at Ninepins every day of the week, so they do.
>
> (II i)
>
> Jealousy, I'm sure theres no such disease in the Receipt Book at home.
>
> (III i)

These pastoral simplicities may tend to obscure her other remarks in the same charming idiom. For the moment it may be adequate to note that from the very start of the play Wycherley presents in Mrs Pinchwife a character not merely incapable of grasping the finer points of etiquette in the fashionable circle to which she is introduced, but incapable of comprehending what—up to and after the Restoration—have been accepted as the basic moral rules of 'civilised' society. 'You shall be my husband now' she announces happily to Horner (V iv), and when this proves difficult she is righteously indignant: 'I'll not lose my second Husband so!' (V iv). 'Pray, Husband, is he a pretty Gentleman that loves me?' she asks the tortured Pinchwife, 'I promise you, I am beholden to him.' (II i)

Mrs Pinchwife has been frequently compared to the figure of Agnès in *L'École des Femmes* (1662) but a quick glance at the two innocents might still prove helpful, for it illuminates the basic differences between two very distinct types of comedy, and in so doing gives a clearer realisation of what Wycherley is trying to demonstrate to the spectator in his *Country Wife.* In *L'École des Femmes* Agnès (significantly Arnolphe's unwitting fiancée, not his wife), represents a moral standard, the norm of nature, of the instincts and senses on which the advice of the detached intellectual norm, Chrysalde, *'le raisonneur'* is based. Both testify to the fact that young girls will naturally fall in love with and wish to marry suitable young men. Arnolphe's frenzied effort to stop this natural happening—to pervert Agnès—is exposed as ludicrous, anti-social, and worst of all as anti-natural, as for instance, in Chrysalde's opening warning:

> Voulez-vous qu'en ami je vous ouvre mon coeur?
> Votre dessin pour vous me fait trembler de peur . . .
> Une femme stupide est donc votre marotte? (I i)

—a warning realized to the full in Agnès's candid exchange with her benefactor on her unshakeable intention to marry Horace:

> ARN: Suivre un galant n'est pas une action infâme?
>
> AGN: C'est un homme qui dit qu'il me veut pour sa femme . . .
>
> ARN: Qui, mais, pour femme, moi, je prétendais vous prendre et je vous l'avais fait, me semble, assez entendre.
>
> AGN: Oui, mais, à vous parler franchement entre nous Il est plus pour cela selon mon goût que vous.
>
> (V iv)

Molière's comedies show a fixed belief in the fundamental rightness of natural law, a belief in the human instincts and senses which, when 'reasonably' controlled, provide a sound base for a morally healthy society. Mrs Margery Pinchwife demonstrates that the Restoration had no such belief in the sweet sanity of nature's laws. She too like Agnès, is a norm of nature, but this is the nature on which the intellectual norm, *le raisonneur*, Horner's 'morals' are based, the Hobbist-libertine's concept of nature, where right and wrong, justice and injustice are relative, or here rather non-existent, where the only laws are those of survival, will and appetite and the senses and instincts, though they form the only practical guide to living, are simultaneously recognised as predatory, ruthless, and to use one of the Restoration's own favourite words—base.

There can be little doubt that such a view was prevalent in certain circles at the time, in the sophisticed London circles through which Wycherley himself moved and which he translated to the stage. As one of the most perceptive modern critics of the period [Samuel I. Mintz in his *The Hunting of Leviathan*, 1962] puts it:

> If the naturalism of the libertine looked one way towards the primitivists' Golden Law of Nature, it looked another towards the naturalism of Machiavelli and later of Hobbes, whose conception of the natural man in moral terms was not greatly different from that of Augustine and the Christian Sceptics . . . the Restoration libertine . . . is always fully and ironically aware of this reality. He insists, in fact, upon man as naturally self-seeking in motivation and ruthless in his means. And while he accepts this as part of a Machiavellian and Hobbesian nature, it is a nature that is never free from the overtones of Christian sin.

This curiously ambivalent attitude, where the rational man simultaneously justifies his beliefs on practical grounds and condemns them as immoral, is peculiarly strong in Restoration literature.

The rake-hero of the comedies is constantly defending his 'right reason', his sceptical commonsense, and, at the same time admitting the intrinsically 'wicked' nature of himself and his practices. When Merryman in Sedley's *The Mistress* (1681) announces that 'in love we are all in a state of nature' (III i), he is deliberately presenting himself to the audience as part of Hobbes's primitive anarchic world as yet unredeemed by 'covenant'. Etherage's Dorimant, while outlining the rationale of desertion to his discarded mistress in *The Man of Mode* admits mockingly that he is, as she says a 'Faithless, inhuman barbarous man . . . Dissembler, damned dissembler.' 'I am so I confess' agrees her ex-lover (II ii). Horner in *The Country Wife* is the most extreme presentation of this kind of thinking on the Restoration stage; the practical man must be immoral, the moral man must be impractical. The most 'depraved' of Restoration comedy's rake-heroes, he is also the most scathing in his denunciations of the corrupt society he is setting out to master and in his sardonic admissions of his own superior 'knavery'. 'In these cases,' he remarks sourly as he betrays his friend to protect and further his own 'project', 'I am always on the Criminals side against the Innocent' (IV iii). This paradox is not confined to the drama, indeed one of its clearest expressions is to be found in another genre, in Rochester's nihilistic tour de

force *A Satyr Against Reason and Mankind* (1675/6) a poem which differs from its accepted model, Boileau's *Eighth Satire,* in very much the same manner as *The Country Wife* differs from *L'École des Femmes.* This tripartite excercise in negation by the foremost of the Hobbist court wits and reputed model for Etherege's Dorimant starts by establishing the libertine sceptic's position. The first section disposes of 'wrong reason', ideals and speculations. The second celebrates the practical Hobbesian credo of 'Right Reason that distinguishes from sense', but the sardonic third section refutes this belief or rather exposes it in turn as valueless in 'moral' terms:

> Thus I hold reason righted but for man
> I'le ne'er recant, defend him if you can . . .
> Be judge yourself, I'll bring it to the test:
> Which is the basest creature, man or beast?
> Birds feed on birds, beasts on each other prey,
> But savage man alone does man betray.
> Pressed by necessity; they kill for food;
> Man undoes man to do himself no good.
> With teeth and claws by nature armed, they hunt
> Nature's allowance, to supply their want.
> But man, with smiles, embraces, friendship, praise,
> Inhumanly his fellow's life betrays . . .
> And honesty's against all common sense:
> Men must be knaves, 'tis in their own defence.
> Mankind's dishonest; if you think it fair
> Amongst known cheats to play upon the square,
> You'll be undone . . .
> The difference lies, as far as I can see,
> Not in the thing itself, but the degree,
> And all the subject matter of debate
> Is only: Who's a knave of the first rate?

Once again human nature and 'civilised' society are shown in a series of graphic examples to be irredeemably corrupt, and worse, knowingly so. Mrs Pinchwife the 'natural' is an integral part of Horner's world, in fact, she represents its basis. She could, quite correctly, be seen as a particularly lively Restoration study in original sin. Her 'natural' instictive actions underline and underlie Horner's intellectual pronouncements on the nature of mankind in general and womankind in particular, a nature which justifies all his 'villainy'. Wycherley presents his innocent as possessed of all the innate vices which, in the first two plays, he tried to explain as the result of a corrupt worldly society. The country wife's basic aims (to deceive her husband and procure Horner for herself) are identical to those of the 'ladies of quality' Squeamish, Dainty and Fidget. From the start, as Pinchwife who 'knows the world' (I iii) suspects, she is already bored with her husband and eager for other conquests. She is shown as naturally promiscuous: 'he would not let me come near the Gentry' she complains to Alithea after her visit to the playhouse, 'he told me none but naughty women sat there, whom they toused and moused. But I would have ventured for all that.' 'He's afraid you should love another Man,' explain Alithea. 'How should he be afraid of my loving another Man when he will not let me see any but himself?' says the country wife with sinister logic (II ii). As soon as she hears Pinchwife's warnings of 'naughty town-women, who only hate their husbands, and love every man man else, love Plays,

Visits, fine Coaches, Fiddles, Balls, Treats' she naturally desires to become one. 'Nay, if to enjoy all these things be a Town Life, London is not so bad a place, dear' (II i). She is delighted at the idea of a lover, 'O gemini is that he that was in love with me? I'm glad on't, I vow, for he's a curious fine Gentleman, and I love him already too' (III ii). Accordingly, to use a phrase from one of Congreve's later ladies [in *The Old Batchelour*] she finds adultery 'as natural as swimming to a Blackamoor.'

> Well, 'tis e'en so, I have got the London disease they call love; I am sick of my Husband and for my Gallant. When I think of my Husband, I tremble, and am in a cold sweat and have inclinations to vomit; but when I think of my Gallant, dear Mr Horner, my hot fit comes, and I am all in a Fever indeed; and as in these Fevers, my own Chamber is tedious to me, and I would fain be removed to his, and then methinks I should be well.
>
> (IV iv)

Mrs Pinchwife is presented as a natural woman without ideals and principles, only desires and appetites. She is openly, and utterly, amoral. Even Horner, whose jaundiced conception of human nature she verifies, is taken aback at her natural abilities to satisfy her prohibited appetites and meet his more than half way: 'How could she contrive it? . . . 'tis an original' (IV iii). Her charm, and Wycherley does present her as charming to the audience, lies not in her morals, for she has none; nor in her innocence. It lies in the one original virture any character in these relentlessly factual plays can possess—her honesty. (Wycherley is to examine this quality again in his next play with Manly, the plain dealer 'on principle', who is as Dryden pointed out on the production of *The Plain Dealer* the only 'truly virtuous hero' in Restoration comedy.) Mrs Pinchwife's honesty sets her apart from Mrs Squeamish, Dainty and Fidget and it is for this that Horner, like the audience, is attracted to her. As opposed to their false prudery she represents frank sensuality. Wycherley spotlights this quality time and again, both linguistically and in terms of action. Placed beside the stale *préciosité* of the 'ladies of quality' their 'dear Jewel of Reputation' and 'the dear Secret' come the letters whose language charms Horner:

> Dear Sweet, Mr Horner,
> My Husband . . . would have me say to you I hate you, poor Mr Horner, but I won't tell a lie for him, for I'm sure if you and I were in the Country at Cards together, I could not help treading under the Table, or rubbing knees with you, and staring in your face till you saw me . . .
> (IV ii)

'Tis the first love letter that ever was, without Flames, Darts, Fates, Destinies, Lying and dissembling in it,' remarks Horner (IV iii). Her language, together with her impulsive displays of feeling—her refusal to leave Horner's company:

> 'I don't know the way home, so I don't . . .
> are you weary of me already? . . .
> you'd make me angry but that I love you so
> mainly'
>
> (V iv)

—make her irresistible to Horner and to the audience alike.

Ironically, and Wycherley is master of this sort of sardonic joke, it is because of her greatest attraction, because of her frankness, her lack of the 'accomplishment' and 'discretion' possessed by the ladies of quality that the country wife is ultimately unsuccessful. She cannot really 'translate her feelings into action' [Norman Holland in his *The First Modern Comedies*, 1959], only wit and sophistication, the manipulation of social convention, the manipulation of language, can see to this. (Every natural-as-primitive in Restoration comedy finally runs into this same trouble no matter how genuine their intentions. Congreve's Brother Ben stalks back, disgusted, to sea; Miss Prue's 'true love' for Tattle is frustrated.) Mrs Pinchwife's triumphant 'you shall be my husband now' tails off into 'I must be a Country Wife still, for I find I can't, like a City one, be rid of my musty old Husband, and do as I list' (V iv). Nor is this all; her generous defence of Horner's virility: 'you shall not disparage poor Mr Horner, for to my certain knowledge . . .' (V ii) nearly ruins not only herself but everyone in the society she frequents, her gallant, Horner, included. Mrs Pinchwife's one original virtue makes her not only personally unsuccessful but publicly dangerous. This scene, with the instant covering clamour that breaks out on all sides, from Lucy's 'Oh, hold', Mrs Squeamish's 'Stop her mouth!' to Alithea's 'Come, Brother, your Wife is yet innocent . . .' is a stage enactment of Halifax's laconic maxim, 'If Men were to say what they think the very Stones in the Street would rise up to cry them down.' The dangerous and anti-social nature of the truth-teller, the breaker through of the polite fictions which keep society going, 'the decorums that the prudent of the world walk by,' (*The Plain Dealer* I iii) was to be explored on stage in full in Wycherley's next play. Here, only if Mrs Pinchwife did away with her sole virtue could she succeed. She cannot keep Horner as her 'second Husband' because her plain dealing makes this impossible, but irony within irony, if she did get rid of it, Horner would no longer care for her. His 'Damned damned loving Changeling' would have become another Mrs Dainty.

In *The Country Wife* Wycherley presents the audience with a moral cul-de-sac. There is indeed 'no single truly virtuous character', no central 'right' standard in the comedy. Looking dispassionately at mankind from the dramatist's version of Hobbes's 'right reason' or commonsense, it is obvious that the more ignorant one is, the more animal, the less successful, *but* the less culpable one will be. The cleverer one is the more successful one will be, *but* the more guilty. The price of success in Wycherley's comedies is high, as is displayed in his maimed hero Horner, who ends the play, lover of the women he loathes, and master of a society he despises, declaring in a *double entendre* during the disillusioned debate on the prospects of becoming 'a Husband' that he 'alas, can't be one' (V iv). There is no practical alternative to the Hobbist rake's practical outlook; but it inexorably dehumanises. *The Country Wife*, despite new critical insights and enthusiasms, celebrates sterility not fertility. In the *dénouement* instead of the betrothal dance of the witty couple that closes almost every

Restoration comedy, a single figure holds the stage. The 'ladies of quality,' their deceived husbands, the hopeful Harcourt and Alithea stand in the background together with the defeated country wife while on the forestage Horner the 'eunuch' speaks the valedictory lines and directs his grotesque 'Dance of Cuckolds.' In their 'Strict Dissection of Human Nature' the Hobbist playwright, his hero and his audience discover nothing but the absurdly deformed, the diseased and the incurable. (pp. 217-30)

> *Harden Jay, "Innocence, Restoration Comedy and Mrs Pinchwife," in* Literature and Learning in Medieval and Renaissance England: Essays Presented to Fitzroy Pyle, *edited by John Scattergood, Irish Academic Press, 1984, pp. 217-33.*

Alice Rayner (essay date 1987)

[*In the following excerpt, Rayner analyzes* The Country Wife *as a drama which challenges social conventions regarding sexuality and persuades its audience to abandon traditional morality.*]

Margery Pinchwife's innocent truth in Wycherley's *The Country Wife* might be a lesson to all critics as well as to all jealous husbands. As an indifferent object collects special interest once it becomes a forbidden object, so Restoration comedies collect special critical questions by exploiting specific moral taboos. The moral issues that *The Country Wife* raises, in brief, are specifically sexual; critics wonder whether we are meant to approve a society

William Wycherley (1640-1716). From a mezzotint after a printing by Sir Peter Lely.

founded on the free exercise of sexual indulgence, or censure it, or simply enjoy the elegant exercise of comic form on a forbidden topic. Knowing that Horner, the self-proclaimed eunuch, should not have his way with other men's wives, we have a curious satisfaction that he does. Knowing that the play ruptures the conventions of sexual morality and punishment, we still delight in it. As a genre, the Restoration comedy habitually appeals to the special delight in forbidden sexuality, plays indulgence against restriction, and leaves the audience in a quandary of satisfaction. As one critic asks [John Harwood, *Critics, Values, and Restoration Comedy,* 1982]: "What happens . . . if the debauched characters seem attractive to the audience, if the satiric punishment is so gentle or ambiguous or incomplete that it is not perceived by the audience?"

If we take Horner as emblematic of the moral and aesthetic problem of Restoration comedy, a character admirable and reprehensible as well as enjoyable, how do we reconcile our enjoyment with our judgment? Part of the answer lies not in the playwright's intent but in the psychology of restriction and desire that Margery Pinchwife mentions. When the play exhibits the pure indulgence of sexuality in Horner's escapades, it is close to a form of wish fulfillment. At the same time, however, the play restrains and restricts that indulgence by formal decorums. I will discuss shortly the specifics of decorum in language, in the narrow society of the play's characters, in the aesthetic enclosure of the world, in the restriction of possible actions. For now, however, I am concerned only to pose a principle of delight that comes to the fore in Restoration comedy. Even in a romantic comedy, our delight in the marriage at the end of the play is heightened by the difficulties and obstacles the young couple overcome in the course of the action: the greater the obstacle, the more impossible it seems to overcome, the greater our interest in their progress and our satisfaction in their success. Our pleasure in the marriages of Olivia and Sebastian, Viola and Orsino, or even Barbara and Cusins is tied to the artificial restrictions imposed by the playwright; and it is partly our pleasure that also defines these marriages as morally good. To put it another way, our sense of aesthetic completion is at least equal to, if not greater than, a prior moral assumption that marriage is a noble estate. Restraints and difficulties serve aesthetic functions to some degree separable from a moral claim that restraint is necessary for social order. Pure wish fulfillment, in other words, is not necessarily delightful; revelry can be boring. If *Twelfth Night* consisted of nothing but songs and dances from a drunken Toby Belch, minus the impositions of Malvolio, it would quickly become tedious.

The closet scene in *The Country Wife* is a case in point. If we were to witness nothing but Horner's perfect success with his ploy, we would quickly lose interest in him. His appetite for married women might easily surfeit in our eyes so we die of boredom. In some measure, his appetite is as one-dimensional and absolute as that of any humored character. In the closet scene, with the sudden appearance of Sir Jasper Fidget, however, that appetite is placed in a restrictive predicament. The complication and restriction of the scene make Horner's apparent success with Lady Fidget more astonishing and aesthetically wonderful because they make it all the more improbable. There is less moral onus on Horner's appetite because of the aesthetically delightful situation, or rather the moral charge in the situation is displaced into aesthetic symmetry as we watch Sir Jasper's glee when Horner and Lady Fidget are together in the "china closet."

That restrictions heighten desire and enjoyment, then, is an aesthetic principle. In drama, however, restrictions and indulgences can never be wholly formal devices. They are almost necessarily tied to further moral implications about human nature or human society. In other art forms, poetry or painting, sculpture or music, even dance, aesthetic elements can become so formal that they lead to our contemplation of a purely aesthetic object. Drama can aspire to such purity, but with human action as its material and the human being as its medium, it can never completely divorce its aesthetic devices from their human, and therefore moral, implications.

With this in mind, one can easily see why Restoration comedies present such difficulties to critics, for it is customary to look at formal, aesthetic, or delightful elements as they serve moral, ideational, or useful elements. The moral critics have complained about the Restoration comedy from its beginning. Jeremy Collier [in his *A Short View of the Immorality and Profaneness of the English Stage,* 1698] called Horner one of the "most remarkable" of the "coarse and slovenly" characters in a genre whose only purpose is "to extinguish shame and make lewdness a diversion. . . . Such licentious discourse tends to no point but to stain the imagination, to awaken folly, and to weaken the defences of virtue." From this perspective, *The Country Wife* might have the same social utility as pornography and might be subject to the same moral debates. Does sexual display, in other words, promote or diffuse sexual license in society? An alternative view—even of pornography—is a moral yawn; the critical version of this view is contained in L. C. Knights's famous dismissal of Restoration comedy [in "Restoration Comedy: The Reality and the Myth," in *Restoration Drama: Modern Essays in Criticism,* edited by John Loftis, 1966] as "trivial, gross and dull" rather than specifically immoral. Just as one might complain of poor photography in erotic pictures, Knights attacks the literary qualities in Restoration comedy.

For other critics Restoration comedies are social documents whose morality simply reflects that of their elite audience in the period of the Restoration. The plays tell us as much about that society as the memoirs of Rochester or the accounts of the escapades of Charles and his mistresses. From this position, the critic neither condemns nor excuses the moral world of plays that simply represent contemporaneous society: an elite Cavalier audience that filled the galleries and formed the models for characters, an audience simply celebrating its release from Puritan oppressions. This perspective offers an answer to moralistic claims against the plays that equate expression with advocacy. It also circumvents the idea that the plays are specifically satirical condemnations of the society, an idea that equates expression with criticism. Another opinion comes from Bonamy Dobrée [in his *Restoration Comedy, 1600-*

1720, 1924], who finds in Wycherley's plays a "deep pessimism and a savage snarl" and in Horner specifically a "grim, nightmare figure." F. W. Bateson, on the other hand [in "L. C. Knights and Restoration Comedy,"] responding to L. C. Knights, finds a "serious social purpose" in Restoration comedies as a whole, a purpose that in "rationalizing . . . the sex instinct" is akin to reconciling Puritans and Royalists.

For some, Restoration comedy as a genre is exempt from any absolute moral representation. "Good morality is not necessarily good art," says John Palmer [in his *The Comedy of Manners,* 1913], and a character like Horner is "immune from the censure of any other period." Other critics establish systems of morality based on such value terms as *wit* or *decorum* or *freedom* or find its moral structures in "right way/wrong way" modes of behavior.

The wide range of critical opinion on Restoration comedy can be explained, perhaps, by the genre's habitual forays into the morally dangerous territory of sexuality without a consistently moral attitude toward that territory. The broad range of appetites that appear in Shakespeare and Jonson is nowhere to be found in the Restoration, where the only appetite seems to be sexual. We rarely find clear censure or clear approval from the playwright. As critics and as audience we want, possibly, both to enjoy the *dulce* and to be irreproachable in that enjoyment, to indulge and to be good; and we seek a system whose terms allow both. If the content of a work seems to divorce itself from a moral scheme, then we come to value the aesthetic, formal, or artificial elements that imply some larger scheme of usefulness or morality. The "*artificielle* critics," according to John Harwood, "hold that literature is an anodyne whose moral effect is to distract the audience from its mundane concerns by immersion in a fictive world." We resist the idea, that is, that any thing can be useless. Part of the difficulty in Restoration comedy is that when we apply criteria of "use," we separate aesthetics from morals. Unlike other comedies that do not disturb our values, Restoration plays send us searching for the terms of value that will allow us to enjoy their license without implying that we are licentious. *The Country Wife* puts us in a particularly difficult position if we find ourselves liking Horner or admiring his manipulation of Pinchwife and Margery; we can admire his skill as we admire that of the Vice figure, but the play never reorders or reassembles society according to values other than Horner's, so our admiration is never superceded by moral righteousness.

On the other hand, *The Country Wife* lets us see how closely aesthetic and formal elements entwine with moral elements, or how we might derive a moral system out of aesthetic features. More specifically, if we accept restriction and indulgence as an aesthetic duality as much as a moral one, we can discover manifestations of that duality in such formal features of the play as language, scene, and character type. The containment or restriction that heightens and enhances our delight operates equally in verbal style and dramatic action. Instead of looking for justice at the end of the play, in other words, we might see how the play is aesthetically self-justified throughout. This perspective is perhaps close to that of the *artificielle* critics

Harwood mentions, but it does not dismiss moral implications as irrelevant. It suggests, however, that any implied moral structure serves the purposes of delight and that we need not look for either approval or censure in the playwright's attitude or our own. *The Country Wife,* in particular, seems to balance the forbidden and the indulgent; it seems to beg for moral interpretation, yet it continually eludes moral definition.

We can, of course, see the Restoration comedies as satires that mock the very values they indulge. But if we do, we must distinguish them in both objects and means from, say, Jonson's satires. Jonson attacks the range of human temperaments that create imbalances in the moral realm of man in society. That is, he attacks moral "essences" through the notion of humors. The rhetoric is artificially constructed, to be sure, but it relies on a presumed connection between language and object. The rhetoric is instrumental, for Jonson, in attacking an imbalance in essences both in the structures of his plays and, by extension, in the structure of society. In Wycherley, the rhetoric is different. It is no accident that the plays of the period are called comedies of manners, for Wycherley and his contemporaries satirize not essences or moral "nature" but styles and their inherent attitudes. His language, moreover, is not instrumental but stylish. In Jonson, words and objects are in some sense coextensive; at the very least Jonson's language takes its qualities from the materiality of the worlds of the play. In the Restoration, objects are virtually nonexistent, as though there were no substance beneath the words at all, as though the decorums and forms of language itself were as brilliant and insubstantial as a gleam of light. If the Restoration world is satirical (and it may well be), still that satire is self-negating. Its rhetoric of highly refined decorum is a "language game" whose rules keep the indulgences of wish fulfillment within bounds. I mean to suggest that the formal elements themselves, as opposed to moral "content," constitute the tension of a moral and aesthetic unity.

Certainly it is difficult, in drama, to isolate strictly formal and aesthetic elements from moral ones. Each character, each moment of action, each speech can be perceived and defined morally, that is to say, in relation to the implicit value of each. If we look for the moment, though, at language and its qualities rather than at specific content, we get some clue about the quality of the play's world. Wycherley's language is typically aphoristic. A quick scan of *The Country Wife* offers a sample.

> A quack is as fit for a pimp as a midwife for a bawd; they are still but in their way both helpers of nature.

> Good wives and private soldiers should be ignorant.

> 'Tis my maxim, he's a fool that marries; but he's a greater that does not marry a fool.

> Mistresses are like books. If you pore upon them too much, they doze you, and make you unfit for company; but if used discreetly, you are the fitter for conversation by 'em.

> Women and fortune are truest still to those that trust 'em.

> And any wild thing grows but the more fierce and hungry for being kept up, and more dangerous to the keeper.

The list could go on. It is easy enough to accept the ironic posture in these statements, and it would undoubtedly be a mistake to boo them off the stage as though they were indications of Restoration misogyny. I am interested in the attitude and manner of such speeches in which irony is an attitude, not a content.

These speeches continually summarize; they are conclusive; although they gain some grace from apt comparisons and witty turns, they are absolute and nonnegotiable nonetheless. They are assertive speeches, expressing no doubt, rarely qualifying themselves, often not moving the action forward. Such language does not advance into action or into sentiment or feeling. The aphorism, as its etymology suggests, "divides a territory" and puts "boundaries on the horizon." That is, the aphorism is the linguistic means of staking out a position. It is the language of the pose that defines a territory, holds all action within its bounds, and makes a spectacle of itself. The aphorism, moreover, is the linguistic version of the Restoration acting style of self-display. Taking a position down front and center, the actor makes a leg, strikes the pose, and delivers.

Our pleasure in the form of aphorism comes from the way that it holds a thought, from its formal restriction of an idea that turns the fluidity of thinking into an object. The wit of the aphorism, in turn, comes from its ability to poise natural likenesses and differences in unnatural balance. An aphorism has the form of an equation that converts natural associations, as in the first of the lines quoted above. The midwife and the bawd are morally different persons, but the same person can be both; the quack doctor and the pimp are likewise morally distinct at first glance, but the suggestion of dishonesty in a doctor makes him liable to any dishonesty and thus makes him fit to be a pimp, as though dishonesty were a mathematical constant that functions according to the distributive principle. The natural, that is, moral, distinctions between midwife and bawd, quack and pimp are equalized by the two-sided signification of "nature," on the one hand biological and on the other, moral. The biological instincts for begetting children are thus wittily turned into a "natural" morality by the careful balance of the aphoristic form. Likewise, good wives and private soldiers are formally joined by ignorance, and one cannot disprove their equation except by separating the terms from the form. But according to the criteria of wit by which it gives us pleasure, the equation is "true" because it is balanced. Similarly, the aphorism puts foolishness and marriage into a self-enclosing proportion that begins and ends with a fool taken in marriage. If one is going to be so foolish as to marry, then the only balance for that action is to marry a fool (in another sense of the word—one who is ignorant), but the result is a marriage of two fools.

The status of the aphorism is both absolute and precarious. It cannot be disproved or even argued except by putting its assertion into some other form, for example, discourse, at which point it loses its identity and its truth. The aphorisms are true only in their form; in the fluidity of discourse or in the flux of real experience, they quickly become nonsense; but their satisfaction comes from the temporary stillness and perfect balance. The wit of the aphorism often comes from making unlikely associations as assertions of truth, as in the following example. Sir Jasper Fidget has just spoken of woman as "that sweet, soft, gentle, tame, noble creature, woman, made for man's companion." Horner replies: "So is that soft, gentle, tame and more noble creature a spaniel, and has all their tricks; can fawn, lie down, suffer beating, and fawn the more; barks at your friends when they come to see you, makes your bed hard, gives you fleas, and the mange sometimes. And all the difference is, the spaniel's the more faithful animal, and fawns but upon one master." This speech is not an aphorism, but it is presented as declarative truth. I am suggesting how the form of the language creates the quality of both the characters we perceive and the world of the play. Like a maxim, *The Country Wife* has very little of the geniality of discussion.

In an essay on La Rochefoucauld, Roland Barthes describes the difference between discourse and maxim in precisely the terms of quality that I am suggesting for the rhetoric of the Restoration. In discourse, he said, there is

> a certain fragility, a certain discursive caution, a language more delicate, more open to kindliness, as if, conversely, the maxim could only be mean—as if the closure of the maxim were also a closing of the heart. . . .
>
> . . . a normal sentence, a *spoken* sentence always tends to dissolve its parts into each other, to equalize the flux of thought; it progresses, in short, according to an apparently unorganized process; in the maxim, the converse is the case; the maxim is a general unit composed of particular units; the skeleton—and bones are hard things—is more than apparent: spectacular.

I am not suggesting that *The Country Wife* is one large sententious maxim but that the world of the play is "hard" like the maxim, pared down to essentials, closed off from the fluctuation of change. In other words, one element of the play that gives us the sense of a heartless world is the aphoristic form of its language. Characters take poses in their speeches and offer proofs of their positions. They do not invite any sympathy from the audience, though the audience may try to give sympathy. Like the maxim, the play closes itself off from feeling by its rational construction of language. It never hesitates or qualifies its presentation. The language is "spectacular" in being more like written speech than spoken thought; it has the conclusiveness and the fixation that customarily belong to writing, not talking.

The brutality that some critics have seen in this world might well be attributed to the hardness of the form of the play itself, not to some deep cynicism or dark satirical purpose that is hidden from view. Brutality comes not simply from amoral or immoral actions or from moral content alone but from the fixture of positions, an absence of the expectation of or desire for change. And the audience is complicitous, neither expecting nor wanting Horner to change; we want and applaud the perpetuation of his seeming/being ploy, though I doubt we would necessarily complain if he were somehow punished, for we have no emotional stake in Horner, or in Pinchwife, or in the Fidgets. We have a stake in the wittiness of the play—the pleasure of form—not in the characters. The particular dystopia of this play, then, does not come from represented world or from the satirical vision of the playwright, as it did in Jonson, although if we imagined this world as real, we would certainly see a dystopian place. This dystopia comes from the hardness of the language itself, from the sense of a purely artificial moral world created out of a form of writing. The dystopias of Wycherley and Shaw share a sense that the world of the play emerges from words, but where Shaw's words are discursive and therefore aimed at utilitarian effectiveness, Wycherley's words fix themselves to the pure formalism of the maxim. The *dulce* element of pure formality helps create an unkind world made out of the brutality of words in mathematical shapes. Shaw's language aims at persuasion; Wycherley's language aims at self-enclosed artifice with no apparent desire to persuade.

From this perspective, we can imagine that wit is a value not simply for the characters in the play but for the play itself. The wit of the aphorism creates value in the artifact as an object. As critics, we often want to get away from the surface to plumb the depths of intention and implication, but this Restoration comedy continually insists on its surfaces and on its spectacle, for even its language is spectacular. The world of the play is dystopian because of its hardness. It refuses to embrace us with the "kindliness" of discourse; morally, it is not a world that "ought" to be, but its artifice suggests that it can be no other way.

The hardness of the world is evident in the wit that perceives a perfect inversion or system of opposites. Horner, for example, says, "Your arrantest cheat is your trustee or executor, your jealous man, the greatest cuckold, your churchman the greatest atheist, and your noisy pert rogue of a wit, the greatest fop, dullest ass, and worst company." We value such a speech only partly for its moral content. We appreciate the extremity and opposition of a moral perception and an artificial formulation. The speech excludes an enormous amount of detail, perhaps, but thus has the essence of a caricature that is minimal but comprehensive. Like the aphorism, it justifies itself, and its very self-completion is satisfying. For some, the speech indicates Horner's cynicism, which it may well show, but it is also an elegant assertion whose value lies in its elegance. It is language that makes a spectacle of itself, to paraphrase Barthes, and that spectacle is inversion. The motive of such inversion is less to arrive at a truth than to display extremities.

The wits of the Restoration world see ironically, not because irony is true but because it is elegant. The oppositions in the speech above suggest the paradoxical irony that Shavian characters see in the world: "My greatest friend is my bravest enemy," says Undershaft. But where Shaw uses his paradoxes to reach toward a larger, almost metaphysical, perception, Wycherley uses his to reach toward the perfection of an artifact, so that we think of Shaw at an extreme of *utile* and of Wycherley at an extreme of *dulce*. Shaw has lessons to teach through pleasurable means; Wycherley would give us simply lessons in pleasure. The world of Wycherley's play is not necessarily a pleasant one: as a representation it resists our liking, our sympathy, and our own kindliness because of its elegant enclosure. We cannot enter its display, nor does it join with us.

The sense of restriction in the scene of **The Country Wife** is only partially dependent on the narrowness of the society the play portrays, a society consisting of young gallants, a sparkish fop, a jealous husband and his wife, ladies of the town, an all-important maid, and a doctor. For the most part this cast belongs to a single social stratum that implies no hierarchical values like those we find in Shakespeare. It may well be true that the play mirrors the elite and narrow audience of the Restoration period and employs recognizable types for its social images. Beyond its immediate imitation or reflection of that society, however, its compression of value tightly encloses its world. One can give that value any one of a number of names, wit or success, style or gallantry, but none has much to do with conventional features of moral value. Hence the difficulty in reconciling the comic delight of the play with any external system of value. The play is compressed by the singleness of its concern. Its inverted world is less than significative in social terms, dangerous in moral ones because it fixates on sexuality as the center of society. Not the class system itself but the domination of all relations and actions by sexuality narrows the world. In some sense, sexuality is the scene of the play even though we move from Horner's lodgings to Pinchwife's house to the New Exchange. The particulars of place are not much more than occasions for variations on sexual gambit. The scene dominates characters and action in such a way that it seems to mirror not an external society but a core of sexual instinct. The range of possible actions is thus narrowed to permutations of that single issue.

In precise terms, Harcourt and Alithea are exceptions because marriage is their promised end. But their marriage is not so much distinct from the scene of sexuality as it is distant from the center. As characters, they both belong in the Restoration scene as opposed, say, to a romantic or sentimental one; and as agents of dramatic structure they provide a moral limit to the world that keeps the Horner excess from spilling over. From the first we see Harcourt as a realist, not a dewy-eyed romantic; he is clearly a member of the wit world in good standing. When he says, "Mistresses are like books," he distinguishes his own sense of balance and proportion in regard to women from Horner's excessive cynicism.

> HORNER: Wine gives you joy; love, grief and tortures, besides the chirurgeon's. Wine makes us witty; love, only sots. Wine makes us sleep; love breaks it.
>
> DORILANT: By the world, he has reason, Harcourt.
>
> HORNER: Wine makes—

> DORILANT: Ay, wine makes us—makes us princes; love makes us beggars, poor rogues, egad—and wine—
>
> HORNER: So, there's one converted.—No, no, love and wine, oil and vinegar.
>
> HARCOURT: I grant it; love will still be uppermost.

However briefly, we are being prepared to value Harcourt as a lover. Granting all the contradictions of women and wine (wine that makes Dorilant stumble and Horner hesitate), love will still be uppermost. Harcourt seems to understand both proportion and love, and we are prepared to believe that he is capable of love beyond lust. We match him with Alithea, the other reasonable creature in the play, who also appears to have a sense of balance and proportion, who is not naive yet takes "the innocent liberty of the town," who values marriage, honor, and commitment.

In a Shakespearean play, Harcourt and Alithea would probably stand at the center of the social and moral order; they would be the heart of the play around which other characters would gather in concentric rings. The romance requires just such a center of value as it replicates an idea of order based on ideal love. At least one critic asserts that Harcourt and Alithea do stand "at the center of the play"; another believes that they at least hint at "true standards of judgement" [Anne Righter and Kenneth Muir, quoted by Robert D. Hume in his *The Development of English Drama in the Late Seventeenth Century,* 1976]. These assessments suggest how eagerly we seek characters who demonstrate a central value on which all others depend and how well a romance pair suits the needs of such centrality. Rosalind and Orlando are central in the world of *As You Like It* and in some measure represent a standard of judgment. But **The Country Wife** does not revolve around Harcourt and Alithea. . . . Their romance is derivative; they set limits on Horner's world in the suggestion of a sound marriage, but they establish no ideal in the play. Their marriage does not represent a conversion of the society out of its dystopia, for the dance at the end is a dance of cuckolds, not of happy couples.

As a dramatic function, the pairing of Harcourt and Alithea propitiates some of our moral objections to the rest of the play. To some extent it diffuses the unrelenting comic energy of the sex farce with sentiment. As critics we perhaps submit to the value of the pairing out of habit and might like to enlarge its significance as the last vestige of romance in a corrupt world, but the comic interest and dramatic energy are elsewhere. The inevitability of Harcourt and Alithea's marriage allows us to enjoy the unexpected turns of Horner's ploy all the more because they are safely contained. And the constraint of Harcourt and Alithea's romance allows us to indulge our pleasure in Horner and his ladies not because that romance is central but because it is peripheral. Harcourt and Alithea offer no renewal of the world, nor is their marriage a ritual celebration of hope that a utopian romantic comedy might offer. They are both realists in this world. The play, however, offers at least one hint of the sentimental dramas to come. "Can there be a greater cheat or wrong done to a man than to give him your person without your heart?" asks Lucy, Alithea's maid. In this small indictment of the Horner-value in the play we can hear the whisper of a sentimental antidote for the sexual scene. The heart is at the core of sentimental sensibilities and develops as a moral force in the later sentimental comedies. Here Lucy offers the "heart" as a value that supersedes Alithea's honorable intent toward Sparkish, her unlovable fiancé. Already it appears as a self-justified moral value, as a higher source of morality than honor. In a Shakespearean romance, for example, it is unnecessary to appeal to the heart as an antidote to a society corrupted by sexuality and acquisitive motives, for Shakespeare's world is not dialectically divided in those terms. The dystopia of a society founded on sexuality, however, calls out for its opposite, for this world has severed the connection between sexual instinct and feeling and, however incidentally, seeks a reconciliation. In a character like Horner, wit and its powers of rational perception and judgment are fully in service to instinct, and the rupture between sexual instinct and feeling is the basis of the satirical strain of the play. I do not mean to suggest that the play is in any way sentimental or that its aim is to reconcile sexual instinct and feeling. But the moral strain against the form is such that the world of the play invites a sentimental deflation.

There are strains of both farce and satire in *The Country Wife*. Pinchwife, Jasper Fidget and his wife, Lady Squeamish, Sparkish, Margery are all set up for us as objects of ridicule, examples of errors, hypocrisy, excess, blindness. We know immediately what their various errors are and how those errors led them to their comic predicaments. Pinchwife is living proof that overzealous protection of one's wife causes and spurs the wife's desire. In an elegant extension of the principle, Pinchwife delivers not only a love letter from his wife to her lover but his wife herself as well. At the other extreme, Sir Jasper Fidget delivers lover to wife out of overzealous interest in business. Lady Fidget and Squeamish, if not punished for their hypocrisy, are at least stuck with it, being forced to keep their knowledge a secret. Like Jonsonian caricatures, these characters typify their obsessions. They are well within the tradition of comic types who exhibit the single dimension of a moral point.

Depending on one's point of view, the play satirizes lust, rigidity, foppish excess, sexual repression, innocence, false seeming, witlessness: the possibilities are extensive. But what sort of errors are these? Do character types and obsessions contain the moral premises of the playwright or do they simply create the foundation for comic possibilities? Obviously there is an overlap between moral premises and comic possibilities, but we seem to keep asking for the playwright's intent beneath the comic uses of moral materials. Rigidity, for example, is a moral problem. It is made to be broken as much as husbands are made to be cuckolds. The dramatic principle is not so much that rigidity or marriage is wrong as that each one carries in it the principle of opposition that makes extreme reversals both necessary and probable.

Sometimes a play offers its own judgment by using the principle of reversal as evidence of retribution, as when

Volpone and Mosca are sent off to prison and the galleys by the Avocatori. Law comes in from the outside to deliver their fate; characters unmask; or disguises are discarded. In *The Country Wife,* however, there is no such imposition of justice, and Horner's disguise slips but is not removed. In another play we might expect that Margery would never reach Horner's closet, or that Pinchwife at some point would become aware of his moral error, or that the wives would be publicly ostracized, or that Horner would be banished. But here there is no holding back from the deed, no public renunciation or revelation. Pinchwife discovers that he has mistakenly delivered his wife to her lover, but he never recognizes that his own moral error made him her purveyor. He chooses further self-deception, as Sir Jasper continues his, as Horner chooses continued public deception for private gains. The play teeters on the edge of revelation but never falls over. It is saved by the complicity of silence among its characters, although Margery would like to reveal all. Since the characters never unmask, since they insist on continuing both public and private deceptions, the play does not leave the world of its artifice; it never emerges from itself but rather turns back on itself. The audience can feel slightly cheated of a conclusion, can feel perhaps the dark implications of continuing deceptions, but the play resists the audience until its epilogue. Until then, it maintains the obdurate surfaces of an artifact seen at a distance. It refuses to acknowledge itself as a fictional deception except in the occasional aside because it is so wholly committed to self-display.

The motive of self-display brings us back to the motives of wit. True wit in characters partly manifests itself in the presentation of an idea as an object rather than as a revelation of the self. Wit is not a communication; it allows no interaction. It exists outside the human being or is like a game that characters play, separate from their persons. Wit is manufactured and set out for all to see. Sparkish is not a wit in part because he continually proclaims himself in his speech. His wish to be accepted, his desire for fellowship, his eagerness to join are all too apparent. Unlike Horner or Harcourt or Dorilant, he cannot divorce himself from his speech and make his speech an object; we see too much of him when he talks, and he thus turns himself into an object for ridicule. Pinchwife, too, reveals too much of himself and his single concern. And Margery reveals too much earnest innocence. The wits separate themselves from what they say and operate at a distance. This gives them less "character" in one way but more power in another. The unwitty characters too often mean what they say, and thus are more available as objects of ridicule. Wit makes characters invulnerable to attack; it protects and contains them. But wit is also the aesthetic element that makes almost any comedy of manners appear shallow; it allows no penetration into character. At the same time, however, because it is a source of delight, it becomes a value in itself.

Wit both helps to make comedy of manners impenetrable and gives it a value. It thus creates an aesthetic surface that resists a sentimental conclusion, for it makes no ap-

> **[This] play constantly provokes our moral sensibilities while it insists that we enjoy its indulgences. Unless we insist on a definitive moral and ethical posture, the play stays alive in the contradiction of desire and forbidden territory, suggesting that the pleasure of form and aesthetic artifice can make even a dystopian world a delight.**
>
> **—Alice Rayner**

peal to the heart. The final summary of the lesson of *The Country Wife* is a formal one, a statement of principle:

> LUCY: And any wild thing grows but the more fierce and hungry for being kept up, and more dangerous to the keeper.
>
> ALITHEA: There's doctrine for all husbands, Mr. Harcourt.
>
> HARCOURT: I edify, madam, so much, that I am impatient till I am one.
>
> DORILANT: And I edify so much by example, I will never be one.
>
> SPARKISH: And because I will not disparage my parts, I'll ne'er be one.
>
> HORNER: And I, alas! can't be one.
>
> PINCHWIFE: But I must be one—against my will to a country wife, with a country murrain to me!
>
> MARGERY: (*Aside*) And I must be a country wife still too, I find; for I can't, like a city one, be rid of my musty husband, and do what I list.

This round of affirmations is more explicitly conclusive than many comic endings. The lesson is clear and all characters acknowledge their relation to it. Perhaps it jars with our knowledge that Horner will continue his deception and that the Pinchwifes will continue a marriage of tension, but it is a clear and formal completion of the doctrine of repression. Its very formality creates the structure of containment that has allowed us to enjoy the indulgence of Horner's exploits. This formal completion asserts an aesthetic value that may be at odds with moral implications, or at least with our feeling about how the world ought to be. That feeling says we ought not to approve of Horner's deception or, further, that the gulf between dissembling and truth ought to be bridged. But aesthetically we admire Horner. The play continually tosses the audience between moral disapproval and astonished admiration, attempting to convert our disapproval by its assertive audacity. It dares the audience to take it seriously but repels all attempts to do so. Like the hard surface of a mirror, it appears to reflect society but is finally only a surface.

This illusion requires a means of convincing the audience or converting it to the truth of the illusion. The character who aids and abets the illusion for the audience, as well as for Horner, is Quack. In narrative terms, he is present simply to spread the rumor of Horner's impotence and to confirm it to the husbands at the end of the play. But for the audience he serves a further function. The doctor helps to assuage our incredulity. He makes Horner's audacity plausible even as he subdues any astonishment at it. The doctor takes the audacity of the ploy as preposterous, "as ridiculous as if we operators in physic should put forth bills to disparage our medicaments, with hopes to gain customers." Finally, though, he is convinced. The doctor verifies for himself, from behind the screen, the efficacy of the ploy, and his own amazement reduces our critical distance, helping to convert us. We agree with him that men are not what they seem and that disguise is the most effective premise for action. We comply with what our moral sense tells us ought not to be true, for the very extremity of the premise is astonishing: the saddest eunuch is the greatest rogue. The collapse of seeming and being into one image is both morally offensive and formally wonderful. And because no justice is finally imposed on Horner, because he will continue the deception, there seems no end to the collapse; the game will continue, breaking all the rules of the real world.

The humor of the play depends heavily on our sense of those rules. We must know that deception, hypocrisy, rampant lust are essentially antisocial or we will not laugh at their rupture. But the play itself will not acknowledge its attitude toward the rules, and we laugh at the doubling of standards as we laugh in the famous china closet scene, in which there is no indication that Horner and Lady Fidget are discussing anything but the sale of china. Horner continually invites retribution, but his skill and the complicity of the doctor repulse the wheels of justice and revelation.

The formal containment of sexual indulgences in *The Country Wife* leaves us with the principle of Margery's statement quoted in the epigraph of this chapter. With a slight alteration, we would say, "I did not care for morality, but when you forbid it, you make me, as 'twere, desire it." For this play constantly provokes our moral sensibilities while it insists that we enjoy its indulgences. Unless we insist on a definitive moral and ethical posture, the play stays alive in the contradiction of desire and forbidden territory, suggesting that the pleasure of form and aesthetic artifice can make even a dystopian world a delight. (pp. 61-80)

Alice Rayner, "Wycherley's Aphorism: Delight in Dystopia," in her Comic Persuasion: Moral Structure in British Comedy from Shakespeare to Stoppard, *University of California Press, 1987, pp. 61-80.*

Edward Burns   (essay date 1987)

[In the excerpt that follows, Burns surveys Wycherley's principal plays, noting the dramatist's adaptation of themes and characterizations prominent in the comedies of George Etherege.]

Wycherley's first play, *Love in a Wood* (1671) is subtitled

St James's Park, a location hailed by the play's three gallants with a litany of its unrespectable functions:

> RANGER. Hang me if I am not pleas'd extreamly with this new fashioned catterwauling, this midnight coursing in the Park.
>
> VINCENT. A man may come after Supper with his three Bottles in his head, reel himself sober, without reproof from his Mother, Aunt, or grave relation.
>
> RANGER. May bring his bashful Wench, and not have her put out of countenance by the impudent honest women of the Town.
>
> DAPPERWIT. And a man of wit may have the better of the dumb shew, of well trim'd Vest, or fair Perruque; no man's now is whitest.
>
> RANGER. And now no woman's modest, or proud, for her blushes are hid, and the rubies on her lips are died, and all sleepy and glimmering eyes have lost their attraction.
>
> VINCENT. And now a man may carry a Bottle under his arm, instead of his Hat, and no observing spruce Fop will miss the Crevat that lies on ones shoulder, or count the pimples on ones face.
>
> DAPPERWIT. And now the brisk reparty ruins the complaisant Cringe, or wise Grimace, something 'twas, we men of virtue always lov'd the night.
>
> RANGER. O blessed season.
>
> VINCENT. For good-Fellows.
>
> RANGER. For Lovers.
>
> DAPPERWIT. And for the Muses.

This is Rochester's St James's, not Waller's. 'In a Wood' means lost, confused, mad. The play's action, to use an image Ranger picks up from *Pastor Fido,* is 'Blind-mans Buff'. 'St James's Park at Night' is not the same place as Etherege's civilized Mall; it stands for an anarchy of desire wiser than self-conscious wit. *Love in a Wood* is often found diffuse. I intend to answer the charge that the play is centreless by pointing out, not, I hope, wholly unpredictably, that its centre is the park.

Wycherley's first attempt at the recreation of Etheregean comedy reduces a cast that previous playwrights would have arranged in careful social and stylistic layers to an equal footing of muddled desire and botched emotional contact. He not only deprives Valentine and Christina of verse but involves them despite themselves in a comic world where the clearest outcome of Christina's cloistered devotion is a lifestyle of alternate mopings on the balcony and squabbles with her maid, where Valentine's passion becomes peevishness and an ignorance both of himself and its object. The dizzy game of blindman's buff is to draw them into its pattern despite their determination to stay aloof; the disguise plot drags them from their own custody as it is to drag Margery from Pinchwife's. Christina and Valentine, Lydia and Ranger, are lost 'in a wood' of self-created fears and doubts, the witty couple levelled from a potential Etheregean poise in Wycherley's disordered

version of the choreography of pursuit and unmasking. *'They all go off together in a huddle, hastily',* as one of the stage directions puts it, aptly summarizing the effect of the equalizing darkness of the park.

Disguise and the doppleganger plot fascinate Wycherley, for they pose in its most flamboyant theatrical from a crisis of desire and identity. His characters cannot have what they want without betraying their sense of who they are. But by the end of the play—and this belies the idea that Wycherley's are dark comedies—they rediscover that identity, having established it for themselves. In so far as Hippolita, for example, or Margery, is the butt of the plot, their 'innocency' is open to question. But the shape of the play transforms them from object to subject, from prize to plotter, and a new paradoxical innocence is discovered. Horner alone of Wycherley's major characters becomes, bewilderingly, the object of a plot he has set in motion himself.

Wycherley remakes the conventions of Etheregean comedy into a personal comic style. As a consequence, he takes care to measure the distance between himself and his predecessors. In *Love in a Wood* Flippant and Dapperwit are a parodistic version of the widow and the wit. The lady is perfectly willing to pursue wit-combat through to a marriage she affects to abhor, but the gentleman deliberately fluffs his cues. At the end of Act I Flippant and the inconstant Ranger are put in suggestive apposition.

> FLIPPANT. . . . pray tell me is your aversion to marriage real?
>
> RANGER. . . . As real as yours.
>
> FLIPPANT. (aside) If it were no more real than mine.

But in the last act Ranger has come to propose marriage, surprising Lydia into doubts that have not apparently slowed her pursuit of him in the past.

> Cou'd you find in your heart to quit all other engagements, and voluntarily turn yourself over to one woman, and she a Wife too? Cou'd you away with the insupportable bondage of Matrimony?

Ranger, who has earlier nudged Valentine into proposing a completion of the line of married couples that span the stage at the end of Act V ('Our Ladies, Sir, I suppose, expect the same promise from us'), ends the play with a reply that seems to me to touch on Wycherley's central concerns.

> You talk of Matrimony as irreverently, as my
> *Lady Flippant;*
> the Bond of Matrimony, no—
> The end of Marriage, now is liberty,
> And two are bound—to set each other free.

Wycherley's prose style links ideas by analogy. His characters are similarly disposed in a pattern of doubles, thus freeing each other from an emotional solitude that may seem heroic to Christina and Valentine (or Alithea) but is in fact the most despairing kind of farce. These characters must find a partner; society is too precarious and cruel a mechanism to answer their needs. The early plays and some of the casts of the later tend towards a freedom found in pairing.

Ranger's romantic adventure with Christina comes to a head just after he tells Dapperwit that he makes '. . . honourable Love, meerly out of necessity; as your Rooks play on the square rather than not play at all'. Woman-chasing is a compulsive, and up till now, a harmless game. It is entirely fitting, when the 'Blind-mans Buff' gets out of hand, that he should choose to give it over. When the 'honourable' romance with Christina dissolves it reveals the reality of his need of Lydia, to which those final lines bear witness. Like wit and heroic virtue, game-playing is a behavioural trap sprung in the night-park.

The resolution of *Love in a Wood* is imaged not, as in classical pastoral, by dawn, but by a shared enjoyment of those private pleasures the characters have tended to pursue, a feast at the Mulberry Garden in which the whole cast takes part. The comic villain of the piece is the niggardly Alderman Gripe, for in aiming to take his pleasure cheaply he contradicts the pull towards a generous and honest acknowledgement of appetite that is the real ethos of the park. His mean self-indulgence is the physical equivalent of the other characters' treasured neuroses, and it is when Mrs Joyner succeeds in lugging him to the Mulberry Garden that the end of the play is signalled. Every character however resistant is pulled into the park; it reforms the entire cast of unlovely individualists into a society of couples, of matches not only just but practical. The end of the play posits not an ideal, but a reality, unrespectable but festive.

The Gentleman Dancing Master (1672), in marked contrast, limits itself to the scope of a single household. Hippolita and her maid Prue may lament their exile from the pleasures of the town, but it does enforce a discipline on the playwright that might well have seemed a necessary curb on the inventive exuberance of his first play. In *The Gentleman Dancing Master* Wycherley shuffles and retests aspects of his dramatic style that seemed to run out of control in *Love in a Wood,* but become crucial to the effect of the two last great plays.

Love in a Wood markedly lacks the kind of double-entendre that makes the style of *The Country-Wife* so lewdly buoyant. Only the mock-innocent Lucy uses the arts learned as Dapperwit's mistress to entice the ponderous lust of Alderman Gripe.

> Are you a Dancing-Master sir? . . . I don't see your Fidle, Sir, where is your little Kitt?

In *The Gentleman Dancing Master* Hippolita's 'innocency' is itself a double meaning at which the other characters probe. She teases her aunt Caution with an account of dreams bred by the lack of a man—

> HIPPOLITA. But I did not only dream Ih . . . (sighs)
>
> CAUTION. How, how! did you more than dream! speak, young Harlotry; confess, did you more than dream? How could you more than dream in this house? speak! confess.
>
> HIPPOLITA. Well! I will then. Indeed, Aunt, I

did not only dream, but I was pleased with my dream when wak'd.

> CAUTION. Oh is that all? nay, if a dream only will please you, you are a modest young woman still; but have a care of a Vision.

Hippolita is too sensible and forthright to join the frustrated dreaming heroines of the period,—Lee's Princess of Clove, for example, or the heroine of Rochester's *Valentinian*—but the parallel is suggestive when one bears in mind 'fair Chloris' of Rochester's mock pastoral, 'innocent and pleased'. Isolation and stress are themes of the times, and the self-sufficient Chloris provided an extreme model of one way of resolving them. The passage from *The Gentleman Dancing Master* is interesting as an example of the way the characters in this piece pick up words carefully as if to see what is lurking underneath. Even in *Love in a Wood* a single word can hammer through a speech, till its meaning becomes almost ominously doubtful. This is characteristically Wycherleyan, in a way that makes him of all Restoration dramatists the most nakedly theatrical, the closest to the bone of dramatic situation. While for Etherege speech and action are 'manner', a mask behind which one deduces a fully imagined reality, for Wycherley they are alive with a theatrical electricity, a potently treacherous communication to whose shifts of meaning one must be continually alert. There is an impulse basic to Wycherley's plays in this sense of the dramatic language as a risky but vital medium of his characters' aims and selfhood. The linguistic double meaning is complemented by the ambiguities of performance, and it is in isolating the idea of performance that *The Gentleman Dancing Master* proved so valuable. *Love in a Wood,* like so many first plays, describes what it cannot enact. Betrayal is an idea implemented by the cast to a mind-boggling cumulation of social chaos but it is not yet implicit in the language. Similarly, those crucially Wycherleyan scenes where x watches y encounter z and makes a very private deduction of what happens between them are all arrived at by accidents, with an undeniably, though to my mind not unappealingly, flustered effect. In *The Dancing Master* Hippolita, by disguising her lover Gerard as the 'master' of the title, involves him in a performance whose meaning is gracefully worked out from act to act. Only the aunt understands what is happening between them, but the fiancé and the father restrain her from revealing it. It is a very funny, rather cruel variation on the process of distanced, botched comprehension that is the best Wycherley's characters can usually manage. Caution knows what is going on in the same way that she felt she understood Hippolita's dreams—' . . . I know by experience what will follow'. Like Olivia at *The Country-Wife.* Caution is exposed by her understanding of the performance, and criticized for her meanly hypocritical reaction.

A firm and sympathetic judgement of Wycherley's work is impossible unless one can characterize a distinctly Wycherleyan mode of comic writing. Perhaps that requires a larger scope. But it is worth pointing out how badly Wycherley comes off even in as sympathetic an account as Anne Righter's, if he is presumed to be attempting to write comedy in the style of Etherege or Moliere. Only *The Gentleman Dancing Master* is left unscathed; other, in many ways more ambitious, pieces come to look like the result of subtle material filtered through a coarse and uncomprehending sensibility. Alithea and Harcourt do not seem to me (as they do to Dr Righter) to be Etherege characters in whom Wycherley cannot believe; I don't believe in them as Etherege characters either. One should see them in the light of what Wycherley was doing in *Love in a Wood,* a play which *The Country-Wife* (1675) to some extent remakes.

The Etherege characters whom Alithea most resembles are those of the 'high' plots. She has a simple 'heroic' concept of love and marriage.

> Love proceeds from esteem; he cannot distrust
> my virtue, besides he loves me, or he wou'd not
> marry me.

But, like Christina and Valentine, Alithea is flung into a vigorously prosaic comic world in which ideals are not safely packaged in that cotton wool of Restoration blank verse. The play's intrigues equalize her with Sparkish and Harcourt; they all live in the same town-world, whose delights Alithea finds herself increasingly called upon to pay for by marriage to Sparkish. That is one view of her predicament, and in that it is her maid Lucy's one can accept it as thoroughly realistic. Alithea's own is that to betray his trust would be to betray her own identity. Like Manly she has found a mirror for her virtue, her 'truth', and like him she finds that mirrors are brittle things that one must learn to do without. Her heroic self-sacrifice is, like his heroic love, self-indulgence and, in a way, cowardice. She has to learn to trust the hazards of intrigue, and to face, sharply but temporarily, the loneliness of slander, of the loss of that externalized 'truth'. Alithea functions deftly, even wittily, in the fashionable world, but she is much less of a heroine à la mode than Etherege's. There is something statuesque and old-fashioned about her. One wonders if she is not a little nearer her brother's age than, say, Arianna and Gatty's. Her wistfully retrospective correction of Pinchwife's 'greasie' comparison puts a personal rather fragile sheen on the plot device that is to bind her story and Margery's together.

> I had a gentle Gallant, us'd to say, a Beauty
> mask'd, like the Sun in Eclipse, gathers together
> more gazers, than if it shin'd out.

Harcourt too is significantly unlike the Etheregean norm, but in rather the opposite direction. He is too light, too playful, for those gentlemen's serious dedication to pleasure. For Harcourt

> Mistresses are like Books; if you pore upon them
> too much, they doze you, and make you unfit for
> Company; but if us'd discreetly, you are the fitter for conversation by 'em.

The wit games with which he tries to break Alithea's contract to Sparkish, like the game in which Hippolita coaches Gerard, are a medium of contact which, like conversation, bridges the gap between wary personalities. Harcourt moves from Horner's world to Alithea's, remaining amicable to both. He has none of the egoistic drive of the Etheregean male; rather, like Ranger, Gerard and Freeman, he offers a shallow, slightly opportunistic, but just

and humane companionship, that effectively rescues others from neurosis, or virtue. The point in which he announces his trust in Alithea is scarcely a great leap of faith, though it does outjump Sparkish—after all Harcourt was one of the first to know of Horner's 'impotence'. Wycherley is content to reduce Harcourt and Alithea back to the compromised truth of the town-world. Their resolution is personal and, characteristically, he refrains from pointing a moral, however delicately Etheregean.

It may seem perverse to start a discussion of the play at Alithea, but I want to stress Wycherley's method of linking his characters by relationship into a kind of lateral, unstratified scheme. If literary critics seem not to realize this, then neither do the play's performers. Wycherley very deliberately put Sparkish and Alithea into relationship, and yet they are always acted in flamboyantly divergent style. To link Alithea, Harcourt, Margery and Horner into the change-of-identity plot is to force opposites into analogies.

Horner is not, I think, a libertine; libertines do not specialize in concealment. He does possess a heightened intelligence, even moral consciousness, of a kind that detaches itself from the rest of the play. The contempt he has for Pinchwife is a case in point. One might characterize his plot, so vague in the infinity of its aims, as an experiment. The Quack serves to point this up. Horner's 'process' is an experiment in natural science, or, more precisely, as it operates on bodies, in medicine. Horner is a true virtuoso, his experiment carried out, in the spirit of the Royal Society, as an exhibition of skill for the knowledgeable few (the assistant quack, and the audience), and as a selfless pursuit of the truth; the truth about the ladies of quality, the suppressed libertinism of his patients. He looks for a cure for 'Love and all other Women's evils'; in a sense the pretence is psychologically apt as Horner, though not fiercely misogynist, is eunuchoid emotionally in a way that Harcourt is not. The indulgence in woman-hating that his pretence allows him is itself to be relished. Aptly enough, when Margery finds herself to be in love with him, she soliloquizes with typical frankness in terms of her physical symptoms.

> I have heard this distemper, call'd a Feaver, but
> methinks tis liker an Ague, for when I think of
> my Husband, I tremble and am in a cold sweat,
> and have inclinations to vomit, but when I think
> of my Gallant, dear Mr. Horner, my hot fit
> comes . . .

When Pinchwife is tricked into bringing her disguised to Horner, Horner enquires of the pox. For him Pinchwife's whoring has led to a kind of moral pox, and the contempt he shows him is more chilling for Pinchwife's inability to be shocked by it. But while this would seem to place the analyst of physical and moral disease in opposition to the passive Margery, by the very end of the play they have come to change places.

The ability of the society for which the town ladies stand to use people simply as things absorbs Horner into its hypocrisies; and thus Horner finds himself a wondrous necessary man to those whom he had seemed to challenge. He becomes a double meaning. China is only the latest craze. In the games of the 'Bacchic' scene he is used among other things as 'thou representative of a Husband' and the real husband, Sir Jasper, achieves what Sir Epicure Mammon only dreamed of; he has made a 'town-stallion' his eunuch. Horner is the victim of a town society with which Margery eventually learns to deal and from whose representative, Sparkish, Alithea is rescued.

Wycherley's farce implodes. It leaves Margery the only character not its puppet; she has the only moral choice to make, and she chooses to lie. The final scene is curiously touching. Perhaps the first lie is the end of childhood; the end of her trust in her own pastoral simplicity, and its attendant concept of fidelity to Horner in an unattainable ideal of a relationship of mutual satisfaction, without economic pressures or social ties; the beginning of responsibility. The reality of rural life to which she returns, to play endless card games, to tell her neighbours of the sights, is as real for us as that of Harriet (another Hampshire girl) but a little more attractive. Margery has the sturdiness to function well in her own world, even, in better times, with her own husband—'You are mine own Dear Bud, and I know you' she says, 'I hate a Stranger.' If the play puts her in apposition to Horner, it is as the reality that the virtuoso seeks. When the play ends, she is liberated into ordinary life and compromise; he is boxed in by the demands of deceit. Just how much china *can* he produce?

Wycherley builds **The Country-Wife** out of the contradictions and tensions in pastoral ideas, with a deepening apprehension of the unattainability of real escape. The play is at once more farcical and more despairing than anything that went before. Margery is herself a locus amoenus, an enclosed pleasure for Pinchwife, as Horner is at the end for his three ladies. When their paths cross in Act III they act out within the enclosed environment of the room off the New Exchange the pastoral game of Orlando and Ganymede (though it must be said that Margery is less of a Rosalind than a Mopsa). The event is enclosed again by her narration of it to the obsessed Pinchwife within their bed-chamber. *The Plain Dealer* (1676) takes this process of enclosure a step further. In exploring pastoral ironies in an increasingly interior and private way Wycherley instigates the pattern to be followed by Congreve, Farquhar and other writers of a limited comic *oeuvre,* who gradually eschew flamboyance and burlesque for a sober, even static discussion of the issues that inform the mode. This is how Olivia in *The Plain Dealer,* expresses her responses to *The Country-Wife.*

> OLIVIA. . . . does it not give you the rank conception, or image of a Goat, a Town-Bull or a Satyr? nay, what is yet a filthier image than all the rest, that of an eunuch?
>
> ELIZA. What then? I can think of a Goat, a Bull, or Satyr, without any hurt.
>
> OLIVIA. I, but, Cousin, one cannot stop there.
>
> ELIZA. I can, Cousin.
>
> OLIVIA. Oh no; for when you have those filthy creatures in your head once, the next thing you think, is what they do; as their defiling of honest Men's Beds and Couches, Rapes upon sleeping

and waking Countrey Virgins, under Hedges and on Haycocks . . .

Pastoral ideas exist within it as prevalent fictions in the characters' world; they serve to expose a mental landscape. Against the dissembled libertinism of Olivia's satyr-haunted description of her reaction to **The Country-Wife**—thus one play may even enclose another—one must set the fantasy world of Manly, the 'plain dealer' of the title;

> Therefore I raher choose to go where honest downright Barbarity is profest; where men devour one another like generous hungry Lyons and Tygers, not like Crocodiles . . .

Between the two of them Wycherley places Fidelia, the girl disguised as a boy, the embodiment of that goal pursued by the other characters, a world to satisfy their inner world. She sums up the problem in a blank verse soliloquy;

> O Heav'ns! is there not punishment enough
> In loving well, if you will have't a Crime;
> But you must add fresh Torments daily to't
> And punish us like peevish Rivals still,
> Because we fain would find a Heaven here?

Fidelia's unreality is the unreality of this ideal.

The Plain Dealer is a pivotal piece in the history of Restoration drama. Were it not for its expansive literary energy, figures like Crowne and Otway might not have been interested in writing comedy at all. It is the watershed between the gentleman amateurs and the professional dramatists who dominate the 1680s. The play is innovative in the relationship of the protagonist to the world it depicts. Manly is goaded into a moral aggression; he is dispossessed and resentful; he makes demands that the world he lives in cannot satisfy. If he is indeed normative in the way his name suggests, it is as a modern hero. This was enormously influential on subsequent comedy, to at least Southerne and early Congreve. Perhaps most important is the way the play redraws the groundplan set out by Etherege. Gambling, used in *The Man of Mode* as a graceful metaphor for kinds of emotional commitment, becomes the way of a relentlessly acquisitive world. For Wycherley the metaphor devalues what it images. 'We women . . .' says Olivia,

> like the rest of the Cheats of the World, when our Cullies or Creditors have found out, and will, or can trust no longer; pay Debts, and satisfie Obligations, with a quarrel; . . . for oftentimes in Love, as at Cards, we are forc'd to play foul, only to give over the game; and use our Lovers, like the Cards, when we can get no more by 'em, throw 'em up in a pet, upon the first dispute.

When in the third act the play moves to Westminster-Hall, the law acquires the image for its own.

> . . .'tis like one of their own Halls, in *Christmas* time, whither, from all parts, Fools bring their Money, to try, by the Dice (not the worst Judges) whether it shall be their own or no.

Love and law are not gambles in metaphor only, real money is involved, and the play admits money as a ruling factor in the comic world. The effect on later comedy is obvious. Even such a dissimilar play as *The Way of the World* (1700) owes its slightly bitter worldly wisdom, as well as its tangled property-motivated plot structure to the **Plain Dealer.** The idea of a densely plotted pursuit of money and love through law, ending in a measured judicial finale, is the new and clearly more ambitious model that Wycherley sets up for the comedy of the next two decades. The play deliberately and finally strips off the glamour of the early Restoration to show the well-oiled financial wheels underneath. As the prologue states, its aim is to cut through the flattering self-image of the age.

> Pictures too like, the Ladies will not please;
> They must be drawn too here, like Goddesses.
> You as at *Lely*'s too, wou'd Truncheon wield
> And look like Heroes, in a painted Field.

Its method is almost excessively literary, a return to classical satire. Oldfox, with his 'feign'd Friend in the Countrey' to write epistles to is a witty image in little of the process by which the author hopes to achieve his hard, Roman disabused view of city-life. But this also points to its claustrophobic futility.

Manly and Freeman stand apart from the life of the town. To put it in simple practical terms, they have no money; but Freeman, he tells us, 'chose to cheat the King, than his subjects' and thus left the law, and Manly realizes (as Horner did not), that 'he that is the Slave in the Mine, has the least propriety in the Ore'. *The Plain Dealer* catches a moment of social disillusion with prophetic acuity. But its claims to be a successful political play are jeopardized by the looming detachment of its hero. As the prologue announces;

> I the *Plain-Dealer* am to Act to Day;
> And my rough Part begins before the Play.

Roles like this are exciting emotionally; this too is Wycherley's legacy to future writers. But he is not, as Otway and Crowne are, primarily a psychological writer, and Manly's outbursts can seem like effects without causes. The fantasy of the Indies creates a pastoral of innocent savagery that links up suggestively with the pre-moral landscape of early heroic tragedy. As an heroic figure Manly has emotional roots in the realm of Zempoalla. But the fact that the only contact he has with a character for whom he can admit fellow feeling is the little scene with Vernish near the end wraps him in an isolation that encourages one to see the play as a kind of blusterer's concerto. Wycherley's approach to character in this play seems very literary, a classical wordy gloss on those patterns of performer and critic, of the self-imprisoned, of meaning, double-meaning and misunderstanding that come to such gorgeous fruition in **The Country-Wife.** To this extent the play fails. The step towards a redefinition of character is made by Otway. But a failure to top **The Country-Wife** is scarcely a disgrace. If one pushes Manly back into the play, a lot of its power reasserts itself. Manly after all is a plain-dealer only till the end of the second act. The discovery that moral outrage and a wounded ego do not in themselves cure love—a step out of childhood, like Margery's—trap him into the dissembling he despises in others. It is a discovery that the brittle Olivia makes before

he does; all she need do to counter his outburst is to echo the last curse:

> May the Curse of loving me still, fall upon your
> proud hard heart.

Olivia has his measure in more ways than one. She has acquired his affection by acting up to his narcissism, and retains it by playing with a sadomasochistic urge he is unaware of in himself. 'He has Cruelty indeed' she remarks to Fidelia, '. . . which is no more Corage, than his Railing is Wit.' That Wycherley lets him see through her as soon as they meet in the play indicates where his true interests lie. It is the emotional tie between these two that gives the play its great tension.

Olivia is something of a generalised figure, like the ladies in **The Country-Wife,** she too has no single identity, as Novel's comparison of her to a mirror suggests; '. . . she stands in the Drawing-room, like the Glass, ready for all Commers to set their Gallantry by her; and, like the Glass too, lets no man go from her, unsatisfi'd with himself'. And like those ladies she tends to the allegorical, in her case by her identification with money. Its influence on her language is curiously elevating in effect.

> I . . . think you do not well to spirit him away
> to Sea, and the Sea is already but too rich with
> the spoils of the shore.

She may see Fidelia here as 'spoil' but she needs a glamour on the idea that partly identifies her as an aspect of the 'shore', as a cold but convincingly attractive embodiment of the town and its need for such as Manly for support. Like all Wycherley's misers she is harshly judged. In a brutally witty parody of *Twelfth Night* it is Olivia, not Malvolio, who exists vowing revenge.

Fidelia is another of those problematic heroic figures who deal so ineptly with the comic world and create such problems for Wycherley's critics. The implied comparison with Viola seems deeply unfair, but, though one might point out that male disguise is as much a convention of Restoration comedy as of romance, that the voyage had only been a short one anyway and that such things happened not infrequently, one must remain dubious not so much of Fidelia herself but of what Wycherley does to her. Like all those other heroines, 'romance' is her grimly farcical trap. As a boy Manly finds her a snivelling bore and is too overbearingly bad-tempered to allow her to explain herself. As she realizes, he would probably be even more bad-tempered if she did. She takes refuge in a Viola-like reliance on time, but the scenes with Olivia in that favourite Wycherley locale, the darkened room, explode into a confusion of sexual identity that not only breaks up Olivia's new marriage but convinces both partners that she is of the opposite sex. Viola has wandered into Orton's *What the Butler Saw.* The problem with Fidelia is an unevenness in the writing; the malice in some of her scenes with Manly brings her much closer to us than the woozy verse or the unearned rhetorical seriousness of the end. To say that this might be resolved in the theatre is not to say it away. I feel sure myself that Fidelia could be taken through the Wycherlean progress from the heroic to the farcical to the real by a sympathetic actress, but it is not in the writing—

the most obvious example of Wycherley's ambitions cracking the bounds of his dramatic skill.

Fidelia is baulked of her chance to rescue Manly. The exorcism of his love for Olivia, comes, uncompromisingly, in the playing out of its meaning. Her stature at the end is kept inviolate by her striking away of the jewels, though soured by her observation that now the whore's fee goes to Fidelia. Manly's rescue is his coaxing by Freeman into a realization of the existence of the real world and the necessity of our compromises with it. His last lines are not merely cynical, they resonate back over the play as a formulation of that problem of desire and identity I mentioned earlier.

> I think most of our quarrels to the World, are just such as we have to handsom Woman; only because we cannot enjoy her, as we wou'd do.

After all, there is one real Plain Dealer in the play, Eliza, and she is cut off from almost everything that goes on in it. Like Vincent in *Love in a Wood* (with a trust in women that no other man in the play shares) or Horner with his hard-won knowledge of the Ladies of quality, she is a lonely, and ultimately, a mysterious figure. If there is an ache at the heart of Wycherley's plays, it is the fear of isolation. Vincent is consoled by his bottle; Horner by his taxing pleasures; and Eliza by the plays of the writer she so admires, the author of *The Country-Wife.* (pp. 48-62)

> Edward Burns, "William Wycherley," in his Restoration Comedy: Crises of Desire and Identity, *The Macmillan Press Ltd., 1987, pp. 48-62.*

Robert Markley   (essay date 1988)

[*In the excerpt below, Markley offers a linguistic and stylistic analysis of Wycherley's works.*]

Wycherley's prose represents an intensification of the linguistic devices—similes, comparatives, and antitheses—that are used by Dryden, Etherege, and their predecessors to signify gentlemanly conversation. The effect that Wycherley achieves in *Love in a Wood, The Country Wife,* and *The Plain Dealer* is more one of ironic overkill than of celebrating the ideals of graceful and dispassionate observation. His language is more aphoristic and epigrammatic than his contemporaries': it is packed with jagged antithetical phrasings and negative constructions as well as images of warfare, disease, and animalistic appetites. Imagistically, Wycherley's language develops from the naturalistic prose of *She Wou'd if She Cou'd,* carrying Etherege's verbal satire to its post-Hobbesian extremes. But his handling of stock devices is characteristically double-edged. Wycherley turns the syntactical and semantic conventions of late seventeenth-century theatre to his own ironic ends, calling attention to disruptions between signs and signifieds and implicating his audience in the open-ended process of defamiliarizing the language of wit.

Wycherley's first play, *Love in a Wood* (1671), like Etherege's *The Comical Revenge,* parodies contemporary theatrical fashions. The differences between the two plays are, in part, historical: Etherege in 1664 targets the excesses of

heroic passion; Wycherley seven years later appropriates the conventions of self-dramatizing wit to turn Etheregean mock-heroic into ironic self-mockery. As its title suggests, *Love in a Wood* comically demonstrates the limits of love and wit in a corrupt society. All of the play's characters—from Valentine and Christina to Sir Simon and Lady Flippant—are victimized by the languages they use to define themselves socially and morally. Yet if language in the play is inherently deceptive, it deceives different characters in different ways. As a comic stylist, Wycherley is fascinated by the ways in which characters violate 'normal' discourse by disrupting 'normal' speech-act conditions. In the low plot, moralistic speech hides moral hypocrisy; in the middle plot, the language of wit becomes self-defeating; and in the high plot, sententious eloquence falls victim to the demands of social comedy. The dramatist plays these idioms against each other: they do not resolve themselves into simple right-way, wrong-way demonstrations of the ethics or morality of language but ask to be judged by both satiric standards of censure and comic standards of accommodation. The ironies that abound in *Love in a Wood* seem Wycherley's way of allowing the audience to gauge and to try to cope with disjunctions between noble ideals and flawed actualities. Satiric and comic languages, then, are dialectically bound, qualifying and undermining each other's generic claims to 'reflect' experience accurately.

The stylistic structure of *Love in a Wood* is associative and parodistic; it depends less on thematic exposition than on theatrical displays of hypocrisy, folly, affectation, and self-deception. Much of the play's verbal comedy results from the ironic discrepancies between characters' announced self-perceptions and the ways in which they appear to the audience. The tavern scene in Act I is characteristic of Wycherley's double-edged use of conventional forms. The exchange among Ranger, Vincent, and Dapperwit sets competing—and corrupted—versions of wit against each other:

> DAPPERWIT. Pray, Mr. *Ranger,* let's have no drinking to night.
>
> VINCENT. Pray, Mr. *Ranger,* let's have no *Dapperwit* to night.
>
> RANGER. Nay, nay, *Vincent.*
>
> VINCENT. A pox, I hate his impertinent Chat more than he does the honest *Burgundy.*
>
> DAPPERWIT. But why shou'd you force Wine upon us? we are not all of your gusto.
>
> VINCENT. But why shou'd you force your chaw'd jests, your damn'd ends of your mouldy Lampoones, and last years Sonnets upon us, we are not all of your gusto?
>
> DAPPERWIT. The Wine makes me sick, let me perish.
>
> VINCENT. Thy Rhymes make me spew.
>
> RANGER. At Reparty already, come *Vincent,* I know you would rather have him pledge you . . . but why are you so eager to have him drink always.

VINCENT. Because he is so eager to talk always, and there is no other way to silence him.

(Act I)

This exchange simultaneously makes and subverts conventional distinctions between true and false wit. Its antithetical clauses emphasize the differences between Vincent and Dapperwit and implicate them in a communal, if antagonistic, discourse. Dapperwit's inability to drink and his 'mouldy Lampoones' brand him as a pretender to the kind of plain-dealing wit that presumably makes Vincent an admirable figure. Yet the language of the scene works against the audience's ability to make clear-cut distinctions between their characters. Vincent's language echoes and mimics Dapperwit's. His 'Reparty' is parasitic; it parodies his antagonist's 'impertinent Chat' without offering an alternative to it. Later in the play, Vincent becomes less irascible, a straight man for Ranger's schemes and Valentine's jealousy. In the tavern scene, however, his wit seems as self-serving as Dapperwit's; it underscores his participation in a comically corrupt society.

Wycherley uses the conventions of wit in this exchange to register the paradoxes of fashionable discourse. In one respect, wit is virtually anonymous—its forms can be appropriated and replicated almost endlessly; yet in another, it is also solipsistic—characters invariably appropriate these common forms for selfish ends. Their utterances become subjective corruptions of fashionable ideals of speech. As this scene demonstrates, wit both demands and forestalls replies: it tries to prolong itself paratactically by calling for more variations on its themes, and it tries to assert definitively the speaker's authority. It seeks a closure that it never achieves, encouraging and frustrating those who attempt to manipulate it. For Dapperwit and Vincent, wit is a form of detraction, a verbal rendering of basic antagonisms between men of the same class who frequent the same company. Yet the 'impertinent Chat' and 'Reparty' that characterize this antagonism also forge a rough sense of community among men who drink and wench together. The language of wit corrupts social relations but, by corrupting them, ironically justifies its existence as the only means available to describe the corruption that it both reflects and helps create. In this respect, wit ensures that within the tavern no counter-discourse emerges to challenge its self-justifying displays.

The result of corrupted wit, for Wycherley, is an endemic hypocrisy which implicates fools and men of apparent sense alike. Dapperwit is a master of abusing his absent friends and fawning on whomever is present. When Vincent leaves the stage, he becomes the target of Dapperwit's insults; when he returns and Ranger exits, the latter is abused:

RANGER. But why has *Vincent* neither courage or wit.

DAPPERWIT. He has no courage because he beat his Wench for giving me *les douces yeux once;* and no wit because he does not comprehend my thoughts; and he is a Son of a Whore for his ignorance; I take ignorance worse from any man

than the Lye, because it is as much as to say I am no Wit.

(I)

VINCENT. You are an ungrateful fellow, I have heard him maintain you had wit, which was more than ere you cou'd do for your self . . .

DAPPERWIT. A pox he cannot but esteem me, 'tis for his honour; but I cannot but be just for all that, without favor or affectation, yet I confess I love him so well, that I wish he had but the hundredth part of your courage.

(I)

Dapperwit, Wycherley's caricature of the Fletcherian gallant, speaks a language that is both corrupted and corrupting. His complaint against Vincent quickly deteriorates into a string of self-serving compliments and haphazard insults. His speech on Ranger similarly falls apart syntactically; his attempt at logic is undermined by the disjunctive 'buts' that ultimately make his fawning praise of Vincent's courage (which a few moments earlier he has denied exists) seem worse than his insults. Yet Dapperwit's hypocrisy does less to isolate him satirically than to implicate all three characters in the failings of their society. Vincent, a prototype of Manly, drinks and complains; Ranger, the play's stand-in for the man of sense, maintains that Dapperwit 'has wit'—less an error in judgement on his part than a measure of his compliance with the fashionably degenerate standards of his age. Dialogical wit seems to have metastasized into a pervasive comic corruption.

As the tavern scene suggests, wit in the play exists only in imperfect manifestations of a debunked ideal. *Love in a Wood* goes farther than either *An Evening's Love* or *She Wou'd* in mocking the equation of social or individual worth with clever similes and ringing aphorisms. Dapperwit, 'Mr. or as' Ranger calls him, turns Dryden's chase of wit into an unthinking pursuit of novelty. His search for 'new thoughts' becomes an ongoing joke. In the final act, Dapperwit keeps Martha waiting and risks discovery by her father while he ponders what 'a Wit without vanity is like'; he eventually completes his simile in three different ways: 'he is like—a Picture without shadows, or, or—a Face without Patches—or a Diamond without a Foyl; these are new thoughts now, these are new'. Dapperwit settles on images of town life that reveal his fascination with appearances. As Martha recognizes, his 'thought' is narcissistic, an excuse to force language into an aesthetically and ideologically sanctioned form. His similes are less attempts at communication than art-objects which, he presumes, demonstrate his social as well as verbal competence. Yet ironically they are not qualitatively different from the wit exhibited by Ranger and Vincent. Immediately before he drags 'Mr. or as' off the stage in Act III, Ranger suggests that ''twou'd be as convenient to buy, Satyrs against women, ready made, as it is to buy Crevats ready ty'd'. Earlier, caught in a lie when he invades Christina's lodging, he falls back on the hackneyed image (which Dapperwit also uses) of the losing gambler: 'my perpetual ill luck in lying, should break me of the quality; but like a loosing Gamster, I am still for pushing on, till none will trust me'. Ranger's simile calls attention to his failure; it does not offer any insight into his character or predicament but merely reasserts his commitment to a game which he cannot win. His wit prevents him from distinguishing between his posing and Christina's sincere, if idealistic, love. Ironically, Ranger becomes the butt of his aside: he can only restate the conventional assumptions of his age and play out his losing hand. Like Dapperwit, he is undone by the very forms he uses.

Wycherley's handling of similes—turning them into the targets as well as the vehicles of linguistic satire—is characteristic of the dialogical bent of his dramatic wit. If Etherege in *The Man of Mode* moves away from conventional syntactical structures, Wycherley, in all of his plays, exploits them with an ironic vengeance. Ranger's ready-made satires might be apt images for the dramatist's concern with exploring—and transgressing—the limits of stylistic convention. *Love in a Wood* seems to take as its goal the ironic defamiliarization of familiar patterns of speech. Rather than trying to create a new comic language, Wycherley reinscribes conventional forms to reveal the ways in which the language of wit compulsively undercuts its idealistic pretensions.

This process exposes the dichotomy of true and false wit as an ideological construct grounded in the upper classes' equation of birth, money, and worth. Wycherley delights in ironically debunking the means—wit, carriage, and honour—by which his society defines and values its members. The comic conventions that set truewits against would-be wits attempt to answer—or forestall—questions about individual worth by judging characters on the basis of their conformity to seemingly inviolable ideals. Historically, the dialectic of true and false wit grows out of the slow collapse of dramatic traditions which defined and valued characters by social rank: noble foundlings in Fletcher's plays, for example, invariably turn out to be princes; worth proves a function of birth. The decay of this theatrical tradition (a process which had been going on since the Renaissance) is exacerbated by the confusion of ranks that resulted from the civil war. The emphasis after 1660 on the distinction between true and false wit, then, suppresses political differences—specifically the problem of social inequality—by promoting the fiction of a homologous aristocratic society capable of judging individual worth by invoking stable and mutually sustaining values. Yet at the same time the true wit/false wit distinction calls attention to the conventional nature of values such as dressing, speaking, and carrying oneself well. The tragicomic form, as McKeon [*The Eighteenth Century: Theory and Interpretation,* 1983] and Canfield [*Journal of English Literary History,* 1984] suggest, is one response to the problem of trying to reconcile 'natural' and conventional descriptions of worth. In *Love in a Wood,* Wycherley offers another by presenting wit as ideologically disruptive: it does not simply undermine its speakers but displays its own arbitrary values and configurations.

The exercise of wit in Wycherley's first play, then, becomes its own critique. Ranger and Dapperwit rail at the follies of the age and thereby demonstrate that railing itself is a kind of folly:

> RANGER. But why do we not do the duty of this
> and other such places, walk, censure, and speak
> ill of all we meet?

DAPPERWIT. 'Tis no fault of mine, let me perish.

VINCENT. Fye, fye, Satyrical gentlemen, this is not your time, you cannot distinguish a Friend from a Fop.

DAPPERWIT. No matter, no matter, they will deserve amongst 'em the worst we can say.

(II)

Friend and fop, satirical gentlemen and their targets, become almost indistinguishable in a play which does as much to suppress as to sustain differences between wits and fools. Ironically, the hierarchy of wit and witlessness exists in seventeenth-century comedy precisely because it is difficult in a duplicitous society to tell one's friends from fops. Once the standards of true and false wit are questioned, the hierarchy totters and wit becomes a comically unstable standard of judgement. Dapperwit's long speech on the various 'Classes of Wits', for example, collapses true and false wit; he makes distinctions without demonstrating any substantive differences. The 'Court Wit', 'Coffee-Wit', 'Poll-Wit', and 'Scribble-Wit' are all characterized by their 'railing'; the 'Judg-Wit or Critick', who 'is all of these together, and yet has the wit to be none of them; . . . rails at all the other Classes of Wits, and his wit lies in damning all but himself: he is your true Wit' (II). For Dapperwit, who proudly puts himself in the last category, wit requires only the lung power necessary to rail constantly. It is a mode of attack that, as his speech indicates, undercuts the speaker as much as it discomfits its target. In this regard, Dapperwit's abuse of wit becomes both a self-fulfilling prophecy and an ironic projection of the playwright's dilemma. As the 'Scribble-Wit' who created *Love in a Wood,* Wycherley finds himself 'railing' against his age in the very conventions that he satirizes. If he is often brutally satiric, he is also aware of the limitations of his satire. His response is to court rather than suppress the ironies of his position: he rails against the wit that he exploits.

Wycherley's ironic critique of wit reflects a general crisis of language in the play: none of the characters can make their words correspond to what they presumably want to describe. Among the dramatist's favourite satiric targets are those characters who testify repeatedly to their false senses of certainty. Wycherley uses characterizing verbal tags, for example, to emphasize the mechanistic, arbitrary nature of the steadfast assertions of fools. Lady Flippant's 'certainly', Joyner's 'in truly', Sir Simon's 'faith and troth', and Dapperwit's 'let me perish' all assert absolute truths or beliefs. But in a play full of night-time wanderings, disguises, mistaken identities, outright lies, and endemic plotting and counter-plotting these expressions become signs of folly. 'Faith and troth' and the rest are the remnants of a Cavalier absolutism repeated to absurdity. Like the hypocritical cant of Gripe and Joyner, these verbal tags imply the opposite of what their speakers intend; instead of stabilizing language, they cast it to the arbitrary winds of deceit and self-deception. An inverse calculus is at work: the more authoritative characters try to sound, the more foolish they appear.

Semantic instability, then, is not an aberration in the play but an enabling condition of its comic discourse. Lady

Flippant's 'honour', like Dapperwit's 'wit', indicates how this instability comically subverts relationships between fact and perception, appearance and nature. When Lady Flippant speaks, decades of linguistic theory disappear into her solipsistic perversion of the language. Her 'honour' suggests the lexical and moral distortions of her society:

> LYDIA. There does not pass a night [in the Park] but many a match is made.
>
> FLIPPANT. That a woman of honour shou'd have the word match in her mouth: but I hope, Madam, the fellows do not make honourable Love here, do they? I abominate honourable Love, upon my Honour.
>
> LYDIA. If they should make honourable Love here, I know you would prevent 'em.
>
> (II)

Even within this brief exchange the meanings of 'honour' and 'honourable'—two key words in Lady Flippant's hypocritical arsenal—do not remain fixed. Lydia apparently uses the phrase 'honourable Love' without intending any suggestive overtones, but then undercuts her literal meaning by implying that Lady Flippant would turn any encounter into a sexual adventure. The Widow of course has no 'honour' (except her title) to swear by; her oath is based ironically on her hypocritical abuse of language. Her calling Lydia 'a woman of honour' could be taken at face value, if we assume that she is feigning horror at her companion's use of 'the word match'. Her exaggerated sensitivity, like Olivia's in *The Plain Dealer*, would then be another of her transparently hypocritical guises. Yet although we may try to reconstruct her meanings at length (unlikely enough in the theatre), the exact transformations that 'honour' and 'honourable' undergo seem less important than their obvious instability. Lady Flippant's 'honour' may begin as unambiguous deceit but becomes more complicated and self-deceiving as she repeatedly invokes it. She has not merely perverted 'honour' into a sign for dishonour but so corrupted the word's moral and lexical significance that she has no way of restoring it to a 'normal', pristine state.

The ironies of a language turned against itself are apparent also in the play's comic abuse of familiar aphorisms. Vincent's terse observations on human frailty, Gripe's proverbs, and Dapperwit's clichés work against what the audience sees occurring on stage. Truisms become true in unexpected and ironic ways: Vincent tells Valentine that 'there is no punishment great enough for jealousie, but jealousie' (II); Gripe borrows the proverb, 'Temperance is the nurse of Chastity' (III); and Dapperwit laments, 'Fortune our foe, we cannot over-wit, / By none but thee, our projects are Cross-bit' (V. iii). Although Valentine's jealousy does prove to be its own torment, it does not cost him Christina's love; she remains loyal to him despite himself. Gripe's 'Temperance', like Lucy's 'Chastity', is a hoax; lust has ironically been the 'nurse' of her prostitution. Dapperwit's couplet might be taken as a refuge for those characters who become victims of their own scheming and are trying to escape or rationalize the consequences of their actions. His couplet is not a tidy 'Moral of the whole [play]', as Congreve says his tag lines are, but an indication of his and his society's short-sightedness. The play's aphoristic language, then, requires a double-take on our part. If epigrammatic wit and hypocritical proverbs work ironically against the characters who voice them, they also undermine the stability of assertively univocal forms. The certainty they promise is compromised by the circumstances in which they are uttered.

The language of the play's high plot is similarly undercut by the action on stage. In creating Christina and Valentine, Wycherley develops a strategy that he returns to in *The Country Wife* and *The Plain Dealer*: virtuous and noble characters are given brief opportunities to demonstrate their admirable qualities but then are forced to participate in actions which turn their sentiments to hash. If Christina's and Valentine's language suggests that other, nobler existences are possible, it also blinds them to each other's 'true' natures. Valentine is humourless, rigid, and obsessed by jealousy. When he first appears on stage, he asks Vincent for 'evidences of [Christina's] love, to clear those doubts I went away with'. Vincent's response to his friend's entreaties is telling: 'Still turning the daggers point on your self' (II). Valentine reacts to Ranger's account of following Christina home by assuming the worst:

> VINCENT. Why, do you believe him?
>
> VALENTINE. Shou'd I believe you?
>
> VINCENT. 'Twere more for your interest, and you wou'd be less deceiv'd; if you believe him, you must doubt the chastity of all the fine Women in Town, and five miles about.
>
> VALENTINE. His reports of them, will little invallidate his testimony with me.
>
> (II)

Valentine is as mistaken about Christina as Ranger is—and with less of an excuse. His language of self-flagellating certainty marks him as the first of Wycherley's neurotics, those jealous husbands or lovers who compulsively predict their own cuckoldings or betrayals. Despite Vincent's assurances, Valentine remains impervious to reason; he has no basis for judging Christina except the anti-feminism of a society obsessed with legitimating patrilineal succession. Although he may carry himself 'heroically', duelling with Clerimont for Christina's love, he has the instincts of a cuckold. He is a dramatic symbol of Restoration idealism undermined by its anxieties.

Christina, the 'Faithful Shepherdess', is a forerunner of Alithea and Fidelia—the worthy woman attached to the worthless or uncaring man. Idealistically committed to her love, she tries unsuccessfully to isolate herself from society. The more steadfast she becomes, the more she is implicated in the fashionable realm of pretence and deception that she wishes to avoid. Her language, like Valentine's, is a redaction of Fletcherian sentiment: passionate, histrionic, and excessive. Her speech in Act V, when she mistakes Valentine for Ranger, demonstrates Wycherley's characteristic manner of presenting and ironically mocking the language of injured idealism:

> Was it because you found me in Mr. *Vincent*'s

lodgings, you took a liberty to use me, like one
of your common Visitants? But know, I came no
more to Mr. *Vincent,* than to you; yet, I confess,
my visit was intended to a man—A brave man,
till you made him use a woman ill, worthy the
love of a Princess; till you made him censure
mine; good as Angels, till you made him unjust;
why—in the name of honour, wou'd you do't?

(V)

Christina's language may be full of fine sentiments, but it
is also inaccurate: Valentine was jealous *before* he learned
of her supposed affair with Ranger. Her speech, however,
is rhetorically effective in ways that she does not intend
or anticipate. Her praise of Valentine, swelled by anapho-
ra ('till you') and amplifications ('a man—A brave man'),
succeeds in convincing him of her innocence where other
'evidences' could not. Ironically, the success of her histrionics depends on their inaccuracy. Her idealistic praise
demonstrates her blindness to Valentine's faults and gives
him the opportunity to respond to the only kind of love
he can understand—his narcissism. Christina's language,
then, manages to be both nobly heroic and unintentionally
mock-heroic, a stirring defence of her injured innocence
and a comic demonstration that she has learned nothing
about Valentine by his treatment of her. Her language, like
Ranger's wit, allows her only to choose her fetters, not to
escape them.

The comic idioms of the high, middle, and low plots represent Wycherley's attempt to integrate stylistically the disparate languages of earlier Restoration tragicomedy. *Love
in a Wood* presents the discourse of fashionable society as
a complex, satirically flawed welter of competing voices.
Wycherley's image for the dialogical style of comedy is the
'Town', a metaphoric embodiment of the ideology as well
as the aesthetics of wit. The 'Town' is not merely a reflection of aristocratic privileges and prejudices but a complex
of competing versions of what social life is or should be.
It is a self-referential standard for the characters, a bat-
tered and imperfect signifier for their attempts to legitimate their experience in language. In effect, the town displaces metaphoric language into figures that confirm re-
flexively the hegemony of fashionable existence:

> RANGER. [Sir Simon] has his fruitless designs
> upon the bed-ridden rich Widow, down to the
> sucking Heiresses in her pissing cloute; He was
> once the sport, but now the publick grievance of
> all the fortunes in Town; for he watches them
> like a younger Brother that is afraid to be
> mump'd of his snip . . .
>
> (I)
>
> FLIPPANT. I shou'd rather make an adventure
> of my honour, with a Gallant, for a Gown, a new
> Coach, a Necklase, than clap my Husbands
> cheeks for them, or sit in his lap; I shou'd be as
> asham'd to be caught in such a posture, with a
> Husband, as a brisk well bred of the Town,
> wou'd be, to be caught on his knees at prayers,
> unless to his Mistress.
>
> (III)

The images that Ranger and Lady Flippant employ do not
exploit differences between experiences or perceptions of
the world, as Etherege's love and war metaphors do, but
compare similar experiences to each other. The self-

referentiality of their figurative language reflects the
closed ideology of the play's society: wit can anatomize itself but it cannot articulate what might lie beyond its
boundaries or suggest alternatives to a society based on the
inequalities of upper-class privilege. The language of wit
in the play dialogically binds ideal and satiric images of
town life; or, to use a different metaphor, the ideal and satiric infect each other. The town becomes at once a comic
ideal and a satiric target, *both* the arbiter of style and fashion *and* the fallen standard of a hypocritical and deceptive
society. (pp. 139-50)

The Country Wife, Wycherley's acknowledged masterpiece, is more stylistically cohesive than . . . *Love in a
Wood.* The dramatist's success in the play lies in his creating a comic hero who extends and redefines the generic
boundaries of wit comedy. In his own way, Horner is as
complex and ambiguous a figure as Dorimant. He is not
unmasked, as Congreve's double-dealers are, or demonstrated to be something other than he first seemed. Nor is
he a project for reformation; there is no equivalent of Harriet in *The Country Wife* to outplay the hero at his own
game. Like Dorimant, Horner elicits a number of partial
or conflicting responses that never resolve themselves into
a single, definitive interpretation. He embodies the ambivalence that the ideology of wit engenders.

Horner is the play's most disturbing verbal paradox. He
is a walking pun: the chief cuckold-maker of his society,
a standard of masculine sexuality, and almost the satyr
that Olivia, in *The Plain Dealer,* accuses him of being. His
name also plays upon the corruption of 'honour'. The
ironic coupling 'Horner/honour' offers paradoxical standards of pretence and honesty, each term defining itself by
the satiric corruption of the other. Zimbardo [in her
*Wycherley's Dream: A Link in the Development of English
Satire,* 1965] describes the hero as a 'parasite-satirist' who
both feeds off and exposes his society's follies and vices;
other critics have advanced similar dualistic interpretations of his character. But the complexities of Horner's
name—and nature—do not necessarily resolve themselves
into a binary opposition. The possible meanings of the pun
'Horner' are never stabilized or dialectically transcended
by a third term. The tensions within his name are sustained by a dramatic action that resists our breaking down
his character into its components: wit, Machiavel, para-
site, satirist, and butt. If Horner can be defined at all, it
is only by the dialogical opposition of forces that his character brings into being.

The tensions between what Horner says and what he does
raise interpretative problems for critics and audiences because neither his language nor his actions can be fully described by the vocabularies of Fletcherian wit or Jonsonian satire. Horner's speech, like Manly's, calls attention to
its ironic contexts as stylistically significant. Familiar des-
ignations in Wycherley's final two plays—truewit, satirist,
plain dealer—do not offer stable standards of judgement;
they tell us what characters think of themselves, not what
figures they cut in the worlds of their plays. In both *The
Country Wife* and *The Plain Dealer* dramatic style becomes the ironic implication of language in action: the
plays present a series of speech acts whose illocutionary

and perlocutionary force can never be reduced to stable re-constructions of intention or meaning. Traditional forms of wit become counters in a game of ironic destabilization that Wycherley plays with his audience; the language of wit that the dramatist had satirized in **Love in a Wood** is, in effect, defamiliarized again. For Wycherley, irony is not simply a rhetorical device—saying one thing and meaning another—but a dialogical process which allows him to anatomize the corruption of society while questioning the very standards that result in moralistic denunciations of vice and hypocrisy. It is a way of distancing himself from the vices he depicts. But as his dedication to **The Plain Dealer** suggests, Wycherley recognizes that irony impli-cates its creator in its provisional, performative utterance: for the ironist, the self-consuming artefact is also a self-implicating joke that undermines his authority. Irony, then, is not simply a quality of a given text or performance but an essential condition that makes possible the multiple pretences of dramatic experience; as Schleifer argues [in his "Irony and the Literary Past," *Kierkegaard and Liter-ature: Irony, Repetition, and Criticism,* 1984], irony ren-ders problematic the relationships between language and identity, between imitation and nature. It is tempting, in this respect, to see Horner and Manly as Wycherley's anti-thetical and ironic self-projections: the satirist as corrupt double-dealer and the satirist as corrupt plain dealer. Both characters, in their own ways, represent the playwright's ironic questioning of the dramatic and ideological implica-tions of wit.

Horner's language marks him as a creature of his age, al-though a more complex and ambiguous one than audi-ences had encountered before 1674. His speech is epigram-matic, almost gnomic; in contrast, Dorilant's and Har-court's language is less tightly structured and more depen-dent on conventional images of town life:

> HARCOURT. . . . Mistresses are like Books; if you pore upon them too much, they doze you, and make you unfit for Company; but if us'd dis-creetly, you are the fitter for conversation by 'em.
>
> DORILANT. A Mistress shou'd be like a little Country retreat near the Town, not to dwell in constantly, but only for a night and away; to tast the Town the better when a Man returns.
>
> HORNER. I tell you, 'tis as hard to be a good Fel-low, a good Friend, and a Lover of Women, as 'tis to be a good Fellow, a good Friend, and a Lover of Money: You cannot follow both, then choose your side; Wine gives you liberty, Love takes it away.
>
> DORILANT. Gad, he's in the right on't.
>
> HORNER. Wine gives you joy, Love grief and tortures, besides the Chirurgeon's. Wine makes us witty, Love only Sots: Wine makes us sleep, Love breaks it.
>
> DORILANT. By the World he has reason, *Har-court.*
>
> HORNER. Wine makes—
>
> DORILANT. Ay, Wine makes us—makes us

> Princes, Love makes us Beggars, poor Rogues, y gad—and Wine—
>
> HORNER. So, there's one converted.—
>
> (I)

Harcourt's and Dorilant's wit assumes familiar syntactical and ideological forms. Both characters employ similes which reduce women to distractions from other requisites of libertine existence, notably drinking. Theirs is wit by the numbers, although perhaps because Harcourt will later fall victim to a kind of love that he does not yet antici-pate Wycherley has him remain silent after the hero's comparisons. In contrast, Horner's language is more con-cise and seemingly more authoritative. After his emphatic opening clause, the hero sets good fellowship against women and money; Dorilant takes the truisms that follow as inspired observations. But Horner's celebration of drinking wine over chasing women, as the audience knows, is a sham; in fact, as the play goes on, he seems to prefer the company of women to that of men. Although Horner drinks with his companions, he enjoys deceiving them almost as much as he delights in abusing the men he cuckolds. Like most of the other characters, Harcourt and Dorilant believe their friend is impotent. Apparently ei-ther one or both of them snicker when Horner mentions love's 'grief and tortures', prompting his next phrase, 'be-sides the Chirurgeon's'. But what they take as grim self-irony is a joke at their expense. For Horner, wit is a means of setting himself apart from the fraternal community of drinking and simile-making that Harcourt and Dorilant represent. He may not treat them with the contempt he shows Sparkish, but neither does he make them his co-conspirators. The tensions that Wycherley creates be-tween Horner and his friends—the tensions between iron-ic and straightforward reconstructions of wit—force the audience constantly to reassess their responses to the hero and the roles that he assumes.

The ironies in Horner's speech make it difficult to take anything that he says unambiguously. His double-edged utterances undercut his role as a satirist out to lash the fol-lies of his age. He begins the play with an aside that offers his working definition of 'Nature': 'A Quack is as fit for a Pimp, as a Midwife for a Bawd; they are still but in their way, both helpers of Nature' (I). Even in the theatre, this line may give some spectators pause. We might assume that 'Nature' has become corrupt; manifest as healing and giving birth on one level, it is debased in both comparisons (quack as pimp, midwife as bawd) to a degraded sexuality. But the aside might also be taken to mean that even after they have become panders the quack and midwife are still serving essential needs. The adverbial construction 'still but' emphasizes the naturalness of the 'helpers'' roles, mit-igating the negative connotations of their procuring. The conversion of 'Nature' to sexual intrigues, then, does not imply a final satiric judgement. The moral corruption im-plicit in 'Pimp' and 'Bawd' is subsumed, to some extent, by Horner's amoral delight in turning Quack into an in-strument for his scheme.

The hero's opening aside, then, marks him as both a plain dealer out to expose society's vices and the instigator of the very corruption he condemns. Horner may hold up affectation and hypocrisy for satiric censure, but his actions render his judgements almost as disturbing as the vices he attacks. Wycherley often seems less concerned with exposing folly than with presenting the ironies of the hero's relationship to the society he both condemns and victimizes. Horner's satiric comments resist straightforward interpretations:

> LADY FIDGET. . . . affectation makes not a Woman more odious to [men of wit], than Virtue.

> HORNER. Because your Virtue is your greatest affectation, Madam.
>
> (I)

If we were to substitute 'plain dealing', 'Man', and 'my' for 'Virtue', 'Woman', and 'your', we might arrive at a fair estimation of Horner's character. Plain dealing for him is an affectation, yet his affectation paradoxically verges on plain dealing. The more fervent his satiric denunciations become, the more difficult his position is to define. In the second act, Horner characterizes the women he plans to seduce as 'pretenders to honour, as criticks [are] to wit, only by censuring others; and as every raw peevish, out-of-humour'd, affected, dull, Tea-drinking, Arithmetical Fop sets up for a wit, by railing at men of sence, so these for honour, by railing at the Court, and Ladies of as great honour, as quality' (II). Although Horner begins by attacking female hypocrisy, he devotes most of his invective to two traditional comic butts, critics and fops. His initial parallels between 'pretenders to honour' and critics get shunted aside when he begins abusing 'the Arithmetical Fop'. He is no longer venting moral disgust at female hypocrisy but offering an aesthetic critique of the male pretender's inept attempts to imitate him. By the end of his comparison, the audience may wonder whether he is levelling much of an attack on the 'pretenders to honour' at all. The words 'honour' and 'quality'—violently divorced from any rational signification moments earlier by Lady Fidget and her 'virtuous gang'—have already been so corrupted in the play that they no longer provide a means to distinguish honesty from hypocrisy. Horner's equating them ironically questions the ideology that they ostensibly support.

Horner's satiric utterances, then, are always ironically qualified: he often speaks in Manly's tones but with Dorimant's awareness of the ambiguities of an actor's existence. When Harcourt observes that 'Most Men are the contraries to that they wou'd seem,' Horner agrees: 'Ay, your errantest cheat is your Trustee, or Executor; your jealous Man, the greatest Cuckold; your Church-man, the greatest Atheist; and your noisy pert Rogue of a wit, the greatest Fop, dullest Ass, and worst Company' (I). His, of course, is the voice of experience. He detests 'those nauseous offerers at wit' who, unlike him, are poor performers: 'A Pox on 'em, and all that force Nature, and wou'd be still what she forbids 'em; Affectation is her greatest Monster' (I). Affectation, by definition, is unsuccessful dissembling, the inability to convince your audience that you are behaving naturally. Horner cannot be accused of forcing nature because his nature, like Dorimant's, is to act. His roles—eunuch, friend, lover, wit—are his means

of trying to control the absurdities of fashionable existence; yet his ironic detachment ultimately proves as much a pose as his feigned impotence. Horner cannot be stripped of his disguises, as the pretenders to wit and honour can, because he has no existence beyond the roles he assumes. Unlike Harcourt, he cannot be recovered by a conventional morality because there is no 'essential' Horner who can be scraped clean of his layers of social varnish and restored to a pristine state. He exists only in the ironies of his acting.

Horner's role as a eunuch, then, is a manifestation rather than a cause of the ambiguities of his existence. Feigning impotence allows the hero to remove himself from the patriarchal circuit of power and to comment ironically on it. His role represents a potentially devastating assault on patriarchal ideology. Horner becomes a random variable in equations of patrilineal power; he could conceivably father most of the heirs to property in his end of the town. Much of the delight the audience takes in his sexual adventures results from the dangers he courts; where Dorimant conquers unmarried women, Horner cuckolds fools of 'business' and substance. In one respect, he seems a Restoration Hamlet whose 'antic disposition' frees him from conventional restraints but traps him in those of his own devising. Like Hamlet, Horner plays his role far better than he justifies it. Early in the play, he responds to Quack's scepticism by defending his 'Stratagem':

> QUACK. Nay, by this means you may be the more acquainted with the Husbands, but less with the Wives.

> HORNER. Let me alone, if I can but abuse the Husbands, I'll soon disabuse the Wives: Stay—I'll reckon you up the advantages, I am like to have by my Stratagem: First, I shall be rid of all my old Acquaintances, the most insatiable sorts of Duns, that invade our Lodgings in a morning: And next, to the pleasure of making a New Mistriss, is that of being rid of an Old One, and of all old Debts; Love when it comes to be so, is paid the most unwillingly.
>
> (I)

The logical structure of Horner's speech begins to break down as soon as he tries to rework Quack's antithesis of husbands and wives. By disabusing the women, the hero puts himself as much in their power as they are in his; he trades his libertine freedom for the thrill of always being on the brink of exposure and the distinction of making fools like Sir Jaspar appear more foolish. Horner is able to reckon up only one advantage of his ploy—ridding himself of 'old Acquaintances'—before he slips into the language of jaded libertinism. By comparing his sexual conquests to 'old Debts', Horner de-eroticizes his pursuit of women and underscores the similarities between his 'Stratagem' and the schemes of unfashionable moneymen. The comma after 'next' is at best ambiguous; the phrasing 'And next' seems to promise a second element in the series of advantages but then quickly attaches itself to the prepositional phrase that follows. His attempt to explain why he is feigning impotence trails off into defensive generalizations about 'starting the game': 'Women of Quality are so civil', he complains, 'you can hardly distinguish love from good breeding' (I). Even as Horner explains the advantages of his 'Strategem' they are already proving illusory. The report of his impotence attracts rather than repels 'the most insatiable sorts of Duns'; Horner accumulates mistresses so quickly that by the time of the China scene he has more women than he can sexually satisfy. By Act V, his four new mistresses have become old ones, and, because they are his co-conspirators, he can no more be rid of them than they can be of him.

Horner, then, ironically becomes the victim of his success. Although his ruse allows him to hunt down those women 'who love the sport', it also ensures that he becomes part of their duplicitous act. 'Your women of Honour', he tells Quack, 'are only chary of their reputations, not their Persons, and 'tis scandal they wou'd avoid, not Men' (I). These antitheses turn the 'women of Honour' into mechanistic figures animated by their hypocritical lust, no more complex than the 'contraries' Horner assails later in the scene. But Horner's bragging that his stratagem will make him the *Pas par tout* of the Town' (I) paradoxically reduces him to their level: his sexual conquests become as mechanical as the women's protestations of their virtue. The ragged logic of Horner's justification for his stratagem—his revelling in means rather than ends—brings him down to the level of the characters he outwits. To put it bluntly, he loses as much as he wins. If we take Horner as a moralistic misogynist who demonstrates his hatred of women by seducing them, he loses; if we take him as the grand manipulator of a patriarchal society who reduces women to objects, he also loses; if we take him as an amoral libertine out to scare up game, he succeeds so well that his triumphs leave him seeming, as Weales puts it, 'more like a chain smoker than a great lover'. Horner's ruse is, then, a mark of his vanity; he is as intrigued by the possibilities of the artistic (and ideological) control it offers him as he is by its sexual rewards. One of Wycherley's telling ironies is that Horner does not need his stratagem to seduce Margery, who values his wit and person, not the safe haven he offers her reputation.

The dominance of so ambiguous a figure in *The Country Wife* inevitably disrupts conventional standards of dramatic judgement. Our reactions to Horner, the women of honour, and the comic stereotypes like Margery, Sparkish and Pinchwife, and Harcourt and Alithea can be defined either morally or aesthetically, but neither system of judgement offers a foolproof means of accounting for what occurs in the play. Brown argues [in her *English Dramatic Form 1660-1760,* 1981] that our moral and aesthetic judgements remain distinct: we applaud Horner's ingenuity but distance ourselves from—or condemn—what he is doing. This distinction, however, works better thematically than it does theatrically. Wycherley plays off the realistic aspects of his play against the fantastic exaggerations of satire to subvert systems of signification that would allow his spectators to remain detached observers, neatly parcelling out their aesthetic praise and moral disapproval. At the beginning of the play, when the audience learn Horner's secret, they become his accomplices and find themselves encouraged to root against the values travestied by the play's fools. Their awareness that they are on his side rather than the cuckolds' discourages reactions of either moralistic horror or unbridled amoral delight. The

audience's complicity prevents them from simply imposing inside the theatre the values they may hold outside it. This complex process of implication works throughout the play to undermine their stock responses to other characters as well—fools, hypocrites, and would-be idealists alike.

Horner's true antagonists in the play are the 'women of honour' who try their best to reduce him to the 'Toad' that he pretends to be. Lady Fidget, for example, is more a mirror image of Horner than a passive counter or cipher in a masculine game of domination. Her alliance with the hero draws him into a feminine world of deceit that parodies the imperfect fraternal community of wit represented in Act I by Dorilant and Harcourt. The women's speech is typically derogatory, fragmented, and prone to the brutally simple inversions of Wycherley's linguistic satire. Like Lady Flippant, the women corrupt an ideally univocal language to serve their sexual desires:

> SQUEAMISH. Well, 'tis an errant shame, [we] Noble Persons shou'd be so wrong'd, and neglected.
>
> LADY FIDGET. But still 'tis an erranter shame for a Noble Person, to neglect her own honour, and defame her own Noble Person, with little inconsiderable Fellows, foh!—
>
> DAINTY. I suppose the crime against our honour, is the same with a Man of quality as with another.
>
> LADY FIDGET. How! no sure the Man of quality is likest one's Husband, and therefore the fault shou'd be the less.
>
> DAINTY. But then the pleasure shou'd be the less.
>
> LADY FIDGET. Fye, fye, fye, for shame Sister, whither shall we ramble? be continent in your discourse, or I shall hate you.
>
> DAINTY. Besides an intrigue is so much the more notorious for the man's quality.
>
> SQUEAMISH. 'Tis true, no body takes notice of a private Man, and therefore with him, 'tis more secret, and the crime's the less, when 'tis not known.
>
> LADY FIDGET. You say true; y faith I think you are in the right on't: 'tis not an injury to a Husband, till it be an injury to our honours; so that a Woman of honour looses no honour with a private Person . . .
>
> (II).

Like Horner's language, this exchange works comically by being both brutally honest and deliberately (if ineptly) evasive. Lady Fidget's reprimand to Dainty, 'be continent in your discourse', reflects satirically on her and on the Fletcherian tradition that elevates purity of diction over the purity of the body. Wycherley's women abuse traditional signs of value—particularly 'noble', 'quality', and 'honour'—past the point of recovery. The more frequently they repeat a word the more suspect its connotations become. 'Quality', for example, subsumes the social prerogatives of birth and the satiric corruption of the ideological order that it designates. The doubling of ideological ideal and its corruption under the sign of 'quality' does not describe a stable irony that measures precisely the divergence from a norm but a subversive, dialogical irony that questions the evaluative standards the term implies.

Yet while this exchange satirizes the 'women of honour', it also counters the fragile, transparent nature of their pretences and unites them in a community of feminine double-dealing. The ironic doubling of ideals and their corruption in 'quality' and 'honour' paradoxically unifies the women in their attempts to deceive male society and each other, much as the wine-and-women exchange among Horner, Dorilant, and Harcourt solidifies their self-perceptions as wits, even as it allows the hero to hoodwink his friends. After Lady Fidget upbraids Dainty, the exchange moves toward an affirmation of a comically corrupt solidarity, an agreement to band together against their husbands and guardians while they continue to try to deceive each other. This closing of ranks behind their half-feigned antipathy to 'men of quality' prefigures the deal that they later cut with Horner. When Lady Fidget learns that he has been Dainty's and Squeamish's 'false rogue' as well as her own, her reaction is simply, 'then there's no remedy, Sister Sharers, let us not fall out, but have a care of our Honour'. The Horner/honour pun binds the hero and 'the virtuous gang' in a debased comic community of Hobbesian self-seeking.

In contrast to the 'women of honour' and their 'Harry Common', the play's abject fools—Sir Jaspar, Sparkish, and Pinchwife—are satirically isolated by their incompetence as speakers and interpreters of their society's languages. As Vieth [in *Papers on Language and Literature*, 1966] and Sedgwick [in *Critical Inquiry*, 1984] argue, these characters provide negative images of masculinity that make Horner appear more sexually attractive; they draw off from him the harsh, satiric condemnations that his actions might otherwise elicit. Sir Jaspar, for example, demonstrates repeatedly that he thoroughly deserves his cuckolding. He shows up initially at Horner's lodgings to plague the hero with his preposterous civility and tasteless jokes: 'come and dine with me, and play at Cards with my Wife after dinner, you are fit for Women at that game yet' (I). But Sir Jaspar, like Wycherley's other fools, is done in by his own language; 'play' and 'fit' take on sexual connotations that he does not intend. Later in the play he literally thrusts his wife into Horner's arms, telling the two of them, 'go, go, to your business, I say, pleasure, whilst I go to my pleasure, business' (II). Although his confounding of business and pleasure reflects ironically on Horner's single-minded pursuit of sex, it also brands Sir Jaspar as a satiric butt, a man of 'business' for whom acquisitiveness has replaced sexual gratification. The ironic confounding of business and pleasure (picked up by Etherege in *The Man of Mode*) turns Sir Jaspar into an image of all that Horner rebels against.

Sparkish and Pinchwife as a comic pair are reminiscent of Monsieur and Don Diego; Wycherley sets the one's self-satisfied stupidity against the other's fanatical jealousy. Sparkish is unconcerned about his fiancée's honour because he is incapable of valuing her as, the audience presumes, he should. His inept stabs at wit are a substitute for action (particularly sexual action) and understanding. He values Alithea, as Sedgwick argues, only because he believes that she validates his status as a man of wit. He shows her off, he tells the incredulous Pinchwife, as he would 'shew fine Clothes, at a Play-house the first day, and count money before poor Rogues', only to be envied (I). From the moment he walks on stage, heralded by Horner as 'the greatest Fop, dullest Ass, and worst Company', he is ridiculed by the other characters—except Alithea. Her loyalty to him, long after everyone else has recognized him for a fool, is one measure of the bankruptcy of the traditional values she holds. Sparkish is also an embodiment of the injustice of a rigidly structured social system that values money and land over individual worth. He condemns himself by complaining that contemporary playwrights turn knights into fools: 'Their Predecessors were contented to make Serving-men only their Stage-Fools, but these Rogues must have Gentlemen, with a Pox to 'em, nay Knights: . . . you shall hardly see a Fool upon the Stage, but he's a Knight.' Dorilant responds, 'Blame 'em not, they must follow their Copy, the Age' (III). Sparkish is not a fop but a caricature of aristocratic presumption. He represents the failure of wit and carriage as measures of social value.

Pinchwife's obsession with what he calls 'honour' travesties the values that Alithea articulates. Pinchwife, the 'old Whoremaster', recognizes that the world is corrupt and duplicitous—his favourite assertion is 'I know the Town'—but his knowledge only aggravates his suffering. His coarse, debasing language reflects his pathological view of women and accurately predicts his eventual cuckolding: 'Cuckolds and Bastards', as he says, 'are generally makers of their own fortune' (III). If Sparkish is almost asexual, Pinchwife has declined to near impotence, obsessed by his libertine past and the warped view of women that it has impressed upon him. He regards the corruption of linguistic signs, like 'honour', with a hypocritical mock-horror. His attempts to reassert control over the troublesome terms 'sister' and 'wife' lead him to debase Alithea and Margery to counters in the masculine game of patrilineal succession: 'Wife and Sister are names which make us expect Love and duty, pleasure and comfort, but we find 'em plagues and torments, and are equally, though differently troublesome to their keeper; for we have as much a-doe to get people to lye with our Sisters, as to keep 'em from lying with our Wives' (V). Although Pinchwife recognizes that 'Wife' and 'Sister' have conventional meanings, he corrupts them into solipsistic 'plagues and torments'. His debasing of women actualizes the metaphors of hunting and gaming that all the male characters—from Horner to Sparkish—use to describe their relationships with women. Pinchwife, by his own account, becomes a 'keeper', an image which reduces him to the ridiculous roles of an aging 'Whoremaster' and ill-bred game warden.

Pinchwife's language, then, crosses the boundary from fashionable forms of misogynistic wit to antisocial, even pathological attacks on women. As Dorilant puts it when Pinchwife first begins verbally abusing his wife, 'He talks as like a Grasier as he looks' (I). His vulgar, sexually abusive language verges on the frustrated violence that is latent in any society which reduces women to objects bartered for land and money. But Pinchwife's readiness to draw his sword is played for laughs by Wycherley:

> PINCHWIFE. I will not be a Cuckold I say, there will be danger in making me a Cuckold.
>
> HORNER. Why, wert thou not well cur'd of thy last clap?
>
> PINCHWIFE. I weare a Sword.
>
> HORNER. It should be taken from thee, lest thou should'st do thy self a mischiefe with it, thou art mad, Man.
>
> (IV)

Horner of course takes Pinchwife's phallic sword away from him in more than one sense. The sexual imagery in this exchange, as in Pinchwife's threatening Margery with his penknife, identifies masculine violence with impotence, frustration, and jealousy. Pinchwife represents the bankrupt values of Don Diego carried to self-torturing extremes: he is, as the hero tells him, 'mad'. Like Sir Jaspar, Pinchwife is rendered ridiculous by his vain attempts to deny or control the sexuality of women—particularly his wife's.

Pinchwife's folly is thrown into satiric relief by the education of his wife. The play is aptly named for Margery because in her the audience sees the processes of initiation—or corruption—that turn her from an 'innocent' into a prototype of Lady Fidget. Alithea's comment upon her sister-in-law's favourite recreation sets the tone for Wycherley's treatment of her: 'A walking, hah, ha; Lord, a Country Gentlewomans leasure is the drudgery of a foot-post; and she requires as much airing as her Husbands Horses' (II). Margery is the product of a rustic upbringing, yet her ingenuousness verges on a kind of plain dealing that cuts through the town's fashionable hypocrisy. Her epistle to Horner, he tells Quack, is 'the first love Letter that ever was without Flames, Darts, Fates, Destinies, Lying and Dissembling in't' (IV). Her naïve, 'country' language of plaintive questions and simple, declarative sentences insulates her from harsh satiric judgements and provides a new vehicle for feminine rebellion: speaking her mind. 'I did not care for going [to the play],' she tells her husband, 'but when you forbid me, you make me as't were desire it' (II). She shares the sexual appetites of the 'woman of honour'; what she learns during the play is the means to act upon them.

The scenes of Margery's initiation encourage the audience to cheer for her unabashedly. As Alithea reminds him throughout the play, Pinchwife brings about his own cuckolding, from his first efforts to silence Margery to his leading her to Horner's lodgings. His treatment of her ensures that her cuckolding an abusive husband appears infinitely preferable to her remaining faithful to him. Pinchwife blames her desire for Horner on 'Love', which he identifies with the corruption of the town: ' 'twas [love] gave women first their craft, their art of deluding; out of natures hands, they came plain, open, silly and fit for slaves, as she and Heaven intended 'em'. Although their 'art' may have to be learned, their natures, in his mind, are predisposed to moral corruption. When he asks himself

why women 'have more invention in love than men', his answer is ready-made misogyny: 'because they have more desires, more solliciting passions, more lust, and more of the Devil' (IV). Pinchwife's invocation of Heaven to justify his view of women as 'slaves' forges a link between traditional—and repressive—sexual ideologies and his fear of being cuckolded. It becomes difficult, then, to separate the values that Pinchwife articulates from the folly of their speaker. Although Wycherley is no crusading reformer or champion of women's equality, he relies on the same patterns—setting language and action against each other—to undermine fashionable ideologies of sexual power as he does to subvert the conventional dictates of wit. Margery's cuckolding of Pinchwife is not an aberration that proves the wisdom of patriarchal rule but a comic lambasting of the values of 'business', money, and anti-feminism that are celebrated by Wycherley's fools.

The corrupted sexual values articulated by Sir Jaspar, Sparkish, and Pinchwife serve as metaphors for the comic degeneration of society. Wycherley casts the generic problems of nature and affectation less in terms of fashion than in those of sexual competence and power. In his final two plays Etherege maintains the separation of feminine wit and sexual experience; in contrast, Wycherley demonstrates that the displacement of sexual pleasure into masculine power—into the myths of women as either 'slaves' or 'devils'—results in 'women of honour' appropriating both the deceptive language of wit and the role of sexual aggressor. Because Margery and Lady Fidget are married, their speech does not mask their essential honesty but marks their involvement in a 'masculine' realm of sexual experience and hypocrisy. The action of the play, in this regard, implicates Horner and the women in each other's deceptions, blurring conventional distinctions between masculine and feminine wit. Wycherley's language both describes the antagonism of the sexes and becomes the means by which Horner and the women forge a community of sexual hypocrisy that parodies and subverts the sexually segregated communities of male wit and female dissembling.

This ironic operation of language structures the action of the deservedly celebrated China scene. At the beginning of the scene Quack asks Horner a question which echoes ironically throughout the rest of the play: 'have you not the luck of all your brother Projectors, to deceive only your self at last' (IV). The action—both within and without Horner's China closet—compromises the hero almost as much as it does Sir Jaspar; we are never quite sure who is bearing the brunt of our laughter. All of the characters believe that they are perpetrating jokes on others, yet all are victims of languages that they finally cannot control. The double—or multiple—meanings of 'China' reflect satirically the corruption of language in fashionable society and comically the dialogical undermining of social discourse: once Horner and Lady Fidget start using the word metaphorically, we can no longer be restored to our 'innocent, literal understanding' (IV), an irony Wycherley plays upon in *The Plain Dealer*.

When Lady Fidget enters, Horner tries to silence her fears for her reputation among her 'censorious' friends by claiming that 'rather than they shall prejudice your Honour, I'll prejudice theirs; and to serve you, I'll lye with 'em all, make the secret their own, and then they'll keep it: I am a *Machiavel* in love Madam' (IV). The hero's styling himself a Machiavel celebrates his virtuosity as an actor and invokes the network of self-interest that holds his society—and his schemes—together. The image joins two of his favourite roles: the satirist who lays bare the workings of the town and the conscientious hypocrite dedicated to serving the desires of the women he seduces. In this respect, Horner is honest about his intentions but dishonest about his motives; his plain dealing complicates rather than clarifies the workings of his 'Stratagem'. Later, when Lady Fidget runs off to the China closet, he prefaces his pursuit of her by attacking female 'impertinency':

> HORNER. . . . Oh women, more impertinent, more cunning, and more mischievous than their Monkeys, and to me almost as ugly—now she is throwing my things about, and rifling all I have, but I'll get into her the back way, and so rifle her for it— . . . Stay her a little, I'll ferret her out to you presently, I warrant.
>
> SIR JASPER. Wife, my Lady *Fidget,* Wife, he is coming into you the back way.
>
> LADY FIDGET. Let him come, and welcome, which way he will.
>
> (IV)

Horner's rhetoric offers an oblique satiric comment on Sir Jaspar's sexual inadequacy, debases Lady Fidget, and provides yet another instance of his ambiguous relationship to women. The satiric image of women as monkeys is both a ruse to fool Sir Jaspar and a misogynistic truism which the hero may half-believe. Yet Horner hardly spares himself. The sexual connotations of 'rifle' and 'ferret' bring him down to the bestial level at which he puts the 'impertinent' Lady Fidget. Double meanings proliferate. When Sir Jaspar unwittingly joins in the sexual innuendo, he is victimized by the dialogical 'impertinency' of a language that seemingly cannot escape being twisted into *double entendre*.

Throughout the scene the language of sexual innuendo super-imposes itself on the 'innocent, literal' meanings of conventional discourse. 'China', appropriated for Horner's designs and the women's desires, becomes a focus for undercurrents of hostility, false intimacy, and hypocrisy. The properties of China—it is made from earth, fragile, finely decorated, and used to serve one's appetite—assume an almost metaphoric status. 'China' ironically is and is not what the characters wish it to be:

> LADY FIDGET. And I have been toyling and moyling, for the pretti'st piece of China, my Dear.
>
> HORNER. Nay she has been too hard for me do what I cou'd.
>
> SQUEAMISH. O Lord I'le have some China too, good Mr. Horner, don't think to give other people China, and me none, come in with me too.
>
> HORNER. Upon my honour I have none left now.

> SQUEAMISH. Nay, nay I have known you deny your China before now, but you shan't put me off so, come—
>
> HORNER. This Lady had the last there.
>
> LADY FIDGET. Yes indeed Madam, to my certain knowledge he has no more left.
>
> SQUEAMISH. O but it may be he may have some you could not find.
>
> LADY FIDGET. What d'y think if he had had any left, I would not have had it too, for we women of quality never think we have China enough.
>
> HORNER. Do not take it ill, I cannot make China for you all, but I will have a Rol-waggon for you too, another time.
>
> SQUEAMISH. Thank you dear Toad.
>
> LADY FIDGET. What do you mean by that promise?
>
> HORNER. Alas, she has an innocent, literal understanding.
>
> (IV)

The uninitiated, Sir Jaspar and Old Lady Squeamish, are the obvious butts of the China pun; but as the dialogue continues the China collectors lose control of their duplicitous code. Squeamish and Lady Fidget half-articulate their doubts about each other's pretence to honour, but the language of their China collecting will not allow them to voice their suspicions openly. Both rely on Horner's complicity and both are deceived by the fiction of the other's 'innocent, literal understanding'. But if the China metaphor becomes the scene of a power struggle between the two women, it also reflects the hero's multiple roles in the exchange. Besides the concealed Quack, only Horner knows how ironic his 'China' has become. Yet his knowledge only emphasizes that he has become a victim of his machinations. In showing Lady Fidget his 'China', he has sexually exhausted himself, becoming, for a short while, what he pretends to be. He has willingly transformed himself into a familiar comic butt—the man who does not have 'China enough' to satisfy his mistresses. The ironies of his position are summed up by Old Lady Squeamish, who describes him as 'a Snake without his teeth' (IV). Her image of Horner as a snake (unknown to her) works in a variety of ways: it reinforces his success in duping the voices of senile or inept authority; it extends and improves upon his phallic punning; it associates the hero with the archetypal hypocrite in the Garden of Eden; and it suggests ironically that Horner has indeed been devenomed by the women. 'I cannot make China for you all' is another of the scene's ironic answers to Quack's initial question: 'have you not the luck . . . to deceive only your self at last'.

It may be possible for the audience to react with moralistic horror to the China scene, but only by admitting that they get the joke, that they are, in fact, Horner's co-conspirators. Implicating the audience in the ironies of a language abused is Wycherley's defence against 'innocent, literal understandings' of his play. But the audience's complicity with Horner and Lady Fidget in the China scene raises potentially difficult questions about how Wycherley intends his spectators to respond to those characters who are neither sexually compromised nor obvious comic butts. Harcourt and Alithea have traditionally fascinated those critics who have sought a moral or ethical centre in the play, or those who believe that the danger of Wycherley's comedy is that we will find ourselves drawn to characters of whom we 'should' disapprove—Horner—and laughing at characters who 'should' be exemplary—Christina and Alithea. Voicing idealism in Wycherley's plays, however, is no guarantee of exemplary status. Like Valentine and Christina, Harcourt and Alithea are subject to the corruption of their comically fallen world.

Both characters are initially presented as members of the play's fashionable society: Harcourt trades witty remarks with Horner and Dorilant; Alithea defends taking 'the innocent liberty of the Town' and fuels Pinchwife's jealousy of his wife. Even after he has set his sights on Alithea, Harcourt continues to speak the fashionable language of debunking wit. Norman Holland suggests [in his *First Modern Comedies*, 1959] that his metaphors somehow escape the 'practical reality' that dominates the figurative language of others, but this observation holds true only for those speeches he addresses to Alithea. When Harcourt speaks about her, he conflates her with the conventional mistresses of libertine wit. He asks Horner for romantic advice in an idiom indistinguishable from Dorilant's: 'I am in love with *Sparkish*'s Mistriss, whom he is to marry to morrow, now how shall I get her' (III). Later, in the midst of duping Sparkish, he remarks in an aside, 'we are hard put to't, when we make our Rival our Procurer; but neither [Alithea], nor her Brother, wou'd let me come near her now: when all's done, a Rival is the best cloak to steal a Mistress under, without suspicion; and when we have once got to her as we desire, we throw him off like other Cloaks' (III). The form and diction of Harcourt's speech are conventionally degrading: Alithea is reduced to an object to be stolen or 'got to' or a woman to be procured: in effect, a prostitute. Harcourt's passion may be genuine but his language is degrading. He has no recourse but to apply an ironic, debunking idiom to the object of his 'honourable' desires.

Harcourt's attempts to talk Alithea out of marrying Sparkish reduce her loyalty to her fiancé to near-farce: the longer she holds out and the more fervently Sparkish pushes her into his rival's arms the more the action recalls the Monsieur-Gerrard-Hippolita scenes in *The Gentleman Dancing Master.* Unlike Hippolita and Christina, however, Alithea is presented as a product of the town. As Pinchwife makes clear, her marriage to Sparkish is a mercenary undertaking: its rationale is money and land, not love. Alithea is a willing participant in the arrangement, conditioned by the values of the town that she has internalized as her own. She declares to Harcourt that she must marry Sparkish because 'my reputation wou'd suffer in the World else' (II). Later she asserts ' 'tis *Sparkish*'s confidence in my truth, that obliges me to be so faithful to him' (IV). Her second rationalization seems an understandable psychological reaction to her brother's jealousy: she remains faithful to Sparkish because he represents the antithesis of Pinchwife. But she deceives herself by elevating

Sparkish's 'want of jealousie' into a justification for her loyalty to him. Although her plight is potentially serious (uncaring husband, tyrannical brother), Wycherley treats it comically by demonstrating that Alithea has only herself to blame. Her exclamation after Sparkish has abused her and broken off their match—'How was I deceiv'd in a man!' (V)—is more a comment on her stupidity than his. It is one thing, then, to cheer for Harcourt and Alithea in the theatre—what dolt would root for Sparkish?—but quite another to suggest that they escape the verbal and ideological limitations of their society.

The conclusion of *The Country Wife* parodies the inclusive, communal endings of festive comedy. Disguises are not thrown off but readjusted, and the country wife is welcomed into the circle of deception when she learns to stifle her expressions of love for Horner and go along with Lucy's improbable fiction. When Pinchwife, Alithea, Harcourt, and Sparkish arrive in Horner's lodgings, he is forced to protect Margery by falsely compromising her sister-in-law. Although some critics have argued that Horner's choice reveals his moral degradation, his behaviour should hardly come as a surprise to the audience. He is doing what he has been doing throughout the play: lying. In an aside he admits wronging 'one woman for anothers sake', but accurately asserts, 'that's no new thing with me; for in these cases I am still on the criminal's side, against the innocent' (V). Horner's dilemma is tactical rather than moral: he must sacrifice Alithea to protect Margery. Harcourt does not challenge his friend openly but talks to him, according to the stage direction, *'Apart'*:

> HARCOURT. This Lady [Alithea] has her Honour, and I will protect it.
>
> HORNER. My Lady has not her Honour, but has given it me to keep, and I will preserve it.
>
> HARCOURT. I understand you not.
>
> HORNER. I wou'd not have you.
>
> (V)

Harcourt's ignorance of Horner's stratagem is an apt image for the conclusion of a play that depends on false pretences being preserved rather than unmasked. The tone of the scene, as this exchange suggests, is comic rather than melodramatic; drawing swords over the ladies' honours is left to Pinchwife, who has trouble deciding whether to run through his wife or Horner. Harcourt, Alithea, and particularly Margery must be reintegrated into the world of dissembling and hypocrisy that circumstances threaten to lay bare. After her honour has been saved, Alithea reassures her brother that his 'Wife is yet innocent' (V); her line may be taken either as evidence that she too has been duped by Lucy's story or that she is, like Horner, lying to protect her sister-in-law. Margery must hide her 'certain knowledge' (the same phrase that Lady Fidget had used in the China scene) of Horner's sexual prowess to join the ranks of the women of 'honour'; her last line in the play is, as she tells the audience, another lie. She has been absorbed into a world of fashionable deceit.

The Country Wife concludes by reaffirming its ironically subversive portrait of society. It leaves its audience caught somewhere between amoral laughter and satiric recognition. It is a comedy about the limitations of comedy, about how far men and women can be made to recognize and acquiesce in the comic corruption of their languages, values, and identities. *The Plain Dealer* is similarly structured on the premise that neither harsh satire nor festive comedy in and of itself adequately represents social reality. But in his final play Wycherley exacerbates the tensions between the languages of moralistic condemnation and comic compliance. The language of wit—which still retains ironic currency in *The Country Wife*—becomes, for Manly, a medium that has played itself out, except in the form of antitheses that violently reject any mediation between their terms.

The language of *The Plain Dealer,* beginning with the dedication, is at once brutally satiric and profoundly ironic. It does not restrict itself to a satiric anatomy of the town but explores the vices and follies of 'the World'. Yet Wycherley, while insisting on the corruption of 'the World', dramatizes the follies of a self-righteous hero who declares himself its staunchest critic. The puns and double-meanings that characterize *The Country Wife* are, for the most part, absent from Wycherley's final play after the dedication. They are replaced by competing jargons and dialects, set pieces of satiric invective, and travesties of conventional wit that destroy all pretences to rational communication. Characters interrupt each other frequently; half-sentences, exclamations, and fragments abound. Oldfox, frustrated in his efforts to impose himself on the Widow, sums up the verbal experience of the play when he exclaims, 'all interruption and no sence between us' (IV). In its stylistic inclusiveness, *The Plain Dealer* occasionally seems the 1670s' answer to *Barthol'mew Fair,* but the corruption it portrays is more absolute, its comedy less tolerant, and its ending fantastic rather than corrective. The cacophony of its languages suggests that Wycherley had virtually written himself out of the conventions of wit comedy. Like *The Libertine* and *The Man of Mode* (both produced earlier in 1676), *The Plain Dealer* challenges and redefines traditional comic idioms.

Many of the interpretative problems that the play creates are foreshadowed (for readers, if not for the audience) in Wycherley's savagely ironic dedication to Mother Bennet, an infamous bawd. In his persona of 'The Plain Dealer' the dramatist burlesques fulsome dedications, attacking 'nice coy Women of Honour', moral hypocrisy, misapplied 'touchstones', and the very genre in which he is writing. Double and multiple meanings, crammed into nearly every clause, parody the generic language of writerly obligation:

> And this Play claims naturally your Protection, since it has lost its Reputation with the Ladies of stricter lives in the Play-house; and (you know) when mens endeavours are discountenanc'd and refus'd, by the nice coy Women of Honour, they come to you, To you the Great and Noble Patroness of rejected and bashful men, of which number I profess my self to be one, though a Poet, a Dedicating Poet; To you I say, Madam, who have as discerning a judgment in what's obscene or not, as any quick-sighted civil Person of 'em all, and can make as much of a double meaning saying as the best of 'em; yet wou'd not, as some do, make nonsense

of a Poet's jest, rather than not make it baudy: by which they show they as little value Wit in a Play, as in a Lover, provided they can bring t'other thing about.

This long, involved sentence seems a normative linguist's nightmare: Wycherley's 'double meaning sayings' are set in a syntactical framework which violates conventional patterns of logical development. 'The Plain Dealer' interrupts himself, interjecting direct addresses and sly parenthetical assertions ('you know') and falling back on comic amplifications and digressions, to erase the distinctions between prostitution and honour. The satire in this mock-epistle is brutally frank, but it works against so many targets—hypocrisy, ignorance, obscenity-mongering, fawning poets, dim-witted patrons, 'Women of Honour', misinterpretation—that its implied moral norms get lost in the cross-fire. Wycherley's irony becomes a destabilizing force which seeks to re-create in the minds of his readers what the audience experiences in the theatre. Ultimately, it undermines the interpretative processes by which we try to make sense of it: 'according to the Rules of Dedications, 'tis no matter whether you understand or no, what I quote or say to you, of Writing; for an Author can as easily make any one a Judge or Critick, in an Epistle, as an Hero in his Play'. The dedication picks up where *The Country Wife* left off; it is less an introduction to the play than an initiation that implicates its readers in the processes of interpreting—and misinterpreting—its ironies.

The 'Dedicating Poet', then, cancels his bets as he makes them. His epistle, like the play that follows it, works against itself as well as its targets, reiterating and undermining its satiric premises. His assertion, 'you . . . Madam, are no more an Hypocrite than I am when I praise you' offers two open-ended possibilities: either 'I am as much a hypocrite as you are' or 'in this hypocritical world, we are the only honest ones around'. These possible interpretations, however, provide no straightforward answers, no authoritative 'meaning'; they offer only the experience of being lost in another of the playwright's woods. His dedication thus poses another paradox: although it delights in lambasting hypocrisy, it does not offer an alternative or correction but provides a series of ironic moments that turn inward upon themselves. It both entices the reader to read on and ironically obviates the need to read further. It is not a polemic against a corrupt world but a demonstration of satire's limitations, its inability to register the ironies and tensions of a dialogical discourse.

The dedication (presumably written after the play was produced) may be taken as the playwright's final attempt to deal with the limitations—or outright failures—of wit and its dialogical double, the satire of wit. If Wycherley's homage to Mother Bennet can be read as a radical deconstruction of the ideologies of servile wit and servile social satire, it also focuses attention on the ironic position of a playwright who must write within a language that he distrusts. By signing the dedication 'The Plain Dealer', Wycherley identifies himself with a hero who seems a cross between Juvenal's persona in the *Satires* and Pinchwife. On one level the identification is a joke; the Manly whom the audience sees in the play might be hard pressed to understand, let alone compose, the indirect, ironic discourse of the dedication. Yet on another level Wycherley seems to want his readers to take the relationships among historical author, dedicating persona, and theatrical character as a paradigm of the interpretative problems that the play, like the dedication, creates. In this respect, the signature is not a guide to meaning but an obstacle. 'The Plain Dealer' is a conventional sign for truth-telling defamiliarized, turned into an ironic construct that sets competing interpretations against each other: the Plain Dealer is the noble playwright exposing the vices of his age, the fallible playwright struggling to represent the vices of his age, the double-minded persona who penned the dedication, the embittered speaker of the prologue, the play's nobly flawed idealistic hero, and the play's foolishly flawed hero—the deserving butt of Wycherley's satire. 'The Plain Dealer', then, is the sum of dialogical possibilities that the signature implies. It represents the playwright's 'self' and his character's fictional 'self' as contradictions, as enigmas. 'The Plain Dealer' is a sign of mediation, a borderline between a noble critique of the world and the often ignoble life that one must lead in it.

Manly is the most stylistically distinct of Wycherley's heroes. His characteristic 'nays' and 'buts' are typical of the age, but he employs them with an atypical vehemence to contradict the world. His language reflects his intolerance and inflexibility, favouring syntactical forms that link curt, epigrammatic assertions into long, often involved diatribes against pretence, hypocrisy, and corruption. In Act I, for example, a series of images characterize his self-righteous indignation: 'counterfeit Honour will not be current with me, I weigh the man, not his title; 'tis not the King's stamp can make the metal better, or heavier: your Lord is a Leaden shilling, which you may bend every way; and debases the stamp he bears, instead of being rais'd by't' (I). Manly's response to the world is to bully it. His language relies heavily on negative phrasings and brief, unambiguous antitheses. It rejects the circumlocutions of the Plausibles of the world and derives its authority from the privileged 'I' who parades his values. Frequently, the hero sets ideals of personal honour and political authority against what he sees as their absolute degradation. In Act III Manly identifies Westminster Hall with the despotic rule of the Turkish Emperor: 'This, the Reverend of the Law wou'd have thought the Palace or Residence of Justice; but, if it be, she lives here with the State of a *Turkish* Emperor, rarely seen; and besieg'd, rather than defended, by her numerous black Guard here' (III). The 'but' becomes the hero's way of trying to separate himself from the corruption around him. It signals the leaps of faith that he routinely makes between general principles and his desires. After a long tirade against the Widow Blackacre, he concludes, 'But, bid her come in . . . she is *Olivia's* Kinswoman, and may make amends for her visit, by some discourse of that dear Woman' (I). Manly's 'But' here links rather than separates clauses, implicating him in the kind of self-serving that he condemns. Whether declaiming against 'counterfeit Honour' or attacking hypocrites, Manly has a way of slipping from satiric criticism into solipsistic defences of his integrity. In his own way, he is as self-dramatizing as Plausible, the fop he condemns for not wearing his heart on his sleeve.

Manly, however, is not without verbal wit. He gets the better of his exchanges with Novel, Plausible, Oldfox, and the hypocrites who accost him in Westminster Hall. In these situations, he becomes a master of derogatory comebacks:

> PLAUSIBLE. I wou'd not have my visits troublesome.
>
> MANLY. The onely way to be sure not to have 'em troublesom, is to make 'em when people are not at home; for your visits, like other good turns, are most obliging, when made, or done to a man, in his absence.
>
> (I)
>
> OLDFOX. Pr'ythee tell me what ill luck you have met with here.
>
> MANLY. You.
>
> (III)
>
> ALDERMAN. . . . but Captain, you are like enough to tell me—
>
> MANLY. Truth, which you wo'nt care to hear . . .
>
> (III)

Although Manly appropriates traditional forms of wit, he uses them less to display his ingenuity than to set himself apart from the fools who pester him with their good graces. His retorts express his exasperation with the duplicity of fashionable language. By using wit to attack wit, Manly unleashes the radical energy of a language turned against the premises and values which define it.

Manly's use of conventional forms underscores the ambiguous position of the moralistic reformer who finds himself trapped in a world he despises. The hero embodies the outraged idealism that any self-styled moralist is bound to feel when confronted by vice, folly, and hypocrisy; yet his rigid judgements turn him into a caricature of the rampaging reformer. In the play's opening scene, Wycherley sets Manly's self-righteousness against Plausible's spineless acceptance of social duplicity. At first, Manly gets the better of the exchange—plain dealing as bluff honesty is always in fashion—by attacking his visitor's '*Decorums,* supercilious *Forms,* and slavish *Ceremonies*' (I). Yet by the end of the scene, having castigated the world's double-dealing, he is reduced to speaking the worst of his insults in asides before he exits, as the stage direction states, '*thrusting out my* Lord Plausible'. Plausible may get what he deserves, but Manley's kicking him down the stairs marks a point at which his language fails. Unable to change the world by condemning it, the hero becomes a bully rather than a satirist. The society we see in ***The Plain Dealer*** is almost as bad as Manly says it is, but his criticism of its faults is qualified by his intolerance, double-dealing, and inability to distinguish his friends from his foes. By the time he decides to seduce Olivia by pretending to be the disguised Fidelia, the audience's capacity for moral indignation has probably been overloaded to the point where his corruption offers as good a laugh as his antagonists' hypocrisy. Ironically, Manly, as both satirist and satiric butt, confirms his assessment of human nature.

Manly's long, satiric set pieces mark him as an emotional,

even irrational critic of public corruption. He levels most of his attacks on social, legal, and political vices rather than on personal foibles. Hypocrisy and double-dealing, for Manly, signify the surrender of the individual to a corrupt and corrupting society. In Act I, he offers Plausible his plain-dealing credo:

> . . . if I ever speak well of people, (which is very seldom indeed) it shou'd be sure to be behind their backs; and if I wou'd say, or do ill to any, it shou'd be to their faces: I wou'd justle a proud, strutting, over-looking Coxcomb, at the head of his Sycophants, rather than put out my tongue at him, when he were past me; wou'd frown in the arrogant, big, dull face of an overgrown Knave of business, rather than vent my spleen against him, when his back were turn'd; wou'd give fauning Slaves the Lye, whil'st they embrace or commend me; Cowards, whil'st they brag; call a Rascal by no other title, though his Father had left him a Duke's; laugh at Fools aloud, before their Mistresses: And must desire people to leave me, when their visits grow at last as troublesom, as they were at first impertinent.
>
> (I)

Manly's speech heaps example upon example, relying on active verbs to energize these familiar satiric tableaux. The hero portrays himself engaged in what he considers heroic acts of negation; he does the jostling, frowning, giving the lie, and laughing while his adversaries are reduced to sticking out their tongues. Manly's language, then, creates an uncompromising alternative to fashionable compliance, a romantic refuge for his antisocial idealism. He tells Fidelia (disguised as a boy) that because s/he is a coward s/he will 'live to be cherish'd by Fortune, and the great ones; for thou may'st easily come to out-flatter a dull Poet, out-lye a Coffee-house, or Gazet-writer, out-swear a Knight of the Post, out-watch a Pimp, out-fawn a Rook, out-promise a Lover, out-rail a Wit, and out-brag a Sea-Captain' (I). These 'out-' formations simultaneously proclaim and undermine the satirist's supposedly privileged position. Manly's last three examples—the lover, the railing wit, and the sea-captain—are, in effect, unintentional critiques of his own excesses. The standards of propriety that the hero tries to maintain are violated by a language that does not allow him to distinguish between general observations and specific instances. He perceives the targets of his satire, including Plausible and Fidelia, as vindications of his compulsive need to demonstrate his moral superiority. Even when Manly praises Vernish and Olivia— 'I have such proofs of their faith, as cannot deceive me' (I)—he values them as demonstrations of his judgement and worth. His language, in this regard, falls into the self-deceptive circularity common to Wycherley's fools. It does not examine the world but forces it to conform to rigid, solipsistic patterns.

Manly's language, then, is satirically incorrigible. It prevents him from learning from his experiences even as it implicates him in its double-dealing. Like Fidelia, Manly sees but refuses to change his views on the basis of what he observes. When he is accosted by several Westminster Hall parasites, he gets rid of them by feigning friendship and then asking them for favours. As a satirist, he suc-ceeds in exposing their hypocrisy: when the Lawyer hears 'in *Forma Pauperis*' and the Alderman learns he is to be bound 'in City security', they hurry off, freeing the hero from their hypocritical professions of friendship. But Manly learns little about either himself or his society by his dissembling. His pose confirms what he already believes: 'You are no more to believe a Professing Friend, than a threatning Enemy; and as no Man hurts you, that tells you he'll do you a mischief, no man, you see, is your Servant, who sayes he is so' (III). Manly refuses to see anything that does not fit his radically idealistic perception of the world. He perceives discrepancies between appearances and natures easily enough but cannot see that such contradictions describe his own character. The paradoxes he embodies—insight and blindness, wisdom and folly, morality and hypocrisy—undermine his attempts at self-definition. The tensions within his nature render him, as Shakespeare says of Coriolanus, 'a kind of nothing', a figure who empties the world of any significance beyond his subjective responses to it.

Manly's harsh, antithetical language displaces traditional forms of wit into the extremes of railing and folly. Robbed of its epistemological significance, wit ironically becomes evidence of moral, intellectual, and emotional bankruptcy. In the prologue, 'Spoken by the PLAIN-DEALER', the audience hears that the playwright 'wou'd not have the Wits pleas'd here to Day' and later that 'His men of Wit, and Pleasure of the Age, / Are as dull Rogues, as ever cumber'd Stage'. This explicit rejection of the ideology of wit by an actor, Charles Hart, who had recently played Horner, comes close to a kind of violent self-effacement on the part of 'The Plain-Dealer' who wrote the play.

One strain of corrupt wit is embodied by Freeman. Taken as the 'adversus' of classical satire by Zimbardo and the spirit of comedy by Birdsall, he is described in the dramatis personae as 'a Complyer with the Age'. His mercenary pursuit of the Widow Blackacre links him with Oldfox, Novel, and Plausible, even as he derives much of his pleasure from 'laughing at Fools, and disappointing Knaves' (III). His language, drawing on the traditions of theatrical wit, celebrates its implication in the corruption it describes. Fending off the Widow's attempts to forestall his advances, he tells her, 'you have no business anights, Widow; and I'll make you pleasanter business than any you have: for anights, I assure you, I am a Man of great business; for the business—' (II). By equating business and sexual pleasure, he makes explicit the anti-eroticism implicit in Sir Jaspar's use of the same metaphor in *The Country Wife.* In Freeman's mouth, verbal wit no longer maintains even the fiction of disinterest. He reduces sex to a mercenary transaction: it is not 'like' business, it *is* business, a way of repairing his fortune. The aristocratic myth of *'Birth & Quality'* has deteriorated to the corrupting pursuit of money; Freeman, the fortune-hunter, unmasks the material bases of these values. His designation of pleasure as business discloses matter-of-factly the corruption that Manly takes pride in exposing. In this respect, Freeman's wit mediates between shop-worn Fletcherian ideals and Manly's intolerant rejection of them; and, corrupted by its mediating function, his wit becomes inseparable from the hypocrisies it attacks.

The comic depths to which wit sinks in *The Plain Dealer* are evident in the speeches of Novel and Plausible. For these characters, particularly Novel, wit is synonymous with hypocritical character assassination, a point that Wycherley hammers home in their scene with Olivia in Act II; when they tire of insulting their acquaintances, they begin surreptitiously insulting each other. By Act V, wit has deteriorated to adolescent vandalism, a farcical parody of Cavalier gentility. For Novel, 'Talking is like Fencing', and as he extends his simile, he apparently dances around the stage, imaginary sword in hand, to drive home his point: 'the quicker the better; run 'em down, run 'em down; no matter for parrying; push on still, sa, sa, sa: no matter whether you argue in form, push in guard, or no'. A few moments later, having established that talking is 'a mark of Wit', he maintains that 'so is Railing, Roaring, and making a noise: for, Railing is Satyr, you know, and Roaring and making a noise, Humor' (V. 500). Wit no longer has to make sense, it merely has to wreak havoc. Novel finds 'Wit and Humor' in 'making a noise, and breaking Windows', and maintains that, 'a Wit is as well known by his Frolick, as by his Simile'. When Oldfox protests, Novel asserts that 'where there is Mischief, there's Wit' (V). Wit and carriage have been satirically conflated into a grotesque caricature of the radical, dialogical questioning which Bakhtin and Cope identify with comedy. It is not so much that Novel is 'wrong' or that his speech is satirically flawed—both should be obvious to the most doltish spectator—but that his nonsense raises questions of who could conceivably be 'right'. His definition of wit is laughably inept, as Manly and Freeman quickly note; yet their criticism of him cannot transcend the mazes of ironic qualification on which the play's language insists. The hero uses the language of wit to attack Novel and Oldfox: 'you have done like Wits now; for you Wits, when you quarrel, never give over, till you prove one another Fools' (V) But Manly's appropriation of wit inadvertently allies him with Novel, even as it sharpens the distinctions between their kinds of folly. Although *The Plain Dealer* offers different varieties of false wit, the distinctions it makes among them are less important than its demonstration that wit is a two-edged weapon.

Wycherley's final play, then, fragments the ideal figure of the true wit into three antagonistic 'selves'—the self-righteous plain dealer, the mercenary complier, and the social vandal—that had previously been suppressed by vague idealizations of polite speech and Cavalier gentility. By dividing wit into three imperfect forms, Wycherley dramatizes its dialogical tensions. This demonstration, however, is less a statement of satiric 'truth' than an ongoing challenge to conventions that the play still exploits. If we are at all versed in the conventions of wit comedy, as Wycherley's original audience was, we expect to see something that we can admire in both the plain dealer and the fashionable rake trying to secure his fortune. Wycherley can undermine these stereotypes at such length and with such force precisely because they are ideologically and theatrically sustained by their positions in the play's fictional society. The ambiguities and interpretative problems that Manly and Freeman present result paradoxically from their lack of pretence, from the boldness with which they proclaim their natures. The radical potential

of their languages lies in the dramatist's continuing disclosure of the self-righteousness, intolerance, hypocrisy, compliance and mercenary single-mindedness that traditionally—on stage and in society—had been covered over by a veneer of manners, breeding, and verbal polish.

Wycherley's depiction of the corruption of wit, in this respect, extends beyond linguistic satire to function as an extended metaphor for his society's moral and ideological corruption. To an extent greater than his contemporaries, Wycherley dramatizes this comic corruption in the strained, hostile, and flawed relationships between the sexes. In *The Country Wife* the playwright broke new ground by letting his adultresses escape punishment; in *The Plain Dealer* he uses four very different female characters—Fidelia, Olivia, the Widow, and Eliza—to offer variations on the feminine languages of ideal faith and corrupt passion that he had previously employed. Like his male characters, his female figures are exaggerated for dramatic effect. They represent radical—and radically unsuitable or unstable—alternatives for dealing with the ways of their world.

As he does in his earlier plays, Wycherley relies on mistaken identities, disguises, and scenes played in the dark to generate the theatrical confusion of sex comedy. But *The Plain Dealer* offers correspondingly few episodes of unmasking or revelation; when they do occur—Olivia's taunting of Manly, for example—they intensify rather than relieve existing tensions. Both male and female characters remain victims of their comically flawed judgements. Fidelia has ample proof of the hero's insensitivity and cruelty but clings absurdly to her initial assessment of his character: 'Sir, your Merit is unspeakable' (I). She sees and does not see, as her unintentionally ironic use of 'unspeakable' suggests. Her idealistic language, like Christina's in *Love in a Wood,* prevents her from perceiving what is obvious to the audience. Yet she is not incapable of dissembling. When Manly commands her to 'speak comfort' to him, she abuses him almost as badly as Olivia does, deliberately repeating the latter's insults: Manly becomes 'ten thousand Ruffians', 'Brutes', 'Sea-Monsters', and finally a 'surly Coward' (IV). The voices of the two women—romantic heroine and unprincipled whore—overlap; Fidelia, like Olivia earlier in the play, is able to outwit Manly at his own game of satiric invective. Yet her verbal domination implies no other victories: after their exchange she remains as blindly loyal to him as before, even waiting for him in Olivia's chambers while he is exacting his sexual 'revenge'. Fidelia's wit, in this respect, is similar to Manly's when he dissembles friendship to rid himself of Oldfox, the lawyer, and the alderman. Although both Manly and Fidelia 'learn' how to deceive others, neither is able to use the knowledge, as Horner does, to further his or her own ends. The hero remains a penniless railer and his disguised admirer kindles his desire for revenge on her rival rather than his respect for her. Fidelia's idealism protects her from the corruption of society precisely because it is a form of blindness. Her nobility and ignorance are, in effect, one and the same.

Although Fidelia faithfully dogs Manly's heels, his true antagonist is Olivia, a nightmare image of the woman as 'a mercenary Jilt' (Prologue). She is a caricature given to preposterous denials of her actions and hypocritical assertions of her virtue. She can be understood, as Eliza says of 'modern' women, only as 'Dreams, Almanacks, and *Dutch Gazets,* by the contrary' (II). Whatever Olivia claims to believe or feel one minute she betrays the next. In her opening scene with Eliza, the two women run through a list of fashionable pleasures, from fine clothes to fine men, all of which Olivia claims are her 'aversion'. She pretends not to know Novel when he is announced, then launches into a satiric character of him as 'a Coxcomb . . . who, rather than not rail, will rail at the dead' (II), before finally greeting him with the kind of flattery that she had earlier claimed was her 'aversion'. Her railing at what she most desires—men, clothing, a place at Court—parodies Manly's plain dealing. What he attacks in earnest she condemns for form's sake alone. Like his language, hers is given to satiric catalogues, self-dramatizing examples of her supposed virtue, and absolute declarations of passion (for the disguised Fidelia), loyalty (for Vernish's benefit), and contempt (for Manly). She is a corrupted version of Hippolita in *The Gentleman Dancing Master,* a satirically exaggerated image of the woman as dissembler and phallic manipulator.

Yet Olivia's double-dealing ironically constitutes a kind of insight in a world given to pretence and hypocrisy. Freeman tells Manly at the beginning of the play that hypocrites 'understand the World' (I). Olivia, in one respect, proves his point: she knows enough to fool those characters she needs to deceive. Significantly, Wycherley distinguishes between the act she performs for women, particularly her cousin, and the roles she assumes for Manly, Vernish, Novel, and Plausible. Olivia's outrageous hypocrisies and inept lying are reserved for her scenes with Eliza: she denies what she has just said, contradicts herself endlessly, and pretends, in Act V, to have no knowledge of what she has admitted to her cousin the previous night. When she is with men, however, she proves an adept dissembler. Her hypocrisy, played for satiric laughs when she is talking to Eliza, becomes an effective weapon. The language of her sexual dissembling is more brutally accurate than farcically self-condemning; it is also less given to the comic repetitions and contradictions that characterize her protestations to her cousin. Her descriptions of Manly, for example, are closer to what the audience sees on stage than Fidelia's account of his virtues. She taunts the hero for a courage 'which most of all appears in your spirit of contradiction, for you dare give all Mankind the Lye' (II). Later she dissects his character for Fidelia: 'I knew he lov'd his own singular moroseness so well, as to dote upon any Copy of it; wherefore I feign'd an hatred to the World too, that he might love me in earnest' (IV). Olivia recognizes that Manly's 'spirit of contradiction' is a romantic negation, not simply a denunciation of real corruption but a self-fueling, idealistic rebellion against a world which refuses to conform to his notion of what it should be. His attacks on society are the products of a divisive self-hatred. But Olivia is hardly free from self-deception. Her knowledge of Manly is undone by her blindness to her self-defeating pretences. Her faith in her ability to evade or outface the consequences of her duplicity, like Manly's naysaying, is a debased form of hubris, a false self-

assurance that Wycherley undermines with a vengeance. Olivia's lust proves her undoing: she ends up, without knowing it, in Manly's arms, loses his fortune, and is trapped in her marriage to Vernish. She falls victim to the deceit she practises.

Olivia's 'aversions', like Novel's 'wit' and Freeman's 'business', make explicit what had been implicit in most comedies before 1676: a corrupt language is the product of a corrupt world, and its corruption undermines the legal, social, and moral values that its speakers ostensibly uphold. The most extreme example of linguistic corruption in the play—the legal jargon of Widow Blackacre and her cohorts—drives home this satiric point almost obsessively. The Widow perverts what ideally should be a language of reason and precise definition into a fragmented, incoherent, and solipsistic medium. In Westminster Hall, language drops all pretences to meaning and truth. Quaint describes his courtroom procedure as pure deception: 'I will . . . extenuate or examplifie Matter of Fact; baffle Truth, with Impudence; answer Exceptions, with Questions, tho' never so impertinent; for Reasons, give 'em Words; for Law and Equity, Tropes and Figures: And so relax and enervate the sinews of their Argument, with the oyl of my Eloquence' (III). When the Widow instructs Blunder on how to prosecute her case, Quaint's 'Eloquence' gives way to 'noise': 'baul soundly for me, at the *Kings-Bench;* bluster, sputter, question, cavil . . . but be sure your tongue never stand still; for your own noise will secure your Sense from Censure: 'tis like coughing or heming when one has got the Belly-ake, which stifles the unmannerly noise' (III). The verbs that replace logical argument in the Widow's catalogue divorce language and sense as thoroughly as Olivia's 'aversions' or Quaint's displacement of 'Law and Equity' into 'Tropes and Figures'. The Widow's forgery and suborning perjury in Act V are logical extensions of her immoral disregard for language. Her language does not pervert the law so much as it reveals that the law inevitably corrupts language to ignoble and mercenary ends. Her cavilling and blustering, in this respect, are dangerous in a way that Lady Fidget's or Lady Flippant's verbal pretences are not. It becomes virtually impossible to work one's way back through her language to even the most tarnished or degraded of ideals. Quaint's acknowledgement that all a lawyer can do for a client is tell a 'fine Story, a long Story' turns the law into a series of fictions by which social and economic power is maintained. The law, for Wycherley (who studied at the Inns of Court), thrives on Quaint's 'poinant and sowre invectives', detraction, obscurity, and character assassination. Its jargon promotes the endless contentiousness and duplicity of Westminster Hall, where lawyers try to sustain conflicts rather than resolve them. In this respect, Wycherley's depiction of the Widow and her coterie of bawling lawyers seems intended less as a satiric corrective than as a Juvenalian nightmare of human greed and selfishness run rampant.

The breakdown of the languages of wit, legal order, and moral authority in *The Plain Dealer* prevents us from typing the play as either incoherent satire or raucous comedy. Wycherley's recognition of the dialogical nature of utterance is broadly comic, but his tendency to identify this dialogical quality with social corruption is harshly satiric. The relationship in the play between comic and satiric impulses is thus profoundly ironic. By repeatedly calling attention to discrepancies between words and actions, Wycherley's stylistic ironies work in two ways: they underscore the severity of his plain-dealing attacks on vice and corruption and they allow both the dramatist and his audience to distance themselves from the play's degenerate society and Manly's diatribes against it. In this respect, **The Plain Dealer's** irony serves an almost exorcistic function by channelling into grim laughter the disillusionment that the hero experiences and that all members of an imperfect society may occasionally feel. Manly can thus be at once a savage critic of the world and its biggest dupe, and the audience can empathize with his idealistic ranting while laughing at his follies. Wycherley's irony, then, is more than a simple defence mechanism: it offers the dramatist and the audience a way of escaping from the viciousness of the play's satire. Yet it also eliminates the middle ground of 'objective' detachment, forcing the audience into an ironic no-man's-land among different forms of radical instability. As Wycherley's attacks on wits, fine women, friends, and lawyers in the prologue and epilogue suggest, the play works rigorously to deny the audience a safe haven from which to pass judgement on its action.

Eliza's role, in this regard, is particularly significant. Most critics see her as a surrogate for the audience, commenting incisively on but remaining aloof from Olivia's hypocrisy. Birdsall [in *Wild Civility,* 1970] describes her as a 'comic realist' who, like Freeman, offers 'believable regenerative possibilities'. In Birdsall's view Eliza becomes a choral figure, an open-minded observer whose attack on her cousin's 'aversion' to 'China' serves as Wycherley's warning against false or narrow interpretations of his art. Yet it seems difficult to accept Eliza as the dramatist's mouthpiece in a play which invariably undercuts its characters' self-perceptions. Like Freeman, she is an uncritical spectator of the world, likening it to 'a constant Keeping Gallant, whom we fail not to quarrel with, when any thing crosses us, yet cannot part with't for our hearts' (II). Her judgements on railing and deception are practical rather than moral. 'Railing', she tells Olivia, 'now is so common, that 'tis no more Malice, but the fashion; and the absent think they are no more the worse for being rail'd at, than the present think they are the better for being flatter'd.' Moments later she tries to talk her cousin out of her fondness for dissembling by claiming that ' 'tis grown of no use to us; for all wise observers understand us now adayes, as they do Dreams, Almanacks, and *Dutch Gazets,* by the contrary' (II). Eliza's images—frequently sexual—are drawn from fashionable life, from her knowledge of the town rather than her disgust at its failings. In this respect, her defence of **The Country Wife** depends paradoxically on her willingness to offer her society as a target for Wycherley's satire, even as she tries to ignore the connotations of 'Horner' and limit language to a one-to-one correspondence between words and things. Eliza opposes Olivia's attack on the play by becoming a passive literalist, a female complier with a simplified—and ineffectual—language of plain dealing. In Act V, while Olivia is denying the events of the previous evening, Eliza implicates herself in the farcical world of lust, betrayal, and deception. Her assurance

to her cousin, 'No, you need not fear yet, I'll keep your secret' (V), suggests more a cynical acceptance of human frailty than an exemplary moral stance. Restricted to Olivia's sitting room, she becomes both critic and accomplice, commenting on and abetting her cousin's performances. In short, whatever 'regenerative possibilities' she may present are themselves fair game for the playwright's irony.

Eliza, then, represents the dangers of trying to turn Wycherley's irony into a stable affirmation of the values of 'common sense'. The dramatist's undermining of the conventions which privilege plain dealers like Manly and Eliza seems designed to disorientate and disturb the audience. If Dennis's account of the play's opening [in his *The Critical Works of John Dennis,* edited by Edward Hooker, 1939-43] is accurate, Wycherley apparently got the reaction he intended: 'And when upon the first representation of the **Plain Dealer,** the Town, as the Authour has often told me, appeared Doubtfull what Judgment to Form of it; [Buckley, Denham, Savil, Waller, Rochester, Villiers, Dorset, and Mulgrave] by their loud approbation of it, gave it both a sudden and lasting reputation'. That Wycherley 'often' retold this story suggests that he took pride in the confusion he created among 'the Town' as well as in the praise he received from literary-minded aristocrats. **The Plain Dealer**'s 'sudden and lasting reputation' demonstrates also that his subversion of the conventions of wit comedy should not be taken as an act of nihilistic vandalism but as a historically significant critique of the ideology and conventions of wit.

In the prologue, 'the Plain Dealer' prepares the audience for a happy ending to his tribulations, although he makes it clear that his rewards are the stuff that theatrical dreams are made on:

> And where else, but on Stages, do we see
> Truth pleasing; or rewarded Honesty?
> Which our bold Poet does this day in me.

The ending of the play is an escapist fantasy that is played as part wish-fulfillment, part joke. It becomes difficult for the audience to fall back on the usual system of rewards and punishments as a guide to interpretation. The one-sided contract between Freeman and the Widow harks back to the grotesque legal satire in Act III, and the marriage between Fidelia and Manly punishes her and rewards him beyond what either of them deserves. The play's funniest lines may be Fidelia's justification for her loyalty, 'I left . . . to follow you, Sir; having in several publick places seen you, and observ'd your actions thoroughly, with admiration', and Manly's characterization of Freeman as 'a Plain Dealer too' (V). If Manly is thoroughly admirable and Freeman a plain dealer, then the previous five acts have gone for nought. Wycherley's conclusion flouts what we know about the characters and the conventions of comedy. His hero is not so much converted as offered bribes to 'stay in this ill World': Fidelia's virtue, love, and money. His closing lines suggest that he has yet to learn much about the world he finds so 'odious':

> I will believe, there are now in the World
> Good-natur'd Friends, who are not Prostitutes,
> And handsom Women worthy to be Friends:

Yet, for my sake, let no one e're confide
In Tears, or Oaths, in Love, or Friend untry'd.
                                              (V)

Manly's closing couplet falls back on the virtue-by-trial mentality that originally led to his misplaced trust in Olivia and Vernish. His language, as Holland suggests [in his *Ornament of Action,* 1979] is still 'imprecise' and 'uncontrollable', a solipsistic projection of values that promise only a false stability. **The Plain Dealer** ends by calling attention yet again to the ironies of its attack on the very forms that it employs. Like Etherege at the end of *The Man of Mode,* Wycherley deliberately, ironically takes leave of the conventions of wit.

Manly's warning to be wary of the duplicity of the world does not signal an end to wit comedy: Behn, D'Urfey, Crowne, Dryden, Ravenscroft, Shadwell, and Southerne all wrote popular comedies in the 1680s. But it does mark the exhaustion of the 1670s' ironic attack on the ideology of restoration and the heroicizing of aristocratic privilege. When wit comedy is revived in the 1690s, it assumes different values and epistemologies, even different teleological purposes. For the playwrights of the 1690s, particularly Congreve, **The Plain Dealer** becomes a cultural icon, both a standard to live up to and a point of departure for their own efforts. Congreve, Pope, Dennis, and many of their contemporaries turn the upright 'Plain Dealer', the 'Manly *Witcherley*' celebrated by Dryden, into a kind of folk hero. This identification of playwright and character perpetuates the ironies that Wycherley began when he signed himself 'The Plain Dealer' to the play's dedication. His signature underscores the paradox of the satirist who recognizes that he is implicated in his satire. As Manly is both fool and reformer, so Wycherley is both a detached observer of hypocrisy and its obsessive anatomist. For Wycherley, signing himself 'The Plain Dealer' is his hedge against the absurdities and contradictions of his society; for his contemporaries, the signature represents an act of moral courage impressive enough to dissuade even Jeremy Collier from attacking him. 'The Plain Dealer', in this respect, signals a recognition that the man of wit cannot wall himself off from the vices of his age; it destroys the myth of dispassionate observation that had, for half a century, been taken as a sign of good breeding. From the vantage point of the 1690s, **The Plain Dealer** demonstrates that, by turning the language of wit against itself, comedy can function as a vehicle for a serious criticism of the ways of an imperfect world. (pp. 159-94)

> *Robert Markley, " 'All interruption and no sence between us': The Language of Wycherley's Plays," in his* Two-Edg'd Weapons: Style and Ideology in the Comedies of Etherege, Wycherley and Congreve, *Oxford at the Clarendon Press, 1988, pp. 138-94.*

Peggy Thompson   (essay date 1992)

[*In the following excerpt, Thompson considers several interpretations of Horner in* The Country Wife, *maintaining that the play is a parody of the myth of Adam and Eve's fall from grace in which Horner represents the seducer.*]

The massive commentary on Wycherley's **The Country Wife** ranges largely between two extremes in its treatment of the infamous Horner, who feigns impotence to gain access to wives and wards. At one end of the interpretive spectrum, Horner is a generous "helper of Nature" striving to release himself and others from corrupt social restraints on their pleasure and freedom. At the other extreme, he is a self-interested "*Machiavel* in love," whose goal of sexual conquest is so debilitatingly narrow and compulsive that he becomes the pathetic monster he pretends to be. This essay will argue that a major force behind these diverse interpretations is Wycherley's ambivalent approach to the myth of a sexual fall and its historical recapitulation in carnal witchcraft.

The myth of a sexual fall is a heretical, yet tremendously influential interpretation of Genesis. It claims that Edenic innocence was asexual and that the original sin was Eve's seduction. Rooted in the Hellenistic Neoplatonists' denigration of sexual passion as part of an inferior physical realm, the myth was quickly accepted by early Christians and competing sects. Church leader Tatian, for example, preached that the devil invented sexual intercourse, while Gnostic Julius Cassianus claimed that Jesus had been sent to earth to save men from copulating. Augustine declared the myth a heresy, but the antagonism toward sex that it embodies continued to flourish both in his writings and in Western culture more generally.

Because of Eve's alleged submission to evil impulses and her consequent seduction of Adam, women's sexuality was especially suspect. This was nowhere more clear than in the European witch hunts of 1480 to 1650. According to many "learned" treatises on witchcraft from that period, "it is not unreasonable that this scum of humanity [witches] should be drawn from the feminine sex" [Nicholas Remy, *Demonolatry,* translated by E. A. Ashwin, 1974]. Satan and demons nearly always collaborate with women because "[a]ll witchcraft comes from carnal lust, which is in women insatiable"; women are reduced to witchcraft because of their "bestial cupidity" [Henry Kramer and James Sprenger, *Malleus Malificarum,* 1948; Jean Bodin, *De la demonomanie des sorciers,* translated by Julia O'Faolain and Lauro Martines, 1973]. Even when denying the existence of witches, disputants in the debate assumed the "abhominable lecheries" of women, which though not the result of demonic pacts, were evidence of sexual depravity.

According to Douglas Duncan [in *Essays in Criticism,* 1981] Wycherley's allusions to witchcraft and a sexual fall in **The Country Wife** parody the myth by championing the satanic seducer Horner as a liberator of confined sexuality and an exposer of hypocritical repression. Thus, characters who attempt to conflate the erotic and diabolic as James I did in his *Daemonologie* (1597) are ridiculed, while Horner, whose sexual activity is as ubiquitous as that of Charles II, is hailed as genial and generous. But that is only half the story. For in **The Country Wife,** the fearful and ascetic assumptions informing the myth are so strong that they subvert the parody and reassert themselves. As a result, two contradictory readings emerge.

Sexual desire is wrongly confined in Horner's world; but

it is also a dangerously overwhelming force of which one ought to be wary. Women are unnaturally inhibited; but they are also devious, undeniable, and exhausting sexual creatures. Male friendship is a cover for the cuckolding of deserving hypocrites; but it is also an attractive foil to threatening relationships with women. Finally, Horner is a witty satiric agent and successful sexual liberator; but he is also an intimidated and ineffective antagonist of sexual desire whose play with language makes him more vulnerable to the snares of carnal irrationality. Together the two readings imply that Wycherley cannot decide whether the Eden his diabolical seducer inhabits is a pleasure garden or a battleground.

Like Eve of the sexual fall, who forfeited paradise in search of gratification (and like the witches willing to consort with demons), the women in *The Country Wife* are insatiable. But because, as Duncan notes, they have also accepted the concept of sexual sin, they emerge as ridiculously incongruous and deluded creatures who interrupt their pursuit of lovers to object to the word "naked" as a modifier for "truth" and to compare obscene wits to "a Picture of *Adam and Eve,* without fig leaves." Even at their notorious dinner party in Act 5, where they seem most open about their sexual desires, they continue to exhibit the grossest sort of self-delusion, calling sexually experienced women "common and cheap." Dainty Fidget's remark in the same conversation—"women are least mask'd, when they have the Velvet Vizard on"—does not simply acknowledge their passions; it also reminds us of the mythic view that women are characteristically indirect and devious, even among themselves, in their efforts to satisfy those passions. At this point in the play, after all, the ladies know Horner is not impotent, and yet for the first 150 lines of the scene, all pretend that he is.

The convoluted sexual behavior of these women is balanced by the naive simplicity of Margery's approach to sex. Utterly innocent of the concept of sexual sin, she is utterly straightforward in expressing her sexual desires—insofar as she recognizes them as such. She ingenuously tells her husband, "I have not been well, since you told me there was a Gallant at the Play in love with me," and she urges him to take her to another play, explaining without apology, "I like to look upon the Player-men, and wou'd see, if I cou'd, the Gallant you say loves me; that's all dear Bud." Margery quickly—if somewhat awkwardly—resorts to deception, however, substituting letters and donning disguises as soon as she realizes that Pinchwife will restrain her from acting on her newly awakened passions.

The compelling desires of both Margery and the ladies of "honor" are responsible for much of the physical action on stage as these women recoil from those who cannot gratify their lust and flock toward those who can. Lady Fidget demonstrates the overwhelming impetus of her passion by insisting, despite her husband's unexpected arrival at Horner's lodging, "I will find it out, and have what I came for yet." Horner's lascivious suggestion, "I'll get into her the back way," and Sir Jaspar's obtuse warning, "Wife, he is coming into you the back way," are lewd allusions to witchcraft, specifically to Satan's doing everything

backward, as Duncan points out. But throughout the scene, the emphasis is not on Horner's "seduction"; it is on the lust of Lady Fidget, who responds heartily, "Let him come, and welcome, which way he will." And just as Margery rages against the locks Pinchwife has put between her and the world of desire and gratification, so Mrs. Squeamish impatiently tries the door behind which Horner and Lady Fidget "admire china." Sexual energy animates these women as they crash through the lies and locks designed to control that energy. Complexly self-deluded or incredibly naive, Wycherley's women are essentially and aggressively sexual.

The obvious exception to this generalization is Alithea, whose characterization as an angelic virgin removes from her the powerful physical forces animating the other women. Harcourt consistently approaches her as a creature "above the World" and all its corruptions, thus justifying his attraction by appealing to the "Heavenly form" her beauty manifests. Although much of Harcourt's Neoplatonic language is tongue-in-cheek, Horner's aspersions on Alithea's purity in Act 5 elicit a shock (both within and without the play) that testifies to the audacity and gravity of the accusation—to the profound corruption her alleged sexual experience represents. Meanwhile, the response of the male characters to the other ladies' gluttonous, earthy appetites reinforces the idea that women cannot be of this world and anything other than carnal beasts. Consequently, despite the frequent comparisons between women and food, it is the men who act as though they are in danger of being consumed.

Female sexuality most obviously threatens Pinchwife, who goes to great lengths to avoid being victimized by woman's lust: marrying an incredibly ignorant country girl, keeping her under lock and key when she is in the city, and even dressing her as a boy when they venture out. He explains his paranoia by implying that all women are sexually insatiable and indiscriminate: "I tell you no woman can be forced." And he identifies "love," by which he means sexual desire, as the source of women's devious and deceptive behavior: "Love, 'twas he gave women first their craft, their art of deluding." From this assumption, Pinchwife moves easily to the heart of the myth of a sexual fall, the equation of sex and sin:

> Why should Women have more invention in
> love than men? It can only be because they have
> more desires, more solliciting passions, more
> lust, and more of the Devil.

Pinchwife's conception of unfallen women, "plain, open, silly, and fit for slaves," is a consistent personal ideal for one who is willing to interpret intellectual and physical bondage as virtue and fidelity in his wife. Sir Jaspar's description of the uncorrupted woman, "that sweet, soft, gentle, tame, noble Creature Woman, made for Man's Companion," also excludes sexual passion from the ideal. Like Pinchwife, Sir Jaspar is so insecure about his ability to satisfy his wife that he settles for a form of physical restraint as a substitute for fidelity: he limits her male companions to the supposed eunuch Horner.

Fearful cuckolds are not, however, the only men in the play who speak of women as a source of evil and women's sexual desires as a burden or a threat. As he explains why he writes songs, the fop Sparkish sweepingly condemns the sex and faintly evokes Eve's alleged responsibility for the primal fall. "Women, women," he laments, "that make men do all foolish things, make 'em write Songs too." Even the starry-eyed Harcourt complains of women's draining and callous insatiability: "[T]he vizard Masques you know never pitty a Man when all's gone, though in their Service." Consistently, the focus is on women's demands and men's struggles to satisfy.

Horner joins the other male characters in assuming that women's sexual appetites are voracious. He sees Pinchwife's marriage as futile because he does not believe Pinchwife can ever satisfy a wife:

> So then you only marry'd to keep a Whore to your self; well, but let me tell you, Women, as you say, are like Souldiers made constant and loyal by good pay, rather than by Oaths and Covenants.

Horner's remark does not simply insult Pinchwife; it also suggests that the sexual demands of women are prodigious. Furthermore, as he denies that Pinchwife has protected himself by marrying a country girl, Horner implies that ravenous feminine lust is universal:

> Pshaw, that's all one, that grave circumspection in marrying a Country Wife, is like refusing a deceitful pamper'd *Smithfield* Jade, to go to be cheated by a Friend in the Country.

Horner thus shares with the other male characters the assumption that the sexual appetites of all women are difficult to contain. But he seems to consider this fact an opportunity rather than a threat, a difference crucial to Duncan's (and others') claim that Wycherley uses Horner to satirize "guilt-ridden attitudes to sex." In *The Country Wife,* however, the myth of a sexual fall and its assumptions about women as sexual beings are not simply inverted and parodied by Horner as liberator of natural sexual desire. Rather, as we have seen, the play conforms to the myth in presenting lust as an intimidating, overpowering force and women as carnal, devious, and demanding Eves whose sexual urges the male characters take seriously, even if the women are themselves ludicrous creatures. Moreover, Horner never refers to his stratagems in terms of sexual gratification or liberation. Instead, he appeals repeatedly to a set of "masculine" values that are distinctly anti-sexual.

When Horner and his friends first gather in the play, he declares his preference for the "lasting, rational and manly pleasures" of "good fellowship and good friendship" and his disgust with "love and wenching." But here Horner is apparently expressing his contempt for the pleasures offered by women as part of a ruse designed to secure them. Furthermore, although he claims "manly" pleasures are "rational," he seems to equate male fellowship with drinking, so that by the end of the conversation, he wants only to be "very drunk, and very slovenly." Finally, as Ronald Berman has pointed out [in *Texas Studies in Literature and Language,* 1967], Horner consistently uses friendship as a blind for betrayal in this play. All these points contradict Horner's profession that he genuinely values rational

male fellowship. But this Classical and Renaissance ideal is an important part of Horner's psyche nonetheless, because it underscores his disdain for the alternative: intimidating, draining, and even diabolical relations with women.

The elevation of men as rational, social beings is as old as the denigration of women as selfish, carnal creatures. All Plato's dialogues enact the ideal of rational male discourse, while Aristotle provides a more systematic and explicit exploration of intellectual friendship in his *Nicomachean Ethics* (viii-ix), a work which heavily but indirectly influenced Cicero's famous discussion of the topic, *de Amicitia.* In the Renaissance, friendship was the subject of essays by Castiglione, Bacon, Machiavelli (who, of course, cynically discusses the appropriation and violation of the ideal), and Montaigne, who makes explicit the assumption that rational fellowship is limited to men: "[T]o tell the truth, the ordinary capacity of women is inadequate for that communion and fellowship which is the nurse of this sacred bond; nor does their soul seem firm enough to endure the strain of so tight and durable a knot. . . . But this sex in no instance has yet succeeded in attaining it, and by the common agreement of the ancient schools is excluded from it."

By approaching friendship as a peculiarly masculine relationship in *The Country Wife,* Wycherley not only perpetuates an ancient Western tradition, he continues a pattern in his own career. His first play, *Love in a Wood* (1671), pits romantic interest against the rigid, codified friendship typical of heroic drama. His last, *The Plain Dealer* (1676), might be described as a study of friendship focused, significantly, on a character named "Manly." In addition, Wycherley wrote a poem, **"Upon Friendship, preferre'd to Love,"** according to which friendship is "The Manly Virtue of the Soul, that's Great, / Love, is a Vice, Mean and Effeminate." In *The Country Wife,* Horner voices similar sentiments, referring to sex as a disease and as distinctly unmanly, even when he is not masquerading as embittered and impotent. Speaking to Quack, he characterizes his feigned impotence as "an Antidote for the future, against that damn'd malady, and that worse distemper, love, and all other Womens evils." Although Horner is here telling Quack what to say to those he would deceive, the language he uses is illuminating, for it reveals, both in Horner and in those with whom Quack might converse, familiarity with—if not conscious acceptance of—a conception of women's sexuality as sick and evil. As he speaks more straightforwardly with Quack, Horner echoes the other male characters in describing his sexual partners as demanding and exhausting rather than gratifying and pleasurable. Old mistresses, he complains, are "the most insatiable sort of Duns." He, too, that is, seems intimidated by and hostile toward women as sexual beings, and his avowed preference for "fellowship" to "wenching" should be read as a part of this intimidation and hostility as well as part of the general deception and drunkenness of the male gathering.

Although being "very drunk and very slovenly" is a debasement of the tradition, Horner's associating wine with male fellowship and rational discourse has precedents ranging from Plato's *Symposium* to Ben Jonson's "Inviting a Friend to Supper." Wycherley reinforces the idea that drinking is a distinctly masculine activity in Horner's and Dorilant's litany, which includes lines such as "Wine gives you liberty, Love takes it away" and "Wine gives you joy, Love grief and tortures." The men here see wine as a preferable alternative to sexual relationships. But at their party, which Berman describes as a "grotesque parody of civilized friendship," the ladies treat wine as another "Gallant," a supplement to the "pittance of Pleasure" they receive from their husbands. The two drinking scenes contrast, not only the conviviality and cynicism James Thompson has observed [in his *Language in Wycherley's Plays: Seventeenth-Century Language Theory and Drama,* 1984], but also their respective sources: male rationality and female carnality.

In Sparkish, Wycherley reinforces and focuses the relationship among reason, wine, and male friendship. The others attempt to exclude Sparkish from their circle of friends both because he lacks sense and because, like the cowardly fool Dapperwit in ***Love in a Wood,*** he cannot drink. It is while discussing those like Sparkish who pretend to wit that Horner voices his well-known lines: "A Pox on'em, and all that force Nature, and wou'd be still what she forbids'em; Affectation is her greatest Monster." Horner is here prompted to condemn affectation, not by women who deny their lust, but by men who pretend to sense they do not have, men who fail even to approximate the ideal of intellectual fellowship.

Rather than condemn sexual repression because it forces nature, Horner implies that he himself would like to repress nature as it consists of sexual activity. In his opening speech, an aside that claims a pimp's quack and a bawd's midwife are both "helpers of Nature," Horner equivocates on the word "nature" to justify appropriations of the sexual drive, pimping and whoring. Because Horner is about to exploit a quack for his own purposes (to declare him impotent), his aside suggests that, like the pimp and the whore, he does not value sexual gratification for itself. It implies, that is, that Horner's goal is not natural fulfillment; it is control and appropriation of nature, particularly the natural forces of female sexuality.

The relationship between women's sexuality and natural forces more generally brings us back to witchcraft, for the witches who consorted with devils were also held responsible for unleashing destructive physical forces such as violent storms and sterilizing diseases. The rapid decline in witch hunts after 1650 has been attributed to a new optimism, among scientists especially, about man's ability to understand and control his environment. Significantly, that environment was conceived as a threateningly sensuous woman. Historian Brian Easlea [in his *Witch Hunting, Magic and the New Philosophy: An Introduction to Debates of the Scientific Revolution 1450-1750,* 1980] voices forcefully and succinctly the relevance of seventeenth-century natural philosophy, described by a secretary of the Royal Society as a "Masculine Philosophy," to the misogynist myth informing ***The Country Wife:*** "The 'new philosophers' saw themselves as men equipped to gain for the first time that so elusive and essentially carnal understanding

of nature's inner and emphatically feminine secrets." Knowledge for these men, however, was a relatively modest goal. As Robert Boyle explained, "[S]ome men care only to know nature, others desire to command her." It is this attitude toward nature, not that of a healthy animal, that Horner exhibits as he seeks out "love," that "Womens evil." He seeks control of intimidating physical forces immemorially associated with women. The affinity between Horner and the new science breaks down, however, over the use of language.

His seductive use of figurative and equivocal language seems to place Horner in a tradition of memorable dramatic characters who use language ambiguously in order to confuse their victims and camouflage their ruthless intentions. This tradition, which includes such characters as Shakespeare's Richard III, Middleton and Rowley's De Flores, and Etherege's Dorimant, dates back to the Medieval Vice, whose clever wordplay violated an ideal sense of language as a God-given art meant to complement a God-given nature. Despite his customary self-conscious, self-serving manipulation of language, Horner pretends to subscribe, not merely to a divinely coordinated relationship between word and referent, but to an intrinsic power in truthful words to destroy falsehood. He complains to Lady Fidget:

> [T]o talk of Honour in the mysteries of Love, is
> like talking of Heaven, or the Deity in an opera-
> tion of Witchcraft, just when you are employing
> the Devil, it makes the charm impotent.

Horner here again alludes to witchcraft, a context that reminds us of the extremes to which women allegedly will go for gratification and that presupposes the power of truthful words to reveal the deformity lurking behind false beauty. But Horner's double-entendre on the devil's "charm" belies his alleged respect for such power as it exemplifies his typically equivocal, amoral use of language.

Two other characters allude to a magical power in language. Pinchwife, who earlier curses Horner and "His simile," dimly draws on the legend that correct labeling will itself expose false virtue as he threatens to write "Whore" with his penknife in Margery's face. But his use of the knife indicates the emptiness of that legend for him; he respects and uses only physical restraint and force. Sparkish refers more explicitly to an intrinsic power in language, which he locates in the pen of poets who use "a *Hocus-Pocus*-trick, they have got, which by virtue of *Hictius Doctius, topsey turvey,* they make a wise and witty Man in the World, a Fool upon the Stage you know not how." The Royal Society would join Wycherley in thus ridiculing Sparkish's defensive belief in the magical power of language, but it would also not approve of Horner's equivocation. For those who found the secularization of nature an invitation to rational understanding, language that was figurative, ornamental, and equivocal threatened to obscure and even usurp their knowledge of nature. Hence, the Society's well-known endorsement of a plain, unornamented style, which members characterized as "masculine" and "manly," terms that once again underscore the sexist lines along which the battle with nature was drawn. By equivocating, Horner sallies into the ladies' irrational, deceptive territory, thereby making himself a likely object of their omnivorous desire and thus recapitulating the larger risk he takes by attempting to control women's sexual energy by engaging them sexually. In the china scene, both risks prove unwise as Mrs. Squeamish and Lady Fidget argue metaphorically over Horner's wares:

> LA. FID. Yes indeed Madam, to my certain knowledge he has no more left.
>
> SQUEAM. O but it may be he may have some you could not find.
>
> LA. FID. What d'y think if he had had any left, I would not have had it too, for we women of quality never think we have China enough.
>
> HOR. Do not take it ill, I cannot make China for you all.

Without mentioning the mythic fall, witchcraft, or the new science, F. W. Bateson long ago noted [in *Essays in Criticism,* 1957] that in this scene Horner is displaced as a human being by the china, a phallic symbol from the perspective of the "possessive feminine lust" embodied in both Lady Fidget and Mrs. Squeamish, one satisfied and one not. Horner, "the would-be aggressively masculine woman hunter," disappears. After venturing to combat the carnal, feminine distemper on its own grounds, he is left defenseless and is annihilated, not only by the ladies' lust, but also by their language.

From one perspective, of course, Horner seems anything but a failed antagonist of female sexuality. By the play's end, he has been granted the favors of several women, and his final speech proclaims a continued willingness to be "despis'd" by the men in order to be "priz'd" by the ladies. Wycherley also continues to remind us, however, that the forbidden fruit this sacrifice brings Horner may well be bitter, if not poisonous. The last visual image in the play is "A Dance of Cuckolds," victims of women's insatiability and deception, and the epilogue taunts men who pursue and keep women for show, but who are afraid to engage them sexually. The final lines are especially powerful in conveying the threat women's appetites pose—not to the image these men would impose on a gullible world—but to the virile and confident image they would impose on themselves.

> The World, which to no man his due will give,
> You by experience know you can deceive,
> And men may still believe you Vigorous,
> But then we Women,—there's no cous'ning us.

Most obviously, the final image and lines of the play ridicule the impotent hypocrites whom Horner as parodic satanic seducer helps expose, but the dance and epilogue also resonate with the threatening power of female sexuality that Horner as hostile and inadequate lover cannot control.

The parody of the myth of a sexual fall encourages us to read **The Country Wife** as a radically defiant celebration of natural desire; the subversion of the parody and reassertion of the myth implies that the play is also a document of conservative embattlement. The myth's double function reflects the dual nature of its central figure, the satanic se-

ducer, who, like the libertine more generally, embodies both exhilarating freedom and potency and fearful aggression and hostility—growing paradoxically out of feelings of imprisonment and inadequacy. Noting the rash of misogynist literature in the Restoration (including Wycherley's poetry), Anthony Kaufman speculates [in *Eighteenth-Century Studies,* 1975-76] that hostile aggression toward women is representative of the entire age: "it may be that the new freedom enjoyed by women of the Restoration and the consequent readjustment of sexual roles may have produced a masculine anxiety which expressed itself in art." This theory can be expanded.

The analogy between Horner's sexual pursuits and contemporary philosopher's assault on nature suggests that the Restoration is characterized most profoundly, not by an extraordinary ambivalence toward women as both pleasurable and threatening, but by a more general ambivalence toward a new world that is exciting yet frightening on several fronts: political and social as well as sexual and scientific. Deadly maneuvering over royal succession, for example, or Hobbesian assumptions about human relations can account for competing senses of opportunity and insecurity as well as newly liberated women can. But women, as is often the case, became the literary embodiment of all kinds of conflicting desires and fears. And the myth of a sexual fall was among the most congenial to expressing the powerful, contradictory emotions men were feeling about their seductive, intimidating new environment. Horner elicits the endless stream of critical commentary he does because he so richly taps the mythic fears and aspirations of his age. As the central agent of Wycherley's parody of a sexual fall, he escorts us into a world that has called a halt to the massive witch hunts of the previous generations, that is shedding superstitions and their moral baggage, and that no longer distrusts human carnality. But the parody itself can be seen as an aggressive attempt at conquest motivated as much by insecurity as by confidence. The limited success of that attempt reminds us this was also an age that covered uncertainty with bravado, that may have replaced witch hunts with science, but that was still animated by the same fear of powerful physical forces. (pp. 100-14)

Peggy Thompson, "The Limits of Parody in 'The Country Wife'," in Studies in Philology, *Vol. LXXXIX, No. 1, Winter, 1992, pp. 100-14.*

FURTHER READING

Auffret, J. M. "*The Man of Mode* and *The Plain Dealer:* Common Origin & Parallels." *Etudes Anglaises* XIX, No. 3 (July-September 1966): 209-22.

> Provides evidence that *The Plain-Dealer*'s Manly is a portrayal of the Earl of Mulgrave.

Beauchamp, Gorman. "The Amorous Machiavellism of *The*

Country Wife." *Comparative Drama* 11, No. 4 (Winter 1977-78): 316-30.

Asserts that Horner, as a Machiavellian prince of sex, is unquestionably the hero of *The Country-Wife.*

Bowman, John S. "Dance, Chant, and Mask in the Plays of Wycherley." *Drama Survey* 3, No. 2 (October 1963): 181-205.

Interesting suggestion that Wycherley's inclusion of "the movement of the dance, the rhythm of the chant, the duality of the mask" both mirrors and complements the meaning of his plays.

Dearing, Vinton A. "Pope, Theobald, and Wycherley's *Posthumous Works.*" *PMLA* LXVIII, No. 1 (March 1953): 223-36.

Gives the background of Alexander Pope's edition of Wycherley's posthumous works and compares it with Lewis Theobald's rival edition.

Donaldson, Ian. " 'Tables Turned': *The Plain Dealer.*" *Essays in Criticism* XVII, No. 3 (July 1967): 304-21.

Analysis of paradoxes and contradictions in *The Plain-Dealer.*

Duncan, Douglas. "Mythic Parody in *The Country Wife.*" *Essays in Criticism* XXI, No. 4 (October 1981): 299-312.

Analyzes Wycherley's use of religious and secular myths in his witty discussion of sexual relations in *The Country-Wife.*

Empson, William. "Honest Man." In his *The Structure of Complex Words,* pp. 185-201. Totowa, N.J.: Rowman and Littlefield, 1979.

Study of the changing meaning of the word "honest" in various works of literature, including its significance in *The Plain-Dealer.*

Friedson, A. M. "Wycherley and Molière: Satirical Point of View in *The Plain Dealer.*" *Modern Philology* 64, No. 3 (February 1967): 189-97.

Comparison of *The Plain-Dealer* with Molière's *Le misanthrope.* The essay pays particular attention to the differences between the two plays to illustrate Friedson's contention that Wycherley's satire is directed at society rather than at Manly.

Fujimura, Thomas H. "William Wycherley." In his *The Restoration Comedy of Wit,* pp. 117-55. 1952. Reprint. New York: Barnes & Noble, 1968.

Criticism of Wycherley's plays in which characters are classified as Truewit, Witwoud, or Witless.

Gosse, Edmund. "Wycherley." In his *Silhouettes,* pp. 63-9. New York: Charles Scribner's Sons, 1925.

Short, mostly biographical discussion of Wycherley. Gosse speculates that Wycherley's sojourn in France furnished him with the models for his dramatic characters, who are "French in essence."

Hughes, Derek. "Naming and Entitlement in Wycherley, Etherege, and Dryden." *Comparative Drama* 21, No. 3 (Fall 1987): 259-89.

Investigates the correlation between the linguistic and the social orders in the dramas of Wycherley, Etherege, and Dryden. Hughes maintains that for these playwrights, language revealed the disunion between subjective experience and reality.

Hume, Robert D. "William Wycherley: Text, Life, Interpretation." *Modern Philology* 78, No. 4 (May 1981): 399-415.

Traces the body of criticism surrounding Wycherley's person and work. Hume asserts that the complexity of the plays allows for a variety of meanings and dramatic interpretations.

Kaufman, Anthony. "Wycherley's *The Country Wife* and the Don Juan Character." *Eighteenth-Century Studies* 9, No. 2 (Winter 1975-76): 216-31.

Classifies the character of *The Country-Wife*'s Horner in terms of the Don Juan archetype and Freudian sexual psychology.

Lamb, Charles. "On the Artificial Comedy of the Last Century." In his *The Essays of Elia,* pp. 172-80. New York: A. L. Burt, 1885?

Defends Restoration comedy from the charge of immorality. Lamb contends that the world of Restoration comedy cannot be subjected to moral criteria because it is "altogether a speculative scene of things, which has no reference whatever to the world that is."

Lynch, Kathleen M. "The Period of Etherege." In her *The Social Mode of Restoration Comedy,* pp. 137-81. New York: Macmillan Co., 1926.

Assesses Wycherley's literary debt to Molière and gauges the attitude toward Restoration society expressed in his plays.

Malekin, Peter. " 'Imparadist in One Anothers Arms' or 'The Ecclesiastical Mouse-trap': Marriage in Restoration Comedy." In his *Liberty and Love: English Literature and Society, 1640-88,* pp. 15-95. New York: St. Martin's Press, 1981.

Study of the sexual mores and social attitudes surrounding love and marriage in the Restoration era. Malekin cites examples from the plays of Wycherley and other Restoration dramatists to illustrate the link between literature and social conditions.

Mann, David D. "The Function of the Quack in *The Country Wife.*" *Restoration* 7, No. 1 (Spring 1983): 19-22.

A re-evaluation of the role of Quack in *The Country-Wife.* Mann contends that the character represents the audience on stage as well as Wycherley's outlook on humanity and the world.

Marshall, W. Gerald. "Wycherley's *Love in a Wood* and the Designs of Providence." *Restoration: Studies in English Literary Culture, 1660-1700* 3, No. 1 (Spring 1979): 8-16.

Considers *Love in a Wood* dramatically illustrative of the workings of divine Providence.

———. "Wycherley's Drama of Madness: *The Plain Dealer.*" *Philological Quarterly* 59, No. 1 (Winter 1980): 26-37.

Views *The Plain-Dealer* as a study of obsessive thinking and behavior.

Matalene, H. W. "What Happens in *The Country-Wife.*" *Studies in English Literature, 1500-1900* 22, No. 3 (Summer 1982): 395-411.

Interpretation of Horner in *The Country-Wife.* Matalene argues that Horner's scheme is motivated not by a wish to express his sexuality but by his "homosocial" desires—that is, Horner pursues sexual liaisons with women in order to achieve status with his male peers.

Matlack, Cynthia. "Parody and Burlesque of Heroic Ideals in Wycherley's Comedies: A Critical Reinterpretation of

Contemporary Evidence." *Papers on Language and Literature* VIII, No. 3 (Summer 1972): 273-86.

> Postulates that Wycherley experimented with a burlesque heroic mode within his comedies "to set in opposition different codes of behavior among characters who accept disparate sets of values."

McCarthy, B. Eugene. *William Wycherley: A Biography.* Athens: Ohio University Press, 1979, 255 p.

> Thorough, straightforward biography. McCarthy states that his design in the book is "to make Wycherley a little more visible, a little more knowable and enjoyable."

Milhous, Judith and Hume, Robert D. *"The Country Wife."* In their *Producible Interpretation: Eight English Plays, 1675-1707,* pp. 73-106. Carbondale: Southern Illinois University Press, 1985.

> Analyzes significant critical readings of *The Country-Wife,* outlining several "stageable interpretations" of the play.

Muir, Kenneth. "William Wycherley." In his *The Comedy of Manners,* pp. 67-83. London: Hutchinson University Library, 1970.

> General discussion of Wycherley's plays—their sources, satire, bawdiness, and value.

Mukherjee, Sujit. "Marriage as Punishment in the Plays of Wycherley." *A Review of English Literature* 7, No. 4 (October 1966): 61-4.

> Concludes that Wycherley had such a negative view of marriage that he used it in his work as "an instrument of poetic justice" to punish his characters.

Payne, Deborah C. "Reading the Signs in *The Country Wife.*" *Studies in English Literature, 1500-1900* 26, No. 3 (Summer 1986): 403-19.

> Interprets *The Country-Wife* as an expression (and perhaps indictment) of the indirect and often duplicitous communication prevalent in Restoration society, wherein language, being an inadequate indicator of meaning, was largely replaced by an intricate system of "cultural codes."

Peters, Julie Stone. " 'Things Govern'd by Words': Late 17th-Century Comedy and the Reformers." *English Studies* 68, No. 2 (April 1987): 142-53.

> Examines Wycherley's, Etherege's, and Congreve's rejection of self-referential, involuted language and their attempt in their principal dramas to give new life to the English language through a purposeful joining of words to concrete realities.

Rundle, James Urvin. "Wycherley and Calderón: A Source for *Love in a Wood.*" *PMLA* LXIV, No. 4 (September 1949): 701-07.

> Details the similarities and differences between *Love in a Wood* and its Spanish source, Pedro Calderón's *Mañanas de abril y mayo.* Rundle concludes that "there is no other Restoration play that assimilates Spanish material so poorly."

Stathis, James J. "Those Admirable Devils: The Heroes of Restoration Comedy." In *All the World: Drama Past and Present,* Vol. II, pp. 107-16. Edited by Karelisa V. Hartigan. Washington, D.C.: University Press of America, 1982.

> Explores the role of the devil as symbol of the human quest for freedom and independence in the dramas of Wycherley, Etherege, and Vanbrugh.

Steiger, Richard. " 'Wit in a Corner': Hypocrisy in *The Country Wife.*" In *Tennessee Studies in Literature,* Vol. XXIV, edited by Allison R. Ensor and Thomas J. A. Heffernan, pp. 56-70. Knoxville: University of Tennessee Press, 1979.

> Defines the hypocrisy so prevalent in *The Country-Wife* as a necessary, morally neutral gap between the requirements of social order and the actual behavior of individuals.

Verdurmen, J. Peter. "Grasping for Permanence: Ideal Couples in *The Country Wife* and *Aureng-Zebe.*" *The Huntingdon Library Quarterly* XLII, No. 4 (Autumn 1979): 329-47.

> Examines the relationship between status and change in *The Country-Wife* and John Dryden's *Aureng-Zebe.*

Vernon, P. F. *William Wycherley.* London: Longmans, Green & Co., 1965, 44 p.

> Short but thorough examination of Wycherley's life and work.

———. "Wycherley's First Comedy and Its Spanish Source." *Comparative Literature* XVIII, No. 2 (Spring 1966): 132-44.

> Comparison of *Love in a Wood* with Pedro Calderón's *Mañanas de abril y mayo.* Vernon argues that Wycherley "borrowed with discrimination" and that "his revisions of his source reveal a consistent awareness of the play's total meaning and effect."

Vieth, David M. "Wycherley's *The Country Wife:* An Anatomy of Masculinity." *Papers on Language and Literature* 2, No. 4 (Fall 1966): 335-50.

> Analysis of *The Country-Wife* which describes the play as "centrally concerned with providing a definition of masculinity." Vieth argues that Pinchwife, Sir Jasper, and Sparkish typify failed masculinity due to sexual and personal inadequacies.

Weber, Harold. "The Rake-Hero in Wycherley and Congreve." *Philological Quarterly* 61, No. 2 (Spring 1982): 143-60.

> Compares *The Country-Wife*'s Horner to William Congreve's libertine heroes, finding Horner unusual in his natural, unadulterated, and "joyous sexuality."

Zimbardo, Rose. "Wycherley: The Restoration's Juvenal." *Forum* 17, No. 1 (Winter 1979): 17-26.

> Contends that Wycherley's plays are not comedies of manners but moral satires after the fashion of Juvenal.

Literature
Criticism from
1400 to 1800
Cumulative Indexes

This Index Includes References to Entries in These Gale Series

Contemporary Literary Criticism Presents excerpts of criticism on the works of novelists, poets, dramatists, short story writers, scriptwriters, and other creative writers who are now living or who have died since 1960.

Twentieth-Century Literary Criticism Contains critical excerpts by the most significant commentators on poets, novelists, short story writers, dramatists, and philosophers who died between 1900 and 1960.

Nineteenth-Century Literature Criticism Offers significant passages from criticism on authors who died between 1800 and 1899.

Literature Criticism from 1400 to 1800 Compiles significant passages from the most noteworthy criticism on authors of the fifteenth through eighteenth centuries.

Classical and Medieval Literature Criticism Offers excerpts of criticism on the works of world authors from classical antiquity through the fourteenth century.

Short Story Criticism Compiles excerpts of criticism on short fiction by writers of all eras and nationalities.

Poetry Criticism Presents excerpts of criticism on the works of poets from all eras, movements, and nationalities.

Drama Criticism Contains excerpts of criticism on dramatists of all nationalities and periods of literary history.

Children's Literature Review Includes excerpts from reviews, criticism, and commentary on works of authors and illustrators who create books for children.

Contemporary Authors Series Encompasses five related series. *Contemporary Authors* provides biographical and bibliographical information on more than 97,000 writers of fiction, nonfiction, poetry, journalism, drama, motion pictures, and other fields. Each new volume contains sketches on authors not previously covered in the series. *Contemporary Authors New Revision Series* provides completely updated information on active authors covered in previously published volumes of *CA*. Only entries requiring significant change are revised for *CA New Revision Series. Contemporary Authors Permanent Series* consists of updated listings for deceased and inactive authors removed from the original volumes 9-36 when these volumes were revised. *Contemporary Authors Autobiography Series* presents specially commissioned autobiographies by leading contemporary writers. *Contemporary Authors Bibliographical Series* contains primary and secondary bibliographies as well as analytical bibliographical essays by authorities on major modern authors.

Dictionary of Literary Biography Encompasses three related series. *Dictionary of Literary Biography* furnishes illustrated overviews of authors' lives and works and places them in the larger perspective of literary history. *Dictionary of Literary Biography Documentary Series* illuminates the careers of major figures through a selection of literary documents, including letters, notebook and diary entries, interviews, book reviews, and photographs. *Dictionary of Literary Biography Yearbook* summarizes the past year's literary activity with articles on genres, major prizes, conferences, and other timely subjects and includes updated and new entries on individual authors.

Concise Dictionary of American Literary Biography A six-volume series that collects revised and updated sketches on major American authors that were originally presented in *Dictionary of Literary Biography*.

Something about the Author Series Encompasses three related series. *Something about the Author* contains well-illustrated biographical sketches on juvenile and young adult authors and illustrators from all eras. *Something about the Author Autobiography Series* presents specially commissioned autobiographies by prominent authors and illustrators of books for children and young adults.

Yesterday's Authors of Books for Children Contains heavily illustrated entries on children's writers who died before 1961. Complete in two volumes.

Literary Criticism Series
Cumulative Author Index

A. E. . . . . TCLC 3, 10
See also Russell, George William
See also DLB 19

A. M.
See Megged, Aharon

Abasiyanik, Sait Faik   1906-1954
See Sait Faik
See also CA 123

Abbey, Edward   1927-1989 . . . . . . CLC 36, 59
See also CA 45-48; 128; CANR 2

Abbott, Lee K(ittredge)   1947- . . . . . . CLC 48
See also CA 124

Abe Kobo   1924- . . . . CLC 8, 22, 53
See also CA 65-68; CANR 24; MTCW

Abell, Kjeld   1901-1961. . . . . CLC 15
See also CA 111

Abish, Walter   1931- . . . . CLC 22
See also CA 101; CANR 37

Abrahams, Peter (Henry)   1919- . . . . . CLC 4
See also BW; CA 57-60; CANR 26;
DLB 117; MTCW

Abrams, M(eyer) H(oward)   1912-. . . CLC 24
See also CA 57-60; CANR 13, 33; DLB 67

Abse, Dannie   1923-. . . . . CLC 7, 29
See also CA 53-56; CAAS 1; CANR 4;
DLB 27

Achebe, (Albert) Chinua(lumogu)
1930- . . . . CLC 1, 3, 5, 7, 11, 26, 51
See also BLC 1; BW; CA 1-4R; CANR 6,
26; CLR 20; DLB 117; MAICYA;
MTCW; SATA 38, 40; WLC

Acker, Kathy   1948- . . . . CLC 45
See also CA 117; 122

Ackroyd, Peter   1949-. . . . . CLC 34, 52
See also CA 123; 127

Acorn, Milton   1923-. . . . . CLC 15
See also CA 103; DLB 53

Adamov, Arthur   1908-1970 . . . . . . CLC 4, 25
See also CA 17-18; 25-28R; CAP 2; MTCW

Adams, Alice (Boyd)   1926- . . . CLC 6, 13, 46
See also CA 81-84; CANR 26; DLBY 86;
MTCW

Adams, Douglas (Noel)   1952- . . . CLC 27, 60
See also AAYA 4; BEST 89:3; CA 106;
CANR 34; DLBY 83

Adams, Francis   1862-1893. . . . . . . NCLC 33

Adams, Henry (Brooks)
1838-1918 . . . . TCLC 4
See also CA 104; 133; DLB 12, 47

Adams, Richard (George)
1920- . . . . CLC 4, 5, 18
See also AITN 1, 2; CA 49-52; CANR 3,
35; CLR 20; MAICYA; MTCW;
SATA 7, 69

Adamson, Joy(-Friederike Victoria)
1910-1980 . . . . CLC 17
See also CA 69-72; 93-96; CANR 22;
MTCW; SATA 11, 22

Adcock, Fleur   1934-. . . . . CLC 41
See also CA 25-28R; CANR 11, 34;
DLB 40

Addams, Charles (Samuel)
1912-1988 . . . . CLC 30
See also CA 61-64; 126; CANR 12

Addison, Joseph   1672-1719 . . . . LC 18
See also CDBLB 1660-1789; DLB 101

Adler, C(arole) S(chwerdtfeger)
1932- . . . . CLC 35
See also AAYA 4; CA 89-92; CANR 19;
MAICYA; SATA 26, 63

Adler, Renata   1938-. . . . . CLC 8, 31
See also CA 49-52; CANR 5, 22; MTCW

Ady, Endre   1877-1919 . . . . TCLC 11
See also CA 107

Afton, Effie
See Harper, Frances Ellen Watkins

Agapida, Fray Antonio
See Irving, Washington

Agee, James (Rufus)
1909-1955. . . . . TCLC 1, 19
See also AITN 1; CA 108;
CDALB 1941-1968; DLB 2, 26

Aghill, Gordon
See Silverberg, Robert

Agnon, S(hmuel) Y(osef Halevi)
1888-1970 . . . . CLC 4, 8, 14
See also CA 17-18; 25-28R; CAP 2; MTCW

Aherne, Owen
See Cassill, R(onald) V(erlin)

Ai   1947-. . . . . CLC 4, 14, 69
See also CA 85-88; CAAS 13; DLB 120

Aickman, Robert (Fordyce)
1914-1981 . . . . CLC 57
See also CA 5-8R; CANR 3

Aiken, Conrad (Potter)
1889-1973 . . . CLC 1, 3, 5, 10, 52; SSC 9
See also CA 5-8R; 45-48; CANR 4;
CDALB 1929-1941; DLB 9, 45, 102;
MTCW; SATA 3, 30

Aiken, Joan (Delano)   1924-. . . . . CLC 35
See also AAYA 1; CA 9-12R; CANR 4, 23,
34; CLR 1, 19; MAICYA; MTCW;
SAAS 1; SATA 2, 30

Ainsworth, William Harrison
1805-1882 . . . . NCLC 13
See also DLB 21; SATA 24

Aitmatov, Chingiz (Torekulovich)
1928- . . . . CLC 71
See also CA 103; CANR 38; MTCW;
SATA 56

Akers, Floyd
See Baum, L(yman) Frank

Akhmadulina, Bella Akhatovna
1937- . . . . CLC 53
See also CA 65-68

Akhmatova, Anna
1888-1966 . . . . CLC 11, 25, 64; PC 2
See also CA 19-20; 25-28R; CANR 35;
CAP 1; MTCW

Aksakov, Sergei Timofeyvich
1791-1859 . . . . NCLC 2

Aksenov, Vassily. . . . . CLC 22
See also Aksyonov, Vassily (Pavlovich)

Aksyonov, Vassily (Pavlovich)
1932-. . . . . CLC 37
See also Aksenov, Vassily
See also CA 53-56; CANR 12

Akutagawa Ryunosuke
1892-1927 . . . . TCLC 16
See also CA 117

Alain   1868-1951 . . . . TCLC 41

Alain-Fournier. . . . . TCLC 6
See also Fournier, Henri Alban
See also DLB 65

Alarcon, Pedro Antonio de
1833-1891 . . . . NCLC 1

Alas (y Urena), Leopoldo (Enrique Garcia)
1852-1901 . . . . TCLC 29
See also CA 113; 131; HW

Albee, Edward (Franklin III)
1928- . . . CLC 1, 2, 3, 5, 9, 11, 13, 25, 53
See also AITN 1; CA 5-8R; CABS 3;
CANR 8; CDALB 1941-1968; DLB 7;
MTCW; WLC

Alberti, Rafael   1902-. . . . . CLC 7
See also CA 85-88; DLB 108

Alcala-Galiano, Juan Valera y
See Valera y Alcala-Galiano, Juan

Alcott, Amos Bronson   1799-1888 . . NCLC 1
See also DLB 1

Alcott, Louisa May   1832-1888 . . . . NCLC 6
See also CDALB 1865-1917; CLR 1;
DLB 1, 42, 79; MAICYA; WLC;
YABC 1

Aldanov, M. A.
See Aldanov, Mark (Alexandrovich)

Aldanov, Mark (Alexandrovich)
1886(?)-1957 . . . . TCLC 23
See also CA 118

Aldington, Richard   1892-1962. . . . . . CLC 49
See also CA 85-88; DLB 20, 36, 100

Aldiss, Brian W(ilson)
1925-. . . . . CLC 5, 14, 40
See also CA 5-8R; CAAS 2; CANR 5, 28;
DLB 14; MTCW; SATA 34

Alegria, Fernando   1918-. . . . . CLC 57
See also CA 9-12R; CANR 5, 32; HW

Aleichem, Sholom . . . . TCLC 1, 35
See also Rabinovitch, Sholem

Aleixandre, Vicente 1898-1984 . . . **CLC 9, 36**
See also CA 85-88; 114; CANR 26;
DLB 108; HW; MTCW

Alepoudelis, Odysseus
See Elytis, Odysseus

Aleshkovsky, Joseph 1929-
See Aleshkovsky, Yuz
See also CA 121; 128

Aleshkovsky, Yuz . . . . **CLC 44**
See also Aleshkovsky, Joseph

Alexander, Lloyd (Chudley) 1924- . . **CLC 35**
See also AAYA 1; CA 1-4R; CANR 1, 24,
38; CLR 1, 5; DLB 52; MAICYA;
MTCW; SATA 3, 49

Alfau, Felipe 1902- . . . . **CLC 66**
See also CA 137

Alger, Horatio Jr. 1832-1899 . . . . . **NCLC 8**
See also DLB 42; SATA 16

Algren, Nelson 1909-1981 . . . . **CLC 4, 10, 33**
See also CA 13-16R; 103; CANR 20;
CDALB 1941-1968; DLB 9; DLBY 81,
82; MTCW

Ali, Ahmed 1910- . . . . **CLC 69**
See also CA 25-28R; CANR 15, 34

Alighieri, Dante 1265-1321 . . . . **CMLC 3**

Allan, John B.
See Westlake, Donald E(dwin)

Allen, Edward 1948- . . . . **CLC 59**

Allen, Roland
See Ayckbourn, Alan

Allen, Woody 1935- . . . . **CLC 16, 52**
See also CA 33-36R; CANR 27, 38;
DLB 44; MTCW

Allende, Isabel 1942- . . . . **CLC 39, 57**
See also CA 125; 130; HW; MTCW

Alleyn, Ellen
See Rossetti, Christina (Georgina)

Allingham, Margery (Louise)
1904-1966 . . . . **CLC 19**
See also CA 5-8R; 25-28R; CANR 4;
DLB 77; MTCW

Allingham, William 1824-1889 . . . **NCLC 25**
See also DLB 35

Allston, Washington 1779-1843 . . . . **NCLC 2**
See also DLB 1

Almedingen, E. M. . . . . **CLC 12**
See also Almedingen, Martha Edith von
See also SATA 3

Almedingen, Martha Edith von 1898-1971
See Almedingen, E. M.
See also CA 1-4R; CANR 1

Alonso, Damaso 1898-1990 . . . . **CLC 14**
See also CA 110; 131; 130; DLB 108; HW

Alta 1942- . . . . **CLC 19**
See also CA 57-60

Alter, Robert B(ernard) 1935- . . . . . . **CLC 34**
See also CA 49-52; CANR 1

Alther, Lisa 1944- . . . . **CLC 7, 41**
See also CA 65-68; CANR 12, 30; MTCW

Altman, Robert 1925- . . . . **CLC 16**
See also CA 73-76

Alvarez, A(lfred) 1929- . . . . **CLC 5, 13**
See also CA 1-4R; CANR 3, 33; DLB 14,
40

Alvarez, Alejandro Rodriguez 1903-1965
See Casona, Alejandro
See also CA 131; 93-96; HW

Amado, Jorge 1912- . . . . **CLC 13, 40**
See also CA 77-80; CANR 35; DLB 113;
MTCW

Ambler, Eric 1909- . . . . **CLC 4, 6, 9**
See also CA 9-12R; CANR 7, 38; DLB 77;
MTCW

Amichai, Yehuda 1924- . . . . . . **CLC 9, 22, 57**
See also CA 85-88; MTCW

Amiel, Henri Frederic 1821-1881 . . **NCLC 4**

Amis, Kingsley (William)
1922- . . . . . . **CLC 1, 2, 3, 5, 8, 13, 40, 44**
See also AITN 2; CA 9-12R; CANR 8, 28;
CDBLB 1945-1960; DLB 15, 27, 100;
MTCW

Amis, Martin (Louis)
1949- . . . . **CLC 4, 9, 38, 62**
See also BEST 90:3; CA 65-68; CANR 8,
27; DLB 14

Ammons, A(rchie) R(andolph)
1926- . . . . **CLC 2, 3, 5, 8, 9, 25, 57**
See also AITN 1; CA 9-12R; CANR 6, 36;
DLB 5; MTCW

Amo, Tauraatua i
See Adams, Henry (Brooks)

Anand, Mulk Raj 1905- . . . . **CLC 23**
See also CA 65-68; CANR 32; MTCW

Anatol
See Schnitzler, Arthur

Anaya, Rudolfo A(lfonso) 1937- . . . . **CLC 23**
See also CA 45-48; CAAS 4; CANR 1, 32;
DLB 82; HW; MTCW

Andersen, Hans Christian
1805-1875 . . . . **NCLC 7; SSC 6**
See also CLR 6; MAICYA; WLC; YABC 1

Anderson, C. Farley
See Mencken, H(enry) L(ouis); Nathan,
George Jean

Anderson, Jessica (Margaret) Queale
. . . . **CLC 37**
See also CA 9-12R; CANR 4

Anderson, Jon (Victor) 1940- . . . . **CLC 9**
See also CA 25-28R; CANR 20

Anderson, Lindsay (Gordon)
1923- . . . . **CLC 20**
See also CA 125; 128

Anderson, Maxwell 1888-1959 . . . . . **TCLC 2**
See also CA 105; DLB 7

Anderson, Poul (William) 1926- . . . . **CLC 15**
See also AAYA 5; CA 1-4R; CAAS 2;
CANR 2, 15, 34; DLB 8; MTCW;
SATA 39

Anderson, Robert (Woodruff)
1917- . . . . **CLC 23**
See also AITN 1; CA 21-24R; CANR 32;
DLB 7

Anderson, Sherwood
1876-1941 . . . . . . **TCLC 1, 10, 24; SSC 1**
See also CA 104; 121; CDALB 1917-1929;
DLB 4, 9, 86; DLBD 1; MTCW; WLC

Andouard
See Giraudoux, (Hippolyte) Jean

Andrade, Carlos Drummond de . . . . . . **CLC 18**
See also Drummond de Andrade, Carlos

Andrade, Mario de 1893-1945 . . . . . **TCLC 43**

Andrewes, Lancelot 1555-1626 . . . . **LC 5**

Andrews, Cicily Fairfield
See West, Rebecca

Andrews, Elton V.
See Pohl, Frederik

Andreyev, Leonid (Nikolaevich)
1871-1919 . . . . **TCLC 3**
See also CA 104

Andric, Ivo 1892-1975 . . . . **CLC 8**
See also CA 81-84; 57-60; MTCW

Angelique, Pierre
See Bataille, Georges

Angell, Roger 1920- . . . . **CLC 26**
See also CA 57-60; CANR 13

Angelou, Maya 1928- . . . . **CLC 12, 35, 64**
See also AAYA 7; BLC 1; BW; CA 65-68;
CANR 19; DLB 38; MTCW; SATA 49

Annensky, Innokenty Fyodorovich
1856-1909 . . . . **TCLC 14**
See also CA 110

Anon, Charles Robert
See Pessoa, Fernando (Antonio Nogueira)

Anouilh, Jean (Marie Lucien Pierre)
1910-1987 . . . . . . **CLC 1, 3, 8, 13, 40, 50**
See also CA 17-20R; 123; CANR 32;
MTCW

Anthony, Florence
See Ai

Anthony, John
See Ciardi, John (Anthony)

Anthony, Peter
See Shaffer, Anthony (Joshua); Shaffer,
Peter (Levin)

Anthony, Piers 1934- . . . . **CLC 35**
See also CA 21-24R; CANR 28; DLB 8;
MTCW

Antoine, Marc
See Proust,
(Valentin-Louis-George-Eugene-)Marcel

Antoninus, Brother
See Everson, William (Oliver)

Antonioni, Michelangelo 1912- . . . . . **CLC 20**
See also CA 73-76

Antschel, Paul 1920-1970 . . . . **CLC 10, 19**
See also Celan, Paul
See also CA 85-88; CANR 33; MTCW

Anwar, Chairil 1922-1949 . . . . **TCLC 22**
See also CA 121

Apollinaire, Guillaume . . . . **TCLC 3, 8**
See also Kostrowitzki, Wilhelm Apollinaris
de

Appelfeld, Aharon 1932- . . . . **CLC 23, 47**
See also CA 112; 133

Apple, Max (Isaac) 1941- . . . . **CLC 9, 33**
See also CA 81-84; CANR 19

Appleman, Philip (Dean) 1926- . . . . . **CLC 51**
See also CA 13-16R; CANR 6, 29

Appleton, Lawrence
See Lovecraft, H(oward) P(hillips)

Author Index

Apuleius, (Lucius Madaurensis)
　125(?)-175(?) . . . . **CMLC 1**

Aquin, Hubert 1929-1977. . . . . **CLC 15**
　See also CA 105; DLB 53

Aragon, Louis 1897-1982. . . . . . . **CLC 3, 22**
　See also CA 69-72; 108; CANR 28;
　DLB 72; MTCW

Arany, Janos 1817-1882. . . . . **NCLC 34**

Arbuthnot, John 1667-1735 . . . . **LC 1**
　See also DLB 101

Archer, Herbert Winslow
　See Mencken, H(enry) L(ouis)

Archer, Jeffrey (Howard) 1940- . . . . **CLC 28**
　See also BEST 89:3; CA 77-80; CANR 22

Archer, Jules 1915- . . . . **CLC 12**
　See also CA 9-12R; CANR 6; SAAS 5;
　SATA 4

Archer, Lee
　See Ellison, Harlan

Arden, John 1930- . . . . **CLC 6, 13, 15**
　See also CA 13-16R; CAAS 4; CANR 31;
　DLB 13; MTCW

Arenas, Reinaldo 1943-1990 . . . . . . **CLC 41**
　See also CA 124; 128; 133; HW

Arendt, Hannah 1906-1975 . . . . . . **CLC 66**
　See also CA 17-20R; 61-64; CANR 26;
　MTCW

Aretino, Pietro 1492-1556 . . . . **LC 12**

Arguedas, Jose Maria
　1911-1969 . . . . **CLC 10, 18**
　See also CA 89-92; DLB 113; HW

Argueta, Manlio 1936- . . . . **CLC 31**
　See also CA 131; HW

Ariosto, Ludovico 1474-1533. . . . . **LC 6**

Aristides
　See Epstein, Joseph

Aristophanes
　450B.C.-385B.C. . . . . **CMLC 4; DC 2**

Arlt, Roberto (Godofredo Christophersen)
　1900-1942 . . . . **TCLC 29**
　See also CA 123; 131; HW

Armah, Ayi Kwei 1939- . . . . **CLC 5, 33**
　See also BLC 1; BW; CA 61-64; CANR 21;
　DLB 117; MTCW

Armatrading, Joan 1950- . . . . **CLC 17**
　See also CA 114

Arnette, Robert
　See Silverberg, Robert

Arnim, Achim von (Ludwig Joachim von
　Arnim) 1781-1831 . . . . **NCLC 5**
　See also DLB 90

Arnim, Bettina von 1785-1859. . . . **NCLC 38**
　See also DLB 90

Arnold, Matthew
　1822-1888 . . . . **NCLC 6, 29; PC 5**
　See also CDBLB 1832-1890; DLB 32, 57;
　WLC

Arnold, Thomas 1795-1842 . . . . . . **NCLC 18**
　See also DLB 55

Arnow, Harriette (Louisa) Simpson
　1908-1986 . . . . **CLC 2, 7, 18**
　See also CA 9-12R; 118; CANR 14; DLB 6;
　MTCW; SATA 42, 47

Arp, Hans
　See Arp, Jean

Arp, Jean 1887-1966. . . . . **CLC 5**
　See also CA 81-84; 25-28R

Arrabal . . . . **CLC 2, 9, 18**
　See also Arrabal, Fernando

Arrabal, Fernando 1932- . . . . **CLC 58**
　See also Arrabal
　See also CA 9-12R; CANR 15

Arrick, Fran . . . . **CLC 30**

Artaud, Antonin 1896-1948 . . . . . **TCLC 3, 36**
　See also CA 104

Arthur, Ruth M(abel) 1905-1979. . . . **CLC 12**
　See also CA 9-12R; 85-88; CANR 4;
　SATA 7, 26

Artsybashev, Mikhail (Petrovich)
　1878-1927 . . . . **TCLC 31**

Arundel, Honor (Morfydd)
　1919-1973 . . . . **CLC 17**
　See also CA 21-22; 41-44R; CAP 2;
　SATA 4, 24

Asch, Sholem 1880-1957 . . . . **TCLC 3**
　See also CA 105

Ash, Shalom
　See Asch, Sholem

Ashbery, John (Lawrence)
　1927- . . . **CLC 2, 3, 4, 6, 9, 13, 15, 25, 41**
　See also CA 5-8R; CANR 9, 37; DLB 5;
　DLBY 81; MTCW

Ashdown, Clifford
　See Freeman, R(ichard) Austin

Ashe, Gordon
　See Creasey, John

Ashton-Warner, Sylvia (Constance)
　1908-1984 . . . . **CLC 19**
　See also CA 69-72; 112; CANR 29; MTCW

Asimov, Isaac
　1920-1992 . . . . **CLC 1, 3, 9, 19, 26**
　See also BEST 90:2; CA 1-4R; 137;
　CANR 2, 19, 36; CLR 12; DLB 8;
　MAICYA; MTCW; SATA 1, 26

Astley, Thea (Beatrice May)
　1925- . . . . **CLC 41**
　See also CA 65-68; CANR 11

Aston, James
　See White, T(erence) H(anbury)

Asturias, Miguel Angel
　1899-1974 . . . . **CLC 3, 8, 13**
　See also CA 25-28; 49-52; CANR 32;
　CAP 2; DLB 113; HW; MTCW

Atares, Carlos Saura
　See Saura (Atares), Carlos

Atheling, William
　See Pound, Ezra (Weston Loomis)

Atheling, William Jr.
　See Blish, James (Benjamin)

Atherton, Gertrude (Franklin Horn)
　1857-1948 . . . . **TCLC 2**
　See also CA 104; DLB 9, 78

Atherton, Lucius
　See Masters, Edgar Lee

Atkins, Jack
　See Harris, Mark

Atticus
　See Fleming, Ian (Lancaster)

Atwood, Margaret (Eleanor)
　1939- . . . . **CLC 2, 3, 4, 8, 13, 15, 25, 44;**
　　　　　　　　　　　　　　　　　　　SSC 2
　See also BEST 89:2; CA 49-52; CANR 3,
　24, 33; DLB 53; MTCW; SATA 50; WLC

Aubigny, Pierre d'
　See Mencken, H(enry) L(ouis)

Aubin, Penelope 1685-1731(?) . . . . **LC 9**
　See also DLB 39

Auchincloss, Louis (Stanton)
　1917- . . . . **CLC 4, 6, 9, 18, 45**
　See also CA 1-4R; CANR 6, 29; DLB 2;
　DLBY 80; MTCW

Auden, W(ystan) H(ugh)
　1907-1973 . . . . . **CLC 1, 2, 3, 4, 6, 9, 11,
　　　　　　　　　　　　　　14, 43; PC 1**
　See also CA 9-12R; 45-48; CANR 5;
　CDBLB 1914-1945; DLB 10, 20; MTCW;
　WLC

Audiberti, Jacques 1900-1965 . . . . . . **CLC 38**
　See also CA 25-28R

Auel, Jean M(arie) 1936-. . . . . **CLC 31**
　See also AAYA 7; BEST 90:4; CA 103;
　CANR 21

Auerbach, Erich 1892-1957 . . . . **TCLC 43**
　See also CA 118

Augier, Emile 1820-1889 . . . . **NCLC 31**

August, John
　See De Voto, Bernard (Augustine)

Augustine, St. 354-430 . . . . **CMLC 6**

Aurelius
　See Bourne, Randolph S(illiman)

Austen, Jane
　1775-1817 . . . . **NCLC 1, 13, 19, 33**
　See also CDBLB 1789-1832; DLB 116;
　WLC

Auster, Paul 1947- . . . . **CLC 47**
　See also CA 69-72; CANR 23

Austin, Mary (Hunter)
　1868-1934 . . . . **TCLC 25**
　See also CA 109; DLB 9, 78

Autran Dourado, Waldomiro
　See Dourado, (Waldomiro Freitas) Autran

Averroes 1126-1198 . . . . **CMLC 7**
　See also DLB 115

Avison, Margaret 1918-. . . . . **CLC 2, 4**
　See also CA 17-20R; DLB 53; MTCW

Ayckbourn, Alan 1939- . . . . **CLC 5, 8, 18, 33**
　See also CA 21-24R; CANR 31; DLB 13;
　MTCW

Aydy, Catherine
　See Tennant, Emma (Christina)

Ayme, Marcel (Andre) 1902-1967. . . **CLC 11**
　See also CA 89-92; CLR 25; DLB 72

Ayrton, Michael 1921-1975. . . . . **CLC 7**
　See also CA 5-8R; 61-64; CANR 9, 21

Azorin. . . . . **CLC 11**
　See also Martinez Ruiz, Jose

Azuela, Mariano 1873-1952. . . . . **TCLC 3**
　See also CA 104; 131; HW; MTCW

Baastad, Babbis Friis
　See Friis-Baastad, Babbis Ellinor

Bab
See Gilbert, W(illiam) S(chwenck)

Babbis, Eleanor
See Friis-Baastad, Babbis Ellinor

Babel, Isaac (Emanuilovich) .... TCLC 13
See also Babel, Isaak (Emmanuilovich)

Babel, Isaak (Emmanuilovich)
1894-1941(?) .... TCLC 2
See also Babel, Isaac (Emanuilovich)
See also CA 104

Babits, Mihaly 1883-1941 .... TCLC 14
See also CA 114

Babur 1483-1530................. LC 18

Bacchelli, Riccardo 1891-1985 ..... CLC 19
See also CA 29-32R; 117

Bach, Richard (David) 1936-....... CLC 14
See also AITN 1; BEST 89:2; CA 9-12R;
CANR 18; MTCW; SATA 13

Bachman, Richard
See King, Stephen (Edwin)

Bachmann, Ingeborg 1926-1973..... CLC 69
See also CA 93-96; 45-48; DLB 85

Bacon, Francis 1561-1626 .... LC 18
See also CDBLB Before 1660

Bacovia, George................. TCLC 24
See also Vasiliu, Gheorghe

Badanes, Jerome 1937-........... CLC 59

Bagehot, Walter 1826-1877 ...... NCLC 10
See also DLB 55

Bagnold, Enid 1889-1981.......... CLC 25
See also CA 5-8R; 103; CANR 5; DLB 13;
MAICYA; SATA 1, 25

Bagrjana, Elisaveta
See Belcheva, Elisaveta

Bagryana, Elisaveta
See Belcheva, Elisaveta

Bailey, Paul 1937- .... CLC 45
See also CA 21-24R; CANR 16; DLB 14

Baillie, Joanna 1762-1851 .... NCLC 2
See also DLB 93

Bainbridge, Beryl (Margaret)
1933- .... CLC 4, 5, 8, 10, 14, 18, 22, 62
See also CA 21-24R; CANR 24; DLB 14;
MTCW

Baker, Elliott 1922- .... CLC 8
See also CA 45-48; CANR 2

Baker, Nicholson 1957- .... CLC 61
See also CA 135

Baker, Ray Stannard 1870-1946... TCLC 47
See also CA 118

Baker, Russell (Wayne) 1925-...... CLC 31
See also BEST 89:4; CA 57-60; CANR 11;
MTCW

Bakshi, Ralph 1938(?)-........... CLC 26
See also CA 112; 138

Bakunin, Mikhail (Alexandrovich)
1814-1876 .... NCLC 25

Baldwin, James (Arthur)
1924-1987 ..... CLC 1, 2, 3, 4, 5, 8, 13,
15, 17, 42, 50, 67; DC 1; SSC 10
See also AAYA 4; BLC 1; BW; CA 1-4R;
124; CABS 1; CANR 3, 24;
CDALB 1941-1968; DLB 2, 7, 33;
DLBY 87; MTCW; SATA 9, 54; WLC

Ballard, J(ames) G(raham)
1930- .... CLC 3, 6, 14, 36; SSC 1
See also AAYA 3; CA 5-8R; CANR 15, 39;
DLB 14; MTCW

Balmont, Konstantin (Dmitriyevich)
1867-1943 .... TCLC 11
See also CA 109

Balzac, Honore de
1799-1850 .... NCLC 5, 35; SSC 5
See also DLB 119; WLC

Bambara, Toni Cade 1939- .... CLC 19
See also AAYA 5; BLC 1; BW; CA 29-32R;
CANR 24; DLB 38; MTCW

Bamdad, A.
See Shamlu, Ahmad

Banat, D. R.
See Bradbury, Ray (Douglas)

Bancroft, Laura
See Baum, L(yman) Frank

Banim, John 1798-1842 .... NCLC 13
See also DLB 116

Banim, Michael 1796-1874 ...... NCLC 13

Banks, Iain
See Banks, Iain M(enzies)

Banks, Iain M(enzies) 1954-....... CLC 34
See also CA 123; 128

Banks, Lynne Reid .... CLC 23
See also Reid Banks, Lynne
See also AAYA 6

Banks, Russell 1940- .... CLC 37, 72
See also CA 65-68; CAAS 15; CANR 19

Banville, John 1945-.............. CLC 46
See also CA 117; 128; DLB 14

Banville, Theodore (Faullain) de
1832-1891 .... NCLC 9

Baraka, Amiri
1934- ... CLC 1, 2, 3, 5, 10, 14, 33; PC 4
See also Jones, LeRoi
See also BLC 1; BW; CA 21-24R; CABS 3;
CANR 27, 38; CDALB 1941-1968;
DLB 5, 7, 16, 38; DLBD 8; MTCW

Barbellion, W. N. P............... TCLC 24
See also Cummings, Bruce F(rederick)

Barbera, Jack 1945-.............. CLC 44
See also CA 110

Barbey d'Aurevilly, Jules Amedee
1808-1889 .... NCLC 1
See also DLB 119

Barbusse, Henri 1873-1935 .... TCLC 5
See also CA 105; DLB 65

Barclay, Bill
See Moorcock, Michael (John)

Barclay, William Ewert
See Moorcock, Michael (John)

Barea, Arturo 1897-1957 .... TCLC 14
See also CA 111

Barfoot, Joan 1946-.............. CLC 18
See also CA 105

Baring, Maurice 1874-1945 .... TCLC 8
See also CA 105; DLB 34

Barker, Clive 1952- .... CLC 52
See also BEST 90:3; CA 121; 129; MTCW

Barker, George Granville
1913-1991 .... CLC 8, 48
See also CA 9-12R; 135; CANR 7, 38;
DLB 20; MTCW

Barker, Harley Granville
See Granville-Barker, Harley
See also DLB 10

Barker, Howard 1946-............ CLC 37
See also CA 102; DLB 13

Barker, Pat 1943-................ CLC 32
See also CA 117; 122

Barlow, Joel 1754-1812 .... NCLC 23
See also DLB 37

Barnard, Mary (Ethel) 1909-....... CLC 48
See also CA 21-22; CAP 2

Barnes, Djuna
1892-1982 ... CLC 3, 4, 8, 11, 29; SSC 3
See also CA 9-12R; 107; CANR 16; DLB 4,
9, 45; MTCW

Barnes, Julian 1946-.............. CLC 42
See also CA 102; CANR 19

Barnes, Peter 1931- .... CLC 5, 56
See also CA 65-68; CAAS 12; CANR 33,
34; DLB 13; MTCW

Baroja (y Nessi), Pio 1872-1956 .... TCLC 8
See also CA 104

Baron, David
See Pinter, Harold

Baron Corvo
See Rolfe, Frederick (William Serafino
Austin Lewis Mary)

Barondess, Sue K(aufman)
1926-1977 .... CLC 8
See also Kaufman, Sue
See also CA 1-4R; 69-72; CANR 1

Baron de Teive
See Pessoa, Fernando (Antonio Nogueira)

Barres, Maurice 1862-1923 .... TCLC 47

Barreto, Afonso Henrique de Lima
See Lima Barreto, Afonso Henrique de

Barrett, (Roger) Syd 1946- .... CLC 35
See also Pink Floyd

Barrett, William (Christopher)
1913- .... CLC 27
See also CA 13-16R; CANR 11

Barrie, J(ames) M(atthew)
1860-1937 .... TCLC 2
See also CA 104; 136; CDBLB 1890-1914;
CLR 16; DLB 10; MAICYA; YABC 1

Barrington, Michael
See Moorcock, Michael (John)

Barrol, Grady
See Bograd, Larry

Barry, Mike
See Malzberg, Barry N(athaniel)

Barry, Philip 1896-1949.......... TCLC 11
See also CA 109; DLB 7

Bart, Andre Schwarz
See Schwarz-Bart, Andre

Barth, John (Simmons)
1930- ...... CLC 1, 2, 3, 5, 7, 9, 10, 14,
27, 51; SSC 10
See also AITN 1, 2; CA 1-4R; CABS 1;
CANR 5, 23; DLB 2; MTCW

Barthelme, Donald
1931-1989 ..... **CLC 1, 2, 3, 5, 6, 8, 13, 23, 46, 59; SSC 2**
See also CA 21-24R; 129; CANR 20; DLB 2; DLBY 80, 89; MTCW; SATA 7, 62

Barthelme, Frederick 1943-........ **CLC 36**
See also CA 114; 122; DLBY 85

Barthes, Roland (Gerard)
1915-1980 .... **CLC 24**
See also CA 130; 97-100; MTCW

Barzun, Jacques (Martin) 1907- .... **CLC 51**
See also CA 61-64; CANR 22

Bashevis, Isaac
See Singer, Isaac Bashevis

Bashkirtseff, Marie 1859-1884 ... **NCLC 27**

Basho
See Matsuo Basho

Bass, Kingsley B. Jr.
See Bullins, Ed

Bassani, Giorgio 1916-............. **CLC 9**
See also CA 65-68; CANR 33; MTCW

Bastos, Augusto (Antonio) Roa
See Roa Bastos, Augusto (Antonio)

Bataille, Georges 1897-1962 .... **CLC 29**
See also CA 101; 89-92

Bates, H(erbert) E(rnest)
1905-1974 .... **CLC 46; SSC 10**
See also CA 93-96; 45-48; CANR 34; MTCW

Bauchart
See Camus, Albert

Baudelaire, Charles
1821-1867 .... **NCLC 6, 29; PC 1**
See also WLC

Baudrillard, Jean 1929-........... **CLC 60**

Baum, L(yman) Frank 1856-1919 ... **TCLC 7**
See also CA 108; 133; CLR 15; DLB 22; MAICYA; MTCW; SATA 18

Baum, Louis F.
See Baum, L(yman) Frank

Baumbach, Jonathan 1933- ...... **CLC 6, 23**
See also CA 13-16R; CAAS 5; CANR 12; DLBY 80; MTCW

Bausch, Richard (Carl) 1945- ...... **CLC 51**
See also CA 101; CAAS 14

Baxter, Charles 1947-............. **CLC 45**
See also CA 57-60

Baxter, James K(eir) 1926-1972 .... **CLC 14**
See also CA 77-80

Baxter, John
See Hunt, E(verette) Howard Jr.

Bayer, Sylvia
See Glassco, John

Beagle, Peter S(oyer) 1939-........ **CLC 7**
See also CA 9-12R; CANR 4; DLBY 80; SATA 60

Bean, Normal
See Burroughs, Edgar Rice

Beard, Charles A(ustin)
1874-1948 .... **TCLC 15**
See also CA 115; DLB 17; SATA 18

Beardsley, Aubrey 1872-1898 ..... **NCLC 6**

Beattie, Ann
1947- .... **CLC 8, 13, 18, 40, 63; SSC 11**
See also BEST 90:2; CA 81-84; DLBY 82; MTCW

Beattie, James 1735-1803 .... **NCLC 25**
See also DLB 109

Beauchamp, Kathleen Mansfield 1888-1923
See Mansfield, Katherine
See also CA 104; 134

Beauvoir, Simone (Lucie Ernestine Marie Bertrand) de
1908-1986 ... **CLC 1, 2, 4, 8, 14, 31, 44, 50, 71**
See also CA 9-12R; 118; CANR 28; DLB 72; DLBY 86; MTCW; WLC

Becker, Jurek 1937-............. **CLC 7, 19**
See also CA 85-88; DLB 75

Becker, Walter 1950-............. **CLC 26**

Beckett, Samuel (Barclay)
1906-1989 ..... **CLC 1, 2, 3, 4, 6, 9, 10, 11, 14, 18, 29, 57, 59**
See also CA 5-8R; 130; CANR 33; CDBLB 1945-1960; DLB 13, 15; DLBY 90; MTCW; WLC

Beckford, William 1760-1844 .... **NCLC 16**
See also DLB 39

Beckman, Gunnel 1910-........... **CLC 26**
See also CA 33-36R; CANR 15; CLR 25; MAICYA; SAAS 9; SATA 6

Becque, Henri 1837-1899........ **NCLC 3**

Beddoes, Thomas Lovell
1803-1849 .... **NCLC 3**
See also DLB 96

Bedford, Donald F.
See Fearing, Kenneth (Flexner)

Beecher, Catharine Esther
1800-1878 .... **NCLC 30**
See also DLB 1

Beecher, John 1904-1980........... **CLC 6**
See also AITN 1; CA 5-8R; 105; CANR 8

Beer, Johann 1655-1700............ **LC 5**

Beer, Patricia 1924-............. **CLC 58**
See also CA 61-64; CANR 13; DLB 40

Beerbohm, Henry Maximilian
1872-1956 .... **TCLC 1, 24**
See also CA 104; DLB 34, 100

Begiebing, Robert J(ohn) 1946-..... **CLC 70**
See also CA 122

Behan, Brendan
1923-1964 .... **CLC 1, 8, 11, 15**
See also CA 73-76; CANR 33; CDBLB 1945-1960; DLB 13; MTCW

Behn, Aphra 1640(?)-1689 .... **LC 1**
See also DLB 39, 80; WLC

Behrman, S(amuel) N(athaniel)
1893-1973 .... **CLC 40**
See also CA 13-16; 45-48; CAP 1; DLB 7, 44

Belasco, David 1853-1931 .... **TCLC 3**
See also CA 104; DLB 7

Belcheva, Elisaveta 1893- .... **CLC 10**

Beldone, Phil "Cheech"
See Ellison, Harlan

Beleno
See Azuela, Mariano

Belinski, Vissarion Grigoryevich
1811-1848 .... **NCLC 5**

Belitt, Ben 1911-................ **CLC 22**
See also CA 13-16R; CAAS 4; CANR 7; DLB 5

Bell, James Madison 1826-1902 ... **TCLC 43**
See also BLC 1; BW; CA 122; 124; DLB 50

Bell, Madison (Smartt) 1957- ...... **CLC 41**
See also CA 111; CANR 28

Bell, Marvin (Hartley) 1937-..... **CLC 8, 31**
See also CA 21-24R; CAAS 14; DLB 5; MTCW

Bell, W. L. D.
See Mencken, H(enry) L(ouis)

Bellamy, Atwood C.
See Mencken, H(enry) L(ouis)

Bellamy, Edward 1850-1898 ...... **NCLC 4**
See also DLB 12

Bellin, Edward J.
See Kuttner, Henry

Belloc, (Joseph) Hilaire (Pierre)
1870-1953 ....**TCLC 7, 18**
See also CA 106; DLB 19, 100; YABC 1

Belloc, Joseph Peter Rene Hilaire
See Belloc, (Joseph) Hilaire (Pierre)

Belloc, Joseph Pierre Hilaire
See Belloc, (Joseph) Hilaire (Pierre)

Belloc, M. A.
See Lowndes, Marie Adelaide (Belloc)

Bellow, Saul
1915- ..... **CLC 1, 2, 3, 6, 8, 10, 13, 15, 25, 33, 34, 63**
See also AITN 2; BEST 89:3; CA 5-8R; CABS 1; CANR 29; CDALB 1941-1968; DLB 2, 28; DLBD 3; DLBY 82; MTCW; WLC

Belser, Reimond Karel Maria de
1929- .... **CLC 14**

Bely, Andrey .... **TCLC 7**
See also Bugayev, Boris Nikolayevich

Benary, Margot
See Benary-Isbert, Margot

Benary-Isbert, Margot 1889-1979... **CLC 12**
See also CA 5-8R; 89-92; CANR 4; CLR 12; MAICYA; SATA 2, 21

Benavente (y Martinez), Jacinto
1866-1954 .... **TCLC 3**
See also CA 106; 131; HW; MTCW

Benchley, Peter (Bradford)
1940- .... **CLC 4, 8**
See also AITN 2; CA 17-20R; CANR 12, 35; MTCW; SATA 3

Benchley, Robert (Charles)
1889-1945 .... **TCLC 1**
See also CA 105; DLB 11

Benedikt, Michael 1935- .... **CLC 4, 14**
See also CA 13-16R; CANR 7; DLB 5

Benet, Juan 1927-................ **CLC 28**

Benet, Stephen Vincent
1898-1943 .... **TCLC 7; SSC 10**
See also CA 104; DLB 4, 48, 102; YABC 1

Benet, William Rose   1886-1950 ... **TCLC 28**
See also CA 118; DLB 45

Benford, Gregory (Albert)   1941-.... **CLC 52**
See also CA 69-72; CANR 12, 24;
DLBY 82

Benjamin, Lois
See Gould, Lois

Benjamin, Walter   1892-1940 ..... **TCLC 39**

Benn, Gottfried   1886-1956........ **TCLC 3**
See also CA 106; DLB 56

Bennett, Alan   1934- .... **CLC 45**
See also CA 103; CANR 35; MTCW

Bennett, (Enoch) Arnold
1867-1931 .... **TCLC 5, 20**
See also CA 106; CDBLB 1890-1914;
DLB 10, 34, 98

Bennett, Elizabeth
See Mitchell, Margaret (Munnerlyn)

Bennett, George Harold   1930-
See Bennett, Hal
See also BW; CA 97-100

Bennett, Hal .... **CLC 5**
See also Bennett, George Harold
See also DLB 33

Bennett, Jay   1912- .... **CLC 35**
See also CA 69-72; CANR 11; SAAS 4;
SATA 27, 41

Bennett, Louise (Simone)   1919-..... **CLC 28**
See also BLC 1; DLB 117

Benson, E(dward) F(rederic)
1867-1940 .... **TCLC 27**
See also CA 114

Benson, Jackson J.   1930-.......... **CLC 34**
See also CA 25-28R; DLB 111

Benson, Sally   1900-1972 .... **CLC 17**
See also CA 19-20; 37-40R; CAP 1;
SATA 1, 27, 35

Benson, Stella   1892-1933........ **TCLC 17**
See also CA 117; DLB 36

Bentham, Jeremy   1748-1832 ..... **NCLC 38**
See also DLB 107

Bentley, E(dmund) C(lerihew)
1875-1956 .... **TCLC 12**
See also CA 108; DLB 70

Bentley, Eric (Russell)   1916-....... **CLC 24**
See also CA 5-8R; CANR 6

Beranger, Pierre Jean de
1780-1857 .... **NCLC 34**

Berger, Colonel
See Malraux, (Georges-)Andre

Berger, John (Peter)   1926- ...... **CLC 2, 19**
See also CA 81-84; DLB 14

Berger, Melvin H.   1927- .... **CLC 12**
See also CA 5-8R; CANR 4; SAAS 2;
SATA 5

Berger, Thomas (Louis)
1924- .... **CLC 3, 5, 8, 11, 18, 38**
See also CA 1-4R; CANR 5, 28; DLB 2;
DLBY 80; MTCW

Bergman, (Ernst) Ingmar
1918- .... **CLC 16, 72**
See also CA 81-84; CANR 33

Bergson, Henri   1859-1941 .... **TCLC 32**

Bergstein, Eleanor   1938- .... **CLC 4**
See also CA 53-56; CANR 5

Berkoff, Steven   1937-............. **CLC 56**
See also CA 104

Bermant, Chaim (Icyk)   1929- ...... **CLC 40**
See also CA 57-60; CANR 6, 31

Bernanos, (Paul Louis) Georges
1888-1948 .... **TCLC 3**
See also CA 104; 130; DLB 72

Bernard, April   1956- .... **CLC 59**
See also CA 131

Bernhard, Thomas
1931-1989 .... **CLC 3, 32, 61**
See also CA 85-88; 127; CANR 32;
DLB 85; MTCW

Berrigan, Daniel   1921-............. **CLC 4**
See also CA 33-36R; CAAS 1; CANR 11;
DLB 5

Berrigan, Edmund Joseph Michael Jr.
1934-1983
See Berrigan, Ted
See also CA 61-64; 110; CANR 14

Berrigan, Ted.................... **CLC 37**
See also Berrigan, Edmund Joseph Michael
Jr.
See also DLB 5

Berry, Charles Edward Anderson   1931-
See Berry, Chuck
See also CA 115

Berry, Chuck..................... **CLC 17**
See also Berry, Charles Edward Anderson

Berry, Jonas
See Ashbery, John (Lawrence)

Berry, Wendell (Erdman)
1934- .... **CLC 4, 6, 8, 27, 46**
See also AITN 1; CA 73-76; DLB 5, 6

Berryman, John
1914-1972 ..... **CLC 1, 2, 3, 4, 6, 8, 10, 13, 25, 62**
See also CA 13-16; 33-36R; CABS 2;
CANR 35; CAP 1; CDALB 1941-1968;
DLB 48; MTCW

Bertolucci, Bernardo   1940- .... **CLC 16**
See also CA 106

Bertrand, Aloysius   1807-1841 .... **NCLC 31**

Bertran de Born   c. 1140-1215 ..... **CMLC 5**

Besant, Annie (Wood)   1847-1933 ... **TCLC 9**
See also CA 105

Bessie, Alvah   1904-1985........... **CLC 23**
See also CA 5-8R; 116; CANR 2; DLB 26

Bethlen, T. D.
See Silverberg, Robert

Beti, Mongo..................... **CLC 27**
See also Biyidi, Alexandre
See also BLC 1

Betjeman, John
1906-1984 .... **CLC 2, 6, 10, 34, 43**
See also CA 9-12R; 112; CANR 33;
CDBLB 1945-1960; DLB 20; DLBY 84;
MTCW

Betti, Ugo   1892-1953 .... **TCLC 5**
See also CA 104

Betts, Doris (Waugh)   1932-.... **CLC 3, 6, 28**
See also CA 13-16R; CANR 9; DLBY 82

Bevan, Alistair
See Roberts, Keith (John Kingston)

Beynon, John
See Harris, John (Wyndham Parkes Lucas)
Beynon

Bialik, Chaim Nachman
1873-1934 .... **TCLC 25**

Bickerstaff, Isaac
See Swift, Jonathan

Bidart, Frank   19(?)- .... **CLC 33**

Bienek, Horst   1930-............ **CLC 7, 11**
See also CA 73-76; DLB 75

Bierce, Ambrose (Gwinett)
1842-1914(?) ..... **TCLC 1, 7, 44; SSC 9**
See also CA 104; CDALB 1865-1917;
DLB 11, 12, 23, 71, 74; WLC

Billings, Josh
See Shaw, Henry Wheeler

Billington, Rachel   1942-........... **CLC 43**
See also AITN 2; CA 33-36R

Binyon, T(imothy) J(ohn)   1936- .... **CLC 34**
See also CA 111; CANR 28

Bioy Casares, Adolfo   1914-.... **CLC 4, 8, 13**
See also CA 29-32R; CANR 19; DLB 113;
HW; MTCW

Bird, C.
See Ellison, Harlan

Bird, Cordwainer
See Ellison, Harlan

Bird, Robert Montgomery
1806-1854 .... **NCLC 1**

Birney, (Alfred) Earle
1904- .... **CLC 1, 4, 6, 11**
See also CA 1-4R; CANR 5, 20; DLB 88;
MTCW

Bishop, Elizabeth
1911-1979 ..... **CLC 1, 4, 9, 13, 15, 32; PC 3**
See also CA 5-8R; 89-92; CABS 2;
CANR 26; CDALB 1968-1988; DLB 5;
MTCW; SATA 24

Bishop, John   1935-............... **CLC 10**
See also CA 105

bissett, bill   1939- .... **CLC 18**
See also CA 69-72; CANR 15; DLB 53;
MTCW

Bitov, Andrei (Georgievich)   1937-... **CLC 57**

Biyidi, Alexandre   1932-
See Beti, Mongo
See also BW; CA 114; 124; MTCW

Bjarme, Brynjolf
See Ibsen, Henrik (Johan)

Bjoernson, Bjoernstjerne (Martinius)
1832-1910 .... **TCLC 7**
See also Bjornson, Bjornstjerne; Bjornson,
Bjornstjerne (Martinius)
See also CA 104

Bjornson, Bjornstjerne .... **TCLC 37**
See also Bjoernson, Bjoernstjerne
(Martinius)

Bjornson, Bjornstjerne (Martinius) ... **TCLC 7**
See also Bjoernson, Bjoernstjerne
(Martinius)

Black, Robert
See Holdstock, Robert P.

Blackburn, Paul 1926-1971 ...... **CLC 9, 43**
See also CA 81-84; 33-36R; CANR 34;
DLB 16; DLBY 81

Black Elk 1863-1950 .... **TCLC 33**

Black Hobart
See Sanders, (James) Ed(ward)

Blacklin, Malcolm
See Chambers, Aidan

Blackmore, R(ichard) D(oddridge)
1825-1900 .... **TCLC 27**
See also CA 120; DLB 18

Blackmur, R(ichard) P(almer)
1904-1965 .... **CLC 2, 24**
See also CA 11-12; 25-28R; CAP 1; DLB 63

Black Tarantula, The
See Acker, Kathy

Blackwood, Algernon (Henry)
1869-1951 .... **TCLC 5**
See also CA 105

Blackwood, Caroline 1931- .... **CLC 6, 9**
See also CA 85-88; CANR 32; DLB 14;
MTCW

Blade, Alexander
See Hamilton, Edmond; Silverberg, Robert

Blair, Eric (Arthur) 1903-1950
See Orwell, George
See also CA 104; 132; MTCW; SATA 29

Blais, Marie-Claire
1939- .... **CLC 2, 4, 6, 13, 22**
See also CA 21-24R; CAAS 4; CANR 38;
DLB 53; MTCW

Blaise, Clark 1940-............... **CLC 29**
See also AITN 2; CA 53-56; CAAS 3;
CANR 5; DLB 53

Blake, Nicholas
See Day Lewis, C(ecil)
See also DLB 77

Blake, William 1757-1827 .... **NCLC 13**
See also CDBLB 1789-1832; DLB 93;
MAICYA; SATA 30; WLC

Blasco Ibanez, Vicente
1867-1928 .... **TCLC 12**
See also CA 110; 131; HW; MTCW

Blatty, William Peter 1928-........ **CLC 2**
See also CA 5-8R; CANR 9

Bleeck, Oliver
See Thomas, Ross (Elmore)

Blessing, Lee 1949-............... **CLC 54**

Blish, James (Benjamin)
1921-1975 .... **CLC 14**
See also CA 1-4R; 57-60; CANR 3; DLB 8;
MTCW; SATA 66

Bliss, Reginald
See Wells, H(erbert) G(eorge)

Blixen, Karen (Christentze Dinesen)
1885-1962
See Dinesen, Isak
See also CA 25-28; CANR 22; CAP 2;
MTCW; SATA 44

Bloch, Robert (Albert) 1917-....... **CLC 33**
See also CA 5-8R; CANR 5; DLB 44;
SATA 12

Blok, Alexander (Alexandrovich)
1880-1921 .... **TCLC 5**
See also CA 104

Blom, Jan
See Breytenbach, Breyten

Bloom, Harold 1930- .... **CLC 24**
See also CA 13-16R; CANR 39; DLB 67

Bloomfield, Aurelius
See Bourne, Randolph S(illiman)

Blount, Roy (Alton) Jr. 1941-...... **CLC 38**
See also CA 53-56; CANR 10, 28; MTCW

Bloy, Leon 1846-1917............. **TCLC 22**
See also CA 121

Blume, Judy (Sussman) 1938-... **CLC 12, 30**
See also AAYA 3; CA 29-32R; CANR 13,
37; CLR 2, 15; DLB 52; MAICYA;
MTCW; SATA 2, 31

Blunden, Edmund (Charles)
1896-1974 .... **CLC 2, 56**
See also CA 17-18; 45-48; CAP 2; DLB 20,
100; MTCW

Bly, Robert (Elwood)
1926- .... **CLC 1, 2, 5, 10, 15, 38**
See also CA 5-8R; DLB 5; MTCW

Bobette
See Simenon, Georges (Jacques Christian)

Boccaccio, Giovanni 1313-1375
See also SSC 10

Bochco, Steven 1943-............. **CLC 35**
See also CA 124; 138

Bodenheim, Maxwell 1892-1954 ... **TCLC 44**
See also CA 110; DLB 9, 45

Bodker, Cecil 1927- .... **CLC 21**
See also CA 73-76; CANR 13; CLR 23;
MAICYA; SATA 14

Boell, Heinrich (Theodor)
1917-1985 ... **CLC 2, 3, 6, 9, 11, 15, 27,
39**
See also Boll, Heinrich (Theodor)
See also CA 21-24R; 116; CANR 24;
DLB 69; DLBY 85; MTCW

Bogan, Louise 1897-1970..... **CLC 4, 39, 46**
See also CA 73-76; 25-28R; CANR 33;
DLB 45; MTCW

Bogarde, Dirk .... **CLC 19**
See also Van Den Bogarde, Derek Jules
Gaspard Ulric Niven
See also DLB 14

Bogosian, Eric 1953- .... **CLC 45**
See also CA 138

Bograd, Larry 1953-.............. **CLC 35**
See also CA 93-96; SATA 33

Boiardo, Matteo Maria 1441-1494 .... **LC 6**

Boileau-Despreaux, Nicolas
1636-1711 .... **LC 3**

Boland, Eavan 1944-.......... **CLC 40, 67**
See also DLB 40

Boll, Heinrich (Theodor)
1917-1985 ... **CLC 2, 3, 6, 9, 11, 15, 27,
39, 72**
See also Boell, Heinrich (Theodor)
See also DLB 69; DLBY 85; WLC

Bolt, Robert (Oxton) 1924-........ **CLC 14**
See also CA 17-20R; CANR 35; DLB 13;
MTCW

Bomkauf
See Kaufman, Bob (Garnell)

Bonaventura.................... **NCLC 35**
See also DLB 90

Bond, Edward 1934-....... **CLC 4, 6, 13, 23**
See also CA 25-28R; CANR 38; DLB 13;
MTCW

Bonham, Frank 1914-1989......... **CLC 12**
See also AAYA 1; CA 9-12R; CANR 4, 36;
MAICYA; SAAS 3; SATA 1, 49, 62

Bonnefoy, Yves 1923-........ **CLC 9, 15, 58**
See also CA 85-88; CANR 33; MTCW

Bontemps, Arna(ud Wendell)
1902-1973 .... **CLC 1, 18**
See also BLC 1; BW; CA 1-4R; 41-44R;
CANR 4, 35; CLR 6; DLB 48, 51;
MAICYA; MTCW; SATA 2, 24, 44

Booth, Martin 1944-.............. **CLC 13**
See also CA 93-96; CAAS 2

Booth, Philip 1925-.............. **CLC 23**
See also CA 5-8R; CANR 5; DLBY 82

Booth, Wayne C(layson) 1921- ..... **CLC 24**
See also CA 1-4R; CAAS 5; CANR 3;
DLB 67

Borchert, Wolfgang 1921-1947 ..... **TCLC 5**
See also CA 104; DLB 69

Borges, Jorge Luis
1899-1986 ... **CLC 1, 2, 3, 4, 6, 8, 9, 10,
13, 19, 44, 48; SSC 4**
See also CA 21-24R; CANR 19, 33;
DLB 113; DLBY 86; HW; MTCW; WLC

Borowski, Tadeusz 1922-1951...... **TCLC 9**
See also CA 106

Borrow, George (Henry)
1803-1881 .... **NCLC 9**
See also DLB 21, 55

Bosschere, Jean de 1878(?)-1953... **TCLC 19**
See also CA 115

Boswell, James 1740-1795.......... **LC 4**
See also CDBLB 1660-1789; DLB 104;
WLC

Bottoms, David 1949-............. **CLC 53**
See also CA 105; CANR 22; DLB 120;
DLBY 83

Boucolon, Maryse 1937-
See Conde, Maryse
See also CA 110; CANR 30

Bourget, Paul (Charles Joseph)
1852-1935 .... **TCLC 12**
See also CA 107

Bourjaily, Vance (Nye) 1922- .... **CLC 8, 62**
See also CA 1-4R; CAAS 1; CANR 2;
DLB 2

Bourne, Randolph S(illiman)
1886-1918 .... **TCLC 16**
See also CA 117; DLB 63

Bova, Ben(jamin William) 1932-.... **CLC 45**
See also CA 5-8R; CANR 11; CLR 3;
DLBY 81; MAICYA; MTCW; SATA 6,
68

Bowen, Elizabeth (Dorothea Cole)
1899-1973 ..... **CLC 1, 3, 6, 11, 15, 22;
SSC 3**
See also CA 17-18; 41-44R; CANR 35;
CAP 2; CDBLB 1945-1960; DLB 15;
MTCW

Bowering, George 1935-........ **CLC 15, 47**
See also CA 21-24R; CAAS 16; CANR 10;
DLB 53

Bowering, Marilyn R(uthe) 1949-... **CLC 32**
See also CA 101

Bowers, Edgar 1924- .... **CLC 9**
See also CA 5-8R; CANR 24; DLB 5

Bowie, David .... **CLC 17**
See also Jones, David Robert

Bowles, Jane (Sydney)
1917-1973 .... **CLC 3, 68**
See also CA 19-20; 41-44R; CAP 2

Bowles, Paul (Frederick)
1910- .... **CLC 1, 2, 19, 53; SSC 3**
See also CA 1-4R; CAAS 1; CANR 1, 19;
DLB 5, 6; MTCW

Box, Edgar
See Vidal, Gore

Boyd, Nancy
See Millay, Edna St. Vincent

Boyd, William 1952-........ **CLC 28, 53, 70**
See also CA 114; 120

Boyle, Kay 1902- .. **CLC 1, 5, 19, 58; SSC 5**
See also CA 13-16R; CAAS 1; CANR 29;
DLB 4, 9, 48, 86; MTCW

Boyle, Mark
See Kienzle, William X(avier)

Boyle, Patrick 1905-1982......... **CLC 19**
See also CA 127

Boyle, T. Coraghessan 1948-.... **CLC 36, 55**
See also BEST 90:4; CA 120; DLBY 86

Brackenridge, Hugh Henry
1748-1816 .... **NCLC 7**
See also DLB 11, 37

Bradbury, Edward P.
See Moorcock, Michael (John)

Bradbury, Malcolm (Stanley)
1932- .... **CLC 32, 61**
See also CA 1-4R; CANR 1, 33; DLB 14;
MTCW

Bradbury, Ray (Douglas)
1920- .... **CLC 1, 3, 10, 15, 42**
See also AITN 1, 2; CA 1-4R; CANR 2, 30;
CDALB 1968-1988; DLB 2, 8; MTCW;
SATA 11, 64; WLC

Bradford, Gamaliel 1863-1932..... **TCLC 36**
See also DLB 17

Bradley, David (Henry Jr.) 1950-... **CLC 23**
See also BLC 1; BW; CA 104; CANR 26;
DLB 33

Bradley, John Ed 1959-.......... **CLC 55**

Bradley, Marion Zimmer 1930-..... **CLC 30**
See also AAYA 9; CA 57-60; CAAS 10;
CANR 7, 31; DLB 8; MTCW

Bradstreet, Anne 1612(?)-1672 .... **LC 4**
See also CDALB 1640-1865; DLB 24

Bragg, Melvyn 1939- .... **CLC 10**
See also BEST 89:3; CA 57-60; CANR 10;
DLB 14

Braine, John (Gerard)
1922-1986 .... **CLC 1, 3, 41**
See also CA 1-4R; 120; CANR 1, 33;
CDBLB 1945-1960; DLB 15; DLBY 86;
MTCW

Brammer, William 1930(?)-1978 .... **CLC 31**
See also CA 77-80

Brancati, Vitaliano 1907-1954..... **TCLC 12**
See also CA 109

Brancato, Robin F(idler) 1936-..... **CLC 35**
See also AAYA 9; CA 69-72; CANR 11;
SAAS 9; SATA 23

Brand, Millen 1906-1980........... **CLC 7**
See also CA 21-24R; 97-100

Branden, Barbara .... **CLC 44**

Brandes, Georg (Morris Cohen)
1842-1927 .... **TCLC 10**
See also CA 105

Brandys, Kazimierz 1916- .... **CLC 62**

Branley, Franklyn M(ansfield)
1915- .... **CLC 21**
See also CA 33-36R; CANR 14, 39;
CLR 13; MAICYA; SATA 4, 68

Brathwaite, Edward (Kamau)
1930- .... **CLC 11**
See also BW; CA 25-28R; CANR 11, 26

Brautigan, Richard (Gary)
1935-1984 .... **CLC 1, 3, 5, 9, 12, 34, 42**
See also CA 53-56; 113; CANR 34; DLB 2,
5; DLBY 80, 84; MTCW; SATA 56

Braverman, Kate 1950- .... **CLC 67**
See also CA 89-92

Brecht, Bertolt
1898-1956 .... **TCLC 1, 6, 13, 35**
See also CA 104; 133; DLB 56; MTCW;
WLC

Brecht, Eugen Berthold Friedrich
See Brecht, Bertolt

Bremer, Fredrika 1801-1865 ..... **NCLC 11**

Brennan, Christopher John
1870-1932 .... **TCLC 17**
See also CA 117

Brennan, Maeve 1917-............. **CLC 5**
See also CA 81-84

Brentano, Clemens (Maria)
1778-1842 .... **NCLC 1**

Brent of Bin Bin
See Franklin, (Stella Maraia Sarah) Miles

Brenton, Howard 1942-........... **CLC 31**
See also CA 69-72; CANR 33; DLB 13;
MTCW

Breslin, James 1930-
See Breslin, Jimmy
See also CA 73-76; CANR 31; MTCW

Breslin, Jimmy .... **CLC 4, 43**
See also Breslin, James
See also AITN 1

Bresson, Robert 1907- .... **CLC 16**
See also CA 110

Breton, Andre 1896-1966... **CLC 2, 9, 15, 54**
See also CA 19-20; 25-28R; CAP 2;
DLB 65; MTCW

Breytenbach, Breyten 1939(?)- .. **CLC 23, 37**
See also CA 113; 129

Bridgers, Sue Ellen 1942- .... **CLC 26**
See also AAYA 8; CA 65-68; CANR 11,
36; CLR 18; DLB 52; MAICYA;
SAAS 1; SATA 22

Bridges, Robert (Seymour)
1844-1930 .... **TCLC 1**
See also CA 104; CDBLB 1890-1914;
DLB 19, 98

Bridie, James.................... **TCLC 3**
See also Mavor, Osborne Henry
See also DLB 10

Brin, David 1950-................ **CLC 34**
See also CA 102; CANR 24; SATA 65

Brink, Andre (Philippus)
1935-...................... **CLC 18, 36**
See also CA 104; CANR 39; MTCW

Brinsmead, H(esba) F(ay) 1922-.... **CLC 21**
See also CA 21-24R; CANR 10; MAICYA;
SAAS 5; SATA 18

Brittain, Vera (Mary)
1893(?)-1970 .... **CLC 23**
See also CA 13-16; 25-28R; CAP 1; MTCW

Broch, Hermann 1886-1951....... **TCLC 20**
See also CA 117; DLB 85

Brock, Rose
See Hansen, Joseph

Brodkey, Harold 1930-........... **CLC 56**
See also CA 111

Brodsky, Iosif Alexandrovich 1940-
See Brodsky, Joseph
See also AITN 1; CA 41-44R; CANR 37;
MTCW

Brodsky, Joseph .... **CLC 4, 6, 13, 36, 50**
See also Brodsky, Iosif Alexandrovich

Brodsky, Michael Mark 1948- ..... **CLC 19**
See also CA 102; CANR 18

Bromell, Henry 1947-............. **CLC 5**
See also CA 53-56; CANR 9

Bromfield, Louis (Brucker)
1896-1956 .... **TCLC 11**
See also CA 107; DLB 4, 9, 86

Broner, E(sther) M(asserman)
1930- .... **CLC 19**
See also CA 17-20R; CANR 8, 25; DLB 28

Bronk, William 1918-............. **CLC 10**
See also CA 89-92; CANR 23

Bronstein, Lev Davidovich
See Trotsky, Leon

Bronte, Anne 1820-1849.......... **NCLC 4**
See also DLB 21

Bronte, Charlotte
1816-1855 .... **NCLC 3, 8, 33**
See also CDBLB 1832-1890; DLB 21; WLC

Bronte, (Jane) Emily
1818-1848 .... **NCLC 16, 35**
See also CDBLB 1832-1890; DLB 21, 32;
WLC

Brooke, Frances 1724-1789 .... **LC 6**
See also DLB 39, 99

Brooke, Henry 1703(?)-1783 .... **LC 1**
See also DLB 39

Brooke, Rupert (Chawner)
1887-1915 .... **TCLC 2, 7**
See also CA 104; 132; CDBLB 1914-1945;
DLB 19; MTCW; WLC

Brooke-Haven, P.
See Wodehouse, P(elham) G(renville)

Brooke-Rose, Christine 1926- ...... **CLC 40**
See also CA 13-16R; DLB 14

Brookner, Anita 1928- ...... **CLC 32, 34, 51**
See also CA 114; 120; CANR 37; DLBY 87;
MTCW

Brooks, Cleanth 1906- .... **CLC 24**
See also CA 17-20R; CANR 33, 35;
DLB 63; MTCW

Brooks, George
See Baum, L(yman) Frank

Brooks, Gwendolyn
1917- .... **CLC 1, 2, 4, 5, 15, 49**
See also AITN 1; BLC 1; BW; CA 1-4R;
CANR 1, 27; CDALB 1941-1968;
CLR 27; DLB 5, 76; MTCW; SATA 6;
WLC

Brooks, Mel..................... **CLC 12**
See also Kaminsky, Melvin
See also DLB 26

Brooks, Peter 1938- .... **CLC 34**
See also CA 45-48; CANR 1

Brooks, Van Wyck 1886-1963...... **CLC 29**
See also CA 1-4R; CANR 6; DLB 45, 63,
103

Brophy, Brigid (Antonia)
1929- .... **CLC 6, 11, 29**
See also CA 5-8R; CAAS 4; CANR 25;
DLB 14; MTCW

Brosman, Catharine Savage 1934-.... **CLC 9**
See also CA 61-64; CANR 21

Brother Antoninus
See Everson, William (Oliver)

Broughton, T(homas) Alan 1936- ... **CLC 19**
See also CA 45-48; CANR 2, 23

Broumas, Olga 1949- .... **CLC 10**
See also CA 85-88; CANR 20

Brown, Charles Brockden
1771-1810 .... **NCLC 22**
See also CDALB 1640-1865; DLB 37, 59,
73

Brown, Christy 1932-1981......... **CLC 63**
See also CA 105; 104; DLB 14

Brown, Claude 1937- .... **CLC 30**
See also AAYA 7; BLC 1; BW; CA 73-76

Brown, Dee (Alexander) 1908- .. **CLC 18, 47**
See also CA 13-16R; CAAS 6; CANR 11;
DLBY 80; MTCW; SATA 5

Brown, George
See Wertmueller, Lina

Brown, George Douglas
1869-1902 .... **TCLC 28**

Brown, George Mackay 1921-.... **CLC 5, 48**
See also CA 21-24R; CAAS 6; CANR 12,
37; DLB 14, 27; MTCW; SATA 35

Brown, Moses
See Barrett, William (Christopher)

Brown, Rita Mae 1944- .... **CLC 18, 43**
See also CA 45-48; CANR 2, 11, 35;
MTCW

Brown, Roderick (Langmere) Haig-
See Haig-Brown, Roderick (Langmere)

Brown, Rosellen 1939-............ **CLC 32**
See also CA 77-80; CAAS 10; CANR 14

Brown, Sterling Allen
1901-1989 .... **CLC 1, 23, 59**
See also BLC 1; BW; CA 85-88; 127;
CANR 26; DLB 48, 51, 63; MTCW

Brown, Will
See Ainsworth, William Harrison

Brown, William Wells
1813-1884 .... **NCLC 2; DC 1**
See also BLC 1; DLB 3, 50

Browne, (Clyde) Jackson 1948(?)-... **CLC 21**
See also CA 120

Browning, Elizabeth Barrett
1806-1861 .... **NCLC 1, 16**
See also CDBLB 1832-1890; DLB 32; WLC

Browning, Robert
1812-1889 .... **NCLC 19; PC 2**
See also CDBLB 1832-1890; DLB 32;
YABC 1

Browning, Tod 1882-1962 .... **CLC 16**
See also CA 117

Bruccoli, Matthew J(oseph) 1931- .. **CLC 34**
See also CA 9-12R; CANR 7; DLB 103

Bruce, Lenny..................... **CLC 21**
See also Schneider, Leonard Alfred

Bruin, John
See Brutus, Dennis

Brulls, Christian
See Simenon, Georges (Jacques Christian)

Brunner, John (Kilian Houston)
1934- .... **CLC 8, 10**
See also CA 1-4R; CAAS 8; CANR 2, 37;
MTCW

Brutus, Dennis 1924- .... **CLC 43**
See also BLC 1; BW; CA 49-52; CAAS 14;
CANR 2, 27; DLB 117

Bryan, C(ourtlandt) D(ixon) B(arnes)
1936- .... **CLC 29**
See also CA 73-76; CANR 13

Bryan, Michael
See Moore, Brian

Bryant, William Cullen
1794-1878 .... **NCLC 6**
See also CDALB 1640-1865; DLB 3, 43, 59

Bryusov, Valery Yakovlevich
1873-1924 .... **TCLC 10**
See also CA 107

Buchan, John 1875-1940 .... **TCLC 41**
See also CA 108; DLB 34, 70; YABC 2

Buchanan, George 1506-1582 .... **LC 4**

Buchheim, Lothar-Guenther 1918- ... **CLC 6**
See also CA 85-88

Buchner, (Karl) Georg
1813-1837 .... **NCLC 26**

Buchwald, Art(hur) 1925-......... **CLC 33**
See also AITN 1; CA 5-8R; CANR 21;
MTCW; SATA 10

Buck, Pearl S(ydenstricker)
1892-1973 .... **CLC 7, 11, 18**
See also AITN 1; CA 1-4R; 41-44R;
CANR 1, 34; DLB 9, 102; MTCW;
SATA 1, 25

Buckler, Ernest 1908-1984......... **CLC 13**
See also CA 11-12; 114; CAP 1; DLB 68;
SATA 47

Buckley, Vincent (Thomas)
1925-1988 .... **CLC 57**
See also CA 101

Buckley, William F(rank) Jr.
1925- .... **CLC 7, 18, 37**
See also AITN 1; CA 1-4R; CANR 1, 24;
DLBY 80; MTCW

Buechner, (Carl) Frederick
1926- .... **CLC 2, 4, 6, 9**
See also CA 13-16R; CANR 11, 39;
DLBY 80; MTCW

Buell, John (Edward) 1927-........ **CLC 10**
See also CA 1-4R; DLB 53

Buero Vallejo, Antonio 1916- ... **CLC 15, 46**
See also CA 106; CANR 24; HW; MTCW

Bugayev, Boris Nikolayevich 1880-1934
See Bely, Andrey
See also CA 104

Bukowski, Charles 1920- .... **CLC 2, 5, 9, 41**
See also CA 17-20R; DLB 5; MTCW

Bulgakov, Mikhail (Afanas'evich)
1891-1940 .... **TCLC 2, 16**
See also CA 105

Bullins, Ed 1935- .... **CLC 1, 5, 7**
See also BLC 1; BW; CA 49-52; CAAS 16;
CANR 24; DLB 7, 38; MTCW

Bulwer-Lytton, Edward (George Earle Lytton)
1803-1873 .... **NCLC 1**
See also DLB 21

Bunin, Ivan Alexeyevich
1870-1953 .... **TCLC 6; SSC 5**
See also CA 104

Bunting, Basil 1900-1985.... **CLC 10, 39, 47**
See also CA 53-56; 115; CANR 7; DLB 20

Bunuel, Luis 1900-1983 .... **CLC 16**
See also CA 101; 110; CANR 32; HW

Bunyan, John 1628-1688 .... **LC 4**
See also CDBLB 1660-1789; DLB 39; WLC

Burford, Eleanor
See Hibbert, Eleanor Burford

Burgess, Anthony
.. **CLC 1, 2, 4, 5, 8, 10, 13, 15, 22, 40, 62**
See also Wilson, John (Anthony) Burgess
See also AITN 1; CDBLB 1960 to Present;
DLB 14

Burke, Edmund 1729(?)-1797........ **LC 7**
See also DLB 104; WLC

Burke, Kenneth (Duva) 1897- .... **CLC 2, 24**
See also CA 5-8R; CANR 39; DLB 45, 63;
MTCW

Burke, Leda
See Garnett, David

Burke, Ralph
See Silverberg, Robert

Burney, Fanny 1752-1840 .... **NCLC 12**
See also DLB 39

Burns, Robert 1759-1796............ **LC 3**
See also CDBLB 1789-1832; DLB 109;
WLC

Burns, Tex
See L'Amour, Louis (Dearborn)

Burnshaw, Stanley 1906-..... **CLC 3, 13, 44**
See also CA 9-12R; DLB 48

Burr, Anne 1937-................. **CLC 6**
See also CA 25-28R

Burroughs, Edgar Rice
1875-1950 .... **TCLC 2, 32**
See also CA 104; 132; DLB 8; MTCW;
SATA 41

Burroughs, William S(eward)
1914-.......... **CLC 1, 2, 5, 15, 22, 42**
See also AITN 2; CA 9-12R; CANR 20;
DLB 2, 8, 16; DLBY 81; MTCW; WLC

Busch, Frederick 1941-... **CLC 7, 10, 18, 47**
See also CA 33-36R; CAAS 1; DLB 6

Bush, Ronald 1946- .... **CLC 34**
See also CA 136

Bustos, F(rancisco)
See Borges, Jorge Luis

Bustos Domecq, H(onorio)
See Bioy Casares, Adolfo; Borges, Jorge
Luis

Bustos Domecq, H(onrio)
See Borges, Jorge Luis

Butler, Octavia E(stelle) 1947-..... **CLC 38**
See also BW; CA 73-76; CANR 12, 24, 38;
DLB 33; MTCW

Butler, Samuel 1612-1680 .... **LC 16**
See also DLB 101

Butler, Samuel 1835-1902 ...... **TCLC 1, 33**
See also CA 104; CDBLB 1890-1914;
DLB 18, 57; WLC

Butor, Michel (Marie Francois)
1926- .... **CLC 1, 3, 8, 11, 15**
See also CA 9-12R; CANR 33; DLB 83;
MTCW

Buzo, Alexander (John) 1944-...... **CLC 61**
See also CA 97-100; CANR 17, 39

Buzzati, Dino 1906-1972 .... **CLC 36**
See also CA 33-36R

Byars, Betsy (Cromer) 1928-....... **CLC 35**
See also CA 33-36R; CANR 18, 36; CLR 1,
16; DLB 52; MAICYA; MTCW; SAAS 1;
SATA 4, 46

Byatt, A(ntonia) S(usan Drabble)
1936- .... **CLC 19, 65**
See also CA 13-16R; CANR 13, 33;
DLB 14; MTCW

Byrne, David 1952-................ **CLC 26**
See also CA 127

Byrne, John Keyes 1926-.......... **CLC 19**
See also Leonard, Hugh
See also CA 102

Byron, George Gordon (Noel)
1788-1824 .... **NCLC 2, 12**
See also CDBLB 1789-1832; DLB 96, 110;
WLC

C.3.3.
See Wilde, Oscar (Fingal O'Flahertie Wills)

Caballero, Fernan 1796-1877..... **NCLC 10**

Cabell, James Branch 1879-1958 ... **TCLC 6**
See also CA 105; DLB 9, 78

Cable, George Washington
1844-1925 .... **TCLC 4; SSC 4**
See also CA 104; DLB 12, 74

Cabrera Infante, G(uillermo)
1929-.................. **CLC 5, 25, 45**
See also CA 85-88; CANR 29; DLB 113;
HW; MTCW

Cade, Toni
See Bambara, Toni Cade

Cadmus
See Buchan, John

Caedmon fl. 658-680............. **CMLC 7**

Caeiro, Alberto
See Pessoa, Fernando (Antonio Nogueira)

Cage, John (Milton Jr.) 1912-...... **CLC 41**
See also CA 13-16R; CANR 9

Cain, G.
See Cabrera Infante, G(uillermo)

Cain, Guillermo
See Cabrera Infante, G(uillermo)

Cain, James M(allahan)
1892-1977 .... **CLC 3, 11, 28**
See also AITN 1; CA 17-20R; 73-76;
CANR 8, 34; MTCW

Caine, Mark
See Raphael, Frederic (Michael)

Caldwell, Erskine (Preston)
1903-1987 .... **CLC 1, 8, 14, 50, 60**
See also AITN 1; CA 1-4R; 121; CAAS 1;
CANR 2, 33; DLB 9, 86; MTCW

Caldwell, (Janet Miriam) Taylor (Holland)
1900-1985 .... **CLC 2, 28, 39**
See also CA 5-8R; 116; CANR 5

Calhoun, John Caldwell
1782-1850 .... **NCLC 15**
See also DLB 3

Calisher, Hortense 1911-.... **CLC 2, 4, 8, 38**
See also CA 1-4R; CANR 1, 22; DLB 2;
MTCW

Callaghan, Morley Edward
1903-1990 .... **CLC 3, 14, 41, 65**
See also CA 9-12R; 132; CANR 33;
DLB 68; MTCW

Calvino, Italo
1923-1985 .... **CLC 5, 8, 11, 22, 33, 39;**
SSC 3
See also CA 85-88; 116; CANR 23; MTCW

Cameron, Carey 1952-............. **CLC 59**
See also CA 135

Cameron, Peter 1959-............. **CLC 44**
See also CA 125

Campana, Dino 1885-1932........ **TCLC 20**
See also CA 117; DLB 114

Campbell, John W(ood Jr.)
1910-1971 .... **CLC 32**
See also CA 21-22; 29-32R; CANR 34;
CAP 2; DLB 8; MTCW

Campbell, Joseph 1904-1987 .... **CLC 69**
See also AAYA 3; BEST 89:2; CA 1-4R;
124; CANR 3, 28; MTCW

Campbell, (John) Ramsey 1946- .... **CLC 42**
See also CA 57-60; CANR 7

Campbell, (Ignatius) Roy (Dunnachie)
1901-1957 .... **TCLC 5**
See also CA 104; DLB 20

Campbell, Thomas 1777-1844 .... **NCLC 19**
See also DLB 93

Campbell, Wilfred................. **TCLC 9**
See also Campbell, William

Campbell, William 1858(?)-1918
See Campbell, Wilfred
See also CA 106; DLB 92

Campos, Alvaro de
See Pessoa, Fernando (Antonio Nogueira)

Camus, Albert
1913-1960 ... **CLC 1, 2, 4, 9, 11, 14, 32,**
63, 69; DC 2; SSC 9
See also CA 89-92; DLB 72; MTCW; WLC

Canby, Vincent 1924-............. **CLC 13**
See also CA 81-84

Cancale
See Desnos, Robert

Canetti, Elias 1905- .... **CLC 3, 14, 25**
See also CA 21-24R; CANR 23; DLB 85;
MTCW

Canin, Ethan 1960-............... **CLC 55**
See also CA 131; 135

Cannon, Curt
See Hunter, Evan

Cape, Judith
See Page, P(atricia) K(athleen)

Capek, Karel
1890-1938 .... **TCLC 6, 37; DC 1**
See also CA 104; WLC

Capote, Truman
1924-1984 ..... **CLC 1, 3, 8, 13, 19, 34,**
38, 58; SSC 2
See also CA 5-8R; 113; CANR 18;
CDALB 1941-1968; DLB 2; DLBY 80,
84; MTCW; WLC

Capra, Frank 1897-1991........... **CLC 16**
See also CA 61-64; 135

Caputo, Philip 1941-.............. **CLC 32**
See also CA 73-76

Card, Orson Scott 1951- .... **CLC 44, 47, 50**
See also CA 102; CANR 27; MTCW

Cardenal (Martinez), Ernesto
1925- .... **CLC 31**
See also CA 49-52; CANR 2, 32; HW;
MTCW

Carducci, Giosue 1835-1907....... **TCLC 32**

Carew, Thomas 1595(?)-1640........ **LC 13**

Carey, Ernestine Gilbreth 1908-.... **CLC 17**
See also CA 5-8R; SATA 2

Carey, Peter 1943-............. **CLC 40, 55**
See also CA 123; 127; MTCW

Carleton, William 1794-1869...... **NCLC 3**

Carlisle, Henry (Coffin) 1926-...... **CLC 33**
See also CA 13-16R; CANR 15

Carlsen, Chris
See Holdstock, Robert P.

Carlson, Ron(ald F.) 1947-......... **CLC 54**
See also CA 105; CANR 27

Carlyle, Thomas 1795-1881...... **NCLC 22**
See also CDBLB 1789-1832; DLB 55

Carman, (William) Bliss
1861-1929 .... **TCLC 7**
See also CA 104; DLB 92

Carpenter, Don(ald Richard)
1931- .... **CLC 41**
See also CA 45-48; CANR 1

Carpentier (y Valmont), Alejo
   1904-1980 . . . . **CLC 8, 11, 38**
   See also CA 65-68; 97-100; CANR 11;
   DLB 113; HW

Carr, Emily 1871-1945 . . . . **TCLC 32**
   See also DLB 68

Carr, John Dickson 1906-1977 . . . . . . **CLC 3**
   See also CA 49-52; 69-72; CANR 3, 33;
   MTCW

Carr, Philippa
   See Hibbert, Eleanor Burford

Carr, Virginia Spencer 1929- . . . . **CLC 34**
   See also CA 61-64; DLB 111

Carrier, Roch 1937- . . . . **CLC 13**
   See also CA 130; DLB 53

Carroll, James P. 1943(?)- . . . . **CLC 38**
   See also CA 81-84

Carroll, Jim 1951- . . . . **CLC 35**
   See also CA 45-48

Carroll, Lewis . . . . **NCLC 2**
   See also Dodgson, Charles Lutwidge
   See also CDBLB 1832-1890; CLR 2, 18;
   DLB 18; WLC

Carroll, Paul Vincent 1900-1968. . . . **CLC 10**
   See also CA 9-12R; 25-28R; DLB 10

Carruth, Hayden 1921- . . . . **CLC 4, 7, 10, 18**
   See also CA 9-12R; CANR 4, 38; DLB 5;
   MTCW; SATA 47

Carson, Rachel Louise 1907-1964 . . . **CLC 71**
   See also CA 77-80; CANR 35; MTCW;
   SATA 23

Carter, Angela (Olive)
   1940-1991 . . . . **CLC 5, 41**
   See also CA 53-56; 136; CANR 12, 36;
   DLB 14; MTCW; SATA 66; SATO 70

Carter, Nick
   See Smith, Martin Cruz

Carver, Raymond
   1938-1988 . . . **CLC 22, 36, 53, 55; SSC 8**
   See also CA 33-36R; 126; CANR 17, 34;
   DLBY 84, 88; MTCW

Cary, (Arthur) Joyce (Lunel)
   1888-1957 . . . . **TCLC 1, 29**
   See also CA 104; CDBLB 1914-1945;
   DLB 15, 100

Casanova de Seingalt, Giovanni Jacopo
   1725-1798 . . . . **LC 13**

Casares, Adolfo Bioy
   See Bioy Casares, Adolfo

Casely-Hayford, J(oseph) E(phraim)
   1866-1930 . . . . **TCLC 24**
   See also BLC 1; CA 123

Casey, John (Dudley) 1939- . . . . **CLC 59**
   See also BEST 90:2; CA 69-72; CANR 23

Casey, Michael 1947- . . . . **CLC 2**
   See also CA 65-68; DLB 5

Casey, Patrick
   See Thurman, Wallace (Henry)

Casey, Warren (Peter) 1935-1988 . . . **CLC 12**
   See also CA 101; 127

Casona, Alejandro . . . . **CLC 49**
   See also Alvarez, Alejandro Rodriguez

Cassavetes, John 1929-1989 . . . . **CLC 20**
   See also CA 85-88; 127

Cassill, R(onald) V(erlin) 1919- . . . **CLC 4, 23**
   See also CA 9-12R; CAAS 1; CANR 7;
   DLB 6

Cassity, (Allen) Turner 1929- . . . . **CLC 6, 42**
   See also CA 17-20R; CAAS 8; CANR 11;
   DLB 105

Castaneda, Carlos 1931(?)- . . . . **CLC 12**
   See also CA 25-28R; CANR 32; HW;
   MTCW

Castedo, Elena 1937- . . . . **CLC 65**
   See also CA 132

Castedo-Ellerman, Elena
   See Castedo, Elena

Castellanos, Rosario 1925-1974 . . . . . **CLC 66**
   See also CA 131; 53-56; DLB 113; HW

Castelvetro, Lodovico 1505-1571 . . . . **LC 12**

Castiglione, Baldassare 1478-1529 . . . **LC 12**

Castle, Robert
   See Hamilton, Edmond

Castro, Guillen de 1569-1631 . . . . **LC 19**

Castro, Rosalia de 1837-1885 . . . . . **NCLC 3**

Cather, Willa
   See Cather, Willa Sibert

Cather, Willa Sibert
   1873-1947 . . . . . . **TCLC 1, 11, 31; SSC 2**
   See also CA 104; 128; CDALB 1865-1917;
   DLB 9, 54, 78; DLBD 1; MTCW;
   SATA 30; WLC

Catton, (Charles) Bruce
   1899-1978 . . . . **CLC 35**
   See also AITN 1; CA 5-8R; 81-84;
   CANR 7; DLB 17; SATA 2, 24

Cauldwell, Frank
   See King, Francis (Henry)

Caunitz, William J. 1933- . . . . **CLC 34**
   See also BEST 89:3; CA 125; 130

Causley, Charles (Stanley) 1917- . . . . . **CLC 7**
   See also CA 9-12R; CANR 5, 35; DLB 27;
   MTCW; SATA 3, 66

Caute, David 1936- . . . . **CLC 29**
   See also CA 1-4R; CAAS 4; CANR 1, 33;
   DLB 14

Cavafy, C(onstantine) P(eter) . . . . . . **TCLC 2, 7**
   See also Kavafis, Konstantinos Petrou

Cavallo, Evelyn
   See Spark, Muriel (Sarah)

Cavanna, Betty . . . . **CLC 12**
   See also Harrison, Elizabeth Cavanna
   See also MAICYA; SAAS 4; SATA 1, 30

Caxton, William 1421(?)-1491(?) . . . . . **LC 17**

Cayrol, Jean 1911- . . . . **CLC 11**
   See also CA 89-92; DLB 83

Cela, Camilo Jose 1916- . . . . . . **CLC 4, 13, 59**
   See also BEST 90:2; CA 21-24R; CAAS 10;
   CANR 21, 32; DLBY 89; HW; MTCW

Celan, Paul . . . . **CLC 53**
   See also Antschel, Paul
   See also DLB 69

Celine, Louis-Ferdinand
   . . . . **CLC 1, 3, 4, 7, 9, 15, 47**
   See also Destouches, Louis-Ferdinand
   See also DLB 72

Cellini, Benvenuto 1500-1571 . . . . **LC 7**

Cendrars, Blaise
   See Sauser-Hall, Frederic

Cernuda (y Bidon), Luis
   1902-1963 . . . . **CLC 54**
   See also CA 131; 89-92; HW

Cervantes (Saavedra), Miguel de
   1547-1616 . . . . **LC 6**
   See also WLC

Cesaire, Aime (Fernand) 1913- . . **CLC 19, 32**
   See also BLC 1; BW; CA 65-68; CANR 24;
   MTCW

Chabon, Michael 1965(?)- . . . . **CLC 55**

Chabrol, Claude 1930- . . . . **CLC 16**
   See also CA 110

Challans, Mary 1905-1983
   See Renault, Mary
   See also CA 81-84; 111; SATA 23, 36

Chambers, Aidan 1934- . . . . **CLC 35**
   See also CA 25-28R; CANR 12, 31;
   MAICYA; SAAS 12; SATA 1, 69

Chambers, James 1948-
   See Cliff, Jimmy
   See also CA 124

Chambers, Jessie
   See Lawrence, D(avid) H(erbert Richards)

Chambers, Robert W. 1865-1933 . . . **TCLC 41**

Chandler, Raymond (Thornton)
   1888-1959 . . . . **TCLC 1, 7**
   See also CA 104; 129; CDALB 1929-1941;
   DLBD 6; MTCW

Chang, Jung 1952- . . . . **CLC 71**

Channing, William Ellery
   1780-1842 . . . . **NCLC 17**
   See also DLB 1, 59

Chaplin, Charles Spencer
   1889-1977 . . . . **CLC 16**
   See also Chaplin, Charlie
   See also CA 81-84; 73-76

Chaplin, Charlie
   See Chaplin, Charles Spencer
   See also DLB 44

Chapman, Graham 1941-1989 . . . . . . **CLC 21**
   See also Monty Python
   See also CA 116; 129; CANR 35

Chapman, John Jay 1862-1933 . . . . . **TCLC 7**
   See also CA 104

Chapman, Walker
   See Silverberg, Robert

Chappell, Fred (Davis) 1936- . . . . **CLC 40**
   See also CA 5-8R; CAAS 4; CANR 8, 33;
   DLB 6, 105

Char, Rene(-Emile)
   1907-1988 . . . . **CLC 9, 11, 14, 55**
   See also CA 13-16R; 124; CANR 32;
   MTCW

Charby, Jay
   See Ellison, Harlan

Chardin, Pierre Teilhard de
   See Teilhard de Chardin, (Marie Joseph)
   Pierre

Charles I 1600-1649 . . . . **LC 13**

Charyn, Jerome 1937- . . . . **CLC 5, 8, 18**
   See also CA 5-8R; CAAS 1; CANR 7;
   DLBY 83; MTCW

Chase, Mary (Coyle) 1907-1981 ...... **DC 1**
See also CA 77-80; 105; SATA 17, 29

Chase, Mary Ellen 1887-1973 .... **CLC 2**
See also CA 13-16; 41-44R; CAP 1;
SATA 10

Chase, Nicholas
See Hyde, Anthony

Chateaubriand, Francois Rene de
1768-1848 .... **NCLC 3**
See also DLB 119

Chatterje, Sarat Chandra 1876-1936(?)
See Chatterji, Saratchandra
See also CA 109

Chatterji, Bankim Chandra
1838-1894 .... **NCLC 19**

Chatterji, Saratchandra .... **TCLC 13**
See also Chatterje, Sarat Chandra

Chatterton, Thomas 1752-1770 ...... **LC 3**
See also DLB 109

Chatwin, (Charles) Bruce
1940-1989 .... **CLC 28, 57, 59**
See also AAYA 4; BEST 90:1; CA 85-88;
127

Chaucer, Daniel
See Ford, Ford Madox

Chaucer, Geoffrey 1340(?)-1400 ..... **LC 17**
See also CDBLB Before 1660

Chaviaras, Strates 1935-
See Haviaras, Stratis
See also CA 105

Chayefsky, Paddy .... **CLC 23**
See also Chayefsky, Sidney
See also DLB 7, 44; DLBY 81

Chayefsky, Sidney 1923-1981
See Chayefsky, Paddy
See also CA 9-12R; 104; CANR 18

Chedid, Andree 1920- .... **CLC 47**

Cheever, John
1912-1982 ..... **CLC 3, 7, 8, 11, 15, 25,**
64; SSC 1
See also CA 5-8R; 106; CABS 1; CANR 5,
27; CDALB 1941-1968; DLB 2, 102;
DLBY 80, 82; MTCW; WLC

Cheever, Susan 1943- .... **CLC 18, 48**
See also CA 103; CANR 27; DLBY 82

Chekhonte, Antosha
See Chekhov, Anton (Pavlovich)

Chekhov, Anton (Pavlovich)
1860-1904 ...... **TCLC 3, 10, 31; SSC 2**
See also CA 104; 124; WLC

Chernyshevsky, Nikolay Gavrilovich
1828-1889 .... **NCLC 1**

Cherry, Carolyn Janice 1942-
See Cherryh, C. J.
See also CA 65-68; CANR 10

Cherryh, C. J. .... **CLC 35**
See also Cherry, Carolyn Janice
See also DLBY 80

Chesnutt, Charles W(addell)
1858-1932 .... **TCLC 5, 39; SSC 7**
See also BLC 1; BW; CA 106; 125; DLB 12,
50, 78; MTCW

Chester, Alfred 1929(?)-1971 .... **CLC 49**
See also CA 33-36R

Chesterton, G(ilbert) K(eith)
1874-1936 .... **TCLC 1, 6; SSC 1**
See also CA 104; 132; CDBLB 1914-1945;
DLB 10, 19, 34, 70, 98; MTCW;
SATA 27

Chiang Pin-chin 1904-1986
See Ding Ling
See also CA 118

Ch'ien Chung-shu 1910- .... **CLC 22**
See also CA 130; MTCW

Child, L. Maria
See Child, Lydia Maria

Child, Lydia Maria 1802-1880 .... **NCLC 6**
See also DLB 1, 74; SATA 67

Child, Mrs.
See Child, Lydia Maria

Child, Philip 1898-1978 .... **CLC 19, 68**
See also CA 13-14; CAP 1; SATA 47

Childress, Alice 1920- .... **CLC 12, 15**
See also AAYA 8; BLC 1; BW; CA 45-48;
CANR 3, 27; CLR 14; DLB 7, 38;
MAICYA; MTCW; SATA 7, 48

Chislett, (Margaret) Anne 1943- .... **CLC 34**

Chitty, Thomas Willes 1926- .... **CLC 11**
See also Hinde, Thomas
See also CA 5-8R

Chomette, Rene Lucien 1898-1981 .. **CLC 20**
See also Clair, Rene
See also CA 103

Chopin, Kate .... **TCLC 5, 14; SSC 8**
See also Chopin, Katherine
See also CDALB 1865-1917; DLB 12, 78

Chopin, Katherine 1851-1904
See Chopin, Kate
See also CA 104; 122

Christie
See Ichikawa, Kon

Christie, Agatha (Mary Clarissa)
1890-1976 ...... **CLC 1, 6, 8, 12, 39, 48**
See also AAYA 9; AITN 1, 2; CA 17-20R;
61-64; CANR 10, 37; CDBLB 1914-1945;
DLB 13, 77; MTCW; SATA 36

Christie, (Ann) Philippa
See Pearce, Philippa
See also CA 5-8R; CANR 4

Christine de Pizan 1365(?)-1431(?) .... **LC 9**

Chubb, Elmer
See Masters, Edgar Lee

Chulkov, Mikhail Dmitrievich
1743-1792 .... **LC 2**

Churchill, Caryl 1938- .... **CLC 31, 55**
See also CA 102; CANR 22; DLB 13;
MTCW

Churchill, Charles 1731-1764 .... **LC 3**
See also DLB 109

Chute, Carolyn 1947- .... **CLC 39**
See also CA 123

Ciardi, John (Anthony)
1916-1986 .... **CLC 10, 40, 44**
See also CA 5-8R; 118; CAAS 2; CANR 5,
33; CLR 19; DLB 5; DLBY 86;
MAICYA; MTCW; SATA 1, 46, 65

Cicero, Marcus Tullius
106B.C.-43B.C. .... **CMLC 3**

Cimino, Michael 1943- .... **CLC 16**
See also CA 105

Cioran, E(mil) M. 1911- .... **CLC 64**
See also CA 25-28R

Cisneros, Sandra 1954- .... **CLC 69**
See also AAYA 9; CA 131; HW

Clair, Rene .... **CLC 20**
See also Chomette, Rene Lucien

Clampitt, Amy 1920- .... **CLC 32**
See also CA 110; CANR 29; DLB 105

Clancy, Thomas L. Jr. 1947-
See Clancy, Tom
See also CA 125; 131; MTCW

Clancy, Tom .... **CLC 45**
See also Clancy, Thomas L. Jr.
See also AAYA 9; BEST 89:1, 90:1

Clare, John 1793-1864 .... **NCLC 9**
See also DLB 55, 96

Clarin
See Alas (y Urena), Leopoldo (Enrique
Garcia)

Clark, (Robert) Brian 1932- .... **CLC 29**
See also CA 41-44R

Clark, Eleanor 1913- .... **CLC 5, 19**
See also CA 9-12R; DLB 6

Clark, J. P.
See Clark, John Pepper
See also DLB 117

Clark, John Pepper 1935- .... **CLC 38**
See also Clark, J. P.
See also BLC 1; BW; CA 65-68; CANR 16

Clark, M. R.
See Clark, Mavis Thorpe

Clark, Mavis Thorpe 1909- .... **CLC 12**
See also CA 57-60; CANR 8, 37; MAICYA;
SAAS 5; SATA 8

Clark, Walter Van Tilburg
1909-1971 .... **CLC 28**
See also CA 9-12R; 33-36R; DLB 9;
SATA 8

Clarke, Arthur C(harles)
1917- ...... **CLC 1, 4, 13, 18, 35; SSC 3**
See also AAYA 4; CA 1-4R; CANR 2, 28;
MAICYA; MTCW; SATA 13, 70

Clarke, Austin C(hesterfield)
1934- .... **CLC 8, 53**
See also BLC 1; BW; CA 25-28R;
CAAS 16; CANR 14, 32; DLB 53

Clarke, Austin 1896-1974 .... **CLC 6, 9**
See also CA 29-32; 49-52; CAP 2; DLB 10,
20

Clarke, Gillian 1937- .... **CLC 61**
See also CA 106; DLB 40

Clarke, Marcus (Andrew Hislop)
1846-1881 .... **NCLC 19**

Clarke, Shirley 1925- .... **CLC 16**

.... **CLC 30**
See also Headon, (Nicky) Topper; Jones,
Mick; Simonon, Paul; Strummer, Joe

Claudel, Paul (Louis Charles Marie)
1868-1955 .... **TCLC 2, 10**
See also CA 104

Clavell, James (duMaresq)
1925- .... **CLC 6, 25**
See also CA 25-28R; CANR 26; MTCW

Cleaver, (Leroy) Eldridge 1935- .... **CLC 30**
See also BLC 1; BW; CA 21-24R;
CANR 16

Cleese, John (Marwood) 1939- ..... **CLC 21**
See also Monty Python
See also CA 112; 116; CANR 35; MTCW

Cleishbotham, Jebediah
See Scott, Walter

Cleland, John 1710-1789 .... **LC 2**
See also DLB 39

Clemens, Samuel Langhorne 1835-1910
See Twain, Mark
See also CA 104; 135; CDALB 1865-1917;
DLB 11, 12, 23, 64, 74; MAICYA;
YABC 2

Clerihew, E.
See Bentley, E(dmund) C(lerihew)

Clerk, N. W.
See Lewis, C(live) S(taples)

Cliff, Jimmy .... **CLC 21**
See also Chambers, James

Clifton, (Thelma) Lucille
1936- .... **CLC 19, 66**
See also BLC 1; BW; CA 49-52; CANR 2,
24; CLR 5; DLB 5, 41; MAICYA;
MTCW; SATA 20, 69

Clinton, Dirk
See Silverberg, Robert

Clough, Arthur Hugh 1819-1861 .. **NCLC 27**
See also DLB 32

Clutha, Janet Paterson Frame 1924-
See Frame, Janet
See also CA 1-4R; CANR 2, 36; MTCW

Clyne, Terence
See Blatty, William Peter

Cobalt, Martin
See Mayne, William (James Carter)

Coburn, D(onald) L(ee) 1938- ...... **CLC 10**
See also CA 89-92

Cocteau, Jean (Maurice Eugene Clement)
1889-1963 .... **CLC 1, 8, 15, 16, 43**
See also CA 25-28; CAP 2; DLB 65;
MTCW; WLC

Codrescu, Andrei 1946- .... **CLC 46**
See also CA 33-36R; CANR 13, 34

Coe, Max
See Bourne, Randolph S(illiman)

Coe, Tucker
See Westlake, Donald E(dwin)

Coetzee, J(ohn) M(ichael)
1940- .... **CLC 23, 33, 66**
See also CA 77-80; MTCW

Cohen, Arthur A(llen)
1928-1986 .... **CLC 7, 31**
See also CA 1-4R; 120; CANR 1, 17;
DLB 28

Cohen, Leonard (Norman)
1934- .... **CLC 3, 38**
See also CA 21-24R; CANR 14; DLB 53;
MTCW

Cohen, Matt 1942- .... **CLC 19**
See also CA 61-64; DLB 53

Cohen-Solal, Annie 19(?)- .... **CLC 50**

Colegate, Isabel 1931- .... **CLC 36**
See also CA 17-20R; CANR 8, 22; DLB 14;
MTCW

Coleman, Emmett
See Reed, Ishmael

Coleridge, Samuel Taylor
1772-1834 .... **NCLC 9**
See also CDBLB 1789-1832; DLB 93, 107;
WLC

Coleridge, Sara 1802-1852 .... **NCLC 31**

Coles, Don 1928- .... **CLC 46**
See also CA 115; CANR 38

Colette, (Sidonie-Gabrielle)
1873-1954 ...... **TCLC 1, 5, 16; SSC 10**
See also CA 104; 131; DLB 65; MTCW

Collett, (Jacobine) Camilla (Wergeland)
1813-1895 .... **NCLC 22**

Collier, Christopher 1930- .... **CLC 30**
See also CA 33-36R; CANR 13, 33;
MAICYA; SATA 16, 70

Collier, James L(incoln) 1928- ..... **CLC 30**
See also CA 9-12R; CANR 4, 33;
MAICYA; SATA 8, 70

Collier, Jeremy 1650-1726 .... **LC 6**

Collins, Hunt
See Hunter, Evan

Collins, Linda 1931- .... **CLC 44**
See also CA 125

Collins, (William) Wilkie
1824-1889 .... **NCLC 1, 18**
See also CDBLB 1832-1890; DLB 18, 70

Collins, William 1721-1759 .... **LC 4**
See also DLB 109

Colman, George
See Glassco, John

Colt, Winchester Remington
See Hubbard, L(afayette) Ron(ald)

Colter, Cyrus 1910- .... **CLC 58**
See also BW; CA 65-68; CANR 10; DLB 33

Colton, James
See Hansen, Joseph

Colum, Padraic 1881-1972 .... **CLC 28**
See also CA 73-76; 33-36R; CANR 35;
MAICYA; MTCW; SATA 15

Colvin, James
See Moorcock, Michael (John)

Colwin, Laurie 1944- .... **CLC 5, 13, 23**
See also CA 89-92; CANR 20; DLBY 80;
MTCW

Comfort, Alex(ander) 1920- .... **CLC 7**
See also CA 1-4R; CANR 1

Comfort, Montgomery
See Campbell, (John) Ramsey

Compton-Burnett, I(vy)
1884(?)-1969 ...... **CLC 1, 3, 10, 15, 34**
See also CA 1-4R; 25-28R; CANR 4;
DLB 36; MTCW

Comstock, Anthony 1844-1915 .... **TCLC 13**
See also CA 110

Conan Doyle, Arthur
See Doyle, Arthur Conan

Conde, Maryse .... **CLC 52**
See also Boucolon, Maryse

Condon, Richard (Thomas)
1915- .... **CLC 4, 6, 8, 10, 45**
See also BEST 90:3; CA 1-4R; CAAS 1;
CANR 2, 23; MTCW

Congreve, William
1670-1729 .... **LC 5, 21; DC 2**
See also CDBLB 1660-1789; DLB 39, 84;
WLC

Connell, Evan S(helby) Jr.
1924- .... **CLC 4, 6, 45**
See also AAYA 7; CA 1-4R; CAAS 2;
CANR 2, 39; DLB 2; DLBY 81; MTCW

Connelly, Marc(us Cook)
1890-1980 .... **CLC 7**
See also CA 85-88; 102; CANR 30; DLB 7;
DLBY 80; SATA 25

Connor, Ralph .... **TCLC 31**
See also Gordon, Charles William
See also DLB 92

Conrad, Joseph
1857-1924 ...... **TCLC 1, 6, 13, 25, 43;**
SSC 9
See also CA 104; 131; CDBLB 1890-1914;
DLB 10, 34, 98; MTCW; SATA 27; WLC

Conrad, Robert Arnold
See Hart, Moss

Conroy, Pat 1945- .... **CLC 30**
See also AAYA 8; AITN 1; CA 85-88;
CANR 24; DLB 6; MTCW

Constant (de Rebecque), (Henri) Benjamin
1767-1830 .... **NCLC 6**
See also DLB 119

Conybeare, Charles Augustus
See Eliot, T(homas) S(tearns)

Cook, Michael 1933- .... **CLC 58**
See also CA 93-96; DLB 53

Cook, Robin 1940- .... **CLC 14**
See also BEST 90:2; CA 108; 111

Cook, Roy
See Silverberg, Robert

Cooke, Elizabeth 1948- .... **CLC 55**
See also CA 129

Cooke, John Esten 1830-1886 ..... **NCLC 5**
See also DLB 3

Cooke, John Estes
See Baum, L(yman) Frank

Cooke, M. E.
See Creasey, John

Cooke, Margaret
See Creasey, John

Cooney, Ray .... **CLC 62**

Cooper, Henry St. John
See Creasey, John

Cooper, J. California .... **CLC 56**
See also BW; CA 125

Cooper, James Fenimore
1789-1851 .... **NCLC 1, 27**
See also CDALB 1640-1865; DLB 3;
SATA 19

Coover, Robert (Lowell)
1932- .... **CLC 3, 7, 15, 32, 46**
See also CA 45-48; CANR 3, 37; DLB 2;
DLBY 81; MTCW

Copeland, Stewart (Armstrong)
1952- .... **CLC 26**
See also The Police

Coppard, A(lfred) E(dgar)
1878-1957 .... **TCLC 5**
See also CA 114; YABC 1

Coppee, Francois 1842-1908 ..... **TCLC 25**

Coppola, Francis Ford 1939-...... **CLC 16**
See also CA 77-80; DLB 44

Corcoran, Barbara 1911-.......... **CLC 17**
See also CA 21-24R; CAAS 2; CANR 11,
28; DLB 52; SATA 3

Cordelier, Maurice
See Giraudoux, (Hippolyte) Jean

Corman, Cid....................... **CLC 9**
See also Corman, Sidney
See also CAAS 2; DLB 5

Corman, Sidney 1924-
See Corman, Cid
See also CA 85-88

Cormier, Robert (Edmund)
1925- .... **CLC 12, 30**
See also AAYA 3; CA 1-4R; CANR 5, 23;
CDALB 1968-1988; CLR 12; DLB 52;
MAICYA; MTCW; SATA 10, 45

Corn, Alfred 1943-............... **CLC 33**
See also CA 104; DLB 120; DLBY 80

Cornwell, David (John Moore)
1931- .... **CLC 9, 15**
See also le Carre, John
See also CA 5-8R; CANR 13, 33; MTCW

Corrigan, Kevin................... **CLC 55**

Corso, (Nunzio) Gregory 1930-... **CLC 1, 11**
See also CA 5-8R; DLB 5,16; MTCW

Cortazar, Julio
1914-1984 ..... **CLC 2, 3, 5, 10, 13, 15,
33, 34; SSC 7**
See also CA 21-24R; CANR 12, 32;
DLB 113; HW; MTCW

Corwin, Cecil
See Kornbluth, C(yril) M.

Cosic, Dobrica 1921- .... **CLC 14**
See also CA 122; 138

Costain, Thomas B(ertram)
1885-1965 .... **CLC 30**
See also CA 5-8R; 25-28R; DLB 9

Costantini, Humberto
1924(?)-1987 .... **CLC 49**
See also CA 131; 122; HW

Costello, Elvis 1955-.............. **CLC 21**

Cotter, Joseph S. Sr.
See Cotter, Joseph Seamon Sr.

Cotter, Joseph Seamon Sr.
1861-1949 .... **TCLC 28**
See also BLC 1; BW; CA 124; DLB 50

Coulton, James
See Hansen, Joseph

Couperus, Louis (Marie Anne)
1863-1923 .... **TCLC 15**
See also CA 115

Court, Wesli
See Turco, Lewis (Putnam)

Courtenay, Bryce 1933-.......... **CLC 59**
See also CA 138

Courtney, Robert
See Ellison, Harlan

Cousteau, Jacques-Yves 1910-...... **CLC 30**
See also CA 65-68; CANR 15; MTCW;
SATA 38

Coward, Noel (Peirce)
1899-1973.............. **CLC 1, 9, 29, 51**
See also AITN 1; CA 17-18; 41-44R;
CANR 35; CAP 2; CDBLB 1914-1945;
DLB 10; MTCW

Cowley, Malcolm 1898-1989 .... **CLC 39**
See also CA 5-8R; 128; CANR 3; DLB 4,
48; DLBY 81, 89; MTCW

Cowper, William 1731-1800....... **NCLC 8**
See also DLB 104, 109

Cox, William Trevor 1928- ... **CLC 9, 14, 71**
See also Trevor, William
See also CA 9-12R; CANR 4, 37; DLB 14;
MTCW

Cozzens, James Gould
1903-1978 .... **CLC 1, 4, 11**
See also CA 9-12R; 81-84; CANR 19;
CDALB 1941-1968; DLB 9; DLBD 2;
DLBY 84; MTCW

Crabbe, George 1754-1832....... **NCLC 26**
See also DLB 93

Craig, A. A.
See Anderson, Poul (William)

Craik, Dinah Maria (Mulock)
1826-1887 .... **NCLC 38**
See also DLB 35; MAICYA; SATA 34

Cram, Ralph Adams 1863-1942.... **TCLC 45**

Crane, (Harold) Hart
1899-1932 .... **TCLC 2, 5; PC 3**
See also CA 104; 127; CDALB 1917-1929;
DLB 4, 48; MTCW; WLC

Crane, R(onald) S(almon)
1886-1967 .... **CLC 27**
See also CA 85-88; DLB 63

Crane, Stephen (Townley)
1871-1900 ..... **TCLC 11, 17, 32; SSC 7**
See also CA 109; CDALB 1865-1917;
DLB 12, 54, 78; WLC; YABC 2

Crase, Douglas 1944-............. **CLC 58**
See also CA 106

Craven, Margaret 1901-1980....... **CLC 17**
See also CA 103

Crawford, F(rancis) Marion
1854-1909 .... **TCLC 10**
See also CA 107; DLB 71

Crawford, Isabella Valancy
1850-1887 .... **NCLC 12**
See also DLB 92

Crayon, Geoffrey
See Irving, Washington

Creasey, John 1908-1973.......... **CLC 11**
See also CA 5-8R; 41-44R; CANR 8;
DLB 77; MTCW

Crebillon, Claude Prosper Jolyot de (fils)
1707-1777 .... **LC 1**

Credo
See Creasey, John

Creeley, Robert (White)
1926- .... **CLC 1, 2, 4, 8, 11, 15, 36**
See also CA 1-4R; CAAS 10; CANR 23;
DLB 5, 16; MTCW

Crews, Harry (Eugene)
1935- .... **CLC 6, 23, 49**
See also AITN 1; CA 25-28R; CANR 20;
DLB 6; MTCW

Crichton, (John) Michael
1942- .... **CLC 2, 6, 54**
See also AITN 2; CA 25-28R; CANR 13;
DLBY 81; MTCW; SATA 9

Crispin, Edmund .... **CLC 22**
See also Montgomery, (Robert) Bruce
See also DLB 87

Cristofer, Michael 1945(?)- .... **CLC 28**
See also CA 110; DLB 7

Croce, Benedetto 1866-1952 ...... **TCLC 37**
See also CA 120

Crockett, David 1786-1836 .... **NCLC 8**
See also DLB 3, 11

Crockett, Davy
See Crockett, David

Croker, John Wilson 1780-1857 .. **NCLC 10**
See also DLB 110

Cronin, A(rchibald) J(oseph)
1896-1981 .... **CLC 32**
See also CA 1-4R; 102; CANR 5; SATA 25,
47

Cross, Amanda
See Heilbrun, Carolyn G(old)

Crothers, Rachel 1878(?)-1958..... **TCLC 19**
See also CA 113; DLB 7

Croves, Hal
See Traven, B.

Crowfield, Christopher
See Stowe, Harriet (Elizabeth) Beecher

Crowley, Aleister.................. **TCLC 7**
See also Crowley, Edward Alexander

Crowley, Edward Alexander 1875-1947
See Crowley, Aleister
See also CA 104

Crowley, John 1942-.............. **CLC 57**
See also CA 61-64; DLBY 82; SATA 65

Crud
See Crumb, R(obert)

Crumarums
See Crumb, R(obert)

Crumb, R(obert) 1943-............. **CLC 17**
See also CA 106

Crumbum
See Crumb, R(obert)

Crumski
See Crumb, R(obert)

Crum the Bum
See Crumb, R(obert)

Crunk
See Crumb, R(obert)

Crustt
See Crumb, R(obert)

Cryer, Gretchen (Kiger) 1935-...... **CLC 21**
See also CA 114; 123

Csath, Geza 1887-1919.......... **TCLC 13**
See also CA 111

Cudlip, David 1933- . . . . CLC 34

Cullen, Countee 1903-1946 . . . . . TCLC 4, 37
  See also BLC 1; BW; CA 108; 124;
  CDALB 1917-1929; DLB 4, 48, 51;
  MTCW; SATA 18

Cum, R.
  See Crumb, R(obert)

Cummings, Bruce F(rederick) 1889-1919
  See Barbellion, W. N. P.
  See also CA 123

Cummings, E(dward) E(stlin)
  1894-1962 . . . . . CLC 1, 3, 8, 12, 15, 68;
                                                  PC 5
  See also CA 73-76; CANR 31;
  CDALB 1929-1941; DLB 4, 48; MTCW;
  WLC 2

Cunha, Euclides (Rodrigues Pimenta) da
  1866-1909 . . . . TCLC 24
  See also CA 123

Cunningham, E. V.
  See Fast, Howard (Melvin)

Cunningham, J(ames) V(incent)
  1911-1985 . . . . CLC 3, 31
  See also CA 1-4R; 115; CANR 1; DLB 5

Cunningham, Julia (Woolfolk)
  1916- . . . . CLC 12
  See also CA 9-12R; CANR 4, 19, 36;
  MAICYA; SAAS 2; SATA 1, 26

Cunningham, Michael 1952- . . . . CLC 34
  See also CA 136

Cunninghame Graham, R(obert) B(ontine)
  1852-1936 . . . . TCLC 19
  See also Graham, R(obert) B(ontine)
  Cunninghame
  See also CA 119; DLB 98

Currie, Ellen 19(?)- . . . . CLC 44

Curtin, Philip
  See Lowndes, Marie Adelaide (Belloc)

Curtis, Price
  See Ellison, Harlan

Czaczkes, Shmuel Yosef
  See Agnon, S(hmuel) Y(osef Halevi)

D. P.
  See Wells, H(erbert) G(eorge)

Dabrowska, Maria (Szumska)
  1889-1965 . . . . CLC 15
  See also CA 106

Dabydeen, David 1955- . . . . CLC 34
  See also BW; CA 125

Dacey, Philip 1939- . . . . CLC 51
  See also CA 37-40R; CANR 14, 32;
  DLB 105

Dagerman, Stig (Halvard)
  1923-1954 . . . . TCLC 17
  See also CA 117

Dahl, Roald 1916-1990 . . . . CLC 1, 6, 18
  See also CA 1-4R; 133; CANR 6, 32, 37;
  CLR 1, 7; MAICYA; MTCW; SATA 1,
  26; SATO 65

Dahlberg, Edward 1900-1977 . . . CLC 1, 7, 14
  See also CA 9-12R; 69-72; CANR 31;
  DLB 48; MTCW

Dale, Colin . . . . TCLC 18
  See also Lawrence, T(homas) E(dward)

Dale, George E.
  See Asimov, Isaac

Daly, Elizabeth 1878-1967 . . . . CLC 52
  See also CA 23-24; 25-28R; CAP 2

Daly, Maureen 1921- . . . . CLC 17
  See also AAYA 5; CANR 37; MAICYA;
  SAAS 1; SATA 2

Daniels, Brett
  See Adler, Renata

Dannay, Frederic 1905-1982 . . . . . . CLC 11
  See also Queen, Ellery
  See also CA 1-4R; 107; CANR 1, 39;
  MTCW

D'Annunzio, Gabriele
  1863-1938 . . . . TCLC 6, 40
  See also CA 104

d'Antibes, Germain
  See Simenon, Georges (Jacques Christian)

Danvers, Dennis 1947- . . . . CLC 70

Danziger, Paula 1944- . . . . CLC 21
  See also AAYA 4; CA 112; 115; CANR 37;
  CLR 20; MAICYA; SATA 30, 36, 63

Dario, Ruben . . . . TCLC 4
  See also Sarmiento, Felix Ruben Garcia

Darley, George 1795-1846 . . . . NCLC 2
  See also DLB 96

Daryush, Elizabeth 1887-1977 . . . . CLC 6, 19
  See also CA 49-52; CANR 3; DLB 20

Daudet, (Louis Marie) Alphonse
  1840-1897 . . . . NCLC 1

Daumal, Rene 1908-1944 . . . . TCLC 14
  See also CA 114

Davenport, Guy (Mattison Jr.)
  1927- . . . . CLC 6, 14, 38
  See also CA 33-36R; CANR 23

Davidson, Avram 1923-
  See Queen, Ellery
  See also CA 101; CANR 26; DLB 8

Davidson, Donald (Grady)
  1893-1968 . . . . CLC 2, 13, 19
  See also CA 5-8R; 25-28R; CANR 4;
  DLB 45

Davidson, Hugh
  See Hamilton, Edmond

Davidson, John 1857-1909 . . . . TCLC 24
  See also CA 118; DLB 19

Davidson, Sara 1943- . . . . CLC 9
  See also CA 81-84

Davie, Donald (Alfred)
  1922- . . . . CLC 5, 8, 10, 31
  See also CA 1-4R; CAAS 3; CANR 1;
  DLB 27; MTCW

Davies, Ray(mond Douglas) 1944- . . CLC 21
  See also CA 116

Davies, Rhys 1903-1978 . . . . CLC 23
  See also CA 9-12R; 81-84; CANR 4

Davies, (William) Robertson
  1913- . . . . CLC 2, 7, 13, 25, 42
  See also BEST 89:2; CA 33-36R; CANR 17;
  DLB 68; MTCW; WLC

Davies, W(illiam) H(enry)
  1871-1940 . . . . TCLC 5
  See also CA 104; DLB 19

Davies, Walter C.
  See Kornbluth, C(yril) M.

Davis, B. Lynch
  See Bioy Casares, Adolfo; Borges, Jorge
  Luis

Davis, Gordon
  See Hunt, E(verette) Howard Jr.

Davis, Harold Lenoir 1896-1960 . . . . CLC 49
  See also CA 89-92; DLB 9

Davis, Rebecca (Blaine) Harding
  1831-1910 . . . . TCLC 6
  See also CA 104; DLB 74

Davis, Richard Harding
  1864-1916 . . . . TCLC 24
  See also CA 114; DLB 12, 23, 78, 79

Davison, Frank Dalby 1893-1970 . . . CLC 15
  See also CA 116

Davison, Lawrence H.
  See Lawrence, D(avid) H(erbert Richards)

Davison, Peter 1928- . . . . CLC 28
  See also CA 9-12R; CAAS 4; CANR 3;
  DLB 5

Davys, Mary 1674-1732 . . . . LC 1
  See also DLB 39

Dawson, Fielding 1930- . . . . CLC 6
  See also CA 85-88

Day, Clarence (Shepard Jr.)
  1874-1935 . . . . TCLC 25
  See also CA 108; DLB 11

Day, Thomas 1748-1789 . . . . LC 1
  See also DLB 39; YABC 1

Day Lewis, C(ecil)
  1904-1972 . . . . CLC 1, 6, 10
  See also Blake, Nicholas
  See also CA 13-16; 33-36R; CANR 34;
  CAP 1; DLB 15, 20; MTCW

Dazai, Osamu . . . . TCLC 11
  See also Tsushima, Shuji

de Andrade, Carlos Drummond
  See Drummond de Andrade, Carlos

Deane, Norman
  See Creasey, John

de Beauvoir, Simone (Lucie Ernestine Marie
  Bertrand)
  See Beauvoir, Simone (Lucie Ernestine
  Marie Bertrand) de

de Brissac, Malcolm
  See Dickinson, Peter (Malcolm)

de Chardin, Pierre Teilhard
  See Teilhard de Chardin, (Marie Joseph)
  Pierre

Dee, John 1527-1608 . . . . LC 20

Deer, Sandra 1940- . . . . CLC 45

De Ferrari, Gabriella . . . . CLC 65

Defoe, Daniel 1660(?)-1731 . . . . LC 1
  See also CDBLB 1660-1789; DLB 39, 95,
  101; MAICYA; SATA 22; WLC

de Gourmont, Remy
  See Gourmont, Remy de

de Hartog, Jan 1914- . . . . CLC 19
  See also CA 1-4R; CANR 1

de Hostos, E. M.
  See Hostos (y Bonilla), Eugenio Maria de

de Hostos, Eugenio M.
See Hostos (y Bonilla), Eugenio Maria de

Deighton, Len . . . . **CLC 4, 7, 22, 46**
See also Deighton, Leonard Cyril
See also AAYA 6; BEST 89:2;
CDBLB 1960 to Present; DLB 87

Deighton, Leonard Cyril 1929-
See Deighton, Len
See also CA 9-12R; CANR 19, 33; MTCW

de la Mare, Walter (John)
1873-1956 . . . . **TCLC 4**
See also CA 110; 137; CDBLB 1914-1945;
CLR 23; DLB 19; MAICYA; SATA 16;
WLC

Delaney, Franey
See O'Hara, John (Henry)

Delaney, Shelagh 1939- . . . . **CLC 29**
See also CA 17-20R; CANR 30;
CDBLB 1960 to Present; DLB 13;
MTCW

Delany, Mary (Granville Pendarves)
1700-1788 . . . . **LC 12**

Delany, Samuel R(ay Jr.)
1942- . . . . **CLC 8, 14, 38**
See also BLC 1; BW; CA 81-84; CANR 27;
DLB 8, 33; MTCW

Delaporte, Theophile
See Green, Julian (Hartridge)

De La Ramee, (Marie) Louise 1839-1908
See Ouida
See also SATA 20

de la Roche, Mazo 1879-1961 . . . . . . **CLC 14**
See also CA 85-88; CANR 30; DLB 68;
SATA 64

Delbanco, Nicholas (Franklin)
1942- . . . . **CLC 6, 13**
See also CA 17-20R; CAAS 2; CANR 29;
DLB 6

del Castillo, Michel 1933- . . . . **CLC 38**
See also CA 109

Deledda, Grazia (Cosima)
1875(?)-1936 . . . . **TCLC 23**
See also CA 123

Delibes, Miguel . . . . **CLC 8, 18**
See also Delibes Setien, Miguel

Delibes Setien, Miguel 1920-
See Delibes, Miguel
See also CA 45-48; CANR 1, 32; HW;
MTCW

DeLillo, Don
1936- . . . . **CLC 8, 10, 13, 27, 39, 54**
See also BEST 89:1; CA 81-84; CANR 21;
DLB 6; MTCW

de Lisser, H. G.
See De Lisser, Herbert George
See also DLB 117

De Lisser, Herbert George
1878-1944 . . . . **TCLC 12**
See also de Lisser, H. G.
See also CA 109

Deloria, Vine (Victor) Jr. 1933- . . . . **CLC 21**
See also CA 53-56; CANR 5, 20; MTCW;
SATA 21

Del Vecchio, John M(ichael)
1947- . . . . **CLC 29**
See also CA 110; DLBD 9

de Man, Paul (Adolph Michel)
1919-1983 . . . . **CLC 55**
See also CA 128; 111; DLB 67; MTCW

De Marinis, Rick 1934- . . . . **CLC 54**
See also CA 57-60; CANR 9, 25

Demby, William 1922- . . . . **CLC 53**
See also BLC 1; BW; CA 81-84; DLB 33

Demijohn, Thom
See Disch, Thomas M(ichael)

de Montherlant, Henry (Milon)
See Montherlant, Henry (Milon) de

de Natale, Francine
See Malzberg, Barry N(athaniel)

Denby, Edwin (Orr) 1903-1983 . . . . . **CLC 48**
See also CA 138; 110

Denis, Julio
See Cortazar, Julio

Denmark, Harrison
See Zelazny, Roger (Joseph)

Dennis, John 1658-1734 . . . . **LC 11**
See also DLB 101

Dennis, Nigel (Forbes) 1912-1989 . . . . **CLC 8**
See also CA 25-28R; 129; DLB 13, 15;
MTCW

De Palma, Brian (Russell) 1940- . . . . **CLC 20**
See also CA 109

De Quincey, Thomas 1785-1859 . . . **NCLC 4**
See also CDBLB 1789-1832; DLB 110

Deren, Eleanora 1908(?)-1961
See Deren, Maya
See also CA 111

Deren, Maya . . . . **CLC 16**
See also Deren, Eleanora

Derleth, August (William)
1909-1971 . . . . **CLC 31**
See also CA 1-4R; 29-32R; CANR 4;
DLB 9; SATA 5

de Routisie, Albert
See Aragon, Louis

Derrida, Jacques 1930- . . . . **CLC 24**
See also CA 124; 127

Derry Down Derry
See Lear, Edward

Dersonnes, Jacques
See Simenon, Georges (Jacques Christian)

Desai, Anita 1937- . . . . **CLC 19, 37**
See also CA 81-84; CANR 33; MTCW;
SATA 63

de Saint-Luc, Jean
See Glassco, John

de Saint Roman, Arnaud
See Aragon, Louis

Descartes, Rene 1596-1650 . . . . **LC 20**

De Sica, Vittorio 1901(?)-1974 . . . . . **CLC 20**
See also CA 117

Desnos, Robert 1900-1945 . . . . **TCLC 22**
See also CA 121

Destouches, Louis-Ferdinand
1894-1961 . . . . **CLC 9, 15**
See also Celine, Louis-Ferdinand
See also CA 85-88; CANR 28; MTCW

Deutsch, Babette 1895-1982 . . . . **CLC 18**
See also CA 1-4R; 108; CANR 4; DLB 45;
SATA 1, 33

Devenant, William 1606-1649 . . . . . . **LC 13**

Devkota, Laxmiprasad
1909-1959 . . . . **TCLC 23**
See also CA 123

De Voto, Bernard (Augustine)
1897-1955 . . . . **TCLC 29**
See also CA 113; DLB 9

De Vries, Peter
1910- . . . . **CLC 1, 2, 3, 7, 10, 28, 46**
See also CA 17-20R; DLB 6; DLBY 82;
MTCW

Dexter, Pete 1943- . . . . **CLC 34, 55**
See also BEST 89:2; CA 127; 131; MTCW

Diamano, Silmang
See Senghor, Leopold Sedar

Diamond, Neil 1941- . . . . **CLC 30**
See also CA 108

di Bassetto, Corno
See Shaw, George Bernard

Dick, Philip K(indred)
1928-1982 . . . . **CLC 10, 30, 72**
See also CA 49-52; 106; CANR 2, 16;
DLB 8; MTCW

Dickens, Charles (John Huffam)
1812-1870 . . . . **NCLC 3, 8, 18, 26**
See also CDBLB 1832-1890; DLB 21, 55,
70; MAICYA; SATA 15

Dickey, James (Lafayette)
1923- . . . . **CLC 1, 2, 4, 7, 10, 15, 47**
See also AITN 1, 2; CA 9-12R; CABS 2;
CANR 10; CDALB 1968-1988; DLB 5;
DLBD 7; DLBY 82; MTCW

Dickey, William 1928- . . . . **CLC 3, 28**
See also CA 9-12R; CANR 24; DLB 5

Dickinson, Charles 1951- . . . . **CLC 49**
See also CA 128

Dickinson, Emily (Elizabeth)
1830-1886 . . . . **NCLC 21; PC 1**
See also CDALB 1865-1917; DLB 1;
SATA 29; WLC

Dickinson, Peter (Malcolm)
1927- . . . . **CLC 12, 35**
See also AAYA 9; CA 41-44R; CANR 31;
DLB 87; MAICYA; SATA 5, 62

Dickson, Carr
See Carr, John Dickson

Dickson, Carter
See Carr, John Dickson

Didion, Joan 1934- . . . . . **CLC 1, 3, 8, 14, 32**
See also AITN 1; CA 5-8R; CANR 14;
CDALB 1968-1988; DLB 2; DLBY 81,
86; MTCW

Dietrich, Robert
See Hunt, E(verette) Howard Jr.

Dillard, Annie 1945- . . . . **CLC 9, 60**
See also AAYA 6; CA 49-52; CANR 3;
DLBY 80; MTCW; SATA 10

Dillard, R(ichard) H(enry) W(ilde)
1937- . . . . **CLC 5**
See also CA 21-24R; CAAS 7; CANR 10;
DLB 5

Dillon, Eilis 1920-............... **CLC 17**
See also CA 9-12R; CAAS 3; CANR 4, 38;
CLR 26; MAICYA; SATA 2

Dimont, Penelope
See Mortimer, Penelope (Ruth)

Dinesen, Isak.......... **CLC 10, 29; SSC 7**
See also Blixen, Karen (Christentze
Dinesen)

Ding Ling....................... **CLC 68**
See also Chiang Pin-chin

Disch, Thomas M(ichael) 1940-... **CLC 7, 36**
See also CA 21-24R; CAAS 4; CANR 17,
36; CLR 18; DLB 8; MAICYA; MTCW;
SATA 54

Disch, Tom
See Disch, Thomas M(ichael)

d'Isly, Georges
See Simenon, Georges (Jacques Christian)

Disraeli, Benjamin 1804-1881..... **NCLC 2**
See also DLB 21, 55

Ditcum, Steve
See Crumb, R(obert)

Dixon, Paige
See Corcoran, Barbara

Dixon, Stephen 1936-............. **CLC 52**
See also CA 89-92; CANR 17

Doblin, Alfred................... **TCLC 13**
See also Doeblin, Alfred

Dobrolyubov, Nikolai Alexandrovich
1836-1861.................. **NCLC 5**

Dobyns, Stephen 1941-............ **CLC 37**
See also CA 45-48; CANR 2, 18

Doctorow, E(dgar) L(aurence)
1931-..... **CLC 6, 11, 15, 18, 37, 44, 65**
See also AITN 2; BEST 89:3; CA 45-48;
CANR 2, 33; CDALB 1968-1988; DLB 2,
28; DLBY 80; MTCW

Dodgson, Charles Lutwidge 1832-1898
See Carroll, Lewis
See also CLR 2; MAICYA; YABC 2

Doeblin, Alfred 1878-1957........ **TCLC 13**
See also Doblin, Alfred
See also CA 110; DLB 66

Doerr, Harriet 1910- .... **CLC 34**
See also CA 117; 122

Domecq, H(onorio) Bustos
See Bioy Casares, Adolfo; Borges, Jorge
Luis

Domini, Rey
See Lorde, Audre (Geraldine)

Dominique
See Proust,
(Valentin-Louis-George-Eugene-)Marcel

Don, A
See Stephen, Leslie

Donaldson, Stephen R. 1947-....... **CLC 46**
See also CA 89-92; CANR 13

Donleavy, J(ames) P(atrick)
1926- .... **CLC 1, 4, 6, 10, 45**
See also AITN 2; CA 9-12R; CANR 24;
DLB 6; MTCW

Donne, John 1572-1631....... **LC 10; PC 1**
See also CDBLB Before 1660; DLB 121;
WLC

Donnell, David 1939(?)-........... **CLC 34**

Donoso (Yanez), Jose
1924-................ **CLC 4, 8, 11, 32**
See also CA 81-84; CANR 32; DLB 113;
HW; MTCW

Donovan, John 1928-1992 .... **CLC 35**
See also CA 97-100; 137; CLR 3;
MAICYA; SATA 29

Don Roberto
See Cunninghame Graham, R(obert)
B(ontine)

Doolittle, Hilda
1886-1961 ... **CLC 3, 8, 14, 31, 34; PC 5**
See also H. D.
See also CA 97-100; CANR 35; DLB 4, 45;
MTCW; WLC

Dorfman, Ariel 1942-............ **CLC 48**
See also CA 124; 130; HW

Dorn, Edward (Merton) 1929-... **CLC 10, 18**
See also CA 93-96; DLB 5

Dorsan, Luc
See Simenon, Georges (Jacques Christian)

Dorsange, Jean
See Simenon, Georges (Jacques Christian)

Dos Passos, John (Roderigo)
1896-1970 ... **CLC 1, 4, 8, 11, 15, 25, 34**
See also CA 1-4R; 29-32R; CANR 3;
CDALB 1929-1941; DLB 4, 9; DLBD 1;
MTCW; WLC

Dossage, Jean
See Simenon, Georges (Jacques Christian)

Dostoevsky, Fedor Mikhailovich
1821-1881.... **NCLC 2, 7, 21, 33; SSC 2**
See also WLC

Doughty, Charles M(ontagu)
1843-1926.................. **TCLC 27**
See also CA 115; DLB 19, 57

Douglas, Gavin 1475(?)-1522........ **LC 20**

Douglas, Keith 1920-1944 .... **TCLC 40**
See also DLB 27

Douglas, Leonard
See Bradbury, Ray (Douglas)

Douglas, Michael
See Crichton, (John) Michael

Douglass, Frederick 1817(?)-1895.. **NCLC 7**
See also BLC 1; CDALB 1640-1865;
DLB 1, 43, 50, 79; SATA 29; WLC

Dourado, (Waldomiro Freitas) Autran
1926-.................... **CLC 23, 60**
See also CA 25-28R; CANR 34

Dourado, Waldomiro Autran
See Dourado, (Waldomiro Freitas) Autran

Dove, Rita (Frances) 1952- .... **CLC 50**
See also BW; CA 109; CANR 27; DLB 120

Dowell, Coleman 1925-1985........ **CLC 60**
See also CA 25-28R; 117; CANR 10

Dowson, Ernest Christopher
1867-1900.................. **TCLC 4**
See also CA 105; DLB 19

Doyle, A. Conan
See Doyle, Arthur Conan

Doyle, Arthur Conan 1859-1930 .... **TCLC 7**
See also CA 104; 122; CDBLB 1890-1914;
DLB 18, 70; MTCW; SATA 24; WLC

Doyle, Conan
See Doyle, Arthur Conan

Doyle, John
See Graves, Robert (von Ranke)

Doyle, Sir A. Conan
See Doyle, Arthur Conan

Doyle, Sir Arthur Conan
See Doyle, Arthur Conan

Dr. A
See Asimov, Isaac; Silverstein, Alvin

Drabble, Margaret
1939- .... **CLC 2, 3, 5, 8, 10, 22, 53**
See also CA 13-16R; CANR 18, 35;
CDBLB 1960 to Present; DLB 14;
MTCW; SATA 48

Drapier, M. B.
See Swift, Jonathan

Drayham, James
See Mencken, H(enry) L(ouis)

Drayton, Michael 1563-1631........ **LC 8**

Dreadstone, Carl
See Campbell, (John) Ramsey

Dreiser, Theodore (Herman Albert)
1871-1945........... **TCLC 10, 18, 35**
See also CA 106; 132; CDALB 1865-1917;
DLB 9, 12, 102; DLBD 1; MTCW; WLC

Drexler, Rosalyn 1926- .... **CLC 2, 6**
See also CA 81-84

Dreyer, Carl Theodor 1889-1968.... **CLC 16**
See also CA 116

Drieu la Rochelle, Pierre(-Eugene)
1893-1945.................. **TCLC 21**
See also CA 117; DLB 72

Drop Shot
See Cable, George Washington

Droste-Hulshoff, Annette Freiin von
1797-1848.................. **NCLC 3**

Drummond, Walter
See Silverberg, Robert

Drummond, William Henry
1854-1907.................. **TCLC 25**
See also DLB 92

Drummond de Andrade, Carlos
1902-1987.................. **CLC 18**
See also Andrade, Carlos Drummond de
See also CA 132; 123

Drury, Allen (Stuart) 1918-........ **CLC 37**
See also CA 57-60; CANR 18

Dryden, John 1631-1700 .... **LC 3, 21**
See also CDBLB 1660-1789; DLB 80, 101;
WLC

Dryden, John 1631-1700 .... **LC 3**

Duberman, Martin 1930-........... **CLC 8**
See also CA 1-4R; CANR 2

Dubie, Norman (Evans) 1945-...... **CLC 36**
See also CA 69-72; CANR 12; DLB 120

Du Bois, W(illiam) E(dward) B(urghardt)
1868-1963........... **CLC 1, 2, 13, 64**
See also BLC 1; BW; CA 85-88; CANR 34;
CDALB 1865-1917; DLB 47, 50, 91;
MTCW; SATA 42; WLC

Dubus, Andre 1936-............ **CLC 13, 36**
See also CA 21-24R; CANR 17

Duca Minimo
See D'Annunzio, Gabriele

Duclos, Charles Pinot 1704-1772 ..... LC 1

Dudek, Louis 1918- .... CLC 11, 19
See also CA 45-48; CAAS 14; CANR 1;
DLB 88

Duerrenmatt, Friedrich
1921-1990 ...... CLC 1, 4, 8, 11, 15, 43
See also Durrenmatt, Friedrich
See also CA 17-20R; CANR 33; DLB 69;
MTCW

Duffy, Bruce (?)- .... CLC 50

Duffy, Maureen 1933- .... CLC 37
See also CA 25-28R; CANR 33; DLB 14;
MTCW

Dugan, Alan 1923- .... CLC 2, 6
See also CA 81-84; DLB 5

du Gard, Roger Martin
See Martin du Gard, Roger

Duhamel, Georges 1884-1966 .... CLC 8
See also CA 81-84; 25-28R; CANR 35;
DLB 65; MTCW

Dujardin, Edouard (Emile Louis)
1861-1949 .... TCLC 13
See also CA 109

Dumas, Alexandre (Davy de la Pailleterie)
1802-1870 .... NCLC 11
See also DLB 119; SATA 18; WLC

Dumas, Alexandre
1824-1895 .... NCLC 9; DC 1

Dumas, Claudine
See Malzberg, Barry N(athaniel)

Dumas, Henry L. 1934-1968 ..... CLC 6, 62
See also BW; CA 85-88; DLB 41

du Maurier, Daphne
1907-1989 .... CLC 6, 11, 59
See also CA 5-8R; 128; CANR 6; MTCW;
SATA 27, 60

Dunbar, Paul Laurence
1872-1906 .... TCLC 2, 12; PC 5; SSC 8
See also BLC 1; BW; CA 104; 124;
CDALB 1865-1917; DLB 50, 54, 78;
SATA 34; WLC

Dunbar, William 1460(?)-1530(?) .... LC 20

Duncan, Lois 1934-............... CLC 26
See also AAYA 4; CA 1-4R; CANR 2, 23,
36; MAICYA; SAAS 2; SATA 1, 36

Duncan, Robert (Edward)
1919-1988 ... CLC 1, 2, 4, 7, 15, 41, 55;
PC 2
See also CA 9-12R; 124; CANR 28; DLB 5,
16; MTCW

Dunlap, William 1766-1839 .... NCLC 2
See also DLB 30, 37, 59

Dunn, Douglas (Eaglesham)
1942- .... CLC 6, 40
See also CA 45-48; CANR 2, 33; DLB 40;
MTCW

Dunn, Katherine (Karen) 1945-..... CLC 71
See also CA 33-36R

Dunn, Stephen 1939- .... CLC 36
See also CA 33-36R; CANR 12; DLB 105

Dunne, Finley Peter 1867-1936.... TCLC 28
See also CA 108; DLB 11, 23

Dunne, John Gregory 1932-........ CLC 28
See also CA 25-28R; CANR 14; DLBY 80

Dunsany, Edward John Moreton Drax
Plunkett 1878-1957
See Dunsany, Lord; Lord Dunsany
See also CA 104; DLB 10

Dunsany, Lord................... TCLC 2
See also Dunsany, Edward John Moreton
Drax Plunkett
See also DLB 77

du Perry, Jean
See Simenon, Georges (Jacques Christian)

Durang, Christopher (Ferdinand)
1949- .... CLC 27, 38
See also CA 105

Duras, Marguerite
1914- ...... CLC 3, 6, 11, 20, 34, 40, 68
See also CA 25-28R; DLB 83; MTCW

Durban, (Rosa) Pam 1947-........ CLC 39
See also CA 123

Durcan, Paul 1944-............ CLC 43, 70
See also CA 134

Durrell, Lawrence (George)
1912-1990 .... CLC 1, 4, 6, 8, 13, 27, 41
See also CA 9-12R; 132;
CDBLB 1945-1960; DLB 15, 27;
DLBY 90; MTCW

Durrenmatt, Friedrich
.... CLC 1, 4, 8, 11, 15, 43
See also Duerrenmatt, Friedrich
See also DLB 69

Dutt, Toru 1856-1877.......... NCLC 29

Dwight, Timothy 1752-1817...... NCLC 13
See also DLB 37

Dworkin, Andrea 1946- .... CLC 43
See also CA 77-80; CANR 16, 39; MTCW

Dylan, Bob 1941-.......... CLC 3, 4, 6, 12
See also CA 41-44R; DLB 16

Eagleton, Terence (Francis) 1943-
See Eagleton, Terry
See also CA 57-60; CANR 7, 23; MTCW

Eagleton, Terry................... CLC 63
See also Eagleton, Terence (Francis)

East, Michael
See West, Morris L(anglo)

Eastaway, Edward
See Thomas, (Philip) Edward

Eastlake, William (Derry) 1917-..... CLC 8
See also CA 5-8R; CAAS 1; CANR 5;
DLB 6

Eberhart, Richard (Ghormley)
1904- .... CLC 3, 11, 19, 56
See also CA 1-4R; CANR 2;
CDALB 1941-1968; DLB 48; MTCW

Eberstadt, Fernanda 1960-........ CLC 39
See also CA 136

Echegaray (y Eizaguirre), Jose (Maria Waldo)
1832-1916 .... TCLC 4
See also CA 104; CANR 32; HW; MTCW

Echeverria, (Jose) Esteban (Antonino)
1805-1851 .... NCLC 18

Echo
See Proust,
(Valentin-Louis-George-Eugene-)Marcel

Eckert, Allan W. 1931- .... CLC 17
See also CA 13-16R; CANR 14; SATA 27,
29

Eckhart, Meister 1260(?)-1328(?) .. CMLC 9
See also DLB 115

Eckmar, F. R.
See de Hartog, Jan

Eco, Umberto 1932-........... CLC 28, 60
See also BEST 90:1; CA 77-80; CANR 12,
33; MTCW

Eddison, E(ric) R(ucker)
1882-1945 .... TCLC 15
See also CA 109

Edel, (Joseph) Leon 1907-...... CLC 29, 34
See also CA 1-4R; CANR 1, 22; DLB 103

Eden, Emily 1797-1869 .... NCLC 10

Edgar, David 1948-............... CLC 42
See also CA 57-60; CANR 12; DLB 13;
MTCW

Edgerton, Clyde (Carlyle) 1944- .... CLC 39
See also CA 118; 134

Edgeworth, Maria 1767-1849...... NCLC 1
See also DLB 116; SATA 21

Edmonds, Paul
See Kuttner, Henry

Edmonds, Walter D(umaux) 1903- .. CLC 35
See also CA 5-8R; CANR 2; DLB 9;
MAICYA; SAAS 4; SATA 1, 27

Edmondson, Wallace
See Ellison, Harlan

Edson, Russell.................... CLC 13
See also CA 33-36R

Edwards, G(erald) B(asil)
1899-1976 .... CLC 25
See also CA 110

Edwards, Gus 1939-.............. CLC 43
See also CA 108

Edwards, Jonathan 1703-1758........ LC 7
See also DLB 24

Efron, Marina Ivanovna Tsvetaeva
See Tsvetaeva (Efron), Marina (Ivanovna)

Ehle, John (Marsden Jr.) 1925- .... CLC 27
See also CA 9-12R

Ehrenbourg, Ilya (Grigoryevich)
See Ehrenburg, Ilya (Grigoryevich)

Ehrenburg, Ilya (Grigoryevich)
1891-1967 .... CLC 18, 34, 62
See also CA 102; 25-28R

Ehrenburg, Ilyo (Grigoryevich)
See Ehrenburg, Ilya (Grigoryevich)

Eich, Guenter 1907-1972 .... CLC 15
See also CA 111; 93-96; DLB 69

Eichendorff, Joseph Freiherr von
1788-1857 .... NCLC 8
See also DLB 90

Eigner, Larry.................... CLC 9
See also Eigner, Laurence (Joel)
See also DLB 5

Eigner, Laurence (Joel) 1927-
See Eigner, Larry
See also CA 9-12R; CANR 6

Eiseley, Loren Corey 1907-1977..... CLC 7
See also AAYA 5; CA 1-4R; 73-76;
CANR 6

Eisenstadt, Jill 1963- .... **CLC 50**

Eisner, Simon
See Kornbluth, C(yril) M.

Ekeloef, (Bengt) Gunnar
1907-1968 .... **CLC 27**
See also Ekelof, (Bengt) Gunnar
See also CA 123; 25-28R

Ekelof, (Bengt) Gunnar............ **CLC 27**
See also Ekeloef, (Bengt) Gunnar

Ekwensi, C. O. D.
See Ekwensi, Cyprian (Odiatu Duaka)

Ekwensi, Cyprian (Odiatu Duaka)
1921- .... **CLC 4**
See also BLC 1; BW; CA 29-32R;
CANR 18; DLB 117; MTCW; SATA 66

Elaine........................ **TCLC 18**
See also Leverson, Ada

El Crummo
See Crumb, R(obert)

Elia
See Lamb, Charles

Eliade, Mircea 1907-1986 .... **CLC 19**
See also CA 65-68; 119; CANR 30; MTCW

Eliot, A. D.
See Jewett, (Theodora) Sarah Orne

Eliot, Alice
See Jewett, (Theodora) Sarah Orne

Eliot, Dan
See Silverberg, Robert

Eliot, George 1819-1880.... **NCLC 4, 13, 23**
See also CDBLB 1832-1890; DLB 21, 35,
55; WLC

Eliot, John 1604-1690 .... **LC 5**
See also DLB 24

Eliot, T(homas) S(tearns)
1888-1965 .... **CLC 1, 2, 3, 6, 9, 10, 13,**
15, 24, 34, 41, 55, 57; PC 5
See also CA 5-8R; 25-28R;
CDALB 1929-1941; DLB 7, 10, 45, 63;
MTCW; WLC 2

Elizabeth 1866-1941............. **TCLC 41**

Elkin, Stanley L(awrence)
1930- .... **CLC 4, 6, 9, 14, 27, 51**
See also CA 9-12R; CANR 8; DLB 2, 28;
DLBY 80; MTCW

Elledge, Scott..................... **CLC 34**

Elliott, Don
See Silverberg, Robert

Elliott, George P(aul) 1918-1980..... **CLC 2**
See also CA 1-4R; 97-100; CANR 2

Elliott, Janice 1931-.............. **CLC 47**
See also CA 13-16R; CANR 8, 29; DLB 14

Elliott, Sumner Locke 1917-1991 ... **CLC 38**
See also CA 5-8R; 134; CANR 2, 21

Elliott, William
See Bradbury, Ray (Douglas)

Ellis, A. E...................... **CLC 7**

Ellis, Alice Thomas............... **CLC 40**
See also Haycraft, Anna

Ellis, Bret Easton 1964-........ **CLC 39, 71**
See also AAYA 2; CA 118; 123

Ellis, (Henry) Havelock
1859-1939 .... **TCLC 14**
See also CA 109

Ellis, Landon
See Ellison, Harlan

Ellis, Trey 1962-................ **CLC 55**

Ellison, Harlan 1934-........ **CLC 1, 13, 42**
See also CA 5-8R; CANR 5; DLB 8;
MTCW

Ellison, Ralph (Waldo)
1914- .... **CLC 1, 3, 11, 54**
See also BLC 1; BW; CA 9-12R; CANR 24;
CDALB 1941-1968; DLB 2, 76; MTCW;
WLC

Ellmann, Lucy (Elizabeth) 1956-.... **CLC 61**
See also CA 128

Ellmann, Richard (David)
1918-1987 .... **CLC 50**
See also BEST 89:2; CA 1-4R; 122;
CANR 2, 28; DLB 103; DLBY 87;
MTCW

Elman, Richard 1934-............ **CLC 19**
See also CA 17-20R; CAAS 3

Elron
See Hubbard, L(afayette) Ron(ald)

Eluard, Paul................ **TCLC 7, 41**
See also Grindel, Eugene

Elyot, Sir Thomas 1490(?)-1546 ..... **LC 11**

Elytis, Odysseus 1911-......... **CLC 15, 49**
See also CA 102; MTCW

Emecheta, (Florence Onye) Buchi
1944- .... **CLC 14, 48**
See also BLC 2; BW; CA 81-84; CANR 27;
DLB 117; MTCW; SATA 66

Emerson, Ralph Waldo
1803-1882 .... **NCLC 1, 38**
See also CDALB 1640-1865; DLB 1, 59, 73;
WLC

Eminescu, Mihail 1850-1889 ..... **NCLC 33**

Empson, William
1906-1984 .... **CLC 3, 8, 19, 33, 34**
See also CA 17-20R; 112; CANR 31;
DLB 20; MTCW

Enchi Fumiko (Ueda) 1905-1986.... **CLC 31**
See also CA 129; 121

Ende, Michael (Andreas Helmuth)
1929- .... **CLC 31**
See also CA 118; 124; CANR 36; CLR 14;
DLB 75; MAICYA; SATA 42, 61

Endo, Shusaku 1923-..... **CLC 7, 14, 19, 54**
See also CA 29-32R; CANR 21; MTCW

Engel, Marian 1933-1985......... **CLC 36**
See also CA 25-28R; CANR 12; DLB 53

Engelhardt, Frederick
See Hubbard, L(afayette) Ron(ald)

Enright, D(ennis) J(oseph)
1920- .... **CLC 4, 8, 31**
See also CA 1-4R; CANR 1; DLB 27;
SATA 25

Enzensberger, Hans Magnus
1929- .... **CLC 43**
See also CA 116; 119

Ephron, Nora 1941- .... **CLC 17, 31**
See also AITN 2; CA 65-68; CANR 12, 39

Epsilon
See Betjeman, John

Epstein, Daniel Mark 1948- .... **CLC 7**
See also CA 49-52; CANR 2

Epstein, Jacob 1956- .... **CLC 19**
See also CA 114

Epstein, Joseph 1937-............. **CLC 39**
See also CA 112; 119

Epstein, Leslie 1938- .... **CLC 27**
See also CA 73-76; CAAS 12; CANR 23

Equiano, Olaudah 1745(?)-1797...... **LC 16**
See also BLC 2; DLB 37, 50

Erasmus, Desiderius 1469(?)-1536.... **LC 16**

Erdman, Paul E(mil) 1932- .... **CLC 25**
See also AITN 1; CA 61-64; CANR 13

Erdrich, Louise 1954-......... **CLC 39, 54**
See also BEST 89:1; CA 114; MTCW

Erenburg, Ilya (Grigoryevich)
See Ehrenburg, Ilya (Grigoryevich)

Erickson, Stephen Michael 1950-
See Erickson, Steve
See also CA 129

Erickson, Steve .... **CLC 64**
See also Erickson, Stephen Michael

Ericson, Walter
See Fast, Howard (Melvin)

Eriksson, Buntel
See Bergman, (Ernst) Ingmar

Eschenbach, Wolfram von
See Wolfram von Eschenbach

Eseki, Bruno
See Mphahlele, Ezekiel

Esenin, Sergei (Alexandrovich)
1895-1925 .... **TCLC 4**
See also CA 104

Eshleman, Clayton 1935-........... **CLC 7**
See also CA 33-36R; CAAS 6; DLB 5

Espriella, Don Manuel Alvarez
See Southey, Robert

Espriu, Salvador 1913-1985......... **CLC 9**
See also CA 115

Esse, James
See Stephens, James

Esterbrook, Tom
See Hubbard, L(afayette) Ron(ald)

Estleman, Loren D. 1952- .... **CLC 48**
See also CA 85-88; CANR 27; MTCW

Evans, Mary Ann
See Eliot, George

Evarts, Esther
See Benson, Sally

Everett, Percival
See Everett, Percival L.

Everett, Percival L. 1956- .... **CLC 57**
See also CA 129

Everson, R(onald) G(ilmour)
1903- .... **CLC 27**
See also CA 17-20R; DLB 88

Everson, William (Oliver)
1912- .... **CLC 1, 5, 14**
See also CA 9-12R; CANR 20; DLB 5, 16;
MTCW

Evtushenko, Evgenii Aleksandrovich
See Yevtushenko, Yevgeny (Alexandrovich)

Ewart, Gavin (Buchanan)
1916- .... **CLC 13, 46**
See also CA 89-92; CANR 17; DLB 40;
MTCW

Ewers, Hanns Heinz 1871-1943 ... **TCLC 12**
See also CA 109

Ewing, Frederick R.
See Sturgeon, Theodore (Hamilton)

Exley, Frederick (Earl) 1929- .... **CLC 6, 11**
See also AITN 2; CA 81-84; 138; DLBY 81

Eynhardt, Guillermo
See Quiroga, Horacio (Sylvestre)

Ezekiel, Nissim 1924-............. **CLC 61**
See also CA 61-64

Ezekiel, Tish O'Dowd 1943- .... **CLC 34**
See also CA 129

Fagen, Donald 1948-............. **CLC 26**

Fainzilberg, Ilya Arnoldovich 1897-1937
See Ilf, Ilya
See also CA 120

Fair, Ronald L. 1932-............. **CLC 18**
See also BW; CA 69-72; CANR 25; DLB 33

Fairbairns, Zoe (Ann) 1948- .... **CLC 32**
See also CA 103; CANR 21

Falco, Gian
See Papini, Giovanni

Falconer, James
See Kirkup, James

Falconer, Kenneth
See Kornbluth, C(yril) M.

Falkland, Samuel
See Heijermans, Herman

Fallaci, Oriana 1930-............. **CLC 11**
See also CA 77-80; CANR 15; MTCW

Faludy, George 1913-............. **CLC 42**
See also CA 21-24R

Faludy, Gyoergy
See Faludy, George

Fanshawe, Ann .... **LC 11**

Fante, John (Thomas) 1911-1983 ... **CLC 60**
See also CA 69-72; 109; CANR 23;
DLBY 83

Farah, Nuruddin 1945-............. **CLC 53**
See also BLC 2; CA 106

Fargue, Leon-Paul 1876(?)-1947 ... **TCLC 11**
See also CA 109

Farigoule, Louis
See Romains, Jules

Farina, Richard 1936(?)-1966 .... **CLC 9**
See also CA 81-84; 25-28R

Farley, Walter (Lorimer)
1915-1989 .... **CLC 17**
See also CA 17-20R; CANR 8, 29; DLB 22;
MAICYA; SATA 2, 43

Farmer, Philip Jose 1918-....... **CLC 1, 19**
See also CA 1-4R; CANR 4, 35; DLB 8;
MTCW

Farquhar, George 1677-1707 .... **LC 21**
See also DLB 84

Farrell, J(ames) G(ordon)
1935-1979 .... **CLC 6**
See also CA 73-76; 89-92; CANR 36;
DLB 14; MTCW

Farrell, James T(homas)
1904-1979 .... **CLC 1, 4, 8, 11, 66**
See also CA 5-8R; 89-92; CANR 9; DLB 4,
9, 86; DLBD 2; MTCW

Farren, Richard J.
See Betjeman, John

Farren, Richard M.
See Betjeman, John

Fassbinder, Rainer Werner
1946-1982 .... **CLC 20**
See also CA 93-96; 106; CANR 31

Fast, Howard (Melvin) 1914- ...... **CLC 23**
See also CA 1-4R; CANR 1, 33; DLB 9;
SATA 7

Faulcon, Robert
See Holdstock, Robert P.

Faulkner, William (Cuthbert)
1897-1962 .... **CLC 1, 3, 6, 8, 9, 11, 14,
18, 28, 52, 68; SSC 1**
See also AAYA 7; CA 81-84; CANR 33;
CDALB 1929-1941; DLB 9, 11, 44, 102;
DLBD 2; DLBY 86; MTCW; WLC

Fauset, Jessie Redmon
1884(?)-1961 .... **CLC 19, 54**
See also BLC 2; BW; CA 109; DLB 51

Faust, Irvin 1924-................. **CLC 8**
See also CA 33-36R; CANR 28; DLB 2, 28;
DLBY 80

Fawkes, Guy
See Benchley, Robert (Charles)

Fearing, Kenneth (Flexner)
1902-1961 .... **CLC 51**
See also CA 93-96; DLB 9

Fecamps, Elise
See Creasey, John

Federman, Raymond 1928- ...... **CLC 6, 47**
See also CA 17-20R; CAAS 8; CANR 10;
DLBY 80

Federspiel, J(uerg) F. 1931-........ **CLC 42**

Feiffer, Jules (Ralph) 1929-.... **CLC 2, 8, 64**
See also AAYA 3; CA 17-20R; CANR 30;
DLB 7, 44; MTCW; SATA 8, 61

Feige, Hermann Albert Otto Maximilian
See Traven, B.

Fei-Kan, Li
See Li Fei-kan

Feinberg, David B. 1956-.......... **CLC 59**
See also CA 135

Feinstein, Elaine 1930-............ **CLC 36**
See also CA 69-72; CAAS 1; CANR 31;
DLB 14, 40; MTCW

Feldman, Irving (Mordecai) 1928-.... **CLC 7**
See also CA 1-4R; CANR 1

Fellini, Federico 1920-............ **CLC 16**
See also CA 65-68; CANR 33

Felsen, Henry Gregor 1916- .... **CLC 17**
See also CA 1-4R; CANR 1; SAAS 2;
SATA 1

Fenton, James Martin 1949-....... **CLC 32**
See also CA 102; DLB 40

Ferber, Edna 1887-1968.......... **CLC 18**
See also AITN 1; CA 5-8R; 25-28R; DLB 9,
28, 86; MTCW; SATA 7

Ferguson, Helen
See Kavan, Anna

Ferguson, Samuel 1810-1886..... **NCLC 33**
See also DLB 32

Ferling, Lawrence
See Ferlinghetti, Lawrence (Monsanto)

Ferlinghetti, Lawrence (Monsanto)
1919(?)-........ **CLC 2, 6, 10, 27; PC 1**
See also CA 5-8R; CANR 3;
CDALB 1941-1968; DLB 5, 16; MTCW

Fernandez, Vicente Garcia Huidobro
See Huidobro Fernandez, Vicente Garcia

Ferrer, Gabriel (Francisco Victor) Miro
See Miro (Ferrer), Gabriel (Francisco
Victor)

Ferrier, Susan (Edmonstone)
1782-1854 .... **NCLC 8**
See also DLB 116

Ferrigno, Robert .... **CLC 65**

Feuchtwanger, Lion 1884-1958 ..... **TCLC 3**
See also CA 104; DLB 66

Feydeau, Georges (Leon Jules Marie)
1862-1921 .... **TCLC 22**
See also CA 113

Ficino, Marsilio 1433-1499 .... **LC 12**

Fiedler, Leslie A(aron)
1917-................... **CLC 4, 13, 24**
See also CA 9-12R; CANR 7; DLB 28, 67;
MTCW

Field, Andrew 1938-.............. **CLC 44**
See also CA 97-100; CANR 25

Field, Eugene 1850-1895 .... **NCLC 3**
See also DLB 23, 42; MAICYA; SATA 16

Field, Gans T.
See Wellman, Manly Wade

Field, Michael .... **TCLC 43**

Field, Peter
See Hobson, Laura Z(ametkin)

Fielding, Henry 1707-1754 .... **LC 1**
See also CDBLB 1660-1789; DLB 39, 84,
101; WLC

Fielding, Sarah 1710-1768 .... **LC 1**
See also DLB 39

Fierstein, Harvey (Forbes) 1954- ... **CLC 33**
See also CA 123; 129

Figes, Eva 1932-................. **CLC 31**
See also CA 53-56; CANR 4; DLB 14

Finch, Robert (Duer Claydon)
1900-..................... **CLC 18**
See also CA 57-60; CANR 9, 24; DLB 88

Findley, Timothy 1930- .... **CLC 27**
See also CA 25-28R; CANR 12; DLB 53

Fink, William
See Mencken, H(enry) L(ouis)

Firbank, Louis 1942-
See Reed, Lou
See also CA 117

Firbank, (Arthur Annesley) Ronald
1886-1926 .... **TCLC 1**
See also CA 104; DLB 36

Fisher, Roy 1930-............... **CLC 25**
See also CA 81-84; CAAS 10; CANR 16;
DLB 40

Fisher, Rudolph 1897-1934 .... **TCLC 11**
See also BLC 2; BW; CA 107; 124; DLB 51,
102

Fisher, Vardis (Alvero) 1895-1968.... **CLC 7**
See also CA 5-8R; 25-28R; DLB 9

Fiske, Tarleton
See Bloch, Robert (Albert)

Fitch, Clarke
See Sinclair, Upton (Beall)

Fitch, John IV
See Cormier, Robert (Edmund)

Fitgerald, Penelope 1916- .... **CLC 61**

Fitzgerald, Captain Hugh
See Baum, L(yman) Frank

FitzGerald, Edward 1809-1883 .... **NCLC 9**
See also DLB 32

Fitzgerald, F(rancis) Scott (Key)
1896-1940 .... **TCLC 1, 6, 14, 28; SSC 6**
See also AITN 1; CA 110; 123;
CDALB 1917-1929; DLB 4, 9, 86;
DLBD 1; DLBY 81; MTCW; WLC

Fitzgerald, Penelope 1916-...... **CLC 19, 51**
See also CA 85-88; CAAS 10; DLB 14

FitzGerald, Robert D(avid)
1902-1987 .... **CLC 19**
See also CA 17-20R

Fitzgerald, Robert (Stuart)
1910-1985 .... **CLC 39**
See also CA 1-4R; 114; CANR 1; DLBY 80

Flanagan, Thomas (James Bonner)
1923- .... **CLC 25, 52**
See also CA 108; DLBY 80; MTCW

Flaubert, Gustave
1821-1880 ..... **NCLC 2, 10, 19; SSC 11**
See also DLB 119; WLC

Flecker, (Herman) James Elroy
1884-1915 .... **TCLC 43**
See also CA 109; DLB 10, 19

Fleming, Ian (Lancaster)
1908-1964 .... **CLC 3, 30**
See also CA 5-8R; CDBLB 1945-1960;
DLB 87; MTCW; SATA 9

Fleming, Thomas (James) 1927- .... **CLC 37**
See also CA 5-8R; CANR 10; SATA 8

Fletcher, John Gould 1886-1950... **TCLC 35**
See also CA 107; DLB 4, 45

Fleur, Paul
See Pohl, Frederik

Flying Officer X
See Bates, H(erbert) E(rnest)

Fo, Dario 1926-.................. **CLC 32**
See also CA 116; 128; MTCW

Fogarty, Jonathan Titulescu Esq.
See Farrell, James T(homas)

Folke, Will
See Bloch, Robert (Albert)

Follett, Ken(neth Martin) 1949- .... **CLC 18**
See also AAYA 6; BEST 89:4; CA 81-84;
CANR 13, 33; DLB 87; DLBY 81;
MTCW

Fontane, Theodor 1819-1898 ..... **NCLC 26**

Foote, Horton 1916-.............. **CLC 51**
See also CA 73-76; CANR 34; DLB 26

Forbes, Esther 1891-1967......... **CLC 12**
See also CA 13-14; 25-28R; CAP 1;
CLR 27; DLB 22; MAICYA; SATA 2

Forche, Carolyn (Louise) 1950-..... **CLC 25**
See also CA 109; 117; DLB 5

Ford, Elbur
See Hibbert, Eleanor Burford

Ford, Ford Madox
1873-1939 .... **TCLC 1, 15, 39**
See also CA 104; 132; CDBLB 1914-1945;
DLB 34, 98; MTCW

Ford, John 1895-1973............. **CLC 16**
See also CA 45-48

Ford, Richard 1944-.............. **CLC 46**
See also CA 69-72; CANR 11

Ford, Webster
See Masters, Edgar Lee

Foreman, Richard 1937-.......... **CLC 50**
See also CA 65-68; CANR 32

Forester, C(ecil) S(cott)
1899-1966 .... **CLC 35**
See also CA 73-76; 25-28R; SATA 13

Forez
See Mauriac, Francois (Charles)

Forman, James Douglas 1932-...... **CLC 21**
See also CA 9-12R; CANR 4, 19;
MAICYA; SATA 8, 70

Fornes, Maria Irene 1930-...... **CLC 39, 61**
See also CA 25-28R; CANR 28; DLB 7;
HW; MTCW

Forrest, Leon 1937- .... **CLC 4**
See also BW; CA 89-92; CAAS 7;
CANR 25; DLB 33

Forster, E(dward) M(organ)
1879-1970 .... **CLC 1, 2, 3, 4, 9, 10, 13,
15, 22, 45**
See also AAYA 2; CA 13-14; 25-28R;
CAP 1; CDBLB 1914-1945; DLB 34, 98;
MTCW; SATA 57; WLC

Forster, John 1812-1876 .... **NCLC 11**

Forsyth, Frederick 1938-...... **CLC 2, 5, 36**
See also BEST 89:4; CA 85-88; CANR 38;
DLB 87; MTCW

Forten, Charlotte L. .... **TCLC 16**
See also Grimke, Charlotte L(ottie) Forten
See also BLC 2; DLB 50

Foscolo, Ugo 1778-1827.......... **NCLC 8**

Fosse, Bob .... **CLC 20**
See also Fosse, Robert Louis

Fosse, Robert Louis 1927-1987
See Fosse, Bob
See also CA 110; 123

Foster, Stephen Collins
1826-1864 .... **NCLC 26**

Foucault, Michel
1926-1984 .... **CLC 31, 34, 69**
See also CA 105; 113; CANR 34; MTCW

Fouque, Friedrich Heinrich Karl) de la Motte
1777-1843 .... **NCLC 2**
See also DLB 90

Fournier, Henri Alban 1886-1914
See Alain-Fournier
See also CA 104

Fournier, Pierre 1916-............ **CLC 11**
See also Gascar, Pierre
See also CA 89-92; CANR 16

Fowles, John
1926- .... **CLC 1, 2, 3, 4, 6, 9, 10, 15, 33**
See also CA 5-8R; CANR 25; CDBLB 1960
to Present; DLB 14; MTCW; SATA 22

Fox, Paula 1923-................ **CLC 2, 8**
See also AAYA 3; CA 73-76; CANR 20,
36; CLR 1; DLB 52; MAICYA; MTCW;
SATA 17, 60

Fox, William Price (Jr.) 1926- ..... **CLC 22**
See also CA 17-20R; CANR 11; DLB 2;
DLBY 81

Foxe, John 1516(?)-1587 .... **LC 14**

Frame, Janet .... **CLC 2, 3, 6, 22, 66**
See also Clutha, Janet Paterson Frame

France, Anatole.................... **TCLC 9**
See also Thibault, Jacques Anatole Francois

Francis, Claude 19(?)- .... **CLC 50**

Francis, Dick 1920- .... **CLC 2, 22, 42**
See also AAYA 5; BEST 89:3; CA 5-8R;
CANR 9; CDBLB 1960 to Present;
DLB 87; MTCW

Francis, Robert (Churchill)
1901-1987 .... **CLC 15**
See also CA 1-4R; 123; CANR 1

Frank, Anne(lies Marie)
1929-1945 .... **TCLC 17**
See also CA 113; 133; MTCW; SATA 42;
WLC

Frank, Elizabeth 1945-........... **CLC 39**
See also CA 121; 126

Franklin, Benjamin
See Hasek, Jaroslav (Matej Frantisek)

Franklin, (Stella Maraia Sarah) Miles
1879-1954 .... **TCLC 7**
See also CA 104

Fraser, Antonia (Pakenham)
1932- .... **CLC 32**
See also CA 85-88; MTCW; SATA 32

Fraser, George MacDonald 1925-.... **CLC 7**
See also CA 45-48; CANR 2

Fraser, Sylvia 1935-.............. **CLC 64**
See also CA 45-48; CANR 1, 16

Frayn, Michael 1933-...... **CLC 3, 7, 31, 47**
See also CA 5-8R; CANR 30; DLB 13, 14;
MTCW

Fraze, Candida (Merrill) 1945-..... **CLC 50**
See also CA 126

Frazer, J(ames) G(eorge)
1854-1941 .... **TCLC 32**
See also CA 118

Frazer, Robert Caine
See Creasey, John

Frazer, Sir James George
See Frazer, J(ames) G(eorge)

Frazier, Ian 1951-................ **CLC 46**
See also CA 130

Frederic, Harold 1856-1898...... **NCLC 10**
See also DLB 12, 23

Frederick the Great 1712-1786 ...... **LC 14**

Fredro, Aleksander 1793-1876..... **NCLC 8**

Freeling, Nicolas 1927- .... **CLC 38**
See also CA 49-52; CAAS 12; CANR 1, 17;
DLB 87

Freeman, Douglas Southall
1886-1953 .... **TCLC 11**
See also CA 109; DLB 17

Freeman, Judith 1946- .... **CLC 55**

Freeman, Mary Eleanor Wilkins
1852-1930 .... **TCLC 9; SSC 1**
See also CA 106; DLB 12, 78

Freeman, R(ichard) Austin
1862-1943 .... **TCLC 21**
See also CA 113; DLB 70

French, Marilyn 1929- ...... **CLC 10, 18, 60**
See also CA 69-72; CANR 3, 31; MTCW

French, Paul
See Asimov, Isaac

Freneau, Philip Morin 1752-1832.. **NCLC 1**
See also DLB 37, 43

Friedman, B(ernard) H(arper)
1926- .... **CLC 7**
See also CA 1-4R; CANR 3

Friedman, Bruce Jay 1930-.... **CLC 3, 5, 56**
See also CA 9-12R; CANR 25; DLB 2, 28

Friel, Brian 1929-........... **CLC 5, 42, 59**
See also CA 21-24R; CANR 33; DLB 13;
MTCW

Friis-Baastad, Babbis Ellinor
1921-1970 .... **CLC 12**
See also CA 17-20R; 134; SATA 7

Frisch, Max (Rudolf)
1911-1991 ..... **CLC 3, 9, 14, 18, 32, 44**
See also CA 85-88; 134; CANR 32;
DLB 69; MTCW

Fromentin, Eugene (Samuel Auguste)
1820-1876 .... **NCLC 10**

Frost, Robert (Lee)
1874-1963 ... **CLC 1, 3, 4, 9, 10, 13, 15,**
26, 34, 44; PC 1
See also CA 89-92; CANR 33;
CDALB 1917-1929; DLB 54; DLBD 7;
MTCW; SATA 14; WLC

Froy, Herald
See Waterhouse, Keith (Spencer)

Fry, Christopher 1907-....... **CLC 2, 10, 14**
See also CA 17-20R; CANR 9, 30; DLB 13;
MTCW; SATA 66

Frye, (Herman) Northrop
1912-1991 .... **CLC 24, 70**
See also CA 5-8R; 133; CANR 8, 37;
DLB 67, 68; MTCW

Fuchs, Daniel 1909- .... **CLC 8, 22**
See also CA 81-84; CAAS 5; DLB 9, 26, 28

Fuchs, Daniel 1934- .... **CLC 34**
See also CA 37-40R; CANR 14

Fuentes, Carlos
1928- ...... **CLC 3, 8, 10, 13, 22, 41, 60**
See also AAYA 4; AITN 2; CA 69-72;
CANR 10, 32; DLB 113; HW; MTCW;
WLC

Fuentes, Gregorio Lopez y
See Lopez y Fuentes, Gregorio

Fugard, (Harold) Athol
1932- .... **CLC 5, 9, 14, 25, 40**
See also CA 85-88; CANR 32; MTCW

Fugard, Sheila 1932- .... **CLC 48**
See also CA 125

Fuller, Charles (H. Jr.)
1939- .... **CLC 25; DC 1**
See also BLC 2; BW; CA 108; 112; DLB 38;
MTCW

Fuller, John (Leopold) 1937-....... **CLC 62**
See also CA 21-24R; CANR 9; DLB 40

Fuller, Margaret .... **NCLC 5**
See also Ossoli, Sarah Margaret (Fuller
marchesa d')

Fuller, Roy (Broadbent)
1912-1991 .... **CLC 4, 28**
See also CA 5-8R; 135; CAAS 10; DLB 15,
20

Fulton, Alice 1952-............... **CLC 52**
See also CA 116

Furphy, Joseph 1843-1912........ **TCLC 25**

Futabatei, Shimei 1864-1909 ...... **TCLC 44**

Futrelle, Jacques 1875-1912 ...... **TCLC 19**
See also CA 113

G. B. S.
See Shaw, George Bernard

Gaboriau, Emile 1835-1873 ...... **NCLC 14**

Gadda, Carlo Emilio 1893-1973 .... **CLC 11**
See also CA 89-92

Gaddis, William
1922- .... **CLC 1, 3, 6, 8, 10, 19, 43**
See also CA 17-20R; CANR 21; DLB 2;
MTCW

Gaines, Ernest J(ames)
1933- .... **CLC 3, 11, 18**
See also AITN 1; BLC 2; BW; CA 9-12R;
CANR 6, 24; CDALB 1968-1988; DLB 2,
33; DLBY 80; MTCW

Gaitskill, Mary 1954-............. **CLC 69**
See also CA 128

Galdos, Benito Perez
See Perez Galdos, Benito

Gale, Zona 1874-1938 .... **TCLC 7**
See also CA 105; DLB 9, 78

Galeano, Eduardo (Hughes) 1940-... **CLC 72**
See also CA 29-32R; CANR 13, 32; HW

Galiano, Juan Valera y Alcala
See Valera y Alcala-Galiano, Juan

Gallagher, Tess 1943-......... **CLC 18, 63**
See also CA 106; DLB 120

Gallant, Mavis
1922- .... **CLC 7, 18, 38; SSC 5**
See also CA 69-72; CANR 29; DLB 53;
MTCW

Gallant, Roy A(rthur) 1924- .... **CLC 17**
See also CA 5-8R; CANR 4, 29; MAICYA;
SATA 4, 68

Gallico, Paul (William) 1897-1976 ... **CLC 2**
See also AITN 1; CA 5-8R; 69-72;
CANR 23; DLB 9; MAICYA; SATA 13

Gallup, Ralph
See Whitemore, Hugh (John)

Galsworthy, John 1867-1933 .... **TCLC 1, 45**
See also CA 104; CDBLB 1890-1914;
DLB 10, 34, 98; WLC 2

Galt, John 1779-1839........... **NCLC 1**
See also DLB 99, 116

Galvin, James 1951-.............. **CLC 38**
See also CA 108; CANR 26

Gamboa, Federico 1864-1939...... **TCLC 36**

Gann, Ernest Kellogg 1910-1991.... **CLC 23**
See also AITN 1; CA 1-4R; 136; CANR 1

Garcia Lorca, Federico
1898-1936 ..... **TCLC 1, 7; DC 2; PC 3**
See also CA 104; 131; DLB 108; HW;
MTCW; WLC

Garcia Marquez, Gabriel (Jose)
1928- ... **CLC 2, 3, 8, 10, 15, 27, 47, 55;**
SSC 8
See also Marquez, Gabriel (Jose) Garcia
See also AAYA 3; BEST 89:1, 90:4;
CA 33-36R; CANR 10, 28; DLB 113;
HW; MTCW; WLC

Gard, Janice
See Latham, Jean Lee

Gard, Roger Martin du
See Martin du Gard, Roger

Gardam, Jane 1928-.............. **CLC 43**
See also CA 49-52; CANR 2, 18, 33;
CLR 12; DLB 14; MAICYA; MTCW;
SAAS 9; SATA 28, 39

Gardner, Herb.................... **CLC 44**

Gardner, John (Champlin) Jr.
1933-1982 .... **CLC 2, 3, 5, 7, 8, 10, 18,**
28, 34; SSC 7
See also AITN 1; CA 65-68; 107;
CANR 33; DLB 2; DLBY 82; MTCW;
SATA 31, 40

Gardner, John (Edmund) 1926-..... **CLC 30**
See also CA 103; CANR 15; MTCW

Gardner, Noel
See Kuttner, Henry

Gardons, S. S.
See Snodgrass, William D(e Witt)

Garfield, Leon 1921-.............. **CLC 12**
See also AAYA 8; CA 17-20R; CANR 38;
CLR 21; MAICYA; SATA 1, 32

Garland, (Hannibal) Hamlin
1860-1940 .... **TCLC 3**
See also CA 104; DLB 12, 71, 78

Garneau, (Hector de) Saint-Denys
1912-1943 .... **TCLC 13**
See also CA 111; DLB 88

Garner, Alan 1934-.............. **CLC 17**
See also CA 73-76; CANR 15; CLR 20;
MAICYA; MTCW; SATA 18, 69

Garner, Hugh 1913-1979 .... **CLC 13**
See also CA 69-72; CANR 31; DLB 68

Garnett, David 1892-1981 .... **CLC 3**
See also CA 5-8R; 103; CANR 17; DLB 34

Garos, Stephanie
See Katz, Steve

Garrett, George (Palmer)
1929- .... **CLC 3, 11, 51**
See also CA 1-4R; CAAS 5; CANR 1;
DLB 2, 5; DLBY 83

Garrick, David 1717-1779 .... **LC 15**
See also DLB 84

Garrigue, Jean 1914-1972 .... **CLC 2, 8**
See also CA 5-8R; 37-40R; CANR 20

Garrison, Frederick
See Sinclair, Upton (Beall)

Garth, Will
See Hamilton, Edmond; Kuttner, Henry

Garvey, Marcus (Moziah Jr.)
1887-1940 .... **TCLC 41**
See also BLC 2; BW; CA 120; 124

Gary, Romain .... **CLC 25**
See also Kacew, Romain
See also DLB 83

Gascar, Pierre .... **CLC 11**
See also Fournier, Pierre

Gascoyne, David (Emery) 1916- .... **CLC 45**
See also CA 65-68; CANR 10, 28; DLB 20;
MTCW

Gaskell, Elizabeth Cleghorn
1810-1865 .... **NCLC 5**
See also CDBLB 1832-1890; DLB 21

Gass, William H(oward)
1924- .... **CLC 1, 2, 8, 11, 15, 39**
See also CA 17-20R; CANR 30; DLB 2;
MTCW

Gasset, Jose Ortega y
See Ortega y Gasset, Jose

Gautier, Theophile 1811-1872 ..... **NCLC 1**
See also DLB 119

Gawsworth, John
See Bates, H(erbert) E(rnest)

Gaye, Marvin (Penze) 1939-1984 ... **CLC 26**
See also CA 112

Gebler, Carlo (Ernest) 1954- .... **CLC 39**
See also CA 119; 133

Gee, Maggie (Mary) 1948- .... **CLC 57**
See also CA 130

Gee, Maurice (Gough) 1931- .... **CLC 29**
See also CA 97-100; SATA 46

Gelbart, Larry (Simon) 1923- ... **CLC 21, 61**
See also CA 73-76

Gelber, Jack 1932- .... **CLC 1, 6, 14**
See also CA 1-4R; CANR 2; DLB 7

Gellhorn, Martha Ellis 1908- ... **CLC 14, 60**
See also CA 77-80; DLBY 82

Genet, Jean
1910-1986 ... **CLC 1, 2, 5, 10, 14, 44, 46**
See also CA 13-16R; CANR 18; DLB 72;
DLBY 86; MTCW

Gent, Peter 1942- .... **CLC 29**
See also AITN 1; CA 89-92; DLBY 82

George, Jean Craighead 1919- ...... **CLC 35**
See also AAYA 8; CA 5-8R; CANR 25;
CLR 1; DLB 52; MAICYA; SATA 2, 68

George, Stefan (Anton)
1868-1933 .... **TCLC 2, 14**
See also CA 104

Georges, Georges Martin
See Simenon, Georges (Jacques Christian)

Gerhardi, William Alexander
See Gerhardie, William Alexander

Gerhardie, William Alexander
1895-1977 .... **CLC 5**
See also CA 25-28R; 73-76; CANR 18;
DLB 36

Gerstler, Amy 1956- .... **CLC 70**

Gertler, T. .... **CLC 34**
See also CA 116; 121

Ghelderode, Michel de
1898-1962 .... **CLC 6, 11**
See also CA 85-88

Ghiselin, Brewster 1903- .... **CLC 23**
See also CA 13-16R; CAAS 10; CANR 13

Ghose, Zulfikar 1935- .... **CLC 42**
See also CA 65-68

Ghosh, Amitav 1956- .... **CLC 44**

Giacosa, Giuseppe 1847-1906 ...... **TCLC 7**
See also CA 104

Gibb, Lee
See Waterhouse, Keith (Spencer)

Gibbon, Lewis Grassic .... **TCLC 4**
See also Mitchell, James Leslie

Gibbons, Kaye 1960- .... **CLC 50**

Gibran, Kahlil 1883-1931 .... **TCLC 1, 9**
See also CA 104

Gibson, William (Ford) 1948- ... **CLC 39, 63**
See also CA 126; 133

Gibson, William 1914- .... **CLC 23**
See also CA 9-12R; CANR 9; DLB 7;
SATA 66

Gide, Andre (Paul Guillaume)
1869-1951 .... **TCLC 5, 12, 36**
See also CA 104; 124; DLB 65; MTCW;
WLC

Gifford, Barry (Colby) 1946- .... **CLC 34**
See also CA 65-68; CANR 9, 30

Gilbert, W(illiam) S(chwenck)
1836-1911 .... **TCLC 3**
See also CA 104; SATA 36

Gilbreth, Frank B. Jr. 1911- .... **CLC 17**
See also CA 9-12R; SATA 2

Gilchrist, Ellen 1935- .... **CLC 34, 48**
See also CA 113; 116; MTCW

Giles, Molly 1942- .... **CLC 39**
See also CA 126

Gill, Patrick
See Creasey, John

Gilliam, Terry (Vance) 1940- .... **CLC 21**
See also Monty Python
See also CA 108; 113; CANR 35

Gillian, Jerry
See Gilliam, Terry (Vance)

Gilliatt, Penelope (Ann Douglass)
1932- .... **CLC 2, 10, 13, 53**
See also AITN 2; CA 13-16R; DLB 14

Gilman, Charlotte (Anna) Perkins (Stetson)
1860-1935 .... **TCLC 9, 37**
See also CA 106

Gilmour, David 1944- .... **CLC 35**
See also Pink Floyd
See also CA 138

Gilpin, William 1724-1804 ...... **NCLC 30**

Gilray, J. D.
See Mencken, H(enry) L(ouis)

Gilroy, Frank D(aniel) 1925- .... **CLC 2**
See also CA 81-84; CANR 32; DLB 7

Ginsberg, Allen
1926- ..... **CLC 1, 2, 3, 4, 6, 13, 36, 69;
PC 4**
See also AITN 1; CA 1-4R; CANR 2;
CDALB 1941-1968; DLB 5, 16; MTCW;
WLC 3

Ginzburg, Natalia
1916-1991 .... **CLC 5, 11, 54, 70**
See also CA 85-88; 135; CANR 33; MTCW

Giono, Jean 1895-1970.......... **CLC 4, 11**
See also CA 45-48; 29-32R; CANR 2, 35;
DLB 72; MTCW

Giovanni, Nikki 1943- ..... **CLC 2, 4, 19, 64**
See also AITN 1; BLC 2; BW; CA 29-32R;
CAAS 6; CANR 18; CLR 6; DLB 5, 41;
MAICYA; MTCW; SATA 24

Giovene, Andrea 1904- .... **CLC 7**
See also CA 85-88

Gippius, Zinaida (Nikolayevna) 1869-1945
See Hippius, Zinaida
See also CA 106

Giraudoux, (Hippolyte) Jean
1882-1944 .... **TCLC 2, 7**
See also CA 104; DLB 65

Gironella, Jose Maria 1917- .... **CLC 11**
See also CA 101

Gissing, George (Robert)
1857-1903 .... **TCLC 3, 24, 47**
See also CA 105; DLB 18

Giurlani, Aldo
See Palazzeschi, Aldo

Gladkov, Fyodor (Vasilyevich)
1883-1958 .... **TCLC 27**

Glanville, Brian (Lester) 1931- ...... **CLC 6**
See also CA 5-8R; CAAS 9; CANR 3;
DLB 15; SATA 42

Glasgow, Ellen (Anderson Gholson)
1873(?)-1945 .... **TCLC 2, 7**
See also CA 104; DLB 9, 12

Glassco, John 1909-1981 .... **CLC 9**
See also CA 13-16R; 102; CANR 15;
DLB 68

Glasscock, Amnesia
See Steinbeck, John (Ernst)

Glasser, Ronald J. 1940(?)- .... **CLC 37**

Glassman, Joyce
See Johnson, Joyce

Glendinning, Victoria 1937- .... **CLC 50**
See also CA 120; 127

Glissant, Edouard 1928- .... **CLC 10, 68**

Gloag, Julian 1930- .... **CLC 40**
See also AITN 1; CA 65-68; CANR 10

Gluck, Louise 1943- .... **CLC 7, 22, 44**
See also Glueck, Louise
See also CA 33-36R; DLB 5

Glueck, Louise .... **CLC 7, 22**
See also Gluck, Louise
See also DLB 5

Gobineau, Joseph Arthur (Comte) de
1816-1882 .... **NCLC 17**

Godard, Jean-Luc 1930- .... **CLC 20**
See also CA 93-96

Godden, (Margaret) Rumer 1907-... **CLC 53**
See also AAYA 6; CA 5-8R; CANR 4, 27,
36; CLR 20; MAICYA; SAAS 12;
SATA 3, 36

Godoy Alcayaga, Lucila 1889-1957
See Mistral, Gabriela
See also CA 104; 131; HW; MTCW

Godwin, Gail (Kathleen)
1937- .... **CLC 5, 8, 22, 31, 69**
See also CA 29-32R; CANR 15; DLB 6;
MTCW

Godwin, William 1756-1836...... **NCLC 14**
See also CDBLB 1789-1832; DLB 39, 104

Goethe, Johann Wolfgang von
1749-1832 .... **NCLC 4, 22, 34; PC 5**
See also DLB 94; WLC 3

Gogarty, Oliver St. John
1878-1957 .... **TCLC 15**
See also CA 109; DLB 15, 19

Gogol, Nikolai (Vasilyevich)
1809-1852 ..... **NCLC 5, 15, 31; DC 1;
SSC 4**
See also WLC

Gold, Herbert 1924-....... **CLC 4, 7, 14, 42**
See also CA 9-12R; CANR 17; DLB 2;
DLBY 81

Goldbarth, Albert 1948-........ **CLC 5, 38**
See also CA 53-56; CANR 6; DLB 120

Goldberg, Anatol 1910-1982 .... **CLC 34**
See also CA 131; 117

Goldemberg, Isaac 1945-.......... **CLC 52**
See also CA 69-72; CAAS 12; CANR 11,
32; HW

Golden Silver
See Storm, Hyemeyohsts

Golding, William (Gerald)
1911- ..... **CLC 1, 2, 3, 8, 10, 17, 27, 58**
See also AAYA 5; CA 5-8R; CANR 13, 33;
CDBLB 1945-1960; DLB 15, 100;
MTCW; WLC

Goldman, Emma 1869-1940...... **TCLC 13**
See also CA 110

Goldman, William (W.) 1931-.... **CLC 1, 48**
See also CA 9-12R; CANR 29; DLB 44

Goldmann, Lucien 1913-1970 ...... **CLC 24**
See also CA 25-28; CAP 2

Goldoni, Carlo 1707-1793 .... **LC 4**

Goldsberry, Steven 1949-.......... **CLC 34**
See also CA 131

Goldsmith, Oliver 1728(?)-1774....... **LC 2**

Goldsmith, Peter
See Priestley, J(ohn) B(oynton)

Gombrowicz, Witold
1904-1969 .... **CLC 4, 7, 11, 49**
See also CA 19-20; 25-28R; CAP 2

Gomez de la Serna, Ramon
1888-1963 .... **CLC 9**
See also CA 116; HW

Goncharov, Ivan Alexandrovich
1812-1891 .... **NCLC 1**

Goncourt, Edmond (Louis Antoine Huot) de
1822-1896 .... **NCLC 7**

Goncourt, Jules (Alfred Huot) de
1830-1870 .... **NCLC 7**

Gontier, Fernande 19(?)- .... **CLC 50**

Goodman, Paul 1911-1972.... **CLC 1, 2, 4, 7**
See also CA 19-20; 37-40R; CANR 34;
CAP 2; MTCW

Gordimer, Nadine
1923- .... **CLC 3, 5, 7, 10, 18, 33, 51, 70**
See also CA 5-8R; CANR 3, 28; MTCW

Gordon, Adam Lindsay
1833-1870 .... **NCLC 21**

Gordon, Caroline
1895-1981 .... **CLC 6, 13, 29**
See also CA 11-12; 103; CANR 36; CAP 1;
DLB 4, 9, 102; DLBY 81; MTCW

Gordon, Charles William 1860-1937
See Connor, Ralph
See also CA 109

Gordon, Mary (Catherine)
1949- .... **CLC 13, 22**
See also CA 102; DLB 6; DLBY 81;
MTCW

Gordon, Sol 1923-................ **CLC 26**
See also CA 53-56; CANR 4; SATA 11

Gordone, Charles 1925-.......... **CLC 1, 4**
See also BW; CA 93-96; DLB 7; MTCW

Gorenko, Anna Andreevna
See Akhmatova, Anna

Gorky, Maxim.................... TCLC 8
See also Peshkov, Alexei Maximovich
See also WLC

Goryan, Sirak
See Saroyan, William

Gosse, Edmund (William)
1849-1928 .... **TCLC 28**
See also CA 117; DLB 57

Gotlieb, Phyllis Fay (Bloom)
1926- .... **CLC 18**
See also CA 13-16R; CANR 7; DLB 88

Gottesman, S. D.
See Kornbluth, C(yril) M.; Pohl, Frederik

Gottschalk, Laura Riding
See Jackson, Laura (Riding)

Gould, Lois .... CLC 4, 10
See also CA 77-80; CANR 29; MTCW

Gourmont, Remy de 1858-1915.... **TCLC 17**
See also CA 109

Govier, Katherine 1948-........... **CLC 51**
See also CA 101; CANR 18

Goyen, (Charles) William
1915-1983 .... **CLC 5, 8, 14, 40**
See also AITN 2; CA 5-8R; 110; CANR 6;
DLB 2; DLBY 83

Goytisolo, Juan 1931- .... **CLC 5, 10, 23**
See also CA 85-88; CANR 32; HW; MTCW

Gozzi, (Conte) Carlo 1720-1806 .. **NCLC 23**

Grabbe, Christian Dietrich
1801-1836 .... **NCLC 2**

Grace, Patricia 1937-............. **CLC 56**

Gracian y Morales, Baltasar
1601-1658 .... **LC 15**

Gracq, Julien................ CLC 11, 48
See also Poirier, Louis
See also DLB 83

Grade, Chaim 1910-1982 .... **CLC 10**
See also CA 93-96; 107

Graduate of Oxford, A
See Ruskin, John

Graham, John
See Phillips, David Graham

Graham, Jorie 1951-.............. **CLC 48**
See also CA 111; DLB 120

Graham, R(obert) B(ontine) Cunninghame
See Cunninghame Graham, R(obert)
B(ontine)
See also DLB 98

Graham, Robert
See Haldeman, Joe (William)

Graham, Tom
See Lewis, (Harry) Sinclair

Graham, W(illiam) S(ydney)
1918-1986 .... **CLC 29**
See also CA 73-76; 118; DLB 20

Graham, Winston (Mawdsley)
1910- .... **CLC 23**
See also CA 49-52; CANR 2, 22; DLB 77

Granville-Barker, Harley
1877-1946 .... **TCLC 2**
See also Barker, Harley Granville
See also CA 104

Grass, Guenter (Wilhelm)
1927- .. **CLC 1, 2, 4, 6, 11, 15, 22, 32, 49**
See also CA 13-16R; CANR 20; DLB 75;
MTCW; WLC

Gratton, Thomas
See Hulme, T(homas) E(rnest)

Grau, Shirley Ann 1929- .... **CLC 4, 9**
See also CA 89-92; CANR 22; DLB 2;
MTCW

Gravel, Fern
See Hall, James Norman

Graver, Elizabeth 1964-........... **CLC 70**
See also CA 135

Graves, Richard Perceval 1945- .... **CLC 44**
See also CA 65-68; CANR 9, 26

Graves, Robert (von Ranke)
1895-1985 ... **CLC 1, 2, 6, 11, 39, 44, 45**
See also CA 5-8R; 117; CANR 5, 36;
CDBLB 1914-1945; DLB 20, 100;
DLBY 85; MTCW; SATA 45

Gray, Alasdair (James) 1934- ...... **CLC 41**
See also CA 126; MTCW

Gray, Amlin 1946- .... **CLC 29**
See also CA 138

Gray, Francine du Plessix 1930-.... **CLC 22**
See also BEST 90:3; CA 61-64; CAAS 2;
CANR 11, 33; MTCW

Gray, John (Henry) 1866-1934 .... **TCLC 19**
See also CA 119

Gray, Simon (James Holliday)
1936-.................... **CLC 9, 14, 36**
See also AITN 1; CA 21-24R; CAAS 3;
CANR 32; DLB 13; MTCW

Gray, Spalding 1941-............. **CLC 49**
See also CA 128

Gray, Thomas 1716-1771....... **LC 4; PC 2**
See also CDBLB 1660-1789; DLB 109;
WLC

Grayson, David
See Baker, Ray Stannard

Grayson, Richard (A.) 1951- ...... **CLC 38**
See also CA 85-88; CANR 14, 31

Greeley, Andrew M(oran) 1928- .... **CLC 28**
See also CA 5-8R; CAAS 7; CANR 7;
MTCW

Green, Brian
See Card, Orson Scott

Green, Hannah
See Greenberg, Joanne (Goldenberg)

Green, Hannah .... **CLC 3**
See also CA 73-76

Green, Henry................... **CLC 2, 13**
See also Yorke, Henry Vincent
See also DLB 15

Green, Julian (Hartridge)
1900- .... **CLC 3, 11**
See also CA 21-24R; CANR 33; DLB 4, 72;
MTCW

Green, Julien
See Green, Julian (Hartridge)

Green, Paul (Eliot) 1894-1981..... **CLC 25**
See also AITN 1; CA 5-8R; 103; CANR 3;
DLB 7, 9; DLBY 81

Greenberg, Ivan 1908-1973
See Rahv, Philip
See also CA 85-88

Greenberg, Joanne (Goldenberg)
1932- .... **CLC 7, 30**
See also CA 5-8R; CANR 14, 32; SATA 25

Greenberg, Richard 1959(?)- .... **CLC 57**
See also CA 138

Greene, Bette 1934- .... **CLC 30**
See also AAYA 7; CA 53-56; CANR 4;
CLR 2; MAICYA; SATA 8

Greene, Gael .... **CLC 8**
See also CA 13-16R; CANR 10

Greene, Graham (Henry)
1904-1991 ... **CLC 1, 3, 6, 9, 14, 18, 27,
37, 70, 72**
See also AITN 2; CA 13-16R; 133;
CANR 35; CDBLB 1945-1960; DLB 13,
15, 77, 100; DLBY 91; MTCW;
SATA 20; WLC

Greer, Richard
See Silverberg, Robert

Greer, Richard
See Silverberg, Robert

Gregor, Arthur 1923- .... **CLC 9**
See also CA 25-28R; CAAS 10; CANR 11;
SATA 36

Gregor, Lee
See Pohl, Frederik

Gregory, Isabella Augusta (Persse)
1852-1932 .... **TCLC 1**
See also CA 104; DLB 10

Gregory, J. Dennis
See Williams, John A(lfred)

Grendon, Stephen
See Derleth, August (William)

Grenville, Kate 1950- .... **CLC 61**
See also CA 118

Grenville, Pelham
See Wodehouse, P(elham) G(renville)

Greve, Felix Paul (Berthold Friedrich)
1879-1948
See Grove, Frederick Philip
See also CA 104

Grey, Zane 1872-1939 .... **TCLC 6**
See also CA 104; 132; DLB 9; MTCW

Grieg, (Johan) Nordahl (Brun)
1902-1943 .... **TCLC 10**
See also CA 107

Grieve, C(hristopher) M(urray)
1892-1978 .... **CLC 11, 19**
See also MacDiarmid, Hugh
See also CA 5-8R; 85-88; CANR 33;
MTCW

Griffin, Gerald 1803-1840 .... **NCLC 7**

Griffin, John Howard 1920-1980.... **CLC 68**
See also AITN 1; CA 1-4R; 101; CANR 2

Griffin, Peter .... **CLC 39**

Griffiths, Trevor 1935- .... **CLC 13, 52**
See also CA 97-100; DLB 13

Grigson, Geoffrey (Edward Harvey)
1905-1985 .... **CLC 7, 39**
See also CA 25-28R; 118; CANR 20, 33;
DLB 27; MTCW

Grillparzer, Franz 1791-1872...... **NCLC 1**

Grimble, Reverend Charles James
See Eliot, T(homas) S(tearns)

Grimke, Charlotte L(ottie) Forten
1837(?)-1914
See Forten, Charlotte L.
See also BW; CA 117; 124

Grimm, Jacob Ludwig Karl
1785-1863 .... **NCLC 3**
See also DLB 90; MAICYA; SATA 22

Grimm, Wilhelm Karl 1786-1859 .. **NCLC 3**
See also DLB 90; MAICYA; SATA 22

Grimmelshausen, Johann Jakob Christoffel
von 1621-1676 .... **LC 6**

Grindel, Eugene 1895-1952
See Eluard, Paul
See also CA 104

Grossman, David................. **CLC 67**
See also CA 138

Grossman, Vasily (Semenovich)
1905-1964 .... **CLC 41**
See also CA 124; 130; MTCW

Grove, Frederick Philip .... **TCLC 4**
See also Greve, Felix Paul (Berthold
Friedrich)
See also DLB 92

Grubb
See Crumb, R(obert)

Grumbach, Doris (Isaac)
1918- .... **CLC 13, 22, 64**
See also CA 5-8R; CAAS 2; CANR 9

Grundtvig, Nicolai Frederik Severin
1783-1872 .... **NCLC 1**

Grunge
See Crumb, R(obert)

Grunwald, Lisa 1959-............. **CLC 44**
See also CA 120

Guare, John 1938- .... **CLC 8, 14, 29, 67**
See also CA 73-76; CANR 21; DLB 7;
MTCW

Gudjonsson, Halldor Kiljan 1902-
See Laxness, Halldor
See also CA 103

Guenter, Erich
See Eich, Guenter

Guest, Barbara 1920-............. **CLC 34**
See also CA 25-28R; CANR 11; DLB 5

Guest, Judith (Ann) 1936-....... **CLC 8, 30**
See also AAYA 7; CA 77-80; CANR 15;
MTCW

Guild, Nicholas M. 1944-.......... **CLC 33**
See also CA 93-96

Guillemin, Jacques
See Sartre, Jean-Paul

Guillen, Jorge 1893-1984.......... **CLC 11**
See also CA 89-92; 112; DLB 108; HW

Guillen (y Batista), Nicolas (Cristobal)
1902-1989 .... **CLC 48**
See also BLC 2; BW; CA 116; 125; 129;
HW

Guillevic, (Eugene) 1907-......... **CLC 33**
See also CA 93-96

Guillois
See Desnos, Robert

Guiney, Louise Imogen
1861-1920 .... **TCLC 41**
See also DLB 54

Guiraldes, Ricardo (Guillermo)
1886-1927 .... **TCLC 39**
See also CA 131; HW; MTCW

Gunn, Bill .... **CLC 5**
See also Gunn, William Harrison
See also DLB 38

Gunn, Thom(son William)
1929- .... **CLC 3, 6, 18, 32**
See also CA 17-20R; CANR 9, 33;
CDBLB 1960 to Present; DLB 27;
MTCW

Gunn, William Harrison 1934(?)-1989
See Gunn, Bill
See also AITN 1; BW; CA 13-16R; 128;
CANR 12, 25

Gunnars, Kristjana 1948-.......... **CLC 69**
See also CA 113; DLB 60

Gurganus, Allan 1947-............ **CLC 70**
See also BEST 90:1; CA 135

Gurney, A(lbert) R(amsdell) Jr.
1930- .... **CLC 32, 50, 54**
See also CA 77-80; CANR 32

Gurney, Ivor (Bertie) 1890-1937... **TCLC 33**

Gurney, Peter
See Gurney, A(lbert) R(amsdell) Jr.

Gustafson, Ralph (Barker) 1909-.... **CLC 36**
See also CA 21-24R; CANR 8; DLB 88

Gut, Gom
See Simenon, Georges (Jacques Christian)

Guthrie, A(lfred) B(ertram) Jr.
1901-1991 .... **CLC 23**
See also CA 57-60; 134; CANR 24; DLB 6;
SATA 62; SATO 67

Guthrie, Isobel
See Grieve, C(hristopher) M(urray)

Guthrie, Woodrow Wilson 1912-1967
See Guthrie, Woody
See also CA 113; 93-96

Guthrie, Woody................... **CLC 35**
See also Guthrie, Woodrow Wilson

Guy, Rosa (Cuthbert) 1928-........ **CLC 26**
See also AAYA 4; BW; CA 17-20R;
CANR 14, 34; CLR 13; DLB 33;
MAICYA; SATA 14, 62

Gwendolyn
See Bennett, (Enoch) Arnold

H. D. .... **CLC 3, 8, 14, 31, 34; PC 5**
See also Doolittle, Hilda

Haavikko, Paavo Juhani
1931- .... **CLC 18, 34**
See also CA 106

Habbema, Koos
See Heijermans, Herman

Hacker, Marilyn 1942- .... **CLC 5, 9, 23, 72**
See also CA 77-80; DLB 120

Haggard, H(enry) Rider
1856-1925 .... **TCLC 11**
See also CA 108; DLB 70; SATA 16

Haig, Fenil
See Ford, Ford Madox

Haig-Brown, Roderick (Langmere)
1908-1976 .... **CLC 21**
See also CA 5-8R; 69-72; CANR 4, 38;
DLB 88; MAICYA; SATA 12

Hailey, Arthur 1920- .... **CLC 5**
See also AITN 2; BEST 90:3; CA 1-4R;
CANR 2, 36; DLB 88; DLBY 82; MTCW

Hailey, Elizabeth Forsythe 1938-... **CLC 40**
See also CA 93-96; CAAS 1; CANR 15

Haines, John (Meade) 1924-....... **CLC 58**
See also CA 17-20R; CANR 13, 34; DLB 5

Haldeman, Joe (William) 1943-..... **CLC 61**
See also CA 53-56; CANR 6; DLB 8

Haley, Alex(ander Murray Palmer)
1921-1992 .... **CLC 8, 12**
See also BLC 2; BW; CA 77-80; 136;
DLB 38; MTCW

Haliburton, Thomas Chandler
1796-1865 .... **NCLC 15**
See also DLB 11, 99

Hall, Donald (Andrew Jr.)
1928- .... **CLC 1, 13, 37, 59**
See also CA 5-8R; CAAS 7; CANR 2;
DLB 5; SATA 23

Hall, Frederic Sauser
See Sauser-Hall, Frederic

Hall, James
See Kuttner, Henry

Hall, James Norman 1887-1951 ... **TCLC 23**
See also CA 123; SATA 21

Hall, (Marguerite) Radclyffe
1886(?)-1943 .... **TCLC 12**
See also CA 110

Hall, Rodney 1935- .... **CLC 51**
See also CA 109

Halliday, Michael
See Creasey, John

Halpern, Daniel 1945- .... **CLC 14**
See also CA 33-36R

Hamburger, Michael (Peter Leopold)
1924- .... **CLC 5, 14**
See also CA 5-8R; CAAS 4; CANR 2;
DLB 27

Hamill, Pete 1935-............... **CLC 10**
See also CA 25-28R; CANR 18

Hamilton, Clive
See Lewis, C(live) S(taples)

Hamilton, Edmond 1904-1977....... **CLC 1**
See also CA 1-4R; CANR 3; DLB 8

Hamilton, Eugene (Jacob) Lee
See Lee-Hamilton, Eugene (Jacob)

Hamilton, Franklin
See Silverberg, Robert

Hamilton, Gail
See Corcoran, Barbara

Hamilton, Mollie
See Kaye, M(ary) M(argaret)

Hamilton, (Anthony Walter) Patrick
1904-1962 .... **CLC 51**
See also CA 113; DLB 10

Hamilton, Virginia 1936-......... **CLC 26**
See also AAYA 2; BW; CA 25-28R;
CANR 20, 37; CLR 1, 11; DLB 33, 52;
MAICYA; MTCW; SATA 4, 56

Hammett, (Samuel) Dashiell
1894-1961 ...... **CLC 3, 5, 10, 19, 47**
See also AITN 1; CA 81-84;
CDALB 1929-1941; DLBD 6; MTCW

Hammon, Jupiter 1711(?)-1800(?).. **NCLC 5**
See also BLC 2; DLB 31, 50

Hammond, Keith
See Kuttner, Henry

Hamner, Earl (Henry) Jr. 1923-.... **CLC 12**
See also AITN 2; CA 73-76; DLB 6

Hampton, Christopher (James)
1946- .... **CLC 4**
See also CA 25-28R; DLB 13; MTCW

Hamsun, Knut................. **TCLC 2, 14**
See also Pedersen, Knut

Handke, Peter 1942- .. **CLC 5, 8, 10, 15, 38**
See also CA 77-80; CANR 33; DLB 85;
MTCW

Hanley, James 1901-1985 ... **CLC 3, 5, 8, 13**
See also CA 73-76; 117; CANR 36; MTCW

Hannah, Barry 1942-.......... **CLC 23, 38**
See also CA 108; 110; DLB 6; MTCW

Hannon, Ezra
See Hunter, Evan

Hansberry, Lorraine (Vivian)
1930-1965 .... **CLC 17, 62; DC 2**
See also BLC 2; BW; CA 109; 25-28R;
CABS 3; CDALB 1941-1968; DLB 7, 38;
MTCW

Hansen, Joseph 1923-............. **CLC 38**
See also CA 29-32R; CANR 16

Hansen, Martin A. 1909-1955..... **TCLC 32**

Hanson, Kenneth O(stlin) 1922- .... **CLC 13**
See also CA 53-56; CANR 7

Hardwick, Elizabeth 1916- .... **CLC 13**
See also CA 5-8R; CANR 3, 32; DLB 6;
MTCW

Hardy, Thomas
1840-1928 ... **TCLC 4, 10, 18, 32; SSC 2**
See also CA 104; 123; CDBLB 1890-1914;
DLB 18, 19; MTCW; WLC

Hare, David 1947- .... **CLC 29, 58**
See also CA 97-100; CANR 39; DLB 13;
MTCW

Harford, Henry
See Hudson, W(illiam) H(enry)

Hargrave, Leonie
See Disch, Thomas M(ichael)

Harlan, Louis R(udolph) 1922-..... **CLC 34**
See also CA 21-24R; CANR 25

Harling, Robert 1951(?)- .... **CLC 53**

Harmon, William (Ruth) 1938-..... **CLC 38**
See also CA 33-36R; CANR 14, 32, 35;
SATA 65

Harper, F. E. W.
See Harper, Frances Ellen Watkins

Harper, Frances E. W.
See Harper, Frances Ellen Watkins

Harper, Frances E. Watkins
See Harper, Frances Ellen Watkins

Harper, Frances Ellen
See Harper, Frances Ellen Watkins

Harper, Frances Ellen Watkins
1825-1911 .... **TCLC 14**
See also BLC 2; BW; CA 111; 125; DLB 50

Harper, Michael S(teven) 1938- .. **CLC 7, 22**
See also BW; CA 33-36R; CANR 24;
DLB 41

Harper, Mrs. F. E. W.
See Harper, Frances Ellen Watkins

Harris, Christie (Lucy) Irwin
1907- .... **CLC 12**
See also CA 5-8R; CANR 6; DLB 88;
MAICYA; SAAS 10; SATA 6

Harris, Frank 1856(?)-1931....... **TCLC 24**
See also CA 109

Harris, George Washington
1814-1869 .... **NCLC 23**
See also DLB 3, 11

Harris, Joel Chandler 1848-1908 ... **TCLC 2**
See also CA 104; 137; DLB 11, 23, 42, 78,
91; MAICYA; YABC 1

Harris, John (Wyndham Parkes Lucas)
Beynon 1903-1969 .... **CLC 19**
See also CA 102; 89-92

Harris, MacDonald
See Heiney, Donald (William)

Harris, Mark 1922- .... **CLC 19**
See also CA 5-8R; CAAS 3; CANR 2;
DLB 2; DLBY 80

Harris, (Theodore) Wilson 1921-.... **CLC 25**
See also BW; CA 65-68; CAAS 16;
CANR 11, 27; DLB 117; MTCW

Harrison, Elizabeth Cavanna 1909-
See Cavanna, Betty
See also CA 9-12R; CANR 6, 27

Harrison, Harry (Max) 1925-...... **CLC 42**
See also CA 1-4R; CANR 5, 21; DLB 8;
SATA 4

Harrison, James (Thomas) 1937-
  See Harrison, Jim
  See also CA 13-16R; CANR 8

Harrison, Jim . . . . **CLC 6, 14, 33, 66**
  See also Harrison, James (Thomas)
  See also DLBY 82

Harrison, Kathryn 1961- . . . . **CLC 70**

Harrison, Tony 1937- . . . . **CLC 43**
  See also CA 65-68; DLB 40; MTCW

Harriss, Will(ard Irvin) 1922- . . . . . . **CLC 34**
  See also CA 111

Harson, Sley
  See Ellison, Harlan

Hart, Ellis
  See Ellison, Harlan

Hart, Josephine 1942(?)- . . . . **CLC 70**
  See also CA 138

Hart, Moss 1904-1961 . . . . **CLC 66**
  See also CA 109; 89-92; DLB 7

Harte, (Francis) Bret(t)
  1836(?)-1902 . . . . **TCLC 1, 25; SSC 8**
  See also CA 104; CDALB 1865-1917;
    DLB 12, 64, 74, 79; SATA 26; WLC

Hartley, L(eslie) P(oles)
  1895-1972 . . . . **CLC 2, 22**
  See also CA 45-48; 37-40R; CANR 33;
    DLB 15; MTCW

Hartman, Geoffrey H. 1929- . . . . **CLC 27**
  See also CA 117; 125; DLB 67

Haruf, Kent 19(?)- . . . . **CLC 34**

Harwood, Ronald 1934- . . . . **CLC 32**
  See also CA 1-4R; CANR 4; DLB 13

Hasek, Jaroslav (Matej Frantisek)
  1883-1923 . . . . **TCLC 4**
  See also CA 104; 129; MTCW

Hass, Robert 1941- . . . . **CLC 18, 39**
  See also CA 111; CANR 30; DLB 105

Hastings, Hudson
  See Kuttner, Henry

Hastings, Selina . . . . **CLC 44**

Hatteras, Amelia
  See Mencken, H(enry) L(ouis)

Hatteras, Owen
  See Mencken, H(enry) L(ouis)

Hatteras, Owen . . . . **TCLC 18**
  See also Nathan, George Jean

Hauptmann, Gerhart (Johann Robert)
  1862-1946 . . . . **TCLC 4**
  See also CA 104; DLB 66, 118

Havel, Vaclav 1936- . . . . **CLC 25, 58, 65**
  See also CA 104; CANR 36; MTCW

Haviaras, Stratis . . . . **CLC 33**
  See also Chaviaras, Strates

Hawes, Stephen 1475(?)-1523(?) . . . . . **LC 17**

Hawkes, John (Clendennin Burne Jr.)
  1925- . . . . . . **CLC 1, 2, 3, 4, 7, 9, 14, 15,
                                          27, 49**
  See also CA 1-4R; CANR 2; DLB 2, 7;
    DLBY 80; MTCW

Hawking, S. W.
  See Hawking, Stephen W(illiam)

Hawking, Stephen W(illiam)
  1942- . . . . **CLC 63**
  See also BEST 89:1; CA 126; 129

Hawthorne, Julian 1846-1934 . . . . . **TCLC 25**

Hawthorne, Nathaniel
  1804-1864 . . . **NCLC 2, 10, 17, 23; SSC 3**
  See also CDALB 1640-1865; DLB 1, 74;
    WLC; YABC 2

Hayaseca y Eizaguirre, Jorge
  See Echegaray (y Eizaguirre), Jose (Maria
    Waldo)

Hayashi Fumiko 1904-1951 . . . . . . **TCLC 27**

Haycraft, Anna
  See Ellis, Alice Thomas
  See also CA 122

Hayden, Robert E(arl)
  1913-1980 . . . . **CLC 5, 9, 14, 37**
  See also BLC 2; BW; CA 69-72; 97-100;
    CABS 2; CANR 24; CDALB 1941-1968;
    DLB 5, 76; MTCW; SATA 19, 26

Hayford, J(oseph) E(phraim) Casely
  See Casely-Hayford, J(oseph) E(phraim)

Hayman, Ronald 1932- . . . . **CLC 44**
  See also CA 25-28R; CANR 18

Haywood, Eliza (Fowler)
  1693(?)-1756 . . . . **LC 1**

Hazlitt, William 1778-1830 . . . . . . **NCLC 29**
  See also DLB 110

Hazzard, Shirley 1931- . . . . **CLC 18**
  See also CA 9-12R; CANR 4; DLBY 82;
    MTCW

Head, Bessie 1937-1986 . . . . **CLC 25, 67**
  See also BLC 2; BW; CA 29-32R; 119;
    CANR 25; DLB 117; MTCW

Headon, (Nicky) Topper 1956(?)- . . . **CLC 30**
  See also The Clash

Heaney, Seamus (Justin)
  1939- . . . . **CLC 5, 7, 14, 25, 37**
  See also CA 85-88; CANR 25;
    CDBLB 1960 to Present; DLB 40;
    MTCW

Hearn, (Patricio) Lafcadio (Tessima Carlos)
  1850-1904 . . . . **TCLC 9**
  See also CA 105; DLB 12, 78

Hearne, Vicki 1946- . . . . **CLC 56**

Hearon, Shelby 1931- . . . . **CLC 63**
  See also AITN 2; CA 25-28R; CANR 18

Heat-Moon, William Least . . . . **CLC 29**
  See also Trogdon, William (Lewis)
  See also AAYA 9

Hebert, Anne 1916- . . . . **CLC 4, 13, 29**
  See also CA 85-88; DLB 68; MTCW

Hecht, Anthony (Evan)
  1923- . . . . **CLC 8, 13, 19**
  See also CA 9-12R; CANR 6; DLB 5

Hecht, Ben 1894-1964 . . . . **CLC 8**
  See also CA 85-88; DLB 7, 9, 25, 26, 28, 86

Hedayat, Sadeq 1903-1951 . . . . **TCLC 21**
  See also CA 120

Heidegger, Martin 1889-1976 . . . . . . **CLC 24**
  See also CA 81-84; 65-68; CANR 34;
    MTCW

Heidenstam, (Carl Gustaf) Verner von
  1859-1940 . . . . **TCLC 5**
  See also CA 104

Heifner, Jack 1946- . . . . **CLC 11**
  See also CA 105

Heijermans, Herman 1864-1924 . . . **TCLC 24**
  See also CA 123

Heilbrun, Carolyn G(old) 1926- . . . . . **CLC 25**
  See also CA 45-48; CANR 1, 28

Heine, Heinrich 1797-1856 . . . . **NCLC 4**
  See also DLB 90

Heinemann, Larry (Curtiss) 1944- . . **CLC 50**
  See also CA 110; CANR 31; DLBD 9

Heiney, Donald (William) 1921- . . . . . **CLC 9**
  See also CA 1-4R; CANR 3

Heinlein, Robert A(nson)
  1907-1988 . . . . . . **CLC 1, 3, 8, 14, 26, 55**
  See also CA 1-4R; 125; CANR 1, 20;
    DLB 8; MAICYA; MTCW; SATA 9, 56,
    69

Helforth, John
  See Doolittle, Hilda

Hellenhofferu, Vojtech Kapristian z
  See Hasek, Jaroslav (Matej Frantisek)

Heller, Joseph
  1923- . . . . **CLC 1, 3, 5, 8, 11, 36, 63**
  See also AITN 1; CA 5-8R; CABS 1;
    CANR 8; DLB 2, 28; DLBY 80; MTCW;
    WLC

Hellman, Lillian (Florence)
  1906-1984 . . . . . **CLC 2, 4, 8, 14, 18, 34,
                                          44, 52; DC 1**
  See also AITN 1, 2; CA 13-16R; 112;
    CANR 33; DLB 7; DLBY 84; MTCW

Helprin, Mark 1947- . . . . . **CLC 7, 10, 22, 32**
  See also CA 81-84; DLBY 85; MTCW

Helyar, Jane Penelope Josephine 1933-
  See Poole, Josephine
  See also CA 21-24R; CANR 10, 26

Hemans, Felicia 1793-1835 . . . . . . **NCLC 29**
  See also DLB 96

Hemingway, Ernest (Miller)
  1899-1961 . . . **CLC 1, 3, 6, 8, 10, 13, 19,
                  30, 34, 39, 41, 44, 50, 61; SSC 1**
  See also CA 77-80; CANR 34;
    CDALB 1917-1929; DLB 4, 9, 102;
    DLBD 1; DLBY 81, 87; MTCW; WLC

Hempel, Amy 1951- . . . . **CLC 39**
  See also CA 118; 137

Henderson, F. C.
  See Mencken, H(enry) L(ouis)

Henderson, Sylvia
  See Ashton-Warner, Sylvia (Constance)

Henley, Beth . . . . **CLC 23**
  See also Henley, Elizabeth Becker
  See also CABS 3; DLBY 86

Henley, Elizabeth Becker 1952-
  See Henley, Beth
  See also CA 107; CANR 32; MTCW

Henley, William Ernest
  1849-1903 . . . . **TCLC 8**
  See also CA 105; DLB 19

Hennissart, Martha
  See Lathen, Emma
  See also CA 85-88

Henry, O............... TCLC 1, 19; SSC 5
See also Porter, William Sydney
See also WLC

Henryson, Robert 1430(?)-1506(?).... LC 20

Henry VIII 1491-1547............. LC 10

Henschke, Alfred
See Klabund

Hentoff, Nat(han Irving) 1925-..... CLC 26
See also AAYA 4; CA 1-4R; CAAS 6;
CANR 5, 25; CLR 1; MAICYA;
SATA 27, 42, 69

Heppenstall, (John) Rayner
1911-1981 .... CLC 10
See also CA 1-4R; 103; CANR 29

Herbert, Frank (Patrick)
1920-1986 .... CLC 12, 23, 35, 44
See also CA 53-56; 118; CANR 5; DLB 8;
MTCW; SATA 9, 37, 47

Herbert, George 1593-1633......... PC 4
See also CDBLB Before 1660

Herbert, Zbigniew 1924-........ CLC 9, 43
See also CA 89-92; CANR 36; MTCW

Herbst, Josephine (Frey)
1897-1969 .... CLC 34
See also CA 5-8R; 25-28R; DLB 9

Hergesheimer, Joseph
1880-1954 .... TCLC 11
See also CA 109; DLB 102, 9

Herlihy, James Leo 1927-.......... CLC 6
See also CA 1-4R; CANR 2

Hermogenes fl. c. 175-........... CMLC 6

Hernandez, Jose 1834-1886...... NCLC 17

Herrick, Robert 1591-1674 .... LC 13

Herriot, James.................... CLC 12
See also Wight, James Alfred
See also AAYA 1

Herrmann, Dorothy 1941-......... CLC 44
See also CA 107

Herrmann, Taffy
See Herrmann, Dorothy

Hersey, John (Richard)
1914-.............. CLC 1, 2, 7, 9, 40
See also CA 17-20R; CANR 33; DLB 6;
MTCW; SATA 25

Herzen, Aleksandr Ivanovich
1812-1870 .... NCLC 10

Herzl, Theodor 1860-1904........ TCLC 36

Herzog, Werner 1942-............ CLC 16
See also CA 89-92

Hesiod c. 8th cent. B.C.-......... CMLC 5

Hesse, Hermann
1877-1962 ... CLC 1, 2, 3, 6, 11, 17, 25,
69; SSC 9
See also CA 17-18; CAP 2; DLB 66;
MTCW; SATA 50; WLC

Hewes, Cady
See De Voto, Bernard (Augustine)

Heyen, William 1940- .... CLC 13, 18
See also CA 33-36R; CAAS 9; DLB 5

Heyerdahl, Thor 1914-........... CLC 26
See also CA 5-8R; CANR 5, 22; MTCW;
SATA 2, 52

Heym, Georg (Theodor Franz Arthur)
1887-1912 .... TCLC 9
See also CA 106

Heym, Stefan 1913-............. CLC 41
See also CA 9-12R; CANR 4; DLB 69

Heyse, Paul (Johann Ludwig von)
1830-1914 .... TCLC 8
See also CA 104

Hibbert, Eleanor Burford 1906-..... CLC 7
See also BEST 90:4; CA 17-20R; CANR 9,
28; SATA 2

Higgins, George V(incent)
1939-................. CLC 4, 7, 10, 18
See also CA 77-80; CAAS 5; CANR 17;
DLB 2; DLBY 81; MTCW

Higginson, Thomas Wentworth
1823-1911 .... TCLC 36
See also DLB 1, 64

Highet, Helen
See MacInnes, Helen (Clark)

Highsmith, (Mary) Patricia
1921-................. CLC 2, 4, 14, 42
See also CA 1-4R; CANR 1, 20; MTCW

Highwater, Jamake (Mamake)
1942(?)-................. CLC 12
See also AAYA 7; CA 65-68; CAAS 7;
CANR 10, 34; CLR 17; DLB 52;
DLBY 85; MAICYA; SATA 30, 32, 69

Hijuelos, Oscar 1951-............ CLC 65
See also BEST 90:1; CA 123; HW

Hikmet, Nazim 1902-1963........ CLC 40
See also CA 93-96

Hildesheimer, Wolfgang
1916-1991 .... CLC 49
See also CA 101; 135; DLB 69

Hill, Geoffrey (William)
1932-................. CLC 5, 8, 18, 45
See also CA 81-84; CANR 21;
CDBLB 1960 to Present; DLB 40;
MTCW

Hill, George Roy 1921-........... CLC 26
See also CA 110; 122

Hill, Susan (Elizabeth) 1942- .... CLC 4
See also CA 33-36R; CANR 29; DLB 14;
MTCW

Hillerman, Tony 1925-............ CLC 62
See also AAYA 6; BEST 89:1; CA 29-32R;
CANR 21; SATA 6

Hilliard, Noel (Harvey) 1929-...... CLC 15
See also CA 9-12R; CANR 7

Hillis, Rick 1956-................ CLC 66
See also CA 134

Hilton, James 1900-1954........ TCLC 21
See also CA 108; DLB 34, 77; SATA 34

Himes, Chester (Bomar)
1909-1984 .... CLC 2, 4, 7, 18, 58
See also BLC 2; BW; CA 25-28R; 114;
CANR 22; DLB 2, 76; MTCW

Hinde, Thomas .... CLC 6, 11
See also Chitty, Thomas Willes

Hindin, Nathan
See Bloch, Robert (Albert)

Hine, (William) Daryl 1936-....... CLC 15
See also CA 1-4R; CAAS 15; CANR 1, 20;
DLB 60

Hinkson, Katharine Tynan
See Tynan, Katharine

Hinton, S(usan) E(loise) 1950- ..... CLC 30
See also AAYA 2; CA 81-84; CANR 32;
CLR 3, 23; MAICYA; MTCW;
SATA 19, 58

Hippius, Zinaida .... TCLC 9
See also Gippius, Zinaida (Nikolayevna)

Hiraoka, Kimitake 1925-1970
See Mishima, Yukio
See also CA 97-100; 29-32R; MTCW

Hirsch, Edward 1950- .... CLC 31, 50
See also CA 104; CANR 20; DLB 120

Hitchcock, Alfred (Joseph)
1899-1980 .... CLC 16
See also CA 97-100; SATA 24, 27

Hoagland, Edward 1932-.......... CLC 28
See also CA 1-4R; CANR 2, 31; DLB 6;
SATA 51

Hoban, Russell (Conwell) 1925- .. CLC 7, 25
See also CA 5-8R; CANR 23, 37; CLR 3;
DLB 52; MAICYA; MTCW; SATA 1, 40

Hobbs, Perry
See Blackmur, R(ichard) P(almer)

Hobson, Laura Z(ametkin)
1900-1986 .... CLC 7, 25
See also CA 17-20R; 118; DLB 28;
SATA 52

Hochhuth, Rolf 1931-........ CLC 4, 11, 18
See also CA 5-8R; CANR 33; MTCW

Hochman, Sandra 1936-.......... CLC 3, 8
See also CA 5-8R; DLB 5

Hochwaelder, Fritz 1911-1986...... CLC 36
See also Hochwalder, Fritz
See also CA 29-32R; 120; MTCW

Hochwalder, Fritz................. CLC 36
See also Hochwaelder, Fritz

Hocking, Mary (Eunice) 1921-..... CLC 13
See also CA 101; CANR 18

Hodgins, Jack 1938-............. CLC 23
See also CA 93-96; DLB 60

Hodgson, William Hope
1877(?)-1918 .... TCLC 13
See also CA 111; DLB 70

Hoffman, Alice 1952-............. CLC 51
See also CA 77-80; CANR 34; MTCW

Hoffman, Daniel (Gerard)
1923-.................. CLC 6, 13, 23
See also CA 1-4R; CANR 4; DLB 5

Hoffman, Stanley 1944-........... CLC 5
See also CA 77-80

Hoffman, William M(oses) 1939- ... CLC 40
See also CA 57-60; CANR 11

Hoffmann, E(rnst) T(heodor) A(madeus)
1776-1822 .... NCLC 2
See also DLB 90; SATA 27

Hofmann, Gert 1931-............. CLC 54
See also CA 128

Hofmannsthal, Hugo von
1874-1929 .... TCLC 11
See also CA 106; DLB 81, 118

Hogarth, Charles
See Creasey, John

Hogg, James   1770-1835 . . . .   **NCLC 4**
See also DLB 93, 116

Holbach, Paul Henri Thiry Baron
1723-1789 . . . .   **LC 14**

Holberg, Ludvig   1684-1754 . . . .   **LC 6**

Holden, Ursula   1921- . . . .   **CLC 18**
See also CA 101; CAAS 8; CANR 22

Holderlin, (Johann Christian) Friedrich
1770-1843 . . . .   **NCLC 16; PC 4**

Holdstock, Robert
See Holdstock, Robert P.

Holdstock, Robert P.   1948- . . . .   **CLC 39**
See also CA 131

Holland, Isabelle   1920- . . . .   **CLC 21**
See also CA 21-24R; CANR 10, 25;
MAICYA; SATA 8, 70

Holland, Marcus
See Caldwell, (Janet Miriam) Taylor
(Holland)

Hollander, John   1929- . . . . . .   **CLC 2, 5, 8, 14**
See also CA 1-4R; CANR 1; DLB 5;
SATA 13

Hollander, Paul
See Silverberg, Robert

Holleran, Andrew   1943(?)- . . . .   **CLC 38**

Hollinghurst, Alan   1954- . . . .   **CLC 55**
See also CA 114

Hollis, Jim
See Summers, Hollis (Spurgeon Jr.)

Holmes, John
See Souster, (Holmes) Raymond

Holmes, John Clellon   1926-1988 . . . .   **CLC 56**
See also CA 9-12R; 125; CANR 4; DLB 16

Holmes, Oliver Wendell
1809-1894 . . . .   **NCLC 14**
See also CDALB 1640-1865; DLB 1;
SATA 34

Holmes, Raymond
See Souster, (Holmes) Raymond

Holt, Victoria
See Hibbert, Eleanor Burford

Holub, Miroslav   1923- . . . .   **CLC 4**
See also CA 21-24R; CANR 10

Homer   c. 8th cent. B.C.- . . . .   **CMLC 1**

Honig, Edwin   1919- . . . .   **CLC 33**
See also CA 5-8R; CAAS 8; CANR 4;
DLB 5

Hood, Hugh (John Blagdon)
1928- . . . .   **CLC 15, 28**
See also CA 49-52; CANR 1, 33; DLB 53

Hood, Thomas   1799-1845 . . . .   **NCLC 16**
See also DLB 96

Hooker, (Peter) Jeremy   1941- . . . . . .   **CLC 43**
See also CA 77-80; CANR 22; DLB 40

Hope, A(lec) D(erwent)   1907- . . . .   **CLC 3, 51**
See also CA 21-24R; CANR 33; MTCW

Hope, Brian
See Creasey, John

Hope, Christopher (David Tully)
1944- . . . .   **CLC 52**
See also CA 106; SATA 62

Hopkins, Gerard Manley
1844-1889 . . . .   **NCLC 17**
See also CDBLB 1890-1914; DLB 35, 57;
WLC

Hopkins, John (Richard)   1931- . . . . . .   **CLC 4**
See also CA 85-88

Hopkins, Pauline Elizabeth
1859-1930 . . . .   **TCLC 28**
See also BLC 2; DLB 50

Horatio
See Proust,
(Valentin-Louis-George-Eugene-)Marcel

Horgan, Paul   1903- . . . .   **CLC 9, 53**
See also CA 13-16R; CANR 9, 35;
DLB 102; DLBY 85; MTCW; SATA 13

Horn, Peter
See Kuttner, Henry

Horovitz, Israel   1939- . . . .   **CLC 56**
See also CA 33-36R; DLB 7

Horvath, Odon von
See Horvath, Oedoen von
See also DLB 85

Horvath, Oedoen von   1901-1938 . . .   **TCLC 45**
See also Horvath, Odon von
See also CA 118

Horwitz, Julius   1920-1986 . . . .   **CLC 14**
See also CA 9-12R; 119; CANR 12

Hospital, Janette Turner   1942- . . . . .   **CLC 42**
See also CA 108

Hostos, E. M. de
See Hostos (y Bonilla), Eugenio Maria de

Hostos, Eugenio M. de
See Hostos (y Bonilla), Eugenio Maria de

Hostos, Eugenio Maria
See Hostos (y Bonilla), Eugenio Maria de

Hostos (y Bonilla), Eugenio Maria de
1839-1903 . . . .   **TCLC 24**
See also CA 123; 131; HW

Houdini
See Lovecraft, H(oward) P(hillips)

Hougan, Carolyn   19(?)- . . . .   **CLC 34**

Household, Geoffrey (Edward West)
1900-1988 . . . .   **CLC 11**
See also CA 77-80; 126; DLB 87; SATA 14,
59

Housman, A(lfred) E(dward)
1859-1936 . . . .   **TCLC 1, 10; PC 2**
See also CA 104; 125; DLB 19; MTCW

Housman, Laurence   1865-1959 . . . . .   **TCLC 7**
See also CA 106; DLB 10; SATA 25

Howard, Elizabeth Jane   1923- . . .   **CLC 7, 29**
See also CA 5-8R; CANR 8

Howard, Maureen   1930- . . . . .   **CLC 5, 14, 46**
See also CA 53-56; CANR 31; DLBY 83;
MTCW

Howard, Richard   1929- . . . . . .   **CLC 7, 10, 47**
See also AITN 1; CA 85-88; CANR 25;
DLB 5

Howard, Robert Ervin   1906-1936 . . .   **TCLC 8**
See also CA 105

Howard, Warren F.
See Pohl, Frederik

Howe, Fanny   1940- . . . .   **CLC 47**
See also CA 117; SATA 52

Howe, Julia Ward   1819-1910 . . . . .   **TCLC 21**
See also CA 117; DLB 1

Howe, Susan   1937- . . . .   **CLC 72**
See also DLB 120

Howe, Tina   1937- . . . .   **CLC 48**
See also CA 109

Howell, James   1594(?)-1666 . . . .   **LC 13**

Howells, W. D.
See Howells, William Dean

Howells, William D.
See Howells, William Dean

Howells, William Dean
1837-1920 . . . .   **TCLC 41, 7, 17**
See also CA 104; 134; CDALB 1865-1917;
DLB 12, 64, 74, 79

Howes, Barbara   1914- . . . .   **CLC 15**
See also CA 9-12R; CAAS 3; SATA 5

Hrabal, Bohumil   1914- . . . .   **CLC 13, 67**
See also CA 106; CAAS 12

Hsun, Lu . . . .   **TCLC 3**
See also Shu-Jen, Chou

Hubbard, L(afayette) Ron(ald)
1911-1986 . . . .   **CLC 43**
See also CA 77-80; 118; CANR 22

Huch, Ricarda (Octavia)
1864-1947 . . . .   **TCLC 13**
See also CA 111; DLB 66

Huddle, David   1942- . . . .   **CLC 49**
See also CA 57-60

Hudson, Jeffery
See Crichton, (John) Michael

Hudson, W(illiam) H(enry)
1841-1922 . . . .   **TCLC 29**
See also CA 115; DLB 98; SATA 35

Hueffer, Ford Madox
See Ford, Ford Madox

Hughart, Barry . . . .   **CLC 39**
See also CA 137

Hughes, Colin
See Creasey, John

Hughes, David (John)   1930- . . . .   **CLC 48**
See also CA 116; 129; DLB 14

Hughes, (James) Langston
1902-1967 . . . .   **CLC 1, 5, 10, 15, 35, 44;**
PC 1; SSC 6
See also BLC 2; BW; CA 1-4R; 25-28R;
CANR 1, 34; CDALB 1929-1941;
CLR 17; DLB 4, 7, 48, 51, 86; MAICYA;
MTCW; SATA 4, 33; WLC

Hughes, Richard (Arthur Warren)
1900-1976 . . . .   **CLC 1, 11**
See also CA 5-8R; 65-68; CANR 4;
DLB 15; MTCW; SATA 8, 25

Hughes, Ted   1930- . . . . .   **CLC 2, 4, 9, 14, 37**
See also CA 1-4R; CANR 1, 33; CLR 3;
DLB 40; MAICYA; MTCW; SATA 27,
49

Hugo, Richard F(ranklin)
1923-1982 . . . .   **CLC 6, 18, 32**
See also CA 49-52; 108; CANR 3; DLB 5

Hugo, Victor (Marie)
1802-1885 . . . .   **NCLC 3, 10, 21**
See also DLB 119; SATA 47; WLC

Huidobro, Vicente
See Huidobro Fernandez, Vicente Garcia

Huidobro Fernandez, Vicente Garcia
1893-1948 .... TCLC 31
See also CA 131; HW

Hulme, Keri 1947- .... CLC 39
See also CA 125

Hulme, T(homas) E(rnest)
1883-1917 .... TCLC 21
See also CA 117; DLB 19

Hume, David 1711-1776............ LC 7
See also DLB 104

Humphrey, William 1924-......... CLC 45
See also CA 77-80; DLB 6

Humphreys, Emyr Owen 1919-..... CLC 47
See also CA 5-8R; CANR 3, 24; DLB 15

Humphreys, Josephine 1945-.... CLC 34, 57
See also CA 121; 127

Hungerford, Pixie
See Brinsmead, H(esba) F(ay)

Hunt, E(verette) Howard Jr. 1918-... CLC 3
See also AITN 1; CA 45-48; CANR 2

Hunt, Kyle
See Creasey, John

Hunt, (James Henry) Leigh
1784-1859 .... NCLC 1

Hunt, Marsha 1946-.............. CLC 70

Hunter, E. Waldo
See Sturgeon, Theodore (Hamilton)

Hunter, Evan 1926- .... CLC 11, 31
See also CA 5-8R; CANR 5, 38; DLBY 82;
MTCW; SATA 25

Hunter, Kristin (Eggleston) 1931-... CLC 35
See also AITN 1; BW; CA 13-16R;
CANR 13; CLR 3; DLB 33; MAICYA;
SAAS 10; SATA 12

Hunter, Mollie 1922-............. CLC 21
See also McIlwraith, Maureen Mollie
Hunter
See also CANR 37; CLR 25; MAICYA;
SAAS 7; SATA 54

Hunter, Robert (?)-1734............ LC 7

Hurston, Zora Neale
1903-1960 .... CLC 7, 30, 61; SSC 4
See also BLC 2; BW; CA 85-88; DLB 51,
86; MTCW

Huston, John (Marcellus)
1906-1987 .... CLC 20
See also CA 73-76; 123; CANR 34; DLB 26

Hutten, Ulrich von 1488-1523...... LC 16

Huxley, Aldous (Leonard)
1894-1963 .. CLC 1, 3, 4, 5, 8, 11, 18, 35
See also CA 85-88; CDBLB 1914-1945;
DLB 36, 100; MTCW; SATA 63; WLC

Huysmans, Charles Marie Georges
1848-1907
See Huysmans, Joris-Karl
See also CA 104

Huysmans, Joris-Karl............. TCLC 7
See also Huysmans, Charles Marie Georges

Hwang, David Henry 1957-........ CLC 55
See also CA 127; 132

Hyde, Anthony 1946-............. CLC 42
See also CA 136

Hyde, Margaret O(ldroyd) 1917-... CLC 21
See also CA 1-4R; CANR 1, 36; CLR 23;
MAICYA; SAAS 8; SATA 1, 42

Hynes, James 1956(?)-............ CLC 65

Ian, Janis 1951- .... CLC 21
See also CA 105

Ibanez, Vicente Blasco
See Blasco Ibanez, Vicente

Ibarguengoitia, Jorge 1928-1983.... CLC 37
See also CA 124; 113; HW

Ibsen, Henrik (Johan)
1828-1906 ..... TCLC 2, 8, 16, 37; DC 2
See also CA 104; WLC

Ibuse Masuji 1898-............... CLC 22
See also CA 127

Ichikawa, Kon 1915-.............. CLC 20
See also CA 121

Idle, Eric 1943-.................. CLC 21
See also Monty Python
See also CA 116; CANR 35

Ignatow, David 1914-...... CLC 4, 7, 14, 40
See also CA 9-12R; CAAS 3; CANR 31;
DLB 5

Ihimaera, Witi 1944- .... CLC 46
See also CA 77-80

Ilf, Ilya........................ TCLC 21
See also Fainzilberg, Ilya Arnoldovich

Immermann, Karl (Lebrecht)
1796-1840 .... NCLC 4

Inclan, Ramon (Maria) del Valle
See Valle-Inclan, Ramon (Maria) del

Infante, G(uillermo) Cabrera
See Cabrera Infante, G(uillermo)

Ingalls, Rachel (Holmes) 1940-..... CLC 42
See also CA 123; 127

Ingamells, Rex 1913-1955 .... TCLC 35

Inge, William Motter
1913-1973 .... CLC 1, 8, 19
See also CA 9-12R; CDALB 1941-1968;
DLB 7; MTCW

Ingram, Willis J.
See Harris, Mark

Innaurato, Albert (F.) 1948(?)- .. CLC 21, 60
See also CA 115; 122

Innes, Michael
See Stewart, J(ohn) I(nnes) M(ackintosh)

Ionesco, Eugene
1912-........ CLC 1, 4, 6, 9, 11, 15, 41
See also CA 9-12R; MTCW; SATA 7; WLC

Iqbal, Muhammad 1873-1938 ..... TCLC 28

Irland, David
See Green, Julian (Hartridge)

Iron, Ralph
See Schreiner, Olive (Emilie Albertina)

Irving, John (Winslow)
1942- .... CLC 13, 23, 38
See also AAYA 8; BEST 89:3; CA 25-28R;
CANR 28; DLB 6; DLBY 82; MTCW

Irving, Washington
1783-1859 .... NCLC 2, 19; SSC 2
See also CDALB 1640-1865; DLB 3, 11, 30,
59, 73, 74; WLC; YABC 2

Irwin, P. K.
See Page, P(atricia) K(athleen)

Isaacs, Susan 1943- .... CLC 32
See also BEST 89:1; CA 89-92; CANR 20;
MTCW

Isherwood, Christopher (William Bradshaw)
1904-1986 .... CLC 1, 9, 11, 14, 44
See also CA 13-16R; 117; CANR 35;
DLB 15; DLBY 86; MTCW

Ishiguro, Kazuo 1954- ...... CLC 27, 56, 59
See also BEST 90:2; CA 120; MTCW

Ishikawa Takuboku
1886(?)-1912 .... TCLC 15
See also CA 113

Iskander, Fazil 1929-.............. CLC 47
See also CA 102

Ivan IV 1530-1584 .... LC 17

Ivanov, Vyacheslav Ivanovich
1866-1949 .... TCLC 33
See also CA 122

Ivask, Ivar Vidrik 1927- .... CLC 14
See also CA 37-40R; CANR 24

Jackson, Daniel
See Wingrove, David (John)

Jackson, Jesse 1908-1983 .... CLC 12
See also BW; CA 25-28R; 109; CANR 27;
CLR 28; MAICYA; SATA 2, 29, 48

Jackson, Laura (Riding) 1901-1991 .. CLC 7
See also Riding, Laura
See also CA 65-68; 135; CANR 28; DLB 48

Jackson, Sam
See Trumbo, Dalton

Jackson, Sara
See Wingrove, David (John)

Jackson, Shirley
1919-1965 .... CLC 11, 60; SSC 9
See also AAYA 9; CA 1-4R; 25-28R;
CANR 4; CDALB 1941-1968; DLB 6;
SATA 2; WLC

Jacob, (Cyprien-)Max 1876-1944 ... TCLC 6
See also CA 104

Jacobs, Jim 1942-................. CLC 12
See also CA 97-100

Jacobs, W(illiam) W(ymark)
1863-1943 .... TCLC 22
See also CA 121

Jacobsen, Jens Peter 1847-1885 .. NCLC 34

Jacobsen, Josephine 1908-......... CLC 48
See also CA 33-36R; CANR 23

Jacobson, Dan 1929- .... CLC 4, 14
See also CA 1-4R; CANR 2, 25; DLB 14;
MTCW

Jacqueline
See Carpentier (y Valmont), Alejo

Jagger, Mick 1944-............... CLC 17

Jakes, John (William) 1932-........ CLC 29
See also BEST 89:4; CA 57-60; CANR 10;
DLBY 83; MTCW; SATA 62

James, Andrew
See Kirkup, James

James, C(yril) L(ionel) R(obert)
1901-1989 .... CLC 33
See also BW; CA 117; 125; 128; MTCW

James, Daniel (Lewis) 1911-1988
See Santiago, Danny
See also CA 125

James, Dynely
See Mayne, William (James Carter)

James, Henry
1843-1916 . . . . . **TCLC 2, 11, 24, 40, 47;**
SSC 8
See also CA 104; 132; CDALB 1865-1917;
DLB 12, 71, 74; MTCW; WLC

James, Montague (Rhodes)
1862-1936 . . . . **TCLC 6**
See also CA 104

James, P. D. . . . . **CLC 18, 46**
See also White, Phyllis Dorothy James
See also BEST 90:2; CDBLB 1960 to
Present; DLB 87

James, Philip
See Moorcock, Michael (John)

James, William 1842-1910 . . . . . **TCLC 15, 32**
See also CA 109

James I 1394-1437 . . . . **LC 20**

Jami, Nur al-Din 'Abd al-Rahman
1414-1492 . . . . **LC 9**

Jandl, Ernst 1925- . . . . **CLC 34**

Janowitz, Tama 1957- . . . . **CLC 43**
See also CA 106

Jarrell, Randall
1914-1965 . . . . **CLC 1, 2, 6, 9, 13, 49**
See also CA 5-8R; 25-28R; CABS 2;
CANR 6, 34; CDALB 1941-1968; CLR 6;
DLB 48, 52; MAICYA; MTCW; SATA 7

Jarry, Alfred 1873-1907. . . . . . . **TCLC 2, 14**
See also CA 104

Jarvis, E. K.
See Bloch, Robert (Albert); Ellison, Harlan;
Silverberg, Robert

Jeake, Samuel Jr.
See Aiken, Conrad (Potter)

Jean Paul 1763-1825 . . . . **NCLC 7**

Jeffers, (John) Robinson
1887-1962 . . . . **CLC 2, 3, 11, 15, 54**
See also CA 85-88; CANR 35;
CDALB 1917-1929; DLB 45; MTCW;
WLC

Jefferson, Janet
See Mencken, H(enry) L(ouis)

Jefferson, Thomas 1743-1826 . . . . **NCLC 11**
See also CDALB 1640-1865; DLB 31

Jeffrey, Francis 1773-1850. . . . . . . **NCLC 33**
See also DLB 107

Jelakowitch, Ivan
See Heijermans, Herman

Jellicoe, (Patricia) Ann 1927- . . . . . . **CLC 27**
See also CA 85-88; DLB 13

Jen, Gish . . . . **CLC 70**
See also Jen, Lillian

Jen, Lillian 1956(?)-
See Jen, Gish
See also CA 135

Jenkins, (John) Robin 1912- . . . . **CLC 52**
See also CA 1-4R; CANR 1; DLB 14

Jennings, Elizabeth (Joan)
1926- . . . . **CLC 5, 14**
See also CA 61-64; CAAS 5; CANR 8, 39;
DLB 27; MTCW; SATA 66

Jennings, Waylon 1937-. . . . . **CLC 21**

Jensen, Johannes V. 1873-1950. . . . **TCLC 41**

Jensen, Laura (Linnea) 1948- . . . . . . **CLC 37**
See also CA 103

Jerome, Jerome K(lapka)
1859-1927 . . . . **TCLC 23**
See also CA 119; DLB 10, 34

Jerrold, Douglas William
1803-1857 . . . . **NCLC 2**

Jewett, (Theodora) Sarah Orne
1849-1909 . . . . **TCLC 1, 22; SSC 6**
See also CA 108; 127; DLB 12, 74;
SATA 15

Jewsbury, Geraldine (Endsor)
1812-1880 . . . . **NCLC 22**
See also DLB 21

Jhabvala, Ruth Prawer
1927- . . . . **CLC 4, 8, 29**
See also CA 1-4R; CANR 2, 29; MTCW

Jiles, Paulette 1943-. . . . . **CLC 13, 58**
See also CA 101

Jimenez (Mantecon), Juan Ramon
1881-1958 . . . . **TCLC 4**
See also CA 104; 131; HW; MTCW

Jimenez, Ramon
See Jimenez (Mantecon), Juan Ramon

Jimenez Mantecon, Juan
See Jimenez (Mantecon), Juan Ramon

Joel, Billy . . . . **CLC 26**
See also Joel, William Martin

Joel, William Martin 1949-
See Joel, Billy
See also CA 108

John of the Cross, St. 1542-1591 . . . . **LC 18**

Johnson, B(ryan) S(tanley William)
1933-1973 . . . . **CLC 6, 9**
See also CA 9-12R; 53-56; CANR 9;
DLB 14, 40

Johnson, Charles (Richard)
1948- . . . . **CLC 7, 51, 65**
See also BLC 2; BW; CA 116; DLB 33

Johnson, Denis 1949-. . . . . **CLC 52**
See also CA 117; 121; DLB 120

Johnson, Diane (Lain)
1934- . . . . **CLC 5, 13, 48**
See also CA 41-44R; CANR 17; DLBY 80;
MTCW

Johnson, Eyvind (Olof Verner)
1900-1976 . . . . **CLC 14**
See also CA 73-76; 69-72; CANR 34

Johnson, J. R.
See James, C(yril) L(ionel) R(obert)

Johnson, James Weldon
1871-1938 . . . . **TCLC 3, 19**
See also BLC 2; BW; CA 104; 125;
CDALB 1917-1929; DLB 51; MTCW;
SATA 31

Johnson, Joyce 1935-. . . . . **CLC 58**
See also CA 125; 129

Johnson, Lionel (Pigot)
1867-1902 . . . . **TCLC 19**
See also CA 117; DLB 19

Johnson, Mel
See Malzberg, Barry N(athaniel)

Johnson, Pamela Hansford
1912-1981 . . . . **CLC 1, 7, 27**
See also CA 1-4R; 104; CANR 2, 28;
DLB 15; MTCW

Johnson, Samuel 1709-1784. . . . . **LC 15**
See also CDBLB 1660-1789; DLB 39, 95,
104; WLC

Johnson, Uwe
1934-1984 . . . . **CLC 5, 10, 15, 40**
See also CA 1-4R; 112; CANR 1, 39;
DLB 75; MTCW

Johnston, George (Benson) 1913-. . . **CLC 51**
See also CA 1-4R; CANR 5, 20; DLB 88

Johnston, Jennifer 1930-. . . . . **CLC 7**
See also CA 85-88; DLB 14

Jolley, (Monica) Elizabeth 1923- . . . **CLC 46**
See also CA 127; CAAS 13

Jones, Arthur Llewellyn 1863-1947
See Machen, Arthur
See also CA 104

Jones, D(ouglas) G(ordon) 1929-. . . . **CLC 10**
See also CA 29-32R; CANR 13; DLB 53

Jones, David (Michael)
1895-1974 . . . . **CLC 2, 4, 7, 13, 42**
See also CA 9-12R; 53-56; CANR 28;
CDBLB 1945-1960; DLB 20, 100; MTCW

Jones, David Robert 1947-
See Bowie, David
See also CA 103

Jones, Diana Wynne 1934- . . . . **CLC 26**
See also CA 49-52; CANR 4, 26; CLR 23;
MAICYA; SAAS 7; SATA 9, 70

Jones, Gayl 1949-. . . . . **CLC 6, 9**
See also BLC 2; BW; CA 77-80; CANR 27;
DLB 33; MTCW

Jones, James 1921-1977. . . . **CLC 1, 3, 10, 39**
See also AITN 1, 2; CA 1-4R; 69-72;
CANR 6; DLB 2; MTCW

Jones, John J.
See Lovecraft, H(oward) P(hillips)

Jones, LeRoi . . . . **CLC 1, 2, 3, 5, 10, 14**
See also Baraka, Amiri

Jones, Louis B. . . . . **CLC 65**

Jones, Madison (Percy Jr.) 1925-. . . . **CLC 4**
See also CA 13-16R; CAAS 11; CANR 7

Jones, Mervyn 1922- . . . . **CLC 10, 52**
See also CA 45-48; CAAS 5; CANR 1;
MTCW

Jones, Mick 1956(?)- . . . . **CLC 30**
See also The Clash

Jones, Nettie (Pearl) 1941- . . . . **CLC 34**
See also CA 137

Jones, Preston 1936-1979 . . . . **CLC 10**
See also CA 73-76; 89-92; DLB 7

Jones, Robert F(rancis) 1934-. . . . . . . **CLC 7**
See also CA 49-52; CANR 2

Jones, Rod 1953- . . . . **CLC 50**
See also CA 128

Jones, Terence Graham Parry
1942- .... **CLC 21**
See also Jones, Terry; Monty Python
See also CA 112; 116; CANR 35; SATA 51

Jones, Terry
See Jones, Terence Graham Parry
See also SATA 67

Jong, Erica 1942- .... **CLC 4, 6, 8, 18**
See also AITN 1; BEST 90:2; CA 73-76;
CANR 26; DLB 2, 5, 28; MTCW

Jonson, Ben(jamin) 1572(?)-1637...... **LC 6**
See also CDBLB Before 1660; DLB 62, 121;
WLC

Jordan, June 1936- .... **CLC 5, 11, 23**
See also AAYA 2; BW; CA 33-36R;
CANR 25; CLR 10; DLB 38; MAICYA;
MTCW; SATA 4

Jordan, Pat(rick M.) 1941- .... **CLC 37**
See also CA 33-36R

Jorgensen, Ivar
See Ellison, Harlan

Jorgenson, Ivar
See Silverberg, Robert

Josipovici, Gabriel 1940- .... **CLC 6, 43**
See also CA 37-40R; CAAS 8; DLB 14

Joubert, Joseph 1754-1824 .... **NCLC 9**

Jouve, Pierre Jean 1887-1976...... **CLC 47**
See also CA 65-68

Joyce, James (Augustine Aloysius)
1882-1941 .... **TCLC 3, 8, 16, 35; SSC 3**
See also CA 104; 126; CDBLB 1914-1945;
DLB 10, 19, 36; MTCW; WLC

Jozsef, Attila 1905-1937......... **TCLC 22**
See also CA 116

Juana Ines de la Cruz 1651(?)-1695 ... **LC 5**

Judd, Cyril
See Kornbluth, C(yril) M.; Pohl, Frederik

Julian of Norwich 1342(?)-1416(?) .... **LC 6**

Just, Ward (Swift) 1935- ...... **CLC 4, 27**
See also CA 25-28R; CANR 32

Justice, Donald (Rodney) 1925- .. **CLC 6, 19**
See also CA 5-8R; CANR 26; DLBY 83

Juvenal c. 55-c. 127 .... **CMLC 8**

Juvenis
See Bourne, Randolph S(illiman)

Kacew, Romain 1914-1980
See Gary, Romain
See also CA 108; 102

Kadare, Ismail 1936- .... **CLC 52**

Kadohata, Cynthia................ **CLC 59**

Kafka, Franz
1883-1924 ...... **TCLC 2, 6, 13, 29, 47;**
SSC 5
See also CA 105; 126; DLB 81; MTCW;
WLC

Kahn, Roger 1927- .... **CLC 30**
See also CA 25-28R; SATA 37

Kain, Saul
See Sassoon, Siegfried (Lorraine)

Kaiser, Georg 1878-1945 .... **TCLC 9**
See also CA 106

Kaletski, Alexander 1946- .... **CLC 39**
See also CA 118

Kalidasa fl. c. 400- .... **CMLC 9**

Kallman, Chester (Simon)
1921-1975 .... **CLC 2**
See also CA 45-48; 53-56; CANR 3

Kaminsky, Melvin 1926-
See Brooks, Mel
See also CA 65-68; CANR 16

Kaminsky, Stuart M(elvin) 1934- ... **CLC 59**
See also CA 73-76; CANR 29

Kane, Paul
See Simon, Paul

Kane, Wilson
See Bloch, Robert (Albert)

Kanin, Garson 1912-............. **CLC 22**
See also AITN 1; CA 5-8R; CANR 7;
DLB 7

Kaniuk, Yoram 1930- .... **CLC 19**
See also CA 134

Kant, Immanuel 1724-1804 ...... **NCLC 27**
See also DLB 94

Kantor, MacKinlay 1904-1977 ...... **CLC 7**
See also CA 61-64; 73-76; DLB 9, 102

Kaplan, David Michael 1946- ...... **CLC 50**

Kaplan, James 1951- .... **CLC 59**
See also CA 135

Karageorge, Michael
See Anderson, Poul (William)

Karamzin, Nikolai Mikhailovich
1766-1826 .... **NCLC 3**

Karapanou, Margarita 1946- .... **CLC 13**
See also CA 101

Karinthy, Frigyes 1887-1938 ...... **TCLC 47**

Karl, Frederick R(obert) 1927- ..... **CLC 34**
See also CA 5-8R; CANR 3

Kastel, Warren
See Silverberg, Robert

Kataev, Evgeny Petrovich 1903-1942
See Petrov, Evgeny
See also CA 120

Kataphusin
See Ruskin, John

Katz, Steve 1935-................. **CLC 47**
See also CA 25-28R; CAAS 14; CANR 12;
DLBY 83

Kauffman, Janet 1945-............ **CLC 42**
See also CA 117; DLBY 86

Kaufman, Bob (Garnell)
1925-1986 .... **CLC 49**
See also BW; CA 41-44R; 118; CANR 22;
DLB 16, 41

Kaufman, George S. 1889-1961..... **CLC 38**
See also CA 108; 93-96; DLB 7

Kaufman, Sue .... **CLC 3, 8**
See also Barondess, Sue K(aufman)

Kavafis, Konstantinos Petrou 1863-1933
See Cavafy, C(onstantine) P(eter)
See also CA 104

Kavan, Anna 1901-1968........ **CLC 5, 13**
See also CA 5-8R; CANR 6; MTCW

Kavanagh, Dan
See Barnes, Julian

Kavanagh, Patrick (Joseph)
1904-1967 .... **CLC 22**
See also CA 123; 25-28R; DLB 15, 20;
MTCW

Kawabata, Yasunari
1899-1972 .... **CLC 2, 5, 9, 18**
See also CA 93-96; 33-36R

Kaye, M(ary) M(argaret) 1909-..... **CLC 28**
See also CA 89-92; CANR 24; MTCW;
SATA 62

Kaye, Mollie
See Kaye, M(ary) M(argaret)

Kaye-Smith, Sheila 1887-1956..... **TCLC 20**
See also CA 118; DLB 36

Kaymor, Patrice Maguilene
See Senghor, Leopold Sedar

Kazan, Elia 1909-........... **CLC 6, 16, 63**
See also CA 21-24R; CANR 32

Kazantzakis, Nikos
1883(?)-1957 .... **TCLC 2, 5, 33**
See also CA 105; 132; MTCW

Kazin, Alfred 1915- .... **CLC 34, 38**
See also CA 1-4R; CAAS 7; CANR 1;
DLB 67

Keane, Mary Nesta (Skrine) 1904-
See Keane, Molly
See also CA 108; 114

Keane, Molly.................... **CLC 31**
See also Keane, Mary Nesta (Skrine)

Keates, Jonathan 19(?)- .... **CLC 34**

Keaton, Buster 1895-1966 .... **CLC 20**

Keats, John 1795-1821...... **NCLC 8; PC 1**
See also CDBLB 1789-1832; DLB 96, 110;
WLC

Keene, Donald 1922- .... **CLC 34**
See also CA 1-4R; CANR 5

Keillor, Garrison................. **CLC 40**
See also Keillor, Gary (Edward)
See also AAYA 2; BEST 89:3; DLBY 87;
SATA 58

Keillor, Gary (Edward) 1942-
See Keillor, Garrison
See also CA 111; 117; CANR 36; MTCW

Keith, Michael
See Hubbard, L(afayette) Ron(ald)

Kell, Joseph
See Wilson, John (Anthony) Burgess

Keller, Gottfried 1819-1890....... **NCLC 2**

Kellerman, Jonathan 1949- .... **CLC 44**
See also BEST 90:1; CA 106; CANR 29

Kelley, William Melvin 1937- ...... **CLC 22**
See also BW; CA 77-80; CANR 27; DLB 33

Kellogg, Marjorie 1922-............ **CLC 2**
See also CA 81-84

Kellow, Kathleen
See Hibbert, Eleanor Burford

Kelly, M(ilton) T(erry) 1947-....... **CLC 55**
See also CA 97-100; CANR 19

Kelman, James 1946- .... **CLC 58**

Kemal, Yashar 1923- .... **CLC 14, 29**
See also CA 89-92

Kemble, Fanny 1809-1893 .... **NCLC 18**
See also DLB 32

Kemelman, Harry 1908-. . . . . **CLC 2**
  See also AITN 1; CA 9-12R; CANR 6;
  DLB 28

Kempe, Margery 1373(?)-1440(?) . . . . . **LC 6**

Kempis, Thomas a 1380-1471 . . . . **LC 11**

Kendall, Henry 1839-1882. . . . . . . **NCLC 12**

Keneally, Thomas (Michael)
  1935- . . . . . . **CLC 5, 8, 10, 14, 19, 27, 43**
  See also CA 85-88; CANR 10; MTCW

Kennedy, Adrienne (Lita) 1931- . . . . **CLC 66**
  See also BLC 2; BW; CA 103; CABS 3;
  CANR 26; DLB 38

Kennedy, John Pendleton
  1795-1870 . . . . **NCLC 2**
  See also DLB 3

Kennedy, Joseph Charles 1929-. . . . . . **CLC 8**
  See also Kennedy, X. J.
  See also CA 1-4R; CANR 4, 30; SATA 14

Kennedy, William 1928-. . . **CLC 6, 28, 34, 53**
  See also AAYA 1; CA 85-88; CANR 14,
  31; DLBY 85; MTCW; SATA 57

Kennedy, X. J. **CLC 42**
  See also Kennedy, Joseph Charles
  See also CAAS 9; CLR 27; DLB 5

Kent, Kelvin
  See Kuttner, Henry

Kenton, Maxwell
  See Southern, Terry

Kenyon, Robert O.
  See Kuttner, Henry

Kerouac, Jack . . . . . **CLC 1, 2, 3, 5, 14, 29, 61**
  See also Kerouac, Jean-Louis Lebris de
  See also CDALB 1941-1968; DLB 2, 16;
  DLBD 3

Kerouac, Jean-Louis Lebris de 1922-1969
  See Kerouac, Jack
  See also AITN 1; CA 5-8R; 25-28R;
  CANR 26; MTCW; WLC

Kerr, Jean 1923-. . . . . **CLC 22**
  See also CA 5-8R; CANR 7

Kerr, M. E. . . . . **CLC 12, 35**
  See also Meaker, Marijane (Agnes)
  See also AAYA 2; SAAS 1

Kerr, Robert . . . . **CLC 55**

Kerrigan, (Thomas) Anthony
  1918- . . . . **CLC 4, 6**
  See also CA 49-52; CAAS 11; CANR 4

Kerry, Lois
  See Duncan, Lois

Kesey, Ken (Elton)
  1935- . . . . **CLC 1, 3, 6, 11, 46, 64**
  See also CA 1-4R; CANR 22, 38;
  CDALB 1968-1988; DLB 2, 16; MTCW;
  SATA 66; WLC

Kesselring, Joseph (Otto)
  1902-1967 . . . . **CLC 45**

Kessler, Jascha (Frederick) 1929-. . . . **CLC 4**
  See also CA 17-20R; CANR 8

Kettelkamp, Larry (Dale) 1933- . . . . **CLC 12**
  See also CA 29-32R; CANR 16; SAAS 3;
  SATA 2

Kherdian, David 1931-. . . . . **CLC 6, 9**
  See also CA 21-24R; CAAS 2; CANR 39;
  CLR 24; MAICYA; SATA 16

Khlebnikov, Velimir . . . . **TCLC 20**
  See also Khlebnikov, Viktor Vladimirovich

Khlebnikov, Viktor Vladimirovich 1885-1922
  See Khlebnikov, Velimir
  See also CA 117

Khodasevich, Vladislav (Felitsianovich)
  1886-1939 . . . . **TCLC 15**
  See also CA 115

Kielland, Alexander Lange
  1849-1906 . . . . **TCLC 5**
  See also CA 104

Kiely, Benedict 1919-. . . . . **CLC 23, 43**
  See also CA 1-4R; CANR 2; DLB 15

Kienzle, William X(avier) 1928- . . . . **CLC 25**
  See also CA 93-96; CAAS 1; CANR 9, 31;
  MTCW

Kierkegaard, Søren 1813-1855. . **NCLC 34**

Killens, John Oliver 1916-1987. . . . . **CLC 10**
  See also BW; CA 77-80; 123; CAAS 2;
  CANR 26; DLB 33

Killigrew, Anne 1660-1685. . . . . **LC 4**

Kim
  See Simenon, Georges (Jacques Christian)

Kincaid, Jamaica 1949-. . . . . **CLC 43, 68**
  See also BLC 2; BW; CA 125

King, Francis (Henry) 1923- . . . . . **CLC 8, 53**
  See also CA 1-4R; CANR 1, 33; DLB 15;
  MTCW

King, Stephen (Edwin)
  1947- . . . . **CLC 12, 26, 37, 61**
  See also AAYA 1; BEST 90:1; CA 61-64;
  CANR 1, 30; DLBY 80; MTCW;
  SATA 9, 55

King, Steve
  See King, Stephen (Edwin)

Kingman, Lee. . . . . **CLC 17**
  See also Natti, (Mary) Lee
  See also SAAS 3; SATA 1, 67

Kingsley, Charles 1819-1875 . . . . . **NCLC 35**
  See also DLB 21, 32; YABC 2

Kingsley, Sidney 1906-. . . . . **CLC 44**
  See also CA 85-88; DLB 7

Kingsolver, Barbara 1955-. . . . . **CLC 55**
  See also CA 129; 134

Kingston, Maxine (Ting Ting) Hong
  1940- . . . . **CLC 12, 19, 58**
  See also AAYA 8; CA 69-72; CANR 13,
  38; DLBY 80; MTCW; SATA 53

Kinnell, Galway
  1927- . . . . **CLC 1, 2, 3, 5, 13, 29**
  See also CA 9-12R; CANR 10, 34; DLB 5;
  DLBY 87; MTCW

Kinsella, Thomas 1928- . . . . **CLC 4, 19**
  See also CA 17-20R; CANR 15; DLB 27;
  MTCW

Kinsella, W(illiam) P(atrick)
  1935- . . . . **CLC 27, 43**
  See also AAYA 7; CA 97-100; CAAS 7;
  CANR 21, 35; MTCW

Kipling, (Joseph) Rudyard
  1865-1936 . . . . **TCLC 8, 17; PC 3; SSC 5**
  See also CA 105; 120; CANR 33;
  CDBLB 1890-1914; DLB 19, 34;
  MAICYA; MTCW; WLC; YABC 2

Kirkup, James 1918- . . . . **CLC 1**
  See also CA 1-4R; CAAS 4; CANR 2;
  DLB 27; SATA 12

Kirkwood, James 1930(?)-1989. . . . . . **CLC 9**
  See also AITN 2; CA 1-4R; 128; CANR 6

Kis, Danilo 1935-1989. . . . . **CLC 57**
  See also CA 109; 118; 129; MTCW

Kivi, Aleksis 1834-1872. . . . . **NCLC 30**

Kizer, Carolyn (Ashley) 1925-. . . **CLC 15, 39**
  See also CA 65-68; CAAS 5; CANR 24;
  DLB 5

Klabund 1890-1928. . . . . **TCLC 44**
  See also DLB 66

Klappert, Peter 1942-. . . . . **CLC 57**
  See also CA 33-36R; DLB 5

Klein, A(braham) M(oses)
  1909-1972 . . . . **CLC 19**
  See also CA 101; 37-40R; DLB 68

Klein, Norma 1938-1989. . . . . **CLC 30**
  See also AAYA 2; CA 41-44R; 128;
  CANR 15, 37; CLR 2, 19; MAICYA;
  SAAS 1; SATA 7, 57

Klein, T(heodore) E(ibon) D(onald)
  1947- . . . . **CLC 34**
  See also CA 119

Kleist, Heinrich von 1777-1811. . . . **NCLC 2**
  See also DLB 90

Klima, Ivan 1931-. . . . . **CLC 56**
  See also CA 25-28R; CANR 17

Klimentov, Andrei Platonovich 1899-1951
  See Platonov, Andrei
  See also CA 108

Klinger, Friedrich Maximilian von
  1752-1831 . . . . **NCLC 1**
  See also DLB 94

Klopstock, Friedrich Gottlieb
  1724-1803 . . . . **NCLC 11**
  See also DLB 97

Knebel, Fletcher 1911-. . . . . **CLC 14**
  See also AITN 1; CA 1-4R; CAAS 3;
  CANR 1, 36; SATA 36

Knickerbocker, Diedrich
  See Irving, Washington

Knight, Etheridge 1931-1991. . . . . . . **CLC 40**
  See also BLC 2; BW; CA 21-24R; 133;
  CANR 23; DLB 41

Knight, Sarah Kemble 1666-1727 . . . . . **LC 7**
  See also DLB 24

Knowles, John 1926- . . . . . . **CLC 1, 4, 10, 26**
  See also CA 17-20R; CDALB 1968-1988;
  DLB 6; MTCW; SATA 8

Knox, Calvin M.
  See Silverberg, Robert

Knye, Cassandra
  See Disch, Thomas M(ichael)

Koch, C(hristopher) J(ohn) 1932- . . . **CLC 42**
  See also CA 127

Koch, Christopher
  See Koch, C(hristopher) J(ohn)

Koch, Kenneth 1925- . . . . **CLC 5, 8, 44**
  See also CA 1-4R; CANR 6, 36; DLB 5;
  SATA 65

Kochanowski, Jan 1530-1584. . . . . . . **LC 10**

Kock, Charles Paul de
 1794-1871 .... NCLC 16

Koda Shigeyuki 1867-1947
 See Rohan, Koda
 See also CA 121

Koestler, Arthur
 1905-1983 ...... CLC 1, 3, 6, 8, 15, 33
 See also CA 1-4R; 109; CANR 1, 33;
 CDBLB 1945-1960; DLBY 83; MTCW

Kohout, Pavel 1928-............... CLC 13
 See also CA 45-48; CANR 3

Koizumi, Yakumo
 See Hearn, (Patricio) Lafcadio (Tessima
 Carlos)

Kolmar, Gertrud 1894-1943...... TCLC 40

Konrad, George
 See Konrad, Gyoergy

Konrad, Gyoergy 1933- .... CLC 4, 10
 See also CA 85-88

Konwicki, Tadeusz 1926-..... CLC 8, 28, 54
 See also CA 101; CAAS 9; CANR 39;
 MTCW

Kopit, Arthur (Lee) 1937- .... CLC 1, 18, 33
 See also AITN 1; CA 81-84; CABS 3;
 DLB 7; MTCW

Kops, Bernard 1926-............. CLC 4
 See also CA 5-8R; DLB 13

Kornbluth, C(yril) M. 1923-1958.... TCLC 8
 See also CA 105; DLB 8

Korolenko, V. G.
 See Korolenko, Vladimir Galaktionovich

Korolenko, Vladimir
 See Korolenko, Vladimir Galaktionovich

Korolenko, Vladimir G.
 See Korolenko, Vladimir Galaktionovich

Korolenko, Vladimir Galaktionovich
 1853-1921 .... TCLC 22
 See also CA 121

Kosinski, Jerzy (Nikodem)
 1933-1991 ... CLC 1, 2, 3, 6, 10, 15, 53,
 70
 See also CA 17-20R; 134; CANR 9; DLB 2;
 DLBY 82; MTCW

Kostelanetz, Richard (Cory) 1940- .. CLC 28
 See also CA 13-16R; CAAS 8; CANR 38

Kostrowitzki, Wilhelm Apollinaris de
 1880-1918
 See Apollinaire, Guillaume
 See also CA 104

Kotlowitz, Robert 1924-............ CLC 4
 See also CA 33-36R; CANR 36

Kotzebue, August (Friedrich Ferdinand) von
 1761-1819 .... NCLC 25
 See also DLB 94

Kotzwinkle, William 1938- ... CLC 5, 14, 35
 See also CA 45-48; CANR 3; CLR 6;
 MAICYA; SATA 24, 70

Kozol, Jonathan 1936-............ CLC 17
 See also CA 61-64; CANR 16

Kozoll, Michael 1940(?)-.......... CLC 35

Kramer, Kathryn 19(?)-........... CLC 34

Kramer, Larry 1935- .... CLC 42
 See also CA 124; 126

Krasicki, Ignacy 1735-1801 .... NCLC 8

Krasinski, Zygmunt 1812-1859 .... NCLC 4

Kraus, Karl 1874-1936........... TCLC 5
 See also CA 104; DLB 118

Kreve (Mickevicius), Vincas
 1882-1954 .... TCLC 27

Kristofferson, Kris 1936-......... CLC 26
 See also CA 104

Krizanc, John 1956-.............. CLC 57

Krleza, Miroslav 1893-1981........ CLC 8
 See also CA 97-100; 105

Kroetsch, Robert 1927- ...... CLC 5, 23, 57
 See also CA 17-20R; CANR 8, 38; DLB 53;
 MTCW

Kroetz, Franz
 See Kroetz, Franz Xaver

Kroetz, Franz Xaver 1946- .... CLC 41
 See also CA 130

Kropotkin, Peter (Aleksieevich)
 1842-1921 .... TCLC 36
 See also CA 119

Krotkov, Yuri 1917-.............. CLC 19
 See also CA 102

Krumb
 See Crumb, R(obert)

Krumgold, Joseph (Quincy)
 1908-1980 .... CLC 12
 See also CA 9-12R; 101; CANR 7;
 MAICYA; SATA 1, 23, 48

Krumwitz
 See Crumb, R(obert)

Krutch, Joseph Wood 1893-1970.... CLC 24
 See also CA 1-4R; 25-28R; CANR 4;
 DLB 63

Krutzch, Gus
 See Eliot, T(homas) S(tearns)

Krylov, Ivan Andreevich
 1768(?)-1844 .... NCLC 1

Kubin, Alfred 1877-1959 .... TCLC 23
 See also CA 112; DLB 81

Kubrick, Stanley 1928-........... CLC 16
 See also CA 81-84; CANR 33; DLB 26

Kumin, Maxine (Winokur)
 1925- .... CLC 5, 13, 28
 See also AITN 2; CA 1-4R; CAAS 8;
 CANR 1, 21; DLB 5; MTCW; SATA 12

Kundera, Milan
 1929- .... CLC 4, 9, 19, 32, 68
 See also AAYA 2; CA 85-88; CANR 19;
 MTCW

Kunitz, Stanley (Jasspon)
 1905- .... CLC 6, 11, 14
 See also CA 41-44R; CANR 26; DLB 48;
 MTCW

Kunze, Reiner 1933-.............. CLC 10
 See also CA 93-96; DLB 75

Kuprin, Aleksandr Ivanovich
 1870-1938 .... TCLC 5
 See also CA 104

Kureishi, Hanif 1954-............. CLC 64

Kurosawa, Akira 1910-........... CLC 16
 See also CA 101

Kuttner, Henry 1915-1958........ TCLC 10
 See also CA 107; DLB 8

Kuzma, Greg 1944-................ CLC 7
 See also CA 33-36R

Kuzmin, Mikhail 1872(?)-1936 .... TCLC 40

Kyprianos, Iossif
 See Samarakis, Antonis

La Bruyere, Jean de 1645-1696...... LC 17

Laclos, Pierre Ambroise Francois Choderlos
 de 1741-1803 .... NCLC 4

Lacolere, Francois
 See Aragon, Louis

La Colere, Francois
 See Aragon, Louis

La Deshabilleuse
 See Simenon, Georges (Jacques Christian)

Lady Gregory
 See Gregory, Isabella Augusta (Persse)

Lady of Quality, A
 See Bagnold, Enid

La Fayette, Marie (Madelaine Pioche de la
 Vergne Comtes 1634-1693....... LC 2

Lafayette, Rene
 See Hubbard, L(afayette) Ron(ald)

Laforgue, Jules 1860-1887....... NCLC 5

Lagerkvist, Paer (Fabian)
 1891-1974 .... CLC 7, 10, 13, 54
 See also CA 85-88; 49-52; MTCW

Lagerkvist, Par
 See Lagerkvist, Paer (Fabian)

Lagerloef, Selma (Ottiliana Lovisa)
 1858-1940 .... TCLC 4, 36
 See also Lagerlof, Selma (Ottiliana Lovisa)
 See also CA 108; CLR 7; SATA 15

Lagerlof, Selma (Ottiliana Lovisa)
 See Lagerloef, Selma (Ottiliana Lovisa)
 See also CLR 7; SATA 15

La Guma, (Justin) Alex(ander)
 1925-1985 .... CLC 19
 See also BW; CA 49-52; 118; CANR 25;
 DLB 117; MTCW

Laidlaw, A. K.
 See Grieve, C(hristopher) M(urray)

Lainez, Manuel Mujica
 See Mujica Lainez, Manuel
 See also HW

Lamartine, Alphonse (Marie Louis Prat) de
 1790-1869 .... NCLC 11

Lamb, Charles 1775-1834........ NCLC 10
 See also CDBLB 1789-1832; DLB 93, 107;
 SATA 17; WLC

Lamb, Lady Caroline 1785-1828.. NCLC 38
 See also DLB 116

Lamming, George (William)
 1927- .... CLC 2, 4, 66
 See also BLC 2; BW; CA 85-88; CANR 26;
 MTCW

L'Amour, Louis (Dearborn)
 1908-1988 .... CLC 25, 55
 See also AITN 2; BEST 89:2; CA 1-4R;
 125; CANR 3, 25; DLBY 80; MTCW

Lampedusa, Giuseppe (Tomasi) di ... TCLC 13
 See also Tomasi di Lampedusa, Giuseppe

Lampman, Archibald 1861-1899 .. NCLC 25
 See also DLB 92

Lancaster, Bruce 1896-1963........ **CLC 36**
    See also CA 9-10; CAP 1; SATA 9

Landau, Mark Alexandrovich
    See Aldanov, Mark (Alexandrovich)

Landau-Aldanov, Mark Alexandrovich
    See Aldanov, Mark (Alexandrovich)

Landis, John 1950-.............. **CLC 26**
    See also CA 112; 122

Landolfi, Tommaso 1908-1979... **CLC 11, 49**
    See also CA 127; 117

Landon, Letitia Elizabeth
    1802-1838 .... **NCLC 15**
    See also DLB 96

Landor, Walter Savage
    1775-1864 .... **NCLC 14**
    See also DLB 93, 107

Landwirth, Heinz 1927-
    See Lind, Jakov
    See also CA 9-12R; CANR 7

Lane, Patrick 1939- .... **CLC 25**
    See also CA 97-100; DLB 53

Lang, Andrew 1844-1912........ **TCLC 16**
    See also CA 114; 137; DLB 98; MAICYA;
    SATA 16

Lang, Fritz 1890-1976 .... **CLC 20**
    See also CA 77-80; 69-72; CANR 30

Lange, John
    See Crichton, (John) Michael

Langer, Elinor 1939- .... **CLC 34**
    See also CA 121

Langland, William 1330(?)-1400(?) ... **LC 19**

Langstaff, Launcelot
    See Irving, Washington

Lanier, Sidney 1842-1881 .... **NCLC 6**
    See also DLB 64; MAICYA; SATA 18

Lanyer, Aemilia 1569-1645 .... **LC 10**

Lao Tzu .... **CMLC 7**

Lapine, James (Elliot) 1949- .... **CLC 39**
    See also CA 123; 130

Larbaud, Valery (Nicolas)
    1881-1957 .... **TCLC 9**
    See also CA 106

Lardner, Ring
    See Lardner, Ring(gold) W(ilmer)

Lardner, Ring W. Jr.
    See Lardner, Ring(gold) W(ilmer)

Lardner, Ring(gold) W(ilmer)
    1885-1933 .... **TCLC 2, 14**
    See also CA 104; 131; CDALB 1917-1929;
    DLB 11, 25, 86; MTCW

Laredo, Betty
    See Codrescu, Andrei

Larkin, Maia
    See Wojciechowska, Maia (Teresa)

Larkin, Philip (Arthur)
    1922-1985 ... **CLC 3, 5, 8, 9, 13, 18, 33,**
                                           39, 64
    See also CA 5-8R; 117; CANR 24;
    CDBLB 1960 to Present; DLB 27;
    MTCW

Larra (y Sanchez de Castro), Mariano Jose de
    1809-1837 .... **NCLC 17**

Larsen, Eric 1941- .... **CLC 55**
    See also CA 132

Larsen, Nella 1891-1964 .... **CLC 37**
    See also BLC 2; BW; CA 125; DLB 51

Larson, Charles R(aymond) 1938-... **CLC 31**
    See also CA 53-56; CANR 4

Latham, Jean Lee 1902-.......... **CLC 12**
    See also AITN 1; CA 5-8R; CANR 7;
    MAICYA; SATA 2, 68

Latham, Mavis
    See Clark, Mavis Thorpe

Lathen, Emma .... **CLC 2**
    See also Hennissart, Martha; Latsis, Mary
    J(ane)

Lathrop, Francis
    See Leiber, Fritz (Reuter Jr.)

Latsis, Mary J(ane)
    See Lathen, Emma
    See also CA 85-88

Lattimore, Richmond (Alexander)
    1906-1984 .... **CLC 3**
    See also CA 1-4R; 112; CANR 1

Laughlin, James 1914-............ **CLC 49**
    See also CA 21-24R; CANR 9; DLB 48

Laurence, (Jean) Margaret (Wemyss)
    1926-1987 .. **CLC 3, 6, 13, 50, 62; SSC 7**
    See also CA 5-8R; 121; CANR 33; DLB 53;
    MTCW; SATA 50

Laurent, Antoine 1952- .... **CLC 50**

Lauscher, Hermann
    See Hesse, Hermann

Lautreamont, Comte de
    1846-1870 .... **NCLC 12**

Laverty, Donald
    See Blish, James (Benjamin)

Lavin, Mary 1912- ...... **CLC 4, 18; SSC 4**
    See also CA 9-12R; CANR 33; DLB 15;
    MTCW

Lavond, Paul Dennis
    See Kornbluth, C(yril) M.; Pohl, Frederik

Lawler, Raymond Evenor 1922- .... **CLC 58**
    See also CA 103

Lawrence, D(avid) H(erbert Richards)
    1885-1930 .... **TCLC 2, 9, 16, 33; SSC 4**
    See also CA 104; 121; CDBLB 1914-1945;
    DLB 10, 19, 36, 98; MTCW; WLC

Lawrence, T(homas) E(dward)
    1888-1935 .... **TCLC 18**
    See also Dale, Colin
    See also CA 115

Lawrence Of Arabia
    See Lawrence, T(homas) E(dward)

Lawson, Henry (Archibald Hertzberg)
    1867-1922 .... **TCLC 27**
    See also CA 120

Laxness, Halldor................... **CLC 25**
    See also Gudjonsson, Halldor Kiljan

Laye, Camara 1928-1980........ **CLC 4, 38**
    See also BLC 2; BW; CA 85-88; 97-100;
    CANR 25; MTCW

Layton, Irving (Peter) 1912- ..... **CLC 2, 15**
    See also CA 1-4R; CANR 2, 33; DLB 88;
    MTCW

Lazarus, Emma 1849-1887........ **NCLC 8**

Lazarus, Felix
    See Cable, George Washington

Lea, Joan
    See Neufeld, John (Arthur)

Leacock, Stephen (Butler)
    1869-1944 .... **TCLC 2**
    See also CA 104; DLB 92

Lear, Edward 1812-1888 .... **NCLC 3**
    See also CLR 1; DLB 32; MAICYA;
    SATA 18

Lear, Norman (Milton) 1922- ...... **CLC 12**
    See also CA 73-76

Leavis, F(rank) R(aymond)
    1895-1978 .... **CLC 24**
    See also CA 21-24R; 77-80; MTCW

Leavitt, David 1961-.............. **CLC 34**
    See also CA 116; 122

Lebowitz, Fran(ces Ann)
    1951(?)- .... **CLC 11, 36**
    See also CA 81-84; CANR 14; MTCW

le Carre, John .... **CLC 3, 5, 9, 15, 28**
    See also Cornwell, David (John Moore)
    See also BEST 89:4; CDBLB 1960 to
    Present; DLB 87

Le Clezio, J(ean) M(arie) G(ustave)
    1940- .... **CLC 31**
    See also CA 116; 128; DLB 83

Leconte de Lisle, Charles-Marie-Rene
    1818-1894 .... **NCLC 29**

Le Coq, Monsieur
    See Simenon, Georges (Jacques Christian)

Leduc, Violette 1907-1972......... **CLC 22**
    See also CA 13-14; 33-36R; CAP 1

Ledwidge, Francis 1887(?)-1917 ... **TCLC 23**
    See also CA 123; DLB 20

Lee, Andrea 1953- .... **CLC 36**
    See also BLC 2; BW; CA 125

Lee, Andrew
    See Auchincloss, Louis (Stanton)

Lee, Don L....................... **CLC 2**
    See also Madhubuti, Haki R.

Lee, George W(ashington)
    1894-1976 .... **CLC 52**
    See also BLC 2; BW; CA 125; DLB 51

Lee, (Nelle) Harper 1926- ...... **CLC 12, 60**
    See also CA 13-16R; CDALB 1941-1968;
    DLB 6; MTCW; SATA 11; WLC

Lee, Julian
    See Latham, Jean Lee

Lee, Lawrence 1903- .... **CLC 34**
    See also CA 25-28R

Lee, Manfred B(ennington)
    1905-1971 .... **CLC 11**
    See also Queen, Ellery
    See also CA 1-4R; 29-32R; CANR 2

Lee, Stan 1922-.................. **CLC 17**
    See also AAYA 5; CA 108; 111

Lee, Tanith 1947-................ **CLC 46**
    See also CA 37-40R; SATA 8

Lee, Vernon.................... **TCLC 5**
    See also Paget, Violet
    See also DLB 57

Lee, William
    See Burroughs, William S(eward)

Lee, Willy
See Burroughs, William S(eward)

Lee-Hamilton, Eugene (Jacob)
1845-1907 .... **TCLC 22**
See also CA 117

Leet, Judith 1935- .... **CLC 11**

Le Fanu, Joseph Sheridan
1814-1873 .... **NCLC 9**
See also DLB 21, 70

Leffland, Ella 1931- .... **CLC 19**
See also CA 29-32R; CANR 35; DLBY 84;
SATA 65

Leger, (Marie-Rene) Alexis Saint-Leger
1887-1975 .... **CLC 11**
See also Perse, St.-John
See also CA 13-16R; 61-64; MTCW

Leger, Saintleger
See Leger, (Marie-Rene) Alexis Saint-Leger

Le Guin, Ursula K(roeber)
1929- .... **CLC 8, 13, 22, 45, 71**
See also AAYA 9; AITN 1; CA 21-24R;
CANR 9, 32; CDALB 1968-1988; CLR 3,
28; DLB 8, 52; MAICYA; MTCW;
SATA 4, 52

Lehmann, Rosamond (Nina)
1901-1990 .... **CLC 5**
See also CA 77-80; 131; CANR 8; DLB 15

Leiber, Fritz (Reuter Jr.) 1910- .... **CLC 25**
See also CA 45-48; CANR 2; DLB 8;
MTCW; SATA 45

Leimbach, Martha 1963-
See Leimbach, Marti
See also CA 130

Leimbach, Marti .... **CLC 65**
See also Leimbach, Martha

Leino, Eino .... **TCLC 24**
See also Loennbohm, Armas Eino Leopold

Leiris, Michel (Julien) 1901-1990 ... **CLC 61**
See also CA 119; 128; 132

Leithauser, Brad 1953-............. **CLC 27**
See also CA 107; CANR 27; DLB 120

Lelchuk, Alan 1938-............... **CLC 5**
See also CA 45-48; CANR 1

Lem, Stanislaw 1921-........ **CLC 8, 15, 40**
See also CA 105; CAAS 1; CANR 32;
MTCW

Lemann, Nancy 1956-............. **CLC 39**
See also CA 118; 136

Lemonnier, (Antoine Louis) Camille
1844-1913 .... **TCLC 22**
See also CA 121

Lenau, Nikolaus 1802-1850 ...... **NCLC 16**

L'Engle, Madeleine (Camp Franklin)
1918- .... **CLC 12**
See also AAYA 1; AITN 2; CA 1-4R;
CANR 3, 21, 39; CLR 1, 14; DLB 52;
MAICYA; MTCW; SATA 1, 27

Lengyel, Jozsef 1896-1975......... **CLC 7**
See also CA 85-88; 57-60

Lennon, John (Ono)
1940-1980 .... **CLC 12, 35**
See also CA 102

Lennox, Charlotte Ramsay
1729(?)-1804 .... **NCLC 23**
See also DLB 39

Lentricchia, Frank (Jr.) 1940-...... **CLC 34**
See also CA 25-28R; CANR 19

Lenz, Siegfried 1926-............. **CLC 27**
See also CA 89-92; DLB 75

Leonard, Elmore (John Jr.)
1925- .... **CLC 28, 34, 71**
See also AITN 1; BEST 89:1, 90:4;
CA 81-84; CANR 12, 28; MTCW

Leonard, Hugh
See Byrne, John Keyes
See also DLB 13

**Leopardi, (Conte) Giacomo (Talegardo
Francesco di Sales Save**
1798-1837 .... **NCLC 22**

Le Reveler
See Artaud, Antonin

Lerman, Eleanor 1952-............. **CLC 9**
See also CA 85-88

Lerman, Rhoda 1936-............. **CLC 56**
See also CA 49-52

Lermontov, Mikhail Yuryevich
1814-1841 .... **NCLC 5**

Leroux, Gaston 1868-1927........ **TCLC 25**
See also CA 108; 136; SATA 65

Lesage, Alain-Rene 1668-1747....... **LC 2**

Leskov, Nikolai (Semyonovich)
1831-1895 .... **NCLC 25**

Lessing, Doris (May)
1919- .... **CLC 1, 2, 3, 6, 10, 15, 22, 40;
SSC 6**
See also CA 9-12R; CAAS 14; CANR 33;
CDBLB 1960 to Present; DLB 15;
DLBY 85; MTCW

Lessing, Gotthold Ephraim
1729-1781 .... **LC 8**
See also DLB 97

Lester, Richard 1932-............. **CLC 20**

Lever, Charles (James)
1806-1872 .... **NCLC 23**
See also DLB 21

Leverson, Ada 1865(?)-1936(?) .... **TCLC 18**
See also Elaine
See also CA 117

Levertov, Denise
1923- ...... **CLC 1, 2, 3, 5, 8, 15, 28, 66**
See also CA 1-4R; CANR 3, 29; DLB 5;
MTCW

Levi, Peter (Chad Tigar) 1931-..... **CLC 41**
See also CA 5-8R; CANR 34; DLB 40

Levi, Primo 1919-1987........ **CLC 37, 50**
See also CA 13-16R; 122; CANR 12, 33;
MTCW

Levin, Ira 1929- .... **CLC 3, 6**
See also CA 21-24R; CANR 17; MTCW;
SATA 66

Levin, Meyer 1905-1981 .... **CLC 7**
See also AITN 1; CA 9-12R; 104;
CANR 15; DLB 9, 28; DLBY 81;
SATA 21, 27

Levine, Norman 1924- .... **CLC 54**
See also CA 73-76; CANR 14; DLB 88

Levine, Philip 1928-.. **CLC 2, 4, 5, 9, 14, 33**
See also CA 9-12R; CANR 9, 37; DLB 5

Levinson, Deirdre 1931-........... **CLC 49**
See also CA 73-76

Levi-Strauss, Claude 1908- .... **CLC 38**
See also CA 1-4R; CANR 6, 32; MTCW

Levitin, Sonia (Wolff) 1934- .... **CLC 17**
See also CA 29-32R; CANR 14, 32;
MAICYA; SAAS 2; SATA 4, 68

Levon, O. U.
See Kesey, Ken (Elton)

Lewes, George Henry
1817-1878 .... **NCLC 25**
See also DLB 55

Lewis, Alun 1915-1944........... **TCLC 3**
See also CA 104; DLB 20

Lewis, C. Day
See Day Lewis, C(ecil)

Lewis, C(live) S(taples)
1898-1963 .... **CLC 1, 3, 6, 14, 27**
See also AAYA 3; CA 81-84; CANR 33;
CDBLB 1945-1960; CLR 3, 27; DLB 15,
100; MAICYA; MTCW; SATA 13; WLC

Lewis, Janet 1899-............... **CLC 41**
See also Winters, Janet Lewis
See also CA 9-12R; CANR 29; CAP 1;
DLBY 87

Lewis, Matthew Gregory
1775-1818 .... **NCLC 11**
See also DLB 39

Lewis, (Harry) Sinclair
1885-1951 .... **TCLC 4, 13, 23, 39**
See also CA 104; 133; CDALB 1917-1929;
DLB 9, 102; DLBD 1; MTCW; WLC

Lewis, (Percy) Wyndham
1884(?)-1957 .... **TCLC 2, 9**
See also CA 104; DLB 15

Lewisohn, Ludwig 1883-1955...... **TCLC 19**
See also CA 107; DLB 4, 9, 28, 102

Lezama Lima, Jose 1910-1976 ... **CLC 4, 10**
See also CA 77-80; DLB 113; HW

L'Heureux, John (Clarke) 1934-.... **CLC 52**
See also CA 13-16R; CANR 23

Liddell, C. H.
See Kuttner, Henry

Lie, Jonas (Lauritz Idemil)
1833-1908(?) .... **TCLC 5**
See also CA 115

Lieber, Joel 1937-1971............. **CLC 6**
See also CA 73-76; 29-32R

Lieber, Stanley Martin
See Lee, Stan

Lieberman, Laurence (James)
1935- .... **CLC 4, 36**
See also CA 17-20R; CANR 8, 36

Lieksman, Anders
See Haavikko, Paavo Juhani

Li Fei-kan 1904-................. **CLC 18**
See also CA 105

Lifton, Robert Jay 1926-.......... **CLC 67**
See also CA 17-20R; CANR 27; SATA 66

Lightfoot, Gordon 1938-.......... **CLC 26**
See also CA 109

Ligotti, Thomas 1953- .... **CLC 44**
See also CA 123

Liliencron, (Friedrich Adolf Axel) Detlev von
1844-1909 .... **TCLC 18**
See also CA 117

Lima, Jose Lezama
See Lezama Lima, Jose

Lima Barreto, Afonso Henrique de
1881-1922 .... **TCLC 23**
See also CA 117

Limonov, Eduard.................. **CLC 67**

Lin, Frank
See Atherton, Gertrude (Franklin Horn)

Lincoln, Abraham 1809-1865..... **NCLC 18**

Lind, Jakov .... **CLC 1, 2, 4, 27**
See also Landwirth, Heinz
See also CAAS 4

Lindsay, David 1878-1945 .... **TCLC 15**
See also CA 113

Lindsay, (Nicholas) Vachel
1879-1931 .... **TCLC 17**
See also CA 114; 135; CDALB 1865-1917;
DLB 54; SATA 40; WLC

Linke-Poot
See Doeblin, Alfred

Linney, Romulus 1930- .... **CLC 51**
See also CA 1-4R

Li Po 701-763 .... **CMLC 2**

Lipsius, Justus 1547-1606 .... **LC 16**

Lipsyte, Robert (Michael) 1938-.... **CLC 21**
See also AAYA 7; CA 17-20R; CANR 8;
CLR 23; MAICYA; SATA 5, 68

Lish, Gordon (Jay) 1934-.......... **CLC 45**
See also CA 113; 117

Lispector, Clarice 1925-1977....... **CLC 43**
See also CA 116; DLB 113

Littell, Robert 1935(?)- .... **CLC 42**
See also CA 109; 112

Littlewit, Humphrey Gent.
See Lovecraft, H(oward) P(hillips)

Litwos
See Sienkiewicz, Henryk (Adam Alexander
Pius)

Liu E 1857-1909................ **TCLC 15**
See also CA 115

Lively, Penelope (Margaret)
1933-.................... **CLC 32, 50**
See also CA 41-44R; CANR 29; CLR 7;
DLB 14; MAICYA; MTCW; SATA 7, 60

Livesay, Dorothy (Kathleen)
1909-.................... **CLC 4, 15**
See also AITN 2; CA 25-28R; CAAS 8;
CANR 36; DLB 68; MTCW

Lizardi, Jose Joaquin Fernandez de
1776-1827 .... **NCLC 30**

Llewellyn, Richard .... **CLC 7**
See also Llewellyn Lloyd, Richard Dafydd
Vivian
See also DLB 15

Llewellyn Lloyd, Richard Dafydd Vivian
1906-1983
See Llewellyn, Richard
See also CA 53-56; 111; CANR 7;
SATA 11, 37

Llosa, (Jorge) Mario (Pedro) Vargas
See Vargas Llosa, (Jorge) Mario (Pedro)

Lloyd Webber, Andrew 1948-
See Webber, Andrew Lloyd
See also AAYA 1; CA 116; SATA 56

Locke, Alain (Le Roy)
1886-1954 .... **TCLC 43**
See also BW; CA 106; 124; DLB 51

Locke, John 1632-1704 .... **LC 7**
See also DLB 101

Locke-Elliott, Sumner
See Elliott, Sumner Locke

Lockhart, John Gibson
1794-1854 .... **NCLC 6**
See also DLB 110, 116

Lodge, David (John) 1935-........ **CLC 36**
See also BEST 90:1; CA 17-20R; CANR 19;
DLB 14; MTCW

Loennbohm, Armas Eino Leopold 1878-1926
See Leino, Eino
See also CA 123

Loewinsohn, Ron(ald William)
1937-...................... **CLC 52**
See also CA 25-28R

Logan, Jake
See Smith, Martin Cruz

Logan, John (Burton) 1923-1987..... **CLC 5**
See also CA 77-80; 124; DLB 5

Lo Kuan-chung 1330(?)-1400(?)...... **LC 12**

Lombard, Nap
See Johnson, Pamela Hansford

London, Jack........ **TCLC 9, 15, 39; SSC 4**
See also London, John Griffith
See also AITN 2; CDALB 1865-1917;
DLB 8, 12, 78; SATA 18; WLC

London, John Griffith 1876-1916
See London, Jack
See also CA 110; 119; MAICYA; MTCW

Long, Emmett
See Leonard, Elmore (John Jr.)

Longbaugh, Harry
See Goldman, William (W.)

Longfellow, Henry Wadsworth
1807-1882 .... **NCLC 2**
See also CDALB 1640-1865; DLB 1, 59;
SATA 19

Longley, Michael 1939-........... **CLC 29**
See also CA 102; DLB 40

Longus fl. c. 2nd cent. - .... **CMLC 7**

Longway, A. Hugh
See Lang, Andrew

Lopate, Phillip 1943- .... **CLC 29**
See also CA 97-100; DLBY 80

Lopez Portillo (y Pacheco), Jose
1920-..................... **CLC 46**
See also CA 129; HW

Lopez y Fuentes, Gregorio
1897(?)-1966 .... **CLC 32**
See also CA 131; HW

Lorca, Federico Garcia
See Garcia Lorca, Federico

Lord, Bette Bao 1938-............ **CLC 23**
See also BEST 90:3; CA 107; SATA 58

Lord Auch
See Bataille, Georges

Lord Byron
See Byron, George Gordon (Noel)

Lord Dunsany .... **TCLC 2**
See also Dunsany, Edward John Moreton
Drax Plunkett

Lorde, Audre (Geraldine)
1934-..................... **CLC 18, 71**
See also BLC 2; BW; CA 25-28R;
CANR 16, 26; DLB 41; MTCW

Lord Jeffrey
See Jeffrey, Francis

Lorenzo, Heberto Padilla
See Padilla (Lorenzo), Heberto

Loris
See Hofmannsthal, Hugo von

Loti, Pierre .... **TCLC 11**
See also Viaud, (Louis Marie) Julien

Louie, David Wong 1954- .... **CLC 70**

Louis, Father M.
See Merton, Thomas

Lovecraft, H(oward) P(hillips)
1890-1937 .... **TCLC 4, 22; SSC 3**
See also CA 104; 133; MTCW

Lovelace, Earl 1935-............. **CLC 51**
See also CA 77-80; MTCW

Lowell, Amy 1874-1925........ **TCLC 1, 8**
See also CA 104; DLB 54

Lowell, James Russell 1819-1891 .. **NCLC 2**
See also CDALB 1640-1865; DLB 1, 11, 64,
79

Lowell, Robert (Traill Spence Jr.)
1917-1977 ... **CLC 1, 2, 3, 4, 5, 8, 9, 11,
15, 37; PC 3**
See also CA 9-12R; 73-76; CABS 2;
CANR 26; DLB 5; MTCW; WLC

Lowndes, Marie Adelaide (Belloc)
1868-1947 .... **TCLC 12**
See also CA 107; DLB 70

Lowry, (Clarence) Malcolm
1909-1957 .... **TCLC 6, 40**
See also CA 105; 131; CDBLB 1945-1960;
DLB 15; MTCW

Lowry, Mina Gertrude 1882-1966
See Loy, Mina
See also CA 113

Loxsmith, John
See Brunner, John (Kilian Houston)

Loy, Mina .... **CLC 28**
See also Lowry, Mina Gertrude
See also DLB 4, 54

Loyson-Bridet
See Schwob, (Mayer Andre) Marcel

Lucas, Craig 1951-............... **CLC 64**
See also CA 137

Lucas, George 1944-.............. **CLC 16**
See also AAYA 1; CA 77-80; CANR 30;
SATA 56

Lucas, Hans
See Godard, Jean-Luc

Lucas, Victoria
See Plath, Sylvia

Ludlam, Charles 1943-1987 ..... **CLC 46, 50**
See also CA 85-88; 122

Ludlum, Robert 1927- .... CLC 22, 43
See also BEST 89:1, 90:3; CA 33-36R;
CANR 25; DLBY 82; MTCW

Ludwig, Ken. .... CLC 60

Ludwig, Otto 1813-1865. .... NCLC 4

Lugones, Leopoldo 1874-1938 ..... TCLC 15
See also CA 116; 131; HW

Lu Hsun 1881-1936 .... TCLC 3

Lukacs, George .... CLC 24
See also Lukacs, Gyorgy (Szegeny von)

Lukacs, Gyorgy (Szegeny von) 1885-1971
See Lukacs, George
See also CA 101; 29-32R

Luke, Peter (Ambrose Cyprian)
1919- .... CLC 38
See also CA 81-84; DLB 13

Lunar, Dennis
See Mungo, Raymond

Lurie, Alison 1926- .... CLC 4, 5, 18, 39
See also CA 1-4R; CANR 2, 17; DLB 2;
MTCW; SATA 46

Lustig, Arnost 1926- .... CLC 56
See also AAYA 3; CA 69-72; SATA 56

Luther, Martin 1483-1546 .... LC 9

Luzi, Mario 1914- .... CLC 13
See also CA 61-64; CANR 9

Lynch, B. Suarez
See Bioy Casares, Adolfo; Borges, Jorge
Luis

Lynch, David (K.) 1946- .... CLC 66
See also CA 124; 129

Lynch, James
See Andreyev, Leonid (Nikolaevich)

Lynch Davis, B.
See Bioy Casares, Adolfo; Borges, Jorge
Luis

Lyndsay, Sir David 1490-1555 .... LC 20

Lynn, Kenneth S(chuyler) 1923- .... CLC 50
See also CA 1-4R; CANR 3, 27

Lynx
See West, Rebecca

Lyons, Marcus
See Blish, James (Benjamin)

Lyre, Pinchbeck
See Sassoon, Siegfried (Lorraine)

Lytle, Andrew (Nelson) 1902- ...... CLC 22
See also CA 9-12R; DLB 6

Lyttelton, George 1709-1773 .... LC 10

Maas, Peter 1929- .... CLC 29
See also CA 93-96

Macaulay, Rose 1881-1958 ..... TCLC 7, 44
See also CA 104; DLB 36

MacBeth, George (Mann)
1932-1992 .... CLC 2, 5, 9
See also CA 25-28R; 136; DLB 40; MTCW;
SATA 4; SATO 70

MacCaig, Norman (Alexander)
1910- .... CLC 36
See also CA 9-12R; CANR 3, 34; DLB 27

MacCarthy, (Sir Charles Otto) Desmond
1877-1952 .... TCLC 36

MacDiarmid, Hugh ..... CLC 2, 4, 11, 19, 63
See also Grieve, C(hristopher) M(urray)
See also CDBLB 1945-1960; DLB 20

MacDonald, Anson
See Heinlein, Robert A(nson)

Macdonald, Cynthia 1928- ...... CLC 13, 19
See also CA 49-52; CANR 4; DLB 105

MacDonald, George 1824-1905 ..... TCLC 9
See also CA 106; 137; DLB 18; MAICYA;
SATA 33

Macdonald, John
See Millar, Kenneth

MacDonald, John D(ann)
1916-1986 .... CLC 3, 27, 44
See also CA 1-4R; 121; CANR 1, 19;
DLB 8; DLBY 86; MTCW

Macdonald, John Ross
See Millar, Kenneth

Macdonald, Ross ..... CLC 1, 2, 3, 14, 34, 41
See also Millar, Kenneth
See also DLBD 6

MacDougal, John
See Blish, James (Benjamin)

MacEwen, Gwendolyn (Margaret)
1941-1987 .... CLC 13, 55
See also CA 9-12R; 124; CANR 7, 22;
DLB 53; SATA 50, 55

Machado (y Ruiz), Antonio
1875-1939 .... TCLC 3
See also CA 104; DLB 108

Machado de Assis, Joaquim Maria
1839-1908 .... TCLC 10
See also BLC 2; CA 107

Machen, Arthur .... TCLC 4
See also Jones, Arthur Llewellyn
See also DLB 36

Machiavelli, Niccolo 1469-1527 ...... LC 8

MacInnes, Colin 1914-1976 ...... CLC 4, 23
See also CA 69-72; 65-68; CANR 21;
DLB 14; MTCW

MacInnes, Helen (Clark)
1907-1985 .... CLC 27, 39
See also CA 1-4R; 117; CANR 1, 28;
DLB 87; MTCW; SATA 22, 44

Mackenzie, Compton (Edward Montague)
1883-1972 .... CLC 18
See also CA 21-22; 37-40R; CAP 2;
DLB 34, 100

Mackintosh, Elizabeth 1896(?)-1952
See Tey, Josephine
See also CA 110

MacLaren, James
See Grieve, C(hristopher) M(urray)

Mac Laverty, Bernard 1942- .... CLC 31
See also CA 116; 118

MacLean, Alistair (Stuart)
1922-1987 .... CLC 3, 13, 50, 63
See also CA 57-60; 121; CANR 28; MTCW;
SATA 23, 50

MacLeish, Archibald
1892-1982 .... CLC 3, 8, 14, 68
See also CA 9-12R; 106; CANR 33; DLB 4,
7, 45; DLBY 82; MTCW

MacLennan, (John) Hugh
1907- .... CLC 2, 14
See also CA 5-8R; CANR 33; DLB 68;
MTCW

MacLeod, Alistair 1936- .... CLC 56
See also CA 123; DLB 60

MacNeice, (Frederick) Louis
1907-1963 .... CLC 1, 4, 10, 53
See also CA 85-88; DLB 10, 20; MTCW

MacNeill, Dand
See Fraser, George MacDonald

Macpherson, (Jean) Jay 1931- ...... CLC 14
See also CA 5-8R; DLB 53

MacShane, Frank 1927- .... CLC 39
See also CA 9-12R; CANR 3, 33; DLB 111

Macumber, Mari
See Sandoz, Mari(e Susette)

Madach, Imre 1823-1864 .... NCLC 19

Madden, (Jerry) David 1933- .... CLC 5, 15
See also CA 1-4R; CAAS 3; CANR 4;
DLB 6; MTCW

Maddern, Al(an)
See Ellison, Harlan

Madhubuti, Haki R. 1942- .... CLC 6; PC 5
See also Lee, Don L.
See also BLC 2; BW; CA 73-76; CANR 24;
DLB 5, 41; DLBD 8

Madow, Pauline (Reichberg) .... CLC 1
See also CA 9-12R

Maepenn, Hugh
See Kuttner, Henry

Maepenn, K. H.
See Kuttner, Henry

Maeterlinck, Maurice 1862-1949 ... TCLC 3
See also CA 104; 136; SATA 66

Maginn, William 1794-1842 .... NCLC 8
See also DLB 110

Mahapatra, Jayanta 1928- .... CLC 33
See also CA 73-76; CAAS 9; CANR 15, 33

Mahfouz, Naguib (Abdel Aziz Al-Sabilgi)
1911(?)-
See Mahfuz, Najib
See also BEST 89:2; CA 128; MTCW

Mahfuz, Najib .... CLC 52, 55
See also Mahfouz, Naguib (Abdel Aziz
Al-Sabilgi)
See also DLBY 88

Mahon, Derek 1941- .... CLC 27
See also CA 113; 128; DLB 40

Mailer, Norman
1923- ...... CLC 1, 2, 3, 4, 5, 8, 11, 14,
28, 39
See also AITN 2; CA 9-12R; CABS 1;
CANR 28; CDALB 1968-1988; DLB 2,
16, 28; DLBD 3; DLBY 80, 83; MTCW

Maillet, Antonine 1929- .... CLC 54
See also CA 115; 120; DLB 60

Mais, Roger 1905-1955 .... TCLC 8
See also BW; CA 105; 124; MTCW

Maitland, Sara (Louise) 1950- ...... CLC 49
See also CA 69-72; CANR 13

Major, Clarence 1936- .... CLC 3, 19, 48
See also BLC 2; BW; CA 21-24R; CAAS 6;
CANR 13, 25; DLB 33

Major, Kevin (Gerald) 1949-....... **CLC 26**
See also CA 97-100; CANR 21, 38;
CLR 11; DLB 60; MAICYA; SATA 32

Maki, James
See Ozu, Yasujiro

Malabaila, Damiano
See Levi, Primo

Malamud, Bernard
1914-1986 ..... **CLC 1, 2, 3, 5, 8, 9, 11,**
18, 27, 44
See also CA 5-8R; 118; CABS 1; CANR 28;
CDALB 1941-1968; DLB 2, 28;
DLBY 80, 86; MTCW; WLC

Malcolm, Dan
See Silverberg, Robert

Malherbe, Francois de 1555-1628..... **LC 5**

Mallarme, Stephane
1842-1898 .... **NCLC 4; PC 4**

Mallet-Joris, Francoise 1930-...... **CLC 11**
See also CA 65-68; CANR 17; DLB 83

Malley, Ern
See McAuley, James Phillip

Mallowan, Agatha Christie
See Christie, Agatha (Mary Clarissa)

Maloff, Saul 1922-................ **CLC 5**
See also CA 33-36R

Malone, Louis
See MacNeice, (Frederick) Louis

Malone, Michael (Christopher)
1942-...................... **CLC 43**
See also CA 77-80; CANR 14, 32

Malory, (Sir) Thomas
1410(?)-1471(?)................ **LC 11**
See also CDBLB Before 1660; SATA 33, 59

Malouf, (George Joseph) David
1934-...................... **CLC 28**
See also CA 124

Malraux, (Georges-)Andre
1901-1976 ...... **CLC 1, 4, 9, 13, 15, 57**
See also CA 21-22; 69-72; CANR 34;
CAP 2; DLB 72; MTCW

Malzberg, Barry N(athaniel) 1939-... **CLC 7**
See also CA 61-64; CAAS 4; CANR 16;
DLB 8

Mamet, David (Alan)
1947-................ **CLC 9, 15, 34, 46**
See also AAYA 3; CA 81-84; CABS 3;
CANR 15; DLB 7; MTCW

Mamoulian, Rouben (Zachary)
1897-1987 .... **CLC 16**
See also CA 25-28R; 124

Mandelstam, Osip (Emilievich)
1891(?)-1938(?)............. **TCLC 2, 6**
See also CA 104

Mander, (Mary) Jane 1877-1949... **TCLC 31**

Mandiargues, Andre Pieyre de....... **CLC 41**
See also Pieyre de Mandiargues, Andre
See also DLB 83

Mandrake, Ethel Belle
See Thurman, Wallace (Henry)

Mangan, James Clarence
1803-1849 .... **NCLC 27**

Maniere, J.-E.
See Giraudoux, (Hippolyte) Jean

Manley, (Mary) Delariviere
1672(?)-1724 .... **LC 1**
See also DLB 39, 80

Mann, Abel
See Creasey, John

Mann, (Luiz) Heinrich 1871-1950... **TCLC 9**
See also CA 106; DLB 66

Mann, (Paul) Thomas
1875-1955 ... **TCLC 2, 8, 14, 21, 35, 44;**
SSC 5
See also CA 104; 128; DLB 66; MTCW;
WLC

Manning, Frederic 1887(?)-1935... **TCLC 25**
See also CA 124

Manning, Olivia 1915-1980...... **CLC 5, 19**
See also CA 5-8R; 101; CANR 29; MTCW

Mano, D. Keith 1942-.......... **CLC 2, 10**
See also CA 25-28R; CAAS 6; CANR 26;
DLB 6

Mansfield, Katherine... **TCLC 2, 8, 39; SSC 9**
See also Beauchamp, Kathleen Mansfield
See also WLC

Manso, Peter 1940-.............. **CLC 39**
See also CA 29-32R

Mantecon, Juan Jimenez
See Jimenez (Mantecon), Juan Ramon

Manton, Peter
See Creasey, John

Man Without a Spleen, A
See Chekhov, Anton (Pavlovich)

Manzoni, Alessandro 1785-1873.. **NCLC 29**

Mapu, Abraham (ben Jekutiel)
1808-1867 .... **NCLC 18**

Mara, Sally
See Queneau, Raymond

Marat, Jean Paul 1743-1793....... **LC 10**

Marcel, Gabriel Honore
1889-1973 .... **CLC 15**
See also CA 102; 45-48; MTCW

Marchbanks, Samuel
See Davies, (William) Robertson

Marchi, Giacomo
See Bassani, Giorgio

Marie de France c. 12th cent. -.... **CMLC 8**

Marie de l'Incarnation 1599-1672.... **LC 10**

Mariner, Scott
See Pohl, Frederik

Marinetti, Filippo Tommaso
1876-1944 .... **TCLC 10**
See also CA 107; DLB 114

Marivaux, Pierre Carlet de Chamblain de
1688-1763 .... **LC 4**

Markandaya, Kamala .... **CLC 8, 38**
See also Taylor, Kamala (Purnaiya)

Markfield, Wallace 1926-.......... **CLC 8**
See also CA 69-72; CAAS 3; DLB 2, 28

Markham, Edwin 1852-1940..... **TCLC 47**
See also DLB 54

Markham, Robert
See Amis, Kingsley (William)

Marks, J
See Highwater, Jamake (Mamake)

Marks-Highwater, J
See Highwater, Jamake (Mamake)

Markson, David M(errill) 1927-.... **CLC 67**
See also CA 49-52; CANR 1

Marley, Bob.................... **CLC 17**
See also Marley, Robert Nesta

Marley, Robert Nesta 1945-1981
See Marley, Bob
See also CA 107; 103

Marlowe, Christopher 1564-1593 ..... **DC 1**
See also CDBLB Before 1660; DLB 62;
WLC

Marmontel, Jean-Francois
1723-1799 .... **LC 2**

Marquand, John P(hillips)
1893-1960 .... **CLC 2, 10**
See also CA 85-88; DLB 9, 102

Marquez, Gabriel (Jose) Garcia...... **CLC 68**
See also Garcia Marquez, Gabriel (Jose)

Marquis, Don(ald Robert Perry)
1878-1937 .... **TCLC 7**
See also CA 104; DLB 11, 25

Marric, J. J.
See Creasey, John

Marrow, Bernard
See Moore, Brian

Marryat, Frederick 1792-1848 .... **NCLC 3**
See also DLB 21

Marsden, James
See Creasey, John

Marsh, (Edith) Ngaio
1899-1982 .... **CLC 7, 53**
See also CA 9-12R; CANR 6; DLB 77;
MTCW

Marshall, Garry 1934-............ **CLC 17**
See also AAYA 3; CA 111; SATA 60

Marshall, Paule 1929-.. **CLC 27, 72; SSC 3**
See also BLC 3; BW; CA 77-80; CANR 25;
DLB 33; MTCW

Marsten, Richard
See Hunter, Evan

Martha, Henry
See Harris, Mark

Martin, Ken
See Hubbard, L(afayette) Ron(ald)

Martin, Richard
See Creasey, John

Martin, Steve 1945-.............. **CLC 30**
See also CA 97-100; CANR 30; MTCW

Martin, Webber
See Silverberg, Robert

Martin du Gard, Roger
1881-1958 .... **TCLC 24**
See also CA 118; DLB 65

Martineau, Harriet 1802-1876.... **NCLC 26**
See also DLB 21, 55; YABC 2

Martines, Julia
See O'Faolain, Julia

Martinez, Jacinto Benavente y
See Benavente (y Martinez), Jacinto

Martinez Ruiz, Jose 1873-1967
See Azorin; Ruiz, Jose Martinez
See also CA 93-96; HW

Martinez Sierra, Gregorio
1881-1947 .... TCLC 6
See also CA 115

Martinez Sierra, Maria (de la O'LeJarraga)
1874-1974 .... TCLC 6
See also CA 115

Martinsen, Martin
See Follett, Ken(neth Martin)

Martinson, Harry (Edmund)
1904-1978 .... CLC 14
See also CA 77-80; CANR 34

Marut, Ret
See Traven, B.

Marut, Robert
See Traven, B.

Marvell, Andrew 1621-1678......... LC 4
See also CDBLB 1660-1789; WLC

Marx, Karl (Heinrich)
1818-1883 .... NCLC 17

Masaoka Shiki................. TCLC 18
See also Masaoka Tsunenori

Masaoka Tsunenori 1867-1902
See Masaoka Shiki
See also CA 117

Masefield, John (Edward)
1878-1967 .... CLC 11, 47
See also CA 19-20; 25-28R; CANR 33;
CAP 2; CDBLB 1890-1914; DLB 10;
MTCW; SATA 19

Maso, Carole 19(?)- .... CLC 44

Mason, Bobbie Ann
1940- .... CLC 28, 43; SSC 4
See also AAYA 5; CA 53-56; CANR 11,
31; DLBY 87; MTCW

Mason, Ernst
See Pohl, Frederik

Mason, Lee W.
See Malzberg, Barry N(athaniel)

Mason, Nick 1945-............... CLC 35
See also Pink Floyd

Mason, Tally
See Derleth, August (William)

Mass, William
See Gibson, William

Masters, Edgar Lee
1868-1950 .... TCLC 2, 25; PC 1
See also CA 104; 133; CDALB 1865-1917;
DLB 54; MTCW

Masters, Hilary 1928- .... CLC 48
See also CA 25-28R; CANR 13

Mastrosimone, William 19(?)-...... CLC 36

Mathe, Albert
See Camus, Albert

Matheson, Richard Burton 1926- ... CLC 37
See also CA 97-100; DLB 8, 44

Mathews, Harry 1930-.......... CLC 6, 52
See also CA 21-24R; CAAS 6; CANR 18

Mathias, Roland (Glyn) 1915-...... CLC 45
See also CA 97-100; CANR 19; DLB 27

Matsuo Basho 1644-1694........... PC 3

Mattheson, Rodney
See Creasey, John

Matthews, Greg 1949- .... CLC 45
See also CA 135

Matthews, William 1942-.......... CLC 40
See also CA 29-32R; CANR 12; DLB 5

Matthias, John (Edward) 1941-...... CLC 9
See also CA 33-36R

Matthiessen, Peter
1927- .... CLC 5, 7, 11, 32, 64
See also AAYA 6; BEST 90:4; CA 9-12R;
CANR 21; DLB 6; MTCW; SATA 27

Maturin, Charles Robert
1780(?)-1824 .... NCLC 6

Matute (Ausejo), Ana Maria
1925- .... CLC 11
See also CA 89-92; MTCW

Maugham, W. S.
See Maugham, W(illiam) Somerset

Maugham, W(illiam) Somerset
1874-1965 .... CLC 1, 11, 15, 67; SSC 8
See also CA 5-8R; 25-28R;
CDBLB 1914-1945; DLB 10, 36, 77, 100;
MTCW; SATA 54; WLC

Maugham, William Somerset
See Maugham, W(illiam) Somerset

Maupassant, (Henri Rene Albert) Guy de
1850-1893 .... NCLC 1; SSC 1
See also WLC

Maurhut, Richard
See Traven, B.

Mauriac, Claude 1914-............. CLC 9
See also CA 89-92; DLB 83

Mauriac, Francois (Charles)
1885-1970 .... CLC 4, 9, 56
See also CA 25-28; CAP 2; DLB 65;
MTCW

Mavor, Osborne Henry 1888-1951
See Bridie, James
See also CA 104

Maxwell, William (Keepers Jr.)
1908- .... CLC 19
See also CA 93-96; DLBY 80

May, Elaine 1932- .... CLC 16
See also CA 124; DLB 44

Mayakovski, Vladimir (Vladimirovich)
1893-1930 .... TCLC 4, 18
See also CA 104

Mayhew, Henry 1812-1887 ...... NCLC 31
See also DLB 18, 55

Maynard, Joyce 1953-............. CLC 23
See also CA 111; 129

Mayne, William (James Carter)
1928- .... CLC 12
See also CA 9-12R; CANR 37; CLR 25;
MAICYA; SAAS 11; SATA 6, 68

Mayo, Jim
See L'Amour, Louis (Dearborn)

Maysles, Albert 1926- .... CLC 16
See also CA 29-32R

Maysles, David 1932-............. CLC 16

Mazer, Norma Fox 1931- .... CLC 26
See also AAYA 5; CA 69-72; CANR 12,
32; CLR 23; MAICYA; SAAS 1;
SATA 24, 67

Mazzini, Guiseppe 1805-1872 .... NCLC 34

Mazzini, Guiseppe 1805-1872 .... NCLC 34

McAuley, James Phillip
1917-1976 .... CLC 45
See also CA 97-100

McBain, Ed
See Hunter, Evan

McBrien, William Augustine
1930- .... CLC 44
See also CA 107

McCaffrey, Anne (Inez) 1926-...... CLC 17
See also AAYA 6; AITN 2; BEST 89:2;
CA 25-28R; CANR 15, 35; DLB 8;
MAICYA; MTCW; SAAS 11; SATA 8,
70

McCann, Arthur
See Campbell, John W(ood Jr.)

McCann, Edson
See Pohl, Frederik

McCarthy, Cormac 1933-........ CLC 4, 57
See also CA 13-16R; CANR 10; DLB 6

McCarthy, Mary (Therese)
1912-1989 ... CLC 1, 3, 5, 14, 24, 39, 59
See also CA 5-8R; 129; CANR 16; DLB 2;
DLBY 81; MTCW

McCartney, (James) Paul
1942- .... CLC 12, 35

McCauley, Stephen 19(?)- .... CLC 50

McClure, Michael (Thomas)
1932- .... CLC 6, 10
See also CA 21-24R; CANR 17; DLB 16

McCorkle, Jill (Collins) 1958-...... CLC 51
See also CA 121; DLBY 87

McCourt, James 1941-............. CLC 5
See also CA 57-60

McCoy, Horace (Stanley)
1897-1955 .... TCLC 28
See also CA 108; DLB 9

McCrae, John 1872-1918......... TCLC 12
See also CA 109; DLB 92

McCreigh, James
See Pohl, Frederik

McCullers, (Lula) Carson (Smith)
1917-1967 .. CLC 1, 4, 10, 12, 48; SSC 9
See also CA 5-8R; 25-28R; CABS 1, 3;
CANR 18; CDALB 1941-1968; DLB 2, 7;
MTCW; SATA 27; WLC

McCulloch, John Tyler
See Burroughs, Edgar Rice

McCullough, Colleen 1938(?)-...... CLC 27
See also CA 81-84; CANR 17; MTCW

McElroy, Joseph 1930- .... CLC 5, 47
See also CA 17-20R

McEwan, Ian (Russell) 1948- ... CLC 13, 66
See also BEST 90:4; CA 61-64; CANR 14;
DLB 14; MTCW

McFadden, David 1940-........... CLC 48
See also CA 104; DLB 60

McFarland, Dennis 1950- .... CLC 65

McGahern, John 1934-........ CLC 5, 9, 48
See also CA 17-20R; CANR 29; DLB 14;
MTCW

McGinley, Patrick (Anthony)
1937- .... CLC 41
See also CA 120; 127

McGinley, Phyllis 1905-1978 ...... CLC 14
See also CA 9-12R; 77-80; CANR 19;
DLB 11, 48; SATA 2, 24, 44

McGinniss, Joe 1942-............ CLC 32
See also AITN 2; BEST 89:2; CA 25-28R;
CANR 26

McGivern, Maureen Daly
See Daly, Maureen

McGrath, Patrick 1950-.......... CLC 55
See also CA 136

McGrath, Thomas (Matthew)
1916-1990 .... CLC 28, 59
See also CA 9-12R; 132; CANR 6, 33;
MTCW; SATA 41; SATO 66

McGuane, Thomas (Francis III)
1939- .... CLC 3, 7, 18, 45
See also AITN 2; CA 49-52; CANR 5, 24;
DLB 2; DLBY 80; MTCW

McGuckian, Medbh 1950-......... CLC 48
See also DLB 40

McHale, Tom 1942(?)-1982....... CLC 3, 5
See also AITN 1; CA 77-80; 106

McIlvanney, William 1936-........ CLC 42
See also CA 25-28R; DLB 14

McIlwraith, Maureen Mollie Hunter
See Hunter, Mollie
See also SATA 2

McInerney, Jay 1955- .... CLC 34
See also CA 116; 123

McIntyre, Vonda N(eel) 1948- ..... CLC 18
See also CA 81-84; CANR 17, 34; MTCW

McKay, Claude .... TCLC 7, 41; PC 2
See also McKay, Festus Claudius
See also BLC 3; DLB 4, 45, 51, 117

McKay, Festus Claudius 1889-1948
See McKay, Claude
See also BW; CA 104; 124; MTCW; WLC

McKuen, Rod 1933-............. CLC 1, 3
See also AITN 1; CA 41-44R

McLoughlin, R. B.
See Mencken, H(enry) L(ouis)

McLuhan, (Herbert) Marshall
1911-1980 .... CLC 37
See also CA 9-12R; 102; CANR 12, 34;
DLB 88; MTCW

McMillan, Terry 1951- .... CLC 50, 61

McMurtry, Larry (Jeff)
1936- .... CLC 2, 3, 7, 11, 27, 44
See also AITN 2; BEST 89:2; CA 5-8R;
CANR 19; CDALB 1968-1988; DLB 2;
DLBY 80, 87; MTCW

McNally, Terrence 1939-...... CLC 4, 7, 41
See also CA 45-48; CANR 2; DLB 7

McNamer, Deirdre 1950-......... CLC 70

McNeile, Herman Cyril 1888-1937
See Sapper
See also DLB 77

McPhee, John (Angus) 1931- ...... CLC 36
See also BEST 90:1; CA 65-68; CANR 20;
MTCW

McPherson, James Alan 1943- ..... CLC 19
See also BW; CA 25-28R; CANR 24;
DLB 38; MTCW

McPherson, William (Alexander)
1933- .... CLC 34
See also CA 69-72; CANR 28

McSweeney, Kerry .... CLC 34

Mead, Margaret 1901-1978....... CLC 37
See also AITN 1; CA 1-4R; 81-84;
CANR 4; MTCW; SATA 20

Meaker, Marijane (Agnes) 1927-
See Kerr, M. E.
See also CA 107; CANR 37; MAICYA;
MTCW; SATA 20, 61

Medoff, Mark (Howard) 1940- ... CLC 6, 23
See also AITN 1; CA 53-56; CANR 5;
DLB 7

Meged, Aharon
See Megged, Aharon

Meged, Aron
See Megged, Aharon

Megged, Aharon 1920-............ CLC 9
See also CA 49-52; CAAS 13; CANR 1

Mehta, Ved (Parkash) 1934-....... CLC 37
See also CA 1-4R; CANR 2, 23; MTCW

Melanter
See Blackmore, R(ichard) D(oddridge)

Melikow, Loris
See Hofmannsthal, Hugo von

Melmoth, Sebastian
See Wilde, Oscar (Fingal O'Flahertie Wills)

Meltzer, Milton 1915-............ CLC 26
See also AAYA 8; CA 13-16R; CANR 38;
CLR 13; DLB 61; MAICYA; SAAS 1;
SATA 1, 50

Melville, Herman
1819-1891 ...... NCLC 3, 12, 29; SSC 1
See also CDALB 1640-1865; DLB 3, 74;
SATA 59; WLC

Menander c. 342B.C.-c. 292B.C.... CMLC 9

Mencken, H(enry) L(ouis)
1880-1956 .... TCLC 13
See also CA 105; 125; CDALB 1917-1929;
DLB 11, 29, 63; MTCW

Mercer, David 1928-1980.......... CLC 5
See also CA 9-12R; 102; CANR 23;
DLB 13; MTCW

Merchant, Paul
See Ellison, Harlan

Meredith, George 1828-1909 ... TCLC 17, 43
See also CA 117; CDBLB 1832-1890;
DLB 18, 35, 57

Meredith, William (Morris)
1919- .... CLC 4, 13, 22, 55
See also CA 9-12R; CAAS 14; CANR 6;
DLB 5

Merezhkovsky, Dmitry Sergeyevich
1865-1941 .... TCLC 29

Merimee, Prosper
1803-1870 .... NCLC 6; SSC 7
See also DLB 119

Merkin, Daphne 1954-........... CLC 44
See also CA 123

Merlin, Arthur
See Blish, James (Benjamin)

Merrill, James (Ingram)
1926- .... CLC 2, 3, 6, 8, 13, 18, 34
See also CA 13-16R; CANR 10; DLB 5;
DLBY 85; MTCW

Merriman, Alex
See Silverberg, Robert

Merritt, E. B.
See Waddington, Miriam

Merton, Thomas
1915-1968 .... CLC 1, 3, 11, 34
See also CA 5-8R; 25-28R; CANR 22;
DLB 48; DLBY 81; MTCW

Merwin, W(illiam) S(tanley)
1927- ...... CLC 1, 2, 3, 5, 8, 13, 18, 45
See also CA 13-16R; CANR 15; DLB 5;
MTCW

Metcalf, John 1938-.............. CLC 37
See also CA 113; DLB 60

Metcalf, Suzanne
See Baum, L(yman) Frank

Mew, Charlotte (Mary)
1870-1928 .... TCLC 8
See also CA 105; DLB 19

Mewshaw, Michael 1943-.......... CLC 9
See also CA 53-56; CANR 7; DLBY 80

Meyer, June
See Jordan, June

Meyer-Meyrink, Gustav 1868-1932
See Meyrink, Gustav
See also CA 117

Meyers, Jeffrey 1939- .... CLC 39
See also CA 73-76; DLB 111

Meynell, Alice (Christina Gertrude Thompson)
1847-1922 .... TCLC 6
See also CA 104; DLB 19, 98

Meyrink, Gustav .... TCLC 21
See also Meyer-Meyrink, Gustav
See also DLB 81

Michaels, Leonard 1933-........ CLC 6, 25
See also CA 61-64; CANR 21; MTCW

Michaux, Henri 1899-1984 ...... CLC 8, 19
See also CA 85-88; 114

Michelangelo 1475-1564............ LC 12

Michelet, Jules 1798-1874....... NCLC 31

Michener, James A(lbert)
1907(?)-.......... CLC 1, 5, 11, 29, 60
See also AITN 1; BEST 90:1; CA 5-8R;
CANR 21; DLB 6; MTCW

Mickiewicz, Adam 1798-1855 ..... NCLC 3

Middleton, Christopher 1926-...... CLC 13
See also CA 13-16R; CANR 29; DLB 40

Middleton, Stanley 1919-........ CLC 7, 38
See also CA 25-28R; CANR 21; DLB 14

Migueis, Jose Rodrigues 1901-..... CLC 10

Mikszath, Kalman 1847-1910 ..... TCLC 31

Miles, Josephine
1911-1985 .... CLC 1, 2, 14, 34, 39
See also CA 1-4R; 116; CANR 2; DLB 48

Militant
See Sandburg, Carl (August)

Mill, John Stuart 1806-1873 ..... NCLC 11
See also CDBLB 1832-1890; DLB 55

Millar, Kenneth 1915-1983 . . . . **CLC 14**
See also Macdonald, Ross
See also CA 9-12R; 110; CANR 16; DLB 2;
    DLBD 6; DLBY 83; MTCW

Millay, E. Vincent
See Millay, Edna St. Vincent

Millay, Edna St. Vincent
    1892-1950 . . . . **TCLC 4**
See also CA 104; 130; CDALB 1917-1929;
    DLB 45; MTCW

Miller, Arthur
    1915- . . . . . . **CLC 1, 2, 6, 10, 15, 26, 47;
                                            DC 1**
See also AITN 1; CA 1-4R; CABS 3;
    CANR 2, 30; CDALB 1941-1968; DLB 7;
    MTCW; WLC

Miller, Henry (Valentine)
    1891-1980 . . . . **CLC 1, 2, 4, 9, 14, 43**
See also CA 9-12R; 97-100; CANR 33;
    CDALB 1929-1941; DLB 4, 9; DLBY 80;
    MTCW; WLC

Miller, Jason 1939(?)- . . . . **CLC 2**
See also AITN 1; CA 73-76; DLB 7

Miller, Sue 19(?)- . . . . **CLC 44**
See also BEST 90:3

Miller, Walter M(ichael Jr.)
    1923- . . . . **CLC 4, 30**
See also CA 85-88; DLB 8

Millett, Kate 1934- . . . . **CLC 67**
See also AITN 1; CA 73-76; CANR 32;
    MTCW

Millhauser, Steven 1943- . . . . **CLC 21, 54**
See also CA 110; 111; DLB 2

Millin, Sarah Gertrude 1889-1968 . . **CLC 49**
See also CA 102; 93-96

Milne, A(lan) A(lexander)
    1882-1956 . . . . **TCLC 6**
See also CA 104; 133; CLR 1, 26; DLB 10,
    77, 100; MAICYA; MTCW; YABC 1

Milner, Ron(ald) 1938- . . . . **CLC 56**
See also AITN 1; BLC 3; BW; CA 73-76;
    CANR 24; DLB 38; MTCW

Milosz, Czeslaw
    1911- . . . . **CLC 5, 11, 22, 31, 56**
See also CA 81-84; CANR 23; MTCW

Milton, John 1608-1674 . . . . **LC 9**
See also CDBLB 1660-1789; WLC

Minehaha, Cornelius
See Wedekind, (Benjamin) Frank(lin)

Miner, Valerie 1947- . . . . **CLC 40**
See also CA 97-100

Minimo, Duca
See D'Annunzio, Gabriele

Minot, Susan 1956- . . . . **CLC 44**
See also CA 134

Minus, Ed 1938- . . . . **CLC 39**

Miranda, Javier
See Bioy Casares, Adolfo

Miro (Ferrer), Gabriel (Francisco Victor)
    1879-1930 . . . . **TCLC 5**
See also CA 104

Mishima, Yukio
    . . . . **CLC 2, 4, 6, 9, 27; DC 1; SSC 4**
See also Hiraoka, Kimitake

Mistral, Gabriela . . . . **TCLC 2**
See also Godoy Alcayaga, Lucila

Mistry, Rohinton 1952- . . . . **CLC 71**

Mitchell, Clyde
See Ellison, Harlan; Silverberg, Robert

Mitchell, James Leslie 1901-1935
See Gibbon, Lewis Grassic
See also CA 104; DLB 15

Mitchell, Joni 1943- . . . . **CLC 12**
See also CA 112

Mitchell, Margaret (Munnerlyn)
    1900-1949 . . . . **TCLC 11**
See also CA 109; 125; DLB 9; MTCW

Mitchell, Peggy
See Mitchell, Margaret (Munnerlyn)

Mitchell, S(ilas) Weir 1829-1914 . . **TCLC 36**

Mitchell, W(illiam) O(rmond)
    1914- . . . . **CLC 25**
See also CA 77-80; CANR 15; DLB 88

Mitford, Mary Russell 1787-1855 . . **NCLC 4**
See also DLB 110, 116

Mitford, Nancy 1904-1973 . . . . **CLC 44**
See also CA 9-12R

Miyamoto, Yuriko 1899-1951 . . . . . **TCLC 37**

Mo, Timothy (Peter) 1950(?)- . . . . . . **CLC 46**
See also CA 117; MTCW

Modarressi, Taghi (M.) 1931- . . . . . . **CLC 44**
See also CA 121; 134

Modiano, Patrick (Jean) 1945- . . . . . **CLC 18**
See also CA 85-88; CANR 17; DLB 83

Moerck, Paal
See Roelvaag, O(le) E(dvart)

Mofolo, Thomas (Mokopu)
    1875(?)-1948 . . . . **TCLC 22**
See also BLC 3; CA 121

Mohr, Nicholasa 1935- . . . . **CLC 12**
See also AAYA 8; CA 49-52; CANR 1, 32;
    CLR 22; HW; SAAS 8; SATA 8

Mojtabai, A(nn) G(race)
    1938- . . . . **CLC 5, 9, 15, 29**
See also CA 85-88

Moliere 1622-1673 . . . . **LC 10**
See also WLC

Molin, Charles
See Mayne, William (James Carter)

Molnar, Ferenc 1878-1952 . . . . **TCLC 20**
See also CA 109

Momaday, N(avarre) Scott
    1934- . . . . **CLC 2, 19**
See also CA 25-28R; CANR 14, 34;
    MTCW; SATA 30, 48

Monroe, Harriet 1860-1936 . . . . **TCLC 12**
See also CA 109; DLB 54, 91

Monroe, Lyle
See Heinlein, Robert A(nson)

Montagu, Elizabeth 1917- . . . . **NCLC 7**
See also CA 9-12R

Montagu, Mary (Pierrepont) Wortley
    1689-1762 . . . . **LC 9**
See also DLB 95, 101

Montague, John (Patrick)
    1929- . . . . **CLC 13, 46**
See also CA 9-12R; CANR 9; DLB 40;
    MTCW

Montaigne, Michel (Eyquem) de
    1533-1592 . . . . **LC 8**
See also WLC

Montale, Eugenio 1896-1981 . . . **CLC 7, 9, 18**
See also CA 17-20R; 104; CANR 30;
    DLB 114; MTCW

Montesquieu, Charles-Louis de Secondat
    1689-1755 . . . . **LC 7**

Montgomery, (Robert) Bruce 1921-1978
See Crispin, Edmund
See also CA 104

Montgomery, Marion H. Jr. 1925- . . . **CLC 7**
See also AITN 1; CA 1-4R; CANR 3;
    DLB 6

Montgomery, Max
See Davenport, Guy (Mattison Jr.)

Montherlant, Henry (Milon) de
    1896-1972 . . . . **CLC 8, 19**
See also CA 85-88; 37-40R; DLB 72;
    MTCW

Python . . . . **CLC 21**
See also Chapman, Graham; Cleese, John
    (Marwood); Gilliam, Terry (Vance); Idle,
    Eric; Jones, Terence Graham Parry; Palin,
    Michael (Edward)
See also AAYA 7

Moodie, Susanna (Strickland)
    1803-1885 . . . . **NCLC 14**
See also DLB 99

Mooney, Edward 1951- . . . . **CLC 25**
See also CA 130

Mooney, Ted
See Mooney, Edward

Moorcock, Michael (John)
    1939- . . . . **CLC 5, 27, 58**
See also CA 45-48; CAAS 5; CANR 2, 17,
    38; DLB 14; MTCW

Moore, Brian
    1921- . . . . **CLC 1, 3, 5, 7, 8, 19, 32**
See also CA 1-4R; CANR 1, 25; MTCW

Moore, Edward
See Muir, Edwin

Moore, George Augustus
    1852-1933 . . . . **TCLC 7**
See also CA 104; DLB 10, 18, 57

Moore, Lorrie . . . . **CLC 39, 45, 68**
See also Moore, Marie Lorena

Moore, Marianne (Craig)
    1887-1972 . . . **CLC 1, 2, 4, 8, 10, 13, 19,
                                            47; PC 4**
See also CA 1-4R; 33-36R; CANR 3;
    CDALB 1929-1941; DLB 45; DLBD 7;
    MTCW; SATA 20

Moore, Marie Lorena 1957-
See Moore, Lorrie
See also CA 116; CANR 39

Moore, Thomas 1779-1852 . . . . **NCLC 6**
See also DLB 96

Morand, Paul 1888-1976 . . . . **CLC 41**
See also CA 69-72; DLB 65

Morante, Elsa 1918-1985....... **CLC 8, 47**
See also CA 85-88; 117; CANR 35; MTCW

Moravia, Alberto....... **CLC 2, 7, 11, 27, 46**
See also Pincherle, Alberto

More, Hannah 1745-1833 .... **NCLC 27**
See also DLB 107, 109, 116

More, Henry 1614-1687............ **LC 9**

More, Sir Thomas 1478-1535 .... **LC 10**

Moreas, Jean.................... **TCLC 18**
See also Papadiamantopoulos, Johannes

Morgan, Berry 1919-............. **CLC 6**
See also CA 49-52; DLB 6

Morgan, Claire
See Highsmith, (Mary) Patricia

Morgan, Edwin (George) 1920-..... **CLC 31**
See also CA 5-8R; CANR 3; DLB 27

Morgan, (George) Frederick
1922-...................... **CLC 23**
See also CA 17-20R; CANR 21

Morgan, Harriet
See Mencken, H(enry) L(ouis)

Morgan, Jane
See Cooper, James Fenimore

Morgan, Janet 1945-............. **CLC 39**
See also CA 65-68

Morgan, Lady 1776(?)-1859...... **NCLC 29**
See also DLB 116

Morgan, Robin 1941-............. **CLC 2**
See also CA 69-72; CANR 29; MTCW

Morgan, Scott
See Kuttner, Henry

Morgan, Seth 1949(?)-1990 .... **CLC 65**
See also CA 132

Morgenstern, Christian
1871-1914 .... **TCLC 8**
See also CA 105

Morgenstern, S.
See Goldman, William (W.)

Moricz, Zsigmond 1879-1942 ..... **TCLC 33**

Morike, Eduard (Friedrich)
1804-1875 .... **NCLC 10**

Mori Ogai .... **TCLC 14**
See also Mori Rintaro

Mori Rintaro 1862-1922
See Mori Ogai
See also CA 110

Moritz, Karl Philipp 1756-1793 ...... **LC 2**
See also DLB 94

Morren, Theophil
See Hofmannsthal, Hugo von

Morris, Julian
See West, Morris L(anglo)

Morris, Steveland Judkins 1950(?)-
See Wonder, Stevie
See also CA 111

Morris, William 1834-1896 .... **NCLC 4**
See also CDBLB 1832-1890; DLB 18, 35, 57

Morris, Wright 1910-... **CLC 1, 3, 7, 18, 37**
See also CA 9-12R; CANR 21; DLB 2;
DLBY 81; MTCW

Morrison, Chloe Anthony Wofford
See Morrison, Toni

Morrison, James Douglas 1943-1971
See Morrison, Jim
See also CA 73-76

Morrison, Jim .... **CLC 17**
See also Morrison, James Douglas

Morrison, Toni 1931-..... **CLC 4, 10, 22, 55**
See also AAYA 1; BLC 3; BW; CA 29-32R;
CANR 27; CDALB 1968-1988; DLB 6,
33; DLBY 81; MTCW; SATA 57

Morrison, Van 1945-............. **CLC 21**
See also CA 116

Mortimer, John (Clifford)
1923-................... **CLC 28, 43**
See also CA 13-16R; CANR 21;
CDBLB 1960 to Present; DLB 13;
MTCW

Mortimer, Penelope (Ruth) 1918-.... **CLC 5**
See also CA 57-60

Morton, Anthony
See Creasey, John

Mosher, Howard Frank .... **CLC 62**

Mosley, Nicholas 1923-........ **CLC 43, 70**
See also CA 69-72; DLB 14

Moss, Howard
1922-1987 .... **CLC 7, 14, 45, 50**
See also CA 1-4R; 123; CANR 1; DLB 5

Motion, Andrew 1952-............ **CLC 47**
See also DLB 40

Motley, Willard (Francis)
1912-1965 .... **CLC 18**
See also BW; CA 117; 106; DLB 76

Mott, Michael (Charles Alston)
1930-.................. **CLC 15, 34**
See also CA 5-8R; CAAS 7; CANR 7, 29

Mowat, Farley (McGill) 1921- ..... **CLC 26**
See also AAYA 1; CA 1-4R; CANR 4, 24;
CLR 20; DLB 68; MAICYA; MTCW;
SATA 3, 55

Mphahlele, Es'kia
See Mphahlele, Ezekiel

Mphahlele, Ezekiel 1919-.......... **CLC 25**
See also BLC 3; BW; CA 81-84; CANR 26

Mqhayi, S(amuel) E(dward) K(rune Loliwe)
1875-1945 .... **TCLC 25**
See also BLC 3

Mr. Martin
See Burroughs, William S(eward)

Mrozek, Slawomir 1930-........ **CLC 3, 13**
See also CA 13-16R; CAAS 10; CANR 29;
MTCW

Mrs. Belloc-Lowndes
See Lowndes, Marie Adelaide (Belloc)

Mtwa, Percy (?)-................ **CLC 47**

Mueller, Lisel 1924-........... **CLC 13, 51**
See also CA 93-96; DLB 105

Muir, Edwin 1887-1959 .... **TCLC 2**
See also CA 104; DLB 20, 100

Muir, John 1838-1914 .... **TCLC 28**

Mujica Lainez, Manuel
1910-1984 .... **CLC 31**
See also Lainez, Manuel Mujica
See also CA 81-84; 112; CANR 32; HW

Mukherjee, Bharati 1940-......... **CLC 53**
See also BEST 89:2; CA 107; DLB 60;
MTCW

Muldoon, Paul 1951-.......... **CLC 32, 72**
See also CA 113; 129; DLB 40

Mulisch, Harry 1927-............. **CLC 42**
See also CA 9-12R; CANR 6, 26

Mull, Martin 1943-.............. **CLC 17**
See also CA 105

Mulock, Dinah Maria
See Craik, Dinah Maria (Mulock)

Munford, Robert 1737(?)-1783 .... **LC 5**
See also DLB 31

Mungo, Raymond 1946-........... **CLC 72**
See also CA 49-52; CANR 2

Munro, Alice
1931-........ **CLC 6, 10, 19, 50; SSC 3**
See also AITN 2; CA 33-36R; CANR 33;
DLB 53; MTCW; SATA 29

Munro, H(ector) H(ugh) 1870-1916
See Saki
See also CA 104; 130; CDBLB 1890-1914;
DLB 34; MTCW; WLC

Murasaki, Lady.................. **CMLC 1**

Murdoch, (Jean) Iris
1919- ...... **CLC 1, 2, 3, 4, 6, 8, 11, 15,
22, 31, 51**
See also CA 13-16R; CANR 8;
CDBLB 1960 to Present; DLB 14;
MTCW

Murphy, Richard 1927-........... **CLC 41**
See also CA 29-32R; DLB 40

Murphy, Sylvia 1937-............. **CLC 34**
See also CA 121

Murphy, Thomas (Bernard) 1935-... **CLC 51**
See also CA 101

Murray, Les(lie) A(llan) 1938- ..... **CLC 40**
See also CA 21-24R; CANR 11, 27

Murry, J. Middleton
See Murry, John Middleton

Murry, John Middleton
1889-1957 .... **TCLC 16**
See also CA 118

Musgrave, Susan 1951- .... **CLC 13, 54**
See also CA 69-72

Musil, Robert (Edler von)
1880-1942 .... **TCLC 12**
See also CA 109; DLB 81

Musset, (Louis Charles) Alfred de
1810-1857 .... **NCLC 7**

My Brother's Brother
See Chekhov, Anton (Pavlovich)

Myers, Walter Dean 1937- .... **CLC 35**
See also AAYA 4; BLC 3; BW; CA 33-36R;
CANR 20; CLR 4, 16; DLB 33;
MAICYA; SAAS 2; SATA 27, 41, 70, 71

Myers, Walter M.
See Myers, Walter Dean

Myles, Symon
See Follett, Ken(neth Martin)

Nabokov, Vladimir (Vladimirovich)
1899-1977 .... **CLC 1, 2, 3, 6, 8, 11, 15, 23, 44, 46, 64; SSC 11**
See also CA 5-8R; 69-72; CANR 20; CDALB 1941-1968; DLB 2; DLBD 3; DLBY 80, 91; MTCW; WLC

Nagy, Laszlo 1925-1978........... **CLC 7**
See also CA 129; 112

Naipaul, Shiva(dhar Srinivasa)
1945-1985 .... **CLC 32, 39**
See also CA 110; 112; 116; CANR 33; DLBY 85; MTCW

Naipaul, V(idiadhar) S(urajprasad)
1932- .... **CLC 4, 7, 9, 13, 18, 37**
See also CA 1-4R; CANR 1, 33; CDBLB 1960 to Present; DLBY 85; MTCW

Nakos, Lilika 1899(?)- .... **CLC 29**

Narayan, R(asipuram) K(rishnaswami)
1906- .... **CLC 7, 28, 47**
See also CA 81-84; CANR 33; MTCW; SATA 62

Nash, (Frediric) Ogden 1902-1971 .. **CLC 23**
See also CA 13-14; 29-32R; CANR 34; CAP 1; DLB 11; MAICYA; MTCW; SATA 2, 46

Nathan, Daniel
See Dannay, Frederic

Nathan, George Jean 1882-1958 ... **TCLC 18**
See also Hatteras, Owen
See also CA 114

Natsume, Kinnosuke 1867-1916
See Natsume, Soseki
See also CA 104

Natsume, Soseki .... **TCLC 2, 10**
See also Natsume, Kinnosuke

Natti, (Mary) Lee 1919-
See Kingman, Lee
See also CA 5-8R; CANR 2

Naylor, Gloria 1950- .... **CLC 28, 52**
See also AAYA 6; BLC 3; BW; CA 107; CANR 27; MTCW

Neihardt, John Gneisenau
1881-1973 .... **CLC 32**
See also CA 13-14; CAP 1; DLB 9, 54

Nekrasov, Nikolai Alekseevich
1821-1878 .... **NCLC 11**

Nelligan, Emile 1879-1941........ **TCLC 14**
See also CA 114; DLB 92

Nelson, Willie 1933-............. **CLC 17**
See also CA 107

Nemerov, Howard (Stanley)
1920-1991 .... **CLC 2, 6, 9, 36**
See also CA 1-4R; 134; CABS 2; CANR 1, 27; DLB 6; DLBY 83; MTCW

Neruda, Pablo
1904-1973 .... **CLC 1, 2, 5, 7, 9, 28, 62; PC 4**
See also CA 19-20; 45-48; CAP 2; HW; MTCW; WLC

Nerval, Gerard de 1808-1855...... **NCLC 1**

Nervo, (Jose) Amado (Ruiz de)
1870-1919 .... **TCLC 11**
See also CA 109; 131; HW

Nessi, Pio Baroja y
See Baroja (y Nessi), Pio

Neufeld, John (Arthur) 1938- ...... **CLC 17**
See also CA 25-28R; CANR 11, 37; MAICYA; SAAS 3; SATA 6

Neville, Emily Cheney 1919- ...... **CLC 12**
See also CA 5-8R; CANR 3, 37; MAICYA; SAAS 2; SATA 1

Newbound, Bernard Slade 1930-
See Slade, Bernard
See also CA 81-84

Newby, P(ercy) H(oward)
1918- .... **CLC 2, 13**
See also CA 5-8R; CANR 32; DLB 15; MTCW

Newlove, Donald 1928- .... **CLC 6**
See also CA 29-32R; CANR 25

Newlove, John (Herbert) 1938-..... **CLC 14**
See also CA 21-24R; CANR 9, 25

Newman, Charles 1938-.......... **CLC 2, 8**
See also CA 21-24R

Newman, Edwin (Harold) 1919- .... **CLC 14**
See also AITN 1; CA 69-72; CANR 5

Newman, John Henry
1801-1890 .... **NCLC 38**
See also DLB 18, 32, 55

Newton, Suzanne 1936-........... **CLC 35**
See also CA 41-44R; CANR 14; SATA 5

Nexo, Martin Andersen
1869-1954 .... **TCLC 43**

Nezval, Vitezslav 1900-1958 ...... **TCLC 44**
See also CA 123

Ngema, Mbongeni 1955- .... **CLC 57**

Ngugi, James T(hiong'o)........ **CLC 3, 7, 13**
See also Ngugi wa Thiong'o

Ngugi wa Thiong'o 1938-.......... **CLC 36**
See also Ngugi, James T(hiong'o)
See also BLC 3; BW; CA 81-84; CANR 27; MTCW

Nichol, B(arrie) P(hillip)
1944-1988 .... **CLC 18**
See also CA 53-56; DLB 53; SATA 66

Nichols, John (Treadwell) 1940- .... **CLC 38**
See also CA 9-12R; CAAS 2; CANR 6; DLBY 82

Nichols, Peter (Richard)
1927- .... **CLC 5, 36, 65**
See also CA 104; CANR 33; DLB 13; MTCW

Nicolas, F. R. E.
See Freeling, Nicolas

Niedecker, Lorine 1903-1970.... **CLC 10, 42**
See also CA 25-28; CAP 2; DLB 48

Nietzsche, Friedrich (Wilhelm)
1844-1900 .... **TCLC 10, 18**
See also CA 107; 121

Nievo, Ippolito 1831-1861 .... **NCLC 22**

Nightingale, Anne Redmon 1943-
See Redmon, Anne
See also CA 103

Nik.T.O.
See Annensky, Innokenty Fyodorovich

Nin, Anais
1903-1977 ..... **CLC 1, 4, 8, 11, 14, 60; SSC 10**
See also AITN 2; CA 13-16R; 69-72; CANR 22; DLB 2, 4; MTCW

Nissenson, Hugh 1933-........... **CLC 4, 9**
See also CA 17-20R; CANR 27; DLB 28

Niven, Larry .... **CLC 8**
See also Niven, Laurence Van Cott
See also DLB 8

Niven, Laurence Van Cott 1938-
See Niven, Larry
See also CA 21-24R; CAAS 12; CANR 14; MTCW

Nixon, Agnes Eckhardt 1927-...... **CLC 21**
See also CA 110

Nizan, Paul 1905-1940........... **TCLC 40**
See also DLB 72

Nkosi, Lewis 1936-............... **CLC 45**
See also BLC 3; BW; CA 65-68; CANR 27

Nodier, (Jean) Charles (Emmanuel)
1780-1844 .... **NCLC 19**
See also DLB 119

Nolan, Christopher 1965-......... **CLC 58**
See also CA 111

Norden, Charles
See Durrell, Lawrence (George)

Nordhoff, Charles (Bernard)
1887-1947 .... **TCLC 23**
See also CA 108; DLB 9; SATA 23

Norman, Marsha 1947- .... **CLC 28**
See also CA 105; CABS 3; DLBY 84

Norris, Benjamin Franklin Jr.
1870-1902 .... **TCLC 24**
See also Norris, Frank
See also CA 110

Norris, Frank
See Norris, Benjamin Franklin Jr.
See also CDALB 1865-1917; DLB 12, 71

Norris, Leslie 1921-............... **CLC 14**
See also CA 11-12; CANR 14; CAP 1; DLB 27

North, Andrew
See Norton, Andre

North, Captain George
See Stevenson, Robert Louis (Balfour)

North, Milou
See Erdrich, Louise

Northrup, B. A.
See Hubbard, L(afayette) Ron(ald)

North Staffs
See Hulme, T(homas) E(rnest)

Norton, Alice Mary
See Norton, Andre
See also MAICYA; SATA 1, 43

Norton, Andre 1912- .... **CLC 12**
See also Norton, Alice Mary
See also CA 1-4R; CANR 2, 31; DLB 8, 52; MTCW

Norway, Nevil Shute 1899-1960
See Shute, Nevil
See also CA 102; 93-96

Norwid, Cyprian Kamil
1821-1883 .... **NCLC 17**

Nosille, Nabrah
See Ellison, Harlan

Nossack, Hans Erich 1901-1978 ..... **CLC 6**
See also CA 93-96; 85-88; DLB 69

Nosu, Chuji
See Ozu, Yasujiro

Nova, Craig 1945-............. **CLC 7, 31**
See also CA 45-48; CANR 2

Novak, Joseph
See Kosinski, Jerzy (Nikodem)

Novalis 1772-1801 .... **NCLC 13**
See also DLB 90

Nowlan, Alden (Albert) 1933-1983 .. **CLC 15**
See also CA 9-12R; CANR 5; DLB 53

Noyes, Alfred 1880-1958 .... **TCLC 7**
See also CA 104; DLB 20

Nunn, Kem 19(?)-................ **CLC 34**

Nye, Robert 1939- .... **CLC 13, 42**
See also CA 33-36R; CANR 29; DLB 14;
MTCW; SATA 6

Nyro, Laura 1947- .... **CLC 17**

Oates, Joyce Carol
1938- ..... **CLC 1, 2, 3, 6, 9, 11, 15, 19,**
33, 52; SSC 6
See also AITN 1; BEST 89:2; CA 5-8R;
CANR 25; CDALB 1968-1988; DLB 2, 5;
DLBY 81; MTCW; WLC

O'Brien, E. G.
See Clarke, Arthur C(harles)

O'Brien, Edna
1936- .. **CLC 3, 5, 8, 13, 36, 65; SSC 10**
See also CA 1-4R; CANR 6; CDBLB 1960
to Present; DLB 14; MTCW

O'Brien, Fitz-James 1828-1862... **NCLC 21**
See also DLB 74

O'Brien, Flann........ **CLC 1, 4, 5, 7, 10, 47**
See also O Nuallain, Brian

O'Brien, Richard 1942- .... **CLC 17**
See also CA 124

O'Brien, Tim 1946-......... **CLC 7, 19, 40**
See also CA 85-88; DLBD 9; DLBY 80

Obstfelder, Sigbjoern 1866-1900... **TCLC 23**
See also CA 123

O'Casey, Sean
1880-1964 .... **CLC 1, 5, 9, 11, 15**
See also CA 89-92; CDBLB 1914-1945;
DLB 10; MTCW

O'Cathasaigh, Sean
See O'Casey, Sean

Ochs, Phil 1940-1976............. **CLC 17**
See also CA 65-68

O'Connor, Edwin (Greene)
1918-1968 .... **CLC 14**
See also CA 93-96; 25-28R

O'Connor, (Mary) Flannery
1925-1964 ... **CLC 1, 2, 3, 6, 10, 13, 15,**
21, 66; SSC 1
See also AAYA 7; CA 1-4R; CANR 3;
CDALB 1941-1968; DLB 2; DLBY 80;
MTCW; WLC

O'Connor, Frank........... **CLC 23; SSC 5**
See also O'Donovan, Michael John

O'Dell, Scott 1898-1989.......... **CLC 30**
See also AAYA 3; CA 61-64; 129;
CANR 12, 30; CLR 1, 16; DLB 52;
MAICYA; SATA 12, 60

Odets, Clifford 1906-1963 .... **CLC 2, 28**
See also CA 85-88; DLB 7, 26; MTCW

O'Donnell, K. M.
See Malzberg, Barry N(athaniel)

O'Donnell, Lawrence
See Kuttner, Henry

O'Donovan, Michael John
1903-1966 .... **CLC 14**
See also O'Connor, Frank
See also CA 93-96

Oe, Kenzaburo 1935-.......... **CLC 10, 36**
See also CA 97-100; CANR 36; MTCW

O'Faolain, Julia 1932-....... **CLC 6, 19, 47**
See also CA 81-84; CAAS 2; CANR 12;
DLB 14; MTCW

O'Faolain, Sean
1900-1991 .... **CLC 1, 7, 14, 32, 70**
See also CA 61-64; 134; CANR 12;
DLB 15; MTCW

O'Flaherty, Liam
1896-1984 .... **CLC 5, 34; SSC 6**
See also CA 101; 113; CANR 35; DLB 36;
DLBY 84; MTCW

Ogilvy, Gavin
See Barrie, J(ames) M(atthew)

O'Grady, Standish James
1846-1928 .... **TCLC 5**
See also CA 104

O'Grady, Timothy 1951-.......... **CLC 59**
See also CA 138

O'Hara, Frank 1926-1966 ..... **CLC 2, 5, 13**
See also CA 9-12R; 25-28R; CANR 33;
DLB 5, 16; MTCW

O'Hara, John (Henry)
1905-1970 .... **CLC 1, 2, 3, 6, 11, 42**
See also CA 5-8R; 25-28R; CANR 31;
CDALB 1929-1941; DLB 9, 86; DLBD 2;
MTCW

O Hehir, Diana 1922- .... **CLC 41**
See also CA 93-96

Okigbo, Christopher (Ifenayichukwu)
1932-1967 .... **CLC 25**
See also BLC 3; BW; CA 77-80; MTCW

Olds, Sharon 1942-............ **CLC 32, 39**
See also CA 101; CANR 18; DLB 120

Oldstyle, Jonathan
See Irving, Washington

Olesha, Yuri (Karlovich)
1899-1960 .... **CLC 8**
See also CA 85-88

Oliphant, Margaret (Oliphant Wilson)
1828-1897 .... **NCLC 11**
See also DLB 18

Oliver, Mary 1935-............ **CLC 19, 34**
See also CA 21-24R; CANR 9; DLB 5

Olivier, Laurence (Kerr)
1907-1989 .... **CLC 20**
See also CA 111; 129

Olsen, Tillie 1913- ..... **CLC 4, 13; SSC 11**
See also CA 1-4R; CANR 1; DLB 28;
DLBY 80; MTCW

Olson, Charles (John)
1910-1970 ..... **CLC 1, 2, 5, 6, 9, 11, 29**
See also CA 13-16; 25-28R; CABS 2;
CANR 35; CAP 1; DLB 5, 16; MTCW

Olson, Toby 1937- .... **CLC 28**
See also CA 65-68; CANR 9, 31

Olyesha, Yuri
See Olesha, Yuri (Karlovich)

Ondaatje, Michael 1943- .... **CLC 14, 29, 51**
See also CA 77-80; DLB 60

Oneal, Elizabeth 1934-
See Oneal, Zibby
See also CA 106; CANR 28; MAICYA;
SATA 30

Oneal, Zibby .... **CLC 30**
See also Oneal, Elizabeth
See also AAYA 5; CLR 13

O'Neill, Eugene (Gladstone)
1888-1953 .... **TCLC 1, 6, 27**
See also AITN 1; CA 110; 132;
CDALB 1929-1941; DLB 7; MTCW;
WLC

Onetti, Juan Carlos 1909-....... **CLC 7, 10**
See also CA 85-88; CANR 32; DLB 113;
HW; MTCW

O Nuallain, Brian 1911-1966
See O'Brien, Flann
See also CA 21-22; 25-28R; CAP 2

Oppen, George 1908-1984 .... **CLC 7, 13, 34**
See also CA 13-16R; 113; CANR 8; DLB 5

Oppenheim, E(dward) Phillips
1866-1946 .... **TCLC 45**
See also CA 111; DLB 70

Orlovitz, Gil 1918-1973 .... **CLC 22**
See also CA 77-80; 45-48; DLB 2, 5

Ortega y Gasset, Jose 1883-1955 ... **TCLC 9**
See also CA 106; 130; HW; MTCW

Ortiz, Simon J(oseph) 1941-....... **CLC 45**
See also CA 134; DLB 120

Orton, Joe .... **CLC 4, 13, 43**
See also Orton, John Kingsley
See also CDBLB 1960 to Present; DLB 13

Orton, John Kingsley 1933-1967
See Orton, Joe
See also CA 85-88; CANR 35; MTCW

Orwell, George .... **TCLC 2, 6, 15, 31**
See also Blair, Eric (Arthur)
See also CDBLB 1945-1960; DLB 15, 98;
WLC

Osborne, David
See Silverberg, Robert

Osborne, George
See Silverberg, Robert

Osborne, John (James)
1929- .... **CLC 1, 2, 5, 11, 45**
See also CA 13-16R; CANR 21;
CDBLB 1945-1960; DLB 13; MTCW;
WLC

Osborne, Lawrence 1958- .... **CLC 50**

Oshima, Nagisa 1932- .... **CLC 20**
See also CA 116; 121

Oskison, John M(ilton)
1874-1947 .... **TCLC 35**

Ossoli, Sarah Margaret (Fuller marchesa d')
1810-1850
See Fuller, Margaret
See also SATA 25

Ostrovsky, Alexander
1823-1886 .... NCLC 30

Otero, Blas de 1916- .... CLC 11
See also CA 89-92

Otto, Whitney 1955-............. CLC 70

Ouida .... TCLC 43
See also De La Ramee, (Marie) Louise
See also DLB 18

Ousmane, Sembene 1923- .... CLC 66
See also BLC 3; BW; CA 117; 125; MTCW

Ovid 43B.C.-18th cent. (?)... CMLC 7; PC 2

Owen, Wilfred 1893-1918 ..... TCLC 5, 27
See also CA 104; CDBLB 1914-1945;
DLB 20; WLC

Owens, Rochelle 1936-............. CLC 8
See also CA 17-20R; CAAS 2; CANR 39

Oz, Amos 1939- ... CLC 5, 8, 11, 27, 33, 54
See also CA 53-56; CANR 27; MTCW

Ozick, Cynthia 1928-...... CLC 3, 7, 28, 62
See also BEST 90:1; CA 17-20R; CANR 23;
DLB 28; DLBY 82; MTCW

Ozu, Yasujiro 1903-1963......... CLC 16
See also CA 112

Pacheco, C.
See Pessoa, Fernando (Antonio Nogueira)

Pa Chin
See Li Fei-kan

Pack, Robert 1929-............. CLC 13
See also CA 1-4R; CANR 3; DLB 5

Padgett, Lewis
See Kuttner, Henry

Padilla (Lorenzo), Heberto 1932-... CLC 38
See also AITN 1; CA 123; 131; HW

Page, Jimmy 1944-............... CLC 12

Page, Louise 1955-............... CLC 40

Page, P(atricia) K(athleen)
1916- .... CLC 7, 18
See also CA 53-56; CANR 4, 22; DLB 68;
MTCW

Paget, Violet 1856-1935
See Lee, Vernon
See also CA 104

Paget-Lowe, Henry
See Lovecraft, H(oward) P(hillips)

Paglia, Camille 1947-............. CLC 68

Pakenham, Antonia
See Fraser, Antonia (Pakenham)

Palamas, Kostes 1859-1943 .... TCLC 5
See also CA 105

Palazzeschi, Aldo 1885-1974...... CLC 11
See also CA 89-92; 53-56; DLB 114

Paley, Grace 1922-.... CLC 4, 6, 37; SSC 8
See also CA 25-28R; CANR 13; DLB 28;
MTCW

Palin, Michael (Edward) 1943-..... CLC 21
See also Monty Python
See also CA 107; CANR 35; SATA 67

Palliser, Charles 1947-............ CLC 65
See also CA 136

Palma, Ricardo 1833-1919....... TCLC 29

Pancake, Breece Dexter 1952-1979
See Pancake, Breece D'J
See also CA 123; 109

Pancake, Breece D'J............ CLC 29
See also Pancake, Breece Dexter

Papadiamantis, Alexandros
1851-1911 .... TCLC 29

Papadiamantopoulos, Johannes 1856-1910
See Moreas, Jean
See also CA 117

Papini, Giovanni 1881-1956....... TCLC 22
See also CA 121

Paracelsus 1493-1541.............. LC 14

Parasol, Peter
See Stevens, Wallace

Parfenie, Maria
See Codrescu, Andrei

Parini, Jay (Lee) 1948- .... CLC 54
See also CA 97-100; CAAS 16; CANR 32

Park, Jordan
See Kornbluth, C(yril) M.; Pohl, Frederik

Parker, Bert
See Ellison, Harlan

Parker, Dorothy (Rothschild)
1893-1967 .... CLC 15, 68; SSC 2
See also CA 19-20; 25-28R; CAP 2;
DLB 11, 45, 86; MTCW

Parker, Robert B(rown) 1932-...... CLC 27
See also BEST 89:4; CA 49-52; CANR 1,
26; MTCW

Parkes, Lucas
See Harris, John (Wyndham Parkes Lucas)
Beynon

Parkin, Frank 1940-............. CLC 43

Parkman, Francis Jr. 1823-1893.. NCLC 12
See also DLB 1, 30

Parks, Gordon (Alexander Buchanan)
1912- .... CLC 1, 16
See also AITN 2; BLC 3; BW; CA 41-44R;
CANR 26; DLB 33; SATA 8

Parnell, Thomas 1679-1718......... LC 3
See also DLB 94

Parra, Nicanor 1914-.............. CLC 2
See also CA 85-88; CANR 32; HW; MTCW

Parson Lot
See Kingsley, Charles

Partridge, Anthony
See Oppenheim, E(dward) Phillips

Pascoli, Giovanni 1855-1912 ..... TCLC 45

Pasolini, Pier Paolo
1922-1975 .... CLC 20, 37
See also CA 93-96; 61-64; MTCW

Pasquini
See Silone, Ignazio

Pastan, Linda (Olenik) 1932- ...... CLC 27
See also CA 61-64; CANR 18; DLB 5

Pasternak, Boris (Leonidovich)
1890-1960 .... CLC 7, 10, 18, 63
See also CA 127; 116; MTCW; WLC

Patchen, Kenneth 1911-1972... CLC 1, 2, 18
See also CA 1-4R; 33-36R; CANR 3, 35;
DLB 16, 48; MTCW

Pater, Walter (Horatio)
1839-1894 .... NCLC 7
See also CDBLB 1832-1890; DLB 57

Paterson, A(ndrew) B(arton)
1864-1941 .... TCLC 32

Paterson, Katherine (Womeldorf)
1932- .... CLC 12, 30
See also AAYA 1; CA 21-24R; CANR 28;
CLR 7; DLB 52; MAICYA; MTCW;
SATA 13, 53

Patmore, Coventry Kersey Dighton
1823-1896 .... NCLC 9
See also DLB 35, 98

Paton, Alan (Stewart)
1903-1988 ....CLC 4, 10, 25, 55
See also CA 13-16; 125; CANR 22; CAP 1;
MTCW; SATA 11, 56; WLC

Paton Walsh, Gillian 1939-
See Walsh, Jill Paton
See also CANR 38; MAICYA; SAAS 3;
SATA 4

Paulding, James Kirke 1778-1860.. NCLC 2
See also DLB 3, 59, 74

Paulin, Thomas Neilson 1949-
See Paulin, Tom
See also CA 123; 128

Paulin, Tom...................... CLC 37
See also Paulin, Thomas Neilson
See also DLB 40

Paustovsky, Konstantin (Georgievich)
1892-1968 .... CLC 40
See also CA 93-96; 25-28R

Pavese, Cesare 1908-1950 .... TCLC 3
See also CA 104

Pavic, Milorad 1929-............. CLC 60
See also CA 136

Payne, Alan
See Jakes, John (William)

Paz, Gil
See Lugones, Leopoldo

Paz, Octavio
1914- ...... CLC 3, 4, 6, 10, 19, 51, 65;
PC 1
See also CA 73-76; CANR 32; DLBY 90;
HW; MTCW; WLC

Peacock, Molly 1947-............. CLC 60
See also CA 103; DLB 120

Peacock, Thomas Love
1785-1866 .... NCLC 22
See also DLB 96, 116

Peake, Mervyn 1911-1968....... CLC 7, 54
See also CA 5-8R; 25-28R; CANR 3;
DLB 15; MTCW; SATA 23

Pearce, Philippa .... CLC 21
See also Christie, (Ann) Philippa
See also CLR 9; MAICYA; SATA 1, 67

Pearl, Eric
See Elman, Richard

Pearson, T(homas) R(eid) 1956- .... CLC 39
See also CA 120; 130

Peck, John 1941- .... CLC 3
See also CA 49-52; CANR 3

Peck, Richard (Wayne) 1934-...... CLC 21
See also AAYA 1; CA 85-88; CANR 19,
38; MAICYA; SAAS 2; SATA 18, 55

Peck, Robert Newton 1928-........ CLC 17
  See also AAYA 3; CA 81-84; CANR 31;
  MAICYA; SAAS 1; SATA 21, 62

Peckinpah, (David) Sam(uel)
  1925-1984 .... CLC 20
  See also CA 109; 114

Pedersen, Knut 1859-1952
  See Hamsun, Knut
  See also CA 104; 119; MTCW

Peeslake, Gaffer
  See Durrell, Lawrence (George)

Peguy, Charles Pierre
  1873-1914 .... TCLC 10
  See also CA 107

Pena, Ramon del Valle y
  See Valle-Inclan, Ramon (Maria) del

Pendennis, Arthur Esquir
  See Thackeray, William Makepeace

Pepys, Samuel 1633-1703.......... LC 11
  See also CDBLB 1660-1789; DLB 101;
  WLC

Percy, Walker
  1916-1990 ... CLC 2, 3, 6, 8, 14, 18, 47,
                                         65
  See also CA 1-4R; 131; CANR 1, 23;
  DLB 2; DLBY 80, 90; MTCW

Perec, Georges 1936-1982 .... CLC 56
  See also DLB 83

Pereda (y Sanchez de Porrua), Jose Maria de
  1833-1906 .... TCLC 16
  See also CA 117

Pereda y Porrua, Jose Maria de
  See Pereda (y Sanchez de Porrua), Jose
  Maria de

Peregoy, George Weems
  See Mencken, H(enry) L(ouis)

Perelman, S(idney) J(oseph)
  1904-1979 ... CLC 3, 5, 9, 15, 23, 44, 49
  See also AITN 1, 2; CA 73-76; 89-92;
  CANR 18; DLB 11, 44; MTCW

Peret, Benjamin 1899-1959 .... TCLC 20
  See also CA 117

Peretz, Isaac Loeb 1851(?)-1915... TCLC 16
  See also CA 109

Peretz, Yitzkhok Leibush
  See Peretz, Isaac Loeb

Perez Galdos, Benito 1843-1920 ... TCLC 27
  See also CA 125; HW

Perrault, Charles 1628-1703 .... LC 2
  See also MAICYA; SATA 25

Perry, Brighton
  See Sherwood, Robert E(mmet)

Perse, Saint-John
  See Leger, (Marie-Rene) Alexis Saint-Leger

Perse, St.-John .... CLC 4, 11, 46
  See also Leger, (Marie-Rene) Alexis
  Saint-Leger

Peseenz, Tulio F.
  See Lopez y Fuentes, Gregorio

Pesetsky, Bette 1932-............ CLC 28
  See also CA 133

Peshkov, Alexei Maximovich 1868-1936
  See Gorky, Maxim
  See also CA 105

Pessoa, Fernando (Antonio Nogueira)
  1888-1935 .... TCLC 27
  See also CA 125

Peterkin, Julia Mood 1880-1961.... CLC 31
  See also CA 102; DLB 9

Peters, Joan K. 1945-............ CLC 39

Peters, Robert L(ouis) 1924-........ CLC 7
  See also CA 13-16R; CAAS 8; DLB 105

Petofi, Sandor 1823-1849........... NCLC 21

Petrakis, Harry Mark 1923-......... CLC 3
  See also CA 9-12R; CANR 4, 30

Petrov, Evgeny .... TCLC 21
  See also Kataev, Evgeny Petrovich

Petry, Ann (Lane) 1908- ...... CLC 1, 7, 18
  See also BW; CA 5-8R; CAAS 6; CANR 4;
  CLR 12; DLB 76; MAICYA; MTCW;
  SATA 5

Petursson, Halligrimur 1614-1674 .... LC 8

Philipson, Morris H. 1926-........ CLC 53
  See also CA 1-4R; CANR 4

Phillips, David Graham
  1867-1911 .... TCLC 44
  See also CA 108; DLB 9, 12

Phillips, Jack
  See Sandburg, Carl (August)

Phillips, Jayne Anne 1952- ..... CLC 15, 33
  See also CA 101; CANR 24; DLBY 80;
  MTCW

Phillips, Richard
  See Dick, Philip K(indred)

Phillips, Robert (Schaeffer) 1938-... CLC 28
  See also CA 17-20R; CAAS 13; CANR 8;
  DLB 105

Phillips, Ward
  See Lovecraft, H(oward) P(hillips)

Piccolo, Lucio 1901-1969.......... CLC 13
  See also CA 97-100; DLB 114

Pickthall, Marjorie L(owry) C(hristie)
  1883-1922 .... TCLC 21
  See also CA 107; DLB 92

Pico della Mirandola, Giovanni
  1463-1494 .... LC 15

Piercy, Marge
  1936- .... CLC 3, 6, 14, 18, 27, 62
  See also CA 21-24R; CAAS 1; CANR 13;
  DLB 120; MTCW

Piers, Robert
  See Anthony, Piers

Pieyre de Mandiargues, Andre 1909-1991
  See Mandiargues, Andre Pieyre de
  See also CA 103; 136; CANR 22

Pilnyak, Boris .... TCLC 23
  See also Vogau, Boris Andreyevich

Pincherle, Alberto 1907-1990 ... CLC 11, 18
  See also Moravia, Alberto
  See also CA 25-28R; 132; CANR 33;
  MTCW

Pineda, Cecile 1942-............. CLC 39
  See also CA 118

Pinero, Arthur Wing 1855-1934 ... TCLC 32
  See also CA 110; DLB 10

Pinero, Miguel (Antonio Gomez)
  1946-1988 .... CLC 4, 55
  See also CA 61-64; 125; CANR 29; HW

Pinget, Robert 1919- .... CLC 7, 13, 37
  See also CA 85-88; DLB 83

Floyd .... CLC 35
  See also Barrett, (Roger) Syd; Gilmour,
  David; Mason, Nick; Waters, Roger;
  Wright, Rick

Pinkney, Edward 1802-1828 ..... NCLC 31

Pinkwater, Daniel Manus 1941- .... CLC 35
  See also Pinkwater, Manus
  See also AAYA 1; CA 29-32R; CANR 12,
  38; CLR 4; MAICYA; SAAS 3; SATA 46

Pinkwater, Manus
  See Pinkwater, Daniel Manus
  See also SATA 8

Pinsky, Robert 1940-........ CLC 9, 19, 38
  See also CA 29-32R; CAAS 4; DLBY 82

Pinta, Harold
  See Pinter, Harold

Pinter, Harold
  1930- ..... CLC 1, 3, 6, 9, 11, 15, 27, 58
  See also CA 5-8R; CANR 33; CDBLB 1960
  to Present; DLB 13; MTCW; WLC

Pirandello, Luigi 1867-1936..... TCLC 4, 29
  See also CA 104; WLC

Pirsig, Robert M(aynard) 1928- ... CLC 4, 6
  See also CA 53-56; MTCW; SATA 39

Pisarev, Dmitry Ivanovich
  1840-1868 .... NCLC 25

Pix, Mary (Griffith) 1666-1709....... LC 8
  See also DLB 80

Plaidy, Jean
  See Hibbert, Eleanor Burford

Plant, Robert 1948- .... CLC 12

Plante, David (Robert)
  1940- .... CLC 7, 23, 38
  See also CA 37-40R; CANR 12, 36;
  DLBY 83; MTCW

Plath, Sylvia
  1932-1963 .... CLC 1, 2, 3, 5, 9, 11, 14,
                         17, 50, 51, 62; PC 1
  See also CA 19-20; CANR 34; CAP 2;
  CDALB 1941-1968; DLB 5, 6; MTCW;
  WLC

Plato 428(?)B.C.-348(?)B.C........ CMLC 8

Platonov, Andrei .... TCLC 14
  See also Klimentov, Andrei Platonovich

Platt, Kin 1911- .... CLC 26
  See also CA 17-20R; CANR 11; SATA 21

Plick et Plock
  See Simenon, Georges (Jacques Christian)

Plimpton, George (Ames) 1927-..... CLC 36
  See also AITN 1; CA 21-24R; CANR 32;
  MTCW; SATA 10

Plomer, William Charles Franklin
  1903-1973 .... CLC 4, 8
  See also CA 21-22; CANR 34; CAP 2;
  DLB 20; MTCW; SATA 24

Plowman, Piers
  See Kavanagh, Patrick (Joseph)

Plum, J.
  See Wodehouse, P(elham) G(renville)

Plumly, Stanley (Ross) 1939- ...... CLC 33
  See also CA 108; 110; DLB 5

Poe, Edgar Allan
1809-1849 ... **NCLC 1, 16; PC 1; SSC 1**
See also CDALB 1640-1865; DLB 3, 59, 73,
74; SATA 23; WLC

Poet of Titchfield Street, The
See Pound, Ezra (Weston Loomis)

Pohl, Frederik 1919- .... **CLC 18**
See also CA 61-64; CAAS 1; CANR 11, 37;
DLB 8; MTCW; SATA 24

Poirier, Louis 1910-
See Gracq, Julien
See also CA 122; 126

Poitier, Sidney 1927- .... **CLC 26**
See also BW; CA 117

Polanski, Roman 1933- .... **CLC 16**
See also CA 77-80

Poliakoff, Stephen 1952- .... **CLC 38**
See also CA 106; DLB 13

.... **CLC 26**
See also Copeland, Stewart (Armstrong);
Summers, Andrew James; Sumner,
Gordon Matthew

Pollitt, Katha 1949- .... **CLC 28**
See also CA 120; 122; MTCW

Pollock, Sharon 1936- .... **CLC 50**
See also DLB 60

Pomerance, Bernard 1940-........ **CLC 13**
See also CA 101

Ponge, Francis (Jean Gaston Alfred)
1899-1988 .... **CLC 6, 18**
See also CA 85-88; 126

Pontoppidan, Henrik 1857-1943 ... **TCLC 29**

Poole, Josephine .... **CLC 17**
See also Helyar, Jane Penelope Josephine
See also SAAS 2; SATA 5

Popa, Vasko 1922- .... **CLC 19**
See also CA 112

Pope, Alexander 1688-1744.......... **LC 3**
See also CDBLB 1660-1789; DLB 95, 101;
WLC

Porter, Connie 1960- .... **CLC 70**

Porter, Gene(va Grace) Stratton
1863(?)-1924 .... **TCLC 21**
See also CA 112

Porter, Katherine Anne
1890-1980 ..... **CLC 1, 3, 7, 10, 13, 15,
27; SSC 4**
See also AITN 2; CA 1-4R; 101; CANR 1;
DLB 4, 9, 102; DLBY 80; MTCW;
SATA 23, 39

Porter, Peter (Neville Frederick)
1929- .... **CLC 5, 13, 33**
See also CA 85-88; DLB 40

Porter, William Sydney 1862-1910
See Henry, O.
See also CA 104; 131; CDALB 1865-1917;
DLB 12, 78, 79; MTCW; YABC 2

Portillo (y Pacheco), Jose Lopez
See Lopez Portillo (y Pacheco), Jose

Post, Melville Davisson
1869-1930 .... **TCLC 39**
See also CA 110

Potok, Chaim 1929- .... **CLC 2, 7, 14, 26**
See also AITN 1, 2; CA 17-20R; CANR 19,
35; DLB 28; MTCW; SATA 33

Potter, Beatrice
See Webb, (Martha) Beatrice (Potter)
See also MAICYA

Potter, Dennis (Christopher George)
1935- .... **CLC 58**
See also CA 107; CANR 33; MTCW

Pound, Ezra (Weston Loomis)
1885-1972 ..... **CLC 1, 2, 3, 4, 5, 7, 10,
13, 18, 34, 48, 50; PC 4**
See also CA 5-8R; 37-40R;
CDALB 1917-1929; DLB 4, 45, 63;
MTCW; WLC

Povod, Reinaldo 1959- .... **CLC 44**
See also CA 136

Powell, Anthony (Dymoke)
1905- .... **CLC 1, 3, 7, 9, 10, 31**
See also CA 1-4R; CANR 1, 32;
CDBLB 1945-1960; DLB 15; MTCW

Powell, Dawn 1897-1965 .... **CLC 66**
See also CA 5-8R

Powell, Padgett 1952-............. **CLC 34**
See also CA 126

Powers, J(ames) F(arl)
1917- .... **CLC 1, 4, 8, 57; SSC 4**
See also CA 1-4R; CANR 2; MTCW

Powers, John J(ames) 1945-
See Powers, John R.
See also CA 69-72

Powers, John R. .... **CLC 66**
See also Powers, John J(ames)

Pownall, David 1938-............. **CLC 10**
See also CA 89-92; DLB 14

Powys, John Cowper
1872-1963 .... **CLC 7, 9, 15, 46**
See also CA 85-88; DLB 15; MTCW

Powys, T(heodore) F(rancis)
1875-1953 .... **TCLC 9**
See also CA 106; DLB 36

Prager, Emily 1952-.............. **CLC 56**

Pratt, Edwin John 1883-1964 ...... **CLC 19**
See also CA 93-96; DLB 92

Premchand...................... **TCLC 21**
See also Srivastava, Dhanpat Rai

Preussler, Otfried 1923-........... **CLC 17**
See also CA 77-80; SATA 24

Prevert, Jacques (Henri Marie)
1900-1977 .... **CLC 15**
See also CA 77-80; 69-72; CANR 29;
MTCW; SATA 30

Prevost, Abbe (Antoine Francois)
1697-1763 .... **LC 1**

Price, (Edward) Reynolds
1933- .... **CLC 3, 6, 13, 43, 50, 63**
See also CA 1-4R; CANR 1, 37; DLB 2

Price, Richard 1949- .... **CLC 6, 12**
See also CA 49-52; CANR 3; DLBY 81

Prichard, Katharine Susannah
1883-1969 .... **CLC 46**
See also CA 11-12; CANR 33; CAP 1;
MTCW; SATA 66

Priestley, J(ohn) B(oynton)
1894-1984 .... **CLC 2, 5, 9, 34**
See also CA 9-12R; 113; CANR 33;
CDBLB 1914-1945; DLB 10, 34, 77, 100;
DLBY 84; MTCW

Prince, F(rank) T(empleton) 1912- .. **CLC 22**
See also CA 101; DLB 20

Prince 1958(?)- .... **CLC 35**

Prince Kropotkin
See Kropotkin, Peter (Aleksieevich)

Prior, Matthew 1664-1721........... **LC 4**
See also DLB 95

Pritchard, William H(arrison)
1932- .... **CLC 34**
See also CA 65-68; CANR 23; DLB 111

Pritchett, V(ictor) S(awdon)
1900- .... **CLC 5, 13, 15, 41**
See also CA 61-64; CANR 31; DLB 15;
MTCW

Private 19022
See Manning, Frederic

Probst, Mark 1925- .... **CLC 59**
See also CA 130

Prokosch, Frederic 1908-1989.... **CLC 4, 48**
See also CA 73-76; 128; DLB 48

Prophet, The
See Dreiser, Theodore (Herman Albert)

Prose, Francine 1947-............. **CLC 45**
See also CA 109; 112

Proudhon
See Cunha, Euclides (Rodrigues Pimenta) da

**Proust,
(Valentin-Louis-George-Eugene-)Marcel**
1871-1922 .... **TCLC 7, 13, 33**
See also CA 104; 120; DLB 65; MTCW;
WLC

Prowler, Harley
See Masters, Edgar Lee

Pryor, Richard (Franklin Lenox Thomas)
1940- .... **CLC 26**
See also CA 122

Przybyszewski, Stanislaw
1868-1927 .... **TCLC 36**
See also DLB 66

Pteleon
See Grieve, C(hristopher) M(urray)

Puckett, Lute
See Masters, Edgar Lee

Puig, Manuel
1932-1990 .... **CLC 3, 5, 10, 28, 65**
See also CA 45-48; CANR 2, 32; DLB 113;
HW; MTCW

Purdy, A(lfred) W(ellington)
1918- .... **CLC 3, 6, 14, 50**
See also Purdy, Al
See also CA 81-84

Purdy, Al
See Purdy, A(lfred) W(ellington)
See also DLB 88

Purdy, James (Amos)
1923- .... **CLC 2, 4, 10, 28, 52**
See also CA 33-36R; CAAS 1; CANR 19;
DLB 2; MTCW

Pure, Simon
See Swinnerton, Frank Arthur

Pushkin, Alexander (Sergeyevich)
1799-1837 .... **NCLC 3, 27**
See also SATA 61; WLC

P'u Sung-ling 1640-1715 .... **LC 3**

Putnam, Arthur Lee
See Alger, Horatio Jr.

Puzo, Mario 1920- .... **CLC 1, 2, 6, 36**
See also CA 65-68; CANR 4; DLB 6;
MTCW

Pym, Barbara (Mary Crampton)
1913-1980 .... **CLC 13, 19, 37**
See also CA 13-14; 97-100; CANR 13, 34;
CAP 1; DLB 14; DLBY 87; MTCW

Pynchon, Thomas (Ruggles Jr.)
1937- .. **CLC 2, 3, 6, 9, 11, 18, 33, 62, 72**
See also BEST 90:2; CA 17-20R; CANR 22;
DLB 2; MTCW; WLC

Qian Zhongshu
See Ch'ien Chung-shu

Qroll
See Dagerman, Stig (Halvard)

Quarrington, Paul (Lewis) 1953-.... **CLC 65**
See also CA 129

Quasimodo, Salvatore 1901-1968 ... **CLC 10**
See also CA 13-16; 25-28R; CAP 1;
DLB 114; MTCW

Queen, Ellery.................. **CLC 3, 11**
See also Dannay, Frederic; Davidson,
Avram; Lee, Manfred B(ennington);
Sturgeon, Theodore (Hamilton); Vance,
John Holbrook

Queen, Ellery Jr.
See Dannay, Frederic; Lee, Manfred
B(ennington)

Queneau, Raymond
1903-1976 .... **CLC 2, 5, 10, 42**
See also CA 77-80; 69-72; CANR 32;
DLB 72; MTCW

Quin, Ann (Marie) 1936-1973 .... **CLC 6**
See also CA 9-12R; 45-48; DLB 14

Quinn, Martin
See Smith, Martin Cruz

Quinn, Simon
See Smith, Martin Cruz

Quiroga, Horacio (Sylvestre)
1878-1937 .... **TCLC 20**
See also CA 117; 131; HW; MTCW

Quoirez, Francoise 1935-........... **CLC 9**
See also Sagan, Francoise
See also CA 49-52; CANR 6, 39; MTCW

Raabe, Wilhelm 1831-1910 .... **TCLC 45**

Rabe, David (William) 1940-... **CLC 4, 8, 33**
See also CA 85-88; CABS 3; DLB 7

Rabelais, Francois 1483-1553 .... **LC 5**
See also WLC

Rabinovitch, Sholem 1859-1916
See Aleichem, Sholom
See also CA 104

Radcliffe, Ann (Ward) 1764-1823 .. **NCLC 6**
See also DLB 39

Radiguet, Raymond 1903-1923 .... **TCLC 29**
See also DLB 65

Radnoti, Miklos 1909-1944 .... **TCLC 16**
See also CA 118

Rado, James 1939-............... **CLC 17**
See also CA 105

Radvanyi, Netty 1900-1983
See Seghers, Anna
See also CA 85-88; 110

Raeburn, John (Hay) 1941-........ **CLC 34**
See also CA 57-60

Ragni, Gerome 1942-1991 .... **CLC 17**
See also CA 105; 134

Rahv, Philip..................... **CLC 24**
See also Greenberg, Ivan

Raine, Craig 1944- .... **CLC 32**
See also CA 108; CANR 29; DLB 40

Raine, Kathleen (Jessie) 1908- ... **CLC 7, 45**
See also CA 85-88; DLB 20; MTCW

Rainis, Janis 1865-1929 .... **TCLC 29**

Rakosi, Carl..................... **CLC 47**
See also Rawley, Callman
See also CAAS 5

Raleigh, Richard
See Lovecraft, H(oward) P(hillips)

Rallentando, H. P.
See Sayers, Dorothy L(eigh)

Ramal, Walter
See de la Mare, Walter (John)

Ramon, Juan
See Jimenez (Mantecon), Juan Ramon

Ramos, Graciliano 1892-1953 ..... **TCLC 32**

Rampersad, Arnold 1941-......... **CLC 44**
See also CA 127; 133; DLB 111

Rampling, Anne
See Rice, Anne

Ramuz, Charles-Ferdinand
1878-1947 .... **TCLC 33**

Rand, Ayn 1905-1982........ **CLC 3, 30, 44**
See also CA 13-16R; 105; CANR 27;
MTCW; WLC

Randall, Dudley (Felker) 1914-...... **CLC 1**
See also BLC 3; BW; CA 25-28R;
CANR 23; DLB 41

Randall, Robert
See Silverberg, Robert

Ranger, Ken
See Creasey, John

Ransom, John Crowe
1888-1974 .... **CLC 2, 4, 5, 11, 24**
See also CA 5-8R; 49-52; CANR 6, 34;
DLB 45, 63; MTCW

Rao, Raja 1909- .... **CLC 25, 56**
See also CA 73-76; MTCW

Raphael, Frederic (Michael)
1931- .... **CLC 2, 14**
See also CA 1-4R; CANR 1; DLB 14

Ratcliffe, James P.
See Mencken, H(enry) L(ouis)

Rathbone, Julian 1935- .... **CLC 41**
See also CA 101; CANR 34

Rattigan, Terence (Mervyn)
1911-1977 .... **CLC 7**
See also CA 85-88; 73-76;
CDBLB 1945-1960; DLB 13; MTCW

Ratushinskaya, Irina 1954- .... **CLC 54**
See also CA 129

Raven, Simon (Arthur Noel)
1927- .... **CLC 14**
See also CA 81-84

Rawley, Callman 1903-
See Rakosi, Carl
See also CA 21-24R; CANR 12, 32

Rawlings, Marjorie Kinnan
1896-1953 .... **TCLC 4**
See also CA 104; 137; DLB 9, 22, 102;
MAICYA; YABC 1

Ray, Satyajit 1921-............... **CLC 16**
See also CA 114; 137

Read, Herbert Edward 1893-1968.... **CLC 4**
See also CA 85-88; 25-28R; DLB 20

Read, Piers Paul 1941- ...... **CLC 4, 10, 25**
See also CA 21-24R; CANR 38; DLB 14;
SATA 21

Reade, Charles 1814-1884 .... **NCLC 2**
See also DLB 21

Reade, Hamish
See Gray, Simon (James Holliday)

Reading, Peter 1946-............. **CLC 47**
See also CA 103; DLB 40

Reaney, James 1926- .... **CLC 13**
See also CA 41-44R; CAAS 15; DLB 68;
SATA 43

Rebreanu, Liviu 1885-1944 .... **TCLC 28**

Rechy, John (Francisco)
1934-.............. **CLC 1, 7, 14, 18**
See also CA 5-8R; CAAS 4; CANR 6, 32;
DLBY 82; HW

Redcam, Tom 1870-1933 .... **TCLC 25**

Reddin, Keith.................... **CLC 67**

Redgrove, Peter (William)
1932- .... **CLC 6, 41**
See also CA 1-4R; CANR 3, 39; DLB 40

Redmon, Anne................... **CLC 22**
See also Nightingale, Anne Redmon
See also DLBY 86

Reed, Eliot
See Ambler, Eric

Reed, Ishmael
1938- .... **CLC 2, 3, 5, 6, 13, 32, 60**
See also BLC 3; BW; CA 21-24R;
CANR 25; DLB 2, 5, 33; DLBD 8;
MTCW

Reed, John (Silas) 1887-1920 ...... **TCLC 9**
See also CA 106

Reed, Lou....................... **CLC 21**
See also Firbank, Louis

Reeve, Clara 1729-1807 .... **NCLC 19**
See also DLB 39

Reid, Christopher 1949-........... **CLC 33**
See also DLB 40

Reid, Desmond
See Moorcock, Michael (John)

Reid Banks, Lynne 1929-
See Banks, Lynne Reid
See also CA 1-4R; CANR 6, 22, 38;
CLR 24; MAICYA; SATA 22

Reilly, William K.
See Creasey, John

Reiner, Max
  See Caldwell, (Janet Miriam) Taylor
  (Holland)

Reis, Ricardo
  See Pessoa, Fernando (Antonio Nogueira)

Remarque, Erich Maria
  1898-1970 .... **CLC 21**
  See also CA 77-80; 29-32R; DLB 56;
  MTCW

Remizov, A.
  See Remizov, Aleksei (Mikhailovich)

Remizov, A. M.
  See Remizov, Aleksei (Mikhailovich)

Remizov, Aleksei (Mikhailovich)
  1877-1957 .... **TCLC 27**
  See also CA 125; 133

Renan, Joseph Ernest
  1823-1892 .... **NCLC 26**

Renard, Jules 1864-1910 .... **TCLC 17**
  See also CA 117

Renault, Mary .... **CLC 3, 11, 17**
  See also Challans, Mary
  See also DLBY 83

Rendell, Ruth (Barbara) 1930- .. **CLC 28, 48**
  See also Vine, Barbara
  See also CA 109; CANR 32; DLB 87;
  MTCW

Renoir, Jean 1894-1979 .... **CLC 20**
  See also CA 129; 85-88

Resnais, Alain 1922- .... **CLC 16**

Reverdy, Pierre 1889-1960 .... **CLC 53**
  See also CA 97-100; 89-92

Rexroth, Kenneth
  1905-1982 ..... **CLC 1, 2, 6, 11, 22, 49**
  See also CA 5-8R; 107; CANR 14, 34;
  CDALB 1941-1968; DLB 16, 48;
  DLBY 82; MTCW

Reyes, Alfonso 1889-1959 .... **TCLC 33**
  See also CA 131; HW

Reyes y Basoalto, Ricardo Eliecer Neftali
  See Neruda, Pablo

Reymont, Wladyslaw (Stanislaw)
  1868(?)-1925 .... **TCLC 5**
  See also CA 104

Reynolds, Jonathan 1942- .... **CLC 6, 38**
  See also CA 65-68; CANR 28

Reynolds, Joshua 1723-1792 .... **LC 15**
  See also DLB 104

Reynolds, Michael Shane 1937- .... **CLC 44**
  See also CA 65-68; CANR 9

Reznikoff, Charles 1894-1976 .... **CLC 9**
  See also CA 33-36; 61-64; CAP 2; DLB 28,
  45

Rezzori (d'Arezzo), Gregor von
  1914- .... **CLC 25**
  See also CA 122; 136

Rhine, Richard
  See Silverstein, Alvin

Rhys, Jean
  1890(?)-1979 .... **CLC 2, 4, 6, 14, 19, 51**
  See also CA 25-28R; 85-88; CANR 35;
  CDBLB 1945-1960; DLB 36, 117; MTCW

Ribeiro, Darcy 1922- .... **CLC 34**
  See also CA 33-36R

Ribeiro, Joao Ubaldo (Osorio Pimentel)
  1941- .... **CLC 10, 67**
  See also CA 81-84

Ribman, Ronald (Burt) 1932- .... **CLC 7**
  See also CA 21-24R

Ricci, Nino 1959- .... **CLC 70**
  See also CA 137

Rice, Anne 1941- .... **CLC 41**
  See also AAYA 9; BEST 89:2; CA 65-68;
  CANR 12, 36

Rice, Elmer (Leopold)
  1892-1967 .... **CLC 7, 49**
  See also CA 21-22; 25-28R; CAP 2; DLB 4,
  7; MTCW

Rice, Tim 1944- .... **CLC 21**
  See also CA 103

Rich, Adrienne (Cecile)
  1929- ..... **CLC 3, 6, 7, 11, 18, 36; PC 5**
  See also CA 9-12R; CANR 20; DLB 5, 67;
  MTCW

Rich, Barbara
  See Graves, Robert (von Ranke)

Rich, Robert
  See Trumbo, Dalton

Richards, David Adams 1950- ...... **CLC 59**
  See also CA 93-96; DLB 53

Richards, I(vor) A(rmstrong)
  1893-1979 .... **CLC 14, 24**
  See also CA 41-44R; 89-92; CANR 34;
  DLB 27

Richardson, Anne
  See Roiphe, Anne Richardson

Richardson, Dorothy Miller
  1873-1957 .... **TCLC 3**
  See also CA 104; DLB 36

Richardson, Ethel Florence (Lindesay)
  1870-1946
  See Richardson, Henry Handel
  See also CA 105

Richardson, Henry Handel .... **TCLC 4**
  See also Richardson, Ethel Florence
  (Lindesay)

Richardson, Samuel 1689-1761 .... **LC 1**
  See also CDBLB 1660-1789; DLB 39; WLC

Richler, Mordecai
  1931- ...... **CLC 3, 5, 9, 13, 18, 46, 70**
  See also AITN 1; CA 65-68; CANR 31;
  CLR 17; DLB 53; MAICYA; MTCW;
  SATA 27, 44

Richter, Conrad (Michael)
  1890-1968 .... **CLC 30**
  See also CA 5-8R; 25-28R; CANR 23;
  DLB 9; MTCW; SATA 3

Riddell, J. H. 1832-1906 .... **TCLC 40**

Riding, Laura .... **CLC 3, 7**
  See also Jackson, Laura (Riding)

Riefenstahl, Berta Helene Amalia 1902-
  See Riefenstahl, Leni
  See also CA 108

Riefenstahl, Leni .... **CLC 16**
  See also Riefenstahl, Berta Helene Amalia

Riffe, Ernest
  See Bergman, (Ernst) Ingmar

Riley, Tex
  See Creasey, John

Rilke, Rainer Maria
  1875-1926 .... **TCLC 1, 6, 19; PC 2**
  See also CA 104; 132; DLB 81; MTCW

Rimbaud, (Jean Nicolas) Arthur
  1854-1891 .... **NCLC 4, 35; PC 3**
  See also WLC

Ringmaster, The
  See Mencken, H(enry) L(ouis)

Ringwood, Gwen(dolyn Margaret) Pharis
  1910-1984 .... **CLC 48**
  See also CA 112; DLB 88

Rio, Michel 19(?)- .... **CLC 43**

Ritsos, Giannes
  See Ritsos, Yannis

Ritsos, Yannis 1909-1990..... **CLC 6, 13, 31**
  See also CA 77-80; 133; CANR 39; MTCW

Ritter, Erika 1948(?)- .... **CLC 52**

Rivera, Jose Eustasio 1889-1928... **TCLC 35**
  See also HW

Rivers, Conrad Kent 1933-1968...... **CLC 1**
  See also BW; CA 85-88; DLB 41

Rivers, Elfrida
  See Bradley, Marion Zimmer

Riverside, John
  See Heinlein, Robert A(nson)

Rizal, Jose 1861-1896........... **NCLC 27**

Roa Bastos, Augusto (Antonio)
  1917- .... **CLC 45**
  See also CA 131; DLB 113; HW

Robbe-Grillet, Alain
  1922- ...... **CLC 1, 2, 4, 6, 8, 10, 14, 43**
  See also CA 9-12R; CANR 33; DLB 83;
  MTCW

Robbins, Harold 1916- .... **CLC 5**
  See also CA 73-76; CANR 26; MTCW

Robbins, Thomas Eugene 1936-
  See Robbins, Tom
  See also CA 81-84; CANR 29; MTCW

Robbins, Tom .... **CLC 9, 32, 64**
  See also Robbins, Thomas Eugene
  See also BEST 90:3; DLBY 80

Robbins, Trina 1938- .... **CLC 21**
  See also CA 128

Roberts, Charles G(eorge) D(ouglas)
  1860-1943 .... **TCLC 8**
  See also CA 105; DLB 92; SATA 29

Roberts, Kate 1891-1985 .... **CLC 15**
  See also CA 107; 116

Roberts, Keith (John Kingston)
  1935- .... **CLC 14**
  See also CA 25-28R

Roberts, Kenneth (Lewis)
  1885-1957 .... **TCLC 23**
  See also CA 109; DLB 9

Roberts, Michele (B.) 1949-........ **CLC 48**
  See also CA 115

Robertson, Ellis
  See Ellison, Harlan; Silverberg, Robert

Robertson, Thomas William
  1829-1871 .... **NCLC 35**

Robinson, Edwin Arlington
  1869-1935 .... **TCLC 5; PC 1**
  See also CA 104; 133; CDALB 1865-1917;
  DLB 54; MTCW

Robinson, Henry Crabb
1775-1867 .... **NCLC 15**
See also DLB 107

Robinson, Jill 1936- .... **CLC 10**
See also CA 102

Robinson, Kim Stanley 1952- ...... **CLC 34**
See also CA 126

Robinson, Lloyd
See Silverberg, Robert

Robinson, Marilynne 1944- .... **CLC 25**
See also CA 116

Robinson, Smokey .... **CLC 21**
See also Robinson, William Jr.

Robinson, William Jr. 1940-
See Robinson, Smokey
See also CA 116

Robison, Mary 1949- .... **CLC 42**
See also CA 113; 116

Roddenberry, Eugene Wesley 1921-1991
See Roddenberry, Gene
See also CA 110; 135; CANR 37; SATA 45

Roddenberry, Gene .... **CLC 17**
See also Roddenberry, Eugene Wesley
See also AAYA 5; SATO 69

Rodgers, Mary 1931- .... **CLC 12**
See also CA 49-52; CANR 8; CLR 20;
MAICYA; SATA 8

Rodgers, W(illiam) R(obert)
1909-1969 .... **CLC 7**
See also CA 85-88; DLB 20

Rodman, Eric
See Silverberg, Robert

Rodman, Howard 1920(?)-1985 ..... **CLC 65**
See also CA 118

Rodman, Maia
See Wojciechowska, Maia (Teresa)

Rodriguez, Claudio 1934- .... **CLC 10**

Roelvaag, O(le) E(dvart)
1876-1931 .... **TCLC 17**
See also CA 117; DLB 9

Roethke, Theodore (Huebner)
1908-1963 ...... **CLC 1, 3, 8, 11, 19, 46**
See also CA 81-84; CABS 2;
CDALB 1941-1968; DLB 5; MTCW

Rogers, Thomas Hunton 1927- ..... **CLC 57**
See also CA 89-92

Rogers, Will(iam Penn Adair)
1879-1935 .... **TCLC 8**
See also CA 105; DLB 11

Rogin, Gilbert 1929- .... **CLC 18**
See also CA 65-68; CANR 15

Rohan, Koda .... **TCLC 22**
See also Koda Shigeyuki

Rohmer, Eric .... **CLC 16**
See also Scherer, Jean-Marie Maurice

Rohmer, Sax .... **TCLC 28**
See also Ward, Arthur Henry Sarsfield
See also DLB 70

Roiphe, Anne Richardson 1935- ... **CLC 3, 9**
See also CA 89-92; DLBY 80

Rolfe, Frederick (William Serafino Austin
Lewis Mary) 1860-1913 ...... **TCLC 12**
See also CA 107; DLB 34

Rolland, Romain 1866-1944 ...... **TCLC 23**
See also CA 118; DLB 65

Rolvaag, O(le) E(dvart)
See Roelvaag, O(le) E(dvart)

Romain Arnaud, Saint
See Aragon, Louis

Romains, Jules 1885-1972 .... **CLC 7**
See also CA 85-88; CANR 34; DLB 65;
MTCW

Romero, Jose Ruben 1890-1952 ... **TCLC 14**
See also CA 114; 131; HW

Ronsard, Pierre de 1524-1585 .... **LC 6**

Rooke, Leon 1934- .... **CLC 25, 34**
See also CA 25-28R; CANR 23

Roper, William 1498-1578 .... **LC 10**

Roquelaure, A. N.
See Rice, Anne

Rosa, Joao Guimaraes 1908-1967 ... **CLC 23**
See also CA 89-92; DLB 113

Rosen, Richard (Dean) 1949- ...... **CLC 39**
See also CA 77-80

Rosenberg, Isaac 1890-1918 ...... **TCLC 12**
See also CA 107; DLB 20

Rosenblatt, Joe .... **CLC 15**
See also Rosenblatt, Joseph

Rosenblatt, Joseph 1933-
See Rosenblatt, Joe
See also CA 89-92

Rosenfeld, Samuel 1896-1963
See Tzara, Tristan
See also CA 89-92

Rosenthal, M(acha) L(ouis) 1917-... **CLC 28**
See also CA 1-4R; CAAS 6; CANR 4;
DLB 5; SATA 59

Ross, Barnaby
See Dannay, Frederic

Ross, Bernard L.
See Follett, Ken(neth Martin)

Ross, J. H.
See Lawrence, T(homas) E(dward)

Ross, (James) Sinclair 1908- .... **CLC 13**
See also CA 73-76; DLB 88

Rossetti, Christina (Georgina)
1830-1894 .... **NCLC 2**
See also DLB 35; MAICYA; SATA 20;
WLC

Rossetti, Dante Gabriel
1828-1882 .... **NCLC 4**
See also CDBLB 1832-1890; DLB 35; WLC

Rossner, Judith (Perelman)
1935- .... **CLC 6, 9, 29**
See also AITN 2; BEST 90:3; CA 17-20R;
CANR 18; DLB 6; MTCW

Rostand, Edmond (Eugene Alexis)
1868-1918 .... **TCLC 6, 37**
See also CA 104; 126; MTCW

Roth, Henry 1906- .... **CLC 2, 6, 11**
See also CA 11-12; CANR 38; CAP 1;
DLB 28; MTCW

Roth, Joseph 1894-1939 .... **TCLC 33**
See also DLB 85

Roth, Philip (Milton)
1933- ...... **CLC 1, 2, 3, 4, 6, 9, 15, 22,**
31, 47, 66
See also BEST 90:3; CA 1-4R; CANR 1, 22,
36; CDALB 1968-1988; DLB 2, 28;
DLBY 82; MTCW; WLC

Rothenberg, Jerome 1931- .... **CLC 6, 57**
See also CA 45-48; CANR 1; DLB 5

Roumain, Jacques (Jean Baptiste)
1907-1944 .... **TCLC 19**
See also BLC 3; BW; CA 117; 125

Rourke, Constance (Mayfield)
1885-1941 .... **TCLC 12**
See also CA 107; YABC 1

Rousseau, Jean-Baptiste 1671-1741 ... **LC 9**

Rousseau, Jean-Jacques 1712-1778... **LC 14**
See also WLC

Roussel, Raymond 1877-1933 ..... **TCLC 20**
See also CA 117

Rovit, Earl (Herbert) 1927- .... **CLC 7**
See also CA 5-8R; CANR 12

Rowe, Nicholas 1674-1718 .... **LC 8**
See also DLB 84

Rowley, Ames Dorrance
See Lovecraft, H(oward) P(hillips)

Rowson, Susanna Haswell
1762(?)-1824 .... **NCLC 5**
See also DLB 37

Roy, Gabrielle 1909-1983 .... **CLC 10, 14**
See also CA 53-56; 110; CANR 5; DLB 68;
MTCW

Rozewicz, Tadeusz 1921- .... **CLC 9, 23**
See also CA 108; CANR 36; MTCW

Ruark, Gibbons 1941- .... **CLC 3**
See also CA 33-36R; CANR 14, 31;
DLB 120

Rubens, Bernice (Ruth) 1923-... **CLC 19, 31**
See also CA 25-28R; CANR 33; DLB 14;
MTCW

Rudkin, (James) David 1936- ...... **CLC 14**
See also CA 89-92; DLB 13

Rudnik, Raphael 1933- .... **CLC 7**
See also CA 29-32R

Ruffian, M.
See Hasek, Jaroslav (Matej Frantisek)

Ruiz, Jose Martinez .... **CLC 11**
See also Martinez Ruiz, Jose

Rukeyser, Muriel
1913-1980 .... **CLC 6, 10, 15, 27**
See also CA 5-8R; 93-96; CANR 26;
DLB 48; MTCW; SATA 22

Rule, Jane (Vance) 1931- .... **CLC 27**
See also CA 25-28R; CANR 12; DLB 60

Rulfo, Juan 1918-1986 .... **CLC 8**
See also CA 85-88; 118; CANR 26;
DLB 113; HW; MTCW

Runyon, (Alfred) Damon
1884(?)-1946 .... **TCLC 10**
See also CA 107; DLB 11, 86

Rush, Norman 1933- .... **CLC 44**
See also CA 121; 126

Rushdie, (Ahmed) Salman
1947- . . . . **CLC 23, 31, 55**
See also BEST 89:3; CA 108; 111;
CANR 33; MTCW

Rushforth, Peter (Scott) 1945- . . . . . **CLC 19**
See also CA 101

Ruskin, John 1819-1900 . . . . **TCLC 20**
See also CA 114; 129; CDBLB 1832-1890;
DLB 55; SATA 24

Russ, Joanna 1937- . . . . **CLC 15**
See also CA 25-28R; CANR 11, 31; DLB 8;
MTCW

Russell, George William 1867-1935
See A. E.
See also CA 104; CDBLB 1890-1914

Russell, (Henry) Ken(neth Alfred)
1927- . . . . **CLC 16**
See also CA 105

Russell, Willy 1947- . . . . **CLC 60**

Rutherford, Mark . . . . **TCLC 25**
See also White, William Hale
See also DLB 18

Ruyslinck, Ward
See Belser, Reimond Karel Maria de

Ryan, Cornelius (John) 1920-1974 . . . **CLC 7**
See also CA 69-72; 53-56; CANR 38

Ryan, Michael 1946- . . . . **CLC 65**
See also CA 49-52; DLBY 82

Rybakov, Anatoli (Naumovich)
1911- . . . . **CLC 23, 53**
See also CA 126; 135

Ryder, Jonathan
See Ludlum, Robert

Ryga, George 1932-1987 . . . . **CLC 14**
See also CA 101; 124; DLB 60

S. S.
See Sassoon, Siegfried (Lorraine)

Saba, Umberto 1883-1957 . . . . **TCLC 33**
See also DLB 114

Sabatini, Rafael 1875-1950 . . . . **TCLC 47**

Sabato, Ernesto (R.) 1911- . . . . . . **CLC 10, 23**
See also CA 97-100; CANR 32; HW;
MTCW

Sacastru, Martin
See Bioy Casares, Adolfo

Sacher-Masoch, Leopold von
1836(?)-1895 . . . . **NCLC 31**

Sachs, Marilyn (Stickle) 1927- . . . . . **CLC 35**
See also AAYA 2; CA 17-20R; CANR 13;
CLR 2; MAICYA; SAAS 2; SATA 3, 68

Sachs, Nelly 1891-1970 . . . . **CLC 14**
See also CA 17-18; 25-28R; CAP 2

Sackler, Howard (Oliver)
1929-1982 . . . . **CLC 14**
See also CA 61-64; 108; CANR 30; DLB 7

Sacks, Oliver (Wolf) 1933- . . . . **CLC 67**
See also CA 53-56; CANR 28; MTCW

Sade, Donatien Alphonse Francois Comte
1740-1814 . . . . **NCLC 3**

Sadoff, Ira 1945- . . . . **CLC 9**
See also CA 53-56; CANR 5, 21; DLB 120

Saetone
See Camus, Albert

Safire, William 1929- . . . . **CLC 10**
See also CA 17-20R; CANR 31

Sagan, Carl (Edward) 1934- . . . . **CLC 30**
See also AAYA 2; CA 25-28R; CANR 11,
36; MTCW; SATA 58

Sagan, Francoise . . . . **CLC 3, 6, 9, 17, 36**
See also Quoirez, Francoise
See also DLB 83

Sahgal, Nayantara (Pandit) 1927- . . . **CLC 41**
See also CA 9-12R; CANR 11

Saint, H(arry) F. 1941- . . . . **CLC 50**
See also CA 127

St. Aubin de Teran, Lisa 1953-
See Teran, Lisa St. Aubin de
See also CA 118; 126

Sainte-Beuve, Charles Augustin
1804-1869 . . . . **NCLC 5**

**Saint-Exupery, Antoine (Jean Baptiste Marie
Roger) de** 1900-1944 . . . . **TCLC 2**
See also CA 108; 132; CLR 10; DLB 72;
MAICYA; MTCW; SATA 20; WLC

St. John, David
See Hunt, E(verette) Howard Jr.

Saint-John Perse
See Leger, (Marie-Rene) Alexis Saint-Leger

Saintsbury, George (Edward Bateman)
1845-1933 . . . . **TCLC 31**
See also DLB 57

Sait Faik . . . . **TCLC 23**
See also Abasiyanik, Sait Faik

Saki . . . . **TCLC 3**
See also Munro, H(ector) H(ugh)

Salama, Hannu 1936- . . . . **CLC 18**

Salamanca, J(ack) R(ichard)
1922- . . . . **CLC 4, 15**
See also CA 25-28R

Sale, J. Kirkpatrick
See Sale, Kirkpatrick

Sale, Kirkpatrick 1937- . . . . **CLC 68**
See also CA 13-16R; CANR 10

Salinas (y Serrano), Pedro
1891(?)-1951 . . . . **TCLC 17**
See also CA 117

Salinger, J(erome) D(avid)
1919- . . . . **CLC 1, 3, 8, 12, 55, 56; SSC 2**
See also AAYA 2; CA 5-8R; CANR 39;
CDALB 1941-1968; CLR 18; DLB 2, 102;
MAICYA; MTCW; SATA 67; WLC

Salisbury, John
See Caute, David

Salter, James 1925- . . . . **CLC 7, 52, 59**
See also CA 73-76

Saltus, Edgar (Everton)
1855-1921 . . . . **TCLC 8**
See also CA 105

Saltykov, Mikhail Evgrafovich
1826-1889 . . . . **NCLC 16**

Samarakis, Antonis 1919- . . . . **CLC 5**
See also CA 25-28R; CAAS 16; CANR 36

Sanchez, Florencio 1875-1910 . . . . . **TCLC 37**
See also HW

Sanchez, Luis Rafael 1936- . . . . **CLC 23**
See also CA 128; HW

Sanchez, Sonia 1934- . . . . **CLC 5**
See also BLC 3; BW; CA 33-36R;
CANR 24; CLR 18; DLB 41; DLBD 8;
MAICYA; MTCW; SATA 22

Sand, George 1804-1876 . . . . **NCLC 2**
See also DLB 119; WLC

Sandburg, Carl (August)
1878-1967 . . . **CLC 1, 4, 10, 15, 35; PC 2**
See also CA 5-8R; 25-28R; CANR 35;
CDALB 1865-1917; DLB 17, 54;
MAICYA; MTCW; SATA 8; WLC

Sandburg, Charles
See Sandburg, Carl (August)

Sandburg, Charles A.
See Sandburg, Carl (August)

Sanders, (James) Ed(ward) 1939- . . . **CLC 53**
See also CA 13-16R; CANR 13; DLB 16

Sanders, Lawrence 1920- . . . . **CLC 41**
See also BEST 89:4; CA 81-84; CANR 33;
MTCW

Sanders, Noah
See Blount, Roy (Alton) Jr.

Sanders, Winston P.
See Anderson, Poul (William)

Sandoz, Mari(e Susette)
1896-1966 . . . . **CLC 28**
See also CA 1-4R; 25-28R; CANR 17;
DLB 9; MTCW; SATA 5

Saner, Reg(inald Anthony) 1931- . . . . **CLC 9**
See also CA 65-68

Sannazaro, Jacopo 1456(?)-1530 . . . . . . **LC 8**

Sansom, William 1912-1976 . . . . **CLC 2, 6**
See also CA 5-8R; 65-68; MTCW

Santayana, George 1863-1952 . . . . . **TCLC 40**
See also CA 115; DLB 54, 71

Santiago, Danny . . . . **CLC 33**
See also James, Daniel (Lewis)

Santmyer, Helen Hooven
1895-1986 . . . . **CLC 33**
See also CA 1-4R; 118; CANR 15, 33;
DLBY 84; MTCW

Santos, Bienvenido N(uqui) 1911- . . . **CLC 22**
See also CA 101; CANR 19

Sapper . . . . **TCLC 44**
See also McNeile, Herman Cyril

Sappho fl. 6th cent. B.C.- . . . . **CMLC 3; PC 5**

Sarduy, Severo 1937- . . . . **CLC 6**
See also CA 89-92; DLB 113; HW

Sargeson, Frank 1903-1982 . . . . **CLC 31**
See also CA 25-28R; 106; CANR 38

Sarmiento, Felix Ruben Garcia 1867-1916
See Dario, Ruben
See also CA 104

Saroyan, William
1908-1981 . . . . . **CLC 1, 8, 10, 29, 34, 56**
See also CA 5-8R; 103; CANR 30; DLB 7,
9, 86; DLBY 81; MTCW; SATA 23, 24;
WLC

Sarraute, Nathalie
1900- . . . . **CLC 1, 2, 4, 8, 10, 31**
See also CA 9-12R; CANR 23; DLB 83;
MTCW

Sarton, (Eleanor) May
1912- . . . . **CLC 4, 14, 49**
See also CA 1-4R; CANR 1, 34; DLB 48;
DLBY 81; MTCW; SATA 36

Sartre, Jean-Paul
1905-1980 . . . **CLC 1, 4, 7, 9, 13, 18, 24,
44, 50, 52**
See also CA 9-12R; 97-100; CANR 21;
DLB 72; MTCW; WLC

Sassoon, Siegfried (Lorraine)
1886-1967 . . . . **CLC 36**
See also CA 104; 25-28R; CANR 36;
DLB 20; MTCW

Satterfield, Charles
See Pohl, Frederik

Saul, John (W. III) 1942- . . . . **CLC 46**
See also BEST 90:4; CA 81-84; CANR 16

Saunders, Caleb
See Heinlein, Robert A(nson)

Saura (Atares), Carlos 1932- . . . . **CLC 20**
See also CA 114; 131; HW

Sauser-Hall, Frederic 1887-1961 . . . . **CLC 18**
See also CA 102; 93-96; CANR 36; MTCW

Savage, Catharine
See Brosman, Catharine Savage

Savage, Thomas 1915- . . . . **CLC 40**
See also CA 126; 132; CAAS 15

Savan, Glenn . . . . **CLC 50**

Saven, Glenn 19(?)- . . . . **CLC 50**

Sayers, Dorothy L(eigh)
1893-1957 . . . . **TCLC 2, 15**
See also CA 104; 119; CDBLB 1914-1945;
DLB 10, 36, 77, 100; MTCW

Sayers, Valerie 1952- . . . . **CLC 50**
See also CA 134

Sayles, John Thomas 1950- . . . **CLC 7, 10, 14**
See also CA 57-60; DLB 44

Scammell, Michael . . . . **CLC 34**

Scannell, Vernon 1922- . . . . **CLC 49**
See also CA 5-8R; CANR 8, 24; DLB 27;
SATA 59

Scarlett, Susan
See Streatfeild, (Mary) Noel

Schaeffer, Susan Fromberg
1941- . . . . **CLC 6, 11, 22**
See also CA 49-52; CANR 18; DLB 28;
MTCW; SATA 22

Schary, Jill
See Robinson, Jill

Schell, Jonathan 1943- . . . . **CLC 35**
See also CA 73-76; CANR 12

Schelling, Friedrich Wilhelm Joseph von
1775-1854 . . . . **NCLC 30**
See also DLB 90

Scherer, Jean-Marie Maurice 1920-
See Rohmer, Eric
See also CA 110

Schevill, James (Erwin) 1920- . . . . . . **CLC 7**
See also CA 5-8R; CAAS 12

Schisgal, Murray (Joseph) 1926- . . . . **CLC 6**
See also CA 21-24R

Schlee, Ann 1934- . . . . **CLC 35**
See also CA 101; CANR 29; SATA 36, 44

Schlegel, August Wilhelm von
1767-1845 . . . . **NCLC 15**
See also DLB 94

Schlegel, Johann Elias (von)
1719(?)-1749 . . . . **LC 5**

Schmidt, Arno (Otto) 1914-1979 . . . . **CLC 56**
See also CA 128; 109; DLB 69

Schmitz, Aron Hector 1861-1928
See Svevo, Italo
See also CA 104; 122; MTCW

Schnackenberg, Gjertrud 1953- . . . . . **CLC 40**
See also CA 116; DLB 120

Schneider, Leonard Alfred 1925-1966
See Bruce, Lenny
See also CA 89-92

Schnitzler, Arthur 1862-1931 . . . . . . **TCLC 4**
See also CA 104; DLB 81, 118

Schor, Sandra (M.) 1932(?)-1990 . . . **CLC 65**
See also CA 132

Schorer, Mark 1908-1977 . . . . **CLC 9**
See also CA 5-8R; 73-76; CANR 7;
DLB 103

Schrader, Paul Joseph 1946- . . . . **CLC 26**
See also CA 37-40R; DLB 44

Schreiner, Olive (Emilie Albertina)
1855-1920 . . . . **TCLC 9**
See also CA 105; DLB 18

Schulberg, Budd (Wilson)
1914- . . . . **CLC 7, 48**
See also CA 25-28R; CANR 19; DLB 6, 26,
28; DLBY 81

Schulz, Bruno 1892-1942 . . . . **TCLC 5**
See also CA 115; 123

Schulz, Charles M(onroe) 1922- . . . . **CLC 12**
See also CA 9-12R; CANR 6; SATA 10

Schuyler, James Marcus
1923-1991 . . . . **CLC 5, 23**
See also CA 101; 134; DLB 5

Schwartz, Delmore (David)
1913-1966 . . . . **CLC 2, 4, 10, 45**
See also CA 17-18; 25-28R; CANR 35;
CAP 2; DLB 28, 48; MTCW

Schwartz, Ernst
See Ozu, Yasujiro

Schwartz, John Burnham 1965- . . . . **CLC 59**
See also CA 132

Schwartz, Lynne Sharon 1939- . . . . . **CLC 31**
See also CA 103

Schwartz, Muriel A.
See Eliot, T(homas) S(tearns)

Schwarz-Bart, Andre 1928- . . . . **CLC 2, 4**
See also CA 89-92

Schwarz-Bart, Simone 1938- . . . . **CLC 7**
See also CA 97-100

Schwob, (Mayer Andre) Marcel
1867-1905 . . . . **TCLC 20**
See also CA 117

Sciascia, Leonardo
1921-1989 . . . . **CLC 8, 9, 41**
See also CA 85-88; 130; CANR 35; MTCW

Scoppettone, Sandra 1936- . . . . **CLC 26**
See also CA 5-8R; SATA 9

Scorsese, Martin 1942- . . . . **CLC 20**
See also CA 110; 114

Scotland, Jay
See Jakes, John (William)

Scott, Duncan Campbell
1862-1947 . . . . **TCLC 6**
See also CA 104; DLB 92

Scott, Evelyn 1893-1963 . . . . **CLC 43**
See also CA 104; 112; DLB 9, 48

Scott, F(rancis) R(eginald)
1899-1985 . . . . **CLC 22**
See also CA 101; 114; DLB 88

Scott, Frank
See Scott, F(rancis) R(eginald)

Scott, Joanna 1960- . . . . **CLC 50**
See also CA 126

Scott, Paul (Mark) 1920-1978 . . . . **CLC 9, 60**
See also CA 81-84; 77-80; CANR 33;
DLB 14; MTCW

Scott, Walter 1771-1832 . . . . **NCLC 15**
See also CDBLB 1789-1832; DLB 93, 107,
116; WLC; YABC 2

Scribe, (Augustin) Eugene
1791-1861 . . . . **NCLC 16**

Scrum, R.
See Crumb, R(obert)

Scudery, Madeleine de 1607-1701 . . . . . **LC 2**

Scum
See Crumb, R(obert)

Scumbag, Little Bobby
See Crumb, R(obert)

Seabrook, John
See Hubbard, L(afayette) Ron(ald)

Sealy, I. Allan 1951- . . . . **CLC 55**

Search, Alexander
See Pessoa, Fernando (Antonio Nogueira)

Sebastian, Lee
See Silverberg, Robert

Sebastian Owl
See Thompson, Hunter S(tockton)

Sebestyen, Ouida 1924- . . . . **CLC 30**
See also AAYA 8; CA 107; CLR 17;
MAICYA; SAAS 10; SATA 39

Sedges, John
See Buck, Pearl S(ydenstricker)

Sedgwick, Catharine Maria
1789-1867 . . . . **NCLC 19**
See also DLB 1, 74

Seelye, John 1931- . . . . **CLC 7**

Seferiades, Giorgos Stylianou 1900-1971
See Seferis, George
See also CA 5-8R; 33-36R; CANR 5, 36;
MTCW

Seferis, George . . . . **CLC 5, 11**
See also Seferiades, Giorgos Stylianou

Segal, Erich (Wolf) 1937- . . . . **CLC 3, 10**
See also BEST 89:1; CA 25-28R; CANR 20,
36; DLBY 86; MTCW

Seger, Bob 1945- . . . . **CLC 35**

Seghers, Anna . . . . **CLC 7**
See also Radvanyi, Netty
See also DLB 69

Seidel, Frederick (Lewis) 1936- . . . . . **CLC 18**
See also CA 13-16R; CANR 8; DLBY 84

Seifert, Jaroslav 1901-1986 . . . . . **CLC 34, 44**
See also CA 127; MTCW

Sei Shonagon c. 966-1017(?) . . . . . . **CMLC 6**

Selby, Hubert Jr. 1928- . . . . . . **CLC 1, 2, 4, 8**
See also CA 13-16R; CANR 33; DLB 2

Sembene, Ousmane
See Ousmane, Sembene

Senancour, Etienne Pivert de
1770-1846 . . . . **NCLC 16**
See also DLB 119

Sender, Ramon (Jose) 1902-1982 . . . . **CLC 8**
See also CA 5-8R; 105; CANR 8; HW;
MTCW

Seneca, Lucius Annaeus
4B.C.-65. . . . . **CMLC 6**

Senghor, Leopold Sedar 1906- . . . . . . **CLC 54**
See also BLC 3; BW; CA 116; 125; MTCW

Serling, (Edward) Rod(man)
1924-1975 . . . . **CLC 30**
See also AITN 1; CA 65-68; 57-60; DLB 26

Serna, Ramon Gomez de la
See Gomez de la Serna, Ramon

Serpieres
See Guillevic, (Eugene)

Service, Robert
See Service, Robert W(illiam)
See also DLB 92

Service, Robert W(illiam)
1874(?)-1958 . . . . **TCLC 15**
See also Service, Robert
See also CA 115; SATA 20; WLC

Seth, Vikram 1952- . . . . **CLC 43**
See also CA 121; 127; DLB 120

Seton, Cynthia Propper
1926-1982 . . . . **CLC 27**
See also CA 5-8R; 108; CANR 7

Seton, Ernest (Evan) Thompson
1860-1946 . . . . **TCLC 31**
See also CA 109; DLB 92; SATA 18

Seton-Thompson, Ernest
See Seton, Ernest (Evan) Thompson

Settle, Mary Lee 1918- . . . . **CLC 19, 61**
See also CA 89-92; CAAS 1; DLB 6

Seuphor, Michel
See Arp, Jean

Sevine, Marquise de Marie de
Rabutin-Chantal 1626-1696 . . . . . **LC 11**

Sevine, Marquise de Marie de
Rabutin-Chantal 1626-1696 . . . . . **LC 11**

Sexton, Anne (Harvey)
1928-1974 . . . **CLC 2, 4, 6, 8, 10, 15, 53;
PC 2**
See also CA 1-4R; 53-56; CABS 2;
CANR 3, 36; CDALB 1941-1968; DLB 5;
MTCW; SATA 10; WLC

Shaara, Michael (Joseph Jr.)
1929-1988 . . . . **CLC 15**
See also AITN 1; CA 102; DLBY 83

Shackleton, C. C.
See Aldiss, Brian W(ilson)

Shacochis, Bob . . . . **CLC 39**
See also Shacochis, Robert G.

Shacochis, Robert G. 1951-
See Shacochis, Bob
See also CA 119; 124

Shaffer, Anthony (Joshua) 1926- . . . . **CLC 19**
See also CA 110; 116; DLB 13

Shaffer, Peter (Levin)
1926- . . . . **CLC 5, 14, 18, 37, 60**
See also CA 25-28R; CANR 25;
CDBLB 1960 to Present; DLB 13;
MTCW

Shakey, Bernard
See Young, Neil

Shalamov, Varlam (Tikhonovich)
1907(?)-1982 . . . . **CLC 18**
See also CA 129; 105

Shamlu, Ahmad 1925- . . . . **CLC 10**

Shammas, Anton 1951- . . . . **CLC 55**

Shange, Ntozake 1948- . . . . . . **CLC 8, 25, 38**
See also AAYA 9; BLC 3; BW; CA 85-88;
CABS 3; CANR 27; DLB 38; MTCW

Shapcott, Thomas William 1935- . . . **CLC 38**
See also CA 69-72

Shapiro, Karl (Jay) 1913- . . **CLC 4, 8, 15, 53**
See also CA 1-4R; CAAS 6; CANR 1, 36;
DLB 48; MTCW

Sharp, William 1855-1905 . . . . **TCLC 39**

Sharpe, Thomas Ridley 1928-
See Sharpe, Tom
See also CA 114; 122

Sharpe, Tom. . . . . **CLC 36**
See also Sharpe, Thomas Ridley
See also DLB 14

Shaw, Bernard . . . . **TCLC 45**
See also Shaw, George Bernard

Shaw, G. Bernard
See Shaw, George Bernard

Shaw, George Bernard
1856-1950 . . . . **TCLC 3, 9, 21**
See also Shaw, Bernard
See also CA 104; 128; CDBLB 1914-1945;
DLB 10, 57; MTCW; WLC

Shaw, Henry Wheeler
1818-1885 . . . . **NCLC 15**
See also DLB 11

Shaw, Irwin 1913-1984 . . . . **CLC 7, 23, 34**
See also AITN 1; CA 13-16R; 112;
CANR 21; CDALB 1941-1968; DLB 6,
102; DLBY 84; MTCW

Shaw, Robert 1927-1978 . . . . **CLC 5**
See also AITN 1; CA 1-4R; 81-84;
CANR 4; DLB 13, 14

Shaw, T. E.
See Lawrence, T(homas) E(dward)

Shawn, Wallace 1943- . . . . **CLC 41**
See also CA 112

Sheed, Wilfrid (John Joseph)
1930- . . . . **CLC 2, 4, 10, 53**
See also CA 65-68; CANR 30; DLB 6;
MTCW

Sheldon, Alice Hastings Bradley
1915(?)-1987
See Tiptree, James Jr.
See also CA 108; 122; CANR 34; MTCW

Sheldon, John
See Bloch, Robert (Albert)

Shelley, Mary Wollstonecraft (Godwin)
1797-1851 . . . . **NCLC 14**
See also CDBLB 1789-1832; DLB 110, 116;
SATA 29; WLC

Shelley, Percy Bysshe
1792-1822 . . . . **NCLC 18**
See also CDBLB 1789-1832; DLB 96, 110;
WLC

Shepard, Jim 1956- . . . . **CLC 36**
See also CA 137

Shepard, Lucius 19(?)- . . . . **CLC 34**
See also CA 128

Shepard, Sam
1943- . . . . **CLC 4, 6, 17, 34, 41, 44**
See also AAYA 1; CA 69-72; CABS 3;
CANR 22; DLB 7; MTCW

Shepherd, Michael
See Ludlum, Robert

Sherburne, Zoa (Morin) 1912- . . . . . . **CLC 30**
See also CA 1-4R; CANR 3, 37; MAICYA;
SATA 3

Sheridan, Frances 1724-1766. . . . . **LC 7**
See also DLB 39, 84

Sheridan, Richard Brinsley
1751-1816 . . . . **NCLC 5; DC 1**
See also CDBLB 1660-1789; DLB 89; WLC

Sherman, Jonathan Marc. . . . . **CLC 55**

Sherman, Martin 1941(?)- . . . . **CLC 19**
See also CA 116; 123

Sherwin, Judith Johnson 1936- . . . **CLC 7, 15**
See also CA 25-28R; CANR 34

Sherwood, Robert E(mmet)
1896-1955 . . . . **TCLC 3**
See also CA 104; DLB 7, 26

Shiel, M(atthew) P(hipps)
1865-1947 . . . . **TCLC 8**
See also CA 106

Shiga, Naoya 1883-1971. . . . . **CLC 33**
See also CA 101; 33-36R

Shimazaki Haruki 1872-1943
See Shimazaki Toson
See also CA 105; 134

Shimazaki Toson . . . . **TCLC 5**
See also Shimazaki Haruki

Sholokhov, Mikhail (Aleksandrovich)
1905-1984 . . . . **CLC 7, 15**
See also CA 101; 112; MTCW; SATA 36

Shone, Patric
See Hanley, James

Shreve, Susan Richards 1939- . . . . . . **CLC 23**
See also CA 49-52; CAAS 5; CANR 5, 38;
MAICYA; SATA 41, 46

Shue, Larry 1946-1985. . . . . **CLC 52**
See also CA 117

Shu-Jen, Chou 1881-1936
See Hsun, Lu
See also CA 104

Shulman, Alix Kates 1932- . . . . . . **CLC 2, 10**
See also CA 29-32R; SATA 7

Shuster, Joe 1914- . . . . **CLC 21**

Shute, Nevil. . . . . **CLC 30**
See also Norway, Nevil Shute

Shuttle, Penelope (Diane) 1947- . . . . . **CLC 7**
See also CA 93-96; CANR 39; DLB 14, 40

Sidney, Mary 1561-1621 . . . . **LC 19**

Sidney, Sir Philip 1554-1586 . . . . **LC 19**
See also CDBLB Before 1660

Siegel, Jerome 1914- . . . . **CLC 21**
See also CA 116

Siegel, Jerry
See Siegel, Jerome

Sienkiewicz, Henryk (Adam Alexander Pius)
1846-1916 . . . . **TCLC 3**
See also CA 104; 134

Sierra, Gregorio Martinez
See Martinez Sierra, Gregorio

Sierra, Maria (de la O'LeJarraga) Martinez
See Martinez Sierra, Maria (de la
O'LeJarraga)

Sigal, Clancy 1926- . . . . **CLC 7**
See also CA 1-4R

Sigourney, Lydia Howard (Huntley)
1791-1865 . . . . **NCLC 21**
See also DLB 1, 42, 73

Siguenza y Gongora, Carlos de
1645-1700 . . . . **LC 8**

Sigurjonsson, Johann 1880-1919 . . . **TCLC 27**

Sikelianos, Angelos 1884-1951 . . . . **TCLC 39**

Silkin, Jon 1930- . . . . **CLC 2, 6, 43**
See also CA 5-8R; CAAS 5; DLB 27

Silko, Leslie Marmon 1948- . . . . **CLC 23**
See also CA 115; 122

Sillanpaa, Frans Eemil 1888-1964 . . . **CLC 19**
See also CA 129; 93-96; MTCW

Sillitoe, Alan
1928- . . . . **CLC 1, 3, 6, 10, 19, 57**
See also AITN 1; CA 9-12R; CAAS 2;
CANR 8, 26; CDBLB 1960 to Present;
DLB 14; MTCW; SATA 61

Silone, Ignazio 1900-1978 . . . . **CLC 4**
See also CA 25-28; 81-84; CANR 34;
CAP 2; MTCW

Silver, Joan Micklin 1935- . . . . **CLC 20**
See also CA 114; 121

Silverberg, Robert 1935- . . . . **CLC 7**
See also CA 1-4R; CAAS 3; CANR 1, 20,
36; DLB 8; MAICYA; MTCW; SATA 13

Silverstein, Alvin 1933- . . . . **CLC 17**
See also CA 49-52; CANR 2; CLR 25;
MAICYA; SATA 8, 69

Silverstein, Virginia B(arbara Opshelor)
1937- . . . . **CLC 17**
See also CA 49-52; CANR 2; CLR 25;
MAICYA; SATA 8, 69

Sim, Georges
See Simenon, Georges (Jacques Christian)

Simak, Clifford D(onald)
1904-1988 . . . . **CLC 1, 55**
See also CA 1-4R; 125; CANR 1, 35;
DLB 8; MTCW; SATA 56

Simenon, Georges (Jacques Christian)
1903-1989 . . . . . . **CLC 1, 2, 3, 8, 18, 47**
See also CA 85-88; 129; CANR 35;
DLB 72; DLBY 89; MTCW

Simic, Charles 1938- . . . **CLC 6, 9, 22, 49, 68**
See also CA 29-32R; CAAS 4; CANR 12,
33; DLB 105

Simmons, Charles (Paul) 1924- . . . . . **CLC 57**
See also CA 89-92

Simmons, Dan . . . . **CLC 44**
See also CA 138

Simmons, James (Stewart Alexander)
1933- . . . . **CLC 43**
See also CA 105; DLB 40

Simms, William Gilmore
1806-1870 . . . . **NCLC 3**
See also DLB 3, 30, 59, 73

Simon, Carly 1945- . . . . **CLC 26**
See also CA 105

Simon, Claude 1913- . . . . **CLC 4, 9, 15, 39**
See also CA 89-92; CANR 33; DLB 83;
MTCW

Simon, (Marvin) Neil
1927- . . . . **CLC 6, 11, 31, 39, 70**
See also AITN 1; CA 21-24R; CANR 26;
DLB 7; MTCW

Simon, Paul 1942(?)- . . . . **CLC 17**
See also CA 116

Simonon, Paul 1956(?)- . . . . **CLC 30**
See also The Clash

Simpson, Harriette
See Arnow, Harriette (Louisa) Simpson

Simpson, Louis (Aston Marantz)
1923- . . . . **CLC 4, 7, 9, 32**
See also CA 1-4R; CAAS 4; CANR 1;
DLB 5; MTCW

Simpson, Mona (Elizabeth) 1957- . . . **CLC 44**
See also CA 122; 135

Simpson, N(orman) F(rederick)
1919- . . . . **CLC 29**
See also CA 13-16R; DLB 13

Sinclair, Andrew (Annandale)
1935- . . . . **CLC 2, 14**
See also CA 9-12R; CAAS 5; CANR 14, 38;
DLB 14; MTCW

Sinclair, Emil
See Hesse, Hermann

Sinclair, Mary Amelia St. Clair 1865(?)-1946
See Sinclair, May
See also CA 104

Sinclair, May . . . . **TCLC 3, 11**
See also Sinclair, Mary Amelia St. Clair
See also DLB 36

Sinclair, Upton (Beall)
1878-1968 . . . . **CLC 1, 11, 15, 63**
See also CA 5-8R; 25-28R; CANR 7;
CDALB 1929-1941; DLB 9; MTCW;
SATA 9; WLC

Singer, Isaac
See Singer, Isaac Bashevis

Singer, Isaac Bashevis
1904-1991 . . . **CLC 1, 3, 6, 9, 11, 15, 23,
38, 69; SSC 3**
See also AITN 1, 2; CA 1-4R; 134;
CANR 1, 39; CDALB 1941-1968; CLR 1;
DLB 6, 28, 52; DLBY 91; MAICYA;
MTCW; SATA 3, 27; SATO 68; WLC

Singer, Israel Joshua 1893-1944 . . . **TCLC 33**

Singh, Khushwant 1915- . . . . **CLC 11**
See also CA 9-12R; CAAS 9; CANR 6

Sinjohn, John
See Galsworthy, John

Sinyavsky, Andrei (Donatevich)
1925- . . . . **CLC 8**
See also CA 85-88

Sirin, V.
See Nabokov, Vladimir (Vladimirovich)

Sissman, L(ouis) E(dward)
1928-1976 . . . . **CLC 9, 18**
See also CA 21-24R; 65-68; CANR 13;
DLB 5

Sisson, C(harles) H(ubert) 1914- . . . . . **CLC 8**
See also CA 1-4R; CAAS 3; CANR 3;
DLB 27

Sitwell, Dame Edith
1887-1964 . . . . **CLC 2, 9, 67; PC 3**
See also CA 9-12R; CANR 35;
CDBLB 1945-1960; DLB 20; MTCW

Sjoewall, Maj 1935- . . . . **CLC 7**
See also CA 65-68

Sjowall, Maj
See Sjoewall, Maj

Skelton, Robin 1925- . . . . **CLC 13**
See also AITN 2; CA 5-8R; CAAS 5;
CANR 28; DLB 27, 53

Skolimowski, Jerzy 1938- . . . . **CLC 20**
See also CA 128

Skram, Amalie (Bertha)
1847-1905 . . . . **TCLC 25**

Skvorecky, Josef (Vaclav)
1924- . . . . **CLC 15, 39, 69**
See also CA 61-64; CAAS 1; CANR 10, 34;
MTCW

Slade, Bernard . . . . **CLC 11, 46**
See also Newbound, Bernard Slade
See also CAAS 9; DLB 53

Slaughter, Carolyn 1946- . . . . **CLC 56**
See also CA 85-88

Slaughter, Frank G(ill) 1908- . . . . . . **CLC 29**
See also AITN 2; CA 5-8R; CANR 5

Slavitt, David R. 1935- . . . . **CLC 5, 14**
See also CA 21-24R; CAAS 3; DLB 5, 6

Slesinger, Tess 1905-1945 . . . . **TCLC 10**
See also CA 107; DLB 102

Slessor, Kenneth 1901-1971 . . . . **CLC 14**
See also CA 102; 89-92

Slowacki, Juliusz 1809-1849 . . . . . **NCLC 15**

Smart, Christopher 1722-1771 . . . . **LC 3**
See also DLB 109

Smart, Elizabeth 1913-1986 . . . . **CLC 54**
See also CA 81-84; 118; DLB 88

Smiley, Jane (Graves) 1949- . . . . **CLC 53**
See also CA 104; CANR 30

Smith, A(rthur) J(ames) M(arshall)
1902-1980 . . . . **CLC 15**
See also CA 1-4R; 102; CANR 4; DLB 88

Smith, Betty (Wehner) 1896-1972 . . . **CLC 19**
See also CA 5-8R; 33-36R; DLBY 82;
SATA 6

Smith, Charlotte (Turner)
1749-1806 . . . . **NCLC 23**
See also DLB 39, 109

Smith, Clark Ashton 1893-1961 . . . . **CLC 43**

Smith, Dave . . . . **CLC 22, 42**
See also Smith, David (Jeddie)
See also CAAS 7; DLB 5

Smith, David (Jeddie) 1942-
See Smith, Dave
See also CA 49-52; CANR 1

Smith, Florence Margaret
1902-1971 .... **CLC 8**
See also Smith, Stevie
See also CA 17-18; 29-32R; CANR 35;
CAP 2; MTCW

Smith, Iain Crichton 1928- .... **CLC 64**
See also CA 21-24R; DLB 40

Smith, John 1580(?)-1631 .... **LC 9**

Smith, Johnston
See Crane, Stephen (Townley)

Smith, Lee 1944-................ **CLC 25**
See also CA 114; 119; DLBY 83

Smith, Martin
See Smith, Martin Cruz

Smith, Martin Cruz 1942-......... **CLC 25**
See also BEST 89:4; CA 85-88; CANR 6, 23

Smith, Mary-Ann Tirone 1944-..... **CLC 39**
See also CA 118; 136

Smith, Patti 1946- .... **CLC 12**
See also CA 93-96

Smith, Pauline (Urmson)
1882-1959 .... **TCLC 25**

Smith, Rosamond
See Oates, Joyce Carol

Smith, Sheila Kaye
See Kaye-Smith, Sheila

Smith, Stevie .... **CLC 3, 8, 25, 44**
See also Smith, Florence Margaret
See also DLB 20

Smith, Wilbur A(ddison) 1933-..... **CLC 33**
See also CA 13-16R; CANR 7; MTCW

Smith, William Jay 1918- .... **CLC 6**
See also CA 5-8R; DLB 5; MAICYA;
SATA 2, 68

Smith, Woodrow Wilson
See Kuttner, Henry

Smolenskin, Peretz 1842-1885.... **NCLC 30**

Smollett, Tobias (George) 1721-1771 .. **LC 2**
See also CDBLB 1660-1789; DLB 39, 104

Snodgrass, William D(e Witt)
1926- .... **CLC 2, 6, 10, 18, 68**
See also CA 1-4R; CANR 6, 36; DLB 5;
MTCW

Snow, C(harles) P(ercy)
1905-1980 .... **CLC 1, 4, 6, 9, 13, 19**
See also CA 5-8R; 101; CANR 28;
CDBLB 1945-1960; DLB 15, 77; MTCW

Snow, Frances Compton
See Adams, Henry (Brooks)

Snyder, Gary (Sherman)
1930- .... **CLC 1, 2, 5, 9, 32**
See also CA 17-20R; CANR 30; DLB 5, 16

Snyder, Zilpha Keatley 1927-...... **CLC 17**
See also CA 9-12R; CANR 38; MAICYA;
SAAS 2; SATA 1, 28

Soares, Bernardo
See Pessoa, Fernando (Antonio Nogueira)

Sobh, A.
See Shamlu, Ahmad

Sobol, Joshua.................... **CLC 60**

Soderberg, Hjalmar 1869-1941 .... **TCLC 39**

Sodergran, Edith (Irene)
See Soedergran, Edith (Irene)

Soedergran, Edith (Irene)
1892-1923 .... **TCLC 31**

Softly, Edgar
See Lovecraft, H(oward) P(hillips)

Softly, Edward
See Lovecraft, H(oward) P(hillips)

Sokolov, Raymond 1941-.......... **CLC 7**
See also CA 85-88

Solo, Jay
See Ellison, Harlan

Sologub, Fyodor .... **TCLC 9**
See also Teternikov, Fyodor Kuzmich

Solomons, Ikey Esquir
See Thackeray, William Makepeace

Solomos, Dionysios 1798-1857 ... **NCLC 15**

Solwoska, Mara
See French, Marilyn

Solzhenitsyn, Aleksandr I(sayevich)
1918- ... **CLC 1, 2, 4, 7, 9, 10, 18, 26, 34**
See also AITN 1; CA 69-72; MTCW; WLC

Somers, Jane
See Lessing, Doris (May)

Sommer, Scott 1951- .... **CLC 25**
See also CA 106

Sondheim, Stephen (Joshua)
1930- .... **CLC 30, 39**
See also CA 103

Sontag, Susan 1933-... **CLC 1, 2, 10, 13, 31**
See also CA 17-20R; CANR 25; DLB 2, 67;
MTCW

Sophocles
496(?)B.C.-406(?)B.C.... **CMLC 2; DC 1**

Sorel, Julia
See Drexler, Rosalyn

Sorrentino, Gilbert
1929- .... **CLC 3, 7, 14, 22, 40**
See also CA 77-80; CANR 14, 33; DLB 5;
DLBY 80

Soto, Gary 1952-................. **CLC 32**
See also CA 119; 125; DLB 82; HW

Soupault, Philippe 1897-1990 ...... **CLC 68**
See also CA 116; 131

Souster, (Holmes) Raymond
1921- .... **CLC 5, 14**
See also CA 13-16R; CAAS 14; CANR 13,
29; DLB 88; SATA 63

Southern, Terry 1926- .... **CLC 7**
See also CA 1-4R; CANR 1; DLB 2

Southey, Robert 1774-1843 .... **NCLC 8**
See also DLB 93, 107; SATA 54

Southworth, Emma Dorothy Eliza Nevitte
1819-1899 .... **NCLC 26**

Souza, Ernest
See Scott, Evelyn

Soyinka, Wole
1934-....... **CLC 3, 5, 14, 36, 44; DC 2**
See also BLC 3; BW; CA 13-16R;
CANR 27, 39; MTCW; WLC

Spackman, W(illiam) M(ode)
1905-1990 .... **CLC 46**
See also CA 81-84; 132

Spacks, Barry 1931-............. **CLC 14**
See also CA 29-32R; CANR 33; DLB 105

Spanidou, Irini 1946-............. **CLC 44**

Spark, Muriel (Sarah)
1918-....... **CLC 2, 3, 5, 8, 13, 18, 40;**
SSC 10
See also CA 5-8R; CANR 12, 36;
CDBLB 1945-1960; DLB 15; MTCW

Spaulding, Douglas
See Bradbury, Ray (Douglas)

Spaulding, Leonard
See Bradbury, Ray (Douglas)

Spence, J. A. D.
See Eliot, T(homas) S(tearns)

Spencer, Elizabeth 1921-.......... **CLC 22**
See also CA 13-16R; CANR 32; DLB 6;
MTCW; SATA 14

Spencer, Leonard G.
See Silverberg, Robert

Spencer, Scott 1945-.............. **CLC 30**
See also CA 113; DLBY 86

Spender, Stephen (Harold)
1909- .... **CLC 1, 2, 5, 10, 41**
See also CA 9-12R; CANR 31;
CDBLB 1945-1960; DLB 20; MTCW

Spengler, Oswald (Arnold Gottfried)
1880-1936 .... **TCLC 25**
See also CA 118

Spenser, Edmund 1552(?)-1599 .... **LC 5**
See also CDBLB Before 1660; WLC

Spicer, Jack 1925-1965 ...... **CLC 8, 18, 72**
See also CA 85-88; DLB 5, 16

Spielberg, Peter 1929-............ **CLC 6**
See also CA 5-8R; CANR 4; DLBY 81

Spielberg, Steven 1947- .... **CLC 20**
See also AAYA 8; CA 77-80; CANR 32;
SATA 32

Spillane, Frank Morrison 1918-
See Spillane, Mickey
See also CA 25-28R; CANR 28; MTCW;
SATA 66

Spillane, Mickey............... **CLC 3, 13**
See also Spillane, Frank Morrison

Spinoza, Benedictus de 1632-1677 .... **LC 9**

Spinrad, Norman (Richard) 1940-... **CLC 46**
See also CA 37-40R; CANR 20; DLB 8

Spitteler, Carl (Friedrich Georg)
1845-1924 .... **TCLC 12**
See also CA 109

Spivack, Kathleen (Romola Drucker)
1938- .... **CLC 6**
See also CA 49-52

Spoto, Donald 1941-.............. **CLC 39**
See also CA 65-68; CANR 11

Springsteen, Bruce (F.) 1949- ...... **CLC 17**
See also CA 111

Spurling, Hilary 1940-............ **CLC 34**
See also CA 104; CANR 25

Squires, Radcliffe 1917-........... **CLC 51**
See also CA 1-4R; CANR 6, 21

Srivastava, Dhanpat Rai   1880(?)-1936
See Premchand
See also CA 118

Stacy, Donald
See Pohl, Frederik

Stael, Germaine de
See Stael-Holstein, Anne Louise Germaine
   Necker Baronn
See also DLB 119

**Stael-Holstein, Anne Louise Germaine Necker
   Baronn**   1766-1817 . . . .   **NCLC 3**
See also Stael, Germaine de

Stafford, Jean   1915-1979 . . .   **CLC 4, 7, 19, 68**
See also CA 1-4R; 85-88; CANR 3; DLB 2;
   MTCW; SATA 22

Stafford, William (Edgar)
   1914- . . . .   **CLC 4, 7, 29**
See also CA 5-8R; CAAS 3; CANR 5, 22;
   DLB 5

Staines, Trevor
See Brunner, John (Kilian Houston)

Stairs, Gordon
See Austin, Mary (Hunter)

Stannard, Martin . . . .   **CLC 44**

Stanton, Maura   1946- . . . .   **CLC 9**
See also CA 89-92; CANR 15; DLB 120

Stanton, Schuyler
See Baum, L(yman) Frank

Stapledon, (William) Olaf
   1886-1950 . . . .   **TCLC 22**
See also CA 111; DLB 15

Starbuck, George (Edwin)   1931- . . . . .   **CLC 53**
See also CA 21-24R; CANR 23

Stark, Richard
See Westlake, Donald E(dwin)

Staunton, Schuyler
See Baum, L(yman) Frank

Stead, Christina (Ellen)
   1902-1983 . . . . **CLC 2, 5, 8, 32**
See also CA 13-16R; 109; CANR 33;
   MTCW

Steele, Richard   1672-1729 . . . .   **LC 18**
See also CDBLB 1660-1789; DLB 84, 101

Steele, Timothy (Reid)   1948- . . . .   **CLC 45**
See also CA 93-96; CANR 16; DLB 120

Steffens, (Joseph) Lincoln
   1866-1936 . . . .   **TCLC 20**
See also CA 117

Stegner, Wallace (Earle)   1909- . . .   **CLC 9, 49**
See also AITN 1; BEST 90:3; CA 1-4R;
   CAAS 9; CANR 1, 21; DLB 9; MTCW

Stein, Gertrude   1874-1946 . . .   **TCLC 1, 6, 28**
See also CA 104; 132; CDALB 1917-1929;
   DLB 4, 54, 86; MTCW; WLC

Steinbeck, John (Ernst)
   1902-1968 . . . . .   **CLC 1, 5, 9, 13, 21, 34,
                                     45; SSC 11**
See also CA 1-4R; 25-28R; CANR 1, 35;
   CDALB 1929-1941; DLB 7, 9; DLBD 2;
   MTCW; SATA 9; WLC

Steinem, Gloria   1934- . . . .   **CLC 63**
See also CA 53-56; CANR 28; MTCW

Steiner, George   1929- . . . .   **CLC 24**
See also CA 73-76; CANR 31; DLB 67;
   MTCW; SATA 62

Steiner, Rudolf   1861-1925 . . . .   **TCLC 13**
See also CA 107

Stendhal   1783-1842 . . . .   **NCLC 23**
See also DLB 119; WLC

Stephen, Leslie   1832-1904 . . . .   **TCLC 23**
See also CA 123; DLB 57

Stephen, Sir Leslie
See Stephen, Leslie

Stephen, Virginia
See Woolf, (Adeline) Virginia

Stephens, James   1882(?)-1950 . . . . . .   **TCLC 4**
See also CA 104; DLB 19

Stephens, Reed
See Donaldson, Stephen R.

Steptoe, Lydia
See Barnes, Djuna

Sterchi, Beat   1949- . . . .   **CLC 65**

Sterling, Brett
See Bradbury, Ray (Douglas); Hamilton,
   Edmond

Sterling, Bruce   1954- . . . .   **CLC 72**
See also CA 119

Sterling, George   1869-1926 . . . .   **TCLC 20**
See also CA 117; DLB 54

Stern, Gerald   1925- . . . .   **CLC 40**
See also CA 81-84; CANR 28; DLB 105

Stern, Richard (Gustave)   1928- . . .   **CLC 4, 39**
See also CA 1-4R; CANR 1, 25; DLBY 87

Sternberg, Josef von   1894-1969 . . . . .   **CLC 20**
See also CA 81-84

Sterne, Laurence   1713-1768 . . . .   **LC 2**
See also CDBLB 1660-1789; DLB 39; WLC

Sternheim, (William Adolf) Carl
   1878-1942 . . . .   **TCLC 8**
See also CA 105; DLB 56, 118

Stevens, Mark   1951- . . . .   **CLC 34**
See also CA 122

Stevens, Wallace
   1879-1955 . . . .   **TCLC 3, 12, 45**
See also CA 104; 124; CDALB 1929-1941;
   DLB 54; MTCW; WLC

Stevenson, Anne (Katharine)
   1933- . . . .   **CLC 7, 33**
See also CA 17-20R; CAAS 9; CANR 9, 33;
   DLB 40; MTCW

Stevenson, Robert Louis (Balfour)
   1850-1894 . . . .   **NCLC 5, 14; SSC 11**
See also CDBLB 1890-1914; CLR 10, 11;
   DLB 18, 57; MAICYA; WLC; YABC 2

Stewart, J(ohn) I(nnes) M(ackintosh)
   1906- . . . .   **CLC 7, 14, 32**
See also CA 85-88; CAAS 3; MTCW

Stewart, Mary (Florence Elinor)
   1916- . . . .   **CLC 7, 35**
See also CA 1-4R; CANR 1; SATA 12

Stewart, Mary Rainbow
See Stewart, Mary (Florence Elinor)

Still, James   1906- . . . .   **CLC 49**
See also CA 65-68; CANR 10, 26; DLB 9;
   SATA 29

Sting
See Sumner, Gordon Matthew

Stirling, Arthur
See Sinclair, Upton (Beall)

Stitt, Milan   1941- . . . .   **CLC 29**
See also CA 69-72

Stockton, Francis Richard   1834-1902
See Stockton, Frank R.
See also CA 108; 137; MAICYA; SATA 44

Stockton, Frank R. . . . .   **TCLC 47**
See also Stockton, Francis Richard
See also DLB 42, 74; SATA 32

Stoddard, Charles
See Kuttner, Henry

Stoker, Abraham   1847-1912
See Stoker, Bram
See also CA 105; SATA 29

Stoker, Bram . . . .   **TCLC 8**
See also Stoker, Abraham
See also CDBLB 1890-1914; DLB 36, 70;
   WLC

Stolz, Mary (Slattery)   1920- . . . .   **CLC 12**
See also AAYA 8; AITN 1; CA 5-8R;
   CANR 13; MAICYA; SAAS 3;
   SATA 10, 70, 71

Stone, Irving   1903-1989 . . . .   **CLC 7**
See also AITN 1; CA 1-4R; 129; CAAS 3;
   CANR 1, 23; MTCW; SATA 3; SATO 64

Stone, Robert (Anthony)
   1937- . . . .   **CLC 5, 23, 42**
See also CA 85-88; CANR 23; MTCW

Stone, Zachary
See Follett, Ken(neth Martin)

Stoppard, Tom
   1937- . . .   **CLC 1, 3, 4, 5, 8, 15, 29, 34, 63**
See also CA 81-84; CANR 39;
   CDBLB 1960 to Present; DLB 13;
   DLBY 85; MTCW; WLC

Storey, David (Malcolm)
   1933- . . . .   **CLC 2, 4, 5, 8**
See also CA 81-84; CANR 36; DLB 13, 14;
   MTCW

Storm, Hyemeyohsts   1935- . . . .   **CLC 3**
See also CA 81-84

Storm, (Hans) Theodor (Woldsen)
   1817-1888 . . . .   **NCLC 1**

Storni, Alfonsina   1892-1938 . . . .   **TCLC 5**
See also CA 104; 131; HW

Stout, Rex (Todhunter)   1886-1975 . . .   **CLC 3**
See also AITN 2; CA 61-64

Stow, (Julian) Randolph   1935- . .   **CLC 23, 48**
See also CA 13-16R; CANR 33; MTCW

Stowe, Harriet (Elizabeth) Beecher
   1811-1896 . . . .   **NCLC 3**
See also CDALB 1865-1917; DLB 1, 12, 42,
   74; MAICYA; WLC; YABC 1

Strachey, (Giles) Lytton
   1880-1932 . . . .   **TCLC 12**
See also CA 110

Strand, Mark   1934- . . . . . .   **CLC 6, 18, 41, 71**
See also CA 21-24R; DLB 5; SATA 41

Straub, Peter (Francis)   1943- . . . . . .   **CLC 28**
See also BEST 89:1; CA 85-88; CANR 28;
   DLBY 84; MTCW

Strauss, Botho   1944- . . . .   **CLC 22**

Streatfeild, (Mary) Noel
   1895(?)-1986 . . . .   **CLC 21**
See also CA 81-84; 120; CANR 31;
   CLR 17; MAICYA; SATA 20, 48

Stribling, T(homas) S(igismund)
    1881-1965 .... CLC 23
    See also CA 107; DLB 9

Strindberg, (Johan) August
    1849-1912 .... TCLC 1, 8, 21, 47
    See also CA 104; 135; WLC

Stringer, Arthur   1874-1950 .... TCLC 37
    See also DLB 92

Stringer, David
    See Roberts, Keith (John Kingston)

Strugatskii, Arkadii (Natanovich)
    1925-1991 .... CLC 27
    See also CA 106; 135

Strugatskii, Boris (Natanovich)
    1933- .... CLC 27
    See also CA 106

Strummer, Joe   1953(?)- .... CLC 30
    See also The Clash

Stuart, Don A.
    See Campbell, John W(ood Jr.)

Stuart, Ian
    See MacLean, Alistair (Stuart)

Stuart, Jesse (Hilton)
    1906-1984 .... CLC 1, 8, 11, 14, 34
    See also CA 5-8R; 112; CANR 31; DLB 9,
    48, 102; DLBY 84; SATA 2, 36

Sturgeon, Theodore (Hamilton)
    1918-1985 .... CLC 22, 39
    See also Queen, Ellery
    See also CA 81-84; 116; CANR 32; DLB 8;
    DLBY 85; MTCW

Styron, William
    1925- .... CLC 1, 3, 5, 11, 15, 60
    See also BEST 90:4; CA 5-8R; CANR 6, 33;
    CDALB 1968-1988; DLB 2; DLBY 80;
    MTCW

Suarez Lynch, B.
    See Bioy Casares, Adolfo; Borges, Jorge
    Luis

Suarez Lynch, B.
    See Borges, Jorge Luis

Su Chien   1884-1918
    See Su Man-shu
    See also CA 123

Sudermann, Hermann   1857-1928 .. TCLC 15
    See also CA 107; DLB 118

Sue, Eugene   1804-1857 .... NCLC 1
    See also DLB 119

Sueskind, Patrick   1949- .... CLC 44

Sukenick, Ronald   1932- ..... CLC 3, 4, 6, 48
    See also CA 25-28R; CAAS 8; CANR 32;
    DLBY 81

Suknaski, Andrew   1942- .... CLC 19
    See also CA 101; DLB 53

Sullivan, Vernon
    See Vian, Boris

Sully Prudhomme   1839-1907 ...... TCLC 31

Su Man-shu .... TCLC 24
    See also Su Chien

Summerforest, Ivy B.
    See Kirkup, James

Summers, Andrew James   1942- ..... CLC 26
    See also The Police

Summers, Andy
    See Summers, Andrew James

Summers, Hollis (Spurgeon Jr.)
    1916- .... CLC 10
    See also CA 5-8R; CANR 3; DLB 6

Summers, (Alphonsus Joseph-Mary Augustus)
    Montague   1880-1948 .... TCLC 16
    See also CA 118

Sumner, Gordon Matthew   1951- .... CLC 26
    See also The Police

Surtees, Robert Smith
    1803-1864 .... NCLC 14
    See also DLB 21

Susann, Jacqueline   1921-1974 ...... CLC 3
    See also AITN 1; CA 65-68; 53-56; MTCW

Suskind, Patrick
    See Sueskind, Patrick

Sutcliff, Rosemary   1920- .... CLC 26
    See also CA 5-8R; CANR 37; CLR 1;
    MAICYA; SATA 6, 44

Sutro, Alfred   1863-1933 .... TCLC 6
    See also CA 105; DLB 10

Sutton, Henry
    See Slavitt, David R.

Svevo, Italo .... TCLC 2, 35
    See also Schmitz, Aron Hector

Swados, Elizabeth   1951- .... CLC 12
    See also CA 97-100

Swados, Harvey   1920-1972 .... CLC 5
    See also CA 5-8R; 37-40R; CANR 6;
    DLB 2

Swan, Gladys   1934- .... CLC 69
    See also CA 101; CANR 17, 39

Swarthout, Glendon (Fred)   1918- ... CLC 35
    See also CA 1-4R; CANR 1; SATA 26

Sweet, Sarah C.
    See Jewett, (Theodora) Sarah Orne

Swenson, May   1919-1989 ..... CLC 4, 14, 61
    See also CA 5-8R; 130; CANR 36; DLB 5;
    MTCW; SATA 15

Swift, Augustus
    See Lovecraft, H(oward) P(hillips)

Swift, Graham   1949- .... CLC 41
    See also CA 117; 122

Swift, Jonathan   1667-1745 .... LC 1
    See also CDBLB 1660-1789; DLB 39, 95,
    101; SATA 19; WLC

Swinburne, Algernon Charles
    1837-1909 .... TCLC 8, 36
    See also CA 105; CDBLB 1832-1890;
    DLB 35, 57; WLC

Swinfen, Ann .... CLC 34

Swinnerton, Frank Arthur
    1884-1982 .... CLC 31
    See also CA 108; DLB 34

Swithen, John
    See King, Stephen (Edwin)

Sylvia
    See Ashton-Warner, Sylvia (Constance)

Symmes, Robert Edward
    See Duncan, Robert (Edward)

Symonds, John Addington
    1840-1893 .... NCLC 34
    See also DLB 57

Symons, Arthur   1865-1945 .... TCLC 11
    See also CA 107; DLB 19, 57

Symons, Julian (Gustave)
    1912- .... CLC 2, 14, 32
    See also CA 49-52; CAAS 3; CANR 3, 33;
    DLB 87; MTCW

Synge, (Edmund) J(ohn) M(illington)
    1871-1909 .... TCLC 6, 37; DC 2
    See also CA 104; CDBLB 1890-1914;
    DLB 10, 19

Syruc, J.
    See Milosz, Czeslaw

Szirtes, George   1948- .... CLC 46
    See also CA 109; CANR 27

Tabori, George   1914- .... CLC 19
    See also CA 49-52; CANR 4

Tagore, Rabindranath   1861-1941 .... TCLC 3
    See also CA 104; 120; MTCW

Taine, Hippolyte Adolphe
    1828-1893 .... NCLC 15

Talese, Gay   1932- .... CLC 37
    See also AITN 1; CA 1-4R; CANR 9;
    MTCW

Tallent, Elizabeth (Ann)   1954- ..... CLC 45
    See also CA 117

Tally, Ted   1952- .... CLC 42
    See also CA 120; 124

Tamayo y Baus, Manuel
    1829-1898 .... NCLC 1

Tammsaare, A(nton) H(ansen)
    1878-1940 .... TCLC 27

Tan, Amy   1952- .... CLC 59
    See also AAYA 9; BEST 89:3; CA 136

Tandem, Felix
    See Spitteler, Carl (Friedrich Georg)

Tanizaki, Jun'ichiro
    1886-1965 .... CLC 8, 14, 28
    See also CA 93-96; 25-28R

Tanner, William
    See Amis, Kingsley (William)

Tao Lao
    See Storni, Alfonsina

Tarassoff, Lev
    See Troyat, Henri

Tarbell, Ida M(inerva)
    1857-1944 .... TCLC 40
    See also CA 122; DLB 47

Tarkington, (Newton) Booth
    1869-1946 .... TCLC 9
    See also CA 110; DLB 9, 102; SATA 17

Tasso, Torquato   1544-1595 .... LC 5

Tate, (John Orley) Allen
    1899-1979 .... CLC 2, 4, 6, 9, 11, 14, 24
    See also CA 5-8R; 85-88; CANR 32;
    DLB 4, 45, 63; MTCW

Tate, Ellalice
    See Hibbert, Eleanor Burford

Tate, James (Vincent)   1943- ... CLC 2, 6, 25
    See also CA 21-24R; CANR 29; DLB 5

Tavel, Ronald   1940- .... CLC 6
    See also CA 21-24R; CANR 33

Taylor, Cecil Philip   1929-1981 ..... CLC 27
    See also CA 25-28R; 105

Taylor, Edward   1642(?)-1729 .... **LC 11**
See also DLB 24

Taylor, Eleanor Ross   1920- .... **CLC 5**
See also CA 81-84

Taylor, Elizabeth   1912-1975 ... **CLC 2, 4, 29**
See also CA 13-16R; CANR 9; MTCW;
SATA 13

Taylor, Henry (Splawn)   1942- ...... **CLC 44**
See also CA 33-36R; CAAS 7; CANR 31;
DLB 5

Taylor, Kamala (Purnaiya)   1924-
See Markandaya, Kamala
See also CA 77-80

Taylor, Mildred D. .... **CLC 21**
See also BW; CA 85-88; CANR 25; CLR 9;
DLB 52; MAICYA; SAAS 5; SATA 15,
70

Taylor, Peter (Hillsman)
1917- ..... **CLC 1, 4, 18, 37, 44, 50, 71;
SSC 10**
See also CA 13-16R; CANR 9; DLBY 81;
MTCW

Taylor, Robert Lewis   1912- .... **CLC 14**
See also CA 1-4R; CANR 3; SATA 10

Tchekhov, Anton
See Chekhov, Anton (Pavlovich)

Teasdale, Sara   1884-1933 .... **TCLC 4**
See also CA 104; DLB 45; SATA 32

Tegner, Esaias   1782-1846 .... **NCLC 2**

Teilhard de Chardin, (Marie Joseph) Pierre
1881-1955 .... **TCLC 9**
See also CA 105

Temple, Ann
See Mortimer, Penelope (Ruth)

Tennant, Emma (Christina)
1937- .... **CLC 13, 52**
See also CA 65-68; CAAS 9; CANR 10, 38;
DLB 14

Tenneshaw, S. M.
See Silverberg, Robert

Tennyson, Alfred   1809-1892 ..... **NCLC 30**
See also CDBLB 1832-1890; DLB 32; WLC

Teran, Lisa St. Aubin de .... **CLC 36**
See also St. Aubin de Teran, Lisa

Teresa de Jesus, St.   1515-1582 ...... **LC 18**

Terkel, Louis   1912-
See Terkel, Studs
See also CA 57-60; CANR 18; MTCW

Terkel, Studs .... **CLC 38**
See also Terkel, Louis
See also AITN 1

Terry, C. V.
See Slaughter, Frank G(ill)

Terry, Megan   1932- .... **CLC 19**
See also CA 77-80; CABS 3; DLB 7

Tertz, Abram
See Sinyavsky, Andrei (Donatevich)

Tesich, Steve   1943(?)- .... **CLC 40, 69**
See also CA 105; DLBY 83

Teternikov, Fyodor Kuzmich   1863-1927
See Sologub, Fyodor
See also CA 104

Tevis, Walter   1928-1984 .... **CLC 42**
See also CA 113

Tey, Josephine .... **TCLC 14**
See also Mackintosh, Elizabeth
See also DLB 77

Thackeray, William Makepeace
1811-1863 .... **NCLC 5, 14, 22**
See also CDBLB 1832-1890; DLB 21, 55;
SATA 23; WLC

Thakura, Ravindranatha
See Tagore, Rabindranath

Tharoor, Shashi   1956- .... **CLC 70**

Thelwell, Michael Miles   1939- ..... **CLC 22**
See also CA 101

Theobald, Lewis Jr.
See Lovecraft, H(oward) P(hillips)

The Prophet
See Dreiser, Theodore (Herman Albert)

Theroux, Alexander (Louis)
1939- .... **CLC 2, 25**
See also CA 85-88; CANR 20

Theroux, Paul (Edward)
1941- .... **CLC 5, 8, 11, 15, 28, 46**
See also BEST 89:4; CA 33-36R; CANR 20;
DLB 2; MTCW; SATA 44

Thesen, Sharon   1946- .... **CLC 56**

Thevenin, Denis
See Duhamel, Georges

Thibault, Jacques Anatole Francois
1844-1924
See France, Anatole
See also CA 106; 127; MTCW

Thiele, Colin (Milton)   1920- .... **CLC 17**
See also CA 29-32R; CANR 12, 28;
CLR 27; MAICYA; SAAS 2; SATA 14

Thomas, Audrey (Callahan)
1935- .... **CLC 7, 13, 37**
See also AITN 2; CA 21-24R; CANR 36;
DLB 60; MTCW

Thomas, D(onald) M(ichael)
1935- .... **CLC 13, 22, 31**
See also CA 61-64; CAAS 11; CANR 17;
CDBLB 1960 to Present; DLB 40;
MTCW

Thomas, Dylan (Marlais)
1914-1953 .... **TCLC 1, 8, 45; PC 2;
SSC 3**
See also CA 104; 120; CDBLB 1945-1960;
DLB 13, 20; MTCW; SATA 60; WLC

Thomas, (Philip) Edward
1878-1917 .... **TCLC 10**
See also CA 106; DLB 19

Thomas, Joyce Carol   1938- .... **CLC 35**
See also BW; CA 113; 116; CLR 19;
DLB 33; MAICYA; MTCW; SAAS 7;
SATA 40

Thomas, Lewis   1913- .... **CLC 35**
See also CA 85-88; CANR 38; MTCW

Thomas, Paul
See Mann, (Paul) Thomas

Thomas, Piri   1928- .... **CLC 17**
See also CA 73-76; HW

Thomas, R(onald) S(tuart)
1913- .... **CLC 6, 13, 48**
See also CA 89-92; CAAS 4; CANR 30;
CDBLB 1960 to Present; DLB 27;
MTCW

Thomas, Ross (Elmore)   1926- ...... **CLC 39**
See also CA 33-36R; CANR 22

Thompson, Francis Clegg
See Mencken, H(enry) L(ouis)

Thompson, Francis Joseph
1859-1907 .... **TCLC 4**
See also CA 104; CDBLB 1890-1914;
DLB 19

Thompson, Hunter S(tockton)
1939- .... **CLC 9, 17, 40**
See also BEST 89:1; CA 17-20R; CANR 23;
MTCW

Thompson, Jim   1906-1976 .... **CLC 69**

Thompson, Judith .... **CLC 39**

Thomson, James   1700-1748 .... **LC 16**

Thomson, James   1834-1882 ...... **NCLC 18**

Thoreau, Henry David
1817-1862 .... **NCLC 7, 21**
See also CDALB 1640-1865; DLB 1; WLC

Thornton, Hall
See Silverberg, Robert

Thurber, James (Grover)
1894-1961 .... **CLC 5, 11, 25; SSC 1**
See also CA 73-76; CANR 17, 39;
CDALB 1929-1941; DLB 4, 11, 22, 102;
MAICYA; MTCW; SATA 13

Thurman, Wallace (Henry)
1902-1934 .... **TCLC 6**
See also BLC 3; BW; CA 104; 124; DLB 51

Ticheburn, Cheviot
See Ainsworth, William Harrison

Tieck, (Johann) Ludwig
1773-1853 .... **NCLC 5**
See also DLB 90

Tiger, Derry
See Ellison, Harlan

Tilghman, Christopher   1948(?)- ..... **CLC 65**

Tillinghast, Richard (Williford)
1940- .... **CLC 29**
See also CA 29-32R; CANR 26

Timrod, Henry   1828-1867 .... **NCLC 25**
See also DLB 3

Tindall, Gillian   1938- .... **CLC 7**
See also CA 21-24R; CANR 11

Tiptree, James Jr. .... **CLC 48, 50**
See also Sheldon, Alice Hastings Bradley
See also DLB 8

Titmarsh, Michael Angelo
See Thackeray, William Makepeace

Tocqueville, Alexis (Charles Henri Maurice
Clerel Comte)   1805-1859 ..... **NCLC 7**

Tolkien, J(ohn) R(onald) R(euel)
1892-1973 .... **CLC 1, 2, 3, 8, 12, 38**
See also AITN 1; CA 17-18; 45-48;
CANR 36; CAP 2; CDBLB 1914-1945;
DLB 15; MAICYA; MTCW; SATA 2,
24, 32; WLC

Toller, Ernst   1893-1939 .... **TCLC 10**
See also CA 107

Tolson, M. B.
See Tolson, Melvin B(eaunorus)

Tolson, Melvin B(eaunorus)
1898(?)-1966 .... **CLC 36**
See also BLC 3; BW; CA 124; 89-92;
DLB 48, 76

Tolstoi, Aleksei Nikolaevich
See Tolstoy, Alexey Nikolaevich

Tolstoy, Alexey Nikolaevich
1882-1945 .... **TCLC 18**
See also CA 107

Tolstoy, Count Leo
See Tolstoy, Leo (Nikolaevich)

Tolstoy, Leo (Nikolaevich)
1828-1910 ..... **TCLC 4, 11, 17, 28, 44;**
SSC 9
See also CA 104; 123; SATA 26; WLC

Tomasi di Lampedusa, Giuseppe 1896-1957
See Lampedusa, Giuseppe (Tomasi) di
See also CA 111

Tomlin, Lily .... **CLC 17**
See also Tomlin, Mary Jean

Tomlin, Mary Jean 1939(?)-
See Tomlin, Lily
See also CA 117

Tomlinson, (Alfred) Charles
1927- .... **CLC 2, 4, 6, 13, 45**
See also CA 5-8R; CANR 33; DLB 40

Tonson, Jacob
See Bennett, (Enoch) Arnold

Toole, John Kennedy
1937-1969 .... **CLC 19, 64**
See also CA 104; DLBY 81

Toomer, Jean
1894-1967 ..... **CLC 1, 4, 13, 22; SSC 1**
See also BLC 3; BW; CA 85-88;
CDALB 1917-1929; DLB 45, 51; MTCW

Torley, Luke
See Blish, James (Benjamin)

Tornimparte, Alessandra
See Ginzburg, Natalia

Torre, Raoul della
See Mencken, H(enry) L(ouis)

Torrey, E(dwin) Fuller 1937- .... **CLC 34**
See also CA 119

Torsvan, Ben Traven
See Traven, B.

Torsvan, Benno Traven
See Traven, B.

Torsvan, Berick Traven
See Traven, B.

Torsvan, Berwick Traven
See Traven, B.

Torsvan, Bruno Traven
See Traven, B.

Torsvan, Traven
See Traven, B.

Tournier, Michel (Edouard)
1924- .... **CLC 6, 23, 36**
See also CA 49-52; CANR 3, 36; DLB 83;
MTCW; SATA 23

Tournimparte, Alessandra
See Ginzburg, Natalia

Towers, Ivar
See Kornbluth, C(yril) M.

Townsend, Sue 1946- .... **CLC 61**
See also CA 119; 127; MTCW; SATA 48,
55

Townshend, Peter (Dennis Blandford)
1945- .... **CLC 17, 42**
See also CA 107

Tozzi, Federigo 1883-1920 .... **TCLC 31**

Traill, Catharine Parr
1802-1899 .... **NCLC 31**
See also DLB 99

Trakl, Georg 1887-1914 .... **TCLC 5**
See also CA 104

Transtroemer, Tomas (Goesta)
1931- .... **CLC 52, 65**
See also CA 117; 129

Transtromer, Tomas Gosta
See Transtroemer, Tomas (Goesta)

Traven, B. (?)-1969 .... **CLC 8, 11**
See also CA 19-20; 25-28R; CAP 2; DLB 9,
56; MTCW

Treitel, Jonathan 1959- .... **CLC 70**

Tremain, Rose 1943- .... **CLC 42**
See also CA 97-100; DLB 14

Tremblay, Michel 1942- .... **CLC 29**
See also CA 116; 128; DLB 60; MTCW

Trevanian (a pseudonym) 1930(?)-... **CLC 29**
See also CA 108

Trevor, Glen
See Hilton, James

Trevor, William
1928- .... **CLC 7, 9, 14, 25, 71**
See also Cox, William Trevor
See also DLB 14

Trifonov, Yuri (Valentinovich)
1925-1981 .... **CLC 45**
See also CA 126; 103; MTCW

Trilling, Lionel 1905-1975 .... **CLC 9, 11, 24**
See also CA 9-12R; 61-64; CANR 10;
DLB 28, 63; MTCW

Trimball, W. H.
See Mencken, H(enry) L(ouis)

Tristan
See Gomez de la Serna, Ramon

Tristram
See Housman, A(lfred) E(dward)

Trogdon, William (Lewis) 1939-
See Heat-Moon, William Least
See also CA 115; 119

Trollope, Anthony 1815-1882 .. **NCLC 6, 33**
See also CDBLB 1832-1890; DLB 21, 57;
SATA 22; WLC

Trollope, Frances 1779-1863 ..... **NCLC 30**
See also DLB 21

Trotsky, Leon 1879-1940 .... **TCLC 22**
See also CA 118

Trotter (Cockburn), Catharine
1679-1749 .... **LC 8**
See also DLB 84

Trout, Kilgore
See Farmer, Philip Jose

Trow, George W. S. 1943- .... **CLC 52**
See also CA 126

Troyat, Henri 1911- .... **CLC 23**
See also CA 45-48; CANR 2, 33; MTCW

Trudeau, G(arretson) B(eekman) 1948-
See Trudeau, Garry B.
See also CA 81-84; CANR 31; SATA 35

Trudeau, Garry B. .... **CLC 12**
See also Trudeau, G(arretson) B(eekman)
See also AITN 2

Truffaut, Francois 1932-1984 ...... **CLC 20**
See also CA 81-84; 113; CANR 34

Trumbo, Dalton 1905-1976 .... **CLC 19**
See also CA 21-24R; 69-72; CANR 10;
DLB 26

Trumbull, John 1750-1831 ...... **NCLC 30**
See also DLB 31

Trundlett, Helen B.
See Eliot, T(homas) S(tearns)

Tryon, Thomas 1926-1991 .... **CLC 3, 11**
See also AITN 1; CA 29-32R; 135;
CANR 32; MTCW

Tryon, Tom
See Tryon, Thomas

Ts'ao Hsueh-ch'in 1715(?)-1763 ...... **LC 1**

Tsushima, Shuji 1909-1948
See Dazai, Osamu
See also CA 107

Tsvetaeva (Efron), Marina (Ivanovna)
1892-1941 .... **TCLC 7, 35**
See also CA 104; 128; MTCW

Tuck, Lily 1938- .... **CLC 70**

Tunis, John R(oberts) 1889-1975 ... **CLC 12**
See also CA 61-64; DLB 22; MAICYA;
SATA 30, 37

Tuohy, Frank .... **CLC 37**
See also Tuohy, John Francis
See also DLB 14

Tuohy, John Francis 1925-
See Tuohy, Frank
See also CA 5-8R; CANR 3

Turco, Lewis (Putnam) 1934- ... **CLC 11, 63**
See also CA 13-16R; CANR 24; DLBY 84

Turgenev, Ivan
1818-1883 .... **NCLC 21; SSC 7**
See also WLC

Turner, Frederick 1943- .... **CLC 48**
See also CA 73-76; CAAS 10; CANR 12,
30; DLB 40

Tusan, Stan 1936- .... **CLC 22**
See also CA 105

Tutuola, Amos 1920- .... **CLC 5, 14, 29**
See also BLC 3; BW; CA 9-12R; CANR 27;
MTCW

Twain, Mark ..... **TCLC 6, 12, 19, 36; SSC 6**
See also Clemens, Samuel Langhorne
See also DLB 11, 12, 23, 64, 74; WLC

Tyler, Anne
1941- .... **CLC 7, 11, 18, 28, 44, 59**
See also BEST 89:1; CA 9-12R; CANR 11,
33; DLB 6; DLBY 82; MTCW; SATA 7

Tyler, Royall 1757-1826 .... **NCLC 3**
See also DLB 37

Tynan, Katharine 1861-1931 ...... **TCLC 3**
See also CA 104

Tytell, John 1939- .... **CLC 50**
See also CA 29-32R

Tyutchev, Fyodor 1803-1873 ..... **NCLC 34**

Tzara, Tristan .... CLC 47
   See also Rosenfeld, Samuel

Uhry, Alfred   1936- .... CLC 55
   See also CA 127; 133

Ulf, Haerved
   See Strindberg, (Johan) August

Ulf, Harved
   See Strindberg, (Johan) August

Unamuno (y Jugo), Miguel de
   1864-1936 .... TCLC 2, 9; SSC 11
   See also CA 104; 131; DLB 108; HW;
   MTCW

Undercliffe, Errol
   See Campbell, (John) Ramsey

Underwood, Miles
   See Glassco, John

Undset, Sigrid   1882-1949 .... TCLC 3
   See also CA 104; 129; MTCW; WLC

Ungaretti, Giuseppe
   1888-1970 .... CLC 7, 11, 15
   See also CA 19-20; 25-28R; CAP 2;
   DLB 114

Unger, Douglas   1952- .... CLC 34
   See also CA 130

Updike, John (Hoyer)
   1932- ...... CLC 1, 2, 3, 5, 7, 9, 13, 15,
                23, 34, 43, 70
   See also CA 1-4R; CABS 1; CANR 4, 33;
   CDALB 1968-1988; DLB 2, 5; DLBD 3;
   DLBY 80, 82; MTCW; WLC

Upshaw, Margaret Mitchell
   See Mitchell, Margaret (Munnerlyn)

Upton, Mark
   See Sanders, Lawrence

Urdang, Constance (Henriette)
   1922- .... CLC 47
   See also CA 21-24R; CANR 9, 24

Uris, Leon (Marcus)   1924- .... CLC 7, 32
   See also AITN 1, 2; BEST 89:2; CA 1-4R;
   CANR 1; MTCW; SATA 49

Urmuz
   See Codrescu, Andrei

Ustinov, Peter (Alexander)   1921- .... CLC 1
   See also AITN 1; CA 13-16R; CANR 25;
   DLB 13

V
   See Chekhov, Anton (Pavlovich)

Vaculik, Ludvik   1926- .... CLC 7
   See also CA 53-56

Valenzuela, Luisa   1938- .... CLC 31
   See also CA 101; CANR 32; DLB 113; HW

Valera y Alcala-Galiano, Juan
   1824-1905 .... TCLC 10
   See also CA 106

Valery, (Ambroise) Paul (Toussaint Jules)
   1871-1945 .... TCLC 4, 15
   See also CA 104; 122; MTCW

Valle-Inclan, Ramon (Maria) del
   1866-1936 .... TCLC 5
   See also CA 106

Vallejo, Antonio Buero
   See Buero Vallejo, Antonio

Vallejo, Cesar (Abraham)
   1892-1938 .... TCLC 3
   See also CA 105; HW

Valle Y Pena, Ramon del
   See Valle-Inclan, Ramon (Maria) del

Van Ash, Cay   1918- .... CLC 34

Vanbrugh, Sir John   1664-1726 ...... LC 21
   See also DLB 80

Van Campen, Karl
   See Campbell, John W(ood Jr.)

Vance, Gerald
   See Silverberg, Robert

Vance, Jack .... CLC 35
   See also Vance, John Holbrook
   See also DLB 8

Vance, John Holbrook   1916-
   See Queen, Ellery; Vance, Jack
   See also CA 29-32R; CANR 17; MTCW

Van Den Bogarde, Derek Jules Gaspard Ulric
   Niven   1921-
   See Bogarde, Dirk
   See also CA 77-80

Vandenburgh, Jane .... CLC 59

Vanderhaeghe, Guy   1951- .... CLC 41
   See also CA 113

van der Post, Laurens (Jan)   1906- ... CLC 5
   See also CA 5-8R; CANR 35

van de Wetering, Janwillem   1931- .. CLC 47
   See also CA 49-52; CANR 4

Van Dine, S. S. .... TCLC 23
   See also Wright, Willard Huntington

Van Doren, Carl (Clinton)
   1885-1950 .... TCLC 18
   See also CA 111

Van Doren, Mark   1894-1972 ..... CLC 6, 10
   See also CA 1-4R; 37-40R; CANR 3;
   DLB 45; MTCW

Van Druten, John (William)
   1901-1957 .... TCLC 2
   See also CA 104; DLB 10

Van Duyn, Mona (Jane)
   1921- .... CLC 3, 7, 63
   See also CA 9-12R; CANR 7, 38; DLB 5

Van Dyne, Edith
   See Baum, L(yman) Frank

van Itallie, Jean-Claude   1936- .... CLC 3
   See also CA 45-48; CAAS 2; CANR 1;
   DLB 7

van Ostaijen, Paul   1896-1928 ..... TCLC 33

Van Peebles, Melvin   1932- ...... CLC 2, 20
   See also BW; CA 85-88; CANR 27

Vansittart, Peter   1920- .... CLC 42
   See also CA 1-4R; CANR 3

Van Vechten, Carl   1880-1964 ...... CLC 33
   See also CA 89-92; DLB 4, 9, 51

Van Vogt, A(lfred) E(lton)   1912- ..... CLC 1
   See also CA 21-24R; CANR 28; DLB 8;
   SATA 14

Vara, Madeleine
   See Jackson, Laura (Riding)

Varda, Agnes   1928- .... CLC 16
   See also CA 116; 122

Vargas Llosa, (Jorge) Mario (Pedro)
   1936- .... CLC 3, 6, 9, 10, 15, 31, 42
   See also CA 73-76; CANR 18, 32; HW;
   MTCW

Vasiliu, Gheorghe   1881-1957
   See Bacovia, George
   See also CA 123

Vassa, Gustavus
   See Equiano, Olaudah

Vassilikos, Vassilis   1933- .... CLC 4, 8
   See also CA 81-84

Vaughn, Stephanie .... CLC 62

Vazov, Ivan (Minchov)
   1850-1921 .... TCLC 25
   See also CA 121

Veblen, Thorstein (Bunde)
   1857-1929 .... TCLC 31
   See also CA 115

Venison, Alfred
   See Pound, Ezra (Weston Loomis)

Verdi, Marie de
   See Mencken, H(enry) L(ouis)

Verdu, Matilde
   See Cela, Camilo Jose

Verga, Giovanni (Carmelo)
   1840-1922 .... TCLC 3
   See also CA 104; 123

Vergil   70B.C.-19B.C. .... CMLC 9

Verhaeren, Emile (Adolphe Gustave)
   1855-1916 .... TCLC 12
   See also CA 109

Verlaine, Paul (Marie)
   1844-1896 .... NCLC 2; PC 2

Verne, Jules (Gabriel)   1828-1905 ... TCLC 6
   See also CA 110; 131; MAICYA; SATA 21

Very, Jones   1813-1880 .... NCLC 9
   See also DLB 1

Vesaas, Tarjei   1897-1970 .... CLC 48
   See also CA 29-32R

Vialis, Gaston
   See Simenon, Georges (Jacques Christian)

Vian, Boris   1920-1959 .... TCLC 9
   See also CA 106; DLB 72

Viaud, (Louis Marie) Julien   1850-1923
   See Loti, Pierre
   See also CA 107

Vicar, Henry
   See Felsen, Henry Gregor

Vicker, Angus
   See Felsen, Henry Gregor

Vidal, Gore
   1925- ..... CLC 2, 4, 6, 8, 10, 22, 33, 72
   See also AITN 1; BEST 90:2; CA 5-8R;
   CANR 13; DLB 6; MTCW

Viereck, Peter (Robert Edwin)
   1916- .... CLC 4
   See also CA 1-4R; CANR 1; DLB 5

Vigny, Alfred (Victor) de
   1797-1863 .... NCLC 7
   See also DLB 119

Vilakazi, Benedict Wallet
   1906-1947 .... TCLC 37

Villiers de l'Isle Adam, Jean Marie Mathias Philippe Auguste Comte
1838-1889 .... NCLC **3**

Vincent, Gabrielle .... CLC **13**
See also CA 126; CLR 13; MAICYA; SATA 61

Vinci, Leonardo da 1452-1519 ...... LC **12**

Vine, Barbara .... CLC **50**
See also Rendell, Ruth (Barbara)
See also BEST 90:4

Vinge, Joan D(ennison) 1948- ...... CLC **30**
See also CA 93-96; SATA 36

Violis, G.
See Simenon, Georges (Jacques Christian)

Visconti, Luchino 1906-1976 .... CLC **16**
See also CA 81-84; 65-68; CANR 39

Vittorini, Elio 1908-1966 ...... CLC **6, 9, 14**
See also CA 133; 25-28R

Vizinczey, Stephen 1933- .... CLC **40**
See also CA 128

Vliet, R(ussell) G(ordon)
1929-1984 .... CLC **22**
See also CA 37-40R; 112; CANR 18

Vogau, Boris Andreyevich 1894-1937(?)
See Pilnyak, Boris
See also CA 123

Voigt, Cynthia 1942- .... CLC **30**
See also AAYA 3; CA 106; CANR 18, 37; CLR 13; MAICYA; SATA 33, 48

Voigt, Ellen Bryant 1943- .... CLC **54**
See also CA 69-72; CANR 11, 29; DLB 120

Voinovich, Vladimir (Nikolaevich)
1932- .... CLC **10, 49**
See also CA 81-84; CAAS 12; CANR 33; MTCW

Voltaire 1694-1778 .... LC **14**
See also WLC

von Daeniken, Erich 1935- .... CLC **30**
See also von Daniken, Erich
See also AITN 1; CA 37-40R; CANR 17

von Daniken, Erich .... CLC **30**
See also von Daeniken, Erich

von Heidenstam, (Carl Gustaf) Verner
See Heidenstam, (Carl Gustaf) Verner von

von Heyse, Paul (Johann Ludwig)
See Heyse, Paul (Johann Ludwig von)

von Hofmannsthal, Hugo
See Hofmannsthal, Hugo von

von Horvath, Odon
See Horvath, Oedoen von

von Horvath, Oedoen
See Horvath, Oedoen von

von Liliencron, (Friedrich Adolf Axel) Detlev
See Liliencron, (Friedrich Adolf Axel) Detlev von

Vonnegut, Kurt Jr.
1922- ...... CLC **1, 2, 3, 4, 5, 8, 12, 22, 40, 60;** SSC **8**
See also AAYA 6; AITN 1; BEST 90:4; CA 1-4R; CANR 1, 25; CDALB 1968-1988; DLB 2, 8; DLBD 3; DLBY 80; MTCW; WLC

Von Rachen, Kurt
See Hubbard, L(afayette) Ron(ald)

von Rezzori (d'Arezzo), Gregor
See Rezzori (d'Arezzo), Gregor von

von Sternberg, Josef
See Sternberg, Josef von

Vorster, Gordon 1924- .... CLC **34**
See also CA 133

Vosce, Trudie
See Ozick, Cynthia

Voznesensky, Andrei (Andreievich)
1933- .... CLC **1, 15, 57**
See also CA 89-92; CANR 37; MTCW

Waddington, Miriam 1917- .... CLC **28**
See also CA 21-24R; CANR 12, 30; DLB 68

Wagman, Fredrica 1937- .... CLC **7**
See also CA 97-100

Wagner, Richard 1813-1883 .... NCLC **9**

Wagner-Martin, Linda 1936- ...... CLC **50**

Wagoner, David (Russell)
1926- .... CLC **3, 5, 15**
See also CA 1-4R; CAAS 3; CANR 2; DLB 5; SATA 14

Wah, Fred(erick James) 1939- ...... CLC **44**
See also CA 107; DLB 60

Wahloo, Per 1926-1975 .... CLC **7**
See also CA 61-64

Wahloo, Peter
See Wahloo, Per

Wain, John (Barrington)
1925- .... CLC **2, 11, 15, 46**
See also CA 5-8R; CAAS 4; CANR 23; CDBLB 1960 to Present; DLB 15, 27; MTCW

Wajda, Andrzej 1926- .... CLC **16**
See also CA 102

Wakefield, Dan 1932- .... CLC **7**
See also CA 21-24R; CAAS 7

Wakoski, Diane
1937- .... CLC **2, 4, 7, 9, 11, 40**
See also CA 13-16R; CAAS 1; CANR 9; DLB 5

Wakoski-Sherbell, Diane
See Wakoski, Diane

Walcott, Derek (Alton)
1930- ...... CLC **2, 4, 9, 14, 25, 42, 67**
See also BLC 3; BW; CA 89-92; CANR 26; DLB 117; DLBY 81; MTCW

Waldman, Anne 1945- .... CLC **7**
See also CA 37-40R; CANR 34; DLB 16

Waldo, E. Hunter
See Sturgeon, Theodore (Hamilton)

Waldo, Edward Hamilton
See Sturgeon, Theodore (Hamilton)

Walker, Alice (Malsenior)
1944- ...... CLC **5, 6, 9, 19, 27, 46, 58;** SSC **5**
See also AAYA 3; BEST 89:4; BLC 3; BW; CA 37-40R; CANR 9, 27; CDALB 1968-1988; DLB 6, 33; MTCW; SATA 31

Walker, David Harry 1911- .... CLC **14**
See also CA 1-4R; 137; CANR 1; SATA 8, 71

Walker, Edward Joseph 1934-
See Walker, Ted
See also CA 21-24R; CANR 12, 28

Walker, George F. 1947- .... CLC **44, 61**
See also CA 103; CANR 21; DLB 60

Walker, Joseph A. 1935- .... CLC **19**
See also BW; CA 89-92; CANR 26; DLB 38

Walker, Margaret (Abigail)
1915- .... CLC **1, 6**
See also BLC 3; BW; CA 73-76; CANR 26; DLB 76; MTCW

Walker, Ted .... CLC **13**
See also Walker, Edward Joseph
See also DLB 40

Wallace, David Foster 1962- .... CLC **50**
See also CA 132

Wallace, Dexter
See Masters, Edgar Lee

Wallace, Irving 1916-1990 .... CLC **7, 13**
See also AITN 1; CA 1-4R; 132; CAAS 1; CANR 1, 27; MTCW

Wallant, Edward Lewis
1926-1962 .... CLC **5, 10**
See also CA 1-4R; CANR 22; DLB 2, 28; MTCW

Walpole, Horace 1717-1797 .... LC **2**
See also DLB 39, 104

Walpole, Hugh (Seymour)
1884-1941 .... TCLC **5**
See also CA 104; DLB 34

Walser, Martin 1927- .... CLC **27**
See also CA 57-60; CANR 8; DLB 75

Walser, Robert 1878-1956 .... TCLC **18**
See also CA 118; DLB 66

Walsh, Jill Paton .... CLC **35**
See also Paton Walsh, Gillian
See also CLR 2; SAAS 3

Walter, Villiam Christian
See Andersen, Hans Christian

Wambaugh, Joseph (Aloysius Jr.)
1937- .... CLC **3, 18**
See also AITN 1; BEST 89:3; CA 33-36R; DLB 6; DLBY 83; MTCW

Ward, Arthur Henry Sarsfield 1883-1959
See Rohmer, Sax
See also CA 108

Ward, Douglas Turner 1930- .... CLC **19**
See also BW; CA 81-84; CANR 27; DLB 7, 38

Warhol, Andy 1928(?)-1987 .... CLC **20**
See also BEST 89:4; CA 89-92; 121; CANR 34

Warner, Francis (Robert le Plastrier)
1937- .... CLC **14**
See also CA 53-56; CANR 11

Warner, Marina 1946- .... CLC **59**
See also CA 65-68; CANR 21

Warner, Rex (Ernest) 1905-1986 .... CLC **45**
See also CA 89-92; 119; DLB 15

Warner, Susan (Bogert)
1819-1885 .... NCLC **31**
See also DLB 3, 42

Warner, Sylvia (Constance) Ashton
See Ashton-Warner, Sylvia (Constance)

Warner, Sylvia Townsend
1893-1978 .... CLC **7, 19**
See also CA 61-64; 77-80; CANR 16;
DLB 34; MTCW

Warren, Mercy Otis 1728-1814... NCLC **13**
See also DLB 31

Warren, Robert Penn
1905-1989 ... CLC **1, 4, 6, 8, 10, 13, 18,
39, 53, 59; SSC 4**
See also AITN 1; CA 13-16R; 129;
CANR 10; CDALB 1968-1988; DLB 2,
48; DLBY 80, 89; MTCW; SATA 46, 63;
WLC

Warshofsky, Isaac
See Singer, Isaac Bashevis

Warton, Thomas 1728-1790........ LC **15**
See also DLB 104, 109

Waruk, Kona
See Harris, (Theodore) Wilson

Warung, Price 1855-1911........ TCLC **45**

Warwick, Jarvis
See Garner, Hugh

Washington, Alex
See Harris, Mark

Washington, Booker T(aliaferro)
1856-1915 .... TCLC **10**
See also BLC 3; BW; CA 114; 125;
SATA 28

Wassermann, (Karl) Jakob
1873-1934 .... TCLC **6**
See also CA 104; DLB 66

Wasserstein, Wendy 1950-...... CLC **32, 59**
See also CA 121; 129; CABS 3

Waterhouse, Keith (Spencer)
1929- .... CLC **47**
See also CA 5-8R; CANR 38; DLB 13, 15;
MTCW

Waters, Roger 1944-............. CLC **35**
See also Pink Floyd

Watkins, Frances Ellen
See Harper, Frances Ellen Watkins

Watkins, Gerrold
See Malzberg, Barry N(athaniel)

Watkins, Paul 1964-............. CLC **55**
See also CA 132

Watkins, Vernon Phillips
1906-1967 .... CLC **43**
See also CA 9-10; 25-28R; CAP 1; DLB 20

Watson, Irving S.
See Mencken, H(enry) L(ouis)

Watson, John H.
See Farmer, Philip Jose

Watson, Richard F.
See Silverberg, Robert

Waugh, Auberon (Alexander) 1939-.. CLC **7**
See also CA 45-48; CANR 6, 22; DLB 14

Waugh, Evelyn (Arthur St. John)
1903-1966 ... CLC **1, 3, 8, 13, 19, 27, 44**
See also CA 85-88; 25-28R; CANR 22;
CDBLB 1914-1945; DLB 15; MTCW;
WLC

Waugh, Harriet 1944- .... CLC **6**
See also CA 85-88; CANR 22

Ways, C. R.
See Blount, Roy (Alton) Jr.

Waystaff, Simon
See Swift, Jonathan

Webb, (Martha) Beatrice (Potter)
1858-1943 .... TCLC **22**
See also Potter, Beatrice
See also CA 117

Webb, Charles (Richard) 1939-...... CLC **7**
See also CA 25-28R

Webb, James H(enry) Jr. 1946- .... CLC **22**
See also CA 81-84

Webb, Mary (Gladys Meredith)
1881-1927 .... TCLC **24**
See also CA 123; DLB 34

Webb, Mrs. Sidney
See Webb, (Martha) Beatrice (Potter)

Webb, Phyllis 1927-.............. CLC **18**
See also CA 104; CANR 23; DLB 53

Webb, Sidney (James)
1859-1947 .... TCLC **22**
See also CA 117

Webber, Andrew Lloyd.............. CLC 21
See also Lloyd Webber, Andrew

Weber, Lenora Mattingly
1895-1971 .... CLC **12**
See also CA 19-20; 29-32R; CAP 1;
SATA 2, 26

Webster, John 1579(?)-1634(?) .... DC **2**
See also CDBLB Before 1660; DLB 58;
WLC

Webster, Noah 1758-1843 .... NCLC **30**

Wedekind, (Benjamin) Frank(lin)
1864-1918 .... TCLC **7**
See also CA 104; DLB 118

Weidman, Jerome 1913-............ CLC **7**
See also AITN 2; CA 1-4R; CANR 1;
DLB 28

Weil, Simone (Adolphine)
1909-1943 .... TCLC **23**
See also CA 117

Weinstein, Nathan
See West, Nathanael

Weinstein, Nathan von Wallenstein
See West, Nathanael

Weir, Peter (Lindsay) 1944- .... CLC **20**
See also CA 113; 123

Weiss, Peter (Ulrich)
1916-1982 .... CLC **3, 15, 51**
See also CA 45-48; 106; CANR 3; DLB 69

Weiss, Theodore (Russell)
1916- .... CLC **3, 8, 14**
See also CA 9-12R; CAAS 2; DLB 5

Welch, (Maurice) Denton
1915-1948 .... TCLC **22**
See also CA 121

Welch, James 1940-........ CLC **6, 14, 52**
See also CA 85-88

Weldon, Fay
1933(?)- .... CLC **6, 9, 11, 19, 36, 59**
See also CA 21-24R; CANR 16;
CDBLB 1960 to Present; DLB 14;
MTCW

Wellek, Rene 1903- .... CLC **28**
See also CA 5-8R; CAAS 7; CANR 8;
DLB 63

Weller, Michael 1942-........ CLC **10, 53**
See also CA 85-88

Weller, Paul 1958-............. CLC **26**

Wellershoff, Dieter 1925-.......... CLC **46**
See also CA 89-92; CANR 16, 37

Welles, (George) Orson
1915-1985 .... CLC **20**
See also CA 93-96; 117

Wellman, Mac 1945- .... CLC **65**

Wellman, Manly Wade 1903-1986 .. CLC **49**
See also CA 1-4R; 118; CANR 6, 16;
SATA 6, 47

Wells, Carolyn 1869(?)-1942 ...... TCLC **35**
See also CA 113; DLB 11

Wells, H(erbert) G(eorge)
1866-1946 ...... TCLC **6, 12, 19; SSC 6**
See also CA 110; 121; CDBLB 1914-1945;
DLB 34, 70; MTCW; SATA 20; WLC

Wells, Rosemary 1943-............ CLC **12**
See also CA 85-88; CLR 16; MAICYA;
SAAS 1; SATA 18, 69

Welty, Eudora
1909- .... CLC **1, 2, 5, 14, 22, 33; SSC 1**
See also CA 9-12R; CABS 1; CANR 32;
CDALB 1941-1968; DLB 2, 102;
DLBY 87; MTCW; WLC

Wen I-to 1899-1946 .... TCLC **28**

Wentworth, Robert
See Hamilton, Edmond

Werfel, Franz (V.) 1890-1945 ...... TCLC **8**
See also CA 104; DLB 81

Wergeland, Henrik Arnold
1808-1845 .... NCLC **5**

Wersba, Barbara 1932-............ CLC **30**
See also AAYA 2; CA 29-32R; CANR 16,
38; CLR 3; DLB 52; MAICYA; SAAS 2;
SATA 1, 58

Wertmueller, Lina 1928- .... CLC **16**
See also CA 97-100; CANR 39

Wescott, Glenway 1901-1987....... CLC **13**
See also CA 13-16R; 121; CANR 23;
DLB 4, 9, 102

Wesker, Arnold 1932- .... CLC **3, 5, 42**
See also CA 1-4R; CAAS 7; CANR 1, 33;
CDBLB 1960 to Present; DLB 13;
MTCW

Wesley, Richard (Errol) 1945-....... CLC **7**
See also BW; CA 57-60; DLB 38

Wessel, Johan Herman 1742-1785 .... LC **7**

West, Anthony (Panther)
1914-1987 .... CLC **50**
See also CA 45-48; 124; CANR 3, 19;
DLB 15

West, C. P.
See Wodehouse, P(elham) G(renville)

West, (Mary) Jessamyn
1902-1984 .... CLC **7, 17**
See also CA 9-12R; 112; CANR 27; DLB 6;
DLBY 84; MTCW; SATA 37

West, Morris L(anglo) 1916-..... CLC **6, 33**
See also CA 5-8R; CANR 24; MTCW

West, Nathanael
1903-1940 . . . . **TCLC 1, 14, 44**
See also CA 104; 125; CDALB 1929-1941;
DLB 4, 9, 28; MTCW

West, Paul 1930- . . . . **CLC 7, 14**
See also CA 13-16R; CAAS 7; CANR 22;
DLB 14

West, Rebecca 1892-1983 . . **CLC 7, 9, 31, 50**
See also CA 5-8R; 109; CANR 19; DLB 36;
DLBY 83; MTCW

Westall, Robert (Atkinson) 1929- . . . **CLC 17**
See also CA 69-72; CANR 18; CLR 13;
MAICYA; SAAS 2; SATA 23, 69

Westlake, Donald E(dwin)
1933- . . . . **CLC 7, 33**
See also CA 17-20R; CAAS 13; CANR 16

Westmacott, Mary
See Christie, Agatha (Mary Clarissa)

Weston, Allen
See Norton, Andre

Wetcheek, J. L.
See Feuchtwanger, Lion

Wetering, Janwillem van de
See van de Wetering, Janwillem

Wetherell, Elizabeth
See Warner, Susan (Bogert)

Whalen, Philip 1923- . . . . **CLC 6, 29**
See also CA 9-12R; CANR 5, 39; DLB 16

Wharton, Edith (Newbold Jones)
1862-1937 . . . . **TCLC 3, 9, 27; SSC 6**
See also CA 104; 132; CDALB 1865-1917;
DLB 4, 9, 12, 78; MTCW; WLC

Wharton, James
See Mencken, H(enry) L(ouis)

Wharton, William (a pseudonym)
. . . . **CLC 18, 37**
See also CA 93-96; DLBY 80

Wheatley (Peters), Phillis
1754(?)-1784 . . . . **LC 3; PC 3**
See also BLC 3; CDALB 1640-1865;
DLB 31, 50; WLC

Wheelock, John Hall 1886-1978 . . . . **CLC 14**
See also CA 13-16R; 77-80; CANR 14;
DLB 45

White, E(lwyn) B(rooks)
1899-1985 . . . . **CLC 10, 34, 39**
See also AITN 2; CA 13-16R; 116;
CANR 16, 37; CLR 1, 21; DLB 11, 22;
MAICYA; MTCW; SATA 2, 29, 44

White, Edmund (Valentine III)
1940- . . . . **CLC 27**
See also AAYA 7; CA 45-48; CANR 3, 19,
36; MTCW

White, Patrick (Victor Martindale)
1912-1990 . . **CLC 3, 4, 5, 7, 9, 18, 65, 69**
See also CA 81-84; 132; MTCW

White, Phyllis Dorothy James 1920-
See James, P. D.
See also CA 21-24R; CANR 17; MTCW

White, T(erence) H(anbury)
1906-1964 . . . . **CLC 30**
See also CA 73-76; CANR 37; MAICYA;
SATA 12

White, Terence de Vere 1912- . . . . . . **CLC 49**
See also CA 49-52; CANR 3

White, Walter
See White, Walter F(rancis)
See also BLC 3

White, Walter F(rancis)
1893-1955 . . . . **TCLC 15**
See also White, Walter
See also CA 115; 124; DLB 51

White, William Hale 1831-1913
See Rutherford, Mark
See also CA 121

Whitehead, E(dward) A(nthony)
1933- . . . . **CLC 5**
See also CA 65-68

Whitemore, Hugh (John) 1936- . . . . . **CLC 37**
See also CA 132

Whitman, Sarah Helen (Power)
1803-1878 . . . . **NCLC 19**
See also DLB 1

Whitman, Walt(er)
1819-1892 . . . . **NCLC 4, 31; PC 3**
See also CDALB 1640-1865; DLB 3, 64;
SATA 20; WLC

Whitney, Phyllis A(yame) 1903- . . . . **CLC 42**
See also AITN 2; BEST 90:3; CA 1-4R;
CANR 3, 25, 38; MAICYA; SATA 1, 30

Whittemore, (Edward) Reed (Jr.)
1919- . . . . **CLC 4**
See also CA 9-12R; CAAS 8; CANR 4;
DLB 5

Whittier, John Greenleaf
1807-1892 . . . . **NCLC 8**
See also CDALB 1640-1865; DLB 1

Whittlebot, Hernia
See Coward, Noel (Peirce)

Wicker, Thomas Grey 1926-
See Wicker, Tom
See also CA 65-68; CANR 21

Wicker, Tom . . . . **CLC 7**
See also Wicker, Thomas Grey

Wideman, John Edgar
1941- . . . . **CLC 5, 34, 36, 67**
See also BLC 3; BW; CA 85-88; CANR 14;
DLB 33

Wiebe, Rudy (H.) 1934- . . . . . . **CLC 6, 11, 14**
See also CA 37-40R; DLB 60

Wieland, Christoph Martin
1733-1813 . . . . **NCLC 17**
See also DLB 97

Wieners, John 1934- . . . . **CLC 7**
See also CA 13-16R; DLB 16

Wiesel, Elie(zer) 1928- . . . . . **CLC 3, 5, 11, 37**
See also AAYA 7; AITN 1; CA 5-8R;
CAAS 4; CANR 8; DLB 83; DLBY 87;
MTCW; SATA 56

Wiggins, Marianne 1947- . . . . **CLC 57**
See also BEST 89:3; CA 130

Wight, James Alfred 1916-
See Herriot, James
See also CA 77-80; SATA 44, 55

Wilbur, Richard (Purdy)
1921- . . . . **CLC 3, 6, 9, 14, 53**
See also CA 1-4R; CABS 2; CANR 2, 29;
DLB 5; MTCW; SATA 9

Wild, Peter 1940- . . . . **CLC 14**
See also CA 37-40R; DLB 5

Wilde, Oscar (Fingal O'Flahertie Wills)
1854(?)-1900 . . . . . . **TCLC 1, 8, 23, 41;**
SSC 11
See also CA 104; 119; CDBLB 1890-1914;
DLB 10, 19, 34, 57; SATA 24; WLC

Wilder, Billy . . . . **CLC 20**
See also Wilder, Samuel
See also DLB 26

Wilder, Samuel 1906-
See Wilder, Billy
See also CA 89-92

Wilder, Thornton (Niven)
1897-1975 . . . . . **CLC 1, 5, 6, 10, 15, 35;**
DC 1
See also AITN 2; CA 13-16R; 61-64;
DLB 4, 7, 9; MTCW; WLC

Wiley, Richard 1944- . . . . **CLC 44**
See also CA 121; 129

Wilhelm, Kate . . . . **CLC 7**
See also Wilhelm, Katie Gertrude
See also CAAS 5; DLB 8

Wilhelm, Katie Gertrude 1928-
See Wilhelm, Kate
See also CA 37-40R; CANR 17, 36; MTCW

Wilkins, Mary
See Freeman, Mary Eleanor Wilkins

Willard, Nancy 1936- . . . . **CLC 7, 37**
See also CA 89-92; CANR 10, 39; CLR 5;
DLB 5, 52; MAICYA; MTCW;
SATA 30, 37, 71

Williams, C(harles) K(enneth)
1936- . . . . **CLC 33, 56**
See also CA 37-40R; DLB 5

Williams, Charles
See Collier, James L(incoln)

Williams, Charles (Walter Stansby)
1886-1945 . . . . **TCLC 1, 11**
See also CA 104; DLB 100

Williams, (George) Emlyn
1905-1987 . . . . **CLC 15**
See also CA 104; 123; CANR 36; DLB 10,
77; MTCW

Williams, Hugo 1942- . . . . **CLC 42**
See also CA 17-20R; DLB 40

Williams, J. Walker
See Wodehouse, P(elham) G(renville)

Williams, John A(lfred) 1925- . . . . **CLC 5, 13**
See also BLC 3; BW; CA 53-56; CAAS 3;
CANR 6, 26; DLB 2, 33

Williams, Jonathan (Chamberlain)
1929- . . . . **CLC 13**
See also CA 9-12R; CAAS 12; CANR 8;
DLB 5

Williams, Joy 1944- . . . . **CLC 31**
See also CA 41-44R; CANR 22

Williams, Norman 1952- . . . . **CLC 39**
See also CA 118

Williams, Tennessee
1911-1983 . . . . **CLC 1, 2, 5, 7, 8, 11, 15,**
19, 30, 39, 45, 71
See also AITN 1, 2; CA 5-8R; 108;
CABS 3; CANR 31; CDALB 1941-1968;
DLB 7; DLBD 4; DLBY 83; MTCW;
WLC

Williams, Thomas (Alonzo)
1926-1990 . . . . **CLC 14**
See also CA 1-4R; 132; CANR 2

Williams, William C.
See Williams, William Carlos

Williams, William Carlos
1883-1963 . . . **CLC 1, 2, 5, 9, 13, 22, 42, 67**
See also CA 89-92; CANR 34;
CDALB 1917-1929; DLB 4, 16, 54, 86;
MTCW

Williamson, David Keith 1942- . . . . . **CLC 56**
See also CA 103

Williamson, Jack . . . . **CLC 29**
See also Williamson, John Stewart
See also CAAS 8; DLB 8

Williamson, John Stewart 1908-
See Williamson, Jack
See also CA 17-20R; CANR 23

Willie, Frederick
See Lovecraft, H(oward) P(hillips)

Willingham, Calder (Baynard Jr.)
1922- . . . . **CLC 5, 51**
See also CA 5-8R; CANR 3; DLB 2, 44;
MTCW

Willis, Charles
See Clarke, Arthur C(harles)

Willy
See Colette, (Sidonie-Gabrielle)

Willy, Colette
See Colette, (Sidonie-Gabrielle)

Wilson, A(ndrew) N(orman) 1950- . . **CLC 33**
See also CA 112; 122; DLB 14

Wilson, Angus (Frank Johnstone)
1913-1991 . . . . **CLC 2, 3, 5, 25, 34**
See also CA 5-8R; 134; CANR 21; DLB 15;
MTCW

Wilson, August
1945- . . . . **CLC 39, 50, 63; DC 2**
See also BLC 3; BW; CA 115; 122; MTCW

Wilson, Brian 1942- . . . . **CLC 12**

Wilson, Colin 1931- . . . . **CLC 3, 14**
See also CA 1-4R; CAAS 5; CANR 1, 22,
33; DLB 14; MTCW

Wilson, Dirk
See Pohl, Frederik

Wilson, Edmund
1895-1972 . . . . **CLC 1, 2, 3, 8, 24**
See also CA 1-4R; 37-40R; CANR 1;
DLB 63; MTCW

Wilson, Ethel Davis (Bryant)
1888(?)-1980 . . . . **CLC 13**
See also CA 102; DLB 68; MTCW

Wilson, John (Anthony) Burgess
1917- . . . . **CLC 8, 10, 13**
See also Burgess, Anthony
See also CA 1-4R; CANR 2; MTCW

Wilson, John 1785-1854 . . . . **NCLC 5**

Wilson, Lanford 1937- . . . . **CLC 7, 14, 36**
See also CA 17-20R; CABS 3; DLB 7

Wilson, Robert M. 1944- . . . . **CLC 7, 9**
See also CA 49-52; CANR 2; MTCW

Wilson, Robert McLiam 1964- . . . . . **CLC 59**
See also CA 132

Wilson, Sloan 1920- . . . . **CLC 32**
See also CA 1-4R; CANR 1

Wilson, Snoo 1948- . . . . **CLC 33**
See also CA 69-72

Wilson, William S(mith) 1932- . . . . . **CLC 49**
See also CA 81-84

Winchilsea, Anne (Kingsmill) Finch Counte
1661-1720 . . . . **LC 3**

Windham, Basil
See Wodehouse, P(elham) G(renville)

Wingrove, David (John) 1954- . . . . . . **CLC 68**
See also CA 133

Winters, Janet Lewis . . . . **CLC 41**
See also Lewis, Janet
See also DLBY 87

Winters, (Arthur) Yvor
1900-1968 . . . . **CLC 4, 8, 32**
See also CA 11-12; 25-28R; CAP 1;
DLB 48; MTCW

Winterson, Jeanette 1959- . . . . **CLC 64**
See also CA 136

Wiseman, Frederick 1930- . . . . **CLC 20**

Wister, Owen 1860-1938 . . . . **TCLC 21**
See also CA 108; DLB 9, 78; SATA 62

Witkacy
See Witkiewicz, Stanislaw Ignacy

Witkiewicz, Stanislaw Ignacy
1885-1939 . . . . **TCLC 8**
See also CA 105

Wittig, Monique 1935(?)- . . . . **CLC 22**
See also CA 116; 135; DLB 83

Wittlin, Jozef 1896-1976 . . . . **CLC 25**
See also CA 49-52; 65-68; CANR 3

Wodehouse, P(elham) G(renville)
1881-1975 . . . **CLC 1, 2, 5, 10, 22; SSC 2**
See also AITN 2; CA 45-48; 57-60;
CANR 3, 33; CDBLB 1914-1945;
DLB 34; MTCW; SATA 22

Woiwode, L.
See Woiwode, Larry (Alfred)

Woiwode, Larry (Alfred) 1941- . . . **CLC 6, 10**
See also CA 73-76; CANR 16; DLB 6

Wojciechowska, Maia (Teresa)
1927- . . . . **CLC 26**
See also AAYA 8; CA 9-12R; CANR 4;
CLR 1; MAICYA; SAAS 1; SATA 1, 28

Wolf, Christa 1929- . . . . **CLC 14, 29, 58**
See also CA 85-88; DLB 75; MTCW

Wolfe, Gene (Rodman) 1931- . . . . **CLC 25**
See also CA 57-60; CAAS 9; CANR 6, 32;
DLB 8

Wolfe, George C. 1954- . . . . **CLC 49**

Wolfe, Thomas (Clayton)
1900-1938 . . . . **TCLC 4, 13, 29**
See also CA 104; 132; CDALB 1929-1941;
DLB 9, 102; DLBD 2; DLBY 85;
MTCW; WLC

Wolfe, Thomas Kennerly Jr. 1930-
See Wolfe, Tom
See also CA 13-16R; CANR 9, 33; MTCW

Wolfe, Tom . . . . **CLC 1, 2, 9, 15, 35, 51**
See also Wolfe, Thomas Kennerly Jr.
See also AAYA 8; AITN 2; BEST 89:1

Wolff, Geoffrey (Ansell) 1937- . . . . . **CLC 41**
See also CA 29-32R; CANR 29

Wolff, Sonia
See Levitin, Sonia (Wolff)

Wolff, Tobias (Jonathan Ansell)
1945- . . . . **CLC 39, 64**
See also BEST 90:2; CA 114; 117

Wolfram von Eschenbach
c. 1170-c. 1220 . . . . **CMLC 5**

Wolitzer, Hilma 1930- . . . . **CLC 17**
See also CA 65-68; CANR 18; SATA 31

Wollstonecraft, Mary 1759-1797 . . . . . . **LC 5**
See also CDBLB 1789-1832; DLB 39, 104

Wonder, Stevie . . . . **CLC 12**
See also Morris, Steveland Judkins

Wong, Jade Snow 1922- . . . . **CLC 17**
See also CA 109

Woodcott, Keith
See Brunner, John (Kilian Houston)

Woodruff, Robert W.
See Mencken, H(enry) L(ouis)

Woolf, (Adeline) Virginia
1882-1941 . . . . **TCLC 1, 5, 20, 43; SSC 7**
See also CA 104; 130; CDBLB 1914-1945;
DLB 36, 100; MTCW; WLC

Woollcott, Alexander (Humphreys)
1887-1943 . . . . **TCLC 5**
See also CA 105; DLB 29

Wordsworth, Dorothy
1771-1855 . . . . **NCLC 25**
See also DLB 107

Wordsworth, William
1770-1850 . . . . **NCLC 12, 38; PC 4**
See also CDBLB 1789-1832; DLB 93, 107;
WLC

Wouk, Herman 1915- . . . . **CLC 1, 9, 38**
See also CA 5-8R; CANR 6, 33; DLBY 82;
MTCW

Wright, Charles (Penzel Jr.)
1935- . . . . **CLC 6, 13, 28**
See also CA 29-32R; CAAS 7; CANR 23,
36; DLBY 82; MTCW

Wright, Charles Stevenson 1932- . . . **CLC 49**
See also BLC 3; BW; CA 9-12R; CANR 26;
DLB 33

Wright, Jack R.
See Harris, Mark

Wright, James (Arlington)
1927-1980 . . . . **CLC 3, 5, 10, 28**
See also AITN 2; CA 49-52; 97-100;
CANR 4, 34; DLB 5; MTCW

Wright, Judith (Arandell)
1915- . . . . **CLC 11, 53**
See also CA 13-16R; CANR 31; MTCW;
SATA 14

Wright, L(aurali) R. . . . . **CLC 44**
See also CA 138

Wright, Richard B(ruce) 1937- . . . . . . **CLC 6**
See also CA 85-88; DLB 53

Wright, Richard (Nathaniel)
1908-1960 . . . **CLC 1, 3, 4, 9, 14, 21, 48;
SSC 2**
See also AAYA 5; BLC 3; BW; CA 108;
CDALB 1929-1941; DLB 76, 102;
DLBD 2; MTCW; WLC

Wright, Rick 1945-.............. **CLC 35**
See also Pink Floyd

Wright, Rowland
See Wells, Carolyn

Wright, Stephen 1946-............ **CLC 33**

Wright, Willard Huntington 1888-1939
See Van Dine, S. S.
See also CA 115

Wright, William 1930-............ **CLC 44**
See also CA 53-56; CANR 7, 23

Wu Ch'eng-en 1500(?)-1582(?)........ **LC 7**

Wu Ching-tzu 1701-1754............ **LC 2**

Wurlitzer, Rudolph 1938(?)- ... **CLC 2, 4, 15**
See also CA 85-88

Wycherley, William 1641-1715.... **LC 8, 21**
See also CDBLB 1660-1789; DLB 80

Wylie, Elinor (Morton Hoyt)
1885-1928 .... **TCLC 8**
See also CA 105; DLB 9, 45

Wylie, Philip (Gordon) 1902-1971... **CLC 43**
See also CA 21-22; 33-36R; CAP 2; DLB 9

Wyndham, John
See Harris, John (Wyndham Parkes Lucas)
Beynon

Wyss, Johann David Von
1743-1818 .... **NCLC 10**
See also MAICYA; SATA 27, 29

Yakumo Koizumi
See Hearn, (Patricio) Lafcadio (Tessima
Carlos)

Yanez, Jose Donoso
See Donoso (Yanez), Jose

Yanovsky, Basile S.
See Yanovsky, V(assily) S(emenovich)

Yanovsky, V(assily) S(emenovich)
1906-1989 .... **CLC 2, 18**
See also CA 97-100; 129

Yates, Richard 1926- .... **CLC 7, 8, 23**
See also CA 5-8R; CANR 10; DLB 2;
DLBY 81

Yeats, W. B.
See Yeats, William Butler

Yeats, William Butler
1865-1939 .... **TCLC 1, 11, 18, 31**
See also CA 104; 127; CDBLB 1890-1914;
DLB 10, 19, 98; MTCW; WLC

Yehoshua, Abraham B. 1936- ... **CLC 13, 31**
See also CA 33-36R

Yep, Laurence Michael 1948- ...... **CLC 35**
See also AAYA 5; CA 49-52; CANR 1;
CLR 3, 17; DLB 52; MAICYA; SATA 7,
69

Yerby, Frank G(arvin)
1916-1991 .... **CLC 1, 7, 22**
See also BLC 3; BW; CA 9-12R; 136;
CANR 16; DLB 76; MTCW

Yesenin, Sergei Alexandrovich
See Esenin, Sergei (Alexandrovich)

Yevtushenko, Yevgeny (Alexandrovich)
1933-............ **CLC 1, 3, 13, 26, 51**
See also CA 81-84; CANR 33; MTCW

Yezierska, Anzia 1885(?)-1970 ..... **CLC 46**
See also CA 126; 89-92; DLB 28; MTCW

Yglesias, Helen 1915-.......... **CLC 7, 22**
See also CA 37-40R; CANR 15; MTCW

Yokomitsu Riichi 1898-1947 ..... **TCLC 47**

York, Jeremy
See Creasey, John

York, Simon
See Heinlein, Robert A(nson)

Yorke, Henry Vincent 1905-1974 ... **CLC 13**
See also Green, Henry
See also CA 85-88; 49-52

Young, Al(bert James) 1939-....... **CLC 19**
See also BLC 3; BW; CA 29-32R;
CANR 26; DLB 33

Young, Andrew (John) 1885-1971.... **CLC 5**
See also CA 5-8R; CANR 7, 29

Young, Collier
See Bloch, Robert (Albert)

Young, Edward 1683-1765........... **LC 3**
See also DLB 95

Young, Neil 1945-................. **CLC 17**
See also CA 110

Yourcenar, Marguerite
1903-1987 .... **CLC 19, 38, 50**
See also CA 69-72; CANR 23; DLB 72;
DLBY 88; MTCW

Yurick, Sol 1925-................. **CLC 6**
See also CA 13-16R; CANR 25

Zamiatin, Yevgenii
See Zamyatin, Evgeny Ivanovich

Zamyatin, Evgeny Ivanovich
1884-1937 .... **TCLC 8, 37**
See also CA 105

Zangwill, Israel 1864-1926....... **TCLC 16**
See also CA 109; DLB 10

Zappa, Francis Vincent Jr. 1940-
See Zappa, Frank
See also CA 108

Zappa, Frank..................... **CLC 17**
See also Zappa, Francis Vincent Jr.

Zaturenska, Marya 1902-1982.... **CLC 6, 11**
See also CA 13-16R; 105; CANR 22

Zelazny, Roger (Joseph) 1937- ..... **CLC 21**
See also AAYA 7; CA 21-24R; CANR 26;
DLB 8; MTCW; SATA 39, 57

Zhdanov, Andrei A(lexandrovich)
1896-1948 .... **TCLC 18**
See also CA 117

Zhukovsky, Vasily 1783-1852.... **NCLC 35**

Ziegenhagen, Eric .... **CLC 55**

Zimmer, Jill Schary
See Robinson, Jill

Zimmerman, Robert
See Dylan, Bob

Zindel, Paul 1936-.............. **CLC 6, 26**
See also AAYA 2; CA 73-76; CANR 31;
CLR 3; DLB 7, 52; MAICYA; MTCW;
SATA 16, 58

Zinov'Ev, A. A.
See Zinoviev, Alexander (Aleksandrovich)

Zinoviev, Alexander (Aleksandrovich)
1922- .... **CLC 19**
See also CA 116; 133; CAAS 10

Zoilus
See Lovecraft, H(oward) P(hillips)

Zola, Emile 1840-1902... **TCLC 1, 6, 21, 41**
See also CA 104; WLC

Zoline, Pamela 1941-............. **CLC 62**

Zorrilla y Moral, Jose 1817-1893.. **NCLC 6**

Zoshchenko, Mikhail (Mikhailovich)
1895-1958 .... **TCLC 15**
See also CA 115

Zuckmayer, Carl 1896-1977....... **CLC 18**
See also CA 69-72; DLB 56

Zuk, Georges
See Skelton, Robin

Zukofsky, Louis
1904-1978 .... **CLC 1, 2, 4, 7, 11, 18**
See also CA 9-12R; 77-80; CANR 39;
DLB 5; MTCW

Zweig, Paul 1935-1984......... **CLC 34, 42**
See also CA 85-88; 113

Zweig, Stefan 1881-1942 .... **TCLC 17**
See also CA 112; DLB 81, 118

Literary Criticism Series
Cumulative Topic Index

This index lists all topic entries in the Gale Literary Criticism Series *Contemporary Literary Criticism, Literature Criticism from 1400 to 1800, Nineteenth-Century Literature Criticism,* and *Twentieth-Century Literary Criticism.*

Age of Johnson LC 15: 1-87
Johnson's London, 3-15
aesthetics of neoclassicism, 15-36
"age of prose and reason," 36-45
clubmen and bluestockings, 45-56
printing technology, 56-62
periodicals: "a map of busy life,"
62-74
transition, 74-86

American Civil War in Literature
NCLC 32: 1-109
overviews, 2-20
regional perspectives, 20-54
fiction popular during the war, 54-79
the historical novel, 79-108

American Frontier in Literature
NCLC 28: 1-103
definitions, 2-12
development, 12-17
nonfiction writing about the frontier,
17-30
frontier fiction, 30-45
frontier protagonists, 45-66
portrayals of Native Americans,
66-86
feminist readings, 86-98
twentieth-century reaction against
frontier literature, 98-100

**American Popular Song, Golden Age
of** TCLC 42: 1-49
background and major figures, 2-34
the lyrics of popular songs, 34-47

American Western Literature TCLC
46: 1-100
definition and development of
American Western literature, 2-7
characteristics of the Western novel,
8-23
Westerns as history and fiction,
23-34
critical reception of American
Western literature, 34-41
the Western hero, 41-73
women in Western fiction, 73-91
later Western fiction, 91-99

Arthurian Revival NCLC 36: 1-77
overviews, 2-12
Tennyson and his influence, 12-43
other leading figures, 43-73
the Arthurian legend in the visual
arts, 73-6

**Beat Generation, Literature of
the** TCLC 42: 50-102
overviews, 51-9
the Beat generation as a social
phenomenon, 59-62
development, 62-5
Beat literature, 66-96
influence, 97-100

***Bildungsroman* in Nineteenth-Century
Literature** NCLC 20: 92-168
surveys, 93-113
in Germany, 113-40
in England, 140-56
female *Bildungsroman,* 156-67

Bloomsbury Group TCLC 34: 1-73
history and major figures, 2-13
definitions, 13-17
influences, 17-27
thought, 27-40
prose, 40-52
and literary criticism, 52-4
political ideals, 54-61
response to, 61-71

**Bly, Robert, *Iron John: A Book about
Men* and Men's Work** CLC 70:414-62

The Book of J CLC 65: 289-311

Businessman in American Literature
TCLC 26: 1-48
portrayal of the businessman, 1-32
themes and techniques in business
fiction, 32-47

Celtic Twilight
See **Irish Literary Renaissance**

Civic Critics, Russian NCLC 20: 402-
46
principal figures and background,
402-09
and Russian Nihilism, 410-16
aesthetic and critical views, 416-45

**Columbus, Christopher, Books on the
Quincentennial of His Arrival in the
New World** CLC 70: 329-60

**Czechoslovakian Literature of the
Twentieth Century** TCLC 42: 103-96
through World War II, 104-35
de-Stalinization, The Prague Spring,
and contemporary literature, 135-
72
Slovak literature, 172-85
Czech science fiction, 185-93

Dadaism TCLC 46: 101-71
background and major figures, 102-
16
definitions, 116-26
manifestos and commentary by
Dadaists, 126-40
theater and film, 140-58
nature and characteristics of Dadaist
writing, 158-70

Darwinism and Literature NCLC 32:
110-206
background, 110-31
direct responses to Darwin, 131-71
collateral effects of Darwinism, 171-
205

de Man, Paul, Wartime Journalism of
CLC 55: 382-424

Detective Fiction, Nineteenth-Century
NCLC 36: 78-148
origins of the genre, 79-100
history of nineteenth-century
detective fiction, 101-33
significance of nineteenth-century
detective fiction, 133-46

Detective Fiction, Twentieth-Century
TCLC 38: 1-96
  genesis and history of the detective
    story, 3-22
  defining detective fiction, 22-32
  evolution and varieties, 32-77
  the appeal of detective fiction, 77-90

Eliot, T. S., Centenary of Birth CLC
55: 345-75

English Caroline Literature LC 13:
221-307
  background, 222-41
  evolution and varieties, 241-62
  the Cavalier mode, 262-75
  court and society, 275-91
  politics and religion, 291-306

**English Decadent Literature of the
1890s** NCLC 28: 104-200
  fin de siècle: the Decadent period,
    105-19
  definitions, 120-37
  major figures: "the tragic
    generation," 137-50
  French literature and English
    literary Decadence, 150-57
  themes, 157-61
  poetry, 161-82
  periodicals, 182-96

English Essay, Rise of the
LC 18: 238-308
  definitions and origins, 239-54
  influences on the essay, 254-69
  historical background, 269-78
  the essay in the seventeenth century,
    279-93
  the essay in the eighteenth century,
    293-307

English Romantic Poetry NCLC 28:
201-327
  overviews and reputation, 202-37
  major subjects and themes, 237-67
  forms of Romantic poetry, 267-78
  politics, society, and Romantic
    poetry, 278-99
  philosophy, religion, and Romantic
    poetry, 299-324

European Romanticism NCLC 36:
149-284
  definitions, 149-77
  origins of the movement, 177-82
  Romantic theory, 182-200
  themes and techniques, 200-23
  Romanticism in Germany, 223-39

  Romanticism in France, 240-61
  Romanticism in Italy, 261-64
  Romanticism in Spain, 264-68
  impact and legacy, 268-82

Existentialism and Literature TCLC
42: 197-268
  overviews and definitions, 198-209
  history and influences, 209-19
  Existentialism critiqued and
    defended, 220-35
  philosophical and religious
    perspectives, 235-41
  Existentialist fiction and drama, 241-
    67

Feminist Criticism in 1990 CLC 65:
312-60

Fifteenth-Century English Literature
LC 17: 248-334
  background, 249-72
  poetry, 272-315
  drama, 315-23
  prose, 323-33

Film and Literature TCLC 38: 97-226
  overviews, 97-119
  film and theater, 119-34
  film and the novel, 134-45
  the art of the screenplay, 145-66
  genre literature/genre film, 167-79
  the writer and the film industry,
    179-90
  authors on film adaptations of their
    works, 190-200
  fiction into film: comparative essays
    200-23

French Enlightenment LC 14: 81-145
  the question of definition, 82-9
  Le siècle des lumières, 89-94
  women and the salons, 94-105
  censorship, 105-15
  the philosophy of reason, 115-31
  influence and legacy, 131-44

Futurism, Italian TCLC 42: 269-354
  principles and formative influences,
    271-79
  manifestos, 279-88
  literature, 288-303
  theater, 303-19
  art, 320-30
  music, 330-36
  architecture, 336-39
  and politics, 339-46
  reputation and significance, 346-51

Gaelic Revival
  See **Irish Literary Renaissance**

**Gates, Henry Louis, Jr., and African-
American Literary Criticism** CLC 65:
361-405

German Exile Literature TCLC 30:
1-58
  the writer and the Nazi state, 1-10
  definition of, 10-14
  life in exile, 14-32
  surveys, 32-50
  Austrian literature in exile, 50-2
  German publishing in the United
    States, 52-7

German Expressionism TCLC 34: 74-
160
  history and major figures, 76-85
  aesthetic theories, 85-109
  drama, 109-26
  poetry, 126-38
  film, 138-42
  painting, 142-47
  music, 147-53
  and politics, 153-58

***Glasnost* and Contemporary Soviet
Literature** CLC 59: 355-97

Gothic Novel NCLC 28: 328-402
  development and major works, 328-
    34
  definitions, 334-50
  themes and techniques, 350-78
  in America, 378-85
  in Scotland, 385-91
  influence and legacy, 391-400

Harlem Renaissance TCLC 26: 49-125
  principal issues and figures, 50-67
  the literature and its audience, 67-74
  theme and technique in poetry,
    fiction, and drama, 74-115
  and American society, 115-21
  achievement and influence, 121-22

**Havel, Václav, Playwright and
President** CLC 65: 406-63

Holocaust, Literature of the TCLC
42: 355-450
  historical overview, 357-61
  critical overview, 361-70
  diaries and memoirs, 370-95
  novels and short stories, 395-425
  poetry, 425-41
  drama, 441-48

Hungarian Literature of the Twentieth Century　TCLC 26: 126-88
　surveys of, 126-47
　Nyugat and early twentieth-century literature, 147-56
　mid-century literature, 156-68
　and politics, 168-78
　since the 1956 revolt, 178-87

Italian Futurism
　See **Futurism, Italian**

Italian Humanism　LC 12: 205-77
　origins and early development, 206-18
　revival of classical letters, 218-23
　humanism and other philosophies, 224-39
　humanisms and humanists, 239-46
　the plastic arts, 246-57
　achievement and significance, 258-76

Irish Literary Renaissance　TCLC 46: 172-287
　overview, 173-83
　development and major figures, 184-202
　influence of Irish folklore and mythology, 202-22
　Irish poetry, 222-34
　Irish drama and the Abbey Theatre, 234-56
　Irish fiction, 256-86

Muckraking Movement in American Journalism　TCLC 34: 161-242
　development, principles, and major figures, 162-70
　publications, 170-79
　social and political ideas, 179-86
　targets, 186-208
　fiction, 208-19
　decline, 219-29
　impact and accomplishments, 229-40

Multiculturalism in Literature and Education　CLC 70: 361-413

Natural School, Russian　NCLC 24: 205-40
　history and characteristics, 205-25
　contemporary criticism, 225-40

Naturalism　NCLC 36: 285-382
　definitions and theories, 286-305
　critical debates on Naturalism, 305-16
　Naturalism in theater, 316-32
　European Naturalism, 332-61
　American Naturalism, 361-72
　the legacy of Naturalism, 372-81

New Criticism　TCLC 34: 243-318
　development and ideas, 244-70
　debate and defense, 270-99
　influence and legacy, 299-315

Newgate Novel　NCLC 24: 166-204
　development of Newgate literature, 166-73
　Newgate Calendar, 173-77
　Newgate fiction, 177-95
　Newgate drama, 195-204

New York Intellectuals and *Partisan Review*　TCLC 30: 117-98
　development and major figures, 118-28
　influence of Judaism, 128-39
　Partisan Review, 139-57
　literary philosophy and practice, 157-75
　political philosophy, 175-87
　achievement and significance, 187-97

Nigerian Literature of the Twentieth Century　TCLC 30: 199-265
　surveys of, 199-227
　English language and African life, 227-45
　politics and the Nigerian writer, 245-54
　Nigerian writers and society, 255-62

Northern Humanism　LC 16: 281-356
　background, 282-305
　precursor of the Reformation, 305-14
　the Brethren of the Common Life, the Devotio Moderna, and education, 314-40
　the impact of printing, 340-56

Nuclear Literature: Writings and Criticism in the Nuclear Age　TCLC 46: 288-390
　overviews, 290-301
　fiction, 301-35
　poetry, 335-38
　nuclear war in Russo-Japanese literature, 338-55
　nuclear war and women writers, 355-67
　the nuclear referent and literary criticism, 367-88

Opium and the Nineteenth-Century Literary Imagination　NCLC 20: 250-301
　original sources, 250-62
　historical background, 262-71
　and literary society, 271-79
　and literary creativity, 279-300

Periodicals, Nineteenth-Century British　NCLC 24: 100-65
　overviews, 100-30
　in the Romantic Age, 130-41
　in the Victorian era, 142-54
　and the reviewer, 154-64

Pre-Raphaelite Movement　NCLC 20: 302-401
　overview, 302-04
　genesis, 304-12
　Germ and *Oxford and Cambridge Magazine*, 312-20
　Robert Buchanan and the "Fleshly School of Poetry," 320-31
　satires and parodies, 331-34
　surveys, 334-51
　aesthetics, 351-75
　sister arts of poetry and painting, 375-94
　influence, 394-99

Psychoanalysis and Literature　TCLC 38: 227-338
　overviews, 227-46
　Freud on literature, 246-51
　psychoanalytic views of the literary process, 251-61
　psychoanalytic theories of response to literature, 261-88
　psychoanalysis and literary criticism, 288-312
　psychoanalysis as literature/literature as psychoanalysis, 313-34

Restoration Drama　LC 21: 184-275
　General overviews, 185-230
　Jeremy Collier Stage Controversy, 230-135
　Other Critical Interpretations, 240-75

Robin Hood, Legend of　LC 19: 205-58
　origins and development of the Robin Hood legend, 206-20
　representations of Robin Hood, 220-44
　Robin Hood as hero, 244-56

Rushdie, Salman, *Satanic Verses* Controversy　CLC 55: 214-63; 59: 404-56

Russian Nihilism　NCLC 28: 403-47
　definitions and overviews, 404-17
　women and Nihilism, 417-27
　literature as reform: the Civic Critics, 427-33
　Nihilism and the Russian novel: Turgenev and Dostoevsky, 433-47

Russian Thaw TCLC 26: 189-247
  literary history of the period, 190-206
  theoretical debate of socialist realism, 206-11
  Novy Mir, 211-17
  Literary Moscow, 217-24
  Pasternak, *Zhivago*, and the Nobel Prize, 224-27
  poetry of liberation, 228-31
  Brodsky trial and the end of the Thaw, 231-36
  achievement and influence, 236-46

Salinger, J. D., Controversy Surrounding *In Search of J. D. Salinger* CLC 55: 325-44

Science Fiction, Nineteenth-Century NCLC 24: 241-306
  background, 242-50
  definitions of the genre, 251-56
  representative works and writers, 256-75
  themes and conventions, 276-305

Scottish Chaucerians LC 20: 363-412

Sherlock Holmes Centenary TCLC 26: 248-310
  Doyle's life and the composition of the Holmes stories, 248-59
  life and character of Holmes, 259-78
  method, 278-79
  Holmes and the Victorian world, 279-92
  Sherlockian scholarship, 292-301
  Doyle and the development of the detective story, 301-07
  Holmes's continuing popularity, 307-09

Slave Narratives, American NCLC 20: 1-91
  background, 2-9
  overviews, 9-24
  contemporary responses, 24-7
  language, theme, and technique, 27-70
  historical authenticity, 70-5
  antecedents, 75-83
  role in development of Black American literature, 83-8

Spanish Civil War Literature TCLC 26: 311-85
  topics in, 312-33
  British and American literature, 333-59
  French literature, 359-62
  Spanish literature, 362-73
  German literature, 373-75
  political idealism and war literature, 375-83

Spasmodic School of Poetry NCLC 24: 307-52
  history and major figures, 307-21
  the Spasmodics on poetry, 321-27
  Firmilian and critical disfavor, 327-39
  theme and technique, 339-47
  influence, 347-51

Steinbeck, John, Fiftieth Anniversary of *The Grapes of Wrath* CLC 59: 311-54

Supernatural Fiction in the Nineteenth Century NCLC 32: 207-87
  major figures and influences, 208-35
  the Victorian ghost story, 236-54
  the influence of science and occultism, 254-66
  supernatural fiction and society, 266-86

Supernatural Fiction, Modern TCLC 30: 59-116
  evolution and varieties, 60-74
  "decline" of the ghost story, 74-86
  as a literary genre, 86-92
  technique, 92-101
  nature and appeal, 101-15

Surrealism TCLC 30: 334-406
  history and formative influences, 335-43
  manifestos, 343-54
  philosophic, aesthetic, and political principles, 354-75
  poetry, 375-81
  novel, 381-86
  drama, 386-92
  film, 392-98
  painting and sculpture, 398-403
  achievement, 403-05

Symbolism, Russian TCLC 30: 266-333
  doctrines and major figures, 267-92
  theories, 293-98
  and French Symbolism, 298-310
  themes in poetry, 310-14
  theater, 314-20
  and the fine arts, 320-32

Symbolist Movement, French NCLC 20: 169-249
  background and characteristics, 170-86
  principles, 186-91
  attacked and defended, 191-97
  influences and predecessors, 197-211
  and Decadence, 211-16
  theater, 216-26
  prose, 226-33
  decline and influence, 233-47

Theater of the Absurd TCLC 38: 339-415
  "The Theater of the Absurd," 340-47
  major plays and playwrights, 347-58
  and the concept of the absurd, 358-86
  theatrical techniques, 386-94
  predecessors of, 394-402
  influence of, 402-13

Tin Pan Alley
  See **American Popular Song, Golden Age of**

Transcendentalism, American NCLC 24: 1-99
  overviews, 3-23
  contemporary documents, 23-41
  theological aspects of, 42-52
  and social issues, 52-74
  literature of, 74-96

Travel Writing in the Twentieth Century TCLC 30: 407-56
  conventions and traditions, 407-27
  and fiction writing, 427-43
  comparative essays on travel writers, 443-54

Ulysses **and the Process of Textual Reconstruction** TCLC 26: 386-416
  evaluations of the new *Ulysses*, 386-94
  editorial principles and procedures, 394-401
  theoretical issues, 401-16

Utopian Literature, Nineteenth-Century NCLC 24: 353-473
  definitions, 354-74
  overviews, 374-88
  theory, 388-408
  communities, 409-26
  fiction, 426-53
  women and fiction, 454-71

Vampire in Literature TCLC 46: 391-454
  origins and evolution, 392-412
  social and psychological perspectives, 413-44
  vampire fiction and science fiction, 445-53

Victorian Novel NCLC 32: 288-454
  development and major characteristics, 290-310
  themes and techniques, 310-58

social criticism in the Victorian
  novel, 359-97
urban and rural life in the Victorian
  novel, 397-406
women in the Victorian novel, 406-
  25
Mudie's Circulating Library, 425-34
the late-Victorian novel, 434-51

World War I Literature   TCLC 34:
392-486
  overview, 393-403
  English, 403-27
  German, 427-50
  American, 450-66
  French, 466-74
  and modern history, 474-82

Yellow Journalism   NCLC 36: 383-456
  overviews, 384-96
  major figures, 396-413
  the role of reporters, 413-28
  the Spanish-American War, 428-48
  Yellow Journalism and society, 448-
    54

Young Playwrights Festival
  1988—CLC 55: 376-81
  1989—CLC 59: 398-403
  1990—CLC 65: 444-48

Topic Index

LC Cumulative Nationality Index

AFGHAN
Bābur 18

AMERICAN
Bradstreet, Anne 4
Edwards, Jonathan 7
Eliot, John 5
Knight, Sarah Kemble 7
Munford, Robert 5
Taylor, Edward 11
Wheatley, Phillis 3

ANGLO-AFRICAN
Equiano, Olaudah 16

CANADIAN
Marie de l'Incarnation 10

CHINESE
Lo Kuan-chung 12
P'u Sung-ling 3
Ts'ao Hsueh-ch'in 1
Wu Ch'eng-En 7
Wu-Ching-tzu 2

DANO-NORWEGIAN
Holberg, Ludvig 6
Wessel, Johan Herman 7

DUTCH
Erasmus, Desiderius 16
Lipsius, Justus 16
Spinoza, Benedictus de 9

ENGLISH
Addison, Joseph 18
Andrewes, Lancelot 5
Arbuthnot, John 1
Aubin, Penelope 9

Bacon, Sir Francis 18
Behn, Aphra 1
Brooke, Frances 6
Bunyan, John 4
Burke, Edmund 7
Butler, Samuel 16
Carew, Thomas 13
Caxton, William 17
Charles I 13
Chatterton, Thomas 3
Chaucer, Geoffrey 17
Churchill, Charles 3
Cleland, John 2
Collier, Jeremy 6
Collins, William 4
Congreve, William 5, 21
Davenant, William 13
Davys, Mary 1
Day, Thomas 1
Dee, John 20
Defoe, Daniel 1
Delany, Mary 12
Dennis, John 11
Donne, John 10
Drayton, Michael 8
Dryden, John 3, 21
Elyot, Sir Thomas 11
Fanshawe, Anne, Lady 11
Farquhar, George 21
Fielding, Henry 1
Fielding, Sarah 1
Foxe, John 14
Garrick, David 15
Goldsmith, Oliver 2
Gray, Thomas 4
Hawes, Stephen 17
Haywood, Eliza 1
Henry VIII 10
Herrick, Robert 13

Howell, James 13
Hunter, Robert 7
Johnson, Samuel 15
Jonson, Ben 6
Julian of Norwich 6
Kempe, Margery 6
Killigrew, Anne 4
Langland, William 19
Lanyer, Aemilia 10
Locke, John 7
Lyttelton, George 10
Malory, Thomas 11
Manley, Mary Delariviere 1
Marvell, Andrew 4
Milton, John 9
Montagu, Mary Wortley, Lady 9
More, Henry 9
More, Sir Thomas 10
Parnell, Thomas 3
Pepys, Samuel 11
Pix, Mary 8
Pope, Alexander 3
Prior, Matthew 4
Reynolds, Sir Joshua 15
Richardson, Samuel 1
Roper, William 10
Rowe, Nicholas 8
Sheridan, Frances 7
Sidney, Mary 19
Sidney, Sir Philip 19
Smart, Christopher 3
Smith, John 9
Spenser, Edmund 5
Steele, Sir Richard 18
Sterne, Laurence 2
Swift, Jonathan 1
Trotter, Catharine 8
Vanbrugh, Sir John 21
Walpole, Horace 2

Warton, Thomas **15**
Winchilsea, Anne Finch, Lady **3**
Wollstonecraft, Mary **5**
Wycherley, William **8, 21**
Young, Edward **3**

FRENCH
Boileau-Despréaux, Nicolas **3**
Christine de Pizan **9**
Crébillon, Claude Prosper Jolyot de, (fils) **1**
Descartes, René **20**
Duclos, Charles Pinot **1**
Holbach, Paul Henri Thiry, Baron d' **14**
La Bruyère, Jean de **17**
La Fayette, Marie-Madelaine, Comtesse de **2**
Lesage, Alain-René **2**
Malherbe, François de **5**
Marat, Jean Paul **10**
Marie de l'Incarnation **10**
Marivaux, Pierre Carlet de Chamblain de **4**
Marmontel, Jean-François **2**
Molière **10**
Montaigne, Michel de **8**
Montesquieu, Charles-Louis, Baron de **7**
Perrault, Charles **2**
Prévost, Antoine François, Abbé **1**
Rabelais, François **5**
Ronsard, Pierre de **6**
Rousseau, Jean-Baptiste **9**
Rousseau, Jean-Jacques **14**
Scudéry, Madeleine de **2**
Sévigné, Marie de Rabutin-Chantal, Marquise de **11**
Voltaire **14**

GERMAN
Beer, Johann **5**
Grimmelshausen, Johann Jakob Christoffel von **6**
Hutten, Ulrich von **16**
Kempis, Thomas á **11**
Lessing, Gotthold Ephraim **8**
Luther, Martin **9**
Moritz, Karl Philipp **2**
Schlegal, Johann Elias **5**

ICELANDIC
Pétursson, Halgrímur **8**

IRISH
Brooke, Henry **1**
Burke, Edmund **7**
Farquhar, George **21**

ITALIAN
Aretino, Pietro **12**
Ariosto, Ludovico **6**
Boiardo, Matteo Maria **6**
Casanova de Seingalt, Giovanni Jacopo **13**
Castelvetro, Lodovico **12**
Castiglione, Baldassare **12**
Cellini, Benvenuto **7**
Ficino, Marsilio **12**
Goldoni, Carlo **4**
Machiavelli, Niccolò **8**
Michelangelo **12**
Pico della Mirandola, Giovanni **15**
Sannazaro, Jacopo **8**
Tasso, Torquato **5**
Vinci, Leonardo da **12**

MEXICAN
Juana Inés de la Cruz **5**
Sigüenza y Góngora, Carlos de **8**

PERSIAN
Jami, Nur ud-din 'Abd-ur-rahman ibn Ahmad **9**

POLISH
Kochanowski, Jan **10**

PRUSSIAN
Frederick the Great **14**

RUSSIAN
Chulkov, Mikhail Dmitrievich **2**
Ivan IV **17**

SCOTTISH
Boswell, James **4**
Buchanan, George **4**
Burns, Robert **3**
Douglas, Gavin **20**
Dunbar, William **20**
Henryson, Robert **20**
Hume, David **7**
James I **20**
Lyndsay, Sir David **20**
Smollett, Tobias **2**
Thomson, James **16**

SPANISH
Castro, Guillén de **19**
Cervantes, Miguel de **6**
Gracían y Morales, Baltasar **15**
John of the Cross, St. **18**
Teresa de Jésus, St. **18**

SWISS
Paracelsus **14**
Rousseau, Jean-Jacques **14**

LC Cumulative Title Index

XCVI Sermons (Andrewes) **5**:19, 22-5, 28, 33, 41

"A Chaulieu" (Rousseau) **9**:344

"A Chretophle de Choiseul" (Ronsard) **6**:433

"A Courtin" (Rousseau) **9**:343-44

"A de Lannoy" (Rousseau) **9**:345

"A Denyse sorciere" (Ronsard) **6**:430

"A Gui Peccate Prieur de Sougé" (Ronsard) **6**:437

"A Guillaume Des Autels" (Ronsard) **6**:433

"A Janet Peintre du Roi" (Ronsard) **6**:433

"A Janne impitoyable" (Ronsard) **6**:419

"A Jean de Morel" (Ronsard) **6**:433

"A la fontaine Bellerie" (Ronsard) **6**:419, 430

"A la paix" (Rousseau) **9**:344

"A la reine sur sa bien-venüe en France" (Malherbe)
   See "Ode à Marie de Médicis, sur sa Bienvenue en France"

"A la reyne mère sur les heureux succez de sa régence" (Malherbe)
   See "Ode pour la Reine Mère du Roy pendant sa Régence"

"A l'ambassadeur de Venise" (Rousseau) **9**:344

"A l'empereur, après la conclusion de la quadruple alliance" (Rousseau) **9**:344

"A l'impératrice Amélie" (Rousseau) **9**:343

"A M. de Grimani" (Rousseau) **9**:340

A Mme Denis nièce de l'auteur, la vie de Paris et de Versailles (Voltaire) **14**:390

"A Monseigneur le Duc de Bellegarde, grand escuyer de France" (Malherbe) **5**:184

"A Philippe de Vendôme" (Rousseau) **9**:344

"A Philomèle" (Rousseau) **9**:345

"A Pierre L'Escot" (Ronsard) **6**:433

"A Robert de La Haye, Conseiller du Roi en son Parlement à Paris" (Ronsard) **6**:433

"A sa Muse" (Ronsard) **6**:430

"A son ame" (Ronsard) **6**:436

"A son livre" (Ronsard) **6**:425-27, 433-34

"A' the Airts" (Burns)
   See "Of A' the Airts"

"A une jeune veuve" (Rousseau)
   See "A une veuve"

"A une veuve" ("A une jeune veuve") (Rousseau) **9**:340, 344

"A Zinzindorf" (Rousseau)
   See "Ode au comte de Sinzendorff"

"Abbatis Eurditae" (Erasmus) **16**:128

"Abbot and the Learned Lady" (Erasmus) **16**:123, 142, 193

L'abbrégé de l'art poétique françois (Art Poétique) (Ronsard) **6**:406, 419, 427

L'A.B.C. (Voltaire) **14**:405

Abdelazer; or, The Moor's Revenge (Behn) **1**:28, 33, 39

Abecedarium Naturae (Bacon) **18**:187

Abhandlung von der Nachahmung (On Imitation) (Schlegel) **5**:274, 282-83

Abhandlung von der Unähnlichkeit in der Nachahmung (Schlegel) **5**:274

Abode of Spring (Jami)
   See *Baháristán*

"Abra; or, The Georgian Sultana" (Collins) **4**:210

Abridgements of the History of Rome and England (Goldsmith) **2**:71

Abridgment of English History (Burke)
   See *An Essay towards an Abridgement of the English History*

Absalom and Achitophel (Dryden) **3**:180, 185, 187, 189-92, 199, 201, 205, 213, 216-22, 225, 228, 231, 234, 240-43, 246; **21**:51, 53-7, 64-5, 86-7, 90-1, 94, 101-03, 111-13

"Absolute Retreat" (Winchilsea)
   See "The Petition for an Absolute Retreat"

Acajou et Zirphile (Duclos) **1**:185, 187

An Accidence; or, The Path-Way to Experience (A Sea Grammar) (Smith) **9**:381-82

The Accomplish'd Rake; or, Modern Fine Gentleman (Davys) **1**:99-100

An Account of a Battel between the Ancient and Modern Books in St. James's Library (Swift)
   See *A Tale of a Tub, Written for the Universal Improvement of Mankind, to Which is Added an Account of a Battel between the Ancient and Modern Books in St. James's Library*

"An Account of the English Poets" (Addison) **18**:6, 16, 38-9, 41, 61

"Account of the Ensuing Poem" (Dryden) **21**:90

The Account of the Fish Pool (Steele) **18**:354

An Account of the Growth of Popery and Arbitrary Power in England (Marvell) **4**:394

An Account of the Life of Mr. Richard Savage, Son of Earl Rivers ("Life of Savage") (Johnson) **15**:188, 195, 199, 203, 206, 287

Account of the Life of Shakespeare (Life of Shakespeare) (Rowe) **8**:296, 303

Act for Abolishing (Six Articles) (Henry VIII) **10**:125, 131, 136-38, 141

"Act Sederunt of the Session" (Burns) **3**:99-100

Actes and Monumentes of these latter perilous dayes touching matters of the Church (The Book of Martyrs; Commentarii; Ecclesiastical History; Monuments of the Martyrs; Rerum in Ecclesia History) (Foxe) **14**:5, 7-10, 12-15, 17, 19-22, 24-29, 32, 36, 38-39, 41, 43, 46-50, 54

Les acteurs de bonnefoi (Marivaux) **4**:369, 377

Ad Caesarem Maximilianum ut bellum in Venetos coeptum prosequatur exhortatorium (Exhortatorium) (Hutten) **16**:238

Adages (Erasmus)
  See *Adagia*
Adagia (*Adages*) (Erasmus) **16**:106, 132, 136, 154, 171, 173, 191, 193, 195-98
Adagiorum chiliades (Erasmus) **16**:132
Adagiorum Opus (Erasmus) **16**:195
Adam; ou, La création de l'homme, sa chûte et sa réparation (Perrault) **2**:256
Additional Articles to the Specimen of an Etimological Vocabulary (Behn) **2**:54
"Address of Beelzebub" (Burns) **3**:78, 95-6
"Address to a Haggis" ("To a Haggis") (Burns) **3**:52, 67, 71, 85
"Address to a Louse" (Burns)
  See "To a Louse, on Seeing One on a Lady's Bonnet at Church"
Address to All the Estates of the German Nation (Hutten) **16**:234
"Address to Edinburgh" (Burns) **3**:83
"Address to Ruin" ("Ruin") (Burns) **3**:48, 67
"Address to Saxham" ("To Saxham") (Carew) **13**:17, 32, 59, 61
"Address to the Atheist" (Wheatley) **3**:424
"Address to the De'il" ("Address to the Devil"; "To the De'il") (Burns) **3**:67, 71, 87, 95-6, 102-03
"Address to the Devil" (Burns)
  See "Address to the De'il"
The Address to the German Nobility (Luther)
  See *An den Christlichen Adel deutscher Nation: Von des Christlichen Standes Besserung*
"An Address to the Soul Occasioned by a Rain" (Taylor) **11**:394
"Address to the Toothache" (Burns)
  See "To the Toothache"
"Address to the Unco Guid, or the Rigidly Righteous" (Burns) **3**:51
Adélaide du Guesclin (Voltaire) **14**:397
Admiralty Letters (Pepys) **11**:238
Admonitioun (Buchanan)
  See *Ane Admonitioun Direct to the Trew Lordis, Maintenaris of Justice and Obedience to the Kingis Grace*
The Advancement and Reformation of Modern Poetry (Dennis) **11**:16, 19, 22-4, 26, 30, 33, 36-8, 40, 43-4, 51-3
The Adventure of the Black Lady (Behn) **1**:34, 38, 46
The Adventures in Madrid (Pix) **8**:262, 269, 271-72, 277
The Adventures of Covent Garden (Farquhar) **21**:135
The Adventures of David Simple (*David Simple, Volume the Last*) (Fielding) **1**:270-75, 278-79
The Adventures of Ferdinand, Count Fathom (Smollett) **2**:319-22, 324, 326, 330-32, 335, 337, 340, 346, 351-52, 354, 356-57, 359
The Adventures of Gargantua and Pantagruel (Rabelais)
  See *Gargantua and Pantagruel*
The Adventures of Gil Blas (Lesage)
  See *Histoire de Gil Blas de Santillane*
The Adventures of Guzman d'Alfarache (Lesage)
  See *Histoire de Guzman d'Alfarache*
The Adventures of Peregrine Pickle (Smollett) **2**:319-21, 324, 326, 328, 330, 332-34, 336-44, 352-57, 359, 361

The Adventures of Rivella (*The History of Rivella*) (Manley) **1**:308, 312, 315-17, 321, 323-24
The Adventures of Roderick Random (Smollett) **2**:319-21, 324-30, 333-34, 336-38, 341-42, 344-47, 351, 353-57, 359-62, 366
The Adventures of Sir Launcelot Greaves (Smollett) **2**:319-20, 322, 324, 329-30, 333, 336-37, 352, 357, 359-60
Adventures of the Chevalier de Beauchêne (Lesage)
  See *Les aventures de Monsieur Robert Chevalier*
The Adventures of the Prince of Clermont, and Madame de Ravezan (Aubin) **9**:6
The Adventurous Simplicissimus's Perpetual Calendar (Grimmelshausen)
  See *Des abenteuerlichen Simplicissimi Ewigwahrender Calender*
"Advertisements" (Garrick) **15**:122
Advertisements for the Unexperienced Planters of New England, or Any Where (Smith) **9**:379, 383-85, 388
Advice (Smollett) **2**:352, 358-59
Advice to a Lady (Lyttelton) **10**:200
Advice to Belinda (Lyttelton) **10**:203
"Ae Fond Kiss" (Burns) **3**:78, 83, 85
Aedes Walpolianae; or, A Description of the Pictures at Houghton Hall in Norfolk (Walpole) **2**:487
"Ælla: A Tragycal Enterlude" ("Dirge in Ælla") (Chatterton) **3**:118-20, 123-24, 127, 129-30, 135
Aesop (Vanbrugh) **21**:284, 287, 294-95, 334
The Affected Ladies (Moliere)
  See *Les précieuses ridicules*
"Affected (Man)" (Butler) **16**:51
"African Eclogues" ("Eclogues") (Chatterton) **3**:121, 123, 132
"After Autumne, Winter" (Herrick) **13**:341
"Afuera, afuera, ansias mías" ("Away, away, my cares") (Juana Ines de la Cruz) **5**:155
Against the Fear of Death (Dryden)
  See *Translation of the Latter Part of the Third Book of Lucretius: Against the Fear of Death*
Agamemnon. A tragedy (Thomson) **16**:385, 396
"Ages" (Bradstreet)
  See "The Four Ages of Man"
Agincourt (Drayton)
  See *The Battaile of Agincourt*
Agnes de Castro (Trotter) **8**:350, 352, 355, 357-59, 363-66, 368, 371-74
Agnes de Castro; or, The Force of Generous Blood (Behn) **1**:42, 44, 50-1
"Agrippina" (Gray) **4**:332
Agudeza de Ingenio (Gracian y Morales)
  See *Agudeza y arte de ingenio*
Agudeza y arte de ingenio (*Agudeza de Ingenio; El Arte de ingenio, tratado de la Agudeza*) (Gracian y Morales) **15**:136, 139, 141, 143-45, 147, 150
Ah, ha, Tumulus thalamus (Howell) **13**:427
"Aire and Angels" (*Twice or thrice had I loved thee*) (Donne) **10**:26, 36, 48, 55, 57-8, 82, 108-09
Akakia (Voltaire) **14**:328
al-Durrah al-Fákhira (*The Precious Pearl*) (Jami) **9**:58, 73
Albovine (Davenant) **13**:175, 196, 216
Alcestis (Buchanan) **4**:134-36

The Alchemist (Jonson) **6**:291, 294-95, 297, 300, 303, 305-07, 310-14, 319-20, 323-24, 328, 330-31, 334-36, 340, 343-44
"Aldarhéttur" ("Ways of the Present World") (Petursson) **8**:252
"Alexander's Feast; or, The Power of Musique. An Ode, in Honour of St. Cecilia's Day" (Dryden) **3**:186-87, 190, 213, 243; **21**:59, 61-4, 83, 88
"Alexandreis" (Killigrew) **4**:350
Alfred. A Masque (Thomson) **16**:396
All for Love; or, The World Well Lost (Dryden) **3**:186, 194, 209-10, 214, 216, 222, 232-35, 237, 242; **21**:52-3, 91
"All Is Vanity" (Winchilsea) **3**:441
"All kings and all their favourites" (Donne)
  See "The Anniversarie"
All Men Are Brothers (Lo Kuan-chung)
  See *Shui Hu Chuan*
"All Saints" (Smart) **3**:378
"Allegoria del poema" (Tasso) **5**:402, 405
"An Allegory on Man" (Parnell) **3**:252, 254
"L'Allegro" (Milton) **9**:177, 192, 197-98, 201, 204, 212, 224-33
"L'Allegro" (Smart) **3**:374
"Alliance" (Gray) **4**:333
All's Right at Last; or, The History of Miss West (Brooke) **6**:119-22
"L'alma, che sparge e versa" (Michelangelo) **12**:370
"Alma; or, The Progress of the Mind" (Prior) **4**:455-56, 459-60, 464, 467-73
Almindelig kirke-historie fra christendommens første begyndelse til Lutheri reformation... (*Church History*) (Holberg) **6**:282
Almyna; or, The Arabian Vow (Manley) **1**:316
"Alt eins og blómstrió eina" ("Eben as a Little Flower") (Petursson) **8**:252, 254
Alzire; ou, Les Américains (Voltaire) **14**:328, 330, 332, 397
"L'amant heureux" (Rousseau) **9**:341
"El amante liberal" ("The Liberal Lover") (Cervantes) **6**:171, 177
Les amants magnifiques (*The Magnificent Lovers*) (Moliere) **10**:283, 313, 320
Amazonum cantilena (Erasmus) **16**:196
"The Amber Bead" (Herrick) **13**:397
The Ambitious Step-Mother (Rowe) **8**:282, 285-86, 292, 295-96, 298, 302-05
Amelia (Fielding) **1**:209-10, 212, 215, 215-18, 224-26, 229, 233-35, 238, 241-42, 249-50, 252, 255, 258-61, 263
Amendments of Mr. Collier's False and Imperfect Citations from the "Old Batchelour," "Double-Dealer," "Love for Love," "Mourning Bride" (Congreve) **5**:104-05
"America" (Wheatley) **3**:435
L'Ami du Peuple (Marat)
  See *Le publiciste parisien, journal politique, libre et impartial . . .*
Aminta (Tasso) **5**:388, 390-92, 401, 407
"Aminta of Tasso" (Winchilsea) **3**:445
El amor constante (Castro) **19**:7-8, 13-15
Amor es más laberinto (*Love, the Greater Labyrinth*) (Juana Ines de la Cruz) **5**:150, 151, 159
L'amor paterno (Goldoni) **4**:261
Amoretti (Spenser) **5**:313, 332, 341-42, 355-56, 363-64
"An Amorist" (Butler) **16**:54

The Amorous Prince; or, The Curious Husband
(Behn)　**1**:33, 39, 52

L'amour de Dieu (Boileau-Despreaux)　**3**:22

"L'amour dévoilé" (Rousseau)　**9**:341

L'amour et la vérité (Marivaux)　**4**:367

L'amour médecin (Moliere)　**10**:282-83, 312-13, 327

"Amourette" (Ronsard)　**6**:427

Amours de Cassandre (Ronsard)　**6**:406, 409, 417

Amours de Marie (Ronsard)　**6**:409, 417

Les amours de Ronsard (Ronsard)　**6**:406, 411, 415-16, 425-27, 430-31

Amphitrion (Dryden)　**3**:180, 210, 222, 230

Amphitryon (Moliere)　**10**:268, 272, 283, 287, 312-13, 323

"Amymone" (Rousseau)　**9**:343

An den Christlichen Adel deutscher Nation: Von des Christlichen Standes Besserung (*The Address to the German Nobility*) (Luther)　**9**:102, 105, 108, 125-27, 134, 140, 143-44, 148

"L'an se rajeunissoit" (Ronsard)　**6**:427

"An Anabaptist" (Butler)　**16**:27

"Anacreontic" (Parnell)　**3**:256

"Anacreontike" (Herrick)　**13**:341

An Anatomie of the World (Donne)
　　See *The First Anniversarie. An Anatomie of the World. Wherein By Occasion of the untimely death of Mistris Elizabeth Drury, the frailtie and decay of this whole World is represented*

"And must I sing? what subject shall I chuse?" (Jonson)　**6**:350

Andreas Hartknopf: Eine Allegorie (Moritz)　**2**:233, 244-46

Andreas Hartknopfs Predigerjahre (Moritz)　**2**:244

"Andrew Turner" (Burns)　**3**:86

Androboros: A Biographical Farce in Three Acts, Viz. The Senate, The Consistory, and The Apotheosis (Hunter)　**7**:209-17

Ane Admonitioun Direct to the Trew Lordis, Maintenaris of Justice and Obedience to the Kingis Grace (*Admonitioun*) (Buchanan)　**4**:118

Ane Opinion anent the University of St. Andrews (Buchanan)
　　See *Opinion Anent the Reformation of the Universities of St Androis*

Anecdotes of Painting in England (Walpole)　**2**:455-56, 487

"Anelida and Arcite" (Chaucer)　**17**:71, 123

Anima magica abscondita (More)　**9**:310

Animadversions upon the Remonstrants Defence (Milton)　**9**:250

Annaei Senecae Philosopli Opera, quae exstant, onmia (Seneca) (Lipsius)　**16**:274

Annales de l'empire (Voltaire)　**14**:338, 411

"Anne Hay" (Carew)
　　See "Obsequies to the Lady Anne Hay"

"Anne Killigrew" (Dryden)
　　See "To the Pious Memory of the Accomplisht Young Lady Mrs. Anne Killigrew"

Annibal (Marivaux)　**4**:366

"The Anniversarie" ("All kings and all their favourites") (Donne)　**10**:18, 36, 48, 52

The Anniversaries (*The First and Second Anniversaries*) (Donne)　**10**:17, 25-6, 39, 53, 63, 67, 74, 83-4, 89, 95, 97-9, 103

Anno 7603 (Wessel)　**7**:390

The Annual Register (*Register*) (Burke)　**7**:63

"The Annuntiation and the Passion" (Donne)　**10**:40, 84

"Annus Mirabilis: The Year of Wonders, 1666" (Dryden)　**3**:178, 190, 192-93, 201, 213, 215-16, 221-24, 226, 234-35, 239-40, 243; **21**:53, 85-6, 88, 91, 107, 111, 116

"Another Grace for a Child" (Herrick)　**13**:357

"The Answer" (Wycherley)　**8**:410

The Answer (Montagu)　**9**:282

An Answer to Some Exceptions in Bishop Burnet's Third Part of the History of the Reformation (Collier)　**6**:209

"Answer to the Guidwife of Wauchope House" (Burns)　**3**:94

Answer to the Poisoned Book (More)　**10**:398, 400, 437

"An Answer to the Rebus" (Wheatley)　**3**:420

"Answer to the Secret Committee" (Prior)　**4**:467

An Answer to the...Book Which a Nameless Heretic hath named: The Supper of the Lord (More)　**10**:370

Anthon Reiser (Moritz)
　　See *Anton Reiser*

Anti-Goeze (Lessing)　**8**:98, 107

Anti-Machiavel (*The Refutation of Machiavelli's Prince*) (Frederick the Great)　**14**:59, 62, 77-8

Antibarbari (*Book against the Barbarians*) (Erasmus)　**16**:134, 142, 145-46

An Antidote Against Atheism (More)　**9**:300, 302, 306, 311

"Antimonopsychia: or, That All Souls are not One" (More)　**9**:313-14, 331

"Antipsychopannychia" (More)　**9**:313, 330-31

The Antiquarian's Family (Goldoni)
　　See *La famiglia dell' antiquario*

"Antiquary" (Donne)　**10**:95

Anton Reiser (*Anthon Reiser*) (Moritz)　**2**:228-48

Antony and Cleopatra (Brooke)　**1**:62

Anzoig (Hutten)　**16**:246

Aphorismi et Consilia, de Auxiliis Mentis, et Accensione (Bacon)　**18**:187

Apologia (Erasmus)　**16**:149

Apologia (Pico della Mirandola)　**15**:321-22, 327

"Apologie de Raimond Sebond" ("An Apology of Raymond Sebond") (Montaigne)　**8**:191-92, 205, 209, 211, 218, 221-22, 225, 228, 230-31, 234, 236-37, 240, 245, 247-48

L'apologie des femmes (*The Vindication of Wives*) (Perrault)　**2**:279

An Apologie for Poetrie (Sidney)
　　See *The Defence of Poesie*

"An Apology" (Bradstreet)　**4**:111

"The Apology" (Churchill)　**3**:144, 150, 152-53, 155-57, 162-63

"The Apology" (Winchilsea)　**3**:446

Apology for Heroic Poetry (Dryden)
　　See *The Author's Apology for Heroic Poetry and Poetic License*

Apology for Smectymnuus (Milton)　**9**:192, 210, 252

"An Apology for the Ladies" (Montagu)　**9**:281

An Apology for the Life of Mrs. Shamela Andrews (*Shamela*) (Fielding)　**1**:238-39, 242-43, 258, 260-61

"An Apology of Raymond Sebond" (Montaigne)
　　See "Apologie de Raimond Sebond"

The apologye of syr Thomas More knyght (More)　**10**:366, 370, 398

Apophthegms New and Old (Bacon)　**18**:136, 192

"Apostate Will" (Chatterton)　**3**:127, 132

Apotheosis of John Reuchlin (Erasmus)　**16**:121

"The Apparition" (Donne)　**10**:34, 36, 52, 73, 82

"The Apparition of his Mistress calling him to Elyzium" (Herrick)　**13**:316, 365

An Appeal from the New, to the Old Whigs in Consequence of Some Late Discussions in Parliament, Relative to the Reflections on the French Revolution (*Appeal to the Old Whigs*) (Burke)　**7**:27, 64

Appeal to the Old Whigs (Burke)
　　See *An Appeal from the New, to the Old Whigs in Consequence of Some Late Discussions in Parliament, Relative to the Reflections on the French Revolution*

Appel à toutes les nations de l'Europe (Voltaire)　**14**:353

Appius and Virginia (Dennis)　**11**:9, 12

"Appleton House" (Marvell)
　　See "Upon Appleton House"

The Apprentice's Vade Mecum (*Vade Mecum*) (Richardson)　**1**:416, 418

"L'apprentie coquette" (Marivaux)　**4**:379

Det arabiske pulver (Holberg)　**6**:277-78

"Arcades" (Milton)　**9**:197, 202-03, 205

Arcadia (Sannazaro)　**8**:322, 326-28, 330-33, 336-37

Arcadia (Sidney)
　　See *The Countess of Pembroke's Arcadia*

Archidoxa (*Archidoxis magica; Nine Books of Archidoxus*) (Paracelsus)　**14**:198, 200

Archidoxis magica (Paracelsus)
　　See *Archidoxa*

"Ardelia's Answer to Ephelia" (Winchilsea)　**3**:449, 451, 456

Areopagitica (Milton)　**9**:191, 195-96, 223-24, 249-57

An Argument against Abolishing Christianity (Swift)　**1**:460, 509, 519

"The Argument of his Book" (Herrick)　**13**:336, 340, 346, 349, 351, 361, 363-64, 374-76, 391, 393, 398

Argumentum de summo bono (Ficino)　**12**:168

Aristomène (Marmontel)　**2**:213, 216

"Aristomenes" (Winchilsea)　**3**:440

Arlequin poli par l'amour (Marivaux)　**4**:365-66, 368, 376

Arminius (Hutten)　**16**:245

Arsace et Isménie (Montesquieu)　**7**:320

"Art above Nature, to Julia" (Herrick)　**13**:351, 369, 393

"Art of Conversation" (Montaigne)
　　See "De l'art de conferer"

The Art of Poetry (Boileau-Despreaux)
　　See *L'art poétique*

"The Art of Sinking in Poetry" (Pope)
　　See "Peri Bathous; or, The Art of Sinking in Poetry"

The Art of War (Machiavelli)
　　See *Libro della arte della guerra*

L'art poétique (*The Art of Poetry*) (Boileau-Despreaux)　**3**:16, 22, 25-35, 39

Art Poétique (Ronsard)
　　See *L'abbrégé de l'art poétique françois*

Artamène; ou, Le Grand Cyrus (*Le Grand Cyrus*) (Marivaux) **4**:365-66, 368, 376

El Arte de ingenio, tratado de la Agudeza (Gracian y Morales)
See *Agudeza y arte de ingenio*

De Arte Versificandi (Hutten) **16**:229

"Artem quaevis alit terra" (Erasmus) **16**:198

The Artful Widow (Goldoni)
See *La vedova scaltra*

"Articles proposed by the Earl of Warwick to the lords and council for their approbation, as preceptor to King Henry VI" **17**:436

Articles . . . to Stabliyshe Christen Quietnes (*Ten Articles*) (Henry VIII) **10**:129-30, 135

'Arud risālesi (Babur) **18**:89-90

"As Love and I, Late Harbour'd in One Inne" (Drayton)
See "Sonnet LIX"

"As Spring the Winter Doth Succeed" (Bradstreet) **4**:99

"As virtuous men pass mildly away" (Donne)
See "A Valediction: forbidding mourning"

"As Weary Pilgrim" ("A Pilgrim") (Bradstreet) **4**:98, 102, 108

"The Ascension of Our Lord Jesus Christ" (Smart) **3**:378

Ascent of Mount Carmel (John of the Cross)
See *Subida del Monte Carmelo*

"Asclepiads" (Sidney) **19**:326

Ash'i'atu 'l Lama'āt (*Rays of the Flashes*) (Jami) **9**:67

"L'asino d'oro" ("The Golden Ass") (Machiavelli) **8**:128, 135, 178-79

"Ask me no more where Jove bestows" (Carew) **13**:11, 20, 28-9, 58

Assertio septem sacramentorum adversus Martinum Lutherum haeresiarchon (*An assertion of the Seven Sacraments, against Martin Luther, Defense of the Seven Sacraments against Martin Luther*) (Henry VIII) **10**:117-118, 120-22, 133-34, 138-39, 141-43, 146-47

An assertion of the Seven Sacraments, against Martin Luther (Henry VIII)
See *Assertio septem sacramentorum adversus Martinum Lutherum haeresiarchon*

The Assignation (Dryden) **3**:230

"The Ass's Skin" (Perrault)
See "Peau d'ane"

"Astrea Redux. A Poem on the Happy Restoration and Return of His Sacred Majesty Charles the Second" (Dryden) **3**:178, 223, 225-26; **21**:85

"Les Astres" ("Hymne des astres") (Ronsard) **6**:410, 422, 429

"Astrologer" (Butler) **16**:55

Astronomia magna, or the Whole Sagacious Philosophy of the Great and Small World (Paracelsus) **14**:199

Astronomical Libra (Siguenza y Gongora)
See *Libra astronomica y philosophica*

"Astrophel: A Pastoral Elegy" (Spenser) **5**:312, 314, 354

Astrophel and Stella (Sidney) **19**:318-19, 329, 334, 345, 352, 354, 358, 360-61, 374-76, 391-97, 406, 409, 413-15, 421-22, 424

Athalie (Voltaire) **14**:354

"The Atheist" (Donne) **10**:30

"The Atheist and the Acorn" (Winchilsea) **3**:451

"Attributes of the Supreme Being" (Smart) **3**:399

"Au beuf qui tout le jour" (Ronsard) **6**:433-34

"Au feu roi sur l'heureux succez du voyage de Sedan" (Malherbe) **5**:184

"Au prince de Vendôme" (Rousseau) **9**:340

"Au prince Eugêne de Savoie, après la paix de Passarowitz" (Rousseau) **9**:340, 344-45

"Au roi de la Grande-Bretagne" (Rousseau) **9**:344

"Au roi de Pologne" (Rousseau) **9**:344

De augmentis scientiarum (*De Dignitate et Augmentis Scientiarum*) (Bacon) **18**:111, 117-18, 120, 126, 146, 152-53, 161-62, 168, 174, 178, 187, 193, 195

Aula (Hutten) **16**:239-41, 246

"The Auld Farmer's New-Year-Morning Salutation" (Burns)
See "The Auld Farmer's New Year's Day Address to His Auld Mare Maggie"

"The Auld Farmer's New Year's Day Address to His Auld Mare Maggie" ("The Auld Farmer's New-Year-Morning Salutation") (Burns) **3**:57, 60, 64, 67, 87, 93

"Auld Lang Syne" (Burns) **3**:561, 62, 66, 78

Aunswere to Frithes Letter agaynst the Blessed Sacramen of the Aulter (*Letter*) (More) **10**:366, 398

Aureng-Zebe (Dryden) **3**:193, 222, 232-33; **21**:72, 75, 88, 120

Aussichten zu einer Experimentalseelenlehre (Moritz) **2**:235-36

The Austrian in Love; or, The Love and Life Story of Sorona, Incomparable in Virtues and Beauty (Beer)
See *Der verliebte Österreicher*

Aut regem aut fatuum (Erasmus) **16**:198

"The Author" (Churchill) **3**:150-51, 155-56, 159-60, 163

"The Author to her Book" (Bradstreet) **4**:107, 112

"Author to His Book" (Beer) **5**:59

"The Author upon Himself" (Swift) **1**:482, 523

The Author's Apology for Heroic Poetry and Poetic License (*Apology for Heroic Poetry*) (Dryden) **3**:197, 236, 238; **21**:66, 85

"The Authors Dreame to the Ladie Marie, the Countesse Dowager of Pembroke" (Lanyer) **10**:184

The Author's Farce and the Pleasures of the Town (Fielding) **1**:203, 219

Autobiography (Cellini)
See *Vita di Benvenuto Cellini*

Autobiography (Fanshawe)
See *Memoirs of Lady Fanshawe*

The Autobiography and Correspondence of Mary Granville (Mrs. Delany) (*Life cnd Correspondence*) (Delany) **12**:135, 140, 143, 148-51, 154

The Autobiography of Venerable Marie of the Incarnation (Marie de l'Incarnation)
See *Relation autobiographique*

Autres balades (Christine de Pizan) **9**:41

"Autumn" (Pope) **3**:334

Autumn (Thomson) **16**:363-64, 372-74, 380-84, 395, 402-05, 411-13, 415, 419, 424-26, 432

"Aux princes chrétiens" (Rousseau) **9**:340, 344

"Aux Suisses" (Rousseau) **9**:344

"Avant-entrée" (Ronsard) **6**:431

L'avare (*The Miser*) (Moliere) **10**:268, 271, 280, 283-85, 287, 290-91, 293, 297, 313, 341, 343, 345-46

Aventure indienne (Voltaire) **14**:346

Les aventures de Monsieur Robert Chevalier (*Adventures of the Chevalier de Beauchêne*) (Lesage) **2**:176, 182

Avision (Christine de Pizan)
See *Lavision-Christine*

Le avventure della villeggiatura (Goldoni) **4**:265-66

L'avvocato veneziano (Goldoni) **4**:262

"Away, away, my cares" (Juana Ines de la Cruz)
See "Afuera, afuera, ansias mías"

"B--, A Song" ("Boswell: A Song") (Boswell) **4**:52, 61

B. D. S. Opera posthuma (*Opera posthuma*) (Spinoza) **9**:397

Bababec (Voltaire) **14**:346

The Babbling Barber (Holberg)
See *Mester Gert Westphaler; eller, Den meget talende barbeer*

The Bābur-nāma (*Memoirs*) (Babur) **18**:84-96

Le bachelier de Salamanque (*The Bachelor of Salamanca*) (Lesage) **2**:177, 179, 182, 184, 202

The Bachelor of Salamanca (Lesage)
See *Le bachelier de Salamanque*

"The bad season makes the Poet sad" (Herrick) **13**:365, 383, 392-93, 396

Badman (Bunyan)
See *The Life and Death of Mr. Badman*

"The Bag Wig and the Tobacco-pipe" (Smart) **3**:366

Baháristán (*Abode of Spring*) (Jami) **9**:61, 63-4, 67-8, 70-1

"Les bains de Thomery" (Rousseau) **9**:343

"Ballad of Down-Hall" ("Down Hall") (Prior) **4**:461, 464, 467

"A Banker" (Butler) **16**:55

The Bankete of Sapience (*The Banquet of Sapience*) (Elyot) **11**:62, 73, 81, 83, 90

"The Banner, or Homage from Prussia" (Kochanowski)
See "Proporzec albo Hold Pruski"

"Bannocks o' Barley Meal" (Burns) **3**:84

Los baños de Argel (Cervantes) **6**:180-81

The Banquet of Sapience (Elyot)
See *The Bankete of Sapience*

Baptistes: sive Calumnia, tragoedia, auctore Georgio Buchanano Scoto (Buchanan) **4**:120, 133-34, 136-37

"La barbe bleue" ("Bluebeard") (Perrault) **2**:254, 258, 260, 267, 280, 284

"The Bard" (Gray) **4**:280, 282-85, 288-89, 292-93, 300-02, 309-10, 312-15, 317-18, 321, 333

"A Bard's Epitaph" (Burns) **3**:67

"Barrenness" (Parnell) **3**:252

The Barrons Wars in the Raigne of Edward the Second (Drayton) **8**:8, 10-11, 14-15, 19-20, 27, 33

Barselstuen (*The Lying-in Room*) (Holberg) **6**:277

Bartholomew Fair (Jonson) **6**:292, 297, 300, 304-06, 313-14, 320, 323-24, 330-31, 334-36, 340, 343

Le baruffe chiozzotte (*The Chioggian Brawls*) (Goldoni) **4**:257, 264, 266, 275

"The Bashful Lover" (Thomson) **16**:427

The Basque Impostor (Cervantes) **6**:190-91

The Battaile of Agincourt (Agincourt)
(Drayton) **8**:8, 14-18, 23, 25-7, 30, 33, 41-2,
44-5
"Battle of Hastings" (Chatterton) **3**:118, 120,
126, 128, 135
"The Battle of Ramellies" (Dennis)
See "The Battle of Ramilla: or, The Power
of Union"
"The Battle of Ramilla: or, The Power of
Union" ("The Battle of Ramellies") (Dennis)
11:13, 15, 26, 49
"The Battle of the Frogs and Mice" (Parnell)
3:251-54
The Beard War (Grimmelshausen)
See *Der Bart-Krieg*
"Beau" (Marmontel) **2**:223
*The Beau Defeated; or, The Lucky Younger
Brother* (Pix) **8**:262, 268-69, 272-73, 276
Beautie (Jonson)
See *Masque of Beauty*
The Beauties of English Poetry (Goldsmith)
2:80
"A Beautiful Young Nymph Going to Bed"
(Swift) **1**:453, 483
"A beautifull Mistris" (Carew) **13**:34
The Beaux' Stratagem (Farquhar) **21**:127-29,
133-35, 138-39, 143-47, 149-54, 158-61, 167-
72, 174-76, 178-79
"Before a Journey" (Andrewes) **5**:35
"Before the Birth of one of her Children"
(Bradstreet) **4**:107
"The Beggar to Mab" (Herrick) **13**:368
"Being once blind, his request to Biancha"
(Herrick) **13**:398
*Beiträge zur Historie und Aufnahme des
Theaters (Contributions to the History and
Improvement of the Theater)* (Lessing)
8:84, 111-12
*Beiträge zur Philosophie des Lebens aus dem
Tagebuch eines Freimaurers* (Moritz) **2**:230,
241-42
"Bel Aubepin" (Ronsard) **6**:425-26
Belfagor (Machiavelli)
See *Favola: Belfagor arcidiavolo che prese
moglie*
Bélisaire (Belisarius) (Marmontel) **2**:208, 213-
14, 217-20
Belisario (Goldoni) **4**:249
Belisarius (Marmontel)
See *Bélisaire*
"La belle au bois dormant" ("Sleeping
Beauty") (Perrault) **2**:253-54, 260-61, 266,
280-84
Bellum Erasmi (Erasmus) **16**:159
"Béni soit le Dieu des armées" (Rousseau)
9:338
"Bermudas" (Marvell) **4**:400, 403-04, 410,
412, 441-42
Bestia Civitatis (Beer) **5**:56
"A Better Answer" (Prior) **4**:466
*Biathanatos. A declaration of that paradoxe, or
thesis, that self-homicide is not so naturally
sinne, that it may never be otherwise.*
(Donne) **10**:11, 36, 77-9
La Bible enfin expliquée (Voltaire) **14**:370
Bibliotheca (Elyot)
See *The Dictionary*
Bibliotheca Eliotae (Elyot)
See *The Dictionary*
"Bid me to live" (Herrick) **13**:332, 338
Le bilboquet (Marivaux) **4**:378
"The Bird" (Winchilsea) **3**:445, 451, 454

"Birth of Love" (Jonson) **6**:326
Bishops' Book (Henry VIII)
See *The Institution of a Christen Man*
The Bitter (Rowe) **8**:292, 299, 310-12
"A Bitter Fate" (Chulkov)
See "Gor'kaia uchast"
Blacknesse (Jonson)
See *Masque of Blacknesse*
Blenheim (Blenheim Castle) (Lyttelton)
10:196, 198, 205, 215
Blenheim Castle (Lyttelton)
See *Blenheim*
"The Blossome" (Donne) **10**:13, 36, 77-9
"Bluebeard" (Perrault)
See "La barbe bleue"
Blunt oder der Gast (Moritz) **2**:228, 242
The Boasting Soldier (Holberg) **6**:259
"Boatmen on Old Dragon River" (P'u Sung-
ling) **3**:345
Bocage royal (Ronsard) **6**:410, 429, 431, 434
"Body and Soul" (More) **9**:298
The Body of Polycye (Christine de Pizan)
See *Le livre du corps de policie*
Boece (Chaucer) **17**:214
The Boke named the Governour (Elyot)
See *The Boke of the Governor, devised by Sir
Thomas Elyot*
The Boke of the Cyte of Ladies (Christine de
Pizan)
See *Le livre de la cité des dames*
*The Boke of the Governor, devised by Sir
Thomas Elyot (The Boke named the
Governour, Book of the Governor, The
Governor, The Governour)* (Elyot) **11**:58-64,
68-9, 71-6, 78-91
"Boldness in Love" (Carew) **13**:15
Bon-Sens (Good Sense) (Holbach) **14**:152,
154, 156-58, 168
Bon Ton; or, High Life Below Stairs (Garrick)
15:91, 93, 101-03, 121
The Bondage of the Will (Luther)
See *De servo arbitrio*
"The Bonniest Lass" (Burns) **3**:98
"Bonny Doon" (Burns) **3**:62, 78
Book against the Barbarians (Erasmus)
See *Antibarbari*
*A Book for Boys and Girls; or, Country Rhimes
for Children* (Bunyan) **4**:170, 172, 182
Book of Essays (Collier) (Collier)
See *Essays upon Several Moral Subjects*
Book of Fame (Chaucer)
See *House of Fame*
The Book of Fayttes of Armes and of Chyvalrye
(Christine de Pizan)
See *Le livre des faits d'armes et de chevalerie*
Book of foundations (Teresa de Jesus)
See *Libro de las fundaciones de Santa Teresa
de Jesús*
*The Book of King Arthur and His Noble
Knights of the Round Table* (Malory)
See *Morte Darthur*
The Book of Margery Kempe (Kempe) **6**:388-
89, 391-93, 395-96, 398-400
The Book of Martyrs (Foxe)
See *Actes and Monumentes of these latter
perilous dayes touching matters of the
Church*
*Book of Saint Valentines Day of the Parlement
of Briddes* (Chaucer)
See *Parlement of Foules*
Book of the Beatific Life (Paracelsus)
See *Vita beata*

The Book of the Courtier (Castiglione)
See *Il libro del cortegiano*
*Book of the Duchess (Book of the Duchesse;
The Death of Blanche the Duchess)*
(Chaucer) **17**:45, 58, 72-9, 91, 97, 105-06,
112-13, 178, 189
Book of the Duchesse (Chaucer)
See *Book of the Duchess*
The Book of the Duke of True Lovers
(Christine de Pizan)
See *Le livre du duc des vrais amans*
Book of the Five and Twenty Ladies (Chaucer)
See *Legend of Good Women*
Book of the Governor (Elyot)
See *The Boke of the Governor, devised by Sir
Thomas Elyot*
Book of the Leon (Chaucer)
See *The Book of the Lion*
The Book of the Lion (Book of the Leon)
(Chaucer) **17**:45, 216
Book of the Reed (Jami)
See *Nay-namá*
Book of Troilus (Chaucer)
See *Troilus and Criseyde*
Books of Hospitals (Paracelsus) **14**:198
Books of the Greater Surgery (Greater Surgery)
(Paracelsus) **14**:199
"Bookworm" (Parnell) **3**:252
The Bores (Moliere)
See *Les fâcheux*
"Borne I Was to meet with Age" (Herrick)
13:341
"Boswell: A Song" (Boswell)
See "B--, A Song"
Boswell on the Grand Tour (The Grand Tour)
(Boswell) **4**:64
Boswell's London Journal (London Journal)
(Boswell) **4**:55, 57-8, 62-3, 71-2
La bottega del caffè (Goldoni) **4**:264, 266
*Le bourgeois gentilhomme (The Bourgeois
Gentleman)* (Moliere) **10**:270, 277-78, 280,
282-83, 286, 288, 290-93, 313
The Bourgeois Gentleman (Moliere)
See *Le bourgeois gentilhomme*
Le bourru bienfaisant (Il burbero benefico)
(Goldoni) **4**:252-53, 255, 268
"The Boy's Piety" (Erasmus) **16**:142
"Breake of Day" (Donne) **10**:32
Breaths of Familiarity (Jami)
See *Nafahát al-uns*
*A Brief Character of the Low Countries under
the States* (Howell) **13**:424
*A Brief Explanation of a Late Pamphlet
Entitled "The Shortest Way with the
Dissenters"* (Defoe) **1**:161
*Brief Notes upon a Late Sermon, Titl'd, "The
Fear of God and the King"* (Milton) **9**:161
Briefe, die neueste Litteratur betreffend
(Lessing) **8**:101
"The Brigs of Ayr" (Burns) **3**:52, 67, 71
"Bristowe Tragedie; or, The Dethe of Syr
Charles Bawdin" (Chatterton) **3**:119, 126,
130, 135
"Britain" (Thomson) **16**:384
"Britannia. A Poem" (Thomson) **16**:375, 384,
393, 395, 423
*Britannia Rediviva: A Poem on the Birth of the
Prince* (Dryden) **21**:65, 82, 87
Britannia Triumphans (Davenant) **13**:189
"Britannia Triumphans: or a Poem on the
Battle of Blenheim" (Dennis)

See "Britannia Triumphans: or, The Empire Sav'd, and Europe Delivered"

"Britannia Triumphans: or, The Empire Sav'd, and Europe Delivered" ("Britannia Triumphans: or a Poem on the Battle of Blenheim") (Dennis) **11**:13, 15, 26, 48

The British Recluse (Haywood) **1**:283

"The Brocaded Gown and the Linen Rag" (Smart) **3**:366

"The broken heart" (Donne) **10**:82

"Brose and Butter" (Burns) **3**:100

"The Brothers" (Young) **3**:467, 487-88

The Brothers at Cross-purposes (Holberg) **6**:259

"Bruar Water" (Burns) **3**:85

Bruder Blau-Mantel (Beer)
See *Der kurtzweilige Bruder Blau-Mantel*

Brutus (Voltaire) **14**:397

Das Buch Paragranum (*Paragranum*) (Paracelsus) **14**:194, 196-99

The Bull Killer (*Bulla*) (Hutten) **16**:225-27, 234, 239-41, 246

Bulla (Hutten)
See *The Bull Killer*

Bulla Decimi Leonis, contra errores Martini Lutheri (Hutten) **16**:233

"Bumpkin or Country Squire" (Butler) **16**:50

La buona famiglia (Goldoni) **4**:251, 260, 265

La buona madre (*The Good Mother*) (Goldoni) **4**:257

La buona moglie (Goldoni) **4**:265-66

"The Bureau of Frauds" (P'u Sung-ling)
See "K'ao-pi ssu"

"Burlesque Lament for Creech" ("Lament for Creech") (Burns) **3**:86

"Busie old foole" (Donne)
See "The Sunne Rising"

"Busiris, King of Egypt" (Young) **3**:467, 485, 487-88

The Busy Idler (Schlegel)
See *Der geschäftige Müssiggänger*

"Buxom Joan of Deptford" (Congreve) **5**:85

C. C. Taciti historiarum et annaliem libri qui exstant (*Tacitus*) (Lipsius) **16**:257, 265, 269, 274

"Ca' the Yowes" (Burns) **3**:81

El caballero bobo (Castro) **19**:8

Le cabinet du philosophe (Marivaux) **4**:359, 376, 378, 380

"Cadenus and Vanessa" (Swift) **1**:481

Caesar's Commentaries (Lipsius) **16**:276

Le café (Rousseau) **9**:337

"The Call of Blood" (Cervantes)
See "La fuerza de la sangre"

"The Calm" (Donne) **10**:4, 97

"Camelion" (Prior)
See "The Chameleon"

Camino de perfección (*The Way of Perfection*) (Teresa de Jesus) **18**:389, 391, 392, 400

The Campaign (Addison) **18**:6, 16, 19, 30-2

"Cancion entre el Alma y el Esposo" (John of the Cross) **18**:202

"Canciones de la Esposa" ("Songs of the Bride") (John of the Cross) **18**:203, 223

"The Candidate" (Churchill) **3**:143-44, 150, 152, 154-55, 158, 160, 162-63, 167-70

"The Candidate" (Gray) **4**:312

The Candidates (Munford)
See *The Candidates; or, The Humors of a Virginia Election*

The Candidates; or, The Humors of a Virginia Election (*The Candidates*) (Munford) **5**:189-92, 195-97

Candide; or, Optimism (Voltaire)
See *Candide; ou, L'optimisme*

Candide; ou, L'optimisme (*Candide; or, Optimism*) (Voltaire) **14**:322, 325, 328, 334, 338, 341-42, 344-46, 353-54, 358-59, 361, 364, 366-67, 373, 378-82, 386-92, 398, 402

"Candidus" (More)
See "To Candidus: How to Choose a Wife"

"The Canonization" ("For Godsake hold your tongue, and let me love") (Donne) **10**:13, 32-3, 36, 49, 58-61, 103

"Canon's Yeoman's Prologue" (Chaucer) **17**:202

"Canon's Yeoman's Tale" ("Chanon's Yeoman's Tale") (Chaucer) **17**:66, 202, 205

Canterburie-Tales (Chaucer)
See *Canterbury Tales*

Canterbury Tales (*Canterburie-Tales*; *Tales*; *Tales of Canterbury*) (Chaucer) **17**:45, 47-50, 57-8, 60, 66-9, 75, 84, 87, 89-90, 98, 105, 112, 121-23, 136, 142, 146-47, 162, 167, 172-80, 183-84, 189, 195-96, 198, 200-02, 204-06, 209-10, 212-18, 220-21, 224-25, 230-33, 236-38, 240-44

"Canticle to Bacchus" (Herrick) **13**:327

"Cántico Espiritual" ("Spiritual Canticle") (John of the Cross) **18**:212-15, 219, 221-24, 232-34

Cántico Espiritual (*The Spiritual Canticle*) (John of the Cross) **18**:206, 213, 229, 230, 234

Canut (*Canut, ein Trauerspiel*) (Schlegel) **5**:273, 281, 283-86, 289

Canut, ein Trauerspiel (Schlegel)
See *Canut*

Capitoli (Aretino) **12**:31

Capricci (Aretino) **12**:20

Le capricieux (Rousseau) **9**:337-38

Captain Carleton (Defoe)
See *The Military Memoirs of Captain Carleton*

"Captain Grose" (Burns)
See "On the Late Captain Grose's Peregrinations Thro' Scotland"

Captain Singleton (Defoe)
See *The Life, Adventures, and Pyracies of the Famous Captain Singleton*

"The Captivated Bee" (Herrick) **13**:367

The Captivity (Goldsmith) **2**:104

Caractères (La Bruyere)
See *The Characters; or, Manners of the Age*

"Caravellers and Peyncters" (Chatterton) **3**:135

"Cardoness" (Burns) **3**:86

"Care and Generosity" (Smart) **3**:366

A Careful and Strict Enquiry into the Modern Prevailing Notions of That Freedom of Will, Which Is Supposed to Be Essential to Moral Agency, Vertue and Vice, Reward and Punishment, Praise and Blame (*The Freedom of the Will*) (Edwards) **7**:91-2, 95-6, 99, 101-03, 118, 121, 124, 126-27

"Carmen Seculare for the Year 1700" (Prior) **4**:454-55, 459, 461, 465, 475

"Caro m' è 'l sonno, e più l' esser di sasso" (Michelangelo) **12**:314

"Carol to St. Peter" (Juana Ines de la Cruz) **5**:146

"Carte de tendre" (Scudery)

See *Clélie: Histoire romaine*

"The Carthusian" ("The Soldier and the Carthusian") (Erasmus) **16**:119, 195

La casa de los celos (Cervantes) **6**:180

La casa nova (*The New House*) (Goldoni) **4**:257, 264, 266

"El casamiento engañoso" (Cervantes) **6**:171-73

The Case is Altered (Jonson) **6**:304

"The Case of Conscience" (Burns) **3**:97-8

La cassaria (Ariosto) **6**:59-61

"Cassinus and Peter" (Swift) **1**:461, 483-84, 502-03, 509-10

Castel of Health (Elyot)
See *The Castel of Helth*

The Castel of Helth (*Castel of Health*; *The Castle of Health*) (Elyot) **11**:58, 60, 62-3, 73, 83

Castillo interior, o las moradas (*The Interior Castle; or, The Mansions*) (Teresa de Jesus) **18**:389, 391-94, 396-99, 400, 402-05, 409

"The Castle Barber's Soliloquu" (Warton) **15**:462

The Castle of Health (Elyot)
See *The Castel of Helth*

The Castle of Indolence: an Allegorical Poem. Written in Immitation of Spenser (Thomson) **16**:367-68, 370, 376-79, 382, 384, 387-88, 392, 395, 398, 406, 416, 418-19, 423-24, 426, 432

The Castle of Otranto (Walpole) **2**:447-52, 456, 458-60, 462, 464, 466-80, 486-89, 495-99, 501, 503-07

Castruccio (Machiavelli)
See *La vita di Castruccio Castracani da Lucca*

A Catalogue of the Royal and Noble Authors of England (Walpole) **2**:456, 486-87

Catechism (Andrewes) **5**:39

Catechistical Doctrine (Andrewes)
See *A Patterne of Catechisticall Doctrine*

Catiline His Conspiracy (*Catiline's Conspiracy*) (Jonson) **6**:291, 294, 296, 300-01, 305-06, 308, 314, 318-20, 323-24, 330-33, 336

Catiline's Conspiracy (Jonson)
See *Catiline His Conspiracy*

The Causes of the Decay and Defects of Dramatick Poetry, and of the Degeneracy of the Public Taste (Dennis) **11**:17

The Cavalier and the Lady (Goldoni)
See *Il cavaliere e la dama*

Cave of Fancy (Wollstonecraft)
See *The Cave of Fancy, a Tale*

The Cave of Fancy, a Tale (*Cave of Fancy*) (Wollstonecraft) **5**:426, 442

The Cave of Salamanca (Cervantes) **6**:189-92

Ce qu'on ne fait pas et ce qu'on pourrait faire (Voltaire) **14**:380

The Celebrated Letter from Samuel Johnson, LL.D. to Philip Dormer Stanhope, Earl of Chesterfield ("Letter to Chesterfield"; "Letter to Lord Chesterfield") (Johnson) **15**:203, 301

A Celebration of Charis in Ten Lyric Pieces ("Triumph of Charis") (Jonson) **6**:305, 326, 336

Célinte: Nouvelle première (Scudery) **2**:307

"El celoso extremeño" ("The Jealous Extremaduran") (Cervantes) **6**:171-72, 177

"Cendrillon" ("Cinderella") (Perrault) **2**:253-54, 260-65, 267, 280-82, 284-85

Les cent balades (Christine de Pizan) **9**:40

Cent balades d'amant et de dame (Christine de Pizan) **9**:48

Cent histoires (Christine de Pizan) **9**:29

Centaur (Young)
  See *The Centaur Not Fabulous, in Six Letters to a Friend on the Life in Vogue*

The Centaur Not Fabulous, in Six Letters to a Friend on the Life in Vogue (*Centaur*) (Young) **3**:488, 492

Centura prima ad Belgas (Lipsius) **16**:269

"Céphale" (Rousseau) **9**:343

Cephise et l'Amour (Montesquieu) **7**:320

El cerco de Numancia (*La Numancia*) (Cervantes) **6**:143, 177-78, 180, 189

"Ceremonies for Christmas" (Herrick) **13**:331, 336

Certain Sonnets (Sidney) **19**:391, 395-96, 424

El cetro de José (Juana Ines de la Cruz) **5**:158

Chain of Gold (Jami)
  See *Silsilatu'dh-Dhahab*

The Chains of Slavery, a Work Wherein the Clandestine and Villainous Attempts of Princes to Ruin Liberty Are Pointed out, and the Dreadful Scenes of Despotism Disclosed . . . (Marat) **10**:226, 231, 236

"The Chameleon" ("Camelion") (Prior) **4**:456, 461

"Chanon's Yeoman's Tale" (Chaucer)
  See "Canon's Yeoman's Tale"

"The Character of a Good Parson" (Dryden) **21**:56

"The Character of Holland" (Marvell) **4**:395, 398, 429

"The Character of Polybius" (Dryden) **3**:237

"Character of St. Evremond" (Dryden) **3**:236

"Characters" (Butler) **16**:18, 26-8, 30, 50-5

Characters and Passages from Note-Books (Butler) **16**:18

Characters Historical and Panegyrical of the Greatest Men (Perrault)
  See *Les hommes illustres qui ont paru en France pendant ce siècle*

The Characters; or, Manners of the Age (*Caractères*) (La Bruyere) **17**:409-15, 417, 419-21, 423-27, 429

"Charity and Humility" (More) **9**:296

Charity and Its Fruits (Edwards) **7**:119

Charms of Study (Marmontel) **2**:213

"Charon" (Erasmus) **16**:114, 116, 132, 142, 155

Chaste Joseph (Grimmelshausen)
  See *Der keusche Joseph*

"Le Chat" (Ronsard) **6**:424, 436

"Che yu" (P'u Sung-ling) **3**:350

"A Cheat" (Butler) **16**:50

The Cheats of Scapin (Moliere)
  See *Les fourberies de Scapin*

"Le chemin de la fortune" (Marivaux) **4**:380

"Ch'eng hsien" ("Ch'eng the Immortal") (P'u Sung-ling) **3**:350, 352

"Cheng the Fairy" (P'u Sung-ling) **3**:344

"Ch'eng the Immortal" (P'u Sung-ling)
  See "Ch'eng hsien"

"Cherche, Cassandre, un poëte nouveau" (Ronsard) **6**:433-34

"Cherry Ripe" (Herrick) **13**:332

"Chiang Ch'eng" (P'u Sung-ling) **3**:346

"Chiao-no" (P'u Sung-ling) **3**:354

"Child-Song" (Sidney) **19**:330

Chiliades (Erasmus) **16**:171

Chin p'ing mei **19**:16-55

The Chioggian Brawls (Goldoni)
  See *Le baruffe chiozzotte*

Chiose (Castelvetro) **12**:67-8

Chirurgia minor quam Bertheoneam intitulaut (*The Little Surgery; Three Bertheonei Books*) (Paracelsus) **14**:198-99

"Chloris Appearing in the Looking-Glass" (Parnell) **3**:255

Choosing a Councilman in Daganzo (Cervantes) **6**:190

Christian Commonwealth (Eliot)
  See *The Christian Commonwealth; or, The Civil Policy of the Rising Kingdom of Jesus Christ. . .*

The Christian Commonwealth; or, The Civil Policy of the Rising Kingdom of Jesus Christ. . . (*Christian Commonwealth*) (Eliot) **5**:129-30, 139-40

Christian Doctrine (Milton)
  See *De doctrina christiana*

Christian Epistle upon Penitence (Perrault) **2**:256

The Christian Hero (Steele) **18**:314, 328-29, 332, 338, 340, 345-46, 348, 350, 353-59, 364-65, 376, 378, 380

"The Christian Militant" (Herrick) **13**:333, 371-72

"Christian Triumph" (Young)
  See "The Complaint; or, Night Thoughts: Night the Fourth"

Christiani Matrimonii Institutio (*Institutio Christiani Matrimoni*) (Erasmus) **16**:154-55, 193

Christianisme dévoilé (*Christianity Unveiled; Dévoilé*) (Holbach) **14**:152-53, 157-59, 166-67

Christianity Unveiled (Holbach)
  See *Christianisme dévoilé*

"The Christians Reply" (Davenant) **13**:204-07

"A Christmas Caroll" (Herrick) **13**:310, 404-05

The Christmas Party (Holberg)
  See *Julestuen*

A Christmas Tale (Garrick) **15**:124

Christographia (Taylor) **11**:369-70, 373-74, 382, 386-88, 390, 398

"Christ's Reply" (Taylor) **11**:361

Christus Triumphans (Foxe) **14**:43, 46-47

"The Chrysanthemum Spirit" (P'u Sung-ling) **3**:348

Church History (Holberg)
  See *Almindelig kirke-historie fra christendommens første begyndelse til Lutheri reformation...*

"Churchwarden" (Butler) **16**:53

"Churchyard" (Gray)
  See "Elegy Written in a Country Churchyard"

Ciceronianus (Erasmus) **16**:175, 177, 182

The Cid (Castro)
  See *Las mocedades del Cid*

"Cinderella" (Perrault)
  See "Cendrillon"

Le cinquième et dernier livre des faictz et dictz heroiques du noble Pantagruel (Rabelais) **5**:215-16, 219, 230, 233, 239, 251

"Circé" (Rousseau) **9**:341-43, 345

The Citizen of the World; or, Letters from a Chinese Philosopher (Goldsmith) **2**:65, 70-1, 74-6, 83-5, 95, 97, 102-05, 107, 116, 127-28

The City Heiress; or, Sir Timothy Treat-all (Behn) **1**:29, 33, 37, 40, 48

City Mouse and Country Mouse (Marvell)
  See *The Hind and the Panther, Transvers'd to the Story of the Country and the City-Mouse*

"A City Night-Piece" (Goldsmith) **2**:103

"A City-Wit" (Butler) **16**:55

De Civilitate (Erasmus) **16**:154

Civility for Boys (Erasmus) **16**:124

The Clandestine Marriage (Garrick) **15**:98, 101-02, 105, 108-09, 111, 114, 116, 121, 124

Clarissa Harlowe (Richardson)
  See *Clarissa; or, The History of a Young Lady*

Clarissa; or, The History of a Young Lady (*Clarissa Harlowe*) (Richardson) **1**:367-69, 371-72, 374, 377-78, 380-82, 385-86, 388-95, 399-413, 415-16, 418

Clélie: Histoire romaine ("Carte de tendre") (Scudery) **2**:293, 300, 302-04, 306-09, 311-14

Clementia; or, The History of an Italian Lady, Who Made Her Escape from a Monastery, for the Love of a Scots Nobleman (Haywood) **1**:283

Cleomenes (Dryden) **3**:222

Cléopâtre (Marmontel) **2**:213, 216-17

"Clerk's Prologue" (Chaucer) **17**:218

"Clerk's Tale" (Chaucer) **17**:65, 142, 195-97, 205, 226, 228, 236-37, 241

The Clever Woman (Goldoni)
  See *La donna di garbo*

"Clifton" (Chatterton) **3**:131

La Clizia (Machiavelli) **8**:126, 170, 176

"Cloe Jealous" (Prior) **4**:463

"Cloe Weeping" (Prior) **4**:459

"Clorinda and Damon" (Marvell) **4**:397, 438

"Clothes do but cheat and cousen us" (Herrick) **13**:369

"Clothes for Continuance" (Herrick) **13**:313

"Coaches" (Montaigne)
  See "Des coches"

"The Cock and the Fox" (Chaucer)
  See "Nun's Priest's Tale"

Codex A (Vinci) **12**:420

Codex Atlanticus (*Codice Atlantico*) (Vinci) **12**:385, 387, 395, 411, 413-14, 417, 419, 433

Codex B (Vinci) **12**:419-20, 422

Codex C (Vinci) **12**:421

Codex E (Vinci) **12**:421

Codex G (Vinci) **12**:421

Codex H (Vinci) **12**:420

Codex Huygens (Vinci) **12**:394

Codex I (Vinci) **12**:420

Codex Trivulziano (*Codicetto Trivulziano*) (Vinci) **12**:386, 420, 422

Codex Urbinas (Vinci) **12**:393, 435

Codice Atlantico (Vinci)
  See *Codex Atlanticus*

Codicetto Trivulziano (Vinci)
  See *Codex Trivulziano*

Codici (Vinci) **12**:419

Coelum Britannicum (Carew) **13**:6-8, 10-11, 13, 20, 24, 26, 38-9, 41-2, 46-7

"Cogitata et Visa" ("Thought and Vision") (Bacon) **18**:153

Cogitationes de Natura Rarum (Bacon) **18**:187

Cogitationes de Scientia Humana (Bacon) **18**:187

"Colin Clout" (Spenser)
  See "Colin Clouts Come Home Againe"

"Colin Clouts Come Home Againe" ("Colin Clout") (Spenser) **5**:313-14, 335, 343, 345-47, 355, 359-62

Collectanea (Erasmus) **16**:171, 195

Collected Works (Lyttelton) **10**:210

Collected Works (Wu Ch'eng-en)
See *She-yan hsien-sheng ts'un-kao*

Collection of Poems (Dennis) **11**:4

A Collection of Several Philosophical Writings (More) **9**:309

A Collection of the Moral and Instructive Sentiments, Maxims, Cautions, and Reflexions, Contained in the Histories of Pamela, Clarissa, and Sir Charles Grandison (Richardson) **1**:416

"College Exercise" (Prior) **4**:455

Colloquia, Familiar Colloquies, Colloquies, Colloquiorum Opus (Erasmus)
See *Familiorum Colloquiorum*

"Colloquium Senile" (Erasmus) **16**:129

"Colloquy of Funerals" (Erasmus)
See "Funus"

The Colonel (Davenant) **13**:175

Colonel Jack (Defoe)
See *The History of the Most Remarkable Life and Extraordinary Adventures of the Truly Honourable Colonel Jacque, Vulgarly Called Colonel Jack*

La colonie (Marivaux) **4**:367, 378

"El coloquio de los perros" (Cervantes) **6**:171-73

Colours of Good and Evil (Table of Colours or Appearance of Good and Evil) (Bacon) **18**:149, 196,

Come and Welcome, to Jesus Christ (Bunyan) **4**:174-75, 177

"Come, thou monarch" (Garrick) **15**:130

Comedy about Life at Court (Aretino)
See *Cortigiana errante*

The Comely Cook (Chulkov)
See *Prigozhaya povarikha*

Comentarius Solutus (Free Commentaries) (Bacon) **18**:133, 153

"Com'esser, donna, può quel c'alcun vede" (Michelangelo) **12**:363, 365

Comfort of Lovers (Hawes) **17**:345-49, 351-54, 362-63

The Comical Gallant (Dennis) **11**:12, 20

"Comme on voit sur la branche" (Ronsard) **6**:425, 435

Commedia di Callimaco: E di Lucretia (Mandragola) (Machiavelli) **8**:126, 131-32, 147, 162-63, 168-72, 175-80

Commentaire sur Corneille (Voltaire) **14**:339

Commentaire sur Desportes (Commentary on Desportes) (Malherbe) **5**:169, 173, 180

Commentarii (Foxe)
See *Actes and Monumentes of these latter perilous dayes touching matters of the Church*

Commentarium in convivium Platonis de amore (Convivium) (Ficino) **12**:184, 197, 201

Commentary (Pico della Mirandola)
See *Commento*

Commentary on Desportes (Malherbe)
See *Commentaire sur Desportes*

Commentary on Prudentius' Hymn to the Nativity (Erasmus) **16**:124

"Commentary on Psalm 118" (Luther) **9**:136

Commentary on the Four Gospels (Taylor) **11**:373

Commentary on the "Lama'át" (Jami) **9**:67

Commentary on the Psalms (Luther)
See *Die sieben Busspsal mit deutscher ausiegung nach dem schrifftlichen synne tzu Christi und gottes gnaden, neben seynes selben, ware erkentniss grundlich gerichtet...*

Commentary on the Symposium (Ficino) **12**:176, 180, 201-03

Commento (Commentary) (Pico della Mirandola) **15**:325, 338-39, 346, 356-58

Comments on Livy (Machiavelli)
See *Discorsi di Nicolo Machiavelli... sopra la prima deca di Tito Livio, a Zanobi Buondelmonte, et a Cosimo Rucellai*

"Companion to the Guide to Oxford" (Warton) **15**:449

Comparative Histories of Heroes (Holberg) **6**:282

Comparative Histories of Heroines (Holberg) **6**:282

"The Comparison" (Carew) **13**:27, 58-9

Comparison of the Arts (Vinci) **12**:416

"Compartlement" (Herrick) **13**:321

"Complaint" (Young)
See "The Complaint; or, Night Thoughts"

"Complaint of Cherwell" (Warton) **15**:431

Complaint of Peace Ejected from All Countries (Erasmus)
See *Querela Pacis*

"The Complaint; or, Night Thoughts" ("Complaint") (Young) **3**:462, 464, 466-78, 480-84, 486-89, 491-500

"The Complaint; or, Night Thoughts: Night the Eighth" ("Night VIII") (Young) **3**:464, 466, 498-99

"The Complaint; or, Night Thoughts: Night the Fifth" ("Night the Fifth") (Young) **3**:464, 466, 480, 491

"The Complaint; or, Night Thoughts: Night the First" ("Night I") (Young) **3**:491, 498

"The Complaint; or, Night Thoughts: Night the Fourth" ("Christian Triumph") (Young) **3**:464, 465, 478, 491, 498-99

"The Complaint; or, Night Thoughts: Night the Ninth" ("The Consolation") (Young) **3**:464, 466, 498-99

"The Complaint; or, Night Thoughts: Night the Second" ("Night II") (Young) **3**:464, 480, 491

"The Complaint; or, Night Thoughts: Night the Seventh" (Young) **3**:464, 466, 498

"The Complaint; or, Night Thoughts: Night the Sixth" ("Night VI") (Young) **3**:466, 498

"The Complaint; or, Night Thoughts: Night the Third" ("Narcissa") (Young) **3**:465, 472, 491

Complaints: Containing Sundrie Small Poemes of the Worlds Vanitie (Spenser) **5**:311-12

A Compleat History of England (Smollett) **2**:342, 344

The Complete Letters of Lady Mary Wortley Montagu, Vol. III: 1752-62 (Montagu) **9**:269

The Complete Vindication (Johnson) **15**:206

"Compleynt of Mars" (Chaucer) **17**:99

La Comtesse de Tende (La Fayette) **2**:138-39, 144, 149-50, 152, 157-59, 165-67, 169

La comtesse d'Escarbagnas (Moliere) **10**:272, 283, 293, 313

El Comulgatorio (Gracian y Morales) **15**:144, 148

Comus: A Maske (Mask of Comus) (Milton) **9**:178, 183, 189, 191-92, 195, 197-99, 202-05, 208, 214-15, 229-30, 234-35, 238, 250-51

Conceptions of Divine Love, Conceptions of the Love of God (Teresa de Jesus)
See *Conceptos del amor de dios sobre algunas palabras de los Cantares de Salomón*

Conceptos del amor de dios sobre algunas palabras de los Cantares de Salomón (Conceptions of Divine Love, Conceptions of the Love of God) (Teresa de Jesus) **18**:389, 392, 409

"Concerning Humour in Comedy" (Congreve)
See "Letter Concerning Humour in Comedy"

Concerning the Christian Religion (Ficino)
See *De religione christiana*

Concerning the End for Which God Created the World (Edwards) **7**:93, 95, 101-03, 117-18, 121

Concerning the Nature of Love (Dryden) **21**:77-8

Concerning the Unity of the Church in Love (Erasmus) **16**:114

Conciones et meditationes (Kempis) **11**:410

Conclusion of the Memoirs of Miss Sidney Bidulph (Sheridan) **7**:371, 378, 383-84

Conclusions (Pico della Mirandola) **15**:321, 324-25, 329, 334

Concord of Plato and Aristotle (Pico della Mirandola) **15**:342

El Conde Alarcos (Count Alarcos) (Castro) **19**:4, 14

The Conduct of the Minority (Burke) **7**:47

The Confederacy (Vanbrugh) **21**:287-89, 292, 295, 301-02, 319-20

"The Conference" (Churchill) **3**:150-52, 155-56, 160, 163

"The Confession of Faith of a Savoyard Vicar" (Rousseau)
See "Profession du vicaire Savoyard"

Les Confessions (Rousseau) **14**:218, 220-23, 226, 247-51, 254, 256-60, 263-64, 267-68, 295, 297, 301, 303-10, 312-14

Les confessions du Comte de *** (Duclos) **1**:187-88, 190-93, 198

The Confutation of Tyndale's Answer (More) **10**:362-63, 366, 370, 396-98, 408-09, 441

Conjectures (Young)
See *Conjectures on Original Composition in a Letter to the Author of Sir Charles Grandison*

Conjectures on Original Composition in a Letter to the Author of Sir Charles Grandison (Conjectures) (Young) **3**:474, 479, 481-82, 484, 489, 492-96, 499

"Conjuration to Electra" (Herrick) **13**:336

"Le connaisseur" ("The Connoisseur") (Marmontel) **2**:214, 221

"The Connoisseur" (Marmontel)
See "Le connaisseur"

"Connubii Flores" (Herrick) **13**:380

The Conquest of Granada by the Spaniards (Dryden) **3**:179, 208, 221, 232

The Conquest of Spain (Pix) **8**:261-63, 269, 271-72, 277

Conquistata (Tasso)
See *Di Gerusalemme conquistata*

The Conscious Lovers (Steele) **18**:320, 330, 345-46, 348, 352-54, 358, 368-75, 377-80, 382-83

De conscribendis Epistolis (Erasmus) **16**:146

"A Consideration upon Cicero" (Montaigne) **8**:232

Considerations on the Causes of the Grandeur and the Decadence of the Romans (Montesquieu)
See *Considérations sur les causes de la grandeur des Romains, et de leur décadence*

Considerations sur le goût (Duclos) **1**:188

Considérations sur les causes de la grandeur des Romains, et de leur décadence (*Considerations on the Causes of the Grandeur and the Decadence of the Romans*) (Montesquieu) **7**:309-12, 319, 321-25, 332, 342, 347, 356-57, 360, 362

Considerations sur les moeurs de ce siècle (Duclos) **1**:184-85, 187-88, 191, 199

Considerations upon Two Bills (Swift) **1**:489

"Consolation" (Malherbe)
See "Consolation à Du Perier"

"The Consolation" (Young)
See "The Complaint; or, Night Thoughts: Night the Ninth"

"Consolation à Du Perier" ("Consolation") (Malherbe) **5**:168, 170

"Consolation au Président de Verdun" (Malherbe) **5**:171

The Consolidator (Defoe) **1**:162

The Constant Couple; or, A Trip to he Jubilee (*Trip to the Jubilee*) (Farquhar) **21**:126, 128-29, 135-36, 139-40, 142, 144, 146, 148, 150, 152-55, 161, 163-64, 170, 176

"Constantia" (Brooke) **1**:62

De Constantia in Publicis Malis (Lipsius)
See *De constantia libri duo*

De constantia libri duo (*De Constantia in Publicis Malis; Of Constancy; On Constancy*) (Lipsius) **16**:252, 257-58, 262, 265-73, 276

Constantine Donation (Hutten)
See *De falso credita et ementita Donatione Constatini Magni*

The Constellation of the Great Bear (Jami)
See *Haft Aurang*

La Constitution ou Projet de déclaration des Droits de l'homme et du citoyen, suivi d'un Plan de constitution juste, sage et libre (*Plan of a Constitution*) (Marat) **10**:221, 226

Constitutions (Teresa de Jesus) **18**:392

Contagion sacrée (*Sacred Contagion; or, The Natural History of Superstition*) (Holbach) **14**:152-53, 157-59, 168-69

"Conte" (Marmontel) **2**:220

"Contemplations" (Bradstreet) **4**:85-6, 90-3, 95-6, 100-04, 108, 112

De contemptu mundi (Erasmus) **16**:133, 144, 146

The Contending Brothers (Brooke) **1**:63

Contes moraux (*Moral Tales*) (Marmontel) **2**:208-15, 220-22, 224

"Continuation of the Yellow Millet" (P'u Sung-ling)
See "Hsu huang-liang"

Le Contrat Social (Rousseau)
See *Du Contrat social*

"Contre les bûcherons de la forêt de Gastine" (Ronsard) **6**:417

"Contre les détracteurs de l'antiquité" (Rousseau) **9**:346

Contributions to the History and Improvement of the Theater (Lessing)
See *Beiträge zur Historie und Aufnahme des Theaters*

"The Conversation" (Prior) **4**:459

Conversations (Jonson) **6**:324

Conversations sur divers sujets (Scudery) **2**:293-94, 303, 307

"Conversion of St. Paul" (Smart) **3**:403

Conversion of St. Paul (Lyttelton)
See *Observations on the Conversion and Apostleship of St. Paul, in a Letter to Gilbert West*

Conversion of Swearers (Hawes) **17**:345-49, 352, 354, 361-62

"The Convert's Love" (Parnell) **3**:255

Convivium (Ficino)
See *Commentarium in convivium Platonis de amore*

Convivium Religiosum (*Religious Symposium*) (Erasmus) **16**:116, 121, 172

"Cook's Prologue" (Chaucer) **17**:206

"Cook's Tale" (Chaucer) **17**:201

"The Copernican System" (Chatterton) **3**:127

De Copia (*Copia*) (Erasmus) **16**:112, 136, 140, 146, 154, 196, 198, 202

Copia (Erasmus)
See *De Copia*

Cordial for Cavaliers (Howell) **13**:420

"Corinna's going a-Maying" (Herrick) **13**:316, 323, 330, 332, 337, 343, 348-51, 357, 361, 364, 366-67, 377, 383-86, 397, 402

Coriolanus (Dennis)
See *The Invader of His Country: or, The Fatal Resentment*

Coriolanus. A Tragedy (Thomson) **16**:396

"Corn Rigs" (Burns) **3**:87

La Corona (Donne) **10**:40, 84

"The Coronet" (Marvell) **4**:396, 403, 426, 437-38, 443

Correction of the Understanding (Spinoza)
See *De intellectus emendatione*

Correspondance (Marie de l'Incarnation)
See *Lettres de la Vénérable Mère Marie de l'Incarnation*

Correspondance (Sevigne)
See *Correspondance de Mme de Sévigné*

Correspondance (Voltaire) **14**:337

Correspondance de Mme de Sévigné (*Correspondance*) (Sevigne) **11**:336-38

Correspondence (Ivan IV) **17**:401

Correspondence (*Der briefwechsel des Spinoza*) (Spinoza) **9**:438

The Correspondence of Swift (Swift) **1**:449

El cortesan o l'uomo di mondo (Goldoni) **4**:249

Cortigiana (Aretino)
See *Cortigiana errante*

Cortigiana errante (*Comedy about Life at Court; Cortigiana; The Courtesan*) (Aretino) **12**:6, 9, 19-20, 23, 26-7, 29-30, 35-6

Corylo (Beer) **5**:56

Cosi-Sancta (Voltaire) **14**:345, 359, 398

"The Cottar's Saturday Night" ("The Cotter's Saturday Night") (Burns) **3**:48, 50, 52, 54-6, 65, 67, 72, 77, 79, 81, 83-5, 93, 102-04

"The Cotter's Saturday Night" (Burns)
See "The Cottar's Saturday Night"

Count Alarcos (Castro)
See *El Conde Alarcos*

Count d'Irlos (Castro) **19**:4

The Counterfeit Bridegroom; or, The Defeated Widow (Behn) **1**:33

The Countess of Dellwyn (Fielding) **1**:273, 278

The Countess of Pembroke's Arcadia (*Arcadia*) (Sidney) **19**:318-27, 329-30, 334-36, 338-45, 347-49, 351-58, 360-62, 364-74, 376-80, 389-91, 396-97, 399-415, 420-30, 432-33

The Country Girl (Garrick) **15**:122-23

The Country House (Vanbrugh) **21**:293, 319

"The Country Lass" (Burns) **3**:85

"The Country Life" (Herrick)
See "The Country life, to the honoured Master Endimion Porter, Groome of the Bed-Chamber to his Majesty"

"A Country Life: To his Brother, Master Thomas Herrick" (Herrick) **13**:377-82

"The Country life, to the honoured Master Endimion Porter, Groome of the Bed-Chamber to his Majesty" ("The Country Life") (Herrick) **13**:327, 364, 368, 377, 395

The Country-Wife (Wycherley) **8**:379-81, 383, 385-92, 394, 396-97, 400-02, 406, 409-16, 419-23, 425-26, 428-29; **21**:347, 355-57, 359-70, 372-76, 379-80, 383, 387-88, 390-91, 393-98

Courage (Grimmelshausen)
See *Die Erzbetrugerin und Landstortzerin Courasche*

"The Court Life. To a Friend, Disswading Him from Attending for Places" (Wycherley) **8**:416

"The Court of Death: a Pindarique Poem, dedicated to the memory of her Most Sacred Majesty, Queen Mary" (Dennis) **11**:14, 49-50

"The Court of Equity" (Burns)
See "Libel Summons"

"Court of Honor" (Addison) **18**:27

The Court of the King of Bantam (Behn) **1**:34, 38, 45-6, 48

Court Poems (*Town Eclogues*) (Montagu) **9**:276

The Courtesan (Aretino)
See *Cortigiana errante*

The Courtier (Castiglione)
See *Il libro del cortegiano*

The Courtier's Library (Donne) **10**:82

"Courtship" (Erasmus) **16**:193

The Cousins (Davys) **1**:97

The Covent-Garden Tragedy (Fielding) **1**:239

"A Covetous Man" (Butler) **16**:50

"The Coy Mistress" (Marvell)
See "To His Coy Mistress"

The Crafty Whore (Aretino) **12**:21, 25

"The Cricket" (P'u Sung-ling)
See "Tsu-chih"

Criminal Legislation (Marat)
See *Plan de législation criminelle, ouvrage dans lequel on traite des délits et des peines, de la force des preuves et des présomptions . . .*

"Cripples" ("On Cripples") (Montaigne) **8**:221

The Crisis (Steele) **18**:352, 354

Crispin, rival de son maître (Lesage) **2**:182, 201

The Critic (Gracian y Morales)
See *El Criticón*

"The Critic and the Writer of Fables" (Winchilsea) **3**:443, 457

Critical Examination of the Apologists of the Christian Religion (Holbach) **14**:167

The Critical History of Jesus Christ; or, Reasoned Analysis of the Gospels (Holbach)

See *Ecce Homo! or, A Critical Inquiry into the History of Jesus of Nazareth; Being a Rational Analysis of the Gospels*

Critical Observations (Dennis)
See *Remarks on a Book, entituled Prince Arthur, an Heroick Poem*

El Criticón (*The Critic; The Master Critic*) (Gracian y Morales) **15**:136-52, 154-55, 157-72, 174-75

La critique de L'école des femmes (*The School for Wives Criticized*) (Moliere) **10**:278, 281, 283, 287, 297, 311, 321

Critique de l'Opera (Perrault) **2**:259

The Critique upon Milton (Addison) **18**:7

Le crocheteur borgne (Voltaire) **14**:359

"Cromwell" (Drayton)
See "Thomas Cromwell, Earle of Essex"

"The Crosse" (Donne) **10**:16, 40, 84

De cruce (Lipsius)
See *De cruce libi tres*

De cruce libi tres (*De cruce*) (Lipsius) **16**:269

The Cruel Brother (Davenant) **13**:175, 216

"The Cruel Mistress" (Carew) **13**:11

"The cruell Maid" (Herrick) **13**:364

The Cruelty of the Spaniards in Peru (Davenant) **13**:190

"The Crusade" (Warton) **15**:432-33, 442, 445, 454

The Cry: A New Dramatic Fable (Fielding) **1**:270, 273

"The Cryer" (Drayton) **8**:27

The Cub at Newmarket. A Letter to the People of Scotland (Boswell) **4**:50, 52-3

"Culex" (Spenser) **5**:312

"A Cully" (Butler) **16**:50

"Cupid and Ganymede" (Prior) **4**:461

"Cupid, I Hate Thee, Which I'de Have Thee Know" (Drayton)
See "Sonnet 48"

"Cupid's Conflict" (More) **9**:298, 302

"A Curious Man" (Butler) **16**:52

"The Curse" (Donne) **10**:52, 82

"The Curse" (Herrick) **13**:341

"A Custom of the Island of Cea" (Montaigne) **8**:238

"Cyclops" (Erasmus) **16**:154

Cymon (Garrick) **15**:124

"Cymon and Iphigenia" (Dryden) **3**:184, 205, 213, 243

"Cynthia" (Jonson) **6**:322

Cynthia's Revels (Jonson) **6**:300, 302, 306, 308, 311, 335-36, 342

The Czar of Muscovy (Pix) **8**:260-61, 263, 269, 271-72, 276

"Czego chcesz od nas, panie?" (Kochanowski)
See "Pieśń"

"Les daimons" ("Demonology") (Ronsard) **6**:407, 411, 422, 424

"Daintie Davie" (Burns) **3**:56

"A Damask Rose Sticking upon a Lady's Breast" ("On a Damaske Rose") (Carew) **13**:18, 30

"Damon the Mower" (Wheatley) **3**:410-11, 441-42

"The Dampe" (Donne) **10**:36-7, 82

The Dancing-Master (Wycherley)
See *The Gentleman Dancing-Master*

The Danger of Priestcraft to Religion and Government (*Priestcraft Dangerous to Religion and Government*) (Dennis) **11**:26

"Dangers wait on Kings" (Herrick) **13**:394

Dannemarks og Norges beskrivelse (*Description of Denmark and Norway*) (Holberg) **6**:266, 281

Dannemarks riges historie (*History of the Kingdom of Denmark*) (Holberg) **6**:266, 278, 281-82

Den danske comoedies ligbegænglese (Holberg) **6**:278

"Daphnaida" (Spenser) **5**:312-13

"Daphnis and Chloe" (Marvell) **4**:408-10

"Dark Night of the Soul" (John of the Cross)
See "Noche Oscura del alma"

The Dark Night of the Soul (John of the Cross)
See *Noche Escura del Alma*

"Um daudans óvíssan tíma" ("On the Uncertain Hour of Death") (Petursson) **8**:253

"The Daughter of the Yen Family" (P'u Sungling)
See "Yen Shih"

"David" (Parnell) **3**:255

David, ou l'Histoire de l'homme selon le cœur de Dieu (Holbach) **14**:153

David Simple, Volume the Last (Fielding)
See *The Adventures of David Simple*

"Dawn of Day and Sunset" (More) **9**:298

"The Day of Judgement" (Swift) **1**:522, 524

Day of Preparation (Bacon)
See *Parasceve*

De IV Novissimis (More) **10**:398-99

De captivitate Babylonica ecclesiae praeludium (*Prelude on the Babylonian Captivity of the Church*) (Luther) **9**:87, 105, 107-08, 125, 141, 151

De Christiana religione (Ficino)
See *De religione christiana*

De disciplina claustralium (Kempis) **11**:411

De doctrina christiana (*Christian Doctrine*) (Milton) **9**:247-48, 250

De felici liberalitate (Paracelsus) **14**:199

De generatione hominis (*On the Origin of Man*) (Paracelsus) **14**:198

De imitatione Christi (*The Imitation of Christ*) (Kempis) **11**:406-13, 415-22, 424-26

De intellectus emendatione (*Correction of the Understanding*) (Spinoza) **9**:402, 423-24, 433, 435, 442-44

De iure regni apud Scotos: dialogus, authore Georgio Buchanano Scoto (Buchanan) **4**:118, 120, 125, 127, 130, 134, 136-37

"De la coustume" (Montaigne) **8**:236-37

"De la cruauté" (Montaigne) **8**:240

De la Littérature Allemande (Frederick the Great) **14**:65, 77

"De la phisionomie" ("Physiognomy") (Montaigne) **8**:221-22, 242

De la politique (Montesquieu) **7**:360-63

"De la praesumption" ("Of Presumption") (Montaigne) **8**:211, 233, 242

"De la vanité" ("Of Vanity") (Montaigne) **8**:197, 211, 232, 240-41

"De l'affection des peres aux enfants" ("On the Resemblance of Children to their Fathers") (Montaigne) **8**:240

"De l'art de conferer" ("Art of Conversation") (Montaigne) **8**:197, 240

"De l'election de son sepulchre" (Ronsard) **6**:417, 430

De l'esprit des loix (Montesquieu) **7**:304-06, 308-13, 315-17, 319-20, 322-29, 331, 333-37, 339, 341-45, 347-50, 356-57, 359-60, 362-64

"De l'excellence de l'esprit de l'homme" (Ronsard) **6**:424

"De l'experience" ("Of Experience") (Montaigne) **8**:211, 221, 236, 239, 241-42

De l'homme (Marat)
See *A Philosophical Essay on Man, Being an Attempt to Investigate the Principles and Laws of the Reciprocal Influence of the Soul on the Body*

"De l'institution des enfans" (Montaigne) **8**:241

De magnificentia (Ficino) **12**:168

De Maria Scotorum regina, totaque ejus contra regem conjuratione (Buchanan) **4**:120, 121, 125-26

"De Monachis S. Antonii" (Buchanan) **4**:122

De morbus amentium (*On the Diseases That Deprive Man of Reason*) (Paracelsus) **14**:198

De musica (Ficino) **12**:197

De Non Plectendis Morte Adulteris (Foxe) **14**:26

De partu virginis (Sannazaro) **8**:320, 322-23, 326-28, 330, 332, 336-37

De prosodia libellus (Buchanan) **4**:129

De Rebus Memorabilibus Angliae (Elyot) **11**:62, 73

De religione christiana (*Concerning the Christian Religion; De Christiana religione; On the Christian Religion*) (Ficino) **12**:172-73, 177, 182, 185, 188-89, 195, 201

De religione perpetua (Paracelsus) **14**:199

De renovatione et restauratione (Paracelsus) **14**:198

De ressurectione et corporum glorificatione (Paracelsus) **14**:199

De sphaera (Buchanan)
See *Sphaera in quinque libros distributa*

De summo bono et aeterno bono (Paracelsus) **14**:199

De testamentis (Casanova de Seingalt) **13**:126

De usynlige (Holberg) **6**:273, 278

De vita (Ficino) **12**:171-72, 180

De vita longa (Paracelsus) **14**:198

"The Dean of the Faculty" (Burns) **3**:96

The Dean's Provocation for Writing the "Lady's Dressing Room " (Montagu) **9**:282

"Death and Daphne" (Swift) **1**:459

"Death and Doctor Hornbook" ("Hornbook") (Burns) **3**:50, 82, 87, 90

"The Death and Dying Words of Poor Mailie" ("Mailie's Dying Words and Elegy"; "Poor Mailie's Elegy") (Burns) **3**:57, 60, 67, 71, 87, 90

"Death of a Favorite Cat" (Gray)
See "Ode on the Death of a Favourite Cat, Drowned in a Tub of Gold Fishes"

"The Death of Astragon" (Davenant) **13**:204, 206

The Death of Blanche the Duchess (Chaucer)
See *Book of the Duchess*

"Death of Sir Roger de Coverley" (Addison) **18**:28

"Death of the Lord Protector" (Marvell)
See "Poem upon the Death of O. C."

Deaths Duell; or, A Consolation to the Soule, against the dying Life, and living Death of the Body (Donne) **10**:64, 85, 102-05

Le debat de deux amans (Christine de Pizan) **9**:28, 42, 48

The Debate of Poissy (Christine de Pizan)
See *Le livre du dit de Poissy*

"Debates in Magna Lilliputia" (Johnson)
  See "Debates in the Senate of Magna
    Lilliputia"
"Debates in the Senate of Magna Lilliputia"
  ("Debates in Magna Lilliputia"; "Reports of
  the Debates of the Senate of Lilliput")
  (Johnson) **15**:194, 206
The Debauchee (Behn) **1**:33
The debellation of Salem and Bizance (More)
  10:366, 370, 398, 408
"Deborah" (Parnell) **3**:255
Decannali (Machiavelli)
  See *Decennale primo*
The Deceiver Deceived (Pix) **8**:259-62, 268-69,
  271-73, 275
Decennale primo (*Decannali*) (Machiavelli)
  8:128
*Declaration of the Articles Condemned by Leo
  X* (Luther) **9**:84
"The Dedication" (Churchill)
  See "Fragment of a Dedication to Dr. W.
    Warburton, Bishop of Gloucester"
"Dedication of Examen Poeticum" (Dryden)
  3:214
"The Dedication of the Aeneis" (Dryden)
  3:242; **21**:109-10, 116
"Dedication to G----- H-----, Esq."
  ("Dedication to Gavin Hamilton") (Burns)
  3:48, 86
"Dedication to Gavin Hamilton" (Burns)
  See "Dedication to G----- H-----, Esq."
"The Dedication to the Sermons" (Churchill)
  3:157
"The Defence" (Chatterton) **3**:133
Defence (Elyot)
  See *The Defence of Good Women*
Defence of an Essay of Dramatic Poesy
  (Dryden) **3**:238; **21**:117
The Defence of Good Women (*Defence*;
  Defense; *Defense of Good Women*;
  Defensorium bonarum mulierum) (Elyot)
  11:58, 61, 68-9, 71, 83-6, 91-2, 95-6
The Defence of Poesie (*An Apologie for Poetrie*)
  (Sidney) **19**:324, 326, 330, 333, 336-37,
  340-41, 345, 352, 355-56, 363-64, 368-69,
  380-81, 393-94, 401-02, 404, 407-13, 415-18,
  420-24, 432-33
"Defence of the Epilogue (to The Conquest of
  Granada)" (Dryden) **3**:238; **21**:116-17
*A Defence of the "Essay of Human
  Understanding"* (Trotter) **8**:353, 355, 358,
  361-63, 365, 370, 374
A Defence of the People of England (Milton)
  See *Pro populo anglicano defensio, contra
    Claudii Anonymi*
*A Defence of the Reasons for Restoring Some
  Prayers and Directions of King Edward the
  Sixth's First Liturgy* (Collier) **6**:209
*A Defence of the Short View of the Profaneness
  and Immorality of the English Stage* (Collier)
  6:229
Defense (Elyot)
  See *The Defence of Good Women*
Défense de "L'esprit des loix" (Montesquieu)
  7:324
La Defense du mondain (Voltaire) **14**:406
Defense of Good Women (Elyot)
  See *The Defence of Good Women*
*Defense of the Seven Sacraments against Martin
  Luther* (Henry VIII)
  See *Assertio septem sacramentorum adversus
    Martinum Lutherum haeresiarchon*

Defensiones (Paracelsus) **14**:200
Defensorium bonarum mulierum (Elyot)
  See *The Defence of Good Women*
"The Definition of Love" (Marvell) **4**:403,
  411, 425, 434, 441-43
"The Deil's Awa' wi' th' Exciseman" (Burns)
  3:96
"Delight in Disorder" (Herrick) **13**:330, 333,
  351, 358, 359, 369, 379-80, 382
Della fortuna (Ficino) **12**:169
"Democritus and Heraclitus" ("Heraclitus")
  (Prior) **4**:464-65
*Democritus plantonissans: or, An Essay upon
  the Infinity of Worlds Out of Platonic
  Principles* (More) **9**:307, 320, 330
"Demonology" (Ronsard)
  See "Les daimons"
*Dendrologia: Dodona's Grove; or, The Vocall
  Forest* (*Dodona's Grove*; *The Vocal Forest*)
  (Howell) **13**:415, 419, 424, 426, 433
Denys le tyran (Marmontel) **2**:213, 215
Le dépit amoureux (*Lovers' Spite*) (Moliere)
  10:275-77, 280, 283, 286, 291, 310, 318
"Deposition from love" (Carew) **13**:11, 15, 61
*Der abenteuerliche Simplicissimus, Teutsch, das
  hist: Die Beschreibun dess Lebens eines
  seltzamen Vaganten, gennant Melchio
  Sternfels von Fuchsheim* (*Simplician
  Writings*) (Grimmelshausen) **6**:235-48, 252
*Der abentheuerliche, wunderbare und unerhörte
  Ritter Hopffen-sack* (*Hopffen-Sack*) (Beer)
  5:54-5
Der Bart-Krieg (*The Beard War*)
  (Grimmelshausen) **6**:247
Der briefwechsel des Spinoza (Spinoza)
  See *Correspondence*
Der erste Beernhäuter (*The First Sluggard*)
  (Grimmelshausen) **6**:247
Der Freygeist (*The Free-Thinker*) (Lessing)
  8:66, 112
Der Geheimnisvolle (Schlegel) **5**:275, 278-79
Der geschäftige Müssiggänger (*The Busy Idler*)
  (Schlegel) **5**:273, 277, 282
Der gute Rat (Schlegel) **5**:278-79
Der junge Gelehrte (*The Young Savant*)
  (Lessing) **8**:63, 94, 98, 113
Der keusche Joseph (*Chaste Joseph*)
  (Grimmelshausen) **6**:247-48
Der kleine Catechismus (*Small Catechism*)
  (Luther) **9**:151
Der kurtzweilige Bruder Blau-Mantel (*Bruder
  Blau-Mantel*) (Beer) **5**:56
Der Narrenspital (Beer) **5**:53-4
Der neu ausgefertigte Jungfer-Hobel (*Jungfer-
  Hobel*) (Beer) **5**:53, 56
Der politische Feuermäuer-kehrer (Beer) **5**:56
Der satyrische Pilgram (*The Satyrical Pilgrim*)
  (Grimmelshausen) **6**:244-48, 251
Der seltsame Springinsfeld (*Heedless Hopalong*)
  (Grimmelshausen) **6**:238, 247, 249-51
Der stoltze Melcher (*Proud Melchio*)
  (Grimmelshausen) **6**:247
*Der symplicianische Welt-Kucker; oder,
  Abentheuerliche Jan Rebhu, Parts I-IV* (*The
  Simplician World-Observer*) (Beer) **5**:52-3,
  55-6, 59-60
Der Teutsche Michel (*German Michael*)
  (Grimmelshausen) **6**:247
Der Triumph der guten Frauen (Schlegel)
  5:275, 278-79

*Der verkehrte Staats-Mann; oder, Nasen-weise
  Secretarius* (*Verkehrter Staatsmann*) (Beer)
  5:57
Der verliebte Österreicher (*The Austrian in
  Love; or, The Love and Life Story of Sorona,
  Incomparable in Virtues and Beauty*) (Beer)
  5:48, 57-9
Les Derniers Vers (Ronsard) **6**:436
*Des abenteuerlichen Simplicissimi Ewig-
  wahrender Calender* (*The Adventurous
  Simplicissimus's Perpetual Calendar*)
  (Grimmelshausen) **6**:248
*Des abentheuerlichen Jan Rebhu Ritter
  Spiridon aus Perusina* (*Ritter Spiridon aus
  Perusina*) (Beer) **5**:54-5
*Des berühmten Spaniers Francisci Sambelle
  wolausgepolirte Weiber-Hächel*
  (*Weiberhächel*) (Beer) **5**:53, 56
"Des cannibales" ("Of Cannibals")
  (Montaigne) **8**:222, 233, 236, 238
"Des coches" ("Coaches") (Montaigne)
  8:197, 204, 236
"Des senteurs" (Montaigne) **8**:234
"The Descent of Odin, an Ode" (Gray)
  4:310, 312, 318
Descriptio Globi Intellectualis (*A Description of
  the Intellectual Globe*) (Bacon) **18**:186-87,
  195
"Description of a City Shower" (Swift) **1**:439,
  458
"Description of a Tapestry at Longleat"
  (Winchilsea) **3**:457
"The Description of a Woman" (Herrick)
  13:398
"Description of an Author's Bedroom"
  (Goldsmith) **2**:74
"A Description of Cannynge's Feast"
  (Chatterton) **3**:135
"The Description of Cooke-ham" (Lanyer)
  10:180-81, 183, 186-88, 192
Description of Denmark and Norway (Holberg)
  See *Dannemarks og Norges beskrivelse*
A Description of New England (Smith) **9**:375,
  382-84
A Description of the Intellectual Globe (Bacon)
  See *Descriptio Globi Intellectualis*
"Description of the Morning" (Swift) **1**:439,
  458, 480-81
The Deserted Village (Goldsmith) **2**:68, 71,
  74-5, 79-80, 82, 90, 94-6, 98, 104-05, 107,
  114
The Desolation of America (Day) **1**:105
"The Despairing Shepherd" (Prior) **4**:461
"Despondency, an Ode" (Burns) **3**:48, 67, 86
Determinations (Taylor)
  See *Gods Determinations touching his Elect:
    and The Elects Combat in their
    Conversion, and Coming up to God in
    Christ: together with the Comfortable
    Effects Thereof*
Deudsch Catechismus (*The Large Catechism*)
  (Luther) **9**:134, 147, 151
Les deux consolés (Voltaire) **14**:398
The Devil is an Ass (Jonson) **6**:297, 304-06,
  311, 314, 320, 327-30, 335
The Devil upon Two Sticks (Lesage)
  See *Le diable boiteux*
Le Devin du village (Rousseau) **14**:287
Dévoilé (Holbach)
  See *Christianisme dévoilé*
"Devotion makes the Deity" (Herrick) **13**:319
Devotions on Sundrie Occasions (Donne)

See *Devotions upon Emergent Occasions, and Severall steps in my sicknes*

Devotions upon Emergent Occasions, and Severall steps in my sicknes (*Devotions on Sundrie Occasions*) (Donne) **10**:31, 40, 64, 84, 89, 103-04

Devout Treatise upon the Pater Noster (Erasmus) **16**:124

Di Gerusalemme conquistata (*Conquistata*) (Tasso) **5**:375-76, 383, 394, 403

Le diable boiteux (*The Devil upon Two Sticks*) (Lesage) **2**:175-77, 181-85, 189, 201-04

A dialogue of comfort against tribulacion (*Of Comfort against Tribulation*) (More) **10**:367, 370, 389, 393-96, 398-99, 404, 407, 409, 413, 431, 435-41

Dialoghi (Aretino)
See *Ragionamento della Nanna e della Antonia*

Dialogi (Hutten) **16**:233

Dialogo del Pietro Aretino nel quale si parla del gioco con moralità piacevole (Aretino) **12**:20

Dialogo nel quale la Nanna insegna a la Pippa (Aretino) **12**:36

"The Dialogue" (Bradstreet)
See "A Dialogue between Old England and New"

A Dialogue (Hume) **7**:184

"The Dialogue between Daphne and Apollo" ("Dialogues of the Dead") (Prior) **4**:466

"Dialogue between Mr. John Lock and Seigneur de Montaigne" ("Dialogues of the Dead") (Prior) **4**:470

"A Dialogue between Old England and New" ("The Dialogue") (Bradstreet) **4**:85, 90, 95, 109

"A Dialogue between the Resolved Soul, and Created Pleasure" (Marvell) **4**:410, 425-27, 442

"A Dialogue between the Soul and Body" (Marvell) **4**:412, 420-23, 426, 429, 439

"Dialogue between the Writer and a Maypole Dresser" (Taylor) **11**:366

"A Dialogue betweene two shepheards, Thenot and Piers, in praise of Astraea" (Sidney) **19**:292-93, 296

A Dialogue Concernynge heresyes and matters of religion (More) **10**:366, 388, 408-09, 438, 441-42

Dialogue de l'Amour et de l'Amitié (Perrault) **2**:280

Dialogue de Sylla et Eucrate (*Sylla et Eucrate*) (Montesquieu) **7**:321, 324

Dialogue des héros de roman (*Les héros de Roman*) (Boileau-Despreaux) **3**:24, 29, 33

Dialogue; ou, Satire X (Boileau-Despreaux) **3**:37-9

"Dialogue with the Nine Sisters" (Ronsard) **6**:412

Dialogues (Aretino)
See *Ragionamento della Nanna e della Antonia*

Dialogues (Eliot)
See *Indian Dialogues, for Their Instruction in that Great Service of Christ, in Calling Home Their Countrymen to the Knowledge of God and of Themselves, and of Jesus Christ*

Dialogues (Lyttelton)
See *Dialogues of the Dead*

Dialogues (More) **10**:370

Dialogues (Reynolds)

See *Johnson & Garrick*

Dialogues avec moi-même (Rousseau)
See *Rousseau juge de Jean Jacques*

Dialogues concerning Natural Religion (Hume) **7**:144, 154-58, 196-98

Dialogues of Freemasons (Lessing)
See *Lessing's Masonic Dialogues*

"Dialogues of the Dead" (Prior) **4**:467-68, 472-73

"Dialogues of the Dead" (Prior)
See "Dialogue between Mr. John Lock and Seigneur de Montaigne"

"Dialogues of the Dead" (Prior)
See "The Dialogue between Daphne and Apollo"

Dialogues of the Dead (*Dialogues*) (Lyttelton) **10**:196, 198-201, 204, 207-10, 212, 214-15

"Dialogues of the Dogs" (Burns)
See "The Twa Dogs"

Dialogues upon Medals (Addison) **18**:6, 8, 30, 39

Dialogus novitiorum (Kempis) **11**:411

"Diane" (Rousseau) **9**:343

Diaries (Johnson) **15**:288

Diary in North Wales (Johnson)
See *A Diary of a Journey into North Wales, in the year 1774*

A Diary of a Journey into North Wales, in the year 1774 (*Diary in North Wales*) (Johnson) **15**:209

The Diary of Samuel Pepys (Pepys) **11**:208-89

"The Dice Box" (Walpole) **2**:500

The Dictionary (*Bibliotheca; Bibliotheca Eliotae; Latin-English Dictionary*) (Elyot) **11**:58, 61-3, 68, 73, 84-5, 87, 90-1

Dictionary (Johnson)
See *Dictionary of the English Language*

Dictionary of the English Language (*Dictionary; English Dictionary*) (Johnson) **15**:182, 195-99, 203, 207-08, 221, 225, 239, 241, 250-51, 270, 276, 278-80, 282-83, 298-302, 306, 310-11, 313

Dictionnaire philosophique (*Portatif*) (Voltaire) **14**:339, 343, 351-53, 358, 367, 369-70, 391-96, 402

Diderich Menschenskræk (*Diderich the Terrible*) (Holberg) **6**:277

Diderich the Terrible (Holberg)
See *Diderich Menschenskræk*

Dido (Schlegel) **5**:280

Dido y Eneas (Castro) **19**:7-8

Dietwald und Amerlinde (Grimmelshausen) **6**:247-48

"The Difference Betwixt Kings and Subjects" (Herrick) **13**:394

The Different Widows; or, Intrigue all-a-Mode (Pix) **8**:260, 269, 271-72, 276

De Dignitate et Augmentis Scientiarum (Bacon)
See *De augmentis scientiarum*

"Dimmi di gratia, Amor, se gli ochi mei" (Michelangelo) **12**:360

"Direct" (Marmontel) **2**:220

"The Dirge" (Sidney) **19**:329

"Dirge for Cymbeline" (Collins)
See "A Song from Cymbeline"

"Dirge in Ælla" (Chatterton)
See "Ælla: A Tragycal Enterlude"

"Dirge of Jephthah's Daughter" (Herrick) **13**:317, 342

"The Disappointment" (Behn) **1**:52, 54

"Discontents in Devon" (Herrick) **13**:387

Discorsi (Tasso) **5**:383, 387, 392-94, 408

Discorsi del poema eroico (*Discorsi Tasso*) (Tasso) **5**:383, 393

Discorsi dell'arte poetica (*Discorsi Tasso*) (Tasso) **5**:383, 392, 394

Discorsi di Nicolo Machiavelli... sopra la prima deca di Tito Livio, a Zanobi Buondelmonte, et a Cosimo Rucellai (*Comments on Livy*) (Machiavelli) **8**:124-28, 130, 133, 135-37, 139, 142, 145, 148-49, 151, 155-56, 158, 160-62, 167, 169-71, 175, 179

Discorsi Tasso (Tasso)
See *Discorsi dell'arte poetica*

Discorsi Tasso (Tasso)
See *Discorsi del poema eroico*

Discours (Ronsard)
See *Discours des misères de ce temps*

"Discours au Roy" (Boileau-Despreaux) **3**:39

Discours des misères de ce temps (*Discours*) (Ronsard) **6**:409-11, 414, 417-18

Discours en vers sur l'homme (Voltaire) **14**:364, 379

Discours sur l'Inégalité (Rousseau)
See *Discours sur l'origine et les fondements de l'inégalité parmi les hommes*

Discours sur l'origine et les fondements de l'inégalité parmi les hommes (*Discours sur l'Inégalité; Discourse on Inequality; Discourse on the Origins of Inequality; Second Discourse*) (Rousseau) **14**:214, 223, 227-28, 239-41, 253, 270, 276, 288-91, 293-95, 297, 306, 309, 313

A Discourse concerning a Guide in Controversies, in Two Letters (Trotter) **8**:355, 362, 370

A Discourse Concerning the Mechanical Operation of the Spirit (Swift) **1**:509, 513-14, 517

A Discourse Concerning the Original and Progress of Satire (*The Original and Progress of Satire*) (Dryden) **3**:210, 214, 231, 237; **21**:111, 133

"Discourse II" (Reynolds)
See "The Second Discourse"

Discourse on Inequality (Rousseau)
See *Discours sur l'origine et les fondements de l'inégalité parmi les hommes*

Discourse on Pastoral Poetry (Pope) **3**:322-23

Discourse on the Arts and Sciences (*First Discourse*) (Rousseau) **14**:255, 276, 286, 288, 297, 305, 309, 313

Discourse on the Changes Which Have Occurred on Our Globe (Voltaire) **14**:390

Discourse on the Origins of Inequality (Rousseau)
See *Discours sur l'origine et les fondements de l'inégalité parmi les hommes*

Discourse on the seven days of the creation (Pico della Mirandola)
See *Heptaplus*

"Discourse Three" (Reynolds)
See "The Third Discourse"

Discourse Upon Comedy (*Essay on Comedy*) (Farquhar) **21**:128, 133, 139, 141-43, 146, 161, 182

A Discourse Upon Gondibert, An Heroic Poem written by Sir William D'Avenant. With an Answer to It by Mr. Hobbes (Davenant) **13**:183, 195, 207

"Discourse XI" (Reynolds)
See "The Eleventh Discourse"

"Discourse XII" (Reynolds)
See "The Twelfth Discourse"

The Discourses (Reynolds)
　See *Discourses on Art*
Discourses on Art (*The Discourses; Fifteen Discourses*) (Reynolds)　15:364, 366, 371-72, 376-77, 379-80, 382, 384-91, 394, 399-402, 404-05, 407-08, 411-18, 420-21, 422
Discoveries (Jonson)
　See *Timber; or, Discoveries*
The Discovery (Sheridan)　7:370, 372-74, 376-77
El Discreto (*The Man of Discretion*) (Gracian y Morales)　15:135-36, 143-45, 165
"Disdaine Returned" ("He that loves a rosy cheek") (Carew)　13:11, 62
The Dismissal of the Grecian Envoys (Kochanowski)
　See *Odprawa posłów grekich*
Disputatio contra iudicium astrologorum (Ficino)　12:171-72, 199-200
Disputatio pro declaratione virtutia indulgentiarum (*Ninety-Five Theses*) (Luther)　9:91, 109, 119, 123-24, 129, 146-47
Disputationes (Pico della Mirandola)　15:354
La dispute (Marivaux)　4:369
"Disquisition" (Davenant)
　See "The Philosophers Disquisition to the Dying Christian"
Dissertatio de libertate christiana per autorem recognita (*The Freedom of a Christian Man*) (Luther)　9:105-06, 108, 123, 125, 134-35, 142
Dissertation (Boileau-Despreaux)
　See *Dissertation sur la Joconde*
Dissertation sur la Joconde (*Dissertation*) (Boileau-Despreaux)　3:29, 33
"The Dissolution" (Donne)　10:58
"A Disswasive to His Mistress on Her Resolving to Turn Nun" (Wycherley)　8:400
Distichs of Cato (Erasmus)　16:123
The Distresses (Davenant)　13:176, 181, 196, 200
Distributio Operis (Bacon)　18:146
Le dit de la pastoure (Christine de Pizan)　9:48
Le dit de la rose (Christine de Pizan)　9:25, 49
"Dithyrambes" (Ronsard)　6:429
Le dittie de Jehanne d'Arc (Christine de Pizan)
　See *Le dittie sur Jeanne d'Arc*
Le dittie sur Jeanne d'Arc (*Le dittie de Jehanne d'Arc*) (Christine de Pizan)　9:39
"Diversion" (Montaigne)　8:221
"Divination by a Daffodil" (Herrick)　13:367
"A Divine and Supernatural Light, Immediately Imparted to the Soul By the Spirit of God, Shown to Be Both a Scriptural, and Rational Doctrine" (Edwards)　7:101, 123, 131
Divine Dialogues (More)　9:293, 297, 300, 307-08
Divine Emblems; or, Temporal Things Spiritualized (*Emblems*) (Bunyan)　4:182
The Divine in Mode (Marvell)
　See *Mr. Smirk; or, The Divine in Mode*
"A Divine Mistris" (Carew)　13:33-4, 62
The Divine Narcissus (Juana Ines de la Cruz)
　See *El divino Narciso*
Divine Poems (Donne)　10:40, 45, 96, 98-99, 106
El divino Narciso (*The Divine Narcissus*) (Juana Ines de la Cruz)　5:143-45, 151-52, 158-59

The Divorce-Court Judge (Cervantes)　6:190-92
Dīwān (Babur)　18:90
"Do Miłłości" ("To Love") (Kochanowski)　10:160
"Do paniej" ("To a Lady") (Kochanowski)　10:160
"Do snu" ("To Sleep") (Kochanowski)　10:161
The Doctor in spite of Himself (Moliere)
　See *Le médecin malgré lui*
The Doctrinal of Princes (Elyot)　11:61, 82, 84-5, 89
Doctrinale seu manuale juvenum (Kempis)　11:411
The Doctrine and Discipline of Divorce (Milton)　9:192, 250, 253
Dodona's Grove (Howell)
　See *Dendrologia: Dodona's Grove; or, The Vocall Forest*
"Does Haughty Gaul" (Burns)　3:81
"The Dolefull Lay of Clorinda" (Sidney)　19:292, 296, 309-10
Don Garcia of Navarre (Moliere)
　See *Don Garcie de Navarre; ou, Le prince jaloux*
Don Garcie de Navarre (Moliere)
　See *Don Garcie de Navarre; ou, Le prince jaloux*
Don Garcie de Navarre; ou, Le prince jaloux (*Don Garcia of Navarre; Don Garcie de Navarre*) (Moliere)　10:277, 280, 283, 291, 297-300, 310, 319-20, 325
Don Giovanni tenorio (Goldoni)　4:262
Don Juan; or, The Banquet of Stone (Moliere)
　See *Don Juan; ou Le festin de Pierre*
Don Juan; ou Le festin de Pierre (*Don Juan; or, The Banquet of Stone; Festin de Pierre*) (Moliere)　10:266, 282-84, 289-91, 298-99, 312, 318-21, 327, 329, 333-34, 345, 347-48
Don Quixote (Castro)　19:2
Don Quixote (Cervantes)
　See *El ingenioso hidalgo Don Quixote de la Mancha*
Don Quixote in England (Fielding)　1:250
Don Ranudo de Colibrados (Holberg)　6:277
Don Sebastian, King of Portugal (Dryden)　3:186, 209-10, 214, 222, 232-33, 235, 241; 21:56, 71
La donna di garbo (*The Clever Woman*) (Goldoni)　4:250, 265, 267
La donna di governo (Goldoni)　4:260
Le donne de casa soa (Goldoni)　4:265-66
Le donne gelose (*The Jealous Women*) (Goldoni)　4:257
Donne's Sermons (Donne)　10:47, 106
"Doris" (Congreve)　5:85, 106-07
"Las dos doncelas" ("The Two Maidens") (Cervantes)　6:171, 177
The Double Dealer (Congreve)　5:64, 66, 68, 71, 74, 76, 78-9, 84, 86-7, 90, 92-3, 96, 98-9, 101, 103, 109-13; 21:3, 5-9, 26-8, 32, 38-41, 45
The Double Distress (Pix)　8:260-63, 269, 271-72, 276
La double inconstance (Marivaux)　4:366-67, 371-72, 376-77, 379-83
Double Supply of Words and Matter (Erasmus)　16:123
Doules sur la religion (Holbach)　14:153
"The Dove" (Prior)　4:467
Dowel, Dobet, and Dobest (Langland)

　See *Piers Plowman*
"Down Hall" (Prior)
　See "Ballad of Down-Hall"
Le doyen de Killérine (Prevost)　1:329-30, 334-37, 343-44, 346-47
Dramatic Works (Garrick)　15:94
The Drapier's Letters (Swift)　1:441, 458, 497, 514, 516
"Draw-Gloves" (Herrick)　13:331
"A Dream" (Burns)　3:87, 96
"Dream" (Juana Ines de la Cruz)
　See "Primero sueño"
"The Dream" (Kochanowski)
　See "Tren XIX"
Dream of the Red Chamber (Ts'ao Hsueh-ch'in)
　See *Hung-lou meng*
"A Dream of Wolves" (P'u Sung-ling)　3:344
"Drink to Me Only with Thine Eyes" (Jonson)
　See "Song to Celia"
The Drummer (Addison)　18:20
Du Contrat social (*Le Contrat Social; The Social Contract*) (Rousseau)　14:215, 223, 227-29, 241, 247-49, 252, 254, 256, 261, 263, 270, 273, 273, 275-78, 284, 288, 292, 297, 300-03, 309, 313-14
"Du repentir" ("Of Repentance") (Montaigne)　8:211, 226, 231, 242
Due Preparations for the Plague (Defoe)　1:168
Due trattati uno intorna alle otto principale arti dell oreficeria. L'altro in materia dell'arte della scultura... (Cellini)　7:74-5, 79
"The Duellist" (Churchill)　3:144-48, 152, 154-55, 158, 160, 163
The Duke of Guise (Dryden)　3:210; 21:53, 55-8, 65, 107
"Duke of Marlborough" (Wycherley)　8:380
Dulce Bellum inexpertis (Erasmus)　16:132, 173, 198
The Dumb Virgin; or, The Force of Imagination (Behn)　1:42-3
"Duncan Gray" (Burns)　3:61, 66, 71
"A Dunce" (Butler)　16:30
"The Dunciad" (Pope)　3:269, 272 , 276-77, 279, 281, 287-91, 295-96, 298-301, 304-07, 313-14, 317-22, 324, 327-31, 333, 336-38
"Dunciad Variorum" (Pope)　3:319-20, 328
The Dupe (Sheridan)　7:370, 373, 377
The Dutch Lover (Behn)　1:29, 33, 39, 52
"Duty to Tyrants" (Herrick)　13:394
"Dweller in Yon Dungeon Dark" (Burns)　3:60
A dyaloge of syr Thomas More knyghte (More)　10:362, 397-98
The Dying Negro (Day)　1:105-07
"The Eagle" (More)　9:298
"The Eagle, the Sow, and the Cat" (Winchilsea)　3:457
The Earl of Essex (Brooke)　1:62
The Earl of Westmoreland (Brooke)　1:62
Eastern Evangelical Planeta (Siguenza y Gongora)
　See *Oriental planeta evangelica epopeya sacro-panegyrica al apostol grande de las Indias S. Francisco Xavier*
"The Ebb and Flow" (Taylor)　11:352, 356, 386
"Eben as a Little Flower" (Petursson)
　See "Alt eins og blómstrió eina"

Title Index

Ecce Homo! or, A Critical Inquiry into the History of Jesus of Nazareth; Being a Rational Analysis of the Gospels (*The Critical History of Jesus Christ; or, Reasoned Analysis of the Gospels*) (Holbach) **14**:148, 168

Ecclesiastes (*The Method of Preaching*) (Erasmus) **16**:115, 154

Ecclesiastical History (Collier)
  See *An Ecclesiastical History of Great Britain*

Ecclesiastical History (Foxe)
  See *Actes and Monumentes of these latter perilous dayes touching matters of the Church*

An Ecclesiastical History of Great Britain (*Ecclesiastical History*) (Collier) **6**:208, 210

Eclogae piscatoriae (*Piscatoriae*) (Sannazaro) **8**:326-27, 332, 334, 336

"Eclogue I" (Drayton) **8**:34-5

"Eclogue II" (Drayton) **8**:35

"Eclogue IV" (Drayton) **8**:35

"Eclogue V" (Drayton) **8**:35

"Eclogue VII" (Drayton) **8**:35

"Eclogue VIII" (Drayton) **8**:35

"Eclogue IX" (Drayton) **8**:35

"Eclogues" (Chatterton)
  See "African Eclogues"

"Eclogues" (Warton)
  See "Five Pastoral Eclogues: The Scenes of Which are Supposed to Lie Among the Shepherds, Oppressed by the War in Germany"

Eclogues (Drayton)
  See *Eglogs*

L'école des femmes (*The School for Wives*) (Moliere) **10**:261-65, 272, 279, 281, 283, 285-88, 297, 300, 302-06, 310, 319, 335, 341

L'école des maris (*The School for Husbands*) (Moliere) **10**:275, 277, 280-81, 283, 286-87, 291, 295, 299-300, 302-04, 310, 312, 341

L'écoles des mères (Marivaux) **4**:354, 365, 368

Ecologues (Dryden) **21**:119

Ecossaise (Voltaire) **14**:338

Écrits spirituels et historiques (Marie de l'Incarnation) **10**:251

"The Ecstasy" (Donne)
  See "The Exstasie"

L'ecumoire; ou, Tanzai et Néadarné, histoire Japonaise (*Tanzai*) (Crebillon) **1**:75, 79, 81, 89-90

"An Eddy" (Carew) **13**:34

The Education of a Christian Prince (Erasmus)
  See *Institutio principis christiani*

The Education of the Human Race (Lessing) **8**:61-2, 84, 100, 105, 107, 112

The Education of Women (Defoe) **1**:148

The Education or bringinge up of Children (Elyot) **11**:61

Edward and Eleonora. A Tragedy (Thomson) **16**:396

Edwin and Angelina (Goldsmith) **2**:74, 104

Les effets surprenants de la sympathie; ou, Les aventures de *** (Marivaux) **4**:361

Les egarements du coeur et de l'esprit; ou, Memoires de Monsieur de Meilcour (Crebillon) **1**:75, 79, 84, 86, 88-95

Eglogs (*Eclogues*) (Drayton) **8**:17, 34-5

Eglogues (Ronsard) **6**:411

Egyptus (Marmontel) **2**:213, 217

Eight Plays and Eight Interludes: New and Never Performed (Cervantes)
  See *Ocho comedias y ocho entremeses*

"The Eighth Discourse" (Reynolds) **15**:382, 396, 403, 405

Eikon Basilike: The Portraicture of His Sacred Majestie in His Solitudes and Sufferings (*Icon Basilike*) (Charles I) **13**:130-54

"Ein' feste Burg ist unser Gott" ("A Mighty Fortress Is Our God") (Luther) **9**:142, 151

Electricity (Marat) **10**:222

"An Elegiac Poem on the Death of George Whitefield" ("On the Death of the Rev. Mr. George Whitefield") (Wheatley) **3**:412, 415, 422, 436

"Elegiarum Liber" (Buchanan) **4**:122

"Elegie I: Jealosie" (Donne) **10**:66-8

"Elegie II: The Anagram" (Donne) **10**:82

"Elegie III: Change" (Donne) **10**:82

"Elegie IV: The Perfume" (Donne) **10**:36, 67-8, 89

"Elegie V: His Picture" (Donne) **10**:67-8

"Elegie VII: 'Nature's lay ideot'" (Donne) **10**:55

"Elegie VIII: The Comparison" (Donne) **10**:10, 82

"Elegie IX: The Autumnall" (Donne) **10**:82

"Elegie XI: The Bracelet" (Donne) **10**:4

"Elegie XII: His parting from her" (Donne) **10**:36, 67-8, 82

"Elegie XIV: A Tale of a Citizen and His Wife" (Donne) **10**:39

"Elegie XV: The Expostulation" (Donne) **10**:67-8

"Elegie XVI: On his mistris" ("On His Mistris") (Donne) **10**:36, 52, 56, 67-8, 82

"Elegie XVII: Variety" (Donne) **10**:81-2

"Elegie XVII: Loves Progress" (Donne) **10**:68

"Elegie XIX: Going to Bed" (Donne) **10**:43, 51-2, 54, 68, 82-4, 88, 103

"Elegie XX: Loves Warr" (Donne) **10**:43, 68

"Elegie a Cassandre" (Ronsard) **6**:432-34

"L'Elégie à Guillaume des Autels sur le Tumulte d'Amboise" (Ronsard) **6**:411

"Elegie A Ian Brinon" (Ronsard) **6**:433

"Elegie A J. De La Peruse" (Ronsard) **6**:433

"Elegie A Loïs Des Masures Tournisien" (Ronsard) **6**:433, 436

"Elégie à Marie" (Ronsard) **6**:426-27, 433

"Elegie A M. A. De Muret" (Ronsard) **6**:433

"Elegie A Tresillustre et Reverendissime Cardinal de Chastillon" (Ronsard) **6**:433

"Elegie Au Seigneur L'Huillier" (Ronsard) **6**:433

"Elegie du Verre à Jan Brinon" (Ronsard) **6**:433

"An Elegie on the La: Pen: sent to my Mistresse out of France" ("La: Pen") (Carew) **13**:50-1

"An Elegie On the Lady Jane Pawlet" (Jonson) **6**:346-47

"Elegie Sur Le Trepas d'Antoine Chateignier" (Ronsard) **6**:432-34

"Elégie (to Mary, Queen of Scots)" (Ronsard) **6**:432

"Elegie Traduite du Grec d'Ergasto" (Ronsard) **6**:433-34

"An Elegie upon that Honourable and renowned Knight Sir Philip Sidney, who was untimely slaine at the Seige of Zutphon, Anno, 1586" (Bradstreet) **4**:94

"An Elegie upon the Death of the Deane of Pauls, Dr. John Donne" (Carew) **13**:19, 26, 28, 52

"Elegie upon the untimely death of the incomparable Prince Henry" (Donne) **10**:4

Elegies (*Love Elegies*) (Donne) **10**:26, 36, 46-7, 50, 54-5, 88-9, 92-3, 96, 98, 106

Elégies (Ronsard) **6**:407, 410-11

Elegies upon Sundry Occasions (Drayton) **8**:7, 17

"Elegy" (Warton) **15**:461

"Elegy on the Death of a Mad Dog" (Goldsmith) **2**:74, 109

"An Elegy on the Death of an Amiable Young Lady" (Boswell) **4**:51

"Elegy on the Marquis of Blanford" (Congreve) **5**:75

"Elegy to an Old Beauty" (Parnell) **3**:252-54

"Elegy to the Memory of an Unfortunate Lady" (Pope) **3**:267-68, 270, 290-91, 302-03, 305, 315-16

"An Elegy Upon the Death of My Lord Francis Villiers" (Marvell) **4**:409

"Elegy Written in a Country Churchyard" ("Churchyard") (Gray) **4**:283, 285, 287-92, 294, 300-05, 308-13, 315-17, 319, 321-23, 326-29, 332, 336-38, 340

"The Elements" (Bradstreet)
  See "The Four Elements"

Eléments de la philosophie de Newton (Voltaire) **14**:366-67

Les éléments de littérature (Marmontel) **2**:213, 220-21, 223

"Elephant in the Moon" (Butler) **16**:4, 16

De elevatione mentis ad acquirendum summum bonum (Kempis) **11**:411

"The Eleventh Discourse" ("Discourse XI") (Reynolds) **15**:383, 397, 403, 416, 421

"Elinoure and Juga" (Chatterton) **3**:118, 135

Den ellefte juni (Holberg) **6**:259, 273, 277

"Eloisa to Abelard" (Pope) **3**:267-68, 271, 273, 276, 290, 296, 307, 315-16

"Eloquence" (Hume) **7**:167

Emblems (Bunyan)
  See *Divine Emblems; or, Temporal Things Spiritualized*

Émile, ou de l'éducation (Rousseau) **14**:220, 235, 237, 240-41, 247-48, 251-53, 260, 269, 273, 276-77, 279-84, 287-88, 291-92, 294-97, 301-02, 306, 308-10, 313-14

Emilia Galotti (Lessing) **8**:58-9, 61-3, 66, 68-70, 72, 85, 88, 94-5, 99, 102, 105, 107, 112, 114, 116

Emily Montague (Brooke)
  See *The History of Emily Montague*

Los empeños de una casa ("The Trials of a Noble House") (Juana Ines de la Cruz) **5**:144, 150-52, 157, 159

The Emperor of the Moon (Behn) **1**:29, 37, 40

Emperor of the Turks (Pix)
  See *Ibrahim, the Thirteenth Emperour of the Turks*

The Empiric (Holberg) **6**:259

"En una Noche escura" (John of the Cross) **18**:201, 224

Enchiridion ethicum (More) **9**:300, 322

Enchiridion metaphysicum (*The Notion of a Spirit*) (More) **9**:305, 307, 325-26

Enchiridion militis christiani (*Handbook of the Militant Christian; Manual of the Christian Knight*) (Erasmus) **16**:106, 110, 135, 137-38, 149-51, 154, 162, 170-71, 179-80, 186-88, 193, 198, 203-04

Encomion musices (Luther) **9**:97

Encomium moriae (Erasmus)

See *Moriae encomium*
End of Life (Jami)
  See *Khátimat al-hayát*
Endimon and Phoebe. Ideas Latmus (Drayton)
  8:19-21, 29, 32, 34, 36-7, 41
Los enemigos hermanos (Castro) **19**:7-8
Englands Heroicall Epistles (*Epistles*) (Drayton)
  8:7-8, 10-12, 14-16, 19, 27-8, 30-1, 33, 43,
  50-1, 53-4
England's Teares for the Present Wars (Howell)
  13:424
English Dictionary (Johnson)
  See *Dictionary of the English Language*
"English Metamorphosis" (Chatterton) **3**:119-
  20
"An English Padlock" (Prior) **4**:461, 464, 467
The Englishman (Steele) **18**:350, 352-53
The Englishman, 9 (Steele) **18**:349
"Ennui without Cause" (Scudery) **2**:294
"Enquiry" (Herrick)
  See "Inquiry"
An Enquiry Concerning Faith (Erasmus)
  See *Inquisitio de Fide*
Enquiry concerning Human Understanding
  (Hume) **7**:170, 176, 179, 183, 185, 192-93,
  199
Enquiry concerning the Principles of Morals
  (Hume) **7**:157-58, 160-61, 163, 176, 188
Enquiry into Human Nature (Hume) **7**:163
Enquiry into the Age of Oil Painting (Lessing)
  8:105
*An Enquiry into the Occasional Conformity of
  Dissenters* (Defoe) **1**:161
*An Enquiry into the Present State of Polite
  Learning in Europe* (Goldsmith) **2**:64-5,
  73-4, 81, 86, 102, 104, 109-11
Enseignemens moraux (*Moral Teachings*)
  (Christine de Pizan) **9**:45, 48
De ente et uno (*On Being and the One*) (Pico
  della Mirandola) **15**:325, 329, 334, 338,
  342, 349, 356
Entertainment (Davenant)
  See *First Day's Entertainment at Rutland
  House*
"Die entführte Dose" (*The Pilfered Snuffbox*)
  (Schlegel) **5**:277, 282
*Enthusiasmus triumphatus: or, A Discourse of
  the Nature, Causes, Kinds, and Cure of
  Enthusiasme* (More) **9**:310-11, 317-20
"Entréme" (John of the Cross) **18**:232-33
La entretenida (Cervantes) **6**:180-81
Epicene (Jonson)
  See *Epicœne; or, the Silent Woman*
Epicœne; or, the Silent Woman (*Epicene*)
  (Jonson) **6**:291, 294-95, 297, 299, 301, 306,
  310-11, 313-14, 318-20, 323-24, 329, 334-36,
  341, 343-45
"The Epicurean" (Hume) **7**:153
Epigrammata (*Epigrammes*) (More) **10**:364,
  372, 374, 426, 428, 430-31
Epigrammes (More)
  See *Epigrammata*
Epigrams (Jonson) **6**:304, 315, 337, 347-48,
  351
Epigrams (Kochanowski) **10**:153, 167
Epilog (Wessel) **7**:390
"An Epilogue Spoken to the King at the
  Opening of the Play-House at Oxford on
  Saturday Last. Being March the Nineteenth
  1681" (Dryden) **21**:82
"Epilogue to Earl Rivers's *Dictes*" (Caxton)
  See "Epilogue to *The Dictes or Sayengs*"

"Epilogue to *Eneydos*" (Caxton) **17**:11
"Epilogue to *The Book of Fame*" (Caxton)
  17:11
"Epilogue to *The Consolation of Philosophy*"
  (Caxton) **17**:11
"Epilogue to *The Dictes or Sayengs*"
  ("Epilogue to Earl Rivers's *Dictes*")
  (Caxton) **17**:6, 11
"Epilogue to *The Order of Chivalry*" (Caxton)
  17:11
Epilogue to the Satires (Pope) **3**:273, 318,
  332-36
"The Epistle" (Chatterton)
  See "Epistle to Catcott"
"Epistle" (Churchill)
  See "An Epistle to William Hogarth"
"Epistle" (Warton) **15**:450
"Epistle III" (Pope) **3**:303
"Epistle IV" (Pope) **3**:303
"An Epistle from Lycidas to Menalcas"
  (Boswell) **4**:51
"Epistle from Mrs. Y[onge] to Her Husband"
  (Montagu) **9**:282
*The Epistle of Othea to Hector; or, The Boke of
  Knyghthode* (Christine de Pizan)
  See *L'epitre d'Othéa*
"The Epistle of Rosamond to King Henry the
  Second" ("Rosamond") (Drayton) **8**:31, 33,
  52
"Epistle to a Lady, Who Desired the Author
  to Make Verses on Her" (Swift) **1**:524
"Epistle to a Young Friend" (Burns) **3**:48, 86
"Epistle to Augustus" (Pope) **3**:332
"Epistle to Blacklock" (Burns) **3**:86
"Epistle to Boileau" (Prior) **4**:455
"Epistle to Catcott" ("The Epistle")
  (Chatterton) **3**:118, 126, 132-33
"Epistle to Colonel de Peyster" (Burns) **3**:85
"Epistle to Davie, a Brother Poet" (Burns)
  See "The Epistles"
"Epistle to Dr. Arbuthnot" (Pope) **3**:273,
  284, 286, 288, 296, 332, 334
"Epistle to Fleetwood Sheppard" (Prior)
  4:465
Epistle to Germanus Brixius (More)
  See *Epistola ad German. Brixium*
"Epistle to Henry Reynolds" (Drayton)
  See "To My Most Dearely-Loved Friend
  Henery Reynolds Esquire, of Poets and
  Poesie"
"Epistle to James Smith" (Burns)
  See "The Epistles"
"Epistle to James Smith" (Wessel)
  See "Smith"
"Epistle to John Lapraik" (Burns)
  See "The Epistles"
"Epistle to John Rankine" (Burns) **3**:67, 85,
  87
"Epistle to Lapraik" (Burns)
  See "The Epistles"
"Epistle to Lord Bathurst" (Pope) **3**:273, 318
"Epistle to Lord Burlington" (Pope) **3**:273,
  317, 332
"Epistle to Monsieur Duhan" (Frederick the
  Great) **14**:62
"An Epistle to Mr. Dryden" (Wycherley)
  21:353
"Epistle to Mr. Jervas, With Dryden's
  Translation of Fresnoy's Art of Painting"
  (Pope) **3**:315
"Epistle to Smith" (Burns)
  See "The Epistles"

"Epistle to the King" (Wycherley) **8**:399
Epistle to the Reader (More) **9**:298
"Epistle to the Vertuous Reader" (Lanyer)
  See "To the Vertuous Reader"
"Epistle to W. S-----n" (Burns)
  See "Epistle to William Simpson"
"An Epistle to William Hogarth" ("Epistle")
  (Churchill) **3**:140, 144, 146, 148, 150, 152,
  154, 157-58, 160, 163-64
"Epistle to William Simpson" ("Epistle to W.
  S-----n") (Burns) **3**:48, 91, 92
*Epistler befattende adskillige historiske,
  politiske, metaphysiske, moralske,
  philosophiske, item skjemtsomme materier...*
  (*Epistles*) (Holberg) **6**:266, 273, 278
"The Epistles" ("Epistle to Davie, a Brother
  Poet"; "Epistle to James Smith"; "Epistle to
  John Lapraik"; "Epistle to Lapraik";
  "Epistle to Smith") (Burns) **3**:53, 72, 77,
  84, 87, 93
Epistles (Drayton)
  See *Englands Heroicall Epistles*
Epistles (Ficino) **12**:165
Epistles (Holberg)
  See *Epistler befattende adskillige historiske,
  politiske, metaphysiske, moralske,
  philosophiske, item skjemtsomme
  materier...*
Epistles for the Ladies (Haywood) **1**:286
Epistles to Mr. Pope (Young) **3**:486, 490
"Epistles to Several Persons" ("Ethick
  Epistles") (Pope) **3**:273
Epistola ad German. Brixium (*Epistle to
  Germanus Brixius*) (More) **10**:364, 431
Epistola contra J. Pomeranum (More)
  See *Epistola in qua...respondet literis
  Pomerani*
Epistola de felicitate (Ficino) **12**:168
*Epistola de tolerantia ad clarissimum virum
  T.A.R.P.T.O.L.A. scripta à P.A.P.O.I.L.A.*
  (Locke) **7**:261
Epistola in qua...respondet literis Pomerani
  (*Epistola contra J. Pomeranum*) (More)
  10:365, 369
*Epistolae Ho-Elianae: Familiar Letters
  Domestic and Forren* (*Familiar Letters*;
  Letters) (Howell) **13**:415-27, 430-34, 436,
  441-46
Epistolæ Obscurorum Vivorum (Hutten)
  See *Literæ obscurorum Vivorum*
Épistre II: À M. de l'Abbé des Roches (Boileau-
  Despreaux) **3**:39
Épistre V: À M. de Guilleragues (Boileau-
  Despreaux) **3**:22
Épistre VI: À M. de Lamoignon, avocat general
  (Boileau-Despreaux) **3**:22
Épistre VII: À M. Racine (Boileau-Despreaux)
  3:19, 21
Épistre IX: À M. le Marquis de Seignelay
  (Boileau-Despreaux) **3**:39
L'epistre au dieu d'amours (*The Letter of
  Cupid*) (Christine de Pizan) **9**:25, 27-8, 38
Épistres (Boileau-Despreaux) **3**:38-9, 42
"Epistulae Obscurorum Virorum" (Buchanan)
  4:123
"An Epitaph" (Prior)
  See "Epitaph on Sauntering Jack and Idle
  Joan"
"Epitaph on Lady Mary Villiers" (Carew)
  13:8
"Epitaph on Miss Elizabeth Stanley"
  (Thomson) **16**:428

"Epitaph on Robert Canynge" (Chatterton) 3:119

"Epitaph on Salathiel Pavy" (Jonson)
See "Epitaph on S(alomon) P(avy)"

"Epitaph on S(alomon) P(avy)" ("Epitaph on Salathiel Pavy") (Jonson) 6:326, 347

"Epitaph on Sauntering Jack and Idle Joan" ("An Epitaph") (Prior) 4:456, 461-62, 470

"Epitaph on the Lady S. Wife to Sir W.S." (Carew) 13:52, 58

"Epitaph on the Marchioness of Winchester" (Milton) 9:205

"An Epitaph upon a child" (Herrick) 13:341

"Epitaphe de Loyse de Mailly" (Ronsard) 6:436

"Epithalamie on Sir Clipseby Crew and his Lady" ("Epithalamion") (Herrick) 13:336-37, 397

"Epithalamion" (Herrick)
See "Epithalamie on Sir Clipseby Crew and his Lady"

"Epithalamion" (Spenser) 5:307, 311, 313-15, 329, 332, 347-49, 355-56, 364

"Epithalamion made at Lincolnes Inne" (Donne) 10:97

"An Epithalamion, or mariage song on the Lady Elizabeth, and Count Palatine being married on St. Valentines day" (Donne) 10:9, 40, 55

"Epithalamium" (Buchanan) 4:122

Épitre XII (On Love for God) (Boileau-Despreaux) 3:38

Epitre à Uranie (Voltaire) 14:369

"Epître aux muses" (Rousseau) 9:346

L'epitre d'Othéa (The Epistle of Othea to Hector; or, The Boke of Knyghthode) (Christine de Pizan) 9:30-1, 37, 48

L'epreuve (Marivaux) 4:358, 364, 369, 371-72

"Equité des Vieux Gaulois" (Ronsard) 6:410

Erasmus Montanus (Holberg) 6:269, 272, 274-77, 283-85

"Êrh-lang Sou-shan-t'u Ko" ("A Song on a Painting Depicting the God Êrh-lang Hunting in the Surrounding Country with His Followers") (Wu Ch'eng-en) 7:397

Eriphyle (Voltaire) 14:397

Eruditissimi viri Guilielmi Rossei opus elegans (Responsio ad Lutherum) (More) 10:365, 369, 409

Die Erzbetrugerin und Landstortzerin Courasche (Courage) (Grimmelshausen) 6:238, 249, 251-52

"La Española inglesa" (Cervantes) 6:171

L'esprit des moeurs (Voltaire) 14:328

Esprit du clergé (Holbach) 14:153

Esprit du judaïsme (Holbach) 14:154

"L'esprit fort" (Perrault) 2:253

Essai sur la poésie épique (Voltaire)
See *Essay upon the Epic Poetry of the European Nations from Homer down to Milton*

Essai sur le goût (Marmontel) 2:214, 222

Essai sur les causes qui peuvent affecter les esprits et les caractères (Montesquieu) 7:348, 358

Essai sur les moeurs (Voltaire) 14:334, 353, 358, 364, 380, 383-88, 395, 402

Essai sur les préjugés (Essay on the Prejudices and the Influence of Opinions on Customs and the Happiness of Mankind) (Holbach) 14:152, 154, 168

Essai sur les révolutions de la musique en France (Marmontel) 2:222

Essai sur les romans (Marmontel) 2:213, 215, 220

Essai sur l'histoire générale et sur les moeurs et l'esprit des nations (Voltaire) 14:411

Essai sur l'origine des langues (Rousseau) 14:292, 294-95

Les essais de Messire Michel Seigneur de Montaigne (Essays) (Montaigne) 8:189, 191-94, 196-97, 199, 201-06, 210, 212-14, 216-20, 223, 225, 229-31, 233-42, 244, 247

"Essay" (Prior)
See "Essay upon Opinion"

An Essay concerning Human Understanding (Locke) 7:236, 238-39, 244, 246-48, 251, 253, 255-56, 258, 266, 269, 271-72, 281, 284-91, 296

An Essay concerning the True Original, Extent, and End of Civil Government (Locke) 7:273

An Essay for the Understanding of St. Paul's Epistles by Consulting St. Paul Himself (Locke) 7:282-83

Essay of Dramatic Poesy (Dryden)
See *Of Dramatick Poesie: An Essay*

"Essay of Heroic Plays" (Dryden)
See "Of Heroic Plays"

"An Essay of Heroic Plays" (Dryden) 3:236

Essay on Comedy (Farquhar)
See *Discourse Upon Comedy*

Essay on Conversation (Fielding) 1:234

"An Essay on Criticism" (Pope) 3:263-64, 267-70, 273, 275-76, 291, 295, 307, 313, 322, 324-28, 337

Essay on Dramatic Discourse Concerning Satire (Dryden) 21:111-12, 115

"Essay on Homer" (Parnell) 3:253

"Essay on Learning" (Prior)
See "Essay upon Learning"

An Essay on Man (Pope) 3:269, 272-73, 276, 279, 287-89, 291, 297, 300, 304, 306-07, 313, 315-16, 318-19, 326, 334, 337

An Essay on publick Spirit (Dennis)
See *An Essay upon Public Spirit; being a Satire in Prose upon the Manners and Luxury of the Times, the chief Sources of our present Parties and Divisions*

"Essay on the Different Styles of Poetry" (Parnell) 3:255

An Essay on the Genius of Shakespear (Letters on the Genius and Writings of Shakespeare; Three Letters on the Genius and Writings of Shakespeare) (Dennis) 11:16, 19, 21, 30, 32, 38-9

"Essay on the Georgics" (Addison) 18:20

An Essay on the Human Soul (Marat) 10:231

"Essay on the Imagination" (Addison) 18:58, 62

Essay on the Knowledge of the Characters of Men (Moritz) 1:234

An Essay on the Navy (Dennis) 11:19

An Essay on the Operas, after the Italian manner, which are about to be established on the English Stage: with some Reflections on the Damage which they may bring to the Public (Dennis) 11:15, 19, 26

Essay on the Prejudices and the Influence of Opinions on Customs and the Happiness of Mankind (Holbach)
See *Essai sur les préjugés*

"Essay on the Real Secret of the Freemasons" (Cleland) 2:53

Essay on the Sublime and Beautiful (Burke)
See *A Philosophical Enquiry into the Origin of Our Ideas of the Sublime and Beautiful*

An Essay on the Theatre (Goldsmith) 2:126

An Essay towards an Abridgement of the English History (Abridgment of English History) (Burke) 7:49

"An Essay upon Acting" (Garrick) 15:122

"Essay upon Learning" ("Essay on Learning") (Prior) 4:465, 467, 474

"Essay upon Opinion" ("Essay") (Prior) 4:467-71

An Essay upon Projects (Defoe) 1:160

An Essay upon Public Spirit; being a Satire in Prose upon the Manners and Luxury of the Times, the chief Sources of our present Parties and Divisions (An Essay on publick Spirit; Publick Spirit) (Dennis) 11:8-9, 15, 17, 19, 26

Essay upon the Civil Wars of France (Voltaire) 14:382

Essay upon the Epic Poetry of the European Nations from Homer down to Milton (Essai sur la poésie épique) (Voltaire) 14:349-50, 352

Essayes in Divinity (Donne) 10:40, 76-7, 83

Essays (Bacon) 18:104, 108, 110, 114-15, 116, 118, 123-24, 128, 132-34, 136-37, 141-42, 146, 149, 178-79, 183, 187, 192

Essays (Hume) 7:145, 167

Essays (Montagu)
See *The Nonsense of Common-Sense*

Essays (Montaigne)
See *Les essais de Messire Michel Seigneur de Montaigne*

Essays and Poems and Simplicity, a Comedy (Montagu) 9:271, 276, 279

Essays and Treatises on Several Subjects (Hume) 7:153

Essays, Moral and Political (Hume) 7:152, 189

Essays Moral, Political, and Literary (Hume) 7:163

Essays upon Several Moral Subjects (Book of Essays (Collier)) (Collier) 6:200, 227

Essays upon Wit (Addison) 18:7, 18, 60

"Eternity" (Herrick) 13:334, 358

"Eternity" (Smart)
See "On the Eternity of the Supreme Being"

Ethic (Spinoza)
See *Ethic ordine geometrico demonstrata*

Ethic ordine geometrico demonstrata (Ethic) (Spinoza) 9:397-99, 402-04, 408, 415-17, 419-26, 428, 431-36, 438-39, 441-42, 444-47

"Ethick Epistles" (Pope)
See "Epistles to Several Persons"

Ethocratie (Holbach) 14:152, 155-56, 160, 174

"Eton" (Gray)
See "Ode on a Distant Prospect of Eton College"

"Eton College Ode" (Gray)
See "Ode on a Distant Prospect of Eton College"

L'étourdi (Moliere) 10:260, 275-77, 280, 283, 286-87, 293, 309-10

Eugenia and Adelaide (Sheridan) 7:371, 378

Eurydice Hiss'd (Fielding) 1:220

"Even now that Care which on thy Crown attends" (Sidney) 19:293-94, 296, 299, 309-10

"Evening" (Parnell)
See "A Hymn for Evening"

"Evening" (Wheatley)
  See "An Hymn to the Evening"
"An Evening Prayer" (Swift) **1**:488
"An Evening Walk in the Abbey-Church of
  Holyroodhouse" (Boswell) **4**:50, 60
An Evening's Love; or, The Mock-Astrologer
  (*The Mock-Astrologer*) (Dryden) **3**:177,
  179, 230, 236, 238
"Evensong" (Herrick) **13**:386
Every Man in his Humour (Jonson) **6**:297,
  300-01, 305-06, 310-12, 320-21, 323, 336,
  342
Every Man out of His Humour (Jonson)
  6:297, 301, 303, 306, 335, 339, 344
"An Evill Spirit Your Beautie Haunts Me
  Still" (Drayton) **8**:27
*Ex Libro de Numphis, Sylvanus, Pygmæs,
  Salamandris et Gigantibus* (Paracelsus)
  14:189
Examen des prophéties (Holbach) **14**:153-54
Examen important de Milord Bolingbroke
  (Voltaire) **14**:370
Examen Poeticum (Dryden) **21**:119
An Examination Concerning Faith (Erasmus)
  See *Inquisitio de Fide*
*An Examination of Dr. Woodward's Account of
  the Deluge, & c.* (Arbuthnot) **1**:15
Example of Vertu (Hawes)
  See *Example of Virtue*
Example of Virtue (*Example of Vertu*) (Hawes)
  17:344-54, 362-63, 365
"The Excellency of Christ" (Edwards) **7**:120,
  122-23
"An Excellente Balade of Charitie as wroten
  bie the gode Prieste Thomas Rowley, 1464"
  (Chatterton) **3**:123-24, 127, 135
Exclamations (Teresa de Jesus) **18**:392
The Excursion (Brooke) **6**:107-08, 110-11,
  115, 117, 119, 121-22
Exemplary Novels (Cervantes)
  See *Novelas exemplares*
Exemplary Stories (Cervantes)
  See *Novelas exemplares*
Exercitia spiritualia (Kempis) **11**:411
"The Exhibition" (Chatterton) **3**:126, 132
Exhortation to Emperor Charles V (Hutten)
  16:234
*Exhortation to the German Princes to
  Undertake War against the Turks* (Hutten)
  16:235
Exhortatorium (Hutten)
  See *Ad Caesarem Maximilianum ut bellum
    in Venetos coeptum prosequatur
    exhortatorium*
"Exorcising Against Jealousy" (P'u Sung-ling)
  3:346
"Exorcism, or The Spectater" (Erasmus)
  16:194-95
The Expedition of Humphry Clinker (*Humphry
  Clinker*) (Smollett) **2**:319-20, 322-26, 329-
  30, 332, 336-37, 341-44, 347-51, 353, 357,
  359, 362-66
"The Experience" (Taylor) **11**:359, 363, 384,
  389, 396
"The Expiration" ("So, so breake off this last
  lamenting kisse") (Donne) **10**:36
*An Explanation of the San-kuo-chih, Done in
  the Popular Style* (Lo Kuan-chung)
  See *San-kuo-chih yeni-i*
Explanations of the 95 Theses (Luther)
  See *Resolutiones disputationum de
    indulgentiarum*

Expositio passionis Christi (More)
  See *Expositio passionis Domini*
Expositio passionis Domini (*Expositio passionis
  Christi*) (More) **10**:365, 413-14
Expostulatio (Hutten) **16**:232, 234-35
"An Expostulation with Inigo Jones" (Jonson)
  6:350
"The Exstasie" ("The Ecstasy") (Donne)
  10:13, 18, 26, 33, 35-6, 46, 51-2, 55, 81-2,
  85, 87, 103
"The Exstasy: A Pindarique Ode to Her
  Majesty the Queen" (Aubin) **9**:4
Extrait des sentiments de Jean Meslier
  (Voltaire) **14**:370
"Eyes and Tears" (Marvell) **4**:397, 403, 439
Eyn Sermon von Ablass und Gnade (*Sermon on
  Indulgences and Grace*) (Luther) **9**:91, 146
"Fable of the Cock and the Fox" (Chaucer)
  See "Nun's Priest's Tale"
*Fables Ancient and Modern; Translated into
  Verse, from Homer, Ovid, Boccace, &
  Chaucer* (Dryden) **3**:184, 187, 190, 204-05,
  216, 221, 237-38, 242-43; **21**:118-19
Les fâcheux (*The Bores*) (Moliere) **10**:275,
  277, 281, 283, 291, 299, 302, 310
*The Faerie Queene, Disposed into Twelve
  Bookes Fashioning XII Morall Vertues*
  (Spenser) **5**:295, 297, 299-302, 304-05, 307-
  25, 328, 331, 333-37, 341-42, 349, 355-56,
  360, 364-66
"Fair copy of my Celia's face" (Carew) **13**:20
"Fair Daffodils" (Herrick)
  See "To Daffadills"
The Fair Favorite (Davenant) **13**:175, 181-82,
  196
"The Fair Hypocrite" (Manley) **1**:306, 308
*The Fair Jilt; or, The History of Prince Tarquin
  and Miranda* (Behn) **1**:30-1, 42-3, 46, 49-
  53, 55
The Fair Penitent (Rowe) **8**:285, 287, 291-
  300, 302-05, 307, 312-14, 316-17
"Fair Recluse" (Smart) **3**:399
"The Fair Singer" (Marvell) **4**:403, 409, 436
"The Fairie Temple: or, Oberons Chappell.
  Dedicated to Mr. John Merrifield,
  Counsellor at Law" ("The Temple")
  (Herrick) **13**:351, 372-73
"The Fairies" (Perrault)
  See "Les Fées"
The Fairies (Garrick) **15**:95-6, 128
"The Fairy Feast" (Parnell) **3**:255
"A Fairy Tale in the Ancient English Style"
  (Parnell) **3**:251, 254, 256-57
*A Faithful Narrative of the Surprizing Work of
  God in the Conversion of Many Hundred
  Souls in Northampton, and the Neighboring
  Towns and Villages* (Edwards) **7**:101, 118
The False Alarm (Johnson) **15**:202, 208
*The False Count; or, A New Way to Play an
  Old Game* (Behn) **1**:34, 37
The False Friend (Vanbrugh) **21**:295, 319
The False Friend; or, The Fate of Disobedience
  (Pix) **8**:259, 261-63, 268-70, 272, 276, 278
"False Knight" (Erasmus) **16**:114
*De falso credita et ementita Donatione
  Constatini Magni* (*Constantine Donation; On
  the Pretended Donation of Constantine*)
  (Hutten) **16**:212, 224, 231, 234, 245
La famiglia dell' antiquario (*The Antiquarian's
  Family*) (Goldoni) **4**:250, 260, 266
Familiar Letters (Howell)

  See *Epistolae Ho-Elianae: Familiar Letters
    Domestic and Forren*
*Familiar Letters between the Principal
  Characters in "David Simple"* (Fielding)
  1:270-73
*Familiar Letters betwixt a Gentleman and a
  Lady* (Davys) **1**:101-02
Familiar Letters on Important Occasions
  (Richardson) **1**:398, 416-17
"Familier" (Marmontel) **2**:221
Familiorum Colloquiorum (*Colloquia, Familiar
  Colloquies, Colloquies, Colloquiorum Opus*)
  (Erasmus) **16**:113-14, 116-17, 121-24, 128,
  132, 139-40, 142-43, 146, 152, 154-57, 162,
  174, 176, 192-95
The Family Instructor (Defoe) **1**:122, 170, 176
"A Famous Prediction of Merlin" (Swift)
  1:516-17
The Fan (Goldoni)
  See *Il ventaglio*
"A Fanatic" (Butler)
  See "A (Puritan) Fanatic"
"Fanatic" (Butler) **16**:52-3
"A Fancy" (Carew) **13**:63
Fanny Hill (Cleland)
  See *Memoirs of a Woman of Pleasure*
"Fanscombe Barn" (Winchilsea) **3**:443, 452,
  457
"Fantastic" (Butler) **16**:51
"A Farewel-Sermon Preached at the First
  Precinct in Northampton after the Peoples'
  Publick Rejection of Their Minister"
  (Edwards) **7**:118
"The Farewell" (Churchill) **3**:151-52, 155-56,
  163
"A Farewell to America" (Wheatley) **3**:416
"Farewel to Eliza" (Burns)
  See "From Thee Eliza"
"Farewell to love" (Donne) **10**:82
"Farewell to Nancy" (Burns) **3**:65
"Farewell to Poetry" ("His farwell vnto
  Poetrie"; "Master Herrick's Farewell unto
  Poetry") (Herrick) **13**:328, 342, 365, 392
*The Farmer's Letters to the Protestants of
  Ireland* (Brooke) **1**:62
The Farmer's Return from London (Garrick)
  15:100
The Farrier (Aretino)
  See *Marescalco*
A Farther Vindication of the Short View
  (Collier) **6**:229-30
"Farwell Frost, or Welcome the Spring"
  (Herrick) **13**:354, 396
Fatal Friendship (Trotter) **8**:352, 355, 357,
  360, 363, 368-69, 371-74
The Fatal Secret; or, Constancy in Distress
  (Haywood) **1**:285
"The Fatal Sisters. An Ode (From the Norse
  Tongue) in the Orcades of Thormodus
  Torfaeus . . . and also in Bartholinus"
  (Gray) **4**:312, 317-18
Fatihat al-shabáb (*Opening of Youth*) (Jami)
  9:65, 68
La fausse suivante (Marivaux) **4**:363, 377
Les fausses confidences (Marivaux) **4**:354,
  358, 360, 365, 368, 371-72
Faust (Lessing) **8**:71, 111-12
Favola: Belfagor arcidiavolo che prese moglie
  (*Belfagor*) (Machiavelli) **8**:126, 128, 137,
  178
Fayerie Court (Drayton)
  See *Nimphidia, the Court of Fayrie*

"A Feaver" ("A Fever"; "Oh do not die")
(Donne) **10**:13, 26-7, 36, 52, 82
Febris II (Fever the Second) (Hutten) **16**:230,
232, 241-42, 246
Febris Prima (Fever the First) (Hutten)
16:230, 232-33, 246
"February" (Chatterton) **3**:131
"Les Fées" ("The Fairies") (Perrault) **2**:254,
260, 280
The Feigned Courtesans; or, A Night's Intrigue
(Behn) **1**:33-4, 37, 39
Félicie (Marivaux) **4**:369
La félicité des temps; ou, Eloge de la France
(Voltaire) **14**:380
"Felix's Behaviour towards Paul" (Sterne)
2:430
The Female Officer (Brooke) **1**:63
"The Female Phaeton" (Prior) **4**:460
The Female Reader (Wollstonecraft) **5**:460
The Female Spectator (Haywood) **1**:286, 288-
89, 300-02
The Female Tatler (Manley) **1**:310
"La femme comme il y en a peu" (Marmontel)
2:212
La femme fidèle (Marivaux) **4**:369
Les femmes savantes (The Learned Ladies)
(Moliere) **10**:268, 272-73, 275, 277, 282-83,
287-88, 291, 293-99, 305, 313, 320-21, 338
*Le femmine puntigliose (The Punctilious
Ladies)* (Goldoni) **4**:258-59, 265
Festin de Pierre (Moliere)
See *Don Juan; ou Le festin de Pierre*
"A Fever" (Donne)
See "A Feaver"
Fever the First (Hutten)
See *Febris Prima*
Fever the Second (Hutten)
See *Febris II*
*A Few Sighs from Hell; or, The Groans of a
Damned Soul* (Bunyan) **4**:172, 175
De fideli dispensatore (Kempis) **11**:411
Fifteen Discourses (Reynolds)
See *Discourses on Art*
"The Fifteenth Discourse" (Reynolds)
15:365, 398, 404-05
"The Fifth Discourse" (Reynolds) **15**:380,
394, 403
"A Fifth-Monarchy Man" (Butler) **16**:27, 54
La figlia obbediente (Goldoni) **4**:260-61
"Le filets de Vulcain" (Rousseau) **9**:343
"Filum Labyrinthi sive Formula Inquisitionis"
(Bacon) **18**:148, 187
Fimmtíu passíusálmar (Hymns of the Passion)
(Petursson) **8**:251-54
"Finjamos que soy feliz" ("Let us pretend I
am happy") (Juana Ines de la Cruz) **5**:155
The First and Second Anniversaries (Donne)
See *The Anniversaries*
*The First Anniversarie. An Anatomie of the
World. Wherein By Occasion of the untimely
death of Mistris Elizabeth Drury, the frailtie
and decay of this whole World is represented
(An Anatomie of the World)* (Donne) **10**:4,
44, 64, 74-7, 83, 89-90, 98
"The First Anniversary of the Government
under O. C." (Marvell) **4**:398, 417, 429-31
*First Day's Entertainment at Rutland House
(Entertainment)* (Davenant) **13**:194-95
"The First Discourse" (Reynolds) **15**:377,
402, 405, 412
First Discourse (Rousseau)
See *Discourse on the Arts and Sciences*

"First Eclogue" (Collins) **4**:229
"First Epistle of the First Book of Horace"
(Pope)
See *Satires and Epistles of Horace, Imitated*
"The First of April" (Warton) **15**:443
The First Sluggard (Grimmelshausen)
See *Der erste Beernhäuter*
"A Fish Diet" (Erasmus)
See "Ichthyophagia"
"Fish-Eating" (Erasmus)
See "Ichthyophagia"
"Five Pastoral Eclogues: The Scenes of Which
are Supposed to Lie Among the Shepherds,
Oppressed by the War in Germany"
("Eclogues") (Warton) **15**:430, 459-60
Five Questions concerning the Mind (Ficino)
12:175
"Flaminica Dialis, or Queen-Priest" (Herrick)
13:353
Flashes of Light (Jami)
See *Lawá'ih*
Le flatteur (Rousseau) **9**:337-38
"The Flea" (Donne) **10**:12, 50, 81-2, 96
"Fleckno" (Marvell) **4**:409
"The Flesh and the Spirit" (Bradstreet) **4**:90,
96
The Flight of Birds (Vinci) **12**:405
Florizel and Perdita (Garrick) **15**:129
"The Flower and the Leaf" (Chaucer) **17**:49,
54, 60
"The Flower and the Leaf" (Dryden) **3**:190
"The Flower Maiden Hsiang-yu" (P'u Sung-
ling) **3**:354
"A Fly that flew into my Mistress her Eye"
(Carew) **13**:18
The Flying Doctor (Moliere)
See *Le médecin volant*
Flying Mercury (Siguenza y Gongora)
See *Mercurio volante con la noticia de la
recuperacion de las provincias del Nuevo
México conseguida por D. Diego de
Vargas, Zapato, y Luxan Ponze de Leon*
Folly (Erasmus)
See *Moriae encomium*
"A Fool" (Butler) **16**:51
*The Fool of Quality; or, The History of Henry,
Earl of Moreland* (Brooke) **1**:59-68, 70-2
"Foolish Men" (Juana Ines de la Cruz)
See "Hombres necios que acusáis"
"For A' That and A' That" (Burns)
See "Is There for Honest Poverty"
"For Deliverance from a Fever" (Bradstreet)
4:100
"For Godsake hold your tongue, and let me
love" (Donne)
See "The Canonization"
"For His Own Epitaph" ("For My Own
Monument") (Prior) **4**:461, 471, 474
"For My Own Monument" (Prior)
See "For His Own Epitaph"
"For Solitude and Retirement against the
Publick Active Life" (Wycherley) **8**:399
"For the Publick Active Life, against Solitude"
(Wycherley) **8**:399
"For the Restoration of My Dear Husband
from a Burning Ague" (Bradstreet) **4**:100
"The Force of Religion; or, Vanquished Love"
(Young) **3**:466, 485, 487
The Forced Marriage (Moliere)
See *Le mariage forcé*
*The Forced Marriage; or, The Jealous
Bridegroom* (Behn) **1**:29, 33, 39

The Forest (Jonson) **6**:304, 312, 315, 325, 337,
347-50
Forest of Forests, Silva Silvarum (Bacon)
See *Sylva Sylvarum: Or a Natural History*
The Forest of Scholars (Wu Ching-tzu)
See *Ju-lin wai-shih*
"Les forges de Lemnos" (Rousseau) **9**:343
"The Fork" (Wessel) **7**:390
"Forma Bonum Fragile" (Prior) **4**:461
"The Fornicator" (Burns) **3**:97
Fortuna (Hutten) **16**:232-33, 241-42
The Fortunate Mistress (Roxana) (Defoe)
1:129, 134, 139-40, 142, 145, 147, 149-50,
173, 177-80
*The Fortunes and Misfortunes of the Famous
Moll Flanders (Moll Flanders)* (Defoe)
1:125, 127, 134-35, 137, 139-40, 142, 145,
147, 151-59, 169, 176-78
"The Four Ages of Man" ("Ages")
(Bradstreet) **4**:89, 94-5, 103
"The Four Elements" ("The Elements")
(Bradstreet) **4**:86, 89, 94, 109, 111
The Four Last Things (More) **10**:370, 415,
430, 435-36
"The Four Monarchies" (Bradstreet) **4**:86,
89-90, 95-6, 102-04, 111
"The Four Seasons of the Year" ("Seasons")
(Bradstreet) **4**:86, 88-9, 94-5, 103-11
*Les fourberies de Scapin (The Cheats of Scapin;
The Rogueries of Scapin; The Tricks of
Scapin)* (Moliere) **10**:268, 272, 275, 283,
285, 293, 297, 299, 313, 335
"The Fourteenth Discourse" (Reynolds)
15:398, 404
"The Fourth Discourse" (Reynolds) **15**:365,
379, 380, 383, 393, 402
Fourth Letter on a Regicide Peace (Burke)
7:64
Fowre Hymnes (Spenser) **5**:313, 323-24, 335,
338, 350, 353-54, 356
The Fox; or, Volpone (Jonson)
See *Volpone; or, the Foxe*
"Fragment" (Chatterton) **3**:123
"Fragment" (Winchilsea) **3**:451
"Fragment of a Dedication to Dr. W.
Warburton, Bishop of Gloucester" ("The
Dedication") (Churchill) **3**:143, 152, 154,
158-67, 169-71
*Fragment of an Original Letter on the Slavery
of the Negroes* (Day) **1**:105
Fragmente eines Ungenannten (Lessing) **8**:105
La Franciade (Ronsard)
See *Les quatre premiers livres de la
Franciade*
Franciscanus (Buchanan)
See *Georgii Buchanani Scoti, franciscanus:
varia eiusdem authoris poemata*
"Franklin's Prologue" (Chaucer) **17**:140
"Franklin's Tale" (Chaucer) **17**:71-2, 133-35,
137, 140-46, 148-49, 153, 201-02, 208, 237
Fraski (Trifles) (Kochanowski) **10**:160-61, 176
"Fratres Fraterrimi" ("Fratres Fraterrimi
XXII") (Buchanan) **4**:120, 122, 134
"Fratres Fraterrimi XXII" (Buchanan)
See "Fratres Fraterrimi"
Free Commentaries (Bacon)
See *Comentarius Solutus*
The Free-Thinker (Lessing)
See *Der Freygeist*
The Freedom of a Christian Man (Luther)
See *Dissertatio de libertate christiana per
autorem recognita*

The Freedom of the Will (Edwards)
  See *A Careful and Strict Enquiry into the Modern Prevailing Notions of That Freedom of Will, Which Is Supposed to Be Essential to Moral Agency, Vertue and Vice, Reward and Punishment, Praise and Blame*
The Freeholder (Addison) **18**:8
A French Grammar, and a Dialogue consisting of all Gallicisms with Additions of the most useful and significant Proverbs (Howell) **13**:427
French Revolution (Wollstonecraft)
  See *An Historical and Moral View of the Origin and Progress of the French Revolution, and the Effect It Has Produced in Europe*
"Friar's Tale" (Chaucer) **17**:198, 205
"The Fribbleriad" (Garrick) **15**:115
The Friend of the People (Marat)
  See *Le publiciste parisien, journal politique, libre et impartial . . .*
"Friendly Reproof to Ben Jonson" (Carew) **13**:9
"Friendship Put to the Test" (Marmontel) **2**:214
"A Frolick" (Herrick) **13**:365
"From Thee Eliza" ("Farewell to Eliza") (Burns) **3**:86
"Frozen Words" (Addison) **18**:27
"The Frozen Zone" (Herrick) **13**:368
The Fruitless Enquiry (Haywood) **1**:284
"La fuerza de la sangre" ("The Call of Blood") (Cervantes) **6**:171, 176-77
The Fundamental Constitutions of Carolina (Locke) **7**:295
"The Funeral" (Erasmus)
  See "Funus"
The Funeral (Steele) **18**:314, 329-30, 332-33, 336-40, 348-49, 352-54, 359, 362-65, 370-72, 374, 383
"The Funerall" ("Who ever comes to shroud me do not harme") (Donne) **10**:26, 36
"The Funerall Rites of the Rose" (Herrick) **13**:348-51, 353, 373, 384
"Funus" ("Colloquy of Funerals"; "The Funeral") (Erasmus) **16**:116, 119, 141, 155
Furioso (Ariosto)
  See *Orlando furioso*
A Further Defence: Being an Answer to a Reply to the Vindication of the Reasons and Defence for Restoring, &c. (Collier) **6**:209
"The Future Punishment of the Wicked Unavoidable and Intolerable" (Edwards) **7**:98, 107
El Galante (Gracian y Morales) **15**:135
La Galatea (Cervantes) **6**:130, 143-44, 151, 160, 164, 174, 177, 189
Das Galgen-Männlin (*The Mandrake*) (Grimmelshausen) **6**:247
El gallardo español (Cervantes) **6**:180
"The Gallery" (Marvell) **4**:403, 408-09, 435
"Gallo crocitanti" ("To a Crowing Cock"; "To a Crowing Gaul") (Kochanowski) **10**:175
"The Game of Chess" (Kochanowski)
  See "Szachy"
"The Garden" (Marvell) **4**:400, 404-07, 410, 412, 426-27, 430, 435, 437, 439, 441-42, 445-48
"Garden of Adonis" (Herrick) **13**:361
Garden of Roses (Kempis)

  See *Hortulus rosarii de valle lachrymarum continens egreias & devotas sentecias*
Gargantua and Pantagruel (*The Adventures of Gargantua and Pantagruel*) (Rabelais) **5**:203, 214-15, 220, 221, 230, 234-35, 244, 248, 250
"The Garland" (Prior) **4**:460-61
"Gather ye rosebuds while ye may" ("To the Virgins, to make much of Time") (Herrick) **13**:319, 337, 354, 357, 361, 367
"Gaveston" (Drayton)
  See "Pierce Gaveston, Earle of Cornwall"
"Gay Bacchus" (Parnell) **3**:251-52
Gedanken zur Aufnahme des dänischen Theaters (Schlegel) **5**:272-74, 279
"General Prologue" ("Prologue") (Chaucer) **17**:60, 67, 69, 84, 98, 133, 141, 147, 162-63, 166, 168, 173-74, 176-78, 189, 194, 197, 200-01, 204-07, 209-10, 213-15, 218, 224-26, 230, 232, 234, 236, 238, 242-43
The Generall Historie of Virginia, New-England, and the Summer Isles (Smith) **9**:352-56, 358-61, 364-66, 373-79, 381-87
Genesis (Aretino) **12**:13, 20, 36
Le Génie (Marmontel) **2**:222, 259
"Gentillesse" (Chaucer) **17**:60, 145, 236, 240
The Gentleman Dancing-Master (*The Dancing-Master*) (Wycherley) **8**:384-86, 388-92, 395, 401, 404-05, 408-09, 411; **21**:342-44, 346, 351-52, 355-56, 359, 361, 372, 387, 392
"Gentleman in the Navy" (Wheatley)
  See "To a Gentleman in the Navy"
The Genuine Remains (*Remains*) (Butler) **16**:4, 11, 50
The Geometrical School (Vinci) **12**:405
George Dandin; or, The Baffled Husband (Moliere)
  See *George Dandin; ou, Le mari confondu*
George Dandin; ou, Le mari confondu (*George Dandin; or, The Baffled Husband*) (Moliere) **10**:275, 280, 283-85, 297, 312-13, 320, 335, 343-45
Georgics (Dryden) **21**:119
Georgii Buchanani Scoti, franciscanus: varia eiusdem authoris poemata (*Franciscanus*) (Buchanan) **4**:118-20, 123, 134-35, 138
German Michael (Grimmelshausen)
  See *Der Teutsche Michel*
German Requiem for the Burnt Bulls and Papal Laws (Hutten) **16**:232
Gerusalemme (Tasso)
  See *La Gierusalemme liberata*
Geschicht und Histori von Land-Graff Ludwig dem Springer (Beer) **5**:52
Die Geschwister in Taurien (*Schlegel*) (Schlegel) **5**:280
Gesprächbüchlein (Hutten) **16**:234
Gesta Grayorum (Bacon) **18**:196
"The Ghost" (Churchill) **3**:143-45, 148, 151, 153-55, 158-60, 162-64
"Ghost of John Dennis" (Gray) **4**:333
Gibraltar, a Comedy (Dennis) **11**:8
La Gierusalemme liberata (*Gerusalemme*) (Tasso) **5**:372-80, 382-88, 392-95, 398-99, 401, 406-08
"The Gift of Poetry" (Parnell) **3**:255
Gift of the Free (Jami)
  See *Tuhfatu'l-Ahrár*
"The Gifts of Jacquet to Isabeau" (Ronsard) **6**:420
"The Girl of Pohsing" (P'u Sung-ling) **3**:347

"Girl Who Did Not Want to Marry" ("The Girl with No Interest in Marriage"; "The Virgin Averse to Marriage") (Erasmus) **16**:123, 141, 193
"The Girl with No Interest in Marriage" (Erasmus)
  See "Girl Who Did Not Want to Marry"
"La gitanilla" (Cervantes) **6**:171-72
Giudizi (*Pasquinades*) (Aretino) **12**:22, 26
"Giudizzio sovra la Gerusalemme" (Tasso) **5**:384
Giunte (Castelvetro) **12**:67-8
"Giunto è già 'l corso della vita mia" (Michelangelo) **12**:368, 375
Giving Alms to Charity and Employing the Poor (Defoe) **1**:124
"The Glass Scholar" (Cervantes)
  See "El licienciado vidriera"
A Glasse of the Truthe: An Argument by Way of Dialoge between a Lawyer and a Divine; That the Marriage of Henry VIII. with Catherine of Aragon Was Unlawful; And That the Cause Ought to Be Heard and Ordered within the Realm (Henry VIII) **10**:119, 127, 129, 142-45
Gl'innamorati (Goldoni) **4**:267-68
Glorias de Querétaro en la neuva congregacion eclecsiastica de María Santissima de Guadalupe (*Glories of Querétaro*) (Siguenza y Gongora) **8**:339-40
Glories of Querétaro (Siguenza y Gongora)
  See *Glorias de Querétaro en la neuva congregacion eclecsiastica de María Santissima de Guadalupe*
"The Glorious Success of Her Majesty's Arms" (Prior)
  See "The Ode on the Glorious Success of Her Majesty's Arms"
"The Glory and Grace in the Church Set Out" (Taylor) **11**:394
Gnothi Seauton (Arbuthnot) **1**:19
God Glorified in the Work of Redemption, by the Greatness of Man's Dependence upon Him in the Whole of It (*Work of Redemption*) (Edwards) **7**:95
God Not the Author of Evil (Collier) **6**:210
"Goddwyn" (Chatterton) **3**:119, 129
"Godly Girzie" (Burns) **3**:97
Gods Determinations touching his Elect: and The Elects Combat in their Conversion, and Coming up to God in Christ: together with the Comfortable Effects Thereof (*Determinations*) (Taylor) **11**:343-45, 350-51, 354, 356, 358-59, 362-63, 368, 373-74, 376, 381-82, 385, 393-94, 401, 403
Godwin & Mary (Wollstonecraft) **5**:444
"Goe, and catche a falling starre" (Donne)
  See "Song. 'Goe, and catche a falling starre'"
"The Golden Ass" (Machiavelli)
  See "L'asino d'oro"
"Goldie" (Burns)
  See "On Commissary Goldie's Brains"
"Goliath of Gath. 1 Sam. Chap. XVII" (Wheatley) **3**:413, 418, 430, 436
Gondibert: An Heroick Poem (Davenant) **13**:158-60, 164, 167-75, 182-83, 185, 195-96, 199, 202-10, 215
"Good and Ill in Every Nation" (Wessel) **7**:391
"The Good Conscience, the Only Certain, Lasting Good" (Wycherley) **8**:399

"Good Counsel" (Petursson)
See "Heilrædauísur"
"Good Counsel to a Young Maid" (Carew)
13:23, 57
"Good Friday" (Donne)
See "Goodfriday 1613: Riding Westward"
"The Good Husband" (Marmontel) **2**:214
"The good-morrow" ("I wonder by my troth")
(Donne) **10**:12, 26, 32, 36, 49, 52, 54, 57-8
The Good Mother (Goldoni)
See *La buona madre*
The Good Natured Man (Goldsmith) **2**:67-8,
70-1, 73, 76, 81, 84, 86-8, 99, 105-06, 112,
114, 119-21, 126-28
Good Sense (Holbach)
See *Bon-Sens*
"Goodfriday 1613: Riding Westward" ("Good
Friday") (Donne) **10**:40, 61, 84, 96, 105,
107
"The Goodness of his God" (Herrick) **13**:358
"Gor'kaia uchast" ("A Bitter Fate") (Chulkov)
2:14, 18
"Gotham" (Churchill) **3**:141, 145, 149, 152-
53, 155-56, 158, 160, 162-63, 172
Gothrika (Schlegel) **5**:273
"Götterlehre; oder, Mythologische Dichtungen
der Alten" (Moritz) **2**:231, 246
The Governess; or, Little Female Academy
(*Little Female Academy*) (Fielding) **1**:273,
275-78
The Governor (Elyot)
See *The Boke of the Governor, devised by Sir
Thomas Elyot*
"Governor Yu" (P'u Sung-ling) **3**:345
The Governour (Elyot)
See *The Boke of the Governor, devised by Sir
Thomas Elyot*
Grace Abounding to the Chief of Sinners
(Bunyan) **4**:149, 152, 159, 164, 166, 169,
172, 174, 180, 196-202
La gran sultana (Cervantes) **6**:180
Le Grand Cyrus (Marivaux)
See *Artamène; ou, Le Grand Cyrus*
"The Grand Question Debated" (Swift) **1**:459
The Grand Tour (Boswell)
See *Boswell on the Grand Tour*
"Grato e felice, a' tuo feroci mali"
(Michelangelo) **12**:369
"The Grave of King Arthur" (Warton)
15:432-33, 442, 445, 454-55
*The Great Christian Doctrine of Original Sin
Defended* (*Original Sin*) (Edwards) **7**:94-6,
98
*The Great Historical, Geographical,
Genealogical and Poetical Dictionary*
(*Historical Dictionary*) (Collier) **6**:208, 210
*Great Works of Nature for the Particular Use
of Mankind* (Bacon)
See *Magnalia naturae praecipue quoad usus
humanos*
Greater Surgery (Paracelsus)
See *Books of the Greater Surgery*
"Green Grow the Rashes O" (Burns) **3**:71,
87
"Grim Grizzle" (Burns) **3**:99
"Griselidis" ("Patient Griselda") (Perrault)
2:253-56, 279
The Grounds of Criticism in Poetry (Dennis)
11:8, 16, 18, 22-6, 30, 33, 36-7, 40-1, 44,
51-3
The Grounds of Criticism in Tragedy (Dryden)
3:236-37; **21**:52, 114-15

The Grub Street Opera (Fielding) **1**:249
The Guardian (Addison) **18**:7, 20-1, 24
The Guardian (Garrick) **15**:93, 98, 101, 105,
121, 124
The Guardian (Steele) **18**:318, 333, 344, 347,
350, 353-54, 369, 372
The Guardian, 15 (Steele) **18**:349
The Guardian, 21 (Steele) **18**:358
The Guardian, 26 (Steele) **18**:346
The Guardian, 45 (Steele) **18**:349
The Guardian, 172 (Steele) **18**:347
"Gude Ale Keeps the Heart Aboon" (Burns)
3:86
"Gude E'en to You, Kimmer" (Burns) **3**:67
La guerro (Goldoni) **4**:262
"Guid Mornin' to your Majesty" (Burns)
3:71
Gustavus Vasa, the Deliverer of His Country
(Brooke) **1**:62, 67
The Gypsies Metamorphosed (*The
Metamorphosed Gipsies*) (Jonson) **6**:317,
337
Gypsy Balladeer (Garcia Lorca)
See *Romancero gitano*
"H:W: in Hiber: 'belligeranti'" (Donne) **10**:39
"Habbakuk" (Parnell) **3**:255
Haft Aurang (*The Constellation of the Great
Bear*) (Jami) **9**:59, 62, 65-8, 71
"The Hag is Astride" (Herrick) **13**:331, 336
"Hallelujah" (Winchilsea) **3**:451
"Hallowe'en" (Burns) **3**:48, 52, 54, 56, 65,
67, 72-3, 84, 86
Hamburg Dramaturgy (Lessing)
See *Die Hamburgische Dramaturgie*
Die Hamburgische Dramaturgie (*Hamburg
Dramaturgy*) (Lessing) **8**:61-3, 65, 67-9, 71,
73-4, 76-8, 80-7, 94, 98-104, 107, 110-11,
114-16
"The Hamlet" (Warton)
See "Hamlet, an Ode written in Whichwood
Forest"
"Hamlet, an Ode written in Whichwood
Forest" ("The Hamlet") (Warton) **15**:432,
434, 443
"Han Fang" (P'u Sung-ling) **3**:344
Handbook of the Militant Christian (Erasmus)
See *Enchiridion militis christiani*
"Hannah" (Parnell) **3**:255
"Hans Carvel" (Prior) **4**:455, 461, 467
Hans Frandsen (Holberg)
See *Jean de France; eller, Hans Frandsen*
"The Happy Fugitives" (Manley) **1**:306-08
"An Haranguer" (Butler) **16**;53
Harlequin's Invasion (Garrick) **15**:100, 104,
114, 124
*The Harmonie of the Church. Containing the
Spirituall Songes and Holy Hymnes, of
Godley Men, Patriarkes and Prophetes: All,
Sweetly Sounding, to the Praise and Glory of
the Highest* (Drayton) **8**:19, 29
"Harmony" (Kochanowski)
See "Zgoda"
"Harriet's Birth Day" (Smart) **3**:366
Le hasard du coin du feu (Crebillon) **1**:76-7,
79
"Hassan; or, The Camel-Driver" (Collins)
4:210
The Haunch of Venison (Goldsmith) **2**:74,
104
The Hawk-Eyed Sentinel (Cervantes) **6**:190
Hazañas del Cid (Castro)
See *Las mocedades del Cid II*

"He Expresses Joy at Finding...Her Whom He
Had Loved as a Mere Boy" (More) **10**:427
"He that loves a rosy cheek" (Carew)
See "Disdaine Returned"
"He that loves a rosy lip" (Carew) **13**:20
"Heads of an Answer to Rymer" (Dryden)
3:236-37; **21**:114-15
"The Heart" (Drayton) **8**:9, 30
"Heart of Oak" (Garrick) **15**:114, 124
Heat (Marat) **10**:222
The Heavenly Footman (Bunyan) **4**:172, 177
Hebrides Journal (Boswell)
See *Journal of a Tour to the Hebrides with
Samuel Johnson, LL. D.*
Heedless Hopalong (Grimmelshausen)
See *Der seltsame Springinsfeld*
"Heilrædauísur" ("Good Counsel")
(Petursson) **8**:253
Heinrich der Löws (Schlegel) **5**:273
Hekuba (Schlegel) **5**:280
"Helter Skelter" (Swift) **1**:459
La Henriade (Marmontel) **2**:222-23
La henriade (Voltaire) **14**:328, 338, 342, 349,
358, 379, 382, 391, 414
Henrich and Pernille (Holberg)
See *Henrik og Pernille*
Henrik og Pernille (*Henrich and Pernille*)
(Holberg) **6**:277, 283
Henry (Lyttelton)
See *The History of the Life of King Henry
the Second and of the Age in Which He
Lived*
Henry II. (Lyttelton)
See *The History of the Life of King Henry
the Second and of the Age in Which He
Lived*
"Henry and Emma" ("Nut-brown Maid")
(Prior) **4**:455, 458, 460, 467, 474-79
Heptaplus (*Discourse on the seven days of the
creation; Septiform Narration of the Six Days
of Creation*) (Pico della Mirandola) **15**:319,
324, 329-30, 334, 338, 340-41, 345, 350-57,
359-60
"Her Man Described by Her Own Dictamen"
(Jonson) **6**:305
"Her Right Name" (Prior) **4**:460-61, 466
Les Héraclides (Marmontel) **2**:213, 216
"Heraclitus" (Prior)
See "Democritus and Heraclitus"
Herbarius (Paracelsus) **14**:198
"Hercule Chrestien" (Ronsard) **6**:437
"Here she lies, a pretty bud" (Herrick)
See "Upon a child that died"
L'héritier du village (Marivaux) **4**:367
Hermann (*Herrmann*) (Schlegel) **5**:273, 280-
81
The Hermetic and Alchmical Writings
(Paracelsus) **14**:185
"An Hermetic Philosopher" (Butler) **16**:28,
52
"The Hermit" (Parnell) **3**:252-54, 256-58
The Hermit (Goldsmith) **2**:68
The Hero (Gracian y Morales)
See *El Héroe*
El Héroe (*The Hero*) (Gracian y Morales)
15:135-36, 143-45, 165
*Heroic Piety of Don Fernando Cortés, Marqués
del Valle* (Siguenza y Gongora) **8**:343
"Heroical Epistle" (Butler)
See "Heroical Epistle of Hudibras to his
Lady"

"Heroical Epistle of Hudibras to his Lady" ("Heroical Epistle") (Butler) **16**:24, 39, 49

"The Heroine" (P'u Sung-ling)
See "Hsieh-nü"

"Heroique Stanzas to the Glorious Memory of Cromwell" (Dryden) **3**:223-26; **21**:85

Héros (Gracian y Morales) **15**:142

Les héros de Roman (Boileau-Despreaux)
See *Dialogue des héros de roman*

Herrmann (Schlegel)
See *Hermann*

"Hesiod; or, The Rise of Woman" ("The Rise of Woman") (Parnell) **3**:251, 254, 257

Hesperides: or, The Works Both Humane & Divine of Robert Herrick, Esq. (Herrick) **13**:310, 312-13, 315-19, 321-22, 326, 328, 331-33, 335, 340-41, 346, 349-54, 356-58, 360-63, 365, 367, 370, 372-75, 378, 389-92, 394-99, 401-04, 408-11

L'heureux stratagème (Marivaux) **4**:359, 368, 370

Hexerei; eller, Blind allarm (Holberg) **6**:273, 277

"Hey Ca; thro'" (Burns) **3**:86

"Hey, the Dusty Miller" (Burns) **3**:81

"Hezekiah" (Parnell) **3**:255

Hieroglyphic Tales (Walpole) **2**:481, 488, 499-501, 507

"Highland Mary" (Burns) **3**:56, 67, 72

"The Hilliad" (Smart) **3**:367, 372, 394, 399

The Hind and the Panther (Dryden) **3**:184, 190-91, 199, 203-04, 208, 220-21, 234-35, 340-42; **21**:67-72, 79-80, 87

The Hind and the Panther, Transvers'd to the Story of the Country and the City-Mouse (*City Mouse and Country Mouse*) (Marvell) **4**:454, 458, 464

"L'hinne de Bacus" (Ronsard) **6**:420, 429

Hirsau Stained Glass Windows (Lessing) **8**:105

"His age, dedicated to his peculiar friend, M. John Wickes, under the name Posthumus" (Herrick) **13**:365, 378, 381-82, 394

"His Answer to a Question" (Herrick) **13**:337

"His Cloe Hunting" (Prior) **4**:459

"His Creed" (Herrick) **13**:342, 366

"His Defence against the Idle Critick" (Drayton) **8**:27

"His Farewell to Sack" (Herrick) **13**:326, 333, 392-93, 397

"His farwell vnto Poetrie" (Herrick)
See "Farewell to Poetry"

"His Grange, or Private Wealth" (Herrick) **13**:335

"His Lachrimae, or Mirth, turn'd to mourning" (Herrick) **13**:387

"His Letanie, to the Holy Spirit" (Herrick)
See "Litany to the Holy Spirit"

"His Litany to the Holy Spirit" (Herrick)
See "Litany to the Holy Spirit"

His Majesties Declaration Defended (Dryden) **21**:57, 65

"His Meditation Upon Death" (Herrick) **13**:342, 391

His Noble Numbers: or, His Pious Pieces, Wherein (amongst other things) he sings the Birth of his Christ: and sighes for his Saviours suffering on the Crosse (*Noble Numbers, or Pious Pieces*) (Herrick) **13**:310, 312-13, 315, 317, 319, 322, 324, 328, 333-35, 338, 340-41, 353-54, 357-58, 361-63, 366-67, 371, 373, 390-91, 397, 401, 404-05, 411

"His Poetry his Pillar" (Herrick) **13**:327, 341

"His Prayer for Absolution" (Herrick) **13**:328

"His request to Julia" (Herrick) **13**:355

"His Returne to London" (Herrick) **13**:352, 387-88

"His Sailing from Julia" (Herrick) **13**:327, 402

"His Saviour's words, going to the Cross" (Herrick) **13**:358

"His tears to Thamasis" (Herrick) **13**:403

"His Winding-Sheet" (Herrick) **13**:352, 354, 357

Histoire de Brandebourg (*History of Brandenburg*) (Frederick the Great) **14**:58, 69

L'histoire de Charles XII (Voltaire) **14**:328, 382, 386-87, 408

L'histoire de Fenni (Voltaire) **14**:359, 361

Histoire de Gil Blas de Santillane (*The Adventures of Gil Blas*) (Lesage) **2**:174-88, 190-202, 204

Histoire de Guzman d'Alfarache (*The Adventures of Guzman d'Alfarache*) (Lesage) **2**:177, 182, 202-03

L'histoire de Jenni (Voltaire) **14**:346

Histoire de la guerre de 1741 (Voltaire) **14**:383

Histoire de l'empire de Russie sous Pierre le Grand (*History of the Russian Empire under Peter the Great*) (Voltaire) **14**:383, 408

Histoire de Louis XI (Duclos) **1**:186, 189

Histoire de ma Vie jusqu'à l'an 1797 (Casanova de Seingalt)
See *Mémoires de J. Casanova de Seingalt écrits par lui-même*

Histoire de Madame de Luz (Duclos) **1**:187-97

Histoire de Madame Henriette d'Angleterre (La Fayette) **2**:156

Histoire de mon temps (Frederick the Great) **14**:64, 69, 71, 75

Histoire d'Edouard et d'Elisabeth qui passèrent quatre vingt un ans chez les Megamicres (Casanova de Seingalt)
See *Icosameron*

Histoire des voyages de Scarmentado (Voltaire) **14**:359, 378, 386

Histoire d'Estevanille Gonzalez (Lesage) **2**:182, 202, 204

Histoire du Chevalier de Grieux et de Manon Lescaut (Prevost) **1**:328-33, 335-38, 340, 343-44, 346-62

Histoire d'une Grecque moderne (Prevost) **1**:330, 334-35, 343-45

Histoire véritable (Montesquieu) **7**:348

Histoires ou Contes du temps passé, avec des moralités: Contes de Ma Mère l'Oye (Perrault) **2**:252-74, 279-86

Historia (Buchanan)
See *Rerum Scoticarum Historia, auctore Georgio Buchanano Scoto*

Historia Densi et Rari (Bacon) **18**:132

Historia Prima (*Primal History*) (Bacon) **18**:149

Historia Ricardi Tertii (More)
See *The Life of Kinge Richarde the Thirde*

Historia Ventorum (*History of Winds*) (Bacon) **18**:132, 149

Historia Vitae et Mortis (*History of Life and Death*) (Bacon) **18**:131-32, 149-50, 187

Historic Doubts on the Life and Reign of King Richard the Third (Walpole) **2**:456, 488

An Historical and Moral View of the Origin and Progress of the French Revolution, and the Effect It Has Produced in Europe (*French Revolution*) (Wollstonecraft) **5**:416, 426, 429, 431, 436, 443, 461

Historical Description of Russian Commerce (*Istoričeskoe opisanie Rossijskoj kommercii*) (Wollstonecraft) **5**:436

Historical Dictionary (Collier)
See *The Great Historical, Geographical, Genealogical and Poetical Dictionary*

Historie di Nicolo Machiavegli (*The History of Florence*) (Machiavelli) **8**:125, 128, 133, 136, 151, 174-75

The Histories and Novels of the Late Ingenious Mrs. Behn (Behn) **1**:48

The History and Adventures of an Atom (Smollett) **2**:319-20, 329, 331-32, 341

History of a Foundling (Fielding)
See *The History of Tom Jones, a Foundling*

History of Brandenburg (Frederick the Great)
See *Histoire de Brandebourg*

The History of Charles Mandeville (Brooke) **6**:111

History of Edward V. and Richard III. (More) **10**:374

The History of Emily Montague (*Emily Montague*) (Brooke) **6**:108-15, 117-22

History of England (Hume) **7**:140, 153, 159, 166-68, 191-93, 199-200

The History of English Poetry (Warton) **15**:429-30, 435-38, 449, 451-54, 457-59

The History of Florence (Machiavelli)
See *Historie di Nicolo Machiavelli*

The History of Genghizcan the Great, First Emperor of the Antient Moguls and Tartars (Aubin) **9**:3, 7

The History of Great Britain, under the House of Stuart (Hume) **7**:138, 151

The History of Henry II (Lyttelton)
See *The History of the Life of King Henry the Second and of the Age in Which He Lived*

History of Henry the Second (Lyttelton)
See *The History of the Life of King Henry the Second and of the Age in Which He Lived*

The History of Jemmy and Jenny Jessamy (Haywood) **1**:283, 287, 294

The History of John Bull (Arbuthnot) **1**:12-17, 20-2

The History of Jonathan Wild the Great (Fielding)
See *The Life of Mr. Jonathan Wild the Great*

The History of Joseph Andrews (*Joseph Andrews*) (Fielding) **1**:204-05, 207, 209-11, 217-19, 221-24, 228, 230-33, 238, 241-43, 246, 249, 251-55, 258-63, 265

The History of Lady Julia Mandeville (*Julia Mandeville*) (Brooke) **6**:107-110, 115, 118-22

History of Life and Death (Bacon)
See *Historia Vitae et Mortis*

The History of Little Jack (Day) **1**:106, 108, 111

History of Louis le Grand (Boileau-Despreaux) **3**:17

The History of Miss Betsy Thoughtless (Haywood) **1**:282-84, 286-87, 291, 293

History of My Life (Casanova de Seingalt)
See *Mémoires de J. Casanova de Seingalt écrits par lui-même*

The History of Nourjahad (*Nourjahad*)
  (Sheridan) 7:373-74, 378-79, 384-85
The History of Ophelia (Fielding) 1:271-73,
  278
The History of Rasselas, Prince of Abissinia
  (*Rasselas*) (Johnson) 15:191-93, 196-99,
  201-02, 204, 207-08, 213-14, 216-17, 225-29,
  233, 237-38, 240, 244-45, 247, 251-61, 267,
  269-70, 273, 286, 298, 305-07
History of Redemption (Edwards)
  See *History of the Work of Redemption*
The History of Richard III (More)
  See *The Life of Kinge Richarde the Thirde*
The History of Rivella (Manley)
  See *The Adventures of Rivella*
The History of Sandford and Merton (*Sanford
  and Merton*) (Day) 1:105-14
The History of Sir Charles Grandison (*Sir
  Charles Grandison*) (Richardson) 1:369-71,
  374-76, 379-80, 383, 388-90, 399-401, 407-
  10, 413-15, 418
The History of Sir Francis Drake (Davenant)
  13:190
*History of the Canons Regular of Mount St.
  Agnes* (Kempis) 11:411
History of the Earth and Animated Nature
  (Goldsmith) 2:68, 72, 76, 80
History of the Kingdom of Denmark (Holberg)
  See *Dannemarks riges historie*
History of the League (Dryden) 21:58, 68, 72
*The History of the Life and Adventures of Mr.
  Duncan Campbell, a Gentleman* (Defoe)
  1:136
*The History of the Life of King Henry the
  Second and of the Age in Which He Lived*
  (*Henry; Henry II.; The History of Henry II;
  History of Henry the Second; Reign of Henry
  the Second*) (Lyttelton) 10:196-97, 199-201,
  209
*The History of the Most Remarkable Life and
  Extraordinary Adventures of the Truly
  Honourable Colonel Jacque, Vulgarly Called
  Colonel Jack* (*Colonel Jack*) (Defoe) 1:125,
  128, 134, 139-40, 142, 147, 176
A History of the Plague (Defoe)
  See *A Journal of the Plague Year*
*The History of the Reign of King Henry the
  Seventh* (Bacon) 18:132, 134, 136, 177, 187
*History of the Russian Empire under Peter the
  Great* (Voltaire)
  See *Histoire de l'empire de Russie sous Pierre
  le Grand*
The History of the Union of Great Britain (*The
  History of the Union with Scotland*) (Defoe)
  1:124, 162
The History of the Union with Scotland (Defoe)
  See *The History of the Union of Great
  Britain*
History of the Work of Redemption (*History of
  Redemption*) (Edwards) 7:117, 119-20
The History of Tom Jones, a Foundling
  (*History of a Foundling; Tom Jones*)
  (Fielding) 1:205-07, 209-13, 215, 217-19,
  221-25, 228, 230-38, 240-48, 254-63
History of Winds (Bacon)
  See *Historia Ventorum*
"The Hock-Cart, or Harvest home" (Herrick)
  13:351, 368-69, 383, 395
*The Holy Bible: Containing the Old Testament
  and the New* (Eliot)

See *Mamusse wunneetupanatamwe Up-
  Biblum God Naneeswe Nukkone
  Testament Kah Wonk Wusku Testament*
The Holy City; or, The New Jerusalem
  (Bunyan) 4:169-70
"The Holy Fair" (Burns) 3:59, 65, 68, 71-2,
  76-8, 84, 86, 95-7, 104-06
"Holy Sonnet VII: At the round earths
  imagin'd corners blow" (Donne) 10:96
"Holy Sonnet XIII: What if this present were
  the world's last night?" (Donne) 10:73
"Holy Sonnet XIV: Batter my heart, three-
  person'd God" (Donne) 10:96
"Holy Sonnet XVII: Since she whom i lov'd
  hath paid her last debt" (Donne) 10:54
"Holy Sonnet XVII: 'Show me deare Christ,
  thy spouse'" (Donne) 10:84
Holy Sonnets (Donne) 10:26, 40, 45, 52, 55,
  63-4, 84, 93, 96, 99
The Holy War (Bunyan) 4:156-57, 159, 161,
  169-70, 172, 180-82, 203-04, 206
"Holy Willie's Prayer" (Burns) 3:67-9, 71-2,
  78, 82, 85, 87, 90, 93, 95, 97-8
"Holyhead" (Swift) 1:482
"Hombres necios que acusáis" ("Foolish
  Men'") (Juana Ines de la Cruz) 5:150, 156
Homer (Pope)
  See *The Odyssey of Homer*
*L'Homère travesti; ou, L'Iliade en vers
  burlesques* (Marivaux) 4:385
De hominis dignitate (Pico della Mirandola)
  See *Oratio de dignitate hominis*
L'homme aux quarante écus (*The Man with
  Forty Ecus*) (Voltaire) 14:338, 346, 359,
  363
*Les hommes illustres qui ont paru en France
  pendant ce siècle* (*Characters Historical and
  Panegyrical of the Greatest Men*) (Perrault)
  2:276, 279, 283
Den honnette ambition (Holberg) 6:267, 275,
  277
The Honorable Girl (Goldoni)
  See *La putta onorata*
"Honored Friend" (Dryden) 21:88
"Honoria" (Dryden)
  See *Theodore and Honoria*
"The Hop-Garden" (Smart) 3:362, 363, 371-
  72, 375, 394, 399
"Hop o' My Thumb" (Perrault)
  See "Le petit poucet"
Hopffen-Sack (Beer)
  See *Der abentheuerliche, wunderbare und
  unerhörte Ritter Hopffen-sack*
Horace (Smart)
  See *The Works of Horace, Translated into
  Verse*
"An Horatian Ode upon Cromwell's Return
  from Ireland" ("Ode") (Marvell) 4:397-98,
  404, 413-17, 425, 430-31, 436, 438, 440, 442
The Horatii (Aretino)
  See *Orazia*
"Hornbook" (Burns)
  See "Death and Doctor Hornbook"
*Les horribles et espouvantables faictz et
  prouesses du tres renommé Pantagruel Roy
  des Dipsodes, filz du grand géant Gargantua*
  (Rabelais) 5:208-09, 216-17, 223, 225-26,
  233, 235-38, 241, 248, 252-54, 257-59, 264-
  68
"Horse-Courser" (Butler) 16:53
The Horse Doctor (Aretino)
  See *Marescalco*

"Horses" (More) 9:298
*Hortulus rosarii de valle lachrymarum
  continens egreias & devotas sentecias* (*Garden
  of Roses; The Little Garden of Roses*)
  (Kempis) 11:410
"Hortus" (Marvell) 4:448
Hospitale pauperum (Kempis) 11:411
Hous of Fame (Chaucer)
  See *House of Fame*
House of Fame (*Book of Fame; Hous of Fame*)
  (Chaucer) 17:45, 58, 78, 87, 97, 108, 178,
  206, 217-19
"Housewifery" (Taylor)
  See "Huswifery"
"How Lilies Came White" (Herrick) 13:346,
  367
"How Marigolds came yellow" (Herrick)
  13:365
"How the Wallflower came first" (Herrick)
  13:365
"Hoy nos viene a redimir" (Teresa de Jesus)
  18:389
"Hsi Fang-ping" (P'u Sung-ling) 3:347
Hsi-yu chi (*The Journey to the West*) (Wu
  Ch'eng-en) 7:395-408, 410-12, 414-15, 417
"Hsia-nü" ("The Lady Knight-Errant") (P'u
  Sung-ling) 3:354
"Hsiang Kao" (P'u Sung-ling) 3:347
"Hsiang-yü" (P'u Sung-ling) 3:354
"Hsieh-nü" ("The Heroine") (P'u Sung-ling)
  3:351
"Hsien-jen tao" ("The Island of Fairies") (P'u
  Sung-ling) 3:354
Hsing-shih yin-yuan chuan (*Marriage as
  Retribution*) (P'u Sung-ling) 3:346, 356
"Hsu huang-liang" ("Continuation of the
  Yellow Millet") (P'u Sung-ling) 3:350
Hudibras (*Hudibras, the first part*) (Butler)
  16:2, 4-12, 14-27, 30-9, 41-8, 50-1
Hudibras (Smart) 3:374
Hudibras, the first part (Butler)
  See *Hudibras*
"Huffing Courtier" (Butler) 16:51, 53
"The Human Nature" (Taylor) 11:370
L'Humanità di Christo (*Humanity of Christ;
  Life of Christ; Vita di Cristo*) (Aretino)
  12:6, 13-4, 20, 35
Humanity of Christ (Aretino)
  See *L'Humanità di Christo*
Humourous Pieces (Warton) 15:434-35
"The Humours" (Bradstreet)
  See "Of the Four Humours in Man's
  Constitution"
Humphry Clinker (Smollett)
  See *The Expedition of Humphry Clinker*
Hung-lou meng (*Dream of the Red Chamber*)
  (Ts'ao Hsueh-ch'in) 1:533-61
"Husbanding Your Will" (Montaigne) 8:221
"The Husband's Resentment" (Manley)
  1:306, 308
"Huswifery" ("Housewifery") (Taylor)
  11:352, 355-56, 360, 386, 393, 402
"L'hymen" (Rousseau) 9:343
Hymenaei (Jonson) 6:315, 349
"A Hymn for Christmas Day" (Chatterton)
  3:127
"A Hymn for Evening" ("Evening") (Parnell)
  3:255
"A Hymn for Morning" ("Morning") (Parnell)
  3:255

"Hymn for the Day of St. Philip and St. James" ("Hymn to St. Philip and St. James") (Smart) **3**:370, 378, 390-91

"Hymn on Solitude" (Thomson) **16**:406

"Hymn on the Nativity of Our Lord and Saviour Jesus Christ" ("The Nativity of Our Lord and Savior Jesus Christ") (Smart) **3**:376, 378, 390, 392

"Hymn on the Power of God" (Thomson) **16**:418

"A Hymn on the Seasons" ("Hymn to the Seasons") (Thomson) **16**:375-76, 384-85, 405-06, 419, 430-31

"Hymn to Adversity" (Gray)
See "Ode to Adversity"

"Hymn to Beauty" (Spenser)
See "An Hymne in Honour of Beautie"

"A Hymn to Contentment" (Parnell) **3**:252-58

"An Hymn to Diana" (Jonson) **6**:325

"An Hymn to God the Father" (Jonson) **6**:326

"An Hymn to Humanity" (Wheatley) **3**:412, 415-16, 420

"Hymn to Ignorance" (Gray) **4**:301, 333

"Hymn to Musique" (Herrick) **13**:324

"Hymn to St. Philip and St. James" (Smart)
See "Hymn for the Day of St. Philip and St. James"

"An Hymn to the Evening" ("Evening") (Wheatley) **3**:413, 418, 420, 430, 435-37

"An Hymn to the Morning" ("Morning") (Wheatley) **3**:413, 418, 435

A Hymn to the Pillory (Defoe) **1**:161

"Hymn to the Seasons" (Thomson)
See "A Hymn on the Seasons"

"Hymn to the Supreme Being, on Recovery from a Dangerous Fit of Illness" (Smart) **3**:366, 371, 375-76, 378, 381-82, 395

"L'Hymne de Henri II" (Ronsard) **6**:439

"Hymne de la Mort" (Ronsard) **6**:422-23, 429, 435-37

"Hymne de la Philosophie" (Ronsard) **6**:422-23, 429

"Hymne de l'autonne" (Ronsard) **6**:429

"L'Hymne de l'Esté" (Ronsard) **6**:438

"Hymne de l'éternité" (Ronsard) **6**:422-23, 429, 437, 439

"Hymne de Mercure" (Ronsard) **6**:429

"Hymne des astres" (Ronsard)
See "Les Astres"

"Hymne des estoilles" (Ronsard) **6**:424

"Hymne du ciel" (Ronsard) **6**:422, 424, 429

"An Hymne in Honour of Beautie" ("Hymn to Beauty") (Spenser) **5**:309, 311, 323-24, 352-53

"An Hymne in Honour of Love" (Spenser) **5**:323, 350-52

"An Hymne of Heavenly Beautie" (Spenser) **5**:309, 311, 351-53

"An Hymne of Heavenly Love" (Spenser) **5**:324, 350-53

"A Hymne to Bacchus" (Herrick) **13**:351, 410

"A Hymne to Christ, at the authors last going into Germany" ("In what torne ship") (Donne) **10**:16, 40, 84

"Hymne to God my God, in my sicknesse" ("Since I am comming") (Donne) **10**:16, 40, 65, 85, 97, 106

"A Hymne to God the Father" ("Wilt thou forgive") (Donne) **10**:16, 40, 65, 85

"A Hymne to His Ladies Birth-Place" (Drayton) **8**:42-3

"An hymne to the Saints, and to Marquesse Hamylton" (Donne) **10**:84

Hymnes (*Hymns*) (Ronsard) **6**:407, 409-11, 424, 431-32, 434

Hymnes retranchées (Ronsard) **6**:410, 422

Hymns (Ronsard)
See *Hymnes*

Hymns and Spiritual Songs for the Fasts and Festivals of the Church of England (Smart) **3**:375-78, 390, 400, 402-04

Hymns for Children (Smart)
See *Hymns for the Amusement of Children*

Hymns for the Amusement of Children (*Hymns for Children*) (Smart) **3**:375, 393, 395, 397

Hymns of the Passion (Petursson)
See *Fimmtíu passíusálmar*

The Hypochondriack (Boswell) **4**:34, 36-8, 57-9, 64, 71-2, 74

L'hypocondre; ou, La femme qui ne parle point (Rousseau) **9**:335-36

"An Hypocrite" (Butler) **16**:27

The Hypocrite (Aretino)
See *Lo ipocrito*

"Hypocrites Deficient in the Duty of Prayer" (Edwards) **7**:113

"An Hypocritical Nonconformist" (Butler) **16**:28, 55

"I dare not ask" (Herrick) **13**:322

"I had eight birds hacht in one nest" (Bradstreet) **4**:106

"I Hae a Wife" (Burns) **3**:81

"I have in me a great care" (Juana Ines de la Cruz) **5**:152

"I Heare Some Say, this Man Is Not in Love" (Drayton)
See "Sonnet 24"

"I' ho gia fatto un gozzo in questo stento" (Michelangelo) **12**:365

"I love unloved" (Henry VIII) **10**:145

"I' mi son caro assai più ch'i' non soglio" (Michelangelo) **12**:367

I pettegolezzi delle donne (*Women's Tittle-Tattle*) (Goldoni) **4**:256

I rusteghi (Goldoni) **4**:257, 261, 265, 268, 274-75

I sette salmi de la penitenzia di David (*Penetential Psalms; Sette Salmi; The Seven Penetential Psalms of David*) (Aretino) **12**:13, 20-1, 25, 35

I suppositi (Pope) **3**:334

"I tell thee, Charmion, could I Time retrieve" (Congreve) **5**:85

"I wonder by my troth" (Donne)
See "The good-morrow"

Ibrahim; ou, L'illustre Bassa (Scudery)
See *Isabelle Grimaldi*

Ibrahim; ou, L'illustre Bassa (Scudery) **2**:306-09, 311

Ibrahim, the Thirteenth Emperour of the Turks (*Emperor of the Turks*) (Pix) **8**:258, 260-61, 263, 265, 267, 269-74, 276-78

"Ichthyophagia" ("A Fish Diet"; "Fish-Eating") (Erasmus) **16**:129, 141, 194-95, 198

Icon Basilike (Charles I)
See *Eikon Basilike: The Portraicture of His Sacred Majestie in His Solitudes and Sufferings*

Iconoclastes (Milton) **9**:161

Icosameron (*Histoire d'Edouard et d'Elisabeth qui passèrent quatre vingt un ans chez les Megamicres*) (Casanova de Seingalt) **13**:98, 112

Idalia; or, The Unfortunate Mistress (Haywood) **1**:283

Idea (*Sonnets to Idea*) (Drayton) **8**:14, 19

"Idea 61" (Drayton)
See "Sonnet 61"

"Idea of a Perfect Commonwealth" (Hume) **7**:189-90

Idea the Shepheards Garland, Fashioned in Nine Eglogs. Rowlands Sacrifice to the Nine Muses (*Shepherd's Garland*) (Drayton) **8**:20-1, 29, 31-2, 34-9, 50, 54

Ideal einer vollkommenen Zeitung (Moritz) **2**:240

Ideas Mirrour. Amours in Quatorzains (Drayton) **8**:19, 32, 37, 52, 54

Idées républicaines (Voltaire) **14**:401, 405-06

"Idleness of Business" (Wycherley) **8**:380

The Idler (Johnson) **15**:196, 199, 207, 225, 261-62, 267, 269, 284, 287, 289

"The Idler, 17" (Johnson) **15**:307

"The Idler, 22" ("Imprisonment of Debtors") (Johnson) **15**:307

"The Idler, 24" (Johnson) **15**:288

"The Idler, 27" (Johnson) **15**:288

"The Idler, 32" (Johnson) **15**:289

"The Idler, 50" (Johnson) **15**:287

"The Idler, 64" (Johnson) **15**:266

"The Idler, 73" (Johnson) **15**:262

"The Idler, 89" (Johnson) **15**:290

"If perchance, my Fabio" (Juana Ines de la Cruz)
See "Si acaso, Fabio mío"

"If yet I have not all thy love" (Donne)
See "Lovers infinitenesse"

Ignatius, His Conclave; or His Inthronisation in a Late Election in Hell: wherein many things are mingled by way of satyr (Donne) **10**:39, 62-3

"Ignorance" (Wycherley) **8**:380

"An Ignorant Man" (Butler) **16**:54

Il burbero benefico (Goldoni)
See *Le bourru bienfaisant*

Il campiello (*The St. Marco Place*) (Goldoni) **4**:251, 264, 267

Il cavaliere e la dama (*The Cavalier and the Lady*) (Goldoni) **4**:250, 265

Il cortegiano (Castiglione)
See *Il libro del cortegiano*

Il festino (Goldoni) **4**:262

Il filosofo (*The Philosopher*) (Aretino) **12**:19, 26-7, 30, 36

Il gondoliere veneziano (*Gli sdegni amorosi*) (Goldoni) **4**:267

Il libro del cortegiano (*The Book of the Courtier; The Courtier; Il cortegiano*) (Castiglione) **12**:76-127

Il libro dello amore (Ficino) **12**:176

Il mondo creato (Tasso)
See *Le sette giornate del mondo creato*

Il negromante (Ariosto) **6**:60-1

"Il Penseroso" (Milton) **9**:177, 192, 198, 204, 212, 224-30, 232

Il principe di Niccholo Machivello (*The Prince*) (Machiavelli) **8**:123, 125-28, 130-37, 139-40, 142, 145-49, 151-55, 157-62, 167-68, 170, 172-73, 175-79

Il ritorno dalla villeggiatura (Goldoni) **4**:265

Il servitore di due padroni (*The Servant of Two Masters*) (Goldoni) 4:272-73

Il teatro comico (Goldoni) 4:266, 268

Il ventaglio (*The Fan*) (Goldoni) 4:255, 264, 266-67

Il vero amico (*The True Friend*) (Goldoni) 4:259

L'ile de la raison; ou, Les petits hommes (Marivaux) 4:367, 377, 388

"Île de Ré" (Malherbe)
  See "Pour le roy allant chastier la rebellion des Rochelois et chasser les Anglois qui en leur faveur estoient descendus en l'îsle de Ré"

L'ile des esclaves (Marivaux) 4:361, 465-68, 377, 388

"Ill Government" (Herrick) 13:395

"I'll tell thee now (dear love) what thou shalt doe" (Donne)
  See "A Valediction: of the booke"

The Illustrious French Lovers: Being the True Histories of the Amours of Several French Persons of Quality (Aubin) 9:3-4

"The Illustrious Serving Wench" (Cervantes)
  See "La ilustre fregona"

"La ilustre fregona" ("The Illustrious Serving Wench") (Cervantes) 6:170-71, 176

Image (Elyot)
  See *The Image of Governance compiled of the actes and sentences notable of the moste noble Emperour Alexander Severus, late translated out of Greke into Englyshe by syr Thomas Elyot, Knight, in the fauour of nobylitie*

The Image of Death in Ancient Art (Lessing) 8:104

The Image of Governance compiled of the actes and sentences notable of the moste noble Emperour Alexander Severus, late translated out of Greke into Englyshe by syr Thomas Elyot, Knight, in the fauour of nobylitie (*Image*) (Elyot) 11:60-1, 68, 71, 73-4, 76, 91

Images and Shadows of Divine Things (Edwards) 7:128

The Imaginary Invalid (Moliere)
  See *Le malade imaginaire*

"Imagination" (Marmontel) 2:221

"Imagination" (Wheatley)
  See "On Imagination"

The Imitation of Christ (Kempis)
  See *De imitatione Christi*

"An Imitation of Some French Verses" (Parnell) 3:257

"Imitations of Horace" (Swift) 1:439, 523

Imitations of Horace (Pope)
  See *Satires and Epistles of Horace, Imitated*

"Imitée d'Horace" (Rousseau) 9:344

The Immortality of the Soul (More) 9:305-06, 314, 323-24, 329

The Impartial Critick (Dennis) 11:5, 20, 30, 39

Impertinent Curiosity (Castro) 19:4

The Imposter (Brooke) 1:62

The Imposter (Moliere)
  See *Tartuffe*

L'imposteur (Moliere)
  See *Tartuffe*

L'impostore (Goldoni) 4:262

Imposture sacerdotale (Holbach) 14:153

"Imprisonment of Debtors" (Johnson)
  See "The Idler, 22"

The Impromptu at Versailles (Moliere)
  See *L'impromptu de Versailles*

L'impromptu de Versailles (*The Impromptu at Versailles*) (Moliere) 10:278, 281, 283, 287, 311, 318, 321

"Impromptu on Lord Holland's House" (Gray)
  See "On Lord Holland's Seat near Margate, Kent"

"In Answer of an Elegiacal Letter, upon the Death of the King of Sweden, from Aurelian Townsend, inviting me to write on that subject" (Carew) 13:22, 42

"In Answer to a Mistress, Who Desir'd Her Lover to Marry Her" (Wycherley) 8:415

"In celebration of the yearely Preserver of the Games" (Davenant) 13:205

"In Honour of that High and Mighty Princess Queen Elizabeth of Happy Memory" (Bradstreet) 4:88, 110, 114

"In Praise of Ignorance" (Wycherley) 21:356

"In Pursuit of Benefices" (Erasmus) 16:194

"In Quintum Novembris" (Milton) 9:204

"In reference to her children" (Bradstreet) 4:94

"In the Due Honor of the Author Master Robert Norton, and His Work" (Smith) 9:382

"In vita humana" (Bacon) 18:192

"In what torne ship" (Donne)
  See "A Hymne to Christ, at the authors last going into Germany"

"In Yonder Grave a Druid Lies" (Collins)
  See "An Ode Occasion'd by the Death of Mr. Thomson"

The Incas (Marmontel)
  See *Les Incas*

Les Incas (*The Incas*) (Marmontel) 2:212-14

Incognita; or, Love and Duty Reconcil'd (Congreve) 5:83, 95, 108-09; 21:11-14, 35-9, 44-5

The Inconstant; or, The Way to Win Him (Farquhar) 21:128-29, 133-36, 139-42, 148, 150, 154, 161, 169

"Independence" (Churchill) 3:141, 150-51, 155-56, 163-64

Indian Dialogues, for Their Instruction in that Great Service of Christ, in Calling Home Their Countrymen to the Knowledge of God and of Themselves, and of Jesus Christ (*Dialogues*) (Eliot) 5:135-36, 138

The Indian Emperour (Dryden) 21:88, 105-07

The Indian Emperour; or, The Conquest of Mexico by the Spaniards, Being the Sequel of the Indian Queen (Dryden) 3:177-78, 232, 235; 21:56, 66, 102

The Indian Grammar Begun; or, An Essay to Bring the Indian Language into Rules, for the Help of Such as Desire to Learn the Same, for the Furtherance of the Gospel Among Them (Eliot) 5:134

The Indian Primer; or, The Way of Training up of Our Indian Youth in the Good Knowledge of God, in the Knowledge of the Scriptures and in an Ability to Read (Eliot) 5:132

The Indian Queen (Dryden) 3:231; 21:104-05, 107

Indian Spring (Siguenza y Gongora) 8:340

"The Indifferent" (Donne) 10:12, 52, 82

L'indigent philosophe (Marivaux) 4:376, 378-80, 386-87

Los infortunios de Alonso Ramírez (Siguenza y Gongora)
  See *Infortunios que Alonso Ramírez natural de la ciudad de S. Juan de Puerto Rico*

Infortunios que Alonso Ramírez natural de la ciudad de S. Juan de Puerto Rico (*Los infortunios de Alonso Ramírez*) (Siguenza y Gongora) 8:341, 344-47

El ingenioso hidalgo Don Quixote de la Mancha (*Don Quixote*) (Cervantes) 6:130-37, 139-53, 157-58, 160-64, 166-72, 174, 177, 180, 183-92

L'ingénu (Voltaire) 14:334, 346, 354, 359, 361, 398, 400

"Ingrateful Beauty Threatened" (Carew) 13:23, 28, 33, 63

The Inhumane Cardinal; or, Innocence Betrayed (Pix) 8:260, 267, 277

The Injured Husband; or, The Mistaken Resentment (Haywood) 1:292

Innamorato (Boiardo)
  See *Orlando innamorato*

The Innocent Mistress (Pix) 8:258, 260-62, 268-69, 271-73, 275

"Inquiry" ("Enquiry") (Herrick) 13:311

Inquisitio de Fide (*An Enquiry Concerning Faith; An Examination Concerning Faith*) (Erasmus) 16:142, 155, 193

"Inscription in a Hermitage" (Warton) 15:444, 454

Inspicientes (Hutten)
  See *The Spectators*

"Installation Ode" (Gray) 4:312

Institute of a Christian Prince (Erasmus)
  See *Institutio principis christiani*

The Institutes of Health (Cleland) 2:50, 54

Institutio Christiani Matrimoni (Erasmus)
  See *Christiani Matrimonii Institutio*

Institutio principis (Erasmus) 16:198

Institutio principis christiani (*The Education of a Christian Prince; Institute of a Christian Prince*) (Erasmus) 16:112, 120-21, 132, 154-55, 186

The Institution of a Christen Man (*Bishops' Book*) (Henry VIII) 10:130-31, 133, 135-39, 141

"Institution pour l'adolescence du Roi, Charles IX" (Ronsard) 6:409, 411

Instructions for Forreine Travel (Howell) 13:420, 424, 427-28, 430, 433, 437

Instructions for the Organization of a Community Chest (Luther) 9:134

The Insufficiency of Reason as a Substitute for Revelation (Edwards) 7:129

Interesting Narrative (Equiano)
  See *The Interesting Narrative of the Life of Olaudah Equiano, or Gustavus Vassa, the African*

The Interesting Narrative of Olaudah Equiano (Equiano)
  See *The Interesting Narrative of the Life of Olaudah Equiano, or Gustavus Vassa, the African*

Interesting Narrative of the Life (Equiano)
  See *The Interesting Narrative of the Life of Olaudah Equiano, or Gustavus Vassa, the African*

Julestuen (The Christmas Party) (Holberg) 6:259, 277

Julia Mandeville (Brooke)
  See *The History of Lady Julia Mandeville*

"Julia's Petticoat" (Herrick) 13:351, 370

Julie, ou La Nouvelle Héloïse (Rousseau)
  See *La Nouvelle Héloïse*

Juliet Grenville; or, The History of the Human Heart (Brooke) 1:62, 67, 70, 72

Julius Excluded from Heaven (Erasmus)
  See *Julius secundus exlusus*

Julius exclusus (Erasmus)
  See *Julius secundus exlusus*

Julius secundus exlusus (Julius Excluded from Heaven; Julius exclusus) (Erasmus) 16:132, 169, 172, 175-76, 182, 191-92

Jungfer-Hobel (Beer)
  See *Der neu ausgefertigte Jungfer-Hobel*

"Jupiter et Europe" (Rousseau) 9:341

Jure Divino (Defoe) 1:162

The Just Italian (Davenant) 13:175

Justi Lipsii Diva Sichemiensis sive Aspricollis: nova ejus beneficia & admiranda (Lipsius) 16:253

Justi Lipsii Diva Virgo Hallensis: beneficia ejus & miracula fide atque ordine descripta (Lipsius) 16:253

The Justice of God in the Damnation of Sinners (Edwards) 7:98, 117

"Juvenilia" (Thomson) 16:418

Juvenilia; or, Certaine paradoxes, and problems (Paradoxes and Problems) (Donne) 10:76, 95-6

"Kalendae Maiae" (Buchanan) 4:120, 122-23

"K'ao-pi ssu" ("The Bureau of Frauds") (P'u Sung-ling) 3:354

Katharine and Petruchio (Garrick) 15:94

"Kew Gardens" (Chatterton) 3:125-26, 132, 134-35

Khátimat al-hayát (End of Life) (Jami) 9:65, 68

Khirad-náma-yi Iskandarí (Wisdom of Alexander) (Jami) 9:68, 70-1

Kierlighed uden strømper (Kjælighed uden Strömper) (Wessel) 7:388-92

Kildereisen (Journey to the Spring) (Holberg) 6:259, 277

Kinderlogik (Moritz)
  See *Versuch einer kleinen praktischen Kinderlogik*

"The King and His Three Daughters" (Walpole) 2:500, 507

"King Arthur; or, The British Worthy" (Dryden) 3:222; 21:88

King Charles's Works (Charles I) 13:134

King's Book (Henry VIII)
  See *A Necessary Doctrine and Erudition for any Christen Man, Sette Furthe by the Kynges Majestie of Englande*

"The Kirk's Alarm" (Burns) 3:71, 78, 96

Kjælighed uden Strömper (Wessel)
  See *Kierlighed uden strømper*

Kleine Schriften (Lessing) 8:82

Kleine Schriften, die deutsche Sprache betreffend (Moritz) 2:241

Kleonnis (Lessing) 8:109

"Knave" (Butler) 16:52, 55

"Knight's" (Chaucer)
  See "Knight's Tale"

"Knight's Tale" ("Knight's"; "Palamon and Arcite") (Chaucer) 17:49, 53, 55, 69-70, 72, 117, 123-28, 130-31, 133-36, 149, 183-84, 195, 202, 205, 214, 218, 226-27, 230, 232-35, 237, 243

"Knight's Tale" ("Palamon and Arcite") (Dryden) 3:184-85, 187, 196, 204, 243

Know Yourself (Arbuthnot) 1:19

The Knowledge that Maketh a Wise Man (Elyot)
  See *Of the Knowledge Which Maketh a Wise Man*

Korte Verhandeling van God, de Mensch und deszelhs Welstand (Short Treatise) (Spinoza) 9:423

Kritische Briefe (Lessing) 8:112

"Kung-sun Hsia" (P'u Sung-ling) 3:352

Die kurtzweiligen Sommer-Täge (Beer) 5:46, 48, 50-2, 57-60

"La: Pen" (Carew)
  See "An Elegie on the La: Pen: sent to my Mistresse out of France"

El laberinto de amor (Cervantes) 6:180-81

Le labyrinthe de Versailles (Perrault) 2:266, 280

Labyrinthus medicorum (Paracelsus) 14:200

Ladies' Library (Steele) 18:347, 349-50, 380

The Ladies Subscription (Cleland) 2:51, 53

"The Ladle" (Prior) 4:455, 461, 467, 473

"The Lady Cornelia" (Cervantes)
  See "La Señora Cornelia"

The Lady in Child-bed (Holberg) 6:259

Lady Juliet Catesby (Brooke)
  See *Letters from Juliet, Lady Catesby, to Her Friend, Lady Henrietta Campley*

"The Lady Knight-Errant" (P'u Sung-ling)
  See "Hsia-nü"

The Lady of May (Sidney) 19:328-29, 374, 391, 393, 396-98, 400, 409-10, 421

"The Lady's Answer To The Knight" (Butler) 16:30, 39, 49

"The Lady's Dressing Room" (Swift) 1:453, 461, 483-84, 502, 510

The Lady's Pacquet of Letters Broke Open (Manley)
  See *The New Atalantis*

The Lady's Tale (Davys) 1:97, 100, 102-03

Lailá u Majnún (Laylá and Majnún) (Jami) 9:66, 70-1

"The Lament" (Burns) 3:48, 52, 86

"Lament I" (Kochanowski) 10:166-68

"Lament II" (Kochanowski) 10:165-67

"Lament III" (Kochanowski) 10:153, 166

"Lament IV" (Kochanowski) 10:153, 166-68, 170

"Lament V" (Kochanowski)
  See "Threnody V"

"Lament VI" (Kochanowski) 10:153, 157, 166, 170

"Lament VII" (Kochanowski)
  See "Tren VII"

"Lament VIII" (Kochanowski)
  See "Tren VIII"

"Lament IX" (Kochanowski)
  See "Tren IX"

"Lament X" (Kochanowski) 10:157-58, 166, 170

"Lament XI" (Kochanowski)
  See "Threnody XI"

"Lament XII" (Kochanowski) 10:153, 157-58, 166-67

"Lament XIII" (Kochanowski) 10:153, 166-67

"Lament XIV" (Kochanowski) 10:153, 159, 165, 169

"Lament XV" (Kochanowski) 10:153, 165-66, 170

"Lament XVI" (Kochanowski)
  See "Tren XVI"

"Lament XVII" (Kochanowski)
  See "Tren XVII"

"Lament XVII" (Kochanowski)
  See "Threnody XVII"

"Lament XIX" (Kochanowski)
  See "Tren XIX"

Lament and Exhortation aginst the excessive un-Christian Power of the Bishop of Rome and the unministerial Ministers (A Remonstrance and a Warning against the Presumptuous, Unchristian Power of the Bishop of Rome and the Unspiritual Spiritual Estate) (Hutten) 16:225, 234

"Lament for Creech" (Burns)
  See "Burlesque Lament for Creech"

"Lament for Glencairn" (Burns)
  See "Lament for James, Earl of Glencairn"

"Lament for James, Earl of Glencairn" ("Lament for Glencairn") (Burns) 3:84

"Lamentation for the Queen" (More) 10:430

"The Lamentations of Jeremy, for the most part according to Tremelius" (Donne) 10:84

Laments (Kochanowski)
  See *Treny*

Lamon's Tale (Sidney) 19:422

Laocoon; or, The Limits of Poetry and Painting (Lessing)
  See *Laokoon; oder, Über die Grenzen der Mahlerey und Poesie*

Laokoon; oder, Über die Grenzen der Mahlerey und Poesie (Laocoon; or, The Limits of Poetry and Painting) (Lessing) 8:59-62, 64, 67, 69-71, 73, 76, 80, 82-4, 86-7, 89, 92-3, 98, 100-02, 104-06, 110-11, 114

"Lapides flere" (Erasmus) 16:198

"Lapraik II" (Burns)
  See "Second Epistle to John Lapraik"

Large Account of the Taste in Poetry (Dennis) 11:22, 28, 30

The Large Catechism (Luther)
  See *Deudsch Catechismus*

"Lark" (Herrick) 13:317

"The Lark now leaves his watry Nest" (Davenant) 13:195

"Les Larmes de Saint Pierre" ("The Tears of St. Peter") (Malherbe) 5:165-66, 175, 178, 181

"Larmes du Sieur Malherbe" (Malherbe) 5:178-79

"The Lass of Balloch myle" (Burns) 3:71

"The Last Day" (Young)
  See "Poem on the Last Day"

"The Last Instructions to a Painter" (Marvell) 4:398, 443-45

"Last May a braw Wooer" (Burns) 3:67, 71, 82, 85

The Last Speech of John Good (Brooke) 1:62

"Late Wars" (Butler) 16:27

The Latest from the Realm of Wit (Lessing) 8:112

Latin-English Dictionary (Elyot)
  See *The Dictionary*

"A Latitudinarian" (Butler) 16:52

The Interesting Narrative of the Life of Olaudah Equiano, or Gustavus Vassa, the African (*Interesting Narrative*; *The Interesting Narrative of Olaudah Equiano*; *Interesting Narrative of the Life*; *Life*; *The Life of Olaudah Equiano*; *Narrative*) (Equiano) **16**:60-71, 75-8, 82, 85, 91, 94, 97-9

The Interior Castle; or, The Mansions (Teresa de Jesus)
See *Castillo interior, o las moradas*

Interludes (Cervantes)
See *Ocho comedias y ocho entremeses*

"De Interpretationae Naturae Proemium" (Bacon) **18**:187-88

De Interpretationae Naturae Sententiae XII (Bacon) **18**:187

"Introduction to the Pardoner's Tale" (Chaucer) **17**:122

Inundación Castálida (Juana Ines de la Cruz) **5**:159

The Invader of His Country: or, The Fatal Resentment (*Coriolanus*) (Dennis) **11**:10, 18

Invective against Aleander (Hutten) **16**:234

Invective against the Luther-chewing Priests (Hutten) **16**:234

"The Inventory" (Burns) **3**:87

The Invisible Spy (Haywood) **1**:292

"An Invocation to Sleep" (Winchilsea) **3**:453

"Io crederrei, se tu fussi di sasso" (Michelangelo) **12**:362

Iphigenia (Dennis) **11**:12, 34-6

Lo ipocrito (*The Hypocrite*) (Aretino) **12**:9, 19, 26, 29-30, 36

Irene: A Tragedy (*Mahomet and Irene*) (Johnson) **15**:187, 195, 207, 224

Irish Widow (Garrick) **15**:93, 101-02, 104

"Is There for Honest Poverty" ("For A' That and A' That") (Burns) **3**:65, 72, 78

Isabelle Grimaldi (*Ibrahim; ou, L'illustre Bassa*) (Scudery) **2**:308

"Isaiah LXII: 1-8" (Wheatley) **3**:434

"The Island of Fairies" (P'u Sung-ling)
See "Hsien-jen tao"

Istoričeskoe opisanie Rossijskoj kommercii (Chulkov) **2**:12-3

Istoričeskoe opisanie Rossijskoj kommercii (Wollstonecraft)
See *Historical Description of Russian Commerce*

"It is Not Growing Like a Tree" (Jonson) **6**:322

Jacob and Tyboe (Holberg)
See *Jacob von Tyboe*

Jacob von Tyboe (*Jacob and Tyboe*) (Holberg) **6**:277, 283-84

La jalousie de Barbouillé (*The Jealousy of Le Barbouillé*) (Moliere) **10**:281-83, 309, 312, 314, 344-45

Jane (Rowe)
See *The Tragedy of Lady Jane Gray*

Jane Shore (Rowe)
See *The Tragedy of Jane Shore*

"January and May" (Chaucer)
See "Miller's Tale"

"Ie ne suis point, ma guerrière Cassandre" (Ronsard) **6**:416

"Je vous envoye un bouquet" (Ronsard) **6**:417

"The Jealous Extremaduran" (Cervantes)
See "El celoso extremeño"

The Jealous Old Husband (Cervantes) **6**:190-92

The Jealous Women (Goldoni)
See *Le donne gelose*

The Jealousy of Le Barbouillé (Moliere)
See *La jalousie de Barbouillé*

Jean de France; eller, Hans Frandsen (*Hans Frandsen*) (Holberg) **6**:258, 277

Jeannot et Colin (Voltaire) **14**:342, 344

Jephtha (Buchanan)
See *Jephthes, sive votum: tragoedia; auctore Georgio Buchanano Scoto*

Jephthes, sive votum: tragoedia; auctore Georgio Buchanano Scoto (*Jephtha*) (Buchanan) **4**:120, 128-30, 133, 136-37

Jeppe of the Hill; or, The Peasant Metamorphosed (Holberg)
See *Jeppe paa bjerget; eller, Den forvandlede bonde*

Jeppe paa bjerget; eller, Den forvandlede bonde (*Jeppe of the Hill; or, The Peasant Metamorphosed*) (Holberg) **6**:258, 271-72, 276, 278, 282, 285-86

Jerusalem Delivered (Brooke) **1**:62

The Jerusalem Sinner Saved (Bunyan) **4**:172

"Jesus Christ Gloriously Exalted" (Edwards) **7**:123

Le jeu de l'amour et du hasard (Marivaux) **4**:354, 359-60, 365, 367-70, 372-73, 377-79

Jewish History (Holberg)
See *Jødiske historie fra verdens begyndelse, fortsatt til disse tider, deelt udi svende parter...*

The Jews (Lessing)
See *Die Juden*

"Jinny the Just" (Marvell) **4**:471

"Job" (Young)
See "A Paraphrase on Part of the Book of Job"

Jødiske historie fra verdens begyndelse, fortsatt til disse tider, deelt udi svende parter... (*Jewish History*) (Holberg) **6**:282

Johann Beer: Sein Leben von ihm selbst erzählt (Beer) **5**:52

"John Anderson, My Jo" (Burns) **3**:52, 62, 78, 85

"John Barleycorn" (Burns) **3**:67

"John Smith of His Friend Master John Taylor and His Armado" (Smith) **9**:382

Johnson & Garrick (*Dialogues*) (Reynolds) **15**:388, 399

"The Jolly Beggars" (Burns) **3**:49, 61, 64, 66-9, 72-3, 75-9, 82, 84, 93, 105-06

"Jonah" (Parnell) **3**:255

Jonathan Wild (Fielding)
See *The Life of Mr. Jonathan Wild the Great*

Joseph Andrews (Fielding)
See *The History of Joseph Andrews*

Joseph Musai (Grimmelshausen) **6**:248

Joseph's Scepter (Juana Ines de la Cruz) **5**:152

"Le jour que la beauté" (Ronsard) **6**:433

Journal (Knight)
See *The Journal of Madam Knight*

Journal (Marat)
See *Le publiciste parisien, journal politique, libre et impartial . . .*

Journal du voyage de Michel de Montaigne en Italie par la Suisse et l'Allemagne en 1580 et 1581 (*Travel Journal*) (Montaigne) **8**:234-37, 246

"The Journal of a Modern Lady" (Swift) **1**:482

Journal of a Tour to the Hebrides with Samuel Johnson, LL. D. (*Hebrides Journal*) (Boswell) **4**:24-6, 31, 47, 54, 60, 75-8

The Journal of a Voyage to Lisbon (*A Voyage to Lisbon*) (Fielding) **1**:203

Journal of his Tour in the Netherlands (Reynolds)
See *Journey to Flanders and Holland in the year 1781*

The Journal of Madam Knight (*Journal*) (Knight) **7**:218-30

A Journal of the Plague Year (*A History of the Plague*) (Defoe) **1**:124, 133, 135, 140, 142, 168-70

"Journal of the Retired Citizen" (Addison) **18**:28

"Journal Sixth" (Chatterton) **3**:123

The Journal to Eliza (Sterne) **2**:393, 396, 402, 413, 422-24, 426-28, 439

The Journal to Stella (Swift) **1**:453, 463, 516-17

"The Journey" (Churchill) **3**:143, 150-51, 155-56, 163

Journey from this World to the Next (Fielding) **1**:211, 219, 221, 234

Journey of Niels Klim to the World Underground (Holberg)
See *Nicolai Klimii iter subterraneum...*

A Journey to Bath (Sheridan) **7**:369-70, 377-78

Journey to Flanders and Holland in the year 1781 (*Journal of his Tour in the Netherlands*) (Reynolds) **15**:386, 388, 390

A Journey to London (*The Provok'd Husband*) (Vanbrugh) **21**:286, 291, 293-96, 298-99, 314, 316, 319-22, 328

Journey to the Hebrides (Johnson)
See *A Journey to the Western Islands of Scotland*

Journey to the Spring (Holberg)
See *Kildereisen*

The Journey to the West (Wu Ch'eng-en)
See *Hsi-yu chi*

A Journey to the Western Islands of Scotland (*Journey to the Hebrides*) (Johnson) **15**:198-99, 208, 246, 248, 250, 297

"The Joy of Church Fellowship rightly attended" (Taylor) **11**:368

A Joyful Meditation (*A Joyful Meditation of the Coronation of Henry the Eyght*) (Hawes) **17**:346-47, 349, 352, 362

A Joyful Meditation of the Coronation of Henry the Eyght (Hawes)
See *A Joyful Meditation*

Ju-lin wai-shih (*The Forest of Scholars*) (Wu Ching-tzu) **2**:511-38

"Jubilate Agno" ("Rejoice in the Lamb") (Smart) **3**:373-74, 376, 378-80, 382, 384-86, 390, 394-400, 403

The Jubilee (Garrick) **15**:100, 122, 126

Jucundi Jucundissimi wunderliche Lebens-Beschreibung (*Jucundus Jucundissimus*) (Beer) **5**:49-51, 56

Jucundus Jucundissimus (Beer)
See *Jucundi Jucundissimi wunderliche Lebens-Beschreibung*

Die Juden (*The Jews*) (Lessing) **8**:79, 95, 112-13

The Judgment of Paris (Congreve) **5**:72

"Le jugement de Pluton" (Rousseau) **9**:345

"Jui-yun" (P'u Sung-ling) **3**:348

Launen und Phantasien (Moritz) 2:243

"Lauretta" (Marmontel) 2:214

Laus philosophiae (Ficino) 12:170, 174

Laus Stultitiae (Erasmus) 16:126-27

Lavision-Christine (*Avision*) (Christine de Pizan) 9:24, 33, 36-8, 48

The Law against Lovers (Davenant) 13:185-86, 192-93, 195, 200

Lawá'ih (*Flashes of Light*) (Jami) 9:61-2, 67-8

"The Lawne" (Herrick) 13:393

"A Lawyer" (Butler) 16:50, 55

Laylá and Majnún (Jami)
  See *Lailá u Majnún*

"The Layman's Lamentations upon the Civil Death of the Late Laborers in the Lord's Vineyard, by way of Dialogue between a Proud Prelate and a Poor Professour Silenced on Bartholomew Day, 1662" (Taylor) 11:365-66

"Laziness" (Wycherley) 8:380

"The Lea-Rig" (Burns) 3:85

The Learned Ladies (Moliere)
  See *Les femmes savantes*

"A Lecture upon the Shadow" (Donne) 10:18, 52

Lectures on Genesis (Luther) 9:136

"The Legacie" (Donne) 10:26

Legend (Chaucer)
  See *Legend of Good Women*

Legend of Good Women (*Book of the Five and Twenty Ladies*; *Legend*; *Legende of Good Women*; *Testament of Love*) (Chaucer) 17:45-6, 71, 87, 97, 106, 108, 123, 201, 213-18, 229

Legende of Good Women (Chaucer)
  See *Legend of Good Women*

The Legends (Drayton) 8:10, 14, 33

"The Legion Club" (Swift) 1:513, 524

Legion's Memorial (Defoe) 1:161

Le legs (Marivaux) 4:354, 358, 363, 365, 368-69

La Lena (Ariosto) 6:61

"Lenvoy de Chaucer a Bukton" (Chaucer) 17:236

Lessing's Masonic Dialogues (*Dialogues of Freemasons*) (Lessing) 8:61

"Let us pretend I am happy" (Juana Ines de la Cruz)
  See "Finjamos que soy feliz"

"Letanie" (Herrick)
  See "Litany"

Lethe, or Esop in the Shades (Garrick) 15:98, 101-02, 111-14

Letter (More)
  See *Aunswere to Frithes Letter agaynst the Blessed Sacramen of the Aulter*

"Letter and Discourse to Henry Sevill Touching Helps for the Intellecual Powers" (Bacon) 18:187

"Letter Concerning Humour in Comedy" ("Concerning Humour in Comedy") (Congreve) 5:92, 97, 104-05

A Letter concerning Toleration, Humbly Submitted (Locke) 7:290

A Letter from Edmund Burke, Esq., One of the Representatives in Parliament for the City of Bristol, to John Farr and John Harris, Esqrs., Sheriffs of That City, on the Affairs of America (Burke) 7:39

Letter from Italy (Addison) 18:19

A Letter from Mr. Burke, to a Member of the National Assembly: In Answer to Some Objections to His Book on French Affairs (*A Letter to a Member of the National Assembly*) (Burke) 7:8, 24, 47, 57

A Letter from the Right Honourable Edmund Burke to a Noble Lord, on the Attacks Made upon Him and His Pension, in the House of Lords (Burke) 7:14, 23, 41-2, 47, 59, 61-2

Letter from Thrasybulus to Leucippus (Holbach) 14:167

Letter Impugning Frith (More) 10:436

Letter of Advice to the Earl of Rutland on His Travels (Bacon) 18:133

The Letter of Cupid (Christine de Pizan)
  See *L'epistre au dieu d'amours*

"Letter on Ancient and Modern Tragedy" (Schlegel)
  See "Schreiben an den Herrn N. N. über die Komödie in Versen"

Letter on French Music (Rousseau) 14:286

Letter on the Present Character of the French Nation (Wollstonecraft) 5:426

A Letter to a Member of the National Assembly (Burke)
  See *A Letter from Mr. Burke, to a Member of the National Assembly: In Answer to Some Objections to His Book on French Affairs*

"Letter to Chesterfield" (Johnson)
  See *The Celebrated Letter from Samuel Johnson, LL.D. to Philip Dormer Stanhope, Earl of Chesterfield*

A Letter to Dr. Holdsworth (Trotter) 8:362

"Letter to G.N. from Wrest" ("To my friend G.N. from Wrest") (Carew) 13:17, 32, 59-61

"Letter to Lord Chesterfield" (Johnson)
  See *The Celebrated Letter from Samuel Johnson, LL.D. to Philip Dormer Stanhope, Earl of Chesterfield*

Letter to M. d'Alembert on the Theatre (Rousseau)
  See *Lettre à d'Alembert sur les spectacles*

A Letter to Mr. Harding (Swift) 1:515

"Letter to Mr. Pope" ("To Mr. Pope") (Parnell) 3:250-51

"Letter to Raleigh" (Spenser) 5:364-65

A Letter to Shopkeepers (Swift) 1:515

Letter to the Reader (Erasmus)
  See *De Utilitate Colloquiorum*

Letter to the Reverend Mr. Douglas, Occasioned by his Vindication of Milton (Johnson) 15:306

A Letter to the Whole People of Ireland (Swift) 1:515

Letter to William Elliot (Burke) 7:23, 61-2

Lettere (Tasso) 5:394

Letters (Aretino) 12:4-6, 18, 31, 34, 36-8

Letters (Dennis)
  See *Original Letters, Familiar, Moral and Critical*

Letters (Erasmus) 16:167

Letters (Ficino) 12:174

Letters (Frederick the Great) 14:58

Letters (Gray)
  See *The Letters of Thomas Gray*

Letters (Howell)
  See *Epistolae Ho-Elianae: Familiar Letters Domestic and Forren*

Letters (Lyttelton)

See *Letters from a Persian in England to His Friend at Ispahan*

Letters (Sevigne)
  See *Lettres de Mme de Sévigné, de sa famille et de ses amis*

Letters (Sevigne)
  See *Lettres choisies de Mme la marquise de Sévignéà Mme de Grignan sa fille qui contiennent beaucoup de particularitiés de l'histoire de Louis XIV*

Letters (Wollstonecraft)
  See *Letters Written during a Short Residence in Sweden, Norway, and Denmark*

The Letters and the Life of Francis Bacon, Including all His Occasional Works (Bacon) 18:188, 190

The Letters and Works of Lady Mary Wortley Montagu (Montagu)
  See *The Works of the Right Honourable Lady Mary Wortley Montague*

Letters between the Honourable Andrew Erskine and James Boswell, Esq. (Boswell) 4:15, 57

Letters concerning Contemporary Literature (Lessing)
  See *Literaturbrief*

Letters concerning the English Nation (*Lettres philosophiques*) (Voltaire) 14:350, 364, 380, 383, 390, 393, 403-04

Letters concerning Toleration (Locke) 7:252, 285, 290

Letters during the Embassy (Montagu)
  See *Letters of the Right Honourable Lady Mary Wortley Montague*

Letters from a Persian in England to His Friend at Ispahan (*Letters*; *The Persian Letters*) (Lyttelton) 10:196, 198, 200, 202-07, 209-10, 212-13

Letters from Juliet, Lady Catesby, to Her Friend, Lady Henrietta Campley (*Lady Juliet Catesby*) (Brooke) 6:108, 110

Letters from Mrs. Delany (Widow of Doctor Patrick Delany) to Mrs. Frances Hamilton (Delany) 12:133-34

"Letters from the Devil" (Munford) 5:192

Letters from the Mountains (Rousseau)
  See *Lettres de la montagne*

Letters from Yorick to Eliza (Sterne) 2:424

Letters of Advice to Queen Elizabeth (Bacon) 18:133

Letters of King Henry VIII: A Selection, with Other Documents (Henry VIII) 10:124

Letters of Obscure Men (Hutten)
  See *Literæ obscurorum Vivorum*

Letters of Sir Joshua Reynolds (Reynolds) 15:400

Letters of the Right Honourable Lady Mary Wortley Montague (*Letters during the Embassy*) (Montagu) 9:273, 276, 283-84, 286

The Letters of Thomas Gray (*Letters*) (Gray) 4:295-96, 310-11

Letters of Two Lovers (Rousseau)
  See *La Nouvelle Héloïse*

Letters on the Genius and Writings of Shakespeare (Dennis)
  See *An Essay on the Genius of Shakespear*

Letters on the History of England (Goldsmith) 2:71

The Letters, Speeches and Proclamations of King Charles I (Charles I) 13:144

Letters to a Young Clergyman (Swift) 1:471

Letters to Clarinda, by Robert Burns (Burns)
3:50

Letters to Eugénie; or, Preservative Against Prejudice (Holbach)
See *Lettres à Eugénie*

Letters to Horace Walpole (Walpole) 2:452, 456, 464-66, 484, 491-94

Letters to Imlay (*Posthumous Works of the Author of a Vindication of the Rights of Woman*) (Wollstonecraft) 5:424, 426, 443-44, 458

Letters to Mrs. Bunbury (Goldsmith) 2:74

Letters to Severall Personages (Donne) 10:53, 83

Letters Written by Mrs. Manley (*A Stage-Coach Journey to Exeter*) (Manley) 1:307-09, 313

Letters Written during a Short Residence in Sweden, Norway, and Denmark (*Letters*) (Wollstonecraft) 5:418, 426, 443, 448, 450-52, 461

Lettre à d'Alembert sur les spectacles (*Letter to M. d'Alembert on the Theatre*) (Rousseau) 14:247, 290-93, 297, 301

Lettre à M. de Beaumont (Rousseau) 14:247

Lettre de l'imposteur (Moliere) 10:316

Lettre d'un Turc (Voltaire) 14:380

Lettres (Sevigne)
See *Lettres de Mme de Sévigné, de sa famille et de ses amis*

Lettres à Eugénie (*Letters to Eugénie; or, Preservative Against Prejudice*) (Holbach) 14:153, 168

Lettres choisies de Mme la marquise de Sévignéà Mme de Grignan sa fille qui contiennent beaucoup de particularitiés de l'histoire de Louis XIV (*Letters*) (Sevigne) 11:301, 315

"Les lettres contenant une aventure" (Marivaux) 4:378-79

Lettres d'Amabed (Voltaire) 14:345-46

Les lettres d'Annabel (Voltaire) 14:359

*Lettres de la Duchesse de*** au Duc de**** (Crebillon) 1:86

*Lettres de la Marquise de M*** au Comte de R**** (Crebillon) 1:86, 88

Lettres de la montagne (*Letters from the Mountains*) (Rousseau) 14:247, 288

Lettres de la Vénérable Mère Marie de l'Incarnation (*Correspondance; Spiritual Letters*) (Marie de l'Incarnation) 10:245, 247, 249, 251

Lettres de Mme de Sévigné, de sa famille et de ses amis (*Letters; Lettres*) (Sevigne) 11:301, 315, 336-38

Lettres persanes (*Persian Letters*) (Montesquieu) 7:309-11, 313, 317, 319-25, 327, 339-40, 342-45, 347-49, 356-58, 360, 362-63

Lettres philosophiques (Holbach) 14:153

Lettres philosophiques (Voltaire)
See *Letters concerning the English Nation*

"Les lettres sur les habitants de Paris" (Marivaux) 4:378

Lexicon Tetraglotton: An English-French-Italian-Spanish Dictionary (Howell) 13:427

Liao-chai chih-i (*Strange Stories from a Chinese Studio*) (P'u Sung-ling) 3:342-49, 353-55

"Libel Summons" ("The Court of Equity") (Burns) 3:99

Libell über die Pest (*Pamphlet on the Plague*) (Paracelsus) 14:199

"The Liberal Lover" (Cervantes)
See "El amante liberal"

De Libero Arbitro (*On Free Will*) (Erasmus) 16:155, 193

Liberty (Thomson) 16:363, 369, 374, 382, 384, 386, 388, 395, 406-07, 421, 423

"Liberty and Peace" (Wheatley) 3:409-11, 416, 432, 435

Liberty Asserted (Dennis) 11:12

Libra astronomica y philosophica (*Astronomical Libra*) (Siguenza y Gongora) 8:339-42

Libro de las fundaciones de Santa Teresa de Jesús (*Book of foundations*) (Teresa de Jesus) 18:389, 391, 393

Libro de su vida (*The Life of the Mother Teresa of Jesus*) (Teresa de Jesus) 18:389, 391, 392, 397-98, 400-03, 405-06, 409-18

Libro della arte della guerra (*The Art of War*) (Machiavelli) 8:128, 133, 171-73, 178

"El licienciado vidriera" ("The Glass Scholar") (Cervantes) 6:171-73, 176-77

"Lien-hua Kung-chu" ("Princess Lotus Bloom") (P'u Sung-ling) 3:350

Life (Casanova de Seingalt)
See *Mémoires de J. Casanova de Seingalt écrits par lui-même*

Life (Equiano)
See *The Interesting Narrative of the Life of Olaudah Equiano, or Gustavus Vassa, the African*

The Life, Adventures, and Pyracies of the Famous Captain Singleton (*Captain Singleton*) (Defoe) 1:126, 133, 139-40, 142, 147, 174-75

The Life and Adventures of the Lady Lucy, the Daughter of an Irish Lord (Aubin) 9:3-4, 8-9, 14-15

The Life and Adventures of the Young Count Albertus, the Son of Count Lewis Augustus, by the Lady Lucy (Aubin) 9:3-4, 8

The Life and Amorous Adventures of Lucinda, an English Lady (Aubin) 9:4, 17

Life and Correspondence (Delany)
See *The Autobiography and Correspondence of Mary Granville (Mrs. Delany)*

The Life and Death of Mr. Badman (*Badman*) (Bunyan) 4:156, 159, 161, 163-64, 166-67, 169, 172, 178-79, 190, 202-03

The Life and Death of Sir Thomas Moore (Roper)
See *The Mirrour of Vertue in Worldly Greatnes; or, The Life of syr Thomas More Knight*

The Life and Opinions of Tristram Shandy, Gentleman (*Tristram Shandy*) (Sterne) 2:372-83, 385-96, 398-426, 428-41

The Life and Strange Surprising Adventures of Robinson Crusoe, of York, Mariner (Defoe) 1:118-19, 122-26, 130-31, 134, 137-40, 142-47, 152, 155, 159, 163-74, 176-78

The Life of Charlotta du Pont, an English Lady (Aubin) 9:4-6, 9, 17-18

Life of Christ (Aretino)
See *L'Humanità di Christo*

"Life of Cowley" (Johnson) 15:215, 231-32, 241

The Life of David Hume, Esq., Written by Himself (Hume) 7:146

Life of Destouches (Lessing) 8:101

"Life of Dryden" (Johnson) 15:270, 312

Life of Johan Picus, Earl of Mirandula (*The Life of Pico della Mirandula; Life of Picus*) (More) 10:366, 429, 431-32, 435

Life of Johnson (Boswell)
See *The Life of Samuel Johnson, LL. D.*

The Life of Kinge Richarde the Thirde (*Historia Ricardi Tertii; The History of Richard III; Life of Richard III; Richarde the thirde*) (More) 10:364, 369-70, 372, 378, 395, 409, 415-16, 419-20, 429-31, 433-34, 450

The Life of Madam de Beaumount, a French Lady Who Lived in a Cave in Wales above Fourteen Years Undiscovered... (Aubin) 9:3, 7, 9-13, 17-18

Life of Marianne (Marivaux)
See *La vie de Marianne; ou, Les aventures de Mme la Comtesse de****

Life of Molière (Voltaire) 14:339

Life of More (Roper)
See *The Mirrour of Vertue in Worldly Greatnes; or, The Life of syr Thomas More Knight*

The Life of Mr. Jonathan Wild the Great (*The History of Jonathan Wild the Great; Jonathan Wild*) (Fielding) 1:211, 214, 216-18, 221-22, 226-30, 233, 242-44, 255, 260-63

The Life of Mrs. Christian Davies (Defoe) 1:146

The Life of Olaudah Equiano (Equiano)
See *The Interesting Narrative of the Life of Olaudah Equiano, or Gustavus Vassa, the African*

The Life of Pico della Mirandula (More)
See *Life of Johan Picus, Earl of Mirandula*

Life of Picus (More)
See *Life of Johan Picus, Earl of Mirandula*

Life of Plautus (Lessing) 8:101

"The Life of Plutarch" (Parnell) 3:237

"Life of Pope" (Johnson) 15:270-71

Life of Richard III (More)
See *The Life of Kinge Richarde the Thirde*

Life of Saint Catherine (Aretino)
See *Vita di santa Caterina da Siena*

Life of Saint Thomas Aquinas (Aretino) 12:13, 36

The Life of Samuel Johnson, LL. D. (*Life of Johnson*) (Boswell) 4:18-19, 21-6, 30, 36-7, 39-41, 46-8, 50, 53-4, 56-60, 65-71, 75, 77-9

"Life of Savage" (Johnson)
See *An Account of the Life of Mr. Richard Savage, Son of Earl Rivers*

Life of Shakespeare (Rowe)
See *Account of the Life of Shakespear*

Life of Sophocles (Lessing) 8:101, 109-10

The Life of the Countess de Gondez (Aubin) 9:6

The Life of the Mother Teresa of Jesus (Teresa de Jesus)
See *Libro de su vida*

"The Life of the Soul" (More)
See "Psychozoia: or, A Christiano-Platonicall Display of Life"

Life of the Virgin Mary (Aretino) 12:13, 36

The Life of Thomas More (Roper)
See *The Mirrour of Vertue in Worldly Greatnes; or, The Life of syr Thomas More Knight*

"Life of Waller" (Johnson) 15:225, 230

"Life of Watts" (Johnson) 15:225

Life's Progress through the Passions; or, The Adventures of Natura (Haywood) 1:291

Lilliput (Garrick) 15:101-03, 123-24

"The Lilly in a Cristal" (Herrick) 13:350-51, 369, 380-82, 392-94

Limberham; or, The Kind Keeper (*Mr. Limberham*) (Dryden)   **3**:222, 229-30; **21**:55

"Lines by Ladgate" (Chatterton)   **3**:119

"Lines to Sour-Faced Gila" (Juana Ines de la Cruz)   **5**:146

"Lines Written in Mezeray" (Prior)
  See "Written in the Beginning of Mezeray's History of France"

"Lisetta's Reply" (Prior)   **4**:461, 466

"The Litanie" (Donne)   **10**:40, 56, 84, 92

"Litany" ("Letanie") (Herrick)   **13**:317, 320, 334, 336-38

Litany to the Germans (Hutten)   **16**:234

"Litany to the Holy Spirit" ("His Letanie, to the Holy Spirit"; "His Litany to the Holy Spirit") (Herrick)   **13**:314, 319, 328, 342, 357

Literæ obscurorum Vivorum (*Epistolæ Obscurorum Vivorum*; *Letters of Obscure Men*; *Obscure Men*) (Hutten)   **16**:212, 214-15, 218-25, 228, 230-33, 235-37, 245

Literaturbrief (*Letters concerning Contemporary Literature*) (Lessing)   **8**:70, 98, 100, 103-04, 106, 109-12, 115

"A Litigious Man" (Butler)   **16**:50

Little Female Academy (Fielding)
  See *The Governess; or, Little Female Academy*

The Little Garden of Roses (Kempis)
  See *Hortulus rosarii de valle lachrymarum continens egreias & devotas sentecias*

"Little Red Riding Hood" (Perrault)
  See "Le petit chaperon rouge"

The Little Surgery (Paracelsus)
  See *Chirurgia minor quam Bertheoneam intitulaut*

"Little T. C." (Marvell)
  See "The Picture of Little T. C. in a Prospect of Flowers"

"La liturgie de Cythère" (Rousseau)   **9**:345

The Lives of Cleopatra and Octavia (Fielding)   **1**:273

Lives of Do-wel, Do-bet, and Do-best (Langland)
  See *Piers Plowman*

The Lives of the Poets (Johnson)
  See *Prefaces, Biographical and Critical, to the Works of the English Poets*

"Living Flame of Love" (John of the Cross)
  See "Llama de amor viva"

The Living Flame of Love (John of the Cross)
  See *Llama de Amor Viva*

Le livre de la cité des dames (*The Boke of the Cyte of Ladies*) (Christine de Pizan)   **9**:23, 25, 28, 33-4, 38-9, 44-5

Le livre de la mutacion de fortune (Christine de Pizan)   **9**:24, 28, 34-5, 38-9, 48

Le livre de la paix (Christine de Pizan)   **9**:25, 48

Livre de la prod'hommie de l'homme (Christine de Pizan)   **9**:48

Le livre des fais et bonnes meurs du sage roy Charles V (Christine de Pizan)   **9**:23-4, 26, 48

Le livre des faits d'armes et de chevalerie (*The Book of Fayttes of Armes and of Chyvalrye*) (Christine de Pizan)   **9**:23, 25, 28-9, 35, 45, 47

Le livre du chemin de long estude (*The Long Road of Learning*) (Christine de Pizan)   **9**:24, 27, 46, 48

Le livre du corps de policie (*The Body of Polycye*) (Christine de Pizan)   **9**:25, 46-8

Le livre du dit de Poissy (*The Debate of Poissy*) (Christine de Pizan)   **9**:28, 41, 43

Le livre du duc des vrais amans (*The Book of the Duke of True Lovers*) (Christine de Pizan)   **9**:27, 42, 48

"Livret de Folastries" (Ronsard)   **6**:417, 431

"Llama de amor viva" ("Living Flame of Love") (John of the Cross)   **18**:213, 216-17, 222, 224

Llama de Amor Viva (*The Living Flame of Love*) (John of the Cross)   **18**:202, 205, 221, 229-30

Loa a los años del rey (Juana Ines de la Cruz)   **5**:159

Loa en las huertas donde fue a divertirse la Excelentísima Señora Condesa de Paredes, Marquesa de la Laguna (Juana Ines de la Cruz)   **5**:159

La locandiera (Goldoni)   **4**:262, 264, 267, 273-74

The Logick Primer (Eliot)
  See *The Logick Primer, Some Logical Notions to Initiate the Indians in Knowledge of the Rule of Reason; and to Know How to Make Use Thereof*

The Logick Primer, Some Logical Notions to Initiate the Indians in Knowledge of the Rule of Reason; and to Know How to Make Use Thereof (*The Logick Primer*) (Eliot)   **5**:132, 134-35

Londinopolis; An Historical Discourse or Perlustration of the City of London (Howell)   **13**:424

"London: A Poem, In Imitation of the Third Satire of Juvenal" (Johnson)   **15**:187-90, 194, 206, 288, 291-95, 302-05

London Journal (Boswell)
  See *Boswell's London Journal*

The Long Road of Learning (Christine de Pizan)
  See *Le livre du chemin de long estude*

"A Long Story" (Gray)   **4**:301, 312, 315-17, 333-34

"Longing for Heaven" (Bradstreet)   **4**:85, 112

"A Looking-Glasse" (Carew)   **13**:28

"Lord Daer" (Burns)
  See "Meeting with Lord Daer"

"The Loss of his Mistresses" (Herrick)   **13**:337

The Lost Lover; or, A Jealous Husband (Manley)   **1**:315

Love and a Bottle (*Love in a Bottle*) (Farquhar)   **21**:128, 135-36, 139-40, 145-46, 148, 150-52, 154, 161-63, 170, 176

Love and Business (Farquhar)   **21**:130, 133, 142

Love and Honor (Davenant)   **13**:175-77, 181, 192, 196, 215

Love at a Loss; or, Most Votes Carry It (Trotter)   **8**:355, 357, 361, 368-69, 372-74

"Love Banish'd Heav'n, in Earth Was Held in Scorne" (Drayton)
  See "Sonnet 23"

"Love-Begotten Daughter" (Burns)
  See "A Poet's Welcome to His Love-Begotten Daughter"

"Love Disarm'd" (Prior)   **4**:459

Love Elegies (Donne)
  See *Elegies*

Love for Love (Congreve)   **5**:66, 68, 70-1, 74, 76, 78-9, 81, 83, 84, 86-90, 92, 94, 96-101, 105-06, 109, 111; **21**:4, 9-10, 15, 17, 22-3, 25-7, 29-32, 40-1, 43

Love in a Bottle (Farquhar)
  See *Love and a Bottle*

"Love, in a Humor, Play'd the Prodigall" (Drayton)
  See "Sonnet 7"

Love in a Wood; or, St. James's Park (Wycherley)   **8**:384, 388, 390-92, 395, 397, 402, 407, 410, 432-34; **21**:351-52, 354, 356, 359-60, 370-73, 376-78, 380-81, 391, 396-97

Love in Excess; or, The Fatal Enquiry (Haywood)   **1**:284-85, 290, 292, 295-300

"Love in Fantastic Triumph Sat" (Behn)   **1**:31, 38

Love in Several Masques (Fielding)   **1**:250

Love Letters between a Nobleman and His Sister (Behn)   **1**:34, 43, 48

Love-Letters from King Henry VIII. to Anne Boleyn (Henry VIII)   **10**:119

Love Letters to a Gentleman (Behn)   **1**:38

"The Love of Fame" (Young)
  See "The Universal Passion; or, The Love of Fame"

Love, the Greater Labyrinth (Juana Ines de la Cruz)
  See *Amor es más laberinto*

Love Triumphant (Dryden)   **3**:230

The Lover (Steele)   **18**:354

"Lover and the Maiden" (Erasmus)   **16**:140

"A Lover's Anger" (Prior)   **4**:460

"Lovers infinitenesse" ("If yet I have not all thy love") (Donne)   **10**:36, 82

Lovers' Spite (Moliere)
  See *Le dépit amoureux*

The Lover's Watch (Behn)   **1**:41

"Loves Alchymie" (Donne)   **10**:82

"Loves Deitie" (Donne)   **10**:26, 81

"Loves Growth" (Donne)   **10**:18, 57

"Loves Usury" (Donne)   **10**:52

"Lu p'an" (P'u Sung-ling)   **3**:350

"Lucia" (Young)   **3**:472

"Lucius" (Prior)   **4**:455

The Luckey Chance; or, An Alderman's Bargain (Behn)   **1**:27-9, 34, 37, 40-1, 47-8

The Lucky Mistake (Behn)   **1**:32, 46, 51-2

Luminalia (Davenant)   **13**:189

Luminis Naturalis (Bacon)   **18**:187

"Lung-fei hsiang Kung" ("Minister Dragon's Flight") (P'u Sung-ling)   **3**:350

Lung-hu feng-yün hui (Lo Kuan-chung)   **12**:282

"Le lutrin" (Boileau-Despreaux)   **3**:16-17, 19, 21-2, 24, 29, 37-43

"The Luxury of Vain Imagination" (Johnson)
  See *The Rambler, 89*

"Lycidas" (Milton)   **9**:177, 197, 199, 203-11, 213, 229-30, 238-41, 243

Lycidus (Behn)   **1**:41

The Lyfe of Sir Thomas Moore, Knighte (Roper)
  See *The Mirrour of Vertue in Worldly Greatnes; or, The Life of syr Thomas More Knight*

The Lying-in Room (Holberg)
  See *Barselstuen*

The Lying Lover (Steele)   **18**:314-15, 330, 333, 338-40, 346, 348, 353-54, 359, 364-66, 371

The Lying Valet (Garrick)   **15**:98, 100-01, 113, 121, 124

Det lykkelige skibbrud (Holberg)   **6**:263, 278

Lykken bedre end Forstanden (Wessel)   **7**:390

"La Lyre" (Ronsard)   **6**:427-28

"A Lyrick to Mirth" (Herrick)   **13**:365

Macbeth (Davenant)   **13**:185-87, 212 214-16

Macbeth (Johnson)
   See *Miscellaneous Observations on the
     Tragedy of Macbeth*

*MacFlecknoe; or, A Satire upon the Trew-Blew-
   Protestant Poet, T. S.* (Dryden)   **3**:189, 192,
   199, 205, 212, 222, 231, 242; **21**:51-2, 66, 83,
   90-2, 94, 111, 113

"Macphersons' Farewell" (Burns)   **3**:60

"The Mad Maid's Song" (Herrick)   **13**:319-20,
   324, 326, 332, 336-37

Madagascar; With Other Poems (Davenant)
   13:204-05

La madre amorosa (Goldoni)   **4**:260

Magazin zur Erfahrungsseelenkunde (Moritz)
   2:236

The Magic Bird's Nest (Grimmelshausen)
   See *Das wunderbarliche Vogelnest (I and II)*

*Magnalia naturae praecipue quoad usus
   humanos (Great Works of Nature for the
   Particular Use of Mankind)* (Bacon)   **18**:152

The Magnetic Lady (Jonson)   **6**:306, 311, 314,
   327, 339

The Magnificent Lovers (Moliere)
   See *Les amants magnifiques*

Mahomet (Defoe)   **1**:162

Mahomet (Voltaire)   **14**:328, 397

Mahomet and Irene (Johnson)
   See *Irene: A Tragedy*

"Mailie's Dying Words and Elegy" (Burns)
   See "The Death and Dying Words of Poor
     Mailie"

"Le maître chat; ou, Le chat botté" (Perrault)
   2:254, 257-58, 260, 266-71, 280-81, 284

Le malade imaginaire (The Imaginary Invalid)
   (Moliere)   **10**:270, 272, 274-75, 282-83, 285-
   86, 290-91, 299, 304, 306, 313, 318, 327-29,
   336, 339

*The Male Coquette (The Modern Fine
   Gentleman)* (Garrick)   **15**:98, 101-03

Malpiglio (Tasso)   **5**:407

*Mamusse wunneetupanatamwe Up-Biblum God
   Naneeswe Nukkone Testament Kah Wonk
   Wusku Testament (The Holy Bible:
   Containing the Old Testament and the New)*
   (Eliot)   **5**:124, 126-28, 130-32, 134

Man (Marat)
   See *A Philosophical Essay on Man, Being an
     Attempt to Investigate the Principles and
     Laws of the Reciprocal Influence of the
     Soul on the Body*

The Man in the Moone (Drayton)   **8**:14, 17,
   27, 32, 34, 36-7

"Man Naturally God's Enemies" (Edwards)
   7:98

The Man of Discretion (Gracian y Morales)
   See *El Discreto*

"Man of Lawe's Tale" (Chaucer)
   See "Man of Law's Tale"

"Man of Law's Prologue" (Chaucer)   **17**:214

"Man of Law's Tale" ("Man of Lawe's Tale")
   (Chaucer)   **17**:60, 63, 83, 119, 176, 196,
   205, 232, 237

"Man Was Made to Mourn" (Burns)   **3**:48,
   52, 67, 74, 87

The Man with Forty Ecus (Voltaire)
   See *L'homme aux quarante écus*

"Manciple's Tale" (Chaucer)   **17**:173

Mandragola (Machiavelli)
   See *Commedia di Callimaco: E di Lucretia*

The Mandrake (Grimmelshausen)
   See *Das Galgen-Männlin*

Manductio ad Stoicam philosophiam (Lipsius)
   See *Manductionis ad philosophiam stoicam
     libri tres*

*Manductionis ad philosophiam stoicam libri tres
   (Manductio ad Stoicam philosophiam; Stoic
   Philosophy)* (Lipsius)   **16**:257-58

Manifest (Siguenza y Gongora)
   See *Manifesto philosophico contra los cometas
     despojados del imperio que tenian sobre los
     timidos*

*Manifesto philosophico contra los cometas
   despojados del imperio que tenian sobre los
   timidos (Manifest)* (Siguenza y Gongora)
   8:341-42

"Manliness" (Donne)   **10**:95

"Manne, Womanne, Syr Rogerre" (Collins)
   4:214, 229, 231, 237, 239-43

"Man's Injustice toward Providence"
   (Winchilsea)   **3**:451

The Man's the Master (Davenant)   **13**:186-87,
   189

Manual of Metaphysics (More)   **9**:297

Manual of the Christian Knight (Erasmus)
   See *Enchiridion militis christiani*

The Manual Oracle and Art of Prudence
   (Gracian y Morales)
   See *Oráculo manual y arte de prudencia*

*Map of the Bay and the Rivers, with an
   Annexed Relation of the Countries and
   Nations That Inhabit Them* (Smith)
   See *A Map of Virginia. With a Description of
     the Countrey, the Commodities, People,
     Government, and Religion*

*A Map of Virginia. With a Description of the
   Countrey, the Commodities, People,
   Government, and Religion (Map of the Bay
   and the Rivers, with an Annexed Relation of
   the Countries and Nations That Inhabit
   Them)* (Smith)   **9**:352, 355, 357, 359, 374,
   380-81, 383

Marcus heroicum (Hutten)   **16**:238, 241

*Marescalco (The Farrier, The Horse Doctor,
   The Stablemaster)* (Aretino)   **12**:19, 26-7,
   29-30, 35-7

Marfisa (Aretino)   **12**:35

"Le mari sylphide" (Marmontel)   **2**:212

Maria (Wollstonecraft)
   See *The Wrongs of Woman; or, Maria*

"Maria Wentworth" (Carew)   **13**:48

Le mariage forcé (The Forced Marriage)
   (Moliere)   **10**:283, 287, 311

Mariamne (Voltaire)   **14**:397

Marian: A Comic Opera, in Two Acts (Brooke)
   6:107-09

Marmor Norfolciense (Johnson)   **15**:206

Marriage-á-la-Mode (Dryden)   **3**:208, 210,
   214, 222, 230-33

Marriage as Retribution (P'u Sung-ling)
   See *Hsing-shih yin-yuan chuan*

A Marriage Booklet for Simple Pastors (Luther)
   9:151

The Marriage Contract (Brooke)   **1**:63

"A Marriage in Name Only, or the Unequal
   Match" (Erasmus)
   See "Marriage that was no Marriage"

"Marriage that was no Marriage" ("A
   Marriage in Name Only, or the Unequal
   Match") (Erasmus)   **16**:141, 193

Martin Mar-All (Dryden)
   See *Sir Martin Mar-All; or, The Feign'd
     Innocence*

El mártir de Sacramento (Juana Ines de la
   Cruz)   **5**:158

Mary: A Fiction (Wollstonecraft)   **5**:426-28,
   442-43, 453, 460-61

"Mary Blaize" (Goldsmith)   **2**:74

"Mary in Heaven" (Burns)
   See "To Mary in Heaven"

"Mary Morison" (Burns)   **3**:71, 78, 87

Mascarade (Maskarade) (Holberg)   **6**:259, 269,
   277

Masculine Birth of Time (Bacon)
   See *Temporis partus masculus*

Mask of Comus (Milton)
   See *Comus: A Maske*

Mask of Semele (Semele) (Congreve)   **5**:72;
   21:44

Maskarade (Holberg)
   See *Mascarade*

"Le masque de Laverne" (Rousseau)   **9**:345

Masque of Beauty (Beautie) (Jonson)   **6**:338

Masque of Blacknesse (Blacknesse) (Jonson)
   6:321, 337-38

The Masque of Queens (Queenes) (Jonson)
   6:315, 337, 339

Masques (Jonson)   **6**:323

Le massere (Goldoni)   **4**:264-66

The Master Critic (Gracian y Morales)
   See *El Criticón*

"Master Herrick's Farewell unto Poetry"
   (Herrick)
   See "Farewell to Poetry"

"The Match" (Marvell)   **4**:403, 408

*Mathematical Bellerophon against the
   Astrological Chimera of Don Martin de la
   Torre, etc.* (Siguenza y Gongora)   **8**:341

"A Mathematician" (Butler)   **16**:50

"Matilda the Faire" (Drayton)   **8**:30, 33

Maximes (Gracian y Morales)   **15**:142

May Day (Garrick)   **15**:121

"The Maypole is up" (Herrick)   **13**:331, 364

"Me Thinks I See Some Crooked Mimicke
   Jeere" (Drayton)
   See "Sonnet 31"

"The Medall. A Satire Against Sedition"
   (Dryden)   **3**:187, 199, 222, 234-35, 240;
   21:51, 57, 59, 65, 68, 86, 90

Medea (Buchanan)
   See *Medea Euripidis poetae tragici Georgio
     Buchanano Scoto interprete*

*Medea Euripidis poetae tragici Georgio
   Buchanano Scoto interprete (Medea)*
   (Buchanan)   **4**:134-35

*Le médecin malgré lui (The Doctor in spite of
   Himself)* (Moliere)   **10**:278, 283, 291, 312,
   327

Le médecin volant (The Flying Doctor)
   (Moliere)   **10**:281, 283, 309, 314, 327

"A Medicine-Taker" (Butler)   **16**:50

Medico olandese (Goldoni)   **4**:259

"Meditation 7" (Taylor)   **11**:360

"Meditation 19" (Taylor)   **11**:360

"Meditation 30" (Taylor)   **11**:360

"Meditation 77" (Taylor)   **11**:359

"Meditation Eight" (Taylor)   **11**:351-52

"A Meditation for his Mistresse" (Herrick)
   13:364

"Meditation One" (Taylor)   **11**:349

"Meditation Six" (Taylor)   **11**:356

Meditationes sobre el Cantar (Teresa de Jesus) **18**:400-05

Meditationis Sacrae (Bacon) **18**:149

"Meditations" (Bradstreet)
See "Meditations Divine and Moral"

Meditations (Taylor) **11**:344, 347-48, 355, 359, 365, 367-68, 373, 376-77, 382-84, 396

"Meditations Divine and Moral" ("Meditations") (Bradstreet) **4**:96-7, 99-100, 114

"Meditations upon an Egg" (Bunyan) **4**:182

The Meeting of the Company; or, Baye's Art of Acting (Garrick) **15**:100, 102, 122

"Meeting with Lord Daer" ("Lord Daer") (Burns) **3**:71, 86

Melampe (Melampus) (Holberg) **6**:259, 277

Melampus (Holberg)
See *Melampe*

Mélanges (Voltaire) **14**:337, 367

"Melibee" (Chaucer)
See "Tale of Melibee"

"Melibeus" (Chaucer) **17**:169

Mélicerte (Moliere) **10**:275, 283

Memnon; ou, La sagesse humaine (Voltaire) **14**:346, 398

"Memoir" (Boswell) **4**:61

Mémoire d'un honnête homme (Mémoires d'un honnête homme) (Prevost) **1**:343-44

Mémoire sur les jugements de Dieu (Duclos) **1**:186

Memoires (Voltaire) **14**:364

Mémoires de J. Casanova de Seingalt écrits par lui-même (Histoire de ma Vie jusqu'à l'an 1797; History of My Life; Life) (Casanova de Seingalt) **13**:76, 78, 80-7, 89-93, 95-6, 98, 103-11, 113-18, 121, 123, 126

Mémoires de ma vie (Perrault) **2**:277, 283

Les Mémoires de M. de Montcal (Prevost) **1**:335, 337

Mémoires de M. Goldoni, pour servir à l'histoire de sa vie, et à celle de son théâtre (Goldoni) **4**:255, 262-64, 268, 275

Mémoires d'un honnête homme (Prevost)
See *Mémoire d'un honnête homme*

Mémoires d'un père pour servir à l'instruction de ses enfans (Memoirs of Marmontel) (Marmontel) **2**:208-12, 221, 223

Mémoires et aventures d'un homme de qualité, qui s'est retiré du monde (Prevost) **1**:327, 329, 333-37, 343-44, 347, 351-52, 356

Memoires of the Last Ten Years of the Reign of George the Second (Walpole) **2**:453-54, 456, 481-82, 485-88, 498

Memoires of the Navy (Pepys)
See *Memoires relating to the State of the Royal Navy*

Memoires of the Royal Navy, 1679-88 (Pepys)
See *Memoires relating to the State of the Royal Navy*

Mémoires pour servir à l'histoire de la Maison de Brandebourg (Frederick the Great) **14**:58, 69

Mémoires pour servir de suite aux "Considérations sur les moeurs de ce siècle" (Duclos) **1**:187, 191-92, 198

Memoires relating to the State of the Royal Navy (Memoires of the Navy; Memoires of the Royal Navy, 1679-88) (Pepys) **11**:208, 230, 238, 240

Mémoires secrets sur le règne de Louis XIV, la règence, et le règne de Louis XV (Duclos) **1**:186, 189

Memoirs (Babur)
See *The Bābur-nāma*

Memoirs (Fanshawe)
See *Memoirs of Lady Fanshawe*

Memoirs (Holberg)
See *Memoirs of Lewis Holberg*

Memoirs and Correspondence of George, Lord Lyttelton, 1734 to 1773 (Lyttelton) **10**:198

Memoirs from Europe Towards the Close of the Eighth Century (Manley)
See *The New Atalantis*

Memoirs of a Cavalier (Defoe) **1**:124, 133, 139-40, 146, 175-76

Memoirs of a Certain Island Adjacent to the Kingdom of Utopia (Haywood) **1**:283, 286, 290

Memoirs of a Coxcomb (Cleland) **2**:33, 42, 50-1, 53-7

The Memoirs of a Protestant (Goldsmith) **2**:101-02

Memoirs of a Woman of Pleasure (Fanny Hill) (Cleland) **2**:32-51, 53-60

Memoirs of Ann Lady Fanshawe (Fanshawe)
See *Memoirs of Lady Fanshawe*

Memoirs of Lady Fanshawe (Autobiography; Memoirs; Memoirs of Ann Lady Fanshawe) (Fanshawe) **11**:100-110

Memoirs of Lewis Holberg (Memoirs) (Holberg) **6**:280

Memoirs of Marmontel (Marmontel)
See *Mémoires d'un père pour servir à l'instruction de ses enfans*

The Memoirs of Martinus Scriblerus (Arbuthnot)
See *The Memoirs of the Extraordinary Life, Works, and Discoveries of Martinus Scriblerus*

Memoirs of Miss Sidney Bidulph, Extracted from Her Own Journal (Sidney Bidulph) (Sheridan) **7**:369, 371-76, 378-79, 381-85

"Memoirs of M. de Voltaire" (Goldsmith) **2**:101-02

The Memoirs of the Extraordinary Life, Works, and Discoveries of Martinus Scriblerus (The Memoirs of Martinus Scriblerus) (Arbuthnot) **1**:12-13, 15, 17-20, 23-4

Memoirs of the Reign of George the Third (Walpole) **2**:456, 481-82, 485-88, 498

"Memoirs of the Shilling" (Addison) **18**:27

La méprise (Marivaux) **4**:368

"Merchant" (Young) **3**:467

"The Merchant to Secure His Treasure" (Prior) **4**:466

"Merchant's Prologue" (Chaucer) **17**:167-68

"Merchant's Tale" (Chaucer) **17**:137, 142, 147-54, 167-68, 170-71, 189, 191, 197-98, 201-02, 209, 217, 236-37, 239, 243

Mercurio volante con la noticia de la recuperacion de las provincias del Nuevo México conseguida por D. Diego de Vargas, Zapato, y Luxan Ponze de Leon (Flying Mercury) (Siguenza y Gongora) **8**:344

"Mercury and Cupid" (Prior) **4**:461

Mercury Vindicated (Jonson) **6**:328

Mercy and Justice (Castro) **19**:2

La mère confidente (Marivaux) **4**:368-69

"A meri iest how a sergeant would learne to playe the frere" (More) **10**:430

Mérope (Voltaire) **14**:328, 332, 338, 358, 397, 415-16, 418-19

"Merry Hae I Been Teething a Heckle" (Burns) **3**:67

The Merry Masqueraders; or, The Humorous Cuckold (Aubin) **9**:6

"The Merry Tales of Lynn" (Boswell) **4**:61

The Merry Wanderer (Davys) **1**:99

"The Messiah" (Pope) **3**:270, 292

Mester Gert Westphaler; eller, Den meget talende barbeer (The Babbling Barber) (Holberg) **6**:258-59, 273, 277

The Metamorphosed Gipsies (Jonson)
See *The Gypsies Metamorphosed*

Metamorphosis (Holberg) **6**:266

Le métempsychosiste (Montesquieu) **7**:348

The Method of Preaching (Erasmus)
See *Ecclesiastes*

Method of Study (Erasmus) **16**:123

Metrical History of Christianity (Taylor) **11**:373-74, 393

"The Metropolis of Great Britain" (Dryden) **3**:239

"Mi Li: A Chinese Fairy Tale" (Walpole) **2**:500

Micromégas (Voltaire) **14**:341, 346, 359-60, 366

"Midas" (Rousseau) **9**:345

Middle of the Necklace (Jami)
See *Wāsiṭat al-Iqd*

"A Mighty Fortress Is Our God" (Luther)
See "Ein' feste Burg ist unser Gott"

"Mignonne, allons voir si la rose" (Ronsard)
See "Ode à Cassandre: 'Mignonne, allon voir'"

Militaire philosophe (The Military Philosopher; or, Difficulties of Religion) (Holbach) **14**:153, 167

The Military Memoirs of Captain Carleton (Captain Carleton) (Defoe) **1**:133, 140, 146

The Military Philosopher; or, Difficulties of Religion (Holbach)
See *Militaire philosophe*

De militia romana libri quinque (Lipsius) **16**:265, 267, 269, 277-78

"Miller's" (Chaucer)
See "Miller's Tale"

"Miller's Prologue" (Chaucer) **17**:183, 204

"Miller's Tale" ("January and May"; "Miller's") (Chaucer) **17**:55, 168, 170, 183-88, 191, 193-94, 197-98, 201-02, 209, 217, 220, 233-35

Milton (Warton) **15**:438

Mind (Edwards)
See *Notes on the Mind*

"Minerva" (Rousseau) **9**:345

"Minister Dragon's Flight" (P'u Sung-ling)
See "Lung-fei hsiang Kung"

Minna von Barnhelm (Lessing) **8**:58, 60-3, 66, 68-70, 72, 74-5, 83, 85, 87-8, 92, 94-5, 98, 105-07, 112, 114, 116

"Minute Philosopher of Bishop Berkley" (Addison) **18**:20

The Mirrour of Vertue in Worldly Greatnes; or, The Life of syr Thomas More Knight (The Life and Death of Sir Thomas Moore; Life of More; The Life of Thomas More; The Lyfe of Sir Thomas Moore, Knighte; Roper's More) (Roper) **10**:459-87

le Misanthrope (Moliere) **10**:268-69, 271-73, 275-78, 280, 282-88, 290-93, 295-99, 308, 312-13, 318-21, 335, 338

"The Misanthrope Corrected" (Marmontel)
See "Le misanthrope corrigé"

"Le misanthrope corrigé" ("The Misanthrope Corrected") (Marmontel) **2**:214, 218

"Miscell. IV" (Buchanan) **4**:134

Miscellaneous Observations (Butler) **16**:26

Miscellaneous Observations on Important Theological Subjects (Edwards) **7**:114

Miscellaneous Observations on the Tragedy of Macbeth (*Macbeth*; *Observations on Macbeth*) (Johnson) **15**:206, 241, 307, 312-13

Miscellaneous Poetry (Dennis)
   See *Miscellanies in Verse and Prose by Mr. Dennis*

Miscellanies (Congreve) **5**:69, 75

Miscellanies (Fielding) **1**:211, 219, 221

Miscellanies (Wycherley)
   See *Miscellany Poems*

Miscellanies in Verse and Prose by Mr. Dennis (*Miscellaneous Poetry*; *Miscellany*) (Dennis) **11**:4-5, 15, 47

Miscellany (Dennis)
   See *Miscellanies in Verse and Prose by Mr. Dennis*

Miscellany Poems (Dryden) **21**:119

Miscellany Poems (*Miscellanies*) (Wycherley) **8**:380, 415-16

Miscellany Poems on Several Occasions, Written by a Lady, 1713 (Winchilsea) **3**:456

"The Miser" (Butler) **16**:50

The Miser (Moliere)
   See *L'avare*

The Miseries of Enforced Marriage (Behn) **1**:49

"The Miseries of Queene Margarite" (Drayton) **8**:8, 17, 33

"Miserly Riches" (Erasmus) **16**:142

"The Misery of Unbelievers" (Edwards) **7**:98

Mismatches in Valencia (Castro) **19**:2

"Miss Chia-no" (P'u Sung-ling) **3**:352

"Miss Huan-niang" (P'u Sung-ling) **3**:352

Miss in Her Teens; or, The Medley of Lovers (Garrick) **15**:93, 98, 101-02, 104, 113, 115, 124

Miss Lucy in Town, A Sequel to the Virgin Unmasked (Fielding) **1**:251

Miss Sara Sampson (*Miss Sarah Sampson*) (Lessing) **8**:58, 66, 70, 72, 80, 85, 94-5, 98, 105, 107-09, 112, 116

Miss Sarah Sampson (Lessing)
   See *Miss Sara Sampson*

The Mistake (Vanbrugh) **21**:293, 295, 319

"Mnemon" (More) **9**:298

Las mocedades del Cid (*The Cid*) (Castro) **19**:3, 8, 11-14

Las mocedades del Cid I (Castro) **19**:5, 8

Las mocedades del Cid II (*Hazañas del Cid*) (Castro) **19**:4-5, 8, 12-15

The Mock-Astrologer (Dryden)
   See *An Evening's Love; or, The Mock-Astrologer*

The Mocker (Chulkov)
   See *Peremešnik*

"A Modern Critic" (Butler) **16**:50

The Modern Fine Gentleman (Garrick)
   See *The Male Coquette*

The Modern Husband (Fielding) **1**:203-04, 250

"A Modern Politician" (Butler) **16**:30

A Modest Proposal for Preventing the Children of the Poor People from Being a Burthen (Swift) **1**:442, 447-48, 459-60, 481-82, 484-85, 490, 497, 513, 517, 519-22

Modus Orandi Deum (Erasmus) **16**:154

La moglie saggia (Goldoni) **4**:261-62

"A Mole in Celia's Bosom" (Carew) **13**:18

Moll Flanders (Defoe)
   See *The Fortunes and Misfortunes of the Famous Moll Flanders*

Le mondain (Voltaire) **14**:364, 379, 406

Le monde comme il va (Voltaire) **14**:364, 398

The Monitor (Hutten) **16**:216, 234, 246

Monitor II (Hutten) **16**:241, 246

"Monk's Prologue" (Chaucer)
   See "Prologue to the Monk's Tale"

"Monk's Tale" (Chaucer) **17**:61, 119, 136, 196, 201, 218, 220-21

Monody (Lyttelton)
   See *To the Memory of a Lady Lately Deceased: A Monody*

"Monody, Written near Stratford upon Avon" (Warton) **15**:442

Monsieur de Pourceaugnac (Moliere) **10**:272, 277-78, 282-84, 286, 290-91, 296, 313, 327

"The Monument: a Poem, Sacred to the Immortal Memory of the Best and Greatest of Kings, William the Third, King of Great Britain, &c." (Dennis) **11**:15, 48-50

Monuments of the Martyrs (Foxe)
   See *Actes and Monumentes of these latter perilous dayes touching matters of the Church*

The Moone-Calfe (Drayton) **8**:9, 17

"Moral Essays" (Pope) **3**:273, 319

Moral Fables (Holberg)
   See *Moralske fabler*

The Moral Law Expounded (Andrewes) **5**:28

Moral Proverbs (Christine de Pizan)
   See *Prouverbes moraux*

Moral Reflections (Holberg)
   See *Moralske tanker*

Moral Tales (Marmontel)
   See *Contes moraux*

Moral Teachings (Christine de Pizan)
   See *Enseignemens moraux*

Morale universelle (Holbach) **14**:152, 155-56, 160, 168, 175

Moralske fabler (*Moral Fables*) (Holberg) **6**:278

Moralske tanker (*Moral Reflections*) (Holberg) **6**:266, 273, 278

Moria (Erasmus)
   See *Moriae encomium*

Moriae encomium (*Encomium moriae*; *Folly*; *Moria*; *The Praise of Folly*) (Erasmus) **16**:107-17, 127, 130-33, 135-39, 142, 149, 152-55, 157-62, 165-73, 175-76, 181-83, 185-92, 194-95, 202-07

"Morning" (Parnell)
   See "A Hymn for Morning"

"Morning" (Smart) **3**:366

"Morning" (Wheatley)
   See "An Hymn to the Morning"

"Morning. The Author confined to College" (Warton) **15**:440, 463

"La morosophie" (Rousseau) **9**:345

Morte Arthur (Malory)
   See *Morte Darthur*

Morte Arthure (Malory)
   See *Morte Darthur*

Le Morte d'Arthur (Malory)
   See *Morte Darthur*

Morte Darthur (*The Book of King Arthur and His Noble Knights of the Round Table*; *Morte Arthur*; *Morte Arthure*; *Le Morte d'Arthur*; *The Noble and Joyous Book Entytled Le Morte Darthur*; *The Works of Sir Thomas Malory*) (Malory) **11**:113-202

Mortimer His Fall (Jonson) **6**:311

Mortimeriados. The Lamentable Civell Warres of Edward the Second and the Barrons (Drayton) **8**:19-20, 30, 33

"Moses" (Parnell) **3**:255

"Mother Hubberd's Tale" (Spenser)
   See "Prosopopoia; or, Mother Hubberds Tale"

"A Mountebank" (Butler) **16**:50

"Mourning" (Marvell) **4**:397, 408-10, 425, 439

The Mourning Bride (Congreve) **5**:68-9, 72, 74-6, 79, 85, 88, 101-02, 110-11; **21**:10

"Mourning Muses" (Congreve) **5**:75

Movements of Water (Vinci)
   See *On the Motion and Power of Water*

"The Mower against gardens" (Marvell) **4**:403, 410, 441-42

"The Mower to the Glo-Worms" (Marvell) **4**:411, 425, 441-42

"The Mower's Song" (Marvell) **4**:411, 442

Mr. Burke's Speech, on the 1st December 1783, upon the Question for the Speaker's Leaving the Chair, in Order for the House to Resolve Itself into a Committee on Mr. Fox's East Indian Bill (*Speech on the East India Bill*) (Burke) **7**:34

Mr. Collier's Dissuasive from the Playhouse (Collier) **6**:229

Mr. Howell's Poems upon divers Emergent Occasions (Howell) **13**:427, 431

Mr. Limberham (Dryden)
   See *Limberham; or, The Kind Keeper*

Mr. Smirk; or, The Divine in Mode (*The Divine in Mode*) (Marvell) **4**:394, 399

Mr. Steele's Apology for Himself and His Writings (Steele) **18**:336, 338, 340

Mubayyan (Babur) **18**:89-91

Mubin (Babur) **18**:87

"Muiopotmos" (Spenser) **5**:305, 312, 329-31, 345, 347-49

"The Murder of the Dog" (Wessel) **7**:391

"Les murs de Troie" (Perrault) **2**:274

"The Muse" (Kochanowski)
   See "Muza"

The Muses Elizium, Lately Discovered, by a New Way over Parnassus. The Passages Therein, Being the Subject of Ten Sundry Nymphalls (Drayton) **8**:21, 28, 31, 34, 37, 40-1, 50

"Musicks Empire" (Marvell) **4**:442-43

"Muza" ("The Muse") (Kochanowski) **10**:160

"My ain kind Dearie" (Burns) **3**:71

"My Daughter Hannah Wiggin Her Recovery from a Dangerous Fever" (Bradstreet) **4**:100

"My Heart Was Slaine, and None But You and I" (Drayton)
   See "Sonnet 2"

"My Luve is Like a Red, Red Rose" ("A Red, Red Rose") (Burns) **3**:76, 78, 83

"My Nanie O" (Burns) **3**:71

"My Noble Lovely Little Peggy" (Prior) **4**:464

"My Picture Left in Scotland" (Jonson) **6**:347

"My Son's Return out of England" (Bradstreet) **4**:100

"My thankful heart with glorying tongue" (Bradstreet) **4**:107

The Mysterious Mother (Walpole) **2**:451, 459-60, 473-75, 486, 488, 501, 505-06

"Mystery of Godliness" (More) **9**:300

"Mystery of Iniquity" (More) **9**:300

"Na lipe" ("To the Linden Tree") (Kochanowski) **10**:161

"Na nabożną" ("The Pious Woman") (Kochanowski) **10**:160

El nacimiento de Montesinos (Castro) **19**:13-15

Nafahát al-uns (*Breaths of Familiarity*) (Jami) **9**:67, 71

"Die Namen" (Lessing) **8**:69

Nanine (Voltaire) **14**:338

"Narcissa" (Young)
    See "The Complaint; or, Night Thoughts: Night the Third"

Narcisse (Rousseau) **14**:309

Narrative (Equiano)
    See *The Interesting Narrative of the Life of Olaudah Equiano, or Gustavus Vassa, the African*

"Narva and Mored" (Chatterton) **3**:123

Nathan der Weise (*Nathan the Wise*) (Lessing) **8**:59, 61-3, 66-9, 71, 77-9, 83-7, 89, 94-100, 106-07, 112, 114-16

Nathan the Wise (Lessing)
    See *Nathan der Weise*

"Nativity Ode" (Milton)
    See "On the Morning of Christ's Nativity"

"The Nativity of Our Lord and Savior Jesus Christ" (Smart)
    See "Hymn on the Nativity of Our Lord and Saviour Jesus Christ"

The Nature of True Virtue (Edwards) **7**:93, 95, 102, 108-09, 118-20, 124, 131

"Naufragium" ("The Shipwreck") (Erasmus) **16**:128, 141, 174, 194

Naval Minutes (Pepys) **11**:239-41

Nay-namá (*Book of the Reed*) (Jami) **9**:66

A Necessary Doctrine and Erudition for any Christen Man, Sette Furthe by the Kynges Majestie of Englande (*King's Book*) (Henry VIII) **10**:131, 133, 135-37, 139, 141

Neck or Nothing (Garrick) **15**:98, 101-02

"Negli anni molti e nelle molte pruove" (Michelangelo) **12**:363, 371

Nemo (*The Nobody*) (Hutten) **16**:224, 230, 232-33, 245

Neptunes Triumph (Jonson) **6**:337-38

Neptuno Alegórico (Juana Ines de la Cruz) **5**:144

"N'ésperons plus, mon âme, aux promesses du monde" (Malherbe) **5**:181

Ein neu Lied (*A New Song*) (Hutten) **16**:242, 247

Die neue Cecilia (Moritz) **2**:244-45

Neues ABC Buch, welches zugleich eine Anleitung zum Denken für Kinderenthält (Moritz) **2**:246

"Ein neues Lied wir heben an" ("We Raise a New Song") (Luther) **9**:143

La neuvaine de Cythère (Marmontel) **2**:213

"A New Arabian Night's Entertainment" (Walpole) **2**:500

The New Atalantis (*The Lady's Pacquet of Letters Broke Open; Memoirs from Europe Towards the Close of the Eighth Century; The Secret Memoirs and Manners of Several Persons of Quality*) (Manley) **1**:306-24

New Atlantis (Bacon)
    See *Nova Atlantis*

New Eloise (Rousseau)
    See *La Nouvelle Héloïse*

New Englands Trials (Smith) **9**:352, 355, 358, 383

A New English Grammar Prescribing as certain Rules as the Language will have for Forrenners to learn English. There is also another Grammar of the Spanish or Castillian Toung. (Howell) **13**:427

The New House (Goldoni)
    See *La casa nova*

The New Inn (Jonson) **6**:302, 304, 306, 311, 314, 339

"A New Psalm" (Burns) **3**:95

A New Song (Hutten)
    See *Ein neu Lied*

A New Voyage Round the World (Defoe) **1**:133, 174, 176

"A New-Yeares Gift sent to Sir Simeon Steward" ("New Year's Gift") (Herrick) **13**:310, 351-52, 365

"A New-yeares gift. To the King" (Carew) **13**:44

"New Year's Gift" (Herrick)
    See "A New-Yeares Gift sent to Sir Simeon Steward"

New Year's Wishes (Hutten) **16**:225

Das newe Testament deutzsche (*September Bibel*) (Luther) **9**:152

"Newmarket, a Satire" (Warton) **15**:440, 449, 462

News from Plymouth (Davenant) **13**:175, 187

Nicolai Klimii iter subterraneum... (*Journey of Niels Klim to the World Underground*) (Holberg) **6**:260-61, 266, 270, 273, 278-79

"Nieh Hsiao-ch'ien" (P'u Sung-ling) **3**:352

Nifo (Tasso) **5**:407

"Night" (Churchill) **3**:148, 150, 153, 155-56, 159, 162-63

"Night" (Smart) **3**:366

"Night I" (Young)
    See "The Complaint; or, Night Thoughts: Night the First"

"Night II" (Young)
    See "The Complaint; or, Night Thoughts: Night the Second"

"Night VI" (Young)
    See "The Complaint; or, Night Thoughts: Night the Sixth"

"Night VIII" (Young)
    See "The Complaint; or, Night Thoughts: Night the Eighth"

"Night-Piece" (Parnell)
    See "Night-Piece on Death"

"Night Piece" (Smart) **3**:399

"Night-Piece on Death" ("Night-Piece") (Parnell) **3**:251-52, 254-59

"The Night-Piece to Julia" (Herrick) **13**:332, 336-37, 360, 403

"Night the Fifth" (Young)
    See "The Complaint; or, Night Thoughts: Night the Fifth"

"The Nightingale" (Winchilsea)
    See "To the Nightingale"

Nimphidia, the Court of Fayrie (*Fayerie Court*) (Drayton) **8**:9, 11, 13-21, 23, 25-6, 28, 33-4, 36-7, 41, 46, 48-50

Nine Books of Archidoxus (Paracelsus)
    See *Archidoxa*

Ninety-Five Theses (Luther)
    See *Disputatio pro declaratione virtutia indulgentiarum*

"The Ninth Discourse" (Reynolds) **15**:396, 403, 411-12, 416

"Niobe in Distress for Her Children Slain by Apollo" (Wheatley) **3**:412, 430

No Abolition of Slavery (Boswell) **4**:52

"No Luck in Love" (Herrick) **13**:327

"No Spouse but a sister" (Herrick) **13**:367

Noahs Floud (Drayton) **8**:31

The Noble and Joyous Book Entytled Le Morte Darthur (Malory)
    See *Morte Darthur*

Noble Numbers, or Pious Pieces (Herrick)
    See *His Noble Numbers: or, His Pious Pieces, Wherein (amongst other things) he sings the Birth of his Christ: and sighes for his Saviours suffering on the Crosse*

The Noble Slaves; or, The Lives and Adventures of Two Lords and Two Ladies Who Were Shipwreck'd upon a desolate Island (Aubin) **9**:3-6, 8, 16-17

The Nobody (Hutten)
    See *Nemo*

Noche Escura del Alma (*The Dark Night of the Soul*) (John of the Cross) **18**:202, 214-15, 220, 229-30, 234-35

"Noche Oscura del alma" ("Dark Night of the Soul") (John of the Cross) **18**:213-14, 216, 222-24, 230, 232-35

"A Nocturnal Reverie" (Winchilsea) **3**:441-42, 444-47, 451-52, 455, 457-58

"A Nocturnal upon S. Lucies day, Being the shortest day" ("St. Lucies Day") (Donne) **10**:26, 36, 48, 50, 78-80, 82, 89

"Non è sempre di colpa aspra e mortale" (Michelangelo) **12**:366

"Non ha l'ottimo artista alcun concetto" (Michelangelo) **12**:314, 366, 371, 373

"Non posso non mancar d'ingegno e d'arte" (Michelangelo) **12**:371

"Non pur d'argento o d'oro" (Michelangelo) **12**:368-69

"Non so se s'è la desiata luce" (Michelangelo) **12**:356

"Nonne Preestes Tale" (Chaucer)
    See "Nun's Priest's Tale"

The Nonsense of Common-Sense (*Essays*) (Montagu) **9**:281

"Noon" (Smart) **3**:366

The Northern Heiress; or, The Humours of York (Davys) **1**:97-8

"Not every day fit for Verse" (Herrick) **13**:382

Notebooks (Vinci) **12**:392-93, 397-401, 404-06, 410, 428-29

Notebooks (Voltaire) **14**:380, 391, 395

Notes on the Mind (*Mind*) (Edwards) **7**:99, 120, 124

The Notion of a Spirit (More)
    See *Enchiridion metaphysicum*

Nourjahad (Sheridan)
    See *The History of Nourjahad*

"Nous ne sommes pas nez de la dure semence" (Ronsard) **6**:433-34

Nouvelle continuation des amours (Ronsard)
  6:425-26, 431, 433

La Nouvelle Héloïse (*Julie, ou La Nouvelle
  Héloïse; Letters of Two Lovers; New Eloise*)
  (Rousseau)   14:216, 218, 220, 235, 237, 239,
  247-49, 251-52, 264, 273, 278, 291, 297, 301,
  309, 311, 313

Nova Atlantis (*New Atlantis*) (Bacon)   18:118,
  121, 126, 129, 132, 136, 141, 143, 153, 157-
  58, 163, 173, 176-77, 179-80, 185, 187, 189-
  92, 196-97

Novelas exemplares (*Exemplary Novels;
  Exemplary Stories*) (Cervantes)   6:144, 148,
  171-72, 174, 176-77, 183

Novum instrumentum (Erasmus)   16:159, 163,
  171

Novum Scientiarum Organum (Bacon)
  18:104-05, 108, 115, 118-20, 130-32, 135-36,
  140, 142-44, 146-47, 149-50, 152-53, 155,
  157, 160-61, 163, 165, 168, 172, 174, 187-88,
  193

*La nuit et le moment; ou, Les matines de
  Cythere* (Crebillon)   1:76-7, 79, 90

La Numancia (Cervantes)
  See *El cerco de Numancia*

Numitor (Marmontel)   2:213, 217

"Nun's Priest's Tale" ("The Cock and the
  Fox"; "Fable of the Cock and the Fox";
  "Nonne Preestes Tale") (Chaucer)   17:55,
  58, 71, 82, 136-37, 140, 185, 195-98, 205,
  220-22, 242

"Nuovo piacere e di maggiore stima"
  (Michelangelo)   12:363

"A Nuptiall Song" (Herrick)   13:350, 352,
  364

The Nuptials of Peleus and Thetis (Howell)
  13:414

"Nut-brown Maid" (Prior)
  See "Henry and Emma"

"Nygelle" (Chatterton)   3:129

"A Nymph" (More)   9:298

"A Nymph and a Swain to Apollo once
  pray'd" (Congreve)   5:85

"The Nymph Complaining for the Death of
  Her Faun" (Marvell)   4:395, 397, 401-02,
  404, 412, 419, 423, 425, 435, 438, 443

Nympha Caledoniæ (Buchanan)   4:117

"A Nymph's Passion" (Jonson)   6:351

"O doktorze Hiszpanie" ("The Spanish
  Doctor") (Kochanowski)   10:160

"O For Ane and Twenty, Tam" (Burns)   3:67

"O hermosura que excedéis" (Teresa de Jesus)
  18:390

"O Kapelanie" ("The Priest") (Kochanowski)
  10:160

"O Lay Thy Loof in Mine, Lass" (Burns)
  3:67

"O Lord the Maker of All Things" (Henry
  VIII)   10:146

"O Madness! terror of mankind" (Prior)   4:60

"O śmierci Jana Tarnowskiego"
  (Kochanowski)   10:173

"O Thou, omnipotent, eternal Lord!" (Boswell)
  4:61

"O Wert Thou in the Cauld, Cauld Blast"
  (Burns)   3:67, 82

"Obedience in Subjects" (Herrick)   13:394

Oberon, the Fairy Prince (Jonson)   6:327

"Oberon's Feast" (Herrick)   13:368

"Oberon's Palace" (Herrick)   13:367

Obras (Juana Ines de la Cruz)   5:144

Los Obras de gracián (Gracian y Morales)
  15:142

Obris Espirituales (John of the Cross)   18:202

Obscure Men (Hutten)
  See *Literæ obscurorum Vivorum*

Obsecratio (Erasmus)   16:106

"Obsequies to the Lady Anne Hay" ("Anne
  Hay") (Carew)   13:31, 48-9, 54, 61

"Obsequies to the Lord Harrington, brother to
  the Lady Lucy, Countesse of Bedford"
  (Donne)   10:97

*Observations, Good or Bad, Stupid or Clever,
  Serious or Jocular, on Squire Foote's
  Dramatic Entertainment entitled "The
  Minor," by a Genius* (*Observations on "The
  Minor"*) (Boswell)   4:51

*Observations on a Late Publication Intituled
  "The Present State of the Nation"* (Burke)
  7:54, 57

Observations on Blackmore's Prince Arthur
  (Dennis)
  See *Remarks on a Book, entituled Prince
  Arthur, an Heroick Poem*

Observations on Macbeth (Johnson)
  See *Miscellaneous Observations on the
  Tragedy of Macbeth*

Observations on Spenser (Warton)
  See *Observations on the Faerie Queene of
  Spenser*

Observations on St. Paul's Conversion
  (Lyttelton)
  See *Observations on the Conversion and
  Apostleship of St. Paul, in a Letter to
  Gilbert West*

*Observations on the Conversion and Apostleship
  of St. Paul, in a Letter to Gilbert West*
  (*Conversion of St. Paul; Observations on St.
  Paul's Conversion*) (Lyttelton)   10:196-97,
  200-03, 207, 214

Observations on the Faerie Queene of Spenser
  (*Observations on Spenser*) (Warton)   15:427,
  429, 436-38, 446-48, 451-53, 457

Observations on the Life of Cicero (Lyttelton)
  10:200

Observations on "The Minor" (Boswell)
  See *Observations, Good or Bad, Stupid or
  Clever, Serious or Jocular, on Squire
  Foote's Dramatic Entertainment entitled
  "The Minor," by a Genius*

Observations upon Anthrophia theomagica
  (More)   9:310

"An Obstinate Man" (Butler)   16:27

Occidental Paradise (Siguenza y Gongora)
  See *Parayso occidental, plantado y cultivado
  por la liberal benefica mano de los muy
  Catholicos*

Occulta philosophia (Paracelsus)   14:200

"Ocean: An Ode" (Young)   3:467, 488

Ocho comedias y ocho entremeses (*Eight Plays
  and Eight Interludes: New and Never
  Performed; Interludes*) (Cervantes)   6:177,
  189

"October, a Poem" (Boswell)   4:50

"Ode" (Killigrew)   4:350

"Ode" (Marvell)
  See "An Horatian Ode upon Cromwell's
  Return from Ireland"

"An Ode" (Prior)   4:465

"Ode XIX" (Warton)   15:454

"Ode à Bonneval" (Rousseau)   9:340, 344

"Ode à Cassandre: 'Mignonne, allon voir'"
  ("Mignonne, allons voir si la rose")
  (Ronsard)   6:408-09, 412-13, 417-18, 425

"Ode à Caumartin" (Rousseau)   9:339, 344

"Ode à Duché" (Rousseau)   9:339, 344

"Ode à Henri II" (Ronsard)   6:439

"Ode à la fare" (Rousseau)   9:339, 344

"Ode à la fortune" (Rousseau)   9:339-40, 344

"Ode à la postérité" (Rousseau)   9:345

"Ode à Malherbe" (Rousseau)   9:340, 345

"Ode à Marie de Médicis, sur sa Bienvenue en
  France" ("A la reine sur sa bien-venüe en
  France") (Malherbe)   5:171, 183

"Ode à Michel de l'Hospital" (Ronsard)
  6:427-30

"Ode à Monseigneur le Dauphin" (Ronsard)
  6:438-39

"Ode au comte de Luc" (Rousseau)   9:340-41,
  343

"Ode au comte de Sinzendorff" ("A
  Zinzindorf") (Rousseau)   9:340, 344

"Ode au marquis d'Ussé" (Rousseau)   9:339,
  344

"Ode by Dr. Samuel Johnson to Mrs. Thrale
  upon their supposed approaching Nuptials"
  (Boswell)   4:50

"Ode de la Paix" (Ronsard)   6:431

"Ode for Music" (Gray)   4:316-17, 332-33

"Ode for Music" (Warton)   15:441, 447, 454,
  461

"Ode for St. Cecilia's Day" (Pope)   3:270,
  290, 292, 295

"Ode for St. Cecilia's Day" ("Ode to St.
  Cecilia") (Smart)   3:366, 374

"An Ode Occasion'd by the Death of Mr.
  Thomson" ("In Yonder Grave a Druid
  Lies") (Collins)   4:218, 220, 227, 229, 231

"Ode on a Distant Prospect of Eton College"
  ("Eton"; "Eton College Ode") (Gray)
  4:284, 287, 289, 310-12, 315, 322, 324, 332,
  334

"Ode on Adversity" (Gray)
  See "Ode to Adversity"

"Ode on Colonel Ross" (Collins)
  See "Ode to a Lady on the Death of Colonel
  Ross in the Action of Fontenoy"

"Ode on Shakespeare" (Garrick)   15:114

"Ode on Solitude" (Pope)   3:268

"Ode on Spring" ("Ode on the Spring") (Gray)
  4:283-84, 300, 302, 311, 315, 319, 322-24,
  332-33

"Ode on St. Cecilia" (Addison)   18:16

"Ode On the Approach of Summer" ("On the
  Approach of Summer") (Warton)   15:434-
  35, 441, 454

The Ode on the Battle of Fontenoy
  (Marmontel)   2:213

"Ode on the Death of a Favourite Cat,
  Drowned in a Tub of Gold Fishes" ("Death
  of a Favorite Cat") (Gray)   4:284, 301, 303,
  309-10, 328-29, 332-33

"Ode on the Death of a Lamb" (Boswell)
  4:52, 61

"An Ode on the Death of Mr. Henry Purcell"
  (Dryden)   21:89

"Ode on the Death of Mr. Pelham" (Garrick)
  15:114

"Ode on the Drop of Dew" (Marvell)   4:396-
  97, 403, 426-27, 438, 441, 443

"The Ode on the Glorious Success of Her
  Majesty's Arms" ("The Glorious Success of
  Her Majesty's Arms") (Prior)   4:466

"Ode on the Music of the Grecian Theatre"
   (Collins)   4:214, 220
"Ode on the New Year" (Drayton)
   See "To the New Yeere"
"Ode on the Pleasure Arising from
   Vicissitude" ("Ode on Vicissitude") (Gray)
   4:301, 315, 332
"Ode on the Poetical Character" (Collins)
   4:211, 214, 216, 220, 229, 234, 236, 242, 245
"An Ode on the Popular Superstitions of the
   Highlands of Scotland, etc." ("The Popular
   Superstitions of the Highlands of Scotland")
   (Collins)   4:214, 217, 219, 223, 226, 231,
   234, 236, 244
"Ode on the Progress of Poesy" (Gray)
   See "The Progress of Poesy"
"Ode on the Spring" (Gray)
   See "Ode on Spring"
"Ode on Vale Royal Abbey" (Warton)
   See "Ode Written at Vale-Royal Abbey in
   Cheshire"
"Ode on Vicissitude" (Gray)
   See "Ode on the Pleasure Arising from
   Vicissitude"
"Ode on Whistling" (Boswell)   4:52
"Ode pour la Reine Mère du Roy pendant sa
   Régence" ("A la reyne mère sur les heureux
   succez de sa régence") (Malherbe)   5:171,
   185
"An Ode, Presented to the King, on His
   Majesty's Arrival in Holland, After the
   Queen's Death, 1695" (Prior)   4:465
"Ode sent to Mr. Upton, on his Edition of the
   Faerie Queene" (Warton)   15:442
"Ode sur la mort du prince de Conti"
   (Rousseau)   9:339, 343
"Ode sur la naissance du duc de Bretagne"
   (Rousseau)   9:339-40, 343
"Ode sur les miseres des hommes" (Ronsard)
   6:437
"Ode to a Grizzle Wig" (Warton)   15:441,
   462
"Ode to a Lady on the Death of Colonel Ross
   in the Action of Fontenoy" ("Ode on
   Colonel Ross") (Collins)   4:226, 229-30
"Ode to Adversity" ("Hymn to Adversity";
   "Ode on Adversity") (Gray)   4:282, 311-12,
   332
"Ode to Ambition" (Boswell)   4:52
"Ode to Evening" (Collins)   4:211-13, 216-19,
   221-22, 225-29, 231-36, 239-40, 242, 244
"Ode to Fear" (Collins)   4:211, 216, 229, 231,
   236, 238, 244
"Ode to His Valentine" (Drayton)
   See "To His Valentine"
"Ode to Ill-Nature" (Smart)   3:361, 366
Ode to Independence (Smollett)   2:332, 359
"Ode to Jesus" (Herrick)   13:317
"Ode to John Rouse" (Milton)   9:241
"Ode to Liberty" (Collins)   4:213, 216, 229,
   232, 234
"Ode to Mæcenas" ("To Mæcenas")
   (Wheatley)   3:408, 412, 415-17, 419-20, 423,
   426, 430, 432, 436
"Ode to Mercy" (Collins)   4:216, 229
"Ode to Neptune" (Wheatley)   3:430
"Ode to Peace" (Collins)   4:229, 234
"Ode to Pity" (Collins)   4:214, 216
"Ode to Simplicity" (Collins)   4:214, 216, 229
"An Ode to Sir Clipsebie Crew" (Herrick)
   13:365
"Ode to Sleep" (Wessel)   7:389

"Ode to Solitude, at an Inn" (Warton)   15:444
"Ode to Spring" (Burns)   3:99
"Ode to St. Cecilia" (Smart)
   See "Ode for St. Cecilia's Day"
"Ode to the Elves" (Boswell)   4:52, 61
"Ode to the Queen" (Prior)   4:462
"Ode to the Spleen" ("The Spleen")
   (Winchilsea)   3:441, 446-47, 449, 451, 453,
   457
Ode to Tragedy (Boswell)   4:51
"An Ode upon Dedicating a Building, and
   Erecting a Statue to Shakespeare, at
   Stratford-upon-Avon" (Garrick)   15:91, 97
"Ode Written at Vale-Royal Abbey in
   Cheshire" ("Ode on Vale Royal Abbey";
   "Written at Vale-Royal Abbey") (Warton)
   15:442, 447, 454
"Ode Written in the Beginning of the Year
   1746" (Collins)   4:216-17, 219, 222, 225-26,
   230-32, 235, 243-44
"An Ode Written in the Peake" (Drayton)
   8:42-3
Odes (Drayton)   8:14, 17-18, 21, 30
Odes (Dryden)   21:76
Odes (Gray)   4:279
Odes (Ronsard)   6:409, 411, 414, 429-31
Odes (Young)   3:476
*Odes on Several Descriptive and Allegoric
   Subjects* (Collins)   4:210, 212, 215-17, 221,
   223, 225, 229, 234, 242-43
Odes with Other Lyrick Poesies (Drayton)
   8:27
Odprawa posłów grekich (*The Dismissal of the
   Grecian Envoys*) (Kochanowski)   10:152-53,
   161, 164, 167, 176-77
The Odyssey of Homer (*Homer*) (Pope)   3:291
The Oeconomy of a Winter's Day (Cleland)
   2:50, 54
Oedipe (Voltaire)   14:352, 397, 401
Oedipus (Dryden)   21:90
Oeuvres choisies (Prevost)   1:343
Oeuvres complètes (Montesquieu)   7:357
"Of a Country Life" (Thomson)   16:418, 432
"Of A' the Airts" ("A' the Airts") (Burns)
   3:71, 85
"Of Age" (Montaigne)   8:239
"Of Books" (Montaigne)   8:232
"Of Cannibals" (Montaigne)
   See "Des cannibales"
Of Comfort against Tribulation (More)
   See *A dialoge of comfort against tribulacion*
"Of Commerce" (Hume)   7:190-91
Of Constancy (Lipsius)
   See *De constantia libri duo*
"Of Death" (Bacon)   18:148
Of Density and Rarity (Bacon)   18:143
Of Dramatick Poesie: An Essay (*Essay of
   Dramatic Poesy*) (Dryden)   3:182, 188, 190,
   197, 202, 211, 214, 222, 229, 236-37, 240;
   21:52, 111
"Of earthly Hope" (Bacon)   18:149
Of Education (Milton)   9:252, 257-59, 261-62
"Of Endless Punishment" (Edwards)   7:98
"Of Experience" (Montaigne)
   See "De l'experience"
"Of Giving the Lie" (Montaigne)   8:230
"Of Glory" (Montaigne)   8:245
Of Heaviness and Lightness (Bacon)   18:143
"Of Heroic Plays" ("Essay of Heroic Plays")
   (Dryden)   3:236-38; 21:114
"Of Interest" (Hume)   7:190
"Of Liberty and Necessity" (Hume)   7:151

Of Life and Death (Bacon)   18:143
"Of Luxury" (Hume)   7:190
"Of Masques and Triumphs" (Bacon)   18:195
"Of Miracles" (Hume)   7:151, 155, 157, 175
"Of Moderation of Cares" (Bacon)   18:149
"Of Money" (Hume)   7:190
"Of Popularity" (Holberg)   6:227
Of Prelatical Episcopacy (Milton)   9:249
"Of Presumption" (Montaigne)
   See "De la praesumption"
"Of Public Credit" (Hume)   7:190-91
*Of Reformation Touching Church-Discipline in
   England* (Milton)   9:252
"Of Repentance" (Montaigne)
   See "Du repentir"
"Of Some Verses of Virgil" (Montaigne)
   See "Sur des vers de Virgile"
Of Sulpher, Mercury, and Salt (Bacon)   18:143
"Of Taxes" (Hume)   7:190
"Of the Academic or Sceptical Philosophy"
   (Hume)   7:164
"Of the Balance of Power" (Hume)   7:190
"Of the Balance of Trade" (Hume)   7:190-91
"Of the First Principles of Government"
   (Hume)   7:188
"Of the Four Humours in Man's Constitution"
   ("The Humours") (Bradstreet)   4:89, 94,
   102, 106, 111
"Of the Idea of Necessary Connexion" (Hume)
   7:164
"Of the Independency of Parliament" (Hume)
   7:152, 199
"Of the Jealousy of Trade" (Hume)   7:190-91
Of the Knowledge Which Maketh a Wise Man
   (*The Knowledge that Maketh a Wise Man*)
   (Elyot)   11:58, 60-1, 71-2, 74-5, 81, 84, 89,
   90, 92
"Of the Liberty of the Press" (Hume)   7:152,
   189
"Of the Modern Philosophy" (Hume)   7:198
"Of the Origin of Government" (Hume)
   7:189
"Of the Origin of Romantic Fiction in
   Europe" (Warton)   15:457
"Of the Original Contract" (Hume)   7:189
"Of the Populousness of Antient Nations"
   (Hume)   7:190
*Of the Proficience and Advancement of
   Learning Divine and Human* (Bacon)
   See *On the Advancement of Learning*
Of the Progres of the Soule (Donne)
   See *The Second Anniversarie. Of the Progres
   of the Soule. Wherein, By Occasion Of the
   Religious death of Mistris Elizabeth Drury,
   the incommodities of the Soule in this life,
   and her exaltation in the next, are
   Contemplated*
"Of the Standard of Taste" (Hume)   7:163,
   201-02
Of the Supreme Mysteries of Nature
   (Paracelsus)   14:182
Of the Sympathy and Antipathy of Things
   (Bacon)   18:143
Of the Use and Abuse of the Tongue (Erasmus)
   16:127
"Of the Worshipping of False Imaginations"
   ("Of the Worshipping of Imaginations")
   (Andrewes)   5:22, 34, 42
"Of the Worshipping of Imaginations"
   (Andrewes)
   See "Of the Worshipping of False
   Imaginations"

Title Index

"Of Three Kinds of Association with Others" (Montaigne) **8**:221, 243

"Of Vanity" (Montaigne)
See "De la vanité"

Of Winds (Bacon) **18**:143

"Of Youth and Age" (Bacon) **18**:194

"Office of a Chaplain" (Collier) **6**:200

"An Officer" (Butler) **16**:52

Offrande (Marat)
See *Offrande à la patrie; ou, Discours au Tiers État de France*

Offrande à la patrie; ou, Discours au Tiers État de France (*Offrande*) (Marat) **10**:225, 228-29, 232-33, 236

"Oh do not die" (Donne)
See "A Feaver"

"Oh Doe Not Wanton with Those Eyes" (Jonson) **6**:346

The Old Bachelor (Congreve)
See *The Old Batchelour*

The Old Batchelour (*The Old Bachelor*) (Congreve) **5**:66, 68, 71, 74, 76, 78, 81, 84, 86-8, 91-3, 95-6, 99, 101, 108-09, 112, 117; **21**:9, 12, 26-7, 29, 32, 34-9, 44

The Old Maid by Mary Singleton, Spinster (Brooke) **6**:108, 114-15

An Old Man Taught Wisdom; Or, The Virgin Unmasked (Fielding) **1**:251

Olinda's Adventures; or, The Amours of a Young Lady (Trotter) **8**:364-65, 368

"Ollas Ostentare" (Erasmus) **16**:166, 173, 175

Olympie (Voltaire) **14**:331

"Omniscience" (Smart)
See "On the Omniscience of the Supreme Being"

"On a Bed of Guernsey Lilies" (Smart) **3**:375

"On a Cherry Stone Sent to Weare in his Mistress' Eare, a Death's Head on the one Side and Her Owne Face on the Other Side" (Herrick) **13**:341

"On a Damaske Rose" (Carew)
See "A Damask Rose Sticking upon a Lady's Breast"

"On a Picture Painted by her self, representing two Nimphs of Diana's, one in a posture to Hunt, the other Batheing" (Killigrew) **4**:349

"On a Scotch Bard Gone to the West Indies" (Burns) **3**:86, 92

"On a Solemn Music" (Milton) **9**:198

"On Affliction" (Winchilsea) **3**:451

On Being and the One (Pico della Mirandola)
See *De ente et uno*

"On Being Brought from Africa to America" (Wheatley) **3**:412-13, 415, 417, 420, 425, 427, 429, 431-32

"On Censure" (Boswell) **4**:36

"On Commissary Goldie's Brains" ("Goldie") (Burns) **3**:86, 92

On Conciliation with the Colonies (Burke)
See *Speech on Moving His Resolutions for Conciliation with the Colonies*

On Constancy (Lipsius)
See *De constantia libri duo*

"On Cripples" (Montaigne)
See "Cripples"

"On Cutting Down an Old Thorn" (Swift) **1**:459

"On Death" (Boswell) **4**:36

"On Desire" (Behn) **1**:52

"On Dreams: An Imitation of Petronius" (Swift) **1**:522

"On Fear" (Boswell) **4**:36

On Free Will (Erasmus)
See *De Libero Arbitro*

"On Gelliflowers begotten" (Herrick) **13**:367

"On Glenriddell's Fox Breaking His Chain" (Burns) **3**:77

"On Great Place" (Bacon) **18**:114-15

"On Hapinesse" (Chatterton) **3**:126

"On Himselfe" (Herrick) **13**:340-41, 370

"On His Mistris" (Donne)
See "Elegie XVI: On his mistris"

"On Imagination" ("Imagination"; "To Imagination") (Wheatley) **3**:412-13, 429-30, 435

On Imitation (Schlegel)
See *Abhandlung von der Nachahmung*

"On Julia's Clothes" (Herrick)
See "Upon Julia's Clothes"

"On Justice and Generosity" (Goldsmith) **2**:87, 128

"On King Arthur's Round Table, at Winchester" (Warton) **15**:442

"On Lord Holland's Seat near Margate, Kent" ("Impromptu on Lord Holland's House") (Gray) **4**:301, 303, 316

"On Love" (Boswell) **4**:36

"On Major General Lee" (Wheatley)
See "Thoughts on His Excellency Major General Lee"

"On Michael Angelo's Famous Piece of the Crucifixion" (Young) **3**:488

"On My First Daughter" (Jonson) **6**:347

"On Observing a lock of Miss B-D-N's Hair separated from her Head-dress, and hanging towards the Author" (Boswell) **4**:61

"On Parents & Children" (Boswell) **4**:36

"On Poetry: A Rapsody" (Swift) **1**:435

On Poetry and Our Relish for the Beauties of Nature (Wollstonecraft) **5**:426, 450

"On Quotations" (Boswell) **4**:35, 37

"On Recollection" ("Recollection") (Wheatley) **3**:413, 415, 419, 432

"On Reserve" (Boswell) **4**:34

"On Seeing a Wounded Hare Limp by Me Which a Fellow Had Just Shot at" ("Wounded Hare") (Burns) **3**:59

"On Sight of a Gentlewoman's Face in the Water" (Carew) **13**:18

"On Similarity among Authors" (Boswell) **4**:35

"On Sleeping in Church" (Swift) **1**:465

"On Suicide" (Boswell) **4**:35-6

"On the Accession of King George to the British Throne" (Dennis)
See "A Poem upon the Death of Her Late Sacred Majesty Queen Anne, and the Most Happy and Most Auspicious Accession of His Sacred Majesty King George"

On the Advancement of Learning (*Of the Proficience and Advancement of Learning Divine and Human*) (Bacon) **18**:104, 108, 113, 131, 133-34, 136-37, 140, 142, 144, 146, 148, 153, 161, 163, 168, 170, 173-75, 177-79, 183, 186-87, 193, 195-96

"On the Approach of Summer" (Warton)
See "Ode On the Approach of Summer"

"On the Birth-Day of Queen Katherine" (Killigrew) **4**:350

On the Birth of Perceptible Things in Reason (Paracelsus) **14**;198

"On the Birth of the Prince of Wales" (Warton) **15**:461

On the Christian Religion (Ficino)
See *De religione christiana*

"On the Coronation of the Most August Monarch K. James II, and Queen Mary" (Prior) **4**:475

On the Creative Imitation of the Beautiful (Moritz)
See *Über die bildende Nachahmung des Schönen*

"On the Death of a Very Young Gentleman" (Dryden) **21**:87

"On the Death of an Infant" (Wheatley) **3**:410

"On the Death of George the Second" (Warton) **15**:461

"On the Death of His Mother" (Thomson) **16**:428-29

"On the Death of Mr. Richard West" (Gray)
See "Sonnet on the Death of Mr. Richard West"

"On the Death of Mr. Snider Killed by Richardson" (Wheatley) **3**:435

"On the Death of Mr. William Aikman, the Painter" (Thomson) **16**:428

"On the Death of the Rev. Mr. George Whitefield" (Wheatley)
See "An Elegiac Poem on the Death of George Whitefield"

"On the Death of the Reverend Dr. Sewall" (Wheatley) **3**:416, 436

On the Diseases That Deprive Man of Reason (Paracelsus)
See *De morbus amentium*

"On the Distresses of the Poor" (Goldsmith) **2**:103

"On the Duke of Buckingham" (Carew) **13**:50

"On the Eternity of the Supreme Being" ("Eternity") (Smart) **3**:366, 379, 394, 402

"On the Famous Voyage" (Jonson) **6**:347

"On the Goodness of the Supreme Being" (Smart) **3**:380, 395-97

"On the Hill and Grove at Billborow" (Marvell)
See "Upon the Hill and Grove at Billborow"

"On the Immensity of the Supreme Being" (Smart) **3**:379, 394, 399, 402

"On the Introduction of Learning into England" (Warton) **15**:458

"On the Last Epiphany, or Christ Coming to Judgment" (Chatterton) **3**:127

"On the Late Captain Grose's Peregrinations Thro' Scotland" ("Captain Grose") (Burns) **3**:71, 85-6

"On the Late Massacre in Piemont" (Milton) **9**:191

"On the Marriage of the King" (Warton) **15**:455; **15**:461

"On the Marriage of T.K. and C.C. the morning stormie" (Carew) **13**:57

On the Medium of Moral Government-- Particularly Conversation (Edwards) **7**:129-30

"On the Morning of Christ's Nativity" ("Nativity Ode") (Milton) **9**:198, 204-05, 228, 230

On the Motion and Power of Water (*Movements of Water*) (Vinci) **12**:385, 405

On the Natural History of Religion (Hume) **7**:154-55, 157-58, 186, 196-99

"On the Omniscience of the Supreme Being" ("Omniscience") (Smart) **3**:366, 380, 394

On the Origin of Man (Paracelsus)
See *De generatione hominis*

On the Papacy in Rome, Against the Most Celebrated Romanist in Leipzig (Luther) **9**:125, 140, 148

"On the Power of the Supreme Being" (Smart) **3**:380, 394

On the Pretended Donation of Constantine (Hutten)
See *De falso credita et ementita Donatione Constatini Magni*

"On the Profession of a Player" (Boswell) **4**:71

"On the Resemblance of Children to their Fathers" (Montaigne)
See "De l'affection des peres aux enfants"

On the Roman Trinity (Hutten)
See *Vadiscus, sive Trias Romana*

On the Sublime (Dennis) **11**:33

"On the Testimony of Conscience" (Swift) **1**:488

"On the Theatre: A Comparison between Laughing and Sentimental Comedy" (Goldsmith) **2**:107

"On the Townes Honest Man" (Jonson) **6**:342

On the Trinity (Swift) **1**:495

"On the Uncertain Hour of Death" (Petursson)
See "Um daudans óvíssan tíma"

On the Usefulness of the Stage (Dennis)
See *The Usefulness of the Stage to the Happiness of Mankind, to Government and to Religion*

"On the Victory Obtained by Blake over the Spaniards" (Marvell) **4**:431

"On Time" (Boswell) **4**:71

"On Tragedy" (Hume) **7**:163, 167

On Translating: An Open Letter (Luther) **9**:150

"On Truth" (Boswell) **4**:37

On Usury (Luther) **9**:134

"On Virtue" ("Virtue") (Wheatley) **3**:412-13, 418, 432

"On Youth and Age" (Boswell) **4**:37

"One that died of the Wind Colic" (Carew) **13**:18

The Onlookers (Hutten)
See *The Spectators*

"Onn Oure Ladies Chyrche" (Chatterton) **3**:130

"Open the Door to Me, O" (Burns) **3**:76

Opening of Youth (Jami)
See *Fatihat al-shabáb*

"Opéra" (Marmontel) **2**:223

"L'opéra de Naples" (Rousseau) **9**:345

Opera Omnia (Lipsius) **16**:271

Opera omnia (More) **9**:312

Opera posthuma (Spinoza)
See *B. D. S. Opera posthuma*

Opere (Machiavelli) **8**:135

Opere Varie Critiche (Castelvetro) **12**:45-6, 71

Opinion Anent the Reformation of the Universities of St Androis (*Ane Opinion anent the University of St. Andrews*) (Buchanan) **4**:129

Opinion par alphabet (Voltaire) **14**:392

Optics (Marat) **10**:222

Opus Paramirum (*Paramirum*) (Paracelsus) **14**:187, 198, 198-99

Opuscula (Andrewes)
See *Opuscula quaedam posthuma*

Opuscula Latina (Holberg) **6**:266

Opuscula quaedam posthuma (*Opuscula*) (Andrewes) **5**:22

Oráculo manual y arte de prudencia (*The Manual Oracle and Art of Prudence*) (Gracian y Morales) **15**:135-36, 139, 141, 143-48

L'oraison Notre Dame (Christine de Pizan)
See *L'oryson Notre Dame*

Oratio de dignitate hominis (*De hominis dignitate*; *Oration on Human Dignity*; *Oration on the Dignity of Man*) (Pico della Mirandola) **15**:321, 324-27, 333-35, 338, 341, 345-46, 348, 350, 354-57, 360

Oration on Human Dignity (Pico della Mirandola)
See *Oratio de dignitate hominis*

Oration on the Dignity of Man (Pico della Mirandola)
See *Oratio de dignitate hominis*

Orazia (*The Horatii*; *The Tragedy of the Horatii*) (Aretino) **12**:6, 19, 26-7, 36

"The Ordination" (Burns) **3**:71, 93, 95-6

Les oreilles du comte de Chesterfield (Voltaire) **14**:346, 359, 360

Orest und Pylades (Schlegel) **5**:280

Oreste (Voltaire) **14**:328

Oriental planeta evangelica epopeya sacropanegyrica al apostol grande de las Indias S. Francisco Xavier (*Eastern Evangelical Planeta*) (Siguenza y Gongora) **8**:340

The Original and Progress of Satire (Dryden)
See *A Discourse Concerning the Original and Progress of Satire*

"An Original Letter from a Gentleman of Scotland to the Earl of * * *in London" (Boswell) **4**:53

Original Letters, Familiar, Moral and Critical (*Letters*) (Dennis) **11**:17

Original Letters written during the reigns of Henry VI., Edward IV., and Richard III.
See *Paston Letters*

The Original Power of the Collective Body of the People of England, Examined and Asserted (Defoe) **1**:121

Original Sin (Edwards)
See *The Great Christian Doctrine of Original Sin Defended*

Original Stories from Real Life; with Conversations, Calculated to Regulate the Affections, and Form the Mind to Truth and Goodness (Wollstonecraft) **5**:426, 460

Orlando furioso (*Furioso*) (Ariosto) **6**:21-3, 25-7, 29-41, 43-6, 48-59, 62-3, 65-6, 68-76, 79, 81-3

Orlando innamorato (*Innamorato*) (Boiardo) **6**:86-91, 93-9, 101-04

Oroonoko; or, The Royal Slave (Behn) **1**:29-32, 34-6, 38, 41-2, 44-6, 49-51, 53-6

L'oryson Notre Dame (*L'oraison Notre Dame*) (Christine de Pizan) **9**:25, 46

Outlaws of the Marshes (Lo Kuan-chung)
See *Shui Hu Chuan*

Ovid's Epistles (Dryden) **21**:72

"The Owl Describing Her Young Ones" (Winchilsea) **3**:456

The Owle (Drayton) **8**:14, 27, 30-1

Oxford Newsman's Verses (Warton) **15**:441, 462

The Oxford Sausage; or, Select Poetical Pieces: Written by the Most Celebrated Wits of the University of Oxford (*Sausage*) (Warton) **15**:441-42, 449-50

Paean (Erasmus) **16**:106

"Palamon and Arcite" (Chaucer)
See "Knight's Tale"

"Palamon and Arcite" (Dryden)
See "Knight's Tale"

Palinodiæ (Buchanan) **4**:119, 138

"Palinodie" (Rousseau) **9**:340, 345

Pamela (Goldoni) **4**:273

Pamela in Her Exalted Condition (Richardson)
See *Pamela; or, Virtue Rewarded*

Pamela; or, Virtue Rewarded (*Pamela in Her Exalted Condition*) (Richardson) **1**:365-66, 368, 371-72, 374, 377, 382-91, 395-99, 401-04, 406-10, 414-15, 418

Pamphlet on the Plague (Paracelsus)
See *Libell über die Pest*

"A Panegerick to Sir Lewis Pemberton" (Herrick) **13**:341, 365, 376

"Panegyric on Oxford Ale" (Warton) **15**:440, 450, 462-63

"A Panegyrick on the Dean" (Swift) **1**:504

Panegyricus (Erasmus) **16**:106, 110

Den pantsatte bondedreng (Holberg) **6**:278

"Pao Chu" (P'u Sung-ling) **3**:348

"Papers on the Imagination" (Addison) **18**:61

"Parables of Our Lord and Saviour Jesus Christ" (Smart) **3**:395

Parabolae (Erasmus) **16**:136

Paraclesis (Erasmus)
See *Paraclesis ad Lectorem Pium*

Paraclesis ad Lectorem Pium (*Paraclesis*) (Erasmus) **16**:138, 149, 154

Paradise Lost (Milton) **9**:165-73, 175-83, 185-93, 196-99, 201, 204, 206, 208, 211-22, 228-30, 233-37, 240-50, 252, 257-58, 260-62

Paradise Regained (Milton) **9**:183, 189, 192, 200, 214, 217, 230, 233, 235-37, 246-49

Paradoxes and Problems (Donne)
See *Juvenilia; or, Certaine paradoxes, and problems*

Paragranum (Paracelsus)
See *Das Buch Paragranum*

A Parallel of Poetry and Painting (Dryden) **3**:236-38; **21**:90

"Parallel with other great cities" (Howell) **13**:424

Parallèle des anciens et des modernes en ce qui regarde les arts et les sciences (Perrault) **2**:259, 274-80, 283

Paramirum (Paracelsus)
See *Opus Paramirum*

"A Paranaeticall, or Advisive Verse, to his friend, Master John Wicks" (Herrick) **13**:378

Paraphrase of Hebrews (Erasmus) **16**:157

Paraphrase of the Psalms (Buchanan)
See *Psalmorum Dauidis paraphrasis poetica, nunc primum edita, authore Georgio Buchanano, Scoto, poetarum nostri saeculi facilè principe*

"A Paraphrase on Part of the Book of Job" ("Job") (Young) **3**:467, 492, 497

"Paraphrase on 'Te Deum'" (Dennis)
See "Part of the 'Te Deum' Paraphras'd, in Pindarick Verse"

Parasceve (*Day of Preparation*) (Bacon) **18**:148, 152, 187

Title Index

Parayso occidental, plantado y cultivado por la liberal benefica mano de los muy Catholicos (*Occidental Paradise*) (Siguenza y Gongora) **8**:343

"Pardoner's Prologue" (Chaucer) **17**:118, 122-23

"Pardoner's Tale" (Chaucer) **17**:98, 118, 121-23, 178, 195-200

Parlament of Foules (Chaucer)
See *Parlement of Foules*

Parlement (Chaucer)
See *Parlement of Foules*

Parlement of Foules (*Book of Saint Valentines Day of the Parlement of Briddes*; *Parlament of Foules*; *Parlement*; *Parlement of Foulys*; *Parliament of Fowls*) (Chaucer) **17**:45, 72, 77-8, 82, 91-7, 105, 108, 114-17, 149, 173, 189, 223, 227

Parlement of Foulys (Chaucer)
See *Parlement of Foules*

Parley of Beasts (Howell) **13**:424

Parley of Trees (Howell) **13**:424

Parliament of Fowls (Chaucer)
See *Parlement of Foules*

"The Parliament of Roses, to Julia" (Herrick) **13**:389, 402

Parliamenti Angliae Declaratio, & c. (Marvell) **4**:395

"The Parlyamente of Sprytes" (Chatterton) **3**:129

"Parson's Prologue" (Chaucer) **17**:215-16

"Parson's Tale" (Chaucer) **17**:47, 119-21, 172-73, 176, 178-80, 189, 200, 209, 213, 220, 241-44

"Part of the 'Te Deum' Paraphras'd, in Pindarick Verse" ("Paraphrase on 'Te Deum'"; "Te Deum") (Dennis) **11**:14, 51

"Partes Instauratio Secundae Delineatio et Argumentum" (Bacon) **18**:187

Parthenopoeia (Howell) **13**:441

Parthian Triumph (Siguenza y Gongora)
See *Triumpho parthenico que en glorias de María Santissima immaculadamente concebida*

"A Particular Providence and a Future State" (Hume) **7**:155

"The Parties of Great Britain" (Hume) **7**:152

The Parvenu Countryman (Marivaux)
See *Le paysan parvenu*

Pasquil the Playne (Elyot) **11**:61, 71-2, 84, 89, 92

Pasquin (Fielding) **1**:249

Pasquinades (Aretino)
See *Giudizi*

"The Passion" (Milton) **9**:204, 206

"Passion of Byblis" (Dennis) **11**:4-5, 15

The Passion of Jesus (Aretino)
See *La Passione di Gesù*

"The Passionate Shepherd to his Love" (Herrick) **13**:318

La Passione di Gesù (*The Passion of Jesus*) (Aretino) **12**:20, 35

"The Passions: An Ode for Music" (Collins) **4**:211-12, 214, 216, 220-22, 232, 234

The Pastime of Pleasure (Hawes) **17**:336-43, 347-59, 361-67

"Pastime with Good Company" (Henry VIII) **10**:145

Paston Correspondence
See *Paston Letters*

Paston Letters (*Original Letters written during the reigns of Henry VI., Edward IV., and Richard III.; Paston Correspondence*) **17**:431-74

"Pastoral Dialogue" (Killigrew) **4**:350

"Pastoral in the Manner of Spenser" (Warton) **15**:441

La pastorale comique (Moliere) **10**:283

"A Pastorall Dialogue" (Carew) **13**:59, 62

"A Pastorall upon the birth of Prince Charles" (Herrick) **13**:395

"Pastorals" (Pope) **3**:266-67, 270, 274, 290, 294, 322, 334-35

Pastorals (Drayton) **8**:10, 31

Pastorals (Lyttelton) **10**:202

"Patient Griselda" (Perrault)
See "Griselidis"

"The Patriarch" (Burns) **3**:98

The Patriot (Johnson) **15**:208

The Patriots (Munford) **5**:189-97

A Patterne of Catechisticall Doctrine (*Catechistical Doctrine*) (Andrewes) **5**:23, 28

"Paulo Purganti" (Prior) **4**:455, 461-62, 467

Pax Vobiscum (Aretino) **12**:16

Le paysan parvenu (*The Parvenu Countryman*) (Marivaux) **4**:353-57, 360-62, 368, 373-75, 379, 387

"The Peace Which Christ Gives His True Followers" (Hume) **7**:119

"The Peach in Brandy" (Walpole) **2**:500, 507

"Peau d'ane" ("The Ass's Skin") (Perrault) **2**:253-57, 261, 279, 286

"A Pedant" (Butler) **16**:52

Peder Paars (Holberg) **6**:258, 265-66, 269-71, 273, 278, 282

Pedro de Urdemalas (Cervantes) **6**:180-81

A Peep behind the Curtain (Garrick) **15**:98, 101-02, 122

La Peinture (Perrault) **2**:259

Penetential Psalms (Aretino)
See *I sette salmi de la penitenzia di David*

Pensées chrétiennes (Perrault) **2**:283

Pensées et fragments inédits de Montesquieu (Montesquieu) **7**:329, 332, 339, 342, 346, 348-49, 357, 361

"Pensées sur la clarté du discours" (Marivaux) **4**:371

Pensées sur le gouvernement (Voltaire) **14**:401

Le père prudent et equitable; ou, Crispin l'heureux forbe (Marivaux) **4**:358

Peremešnik (*The Mocker*) (Chulkov) **2**:14-15, 17-24, 26-7

Perfect Description of the People and Country of Scotland (Howell) **13**:420, 424

El perfecto caballero (Castro) **19**:13-14

"Peri Bathous; or, The Art of Sinking in Poetry" ("The Art of Sinking in Poetry") (Pope) **3**:317, 321, 323-24, 328-29

"The Perjured Beauty" (Manley) **1**:306-08

Pernille's Brief Ladyship (Holberg)
See *Pernilles korte frøikenstand*

Pernilles korte frøikenstand (*Pernille's Brief Ladyship*) (Holberg) **6**:263, 277

Persian Eclogues (Collins) **4**:209-11, 215, 217, 229, 233

The Persian Letters (Lyttelton)
See *Letters from a Persian in England to His Friend at Ispahan*

Persian Letters (Montesquieu)
See *Lettres persanes*

Persiles y Sigismunda (Cervantes)

See *Los trabajos de Persiles y Sigismunda*

Personal Narrative (Edwards) **7**:98, 101, 116

"The Personal Union" (Taylor) **11**:370

"Persuasions to Love" (Carew)
See "To A.L. Perswasions to Love"

"Perswasions to Enjoy" (Carew) **13**:59

"Pervigilium Veneris" (Parnell) **3**:251, 253-54

"The Peter-Penny" (Herrick) **13**:331

"Le petit chaperon rouge" ("Little Red Riding Hood") (Perrault) **2**:254-55, 257-58, 260, 262, 266-67, 271-74, 280, 282, 285

Le petit maître corrigé (Marivaux) **4**:368, 378

"Le petit poucet" ("Hop o' My Thumb") (Perrault) **2**:254-56, 258, 260-61, 266, 280-81, 284

"The Petition for an Absolute Retreat" ("Absolute Retreat") (Winchilsea) **3**:451-52, 454-56, 458

"Phaedra" (Prior) **4**:455

Phaenomena Universi (Bacon) **18**:187

"The Phaeton and the One-Horse Chair" (Warton) **15**:441, 462

Phaeton in the Suds (Fielding) **1**:220

Phalarismus (Hutten) **16**:239-41, 245

Pharsamon; ou, Les nouvelles folies romanesques (Marivaux) **4**:378, 385-86

"Philander" (Young) **3**:472

Philebus Commentary (Ficino) **12**:194

Philidore and Placentia (Haywood) **1**:283

"Phillis's Age" (Prior) **4**:461

"Phillis's Reply to the Answer..." ("Reply") (Wheatley) **3**:437

"Philomela" (Sidney) **19**:329

Le philosophe anglais; ou, Histoire de Monsieur Cléveland, Fils naturel de Cromwell (Prevost) **1**:328-29, 333-35, 337-39, 341, 343, 347, 352, 357-59

"A Philosopher" (Butler) **16**:50

The Philosopher (Aretino)
See *Il filosofo*

"The Philosopher and the Lover; to a Mistress dying" (Davenant) **13**:195, 205

"The Philosopher's Devotion" (More) **9**:296

"The Philosophers Disquisition to the Dying Christian" ("Disquisition") (Davenant) **13**:204-06

Philosophia Christi (Erasmus) **16**:142

Philosophia sagax (Paracelsus) **14**:200, 203

A Philosophical Enquiry into the Origin of Our Ideas of the Sublime and Beautiful (*Essay on the Sublime and Beautiful*) (Burke) **7**:4, 6, 39

A Philosophical Essay on Man, Being an Attempt to Investigate the Principles and Laws of the Reciprocal Influence of the Soul on the Body (*De l'homme; Man*) (Marat) **10**:220, 222-23, 231, 239

Philosophical Essays (Hume) **7**:138, 154

Philosophical Essays concerning Human Understanding (Hume) **7**:164

Philosophical Poems (*Poems*) (More) **9**:295, 298, 303, 306, 308, 320

La philosophie de l'histoire (Voltaire) **14**:357, 383, 387

"Philosophy and Religion Are Sisters" (Ficino) **12**:174

Philotas (Lessing) **8**:66, 109

"The Physician's Stratagem" (Manley) **1**:306-08

"Physician's Tale" (Chaucer) **17**:117, 196-97, 200

"Physiognomy" (Montaigne)

See "De la phisionomie"
Physiologia (Lipsius) **16**:258
"The Picture of Little T. C. in a Prospect of
  Flowers" ("Little T. C.") (Marvell) **4**:427,
  434-35, 438, 442
Pieces (Howell) **13**:437
"Pierce Gaveston, Earle of Cornwall"
  ("Gaveston") (Drayton) **8**:29-30, 33
Piers Plowman (*Dowel, Dobet, and Dobest;
  Lives of Do-wel, Do-bet, and Do-best; Visio de
  Petro Plowman, Vita de Dowel, Vita de
  Dobet, Vita de Dobest; Vision of William
  concerning Piers the Plowman*) (Langland)
  19:56-204
"Pieśń" ("Czego chcesz od nas, panie?";
  "What Do You Want from Us, Lord?";
  "What Do You Wish, O Lord, In Return
  For Your Bounteous Gifts?"; "What wilt
  Thou from us, Lord?") (Kochanowski)
  10:154, 156, 160-61, 170, 175-76
"Pieśń Swiętojańska o Sobótce" ("St. John's
  Eve") (Kochanowski) **10**:151-54, 161
Pieśni (*Songs*) (Kochanowski) **10**:161, 167,
  176
"Piety, a Vision" (Parnell)
  See "Piety; or, The Vision"
"Piety; or, The Vision" ("Piety, a Vision")
  (Parnell) **3**:255, 257-58
"The Pig, the Goat, and the Sheep" (Dennis)
  11:47
"The Pigmies and the Cranes" (Addison)
  18:29
The Pilfered Snuffbox (Schlegel)
  See "Die entführte Dose"
"A Pilgrim" (Bradstreet)
  See "As Weary Pilgrim"
"A Pilgrimage for Religion's Sake" (Erasmus)
  See "Religious Pilgrimage"
*The Pilgrim's Progress from This World to That
  Which Is to Come* (Bunyan) **4**:143-73, 178-
  99, 202
"The Pillar of Fame" (Herrick) **13**:358, 391
"A Pimp" (Butler) **16**:54
Pindaric Odes (Ronsard) **6**:411
"A Pindarick Ode on the King...Occasion'd by
  the Victory at Aghrim" (Dennis) **11**:48
"A Pindarick Poem upon the Hurricane"
  (Winchilsea) **3**:451, 454
"A Pindarique on His Majesties Birth-Day"
  (Prior) **4**:475
"Pious Selinda" (Congreve) **5**:85
"The Pious Woman" (Kochanowski)
  See "Na nabożną"
"Piscatoria II" (Sannazaro) **8**:334-35
"Piscatoria III" (Sannazaro) **8**:332, 335
Piscatoriae (Sannazaro)
  See *Eclogae piscatoriae*
Piscatura (Hutten)
  See *De piscatura Venetorum heroicum*
De piscatura Venetorum heroicum (*Piscatura*)
  (Hutten) **16**:238, 241
Placets au roi (Moliere) **10**:281
The Plain-Dealer (Wycherley) **8**:380, 382,
  384-97, 402-03, 406, 409, 415, 420, 423-26,
  429-30, 432; **21**:346-49, 354, 359-60, 363,
  374-76, 379-81, 385, 388-89, 391-94, 396
"Plaine-Path'd Experience, th'Unlearneds
  Guide" (Drayton)
  See "Sonnet 46"
"Plainte pour une Absence" (Malherbe) **5**:171
Plaisirs de l'île enchantée (Moliere) **10**:311

*Plan de législation criminelle, ouvrage dans
  lequel on traite des délits et des peines, de la
  force des preuves et des présomptions . . .*
  (*Criminal Legislation*) (Marat) **10**:221
Plan of a Constitution (Marat)
  See *La Constitution ou Projet de déclaration
    des Droits de l'homme et du citoyen, suivi
    d'un Plan de constitution juste, sage et
    libre*
*The Plan of a Dictionary of the English
  Language; Addressed to the Right
  Honourable Philip Dormer, Earl of
  Chesterfield* ("Prospectus") (Johnson)
  15:197, 206, 250-51
The Platonic Lovers (Davenant) **13**:175-76,
  181, 187, 196-200, 215
Platonic Theology (Ficino)
  See *Theologia platonica de immortalitate
    animorum*
"The Platonist" (Hume) **7**:153
"A Player" (Butler) **16**:26
A Playhouse to Let (Davenant) **13**:190
*The Plays, Histories, and Novels of the Late
  Ingenious Mrs. Behn* (Behn) **1**:29
*The Plays of William Shakespeare, in Eight
  Volumes, with the Corrections and
  Illustrations of Various Commentators; To
  which are added Notes by Sam Johnson*
  (*Shakespeare*) (Johnson) **15**:197, 225, 307,
  313
Pleasure Reconcild to Vertue (Jonson) **6**:337
"The Pleasures of Melancholy" (Warton)
  15:431, 433, 435, 439, 445, 448, 454, 456,
  460
The Pleasures of the Imagination (Addison)
  18:7, 18, 20, 37, 61
The Plebian (Steele) **18**:352-54
A Plot and No Plot (Dennis) **11**:5, 12, 14
"The Plots" (Davenant) **13**:205
"Plutarch's Lives" (Dryden) **21**:52, 58
Plutus's Council-Chamber (Grimmelshausen)
  See *Rathstübel Plutonis*
"A Poem as the Corpus Delicti" (P'u Sung-
  ling)
  See "Shih-yen"
Poem on the Disaster of Lisbon (Voltaire)
  See *Poème sur le désastre de Lisbonne*
"Poem on the Last Day" ("The Last Day")
  (Young) **3**:466-69, 483, 485, 487, 497
*A Poem Sacred to the Memory of Sir Isaac
  Newton* (*To the Memory of Sir Isaac Newton*)
  (Thomson) **16**:384-85, 399, 401, 406, 419,
  421, 423, 425, 428
"A Poem to the Memory of Mr. Congreve"
  (Thomson)
  See "To the Memory of Mr. Congreve"
"A Poem upon the Death of Her Late Sacred
  Majesty Queen Anne, and the Most Happy
  and Most Auspicious Accession of His
  Sacred Majesty King George" ("On the
  Accession of King George to the British
  Throne") (Dennis) **11**:15, 26, 50
"Poem upon the Death of O. C." ("Death of
  the Lord Protector") (Marvell) **4**:398, 417,
  431
"Poème lyrique" (Marmontel) **2**:223
Poème sur la loi naturelle (Voltaire) **14**:378,
  380
Poème sur le désastre de Lisbonne (*Poem on the
  Disaster of Lisbon*) (Voltaire) **14**:364, 378,
  381, 388, 390
Poèmes (*Poems*) (Ronsard) **6**:407, 410, 427

Poems (Bradstreet) **4**:87
Poems (Drayton) **8**:18, 26, 42
Poems (Winchilsea) **3**:448
Poems (Killigrew) **4**:347
Poems (Milton) **9**:262
Poems (More)
  See *Philosophical Poems*
Poems (Ronsard)
  See *Poèmes*
Poems (Taylor) **11**:381
Poems and Letters by Mr. Dennis (Dennis)
  11:4
*Poems Ascribed to Robert Burns, the Ayrshire
  Bard* (Burns) **3**:49
Poems by Christopher Smart (Smart) **3**:392
Poems by Thomas Carew, Esquire (Carew)
  13:9, 27-8, 30, 52
Poems, Chiefly in the Scottish Dialect (Burns)
  3:47-8
Poems for Young Ladies, in Three Parts
  (Goldsmith) **2**:81
Poems in Burlesque (Dennis) **11**:47
Poems Lyrick and Pastorall (Drayton) **8**:17
The Poems of Phillis Wheatley (Wheatley)
  3:421
*The Poems of the Late Christopher Smart, M.
  A., Fellow of Pembroke College, Cambridge,
  Consisting of His Prize Poems, Odes, Sonnets,
  and Fables, Latin and English Translations*
  (Smart) **3**:371
Poems on Several Occasions (Parnell) **3**:258
Poems on Several Occasions (Prior) **4**:466
Poems on Several Occasions (Smart) **3**:375
*Poems on Several Occasions, Never Before
  Printed* (Davenant) **13**:206
*Poems on Various Subjects, Religious and
  Moral, by Phillis Wheatley, Negro Servant to
  Mr. John Wheatley of Boston, in New
  England, 1773* (Wheatley) **3**:407, 409-11,
  417, 421, 431
*Poems upon Several Occasions, with a Voyage to
  the Island of Love* (Behn) **1**:29
The Poetaster (Jonson) **6**:302, 304, 306, 335-
  36
Poetica d'Aristotele vulgarizzata et sposta
  (Castelvetro) **12**:46, 50, 62, 69, 71
"Poetical Banquet" (Erasmus) **16**:140
The Poetical Works of David Garrick, Esq.
  (Garrick) **15**:97, 114
The Poetical Works of Edward Taylor (Taylor)
  11:343, 355
Poetics (Dennis) **11**:33
Poétique française (Marmontel) **2**:223
"A Poet's Welcome to His Love-Begotten
  Daughter" ("Love-Begotten Daughter")
  (Burns) **3**:85, 87
Pokazi (Beer) **5**:56
Politica (Lipsius)
  See *Politicorum sive civilis doctrinae libri sex,
    qui ad principatum maxime spectant*
Political Discourses (Hume) **7**:190
The Political History of the Devil (Defoe)
  1:136
Political Tracts (Johnson) **15**:208
Political Treatise (Spinoza) **9**:423
The Politician (Gracian y Morales)
  See *El Político Don Fernando el Católico*
Político (Gracian y Morales)
  See *El Político Don Fernando el Católico*
El Político Don Fernando el Católico (*The
  Politician; Político*) (Gracian y Morales)
  15:143-45, 165

Politicorum libri sex (Lipsius)
　See *Politicorum sive civilis doctrinae libri sex, qui ad principatum maxime spectant*
Politicorum sive civilis doctrinae libri sex, qui ad principatum maxime spectant (*Politica; Politicorum libri sex; Politics; Six Bookes of Politickes or Civil Doctrine*) (Lipsius) **16**:251, 254, 262, 265-66, 268-69, 277-79
Politics (Lipsius)
　See *Politicorum sive civilis doctrinae libri sex, qui ad principatum maxime spectant*
Politique naturelle (Holbach) **14**:152, 154-56, 160, 162, 168
Den politiske kandestøber (Holberg) **6**:258, 273, 276, 282-83
Poly-Olbion (*The Second Part; or, A Continuance of Poly-Olbion from the Eighteenth Song.*) (Drayton) **8**:5-8, 10-15, 17-21, 24-6, 29, 40-3, 45-7
"Poor Mailie's Elegy" (Burns)
　See "The Death and Dying Words of Poor Mailie"
Pope ein Metaphysiker (Lessing) **8**:98
"Popish Pamphlet cast in London streets not long after the city was burned" (Taylor) **11**:366
"A Popish Priest" (Butler) **16**:50, 53
Popular Elaboration of the Chronicle of the Three Kingdoms (Lo Kuan-chung)
　See *San-kuo-chih yeni-i*
"The Popular Superstitions of the Highlands of Scotland" (Collins)
　See "An Ode on the Popular Superstitions of the Highlands of Scotland, etc."
Portatif (Voltaire)
　See *Dictionnaire philosophique*
Portefeuille de J.-B. Rousseau (Rousseau) **9**:335
Portraits (Reynolds) **15**:407, 419
The Posthumous Poems of Dr. Thomas Parnell Containing Poems Moral and Divine (Parnell) **3**:257
Posthumous Works (Butler) **16**:30
Posthumous Works of the Author of a Vindication of the Rights of Woman (Wollstonecraft)
　See *Letters to Imlay*
The Posthumous Works of William Wycherley, Esq., in Prose and Verse (Wycherley) **8**:416
"Posting" (Montaigne) **8**:203
"Pour le roy allant chastier la rebellion des Rochelois et chasser les Anglois qui en leur faveur estoient descendus en l'îsle de Ré" ("Île de Ré") (Malherbe) **5**:166, 168, 171, 185
"Pour le Sonnet de Cassandre" (Malherbe) **5**:171
"Pour Mme la D... de N... sur le gain d'un procès" (Rousseau) **9**:344
"Pour une personne convalescente" (Rousseau) **9**:342-43
"The power in the people" (Herrick) **13**:395
The Power of Love (Manley) **1**:306, 308, 312
Die Pracht zu Landheim (Schlegel) **5**:277-79
Practica (Paracelsus) **14**:199
Praedones (Hutten)
　See *The Robbers*
De Praeparatione ad Mortem (Erasmus) **16**:154-55
Praescriptio (Lipsius) **16**:271-73
The Praise of Folly (Erasmus)
　See *Moriae encomium*

Praise of Matrimony (Erasmus) **16**:146
Prayer (Andrewes)
　See *Scala coeli: Nineteene Sermons concerning Prayer*
"Prayer before Sermon" (Andrewes) **5**:42-3
"Prayer for the King on his going to Limoges" (Malherbe) **5**:167
"Prayer to Ben Jonson" (Herrick) **13**:323
"A Prayer to the Wind" (Carew) **13**:28
Prayers and Meditations (Johnson) **15**:209, 225, 240, 243, 246
Preces (Andrewes)
　See *Preces privatae, graece, et latine*
Preces privatae, graece, et latine (*Preces*) (Andrewes) **5**:21-4, 26-7, 33-6, 38, 42
Les précieuses ridicules (*The Affected Ladies*) (Moliere) **10**:275, 277, 280-81, 283, 286, 290-93, 299-300, 310, 316-20
The Precious Pearl (Jami)
　See *al-Durrah al-Fákhira*
"Predestination" (Prior) **4**:473
"The Preexistence of the Soul" (More) **9**:313, 330-31
"Preface" (Luther) **9**:118
"The Preface" (Taylor) **11**:393, 401-03
Preface (Schlegel)
　See *Vorrede des Uebersetzers zu Der Ruhmredige*
"Preface to *Eneydos*" (Caxton) **17**:13
Preface to Gondibert (Davenant) **13**:202-03, 207, 209-10, 212
Preface to Ovid's Epistles (Dryden) **3**:217; **21**:113
"Preface to *Polychronicon*" ("Prohemye to *Polychronicon*") (Caxton) **17**:22, 25-6
"Preface to Shakespeare" (Johnson) **15**:214-15, 220, 236, 270, 307-08, 310-13
"Preface (to the Dictionary)" (Johnson) **15**:250-51
"Preface to the Fables" (Dryden) **3**:217; **21**:112
Prefaces, Biographical and Critical, to the Works of the English Poets (*The Lives of the Poets*) (Johnson) **15**:199-200, 203-04, 209-10, 220-21, 229, 231, 237, 241, 243, 251, 270, 285, 287, 298
Le Préjugé vaincu (Marivaux) **4**:364, 369
Prelude on the Babylonian Captivity of the Church (Luther)
　See *De captivitate Babylonica ecclesiae praeludium*
"A Preparation to Prayer" (Winchilsea) **3**:451
Preparatory Meditations before my Approach to the Lords Supper. Chiefly upon the Doctrin preached upon the Day of administration. (*The Sacramental Meditations*) (Taylor) **11**:343-44, 346, 351, 354-55, 358-59, 363, 367-68, 372-73, 377-78, 380-82, 384-86, 392, 394-95, 397-400
"The Present" (Herrick) **13**:317
Present Discontents (Burke)
　See *Thoughts on the Cause of the Present Discontents*
A Present for a Serving Maid (Haywood) **1**:293
The Present Means and Brief Delineation of a Free Commonwealth (Milton) **9**:185
The Present State of Affairs (Burke) **7**:47
"The Presentation of Christ in the Temple" (Smart) **3**:376, 378, 401-02

A Preservative agaynste Deth (Elyot) **11**:62, 71, 83
Prêtres démasqués (Holbach) **14**:153
"The Priest" (Kochanowski)
　See "O Kapelanie"
Priestcraft Dangerous to Religion and Government (Dennis)
　See *The Danger of Priestcraft to Religion and Government*
Priestcraft distinguished from Christianity (Dennis) **11**:15, 26
Prigozhaya povarikha (*The Comely Cook*) (Chulkov) **2**:13-18, 23-5
Primal History (Bacon)
　See *Historia Prima*
"Primero sueño" ("Dream") (Juana Ines de la Cruz) **5**:146-54, 156
"The Primrose" (Carew) **13**:30
"The Primrose" (Donne) **10**:13, 33, 36-7
"Primrose" (Herrick) **13**:311
The Prince (Machiavelli)
　See *Il principe di Niccholo Machivello*
Le prince travesti (Marivaux) **4**:366-67
"The Princess Lily" (Pope) **3**:335
"Princess Lotus Bloom" (P'u Sung-ling)
　See "Lien-hua Kung-chu"
The Princess of Clèves (La Fayette)
　See *La Princesse de Clèves*
The Princess of Elis (Moliere)
　See *La princesse d'Élide*
La princesse de Babylon (Voltaire) **14**:346, 359
La Princesse de Clèves (*The Princess of Clèves*) (La Fayette) **2**:136-40, 142-51, 153-71
La Princesse de Montpensier (La Fayette) **2**:138-39, 144, 151-52, 155-58, 161, 165-66
La princesse d'Élide (*The Princess of Elis*) (Moliere) **10**:282-83, 291, 311, 320, 325, 327
De principiis (Gray)
　See *De principiis cogitandi*
De Principiis atque Originibus (Bacon) **18**:187
De principiis cogitandi (*De principiis*) (Gray) **4**:329
The Principles of Descartes (Spinoza)
　See *Renati Des cartes principiorum philosophiae pars I. et II. more geometrico demonstratae per Benedictum de Spinoza*
Printz Adimantus und der königlichen Princessin Ormizella Liebes-Geschict (Beer) **5**:52, 54-5
"Prioress's Tale" (Chaucer) **17**:60, 68, 119, 177-78
Private Correspondence (Pepys) **11**:241
"Pro Lena apologia" (Buchanan)
　See "Pro Lena apologia, Eleg. III"
"Pro Lena apologia, Eleg. III" ("Pro Lena apologia") (Buchanan) **4**:134-35
Pro populo anglicano defensio, contra Claudii Anonymi (*A Defence of the People of England*) (Milton) **9**:159, 163, 201, 252
"The Prodigal Son" (Marvell) **4**:431
Prodromi sive Anticipatationes Philosophiae Secundae (Bacon) **18**:187
Profane Feast (Erasmus) **16**:143, 145
"Profession du vicaire Savoyard" ("The Confession of Faith of a Savoyard Vicar"; "Profession of Faith") (Rousseau) **14**:247, 260, 301, 310
"Profession of Faith" (Rousseau)
　See "Profession du vicaire Savoyard"

Profitable Meditations Fitted to Man's Different Condition (Bunyan)   **4**:167-68

Progne y Filomena (Castro)   **19**:7-8

Prognostications (Paracelsus)   **14**:187

"The Progress of Beauty" (Swift)   **1**:458, 461, 483-84

"The Progress of Discontent" (Warton)   **15**:434, 440, 463

The Progress of Love, in Four Eclogues (Lyttelton)   **10**:196-97, 200, 203-05

"The Progress of Marriage" (Swift)   **1**:453

"The Progress of Poesy" ("Ode on the Progress of Poesy"; "The Progress of Poetry") (Gray)   **4**:280-81, 283-84, 291-92, 300-02, 309, 312-13, 317, 321, 332-33

"The Progress of Poetry" (Gray)
   See "The Progress of Poesy"

"The Progress of Virtue" (Swift)   **1**:458

The Progresse of the Soule (Donne)   **10**:4, 14, 19-23, 52-3, 62

"Progymnasmata" (More)   **10**:430

"Prohemye to *Polychronicon*" (Caxton)
   See "Preface to *Polychronicon*"

"The Prohibition" ("Take heed of loving mee") (Donne)   **10**:36

A Project for the Advancement of Religion (Swift)   **1**:492

Prólogo (Gracian y Morales)   **15**:171

"The Prologue" (Bradstreet)   **4**:95, 105-06, 110, 114

"Prologue" (Chaucer)
   See "General Prologue"

"Prologue" (Taylor)   **11**:384, 394, 401-03

"Prologue before the Queen" (Prior)   **4**:455

"Prologue of the Nun's Priest's Tale" (Chaucer)   **17**:137

"Prologue on the Old Winchester Playhouse" (Warton)   **15**:462

"Prologue to *Blanchardin and Eglantine*" (Caxton)   **17**:29

"Prologue to *Charles the Great*" (Caxton)   **17**:16, 23

"Prologue to *Eneydos*" (Caxton)   **17**:7, 10, 16-17, 19

"Prologue to *Le Morte d'Arthur*" (Caxton)   **17**:30-1, 33

"Prologue to the *Golden Legend*" (Caxton)   **17**:14

"Prologue to the Monk's Tale" ("Monk's Prologue") (Chaucer)   **17**:122, 137

"Prologue to *The Recuyell*" (Caxton)   **17**:7

"Prologue to the University of Oxford" ("University of Oxon.") (Dryden)   **21**:83, 88

"Prologue to the Wife of Bath's Tale" ("Wife of Bath's Prologue") (Chaucer)   **17**:55, 81, 122, 181, 189, 202, 206, 210-11, 213, 229-31, 236-38, 240-41

Promus of Formularies and Elegancies (Bacon)   **18**:133

Prophecies (Vinci)   **12**:418

"The Prophecy" (Chatterton)   **3**:123

"The Prophecy of Famine" (Churchill)   **3**:140, 142-46, 148, 152-56, 160, 163

"Proporzec albo Hold Pruski" ("The Banner, or Homage from Prussia") (Kochanowski)   **10**:175

A Proposal for Putting a Speedy End to the War (Dennis)   **11**:19

A Proposal for the Universal Use of Irish Manufacture (Swift)   **1**:513-14

Proposals for Printing the Dramatick Works of William Shakespeare (Johnson)   **15**:311, 313

Prose Observations (Butler)   **16**:50

"A Proselite" (Butler)   **16**:50

"Prosopopoia; or, Mother Hubberds Tale" ("Mother Hubberd's Tale") (Spenser)   **5**:312, 329, 345, 356

The Prospect: being the Fifth Part of Liberty (Thomson)   **16**:374

"Prospectus" (Johnson)
   See *The Plan of a Dictionary of the English Language; Addressed to the Right Honourable Philip Dormer, Earl of Chesterfield*

"The Protégé" (Chulkov)
   See "Stavlennik"

"Protestation to Julia" (Herrick)   **13**:327

"Prothalamion; or, A Spousall Verse" (Spenser)   **5**:311, 313, 329, 332, 347, 349, 356

"Protogenes and Apelles" (Prior)   **4**:455

Proud Melchio (Grimmelshausen)
   See *Der stoltze Melcher*

Prouverbes moraux (*Moral Proverbs*) (Christine de Pizan)   **9**:45

La provinciale (Marivaux)   **4**:369

The Provok'd Husband (Vanbrugh)
   See *A Journey to London*

The Provok'd Wife (*The Provoked Wife*) (Vanbrugh)   **21**:278, 281-84, 287, 289-90, 292-94, 296, 298-99, 301, 314-15, 318-20, 322-28, 333-36

The Provoked Wife (Vanbrugh)
   See *The Provok'd Wife*

Proximus and Lympida (Grimmelshausen)
   See *Proximus und Lympida*

Proximus und Lympida (*Proximus and Lympida*) (Grimmelshausen)   **6**:247-48

The Prudent Man (Goldoni)   **4**:250

Psałterz Dawidów (*Psalter of David*) (Kochanowski)   **10**:151, 155, 158, 161-62, 167, 170, 173-74

"A Psalme or Hymne to the Graces" (Herrick)   **13**:391

Psalmes (Sidney)   **19**:309-10, 312, 315

Psalmorum Dauidis paraphrasis poetica, nunc primum edita, authore Georgio Buchanano, Scoto, poetarum nostri saeculi facilè principe (*Paraphrase of the Psalms*) (Buchanan)   **4**:119, 124, 130

"Psalms" (Smart)
   See *A Translation of the Psalms of David, Attempted in the Spirit of Christianity, and Adapted to the Divine Service*

Psalms (Kochanowski)   **10**:172

Psalter of David (Kochanowski)
   See *Psałterz Dawidów*

Pseudo-Martyr: Wherein Out of Certaine Propositions and Gradations, This Conclusion is evicted. That Those Which Are of the Romane Religion in this Kingdome, may and ought to take the Oath of Allegiance (Donne)   **10**:11, 39, 89

Psiché (Moliere)   **10**:275, 283

"Psychathanasia platonica: or, A Platonicall Poem of the Immortality of Souls" (More)   **9**:295, 311-15, 327-31

"Psyche's Song" (More)   **9**:320

Psychodia platonica: or, A Platonicall Song of the Soul (More)   **9**:294, 296, 302, 312, 320, 330-31

"Psychozoia: or, A Christiano-Platonicall Display of Life" ("The Life of the Soul") (More)   **9**:302-04, 309, 312-13, 315, 320-21, 327-28, 330

Publiciste de la Révolution française (Marat)
   See *Le publiciste parisien, journal politique, libre et impartial . . .*

Le Publiciste parisien (Marat)
   See *Le publiciste parisien, journal politique, libre et impartial . . .*

Le publiciste parisien, journal politique, libre et impartial . . . (*L'Ami du Peuple; The Friend of the People; Journal; Publiciste de la Révolution française; Le Publiciste parisien*) (Marat)   **10**:220-21, 227-29, 232, 234, 236

Publick Spirit (Dennis)
   See *An Essay upon Public Spirit; being a Satire in Prose upon the Manners and Luxury of the Times, the chief Sources of our present Parties and Divisions*

La pucelle (Voltaire)   **14**:328, 338, 354, 396-97, 399-400, 413

"De pueris" (Erasmus)   **16**:198-202

The Punctilious Ladies (Goldoni)
   See *Le femmine puntigliose*

"A (Puritan) Fanatic" ("A Fanatic") (Butler)   **16**:27

La putta onorata (*The Honorable Girl*) (Goldoni)   **4**:250, 256, 265-67, 269-70, 272-73

Le Pyrrhonisme de l'histoire (Voltaire)   **14**:383

"Qua si fa elmi di calici e spade" (Michelangelo)   **12**:369

Quæstiones Epistolicæ (Lipsius)   **16**:263

"Quam Pulchra Es" (Henry VIII)   **10**:146

"Quand je suis vingt ou trente mois sans retourner en Vendômois" (Ronsard)   **6**:417

"Quand j'estois libre" (Ronsard)   **6**:432-33

"Quand vous serez bien vieille" (Ronsard)   **6**:409, 417

"A Quarreler" (Butler)   **16**:27

Le quart livre des faictz et dictz heroiques du noble Pantagruel (Rabelais)   **5**:215-16, 224-25, 233-35, 238-40, 249-50, 252, 255-56, 258-59

Les quatre premiers livres de la Franciade (*La Franciade*) (Ronsard)   **6**:406-07, 409-10, 414, 416-17, 420-22, 424, 431-32

"Que philosopher, c'est apprendre à mourir" ("That to Philosophize Is to Learn to Die") (Montaigne)   **8**:236, 238

"Queen and Huntress" (Jonson)   **6**:305

Queen Catharine; or, The Ruines of Love (Pix)   **8**:257, 260-63, 268-69, 271-72, 275

Queenes (Jonson)
   See *The Masque of Queens*

Querela Pacis (*Complaint of Peace Ejected from All Countries; Querimonia Pacis*) (Erasmus)   **16**:132, 154-55, 173, 182, 198

Querelae (Hutten)   **16**:229

Querimonia Pacis (Erasmus)
   See *Querela Pacis*

The Quest of Cynthia (Drayton)   **8**:9, 17, 34

"The Question" (Prior)
   See "The Question, to Lisetta"

"The Question, to Lisetta" ("The Question") (Prior)   **4**:460-61, 466

Questions sur l'Encyclopédie (Voltaire)   **14**:367, 370, 380, 392

Quis aberret a janua (Erasmus)   **16**:196

"A Rabble" (Butler)   **16**:54

Ragionamenti (Aretino)

See *Ragionamento della Nanna e della Antonia*

Ragionamento de le Corti (Aretino) **12**:20

Ragionamento della Nanna e della Antonia (Dialoghi; Dialogues; Ragionamenti; Sei giornate) (Aretino) **12**:4-6, 12, 14, 20-1, 23-6, 31-2, 35-7

La raison par alphabet (Voltaire) **14**:392

The Rambler (Johnson) **15**:189-91, 195-96, 198-201, 207, 218, 251, 259-61, 266-67, 273-74, 285, 287, 289, 306-07, 309

The Rambler, 4 (Johnson) **15**:237

The Rambler, 20 (Johnson) **15**:262

The Rambler, 32 (Johnson) **15**:243

The Rambler, 68 (Johnson) **15**:309

The Rambler, 73 (Johnson) **15**:267

The Rambler, 76 (Johnson) **15**:268

The Rambler, 78 (Johnson) **15**:266

The Rambler, 86 (Johnson) **15**:239

The Rambler, 89 ("The Luxury of Vain Imagination") (Johnson) **15**:213, 240

The Rambler, 92 (Johnson) **15**:239

The Rambler, 125 (Johnson) **15**:309

The Rambler, 154 (Johnson) **15**:237

The Rambler, 159 (Johnson) **15**:268

The Rambler, 167 (Johnson) **15**:309

The Rambler, 168 (Johnson) **15**:239

The Rambler, 177 (Johnson) **15**:241

The Rambler, 183 (Johnson) **15**:267

The Rambler, 188 (Johnson) **15**:266

The Rambler, 190 (Johnson) **15**:244

The Rambler, 203 (Johnson) **15**:291

"A Ranter" (Butler) **16**:52

"The Rantin' Dog the Daddy o't" (Burns) **3**:86

The Rape of the Lock (Pope) **3**:267-71, 273, 275-76, 279-82, 287, 289-91, 295-96, 298-99, 304, 307, 310-14, 317, 335

Rape upon Rape; Or, The Justice Caught in His Own Trap (Fielding) **1**:250

"A Rapture" (Carew) **13**:11-12, 19-20, 24, 26, 28, 30-1, 34-7, 39, 56-60

The Rash Resolve (Haywood) **1**:292

Rasselas (Johnson)
See *The History of Rasselas, Prince of Abissinia*

Rathstübel Plutonis (Plutus's Council-Chamber) (Grimmelshausen) **6**:247

Ratio seu Methodus compendio perveniendi ad veram theologiam (Erasmus) **16**:149, 151

Ratio Status (Grimmelshausen) **6**:247-48

Ratio Verea Theologiae (Erasmus) **16**:154

Rational Account of the Main Doctrines of the Christian Religion Attempted (Edwards) **7**:128

De ratione studii (Erasmus) **16**:136, 146-47, 154, 187

"Rattlin' Roarin' Willie" (Burns) **3**:67, 86

Rays of the Flashes (Jami)
See *Ash'i'atu 'l Lama'át*

The Reader (Steele) **18**:354

The Readie and Easie Way to Establish a Free Commonwealth (Milton) **9**:162-63, 184

The Reason of Church Government (Milton) **9**:192, 203, 250, 252

The Reasonableness of Christianity, as Delivered in the Scriptures (Locke) **7**:259, 281-82, 290

Reasons for Restoring Some Prayers and Directions as They Stand in the Communion Service of the First English Reformed Liturgy (Collier) **6**:209

"Rebel Families" (P'u Sung-ling)
See "Tao-hu"

"A Rebus by I. B." (Wheatley) **3**:4ll, 433

"Recollection" (Wheatley)
See "On Recollection"

The Recruiting Officer (Farquhar) **21**:126, 128-29, 132-33, 135, 138-39, 143-44, 149-54, 157-58, 161, 166-69, 171-72, 176, 178-81

"Red and white roses" (Carew) **13**:11

"A Red, Red Rose" (Burns)
See "My Luve is Like a Red, Red Rose"

Redargutio philosophiarum (Refutation of Philosophies) (Bacon) **18**:153-54, 187

"Redemption" (Brooke) **1**:62

"Reeve's Tale" (Chaucer) **17**:171, 193, 201-02

Reflections Critical and Satyrical, upon a Late Rhapsody call'd An Essay upon Criticism (Reflections upon an Essay on Criticism) (Dennis) **11**:22

Reflections on the French Revolution (Burke)
See *Reflections on the Revolution in France and on the Proceedings in Certain Societies in London Relative to That Event*

Reflections on the Revolution in France and on the Proceedings in Certain Societies in London Relative to That Event (Reflections on the French Revolution) (Burke) **7**:7-9, 14, 20, 23, 26-7, 32, 34, 37, 41, 50-1, 55, 60-2

Reflections upon an Essay on Criticism (Dennis)
See *Reflections Critical and Satyrical, upon a Late Rhapsody call'd An Essay upon Criticism*

Reflections upon the Present State of England, and the Independence of America (Day) **1**:106, 108

"The Reflexion" (Taylor) **11**:352, 360, 363, 384

Réflexions critiques sur Longin (Réflexions sur Longin) (Boileau-Despreaux) **3**:29, 39

Réflexions sur le caractère de quelques princes et sur quelques événements de leur vie (Montesquieu) **7**:360-62

"Réflexions sur les coquettes" (Marivaux) **4**:380

Réflexions sur Longin (Boileau-Despreaux)
See *Réflexions critiques sur Longin*

Reformation Writings (Luther)
See *Die Reformationsschriften*

Die Reformationsschriften (Reformation Writings) (Luther) **9**:140

The Reform'd Coquet; or, The Memoirs of Amoranda (Davys) **1**:98-102

The Refutation of Machiavelli's Prince (Frederick the Great)
See *Anti-Machiavel*

Refutation of Philosophies (Bacon)
See *Redargutio philosophiarum*

The Regicide (Perrault) **2**:357-58

Register (Burke)
See *The Annual Register*

Rehabilitations of Horace (Lessing)
See *Rettungen des Horaz*

The Rehearsall Transpros'd (Marvell) **4**:394, 399-400, 429, 455

Reign of Henry the Second (Lyttelton)
See *The History of the Life of King Henry the Second and of the Age in Which He Lived*

Reisen eines Deutschen in England im Jahr 1782 (Travels, Chiefly on Foot, through Several Parts of England in 1782) (Moritz) **2**:227, 229, 233-34, 244-46

Reisen eines Deutschen in Italien in den Jahren 1786 bis 1788 (Moritz) **2**:233, 246

Rejectiuncula (Lipsius) **16**:254

"Rejoice in the Lamb" (Smart)
See "Jubilate Agno"

The Relapse; or, Vertue in Danger (Vanbrugh)
See *The Relapse; or, Virtue in Danger*

The Relapse; or, Virtue in Danger (The Relapse; or, Vertue in Danger; The Relapser) (Vanbrugh) **21**:278-84, 286, 288-90, 293-94, 296-306, 308-11, 313-14, 316, 318-24, 326-29, 331-36

The Relapser (Vanbrugh)
See *The Relapse; or, Virtue in Danger*

Relation autobiographique (The Autobiography of Venerable Marie of the Incarnation; Relations) (Marie de l'Incarnation) **10**:251-54

Relation du banissement des Jésuites de la Chine (Voltaire) **14**:370

Relations (Marie de l'Incarnation)
See *Relation autobiographique*

Relazioni (Machiavelli) **8**:128

Religio Laici; or, A Layman's Faith (Dryden) **3**:184, 188, 191, 196, 204, 208, 216, 221, 235, 240-43; **21**:51, 56, 58, 67-9, 71-2, 88, 115, 120

Religious Affections (Edwards)
See *A Treatise concerning Religious Affections*

"Religious Banquet" (Erasmus)
See "Religious Treat"

Religious Courtship (Defoe) **1**:122

"Religious Pilgrimage" ("A Pilgrimage for Religion's Sake") (Erasmus) **16**:118, 141, 194-95

Religious Symposium (Erasmus)
See *Convivium Religiosum*

"Religious Treat" ("Religious Banquet") (Erasmus) **16**:117-18, 142

"The Relique" (Donne) **10**:13, 18, 36, 55, 62, 103

Reliques of Robert Burns, Consisting Chiefly of Original Letters, Poems, and Critical Observations on Scottish Songs (Burns) **3**:49

Remains (Butler)
See *The Genuine Remains*

Remarks (Dennis)
See *Remarks on a Book, entituled Prince Arthur, an Heroick Poem*

Remarks on a Book, entituled Prince Arthur, an Heroick Poem (Critical Observations; Observations on Blackmore's Prince Arthur; Remarks; Remarks on Prince Arthur) (Dennis) **11**:5, 8-9, 15, 17, 19, 22, 30, 36-7, 39, 41, 46

Remarks on Italy (Addison) **18**:39

"Remarks on Ovid" (Addison) **18**:18

Remarks on Prince Arthur (Dennis)
See *Remarks on a Book, entituled Prince Arthur, an Heroick Poem*

Remarks on the Policy of the Allies (Burke) **7**:23

Remarks on the Rape of the Lock (Dennis) **11**:21

Remarks upon Cato, a Tragedy (Dennis) **11**:22, 30

Remarks upon Mr. Pope's Translation of Homer (Dennis) **11**:22

Remarks upon Some Writers in the Controversy concerning the Foundation of Moral Duty and Moral Obligation (Trotter) **8**:363

Remarks upon the Principles and Reasonings of Dr. Rutherforth's "Essay on the Nature and Obligations of Virtue" (Trotter) **8**:362-63, 370

Remedy of Affliction for the Loss of Our Friends (Fielding) **1**:234

"The Remedy worse than the Disease" (Prior) **4**:459

A Remonstrance and a Warning against the Presumptuous, Unchristian Power of the Bishop of Rome and the Unspiritual Spiritual Estate (Hutten)
See *Lament and Exhortation aginst the excessive un-Christian Power of the Bishop of Rome and the unministerial Ministers*

Remonstrance au Peuple de France (Ronsard) **6**:411, 418

Renati Des cartes principiorum philosophiae pars I. et II. more geometrico demonstratae per Benedictum de Spinoza (*The Principles of Descartes*) (Spinoza) **9**:396, 402, 423, 433, 442, 444

"The Repentant Girl" (Erasmus)
See "Virgin Repentant"

"Reply" (Wheatley)
See "Phillis's Reply to the Answer..."

"Reply to a Tailor" (Burns) **3**:92

Reply to Burke (Wollstonecraft)
See *A Vindication of the Rights of Men, in a Letter to the Right Honourable Edmund Burke; Occasioned by His Reflections on the Revolution in France*

"Reponse à quelque ministre de Génève" (Ronsard) **6**:417

Report of the Jesuit Berthier's Illness, Confession, Death and Revelation (Voltaire) **14**:340

"Reports of the Debates of the Senate of Lilliput" (Johnson)
See "Debates in the Senate of Magna Lilliputia"

The Reprisal (Smollett) **2**:358

Reproof (Smollett) **2**:352, 358-59

"Republican" (Butler) **16**:51

"A request to the Graces" (Herrick) **13**:393

Rerum in Ecclesia History (Foxe)
See *Actes and Monumentes of these latter perilous dayes touching matters of the Church*

De Rerum Natura (Dryden) **21**:78-9

Rerum Scoticarum Historia, auctore Georgio Buchanano Scoto (*Historia*) (Buchanan) **4**:118-23, 125-27, 129-30, 136-37

"The Resignation" (Chatterton) **3**:125-27, 135

"Resignation" (Young) **3**:467, 477, 490, 492

"Resolution" (More) **9**:296

Resolutiones disputationum de indulgentiarum (*Explanations of the 95 Theses*) (Luther) **9**:91, 109, 146-47

Responde stulto secundum stultitiam eius (More) **10**:365

Responsio ad Lutherum (More)
See *Eruditissimi viri Guilielmi Rossei opus elegans*

"Respuesta a Sor Filotea de la Cruz" (Juana Ines de la Cruz) **5**:147, 150, 152, 156

"Resurrection" (Donne) **10**:17

Retaliation (Goldsmith) **2**:70-1, 74, 104

"Retraction" ("Retractions") (Chaucer) **17**:209, 213, 216, 242

"Retractions" (Chaucer)
See "Retraction"

Rettungen des Horaz (*Rehabilitations of Horace*) (Lessing) **8**:105, 112

"The Return" (Taylor) **11**:363, 368, 384, 389, 396

La réunion des amours (Marivaux) **4**:367

Revelations (Julian of Norwich)
See "Revelations of Divine Love"

"Revelations of Divine Love" (*Revelations*) (Julian of Norwich) **6**:357-59, 362, 366, 369, 373-74, 376, 379-82

"The Revenge" (Chatterton)
See "The Revenge, a Burletta"

"The Revenge" (Young) **3**:467, 485, 487-88

"The Revenge, a Burletta" ("The Revenge") (Chatterton) **3**:123, 132

"A Reverie at the Boar's-Head Tavern" (Goldsmith) **2**:84

Rêveries du promeneur solitaire (Rousseau) **14**:222, 257, 249, 254-55, 266-68, 303-04, 306, 312, 314

"The Reverse: or, The Tables Turn'd" (Dennis) **11**:51-2

"The Review" (Defoe) **1**:137, 155, 161-62

"The Revolution in Low Life" (Goldsmith) **2**:105

The Revolution of Sweden (Trotter) **8**:354-55, 358, 361, 363, 369-70, 372, 374

"The Rich Beggars" (Erasmus) **16**:118, 143

"Richard Cromwell" (Marvell) **4**:398

Richarde the thirde (More)
See *The Life of Kinge Richarde the Thirde*

"Ricky with the Tuft" (Perrault)
See "Riquet à la houppe"

"The Ridiculous Wishes" (Perrault)
See "Les souhaits ridicules"

Rights of Woman (Wollstonecraft)
See *A Vindication of the Rights of Woman, with Strictures on Political and Moral Subjects*

"Rigs o'Barley" ("Rigs of Barley") (Burns) **3**:67, 71

"Rigs of Barley" (Burns)
See "Rigs o'Barley"

Rime (Michelangelo) **12**:354, 356-60, 362-63, 365-68, 371, 374-76

Le Rime del Petrarca brevemente sposte per Ludovico Castelvetro (Castelvetro) **12**:68

Rinaldo (Tasso) **5**:375, 383-84, 392

Rinaldo and Armida (Dennis) **11**:12, 34

"Rinconete y Cortadillo" (Cervantes) **6**:171-72

"Riquet à la houppe" ("Ricky with the Tuft") (Perrault) **2**:254, 257, 260, 280

Risâle-i aruz (Babur) **18**:91

"Rise of Peyncteynge in Englande" ("Ryse of Peyncteynge in Englande") (Chatterton) **3**:119

"The Rise of Woman" (Parnell)
See "Hesiod; or, The Rise of Woman"

Ritter Spiridon aus Perusina (Beer)
See *Des abentheuerlichen Jan Rebhu Ritter Spiridon aus Perusina*

The Rival Ladies (Dryden) **3**:230-31

The Rivals (Davenant) **13**:185-87, 200

The Robbers (*Praedones*) (Hutten) **16**:216, 225, 227, 234, 241, 246

"Robert and Raufe" (Chatterton) **3**:129

"Robert, Duke of Normandie" ("Robert of Normandy") (Drayton) **8**:30, 33

"Robert of Normandy" (Drayton)
See "Robert, Duke of Normandie"

"Robin Shure in Hairst" (Burns) **3**:86

"The Rock of Rubies and the Quarry of Pearls" (Herrick) **13**:312, 338

The Rogueries of Scapin (Moliere)
See *Les fourberies de Scapin*

Roman Triads (Hutten)
See *Vadiscus, sive Trias Romana*

The Romance of a Morning (Cleland) **2**:52

The Romance of a Night; or, A Covent-Garden-Adventure (Cleland) **2**:52

The Romance of an Evening (Cleland) **2**:52

"Romance of the Knight" ("Romaunte of the Cnyghte") (Chatterton) **3**:118, 124

The Romance of Three Kingdoms (Lo Kuan-chung)
See *San-kuo-chih yeni-i*

The Romance of Yúsuf (*Joseph*) *and Zulaykhá* (*Potiphar's Wife*) (Jami)
See *Yúsuf u Zulaikhá*

Romans (Voltaire) **14**:337

Romaunt (Chaucer)
See *Romaunt of the Rose*

Romaunt of the Rose (*Romaunt*) (Chaucer) **17**:47, 58, 116, 195

"Romaunte of the Cnyghte" (Chatterton)
See "Romance of the Knight"

Roper's More (Roper)
See *The Mirrour of Vertue in Worldly Greatnes; or, The Life of syr Thomas More Knight*

"Rosamond" (Drayton)
See "The Epistle of Rosamond to King Henry the Second"

Rosamond (Addison) **18**:7, 17, 19, 32

Rosary of the Pious (Jami)
See *Tuhfat al-ahrár*

"The Rosciad" (Churchill) **3**:139, 143-45, 148-49, 151, 153, 157-59, 161-63, 171-73

"The Rosemarie Branch" (Herrick) **13**:352

Rosina; or, Love in a Cottage: A Comic Opera, in Two Acts (Brooke) **6**:107, 109

The Roundheads; or the Good Old Cause (Behn) **1**:29, 33, 37, 40

Rousseau juge de Jean Jacques (*Dialogues avec moi-même*) (Rousseau) **14**:225, 247, 254, 256, 267, 303-04, 312

The Rover; or, The Banished Cavalier, Parts I and II (Behn) **1**:28, 33-4, 37, 39-40

Rowley Poems (Chatterton) **3**:126-27

Roxana (Defoe)
See *The Fortunate Mistress*

The Royal Convert (Rowe) **8**:292, 299-302, 305, 308

"The Royal Man" (P'u Sung-ling)
See "Wang-che"

The Royal Mischief (Manley) **1**:315-16

"Rubelet" (Herrick) **13**:321

El rufián dichoso (Cervantes) **6**:180

"A Ruful Lamentacion" (More) **10**:428-29

"Ruin" (Burns)
See "Address to Ruin"

"The Ruines of Time" (Spenser) **5**:312, 314

"Rule Brittania" (Thomson) **16**:374, 385, 396

Rules of a Christian Life (Elyot)
See *The Rules of a Christian lyfe made by Picus erle of Mirandula*

The Rules of a Christian lyfe made by Picus erle of Mirandula (*Rules of a Christian Life*) (Elyot)   **11**:62, 84

"Ruth's Resolution" (Edwards)   **7**:119

"Ryse of Peyncteynge in Englande" (Chatterton)
See "Rise of Peyncteynge in Englande"

Sab'a (*Septet*) (Jami)   **9**:65-7, 72

The Sacramental Meditations (Taylor)
See *Preparatory Meditations before my Approach to the Lords Supper. Chiefly upon the Doctrin preached upon the Day of administration.*

Sacred Contagion; or, The Natural History of Superstition (Holbach)
See *Contagion sacrée*

"The Sacrifice, by way of Discourse betwixt himselfe and Julia" (Herrick)   **13**:403

"The Sacrifice to Apollo" (Drayton)   **8**:41

The Sad Shepherd (Jonson)   **6**:304-06, 309, 311, 321-22, 325

"The sadnesse of things for Sapho's sicknesse" (Herrick)   **13**:365

Saint Cyprian (Elyot)
See *A Swete and devoute Sermon of Holy saynt Ciprian of Mortalitie of Man*

Saint Paulin (Perrault)   **2**:260

Salámán and Absál (Jami)
See *Salámán u Absál*

Salámán u Absál (*Salámán and Absál*) (Jami)   **9**:59, 62, 65, 68, 71-2

Salmacida Spolia (Davenant)   **13**:182, 189

Salve Deorum Rex Iudeorum (Lanyer)
See *Salve deus rex judæorum*

Salve deus rex judæorum (*Salve Deorum Rex Iudeorum*) (Lanyer)   **10**:180-83, 186-90, 192

Samson Agonistes (Milton)   **9**:183, 189, 192-93, 198, 200, 204, 217, 229-30, 236-38, 243, 249

Samuel Henzi (Lessing)   **8**:105, 114

San Hermenegildo (Juana Ines de la Cruz)   **5**:158

San Kuo (Lo Kuan-chung)
See *San-kuo-chih yeni-i*

San-kuo-chih yeni-i (*An Explanation of the San-kuo-chih, Done in the Popular Style; Popular Elaboration of the Chronicle of the Three Kingdoms; The Romance of Three Kingdoms; San Kuo; The Three Kingdoms*) (Lo Kuan-chung)   **12**:279-80, 282, 284-97

San-Sui p'ing-yao chuan (Lo Kuan-chung)   **12**:282

Sanford and Merton (Day)
See *The History of Sandford and Merton*

Santa Bárbara, or the Mountain Miracle and Heaven's Martyr (Castro)   **19**:2

De sapienta veterum (*The Wisdom of the Ancients*) (Bacon)   **18**:117, 132, 174, 185, 195

Satire (*Satires*) (Ariosto)   **6**:31-3, 59, 71-2

Satire II: À M. de Molière (Boileau-Despreaux)   **3**:39

Satire III (Boileau-Despreaux)   **3**:37

Satire IV (On Human Folly) (Boileau-Despreaux)   **3**:39

Satire VI (Boileau-Despreaux)   **3**:23, 37-8

Satire VIII: A M. Morel, Docteur en Sorbonne (Boileau-Despreaux)   **3**:25

Satire IX (Boileau-Despreaux)   **3**:35

Satire XII: Sur l'équivoque (Boileau-Despreaux)   **3**:22, 25

Satire of Truth (Boileau-Despreaux)   **3**:21

Satires (Ariosto)
See *Satire*

Satires (Boileau-Despreaux)   **3**:38-9, 42-3

Satires (Young)   **3**:474, 478, 492-93

Satires and Epistles of Horace, Imitated ("First Epistle of the First Book of Horace"; *Imitations of Horace*) (Pope)   **3**:273, 289, 296, 314, 319

Satires and Epistles of Horace, Imitated and Satires of Dr. Donne Versified (Pope)   **3**:289, 292, 302-03

Satires of Dr. Donne Versified (Pope)   **3**:289, 292, 302-03

"Satyr albo Dziki Mąż" ("The Satyr, or The Wild Man") (Kochanowski)   **10**:175

"The Satyr, or The Wild Man" (Kochanowski)
See "Satyr albo Dziki Mąż"

"Satyr upon the Licentious Age of Charles 2D" (Butler)   **16**:52

"Satyre I" (Donne)   **10**:100-02

"Satyre II" (Donne)   **10**:38, 100-02

"Satyre III" (Donne)   **10**:12, 38, 48-9, 84, 93, 100-02

"Satyre IV" (Donne)   **10**:100-02

"Satyre V" (Donne)   **10**:99-102

Satyres (Donne)   **10**:7, 24-5, 38, 42, 47, 98-102

The Satyrical Pilgrim (Grimmelshausen)
See *Der satyrische Pilgram*

Sausage (Warton)
See *The Oxford Sausage; or, Select Poetical Pieces: Written by the Most Celebrated Wits of the University of Oxford*

Sayings of Light and Love (John of the Cross)   **18**:229

Scala coeli: Nineteene Sermons concerning Prayer (*Prayer*) (Andrewes)   **5**:23

Scala Intellectualis (Bacon)   **18**:187

Scarabaeus (Erasmus)   **16**:176

"Sceptic" (Butler)   **16**:53

"The Sceptic" (Hume)   **7**:153, 188

De Schismate extinguendo, et de vera Ecclesiastica Libertate adverenda (Hutten)   **16**:213, 233

"The School for Fathers" (Marmontel)   **2**:214

The School for Husbands (Moliere)
See *L'école des maris*

The School for Wives (Moliere)
See *L'école des femmes*

The School for Wives Criticized (Moliere)
See *La critique de L'école des femmes*

"The School or Perl of Putney" (Herrick)   **13**:353

"Schoolmaster" (Butler)   **16**:50

"Schreiben an den Herrn N. N. über die Komödie in Versen" ("Letter on Ancient and Modern Tragedy") (Schlegel)   **5**:272, 282

"Scotch Drink" (Burns)   **3**:52, 67, 84-5, 87

"Scots wha hae" (Burns)
See "Scots Wha Hae wi' Wallace Bled"

"Scots Wha Hae wi' Wallace Bled" ("Scots wha hae") (Burns)   **3**:52, 60-1, 67, 72, 78, 83

Scriptorum philosophicum (More)   **9**:311

Gli sdegni amorosi (Goldoni)
See *Il gondoliere veneziano*

"Se ben concetto ha la divina parte" (Michelangelo)   **12**:372

A Sea Grammar (Smith)
See *An Accidence; or, The Path-Way to Experience*

"The Sea Marke" (Smith)   **9**:382-83

"Search All the World About" (Davenant)   **13**:204

A Seasonable Argument to Persuade All the Grand Juries in England to Petition for a New Parliament (Marvell)   **4**:394

A Seasonable Question, & c. (Marvell)   **4**:394

"Seasons" (Bradstreet)
See "The Four Seasons of the Year"

The Seasons (Thomson)   **16**:359, 361-63, 365-76, 378-79, 381-86, 388-89, 391-95, 397-98, 401-09, 411-15, 418-19, 421-26, 429-34

The Second Anniversarie. Of the Progres of the Soule. Wherein, By Occasion Of the Religious death of Mistris Elizabeth Drury, the incommodities of the Soule in this life, and her exaltation in the next, are Contemplated (*Of the Progres of the Soule*) (Donne)   **10**:39, 44, 74-5, 77, 89, 95, 98

Second Defence of the English People (Milton)   **9**:235, 250

A Second Defense of the Prophaneness and Immorality of the English Stage (Collier)   **6**:222, 229

Second Diary (Pepys)   **11**:246

"The Second Discourse" ("Discourse II") (Reynolds)   **15**:377, 389, 391, 397, 402, 418-19

Second Discourse (Rousseau)
See *Discours sur l'origine et les fondements de l'inégalité parmi les hommes*

"Second Epistle to John Lapraik" ("Lapraik II") (Burns)   **3**:87, 92-3

"Second Nun's Tale" (Chaucer)   **17**:189, 214, 220, 237

The Second Part; or, A Continuance of Poly-Olbion from the Eighteenth Song. (Drayton)
See *Poly-Olbion*

"The Second Rapture" (Carew)   **13**:26, 34, 57

Second Treatise of Government (Locke)   **7**:277-78, 291, 296

La seconde surprise de l'amour (Marivaux)   **4**:367, 368, 381

"Secresie Protected" (Carew)   **13**:26

The Secret History of Queen Zarah and the Zarazians (Manley)   **1**:307, 309, 311, 313, 316, 319-23

The Secret History of the Present Intrigues of the Court of Caramania (Haywood)   **1**:290

Secret Love; or, The Maiden Queen (Dryden)   **3**:177, 193, 197, 210, 230

The Secret Memoirs and Manners of Several Persons of Quality (Manley)
See *The New Atalantis*

"The Secretary" (Prior)   **4**:460-62, 466

Secular Authority, To What Extent It Should Be Obeyed (Luther)   **9**:134, 151

"The Secular Masque" (Dryden)   **3**:199; **21**:64

"Secular Ode on the Jubilee at Pembroke College, Cambridge, in 1743" (Smart)   **3**:394

"See the Chariot at Hand" (Jonson)   **6**:305

"S'egli è, donna, che puoi" (Michelangelo)   **12**:366

Sei giornate (Aretino)
See *Ragionamento della Nanna e della Antonia*

Sejanus His Fall (Jonson)   **6**:291, 294, 296, 300-01, 305-06, 308, 314, 318, 323, 327, 329-32, 334, 336, 341

The Select Works of Mr. John Dennis (Dennis)   **11**:15-6, 20, 50

"A Self Accuser" (Donne)   **10**:95

The Self Rival (Davys) **1**:97-8

Selfishness of a False Philosophy (Marmontel)
2:213

"Selim; or, The Shepherd's Moral" (Collins)
4:210

Semele (Congreve)
See *Mask of Semele*

Sémiramis (Voltaire) **14**:397

Seneca (Lipsius)
See *Annaei Senecae Philosopli Opera, quae exstant, onmia*

"La Señora Cornelia" ("The Lady Cornelia")
(Cervantes) **6**:171, 177

"Sensibility" (Burns) **3**:83-4

A Sentimental Journey through France and Italy (Sterne) **2**:377, 384-86, 389, 391, 393-96, 398, 400, 402, 411, 413-14, 426-28, 439

"Separation of Lovers" (Carew) **13**:62

September Bibel (Luther)
See *Das newe Testament deutzsche*

Septet (Jami)
See *Sab'a*

Septiform Narration of the Six Days of Creation (Pico della Mirandola)
See *Heptaplus*

Les serments indiscrets (Marivaux) **4**:358-59, 363, 368, 378-79

"Sermon" (Erasmus) **16**:142

"Sermon 4 Of Repentance" (Andrewes) **5**:34

"Sermon 6 Of the Resurrection" (Andrewes)
5:33

"Sermon 7" (Andrewes) **5**:33

"Sermon 9 Of the Nativitie" (Andrewes) **5**:33

"Sermon 11 Of the Nativitie" (Andrewes)
5:34

"Sermon 14 Of the Resurrection" (Andrewes)
5:34

"Sermon 15 Of the Nativitie" (Andrewes)
5:34

"Sermon 17 Of the Resurrection" (Andrewes)
5:34

Sermon de J. Rossette (Voltaire) **14**:357

Sermon des cinquante (Voltaire) **14**:369, 370

The Sermon on Good Works (Luther)
See *Von den guten Wercken*

Sermon on Indulgences and Grace (Luther)
See *Eyn Sermon von Ablass und Gnade*

"A Sermon on Painting" (Walpole) **2**:487

Sermons (Churchill) **3**:141, 167, 169

Sermons (Johnson) **15**:209, 289-90

The Sermons of Mr. Yorick (Sterne) **2**:374, 429-30, 433, 34

Sermons to Novices (Kempis) **11**:410

La serva amorosa (Goldoni) **4**:261, 265

La serva reconoscente (Goldoni) **4**:261

The Servant of Two Masters (Goldoni)
See *Il servitore di due padroni*

De servo arbitrio (*The Bondage of the Will*)
(Luther) **9**:138

Le sette giornate del mondo creato (*Il mondo creato*) (Tasso) **5**:375, 398

Sette Salmi (Aretino)
See *I sette salmi de la penitenzia di David*

The Seven Penetential Psalms of David (Aretino)
See *I sette salmi de la penitenzia di David*

Seventeen Sermons on the Nativity (Andrewes)
5:27

"The Seventh Discourse" (Reynolds) **15**:381, 395, 403

Several Discourses upon Practical Subjects (Collier) **6**:210

Sganarelle; or, The Cuckold in His Own Imagination (Moliere)
See *Sganarelle, ou le cocu imaginaire*

Sganarelle, ou le cocu imaginaire (*Sganarelle; or, The Cuckold in His Own Imagination*)
(Moliere) **10**:277, 280, 283, 286, 302, 306, 310

Shakespeare (Johnson)
See *The Plays of William Shakespeare, in Eight Volumes, with the Corrections and Illustrations of Various Commentators; To which are added Notes by Sam Johnson*

Shamela (Fielding)
See *An Apology for the Life of Mrs. Shamela Andrews*

She Stoops to Conquer (Goldsmith) **2**:67, 69, 72-4, 76, 79-81, 86-7, 89, 98-9, 105-07, 112, 119-21, 126-28

She-yan hsien-sheng ts'un-kao (*Collected Works*) (Wu Ch'eng-en) **7**:396-99

"Shephardling" (Herrick) **13**:321

The Shepheardes Calender: Conteyning Twelve Æglogues Proportionable to the Twelve Monethes (Spenser) **5**:294, 297, 304, 311-12, 323, 326, 329, 354, 359-62

The Shepheards Sirena (Drayton) **8**:9, 17-19, 21, 33-4, 36-7

"The Shepherdess of the Alps" (Marmontel)
2:214

Shepherd's Garland (Drayton)
See *Idea the Shepheards Garland, Fashioned in Nine Eglogs. Rowlands Sacrifice to the Nine Muses*

"Shih Ch'ing-hsu" ("Stone from Heaven") (P'u Sung-ling) **3**:350

"Shih-yen" ("A Poem as the Corpus Delicti")
(P'u Sung-ling) **3**:350

"Shipman's" (Chaucer)
See "Shipman's Tale"

"Shipman's Tale" ("Shipman's") (Chaucer)
17:170, 194, 201-02, 212, 214, 225, 239

"The Shipwreck" (Erasmus)
See "Naufragium"

"The Shoe-tying" (Herrick) **13**:367

"A Shopkeeper" (Butler) **16**:55

A Short Historical Essay Touching General Councils, Creeds, and Impositions in Religion (Marvell) **4**:394

Short Treatise (Spinoza)
See *Korte Verhandeling van God, de Mensch und deszelhs Welstand*

A Short View (Collier)
See *A Short View of the Immorality and Profaneness of the English Stage, Together with the Sense of Antiquity upon This Argument*

A Short View of the Immorality and Profaneness of the English Stage, Together with the Sense of Antiquity upon This Argument (*A Short View*) (Collier) **6**:204-08, 210-12, 215, 217-18, 220-31

A Short Vindication of The Relapse and The Provok'd Wife from Immorality and Prophaneness (*Vindication of the Relapse and the Provok'd Wife from Immorality and Prophaneness*) (Vanbrugh) **21**:289, 292, 297, 321, 324, 326-27, 334

The Shortest Way with the Dissenters; or, Proposals for the Establishment of the Church (Defoe) **1**:118, 121, 144, 161, 163, 166

The Showing forth of Christ: Sermons of John Donne (Donne) **10**:92

"The Shrew-Wife" (More) **9**:298

"Shu'hsi" (P'u Sung-ling) **3**:352

Shui Hu Chuan (*All Men Are Brothers; Outlaws of the Marshes; The Water Margin*)
(Lo Kuan-chung) **12**:279-84, 286, 291-94, 296-97

"Si acaso, Fabio mío" ("If perchance, my Fabio") (Juana Ines de la Cruz) **5**:155

"Si come nella penna e nell'inchiosto"
(Michelangelo) **12**:360

"Sì come per levar, Donna, si pone"
(Michelangelo) **12**:338, 373

"Sic a Wife as Willie Had" (Burns) **3**:86

The Sicilian; or, Love the Painter (Moliere)
See *Le sicilien; ou, L'amour peintre*

Le sicilien; ou, L'amour peintre (*The Sicilian; or, Love the Painter*) (Moliere) **10**:283-84, 291, 312, 328

The Sick Monkey (Garrick) **15**:122

Sidney Bidulph (Sheridan)
See *Memoirs of Miss Sidney Bidulph, Extracted from Her Own Journal*

Die sieben Busspsal mit deutscher au-siegung nach dem schrifftlichen synne tzu Christi und gottes gnaden, neben seynes selben, ware erkentniss grundlich gerichtet... (*Commentary on the Psalms*) (Luther) **9**:79, 119-21, 123

Le siècle de Louis le Grand (Perrault) **2**:259, 274, 276

Le siècle de Louis XIV (Voltaire) **14**:338-39, 352, 364, 372, 383, 388, 409-11

Le siècle de Louis XV (Voltaire) **14**:338-39, 383

The Siege of Rhodes (Davenant) **13**:175-83, 185, 189-90, 192, 194, 215

The Siege of Sinope: A Tragedy (Brooke)
6:109

"A Sigh" (Winchilsea) **3**:447

"Sigismunda and Guiscardo" (Dryden) **3**:184, 204, 216

"The Sign" (Winchilsea) **3**:447

Silenei Alcibia dis (Erasmus) **16**:198

The Silent Woman (Dryden) **3**:236

Silsilatu'dh-Dhahab (*Chain of Gold*) (Jami)
9:65, 68, 71

Silvae (Buchanan) **4**:133, 135

"The Silver Tassie" (Burns) **3**:77-8, 85

"A Simile" (Prior) **4**:460, 475

The Simplician World-Observer (Beer)
See *Der symplicianische Welt-Kucker; oder, Abentheuerliche Jan Rebhu, Parts I-IV*

Simplician Writings (Grimmelshausen)
See *Der abenteuerliche Simplicissimus, Teutsch, das hist: Die Beschreibun dess Lebens eines seltzamen Vaganten, gennant Melchio Sternfels von Fuchsheim*

Simplicissimi wunderliche Gauckel-Tasche (*Simplicissimus's Bag of Tricks*)
(Grimmelshausen) **6**:247

Simplicissimus's Bag of Tricks (Grimmelshausen)
See *Simplicissimi wunderliche Gauckel-Tasche*

"Simplicity and Refinement in Writing" (Hume) **7**:163, 167

"Simulation and Dissimulation" (Bacon)
18:124, 128

"Since I am comming" (Donne)
See "Hymne to God my God, in my sicknesse"

Les sincères (Marivaux)   4:369-70, 372

"Sinners in the Hands of an Angry God"
  (Edwards)   7:92, 98, 102-08, 110, 117-18

Sir Charles Grandison (Richardson)
  See *The History of Sir Charles Grandison*

*Sir Harry Wildair: Being the Sequel of The
  Trip to the Jubilee* (Farquhar)   21:132, 135-
  36, 139-40, 146, 150, 153-54, 161, 163, 170,
  176

Sir Martin Mar-All; or, The Feign'd Innocence
  (*Martin Mar-All*) (Dryden)   3:179, 210, 230

Sir Patient Fancy (Behn)   1:33, 37, 39, 41

"Sir Roger at Church" (Addison)   18:56

Sir Roger de Coverley Papers (Addison)
  18:43, 70

"Sir Tho, Southwell" (Herrick)   13:368

"Sir Thopas" (Chaucer)   17:61, 177, 201-02,
  205

Six Articles (Henry VIII)
  See *Act for Abolishing*

Six Bookes of Politickes or Civil Doctrine
  (Lipsius)
  See *Politicorum sive civilis doctrinae libri sex,
    qui ad principatum maxime spectant*

"The Sixth Discourse" (Reynolds)   15:380,
  394, 397, 403

"Skazka o roždenii taftjanoj muški" (Chulkov)
  2:22-3, 26-9

"The Skylark" (Ronsard)   6:408

"Sleeping Beauty" (Perrault)
  See "La belle au bois dormant"

Small Catechism (Luther)
  See *Der kleine Catechismus*

"A Small Poet" (Butler)   16:23, 54-5

Le smanie della villeggiatura (Goldoni)   4:268

"Smith" ("Epistle to James Smith") (Wessel)
  7:391-92

"So, so breake off this last lamenting kisse"
  (Donne)
  See "The Expiration"

Sober and Seasonable Memorandum (Howell)
  13:440

Sober Inspections (Howell)
  See *Some Sober Inspections Made into the
    Carriage and Consults of the Late Long
    Parliament*

The Social Contract (Rousseau)
  See *Du Contrat social*

"The Soldier" ("The Soldier and the
  Carthusian") (Erasmus)   16:119, 195

"The Soldier and the Carthusian" (Erasmus)
  See "The Soldier"

"The Soldier and the Carthusian" (Erasmus)
  See "The Carthusian"

"The Soldier going to the Field" (Davenant)
  13:195

The Soldier's Fortune (Behn)   1:33

Soliloquium animae (Kempis)   11:410

Soliloquy of a Beauty in the Country
  (Lyttelton)   10:197, 203

De solitudine et silentio (Kempis)   11:411

"Solomon" (Parnell)   3:255

"Solomon" (Prior)
  See "Solomon on the Vanity of the World"

"Solomon on the Vanity of the World"
  ("Solomon") (Prior)   4:455-56, 458-62, 464,
  466-68, 470-73

"Solving a Difficult Case" (P'u Sung-ling)
  3:345

*Some Considerations on Doctor Kennet's Second
  and Third Letters* (Collier)   6:209

"Some Reflections" (Winchilsea)   3:451

*Some Sober Inspections Made into the Carriage
  and Consults of the Late Long Parliament*
  (*Sober Inspections*) (Howell)   13:419-20

Some Thoughts concerning Education (Locke)
  7:271, 280-81

Somnium (Buchanan)   4:119, 123, 134, 138

"The Son of God" (More)   9:298

Sonets amoureux (Ronsard)   6:426

Sonetti Lussuriosi (*Sonnets*) (Aretino)   12:14,
  18, 21-2, 25

"Song" (Herrick)
  See "To the Rose. Song"

"A Song" (Prior)   4:465

"Song 1" (Drayton)   8:46

"Song III" (Kochanowski)   10:161

"Song 5" (Drayton)   8:46

"Song IX" (Kochanowski)   10:161

"Song 18" (Drayton)   8:46

"Song 26" (Drayton)   8:48

"Song 30" (Drayton)   8:48

"Song. Endymion Porter and Olivia"
  (Davenant)   13:195

"A Song from Cymbeline" ("Dirge for
  Cymbeline") (Collins)   4:214, 217, 224, 230

"Song. 'Goe, and catche a falling starre'"
  ("Goe, and catche a falling starre") (Donne)
  10:50, 52

"Song: My Days Have Been so Wondrous
  Free" (Parnell)   3:255

"Song of Death" (Burns)   3:81

"The Song of the Spirit" (John of the Cross)
  18:209-11

"A Song on a Painting Depicting the God
  Êrh-lang Hunting in the Surrounding
  Country with His Followers" (Wu Ch'eng-
  en)
  See "Êrh-lang Sou-shan-t'u Ko"

"Song. 'Sweetest love, I do not goe'"
  ("Sweetest love, I do not goe") (Donne)
  10:12, 26, 31-2, 36, 52, 58, 82, 96

"Song to Celia" ("Drink to Me Only with
  Thine Eyes") (Jonson)   6:304-05, 317, 322-
  23, 346, 349

"A Song to David" (Smart)   3:365, 369-82,
  285-89, 391, 393, 395-401, 403

"A Song to the Maskers" (Herrick)   13:351,
  399, 401

"Song, To Two Lovers Condemn'd to Die"
  (Davenant)   13:205

"A Song upon Sylvia" (Herrick)   13:367

Songs (Kochanowski)
  See *Pieśni*

Songs and Sonets (Donne)   10:32-3, 35-6, 47,
  50, 52, 54-5, 57, 63, 66, 81-2, 84, 88, 92-3,
  96, 98, 106

"Songs of the Bride" (John of the Cross)
  See "Canciones de la Esposa"

"Songs of the Soul" (John of the Cross)
  18:216

"Sonnet 2" ("My Heart Was Slaine, and None
  But You and I") (Drayton)   8:39

"Sonnet 7" ("Love, in a Humor, Play'd the
  Prodigall") (Drayton)   8:39

"Sonnet VIII" ("There's Nothing Grieves Me,
  But that Age Should Haste") (Drayton)
  8:23

"Sonnet 22" ("With Fooles and Children Good
  Discretion Beares") (Drayton)   8:39

"Sonnet 23" ("Love Banish'd Heav'n, in Earth
  Was Held in Scorne") (Drayton)   8:39

"Sonnet 24" ("I Heare Some Say, this Man Is
  Not in Love") (Drayton)   8:38

"Sonnet 31" ("Me Thinks I See Some Crooked
  Mimicke Jeere") (Drayton)   8:38

"Sonnet 36" ("Thou Purblind Boy, since Thou
  Hast Beene So Slacke") (Drayton)   8:39

"Sonnet XLII" (Ronsard)   6:413

"Sonnet XLIII" (Ronsard)   6:413

"Sonnet 46" ("Plaine-Path'd Experience,
  th'Unlearneds Guide") (Drayton)   8:39

"Sonnet 48" ("Cupid, I Hate Thee, Which I'de
  Have Thee Know") (Drayton)   8:39

"Sonnet LVII" (Ronsard)   6:430

"Sonnet LIX" ("As Love and I, Late
  Harbour'd in One Inne") (Drayton)   8:23

"Sonnet 61" ("Idea 61") (Drayton)   8:39

"Sonnet 62" ("When First I Ended, Then I
  First Began") (Drayton)   8:39

"Sonnet LXVI" (Spenser)   5:363

"Sonnet LXXVI" (Ronsard)   6:430

"Sonnet CLXXIV" (Ronsard)   6:431

"Sonnet CXXVII" (Ronsard)   6:430

"Sonnet on Bathing" (Warton)   15:441

"Sonnet on Hope" (Juana Ines de la Cruz)
  5:144

"Sonnet on the Death of Mr. Richard West"
  ("On the Death of Mr. Richard West")
  (Gray)   4:286, 294, 296, 314-15, 322-23

"Sonnet Written after seeing Wilton-House"
  (Warton)   15:444

"Sonnet Written at Winslade in Hampshire"
  (Warton)   15:441

"Sonnet Written in a Blank Leaf of Dugdale's
  'Monasticon'" (Warton)   15:435, 443, 455

Sonnets (Aretino)
  See *Sonetti Lussuriosi*

Sonnets (Warton)   15:435

Sonnets for Hélène (Ronsard)
  See *Sonnets pour Hélène*

Sonnets pour Hélène (*Sonnets for Hélène*)
  (Ronsard)   6:413, 417

Sonnets to Idea (Drayton)
  See *Idea*

Le Sopha (Crebillon)   1:75-7, 79, 81, 88-9

Sophonisba (Thomson)
  See *The Tragedy of Sophonisba*

Sophonisbas (Thomson)   16:393, 395

"Sophronyme" (Rousseau)   9:345

"Sot" (Butler)   16:50-1

"Les souhaits ridicules" ("The Ridiculous
  Wishes") (Perrault)   2:253-56, 261, 266,
  279-80

"The soul is the salt" (Herrick)   13:341

"The Spanish Doctor" (Kochanowski)
  See "O doktorze Hiszpanie"

The Spanish Friar (Behn)   1:47

The Spanish Friar (*The Spanish Fryar*)
  (Dryden)   3:186, 193, 210, 214, 229-30, 233;
  21:55-7

The Spanish Fryar (Dryden)
  See *The Spanish Friar*

The Spanish Lovers (Davenant)   13:176

The Spanish Wives (*Wives*) (Pix)   8:259-61,
  263, 265, 267-69, 271-72, 274-77

Spartam nactus es (Erasmus)   16:198

"A speach according to Horace" (Jonson)
  6:350

Specimen of an Etimological Vocabulary
  (Cleland)   2:53

Le spectateur Français (Marivaux)   4:358-60,
  371-72, 378-80

The Spectator (Addison)   18:4, 7, 13-15, 20-1,
  24, 26-8, 32-7, 39, 42-4, 46-9, 50-1, 53-4, 58,
  60, 63-8, 69-71, 72-6, 78

The Spectator (Steele)   **18**:313, 318, 320-22, 330-31, 333-37, 340-44, 348, 351-55, 359, 368-70, 372, 376-77, 384-85
The Spectator, 5 (Addison)   **18**:51
The Spectator, 10 (Addison)   **18**:50, 65
The Spectator, 26 (Addison)   **18**:54
The Spectator, 26 (Steele)   **18**:324
The Spectator, 35 (Addison)   **18**:77
The Spectator, 38 (Addison)   **18**:74
The Spectator, 39 (Addison)   **18**:8, 39
The Spectator, 40 (Addison)   **18**:39, 77
The Spectator, 42 (Addison)   **18**:39
The Spectator, 42 (Steele)   **18**:326
The Spectator, 44 (Addison)   **18**:39
The Spectator, 45 (Addison)   **18**:39
The Spectator, 47 (Steele)   **18**:372
The Spectator, 58-63 (Addison)   **18**:39, 65
The Spectator, 62 (Addison)   **18**:56
The Spectator, 65 (Steele)   **18**:372, 383
The Spectator, 66 (Steele)   **18**:347
The Spectator, 69 (Addison)   **18**:35
The Spectator, 70 (Addison)   **18**:56
The Spectator, 74 (Addison)   **18**:56
The Spectator, 79 (Steele)   **18**:318
The Spectator, 84 (Steele)   **18**:318
The Spectator, 85 (Addison)   **18**:77
The Spectator, 94 (Addison)   **18**:57
The Spectator, 120 (Addison)   **18**:57
The Spectator, 125 (Addison)   **18**:33, 35
The Spectator, 126 (Addison)   **18**:55
The Spectator, 144 (Steele)   **18**:346
The Spectator, 158 (Addison)   **18**:35
The Spectator, 160 (Addison)   **18**:57
The Spectator, 219 (Addison)   **18**:71
The Spectator, 237 (Addison)   **18**:57
The Spectator, 249 (Steele)   **18**:372
The Spectator, 259 (Steele)   **18**:318
The Spectator, 267 (Addison)   **18**:40, 78
The Spectator, 290 (Steele)   **18**:318
The Spectator, 315 (Addison)   **18**:78
The Spectator, 342 (Steele)   **18**:350
The Spectator, 356 (Steele)   **18**:358
The Spectator, 381 (Addison)   **18**:54
The Spectator, 399 (Addison)   **18**:34
The Spectator, 409 (Addison)   **18**:60, 76
The Spectator, 411 (Addison)   **18**:40
The Spectator, 414 (Addison)   **18**:37
The Spectator, 428 (Steele)   **18**:379
The Spectator, 434 (Addison)   **18**:35
The Spectator, 445 (Addison)   **18**:50
The Spectator, 446 (Addison)   **18**:34
The Spectator, 449 (Steele)   **18**:382
The Spectator, 466 (Steele)   **18**:318
The Spectator, 489 (Addison)   **18**:57
The Spectator, 502 (Steele)   **18**:372
The Spectator, 525 (Addison)   **18**:34
The Spectators (*Inspicientes; The Onlookers*) (Hutten)   **16**:225-27, 230, 233, 239, 241, 247
Speech on Moving His Resolutions for Conciliation with the Colonies (*On Conciliation with the Colonies*) (Burke)   **7**:39, 63
Speech on the East India Bill (Burke)
   See *Mr. Burke's Speech, on the 1st December 1783, upon the Question for the Speaker's Leaving the Chair, in Order for the House to Resolve Itself into a Committee on Mr. Fox's East Indian Bill*
Speech on the Nabob of Arcot's Debts (Burke)   **7**:62

Speech...on Presenting, on the 11 of February 1780--a Plan for the Better Security of the Independence of Parliament and the Economical Reformation of the Civil and Other Establishments (Burke)   **7**:15-16, 26, 46
Sphaera in quinque libros distributa (*De sphaera*) (Buchanan)   **4**:123-25, 129, 134-37
"Spiritual Canticle" (John of the Cross)   **18**:216
"Spiritual Canticle" (John of the Cross)
   See "Cántico Espiritual"
The Spiritual Canticle (John of the Cross)
   See *Cántico Espiritual*
Spiritual Letters (Marie de l'Incarnation)
   See *Lettres de la Vénérable Mère Marie de l'Incarnation*
Spiritual Relations (Teresa de Jesus)   **18**:393, 410
"The Spleen" (Winchilsea)
   See "Ode to the Spleen"
Sposizione ai primi XXIX canti dell'Inferno dantesco (Castelvetro)   **12**:67-8
"The Spring" (Carew)   **13**:20, 32-3
"Spring" (More)   **9**:298
"Spring" (Pope)   **3**:334
Spring. A Poem (Thomson)   **16**:363-64, 373, 381-83, 393, 401, 405-06, 410, 414-15, 423-24, 426, 430-32
"Squieres Tale" (Chaucer)
   See "Squire's Tale"
"Squire's Tale" ("Squieres Tale") (Chaucer)   **17**:71, 81, 201, 205
"St. John's Eve" (Kochanowski)
   See "Pieśń Świętojańska o Sobótce"
"St. Lucies Day" (Donne)
   See "A Nocturnal upon S. Lucies day, Being the shortest day"
The St. Marco Place (Goldoni)
   See *Il campiello*
The Stablemaster (Aretino)
   See *Marescalco*
The Stage Coach (Farquhar)   **21**:151, 169
A Stage-Coach Journey to Exeter (Manley)
   See *Letters Written by Mrs. Manley*
"Stanzas by Mr. Prior" (Prior)   **4**:465
"Stanzas to Alcandre on the Return of Oranthe to Fontainebleau" (Malherbe)   **5**:168
The Staple of News (Jonson)   **6**:300, 306, 308, 310-12, 314, 328, 336
The State of Innocence, and Fall of Man (Dryden)   **3**:206, 221, 233; **21**:66
De Statv Romano (Hutten)   **16**:231
"Stavlennik" ("The Protégé") (Chulkov)   **2**:22
"Steer Her Up" (Burns)   **3**:86
"Stella's Birthday, March 13, 1727" (Swift)   **1**:481, 523
"Still to Be Neat" (Jonson)   **6**:305
"The Stoic" (Hume)   **7**:153
Stoic Philosophy (Lipsius)
   See *Manductionis ad philosophiam stoicam libri tres*
"Stone from Heaven" (P'u Sung-ling)
   See "Shih Ch'ing-hsu"
"The Storm" (Donne)   **10**:97
The Storm (Defoe)   **1**:162
Story of Unnion and Valentine (Steele)   **18**:335
The Strait Gate; or, Great Difficulty of Going to Heaven (Bunyan)   **4**:175

The Strange Adventures of the Count de Vinevil and His Family. Being an Account of What Happen'd to Them Whilst They Resided at Constantinople (Aubin)   **9**:3-5, 7, 10, 13-14, 16-17
Strange Stories from a Chinese Studio (P'u Sung-ling)
   See *Liao-chai chih-i*
"A Strange Tale of Pigeons" (P'u Sung-ling)   **3**:348
"Strephon and Chloe" (Swift)   **1**:453, 484, 502-03, 510
Stricturae Politicae (Lipsius)   **16**:254
"The Stuarts: A Pindarique Ode" (Aubin)   **9**:4
Gli studenti (Ariosto)   **6**:61
Stultatia (Erasmus)   **16**:169
Die stumme Schönheit (Schlegel)   **5**:275, 278
Den stundesløse (Holberg)   **6**:264, 267, 273, 276-77
Subhat al-abrár (Jami)   **9**:66, 68, 71
Subida del Monte Carmelo (*Ascent of Mount Carmel*) (John of the Cross)   **18**:202-03, 214, 229-30, 233-36
Sui-T'ang chih-chuan (Lo Kuan-chung)   **12**:282
Sui-T'ang liang-ch'ao chih-chuan (Lo Kuan-chung)   **12**:282
"The Suicide" (Warton)
   See "To Suicide"
Summer. A Poem (Thomson)   **16**:363-64, 369, 373, 375, 381-83, 400-03, 405-06, 409-10, 412, 415, 423-24, 426, 430-32
"Summoner's Tale" (Chaucer)   **17**:169-70, 194, 197, 202, 231, 243
"The Sun Rising" (Donne)
   See "The Sunne Rising"
"The Sunbeams" (More)   **9**:298, 314
"The Sunne Rising" ("Busie old foole"; "The Sun Rising") (Donne)   **10**:12, 18, 32, 34, 49, 55
The Supplication of Souls (More)   **10**:362, 370, 397-99, 408-09
"Sur des vers de Virgile" ("Of Some Verses of Virgil") (Montaigne)   **8**:204, 221, 231, 235, 242
"Sur la bataille de Peterwardein" (Rousseau)   **9**:340, 344
"Sur l'attentat commis en la personne de sa majesté le 19 de Décembre 1605" (Malherbe)   **5**:183
"Sur l'aveuglement des hommes du siècle" (Rousseau)   **9**:342, 345
"Sur le devoir et le sort des grands hommes" (Rousseau)   **9**:344
"Sur les divinités poétiques" (Rousseau)   **9**:345
"Sur un arbrisseau" (Rousseau)   **9**:341
"Sur un baiser" (Rousseau)   **9**:341
"Sur un commencement d'année" (Rousseau)   **9**:344
La surprise de l'amour (Marivaux)   **4**:354, 366-68, 370, 376-78, 381
The Surprises of Love, Exemplified in the Romance of a Day (Cleland)   **2**:52-4
"Sweet Afton" (Burns)   **3**:76, 86
"Sweet lover of the soul" (Juana Ines de la Cruz)   **5**:152
"Sweetest love, I do not goe" (Donne)
   See "Song. 'Sweetest love, I do not goe'"
"Sweetly breathing vernal air" (Carew)   **13**:20

Title Index

*A Swete and devoute Sermon of Holy saynt
    Ciprian of Mortalitie of Man (Saint Cyprian)*
    (Elyot) **11**:62, 84
Sylla et Eucrate (Montesquieu)
    See *Dialogue de Sylla et Eucrate*
"The Sylph Husband" (Marmontel) **2**:214
*Sylva Sylvarum: Or a Natural History (Forest of
    Forests, Silva Silvarum)* (Bacon) **18**:115,
    132, 137, 143, 149-50, 187
Sylvae (Dryden) **21**:72, 74-5, 77, 79-80, 119-
    20
System of Nature (Holbach)
    See *Système de la nature*
Système de la nature (System of Nature)
    (Holbach) **14**:152, 154-56, 158-59, 166,
    168-71, 175
Système social (Holbach) **14**:152, 154-56, 175
"Szachy" ("The Game of Chess")
    (Kochanowski) **10**:175
*Table of Colours or Appearance of Good and
    Evil* (Bacon)
    See *Colours of Good and Evil*
Table Talk (Luther)
    See *Tischreden; oder, Colloquia ...*
Tableau des vices de la Constitution anglaise
    (Marat) **10**:226
Tacitus (Lipsius)
    See *C. C. Taciti historiarum et annaliem libri
    qui exstant*
"Take heed of loving mee" (Donne)
    See "The Prohibition"
Talanta (Aretino) **12**:19, 26, 30, 36
Tale of a Tub (Jonson) **6**:300, 306, 311, 314
*A Tale of a Tub, Written for the Universal
    Improvement of Mankind, to Which is Added
    an Account of a Battel between the Ancient
    and Modern Books in St. James's Library
    (An Account of a Battel between the Ancient
    and Modern Books in St. James's Library)*
    (Swift) **1**:425, 431, 435, 437, 439-40, 449,
    453-59, 470-71, 473, 484-85, 490-91, 495,
    497, 504, 509, 513-17, 524
"Tale of Melibee" ("Melibee") (Chaucer)
    17:137, 177, 202, 205, 227, 237, 241, 243-44
"A Tale of the Miser and the Poet"
    (Winchilsea) **3**:457
"Tales" (Prior) **4**:460, 464
Tales (Chaucer)
    See *Canterbury Tales*
Tales of Canterbury (Chaucer)
    See *Canterbury Tales*
"Tam Glen" (Burns) **3**:66, 74, 78
"Tam o' Shanter" (Burns) **3**:49, 52, 55-6, 61,
    64, 66-7, 69, 71-2, 75-6, 78-9, 82-3, 85, 87,
    89-91, 96, 106
Tamerlane (Rowe) **8**:282, 285, 289, 292, 298,
    302-04, 308
"Tancred and Sigismunda" (Dryden) **3**:190
Tancred and Sigismunda. A Tragedy
    (Thomson) **16**:369, 396
Tancréde (Voltaire) **14**:358
Tangier Journal (Pepys) **11**:238
Tanzai (Crebillon)
    See *L'ecumoire; ou, Tanzai et Néadarné,
    histoire Japonaise*
"Tao-hu" ("Rebel Families") (P'u Sung-ling)
    3:351
Tartuffe (The Imposter; L'imposteur) (Moliere)
    10:265, 267-69, 272-73, 275, 277-91, 293-94,
    296-99, 304, 307-08, 311-13, 319-21, 325,
    329-30, 332-35, 338-40
Tartuffe: or, The Impostor (Moliere)

    See "The Teares of the Muses"
"Taste" (Smart) **3**:393
The Tatler (Addison) **18**:7, 13-14, 16, 21, 24,
    26-7, 31, 35, 37, 39, 42, 46-7, 49, 54, 65, 69
The Tatler (Steele) **18**:312-13, 315-18, 320-29,
    331-37, 340-44, 346-49, 351-55, 359-61, 367-
    69, 372, 376-78, 380-85
The Tatler, 1 (Steele) **18**:334, 383
The Tatler, 3 (Steele) **18**:376
The Tatler, 4 (Steele) **18**:341
The Tatler, 5 (Steele) **18**:317
The Tatler, 8 (Steele) **18**:381
The Tatler, 11 (Steele) **18**:326
The Tatler, 33 (Steele) **18**:349
The Tatler, 45 (Steele) **18**:381
The Tatler, 49 (Steele) **18**:326
The Tatler, 53 (Steele) **18**:326
The Tatler, 63 (Steele) **18**:349
The Tatler, 68 (Steele) **18**:371, 381
The Tatler, 79 (Steele) **18**:345
The Tatler, 82 (Steele) **18**:381
The Tatler, 113 (Steele) **18**:384
The Tatler, 118 (Steele) **18**:384
The Tatler, 141 (Steele) **18**:347
The Tatler, 144 (Steele) **18**:377
The Tatler, 149 (Steele) **18**:381
The Tatler, 163 (Addison) **18**:79
The Tatler, 165 (Addison) **18**:76
The Tatler, 172 (Steele) **18**:345, 382
The Tatler, 178 (Steele) **18**:318
The Tatler, 181 (Steele) **18**:384
The Tatler, 188 (Steele) **18**:318
The Tatler, 198 (Steele) **18**:382
The Tatler, 199 (Steele) **18**:318
The Tatler, 201 (Steele) **18**:346
The Tatler, 219 (Steele) **18**:372
The Tatler, 244 (Steele) **18**:318
The Tatler, 248 (Steele) **18**:347
The Tatler, 271 (Steele) **18**:335, 378
Le taureau blanc (Voltaire) **14**:346, 359
Taxation No Tyranny (Johnson) **15**:198, 203,
    208, 276
"Te Deum" (Dennis)
    See "Part of the 'Te Deum' Paraphras'd, in
    Pindarick Verse"
"The Tea-pot and the Scrubbing-brush"
    (Smart) **3**:366
"The Teares of the Muses" (*Tartuffe: or, The
    Impostor*) (Spenser) **5**:312
"The Tears of Scotland" (Smollett) **2**:332-33,
    358
"The Tears of St. Peter" (Malherbe)
    See "Les Larmes de Saint Pierre"
Teatro (Aretino) **12**:19
"Tedious Man" (Butler) **16**:55
Le télémaque travesti (Marivaux) **4**:385-87
The Tempest (Dryden) **21**:88, 107
The Tempest; or, The Enchanted Island
    (Davenant) **13**:185-87, 216-19
"The Temple" (Herrick)
    See "The Fairie Temple: or, Oberons
    Chappell. Dedicated to Mr. John
    Merrifield, Counsellor at Law"
The Temple Beau (Dryden) **3**:219, 250
Le tèmple de Gnide (The Temple of Gnidus)
    (Montesquieu) **7**:320, 324, 342, 348
The Temple of Gnidus (Montesquieu)
    See *Le temple de Gnide*
The Temple of Love (Davenant) **13**:175, 181,
    189, 196-97

*Temporis partus masculus (Masculine Birth of
    Time)* (Bacon) **18**:121, 144, 154, 187
"Le tems" (Rousseau) **9**:345
Ten Articles (Henry VIII)
    See *Articles ... to Stabliyshe Christen
    Quietnes*
The Tender Husband (Steele) **18**:314-15, 329-
    30, 339-40, 343, 353-54, 359, 365, 367
"The Tenth Discourse" (Reynolds) **15**:382,
    388, 396, 403
The Tenth Muse Lately sprung up in America
    (Bradstreet) **4**:84-7, 89-90, 94, 102, 107,
    109-11, 114
The Tenure of Kings and Magistrates (Milton)
    9:161
"A Ternary of Littles" (Herrick) **13**:356
Testament of Love (Chaucer)
    See *Legend of Good Women*
Tetrachordon (Milton) **9**:163, 208
"The Thanksgiving" (Herrick) **13**:317, 319,
    362
"The Thanksgiving to God" (Herrick) **13**:324
"Thanksgiving to God for his House"
    (Herrick) **13**:333, 358, 362
"That Politics May Be Reduced to a Science"
    (Hume) **7**:188, 204
"That to Philosophize Is to Learn to Die"
    (Montaigne)
    See "Que philosopher, c'est apprendre à
    mourir"
Theatralische Bibliothek (Lessing) **8**:100
Theatralische Werke (Schlegel) **5**:273
The Theatre (Steele) **18**:346, 354, 372-73
The Theatre, 19 (Steele) **18**:372
The Theatrical Candidates (Garrick) **15**:100
Theodore and Honoria ("Honoria") (Dryden)
    3:184, 190, 204-05, 216
Theologia (Ficino)
    See *Theologia platonica de immortalitate
    animorum*
Theologia Platonica (Ficino)
    See *Theologia platonica de immortalitate
    animorum*
*Theologia platonica de immortalitate animorum
    (Platonic Theology; Theologia; Theologia
    Platonica)* (Ficino) **12**:166-68, 170-72, 174,
    177, 182, 185-87, 189, 191, 193, 195, 197-98,
    200
Theological-Political Treatise (Spinoza)
    See *Tractatus theologico-politicus continens
    dissertationes all quot, quibus ostenditur
    libertatem philosophandi non tantum salva
    pietate, & reipublicae*
Theological Works (More) **9**:309
Théologie portative (Holbach) **14**:152-53
"There Was a Lad" (Burns) **3**:87, 92
"There's Nothing Grieves Me, But that Age
    Should Haste" (Drayton)
    See "Sonnet VIII"
"Thermometer of Zeal" (Addison) **18**:27
"Thétis" (Rousseau) **9**:343
"The Third Discourse" ("Discourse Three")
    (Reynolds) **15**:368, 378-80, 383, 391, 395-
    96, 402, 412, 422
"The Thirteenth Discourse" (Reynolds)
    15:398, 404
This and That (Chulkov) **2**:19
This Is My Body: These Words Still Stand
    (Luther) **9**:136
"Thomas Cromwell, Earle of Essex"
    ("Cromwell") (Drayton) **8**:30, 33
"Thou Lingering Star" (Burns) **3**:56

"Thou Purblind Boy, since Thou Hast Beene So Slacke" (Drayton)
  See "Sonnet 36"
"Thought and Vision" (Bacon)
  See "Cogitata et Visa"
Thoughts (Wollstonecraft)
  See *Thoughts on the Education of Daughters: With Reflections on Female Conduct, in the More Important Duties of Life*
Thoughts and Details on Scarcity (Burke)
  See *Thoughts and Details on Scarcity Originally Presented to the Right Hon. William Pitt in the Month of November, 1795*
Thoughts and Details on Scarcity Originally Presented to the Right Hon. William Pitt in the Month of November, 1795 (*Thoughts and Details on Scarcity*) (Burke)   7:57, 59-60
"Thoughts on His Excellency Major General Lee" ("On Major General Lee") (Wheatley)   3:411, 413, 437
Thoughts on Religion (Swift)   1:486, 491
Thoughts on the Cause of the Present Discontents (*Present Discontents*) (Burke)   7:14, 26, 46, 49, 57, 60-3
Thoughts on the Education of Daughters: With Reflections on Female Conduct, in the More Important Duties of Life (*Thoughts*) (Wollstonecraft)   5:425, 427, 441-42, 460
Thoughts on the late Transactions respecting the Falkland Islands (Johnson)   15:208
Thoughts on Various Subjects (Swift)   1:480
"Thoughts Upon Various Subjects" (Butler)   16:49
Thraseas (Lipsius)   16:254
Three Bertheonei Books (Paracelsus)
  See *Chirurgia minor quam Bertheoneam intituluat*
Three Essays, Moral and Political (Hume)   7:189
Three Hours after Marriage (Arbuthnot)   1:17-19
The Three Kingdoms (Lo Kuan-chung)
  See *San-kuo-chih yeni-i*
Three Letters on the Genius and Writings of Shakespeare (Dennis)
  See *An Essay on the Genius of Shakespear*
Threnodia Augustalis (Dryden)   3:186, 216; 21:65, 67, 82, 86-7
Threnodia Augustalis (Goldsmith)   2:104
The Threnodies (Kochanowski)
  See *Treny*
"Threnody V" ("Lament V") (Kochanowski)   10:153, 163, 166-67, 169
"Threnody VIII" (Kochanowski)
  See "Tren VIII"
"Threnody XI" ("Lament XI") (Kochanowski)   10:157-58, 163
"Threnody XVII" (Kochanowski)
  See "Tren XVII"
"Threnody XVII" ("Lament XVII") (Kochanowski)   10:153, 158-59, 163, 165, 173
"Thumbs" (Montaigne)   8:203
"Thy Human Frame, My Glorious Lord, I Spy" (Taylor)   11:402
"La tía fingida" (Cervantes)   6:171
Le tiers livre des faictz et dictz heroiques du noble Pantagruel (Rabelais)   5:216-19, 233-34, 239-41, 243-44, 249, 255-56, 258-59, 267

Timber; or, Discoveries (*Discoveries*) (Jonson)   6:291, 312-13, 316, 322, 324, 328, 343, 347, 349-50
"The Times" (Churchill)   3:141, 143, 155, 162-63
Timon (Boiardo)
  See *Timone*
Timone (*Timon*) (Boiardo)   6:88
"Tinker's Song" (Herrick)   13:331
Tischreden; oder, Colloquia ... (*Table Talk*) (Luther)   9:110, 127-28
Titus et Gesippus (Foxe)   14:42-44, 46-47
Titus Vespasian (Cleland)   2:51
"To a Child of Quality Five Years Old, the Author Forty, Written in 1704" ("To a Child of Quality of Five Years Old, the Author Suppos'd Forty") (Prior)   4:460, 463, 465-66, 475
"To a Child of Quality of Five Years Old, the Author Suppos'd Forty" (Prior)
  See "To a Child of Quality Five Years Old, the Author Forty, Written in 1704"
"To a Clergyman on the Death of His Lady" (Wheatley)   3:433
"To a Crowing Cock" (Kochanowski)
  See "Gallo crocitanti"
"To a Crowing Gaul" (Kochanowski)
  See "Gallo crocitanti"
"To a Fine Young Woman, Who, Being Asked by Her Lover, Why She Kept So Filthy a Thing as a Snake in Her Bosom; Answer'd, 'Twas to Keep a Filthier Thing out of it, His Hand'" (Wycherley)   8:415
"To a Gentleman in the Navy" ("Gentleman in the Navy") (Wheatley)   3:420
"To a Girl" (Kochanowski)   10:160
"To a Haggis" (Burns)
  See "Address to a Haggis"
"To a Kiss" (Burns)   3:86
"To a Lady" (Kochanowski)
  See "Do paniej"
"To a Lady" (Prior)   4:466
"To a Lady on Her Remarkable Preservation in an Hurricane in North Carolina" (Wheatley)   3:430-31
"To a Lady on the Death of Three Relations" (Wheatley)   3:422, 428
"To a Lady, Who Wore Drawers in an Ill Hour" (Wycherley)   8:399
"To a Louse, on Seeing One on a Lady's Bonnet at Church" ("Address to a Louse") (Burns)   3:63, 67, 71, 87, 94-5
"To a Mountain Daisy, on Turning One Down with the Plough in April, 1786" (Burns)   3:48, 67, 87, 94-5
"To a Mouse, on Turning Her Up in Her Nest with the Plough, November, 1785" (Burns)   3:48, 60, 67, 71, 77, 79, 87, 73-5
"To a Vain Young Courtier" (Wycherley)   21:342
"To a Young Gentleman, Who Was Blam'd for Marrying Young" (Dennis)   11:47
"To a Young Lady Fond of Fortune Telling" (Prior)   4:461
"To A.D., unreasonable distrustfull of her owne beauty" (Carew)   13:37
"To A.L. Perswasions to Love" ("Persuasions to Love") (Carew)   13:11, 18, 21, 27, 29-30, 34, 54-7
"To all vertuous Ladies in generall" (Lanyer)   10:183, 188-89

"To an University Wit, or Poet; Who Had Written Some Ill Verses, with an Ill Play or Two; Which, Not Succeeding, He Resolv'd to Turn Parson" (Wycherley)   8:399
"To Anthea" (Herrick)   13:336, 341, 351-52, 365
"To Anthea Lying in Bed" (Herrick)   13:351
"To Anthea, who may command him any thing" (Herrick)   13:355
"To Ben Jonson Upon occasion of his Ode of defiance annext to his play of the new Inne" ("Upon occasion of his Ode of defiance annext to his Play of the new Inne") (Carew)   13:32, 65
"To Blossoms" (Herrick)   13:336
"To Candidus: How to Choose a Wife" ("Candidus") (More)   10:428-29
"To Cherry-Blossomes" (Herrick)   13:350
"To Cupid" (Herrick)   13:341
"To Daffadills" ("Fair Daffodils") (Herrick)   13:336-37, 349-50, 353-54, 364, 402
"To Deanbourn, a rude River in Devon" (Herrick)   13:387-88
"To Dianeme" (Herrick)   13:389
"To Dr. Sherlock, on His Practical Discourse Concerning Death" (Prior)   4:466
"To drink is a Christian diversion" (Congreve)   5:85
"To Electra" (Herrick)   13:337, 353
"To fair Fidelle's grassy tomb" (Collins)   4:218
"To find God" (Herrick)   13:319, 374
"To Flavia Who Fear'd She Was Too Kind" (Dennis)   11:48
"To Flowers" (Herrick)   13:364
"To God" (Herrick)   13:317
"To Henry Jarmin" (Davenant)   13:206
"To his Book" (Herrick)   13:393
"To his Conscience" (Herrick)   13:319
"To His Coy Love" (Drayton)   8:27
"To His Coy Mistress" ("The Coy Mistress") (Marvell)   4:397, 400-01, 403-4, 411, 425, 427, 430, 432-34, 439, 441-42, 445-57
"To his Dying Brother, Master William Herrick" (Herrick)   13:353
"To His Excellency General George Washington" (Wheatley)   3:416
"To His Honor the Lieutenant Governor on the Death of His Lady" (Wheatley)   3:415
"To his Kinswoman, Mistresse Penelope Wheeler" (Herrick)   13:391
"To his Mistress confined" (Carew)   13:10
"To his Mistresses" (Herrick)   13:393
"To his Muse" (Herrick)   13:393
"To His Rivall" (Drayton)   8:27
"To His Sacred Majesty, A Panegyrick on His Coronation" (Dryden)   3:223; 21:81-2, 85
"To His Valentine" ("Ode to His Valentine") (Drayton)   8:17
"To his Valentine" (Herrick)   13:338
"To his worthy Kinsman, Master Stephen Soame" (Herrick)   13:391
"To Honor Dryden" (Dryden)   3:239
"To Imagination" (Wheatley)
  See "On Imagination"
"To John Hoddesdon, on His Divine Epigrams" (Dryden)   3:223
"To John I Ow'd Great Obligation" (Prior)   4:459
"To Julia" (Herrick)   13:340, 353, 391, 403-04
"To Julia, in her Dawne, or Day-breake" (Herrick)   13:403

"To Laurels" (Herrick) **13**:341

"To Live Merrily, and to Trust to Good Verses" (Herrick) **13**:350, 365-67, 382

"To Love" (Kochanowski) See "Do Miłości"

"To Love" (Wycherley) **8**:399

"To Mæcenas" (Wheatley) See "Ode to Mæcenas"

"To Mary in Heaven" ("Mary in Heaven") (Burns) **3**:61, 72, 74

"To Marygolds" (Herrick) **13**:353

To Matthew Prior, Esq; Upon the Roman Satirists (Dennis) **11**:40

"To Meadows" (Herrick) **13**:337

"To Mr. and Mrs. ******* on the Death of Their Infant Son" (Wheatley) **3**:436

"To Mr. E. H. Physician and Poet" (Dennis) **11**:47

"To Mr. Gray" (Warton) **15**:442

"To Mr. Gray, on the Publication of His Odes" (Garrick) **15**:114, 125

"To Mr. Pope" (Parnell) See "Letter to Mr. Pope"

"To Mr R. W. 'If as mine is'" (Donne) **10**:9, 39

"To Mr S. B. 'O Thou which'" (Donne) **10**:97

"To Mr T. W. 'All haile sweet Poet'" (Donne) **10**:97

"To Mr. Waller in His Old Age" (Wycherley) **8**:380

To Mr. West at Wickham (Lyttelton) **10**:199

"To Mrs M. H. 'Mad paper, stay'" (Donne) **10**:83

"To Music" (Herrick) **13**:317

"To Musique, to becalme his Fever" (Herrick) **13**:336

"To My Booke" (Jonson) **6**:351

"To My Booke-seller" (Jonson) **6**:352

"To my Cousin, C.R., Marrying my Lady A" (Carew) **13**:15

"To my Dear and loving Husband" (Bradstreet) **4**:94

"To My Dear Children" (Bradstreet) **4**:104

"To my friend G.N. from Wrest" (Carew) See "Letter to G.N. from Wrest"

"To my Friend Mr. Ogilby Upon the Fables of Aesop Paraphras'd in Verse" (Davenant) **13**:204, 206

"To My Honored Friend, Dr. Charleton" (Dryden) **3**:223

"To My Honored Friend, Sir Robert Howard" (Dryden) **3**:223

"To My Honour'd Kinsman, John Driden, of Chesterton, in the County of Huntingdon, Esq." (Dryden) **3**:246

"To my Honoured friend, Master Thomas May, upon his Comedie, The Heire" (Carew) **13**:45

"To my Inconstant Mistress" (Carew) **13**:13, 33

"To My Lord Chancellor" (Dryden) **3**:223; **21**:85, 87

"To My Lord Colrane" (Killigrew) **4**:350

To my Lord Hervey (Lyttelton) **10**:215

"To My Mistresse in Absence" (Carew) **13**:62

"To My Most Dearely-Loved Friend Henery Reynolds Esquire, of Poets and Poesie" ("Epistle to Henry Reynolds") (Drayton) **8**:9, 25

"To my much honoured Friend, Henry Lord Carey of Lepington, upon his translation of Malvezzi" (Carew) **13**:54, 65

"To My Noble Friend Master William Browne, of the Evill Time" (Drayton) **8**:9

"To My Reader" (Jonson) **6**:352

"To my worthy Friend, M. D'Avenant, Upon his Excellent Play, The Just Italian" (Carew) **13**:66

"To my Worthy Friend Master George Sandys, on his Translation of the Psalms" (Carew) **13**:25, 31

"To Nath. Lee, in Bethlem" (Wycherley) **21**:344

"To Penshurst" (Jonson) **6**:342, 347

"To Perilla" (Herrick) **13**:350, 352

"To Phyllis, to Love and Live with Him" (Herrick) **13**:323, 332, 360

"To Primroses fill'd with Morning-Dew" (Herrick) **13**:350

"To S. M., A Young African Painter, on Seeing His Works" (Wheatley) **3**:412, 420, 423, 436

"To Saxham" (Carew) See "Address to Saxham"

"To Silvia" (Herrick) **13**:313

"To Sir Clipesby Crew" (Herrick) **13**:368, 392-93

"To Sir Edward Herbert, at Julyers. 'Man is a lumpe'" (Donne) **10**:103

"To Sir Godfrey Knelles" (Dryden) **21**:89

"To Sir Henry Wotton. 'Here's no more newes'" (Donne) **10**:39

"To Sir Henry Wotton. 'Sir, more then kisses'" (Donne) **10**:39

"To Sleep" (Kochanowski) See "Do snu"

"To Sleep" (Warton) **15**:444

"To Suicide" ("The Suicide") (Warton) **15**:444, 447

"To the Angell spirit of the most excellent Sir Phillip Sidney" (Sidney) **19**:296, 299, 303, 309-10

"To the Author of The Touchstone of Truth" (Jonson) **6**:325

"To the Countess of Anglesie upon the immoderately-by-her lamented death of her Husband" (Carew) **13**:49-50

"To the Countess of Burlington" (Garrick) **15**:97

"To the Countesse of Bedford. 'Madame, reason is'" (Donne) **10**:9

"To the Countesse of Bedford. 'Madame, You have refin'd'" (Donne) **10**:83

"To the Countesse of Bedford. 'This twilight of'" (Donne) **10**:9

"To the Countesse of Huntingdon. 'That unripe side'" (Donne) **10**:36

"To the De'il" (Burns) See "Address to the De'il"

"To the Duchess of Ormond" (Dryden) **3**:243; **21**:87

"To the Earle of Portland, Lord Treasurer; on the marriage of his Sonne" (Davenant) **13**:205

"To the Eccho" (Winchilsea) **3**:454

"To the Honour of Pimps and Pimping; dedicated to the Court; and written at a Time when such were most considerable there" (Wycherley) **21**:348

"To the Honourable Charles Montague, Esq." (Prior) **4**:461, 465

"To the King" (Herrick) **13**:395

"To the King" (Young) **3**:488

"To the King at his entrance into Saxham" (Carew) **13**:61

"To the King on New-yeares day 1630" (Davenant) **13**:205

"TO THE KING, to cure the Evill" (Herrick) **13**:395-96

"TO THE KING, Upon his comming with his Army into the West" (Herrick) **13**:389

"To the Lady Castlemaine, upon Her Incouraging His First Play" (Dryden) **3**:223

"To the Lady Crew, upon the Death of her Child" (Herrick) **13**:353, 366

"To the Linden Tree" (Kochanowski) See "Na lipe"

"To the little Spinners" (Herrick) **13**:374

"To the Lord Cary of Lepington" (Davenant) **13**:206

"To the Maids to walk abroad" (Herrick) **13**:360

"To the Majestie of King James" (Drayton) **8**:30

To the Memory of a Lady Lately Deceased: A Monody (*Monody*) (Lyttelton) **10**:198-99, 201, 203, 207, 209-10, 215

"To the Memory of Master Newbery" (Smart) **3**:374

"To the Memory of Mr. Congreve" ("A Poem to the Memory of Mr. Congreve") (Thomson) **16**:428-29

"To the Memory of Mr. Oldham" (Dryden) **3**:201

"To the Memory of My Beloved, the Author, Mr. William Shakespeare, and What He Hath Left Us" (Jonson) **6**:348, 350

To the Memory of Sir Isaac Newton (Thomson) See *A Poem Sacred to the Memory of Sir Isaac Newton*

"To the Memory of the Right Honourable the Lord Talbot" (Thomson) **16**:428

"To the New Yeere" ("Ode on the New Year") (Drayton) **8**:17, 27

"To the Nightengale" (Thomson) **16**:427

"To the Nightingale" ("The Nightingale") (Winchilsea) **3**:441-42, 444, 447, 451, 454

"To the Painter" (Carew) **13**:63

"To the Pious Memory of the Accomplisht Young Lady Mrs. Anne Killigrew" ("Anne Killigrew") (Dryden) **3**:186, 216, 223

"To the Queen" (Carew) **13**:59

"To the Queenes most Excellent Majestie" (Lanyer) **10**:183

"To the Reader of Master William Davenant's Play" (Carew) **13**:67

"To the Reader of These Sonnets" (Drayton) **8**:37

"To the Reverend Shade of his Religious Father" (Herrick) **13**:350

"To the Right Honorable William, Earl of Dartmouth, His Majesty's Principal Secretary of State for North America" (Wheatley) **3**:415, 423, 427, 429, 434

"To the River Lodon" (Warton) **15**:435, 443

"To the Rose" (Herrick) **13**:334

"To the Rose. Song" ("Song") (Herrick) **13**:398

"To the Same (i.e., to Celia)" (Jonson) **6**:349

"To the Toothache" ("Address to the Toothache") (Burns) **3**:67, 85

"To the University of Cambridge, in New England" (Wheatley)   **3**:413, 415-16, 423, 427, 429

"To the Vertuous Reader" ("Epistle to the Vertuous Reader") (Lanyer)   **10**:181-82, 184, 190

"To the Virginian Voyage" ("Virginian Ode") (Drayton)   **8**:18, 25-7, 30, 42-5

"To the Virgins, to make much of Time" (Herrick)
See "Gather ye rosebuds while ye may"

"To the Woodlark" (Burns)   **3**:81

"To Violets" (Herrick)   **13**:337

Tom Jones (Fielding)
See *The History of Tom Jones, a Foundling*

"Tom May's Death" (Marvell)   **4**:439

Tombeau de Marguerite de Valois (Ronsard)   **6**:434

"Le Tombeau du feu Roy Tres-Chrestien Charles IX" (Ronsard)   **6**:437

Tombo-Chiqui; or, The American Savage (Cleland)   **2**:51, 53

"The Toothache cured by a Kiss" (Carew)   **13**:18

The Topsy-Turvy World (Grimmelshausen)
See *Die Verkehrte Welt*

"Torticolis" (Rousseau)   **9**:345

A Tour through the Whole Island of Great Britain (Defoe)   **1**:173-74

"The Tournament" (Chatterton)   **3**:124, 135

Town Eclogues (Montagu)
See *Court Poems*

The Town Fop; or, Sir Timothy Tawdrey (Behn)   **1**:33, 39, 46-7

Los trabajos de Persiles y Sigismunda (*Persiles y Sigismunda*) (Cervantes)   **6**:142-43, 151, 169-70, 174-76, 178, 180

"Tract on the Popery Laws" (Burke)   **7**:46

Tractatus theologico-politicus continens dissertationes all quot, quibus ostenditur libertatem philosophandi non tantum salva pietate, & reipublicae (*Theological-Political Treatise*) (Spinoza)   **9**:393, 397-98, 402, 408-09, 418-19, 423-24, 431, 436, 438-40

La tragedia por los celos (Castro)   **19**:7-8

Tragedy of Cato (Addison)   **18**:7, 10-11, 14-15, 17-19, 31-2, 46-7, 76-7

The Tragedy of Jane Shore (*Jane Shore*) (Rowe)   **8**:285, 287, 292-97, 299-302, 304-08, 314, 316

The Tragedy of Lady Jane Gray (*Jane*) (Rowe)   **8**:293, 297, 300, 302, 305, 307-08

The Tragedy of Sophonisba (*Sophonisba*) (Thomson)   **16**:387

The Tragedy of the Horatii (Aretino)
See *Orazia*

The Tragedy of Tom Thumb (Fielding)   **1**:203, 239

Traité de métaphysique (Voltaire)   **14**:339, 366-67, 379

Traité des devoirs (Montesquieu)   **7**:339, 356, 360

Traité sur la tolérance (Voltaire)   **14**:370, 379, 402

Trampagos, the Pimp Who Lost His Moll (Cervantes)   **6**:190-92

"The Transfiguration" (Herrick)   **13**:353, 403

Translation of the Latter Part of the Third Book of Lucretius: Against the Fear of Death (*Against the Fear of Death*) (Dryden)   **21**:72-4, 76-7

A Translation of the Psalms of David, Attempted in the Spirit of Christianity, and Adapted to the Divine Service ("Psalms") (Smart)   **3**:371, 376-78, 382, 395, 398

"Transmigrations of Pug the Monkey" (Addison)   **18**:28

El trato de Argel (*Los tratos de Argel*) (Cervantes)   **6**:177-78, 180-81

Los tratos de Argel (Cervantes)
See *El trato de Argel*

Trattato della Pittura (*Treatise on Painting*) (Vinci)   **12**:384, 391, 393-96, 406, 412, 417-18, 420-21, 423-25, 427

Travel Journal (Montaigne)
See *Journal du voyage de Michel de Montaigne en Italie par la Suisse et l'Allemagne en 1580 et 1581*

The Traveller (Goldsmith)   **2**:66, 68, 71-5, 80-2, 94-5, 97, 102, 104-05, 112-15, 128-31

Travels (Addison)   **18**:30

Travels, Chiefly on Foot, through Several Parts of England in 1782 (Moritz)
See *Reisen eines Deutschen in England im Jahr 1782*

Travels into Several Remote Nations of the World, in Four Parts; By Lemuel Gulliver (Swift)   **1**:426-29, 432-37, 439-42, 444-52, 456, 460-79, 483-91, 497-502, 504-10, 513-17, 519, 527-29

Travels through France and Italy (Smollett)   **2**:322, 329, 331, 344, 363, 365-67

The Treasure (Lessing)   **8**:112

The Treasure of the City of Ladies, or, The Book of the Three Virtues (Christine de Pizan)
See *La trésor de la cité des dames; or, Le livre des trois vertus*

Treatise (Taylor)
See *Treatise Concerning the Lord's Supper*

Treatise Concerning Enthusiasm (More)   **9**:318

A Treatise concerning Religious Affections (*Religious Affections*) (Edwards)   **7**:94, 96, 101-02, 118-21

Treatise Concerning the Lord's Supper (*Treatise*) (Taylor)   **11**:373, 385-86

A Treatise Historical containing the Bitter Passion of our Saviour Christ (More)   **10**:370

Treatise of Civil Government (Locke)   **7**:269, 273

A Treatise of Human Nature: Being an Attempt to Introduce the Experimental Method of Reasoning into Moral Subjects (Hume)   **7**:136-41, 154-55, 157-58, 160-61, 163, 165-66, 168, 171, 174, 176, 178, 183, 188, 197-99, 202

A Treatise of the Art of Political Lying (Arbuthnot)   **1**:15

Treatise on Painting (Vinci)
See *Trattato della Pittura*

A Treatise on Polite Conversation (Swift)   **1**:437

Treatise on Religion and the State (Spinoza)   **9**:421

Treatise on Shadows (Vinci)   **12**:405

A Treatise on the Astrolabe (Chaucer)   **17**:214-15

Treatise on the Fable (Lessing)   **8**:104

Treatise on the New Testament (Luther)   **9**:140

A Treatise to Receaue the Blessed Sacrament (More)   **10**:367

Treatise upon the Christian Religion (Addison)   **18**:8

A Treatise upon the Passion (More)   **10**:367, 399-400, 405, 436, 440

"The Tree" (Winchilsea)   **3**:442, 444, 451, 454

"Tren VII" ("Lament VII") (Kochanowski)   **10**:153, 157, 166-67, 170

"Tren VIII" ("Lament VIII"; "Threnody VIII") (Kochanowski)   **10**:153, 157, 159, 163, 166-67, 170

"Tren IX" ("Lament IX") (Kochanowski)   **10**:158, 170, 174

"Tren XVI" ("Lament XVI") (Kochanowski)   **10**:153, 158, 165, 170, 174

"Tren XVII" ("Lament XVII"; "Threnody XVII") (Kochanowski)   **10**:153, 157-59, 165, 173-74

"Tren XIX" ("The Dream"; "Lament XIX") (Kochanowski)   **10**:153, 157-58, 165, 170, 173

Treny (*Laments; The Threnodies*) (Kochanowski)   **10**:151-53, 156-59, 162, 164-65, 167-76

La trésor de la cité des dames; or, Le livre des trois vertus (*The Treasure of the City of Ladies, or, The Book of the Three Virtues*) (Christine de Pizan)   **9**:25, 33-5, 38-9, 45, 47

"The Trials of a Noble House" (Juana Ines de la Cruz)
See *Los empeños de una casa*

Trias Romana (Hutten)
See *Vadiscus, sive Trias Romana*

De tribus tabernaculis (Kempis)   **11**:411

The Tricks of Scapin (Moliere)
See *Les fourberies de Scapin*

Trifles (Kochanowski)
See *Fraski*

La trilogia della villeggiatura (Goldoni)   **4**:275

"Triomphe de l'amour" (Rousseau)   **9**:343

Le triomphe de l'amour (Marivaux)   **4**:367, 377

"Le Triomphe de l'Hiver" (Ronsard)   **6**:438

Le triomphe de Plutus (Marivaux)   **4**:367

Trip to the Jubilee (Farquhar)
See *The Constant Couple; or, A Trip to he Jubilee*

"The Triple Fool" (Donne)   **10**:12, 82

De Tristitia Christi (More)   **10**:436

Tristram Shandy (Sterne)
See *The Life and Opinions of Tristram Shandy, Gentleman*

"Triumph of Charis" (Jonson)
See *A Celebration of Charis in Ten Lyric Pieces*

"The Triumph of Isis" (Warton)   **15**:431, 433, 440, 449, 460-61

Triumph of the Four Foster Childern of Desire (Sidney)   **19**:421

Triumpho parthenico que en glorias de María Santissima immaculadamente concebida (*Parthian Truimph*) (Siguenza y Gongora)   **8**:340

"The Triumphs of Owen. A Fragment" (Gray)   **4**:312-13, 318

Triumphus Capnionis (Hutten)   **16**:220, 231, 238-41

Troilus (Chaucer)
See *Troilus and Criseyde*

Troilus and Cressida; or, Truth Found Too Late (Dryden)   **3**:197, 233; **21**:52-4, 56, 114

Title Index

Troilus and Criseyde (*Book of Troilus; Troilus; Troilus and Cryseide*) (Chaucer) **17**:45, 47, 58, 78, 84, 92, 99-100, 104-05, 117, 124, 131-32, 138, 154, 156, 159, 178, 194, 204-05, 213-14, 216-19

Troilus and Cryseide (Chaucer)
See *Troilus and Criseyde*

Trois Livres des nouvelles poesies (Ronsard) **6**:432

Die Trojanerinnen (Schlegel) **5**:273, 280-81

Trophy of Spanish Justice (Siguenza y Gongora) **8**:343

The True-Born Englishman (Defoe) **1**:118, 160

"A True Estimate" (Young) **3**:491

The True Friend (Goldoni)
See *Il vero amico*

"A True Love Story" (Walpole) **2**:500

The True Patriot (Fielding) **1**:234

A True Relation of Such Occurrences and Accidents of Noate As Hath Hapned in Virginia (Smith) **9**:352-55, 357-60, 365-66, 369-71, 380-81, 383, 385-87

A True Relation of the Apparition of One Mrs. Veal (Defoe) **1**:144, 163

The True Travels, Adventures, and Observations of Captaine John Smith (Smith) **9**:352-53, 361-62, 365, 367, 372, 375, 381-84, 388

The Tryal of the Cause of the Roman Catholics (Brooke) **1**:62

Ts'an-T'ang wu-tai-shih yen-i (Lo Kuan-chung) **12**:282

"Tsu-chih" ("The Cricket") (P'u Sung-ling) **3**:347, 350

"Tsui Meng" (P'u Sung-ling) **3**:345

"Tu ha' 'l uiso" (Michelangelo) **12**:362

Tuḥfat al-aḥrár (*Rosary of the Pious*) (Jami) **9**:68

Tuḥfatu'l-Ahrár (*Gift of the Free*) (Jami) **9**:66, 68, 70-1

Tumble-Down Dick (Fielding) **1**:239

Turcaret (Lesage) **2**:175, 180, 182-85, 188, 201-02

Tusculan Disputations (Erasmus) **16**:172

"The Twa Dogs" ("Dialogues of the Dogs") (Burns) **3**:48, 52, 57, 64, 71, 73, 77, 84-5, 96, 103-05

"The Twa Herds" (Burns) **3**:78, 87, 93, 95-6

"The Twelfth Discourse" ("Discourse XII") (Reynolds) **15**:383, 389, 397, 403, 405, 419

"Twelfth-Night, or King and Queen" (Herrick) **13**:331

"Twenty-Four Songs Set to Music by Several Eminent Masters" (Prior) **4**:466-67

Twice or thrice had I loved thee (Donne)
See "Aire and Angels"

"Twicknam Garden" (Donne) **10**:10, 36, 50

The Twin Rivals (Farquhar) **21**:128-29, 132, 135-36, 139-42, 144, 146-47, 149-54, 156-57, 161-66, 169-71, 176

Two Letters...on the Proposals for Peace, with the Regicide Directory of France (Burke) **7**:14, 23, 26, 39, 46, 53, 61

"The Two Maidens" (Cervantes)
See "Las dos doncelas"

"Two Pastoralls" (Sidney) **19**:393

Two Treatises of Government (Locke) **7**:263, 273, 295-96

Tyrannick Love; or, The Royal Martyr (Dryden) **3**:210, 232-33, 235, 237; **21**:88, 102, 105-07

Über den märkischen Dialekt (Moritz) **2**:241

Über die bildende Nachahmung des Schönen (*On the Creative Imitation of the Beautiful*) (Moritz) **2**:234, 243, 245

Uden hoved og hale (*Without Head or Tail*) (Holberg) **6**:277

"Ugadčiki" (Chulkov) **2**:22

"La uita del me amor" (Michelangelo) **12**:360

Ulysses (Rowe) **8**:285, 287, 292, 295, 299, 302, 305

Ulysses von Ithacia; eller, En tysk comoedie (Holberg) **6**:259, 263, 277

Una delle ultime sere di carnovale (Goldoni) **4**:264, 266

"Underneath This Sable Hearse" (Jonson) **6**:304-05

"The undertaking" (Donne) **10**:18, 26, 51, 54-5

The Underwood (Jonson) **6**:304, 312, 315, 325, 337, 348, 350

"An Undeserving Favourite" (Butler) **16**:54

The Unfortunate Happy Lady (Behn) **1**:34, 38, 42, 46, 49, 51-2, 55

"The Unfortunate Lover" (Marvell) **4**:408-10, 442-43

The Unfortunate Lovers (Davenant) **13**:176, 181-82, 196

The Unfortunate Princess (Haywood) **1**:290-91

The Unhappy Mistake; or, The Impious Vow Punished (Behn) **1**:51

The Unhappy Penitent (Trotter) **8**:355, 357, 361, 363, 369, 371-74

The Union: or Select Scots and English Poems (Warton) **15**:441

De unitate ecclesia conservanda (Hutten) **16**:213, 231, 233

Universal Beauty (Brooke) **1**:62, 64-5, 68-9

The Universal Gallant; or, The Different Husbands (Fielding) **1**:250

"The Universal Passion; or, The Love of Fame" ("The Love of Fame") (Young) **3**:467, 476-77, 486

"The Universal Prayer" (Pope) **3**:284

"University of Oxon." (Dryden)
See "Prologue to the University of Oxford"

Unterhaltungen mit seinen Schülern (Moritz) **2**:240

"Up Tails All" (Herrick) **13**:331

"Upon a Child" (Herrick) **13**:340

"Upon a child that died" ("Here she lies, a pretty bud") (Herrick) **13**:340, 367, 409

"Upon a fit of Sickness, Anno 1632" (Bradstreet) **4**:90

"Upon a Lady that Died in Childbirth" (Herrick) **13**:409

"Upon a Lady's Fall over a Stile, Gotten by Running from Her Lover; by Which She Show'd Her Fair Back-Side, Which Was Her Best Side, and Made Him More Her Pursuer than He Was Before" (Wycherley) **8**:415

"Upon a Ribband" (Carew) **13**:33-4

"Upon a Spider Catching a Fly" (Taylor) **11**:356, 369, 385, 394

"Upon a Wasp Child with Cold" (Taylor) **11**:369, 386

"Upon a Wife that dyed mad with Jealousie" (Herrick) **13**:340

"Upon an Old Worn-Out Picture of Justice, Hung... in a Court of Judicature" (Wycherley) **8**:416

"Upon Appleton House" ("Appleton House") (Marvell) **4**:397, 401-04, 409-10, 412, 425, 429, 435-36, 438-41, 448

"Upon Electra" (Herrick) **13**:369

"Upon Friendship, preferre'd to Love" (Wycherley) **21**:396

"Upon Gut" (Herrick) **13**:356

"Upon Happiness" (Thomson) **16**:418

"Upon himself" (Herrick) **13**:387

"Upon His Departure Hence" (Herrick) **13**:333

"Upon his Verses" (Herrick) **13**:392

"Upon Julia's Clothes" ("On Julia's Clothes") (Herrick) **13**:338-39, 351, 368-70, 402

"Upon Julia's Fall" (Herrick) **13**:367

"Upon Julia's Recovery" (Herrick) **13**:349-50, 365, 388-89, 402

"Upon Julia's Voice" (Herrick) **13**:397

"Upon Julia's washing her self in the river" (Herrick) **13**:393

"Upon occasion of his Ode of defiance annext to his Play of the new Inne" (Carew)
See "To Ben Jonson Upon occasion of his Ode of defiance annext to his play of the new Inne"

"Upon our Victory at Sea, and Burning the French Fleet at La Hogu" (Dennis) **11**:48

"Upon Roses" (Herrick) **13**:389

"Upon some verses of Vergil" (Donne) **10**:81

"Upon Sudds" (Herrick) **13**:398

"Upon the Burning of our House" (Bradstreet)
See "Verses Upon the Burning of Our House, July 10th, 1666"

"Upon the death of his Sparrow" (Herrick) **13**:340

"Upon the Death of that Holy and Reverend Man of God, Mr. Samuel Hooker" (Taylor) **11**:368

"Upon the Death of the Lord Hastings" (Dryden) **3**:223, 239

"Upon the Discretion of Folly" (Wycherley) **21**:356

Upon the Excellency of Christianity (Swift) **1**:487

"Upon the Hill and Grove at Billborow" ("On the Hill and Grove at Billborow") (Marvell) **4**:397, 403, 429, 440

"Upon the Idleness of Business: A Satyr. To One, Who Said, a Man Show'd His Sense, Spirit, Industry, and Parts, by His Love of Bus'ness" (Wycherley) **8**:416

"Upon the Impertinence of Knowledge, the Unreasonableness of Reason, and the Brutality of Humanity; Proving the Animal Life the Most Reasonable Life, since the Most Natural, and Most Innocent" (Wycherley) **8**:399, 415; **21**:356

"Upon the Nipples of Julia's Breast" (Herrick) **13**:368, 393

"Upon the troublesome times" (Herrick) **13**:396

Upon the Types of the Old Testament (Taylor) **11**:399-400

"Upon Wedlock and Death of Children" (Taylor) **11**:367-68

Ursus Murmurat (Beer) **5**:52

"The Use and Objects of the Faculties of the Mind" (Bacon) **18**:105

The Usefullness of the Colloquies (Erasmus)
See *De Utilitate Colloquiorum*

The Usefulness of the Stage to the Happiness of Mankind, to Government and to Religion (*On the Usefulness of the Stage*) (Dennis) **11**:20, 30, 37

De Utilitate Colloquiorum (*Letter to the Reader; The Usefullness of the Colloquies*) (Erasmus) **16**:122, 156, 194

Utopia (More) **10**:357-58, 360, 365, 368-69, 373-75, 377-83, 385-97, 400-01, 404-06, 409-15, 420-26, 430-31, 434-36, 441, 443, 449-54

Utrum Hebraei possint construere novas synagogas (Casanova de Seingalt) **13**:126

Vade Mecum (Richardson)
See *The Apprentice's Vade Mecum*

Vadiscus, sive Trias Romana (*On the Roman Trinity; Roman Triads; Trias Romana*) (Hutten) **16**:213, 218, 230-31, 233, 235, 246

Den vægelsindede (Holberg) **6**:258, 263, 267, 273, 277

"A Valediction: forbidding mourning" ("As virtuous men pass mildly away") (Donne) **10**:6, 10-11, 13, 18, 31, 36, 51, 54, 58, 67, 69, 94, 105

"A Valediction: of my name, in the window" (Donne) **10**:31, 82

"A Valediction: of the booke" ("I'll tell thee now (dear love) what thou shalt doe") (Donne) **10**:31, 36

"A Valediction: of weeping" (Donne) **10**:9, 26, 31, 36, 50, 58, 71

Valerius Terminus of the Interpretation of Nature (Bacon) **18**:131, 161, 186-87

The Valley of Lilies (Kempis) **11**:410

"The Vanity of All Worldly Creatures" (Bradstreet)
See "The Vanity of All Worldly Things"

"The Vanity of All Worldly Things" ("The Vanity of All Worldly Creatures") (Bradstreet) **4**:90, 99, 109

"The Vanity of Human Wishes, being the Tenth Satire of Juvenal imitated" (Johnson) **15**:186-89, 194-96, 199, 201, 204, 206, 217, 219, 228, 233-36, 242, 244, 268-75, 277-81, 291-93

Variae Lectiones (Lipsius) **16**:262

El Varon Atento (Gracian y Morales) **15**:135

La vedova scaltra (*The Artful Widow*) (Goldoni) **4**:250, 266-67

La vedova spiritosa (Goldoni) **4**:261

"Veggio co be uostr'ochi" (Michelangelo)
See "Veggio co bei vostr'occhi un dolce lume"

"Veggio co bei vostr'occhi un dolce lume" ("Veggio co be uostr'ochi") (Michelangelo) **12**:360, 367

"Veggio nel tuo bel uiso" (Michelangelo) **12**:360

De vera compunctione animae (Kempis) **11**:411

Vergleichung Shakespears und Andreas Gryphs (Schlegel) **5**:273

"La vérité" (Rousseau) **9**:345

Die Verkehrte Welt (*The Topsy-Turvy World*) (Grimmelshausen) **6**:247

Verkehrter Staatsmann (Beer)
See *Der verkehrte Staats-Mann; oder, Nasenweise Secretarius*

"Verses Intended to Be Written Below a Noble Earl's Picture" (Burns) **3**:86

"Verses Made for Women Who Cry Apples" (Swift) **1**:459

"Verses on Reynold's Window" (Warton)

See "Verses on Sir Joshua's Painted Window at New College"

"Verses on Sir Joshua's Painted Window at New College" ("Verses on Reynold's Window"; "Verses to Sir Joshua Reynolds") (Warton) **15**:432-33, 444, 448, 456

"Verses on the Death of Dr. Swift" (Swift) **1**:439, 475, 482, 523-24

"Verses to a Lady" (Chatterton) **3**:123

"Verses to Collector Mitchell" (Burns) **3**:85

"Verses to Sir Joshua Reynolds" (Warton)
See "Verses on Sir Joshua's Painted Window at New College"

"Verses Upon the Burning of Our House, July 10th, 1666" ("Upon the Burning of our House") (Bradstreet) **4**:90, 98, 112, 114

"Verses Written at the Age of Fourteen, and Sent to Mr. Beville Higgons, on His Sickness and Recovery from the Small-Pox" (Trotter) **8**:358, 368

Versuch einer deutschen Prosodie (Moritz) **2**:231, 242-43, 245

Versuch einer kleinen praktischen Kinderlogik (*Kinderlogik*) (Moritz) **2**:240-41, 246

"La veuve et le magicien" (Marivaux) **4**:380

"Viage del Parnaso" ("Voyage to Parnassus") (Cervantes) **6**:148, 174

The Vicar of Wakefield (Goldsmith) **2**:66-7, 69-72, 74-6, 79-86, 89-94, 98-102, 104-09, 111-12, 114, 116-19, 121-28

Vice and Luxury Public Mischiefs (*Vice and Luxury Public Mishaps*) (Dennis) **11**:19, 26

Vice and Luxury Public Mishaps (Dennis)
See *Vice and Luxury Public Mischiefs*

Vidua Christiana (Erasmus) **16**:193

La vie de Marianne; ou, Les aventures de Mme la Comtesse de*** (*Life of Marianne*) (Marivaux) **4**:353-56, 359-60, 362, 368, 372-75, 378-81, 383-84, 387

La vie inestimable du grand Gargantua, père de Pantagruel (Rabelais) **5**:216-17, 223, 226, 233, 235, 239-41, 249, 251, 254, 256-58, 260

A View of the Edinburgh Theatre during the Summer Season, 1759 (Boswell) **4**:50

"Vigil of Venus" (Parnell) **3**:258

"Vindication" (Dryden) **3**:210

A Vindication of Mr. Locke's Christian Principles from the Injurious Imputations of Dr. Holdsworth (Trotter) **8**:362

A Vindication of Natural Society (Burke)
See *A Vindication of Natural Society; or, A View of the Miseries and Evils Arising to Mankind from Every Species of Artificial Society*

A Vindication of Natural Society; or, A View of the Miseries and Evils Arising to Mankind from Every Species of Artificial Society (*A Vindication of Natural Society*) (Burke) **7**:57, 61

A Vindication of the Reasonableness of Christianity (Locke) **7**:281

A Vindication of the Reasons and Defence, &c. Part I being a Reply to the First Part of No Sufficient Reason. Part II being a Reply to the Second Part of No Sufficient Reason (Collier) **6**:209

Vindication of the Relapse and the Provok'd Wife from Immorality and Prophaneness (Vanbrugh)
See *A Short Vindication of The Relapse and The Provok'd Wife from Immorality and Prophaneness*

A Vindication of the Rights of Men, in a Letter to the Right Honourable Edmund Burke; Occasioned by His Reflections on the Revolution in France (*Reply to Burke*) (Wollstonecraft) **5**:415, 417, 426, 428, 432, 435-41, 444, 451-53, 460-61

A Vindication of the Rights of Woman, with Strictures on Political and Moral Subjects (*Rights of Woman*) (Wollstonecraft) **5**:415-16, 418, 420-29, 431-34, 437, 439-41, 443-44, 446, 448-53, 456-61

The Vindication of Wives (Perrault)
See *L'apologie des femmes*

Vindications (Lessing) **8**:79

"Vine" (Herrick) **13**:320

"A Vintner" (Butler) **16**:55

Violenta; or, The Rewards of Virtue (Pix) **8**:277-78

Virelays (Christine de Pizan) **9**:43

"Virgils Gnat" (Spenser) **5**:312

"The Virgin Averse to Marriage" (Erasmus)
See "Girl Who Did Not Want to Marry"

"Virgin Repentant" ("The Repentant Girl") (Erasmus) **16**:141, 193

Virginia: A Tragedy, with Odes, Pastorals, and Translations (Brooke) **6**:108-09

"Virginian Ode" (Drayton)
See "To the Virginian Voyage"

"The Virgin's Choice" (Chatterton) **3**:132

Virgo Aspricollis (Lipsius) **16**:254

Virgo Sichemiensis (Lipsius) **16**:254

"Virtue" (Wheatley)
See "On Virtue"

"A Virtuoso" (Butler) **16**:50-2

"The Visible and Invisible: Soul and Sense" (More) **9**:298

Visio de Petro Plowman, Vita de Dowel, Vita de Dobet, Vita de Dobest (Langland)
See *Piers Plowman*

"The Vision" (Burns) **3**:47, 50, 71, 86

"A Vision" (Herrick) **13**:351, 367, 393

La vision de Babouc (Voltaire) **14**:359, 360

"Vision of Beauty" (Jonson) **6**:326

"Vision of Mirza" (Addison) **18**:28

Vision of Noah (Aretino) **12**:13

Vision of William concerning Piers the Plowman (Langland)
See *Piers Plowman*

"Visions of the Worlds Vanitie" (Spenser) **5**:312

"Visit to the Exchange" (Addison) **18**:28

"Visits to the Abbey" (Addison) **18**:28

Vita beata (*Book of the Beatific Life*) (Paracelsus) **14**:199

Vita di Benvenuto Cellini (*Autobiography*) (Cellini) **7**:68-74, 76-85

La vita di Castruccio Castracani da Lucca (*Castruccio*) (Machiavelli) **8**:133, 161, 174-75

Vita di Cristo (Aretino)
See *L'Humanità di Christo*

Vita di santa Caterina da Siena (*Life of Saint Catherine*) (Aretino) **12**:6, 8, 13, 36

The Vocal Forest (Howell)
See *Dendrologia: Dodona's Grove; or, The Vocall Forest*

La voiture embourbée (Marivaux) **4**:385-87

La voix du sage et du peuple (Voltaire) **14**:403

"La volière" (Rousseau) **9**:345

Title Index

Volpone; or, the Foxe (The Fox; or, Volpone)
(Jonson) **6**:291, 294-95, 297, 299-300, 303,
306, 308, 310-13, 319-20, 322-24, 328, 330-
36, 339-41, 343, 349-50

Volumen Paramirum (Paracelsus) **14**:199

*Von den guten Wercken (The Sermon on Good
Works)* (Luther) **9**:125, 134-35, 139, 147,
150

Von den hinfallenden Siechtagen (Paracelsus)
14:199

Von den hinfallenden Siechtagen der Mutter
(Paracelsus) **14**:199

Vorlesungen über den Stil (Moritz) **2**:244

*Vorrede des Uebersetzers zu Der Ruhmredige
(Preface)* (Schlegel) **5**:283

"Vorrei voler, Signor, quel ch'io non voglio"
(Michelangelo) **12**:367

Le voyage à Paphos (Montesquieu) **7**:320, 324,
348

"Voyage de Tours" (Ronsard) **6**:426-27

A Voyage to Lisbon (Fielding)
See *The Journal of a Voyage to Lisbon*

"Voyage to Parnassus" (Cervantes)
See "Viage del Parnaso"

"Le voyageur dans le nouveau monde"
(Marivaux) **4**:376, 380

"Wa-ch'u" (P'u Sung-ling) **3**:352

The Wandering Beauty (Behn) **1**:42, 46, 51,
53

"Wang-che" ("The Royal Man") (P'u Sung-
ling) **3**:351

"Wang Ch'eng" (P'u Sung-ling) **3**:350-51

"Wang Tzu-an" (P'u Sung-ling) **3**:345

"War" (Butler) **16**:50

The Warners (Hutten) **16**:228

"A Warning to Professors" (Edwards) **7**:98

Wásitat al-Iqd (Middle of the Necklace) (Jami)
9:65, 68

"The Wassaile" (Herrick) **13**:366

The Water Margin (Lo Kuan-chung)
See *Shui Hu Chuan*

"A Waukrife Minnie" (Burns) **3**:86

The Way of Perfection (Teresa de Jesus)
See *Camino de perfección*

The Way of the World (Congreve) **5**:70-1, 73,
75-6, 78-88, 90-5, 97-100, 103-05, 107, 109-
11, 113, 117; **21**:4-5, 8-10, 13, 15-18, 20, 23,
26-8, 32-4, 43-4

*The Way to Things by Words and to Words by
Things* (Cleland) **2**:53

"Ways of the Present World" (Petursson)
See "Aldarhéttur"

"We Raise a New Song" (Luther)
See "Ein neues Lied wir heben an"

The Wedding Day (Fielding) **1**:208, 220, 250

Weiberhächel (Beer)
See *Des berühmten Spaniers Francisci
Sambelle wolausgepolirte Weiber-Hächel*

"The Welcome: A Poem to His Grace the
Duke of Marlborough" (Aubin) **9**:4

"The Welcome to Sack" (Herrick) **13**:365,
397

"Wha Is That at My Bower-Door" (Burns)
3:100

"Wha'll Mow Me Now" (Burns) **3**:100

"What Do You Want from Us, Lord?"
(Kochanowski)
See "Pieśń"

"What Do You Wish, O Lord, In Return For
Your Bounteous Gifts?" (Kochanowski)
See "Pieśń"

"What Kind of Mistresse He Would Have"
(Herrick) **13**:351, 359, 393

"What wilt Thou from us, Lord?"
(Kochanowski)
See "Pieśń"

"When First I Ended, Then I First Began"
(Drayton)
See "Sonnet 62"

"When He Would Have his Verses Read"
(Herrick) **13**:349, 351, 393, 402

"When Laurell spirts 'ith fire" (Herrick)
13:360

"When Lovely Woman Stoops to Folly"
(Goldsmith) **2**:104

"When Phoebe formed a wanton smile"
(Collins) **4**:225

"When Spring Came on with Fresh Delight"
(Parnell)
See "When Spring Comes On"

"When Spring Comes On" ("When Spring
Came on with Fresh Delight") (Parnell)
3:251-52

"Whether Day or Night Is the More
Excellent" (Milton) **9**:225

"Whether the British Government Inclines
More to Absolute Monarchy, or to a
Republic" (Hume) **7**:189

"While Grace doth stir me" (Juana Ines de la
Cruz) **5**:152

"Whistle and I'll Come tae Ye, My Lad"
(Burns) **3**:66, 74, 78

"The White Island: or place of the Blest"
(Herrick) **13**:319-20, 330, 334, 336, 338,
374, 401

"Who ever comes to shroud me do not harme"
(Donne)
See "The Funerall"

"The Whore" (Chatterton)
See "The Whore of Babylon"

"The Whore of Babylon" ("The Whore")
(Chatterton) **3**:126, 133-34

"Why Doth the Pox so much Affect to
Undermine the Nose?" (Donne) **10**:96

"Why Hath the Common Opinion Afforded
Women Souls?" (Donne) **10**:96

"Why I Write Not of Love" (Jonson) **6**:347-
48

"Wicked Men Useful in Their Destruction
Only" (Edwards) **7**:93, 122

The Widow Ranter (Behn) **1**:35

"The Widow's Tears; or Dirge of Dorcas"
(Herrick) **13**:317

Wie die Alten den Tod gebildeten (Lessing)
8:82

"Wife of Bath" (Pope) **3**:269

"Wife of Bath's Prologue" (Chaucer)
See "Prologue to the Wife of Bath's Tale"

"Wife of Bath's Tale" ("Wife's Tale")
(Chaucer) **17**:142, 145, 181, 189, 191, 202,
213, 229-33, 236-37, 240-41

"A Wife of Ten Thousand" (Marmontel)
2:214

"The Wife's Resentment" (Manley) **1**:306-08

"Wife's Tale" (Chaucer)
See "Wife of Bath's Tale"

The Wild Gallant (Dryden) **3**:193, 230-31

"The Will" (Donne) **10**:13, 18, 50

Willenhag-Romane (Beer) **5**:47-8

"Willie Brew'd a Peck o' Maut" (Burns)
3:61, 78

"The Willing Mistress" (Behn) **1**:52, 54

"Wilt thou forgive" (Donne)
See "A Hymn to God the Father"

"Windsor-Forest" (Pope) **3**:268, 270, 273-74,
290, 292, 306-07, 315-16, 334, 336-38

"Winter" (Pope) **3**:334

"Winter, a Dirge" (Burns) **3**:48

Winter. A Poem (Thomson) **16**:363-64, 366,
369, 372-73, 381, 383, 385, 387, 393, 397-98,
402-03, 405, 409, 413, 415, 419-24, 426, 429,
431, 433

"A Winter Night" (Burns) **3**:86

Wisdom of Alexander (Jami)
See *Khirad-náma-yi Iskandarí*

The Wisdom of the Ancients (Bacon)
See *De sapienta veterum*

"With Fooles and Children Good Discretion
Beares" (Drayton)
See "Sonnet 22"

Without Head or Tail (Holberg)
See *Uden hoved og hale*

The Wits (Davenant) **13**:175, 187

Wives (Pix)
See *The Spanish Wives*

Wolfenbüttel Fragments (Lessing) **8**:64, 79

The Woman of Honor (Cleland) **2**:53-4

"The Woman with a Sausage on Her Nose"
(Perrault) **2**:255

"Woman's Constancy" (Donne) **10**:12, 50, 52

"Women" (Butler) **16**:47

Women's Tittle-Tattle (Goldoni)
See *I pettegolezzi delle donne*

The Wonder Show (Cervantes) **6**:190-91

Wonders of Babylon (Castro) **19**:4

Work of Redemption (Edwards)
See *God Glorified in the Work of
Redemption, by the Greatness of Man's
Dependence upon Him in the Whole of It*

Works (Jonson) **6**:323, 347

"The Works and Wonders of Almighty
Power" (Thomson) **16**:418

The Works of George Lord Lyttelton
(Lyttelton) **10**:196

*The Works of Henry Fielding, Esq.; With the
Life of the Author* (Fielding) **1**:208, 219

The Works of Horace, Translated into Verse
(Horace) (Smart) **3**:397-98

The Works of Michael Drayton (Drayton)
8:48

The Works of Mrs. Davys (Davys) **1**:97-8

The Works of Sir Thomas Malory (Malory)
See *Morte Darthur*

The Works of Sir Thomas More Knyght (More)
10:370

*The Works of the Right Honourable Lady
Mary Wortley Montague (The Letters and
Works of Lady Mary Wortley Montagu)*
(Montagu) **9**:270, 272

*The Works of Virgil...Translated into English
Verse* (Dryden) **3**:201

"Would you know what's soft?" (Carew)
13:11

"Wounded Hare" (Burns)
See "On Seeing a Wounded Hare Limp by
Me Which a Fellow Had Just Shot at"

"The Wounded Heart" (Herrick) **13**:337

"Wrath upon the Wicked to the Uttermost"
(Edwards) **7**:98

"Written at Vale-Royal Abbey" (Warton)
See "Ode Written at Vale-Royal Abbey in
Cheshire"

"Written in the Beginning of Mezeray's
History of France" ("Lines Written in
Mezeray") (Prior) **4**:466, 472

The Wrongs of Woman; or, Maria (Maria)
  (Wollstonecraft)   **5**:416, 424, 426-27, 429-
  31, 443-44, 453-56, 461
*Das wunderbarliche Vogelnest (I and II) (The
  Magic Bird's Nest)* (Grimmelshausen)
  6:238, 247
"Ye have been fresh and green" (Herrick)
  13:319
"Yen Shih" ("The Daughter of the Yen
  Family") (P'u Sung-ling)   **3**:354
"Ying-ning" (P'u Sung-ling)   **3**:348, 352, 354
"Young Damon of the vale is dead" (Collins)
  4:225
"The Young Gentleman in Love" (Prior)
  4:455, 461
The Young King; or, The Mistake (Behn)
  1:33, 39
"Young Love" (Marvell)   **4**:435
The Young Savant (Lessing)
  See *Der junge Gelehrte*
The Younger Brother; or, The Amorous Jilt
  (Behn)   **1**:56
"Youthful Piety" (Erasmus)   **16**:195
"Yu Chu-ngo" (P'u Sung-ling)   **3**:345
*Yúsuf u Zulaikhá (The Romance of Yúsuf
  (Joseph) and Zulaykhá (Potiphar's Wife))*
  (Jami)   **9**:60, 62, 66-7, 70-1
Zadig (Voltaire)   **14**:328, 338, 345, 358-60,
  378, 389, 397
Zaïde (Zayde) (La Fayette)   **2**:138-39, 151-52,
  157-58, 160, 168-69
Zaïre (Voltaire)   **14**:323-25, 328, 338, 342,
  358, 397
Zayde (La Fayette)
  See *Zaïde*
"Zealot" (Butler)   **16**:53
Zelmane; or, The Corinthian Queen (Pix)
  8:276
*Zendorii à Zendoriis teutsche Winternächte;
  oder, Die ausführliche und denckwürdige
  Beschreibung seiner Lebens-Geschict* (Beer)
  5:47-8, 50, 54, 57-8, 60
"Zgoda" ("Harmony") (Kochanowski)
  10:175
Zulime (Voltaire)   **14**:397

Title Index

ISBN 0-8103-7963-5

90000

9 780810 379633